Proportionality: The evil that will be brought about by the action is not out of proportion to the good being aimed at.

A violation that satisfies all of the provisions of the DDE counts as an indirect violation and is thus not prohibited by NLT.

C. KANTIAN MORAL THEORY

Humanity formulation of Kant's fundamental principle, the categorical imperative:

H An action is right if and only if (and because) the action treats persons (including oneself) as ends in themselves and not merely as a means.

Universal Law formulation

UL An action is right if and only if one can both (a) consistently conceive of everyone adopting and acting on the general policy (that is, the maxim) of one's action, and also (b) consistently will that everyone act on that maxim.

D. RIGHTS-BASED MORAL THEORY

As the name suggests, a rights-based moral theory takes the notion of moral rights as basic and defines or characterizes the rightness or wrongness of actions in terms of moral rights.

R An action is right if and only if (and because) in performing it either (a) one does not violate the fundamental moral rights of others, or (b) in cases in which it is not possible to respect all such rights because they are in conflict, one's action is among the best ways to protect the most important rights in the case at hand.

Typical moral rights taken as fundamental include the Jeffersonian rights to life, various liberties, and the freedom to pursue one's own happiness.

E. VIRTUE ETHICS

A type of moral theory that takes considerations of virtue and vice to be the basis for defining or characterizing the rightness and wrongness of actions.

VE An action is right if and only if (and because) it is what a virtuous agent (acting in character) might choose to do in the circumstances under consideration.

Commonly recognized virtues include honesty, courage, justice, temperance, beneficence, humility, loyalty, and gratitude.

F. ETHICS OF PRIMA FACIE DUTY

This sort of moral theory features a plurality of principles of prima facie duty. To reach an all-things-considered moral verdict in cases in which two or more principles apply and favor conflicting actions, one must use moral judgment to figure out which duty is most stringent.

Ross's list of prima facie duties:

Justice:	prima facie, one ought to ensure that pleasure is distributed according to merit.
Beneficence:	prima facie, one ought to help those in need and, in general, increase the virtue, pleasure, and knowledge of others.
Self-improvement:	prima facie, one ought to improve oneself with respect to one's own virtue and knowledge.
Nonmaleficence:	prima facie, one ought to refrain from harming others.
Fidelity:	prima facie, one ought to keep one's promises.
Reparation:	prima facie, one ought to make amends to others for any past wrongs one has done them.
Gratitude:	prima facie, one ought to show gratitude toward one's benefactors.

Audi's proposed additions to Ross's list:

Veracity:	prima facie, one ought not to lie.
Enhancement and preservation of freedom:	prima facie, one ought to contribute to increasing or at least preserving the freedom of others with priority given to removing constraints over enhancing opportunities.
Respectfulness:	prima facie, one ought, in the manner of our relations with other people, treat others respectfully.

G. SOCIAL CONTRACT THEORY

BASIC IDEA:

SC An action is morally right if and only if (and because) it is permitted by a set of moral principles that hypothetical agents would agree to under conditions that are ideal for choosing moral principles (the precise characteristics of the hypothetical agents and ideal conditions to be spelled out.)

RAWLS'S TWO PRINCIPLES OF JUSTICE:

In the context of developing a theory of social justice governing social and political institutions, John Rawls proposed two basic principles of justice that he argued would be chosen by agents (under certain specified conditions) who are deciding on basic principles for mutual governance.

The principle of greatest equal liberty: Each person is to have an equal right to the most extensive basic liberty compatible with a similar liberty for others.

The difference principle: Social and economic inequalities are to be arranged so that they are both (a) reasonably expected to be to everyone's advantage and (b) attached to positions and offices open to all.

DISPUTED MORAL ISSUES

A Reader

Fourth Edition

Mark Timmons
University of Arizona

New York   Oxford
OXFORD UNIVERSITY PRESS

Oxford University Press is a department of the University of Oxford.
It furthers the University's objective of excellence in research,
scholarship, and education by publishing worldwide.

Oxford   New York
Auckland   Cape Town   Dar es Salaam   Hong Kong   Karachi
Kuala Lumpur   Madrid   Melbourne   Mexico City   Nairobi
New Delhi   Shanghai   Taipei   Toronto

With offices in
Argentina   Austria   Brazil   Chile   Czech Republic   France   Greece
Guatemala   Hungary   Italy   Japan   Poland   Portugal   Singapore
South Korea   Switzerland   Thailand   Turkey   Ukraine   Vietnam

For titles covered by Section 112 of the US Higher Education Opportunity
Act, please visit www.oup.com/us/he for the latest information about
pricing and alternate formats.

Published by Oxford University Press
198 Madison Avenue, New York, NY 10016
http://www.oup.com

Library of Congress Cataloging-in-Publication Data
Names: Timmons, Mark, 1951- editor.
Title: Disputed moral issues : a reader / [edited by] Mark Timmons,
   University of Arizona.
Description: Fourth Edition. | New York : Oxford University Press USA, 2016.
Identifiers: LCCN 2016038175| ISBN 9780190490027 (student edition) | ISBN
   9780190490034 (instructor edition) | ISBN 9780190650308 (loose leaf)
Subjects: LCSH: Ethics–Textbooks. | Ethical problems–Textbooks.
Classification: LCC BJ1012 .D57 2016 | DDC 170–dc23 LC record available at https://lccn.loc.gov/2016038175

Printing number: 9 8 7 6 5 4 3 2 1 0

Printed by LSC Communications, United States of America

CONTENTS

PREFACE

The guiding aim of this anthology is to connect various disputed moral issues with moral theory in order to help students better understand the nature of these disputes. The issues featured in this book include questions about the morality of various forms of sexual behavior; pornography, hate speech, and censorship; drugs and addiction; sexism, racism, and reparations; immigration; euthanasia and physician-assisted suicide; the ethical treatment of animals; abortion; cloning and genetic enhancement; the death penalty; war, terrorism, and torture; world hunger and poverty; and ethical questions that relate to consumption, climate change, and the environment in general.

The connection between moral disputes over such issues and moral theory is that opposing moral viewpoints on some topics are very often grounded in one or another moral theory. Thus, to understand an author's arguments for her or his favored position, one must be able to recognize the author's deepest moral assumptions, which are reflected in the moral theory from which the author proceeds in reasoning about particular moral issues.

In editing this anthology, I have attempted to help readers connect moral issues with theory in the following ways:

- *A moral theory primer.* One way to connect issues and theory is to have students read compact summaries of the various moral theories—summaries that convey just enough detail about a moral theory to aid understanding without overwhelming the reader. This is what I have tried to do in the first chapter, "A Moral Theory Primer," in which I first explain what a moral theory is all about—its main concepts and guiding aims—and then proceed to present seven types of moral theory that are essential for understanding moral disputes over the sorts of issues featured in this book. In the brief introduction and "User's Guide" immediately following this preface, I explain how one might integrate the moral theory primer into a moral problems course.
- *Chapter introductions.* In addition to the primer, I have also written introductions to each chapter that go over certain conceptual, historical, and theoretical issues that students must have in beginning their study of moral issues. These introductions include remarks about how the moral theories presented in the primer relate to the arguments of the authors whose writings are featured in the chapter.
- *Selection summaries.* Again, in order to aid one's understanding of the articles, each selection is preceded by a short summary of the article. Immediately after the summary I have, where relevant, included a cue to readers that indicates the relevant part of the moral theory primer that will aid in understanding the article in question.

- *Reading and discussion questions.* Following each selection, I have included a set of reading and discussion questions. The reading questions are meant to prompt students' understanding of each selection's content, whereas the discussion questions are meant to help stimulate critical thought about the issues and arguments in the selections.
- *Quick guide to moral theories.* I have also included a "Quick Guide to Moral Theories," which lists the various principles featured in each of the seven theories featured in the primer. This is for readers who need a brief reminder of the key elements of one or more of the featured moral theories.

In addition, this anthology includes the following features that many will find useful:

- *Glossary.* For ease of reference, I have included a glossary of important terms that are defined in the moral theory primer and in the chapter introductions. Each term in the glossary appears in boldface type when it is first introduced in the text. The glossary entry for each term specifies the chapter and section in which the term is first introduced.
- *Additional resources.* Finally, at the end of each chapter, I have included a short list of resources, broken down into Web resources, authored books and articles, and edited collections. These resources are recommended to those who wish to explore a topic in more detail.

As mentioned earlier, the following "User's Guide" makes a few suggestions about integrating the study of moral theory and moral issues.

New to the Fourth Edition

Here is a summary of the changes I've made in this edition:

- In the chapter featuring classic selections on moral theory, I have replaced the selection from Bentham with one from J. S. Mill's *Utilitarianism.*
- In the chapter on sexual morality, I have replaced "Why Shouldn't Tommy and Jim Have Sex" by John Corvino with an excerpt from his recent 2013 book, *What's Wrong with Homosexuality?* The third edition of this book included two articles debating gay marriage. On the advice of some users, and the fact that many students report to me that for them gay marriage is no longer an issue, I have dropped the two articles in question and have not replaced them.
- I have added two new selections to the chapter on pornography, hate speech, and censorship. Susan Dwyer in "Enter Here—At Your Own Risk: The Moral Dangers of Cyberporn" tackles the question of internet pornography from the perspective of virtue ethics. Andrew Altman defends the justification of hate speech codes in his "Speech Codes and Expressive Harm."
- The chapter on sexism, racism, and reparation now includes "Sexism" by Ann E. Cudd and Leslie E. Jones.
- For the chapter on euthanasia and physician-assisted suicide, I have added David Velleman's "Against the Right to Die," which presents a unique perspective on the dangers of a legal right to die.
- I have made a few changes in the chapter on the ethical treatment of animals. I have replaced three of the articles from the third edition, adding Peter Singer's classic, "All

Animals Are Equal," Peter Carruthers's "Against the Moral Standing of Animals," in which he addresses the issue from a contractualist perspective, and finally, Alastair Norcross's spirited critique of the practice of meat-eating in his "Puppies, Pigs, and People: Eating Meat and Marginal Cases."

- On the good advice of one of the reviewers for this edition of the book, I have added a selection by Stephen M. Gardiner, "A Perfect Moral Storm: Climate Change, Intergenerational Ethics, and the Problem of Moral Corruption," to the chapter on the environment, consumption, and climate change.

Finally, this third edition features an updated Instructor's Manual and Testbank on CD and a companion website for both students and instructors that I describe in more detail in the "User's Guide" following this preface.

Acknowledgments

Thanks to Robert Miller, my editor at Oxford University Press, for encouraging me to do a new edition of this anthology, and to the folks at OUP involved in the production of this volume. I am especially grateful to the following philosophers for their extremely helpful advice for this edition: Jacob Affolter (Arizona State University), Adam Cureton (University of Tennessee, Knoxville), Bob Fischer (Texas State University), Matthew Fitzsimmons (University of North Alabama), Frank Schalow (University of New Orleans), Barbara Tucker (Trident Technical College), and four anonymous reviewers for Oxford University Press.

Dedication

Finally, I wish to dedicate this fourth edition of *Disputed Moral Issues* to Betsy Timmons for her generous research assistance in helping to update many of the chapter introductions and for her cheerful encouragement during my work on this edition.

Mark Timmons
Tucson, AZ

User's Guide

In what follows, I suggest how instructors might approach teaching a course that is primarily focused on particular moral disputes but also integrates moral theory into the teaching of those disputes. Following this discussion is a description of the various resources for both students and instructors that come with this book.

As mentioned in the preface, a central aim of this anthology is to connect a range of contemporary disputed moral issues to moral theory. Much of the philosophical literature on the morality of abortion, homosexuality, pornography, cloning, and the death penalty approaches these and other issues from the perspective of some *moral theory*. As I will explain more fully in the next chapter, a moral theory purports to answer general moral questions about the nature of the right and the good. So one way in which philosophers tackle disputed moral issues is by appealing to a moral theory—appealing, that is, to a general conception of the right and the good in examining some particular moral issue.

But this presents a challenge for students who are trying to understand and think about the moral controversies featured in this book and presents an associated challenge for instructors. Because of the important role that moral theory plays in the writings of both professional philosophers and nonphilosophers who write about contemporary moral issues, a full understanding of most of the readings in this book requires that one have a basic grasp of the various moral theories to which authors appeal in their writings. Some authors take the time to briefly explain whatever moral theory they are using in approaching some moral issue, but many do not—they assume a basic acquaintance with moral theory. And this means that a student not previously acquainted with moral theory is often at a disadvantage in trying to understand the position and arguments of an author. The associated challenge for an instructor is to teach just enough moral theory to aid students' understanding in a course devoted primarily to disputed moral issues.

In this anthology, I try to address this challenge in a number of related ways. First, I have written an introductory overview of moral theory, "A Moral Theory Primer," in which I first explain what a moral theory is all about and then present the basic elements of seven types of moral theory that are featured throughout the readings in this book. These theories include the following:

- *Consequentialism* (including utilitarianism)
- *Natural law theory* (including the doctrine of double effect)
- *Kantian moral theory* (including Kant's Humanity and Universal Law formulations of the categorical imperative—Kant's fundamental moral principle)

- *Rights-based theory* (including an explanation of "rights-focused" approaches to moral problems that are very common but importantly distinct from a genuinely rights-*based* theory)
- *Virtue ethics* (including an explanation of the concepts of virtue and vice)
- *Ethics of prima facie duty* (including W. D. Ross's classic version and the more recent version defended by Robert Audi)
- *Social contract theory* (featuring John Rawls's influential contract theory of justice)

The moral theory primer, then, is meant to get readers up to basic speed on seven essential moral theories, with an eye on their application to disputed moral issues.

The moral theory primer can be read straight through. But let me make a suggestion about how it might be used in a course devoted mainly to contemporary moral problems—a suggestion that incorporates additional ways in which I have tried to address the previously mentioned challenge. (What I am about to say reflects my own approach to teaching a contemporary moral problems course.)

The basic idea is to incorporate select readings from the moral theory primer as one proceeds to work through the readings in the chapters that follow. The motto here is: *Teach moral theory as needed* in working through the readings. I have written the primer so that the segments on each of the seven types of moral theory are largely self-standing; they can be consulted as needed in learning about and teaching moral issues. I find that teaching moral theory as needed helps students to better digest and understand the somewhat abstract nature of a moral theory by immediately relating it to some concrete moral issue. And, of course, their coming to understand moral theory helps them more fully understand the readings.

Let me further suggest a way of implementing the teaching of theory on an as-needed approach.

- *Getting started.* Read the introduction and section 1 of the moral theory primer in which I provide a brief overview of what a moral theory is all about. That will be enough to get readers started.
- *Moving ahead to the moral issues.* Then I recommend proceeding to one of the chapters on a disputed moral issue—they can be taught in any order.[1]
- *Chapter introductions.* Read the chapter introduction on the selected topic; it will explain basic concepts relevant to the chapter topic. Each of these chapters ends with a subsection entitled "Theory Meets Practice," in which I briefly relate the moral theories that are used in that chapter's readings to the topic of the chapter.
- *Cues for the integrated use of the moral theory primer.* Then proceed to work through the readings in the selected chapter. Each reading begins with a brief summary of the article and, in those cases in which an author is appealing to, or relying on, some moral theory, the summaries are followed by a recommended reading, *which cues readers to go back (if needed) to the relevant sections of the moral theory primer where the theory in question is presented.* This is how I incorporate the teaching of various moral theories into the course as needed.

    Let me add that not every reading appeals to one or another moral theory. Some articles are mainly concerned with conveying an understanding of some disputed concept like "sexism" or "racism." One of the articles in the chapter on the death penalty is concerned entirely with statistical evidence about error rates in capital cases, an issue that, of course, bears importantly on the morality of the death penalty. And in a few other cases, the readings do not clearly proceed from some moral theory. So, not every article summary includes a recommendation to consult the moral theory primer. But most of the reading selections do connect directly with one or more of the moral theories explained in the primer.

- *Quick reference guide to moral theories.* In order to make it easy to review the fundamental principles of each of the theories, I have placed a "Quick Guide to Moral Theories" at the front of the book. Once one has read the relevant sections of the moral theory primer, this guide may be consulted to refresh one's memory of the basics.

Again, the preceding steps reflect how I like to proceed. Users are invited to find ways that best fit their own style of teaching.

Resources for Students and Instructors

This fourth edition includes an "Instructor's Manual" and "Computerized Testbank" on CD and a Companion Website (www.oup.com/us/timmons) that offers resources for both students and instructors.

Instructor Resources both in the Instructor's Manual and in the Companion Website include the following:

- Sample syllabi
- Lecture notes in PowerPoint format
- Chapter goals and summaries
- A Testbank that includes essay, multiple-choice, true/false, and fill-in-the-blank questions

Student Resources on the Companion Website include the following:

- Self-quizzes, which include multiple-choice, true/false, and fill-in-the-blank questions
- Helpful Web links
- Suggested readings and media (articles, films, etc.)

Learning Management System (LMS) cartridges are available in formats compatible with any LMS in use at your college or university and include the Instructor's Manual and Computerized Testbank and student resources from the companion website.

NOTE

1. Of course, some topics naturally go well together because the moral issues they raise are deeply connected. For instance, chapter 4 on pornography, hate speech, and censorship raises issues about the morality of government interference in the lives of its citizens. The same sort of issue comes up in chapter 5 on drugs and addiction. Chapters 9 and 10 on animals and abortion, respectively, go together because they raise important questions about the scope of moral standing, that is, about the boundaries of what should count in our moral deliberations.

1 } A Moral Theory Primer

In 1998, Dr. Jack Kevorkian helped Thomas Youk end his life by giving him a lethal injection of drugs—an incident that was videotaped and later broadcast on CBS's *60 Minutes*.[1] Youk had been suffering from amyotrophic lateral sclerosis (often called Lou Gehrig's disease), a progressive neurodegenerative disease that attacks nerve cells in the brain and spinal cord, eventually leading to death. In the later stages of the disease, its victims are completely paralyzed, as was Youk at the time of his death.

Kevorkian's killing Youk was a case of euthanasia, which is defined as the act of killing (or allowing to die) on grounds of mercy for the victim. In this case, because Youk consented to his own death and because Kevorkian brought about Youk's death by an act of lethal injection, Kevorkian's action was an instance of voluntary active euthanasia. Kevorkian was eventually tried and convicted of second degree murder for his active role in bringing about Youk's death. But even if Kevorkian did violate the law, was his action morally wrong? Youk's immediate family and many others saw nothing morally wrong with Youk's decision or with Kevorkian's act. They argued, for example, that proper respect for an individual's freedom of choice means that people in Youk's situation have a moral right to choose to die and that, therefore, Kevorkian was not acting immorally in helping Youk end his life. Of course, many others disagreed, arguing, for example, that euthanasia is morally wrong because of its possible bad effects over time on society, including the possibility that the practice of euthanasia could be abused, and vulnerable persons might be put to death without their consent. Which side of this moral dispute is correct? Is euthanasia at least sometimes morally right, or is this practice morally wrong?

Disputes over moral issues are a fact of our social lives. Most people, through television, the Internet, magazines, and conversing with others, are familiar with some of the general contours of such disputes—disputes, for example, over the death penalty, the ethical treatment of animals, human cloning, abortion. The same sort of moral question raised about the actions of Kevorkian can be raised about these and other moral issues. Thinking critically about such moral issues is where philosophy becomes especially important.

A *philosophical* approach to moral issues has as its guiding aim arriving at correct or justified answers to questions about the morality of the death penalty, the ethical treatment of animals, human cloning, abortion, and other issues of moral concern. Given the contested nature of such practices as cloning and abortion, one needs to be able to defend one's position with *reasons*. Just as those who dispute questions about, say, science or history are expected to give reasons for the scientific and historical beliefs they hold, those who seriously dispute moral questions are expected to give reasons for whatever moral position they take on a certain issue. If we examine how philosophers go about providing reasons for the moral positions they take on certain issues, we find that very often they appeal to a **moral theory.** That is, in arguing for a particular position on the topic of, say, euthanasia, philosophers often make their case by applying a moral theory to the practice of euthanasia. Applying moral theory to issues of practical concern—practical issues—is one dominant way in which reasoning in ethics proceeds. This way of tackling moral issues by applying theory to cases is featured in this book of readings.

But what is a moral theory? What are its guiding aims? What moral theories are there? How is a moral theory used in reasoning about disputed moral issues? These are the main questions of concern in this moral theory primer.

1.   WHAT IS A MORAL THEORY?

According to philosopher John Rawls, "The two main concepts of ethics are those of the right and the good. . . . The structure of an ethical theory is, then, largely determined by how it defines and connects these two basic notions."[2]

In explaining what a moral theory is, then, the place to begin is by clarifying the two main concepts featured in such a theory.

The Main Concepts: The Right and the Good

In ethics, the terms "right" and "wrong" are used primarily to evaluate the morality of actions, and in this chapter we are mainly concerned with moral theories that address the nature of right and wrong action (or right action, for short). Here, talk of right action in contrast to wrong action involves using the term "right" broadly to refer to actions that aren't wrong. Used in this broad sense, to say of an action that it is right is to say that it is "all right" (not wrong) to perform, and we leave open the question of whether the act, in addition to being all right, is an action that we morally ought to perform—an obligation or duty. But we sometimes find "right" being used narrowly to refer to actions that are "the" morally right action for one to perform, and when so used, it refers to actions that are morally required or obligatory (one's obligation or duty). Actions that are all right to perform (right in the sense of merely being not wrong) and that are also not one's moral obligation to perform—actions that are all right to perform and all right not to perform—are morally optional. So, we have three basic categories of moral evaluation into which an action may fall: an action may be morally obligatory (something one morally ought to do, is morally required to do, is one's duty), or morally optional, or morally wrong. To help keep this terminology straight, I have summarized what I have been saying in Figure 1.1.

Again, in ethics, the terms "good" and "bad" are used primarily in assessing the value of persons (their character) as well as experiences, things, and states of affairs. Philosophers distinguish between something's having **intrinsic value** (that is, being intrinsically good or bad) and something's having **extrinsic value** (that is, being extrinsically good or bad). Something has intrinsic value when its value depends on features that are *inherent* to it,

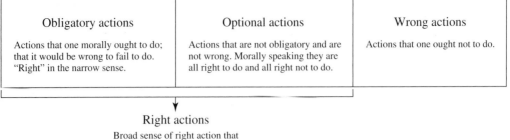

FIGURE 1.1   Basic Categories of Right Conduct

whereas something is extrinsically good when its goodness is a matter of how it is related to something else that is intrinsically good. For instance, some philosophers maintain that happiness is intrinsically good—its goodness depends on the inherent nature of happiness—and that things like money and power, while not intrinsically good, are nevertheless extrinsically good because they can be used to bring about or contribute to happiness. Thus, the notion of intrinsic value is the more basic of the two notions, and so philosophical accounts of value are concerned with the nature of intrinsic value. And here we can recognize three basic value categories: the *intrinsically good,* the *intrinsically bad* (also referred to as the intrinsically *evil*), and what we may call the *intrinsically value-neutral*—that is, the category of all those things that are neither intrinsically good nor bad (though they may have extrinsic value).[3]

A moral theory, then, is a theory about the nature of the right and the good and about the proper method for making correct or justified moral decisions. Accordingly, here are some of the main questions that a moral theory attempts to answer:

1. What *makes* an action right or wrong—what *best explains why* right acts are right and wrong acts are wrong?
2. What *makes* something good or bad—what *best explains why* intrinsically good things are intrinsically good (and similarly for things that are intrinsically bad or evil)?
3. What is the *proper method* for reasoning our way to correct or justified moral conclusions about the rightness and wrongness of actions and the goodness and badness of persons, and other items of moral evaluation?

In order to understand more fully what a moral theory is and how it attempts to answer these questions, let us relate what has just been said to the two guiding aims of moral theory.

Two Main Aims of a Moral Theory

Corresponding to the first two questions about the nature of the right and the good is what we may call the theoretical aim of a moral theory:

The **theoretical aim** of a moral theory is to discover those underlying features of actions, persons, and other items of moral evaluation that *make* them right or wrong, good or bad and thus *explain why* such items have the moral properties they have. Features of this sort serve as *moral criteria* of the right and the good.

Our third main question about proper methodology in ethics is the basis for the practical aim of a moral theory:

> The **practical aim** of a moral theory is to offer *practical guidance* for how we might arrive at correct or justified moral verdicts about matters of moral concern—verdicts which we can then use to help guide choice.

Given these aims, we can evaluate a moral theory by seeing how well it satisfies them. We will return to the issue of evaluating moral theories in section 3. For the time being, we can gain a clearer understanding of these aims by considering the role that principles typically play in moral theories.

The Role of Moral Principles

In attempting to satisfy these two aims, philosophers typically propose **moral principles**—very general moral statements that specify conditions under which an action is right (or wrong) and something is intrinsically good (or bad). Principles that state conditions for an action's being right (or wrong) are **principles of right conduct,** and those that specify conditions under which something has intrinsic value are **principles of value.** Here is an example of a principle of right conduct (where "right" is being used in its broad sense to mean "not wrong"):

> P   An action is right if and only if (and because) it would, if performed, likely bring about at least as much overall happiness as would any available alternative action.[4]

This principle, understood as a moral criterion of right action, purports to reveal the underlying nature of right action—what *makes* a right action right. According to P, facts about how much overall happiness an action would bring about were it to be performed are what determine whether it is morally right. Although P addresses the rightness of actions, it has implications for wrongness as well. From P, together with the definitional claim that if an action is not morally right (in the broad sense of the term) then it is morally wrong, we may infer the following:

> P*   An action is wrong if and only if (and because) it would, if performed, likely not bring about at least as much overall happiness as would some available alternative action.

Since, as we have just seen, principles about moral wrongness can be derived from principles of rightness, I shall, in explaining a moral theory's account of right and wrong, simply formulate a theory's principles (there may be more than one) for right action.

In addition to serving as moral criteria, principles like P are typically intended to provide some practical guidance for coming to correct or justified moral verdicts about particular issues, thus addressing the practical aim of moral theory. The idea is that if P is a correct moral principle, then we should be able to use it to guide our moral deliberations in coming to correct conclusions about the rightness of actions, thus serving as a basis for moral decision making. In reasoning our way to moral conclusions about what to do, P has us focus on the consequences of actions and instructs us to consider in particular how much overall happiness actions would likely bring about.

To sum up, a moral theory can be understood as setting forth moral principles of right conduct and value that are supposed to explain what makes an action or other object of evaluation right or wrong, good or bad (thus satisfying the theoretical aim), as well as principles that can be used to guide moral thought in arriving at correct or justified decisions about what to do (thus satisfying the practical aim).

The Structure of a Moral Theory

Finally, what Rawls calls the "structure" of a moral theory is a matter of how a theory connects the right and the good. As we shall see, some theories take the concept of the good to be more basic than the concept of the right and thus define or characterize the rightness of actions in terms of considerations of intrinsic goodness. Call such theories value-based moral theories. **Value-based moral theories** include versions of consequentialism, natural law theory, and virtue ethics. However, some moral theories do not define rightness in terms of goodness. Some theories are **duty-based moral theories**—theories that take the concept of duty to be basic and so define or characterize the rightness of actions independently of considerations of goodness. These theories are often called "deontological" moral theories (from *deon,* the Greek term for duty). The moral theory of Immanuel Kant (see later in this chapter) and theories inspired by Kant (Kantian moral theories) are arguably deontological.[5] And what is called the ethics of prima facie duty, if not a pure deontological theory, contains deontological elements, as we shall see when we discuss this theory later in section 2.

Brief Summary

Now that we have reviewed a few basic elements of moral theory, let us briefly sum up.

- *Main concepts of moral theory.* The two main concepts featured in moral theory are the concepts of the right (and wrong) and the good (and bad).
- *Two aims of moral theory.* A moral theory can be understood as having two central aims. The theoretical aim is to explain the underlying nature of the right and the good—specifying those features of actions or other items of evaluation that *make* an action or whatever right or wrong, good or bad. We call such features "**moral criteria**." The practical aim is to offer practical guidance for how we might arrive at correct or justified moral verdicts about matters of moral concern.
- *The role of moral principles.* A moral theory is typically composed of moral principles (sometimes a single, fundamental principle) that are intended to serve as criteria of the right and the good (thus satisfying the theoretical aim) and are also intended to be useful in guiding moral thinking toward correct, or at least justified conclusions about some moral issue.
- *The structure of a moral theory.* Considerations of structure concern how a moral theory connects the concepts of the right and the good. Value-based theories make the good (intrinsic value) more basic than the right and define or characterize the right in terms of the good. Duty-based theories characterize the right independently of considerations of value.

In the next section, we briefly examine seven moral theories that play a large role in philosophical discussions of disputed moral issues. After presenting these theories, I devote the remaining section and an appendix to questions that are likely to occur to readers. First, there is the question of why studying moral theories is helpful in thinking about disputed moral issues when there is no *one* moral theory that is accepted by all those who study moral theory. Rather, we find a variety of apparently competing moral theories that sometimes yield conflicting moral verdicts about the same issue. So, how can appealing to moral theory really help in trying to think productively about moral issues? This is a fair question that I address in section 3. However, before going on, let me say something about how one might use this chapter in studying the moral issues featured in this book.

User's Guide Interlude

In the "User's Guide," I suggested that although this chapter can be read straight through, readers may want to stop here and go on to one of the following chapters and begin their study of disputed moral issues. In the chapter introductions and the brief article summaries that precede each reading selection, I prompt readers to read (or reread) my presentations of one or more of the moral theories described in the next section. For those who wish to consult primary sources corresponding to the moral theories in question, there are the selections in the next chapter.

As I explained in the user's guide, I like to teach moral theory along with the readings. Seeing how a moral theory applies to a particular moral issue is helpful for understanding an author's position on the issue, which in turn helps readers gain a deeper understanding of and appreciation for moral theory. As for integrating section 3, I recommend consulting this part of the chapter when the questions it addresses are prompted by one's thinking about and discussing the book's readings.

2.   SEVEN ESSENTIAL MORAL THEORIES

Seven types of moral theory are prominently represented in our readings: consequentialism, natural law theory, Kantian moral theory, rights-based moral theory, virtue ethics, the ethics of prima facie duty, and social contract theory. Here, then, is an overview of these various theories that will provide useful background for understanding our readings.

A. Consequentialism

In thinking about moral issues, one obvious thing to do is to consider the consequences or effects of various actions—the consequences or effects on matters that are of concern to us. **Consequentialism** is a type of moral theory according to which consequences of actions are all that matter in determining the rightness and wrongness of actions. Its guiding idea is this:

C   Right action is to be understood entirely in terms of the overall intrinsic value of the consequences of the action compared to the overall intrinsic value of the consequences associated with alternative actions an agent might perform instead. An action is right if and only if (and because) its consequences would be at least as good as the consequences of any alternative action that the agent might instead perform.

A number of important ideas are packed into C that we need to unpack—ideas that are present in the varieties of consequentialist moral theory presented next. Let us sort them out.

- First, consequentialist moral theory is a *value-based moral theory*: it characterizes or defines right action in terms of intrinsic value.
- Second, this sort of theory involves the fairly intuitive idea of *alternative actions* open to an agent: in circumstances calling for a moral choice, an agent is confronted by a range of alternative actions, any one of which she might choose to perform.
- Third (and relatedly), consequentialism is a *comparative* theory of right action: the rightness (or wrongness) of an action depends on how much intrinsic value it would likely produce (if performed) compared to how much intrinsic value alternative actions would likely produce (if performed).
- Fourth, the consequentialist account of right action is a *maximizing* conception: we are to perform that action, from among the alternatives, whose consequences will have *at least as much* overall value as any other.
- Fifth, and finally, consequentialism is a strongly *impartialist* moral theory in the sense that the rightness or wrongness of an action is made to depend on the values of the consequences for *everyone* who is affected by the action, where everyone affected counts *equally.* (This fifth point will become clearer when we consider particular versions of consequentialism.)

Consequentialism, we have noted, is a *general type* of moral theory that has a variety of species. For instance, consequentialists may differ over the issue of what has intrinsic value. Those versions that take happiness or welfare alone to have intrinsic value are versions of utilitarianism, whereas those that take human perfection to have intrinsic value are versions of perfectionism. Again, consequentialists may differ over the primary focus of consequentialist evaluation. Some versions focus on individual actions, other versions focus on rules. So, we can distinguish four main species of consequentialism. Let us explore further.

Utilitarianism has been perhaps the most prominent form of consequentialism, so let us begin with it.

Utilitarianism

Utilitarianism was originally developed and defended by Jeremy Bentham (1748–1832) and later refined by John Stuart Mill (1806–1873).[6] Their basic idea is that it is *human welfare* or *happiness* that alone is intrinsically valuable and that the rightness or wrongness of actions depends entirely on how they affect human welfare or happiness. As a consequentialist theory, utilitarianism requires that one *maximize* welfare where the welfare of *all* individuals who will be affected by some action counts. We can sharpen our characterization of this theory by introducing the technical term "utility," which refers to the *net value* of the consequences of actions. The net value of an act's consequences refers to how much overall welfare or happiness would likely result from an action, taking into account both the short-term and long-term effects of the action on the welfare of all who will be affected. The basic idea is that an action's rightness or wrongness depends both on how much happiness (if any) it would likely produce for each individual affected were it to be performed, as well as how much unhappiness (if any) it would likely produce for each affected person were it to be performed. For each alternative action, then, we can consider the *net balance* of overall happiness versus unhappiness associated with that action. Call this overall net value the **utility** of an action. We can now formulate a generic statement of the basic utilitarian principle—the **principle of utility:**

> **U**   An action is right if and only if (and because) it would (if performed) likely produce at least as high a utility (net overall balance of happiness versus unhappiness) as would any other alternative action one might perform instead.[7]

Notice that the utility of an action might be negative. That is, all things considered, an action may produce a net balance of unhappiness over happiness were it to be performed. Moreover, since U (like all versions of C) is comparative, it may turn out that the right action in some unfortunate circumstance is the one that would likely bring about the least amount of overall negative utility. This would be where *all* of one's options have a negative utility.

As formulated, U leaves open questions about the nature of happiness and unhappiness about which there are different philosophical theories.[8] Bentham and (apparently) Mill held that happiness is entirely constituted by experiences of pleasure and unhappiness by experiences of displeasure or pain. And so their theory of intrinsic value is called **value hedonism;** *only* states of pleasure have positive intrinsic value and *only* states of pain have intrinsic negative value; anything else of value is of mere extrinsic value. So, for instance, for the value hedonist, any positive value that knowledge may have is extrinsic: it is only of positive value when it contributes to bringing about what has intrinsic value, namely pleasure (or the alleviation of pain). It should be noted that a value hedonist need not (and should not) take an excessively narrow view of pleasure and pain; the hedonist can follow Bentham and Mill in holding that in addition to such bodily pleasures of the sort one gets from eating delicious food or having a massage, there are aesthetic and intellectual pleasures such as appreciating a beautifully written poem. Moreover, the value hedonist will recognize not only passive pleasures of the sort just mentioned, but also active pleasures as when one plays a game or is involved in some creative activity. So value hedonism can recognize a broad range of pleasurable experiences that have positive intrinsic value and a broad range of painful experiences that have negative intrinsic value.

If we now combine the principle of utility (U) with value hedonism, we obtain **hedonistic utilitarianism:**

> **HU**   An action is right if and only if (and because) it would likely produce (if performed) at least as high a net balance of pleasure (or less pain) as would any other alternative action one might do instead.

But as I hope my presentation has made clear, one need not accept hedonism as a theory of value in order to be a utilitarian. In fact, many contemporary utilitarians reject value hedonism and accept some other conception of happiness or welfare. But, again, what makes a theory a version of utilitarianism is that the theory accepts the basic consequentialist claim, C, together with the idea that it is human happiness or human well-being that has intrinsic value and is to be promoted in what we do.

Perfectionist Consequentialism

But a consequentialist need not be a utilitarian. She might hold that there are items having intrinsic value other than happiness that are important in determining the rightness or wrongness of action. To illustrate, I have chosen what is called **perfectionist consequentialism**—a species of the generic view that accepts a perfectionist theory of value.[9] According to a **value perfectionist,** it is states of human perfection, including knowledge and achievement that have intrinsic value.[10] One might come to have a great deal of knowledge and achievement in one's life, yet not be happy. So a perfectionist theory of the good is not the same as a happiness theory of the good. We might formulate the basic principle of perfectionist consequentialism as follows:

> **PC**　An action is right if and only if (and because) it would (if performed) likely bring about a greater net balance of perfectionist goods than would any alternative action one might perform instead.

The distinction between utilitarianism and perfectionist consequentialism has to do with differences over what has intrinsic value for purposes of morally evaluating actions. And notice that the consequentialist principles presented thus far refer to particular concrete actions and their consequences, so the views (expressed in principles U, HU, and PC) are versions of **act consequentialism.** However, as mentioned at the outset, another important division within the ranks of consequentialists is between act and rule versions of the view. So let us turn from act versions to rule versions.

Rule Consequentialism

Moral rules—rules, for example, against lying, theft, and killing—are generally thought to be significant in thinking about particular moral issues. The importance of moral rules is emphasized by rule consequentialists. Act consequentialism is the view that the rightness of a particular, concrete action—an actual or possible doing by a person at a time—depends on the value of its consequences. **Rule consequentialism** is the view that the rightness or wrongness of an action depends on whether it is required, permitted, or prohibited by a rule whose consequences are best.[11] So rule consequentialism involves two levels of evaluation: first, rules that require, permit, or prohibit various courses of action are evaluated by reference to the values of their consequences, and second, a particular action is evaluated by determining whether it is required, permitted, or prohibited by a rule whose consequences are best. Let us explore this view a bit further.

The sense in which a rule can have consequences has to do with the fact that were people to accept the rule in question, this would influence what they do. So, we can evaluate a rule by asking what consequences would likely be brought about were it to be generally accepted in society. Call the value associated with rules their **acceptance value.** This idea is familiar. Think of debates in the sporting world about changing the rules of some sport. The focus in such debates is on the likely effects the proposed rule change would have on the game, were it to be accepted.

According to rule consequentialism, then, the morality of a particular action in some situation depends upon the acceptance values of various competing rules that are relevant to the situation in question. We can thus formulate this theory with the following principle of right conduct:

> **RC**   An action is right if and only if (and because) it is permitted by a rule whose associated acceptance value is at least as high as the acceptance value of any other rule applying to the situation.

In order to better understand this principle, let us illustrate its application with a simple example.

Suppose that I have promised to help you move next Friday morning. Friday morning arrives, and many alternative courses of action are open to me. Among them are these:

A1. Keep my promise (and show up at your place),
A2. Break my promise (and do something else).

Corresponding to each of these alternative actions, we have these rules:

R1. Whenever one makes a promise, keep it,
R2. Whenever one makes a promise, break it if one feels like it.

Now consider the acceptance values associated with these rules. I think we can all agree that the acceptance value of R1 is far greater than that of R2. So (ignoring for the moment that there may be other competing rules to be considered in this situation) rule consequentialism implies that one ought to keep one's promise.

Finally notice that act and rule consequentialism may diverge in their moral implications. To stick with the previous example, suppose that breaking my promise and instead hanging out with some friends at the local pool hall will likely produce a greater level of overall intrinsic value than would the backbreaking work of helping you move. Besides, you've lined up plenty of help; I won't be missed that much. Act consequentialism implies that it would be morally permissible to go ahead and break the promise. Rule consequentialism by contrast implies that I am morally obliged to keep my promise.

Brief Summary

Let us pause for a moment to summarize (see Fig. 1.2) what we have covered. As we have seen, the basic consequentialist idea (C) can be developed in a variety of ways; we have considered four versions of this generic approach to ethics.

For now, the main idea to take away from this discussion is that for all varieties of consequentialism, the rightness or wrongness of an action depends entirely on the net intrinsic value of the consequences of either individual actions or rules. Consequentialist theories

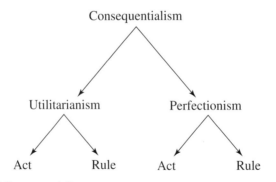

FIGURE 1.2   Some Forms of Consequentialism

(and especially utilitarianism) are often discussed in articles and books about disputed moral issues. Some authors appeal to consequentialism to justify their particular views on some moral issue; other authors will contrast their approach with consequentialism.

Applying consequentialism

To convey a sense of how one is to go about applying consequentialism to a particular moral issue, let us work with act utilitarianism as expressed earlier in U. And to make things fairly manageable, let us consider a rather simple case.

Suppose that I am in charge of inviting a guest philosopher to speak at my university and that I've narrowed the choices to two. On the one hand, I can invite Dr. Brilliant, a very well-known and innovative philosopher but whose manner of presentation is decidedly dull. The philosophy faculty will no doubt take pleasure in his presentation and will benefit intellectually from what he has to say, but others will be bored stiff and get little out of the talk. On the other hand, I can invite Dr. Flash, who is not nearly as accomplished as Dr. Brilliant but who I know is an extremely engaging speaker. Suppose that five professional philosophers and forty-five students are expected to attend the lecture no matter which of these two philosophers I invite.

Now if I apply U to my situation, it would have me invite the speaker whose talk will produce the greatest amount of overall happiness. A careful application of U would require that I consider each person who will be affected by the lecture of Dr. Brilliant and determine how much happiness (if any) that person would experience as a result of this lecture and then determine how much unhappiness (if any) that person would experience as a result of this lecture. Once I have done this calculation for each person, I then calculate how much total happiness the lecture would cause and how much total unhappiness it would cause in order to arrive at the overall net value associated with Dr. Brilliant's lecture. I do the same for Dr. Flash. The lecture I ought to sponsor and hence the philosopher I ought to invite depends on which talk will result in the greatest amount of intrinsic value.

Obviously, to apply U to one's own choices with any precision would require much factual information: information (1) about one's circumstances, (2) about the various alternative actions one might perform in one's particular circumstances, (3) about the individuals who will be affected either negatively or positively were one to perform a particular action, and (4) about the overall amount of happiness or unhappiness, both short term and long term, that would likely result from each of the various alternative actions. Some critics of consequentialism argue that when it comes to satisfying the practical aim of moral theory—the aim of providing practical guidance for arriving at correct or justified verdicts—consequentialism makes implausible demands on what one needs to know in order to apply it to particular cases. Defenders reply that even if *precise* application of this sort of moral theory is not feasible, we can and do make rough estimates of the values of the consequences of various alternative actions, and that in doing so we must realize that the moral verdicts we reach as a result are likely to be highly fallible. But this, say the defenders, is something we just have to live with given our limited information about the effects of our actions.

B. Natural Law Theory

The idea that certain actions or practices are "natural" while others are "unnatural" is commonly offered as a reason why certain "unnatural" actions are wrong and that we ought to do what is natural. Think of popular arguments against homosexuality. This idea of morality being natural is associated with the **natural law theory**.[12]

This type of moral theory is often traced to the thirteenth-century philosopher and theologian St. Thomas Aquinas (1225–1274). It gets its name from the guiding idea that there are objectively true moral principles that are grounded in human nature.[13] Because there are objective facts about human nature that determine what our good consists in, and because moral requirements have to do with maintaining and promoting the human goods, these requirements, unlike the rules of some club or made-up game, are part of the natural order. Because the natural law theory bases right action on considerations of intrinsic value, it is a value-based theory of right conduct, as is consequentialism. However, as we shall see in setting out this theory, natural law theory is opposed to consequentialism—it denies that the *only* considerations that matter when it comes to right action are consequences. So, to understand this theory let us proceed by first presenting its theory of intrinsic value and then presenting its theory of right conduct in two parts: (a) first, the "core" of theory and then (b) the doctrine of double effect.

Theory of Intrinsic Value[14]

According to Aquinas's version of natural law theory, there are four basic intrinsic goods:

- Human life
- Human procreation (which includes raising children)
- Human knowledge
- Human sociability (this value has to do with associations and bonds with others, including friendship, social organizations, and political organizations)

Each of these items, then, has intrinsic value and its destruction is intrinsically bad or evil. These four values are the basis for the core of natural law theory.

The Core

We can state the basic principle of natural law theory roughly as follows:

> **NLT**   An action is right if and only if (and because) in performing the action one does not directly violate any of the basic values.

Thus, killing a human being (with some exceptions explained later) is morally wrong. If we suppose, as many natural law theorists do, that the use of contraceptives thwarts human procreation, then their use is morally wrong. Interfering with the good of knowledge by distorting information or by lying is morally wrong. Destroying legitimate social bonds through the advocacy of anarchy is morally wrong.

But what about hard cases in which no matter what one does, one will violate at least one of the basic values and thus bring about evil through whichever action one chooses? Let us consider a much discussed case involving abortion. Suppose that a pregnant woman has cancer of the uterus and must have a hysterectomy (removal of her uterus) to save her life. Human life is one of the intrinsic goods, so having the operation will have at least one good effect. But suppose (just for the sake of the example) that from conception the fetus counts as a human life and so having the hysterectomy would bring about the death of the unborn human life. This effect, because it involves the destruction of something having intrinsic value—human life—is an evil. And let us suppose that this moral dilemma is unavoidable in this case because there is no way to save the woman's life while also preserving the life of her fetus. How does the natural law theory deal with this kind of case? After all, the core of the theory seems to say that any action that violates one or more of the basic goods is wrong, period. But if it really does say this, then we have to conclude that her having the operation is wrong, but also her not having the operation is wrong (because she will fail to preserve her own life). How can natural law theory deal with this moral dilemma?

If we go back and inspect the basic principle of natural law theory, NLT, we notice that what it prohibits are actions that *directly* violate one or more of the basic goods, thereby bringing about evil. But what counts as a direct violation? Can there be morally permissible "indirect" violations? These questions bring us to the next major component of natural law ethics—the doctrine of double effect.

The Doctrine of Double Effect

In addition to the core principle (NLT), the natural law theory also embraces the following set of provisions that compose the **doctrine of double effect**. It is so named because it concerns cases in which performing an action would have at least one good effect and one bad effect, where good and bad have to do with the theory's list of intrinsic goods. So this doctrine is meant to address the question of whether it is ever morally permissible to knowingly bring about bad or evil consequences where one's aim in action is to bring about or preserve one or more of the basic human goods. Here, then, is a statement of the various provisions making up the doctrine:

> **DDE** An action that would bring about at least one evil effect and at least one good effect is morally permissible if (and only if) the following conditions are satisfied:

> *Intrinsic permissibility:* The action in question, apart from its effects, is morally permissible;
> *Necessity:* It is not possible to bring about the good effect except by performing an action that will bring about the evil effect in question;
> *Nonintentionality:* The evil effect is not intended—it is neither one's end nor a chosen means for bringing about some intended end;
> *Proportionality:* The evil that will be brought about by the action is not out of proportion to the good being aimed at.

What this principle does is help define the idea of a direct violation of a human good which is the central idea in the core principle, NLT. We shall return to this point in a moment. For the time being, let us explain DDE by showing how it would apply to the case just described.

In applying DDE to our moral dilemma, we must ask whether all four of the doctrine's provisions are satisfied. Let us take them in order. (1) First, since having a hysterectomy is not an intrinsically wrong action, the first requirement is satisfied. (2) Furthermore, given my description of the case, the second requirement of DDE is met because having a hysterectomy is the *only* way to save her life. Were there some other operation or some medication that would both save the woman's life and preserve the life of the fetus, then the necessity condition would not be met and the hysterectomy would be wrong. But we are supposing that there are no such options in this case.

(3) The third requirement rests on the distinction between effects that one intends in action and effects that may be foreseen but are unintended. One intends some consequence or effect when either it is something one is aiming to bring about (an end) or it is one's chosen means for bringing about some desired end. Here is a simple, everyday example. I fire a rifle in order to hit the paper target, but in so doing I know that the noise from the rifle will frighten nearby wildlife. But even though I can foresee that my act of pulling the trigger will frighten those animals, this effect is not intended: it is not my purpose. My purpose is to hit the target, and their being frightened is not a means for achieving my end—the means is taking aim and firing. So the effect of my act of firing—frightening those animals—is not something I intend, rather it is a foreseen but unintended side effect of what I do.

Returning now to our example, we find that this third provision is satisfied because although the death of the unborn child is a foreseen effect of the hysterectomy, its death is not her chief aim or end (saving her own life). Moreover, it is not a means by which her life will be saved. After all, were she not pregnant, she would still have the operation to save her life, and so the death of the unborn is a mere unintended and unfortunate side effect of the operation. Removing the cancer is what will save her life.

(4) Finally, the evil that will result from the operation (loss of one innocent human life) is not grossly out of proportion to the good that will result (saving an innocent human life). (When DDE is applied to the morality of war activities, considerations of proportionality of evil to good become especially relevant. See the introduction to chapter 13 and the article in that chapter by Andrew Valls.)

Having explained the DDE, we can now return to the core principle, NLT, and explain how these two elements are related in natural law ethics. The idea is that, according to NLT, we are not to *directly* violate any of the basic human goods. The DDE helps define what counts as a direct violation: direct violations are those that cannot be justified by the doctrine of double effect.

Before going on, it will be useful to pause for a moment to compare the natural law theory with consequentialism. In response to our moral dilemma involving the hysterectomy, an act consequentialist will say that we should consider the value of the consequences of the alternative actions (having a hysterectomy or refraining from this operation) and choose the action with the best consequences. In short, for the act consequentialist good results justify the means. But not for the natural law theorist, because on her theory one may not act in direct violation of the basic goods even if by doing so one would produce better consequences. Good ends do not always justify an action that is a means to those ends. For instance, I am not permitted to intentionally kill one innocent human being (do evil) even if by doing so I can save five others (bring about good). To see how consequentialism and natural law theory yield different verdicts about a difficult moral case, consider the case of a woman who is pregnant, but this time she is suffering from a "tubal" pregnancy, which means that her fetus is lodged in her fallopian tube and thus has not implanted itself into the uterine wall. If nothing is done, both fetus and woman will die. The only thing that can be done to save the woman is to remove the fetus, which will bring about its death. Exercise: Apply act consequentialism and the natural law theory to this case to see whether they differ in their moral implications.

Applying Natural Law Theory

In applying the natural law theory to some case in order to determine whether a particular course of action is morally right, one begins with the core principle, NLT, and asks whether the action in question would violate any of the basic goods. If not, then the action is not wrong. But if it would violate one or more of the basic goods, then one has to determine whether the action would constitute a *direct* violation. And to do that, one makes use of the DDE. If the action satisfies all four provisions of DDE, then the violation is not direct and the action is morally permissible. If the action does not pass DDE, then the action involves a direct violation of one or more of the intrinsic goods and is, therefore, wrong.

Of course, as with all moral theories, applying the natural law theory is not a mechanical process. For one thing, one must address questions about the proper interpretation of the four basic human goods. Surely coming to have knowledge of the basic laws that govern the physical universe is intrinsically valuable, if any knowledge is. But what if, for example, I spend my time counting the number of needles on a cactus plant for no particular reason. Is the knowledge I acquire about the number of needles really of any intrinsic value? One can raise similar questions about the other three basic human goods. Furthermore, applying the doctrine of double effect raises questions of interpretation. For instance, the proportionality provision requires that the evil caused by an action not be "out of proportion" to the good effects of that action. But, of course, determining when things are out of proportion requires sensitivity to particular cases and the use of good judgment.

These points about interpretation are not meant as a criticism of natural law theory; rather they call attention to the fact that applying it to particular moral issues requires that we interpret its various elements. As we shall see, a similar point applies to Kantian moral theory.

C. Kantian Moral Theory

Most everyone has come across moral arguments that appeal to the **golden rule:** do unto others as you would have them do unto you. This rule encapsulates a kind of test for thinking about the morality of actions: it asks the individual making a moral choice that will affect others to consider how one would like it were one on the receiving end of the action in question. In the case of Thomas Youk with which we began the chapter, the golden rule would have Kevorkian consider what he would want done to (or for) him were he in Youk's situation. Various objections have been made to the golden rule—for instance, it suggests that the rightness or wrongness of an action depends simply on what one does or would desire. But people can have crazy desires. A masochist who inflicts pain on others might cheerfully say that he would have others do unto him as he is doing to them. Do we want to conclude that his causing others pain is morally right? Perhaps there is some interpretation of the golden rule that does not yield the wrong result in the case of the masochist or other examples that have been used against it. Nevertheless, there is something about the *spirit* of the golden rule that seems right. The idea suggested by this rule is that morality requires that we not treat people unfairly, that we respect other persons by taking them into account in our moral deliberations. This suggestion is quite vague but finds one articulation in Kantian moral theory to which we now turn.

Kantian moral theory derives from the moral writings of the German philosopher Immanuel Kant (1724–1804), which continue to have an enormous influence on contemporary ethics.[15] Central to Kant's moral theory is the idea that moral requirements can be expressed as commands or imperatives that categorically bid us to perform certain actions—requirements that apply to us regardless of what we might happen to want or desire, or how such actions bear on the production of our own happiness. Kant thought that specific moral requirements could be derived from a fundamental moral principle that he called the **categorical imperative.** Moreover, Kant offered various alternative formulations of his fundamental moral principle. The two I will consider are the ones that are most often applied to moral issues.

The Humanity Formulation

One of Kant's formulations of his categorical imperative is called the **Humanity formulation:**

> **H**   An action is right if and only if (and because) the action treats persons (including oneself) as ends in themselves and not merely as a means.

Obviously, to make use of this principle, we need to know what it means to treat someone as an end and what it means to treat someone merely as a means. Space does not permit a thorough discussion of these ideas, so a few illustrations will have to suffice.[16]

Deception and coercion are two ways in which one can treat another person merely as a means—as an object to be manipulated. Deceiving someone in order to get him or her to do something he or she would otherwise not agree to do constitutes using the person as though that person were a mere instrument at one's disposal for promoting one's own ends. Again, many cases of coercing someone by threats involve attempting to manipulate that person for one's own purposes and hence constitute an attempt to use him or her merely as a means to one's own ends.

But Kant's Humanity formulation requires not only that we not treat others merely as means to our own ends (a negative requirement), but also that we treat them as ends in themselves (a positive requirement). For Kant, to say that persons are ends in themselves is to say that they have a special worth or value that demands of us that we have a certain positive regard for them. Kant refers to this special worth as *dignity.*[17] So, for instance, if I fail to help those who need and deserve my help, I don't treat them merely as means, but I do fail to have a positive regard for their welfare and thus fail to properly recognize their worth as persons.

Applying Kant's Humanity Formulation

As just explained, applying the Humanity formulation requires consideration of the dual requirements that we not treat people merely as means and that we also not fail to treat them as ends in themselves—as individuals who have dignity. Interpreting these requirements is where the hard work comes in. What are the boundaries when it comes to treating people *merely* as a means? If, in walking by, I see that you are wearing a watch and ask you for the time, I am using you as a means for finding out what time it is, but I am not thereby using you *merely* as a means to my own ends. We have noted that deception and coercion represent main ways in which one might use someone merely as a means, as something to be manipulated. So we have a good start on interpreting the idea of such treatment. Here is not the place to consider other ways in which our actions might involve treating someone this way. Rather, the point I wish to make is that we have some idea of what it means to treat someone merely as a means, and we must build on this understanding to apply the Humanity formulation to a range of moral issues.

Similar remarks apply to the requirement that we positively treat others as ends in themselves. Here it is interesting to note that Kant argued that in satisfying this requirement, we are obligated to adopt two very general goals—the goal of promoting the (morally permissible) ends of others and the goal of self-perfection. Such wide-open goals allow a person much latitude in deciding in what ways and on what occasions to promote the ends of others and one's own self-perfection. For Kant, then, applying the positive requirement embedded in H is a matter of figuring out how best to integrate the promotion of the well-being of others and one's own self-perfection into a moral life.

The Universal Law Formulation

Kant's other main formulation of the categorical imperative, the **Universal Law formulation**, expresses a test whereby we can determine whether our actions are right or wrong.

> **UL** An action is right if and only if one can both (a) consistently conceive of everyone adopting and acting on the general policy (that is, the maxim) of one's action, and also (b) consistently will that everyone act on that maxim.[18]

This formulation will remind readers of the golden rule, though notice that UL does not refer to an agent's wants; rather it represents a kind of consistency test.[19] Unfortunately, interpreting Kant's two-part test requires some explanation. So let me say a bit more about UL and then, using some of Kant's own examples, show how it can be applied.

According to Kant, when we act, we act on a general policy that is called a "maxim." To determine the morality of an action, one formulates the general policy of one's action and asks whether one could consistently both conceive of and will that everyone act on the same policy. To put it in Kant's terms, one asks whether one could consistently conceive and will that the maxim of one's action become a "universal law" governing everyone's behavior. If so, then the action is right; if not, then the action is wrong. So UL expresses a two-part test one can use to determine the rightness or wrongness of actions. To make Kant's tests more concrete, let us consider a few of Kant's own sample applications of UL.

One of Kant's examples involves making a lying promise—that is, a promise that one has no intention of keeping. Consider a case in which I desperately need money right away and the only way I can get it is by getting a loan which I must promise to repay. I know, however, that I won't be able to repay the loan. The maxim corresponding to the action I am considering is:

> **M1** Whenever I need money and can get it only by making a lying promise, I will borrow the money by making a lying promise.

Kant's principle, UL, would have me test the morality of making a lying promise by asking whether I could *consistently conceive* and *will* that everyone act on M1—that everyone who needs money in such circumstances as mine make a lying promise. Let us first ask whether this is something I can consistently conceive. If it isn't, then I certainly can't consistently will that everyone adopt and act on it.

Kant claims that when I think through what would be involved in everyone acting on M1, I realize that I cannot even consistently conceive of a world in which everyone in need of money successfully makes lying promises. After all, a world in which everyone in need of money goes around trying to get the money by making a lying promise is one in which successful promising becomes impossible since, as Kant observes, "no one would believe what was promised him but would laugh at all such expressions as vain pretenses."[20] Thus, trying to even conceive of a world in which everyone in need of money acts on M1 involves an inconsistency: it is a world in which (1) *everyone* in need gets money by making a lying promise; but because of the breakdown in the institution of promising that would result, it is a world in which (2) *not everyone* in need gets money by making a lying promise for the reason Kant gives. But if I can't consistently conceive of everyone acting on M1, then my maxim fails the first test mentioned in UL. And if I can't consistently conceive that everyone act on M1, this shows me that, in making a lying promise, I am acting on an immoral policy and that my action is wrong.

But why is the fact that one cannot consistently conceive that everyone act on one's maxim an indication that the action in question is wrong? Kant's idea here seems to be that in performing an action whose maxim I cannot consistently conceive everyone adopting, I am, in effect, proposing to make an exception of myself—an exception that I cannot justify. In making an exception of myself, I am failing to respect others because I'm taking advantage of the fact that many others do not make lying promises. And so these reflections lead us to conclude that making a lying promise is morally wrong.

Here is another example Kant uses to illustrate the application of UL that has to do with clause (b) of UL. Suppose I am in a position to help someone in need but would rather not be bothered. The maxim Kant has us consider is:

M2   Whenever I am able to help others in need, I will refrain from helping them.

Using UL, I am to consider whether I can consistently conceive of a world in which everyone adopts and acts on this maxim. Is such a world conceivable? It would seem so. Granted, a world in which people in need did not receive help from others would be a very unpleasant place. Perhaps the human race would not survive in such a world. But we can certainly conceive of a world in which the human race ceases to exist. So, M2 passes the first part of Kant's UL test.

But can one *will* that M2 be adopted and acted upon by everyone? Upon reflection I realize that if I will that everyone adopt and act on M2, I am thereby willing that others refuse to help me when I am in need. But willing that others refuse to help me is inconsistent with the fact that as a rational agent I do will that others help me when I am in need. That is, as a rational agent, I embrace the following maxim:

RM   I will that others who are able to do so help me when I am in need.

But an implication of my willing that everyone adopt and act on M2 would be:

IM   I will that others who are able to help me refuse to do so when I am in need.

RM is inconsistent with IM—and IM is an implication of willing that everyone adopt and act on M2. Thus, I cannot consistently will that everyone adopt and act on M2. Since I cannot consistently will that everyone adopt M2, then according to clause (b) of Kant's UL, my action of refusing to help others in need is morally wrong.

What is the point of Kant's UL formulation involving two tests? Kant thought that these two tests could distinguish between what he called "narrow" or "perfect" duty and "wide" or "imperfect" duty: maxims that one cannot consistently conceive as adopted and acted on by everyone involve actions that are contrary to narrow duty, whereas those that can be so conceived but which one cannot consistently will involve actions that are contrary to wide duty. The realm of narrow duty concerns those actions and omissions regarding which one has comparatively little room for when and how one complies with the duty. If I have promised to do something for you on a particular occasion—drive you to the airport—then to fulfill my obligation I must perform some rather specific action (driving you) at a certain time. By contrast, a wide duty is one which can be fulfilled in a variety of ways and situations, giving one much leeway in how and when to fulfill the duty. Duties of charity—helping others—are like this.

It is important to notice that in his examples, Kant is not arguing that if everyone went around making lying promises the consequences would be bad and therefore making a lying promise is wrong. Again, he does not argue that the consequences of everyone refusing to help others in need would be bad and therefore refusing help to others is wrong. Such ways of arguing are characteristic of consequentialism, but Kant rejects consequentialism. He has us consider the implications of everyone acting on the general policy behind one's own action because he thinks doing so is a way of revealing any inconsistencies in what one wills, which in turn indicates whether an action fails to respect persons. So the test involved in the categorical imperative is meant to reveal whether one's action shows a proper respect for persons.

Applying the Universal Law Formulation

Since this formulation expresses tests for determining the rightness or wrongness of actions, I have been illustrating how it is to be applied in thinking through moral issues. If we step back from these illustrations, we can summarize the basic procedure to be followed. In applying UL to some actual or contemplated action of yours, here are the basic steps to follow:

- Formulate the maxim on which you are proposing to act, which will have the form "I will ____ whenever ____," where the blanks are filled with a description of your action and circumstances, respectively.
- Next, you consider the possibility of everyone in your circumstances adopting and acting on that same maxim. In particular, you ask yourself whether you can consistently *conceive* of a world in which everyone adopts and acts on the maxim in question. This is the test expressed in clause (a) of UL.
- If you cannot even conceive of such a world, then action on the maxim is morally wrong—a violation of narrow duty. The lying promise example illustrates this result.
- If you can consistently conceive of a world in which everyone adopts and acts on the maxim, then you are to ask yourself whether you could, even so, consistently will that everyone adopt and act on the maxim. This is the test expressed in clause (b) of UL.
- If you cannot consistently will that everyone adopt and act on that maxim, then action on the maxim is wrong—a violation of wide duty. The case of refusing to help others illustrates this result.
- Finally, if your maxim is such that you can both consistently conceive of a world in which everyone adopts and acts on your maxim and consistently will this to be the case—if the maxim passes both tests—then action on the maxim is morally right.

The two main challenges for anyone applying the UL formulation to a particular issue is to correctly formulate one's maxim and then carefully think through Kant's two consistency tests.

How are the two formulations of the categorical imperative—H and UL—related? They are supposed to be alternative formulations of the same basic principle, rather than two entirely distinct principles. One way to see how this might be so is to notice that in cases in which I cannot consistently conceive or will that my maxim be adopted by everyone, I am making an exception of myself, and in doing so either I am treating someone merely as a means or I am failing to treat others as ends in themselves. And, of course, treating others merely as means and failing to treat them as ends in themselves is precisely what the Humanity formulation rules out.

D. Rights-Based Moral Theory

In our brief survey of moral theories up to this point, we have seen how those theories attempt to give accounts of the nature of right (and wrong) action, where "right" is being used in its adjectival sense. Nothing so far has been said about the notion of *a right* or *rights*. However, in moral theory we distinguish between the adjectival use of "right" as in *right action* and its use as a noun as in *a right to life*. One can hold that actions may or may not be right—actions that are either permissible or impermissible to do—without also holding that there are things called rights. Perhaps the most basic idea of a **right** is that of an *entitlement* to be free to engage in some activity, to exercise a certain power, or to be provided with some benefit. One's having such an entitlement typically imposes duties on others (including governments) either to refrain from interfering with one's freedom (or exercise of power) or to provide one with some benefit, depending on the right in question. In explaining the idea of a right and how it figures both in moral theory and in moral controversies, it will be useful to briefly discuss the following topics: (1) some basic elements of a right, (2) categories of rights, (3) rights and moral theory, (4) the idea of a rights-based moral theory, (5) the application of rights-based theories in practice, and (6) so-called rights-focused approaches to moral issues.[21]

Rights: Some Basic Elements

A right has the following characteristics. First, there is the **rights holder**, the party who has or "holds" the right. If you own property, then as a property owner you hold a property right. A rights holder may be an individual or a group. Minority rights are one type of group rights. One of the most important philosophical questions about rights concerns the *scope* of rights holders—those beings that *have* rights. According to some views that would restrict the scope of rights holders, only those creatures that have a developed capacity to reason can be the holders of rights. Less restrictive views would allow that anything having interests, including certain nonhuman animals, can be rights holders. Among those who approach moral issues from the perspective of rights—including the issues of abortion, animals, and the environment—we find important differences in views about the requirements for holding rights and thus differences in views about the scope of rights holders.

A second element of a right is what we might call the **rights addressee**, that is, the individual or group with regard to whom the rights holder is entitled to certain treatment. If I have entered into a contract with you to provide you a service, then I am the addressee of your right; you are entitled to demand that I provide that service. The relationship between a rights holder and the corresponding rights addressee can most often be understood in terms of the idea of a *claim*. For instance, in light of a rights holder being entitled to certain treatment by others, we may say that the former has a valid *claim* on the behavior of the latter. And so, corresponding to a rights holder's claim, the addressee of a right has an obligation or duty to either perform or refrain from performing actions that would affect the rights holder and the treatment to which he or she is entitled. Thus, at least for most rights, there is a correlation between the rights of rights holders and certain duties on the part of addressees.

A third element is the **content** of a right, which refers to whatever action, states, or objects the right concerns. The right to freedom of expression differs in content from the right to life. And, of course, these rights differ in content from property rights, and so on.

Finally, another dimension of rights is that of **strength**. Think of a right as a claim on others that has a certain degree of strength in the sense that the stronger right, the stronger the justification needed to defeat the right in question. For instance, some hold the view that nonhuman animals as well as human beings have a right to life. Suppose this is correct. It may still be the case that the right to life of a human being is stronger than the right to life of, say, a dog or cat. The difference in strength here would be reflected, for example, by the fact that one would be arguably justified in euthanizing a dog or cat if the animal were no longer able to walk, while this same sort of reason would not be strong enough to euthanize a human being.

Related to the fact that rights come in degrees of strength is the fact that in some situations someone might be morally justified in performing an action that "goes against" another person's right. And when this occurs, let us say that the person's right has been infringed. So, for instance, suppose my property rights involve the claim that no one may enter my house and use my property without my consent. Now suppose that my next door neighbor's child has been seriously hurt and needs immediate medical attention, and so calling an ambulance is in order. Suppose also that the closest phone available to my neighbor is the one in my house, but I am not at home. Were the neighbor to break into my house to use my phone, he or she would be infringing upon my property rights. But assuming that the neighbor is morally justified in doing this, we may call this case of "going against" my right, a **rights infringement**. By contrast, **rights violations** involve cases where someone goes against another person's rights but is not morally justified in doing so. Thus, as we are using these terms, rights infringements involve actions that are not morally wrong given the circumstances, while rights violations involve actions that are morally wrong.

Categories of Rights

It is common to recognize both negative and positive rights. A **negative right** is an entitlement of noninterference and thus involves a claim by the rights holder that others refrain from interfering with her engaging in some activity. Because such rights require that others *not* act in certain ways, they impose what are called negative duties. Rights that are correlated with negative duties are called negative rights. A right to certain liberties such as free speech is an example of a negative right—a right that imposes a duty on others not to interfere with one's expressing one's ideas. A **positive right**, by contrast, involves the rights holder being entitled to something and thus having a valid claim that some other party do or provide something (some service or some good) to that rights holder. Because the duty in question requires positive action on the part of the addressee, the corresponding right is called a positive right. For instance, Article 25 of the United Nations 1948 *Universal Declaration of Human Rights* states:

> Everyone has a right to a standard of living adequate for the health and well-being of himself and of his family, including food, clothing, housing, and medical care and necessary social services, and the right to security in the event of unemployment, sickness, disability, widowhood, old age, or other lack of livelihood in circumstances beyond his control.

This (alleged) right is supposed to be held by all human beings and presumably it is a right that one be provided certain necessities by one's nation or perhaps other nations in a position to provide such goods.

In addition to the distinction between negative and positive rights, it is also important to distinguish **moral rights** from legal rights. This distinction has to do with the source of a right. A so-called moral right is a right that a being has independently of any legal system or other set of conventions.[22] So, for instance, it is often claimed that all human beings, in virtue of facts about humanity, have certain rights, including the rights to life, liberty, and well-being. Such alleged universal rights of humanity[23] are typically referred to as **human rights**. A **legal right** is something that comes into existence as the result of a legal statute or some other form of governmental activity. One reason it is important to distinguish moral from legal rights is that controversies over moral issues are often framed in terms of whether some individual (including nonhumans) or group has certain moral rights—rights that may or may not be recognized by some particular legal system and thus do not (at the time in question) count as legal rights within the system in question. So, in debates over the morality of various activities and practices where talk of rights enter the discussion, one is mainly concerned with moral rights.

Another common distinction, often associated with human rights, is the distinction between "basic" and "nonbasic" rights. Roughly speaking, a **basic right** is a universal right that is especially important in the lives of individuals. These include the rights to life and to liberty, which arguably must be met in order to live a decent life. One's right to life and freedom from torture is clearly more important compared with one's right to be repaid a sum of money by a borrower. Just how to distinguish basic from nonbasic rights is controversial, and we need not examine various proposals here. It is enough for our purposes to leave the distinction at a more or less intuitive level and recognize that rights differ in their importance and thus in their comparative strengths.

Let us now turn from our general discussion of rights to their place in moral theory and in contemporary debates over particular moral issues.

Rights and Moral Theory

A great deal of contemporary discussion about moral issues is couched in terms of rights. Does a human fetus have a moral right to life? Does a terminally ill patient in severe pain have a moral right to die? Do people have a moral right to reproduce by cloning? Do animals have moral rights? In this subsection and the next, I explain how rights figure in moral theories. In doing so, I will make two main points: (1) All of the moral theories we have already surveyed (as well as the two that follow) can recognize moral rights. (2) However, what is distinctive of a rights-based moral theory is that it takes rights to be in some sense more basic than such notions as value (including utility), dignity, and right action (including duty). Let us take these points one by one.

First, a utilitarian who recognizes moral rights will attempt to explain rights on the basis of utility by claiming that a moral right is a kind of entitlement that imposes various claims on addressees justified by the fact that its recognition will contribute to the maximization of overall welfare. This means that for the utilitarian—who, as a consequentialist, embraces a value-based moral theory—rights are derivative rather than basic in her moral theory. Similar remarks apply to the moral theories featured in this chapter. For instance, according to Kantian ethics, all human beings possess moral rights in virtue of having a certain status—being the sort of creature that possesses dignity. Having this sort of status, according to the Kantian, demands that persons be treated in certain ways and thus that they enjoy certain moral rights. Thus, utilitarians and Kantians can agree that persons have moral rights. They disagree in how they explain the basis of such rights. And notice that because utilitarians and Kantians purport to explain moral rights in terms of more basic elements—utility in the case of utilitarianism, the possession of dignity in the case of Kantians—it would be incorrect to think of these theories as rights-*based*.

Rights-Based Moral Theory

Might there be a **rights-based moral theory**—a moral theory according to which rights are more basic than utility, dignity, and even duty? Unlike the other theories featured in this chapter, rights-based theories are relatively underdeveloped despite the fact that appeals to rights are very common in discussions of moral issues. What we find in the writings of authors who appeal to rights in discussing particular moral issues is that they often fail to indicate the nature of rights—whether they have a consequentialist, natural law, Kantian, or some other basis on one hand, or whether, on the other hand, they are conceived as basic in the theory. So let us consider the idea of a rights-*based* moral theory.

According to such a theory, rights are even more basic than right action and duty. But one might think that duties must be more basic than rights and so there cannot be a rights-based moral theory. After all, as explained above, a typical moral right is a claim one party has against others that they do or refrain from some activity, and it is natural to think of these burdens as duties or obligations that are owed to the rights-holder. If I have a right to free speech, then this seems to entail that others have a duty not to interfere with me in certain ways and thus that the concept of duty must be used to explain what a right is. If so, then duty is more basic than a right and so a rights-based theory is conceptually impossible.

Granted, it is common to explain the idea of a moral right of one party in terms of certain corresponding duties on the part of others. But as J. L. Mackie, a defender of rights-based moral theory explains, instead of thinking of rights in terms of duties, "we could look at it the other way round: what is primary is A's having this right in a sense indicated by the pre-scription 'Let A be able to do X if he chooses,' and the duty of others not to interfere follows from this."[24]

So let us follow Mackie and suppose that there is no conceptual barrier to there being a rights-based theory of right and wrong action. How might it be developed? The idea would be to begin with a list of moral rights, perhaps distinguishing such basic rights, including for instance the rights to life and to liberty, from nonbasic rights. Once one has identified the various moral rights, one could then proceed to define or characterize the concepts of right and wrong action in terms of moral rights. Here, then, is how one might express the basic idea of right conduct for a rights-based theory:

> R   An action is right if and only if (and because) in performing it either (a) one does not violate the moral rights of others, or (b) in cases where it is not possible to respect all such rights because they are in conflict, one's action is among the best ways to protect the most important rights in the case at hand.

This principle—it is more of a *scheme*—all by itself is too abstract to be of any practical use. What needs to be added, of course, is a specification of the moral rights that figure in this scheme and their relative importance. Mackie proposes a single basic moral right: the right of persons to "choose how they shall live."[25] But this right to choose is wide open, and to work our way from it to specific moral obligations, we will need to specify what sorts of more specific rights people have in virtue of having this most basic right. Perhaps we can begin by recognizing the Jeffersonian moral rights to life, liberty, and the pursuit of happiness. And then, for each of these general rights, we might specify them further by recognizing a set of specific moral rights including, for example, a right to free speech.

So, specifying a single basic and perhaps very general moral right (or set of them) and working toward a specification of more specific moral rights is one task of a rights-based moral theory. However one works out the details of what the moral rights are, we must keep in mind the obvious fact that in some contexts moral rights will come into conflict. My right of free speech may conflict with the rights that others have to be safe from harm. Suppose, for instance, that on some occasion, my speaking out would seriously jeopardize the personal safety of others. If so, then in such circumstances, it is plausible to suppose that people's right of personal safety overrides a person's right to free speech. How is one to determine whether one right overrides another in cases of conflict? This question brings us to the issue of applying a rights-based theory to moral issues.

Applying a Rights-Based Moral Theory

Principle (or scheme) R purports to explain an action's being morally right (and by implication morally wrong) in terms of respecting fundamental moral rights. Clause (a) of R covers the easy case in which one's action simply does not come into contact with the moral rights of others. I get up in the morning and decide to eat Cheerios for breakfast. Unusual cases aside, this action has nothing to do with the moral rights of others—I'm morally free to eat the Cheerios or not. Clause (b), however, is where a rights-based approach to moral problems is most relevant: one can frame many of the disputed moral issues featured in this book as a conflict of rights: right to life versus right to choice; right to express oneself in speech and writing versus right to public safety, and so on.

So in applying R (supplemented with a theory of rights) to moral issues, the challenge is to find the best way of properly balancing competing rights claims in arriving at a moral verdict about what ought to be done. As I will explain more thoroughly below in connection with the ethics of prima facie duty, it is very doubtful that there is some fixed mechanical procedure that one can use in arriving at a correct or justified moral verdict in particular cases based on a consideration of competing rights. Rather, what one needs is what philosophers call **moral judgment**. This is to be understood as an acquired skill at discerning what matters the most morally and coming to an all-things-considered moral verdict where this skill cannot be entirely captured by a set of rules. The point to stress here is that, as with the other moral theories we are considering, applying a moral theory—its principles—to particular issues is not a mechanical process. But this does not take away from the value of such theories in guiding one's moral deliberations and subsequent choices.

Rights-Focused Approaches to Moral Issues

We have noted that talk of rights is very common in moral thought and discussion. However, we have also noted that in thinking about a moral issue in terms of competing rights claims, one need not accept a rights-based moral theory as just described. As noted earlier, consequentialists, Kantians, and natural law theorists can and do recognize rights—although on these theories rights are not what is basic in the theory. So, because one may appeal to rights in discussing a moral issue without accepting a rights-based moral theory, we must recognize what we may call **rights-focused approaches** to moral issues. To say that an author's approach to a moral issue is rights-focused is simply to say that the author appeals to rights as a basis for taking a stand on the issue at hand—the author may or may not also embrace a rights-based moral theory. In my article introductions, I have chosen to use the term "rights-focused" in summarizing the views of those authors who appeal primarily to rights in their article, unless the author makes it clear that he or she embraces a rights-based moral theory.

E. Virtue Ethics

Sometimes our moral thinking is dominated by thoughts about what sort of person one would be if one were to perform some action. The thought of living up to certain ideals or virtues of what a morally good person is like is crucial here. Being an unselfish person is an ideal that we may use in evaluating some course of action, and sometimes we may think, "Not helping her would be selfish on my part, so I'm going to help." When our moral thinking takes this turn, we are evaluating actions in terms of virtue and vice. The ideas of virtue and vice have played a negligible role in the moral theories we have surveyed (at least as I have presented them).[26] However, inspired primarily by the ethical views of the ancient Greek philosophers Plato and Aristotle, **virtue ethics** makes the concepts of virtue and vice central in moral theory. Such theories, as I will understand them, take the concepts of virtue and vice to be more basic than the concepts of right and wrong, and thus propose to define or characterize the latter in terms of the former.[27]

One might characterize right and wrong in terms of virtue and vice in different ways, but here (roughly) is how Rosalind Hursthouse, whose article on abortion is included in chapter 10, formulates a virtue ethical principle of right action:

> **VE**   An action is right if and only if (and because) it is what a virtuous agent (acting in character) would not avoid doing in the circumstances under consideration.

How are we to understand the concept of a virtuous agent featured in this principle? One straightforward way is to say that the virtuous agent is one who has the virtues. But what is a virtue? And which ones does the virtuous agent have?

A **virtue** is a trait of character or mind that typically involves dispositions to act, feel, and think in certain ways and that is central in the *positive* evaluation of persons. Honesty and loyalty are two commonly recognized virtues. The trait of honesty, for instance, involves at a minimum being disposed to tell the truth and avoid lying, as well as the disposition to have certain feelings about truth telling (positive ones) and about lying (negative ones). Honesty, as a virtue, is a trait that has positive value and contributes to what makes someone a good person. In contrast to a virtue, a **vice** is a trait of character or mind which typically involves dispositions to act, feel, and think in certain ways, and that is central in the *negative* evaluation of persons. So, for instance, opposed to the virtue of honesty is the vice of dishonesty, which may be understood as having inappropriate dispositions of action and feeling regarding truth telling and lying. Furthermore, as a vice, dishonesty has negative value and contributes to what makes someone a morally bad person. So, in general, virtues and vices are character traits that are manifested in having certain dispositions to act and feel in certain ways and that bear on what makes a person morally good or bad. Here, then, is a short (and by no means complete) list of fairly commonly recognized moral virtues and their corresponding vices:[28]

- Honesty/Dishonesty
- Courage/Cowardice
- Justice/Injustice
- Temperance/Intemperance
- Beneficence/Selfishness
- Humility/Arrogance
- Loyalty/Disloyalty
- Gratitude/Ingratitude

Applying Virtue Ethics

To apply VE to a particular case, then, we must first determine which character traits are the virtues that are possessed by the virtuous agent (we may begin with the previous list). We then determine how, on the basis of such traits, this agent would be disposed to act in the circumstances in question. An action that a virtuous agent, acting in character, would not fail to perform in some circumstance is morally required; an action she might or might not do at her discretion is morally optional, and one that she would avoid doing is morally wrong.

Of course, in applying virtue ethics to disputed moral issues, we encounter the fact that more than one virtue is relevant to the case at hand and that one of them—say, honesty—favors telling the truth, whereas one of the others—say, loyalty—favors telling a lie. In such cases of conflict among the virtues, we must examine the particular details of the case at hand and ask such questions as, "What is at stake here?" "How important is telling the truth in this case?" "How important is loyalty to an organization?" It is only by examining the details of such cases of conflict that we can come to an all-things-considered moral evaluation of some particular action based on considerations of virtue. This point is reflected in VE's reference to a virtuous agent *acting in character.* Presumably, such an ideal agent has the sort of practical wisdom or judgment that is required in order for her to discern which virtue consideration, from among the competing virtue considerations in a particular case, has the most weight. As I have been noting all along in presenting the various moral theories—something that we explore a bit further in the next subsection—the application of moral theories to particular issues requires moral judgment.

F. Ethics of Prima Facie Duty

Whereas consequentialism, for instance, features a single moral principle of right conduct, what I am calling the **ethics of prima facie duty** features a plurality of basic moral principles of right conduct. The most famous version of this kind of view was developed by the twentieth-century British philosopher W. D. Ross (1877–1971). To understand the elements of Ross's view, we need to do the following: (1) explain what he means by talk of "prima facie duty"; (2) present his basic principles of prima facie duty; and then (3) explain the role of moral judgment in applying them in practice.

The Concept of a Prima Facie Duty

To say that one has a **prima facie duty** to perform some action is to say that one has *some* moral reason to perform the action, but the reason in question might be *overridden* by some other moral reason that favors not performing the action. The best way to understand the concept is with an example. Suppose I have promised to pick you up on Saturday by 10:00 A.M. so that you can get to a very important job interview (your car is in the shop). Ross would say that because of my having made a promise to you, I have a prima facie duty (of fidelity—see later discussion) to do what I said I would do: pick you up by 10:00 A.M. on Saturday. But now suppose that as I am about to leave to pick you up, my child falls off the roof of my house and needs immediate medical attention. Ross would say that here I have a prima facie duty to take my child to the emergency ward of the hospital. So, I have a prima facie duty to start out for your place and a conflicting prima facie duty to attend to my child: as things have turned out, I am not able to fulfill both prima facie duties. Now the point of calling a duty "prima facie" is that the moral reasons provided by such facts as that I've made a promise or that my child needs my help can be outweighed by other moral reasons that favor doing some other action. Ross puts this point by saying that a prima facie duty can be overridden—beat out—by a competing prima facie duty. In the case I've described, because it is my child and because she needs immediate medical attention, my prima facie duty to help her overrides my prima facie duty to come pick you up. When one prima facie duty prevails in some conflict of duties situation, it becomes one's *all-things-considered duty*—it is what you ought, all things considered, to do in that circumstance. So, for Ross, to say that one has a prima facie duty to perform action *A* on some occasion is to say that one has a moral reason to do *A,* and unless something comes up that is morally more important, one has an all-things-considered duty to do *A* on that occasion.

Ross's theory of right conduct, which is our main concern, is based partly on his theory of intrinsic value to which we now turn.

Ross's Theory of Intrinsic Value

Ross held that there are four basic intrinsic goods:

1. *Virtue*. The disposition to act from certain desires, including the desire to do what is morally right, is intrinsically good.
2. *Pleasure*. States of experiencing pleasure are intrinsically good.
3. *Pleasure in proportion to virtue*. The state of experiencing pleasure in proportion to one's level of virtue is intrinsically good.
4. *Knowledge*. Having knowledge (at least of a nontrivial sort) is intrinsically good.

The items on this list are the basis for some of Ross's basic prima facie duties—call them "value-based" prima facie duties. What Ross calls duties of "special obligation" are not based on his theory of intrinsic value.

Ross's Prima Facie Duties

Here, then, is Ross's list of basic prima facie duties, organized into the two categories just mentioned:

Basic Value-Based Prima Facie Duties

1. Justice: prima facie, one ought to help ensure that pleasure is distributed according to merit.
2. Beneficence: prima facie, one ought to help those in need and, in general, increase the virtue, pleasure, and knowledge of others.
3. Self-improvement: prima facie, one ought to improve oneself with respect to one's own virtue and knowledge.
4. Nonmaleficence: prima facie, one ought to refrain from harming others.

Basic Prima Facie Duties of Special Obligation

5. Fidelity: prima facie, one ought to keep one's promises (including the implicit promise to be truthful).
6. Reparation: prima facie, one ought to make amends to others for any past wrongs one has done them.
7. Gratitude: prima facie, one ought to show gratitude toward one's benefactors.

The first four basic prima facie duties, then, make reference to what has intrinsic value according to Ross's theory of value. Ross himself points out that the prima facie duties of justice, beneficence, and self-improvement "come under the general principle that we should produce as much good as possible."[29] This part of Ross's theory fits the characterization of consequentialism.

The duties of special obligation do not make reference to what has intrinsic value: the duties of fidelity, reparation, and gratitude do not depend for their prima facie rightness on the values of the consequences of those actions. This part of Ross's theory is clearly duty-based or deontological. Overall, then, Ross's theory represents a hybrid: part consequentialist, part deontological.

Applying the Ethics of Prima Facie Duties

But how, on Ross's view, does one determine in some particular case that one prima facie duty overrides another, competing prima facie duty? Ross denies that there is any correct super-principle like the principle of utility or Kant's categorical imperative to which one might appeal to determine one's all-things-considered duty in cases of conflict. Nor is there any fixed ranking of the various prima facie duties such that the duty higher up on the list always beats out duties below it. Rather, according to Ross, in determining which prima facie duty is most "stringent" in some particular case and thus represents one's all-things-considered duty, one must examine the details of the case by using one's *judgment* about which of the competing duties is (in that situation) strongest. As mentioned earlier, moral judgment is a matter of discerning the morally important features of a situation and determining what ought or ought not to be done, where doing so cannot be fully captured in a set of rules. Judgment is largely a matter of skill that one may acquire through experience.

One final remark. One need not agree with Ross's own list of basic prima facie duties in order to accept the other tenets of Ross's view. For instance, Robert Audi has recently defended an ethic of prima facie duties that features ten basic prima facie duties.[30] Audi, unlike Ross, distinguishes duties not to lie from duties of fidelity, and he adds two additional duties to Ross's list. So were we to make the additions Audi proposes, we would have the following:

8. Veracity: prima facie, one ought not to lie.
9. Enhancement and preservation of freedom: prima facie, one ought to contribute to increasing or at least preserving the freedom of others with priority given to removing constraints over enhancing opportunities.
10. Respectfulness: prima facie, one ought, in the manner of our relations with other people, treat others respectfully.

The main point I wish to make here is that Ross's version of an ethic of prima facie duties is one version of this general sort of view. Audi's view attempts to build upon and improve Ross's view.

G. Social Contract Theory

The basic idea of **social contract theories of morality** is that correct or justified moral rules or principles are ones that result from some sort of social agreement—whether the agreement is conceived as having actually taken place or (more likely) the agreement in question is hypothetical. Philosophers Thomas Hobbes (1588–1679) and Jean-Jacques Rousseau (1712–1778) developed influential versions of social contract theory. But the view has found its most powerful contemporary development in the writings of John Rawls (*A Theory of Justice*, 1971), David Gauthier (*Morals by Agreement*, 1986), and T. M. Scanlon (*What We Owe to Each Other*, 1998). The selection featured in the next chapter representing this type of theory is an excerpt from Rawls's 1971 book, about which I will say more in a moment. But first I will formulate a representative statement of the theory of right conduct that is characteristic of social contract theory.

Begin with the assumption that parties to the (hypothetical) agreement are conceived to be free and equal and that each is motivated to reach an agreement on the fundamental rules and principles governing conduct. There are various ways of filling in the details that would lead these hypothetical agents to reach such an agreement, and different social contract theorists do so in distinctive and somewhat different ways. And, of course, such details will matter greatly in getting from the idea of individuals involved in the hypothetical agreement to a single set of moral rules and principles that are supposed to emerge from some process involved in reaching an agreement. But putting aside such details for the time being, here is a generic formulation of a social contract theory of right action:

> **SC**   An action is morally right if and only if (and because) it is permitted by a set of moral principles that hypothetical agents would agree to under conditions that are ideal for choosing moral principles (the precise characteristics of the hypothetical agents and ideal conditions to be spelled out).

Of course, SC does not say anything substantive about the agents or the conditions that ground the agreement, and so, as stated, it is useless as a criterion of right action until details are provided. And as I've said, there are different ways of filling out the details. To put some flesh on this bare-bones formulation of social contract theory, let us briefly consider the view of Rawls.

As the preceding formula indicates, in order to develop a social contract theory, one must specify the characteristics, including the motivations of the hypothetical agents who are party to the agreement, as well as the ideal conditions under which the agreement is hypothesized to take place. This is the first general task of such theories. The second task is to argue that some determinate set of moral principles would be favored over competing moral principles under the specified ideal conditions. In *A Theory of Justice*, Rawls is primarily interested in a social contract account of the justification of principles of justice governing the basic institutions of a well-ordered society. The gist of Rawls's theory is nicely expressed in the first paragraph of our selection in the next chapter:

> [T]he guiding idea is that the principles of justice for the basic structure of society are the object of an original agreement. They are the principles that free and rational persons concerned to further their own interests would accept in an initial position of equality as defining the fundamental terms of their associations. These principles are to regulate all further agreements that specify the kinds of social cooperation that can be entered into and the forms of government that can be established. This way of regarding the principles of justice I shall call justice as fairness. (Rawls 1971, 11)

Rawls uses the term *original position* to describe the hypothetical situation—the ideal circumstances—in which persons are to decide on basic principles of justice. As hypothetical, it is not presented as an actual historical state of affairs; instead, it is supposed to represent circumstances for choosing moral principles that capture the idea of fair terms of cooperation. The individuals occupying the original position are understood to be free and equal human beings who each have a rational conception of what constitutes his or her own good. But to ensure that the selection process is as unbiased and thus as fair as possible, the occupants are to choose principles of justice under a "veil of ignorance." That is, they are to choose principles without knowing their own place in society, their class or social position, or anything about their natural talents, abilities, and strength. As Rawls observes, "since all are similarly situated and no one is able to design principles to favor his particular condition, the principles of justice are the result of a fair agreement or bargain" (Ibid., 12). Further details about the original position and its rationale are provided in our reading from Rawls.

Once Rawls has described the hypothetical choice situation, the remaining question is, "Which set of principles will be agreed to by those in the original position?" Rawls argues that two lexically ordered principles would likely be chosen.

> *The principle of greatest equal liberty:* Each person is to have an equal right to the most extensive basic liberty compatible with a similar liberty for others.

The basic liberties in question include such political liberties as the right to vote and run for public office, freedom of assembly, and freedom of speech and conscience.

> *The difference principle:* Social and economic inequalities are to be arranged so that they are both (a) reasonably expected to be to everyone's advantage and (b) attached to positions and offices open to all.

This principle, as Rawls explains, applies primarily to the distribution of wealth and income as well as to the design of organizations having to do with differences in authority and responsibility.

Roughly speaking, the lexical ordering of these principles means that the first is prior to the second, and so social and economic inequalities cannot be legitimately obtained at the expense of compromising the equal liberties of individuals. As Rawls remarks, "The distribution of wealth and income, and the hierarchies of authority, must be consistent with both the liberties of equal citizenship and equality of opportunity" (Ibid., 61). More detail about these principles and Rawls's particular version of social contract are provided in our next chapter's reading. Hopefully, enough has been said here to convey the basic idea of Rawls's version of social contract theory.

It is worth noting that Rawls's theory of justice has had an enormous impact on moral and political philosophy. Although most of the articles in this anthology are not about matters of social justice, or at least many of our authors do not approach their topics from this angle, readers will note many references to the work of Rawls in the book's selections.

Applying Social Contract Theory

Rawls uses the label *justice as fairness* for his conception of justice, and though he admits that his theory is not intended as a complete social contract account of morality, he does note, in our selection from his book, that his social contract theory could be extended to provide a general account of morality, a view appropriately labeled *rightness as fairness*. More recently, T. M. Scanlon (1998) developed the social contract account of morality he calls "contractualism," which is intended to provide a general account of interpersonal moral obligation and so represents a view that is not restricted to principles of social justice. Again, the basic idea of right action that such a view is meant to capture is expressed by SC. But, as noted earlier, in order for a social contract principle of right conduct to have any implications for what is right or wrong, one must first specify in sufficient detail the hypothetical choice situation from which moral principles are to be chosen and then use those more specific principles to address particular moral issues. We have one such version, featuring two fundamental principles of justice, in the work of Rawls.

This completes our survey of some of the leading moral theories that figure importantly in many of this book's readings. As mentioned earlier, I recommend using these summaries as an aid in understanding those writings in which an author appeals to one or another moral theory. In the final section of this chapter, we take up the following question:

What is the point of moral theory in thinking about disputed moral issues in light of the existence of a variety of competing moral theories?

3.   COPING WITH MANY MORAL THEORIES

This chapter began with a brief overview of the central concepts and guiding aims of moral theory and then proceeded to survey some types of moral theory. In working through the various moral problems featured in this book, one will find that different moral theories often yield different and conflicting answers to questions about the morality of some action. The natural law theory, for instance, arguably condemns all homosexual behavior as morally wrong; a consequentialist approach does not. So the application of one theory to an issue may yield one moral verdict, while the application of another theory may yield a conflicting moral verdict. What, then, a student may ask, is the point of thinking about disputed moral issues from the perspective of moral theory? It all seems rather arbitrary.

This is a completely understandable question whose answer requires that one move from a focus on particular moral issues to questions about the nature and evaluation of moral theories. It is not possible to fully address such questions in a chapter whose aim is to provide students with a basic understanding of a range of moral theories. But because of its importance, the question does deserve to be addressed, even if briefly. In so doing, I will first offer some remarks about evaluating a moral theory, and then I will suggest a way of looking at the various moral theories for the illumination I think they provide in thinking about moral issues.

Evaluating a Moral Theory

Philosophers who develop a moral theory do not just state some moral principle or other and leave it at that; rather, they *argue* for whatever principles they are proposing. And we can critically evaluate their arguments. So the first point I wish to make is that there can be rational debate about a moral theory—not any old moral theory is as good as any other.

Furthermore, there are standards for evaluating a moral theory—standards that are not arbitrary but rather have to do with the guiding aims of a moral theory that we discussed in section 1 of this chapter. Corresponding to the theoretical aim of moral theory—the aim of explaining what makes something right or wrong, good or bad—is the principle of **explanatory power:**

> A moral theory should feature principles that explain our more specific considered moral beliefs, thus helping us understand *why* actions, persons, and other objects of moral evaluation are right or wrong, good or bad. The better a theory's principles in providing such explanations, the better the theory.

This principle appeals to our "considered" moral beliefs, which may be defined as those moral beliefs that are *deeply held* and *very widely shared.* I hope that everyone reading this text believes that murder is wrong, that rape is wrong, and that child molestation is wrong. The list could be extended. Moreover, such moral beliefs are (for those who have them) very likely deeply held convictions. The principle of explanatory power tells us to evaluate a moral theory by determining whether its principles properly explain why such actions are morally wrong. Similar remarks apply to widely shared and deeply held beliefs about our obligations. So we can help confirm a moral theory by showing that it can properly explain the rightness or wrongness of actions about whose moral status we are virtually certain. Correlatively, we can criticize a moral theory by showing that it does not properly explain the rightness or wrongness of actions about whose moral status we are virtually certain. Applying this principle requires that we can tell what counts as a good explanation of the rightness or wrongness of actions. This is a topic of lively and ongoing philosophical inquiry whose study would take us far beyond the scope of this book. But in thinking about moral issues from the perspective of moral theory, the reader is invited to consider not only what a theory implies about some action or practice, but also what explanation it provides for whatever verdict it reaches about the action or practice under consideration. (I return briefly to this matter toward the end of this section.)

According to the practical aim of moral theory, we want moral principles that will help guide our moral deliberations and subsequent choices. Corresponding to this aim is the principle of **practical guidance**:

> A moral theory should feature principles that are useful in guiding moral deliberation toward correct or justified moral verdicts about particular issues which we can then use to help guide choice. The better a theory's principles are in providing practical guidance, the better the theory.

Any moral theory that would yield inconsistent verdicts about some particular concrete action is obviously of no practical help on the issue at hand. Furthermore, a moral theory whose principles are so vague that it fails to have clear implications for a range of moral issues is again of no help in guiding thought about those issues. Finally, a moral theory whose principles are extremely difficult to apply because, for example, applying them requires a great deal of factual information that is humanly impossible to acquire, is at odds with the principle of practical guidance. These are three measures to consider in evaluating how well a moral theory does in satisfying the principle of practical guidance and thus how well it does in satisfying the practical aim of moral theory.

These brief remarks are only meant to indicate how one can begin to evaluate a moral theory. Hopefully, what I have said is enough to make a start on answering the challenge that began this section. Let us now move on to the second point I wish to make in response to the challenge.

Moral Theory and Moral Illumination[31]

I conclude with a plea for the importance of moral theory, even if there is no one theory that currently commands the allegiance of all philosophers who specialize in ethics. The plea is that moral theory can help focus and sharpen our moral thinking about particular issues, and it can thereby provide a kind of insight and illumination of moral issues that is otherwise easily missed. Let me explain.

No doubt readers of this chapter will have noticed that the various moral theories we have surveyed build on ideas that are very familiar. To see this, let us return to the case of euthanasia with which this chapter began. You may recall that in that case, Dr. Jack Kevorkian brought about the death of his patient Thomas Youk by a lethal injection. We described Kevorkian's action as an instance of voluntary active euthanasia. Now if one pays attention to on-line discussions and newspaper editorials that focus on this moral issue, and listens to the views of politicians and other social activists who discuss it, we find that some arguments appeal to the likely effects or consequences of allowing this practice. And of course, the idea that an action's rightness or wrongness is to be explained by reference to its likely consequences is the main idea of the various varieties of consequentialist moral theory. Similar remarks can be made about the other types of moral theory presented in section 2. Some arguments over euthanasia focus on the intrinsic value of human life—one of the four basic human goods featured in natural law ethics. Related to questions about end-of-life moral decisions, some have argued that providing a terminal patient with painkilling drugs that will knowingly cause the patient to die of liver failure before succumbing to cancer is nevertheless permissible because death in this case is merely a foreseen side effect of the painkilling drug. Here we have a tacit appeal to the doctrine of double effect. Again, we find arguments that appeal to the special dignity and worth of human beings, as well as arguments that appeal to such alleged rights as the right to die or the right to die with dignity. Such arguments tacitly appeal, respectively, to elements of Kantian moral theory and to rights-based moral theory (or at least rights-focused approaches to moral issues). Similar points can be made about virtue ethics, the ethics of prima facie duties, and social contract theory.

So the first point I wish to make about studying moral issues from the perspective of moral theory is that one thereby gains greater insight and clarity into the kinds of arguments that one commonly reads and hears over disputed moral issues. In fact, one may think of the various moral theories we have surveyed as attempts to develop such familiar ideas from moral thought and discourse in a rigorous philosophical manner. To really understand some moral issue for purposes of making up your own mind about it, you first have to understand the issue, which in turn requires that you consider the various reasons that reflective people bring to bear in thinking and debating the issue at hand. Such reasons, as I have just indicated, are often developed systematically in a moral theory. So coming to understand moral theory helps provide a kind of moral illumination or insight into moral issues.

The further point is this. Different moral theories differ partly because of how they propose to *organize* our moral thinking about practical issues. For instance, utilitarianism has us organize our moral thinking about some issue in terms of its likely effects on well-being or happiness. Virtue ethics, by contrast, has us organize our moral thinking around considerations of virtue and vice, asking us, for example, to view a proposed course of action in terms of what it would express about our characters. Rights-based moral theories have us think about an issue in terms of competing moral claims that can be made by various involved parties. Similar remarks apply to Kantian moral theory, natural law theory, the ethics of prima facie duty, and social contract theory.

However, let us put aside for the moment the fact that the various moral theories in question offer competing answers to questions about the underlying nature of right and wrong, good and bad. If we do, we might then view these theories as providing different ways of diagnosing and thinking about a moral problem. In some cases the best approach is utilitarian, whereas in others the best approach is from a virtue ethics perspective, and still in others, some other moral theory best gets at what is morally most important to consider. In other words, it strikes me that some practical moral questions are best approached from, say, the perspective of act utilitarianism, others not. Here is an example that comes up in the chapter on war, terrorism, and torture and is discussed in the reading from Alan M. Dershowitz. He considers a "ticking bomb" scenario in which a captured terrorist very likely knows the whereabouts of a powerful explosive set to go off in a heavily populated city. Would it be morally permissible to torture this (uncooperative) individual in an attempt to extract information that might be used to locate and defuse the explosive? Given what is at stake in *this* particular case, I can well understand why one's moral thinking would be guided by essentially act utilitarian reasoning. But in other cases, thinking in these terms seems morally askew. Thomas E. Hill Jr., in his article included in chapter 15, argues that in thinking about how we ought to relate to the environment, utilitarianism fails to properly diagnose what is wrong with certain ways of treating the environment. He also argues that thinking in terms of rights fails to get at what is really morally important about our dealings with the environment. His proposal is to think in terms of virtue—ideals of excellence—rather than in terms of utility or rights. As explained in section 1 of this chapter, a moral theory is partly in the business of providing practical guidance for moral thinking and decision making.

My suggestion is that in some contexts it makes sense to think as an act utilitarian, in other contexts it makes most sense to think in terms of rights, and in still other contexts, thinking in terms of virtue and excellence seems most illuminating. The same can be said about the other moral theories we have surveyed. Thinking exclusively about all moral issues in terms of some one particular moral theory assumes a *one-size-fits-all* approach to moral thinking. I am suggesting that this probably isn't the best way to use theory to illuminate practice.[32]

Returning now to the challenge that began this section, I have tried to address it in two ways. First, moral theory is not arbitrary in the sense that you can just pick and choose your favorite or make up your own: there are standards for evaluating moral theories that have to do with the theoretical and practical aims of moral theory. Second, the variety of moral theories on offer can positively aid in one's moral thinking about controversial moral issues in two ways. First, it can do so by providing rigorous articulations of common ideas about morality. And second, it can do so if one views these theories as diagnostic tools for getting to the heart of moral problems. Some tools are better for some jobs than other tools. My suggestion is that a particular moral theory may be a better tool than others when it comes to thinking through some particular issue, though a different theory may be better at helping one think through other issues.

NOTES

1. A few paragraphs of material in this essay are taken from my "Ethics" in *Reflections on Philosophy,* 2nd ed., ed. L. McHenry and T. Yagisowa (New York: Longman's Publishers, 2003), 103–25.
2. John Rawls, *A Theory of Justice* (Cambridge, MA: Harvard University Press, 1971), 24.
3. Given this understanding of the notions of intrinsic and extrinsic value, it is possible for something to have value of both sorts. Suppose, for example, that both happiness and knowledge have intrinsic positive value. Since knowledge can be of use in promoting happiness, knowledge can also have extrinsic value.
4. The "if and only if (and because) . . ." is meant to make clear that what follows the "and because" is meant to be a moral criterion that explains *why* the item being evaluated has whatever moral property (e.g., rightness) is mentioned in the first part of the principle.
5. To categorize Kant's ethical theory as deontological in the sense of being fundamentally duty-based may be inaccurate. Arguably, the notion of dignity—a kind of status that all persons have—is the explanatory basis of duties in Kant's ethical theory. Since dignity is a kind of value, this would make Kant's theory a certain kind of value-based theory, but nevertheless distinct from consequentialist views.
6. See Jeremy Bentham, *An Introduction to the Principles of Morals and Legislation* (New York: Hafner Press, 1948, originally published in 1789), and J. S. Mill, *Utilitarianism* (Indianapolis, IN: Hackett Publishing, 1979, originally published in 1861).
7. Another important distinction within consequentialism is between versions that appeal to the *actual* consequences (and associated value) that would occur were some action to be performed and versions that appeal to the *likely* consequences (and associated value) of actions—those consequences and their associated value that can be reasonably expected to follow from an action were it to be performed. I have chosen to formulate consequentialist principles in terms of likely consequences, since in applying a consequentialist theory to practice, we have to rely on our *estimates* of the consequences and associated value of actions.
8. I have explained utilitarianism in terms of *human* happiness or welfare, but a utilitarian may expand the scope of moral concern to all creatures for whom it makes sense to talk about their happiness or welfare.

9. For a defense of perfectionist consequentialism, see Tom Hurka, *Perfectionism* (Oxford: Oxford University Press, 1993).

10. What I am describing is a pure perfectionist account of value. It is, of course, possible to accept a hybrid view of intrinsic value according to which both happiness and perfectionist goods such as knowledge and achievement have intrinsic value.

11. For a recent defense of rule consequentialism, see Brad Hooker, *Ideal Code, Real World* (Oxford: Oxford University Press, 2000).

12. This is not to say that the best form of the natural law theory embraces the idea that "unnatural" actions are wrong and "natural" actions are right. The version I am about to present does not feature such ideas.

13. For a defense of natural law theory, see John Finnis, *Natural Law and Natural Rights* (Oxford: Oxford University Press, 1980).

14. Here is an appropriate place to clarify what I am calling theories of intrinsic value that figure importantly in those moral theories which feature value-based theories of right conduct. Ideally, a complete theory of intrinsic value would accomplish two related tasks: (1) provide a complete list of those types of things that have intrinsic value and also (2) specify those underlying features of intrinsically good and bad things *in virtue of which* they have whatever intrinsic value they do have. However, since our main concern in this chapter is with that part of a moral theory having to do with right and wrong action, we need only consider how a theory of intrinsic value responds to the first task—a specification of the types of things that have intrinsic value. So, for example, in what immediately follows, I will simply list the most basic types of items that have positive intrinsic value according to the natural law theory.

15. Kant's major writings in ethics include *Groundwork of the Metaphysics of Morals* (1785), *Critique of Practical Reason* (1790), and *The Metaphysics of Morals* (1797). All of these writings are included in Mary E. Gregor, trans., *Kant's Practical Philosophy* (Cambridge: Cambridge University Press, 1997). Page references to Kant's writings are to this edition. For a recent defense of Kantian ethics, see Onora O'Neill, *Towards Justice and Virtue* (Cambridge: Cambridge University Press, 1996).

16. In her article on a Kantian approach to world hunger included in chapter 14, Onora O'Neill develops these ideas in more detail.

17. See *Groundwork of the Metaphysics of Morals,* section II, 84–85.

18. I have left out the "and because" since arguably this formulation does not purport to express a moral criterion of right action—what *makes* an action right for Kant is expressed by the Humanity formulation; a *test* of an action's rightness is provided by the Universal Law formulation. For more on this, see my *Moral Theory: An Introduction,* 2nd ed. (Lanham, MD: Rowman & Littlefield, 2013), chap. 8.

19. In *Groundwork,* section II, in the footnote on p. 80, Kant raises objections to the golden rule.

20. *Practical Philosophy,* 74.

21. Readers should be aware that the topic of rights is extremely complex and contentious. In what follows, my aim is to introduce readers to some distinctions and to some observations about rights, moral theory, and moral controversies which, although elementary and perhaps contentious, are useful for understanding moral disputes that are framed in terms of rights.

22. Such rights are sometimes referred to as "natural rights."

23. *Universal* human rights are rights that are enjoyed by all human beings regardless of nationality, sex, race, religion, or other such distinctions. Universal rights, as universal, are contrasted with the particular rights of particular individuals, such as the rights that come with owning a house or having a certain occupation.

24. J. L. Mackie, "Can There Be a Rights-Based Moral Theory?" *Midwest Studies in Philosophy* 3 (1978): 351.

25. Mackie, "Rights-Based Moral Theory," 355.
26. This does not mean that such theories have little to say about such matters. For instance, Kant elaborates a theory of virtue in the "Doctrine of Virtue" which makes up part 2 of his 1797 *Metaphysics of Morals.*
27. For a defense of virtue ethics, see Rosalind Hursthouse, *On Virtue Ethics* (Oxford: Oxford University Press, 1999).
28. Defenders of virtue ethics often attempt to explain the basis of the virtues and vices (why some trait is a virtue or a vice) by appealing to the idea of human flourishing. The idea is that a trait of character or mind is a virtue because it contributes to or partly constitutes the flourishing of its possessor. For more on this point, see Hursthouse's "Virtue Theory and Abortion" included in chapter 10.
29. W. D. Ross, *The Right and the Good* (Oxford: Oxford University Press, 1930), 27.
30. See Audi's *The Good in the Right* (Princeton, NJ: Princeton University Press, 2004) for a recent defense of an ethic of prima facie duty that attempts to integrate this sort of view into a basically Kantian framework.
31. Special thanks to Jason Brennan and to Dave Schmidtz for very helpful conversations about moral theory and illumination.
32. These remarks suggest the possibility of combining certain elements from the various theories into one big super-theory featuring a plurality of principles, some having to do with duties, others with virtuous actions, others with rights, others with utility, and perhaps all of them unified by the Kantian idea of respect for persons, animals, and the environment. Doing so would still leave open the question of whether some one element of the theory—duties, virtues, rights, etc.—is most basic in the theory. One possibility (and the one that strikes me as initially plausible) is a theory according to which these notions are "interpenetrating"—a full understanding of any one of them requires appeal to the others.

2 } Moral Theory Selections

The following sections are from the writings of J. S. Mill, St. Thomas Aquinas, Immanuel Kant, John Locke, Aristotle, W. D. Ross, and John Rawls. Each selection focuses on key aspects of the philosopher's theory of morality. In each selection, one or both of the following questions are being addressed:

- What makes an action or practice morally right or morally wrong?
- What kind of life is best for human beings to lead?

Mill presents a classic utilitarian version of consequentialism. Aquinas sets forth the elements of natural law theory. Kant explains and illustrates what he takes to be the supreme moral principle of right conduct: the so-called categorical imperative. Locke articulates a conception of natural rights. Aristotle explains the connection between a flourishing life and virtuous action. Ross defends his ethic of prima facie duties. Finally, Rawls defends a social contract theory of the principles of social justice.

An overview of the main concepts and aims of moral theory, in addition to brief overviews of the various types of moral theory featured in each of these selections, can be found in the previous chapter, "A Moral Theory Primer."

(J. S. MILL

Utilitarianism

In the following excerpt from his 1863 book, *Utilitarianism*, Mill introduces the "Greatest Happiness" principle (also called the Principle of Utility) as the foundation or basis for distinguishing morally right from morally wrong action. He then proceeds to answer three objections to his principle, and concludes with a "proof" of the Principle of Utility.

From John Stuart Mill, *Utilitarianism* (1863).

Recommended Reading: See consequentialism, chap. 1, sec. 2A, for more detail on varieties of consequentialism (including utilitarianism).

The creed which accepts as the foundation of morals, Utility, or the Greatest Happiness Principle, holds that actions are right in proportion as they tend to promote happiness, wrong as they tend to produce the reverse of happiness. By happiness is intended pleasure, and the absence of pain; by unhappiness, pain, and the privation of pleasure. To give a clear view of the moral standard set up by the theory, much more requires to be said; in particular, what things it includes in the ideas of pain and pleasure; and to what extent this is left an open question. But these supplementary explanations do not affect the theory of life on which this theory of morality is grounded—namely, that pleasure, and freedom from pain, are the only things desirable as ends; and that all desirable things (which are as numerous in the utilitarian as in any other scheme) are desirable either for the pleasure inherent in themselves, or as means to the promotion of pleasure and the prevention of pain.

Now, such a theory of life excites in many minds, and among them in some of the most estimable in feeling and purpose, inveterate dislike. To suppose that life has (as they express it) no higher end than pleasure—no better and nobler object of desire and pursuit—they designate as utterly mean and grovelling; as a doctrine worthy only of swine, to whom the followers of Epicurus were, at a very early period, contemptuously likened; and modern holders of the doctrine are occasionally made the subject of equally polite comparisons by its German, French, and English assailants.

When thus attacked, the Epicureans have always answered, that it is not they, but their accusers, who represent human nature in a degrading light; since the accusation supposes human beings to be capable of no pleasures except those of which swine are capable. If this supposition were true, the charge could not be gainsaid, but would then be no longer an imputation; for if the sources of pleasure were precisely the same to human beings and to swine, the rule of life which is good enough for the one would be good enough for the other. The comparison of the Epicurean life to that of beasts is felt as degrading, precisely because a beast's pleasures do not satisfy a human being's conceptions of happiness. Human beings have faculties more elevated than the animal appetites, and when once made conscious of them, do not regard anything as happiness which does not include their gratification. I do not, indeed, consider the Epicureans to have been by any means faultless in drawing out their scheme of consequences from the utilitarian principle. To do this in any sufficient manner, many Stoic, as well as Christian, elements require to be included. But there is no known Epicurean theory of life which does not assign to the pleasures of the intellect, of the feelings and imagination, and of the moral sentiments, a much higher value as pleasures than to those of mere sensation. It must be admitted, however, that utilitarian writers in general have placed the superiority of mental over bodily pleasures chiefly in the greater permanency, safety, uncostliness, etc., of the former—that is, in their circumstantial advantages rather than in their intrinsic nature. And on all these points utilitarians have fully proved their case; but they might have taken the other, and, as it may be called, higher ground, with entire consistency. It is quite compatible with the principle of utility to recognize the fact, that some *kinds* of pleasure are more desirable and more valuable than others. It would be absurd that while, in estimating all other things, quality is considered as well as quantity, the estimation of pleasures should be supposed to depend on quantity alone.

If I am asked, what I mean by difference of quality in pleasures, or what makes one pleasure more valuable than another, merely as a pleasure, except its being greater in amount, there is but one possible answer. Of two pleasures, if there be one to which all or almost all who have experience of both give a decided preference, irrespective of any feeling of moral obligation to prefer it, that is the more desirable pleasure. If one of the two is, by those who are competently acquainted with both, placed so far above the other that they prefer it, even though knowing it to be attended with a greater amount of discontent, and would not resign it for any quantity of the other pleasure which their nature is capable of, we are justified in ascribing to the preferred enjoyment a superiority in quality, so far outweighing quantity as to render it, in comparison, of small account.

Now it is an unquestionable fact that those who are equally acquainted with, and equally capable of appreciating and enjoying, both, do give a most marked preference to the manner of existence which employs their higher faculties. Few human creatures would consent to be changed into any of the lower animals, for a promise of the fullest allowance of a beast's pleasures; no intelligent human being would consent to be a fool, no instructed person would be an ignoramus, no person of feeling and conscience would be selfish and base, even though they should be persuaded that the fool, the dunce, or the rascal is better satisfied with his lot than they are with theirs. They would not resign what they possess more than he for the most complete satisfaction of all the desires which they have in common with him. If they ever fancy they would, it is only in cases of unhappiness so extreme, that to escape from it they would exchange their lot for almost any other, however undesirable in their own eyes. A being of higher faculties requires more to make him happy, is capable probably of more acute suffering, and is certainly accessible to it at more points than one of an inferior type; but in spite of these liabilities, he can never really wish to sink into what he feels to be a lower grade of existence. We may give what explanation we please of this unwillingness; we may attribute it to pride, a name which is given indiscriminately to some of the most and to some of the least estimable feelings of which mankind are capable; we may refer it to the love of liberty and personal independence, an appeal to which was with the Stoics one of the most effective means for the inculcation of it; to the love of power, or to the love of excitement, both of which do really enter into and contribute to it: but its most appropriate appellation is a sense of dignity, which all human beings possess in one form or other, and

in some, though by no means in exact, proportion to their higher faculties, and which is so essential a part of the happiness of those in whom it is strong, that nothing which conflicts with it could be, otherwise than momentarily, an object of desire to them. Whoever supposes that this preference takes place at a sacrifice of happiness—that the superior being, in anything like the equal circumstances, is not happier than the inferior— confounds the two very different ideas, of happiness, and content. It is indisputable that the being whose capacities of enjoyment are low, has the greatest chance of having them fully satisfied; and a highly-endowed being will always feel that any happiness which he can look for, as in the world is constituted, is imperfect. But he can learn to bear its imperfections, if they are at all bearable; and they will not make him envy the being who is indeed unconscious of the imperfections, but only because he feels not at all the good which those imperfections qualify. It is better to be a human being dissatisfied than a pig satisfied; better to be Socrates dissatisfied than a fool satisfied. And if the fool, or the pig, is of a different opinion, it is because they only know their own side of the question. The other party to the comparison knows both sides. . . .

. . . The objectors to utilitarianism cannot always be charged with representing it in a discreditable light. On the contrary, those among them who entertain anything like a just idea of its disinterested character, sometimes find fault with its standard as being too high for humanity. They say it is exacting too much to require that people shall always act from the inducement of promoting the general interests of society. But this is to mistake the very meaning of a standard of morals, and to confound the rule of action with the motive of it. It is the business of ethics to tell us what are our duties, or by what test we may know them; but no system of ethics requires that the sole motive of all we do shall be a feeling of duty; on the contrary, ninety-nine hundredths of all our actions are done from other motives, and rightly so done, if the rule of duty does not condemn them. It is the more unjust to utilitarianism that this particular misapprehension should be made a ground of objection to it, inasmuch as utilitarian moralists have gone beyond almost all others in affirming that the motive has nothing to do with the morality of the action, though much with the worth of the agent. He who saves a fellow creature from drowning does what is morally right, whether his motive be duty, or the hope of being paid for his trouble: he who betrays the friend that trusts him is guilty of a crime, even if his object be to serve another friend to whom he is under greater obligations. But to speak only of actions done from the motive of duty, and in direct obedience to principle: it is a misapprehension of the utilitarian mode of thought, to conceive it as implying that people should fix their minds upon so wide a generality as the world, or society at large. The great majority of good actions are intended, not for the benefit of the world, but for that of individuals, of which the good of the world is made up; and the thoughts of the most virtuous man need not on these occasions travel beyond the particular persons concerned, except so far as is necessary to assure himself that in benefiting them he is not violating the rights—that is, the legitimate and authorized expectations—of any one else. The multiplication of happiness is, according to the utilitarian ethics, the object of virtue: the occasions on which any person (except one in a thousand) has it in his power to do this on an extended scale, in other words, to be a public benefactor, are but exceptional; and on these occasions alone is he called on to consider public utility; in every other case, private utility, the interest or happiness of some few persons, is all he has to attend to. Those alone the influence of whose actions extends to society in general, need concern themselves habitually about so large an object. In the case of abstinences indeed—of things which people forbear to do, from moral considerations, though the consequences in the particular case might be beneficial—it would be unworthy of an intelligent agent not to be consciously aware that the action is of a class which, if practiced generally, would be generally injurious, and that this is the ground of the obligation to abstain from it. The amount of regard for the public interest implied in this recognition, is no greater than is demanded by every system of morals; for they all enjoin to abstain from whatever is manifestly pernicious to society. . . .

. . . Again, defenders of utility often find themselves called upon to reply to such objections as this—that there is not time, previous to action, for calculating and weighing the effects of any line of conduct on the general happiness. This is exactly as if any one were to say that it is impossible to guide our conduct by Christianity, because there is not time, on every occasion on which anything has to be done, to read through the Old and New Testaments. The answer to the objection is, that there has been ample time, namely, the whole past duration of . . . the human species. During all that time mankind have been learning by experience the tendencies of actions; on which experience all the prudence, as well as all the morality of life, is dependent. People talk as if the commencement of this course of experience had hitherto been put off, and as if, at the moment when some man feels tempted to meddle with the property or life of another, he had to begin considering for the first time whether murder and theft are injurious to human happiness. Even then I do not think that he would find the question very puzzling; but, at all events, the matter is now done to his hand. It is truly a whimsical supposition that if mankind were agreed in considering utility to be the test of morality, they would remain without any agreement as to what is useful, and would take no measures for having their notions on the subject taught to the young, and enforced by law and opinion. There is no difficulty in proving any ethical standard whatever to work ill, if we suppose universal idiocy to be conjoined with it, but on any hypothesis short of that, mankind must by this time have acquired positive beliefs as to the effects of some actions on their happiness; and the beliefs which have thus come down are the rules of morality for the multitude, and for the philosopher until he has succeeded in finding better. That philosophers might easily do this, even now, on many subjects; that the received code of ethics is by no means of divine right; and that mankind have still much to learn as to the effects of actions on the general happiness, I admit, or rather, earnestly maintain. The corollaries from the principle of utility, like the precepts of every practical art, admit of indefinite improvement, and, in a progressive state of the human mind, their improvement is perpetually going on. But to consider the rules of morality as improvable, is one thing; to pass over the intermediate generalizations entirely, and endeavor to test each individual action directly by the first principle, is another. It is a strange notion that the acknowledgment of a first principle is inconsistent with the admission of secondary ones. To inform a traveller respecting the place of his ultimate destination, is not to forbid the use of landmarks and direction-posts on the way. The proposition that happiness is the end and aim of morality, does not mean that no road ought to be laid down to that goal, or that persons going thither should not be advised to take one direction rather than another. Men really ought to leave off talking a kind of nonsense on this subject, which they would neither talk nor listen to in other matters of practical concernment. Nobody argues that the art of navigation is not founded on astronomy, because sailors cannot wait to calculate the Nautical Almanack. Being rational creatures, they go to sea with it ready calculated; and all rational creatures go out upon the sea of life with their minds made up on the common questions of right and wrong, as well as on many of the far more difficult questions of wise and foolish. And this, as long as foresight is a human quality, is to be presumed they will continue to do. Whatever we adopt as the fundamental principle of morality, we require subordinate principles to apply it by: the impossibility of doing without them, being common to all systems, can afford no argument against any one in particular: but gravely to argue as if no such secondary principles could be had, and as if mankind had remained till now, and always must remain, without drawing any general conclusions from the experience of human life, is as high a pitch, I think, as absurdity has ever reached in philosophical controversy. . . .

OF WHAT SORT OF PROOF THE PRINCIPLE OF UTILITY IS SUSCEPTIBLE

It has already been remarked, that questions of ultimate ends do not admit of proof, in the ordinary acceptation of the term. To be incapable of proof by reasoning is common to all first principles; to the first premises of our knowledge, as well as to those of our conduct. But the former, being matters of fact, may be the subject of a direct appeal to the faculties which judge of fact— namely, our senses, and our internal consciousness. Can an appeal be made to the same faculties on questions of practical ends? Or by what other faculty is cognizance taken of them?

Questions about ends are, in other words, questions what things are desirable. The utilitarian doctrine is, that happiness is desirable, and the only thing desirable, as an end; all other things being only desirable as means to that end. What ought to be required of this doctrine—what conditions is it requisite that the doctrine should fulfill—to make good its claim to be believed?

The only proof capable of being given that an object is visible, is that people actually see it. The only proof that a sound is audible, is that people hear it: and so of the other sources of our experience. In like manner, I apprehend, the sole evidence it is possible to produce that anything is desirable, is that people do actually desire it. If the end which the utilitarian doctrine proposes to itself were not, in theory and in practice, acknowledged to be an end, nothing could ever convince any person that it was so. No reason can be given why the general happiness is desirable, except that each person, so far as he believes it to be attainable, desires his own happiness. This, however, being a fact, we have not only all the proof which the case admits of, but all which it is possible to require, that happiness is a good: that each person's happiness is a good to that person, and the general happiness, therefore, a good to the aggregate of all persons. Happiness has made out its title as *one* of the ends of conduct, and consequently one of the criteria of morality.

But it has not, by this alone, proved itself to be the sole criterion. To do that, it would seem, by the same rule, necessary to show, not only that people desire happiness, but that they never desire anything else. Now it is palpable that they do desire things which, in common language, are decidedly distinguished from happiness. They desire, for example, virtue, and the absence of vice, no less really than pleasure and the absence of pain. The desire of virtue is not as universal, but it is as authentic a fact, as the desire of happiness. And hence the opponents of the utilitarian standard deem that they have a right to infer that there are other ends of human action besides happiness, and that happiness is not the standard of approbation and disapprobation.

But does the utilitarian doctrine deny that people desire virtue, or maintain that virtue is not a thing to be desired? The very reverse. It maintains not only that virtue is to be desired, but that it is to be desired disinterestedly, for itself. Whatever may be the opinion of utilitarian moralists as to the original conditions by which virtue is made virtue; however they may believe (as they do) that actions and dispositions are only virtuous because they promote another end than virtue; yet this being granted, and it having been decided, from considerations of this description, what is virtuous, they not only place virtue at the very head of the things which are good as means to the ultimate end, but they also recognize as a psychological fact the possibility of its being, to the individual, a good in itself, without looking to any end beyond it; and hold, that the mind is not in a right state, not in a state conformable to Utility, not in the state most conducive to the general happiness, unless it does love virtue in this manner—as a thing desirable in itself, even although, in the individual instance, it should not produce those other desirable consequences which it tends to produce, and on account of which it is held to be virtue. This opinion is not, in the smallest degree, a departure from the Happiness principle. The ingredients of happiness are very various, and each of them is desirable in itself, and not merely when considered as swelling an aggregate. The principle of utility does not mean that any given pleasure, as music, for instance, or any given exemption from pain, as for example health, are to be looked upon as a means to a collective something termed happiness, and to be desired on that account. They are desired and desirable in and for themselves; besides being means, they are a part of the end. Virtue, according to the utilitarian doctrine, is not naturally and originally part of the end, but it is capable of becoming so; and in those who love it disinterestedly it has become so, and is desired and cherished, not as a means to happiness, but as a part of their happiness. . . .

READING QUESTIONS

1. What is Mill's "Greatest Happiness" principle?
2. How does Mill understand happiness?
3. How does Mill propose to distinguish higher from lower pleasures?
4. How does Mill reply to the objection that in many circumstances there is no time to apply the Principle of Utility in deciding what to do?

DISCUSSION QUESTIONS

1. Is Mill's proposal for distinguishing higher from lower pleasures plausible?
2. Is there a place in Mill's utilitarianism for individual rights, such as the right to life?
3. According to Mill's Principle of Utility, actions are right "in proportion as they tend to promote happiness, wrong as they tend to produce the reverse of happiness." Does Mill's principle include the happiness of nonhuman animals? Should it?

Treatise on Law

In the following selection from his *Summa Theologiae* (Summary of Theology), thirteenth-century philosopher and theologian St. Thomas Aquinas presents a classical version of the natural law theory of morality. He defines law as "an ordinance of reason for the common good, promulgated by him who has care of the community." *Natural* law is that part of God's eternal law that concerns how human beings ought to conduct themselves. The first precept of natural law is that "good is to be done, evil is to be avoided." Human beings have natural inclinations to seek various ends that (according to Aquinas) indicate what has intrinsic value and thus ought to be protected and cultivated. Thus, for Aquinas, morality is ultimately grounded in facts about human nature that can be discovered by inquiring into the nature of human beings. Hence, the label, "natural law theory."

Recommended Reading: See natural law theory, chap. 1, sec. 2B, for an elaboration of the basic concepts and principles of Aquinas's version of natural law theory, including a presentation of the doctrine of double effect.

WHETHER LAW IS SOMETHING PERTAINING TO REASON?

...It belongs to the law to command and to forbid. But it belongs to reason to command, as was stated above. Therefore law is something pertaining to reason....Law is a rule and measure of acts, whereby man is induced to act or is restrained from acting; for *lex (law)* is derived from *ligare (to bind),* because it binds one to act. Now the rule and measure of human acts is the reason, which is the first principle of human acts, as is evident from what has been stated above. For it belongs to the reason to direct to the end, which is the first principle in all matters of action....

WHETHER LAW IS ALWAYS DIRECTED TO THE COMMON GOOD?

...As we have stated above, law belongs to that which is a principle of human acts, because it is their rule and measure. Now as reason is a principle of human acts, so in reason itself there is something which is the principle in respect of all the rest. Hence to this principle chiefly and mainly law must needs be referred. Now the first principle in practical matters, which are the object of the practical reason, is the last end: and the last end of human life is happiness or beatitude, as we have stated above. Consequently, law must needs concern itself mainly with the order that is in beatitude. Moreover, since every part is ordained to the whole as the imperfect to the perfect, and since one man is a part of the perfect community, law must needs concern itself properly with the order directed to universal happiness.... Since law is chiefly ordained to the common good, any other precept in regard to some individual work must needs be devoid of the nature of a law, save in so far as it regards the common good. Therefore every law is ordained to the common good....

the divine reason. Therefore the very notion of the government of things in God, the ruler of the universe, has the nature of a law. And since the divine reason's conception of things is not subject to time, but is eternal, according to *Prov.* 8:23, therefore it is that this kind of law must be called eternal....

Promulgation is made by word of mouth or in writing, and in both ways the eternal law is promulgated, because both the divine Word and the writing of the Book of Life are eternal....

WHETHER PROMULGATION IS ESSENTIAL TO LAW?

... As was stated above, a law is imposed on others as a rule and measure. Now a rule or measure is imposed by being applied to those who are to be ruled and measured by it. Therefore, in order that a law obtain the binding force which is proper to a law, it must needs be applied to the men who have to be ruled by it. But such application is made by its being made known to them by promulgation. Therefore promulgation is necessary for law to obtain its force.... Law is nothing else than an ordinance of reason for the common good, promulgated by him who has the care of the community....

The natural law is promulgated by the very fact that God has instilled it into man's mind so as to be known by him naturally....

WHETHER THERE IS AN ETERNAL LAW?

... As we have stated above, law is nothing else but a dictate of practical reason emanating from the ruler who governs a perfect community. Now it is evident, granted that the world is ruled by divine providence, as was stated in the First Part, that the whole community of the universe is governed by

WHETHER THERE IS IN US A NATURAL LAW?

... As we have stated above, law, being a rule and measure, can be in a person in two ways: in one way, as in him that rules and measures; in another way, as in that which is ruled and measured, since a thing is ruled and measured in so far as it partakes of the rule or measure. Therefore, since all things subject to divine providence are ruled and measured by the eternal law, as was stated above, it is evident that all things partake in some way in the eternal law, in so far as, namely, from its being imprinted on them, they derive their respective inclinations to their proper acts and ends. Now among all others, the rational creature is subject to divine providence in a more excellent way, in so far as it itself partakes of a share of providence, by being provident both for itself and for others. Therefore it has a share of the eternal reason, whereby it has a natural inclination to its proper act and end; and this participation of the eternal law in the rational creature is called the natural law. Hence the Psalmist, after saying (Ps. 4:6): *Offer up the sacrifice of justice,* as though someone asked what the works of justice are, adds: *Many say, Who showeth us good things?* in answer to which question he says: *The light of Thy countenance, O Lord, is signed upon us.* He thus implies that the light of natural reason, whereby we discern what is good and what is evil, which is the function of the natural law, is nothing else than an imprint on us of the divine light. It is therefore evident that the natural law is nothing else than the rational creature's participation of the eternal law....

WHETHER THE NATURAL LAW CONTAINS SEVERAL PRECEPTS, OR ONLY ONE?

. . . The precepts of the natural law are to the practical reason what the first principles of demonstrations are to the speculative reason, because both are self-evident principles. Now a thing is said to be self-evident in two ways: first, in itself; secondly, in relation to us. Any proposition is said to be self-evident in itself, if its predicate is contained in the notion of the subject; even though it may happen that to one who does not know the definition of the subject, such a proposition is not self-evident. For instance, this proposition, *Man is a rational being,* is, in its very nature, self-evident, since he who says *man,* says *a rational being*; and yet to one who does not know what a man is, this proposition is not self-evident. Hence it is that, as Boethius says, certain axioms or propositions are universally self-evident to all; and such are the propositions whose terms are known to all, as, *Every whole is greater than its part,* and *Things equal to one and the same are equal to one another.* But some propositions are self-evident only to the wise, who understand the meaning of the terms of such propositions. Thus to one who understands that an angel is not a body, it is self-evident that an angel is not circumscriptively in a place. But this is not evident to the unlearned, for they cannot grasp it.

Now a certain order is to be found in those things that are apprehended by men. For that which first falls under apprehension, is *being*, the understanding of which is included in all things whatsoever a man apprehends. Therefore the first indemonstrable principle is that *the same thing cannot be affirmed and denied at the same time*, which is based on the notion of *being and not-being*: and on this principle all others are based. . . . Now as *being* is the first thing that falls under the apprehension absolutely, so *good* is the first thing that falls under the apprehension of the practical reason, which is directed to action (since every agent acts for an end, which has the nature of good). Consequently, the first principle in the practical reason is one founded on the nature of good, viz., that *good is that which all things seek after.* Hence, this is the first precept of law, that *good is to be done and promoted, and evil is to be avoided.* All other precepts of the natural law are based upon this; so that all the things which the practical reason naturally apprehends as man's good belong to the precepts of the natural law under the form of things to be done or avoided.

Since, however, good has the nature of an end, and evil, the nature of the contrary, hence it is that all those things to which man has a natural inclination are naturally apprehended by reason as being good, and consequently as objects of pursuit, and their contraries as evil, and objects of avoidance. Therefore, the order of the precepts of the natural law is according to the order of natural inclinations. For there is in man, first of all, an inclination to good in accordance with the nature which he has in common with all substances, inasmuch, namely, as every substance seeks the preservation of its own being, according to its nature; and by reason of this inclination, whatever is a means of preserving human life, and of warding off its obstacles, belongs to the natural law. Secondly, there is in man an inclination to things that pertain to him more specially, according to that nature which he has in common with other animals; and in virtue of this inclination, those things are said to belong to the natural law *which nature has taught to all animals,* such as sexual intercourse, the education of offspring, and so forth. Thirdly, there is in man an inclination to good according to the nature of his reason, which nature is proper to him. Thus man has a natural inclination to know the truth about God, and to live in society; and in this respect, whatever pertains to this inclination belongs to the natural law: *e.g.,* to shun ignorance, to avoid offending those among whom one has to live, and other such things regarding the above inclination. . . .

All these precepts of the law of nature have the character of one natural law, inasmuch as they flow from one first precept. . . .

WHETHER THE NATURAL LAW IS THE SAME IN ALL MEN?

. . . As we have stated above, to the natural law belong those things to which a man is inclined naturally; and among these it is proper to man to be inclined to act according to reason. Now it belongs to the reason to proceed from what is common to what is proper. . . . The speculative reason, however, is differently situated, in this matter, from the practical reason. For, since the speculative reason is concerned chiefly with necessary things, which cannot be otherwise than they are, its proper conclusions, like the universal principles, contain the truth without fail. The practical reason, on the other hand, is concerned with contingent matters, which is the domain of human actions; and, consequently, although there is necessity in the common principles, the more we descend towards the particular, the more frequently we encounter defects. Accordingly, then, in speculative matters truth is the same in all men, both as to principles and as to conclusions; although the truth is not known to all as regards the conclusions, but only as regards the principles which are called *common notions*. But in matters of action, truth or practical rectitude is not the same for all as to what is particular, but only as to the common principles; and where there is the same rectitude in relation to particulars, it is not equally known to all.

It is therefore evident that, as regards the common principles whether of speculative or of practical reason, truth or rectitude is the same for all, and is equally known by all. But as to the proper conclusions of the speculative reason, the truth is the same for all, but it is not equally known to all. Thus, it is true for all that the three angles of a triangle are together equal to two right angles, although it is not known to all. But as to the proper conclusions of the practical reason, neither is the truth or rectitude the same for all, nor, where it is the same, is it equally known by all. Thus, it is right and true for all to act according to reason, and from this principle it follows, as a proper conclusion, that goods entrusted to another should be restored to their owner. Now this is true for the majority of cases. But it may happen in a particular case that it would be injurious, and therefore unreasonable, to restore goods held in trust; for instance, if they are claimed for the purpose of fighting against one's country. And this principle will be found to fail the more, according as we descend further towards the particular, *e.g.*, if one were to say that goods held in trust should be restored with such and such a guarantee, or in such and such a way; because the greater the number of conditions added, the greater the number of ways in which the principle may fail, so that it be not right to restore or not to restore.

Consequently, we must say that the natural law, as to the first common principles, is the same for all, both as to rectitude and as to knowledge. But as to certain more particular aspects, which are conclusions, as it were, of those common principles, it is the same for all in the majority of cases, both as to rectitude and as to knowledge; and yet in some few cases it may fail, both as to rectitude, by reason of certain obstacles (just as natures subject to generation and corruption fail in some few cases because of some obstacle), and as to knowledge, since in some the reason is perverted by passion, or evil habit, or an evil disposition of nature. Thus at one time theft, although it is expressly contrary to the natural law, was not considered wrong among the Germans, as Julius Caesar relates.

READING QUESTIONS

1. What is "natural" about the natural law?
2. What are the fundamental human goods according to Aquinas? How does Aquinas attempt to support his claims that these are goods?
3. What moral obligations does Aquinas mention as following from each of the human goods?

DISCUSSION QUESTIONS

1. Do you think that Aquinas's list of fundamental human goods is complete? Why or why not?
2. Do you think that Aquinas's natural law theory allows for killing in self-defense? Why or why not?

IMMANUEL KANT

The Moral Law

Kant is one of the most important philosophers of the Western world. In the selection below from his 1785 *Groundwork (Foundations) of the Metaphysics of Morals,* he presents and illustrates what he takes to be the fundamental principle of morality, the Categorical Imperative. He claims that this principle is implicit in the moral thinking of ordinary men and women and argues that this principle can be made explicit by reflecting on the concept of a good will. Kant then proceeds to explain the difference between two types of imperatives—hypothetical and categorical—the latter being distinctive of morality. Then, having explained the very idea of a categorical imperative, Kant formulates his fundamental principle in a variety of ways—in terms of *universal law, humanity as an end in itself,* and *the kingdom of ends*, providing sample applications of the Categorical Imperative to questions about the morality of suicide, making false promises, allowing one's talents to rust, and helping others in need.

Recommended Reading: See Kantian moral theory, chap. 1, sec. 2C, for further explanation of Kant's theory.

THE GOOD WILL

Nothing can possibly be conceived in the world, or even out of it, which can be called good, without qualification, except a Good Will. Intelligence, wit, judgment, and the other *talents* of the mind, however they may be named, or courage, resolution, perseverance, as qualities of temperament, are undoubtedly good and desirable in many respects; but these gifts of nature may also become extremely bad and mischievous if the will which is to make use of them, and which, therefore constitutes what is called *character,* is not good. It is the same with the *gifts of fortune.* Power, riches, honor, even health, and the general well-being and contentment with one's condition which is called *happiness*, inspire pride, and often presumption, if there is not a good will to correct the influence of these on the mind, and with this also to rectify the whole principle of acting, and adapt it to its end. The sight of a being who is not adorned with a single feature of a pure and good will, enjoying unbroken prosperity, can never give pleasure to an impartial rational spectator. Thus a good will appears to constitute the indispensable condition even of being worthy of happiness.

There are even some qualities which are of service to this good will itself, and may facilitate its action, yet which have no intrinsic unconditional value, but always presuppose a good will, and this qualifies the esteem that we justly have for them, and does not permit us to regard them as absolutely good. Moderation in the affections and passions, self-control, and calm deliberation are not only good in many respects, but even seem to constitute part of the intrinsic worth of the person; but they are far from deserving to be called good without qualification, although they have been so unconditionally praised by the ancients. For without the principles of a good will, they may become extremely bad; and the coolness of a villain not only makes him far more dangerous, but also

From I. Kant, *The Foundations of the Metaphysics of Morals*, T. K. Abbott, trans. First published in 1873.

directly makes him more abominable in our eyes than he would have been without it.

A good will is good not because of what it performs or effects, not by its aptness for the attainment of some proposed end, but simply by virtue of the volition, that is, it is good in itself, and considered by itself is to be esteemed much higher than all that can be brought about by it in favor of any inclination, nay, even of the sum-total of all inclinations. Even if it should happen that, owing to special disfavor of fortune, or the niggardly provision of a step-motherly nature, this will should wholly lack power to accomplish its purpose, if with its greatest efforts it should yet achieve nothing, and there should remain only the good will (not, to be sure, a mere wish, but the summoning of all means in our power), then, like a jewel, it would still shine by its own light, as a thing which has its whole value in itself. Its usefulness or fruitlessness can neither add to nor take away anything from this value. . . . .

. . . Thus the moral worth of an action does not lie in the effect expected from it, nor in any principle of action which requires to borrow its motive from this expected effect. For all these effects—agreeableness of one's condition, and even the promotion of the happiness of others—could have been also brought about by other causes, so that for this there would have been no need of the will of a rational being; whereas it is in this alone that the supreme and unconditional good can be found. The pre-eminent good which we call moral can therefore consist in nothing else than *the conception of law* in itself, *which certainly* is *only possible in a rational being*, in so far as this conception, and not the expected effect, determines the will. This is a good which is already present in the person who acts accordingly, and we have not to wait for it to appear first in the result.

THE SUPREME PRINCIPLE OF MORALITY: THE CATEGORICAL IMPERATIVE

But what sort of law can that be, the conception of which must determine the will, even without paying any regard to the effect expected from it, in order that this will may be called good absolutely and without qualification? As I have deprived the will of every impulse which could arise to it from obedience to any law, there remains nothing but the universal conformity of its actions to law in general, which alone is to serve the will as a principle, *i.e.* I am never to act otherwise than *so that I could also will that my maxim should become a universal law*. Here, now, it is the simple conformity to law in general, without assuming any particular law applicable to certain actions, that serves the will as its principle, and must so serve it, if duty is not to be a vain delusion and a chimerical notion. The common reason of men in its practical judgments perfectly coincides with this, and always has in view the principle here suggested. Let the question be, for example: May I when in distress make a promise with the intention not to keep it? I readily distinguish here between the two significations which the question may have: Whether it is prudent, or whether it is right, to make a false promise? The former may undoubtedly often be the case. I see clearly indeed that it is not enough to extricate myself from a present difficulty by means of this subterfuge, but it must be well considered whether there may not hereafter spring from this lie much greater inconvenience than that from which I now free myself, and as, with all my supposed *cunning,* the consequences cannot be so easily foreseen but that credit once lost may be much more injurious to me than any mischief which I seek to avoid at present, it should be considered whether it would not be more *prudent* to act herein according to a universal maxim, and to make it a habit to promise nothing except with the intention of keeping it. But it is soon clear to me that such a maxim will still only be based on the fear of consequences. Now it is a wholly different thing to be truthful from duty, and to be so from apprehension of injurious consequences. In the first case, the very notion of the action already implies a law for me; in the second case, I must first look about elsewhere to see what results may be combined with it which would affect myself. For to deviate from the principle of duty is beyond all doubt wicked; but to be unfaithful to my maxim of prudence may often be very advantageous to me, although to abide by it is certainly safer. The shortest way, however, and an unerring one, to discover the answer to this question whether a lying promise is consistent with duty, is to ask myself, Should I be content that my maxim (to extricate myself from difficulty by a false promise) should hold good as a universal law, for myself as well as for others? and should I be able to say to myself, "Every one may make a deceitful promise when he finds himself in a difficulty from which he cannot otherwise extricate himself"? Then I presently become aware that while I can will the lie, I can by no means will that lying should be a universal law. For with such a law there would be no promises at all, since it would be in vain to allege my intention in regard to my future actions to those who would not believe this allegation, or if they over-hastily did so, would pay me back in my own coin. Hence my maxim, as soon as it should be made a universal law, would necessarily destroy itself. . . .

IMPERATIVES: HYPOTHETICAL AND CATEGORICAL

Everything in nature works according to laws. Rational beings alone have the faculty of acting according *to the conception of laws*, that is according to principles, *i.e.*, have a *will*. Since the deduction of actions from principles requires *reason,* the will is nothing but practical reason. If reason infallibly determines the will, then the actions of such a being which are recognized as objectively necessary are subjectively necessary also, *i.e.*, the will is a faculty to choose *that only* which reason independent of inclination recognizes as practically necessary, *i.e., as* good. But if reason of itself does not sufficiently determine the will, if the latter is subject also to subjective conditions (particular impulses) which do not always coincide with the objective conditions; in a word, if the will does not *in itself* completely accord with reason (which is actually the case with men), then the actions which objectively are recognized as necessary are subjectively contingent, and the determination of such a will according to objective laws is *obligation,* that is

to say, the relation of the objective laws to a will that is not thoroughly good is conceived as the determination of the will of a rational being by principles of reason, but which the will from its nature does not of necessity follow.

The conception of an objective principle, in so far as it is obligatory for a will, is called a command (of reason), and the formula of the command is called an Imperative.

All imperatives are expressed by the word *ought* [or *shall*], and thereby indicate the relation of an objective law of reason to a will, which from its subjective constitution is not necessarily determined by it (an obligation). They say that something would be good to do or to forbear, but they say it to a will which does not always do a thing because it is conceived to be good to do it. That is practically *good*, however, which determines the will by means of the conceptions of reason, and consequently not from subjective causes, but objectively, that is on principles which are valid for every rational being as such. It is distinguished from the *pleasant*, as that which influences the will only by means of sensation from merely subjective causes, valid only for the sense of this or that one, and not as a principle of reason, which holds for every one.

A perfectly good will would therefore be equally subject to objective laws (*viz.*, laws of good), but could not be conceived as *obliged* thereby to act lawfully, because of itself from its subjective constitution it can only be determined by the conception of good. Therefore no imperatives hold for the Divine will, or in general for a *holy* will; *ought* is here out of place, because the volition is already of itself necessarily in unison with the law. Therefore imperatives are only formulae to express the relation of objective laws of all volition to the subjective imperfection of the will of this or that rational being, *e.g.*, the human will.

Now all *imperatives* command either *hypothetically* or *categorically*. The former represent the practical necessity of a possible action as means to something else that is willed (or at least which one might possibly will). The categorical imperative would be that which represented an action as necessary of itself without reference to another end, *i.e.*, as objectively necessary. . . .

FIRST FORMULATION OF THE CATEGORICAL IMPERATIVE: UNIVERSAL LAW

There is therefore but one categorical imperative, namely, this: *Act only on that maxim whereby thou canst at the same time will that it should become a universal law.*

Now if all imperatives of duty can be deduced from this one imperative as from their principle, then, although it should remain undecided whether what is called duty is not merely a vain notion, yet at least we shall be able to show what we understand by it and what this notion means.

Since the universality of the law according to which effects are produced constitutes what is properly called *nature* in the most general sense (as to form), that is the existence of things so far as it is determined by general laws, the imperative of duty may be expressed thus: *Act as if the maxim of thy action were to become by thy will a universal law of nature.*

FOUR ILLUSTRATIONS

We will now enumerate a few duties, adopting the usual division of them into duties to ourselves and to others, and into perfect and imperfect duties.

1. A man reduced to despair by a series of misfortunes feels wearied of life, but is still so far in possession of his reason that he can ask himself whether it would not be contrary to his duty to himself to take his own life. Now he inquires whether the maxim of his action could become a universal law of nature. His maxim is: From self-love I adopt it as a principle to shorten my life when its longer duration is likely to bring more evil than satisfaction. It is asked then simply whether this principle founded on self-love can become a universal law of nature. Now

we see at once that a system of nature of which it should be a law to destroy life by means of the very feeling whose special nature it is to impel to the improvement of life would contradict itself, and therefore could not exist as a system of nature; hence that maxim cannot possibly exist as a universal law of nature, and consequently would be wholly inconsistent with the supreme principle of all duty.

2. Another finds himself forced by necessity to borrow money. He knows that he will not be able to repay it, but sees also that nothing will be lent to him, unless he promises stoutly to repay it in a definite time. He desires to make this promise, but he has still so much conscience as to ask himself: Is it not unlawful and inconsistent with duty to get out of a difficulty in this way? Suppose, however, that he resolves to do so, then the maxim of his action would be expressed thus: When I think myself in want of money, I will borrow money and promise to repay it, although I know that I never can do so. Now this principle of self-love or of one's own advantage may perhaps be consistent with my whole future welfare; but the question now is, Is it right? I change then the suggestion of self-love into a universal law, and state the question thus: How would it be if my maxim were a universal law? Then I see at once that it could never hold as a universal law of nature, but would necessarily contradict itself. For supposing it to be a universal law that everyone when he thinks himself in a difficulty should be able to promise whatever he pleases, with the purpose of not keeping his promise, the promise itself would become impossible, as well as the end that one might have in view in it, since no one would consider that anything was promised to him, but would ridicule all such statements as vain pretenses.

3. A third finds in himself a talent which with the help of some culture might make him a useful man in many respects. But he finds himself

in comfortable circumstances, and prefers to indulge in pleasure rather than to take pains in enlarging and improving his happy natural capacities. He asks, however, whether his maxim of neglect of his natural gifts, besides agreeing with his inclination to indulgence, agrees also with what is called duty. He sees then that a system of nature could indeed subsist with such a universal law although men (like the South Sea islanders) should let their talents rust, and resolve to devote their lives merely to idleness, amusement, and propagation of their species—in a word, to enjoyment; but he cannot possibly will that this should be a universal law of nature, or be implanted in us as such by a natural instinct. For, as a rational being, he necessarily wills that his faculties be developed, since they serve him, and have been given him, for all sorts of possible purposes.

4. A fourth, who is in prosperity, while he sees that others have to contend with great wretchedness and that he could help them, thinks: What concern is it of mine? Let everyone be as happy as Heaven pleases, or as he can make himself; I will take nothing from him nor even envy him, only I do not wish to contribute anything to his welfare or to his assistance in distress! Now no doubt if such a mode of thinking were a universal law, the human race might very well subsist, and doubtless even better than in a state in which everyone talks of sympathy and goodwill, or even takes care occasionally to put it into practice, but, on the other side, also cheats when he can, betrays the rights of men, or otherwise violates them. But although it is possible that a universal law of nature might exist in accordance with that maxim, it is impossible to *will* that such a principle should have the universal validity of a law of nature. For a will which resolved this would contradict itself, inasmuch as many cases might occur in which one would have need of the love and sympathy of others, and in which, by such a law of nature, sprung from his own will, he would deprive himself of all hope of the aid he desires....

SECOND FORMULATION OF THE CATEGORICAL IMPERATIVE: HUMANITY AS AN END IN ITSELF

...Now I say: man and generally any rational being *exists* as an end in himself, *not merely as a means* to be arbitrarily used by this or that will, but in all his actions, whether they concern himself or other rational beings, must be always regarded at the same time as an end. All objects of the inclinations have only a conditional worth; for if the inclinations and the wants founded on them did not exist, then their object would be without value. But the inclinations themselves being sources of want are so far from having an absolute worth for which they should be desired, that, on the contrary, it must be the universal wish of every rational being to be wholly free from them. Thus the worth of any object which is *to be acquired* by our action is always conditional. Beings whose existence depends not on our will but on nature's, have nevertheless, if they are nonrational beings, only a relative value as means, and are therefore called *things;* rational beings, on the contrary, are called *persons,* because their very nature points them out as ends in themselves, that is as something which must not be used merely as means, and so far therefore restricts freedom of action (and is an object of respect). These, therefore, are not merely subjective ends whose existence has a worth *for us* as an effect of our action, but *objective ends,* that is things whose existence is an end in itself: an end moreover for which no other can be substituted, which they should subserve *merely* as means, for otherwise nothing whatever would possess *absolute worth*; but if all worth were conditioned and therefore contingent, then there would be no supreme practical principle of reason whatever.

If then there is a supreme practical principle or, in respect of the human will, a categorical imperative, it must be one which, being drawn from the conception of that which is necessarily an end for everyone because it is *an end in itself,* constitutes an *objective* principle of will, and can therefore serve as a universal practical law. The foundation of this principle is: *rational nature exists as an end in itself.* Man necessarily conceives his own existence as being so: so far then this is a *subjective* principle of human actions. But every other rational being regards its existence similarly, just on the same rational principle that holds for me: so that it is at the same time an objective principle from which as a supreme practical law all laws of the will must be capable of being deduced. Accordingly the practical imperative will be as follows: *So act as to treat humanity, whether in thine own person or in that of any other, in every case as an end withal, never as means only....*

We will now inquire whether this can be practically carried out.

To abide by the previous examples:

Firstly, under the head of the necessary duty to oneself: He who contemplates suicide should ask himself whether his action can be consistent with the idea of humanity *as an end in itself.* If he destroys himself in order to escape from painful circumstances, he uses a person merely as *a mean* to maintain a tolerable condition up to the end of life. But a man is not a thing, that is to say, something which can be used merely as a means, but must in all his actions be always considered as an end in himself. I cannot, therefore, dispose in any way of a man in my own person so as to mutilate him, to damage or kill him. (It belongs to ethics proper to define this principle more precisely so as to avoid all misunderstanding, *e.g.*, as to the amputation of the limbs in order to preserve myself; as to exposing my life to danger with a view to preserve it, &c. This question is therefore omitted here.)

Secondly, as regards necessary duties, or those of strict obligation, towards others; he who is thinking of making a lying promise to others will see at once that he would be using another man *merely as a mean,* without the latter containing at the same time the end in himself. For he whom I propose by such a promise to use for my own purposes cannot possibly assent to my mode of acting towards him, and therefore cannot himself contain the end of this action. This violation of the principle of humanity in other men is more

obvious if we take in examples of attacks on the freedom and property of others. For then it is clear that he who transgresses the rights of men, intends to use the person of others merely as means, without considering that as rational beings they ought always to be esteemed also as ends, that is, as beings who must be capable of containing in themselves the end of the very same action.

Thirdly, as regards contingent (meritorious) duties to oneself; it is not enough that the action does not violate humanity in our own person as an end in itself, it must also *harmonize with* it. Now there are in humanity capacities of greater perfection which belong to the end that nature has in view in regard to humanity in ourselves as the subject: to neglect these might perhaps be consistent with the *maintenance* of humanity as an end in itself, but not with the *advancement* of this end.

Fourthly, as regards meritorious duties towards others: the natural end which all men have is their own happiness. Now humanity might indeed subsist, although no one should contribute anything to the happiness of others, provided he did not intentionally withdraw anything from it; but after all, this would only harmonize negatively not positively with *humanity as an end in itself,* if everyone does not also endeavor, as far as in him lies, to forward the ends of others. For the ends of any subject which is an end in himself, ought as far as possible to be *my* ends also, if that conception is to have its *full* effect with me.

...Looking back now on all previous attempts to discover the principle of morality, we need not wonder why they all failed. It was seen that man was bound to laws by duty, but it was not observed that the laws to which he is subject are *only those of his own giving,* though at the same time they are *universal,* and that he is only bound to act in conformity with his own will; a will, however, which is designed by nature to give universal laws. For when one has conceived man only as subject to a law (no matter what), then this law required some interest, either by way of attraction or constraint, since it did not originate as a law from his *own* will, but this will was according to a law obliged by *something else* to act in a certain manner. Now by this necessary consequence all the labor spent in finding a supreme principle of *duty* was irrevocably lost. For men never elicited duty, but only a necessity of acting from a certain interest. Whether this interest was private or otherwise, in any case the imperative must be conditional, and could not by any means be capable of being a moral command. I will therefore call this the principle of *Autonomy* of the will, in contrast with every other which I accordingly reckon as *Heteronomy*.

THE KINGDOM OF ENDS

The conception of every rational being as one which must consider itself as giving in all the maxims of its will universal laws, so as to judge itself and its actions from this point of view—this conception leads to another which depends on it and is very fruitful, namely, that of a *kingdom of ends*.

By a *kingdom* I understand the union of different rational beings in a system by common laws. Now since it is by laws that ends are determined as regards their universal validity, hence, if we abstract from the personal differences of rational beings, and likewise from all the content of their private ends, we shall be able to conceive all ends combined in a systematic whole (including both rational beings as ends in themselves, and also the special ends which each may propose to himself), that is to say, we can conceive a kingdom of ends, which on the preceding principles is possible.

For all rational beings come under the *law* that each of them must treat itself and all others *never merely as means*, but in every case *at the same time as ends in themselves*. Hence results a systematic union of rational beings by common objective laws, i.e., a kingdom which may be called a kingdom of ends, since what these laws have in view is just the relation of these beings to one another as ends and means....

READING QUESTIONS

1. Explain in your own words Kant's distinction between hypothetical and categorical imperatives. What makes an imperative hypothetical? What makes an imperative categorical?
2. The Universal Law formulation of the categorical imperative involves testing maxims, which Kant proceeds to illustrate with four examples. For each of his examples, try explaining in your own words how Kant's test is supposed to work in showing that certain maxims cannot be consistently willed as universal law.
3. Kant also applies the Humanity as an End in Itself formulation to the same four examples. For each of these examples, how does Kant use his principle to establish claims about the morality of type of action he considers?

DISCUSSION QUESTIONS

1. Suppose someone proposes to act on the following maxim: *Whenever I know that other athletes against whom I am competing are using performance-enhancing drugs, I too will take such drugs in order to have a chance at winning.* Apply Kant's Universal Law formula to this maxim to determine whether the action being proposed is morally right or wrong.
2. Suppose that Jones is terminally ill and he and his physicians are reasonably certain that he only has about a week to live. But his life during his remaining time will be *very* painful and misery-ridden. Jones and his family agree that it would be preferable for Jones to die a drug-induced painless death now than for him to linger on in misery for the next week or so. His physicians agree. Apply Kant's Universal Law and Humanity formulations to this case in order to determine whether (according to Kant's moral theory) it would be permissible for Jones to allow himself to be put to death in these circumstances.

JOHN LOCKE

Natural Rights

According to Locke, all men (humans) are created by God as equal and free, but subject to "the law of nature" which "teaches all mankind who will but consult it that, being all equal and independent, no one ought to harm another in his life, health, liberty, or possessions." Thus Locke, like Aquinas, accepts a natural law conception of morality. However, in the following selection from *Two Treatises of Government*, Locke emphasizes the "natural" rights that correspond to the obligations just mentioned.

Recommended Reading: See rights-based moral theory, chap. 1, sec. 2D, for further discussion of moral rights and how they figure in moral theory.

To understand political power aright, and derive it from its original, we must consider what state all men are naturally in, and that is a state of perfect freedom to order their actions and dispose of their possessions and persons as they think fit, within the bounds of the law of nature, without asking leave, or depending upon the will of any other man.

A state also of equality, wherein all the power and jurisdiction is reciprocal, no one having more than another; there being nothing more evident than that creatures of the same species and rank, promiscuously born to all the same advantages of nature, and the use of the same faculties, should also be equal one amongst another without subordination or subjection, unless the Lord and Master of them all should by any manifest declaration of His will set one above another, and confer on him by an evident and clear appointment an undoubted right to dominion and sovereignty....

But though this be a state of liberty, yet it is not a state of license; though man in that state have an uncontrollable liberty to dispose of his person or possessions, yet he has not liberty to destroy himself, or so much as any creature in his possession, but where some nobler use than its bare preservation calls for it. The state of nature has a law of nature

to govern it, which obliges everyone; and reason, which is that law, teaches all mankind who will but consult it, that, being all equal and independent, no one ought to harm another in his life, health, liberty, or possessions. For men being all the workmanship of one omnipotent and infinitely wise Maker—all the servants of one sovereign Master, sent into the world by His order, and about His business—they are His property, whose workmanship they are, made to last during His, not one another's pleasure; and being furnished with like faculties, sharing all in one community of nature, there cannot be supposed any such subordination among us, that may authorize us to destroy one another, as if we were made for one another's uses, as the inferior ranks of creatures are for ours. Everyone, as he is bound to preserve himself, and not to quit his station willfully, so, by the like reason, when his own preservation comes not in competition, ought he, as much as he can, to preserve the rest of mankind, and not, unless it be to do justice on an offender, take away or impair the life, or what tends to the preservation of the life, the liberty, health, limb, or goods of another.

And that all men be restrained from invading other rights, and from doing hurt to one another, and the

From John Locke, *Two Treatises of Government* (1690).

law of nature be observed, which willeth the peace and preservation of all mankind, the execution of the law of nature is in that state put into every man's hand, whereby everyone has a right to punish the transgressors of that law to such a degree as may hinder its violation. For the law of nature would, as all other laws that concern men in this world, be in vain if there were nobody that, in the state of nature, had a power to execute that law, and thereby preserve the innocent and restrain offenders. And if anyone in the state of nature may punish another for any evil he has done, everyone may do so. For in that state of perfect equality, where naturally there is no superiority or jurisdiction of one over another, what any may do in prosecution of that law, everyone must needs have a right to do.

And thus in the state of nature one man comes by a power over another; but yet no absolute or arbitrary power, to use a criminal, when he has got him in his hands, according to the passionate heats or boundless extravagance of his own will; but only to retribute to him so far as calm reason and conscience dictate what is proportionate to his transgression, which is so much as may serve for reparation and restraint. For these two are the only reasons why one man may lawfully do harm to another, which is that we call punishment. In transgressing the law of nature, the offender declares himself to live by another rule than that of common reason and equity, which is that measure God has set to the actions of men, for their mutual security; and so he becomes dangerous to mankind, the tie which is to secure them from injury and violence being sighted and broken by him. Which, being a trespass against the whole species, and the peace and safety of it, provided for by the law of nature, every man upon this score, by the right he hath to preserve mankind in general, may restrain, or, where it is necessary, destroy things noxious to them, and so may bring such evil on anyone who hath transgressed that law, as may make him repent the doing of it, and thereby deter him, and by his example others, from doing the like mischief. And in this case, and upon this ground, every man hath a right to punish the offender, and be executioner of the law of nature.

I doubt not but this will seem a very strange doctrine to some men: but before they condemn it, I desire them to resolve me by what right any prince or state can put to death or punish an alien, for any crime he commits in their country. 'Tis certain their laws, by virtue of any sanction they receive from the promulgated will of the legislative, reach not a stranger: they speak not to him, nor, if they did, is he bound to hearken them. The legislative authority, by which they are in force over the subjects of that commonwealth, hath no power over him. Those who have the supreme power of making laws in England, France, or Holland, are to an Indian but like the rest of the world—men without authority. And, therefore, if by the law of nature every man hath not a power to punish offenses against it, as he soberly judges the case to require, I see not how the magistrates of any community can punish an alien of another country; since in reference to him they can have no more power than what every man naturally may have over another.

Besides the crime which consists in violating the law, and varying from the right rule of reason, whereby a man so far becomes degenerate, and declares himself to quit the principles of human nature, and to be a noxious creature, there is commonly injury done, and some person or other, some other man receives damage by his transgression, in which case he who hath received any damage, has, besides the right of punishment common to him with other men, a particular right to seek reparation from him that has done it. And any other person who finds it just, may also join with him that is injured, and assist him in recovering from the offender so much as many make satisfaction for the harm he has suffered.

From these two distinct rights—the one of punishing the crime for restraint and preventing the like offense, which right of punishing is in everybody; the other of taking reparation, which belongs only to the injured party—comes it to pass that the magistrate, who by being magistrate hath the common right of punishing put into his hands, can often, where the public good demands not the execution of the law, remit the punishment of criminal offenses by his own authority, but yet cannot remit the satisfaction due to any private man for the damage he has received. That he who has suffered the damage has a right to demand in his own name, and he alone can remit. The damnified person has this power of appropriating to himself the goods or service of the offender, by right of self-preservation, as every man has a power to punish the crime, to prevent its being committed again, by the right he has of preserving all mankind, and doing all reasonable things he can in order to that end. And thus it is that every man in the state of nature has a power to kill a murderer, both to deter others from doing the like injury which no reparation can compensate, by the example of the punishment that attends it from everybody, and also to secure men from the attempts of a criminal who having renounced reason, the common rule and measure God hath given to mankind, hath by the unjust violence and slaughter he hath committed upon one, declared war against all mankind, and therefore may be destroyed as a lion or a tiger, one of those wild savage beasts with whom men can have no society nor security. And upon this is grounded that great law of nature. "Whoso sheddeth man's blood, by man shall his blood be shed." And Cain was so fully convinced that everyone had a right to destroy such a criminal, that after the murder of his brother he cries out, "Every one that findeth me shall slay me"; so plain was it writ in the hearts of mankind.

By the same reason may a man in the state of nature punish the lesser breaches of that law. It will perhaps be demanded, With death? I answer, each transgression may be punished to that degree, and with so much severity, as will suffice to make it an ill bargain to the offender, give him cause to repent, and terrify others from doing the like. Every offense that can be committed in the state of nature, may in the state of nature be also punished equally, and as far forth as it may, in a commonwealth. For though it would be beside my present purpose to enter here into the particulars of the law of nature, or its measures of punishment, yet it is certain there is such a law, and that, too, as intelligible and plain to a rational creature and a studier of that law as the positive laws of commonwealth; nay, possibly plainer, as much as reason is easier to be understood than the fancies and intricate contrivances of men, following contrary and hidden interests put into words; for truly so are a great part of the municipal laws of countries, which are only so far right as they are founded on the law of nature, by which they are to be regulated and interpreted.

To this strange doctrine—viz., that in the state of nature everyone has the executive power of the law of nature—I doubt not but it will be objected that it is unreasonable for men to be judges in their own cases, that self-love will make men partial to themselves and their friends. And on the other side, that ill-nature, passion, and revenge will carry them too far in punishing others; and hence nothing but confusion and disorder will follow; and that therefore God hath certainly appointed government to restrain the partiality and violence of men. I easily grant that civil government is the proper remedy for the inconveniences of the state of nature, which must certainly be great where men may be judges in their own case, since 'tis easy to be imagined that he who was so unjust as to do his brother an injury, will scarce be so just as to condemn himself for it. But I shall desire those who make this objection, to remember that absolute monarchs are but men, and if government is to be the remedy of those evils which necessarily follow from men's being judges in their own cases, and the state of nature is therefore not to be endured, I desire to know what kind of government that is, and how much better it is than the state of nature, where one man commanding a multitude, has the liberty to be judge in his own case, and may do to all his subjects whatever he pleases, without the least question or control of those who execute his pleasure; and in whatsoever he doth, whether led by reason, mistake, or passion, must be submitted to, which men in the state of nature are not bound to do one to another? And if he that judges, judges amiss in his own or any other case, he is answerable for it to the rest of mankind.

'Tis often asked as a mighty objection, Where are, or ever were there, any men in such a state of nature? To which it may suffice as an answer at present: That since all princes and rulers of independent governments all through the world are in a state of nature, 'tis plain the world never was, nor ever will be, without numbers of men in that state. I have named all governors of independent communities, whether they are or are not in league with others. For 'tis not every compact that puts an end to the state of nature between men, but only this one of agreeing together mutually to enter into one community, and make one body politic; other promises and compacts men may make one with another, and yet still be in the state of nature. The promises and bargains for truck, etc., between the two men in Soldania, in or between a Swiss and an Indian, in the woods of America, are binding to them, though they are perfectly in a state of nature in reference to one another. For truth and keeping of faith belong to men as men, and not as members of society.

To those that say there were never any men in the state of nature, I will not only oppose the authority of the judicious Hooker—(Eccl. Pol., lib. i., sect. 10), where he says, "The laws which have been hitherto mentioned," i.e., the laws of nature, "do bind men absolutely, even as they are men, although they have never any settled fellowship, and never any solemn agreement amongst themselves what to do or not to do; but forasmuch as we are not by ourselves sufficient to furnish ourselves with competent store of things needful for such a life as our nature doth desire—a life fit for the dignity of man—therefore to supply those defects and imperfections which are in us, as living single and solely by ourselves, we are naturally induced to seek communion and fellowship with others; this was the cause of men's uniting themselves at first in politic societies"—but I moreover affirm that all men are naturally in that state, and remain so, till by their own consents they make themselves members of some politic society; and I doubt not, in the sequel of this discourse, to make it very clear.

READING QUESTIONS

1. Explain in your own words the idea of a natural right.
2. In addition to the rights to life, health, liberty, and possession, what rights does Locke discuss in this selection?

DISCUSSION QUESTIONS

1. Assuming that there are natural rights, are there any such rights not mentioned by Locke in our selection?
2. Both Aquinas and Locke accept a natural law conception of morality. Does Locke's appeal to natural rights add anything to the natural law theory that is lacking in Aquinas?

ARISTOTLE

Virtue and Character

The writings of Aristotle have made a tremendous impact on the history of philosophy and continue to do so. The following selection is from *Nichomachean Ethics*, in which Aristotle begins by arguing that a happy or good life essentially involves a life of activity in accordance with virtue. He then goes on to define virtue as a disposition to avoid extremes in feeling and action. For example, in matters relating to money, the virtue of generosity stands between the extremes of extravagance and stinginess.

Recommended Reading: See virtue ethics, chap. 1, sec. 2E, for a presentation of a contemporary version of a virtue-based account of right and wrong action that is inspired by the work of Aristotle.

CHARACTERISTICS OF THE GOOD

1. The good is the end of action.

But let us return once again to the good we are looking for, and consider just what it could be, since it is apparently one thing in one action or craft, and another thing in another; for it is one thing in medicine, another in generalship, and so on for the rest.

What, then, is the good in each of these cases? Surely it is that for the sake of which the other things are done; and in medicine this is health, in generalship victory, in house-building a house, in another case something else, but in every action and decision it is the end, since it is for the sake of the end that everyone does the other things.

And so, if there is some end of everything that is pursued in action, this will be the good pursued in action; and if there are more ends than one, these will be the goods pursued in action.

Our argument has progressed, then, to the same conclusion [as before, that the highest end is the good]; but we must try to clarify this still more.

2. The good is complete.

Though apparently there are many ends, we choose some of them, e.g., wealth, flutes and, in general, instruments, because of something else; hence it is clear that not all ends are complete. But the best good is apparently something complete. Hence, if only one end is complete, this will be what we are looking for; and if more than one are complete, the most complete of these will be what we are looking for.

CRITERIA FOR COMPLETENESS

An end pursued in itself, we say, is more complete than an end pursued because of something else; and an end that is never choiceworthy because of something else is more complete than ends that are choiceworthy both in themselves and because of this end; and hence an end that is always [choiceworthy, and also] choiceworthy in itself, never because of something else, is unconditionally complete.

3. Happiness meets the criteria for completeness, but other goods do not.

Now happiness more than anything else seems unconditionally complete, since we always [choose it, and also] choose it because of itself, never because of something else. Honor, pleasure, understanding and every virtue we certainly choose because of themselves, since we would choose each of them even if it had no further result, but we also choose them for the sake of happiness, supposing that through them we shall be happy. Happiness, by contrast, no one ever chooses for their sake, or for the sake of anything else at all.

4. The good is self-sufficient; so is happiness.

The same conclusion [that happiness is complete] also appears to follow from self-sufficiency, since the complete good seems to be self-sufficient.

Now what we count as self-sufficient is not what suffices for a solitary person by himself, living an isolated life, but what suffices also for parents, children, wife and in general for friends and fellow-citizens, since a human being is a naturally political [animal]. Here, however, we must impose some limit; for if we extend the good to parents' parents and children's children and to friends of friends, we shall go on without limit; but we must examine this another time.

Anyhow, we regard something as self-sufficient when all by itself it makes a life choiceworthy and lacking nothing; and that is what we think happiness does.

5. The good is most choiceworthy; so is happiness.

Moreover, [the complete good is most choiceworthy, and] we think happiness is most choiceworthy of all goods, since it is not counted as one good among

many. If it were counted as one among many, then, clearly, we think that the addition of the smallest of goods would make it more choiceworthy; for [the smallest good] that is added becomes an extra quantity of goods [so creating a good larger than the original good], and the larger of two goods is always more choiceworthy. [But we do not think any addition can make happiness more choiceworthy; hence it *is* most choiceworthy.]

Happiness, then, is apparently something complete and self-sufficient, since it is the end of the things pursued in action.

A clearer account of the good: the human soul's activity expressing virtue.

But presumably the remark that the best good is happiness is apparently something [generally] agreed, and what we miss is a clearer statement of what the best good is.

1. If something has a function, its good depends on its function.

Well, perhaps we shall find the best good if we first find the function of a human being. For just as the good, i.e., [doing] well, for a flautist, a sculptor, and every craftsman, and, in general, for whatever has a function and [characteristic] action, seems to depend on its function, the same seems to be true for a human being, if a human being has some function.

2. What sorts of things have functions?

Then do the carpenter and the leatherworker have their functions and actions, while a human being has none, and is by nature idle, without any function? Or, just as eye, hand, foot and, in general, every [bodily] part apparently has its functions, may we likewise ascribe to a human being some functions besides all of theirs?

3. The human function.

What, then, could this be? For living is apparently shared with plants, but what we are looking for is the special function of a human being; hence we should set aside the life of nutrition and growth. The life next in order is some sort of life of sense-perception; but this too is apparently shared, with horse, ox and every animal. The remaining possibility, then, is some sort of life of action of the [part of the soul] that has reason.

Clarification of "has reason" and "life."

Now this [part has two parts, which have reason in different ways], one as obeying the reason [in the other part], the other as itself having reason and thinking. [We intend both.] Moreover, life is also spoken of in two ways [as capacity and as activity], and we must take [a human being's special function to be] life as activity, since this seems to be called life to a fuller extent.

4. The human good is activity expressing virtue.

(a) We have found, then, that the human function is the soul's activity that expresses reason [as itself having reason] or requires reason [as obeying reason]. (b) Now the function of F, e.g., of a harpist, is the same in kind, so we say, as the function of an excellent F, e.g., an excellent harpist. (c) The same is true unconditionally in every case, when we add to the function the superior achievement that expresses the virtue; for a harpist's function, e.g., is to play the harp, and a good harpist's is to do it well. (d) Now we take the human function to be a certain kind of life, and take this life to be the soul's activity and actions that express reason. (e) [Hence by (c) and (d)] the excellent man's function is to do this finely and well. (f) Each function is completed well when its completion expresses the proper virtue. (g) Therefore [by (d), (e) and (f)] the human good turns out to be the soul's activity that expresses virtue.

5. The good must also be complete.

And if there are more virtues than one, the good will express the best and most complete virtue. Moreover, it will be in a complete life. For one swallow does not make a spring, nor does one day; nor, similarly, does one day or a short time make us blessed and happy....

VIRTUES OF CHARACTER IN GENERAL

How a Virtue of Character Is Acquired

Virtue, then, is of two sorts, virtue of thought and virtue of character. Virtue of thought arises and grows mostly from teaching, and hence needs experience and time. Virtue of character [i.e., of *ethos*] results from habit [*ethos*]; hence its name "ethical," slightly varied from "*ethos.*"

Virtue comes about, not by a process of nature, but by habituation.

Hence it is also clear that none of the virtues of character arises in us naturally.

1. What is natural cannot be changed by habituation.

For if something is by nature [in one condition], habituation cannot bring it into another condition. A stone, e.g., by nature moves downwards, and habituation could not make it move upwards, not even if you threw it up ten thousand times to habituate it; nor could habituation make fire move downwards, or bring anything that is by nature in one condition into another condition.

Thus the virtues arise in us neither by nature nor against nature, but we are by nature able to acquire them, and reach our complete perfection through habit.

2. Natural capacities are not acquired by habituation.

Further, if something arises in us by nature, we first have the capacity for it, and later display the activity. This is clear in the case of the senses; for we did not acquire them by frequent seeing or hearing, but already had them when we exercised them, and did not get them by exercising them.

Virtues, by contrast, we acquire, just as we acquire crafts, by having previously activated them. For we learn a craft by producing the same product that we must produce when we have learned it, becoming builders, e.g., by building and harpists by playing the harp; so also, then, we become just by doing just actions, temperate by doing temperate actions, brave by doing brave actions.

3. Legislators concentrate on habituation.

What goes on in cities is evidence for this also. For the legislator makes the citizens good by habituating them, and this is the wish of every legislator; if he fails to do it well he misses his goal. [The right] habituation is what makes the difference between a good political system and a bad one.

4. Virtue and vice are formed by good and bad actions.

Further, just as in the case of a craft, the sources and means that develop each virtue also ruin it. For playing the harp makes both good and bad harpists, and it is analogous in the case of builders and all the rest; for building well makes good builders, building badly, bad ones. If it were not so, no teacher would be needed, but everyone would be born a good or a bad craftsman.

It is the same, then, with the virtues. For actions in dealings with [other] human beings make some people just, some unjust; actions in terrifying situations and the acquired habit of fear or confidence make some brave and others cowardly. The same is true of situations involving appetites and anger; for one or another sort of conduct in these situations makes some people temperate and gentle, others intemperate and irascible.

Conclusion: The Importance of Habituation.

To sum up, then, in a single account: A state [of character] arises from [the repetition of] similar activities. Hence we must display the right activities, since differences in these imply corresponding differences in the states. It is not unimportant, then, to acquire one sort of habit or another, right from our youth; rather, it is very important, indeed all-important....

But our claims about habituation raise a puzzle: How can we become good without being good already?

However, someone might raise this puzzle: "What do you mean by saying that to become just we must first do just actions and to become temperate we must first do temperate actions? For if we do what is grammatical or musical, we must already be grammarians or musicians. In the same way, then, if we do what is just or temperate, we must already be just or temperate."

First reply: Conformity versus understanding.

But surely this is not so even with the crafts, for it is possible to produce something grammatical by chance or by following someone else's instructions. To be a grammarian, then, we must both produce something grammatical and produce it in the way in which the grammarian produces it, i.e., expressing grammatical knowledge that is in us.

Second reply: Crafts versus virtues.

Moreover, in any case what is true of crafts is not true of virtues. For the products of a craft determine by their own character whether they have been produced well; and so it suffices that they are in the right state when they have been produced. But for actions expressing virtue to be done temperately or justly [and hence well] it does not suffice that they are themselves in the right state. Rather, the agent must also be in the right state when he does them. First, he must know [that he is doing virtuous actions]; second, he must decide on them, and decide on them for themselves; and, third, he must also do them from a firm and unchanging state.

As conditions for having a craft these three do not count, except for the knowing itself. As a condition for having a virtue, however, the knowing counts for nothing, or [rather] for only a little, whereas the other two conditions are very important, indeed all-important. And these other two conditions are achieved by the frequent doing of just and temperate actions.

Hence actions are called just or temperate when they are the sort that a just or temperate person would do. But the just and temperate person is not the one who [merely] does these actions, but the one who also does them in the way in which just or temperate people do them.

It is right, then, to say that a person comes to be just from doing just actions and temperate from doing temperate actions; for no one has even a prospect of becoming good from failing to do them.

Virtue requires habituation, and therefore requires practice, not just theory.

The many, however, do not do these actions but take refuge in arguments, thinking that they are doing philosophy, and that this is the way to become excellent people. In this they are like a sick person who listens attentively to the doctor, but acts on none of his instructions. Such a course of treatment will not improve the state of his body; any more than will the many's way of doing philosophy improve the state of their souls.

A VIRTUE OF CHARACTER IS A STATE INTERMEDIATE BETWEEN TWO EXTREMES, AND INVOLVING DECISION

The Genus

Feelings, capacities, states. Next we must examine what virtue is. Since there are three conditions arising in the soul—feelings, capacities and states—virtue must be one of these.

By feelings I mean appetite, anger, fear, confidence, envy, joy, love, hate, longing, jealousy, pity, in general whatever implies pleasure or pain.

By capacities I mean what we have when we are said to be capable of these feelings—capable of, e.g., being angry or afraid or feeling pity.

By states I mean what we have when we are well or badly off in relation to feelings. If, e.g., our feeling is too intense or slack, we are badly off in relation to

anger, but if it is intermediate, we are well off; and the same is true in the other cases.

Virtue is not a feeling...

First, then, neither virtues nor vices are feelings. (a) For we are called excellent or base in so far as we have virtues or vices, not in so far as we have feelings. (b) We are neither praised nor blamed in so far as we have feelings; for we do not praise the angry or the frightened person, and do not blame the person who is simply angry, but only the person who is angry in a particular way. But we are praised or blamed in so far as we have virtues or vices. (c) We are angry and afraid without decision; but the virtues are decisions of some kind, or [rather] require decision. (d) Besides, in so far as we have feelings, we are said to be moved; but in so far as we have virtues or vices, we are said to be in some condition rather than moved.

Or a capacity...

For these reasons the virtues are not capacities either; for we are neither called good nor called bad in so far as we are simply capable of feelings. Further, while *we* have capacities by nature, we do not become good or bad by nature; we have discussed this before.

But a state

If, then, the virtues are neither feelings nor capacities, the remaining possibility is that they are states. And so we have said what the genus of virtue is.

The Differentia

But we must say not only, as we already have, that it is a state, but also what sort of state it is.

Virtue and the Human Function

It should be said, then, that every virtue causes its possessors to be in a good state and to perform their functions well; the virtue of eyes, e.g., makes the eyes and their functioning excellent, because it makes us see well; and similarly, the virtue of a horse makes the horse excellent, and thereby good at galloping, at carrying its rider and at standing steady in the face of the enemy. If this is true in every case, then the virtue of a human being will likewise be the state that makes a human being good and makes him perform his function well . . . .

The Numerical Mean and the Mean Relative to Us

In everything continuous and divisible we can take more, less and equal, and each of them either in the object itself or relative to us; and the equal is some intermediate between excess and deficiency.

By the intermediate in the object I mean what is equidistant from each extremity; this is one and the same for everyone. But relative to us the intermediate is what is neither superfluous nor deficient; this is not one, and is not the same for everyone.

If, e.g., ten are many and two are few, we take six as intermediate in the object, since it exceeds [two] and is exceeded [by ten] by an equal amount, [four]; this is what is intermediate by numerical proportion. But that is not how we must take the intermediate that is relative to us. For if, e.g., ten pounds [of food] are a lot for someone to eat, and two pounds a little, it does not follow that the trainer will prescribe six, since this might also be either a little or a lot for the person who is to take it—for Milo [the athlete] a little, but for the beginner in gymnastics a lot; and the same is true for running and wrestling. In this way every scientific expert avoids excess and deficiency and seeks and chooses what is intermediate—but intermediate relative to us, not in the object.

Virtue seeks the mean relative to us: Argument from craft to virtue.

This, then, is how each science produces its product well, by focusing on what is intermediate and making the product conform to that. This, indeed, is why people regularly comment on well-made products that nothing could be added or subtracted, since they assume that excess or deficiency ruins a good [result] while the mean preserves it. Good craftsmen also, we

say, focus on what is intermediate when they produce their product. And since virtue, like nature, is better and more exact than any craft, it will also aim at what is intermediate.

Arguments from the Nature of Virtue of Character

By virtue I mean virtue of character; for this [pursues the mean because] it is concerned with feelings and actions, and these admit of excess, deficiency and an intermediate condition. We can be afraid, e.g., or be confident, or have appetites, or get angry, or feel pity, in general have pleasure or pain, both too much and too little, and in both ways not well; but [having these feelings] at the right times, about the right things, towards the right people, for the right end, and in the right way, is the intermediate and best condition, and this is proper to virtue. Similarly actions also admit of excess, deficiency and the intermediate condition.

Now virtue is concerned with feelings and actions, in which excess and deficiency are in error and incur blame, while the intermediate condition is correct and wins praise, which are both proper features of virtue. Virtue, then, is a mean, in so far as it aims at what is intermediate.

Moreover, there are many ways to be in error, since badness is proper to what is unlimited, as the Pythagoreans pictured it, and good to what is limited; but there is only one way to be correct. That is why error is easy and correctness hard, since it is easy to miss the target and hard to hit it. And so for this reason also excess and deficiency are proper to vice, the mean to virtue; "for we are noble in only one way, but bad in all sorts of ways."

Definition of Virtue

Virtue, then, is (a) a state that decides, (b) [consisting] in a mean, (c) the mean relative to us, (d) which is defined by reference to reason, (e) i.e., to the reason by reference to which the intelligent person would define it. It is a mean between two vices, one of excess and one of deficiency.

It is a mean for this reason also: Some vices miss what is right because they are deficient, others because they are excessive, in feelings or in actions, while virtue finds and chooses what is intermediate.

Hence, as far as its substance and the account stating its essence are concerned, virtue is a mean; but as far as the best [condition] and the good [result] are concerned, it is an extremity.

The definition must not be misapplied to cases in which there is no mean.

But not every action or feeling admits of the mean. For the names of some automatically include baseness, e.g., spite, shamelessness, envy [among feelings], and adultery, theft, murder, among actions. All of these and similar things are called by these names because they themselves, not their excesses or deficiencies, are base.

Hence in doing these things we can never be correct, but must invariably be in error. We cannot do them well or not well—e.g., by committing adultery with the right woman at the right time in the right way; on the contrary, it is true unconditionally that to do any of them is to be in error.

[To think these admit of a mean], therefore, is like thinking that unjust or cowardly or intemperate action also admits of a mean, an excess and a deficiency. For then there would be a mean of excess, a mean of deficiency, an excess of excess and a deficiency of deficiency.

Rather, just as there is no excess or deficiency of temperance or of bravery, since the intermediate is a sort of extreme [in achieving the good], so also there is no mean of these [vicious actions] either, but whatever way anyone does them, he is in error. For in general there is no mean of excess or of deficiency, and no excess or deficiency of a mean.

The Definition of Virtue as a Mean Applies to the Individual Virtues

However, we must not only state this general account but also apply it to the particular cases. For among accounts concerning actions, though the general ones are common to more cases, the specific ones are truer, since actions are about particular cases, and our account must accord with these. Let us, then, find these from the chart.

CLASSIFICATION OF VIRTUES OF CHARACTER

Virtues Concerned with Feelings

1. First in feelings of fear and confidence the mean is bravery. The excessively fearless person is nameless (and in fact many cases are nameless), while the one who is excessively confident is rash; the one who is excessively afraid and deficient in confidence is cowardly.
2. In pleasures and pains, though not in all types, and in pains less than in pleasures, the mean is temperance and the excess intemperance. People deficient in pleasure are not often found, which is why they also lack even a name; let us call them insensible.

Virtues Concerned with External Goods

3. In giving and taking money the mean is generosity, the excess wastefulness and the deficiency ungenerosity. Here the vicious people have contrary excesses and defects; for the wasteful person spends to excess and is deficient in taking, whereas the ungenerous person takes to excess and is deficient in spending. At the moment we are speaking in outline and summary....
4. In questions of money there are also other conditions. Another mean is magnificence; for the magnificent person differs from the generous by being concerned with large matters, while the generous person is concerned with small. The excess is ostentation and vulgarity, and the deficiency niggardliness, and these differ from the vices related to generosity....
5. In honor and dishonor the mean is magnanimity, the excess something called a sort of vanity, and the deficiency pusillanimity.
6. And just as we said that generosity differs from magnificence in its concern with small matters, similarly there is a virtue concerned with small honors, differing in the same way from magnanimity, which is concerned with great honors. For honor can be desired either in the right way

or more or less than is right. If someone desires it to excess, he is called an honor-lover, and if his desire is deficient he is called indifferent to honor, but if he is intermediate he has no name. The corresponding conditions have no name either, except the condition of the honor-lover, which is called honor-loving.

This is why people at the extremes claim the intermediate area. Indeed, we also sometimes call the intermediate person an honor-lover, and sometimes call him indifferent to honor; and sometimes we praise the honor-lover, sometimes the person indifferent to honor....

Virtues Concerned with Social Life

7. Anger also admits of an excess, deficiency and mean. These are all practically nameless; but since we call the intermediate person mild, let us call the mean mildness. Among the extreme people let the excessive person be irascible, and the vice be irascibility, and let the deficient person be a sort of inirascible person, and the deficiency be inirascibility.

There are three other means, somewhat similar to one another, but different. For they are all concerned with association in conversations and actions, but differ in so far as one is concerned with truth-telling in these areas, the other two with sources of pleasure, some of which are found in amusement, and the others in daily life in general. Hence we should also discuss these states, so that we can better observe that in every case the mean is praiseworthy, while the extremes are neither praiseworthy nor correct, but blameworthy. Most of these cases are also nameless, and we must try, as in the other cases also, to make names ourselves, to make things clear and easy to follow.

8. In truth-telling, then, let us call the intermediate person truthful, and the mean truthfulness;

pretense that overstates will be boastfulness, and the person who has it boastful; pretense that understates will be self-deprecation, and the person who has it self-deprecating.

9. In sources of pleasure in amusements let us call the intermediate person witty, and the condition wit; the excess buffoonery and the person who has it a buffoon; and the deficient person a sort of boor and the state boorishness.

10. In the other sources of pleasure, those in daily life, let us call the person who is pleasant in the right way friendly, and the mean state friendliness. If someone goes to excess with no [further] aim he will be ingratiating; if he does it for his own advantage, a flatterer. The deficient person, unpleasant in everything, will be a sort of quarrelsome and ill-tempered person.

Mean States That Are Not Virtues

11. There are also means in feelings and concerned with feelings: shame, e.g., is not a virtue, but the person prone to shame as well as the virtuous person we have described receives praise. For here also one person is called intermediate, and another—the person excessively prone to shame, who is ashamed about everything— is called excessive; the person who is deficient in shame or never feels shame at all is said to have no sense of disgrace; and the intermediate one is called prone to shame.

12. Proper indignation is the mean between envy and spite; these conditions are concerned with pleasure and pain at what happens to our neighbors. For the properly indignant person feels pain when someone does well undeservedly; the envious person exceeds him by feeling pain when anyone does well, while the spiteful person is so deficient in feeling pain that he actually enjoys [other people's misfortunes].

READING QUESTIONS

1. How does Aristotle defend the claim that the good for human beings is happiness?
2. According to Aristotle, how is virtue acquired?

3. How does Aristotle define virtue? What role does the idea of a "mean" play in his definition?
4. Review the various traits of character Aristotle lists.

DISCUSSION QUESTIONS

1. Are there any virtues that you think are missing from Aristotle's discussion?
2. Which of the virtues and vices Aristotle discusses strike you as distinctively ethical or moral virtues and vices? If you think that some of the virtue and vices are not ethical, what is the basis for distinguishing ethical from other types of virtue and vice?

W. D. Ross

What Makes Right Actions Right?

In contrast to the views of Bentham and Kant, Ross (1877–1971) denies that there is some single moral principle that can be used to derive more specific moral obligations. Rather, he defends a version of moral pluralism, according to which there is a plurality of irreducible moral rules that are basic in moral thought. These rules express what Ross calls *prima facie duties*—duties such as keeping promises and avoiding injury to others. Such duties may come into conflict in particular circumstances, and when they do, what is demanded (according to Ross) is that we use moral judgment in order to determine which prima facie duty is (in that circumstance) weightiest and should be obeyed.

Recommended Reading: See ethics of prima facie duty, chap. 1, sec. 2F, for an explication of Ross's moral theory, plus some remarks about how some contemporary philosophers have developed Ross's theory.

When a plain man fulfills a promise because he thinks he ought to do so, it seems clear that he does so with no thought of its total consequences, still less with any opinion that these are likely to be the best possible. He thinks in fact much more of the past than of the future. What makes him think it right to act in a certain way is the fact that he has promised to do so—that and, usually, nothing more. That his act will produce the best possible consequences is not his reason for calling it right. What lends color to the theory we are examining, then, is not the actions (which form probably a great majority of our actions) in which some such reflection as "I have promised" is the only reason we give ourselves for thinking a certain action right, but the exceptional cases in which the consequences of fulfilling a promise (for

From *The Right and the Good* by W. D. Ross (Oxford: Oxford University Press, 1930). Reprinted by permission of the publisher.

instance) would be so disastrous to others that we judge it right not to do so. It must of course be admitted that such cases exist. If I have promised to meet a friend at a particular time for some trivial purpose, I should certainly think myself justified in breaking my engagement if by doing so I could prevent a serious accident or bring relief to the victims of one. And the supporters of the view we are examining hold that my thinking so is due to my thinking that I shall bring more good into existence by the one action than by the other. A different account may, however, be given of the matter, an account which will, I believe, show itself to be the true one. It may be said that besides the duty of fulfilling promises I have and recognize a duty of relieving distress, and that when I think it right to do the latter at the cost of not doing the former, it is not because I think I shall produce more good thereby but because I think it the duty which is in the circumstances more of a duty. This account surely corresponds much more closely with what we really think in such a situation. If, so far as I can see, I could bring equal amounts of good into being by fulfilling my promise and by helping someone to whom I had made no promise, I should not hesitate to regard the former as my duty. Yet on the view that what is right is right because it is productive of the most good I should not so regard it....

In fact the theory of... utilitarianism... seems to simplify unduly our relations to our fellows. It says, in effect, that the only morally significant relation in which my neighbors stand to me is that of being possible beneficiaries by my action. They do stand in this relation to me, and this relation is morally significant. But they may also stand to me in the relation of promisee to promiser, of creditor to debtor, of wife to husband, of child to parent, of friend to friend, of fellow countryman to fellow countryman, and the like; and each of these relations is the foundation of a *prima facie* duty, which is more or less incumbent on me according to the circumstances of the case. When I am in a situation, as perhaps I always am, in which more than one of these *prima facie* duties is incumbent on me, what I have to do is to study the situation as fully as I can until I form the considered opinion (it is never more) that in the circumstances one of them is more incumbent than any other; then I am bound to think that to do this *prima facie* duty is my duty *sans phrase* in the situation.

I suggest "*prima facie* duty" or "conditional duty" as a brief way of referring to the characteristic (quite distinct from that of being a duty proper) which an act has, in virtue of being of a certain kind (e.g., the keeping of a promise), of being an act which would be a duty proper if it were not at the same time of another kind which is morally significant. Whether an act is a duty proper or actual duty depends on *all* the morally significant kinds it is an instance of....

There is nothing arbitrary about these *prima facie* duties. Each rests on a definite circumstance which cannot seriously be held to be without moral significance. Of *prima facie* duties I suggest, without claiming completeness or finality for it, the following division.

(1) Some duties rest on previous acts of my own. These duties seem to include two kinds, (*a*) those resting on a promise or what may fairly be called an implicit promise, such as the implicit undertaking not to tell lies which seems to be implied in the act of entering into conversation (at any rate by civilized men), or of writing books that purport to be history and not fiction. These may be called the duties of fidelity. (*b*) Those resting on a previous wrongful act. These may be called the duties of reparation. (2) Some rest on previous acts of other men, i.e., services done by them to me. These may be loosely described as the duties of gratitude. (3) Some rest on the fact or possibility of a distribution of pleasure or happiness (or of the means thereto) which is not in accordance with the merit of the persons concerned; in such cases there arises a duty to upset or prevent such a distribution. These are the duties of justice. (4) Some rest on the mere fact that there are other beings in the world whose condition we can make better in respect of virtue, or of intelligence, or of pleasure. These are the duties of beneficence. (5) Some rest on the fact that we can improve our own condition in respect of virtue or of intelligence. These are the duties of self-improvement. (6) I think that we should distinguish from (4) the duties that may be summed up under the title of "not injuring others." No doubt to injure others is incidentally to fail to do them good; but it seems to me clear that nonmaleficence is apprehended as a duty distinct from

that of beneficence, and as a duty of a more stringent character. It will be noticed that this alone among the types of duty has been stated in a negative way. An attempt might no doubt be made to state this duty, like the others, in a positive way. It might be said that it is really the duty to prevent ourselves from acting either from an inclination to harm others or from an inclination to seek our own pleasure, in doing which we should incidentally harm them. But on reflection it seems clear that the primary duty here is the duty not to harm others, this being a duty whether or not we have an inclination that if followed would lead to our harming them; and that when we have such an inclination the primary duty not to harm others gives rise to a consequential duty to resist the inclination. The recognition of this duty of non-maleficence is the first step on the way to the recognition of the duty of beneficence; and that accounts for the prominence of the commands "thou shalt not kill," "thou shalt not commit adultery," "thou shalt not steal," "thou shalt not bear false witness," in so early a code as the Decalogue. But even when we have come to recognize the duty of beneficence, it appears to me that the duty of non-maleficence is recognized as a distinct one, and as *prima facie* more binding. We should not in general consider it justifiable to kill one person in order to keep another alive, or to steal from one in order to give alms to another....

The essential defect of the...utilitarian theory is that it ignores, or at least does not do full justice to, the highly personal character of duty. If the only duty is to produce the maximum of good, the question who is to have the good—whether it is myself, or my benefactor, or a person to whom I have made a promise to confer that good on him, or a mere fellow man to whom I stand in no such special relation—should make no difference to my having a duty to produce that good. But we are all in fact sure that it makes a vast difference....

...That an act, *qua* fulfilling a promise, or *qua* effecting a just distribution of good, or *qua* returning services rendered, or *qua* promoting the good of others, or *qua* promoting the virtue or insight of the agent, is *prima facie* right, is self-evident; not in the sense that it is evident from the beginning of our lives, or as soon as we attend to the proposition for the first time, but in the sense that when we have reached sufficient mental maturity and have given sufficient attention to the proposition it is evident without any need of proof, or of evidence beyond itself. It is self-evident just as a mathematical axiom, or the validity of a form of inference, is evident. The moral order expressed in these propositions is just as much part of the fundamental nature of the universe (and, we may add, of any possible universe in which there were moral agents at all) as is the spatial or numerical structure expressed in the axioms of geometry or arithmetic. In our confidence that these propositions are true there is involved the same trust in our reason that is involved in our confidence in mathematics; and we should have no justification for trusting it in the latter sphere and distrusting it in the former. In both cases we are dealing with propositions that cannot be proved, but that just as certainly need no proof....

Our judgments about our actual duty in concrete situations have none of the certainty that attaches to our recognition of the general principles of duty. A statement is certain, i.e., is an expression of knowledge, only in one or other of two cases: when it is either self-evident, or a valid conclusion from self-evident premises.

And our judgments about our particular duties have neither of these characters. (1) They are not self-evident. Where a possible act is seen to have two characteristics, in virtue of one of which it is *prima facie* right, and in virtue of the other *prima facie* wrong, we are (I think) well aware that we are not certain whether we ought or ought not to do it; that whether we do it or not, we are taking a moral risk. We come in the long run, after consideration, to think one duty more pressing than the other, but we do not feel certain that it is so. And though we do not always recognize that a possible act has two such characteristics, and though there *may* be cases in which it has not, we are never certain that any particular possible act has not, and therefore never certain that it is right, nor certain that it is wrong. For, to go no further in the analysis, it is enough to point out that any particular act will in all probability in the course of time contribute to the bringing about of good or of evil for many human beings, and thus have a *prima facie* rightness or wrongness of which we know nothing. (2) Again, our judgments about our particular duties are not logical conclusions from self-evident premises. The only possible premises would be the general principles stating their *prima facie* rightness or wrongness *qua* having the different characteristics they do have; and even if we could (as we cannot) apprehend the extent to which an act will tend on the one hand, for example, to bring about advantages for our benefactors, and on the other hand to bring about disadvantages for fellow men who are not our benefactors, there is no principle by which we can draw the conclusion that it is on the whole right or on the whole wrong. In this respect the judgment as to the rightness of a particular act is just like the judgment as to the beauty of a particular natural object or work of art. A poem is, for instance, in respect of certain qualities beautiful and in respect of certain others not beautiful; and our judgment as to the degree of beauty it possesses on the whole is never reached by logical reasoning from the apprehension of its particular beauties or particular defects. Both in this and in the moral case we have more or less probable opinions which are not logically justified conclusions from the general principles that are recognized as self-evident.

There is therefore much truth in the description of the right act as a fortunate act. If we cannot be certain that it is right, it is our good fortune if the act we do is the right act. This consideration does not, however, make the doing of our duty a mere matter of chance. There is a parallel here between the doing of duty and the doing of what will be to our personal advantage. We never *know* what act will in the long run be to our advantage. Yet it is certain that we are more likely in general to secure our advantage if we estimate to the best of our ability the probable tendencies of our actions in this respect, than if we act on caprice. And similarly we are more likely to do our duty if we reflect to the best of our ability on the *prima facie* rightness or wrongness of various possible acts in virtue of the characteristics we perceive them to have, than if we act without reflection. With this greater likelihood we must be content....

In what has preceded, a good deal of use has been made of "what we really think" about moral questions....

...It might be said that this is in principle wrong; that we should not be content to expound what our present moral consciousness tells us but should aim at a criticism of our existing moral consciousness in the light of theory. Now I do not doubt that the moral consciousness of men has in detail undergone a good deal of modification as regards the things we think right, at the hands of moral theory. But...we have to ask ourselves whether we really, when we reflect, *are* convinced that this is self-evident, and whether we really *can* get rid of our view that promise-keeping has a bindingness independent of productiveness of maximum good. In my own experience I find that I cannot, in spite of a very genuine attempt to do so....

I would maintain, in fact, that what we are apt to describe as "what we think" about moral questions contains a considerable amount that we do not think but know, and that this forms the standard by reference to which the truth of any moral theory has to be tested, instead of having itself to be tested by reference to any theory. I hope that I have in what precedes indicated what in my view these elements of knowledge are that are involved in our ordinary moral consciousness.

It would be a mistake to found a natural science on "what we really think," i.e., on what reasonably thoughtful and well-educated people think about the subjects of the science before they have studied them scientifically. For such opinions are interpretations, and often misinterpretations, of sense-experience; and the man of science must appeal from these to sense-experience itself, which furnishes his real data. In ethics no such appeal is possible. We have no more direct way of access to the facts about rightness and goodness and about what things are right or good, than by thinking about them; the moral convictions of thoughtful and well-educated people are the data of ethics just as sense-perceptions are the data of a natural science. Just as some of the latter have to be rejected as illusory, so have some of the former; but as the latter are rejected only when they are in conflict with other more accurate sense-perceptions, the former are rejected only when they are in conflict with other convictions which stand better the test of reflection. The existing body of moral convictions of the best people is the cumulative product of the moral reflection of many generations, which has developed an extremely delicate power of appreciation of moral distinctions; and this the theorist cannot afford to treat with anything other than the greatest respect. The verdicts of the moral consciousness of the best people are the foundation on which he must build; though he must first compare them with one another and eliminate any contradictions they may contain.

READING QUESTIONS

1. Explain in your own words what Ross means by "prima facie duty."
2. Ross claims that the utilitarian theory "ignores, or at least does not do full justice to, the highly personal character of duty." What does he mean by this?
3. What does Ross say about the need to prove his principles of prima facie duty? Do you find his claim plausible? Explain.

DISCUSSION QUESTIONS

1. What conclusions do you think follow from Ross's ethic of prima facie duty about the morality of meat eating?
2. What implications do you think Ross's theory has for certain sexual issues including homosexuality, adultery, and prostitution?

JOHN RAWLS

A Theory of Justice

In this selection from his influential book *A Theory of Justice*, published in 1971, John Rawls presents the elements of a social contract account of the principles of social justice. In the first part of the selection, Rawls explains the main ideas that make up his theory including what he calls the "original position," which represents ideal circumstances within which hypothetical contractors are to choose principles of justice. He then proceeds to explain the two fundamental principles of justice—the principle of equal liberty and the difference principle—which, he argues, would be chosen by occupants from within the original position.

Recommended Reading: See social contract theory, chap. 1, sec. 2G, for an exposition of social contract theories, including a brief overview of Rawls's version.

From *A Theory of Justice* by John Rawls (Cambridge, MA: Harvard University Press, 1971), pp. 11–12, 60–65, 100–105. Reprinted by permission of the publisher. Bracketed section titles by James Fieser from his edited version of this same selection in his *Metaethics, Normative Ethics, and Applied Ethics* (Belmont, CA: Wadsworth, 2000).

THE MAIN IDEA OF THE THEORY OF JUSTICE

My aim is to present a conception of justice which generalizes and carries to a higher level of abstraction the familiar theory of the social contract as found, say, in Locke, Rousseau, and Kant. In order to do this we are not to think of the original contract as one to enter a particular society or to set up a particular form of government. Rather, the guiding idea is that the principles of justice for the basic structure of society are the object of the original agreement. They are the principles that free and rational persons concerned to further their own interests would accept in an initial position of equality as defining the fundamental terms of their association. These principles are to regulate all further agreements that specify the kinds of social cooperation that can be entered into and the forms of government that can be established. This way of regarding the principles of justice I shall call justice as fairness.

Thus we are to imagine that those who engage in social cooperation choose together, in one joint act, the principles which are to assign basic rights and duties and to determine the division of social benefits. Men are to decide in advance how they are to regulate their claims against one another and what is to be the foundation charter of their society. Just as each person must decide by rational reflection what constitutes his good, that is, the system of ends which it is rational for him to pursue, so a group of persons must decide once and for all what is to count among them as just and unjust. The choice which rational men would make in this hypothetical situation of equal liberty, assuming for the present that this choice problem has a solution, determines the principles of justice.

In justice as fairness the original position of equality corresponds to the state of nature in the traditional theory of the social contract. This original position is not, of course, thought of as an actual historical state of affairs, much less as a primitive condition of culture. It is understood as a purely hypothetical situation characterized so as to lead to a certain conception of justice. Among the essential features of this situation is that no one knows his place in society, his class position or social status, nor does any one know his fortune in the distribution of natural assets and abilities, his intelligence, strength, and the like. I shall even assume that the parties do not know their conceptions of the good or their special psychological propensities. The principles of justice are chosen behind a veil of ignorance. This ensures that no one is advantaged or disadvantaged in the choice of principles by the outcome of natural chance or the contingency of social circumstances. Since all are similarly situated and no one is able to design principles to favor his particular condition, the principles of justice are the result of a fair agreement or bargain. For given the circumstances of the original position, the symmetry of everyone's relations to each other, this initial situation is fair between individuals as moral persons, that is, as rational beings with their own ends and capable, I shall assume, of a sense of justice. The original position is, one might say, the appropriate initial status quo, and thus the fundamental agreements reached in it are fair. This explains the propriety of the name "justice as fairness": it conveys the idea that the principles of justice are agreed to in an initial situation that is fair. The name does not mean that the concepts of justice and fairness are the same, any more than the phrase "poetry as metaphor" means that the concepts of poetry and metaphor are the same.

[Further Principles Derived from Justice]

Justice as fairness begins, as I have said, with one of the most general of all choices which persons might make together, namely, with the choice of the first principles of a conception of justice which is to regulate all subsequent criticism and reform of institutions. Then, having chosen a conception of justice, we can suppose that they are to choose a constitution and a legislature to enact laws, and so on, all in accordance with the principles of justice initially agreed upon. Our social situation is just if it is such that by this sequence of hypothetical agreements we would have contracted into the general system of rules which defines it. Moreover, assuming that the original position does determine a set of principles (that is, that a particular conception of justice would be chosen), it will then be true that whenever social institutions satisfy these principles those engaged in them can say to one another that they are cooperating, on terms to which they would agree if they were free and equal persons whose relations with respect to one another were fair. They could all view their arrangements as meeting the stipulations which they would acknowledge in an initial situation that embodies widely accepted and reasonable constraints on the choice of principles. The general recognition of this fact would provide the basis for a public acceptance of the corresponding principles of justice. No society can, of course, be a scheme of cooperation which men enter voluntarily in a literal sense; each person finds himself placed at birth in some particular position in some particular society, and the nature of this position materially affects his life prospects. Yet a society satisfying the principles of justice as fairness comes as close as a society can to being a voluntary scheme, for it meets the principles which free and equal persons would assent to under circumstances that are fair. In this sense its members are autonomous and the obligations they recognize self-imposed.

One feature of justice as fairness is to think of the parties in the initial situation as rational and mutually disinterested. This does not mean that the parties are egoists, that is, individuals with only certain kinds of interests, say in wealth, prestige, and domination. But they are conceived as not taking an interest in one another's interests. They are to presume that even their spiritual aims may be opposed, in the way that the aims of those of different religions may be opposed. Moreover, the concept of rationality must be interpreted as far as possible in the narrow sense, standard in economic theory, of taking the most effective means to given ends. I shall modify this concept to some extent, . . . but one must try to avoid introducing into it any controversial ethical elements. The initial situation must be characterized by stipulations that are widely accepted.

[Deriving Justice from the Original Position]

In working out the conception of justice as fairness one main task clearly is to determine which principles of justice would be chosen in the original position. To do this we must describe this situation in some detail and formulate with care the problem of choice which it presents. . . . It may be observed, however, that once the principles of justice are thought of as arising from an original agreement in a situation of equality, it is an open question whether the principle of utility would be acknowledged. Offhand it hardly seems likely that persons who view themselves as equals, entitled to press their claims upon one another, would agree to a principle which may require lesser life prospects for some simply for the sake of a greater sum of advantages enjoyed by others. Since each desires to protect his interests, his capacity to advance his conception of the good, no one has a reason to acquiesce in an enduring loss for himself in order to bring about a greater net balance of satisfaction. In the absence of strong and lasting benevolent impulses, a rational man would not accept a basic structure merely because it maximized the algebraic sum of advantages irrespective of its permanent effects on his own basic rights and interests. Thus it seems that the principle of utility is incompatible with the conception of social cooperation among equals for mutual advantage. It appears to be inconsistent with the idea of reciprocity implicit in the notion of a well-ordered society. Or, at any rate, so I shall argue.

I shall maintain instead that the persons in the initial situation would choose two rather different principles: the first requires equality in the assignment of basic rights and duties, while the second holds that social and economic inequalities, for example inequalities of wealth and authority, are just only if they result in compensating benefits for everyone, and in particular for the least advantaged members of society. These principles rule out justifying institutions on the grounds that the hardships of some are offset by a greater good in the aggregate. It may be expedient but it is not just that some should have less in order that others may prosper. But there is no injustice in the greater benefits earned by a few provided that the situation of persons not so fortunate is thereby improved. The intuitive idea is that since everyone's well-being depends upon a scheme of cooperation without which no one could have a satisfactory life, the division of advantages should be such as to draw forth the willing cooperation of everyone taking part in it, including those less well situated. Yet this can be expected only if reasonable terms are proposed. The two principles mentioned seem to be a fair agreement on the basis of which those better endowed, or more fortunate in their social position, neither of which we can be said to deserve, could expect the willing cooperation of others when some workable scheme is a necessary condition of the welfare of all. Once we decide to look for a conception of justice that nullifies the accidents of natural endowment and the contingencies of social circumstance as counters in quest for political and economic advantage, we are led to these principles. They express the result of leaving aside those aspects of the social world that seem arbitrary from a moral point of view.

The problem of the choice of principles, however, is extremely difficult. I do not expect the answer I shall suggest to be convincing to everyone. It is, therefore, worth noting from the outset that justice as fairness, like other contract views, consists of two parts: (1) an interpretation of the initial situation and of the problem of choice posed there, and (2) a set of principles which, it is argued, would be agreed to. One may accept the first part of the theory (or some variant thereof), but not the other, and conversely.

The concept of the initial contractual situation may seem reasonable although the particular principles proposed are rejected. To be sure, I want to maintain that the most appropriate conception of this situation does lead to principles of justice contrary to utilitarianism and perfectionism, and therefore that the contract doctrine provides an alternative to these views. Still, one may dispute this contention even though one grants that the contractarian method is a useful way of studying ethical theories and of setting forth their underlying assumptions.

[Contract Theory]

Justice as fairness is an example of what I have called a contract theory. Now there may be an objection to the term "contract" and related expressions, but I think it will serve reasonably well. Many words have misleading connotations which at first are likely to confuse. The terms "utility" and "utilitarianism" are surely no exception. They too have unfortunate suggestions which hostile critics have been willing to exploit; yet they are clear enough for those prepared to study utilitarian doctrine. The same should be true of the term "contract" applied to moral theories. As I have mentioned, to understand it one has to keep in mind that it implies a certain level of abstraction. In particular, the content of the relevant agreement is not to enter a given society or to adopt a given form of government, but to accept certain moral principles. Moreover, the undertakings referred to are purely hypothetical: a contract view holds that certain principles would be accepted in a well-defined initial situation.

The merit of the contract terminology is that it conveys the idea that principles of justice may be conceived as principles that would be chosen by rational persons, and that in this way conceptions of justice may be explained and justified. The theory of justice is a part, perhaps the most significant part, of the theory of rational choice. Furthermore, principles of justice deal with conflicting claims upon the advantages won by social cooperation; they apply to the relations among several persons or groups. The word "contract" suggests this plurality as well as the condition that the appropriate division of advantages must be in accordance with principles acceptable to all parties. The condition of publicity for principles of justice is also connoted by the contract phraseology. Thus, if these principles are the outcome of an agreement, citizens have a knowledge of the principles that others follow. It is characteristic of contract theories to stress the public nature of political principles. Finally there is the long tradition of the contract doctrine. Expressing the tie with this line of thought helps to define ideas and accords with natural piety. There are then several advantages in the use of the term "contract." With due precautions taken, it should not be misleading.

A final remark. Justice as fairness is not a complete contract theory. For it is clear that the contractarian idea can be extended to the choice of more or less an entire ethical system, that is, to a system including principles for all the virtues and not only for justice. Now for the most part I shall consider only principles of justice and others closely related to them; I make no attempt to discuss the virtues in a systematic way. Obviously if justice as fairness succeeds reasonably well, a next step would be to study the more general view suggested by the name "rightness as fairness." But even this wider theory fails to embrace all moral relationships, since it would seem to include only our relations with other persons and to leave out of account how we are to conduct ourselves toward animals and the rest of nature. I do not contend that the contract notion offers a way to approach these questions which are certainly of the first importance; and I shall have to put them aside. We must recognize the limited scope of justice as fairness and of the general type of view that it exemplifies. How far its conclusions must be revised once these other matters are understood cannot be decided in advance.

THE ORIGINAL POSITION AND JUSTIFICATION

I have said that the original position is the appropriate initial status quo which insures that the fundamental agreements reached in it are fair. This fact yields the name "justice as fairness." It is clear, then, that I want to say that one conception of justice is more reasonable than another, or justifiable with respect to it, if rational persons in the initial situation would choose its principles over those of the other for the role of justice. Conceptions of justice are to be ranked by their acceptability to persons so circumstanced. Understood in this way the question of justification is settled by working out a problem of deliberation: we have to ascertain which principles it would be rational to adopt given the contractual situation. This connects the theory of justice with the theory of rational choice.

If this view of the problem of justification is to succeed, we must, of course, describe in some detail the nature of this choice problem. A problem of rational decision has a definite answer only if we know the beliefs and interests of the parties, their relations with respect to one another, the alternatives between

which they are to choose, the procedure whereby they make up their minds, and so on. As the circumstances are presented in different ways, correspondingly different principles are accepted. The concept of the original position, as I shall refer to it, is that of the most philosophically favored interpretation of this initial choice situation for the purposes of a theory of justice.

But how are we to decide what is the most favored interpretation? I assume, for one thing, that there is a broad measure of agreement that principles of justice should be chosen under certain conditions. To justify a particular description of the initial situation one shows that it incorporates these commonly shared presumptions. One argues from widely accepted but weak premises to more specific conclusions. Each of the presumptions should by itself be natural and plausible; some of them may seem innocuous or even trivial. The aim of the contract approach is to establish that taken together they impose significant bounds on acceptable principles of justice. The ideal outcome would be that these conditions determine a unique set of principles; but I shall be satisfied if they suffice to rank the main traditional conceptions of social justice.

[Equality and the Veil of Ignorance]

One should not be misled, then, by the somewhat unusual conditions which characterize the original position. The idea here is simply to make vivid to ourselves the restrictions that it seems reasonable to impose on arguments for principles of justice, and therefore on these principles themselves. Thus it seems reasonable and generally acceptable that no one should be advantaged or disadvantaged by natural fortune or social circumstances in the choice of principles. It also seems widely agreed that it should be impossible to tailor principles to the circumstances of one's own case. We should insure further that particular inclinations and aspirations, and persons' conceptions of their good do not affect the principles adopted. The aim is to rule out those principles that it would be rational to propose for acceptance, however little the chance of success, only if one knew certain things that are irrelevant from the standpoint of justice. For example, if a man knew that he was wealthy, he might find it rational to advance the principle that various taxes for welfare measures be counted unjust; if he knew that he was poor, he would most likely propose the contrary principle. To represent the desired restrictions one imagines a situation in which everyone is deprived of this sort of information. One excludes the knowledge of those contingencies which sets men at odds and allows them to be guided by their prejudices. In this manner the veil of ignorance is arrived at in a natural way. This concept should cause no difficulty if we keep in mind the constraints on arguments that it is meant to express. At any time we can enter the original position, so to speak, simply by following a certain procedure, namely, by arguing for principles of justice in accordance with these restrictions.

It seems reasonable to suppose that the parties in the original position are equal. That is, all have the same rights in the procedure for choosing principles; each can make proposals, submit reasons for their acceptance, and so on. Obviously the purpose of these conditions is to represent equality between human beings as moral persons, as creatures having a conception of their good and capable of a sense of justice. The basis of equality is taken to be similarity in these two respects. Systems of ends are not ranked in value; and each man is presumed to have the requisite ability to understand and to act upon whatever principles are adopted. Together with the veil of ignorance, these conditions define the principles of justice as those which rational persons concerned to advance their interests would consent to as equals when none are known to be advantaged or disadvantaged by social and natural contingencies.

[Reflective Equilibrium]

There is, however, another side to justifying a particular description of the original position. This is to see if the principles which would be chosen match our considered convictions of justice or extend them in an acceptable way. We can note whether applying these principles would lead us to make the same judgments about the basic structure of society which we now make intuitively and in which we have the greatest confidence; or whether, in cases where our present judgments are in doubt and given with hesitation, these principles offer a resolution which we can affirm on reflection. There are questions which we feel sure must be answered in a certain way. For example, we are confident that religious intolerance and racial discrimination are unjust. We think that we have examined these things with care and have reached what we believe is an impartial judgment not likely to be distorted by an excessive attention to our own interests. These convictions are provisional fixed points which we presume any conception of justice must fit. But we have much less assurance as to what is the correct distribution of wealth and authority. Here we may be looking for a way to remove our doubts. We can check an interpretation of the initial situation, then, by the capacity of its principles to accommodate our firmest convictions and to provide guidance where guidance is needed.

In searching for the most favored description of this situation we work from both ends. We begin by describing it so that it represents generally shared and preferably weak conditions. We then see if these conditions are strong enough to yield a significant set of principles. If not, we look for further premises equally reasonable. But if so, and these principles match our considered convictions of justice, then so far well and good. But presumably there will be discrepancies. In this case we have a choice. We can either modify the account of the initial situation or we can revise our existing judgments, for even the judgments we take provisionally as fixed points are liable to revision. By going back and forth, sometimes altering the conditions of the contractual circumstances, at others withdrawing our judgments and conforming them to principle, I assume that eventually we shall find a description of the initial situation that both expresses reasonable conditions and yields principles which match our considered judgments duly pruned and adjusted. This state of affairs I refer to as reflective equilibrium. It is an equilibrium because at last our principles and judgments coincide; and it is reflective since we know to what principles our judgments conform and the premises of their derivation. At the moment everything is in order. But this equilibrium is not necessarily stable. It is liable to be upset by further examination of the conditions which should be imposed on the contractual situation and by particular cases which may lead us to revise our judgments. Yet for the time being we have done what we can to render coherent and to justify our convictions of social justice. We have reached a conception of the original position.

I shall not, of course, actually work through this process. Still, we may think of the interpretation of the original position that I shall present as the result of such a hypothetical course of reflection. It represents the attempt to accommodate within one scheme both reasonable philosophical conditions on principles as well as our considered judgments of justice. In arriving at the favored interpretation of the initial situation there is no point at which an appeal is made to self-evidence in the traditional sense either of general conceptions or particular convictions. I do not claim for the principles of justice proposed that they are necessary truths or derivable from such truths. A conception of justice cannot be deduced from self-evident premises or conditions on principles; instead, its justification is a matter of the mutual support of many considerations, of everything fitting together into one coherent view.

A final comment. We shall want to say that certain principles of justice are justified because they would be agreed to in an initial situation of equality. I have emphasized that this original position is purely hypothetical. It is natural to ask why, if this agreement is never actually entered into, we should take any interest in these principles, moral or otherwise. The answer is that the conditions embodied in the description of the original position are ones that we do in fact accept. Or if we do not, then perhaps we can be persuaded to do so by philosophical reflection. Each aspect of the contractual situation can be given supporting grounds. Thus what we shall do is to collect together into one conception a number of conditions on principles that we are ready upon due consideration to recognize as reasonable. These constraints express what we are prepared to regard as limits on fair terms of social cooperation. One way to look at the idea of the original position, therefore,

is to see it as an expository device which sums up the meaning of these conditions and helps us to extract their consequences. On the other hand, this conception is also an intuitive notion that suggests its own elaboration, so that led on by it we are drawn to define more clearly the standpoint from which we can best interpret moral relationships. We need a conception that enables us to envision our objective from afar: the intuitive notion of the original position is to do this for us. . . .

TWO PRINCIPLES OF JUSTICE

I shall now state in a provisional form the two principles of justice that I believe would be chosen in the original position. In this section I wish to make only the most general comments, and therefore the first formulation of these principles is tentative. As we go on I shall run through several formulations and approximate step by step the final statement to be given much later. I believe that doing this allows the exposition to proceed in a natural way.

The first statement of the two principles reads as follows.

> First: Each person is to have an equal right to the most extensive basic liberty compatible with a similar liberty for others.
>
> Second: Social and economic inequalities are to be arranged so that they are both (a) reasonably expected to be to everyone's advantage, and (b) attached to positions and offices open to all.

There are two ambiguous phrases in the second principle, namely "everyone's advantage" and "open to all." . . .

By way of general comment, these principles primarily apply, as I have said, to the basic structure of society. They are to govern the assignment of rights and duties and to regulate the distribution of social and economic advantages. As their formulation suggests, these principles presuppose that the social structure can be divided into two more or less distinct parts, the first principle applying to the one, the second to the other. They distinguish between those aspects of the social system that define and secure the equal liberties of citizenship and those that specify and establish social and economic inequalities. The basic liberties of citizens are, roughly speaking, political liberty (the right to vote and to be eligible for public office) together with freedom of speech and assembly; liberty of conscience and freedom of thought; freedom of the person along with the right to hold (personal) property; and freedom from arbitrary arrest and seizure as defined by the concept of the rule of law. These liberties are all required to be equal by the first principle, since citizens of a just society are to have the same basic rights.

The second principle applies, in the first approximation, to the distribution of income and wealth and to the design of organizations that make use of differences in authority and responsibility, or chains of command. While the distribution of wealth and income need not be equal, it must be to everyone's advantage, and at the same time, positions of authority and offices of command must be accessible to all. One applies the second principle by holding positions open, and then, subject to this constraint, arranges social and economic inequalities so that everyone benefits.

These principles are to be arranged in a serial order with the first principle prior to the second. This ordering means that a departure from the institutions of equal liberty required by the first principle cannot be justified by, or compensated for, by greater social and economic advantages. The distribution of wealth and income, and the hierarchies of authority, must be consistent with both the liberties of equal citizenship and equality of opportunity.

It is clear that these principles are rather specific in their content, and their acceptance rests on certain assumptions that I must eventually try to explain and justify. A theory of justice depends upon a theory of society in ways that will become evident as we proceed. For the present, it should be observed that the two principles (and this holds for all formulations) are a special case of a more general conception of justice that can be expressed as follows.

All social values—liberty and opportunity, income and wealth, and the bases of self-respect—are to be distributed equally unless an unequal distribution of any, or all, of these values is to everyone's advantage.

Injustice, then, is simply inequalities that are not to the benefit of all. Of course, this conception is extremely vague and requires interpretation.

[How the Principles Work]

As a first step, suppose that the basic structure of society distributes certain primary goods, that is, things that every rational man is presumed to want. These goods normally have a use whatever a person's rational plan of life. For simplicity, assume that the chief primary goods at the disposition of society are rights and liberties, powers and opportunities, income and wealth. . . . These are the social primary goods. Other primary goods such as health and vigor, intelligence and imagination, are natural goods; although their possession is influenced by the basic structure, they are not so directly under its control. Imagine, then, a hypothetical initial arrangement in which all the social primary goods are equally distributed: everyone has similar rights and duties, and income and wealth are evenly shared. This state of affairs provides a benchmark for judging improvements. If certain inequalities of wealth and organizational powers would make everyone better off than in this hypothetical starting situation, then they accord with the general conception.

Now it is possible, at least theoretically, that by giving up some of their fundamental liberties men are sufficiently compensated by the resulting social and economic gains. The general conception of justice imposes no restrictions on what sort of inequalities are permissible; it only requires that everyone's position be improved. We need not suppose anything so drastic as consenting to a condition of slavery. Imagine instead that men forego certain political rights when the economic returns are significant and their capacity to influence the course of policy by the exercise of these rights would be marginal in any case. It is this kind of exchange which the two principles as stated rule out; being arranged in serial order they do not permit exchanges between basic liberties and economic and social gains. The serial ordering of principles expresses an underlying preference among primary social goods. When this preference is rational so likewise is the choice of these principles in this order. . . .

The fact that the two principles apply to institutions has certain consequences. Several points illustrate this. First of all, the rights and liberties referred to by these principles are those which are defined by the public rules of the basic structure. Whether men are free is determined by the rights and duties established by the major institutions of society. Liberty is a certain pattern of social forms. The first principle simply requires that certain sorts of rules, those defining basic liberties, apply to everyone equally and that they allow the most extensive liberty compatible with a like liberty for all. The only reason for circumscribing the rights defining liberty and making men's freedom less extensive than it might otherwise be is that these equal rights as institutionally defined would interfere with one another. . . .

Now the second principle insists that each person benefit from permissible inequalities in the basic structure. This means that it must be reasonable for each relevant representative man defined by this structure, when he views it as a going concern, to prefer his prospects with the inequality to his prospects without it. One is not allowed to justify differences in income or organizational powers on the ground that the disadvantages of those in one position are outweighed by the greater advantages of those in another. Much less can infringements of liberty be counterbalanced in this way. Applied to the basic structure, the principle of utility would have us maximize the sum of expectations of representative men (weighted by the number of persons they represent, on the classical view); and this would permit us to compensate for the losses of some by the gains of others. Instead, the two principles require that everyone benefit from economic and social inequalities. It is obvious, however, that there are indefinitely many ways in which all may be advantaged when the initial arrangement of equality is taken as a benchmark. How then are we to choose among these possibilities? The principles must be specified so that they yield a determinate conclusion. . . .

THE TENDENCY TO EQUALITY

I wish to conclude this discussion of the two principles by explaining the sense in which they express an egalitarian conception of justice. Also I should like to forestall the objection to the principle of fair opportunity that it leads to a callous meritocratic society. In order to prepare the way for doing this, I note several aspects of the conception of justice that I have set out.

[Natural Assets and the Principle of Redress]

First we may observe that the difference principle gives some weight to the considerations singled out by the principle of redress. This is the principle that undeserved inequalities call for redress; and since inequalities of birth and natural endowment are undeserved, these inequalities are to be somehow compensated for. Thus the principle holds that in order to treat all persons equally, to provide genuine equality of opportunity, society must give more attention to those with fewer native assets and to those born into the less favorable social positions. The idea is to redress the bias of contingencies in the direction of equality. In pursuit of this principle greater resources might be spent on the education of the less rather than the more intelligent, at least over a certain time of life, say the earlier years of school.

Now the principle of redress has not to my knowledge been proposed as the sole criterion of justice, as the single aim of the social order. It is plausible as most such principles are only as a prima facie principle, one that is to be weighed in the balance with others. For example, we are to weigh it against the principle to improve the average standard of life, or to advance the common good. But whatever other principles we hold, the claims of redress are to be taken into account. It is thought to represent one of the elements in our conception of justice. Now the difference principle is not of course the principle of redress. It does not require society to try to even out handicaps as if all were expected to compete on a fair basis in the same race. But the difference principle would allocate resources in education, say, so as to improve the long-term expectation of the least favored. If this end is attained by giving more attention to the better endowed, it is permissible; otherwise not. And in making this decision, the value of education should not be assessed solely in terms of economic efficiency and social welfare. Equally if not more important is the role of education in enabling a person to enjoy the culture of his society and to take part in its affairs, and in this way to provide for each individual a secure sense of his own worth.

Thus although the difference principle is not the same as that of redress, it does achieve some of the intent of the latter principle. It transforms the aims of the basic structure so that the total scheme of institutions no longer emphasizes social efficiency and technocratic values. We see then that the difference principle represents, in effect, an agreement to regard the distribution of natural talents as a common asset and to share in the benefits of this distribution whatever it turns out to be. Those who have been favored by nature, whoever they are, may gain from their good fortune only on terms that improve the situation of those who have lost out. The naturally advantaged are not to gain merely because they are more gifted, but only to cover the costs of training and education and for using their endowments in ways that help the less fortunate as well. No one deserves his greater natural capacity nor merits a more favorable starting place in society. But it does not follow that one should eliminate these distinctions. There is another way to deal with them. The basic structure can be arranged so that these contingencies work for the good of the least fortunate. Thus we are led to the difference principle if we wish to set up the social system so that no one gains or loses from his arbitrary place in the distribution of natural assets or his initial position in society without giving or receiving compensating advantages in return.

In view of these remarks we may reject the contention that the ordering of institutions is always defective because the distribution of natural talents and the contingencies of social circumstance are unjust, and this injustice must inevitably carry over to human arrangements. Occasionally this reflection is offered as an excuse for ignoring injustice, as if the refusal to acquiesce in injustice is on a par with being unable to accept death. The natural distribution is neither just nor unjust; nor is it unjust that persons are born into society at some particular position. These are simply natural facts. What is just and unjust is the way that institutions deal with these facts. Aristocratic and caste societies are unjust because they make these contingencies the ascriptive basis for belonging to more or less enclosed and privileged social classes. The basic structure of these societies incorporates the arbitrariness found in nature. But there is no necessity for men to resign themselves to these contingencies. The social system is not an unchangeable order beyond human control but a pattern of human action. In justice as fairness men agree to share one another's fate. In designing institutions they undertake to avail themselves of the accidents of nature and social circumstance only when doing so is for the common benefit. The two principles are a fair way of meeting the arbitrariness of fortune; and while no doubt imperfect in other ways, the institutions which satisfy these principles are just.

[Mutual Benefit Through Cooperation]

A further point is that the difference principle expresses a conception of reciprocity. It is a principle of mutual benefit. We have seen that, at least when chain connection holds, each representative man can accept the basic structure as designed to advance his interests. The social order can be justified to everyone, and in particular to those who are least favored; and in this sense it is egalitarian. But it seems necessary to consider in an intuitive way how the condition of mutual benefit is satisfied. Consider any two representative men A and B, and let B be the one who is less favored. Actually, since we are most interested in the comparison with the least favored man, let us assume that B is this individual. Now B can accept A's being better off since A's advantages have been gained in ways that improve B's prospects. If A were not allowed his better position, B would be even worse off than he is. The difficulty is to show that A has no grounds for complaint. Perhaps he is required to have less than he might since his having more would result in some loss to B. Now what can be said to the more favored man? To begin with, it is clear that the well-being of each depends on a scheme of social cooperation without which no one could have a satisfactory life. Secondly, we can ask for the willing cooperation of everyone only if the terms of the scheme are reasonable. The difference principle, then, seems to be a fair basis on which those better endowed, or more fortunate in their social circumstances, could expect others to collaborate with them when some workable arrangement is a necessary condition of the good of all.

There is a natural inclination to object that those better situated deserve their greater advantages whether or not they are to the benefit of others. At this point it is necessary to be clear about the notion of desert. It is perfectly true that given a just system of cooperation as a scheme of public rules and the expectations set up by it, those who, with the prospect of improving their condition, have done what the system announces that it will reward are entitled to their advantages. In this sense the more fortunate have a claim to their better situation; their claims are legitimate expectations established by social institutions, and the community is obligated to meet them. But this sense of desert presupposes the existence of the cooperative scheme; it is irrelevant to the question whether in the first place the scheme is to be designed in accordance with the difference principle or some other criterion.

Perhaps some will think that the person with greater natural endowments deserves those assets and the superior character that made their development possible. Because he is more worthy in this sense, he deserves the greater advantages that he could achieve with them. This view, however, is surely incorrect. It seems to be one of the fixed points of our considered judgments that no one deserves his place in the distribution of native endowments, any more than one deserves one's initial starting place in society. The assertion that a man deserves the superior character that enables him to make the effort to cultivate his abilities is equally problematic; for his character depends in large part upon fortunate family and social circumstances for which he can claim no credit. The notion of desert seems not to apply to these cases. Thus the more advantaged representative man cannot say that he deserves and therefore has a right to a scheme of cooperation in which he is permitted to acquire benefits in ways that do not contribute to the welfare of others. There is no basis for his making this claim. From the standpoint of common sense, then, the difference principle appears to be acceptable both to the more advantaged and to the less advantaged individual. Of course, none of this is strictly speaking an argument for the principle, since in a contract theory arguments are made from the point of view of the original position. But these intuitive considerations help to clarify the nature of the principle and the sense in which it is egalitarian.

READING QUESTIONS

1. What role does the so-called veil of ignorance play in Rawls's theory?
2. Why does Rawls think that a consequentialist principle like the principle of utility will not be chosen by occupants of the original position?
3. What advantages does Rawls cite in favor of his use of the term "contract" to characterize his theory?
4. What reasons does Rawls offer for the claim that his theory represents an "egalitarian" conception of justice?

DISCUSSION QUESTIONS

1. How (if at all) might a social contract theory of morality account for obligations toward nonhuman animals? Do you find this account (assuming you think there is one) plausible?
2. Explain why you agree or disagree with Rawls's claim that such undeserved inequalities of birth and natural endowments are to be compensated for in a theory of justice.

ADDITIONAL RESOURCES

Web Resources

Stanford Encyclopedia of Philosophy, <http://plato.stanford.edu/>. An excellent resource. See in particular the following entries:

- Aquinas's Moral, Political, and Legal Philosophy by John Finnis
- The Natural Law Tradition in Ethics by Mark Murphy
- Doctrine of Double Effect by Alison McIntyre
- Consequentialism by Walter Sinnott-Armstrong
- The History of Utilitarianism by Julia Driver
- Kant's Moral Theory by Robert Johnson
- Locke's Political Philosophy by Alex Tuckness
- Rights by Leif Wenar
- Aristotle's Ethics by Richard Kraut
- Contemporary Approaches to the Social Contract by Fred D'Agostino, Gerald Gaus, and John Thrasher

Authored Books

The following are introductory texts.

Darwall, Stephen, *Philosophical Ethics* (Boulder, CO: Westview Press, 1998). Parts III and IV of this text include two chapters on Mill, two on Kant, and one on Aristotle.

Driver, Julia, *Ethics: The Fundamentals* (Oxford: Blackwell Publishing Ltd, 2007). Includes chapters on God, morality and human nature, utilitarianism, consequentialism, Kant's ethics, virtue ethics, and feminist ethics, social contract theory, intuitionism, and moral nihilism.

Harris, C. E., *Applying Moral Theories,* 5th ed. (Belmont, CA: Wadsworth, 2005). A text featuring chapters on egoism, natural law, utilitarianism, respect for persons, and virtue ethics with a special focus on the application of these theories to moral problems.

Timmons, Mark, *Moral Theory: An Introduction,* 2nd ed. (Lanham, MD: Rowman & Littlefield, 2013). A text entirely devoted to normative ethical theory. Includes chapters on divine command theory, relativism, natural law theory, consequentialism (both classical and contemporary), ethical egoism, Kantian moral theory, ethical pluralism (Ross), virtue ethics, and ethical particularism.

Edited Collections

There are many ethics anthologies that are either dedicated to or feature readings in moral theory. Here are two of them.

Shafer-Landau, Russ, *Ethical Theory: An Anthology,* 2nd ed. (Malden, MA: Wiley-Blackwell, 2013). Approaching 800 pages, this anthology includes a wide range of classical and contemporary selections in both moral theory and applied ethics.

Timmons, Mark, *Conduct and Character: Readings in Moral Theory*, 6th ed. (Belmont, CA: Thomson Wadsworth, 2011). A compact reader with selections from classical and contemporary sources covering a wide variety of moral theories, including the seven featured in chapters 1 and 2 of this anthology.

3) Sexual Morality

Moral questions about sexual activity including contraception, masturbation, simultaneous sex with multiple partners, homosexuality, adultery, premarital sex, and prostitution seem to be a permanent source of dispute. Some think that all such actions are inherently morally wrong; others disagree. Debates over the morality of various forms of sexual behavior raise the following questions:

- For each type of sexual activity in question, are there any conditions under which it is morally wrong?
- For those sexual activities and practices that are morally wrong, what is the best explanation of their wrongness?

1. A SPECTRUM OF VIEWS

Often the terms **"conservative,"** **"liberal,"** and **"moderate"** are used to characterize different positions one might take on some moral issue. Let us first explain these labels as they tend to be used in connection with issues about sexual behavior, and then I will issue a couple of warnings about their use.

The differences among conservative, liberal, and moderate views on most any moral issue have to do with the range of behavior that is taken to be morally permissible: conservative views restrict the range to a greater degree than do moderate or liberal views, and, of course, a moderate view imposes more restrictions than does a liberal one. When it comes to questions of sexual behavior, moral restrictions focus on the nature of the relationship that exists among those engaged in sexual activity. The motto of the conservative is "no sex without legal marriage," where it is assumed that marriage partners are of the opposite sex and that they are restricted in their sexual activity to having sex with each other and not, say, with partners from another marriage. Most obviously, a conservative sexual ethic rules out a number of sexual activities including premarital sex, adultery, prostitution, and homosexual behavior.

By contrast, a liberal on matters of sexual morality will hold that limits on sex have to do with the moral restrictions on human relationships generally—restrictions that are not specifically about sex. So, for example, on a standard liberal view, sexual behavior by an individual that is based on deceiving a sexual partner is wrong because it involves deception.

Lying to someone about having a sexually transmittable disease in order to get them to agree to sexual intercourse is wrong because, lying in general is wrong. Again, sex involving coercion is wrong on a liberal view because such coercion is wrong. A conservative will agree with the liberal about cases involving deception and coercion, but where they differ is that the conservative holds that there are further restrictions on morally permissible sex besides those having to do with general moral rules that apply to all behavior. For a liberal, then, there is nothing inherently morally wrong with homosexuality, premarital sex, prostitution, simultaneous sex with multiple partners, and adultery—individual instances of all of these activities are permissible *so long as they are not in violation of general moral rules applying to all sorts of behavior—sexual and nonsexual.*

Finally, a moderate is someone who disagrees with a conservative in restricting morally permissible sex to partners who are legally married, but also disagrees with a liberal who thinks that the only moral restrictions on sex have to do with general moral rules. Rather, a typical moderate position claims that in order for sexual activity by an individual to be morally legitimate, that person must have a certain "bond" with her or his partner. Sometimes this view is expressed in the motto "no sex without love." Were a moderate to stick to this motto, her view would still allow many forms of sexual interaction ruled out by the typical conservative. For instance, going by this motto, homosexual behavior between gays or lesbians who love each other is morally permitted.

But let me issue two warnings about the use of these labels. First, speaking now about moral issues generally, these labels are here being used for general positions on the morality of some activity that differ in *the range of sexual activities that are thought to be morally permissible.* In other contexts, these same labels are used to classify views over economic policy and more generally over the role of government in the lives of its citizens.[1] And so the first warning is this: when using such labels, remember that it is possible to be, for example, a conservative about economic issues, but a liberal or moderate about moral issues. Additionally, if one is a liberal, say, about the morality of euthanasia, one need not be a liberal about all other moral issues. In short, taking a so-called liberal or conservative or moderate position on one issue need not commit you to taking the same type of position on other issues.

The second warning is this. There is no *one* conservative or liberal or moderate position on any one topic. These labels are names for general types of views, and within each type there will be a variety of more specific versions of the general type. Thus, two individuals might hold a conservative position with respect to sexual morality, but one of these positions may be more conservative than the other. For instance, in addition to holding that sexual partners must be legally married to each other, one might hold that there are moral limits to what sorts of sexual activity they may engage in. One possible further restriction might rule out anal intercourse or mutual masturbation or sexual intercourse that does not aim at producing children. Within each camp, we find a variety of possible views that are more or less restrictive. So, if one is going to use these labels, then it is best to think of there being a spectrum of views that blend into one another. Here is a simple visual aid:

Liberal	Moderate	Conservative

Let the farthest point on the left of the horizontal line represent the most extreme liberal view, and let the farthest point on the right of the same line represent the most extreme conservative view. A line is a series of points, and so think of there being possible views about the morality of sexual behavior that may be positioned anywhere along this line. Using these labels, one might hold an extremely conservative view, or instead one might hold a moderately conservative view, or perhaps a moderately liberal view, and so on. The view one holds on any moral issue should be based on one's assessment of the quality of the moral arguments that concern the issue in question, rather than based on whichever label applies to that view.

Let us now turn to the sorts of arguments featured in our readings. It is useful to sort the readings into two groups. First, there are "general approaches" to sexual morality that attempt to provide a general ethical framework for thinking about matters of sex. Second, there are "selected topics" including adultery and homosexuality that are discussed in our readings.

2. THEORY MEETS PRACTICE: GENERAL APPROACHES

In the first and third readings that follow, we find sharply contrasting approaches to sexual morality. The "Vatican Declaration" presents a conservative sexual ethic based on some elements of natural law theory. In the third article, Thomas A. Mappes defends a liberal view based on one leading idea of Kant's ethics. And in his article on adultery, Raja Halwani embraces a version of virtue ethics. Let us briefly consider the natural law and Kantian approaches, saving the virtue ethics approach for our discussion of special topics.

Natural Law Theory

You may recall from chapter 1 that the basic idea of natural law ethics is that there is an objective human good, and the rightness or wrongness of actions is evaluated in terms of how they bear on the production and maintenance of what is good. According to Aquinas, one of the four basic human goods is procreation, proper respect for which imposes obligations regarding the use of sexual organs as well as obligations regarding the "natural" outcome of sexual intercourse, namely, child rearing.

Sometimes natural law theory is associated with the idea that an action is morally wrong if performing it would somehow go against nature. The idea is summed up in the formula: *an action is wrong if it is unnatural,* and it is the basis of the often-heard "unnaturalness" argument against homosexuality and other forms of sexual behavior. Problems with the unnaturalness argument are discussed in the reading from John Corvino. However, one should not suppose that all versions of natural law theory commit one to questionable ideas about what is and is not natural.

Kantian Moral Theory

One of the leading ideas of Kant's ethics is the general requirement to treat all persons as ends in themselves and never *merely* as means to an end. This is Kant's Humanity formulation of his fundamental moral principle—the categorical imperative. This principle was discussed briefly in the first chapter and is the basis of a liberal view on sexual morality defended by Mappes. What Mappes does is provide a characterization of what it means to treat someone as merely a means, and on that basis he proceeds to draw out various moral implications for sexual activity. It should be noted that Kant himself held a fairly conservative view of sexual morality because he thought that sexual behavior outside the confines of marriage was inherently degrading to the worth or dignity of human beings. On this point Kant and Mappes differ significantly.

3. THEORY MEETS PRACTICE: SPECIAL TOPICS

Adultery

Adultery is the act of voluntary sexual intercourse between a married person and someone other than his or her legal spouse. Adulterous actions are widely considered to be morally wrong—either in all, or at least most, cases. But how can we understand the wrongness of such actions—what best explains the wrongness of adulterous actions? This same question can be asked of infidelity between couples who are not legally married but who are involved in a romantic relationship that is understood by the partners to be sexually exclusive. Consequentialists will appeal to the overall badness of the consequences of sexual infidelity, while Kantians like Mappes will stress the fact that cases of infidelity where one partner deceives the other violate the requirement that partners treat each other not merely as a means but as ends in themselves. By contrast, virtue ethics approaches the morality of adultery in particular and sexual fidelity in general by focusing on ideals toward which a virtuous person would aspire. This is the approach that is defended by Raja Halwani in our readings. He argues that virtue ethics provides a better understanding of the morality of sexual fidelity than does either consequentialist or Kantian approaches.

Homosexuality

The morality of **homosexual behavior**—sexual activity, particularly intercourse, between members of the same sex—is a continuing source of moral and legal dispute. As noted above, one familiar kind of argument for the claim that homosexuality is morally wrong is that such sex is "unnatural." In addition, some critics argue that homosexuality (compared to heterosexuality) is harmful to those who engage in it as well as to other members of society. In addition to his critique of unnaturalness arguments concerning homosexuality, John Corvino also discusses arguments that allege various sorts of harm.

NOTE

1. This usage of "liberal" and "conservative" should not be confused with the political ideologies that are referred to by the labels "Liberal*ism*" and "Conservat*ism.*" These views are briefly described in the introduction to the chapter on pornography, hate speech, and censorship, section 2.

SACRED CONGREGATION FOR THE DOCTRINE OF FAITH, APPROVED BY POPE PAUL VI

Vatican Declaration on Some Questions of Sexual Ethics

This declaration affirms the traditional teachings of the Catholic Church on matters of sexual behavior. The basis of the church's teachings is the natural law approach to ethics, according to which there are objective standards of human behavior that are grounded in facts about human nature and are thus "perennial"—principles that can be known either through revelation or through the use of reason. The fundamental principles of sexual morality concern, then, the nature of the human being and the proper function of sexual behavior, which includes "mutual self-giving and human procreation in the context of true love." This principle is then used as a basis for arguing that premarital sex, homosexuality, and masturbation are morally wrong.

Recommended Reading: natural law theory, chap. 1, sec. 2B.

INTRODUCTION

Importance of Sexuality

1. The human person, according to the scientific disciplines of our day, is so deeply influenced by his sexuality that this latter must be regarded as one of the basic factors shaping human life. The person's sex is the source of the biological, psychological and spiritual characteristics which make the person male or female, and thus are extremely important and influential in the maturation and socialization of the individual. It is easy to understand, therefore, why matters pertaining to sex are frequently and openly discussed in books, periodicals, newspapers and other communications media.

Meanwhile, moral corruption is on the increase. One of the most serious signs of this is the boundless exaltation of sex. In addition, with the help of the mass media and the various forms of entertainment, sex has even invaded the field of education and infected the public mind.

In this situation, some educators, teachers and moralists have been able to contribute to a better understanding and vital integration of the special values and qualities proper to each sex. Others, however, have defended views and ways of acting which are in conflict with the true moral requirements of man, and have even opened the door to a licentious hedonism.

The result is that, within a few years' time, teachings, moral norms and habits of life hitherto faithfully preserved have been called into doubt, even by Christians. Many today are asking what they are to regard as true when so many current views are at odds with what they learned from the Church.

Occasion for This Declaration

2. In the face of this intellectual confusion and moral corruption the Church cannot stand by and do nothing.

The issue here is too important in the life both of the individual and of contemporary society.[1]

Bishops see each day the ever increasing difficulties of the faithful in acquiring sound moral teaching, especially in sexual matters, and of pastors in effectively explaining that teaching. The bishops know it is their pastoral duty to come to the aid of the faithful in such a serious matter. Indeed, some outstanding documents have been published on the subject by some bishops and some episcopal conferences. But, since erroneous views and the deviations they produce continue to be broadcast everywhere, the Sacred Congregation for the Doctrine of the Faith in accordance with its role in the universal Church[2] and by mandate of the Supreme Pontiff, has thought it necessary to issue this Declaration.

I. GENERAL CONSIDERATIONS

The Sources of Moral Knowledge

3. The men of our day are increasingly persuaded that their dignity and calling as human beings requires them to use their minds to discover the values and powers inherent in their nature, to develop these without ceasing and to translate them into action, so that they may make daily greater progress.

When it comes to judgments on moral matters, however, man may not proceed simply as he thinks fit. "Deep within, man detects the law of conscience—a law which is not self-imposed but which holds him to obedience. . . . For man has in his heart a law written by God. To obey it is the very dignity of man; according to it he will be judged."[3]

To us Christians, moreover, God has revealed his plan of salvation and has given us Christ, the Savior and sanctifier, as the supreme and immutable norm of life through his teaching and example. Christ himself has said: "I am the light of the world. No follower of mine shall ever walk in darkness; no, he shall possess the light of life."[4]

The authentic dignity of man cannot be promoted, therefore, except through adherence to the order which

is essential to his nature. There is no denying, of course, that in the history of civilization many of the concrete conditions and relationships of human life have changed and will change again in the future but every moral evolution and every manner of life must respect the limits set by the immutable principles which are grounded in the constitutive elements and essential relations proper to the human person. These elements and relations are not subject to historical contingency.

The basic principles in question can be grasped by man's reason. They are contained in "the divine law—eternal, objective and universal—whereby God orders, directs and governs the entire universe and all the ways of the human community by a plan conceived in wisdom and love. God has made man a participant in this law, with the result that, under the gentle disposition of divine Providence, he can come to perceive ever more fully the truth that is unchanging."[5] This divine law is something we can know.

The Principles of Morality Are Perennial

4. Wrongly, therefore, do many today deny that either human nature or revealed law furnishes any absolute and changeless norm for particular actions except the general law of love and respect for human dignity. To justify this position, they argue that both the so-called norms of the natural law and the precepts of Sacred Scripture are simply products of a particular human culture and its expressions at a certain point in history.

But divine revelation and, in its own order, natural human wisdom show us genuine exigencies of human nature and, as a direct and necessary consequence, immutable laws which are grounded in the constitutive elements of human nature and show themselves the same in all rational beings. . . .

The Fundamental Principles of Sexual Morality

5. Since sexual morality has to do with values which are basic to human and Christian life, the general doctrine we have been presenting applies to it. In this area there are principles and norms which the Church has always unhesitatingly transmitted as part

of her teaching, however opposed they might be to the mentality and ways of the world. These principles and norms have their origin, not in a particular culture, but in knowledge of the divine law and human nature. Consequently, it is impossible for them to lose their binding force or to be called into doubt on the grounds of cultural change.

These principles guided Vatican Council II when it provided advice and directives for the establishment of the kind of social life in which the equal dignity of man and woman will be respected, even while the differences between them also are preserved.[6]

In speaking of the sexual nature of the human being and of the human generative powers, the Council observes that these are "remarkably superior to those found in lower grades of life."[7] Then it deals in detail with the principles and norms which apply to human sexuality in the married state and are based on the finality of the function proper to marriage.

In this context the Council asserts that the moral goodness of the actions proper to married life, when ordered as man's true dignity requires, "does not depend only on a sincere intention and the evaluating of motives, but must be judged by objective standards. These are drawn from the nature of the human person and of his acts, and have regard for the whole meaning of mutual self-giving and human procreation in the context of true love."[8]

These last words are a brief summation of the Council's teaching (previously set forth at length in the same document[9]) on the finality of the sexual act and on the chief norm governing its morality. It is respect for this finality which guarantees the moral goodness of the act.

The same principle, which the Church derives from divine revelation and from her authentic interpretation of the natural law, is also the source of her traditional teaching that the exercise of the sexual function has its true meaning and is morally good only in legitimate marriage.[10]

Limits of This Declaration

6. It is not the intention of this declaration to treat all abuses of the sexual powers nor to deal with all that is involved in the practice of chastity but rather to recall the Church's norms on certain specific points, since there is a crying need of opposing certain serious errors and deviant forms of behavior.

II. SPECIFIC APPLICATIONS

Premarital Relations

7. Many individuals at the present time are claiming the right to sexual union before marriage, at least when there is a firm intention of marrying and when a love which both partners think of as already conjugal demands this further step which seems to them connatural. They consider this further step justified especially when external circumstances prevent the formal entry into marriage or when intimate union seems necessary if love is to be kept alive.

This view is opposed to the Christian teaching that any human genital act whatsoever may be placed only within the framework of marriage. For, however firm the intention of those who pledge themselves to each other in such premature unions, these unions cannot guarantee the sincerity and fidelity of the relationship between man and woman, and, above all, cannot protect the relationship against the changeableness of desire and determination.

Yet, Christ the Lord willed that the union be a stable one and he restored it to its original condition as founded in the difference between the sexes. "Have you not read that at the beginning the Creator made them male and female and declared., 'For this reason a man shall leave his father and mother and cling to his wife and the two shall become as one'? Thus they are no longer two but one flesh. Therefore, let no man separate what God has joined."[11] . . .

Such has always been the Church's understanding of and teaching on the exercise of the sexual function.[12] She finds, moreover, that natural human wisdom and the lessons of history are in profound agreement with her.

Experience teaches that if sexual union is truly to satisfy the requirements of its own finality and of human dignity, love must be safeguarded by the stability marriage gives. These requirements necessitate a contract which is sanctioned and protected by society: the contract gives rise to a new state of life and is of exceptional importance for the exclusive union of man and woman as well as for the good of their family and the whole of human society. Premarital relations, on the other hand, most often exclude any prospect of children. Such love claims in vain to be conjugal since it cannot, as it certainly should, grow into a maternal and paternal love; or, if the pair do become parents, it will be to the detriment of the children, who are deprived of a stable environment in which they can grow up in a proper fashion and find the way and means of entering into the larger society of men.

Therefore, the consent of those entering into marriage must be externally manifested, and this in such a way as to render it binding in the eyes of society. The faithful, for their part, must follow the laws of the Church in declaring their marital consent: it is this consent that makes their marriage a sacrament of Christ.

Homosexuality

8. Contrary to the perennial teaching of the Church and the moral sense of the Christian people, some individuals today have, on psychological grounds, begun to judge indulgently or even simply to excuse homosexual relations for certain people.

They make a distinction which has indeed some foundation: between homosexuals whose bent derives from improper education or a failure of sexual maturation or habit or bad example or some similar cause and is only temporary or at least is not incurable; and homosexuals who are permanently such because of some innate drive or a pathological condition which is considered incurable.

The propensity of those in the latter class is—it is argued—so natural that it should be regarded as justifying homosexual relations within a sincere and loving communion of life which is comparable to marriage inasmuch as those involved in it deem it impossible for them to live a solitary life.

Objective Evil of Such Acts

As far as pastoral care is concerned, such homosexuals are certainly to be treated with understanding and encouraged to hope that they can some day overcome their difficulties and their inability to fit into society in a normal fashion. Prudence, too, must be exercised in judging their guilt. However, no pastoral approach may be taken which would consider these individuals morally justified on the grounds that such acts are in accordance with their nature. For, according to the objective moral order, homosexual relations are acts deprived of the essential ordination they ought to have.

In Sacred Scripture such acts are condemned as serious deviations and are even considered to be the lamentable effect of rejecting God.[13] This judgment on the part of the divinely inspired Scriptures does not justify us in saying that all who suffer from this anomaly are guilty of personal sin but it does show that homosexual acts are disordered by their very nature and can never be approved.

Masturbation

9. Frequently today we find doubt or open rejection of the traditional Catholic teaching that masturbation is a serious moral disorder. Psychology and sociology (it is claimed) show that masturbation, especially in adolescents, is a normal phase in the process of sexual maturation and is, therefore, not gravely sinful unless the individual deliberately cultivates a solitary pleasure that is turned in upon itself ("ipsation"). In this last case, the act would be radically opposed to that loving communion between persons of different sexes which (according to some) is the principal goal to be sought in the use of the sexual powers.

This opinion is contrary to the teaching and pastoral practice of the Catholic Church. Whatever be the validity of certain arguments of a biological and philosophical kind which theologians sometimes use, both the magisterium of the Church (following a constant tradition) and the moral sense of the faithful have unhesitatingly asserted that masturbation is an intrinsically and seriously disordered act.[14] The chief reason for this stand is that, whatever the motive, the deliberate use of the sexual faculty outside of normal conjugal relations essentially contradicts its finality. In such an act there is lacking the sexual relationship which the moral order requires, the kind of relationship in which "the whole meaning of mutual self-giving and human procreation" is made concretely real "in the context of true love."[15] Only within such a relationship may the sexual powers be deliberately exercised.

Even if it cannot be established that Sacred Scripture condemns this sin under a specific name, the Church's tradition rightly understands it to be condemned in the New Testament when the latter speaks of "uncleanness" or "unchasteness" or the other vices contrary to chastity and continence.

Sociological research can show the relative frequency of this disorder according to places, types of people and various circumstances which may be taken into account. It thus provides an array of facts. But facts provide no norm for judging the morality of human acts.[16] The frequency of the act here in question is connected with innate human weakness deriving from original sin, but also with the loss of the sense of God, with the moral corruption fostered by the commercialization of vice, with the unbridled license to be found in so many books and forms of public entertainment and with the forgetfulness of modesty, which is the safeguard of chastity.

In dealing with masturbation, modern psychology provides a number of valid and useful insights which enable us to judge more equitably of moral responsibility. They can also help us understand how adolescent immaturity (sometimes prolonged beyond the adolescent years) or a lack of psychological balance or habits can affect behavior, since they may make an action less deliberate and not always a subjectively serious sin. But the lack of serious responsibility should not be generally presumed; if it is, there is simply a failure to recognize man's ability to act in a moral way.

In the pastoral ministry, in order to reach a balanced judgment in individual cases account must be taken of the overall habitual manner in which the person acts, not only in regard to charity and justice, but also in regard to the care with which he observes the precept of chastity in particular. Special heed must be paid to whether he uses the necessary natural and supernatural helps which Christian asceticism recommends, in the light of long experience, for mastering the passions and attaining virtue. . . .

NOTES

1. See Vatican II, *Pastoral Constitution on the Church in the World of Today,* no. 47: *Acta Apostolicae Sedis* 58 (1966) 1067 [*The Pope Speaks* XI, 289–290].

2. See the Apostolic Constitution *Regimini Ecclesiae universae* (August 15, 1967), no. 29: *AAS* 59 (1967) 897 [*TPS* XII, 401–402].

3. *Pastoral Constitution on the Church in the World of Today,* no. 16: *AAS* 58 (1966) 1037 [*TPS* XI, 268].

4. *Jn* 8, 12.

5. *Declaration on Religious Freedom,* no. 3: *AAS* 58 (1966) 931 [*TPS* XI, 86].

6. See Vatican II, *Declaration on Christian Education,* nos. 1 and 8: *AAS* 58 (1966) 729–730, 734–736 [*TPS* XI, 201–202, 206–207]; *Pastoral Constitution on the Church in the World of Today,* nos. 29, 60, 67: *AAS* 58 (1966) 1048–1049, 1080–1081, 1088–1089 [*TPS* XI, 276 277, 299–300, 304–305].

7. *Pastoral Constitution on the Church in the World of Today,* no. 51: *AAS* 58 (1966) 1072 [*TPS* XI, 293].

8. Loc. cit.: see also no. 49: *AAS* 58 (1966) 1069–1070 [*TPS* XI, 291–292].

9. See *Pastoral Constitution on the Church in the World of Today,* nos. 49–50: *AAS* 58 (1966) 1069–1072 [*TPS* XI, 291–293].

10. The present Declaration does not review all the moral norms for the use of sex, since they have already been set forth in the encyclicals *Casti Connubii* and *Humanae Vitae.*

11. *Mt* 19, 4–6.

12. See Innocent IV, Letter *Sub Catholicae professione* (March 6, 1254) (*DS* 835); Pius II. Letter *Cum sicut accepimus* (November 14, 1459) (*DS* 1367); Decrees of the Holy Office on September 24, 1665 (*DS* 2045) and March 2, 1679 (*DS* 2148); Pius XI, Encyclical *Casti Connubii* (December 31, 1930): *AAS* 22 (1930) 538–539.

13. *Rom* 1:24–27: "In consequence, God delivered them up in their lusts to unclean practices; they engaged in the mutual degradation of their bodies, these men who

exchanged the truth of God for a lie and worshiped and served the creature rather than the Creator—blessed be he forever, amen! God therefore delivered them to disgraceful passions. Their women exchanged natural intercourse for unnatural, and the men gave up natural intercourse with women and burned with lust for one another. Men did shameful things with men, and thus received in their own persons the penalty for their perversity." See also what St. Paul says of sodomy in *1 Cor* 6, 9; *1 Tm* 1, 10.

14. See Leo IX, Letter *Ad splendidum nitentes* (1054) (*DS* 687–688); Decree of the Holy Office on March 2, 1679 (*DS* 2149); Pius XII, Addresses of October 8, 1953: *AAS*

45 (1953) 677–678, and May 19, 1956: *AAS* 48 (1956) 472–473.

15. *Pastoral Constitution on the Church in the World of Today,* no. 51: *AAS* 58 (1966) 1072 [*TPS* XI, 293].

16. See Paul VI, Apostolic Exhortation *Quinque iam anni* (December 8, 1970): *AAS* 63 (1971) 102 [*TPS* XV, 329]: "If sociological surveys are useful for better discovering the thought patterns of the people of a particular place, the anxieties and needs of those to whom we proclaim the word of God, and also the oppositions made to it by modern reasoning through the widespread notion that outside science there exists no legitimate form of knowledge, still the conclusions drawn from such surveys could not of themselves constitute a determining criterion of truth."

READING QUESTIONS

1. Explain the sources of moral knowledge according to the Vatican.
2. How does the Vatican characterize morally good sexual activity?
3. Why does the Vatican object to premarital sexual relations? How is marriage intended to stabilize the relationship between two individuals?
4. What is the distinction recognized by the Vatican regarding the cause of homosexual behavior?
5. Why does the Vatican believe that homosexuality is objectively evil? How should pastors address specific cases of individual engagement in homosexual behavior according to the Vatican?

DISCUSSION QUESTIONS

1. The Vatican claims that the institution of marriage is designed to encourage stable relationships. Consider whether marriages generally succeed or fail in this regard. Can individuals that engage in sexual relations outside of the bonds of marriage maintain stable and lasting commitments to one another?
2. How might persons in the secular and scientific communities respond to the Vatican's objections to homosexuality and masturbation?

JOHN CORVINO

What's Wrong with Homosexuality?

In the following excerpts from his 2013 book, *What's Wrong with Homosexuality?*, John Corvino examines two prominent kinds of anti-homosexuality arguments: harm arguments and "unnaturalness" arguments. He argues that such arguments fail.

Recommended Reading: natural law theory, chap. 1, sec. 2B.

I. "A RISKY LIFESTYLE"

In his essay, "Homosexuality in American Life," Christopher Wolfe "notes some very substantial costs associated with living as a homosexual," including "a very dramatic decrease in life expectancy—in some studies, for male homosexuals, on the order of twenty-five to thirty years," various diseases, higher rates of suicide, and so on. He then asked:

> On the basis of health considerations alone, is it unreasonable to ask if it is better not to be an active homosexual? At the very least, don't the facts suggest that it is desirable to prevent the formation of a homosexual orientation and to bring people out of it when we can?[1]

. . . Harm arguments constitute one of the two major strands of secular arguments against homosexuality. (The other is natural law arguments, which I'll cover in the next Section.) In the debate over same-sex marriage, for example, many people allege harm to the traditional family and particularly to children; in the (now seemingly settled) debate over gays in the military, many alleged harm to combat effectiveness, and so on. . . . Invoking statistics and other empirical data, such arguments can have a compelling scientific ring. And they're based on an unassailable premise: all else being equal, it's bad to hurt oneself or others.

That's why Wolfe's question seems so reasonable, and even compassionate, on the surface: on the basis of health considerations alone, shouldn't we try to discourage homosexuality? And that's why it's tempting for those who believe Wolfe's disease statistics to answer "yes." But the correct answer, even if we assume the statistics to be accurate (which they are not) isn't so simple. It depends on the answers to a number of other questions, none of which Wolfe—or most opponents of homosexuality—bother to ask very carefully. In this chapter I'll explore those questions.

The First Question: Are the Allegations of Harm Accurate?

This question is elementary but crucial. When studying human behavior, it is difficult to isolate relevant factors from other influences. The study of sexuality is especially challenging, since shyness, fear, and the powerful phenomenon of the closet make it notoriously difficult to get adequate representative samples. Even in today's more "accepting" climate, many gay and lesbian people are not prepared to come out to themselves, much less to researchers. This fact complicates an already complicated endeavor.

Of course, some studies are better than others. The problem is that most studies cited by gay-rights

From John Corvino, *What's Wrong with Homosexuality?* (Oxford: Oxford University Press, 2013). Notes have been renumbered and edited.

opponents are abysmally bad. Consider Wolfe's claim, taken from Jeffrey Satinover, that homosexuals suffer "a very dramatic decrease in life expectancy—in some studies, for male homosexuals, on the order of twenty-five to thirty years."[2] Satinover supports this jarring statistic by citing a 1993 paper, "The Homosexual Lifespan."[3] In their study, psychologist Paul Cameron and his colleagues argued that the average lifespan for gay males was between 39 years of age (for those who die of AIDS-related causes) and 42 years of age (for those who die of other causes). In other words, they claimed that *even apart from AIDS,* gay men on average die over 30 years sooner than their straight counterparts.

How did they reach this startling conclusion? By comparing obituaries in 16 gay publications with those in two mainstream newspapers.

Just to be clear: I am not making this up. The methodology in this study is laughable even to those with no formal training in statistics. First, newspaper obituaries, which are typically written by relatives, hardly constitute a reliable scientific source. Second, obituaries that appeared in gay publications during the 1980s were not likely to be representative of the gay community at large, both because of their target demographic and because older gays were (and still are) more likely to be closeted. Remember that obituaries are submitted by survivors, and the survivors of elderly gays are often their heterosexual nieces and nephews. . . . Third, there was no genuine control group: gay people have obituaries in mainstream publications too, and unless a partner or "longtime companion" is mentioned, these are often indistinguishable from those of straight people. Fourth, and perhaps most bizarrely, the study included no *living* people. (It should go without saying, but one cannot do a comparative study of life expectancy without recording the ages of the living.) And so on. It should come as no surprise that a decade earlier Cameron was expelled from the American Psychological Association for "a violation of the Preamble to the Ethical Principles of Psychologists."[4] He was later condemned by the Nebraska Psychological Association and the American Sociological Association for his misrepresentations of scientific research on sexuality.[5]

Even Satinover, from whom Wolfe cited the data, had reservations about Cameron: "Because of the researcher's rough and ready methodology, these findings must be considered preliminary."[6] Rough and ready? Preliminary? Try useless.

Actually, "useless" isn't quite right. Paul Cameron's "research" continues to be useful to those who want to paint a certain picture of gay life regardless of the facts. It is also useful for another reason. As Dr. Morton Frisch, senior epidemiologist at Copenhagen's Statens Serum Institut, put it (discussing a similar study by Cameron and Cameron's son on Danish gay life expectancy): "Although the Camerons' report has no objective scientific value, the authors should be acknowledged for providing teachers with a humorous example of agenda-driven, pseudo-scientific gobbledygook that will make lessons in elementary study design and scientific inference much more amusing for future epidemiology students."[7]

Why worry about a charlatan like Cameron? Because he continues to get cited by serious scholars like Wolfe and in this manner, bizarre myths about gays get passed around as serious research. . . .

What does the best available current research say about the life expectancy of gay or bisexual men? The truth is that there is scant research addressing this question in a general way, rather than looking at a more specific issue, such as AIDS in urban centers or suicide among gay youth. And there's hardly anything at all on lesbians. Wolfe's allegation about homosexual life expectancy remains essentially baseless.

. . . Wolfe claims that even if my critique of Cameron "is correct, that would only leave us without any evidence one way or the other on the allegations of the dangers."[8] That's true as far as it goes. Indeed, I conceded as much in my paper, where I wrote, "Of course, discrediting Cameron's obituary studies is not tantamount to discrediting the right-wing's entire case (though, frankly, it does not help their credibility). So let me shift gears a bit. Suppose, *purely for the sake of argument,* we were to grant the allegations of harm cited by gay-rights opponents."[9]

The problem is that Wolfe just ignores this step in the argument. My overall argument against Wolfe was a layered one, where no step required accepting the previous layer. Step one: Rebut Wolfe's central evidence about the dangers of the homosexual lifestyle. Step two: Argue that, even if Wolfe were right about the dangers, it doesn't automatically follow that homosexuality should be discouraged. Why? Because we still need to ask another question.

The Second Question: Are the Alleged Harms Caused by Homosexuality Itself, or Some Extrinsic Factor?

The focus on AIDS makes it pretty easy to demonstrate this problem: gay sex doesn't kill people, AIDS does. And if the HIV virus isn't present, people can have as much gay sex as they like without worrying about AIDS. (Fatigue, yes; AIDS, no.)

But of course this answer is too easy. (Much like "Guns don't kill people . . .") Wolfe would doubtless respond that, for men, sex with men is statistically more likely to transmit the HIV virus than sex with women. As a general matter this claim is true (given various significant qualifications), but it is unclear what follows. Consider the fact that, for women, heterosexual sex is statistically more likely to transmit the HIV virus than homosexual sex. (One could make a similar argument from the premise that, prior to modern medicine, childbirth could be quite risky for any woman.) Yet no one concludes that the Surgeon General ought to recommend lesbianism, or that, on the basis of health considerations alone, female heterosexuality should be discouraged. There are simply too many missing steps.

AIDS is associated with homosexuality in this country because gay men were the population hit first, and hardest, by the disease. But it bears repeating that gay sex, like straight sex, can happen in many different ways (different positions, occasions, partners, and so on) and that many of them place people at relatively low risk of AIDS. So even If Wolfe's data were accurate, it would not be *homosexuality* we should discourage on the basis of health considerations, but risky sexual practices, including any sex (heterosexual or homosexual) involving a partner of unknown or positive HIV-status ejaculating into another.

As a gay man who is HIV-negative and doesn't engage in practices that would put me at any significant risk for contracting HIV, I find the right wing's obsessive focus on AIDS and other sexually transmitted diseases tiresome. I have a greater risk of being hit by a runaway school bus than of developing AIDS. So given the choice between staying home to have sex with my HIV-negative partner and leaving the house to do anything, it's probably safer for me to stay home and have sex. . . . AIDS doesn't just "happen" in gay sex as a matter of course: The virus must be present. No virus, no AIDS risk.

AIDS is not the only case where opponents display a "blame the victim" mentality. Consider Wolfe's inclusion of "higher rates of suicide" among his reasons for opposing homosexuality. This item is surprising, given that the most plausible explanation for such rates is anti-gay sentiment and the resulting isolation, particularly among gay and lesbian youth. A recent study in the journal *Pediatrics* reports that "lesbian, gay, and bisexual young adults who reported higher levels of family rejection during adolescence were 8.4 times more likely to report having attempted suicide, 5.9 times more likely to report high levels of depression, 3.4 times more likely to use illegal drugs, and 3.4 times more likely to report having engaged in unprotected sexual intercourse compared with peers from families that reported no or low levels of family rejection."[10] Here we have a vicious circle: Opponents of homosexuality base their opposition on factors caused by that very opposition—in other words, blaming the victim. It's like the bully on the playground who teases his classmate, causing him to cry, and then justifies the teasing on the grounds that his classmate is a crybaby. . . .

But suppose I'm wrong. Suppose I were to grant—again, purely for the sake of argument—both that the alleged harms exist and that they are caused by homosexuality itself, rather than some external, separable factor. There is still another question that must be asked.

The Third Question: What Follows?

This question is almost universally ignored. The hidden assumption in arguments like these is that if a particular practice is riskier than the alternatives, it follows that the practice is immoral, imprudent, or otherwise to be avoided. But the assumption is pretty obviously false as stated.

Consider some counterexamples: Driving is riskier than walking. Being a coal miner is riskier than being a philosophy professor. Football is riskier than checkers. In each case, the former activity poses a far greater risk of injury (even fatal injury) than the latter. Yet no one believes that driving, coal mining, and football are therefore wrong, or that they should always and everywhere be discouraged by reasonable people. Why not? Because related to the third question is a fourth.

The Fourth Question: Are the Risks in a Given Case Worth It?

Notice that we normally leave this question to competent adults taking the risks. My dental hygienist races cars in her spare time. I think she's nuts for doing so, but I also think it's none of my business. That said, Wolfe is right that society has a stake in its members' behavior and that people should at times vocally oppose others' risk-taking. There's a big leap, however, from that position to the conclusion that we ought to condemn any and all forms of homosexual conduct.

To see why, let's return to the football analogy. Football is responsible for nunerous injuries, including serious (occasionally even fatal) head trauma. Now on Wolfe's logic, we ought to ask:

> On the basis of health considerations alone, is it unreasonable to ask if it is better not to be [a football player] ? At the very least, don't the facts suggest that it is desirable to prevent the formation of [an interest in football] and to bring people out of it when we can?

After all, there are much safer games, like checkers!

Well, sure. But football players don't want to play checkers; they want to play football. The argument reminds me of an old joke:

QUESTION: What's the best way to avoid spilling your coffee while driving?
ANSWER: Drink tea.

The problem here is not just that the advice is unrealistic or unlikely to be followed. It's that it misses the point. Generally speaking, people choose alternatives they find fulfilling. When those alternatives involve risks, they can take steps to minimize them (like wearing helmets). Some football players, drivers, and coal miners are indeed more reckless than others. So are some sexually active heterosexuals, for that matter. But we don't cite statistics about their problems and conclude that no one should ever engage in any of these activities in any form.

Wolfe responded to my football analogy . . .

> Corvino's argument that [the risks of homosexual activity] are equivalent to playing football is unpersuasive. Moreover, the idea that a person, by his own activity, might contribute to not just his own early death, but the early death of someone else—especially someone he loves—makes this situation very different from other "high-risk" activities.[11]

. . .Wolfe completely misses the point of the football analogy. The point is not that football is more or less risky than gay sex. The point is that "riskier than the alternatives" does not entail "morally wrong." If it did, then no one should ever drive when they could walk, play football when they could play checkers, or have sex of any sort when they could remain celibate.

Most gay people cannot choose to have fulfilling heterosexual relationships. Their choice is not between homosexuality and heterosexuality, but between same-sex relationships and celibacy. Yet within that framework, they also have many other choices: choices about when to have sex, with whom to have sex, how to have sex, and so on. And gays, like everyone else, can make such choices carefully or recklessly.

The only way for Wolfe's argument to work is to assume that homosexual sex in any form is likely to shorten one's lifespan by several decades. In that case, I would agree that celibacy would be the best option for gays. But not even Wolfe believes that assumption. Even if you accepted the ridiculous (or in Wolfe's words, "concededly problematic") Cameron study, and even if you completely ignored the effectiveness of condoms, the most you could conclude is that gay *men* should forgo *anal* sex—which brings me to my next topic.

Anal Sex

In the early 1990s I lived next door to a guy named Jason, who was a born-again Christian rock singer. (Yes, I know this sounds like the premise for a bad sitcom.) While Jason vocally disapproved of my being gay, he was also fascinated by it, and he constantly asked me questions.

One day I revealed to him that I had never had anal sex. His face brightened. "That's awesome!" he shouted.

"Why, pray tell, is it awesome?" I asked.

"Because maybe you'll try it, and then realize you don't like it, and then you won't be gay."

For Jason, being gay meant liking anal sex. He found it strange that the equivalence had never occurred to me. For me, being gay means that I like guys. It means that I have crushes on them, I fall in love with them (one in particular), and I want to "get physical" with them. But it doesn't specify how I should do this.

I suppose the mistake is understandable. Most people would find it bizarre for a heterosexual *not* to desire penile-vaginal intercourse. It's "standard." For some gay men, anal sex is functionally similar— it's what they might call "the real thing." But that's not true for all of us. A guy who's into other guys but prefers oral sex, mutual masturbation, or frottage (look it up) is still gay. Sorry Jason.

Many critics of homosexuality focus on male homosexuality, and particularly anal sex, when discussing the alleged dangers of gay life. This is not surprising. Unprotected anal sex is a particularly apt way of transmitting the HIV virus, a virus that has been responsible for the deaths of legions of gay men and others over the last few decades. These critics needn't embellish the data: I came out in the late 1980s and found AIDS sufficiently frightening. Unlike today, AIDS was then a near-certain death sentence, one that often marked its bearers in visible ways. I am old enough (though just barely) to remember watching acquaintances go from being healthy-looking, to gaunt and lesion-marked, to gone—all in a matter of weeks. While HIV-disease has become far more manageable in the last decade with modern antiretroviral therapies, it is still something I take every precaution to avoid.

Or rather, I *would* take every precaution to avoid HIV if I were in situations that potentially exposed me to it. But as someone who is in a long-term relationship with an HIV-negative partner and doesn't much care for anal sex anyway, HIV is something I seldom think about in a personal way. That's one reason why Wolfe's discussion of fatal diseases . . . seems so remote and inapplicable to me.

To be fair, Wolfe refers to costs "that are often, *though not always,* associated with living as a homosexual," so he recognizes that the connection is not automatic. But the problem remains: Such allegations—even if they were true, or even plausible—provide no reason for me to stop being intimate with Mark, any more than pointing to the town drunk provides me (or any other temperate individual) reason to forgo an occasional glass of wine. It is doubtful that homosexuality is harmful in the ways alleged, and to the extent that it involves risk, it is not clear that those risks are unavoidable, unreasonable, or wrong-making.

Keep in mind that we're not talking about a sport, like football—we're talking about the means for deep human intimacy. So if there's a disanalogy between football and gay sex, it may well be in my favor: I can imagine a life without sports more easily than one without physical intimacy. . . .

In recent years, harm arguments against same-sex relationships have fallen largely out of favor—although they surface from time to time among right-wing bloggers, pastors, and pundits, especially whenever some new junk science is released. Instead, we are seeing a resurgence of natural law arguments, which are the focus of our next section.

Meanwhile, mainstream Americans have become more attuned to the harms of homophobia. A substantial body of research suggests that lesbian, gay, and bisexual youth are significantly more likely to attempt suicide than their heterosexual peers, and that stigma and discrimination are significant risk factors.[12] Even those who survive such treatment often carry long-term emotional scars. There is something perverse about using moral arguments to inflict harm rather than to alleviate it—and sadly, the harm arguments are more often experienced as weapons than as points of insight.

II. "ITS NOT NATURAL"

. . . Natural law theorists such as St. Thomas Aquinas (1225–1274) hold that *all* sin is unnatural, because sin is against reason, which is distinctive to human nature. Nevertheless, among sexual acts Aquinas reserves the term "unnatural" for those that are deliberately non-procreative (and thus against our animal nature), and he labels these "the gravest kind of sin."[13] His list includes not only homosexuality and bestiality but also masturbation and oral sex—in other words, acts that few people today would think twice about, let alone label unnatural.

The looseness of the term "unnatural" may be part of its rhetorical appeal: it can be tossed around to evoke disgust, without much worry about consistency. Why do many people consider masturbation natural but not homosexual conduct? Why do they consider heterosexual oral sex natural but not homosexual oral sex? Why is it fine for me to use my mouth for licking envelopes, chewing gum, or blowing a horn, but not to use it for romantically kissing a man? And if the answers have something to do with statistical norms ("Well, that's not what most people do") then why don't people consider left-handed writing unnatural, as previous generations did? At times, "unnatural" appears to be nothing more than a rhetorical flourish, invoked to smear things that the speaker finds abhorrent.

If the unnaturalness charge is to carry any moral weight, those who level it should be able to do two things. First, they should be able to specify what exactly they mean, explaining why the label applies to homosexuality but not to other acts that they don't similarly wish to smear.

Second, they should be able to explain why unnaturalness matters morally. Many perfectly innocent actions are unnatural in some sense: wearing eyeglasses, flying planes, cooking food, using iPhones, and so on. When people say that homosexuality is unnatural, presumably they mean that we morally ought to avoid it. But why?

Sometimes the implied normative sense of "unnatural" is pretty clear. For example, when someone says, "Don't eat those potato chips, they're loaded with unnatural ingredients;" there's an understood connection between unnaturalness and poor health. But that's not the kind of argument I'll he considering in this chapter. If "unnatural" is just a stand-in for "harmful," then we can lump unnaturalness arguments together with the harm arguments considered in the last section. But many who levy the unnaturalness charge want to claim that homosexuality is wrong regardless of whether it's harmful: unnaturalness is in this case an independent moral assessment. In what follows, I'll consider some possible meanings of "unnatural," examine whether they apply to homosexual conduct, and evaluate their moral significance.[14]

What Is Unusual or Unconventional Is Unnatural

Let's start with an easy one: unnaturalness in the sense of *statistical abnormality*. It is certainly true that most human beings don't engage in homosexual conduct (unless one considers solitary masturbation homosexual conduct). But so what? Most people don't write with their left hands, join monasteries, play the didgeridoo, or put their faces on billboards, either—yet none of these activities are considered wrong simply because they are rare. This sense of "unnatural" misses the term's normative force: to call something "unnatural" is not to *describe* its infrequency but to *prescribe* its avoidance.

This is one reason why it's a mistake for gay-rights activists to place so much emphasis on the oft-cited (and surely exaggerated) claim that gays make up 10% of the population: our numbers are irrelevant when determining whether homosexuality is natural in any morally significant sense. . . .

What Is Not Practiced by Other Animals Is Unnatural

I have heard some people—including a number of elected officials—argue, "Even animals know better than to behave homosexually; homosexuality must be wrong." This argument is doubly flawed. First, it rests on a false premise: Homosexual behavior has been documented in hundreds of species, from insects and worms to apes and dolphins, and some animals form long-term same-sex pair-bonds.[15] (There's even a charming children's book based on the true story of a male-male penguin couple in the Central Park Zoo who hatched and raised a chick: *And Tango Makes Three*—amazingly, one of the most frequently "banned" books in U.S. libraries.) True, it's unusual for animals to have an *exclusive* homosexual orientation over a long period, although this phenomenon has been observed, interestingly, in domesticated rams.

The argument's second flaw is more important: Even if the premise about animal behavior were true—which it is not—it would not show that homosexuality is immoral. After all, animals don't cook their food, brush their teeth, attend college, or read books; human beings do all these without moral fault. The notion that we ought to look to animals for moral standards is supply facetious, as anyone with house pets will readily attest.

What Does Not Proceed from Innate Desires Is Unnatural

Some people argue that gays are "born that way" and that it is therefore natural and good for them to form homosexual relationships. Others insist that homosexuality is a "lifestyle choice," which is therefore unnatural and wrong. Both sides assume a connection between the origin of homosexual orientation and the moral value of homosexual activity. And insofar as they share that assumption, both sides are wrong.

The idea that all innate desires are good ones is obviously false. Research suggests that some people may be born with a predisposition toward violence, but such people have no more right to strangle their neighbors than anyone else. So even though some people may be born with a homosexual orientation, it doesn't follow that they ought to act on it.

Nor does it follow that they ought *not* to act on it, even if it is not innate. I probably do not have an innate tendency to write with my left hand (since I, like everyone else in my family, have always been right-handed), but it doesn't follow that it would be immoral for me to do so. So even if homosexuality were a "lifestyle choice," it wouldn't follow that it's an immoral lifestyle choice.

The thing to remember is this: There's a difference between something's being natural in the sense of resulting from innate disposition and its being natural in the sense of being morally good. The nature/nurture debate may tell us something about how people come to have the sexual desires they have, but it will not tell us whether it's good for them to satisfy those desires, let alone whether they can—or should—change those desires. . . .

What Violates an Organ's Principal Purpose Is Unnatural

Perhaps when people claim that homosexual sex is "unnatural" they mean that it cannot result in procreation. The idea behind the argument is that human organs have various natural or intended purposes: eyes are for seeing, ears are for hearing, genitals are for procreating. According to this position, it is unmoral to use an organ in a way that violates its purpose.

This position finds its fullest premodern elaboration in St. Thomas Aquinas, whose teaching forms the basis of much of Roman Catholic moral theology. Aquinas recognizes procreation as sex's purpose and thus labels "unnatural" any intentionally non-procreative sexual acts. He ranks bestiality as the worst of these, morally speaking, followed by homosexual acts, then "not observing the natural manner of copulation" (e.g., heterosexual oral or anal sex), and finally masturbation. He argues that unnatural sexual acts are the "greatest sin among the species of lust": Whereas ordinary sexual sins such as fornication and adultery are merely violations of right reason, unnatural sexual acts violate nature itself.

Aquinas's position has some hard-to-swallow implications. For example, consider an objection that Aquinas himself anticipates:

It would seem that the unnatural vice is not the greatest sin among the species of lust. For the more a sin is contrary to charity the graver it is. Now adultery, seduction and rape, which are injuries to our neighbor, are seemingly more contrary to the love of our neighbor than unnatural sins, by which no other person is injured.[16]

In response, Aquinas simply bites the bullet and insists that unnatural vices are indeed worse. Whereas rape, fornication, and adultery merely injure human persons, unnatural acts injure God the Author of nature—himself.

Let us pause to digest this conclusion: According to St. Thomas Aquinas, the authority behind much of Roman Catholic moral teaching, *masturbation is worse than rape.*

One might try to rescue Aquinas here by arguing that a sin's being the worst *among the species of lust* is not the same as its being the worst, period. Unlike masturbation, rape is not just a sin against chastity (i.e., a species of lust) but also a sin against justice. But this move won't work in light of what Aquinas writes here, for according to Aquinas, sins against (human) justice can never outweigh those "whereby the very order of nature is violated" and which thus injure God himself.

Alternatively, one might reject Aquinas's stance on masturbation as a function of his mistaken views about human biology, which he largely inherits from Aristotle (384–322 B.C.). Aristotle believed that semen contains the human soul. Aquinas rejects this view (claiming instead that God provides the soul some time after conception) but still believes that the male's "seed" provides the form of the new human being, whereas the female provides only the raw material. The problem with taking this route is that it casts doubt on Aquinas's teachings, not only about masturbation, but also about other "unnatural acts" as well: If "spilling seed" is not next in gravity to homicide, as Aquinas held,[17] then the entire prohibition on non-procreative sexual acts may need to be rethought.

Aquinas's philosophy is more nuanced than his critics (and indeed many of his supporters) sometimes recognize. For example, he rejects the simplistic mapping of human morality onto animal behavior, acknowledges that nature is highly variable, and concedes that humans may permissibly use organs for purposes other than their "natural" ones—it is permissible to walk on one's hands, for instance. Unfortunately, he does not seem to see how such concessions undermine his case against same-sex relations.

In response to the example of walking on one's hands, Aquinas claims that "man's good is not much opposed by such inordinate use";[18] homosexual acts, by contrast, undermine the great good of procreation. There are two problems with this response. The first is that it is by no means clear that procreation is the only legitimate good achieved in sex, or that it is morally necessary for every sexual act to aim at it. Heterosexual couples often have sex even when they don't want children, don't want more children, or can't have children. Most people recognize that sex has other valuable purposes, including the expression of affection; the pursuit of mutual pleasure; and the building, replenishing, and celebrating of a special kind of intimacy. In order to maintain Aquinas's position, one would have to contend either that those purposes are not genuine goods or that homosexual acts cannot achieve them. These contentions both seem false on their face. . . .

The second problem is that the failure to pursue a good—in this case, procreation—is not equivalent to undermining or attacking that good. Aquinas himself was a celibate monk, after all. As the utilitarian philosopher Jeremy Bentham sharply observed over 200 years ago, if gays should be burned at the stake for the failure to procreate, then "monks ought to be roasted alive by a slow fire."[19] The issue of celibacy aside, there are plenty of heterosexuals who procreate abundantly while also occasionally enjoying, say, mutual masturbation or oral sex to orgasm. Such persons can hardly be said to *undermine* the good of procreation any more than Aquinas himself did.

Incidentally, the argument that gays undermine the good of procreation is sometimes mistakenly attributed to Immanuel Kant (1724–1804 A.D.) in the following form: Homosexuality must be bad for society, because *if everyone were homosexual there would be no society.* But, first, if everyone were celibate—like both Kant and Aquinas—there would be no society either. Second, the argument doesn't work against people who engage in both homosexual and heterosexual conduct, or who procreate in some other way, such as in vitro fertilization.

NOTES

1. In Christopher Wolfe, ed., *Same-Sex Matters: The Challenge of Homosexuality* (Dallas: Spence, 2000).

2. Cited in Wolfe 2000, p. 12.

3. Presentation to the Eastern Psychological Association, April 1993. Later published as "The Longevity of Homosexuals: Before and After the AIDS Epidemic," *Omega* 29 (1994): 51–59.

4. Letter from the American Psychological Association to Paul Cameron, December 2, 1983. Cameron has since circulated the letter and claimed that he had resigned prior to its issuance. But APA rules prohibit members from resigning while under investigation.

5. "Minutes of the Nebraska Psychological Association," October 19, 1984, and *ASA footnotes,* Feb. 1987, p. 14.

6. Cited in Wolfe 2000, p. 12.

7. http://wthrockmorton.com/2007/04/13/only-the-gay-die-young-part-2-danish-epidemiologist-reviews-the-cameron-smdy/.

8. Christopher Wolfe, "Homosexual Acts, Morality, and Public Discourse," in L.- Thomas, ed., *Contemporary Debates in Social Philosophy* (Malden: Blackwell, 2007), 94–110.

9. John Corvino, "Homosexuality, Harm, and Moral Principles," in L. Thomas, ed., *Contemporary Debates in Social philosophy* (Malden: Blackwell, 2007), 79–93.

10. Ryan et al., "Family Rejection as a Predictor of Negative Health Outcomes in White and Latino, Lesbian, Gay, and Bisexual Young Adults" *Pediatrics* 123 (2009): 346–352.

11. Wolfe 2007, p.106.

12. Ryan et al.

13. Aquinas, *Summa Theological* II–II, q. 154, a.12.

14. This section builds on a similar section from my essay "Why Shouldn't Tommy and Jim Have Sex?" in J. Corvino, ed., *Same Sex: Debating the Ethics, Science and Culture of Homosexuality* (Lantham, MD: Rowman & Little field. 1997), which itself builds on an older essay from Burton Leiser. I'm also indebted to Richard Mohr here and elsewhere for his pioneering work on ethics and homosexuality.

15. For a review of some studies see N. W. Bailey, and M. Zuk, "Same-Sex Sexual Behavior and Evolution" *Trends in Ecology & Evolution* 24 (2009): 439–46. For a more thorough (but older) treatment see B. Bagemihl, *Biological Exuberance*: *Animal Homosexuality and Natural Diversity*, (New York: St. Martin's Press, 1999).

16. Aquinas, *Summa Theological* II–II, q. 154, a.12.

17. Aquinas, *Summa Contra Gentiles* 3.22.9.

18. Aquinas, *Summa Contra Gentiles* 3.22.9.

19. J. Bentham "An Essay on Paederasty," in R. Baker and F. Elliston, eds., *The Philosophy of Sex* (Buffalo, NY: Prometheus, 1984).

READING QUESTIONS

1. What is the harm argument against homosexuality, and how does Corvino reply to it?
2. Corvino considers various versions of unnaturalness argument against homosexuality. What are the versions, and how does Corvino reply to each one?

DISCUSSION QUESTIONS

1. Are there other ways to understand the term "unnatural" other than the ones considered by Corvino that might be used by an opponent of homosexuality to defend the claim that the behavior and life-style are morally wrong?
2. Suppose, for the sake of argument, that although homosexuality does not pose a harm to anyone, it is morally wrong because it is in some sense unnatural. Would the (supposed) fact that it is morally wrong justify passing laws that would criminalize homosexual behavior? Why or why not? (Relevant to this question are the various "liberty-limiting principles" explained in the introduction to the next chapter.)

THOMAS A. MAPPES

A Liberal View of Sexual Morality and the Concept of Using Another Person

Mappes develops an essentially Kantian sexual ethic by appealing to the idea that in our dealings with others, we ought never to treat someone merely as a means to our own ends; to so treat them is to immorally *use* them. Mappes defines using someone as intentionally treating them in a way that violates the requirement that our involvement with others be based on their *voluntary* and *informed* consent. If we focus on sexual behavior, we arrive at a basic principle of sexual morality according to which A's sexual interaction with B is morally permissible only if A does not sexually treat B in a way that intentionally interferes with B's voluntary and informed consent. Since coercion is a main vehicle for interfering with someone's actions being voluntary, and deception is the means by which one interferes with another's actions being informed, we can use the basic principle just formulated to arrive at moral verdicts about certain forms of sexual behavior. In his article, Mappes develops this Kantian view by investigating specific cases of sexual interaction involving deception, coercion, and offers.

Recommended Reading: Kantian moral theory, chap. 1, sec. 2C.

The central tenet of *conventional* sexual morality is that nonmarital sex is immoral. A somewhat less restrictive sexual ethic holds that *sex without love* is immoral. If neither of these positions is philosophically defensible, and I would contend that neither is, it does not follow that there are no substantive moral restrictions on human sexual interaction. *Any* human interaction, including sexual interaction, may be judged morally objectionable to the extent that it transgresses a justified moral rule or principle. The way to construct a detailed account of sexual morality, it would seem, is simply to work out the implications of relevant moral rules or principles in the area of human sexual interaction.

As one important step in the direction of such an account, I will attempt to work out the implications of an especially relevant moral principle, the principle that it is wrong for one person to use another person. However ambiguous the expression "using another person" may seem to be, there is a determinate and clearly specifiable sense according to which using another person is morally objectionable. Once this morally significant sense of "using another person" is identified and explicated, the concept of using another person can play an important role in the articulation of a defensible account of sexual morality.

I. THE MORALLY SIGNIFICANT SENSE OF "USING ANOTHER PERSON"

Historically, the concept of using another person is associated with the ethical system of Immanuel Kant.

According to a fundamental Kantian principle, it is morally wrong for A to use B *merely as a means* (to achieve A's ends). Kant's principle does not rule out A using B as a means, only A using B *merely* as a means, that is, in a way incompatible with respect for B as a person. In the ordinary course of life, it is surely unavoidable (and morally unproblematic) that each of us in numerous ways uses others as a means to achieve our various ends. A college teacher uses students as a means to achieve his or her livelihood. A college student uses instructors as a means of gaining knowledge and skills. Such human interactions, presumably based on the voluntary participation of the respective parties, are quite compatible with the idea of respect for persons. But respect for persons entails that each of us recognize the rightful authority of other persons (as rational beings) to conduct their individual lives as they see fit. We may legitimately recruit others to participate in the satisfaction of our personal ends, but they are used merely as a means whenever we undermine the voluntary or informed character of their consent to interact with us in some desired way. A coerces B at knife point to hand over $200. A uses B merely as a means. If A had requested of B a gift of $200, leaving B free to determine whether or not to make the gift, A would have proceeded in a manner compatible with respect for B as a person. C deceptively rolls back the odometer of a car and thereby manipulates D's decision to buy the car. C uses D merely as a means.

On the basis of these considerations, I would suggest that the morally significant sense of "using another person" is best understood by reference to the notion of *voluntary informed consent.* More specifically, A immorally uses B if and only if A intentionally acts in a way that violates the requirement that B's involvement with A's ends be based on B's voluntary informed consent. If this account is correct, using another person (in the morally significant sense) can arise in at least two important ways: via *coercion,* which is antithetical to voluntary consent, and via *deception,* which undermines the informed character of voluntary consent. . . .

To illuminate the concept of using that has been proposed, I will consider . . . the matter of research involving human subjects. In the sphere of researcher-subject interaction, just as in the sphere of human sexual interaction, there is ample opportunity for immorally using another person. If a researcher is engaged in a study that involves human subjects, we may presume that the "end" of the researcher is the successful completion of the study. (The researcher may desire this particular end for any number of reasons: the speculative understanding it will provide, the technology it will make possible, the eventual benefit of humankind, increased status in the scientific community, a raise in pay, etc.) The work, let us presume, strictly requires the use (employment) of human research subjects. The researcher, however, immorally uses other people only if he or she intentionally acts in a way that violates the requirement that the participation of research subjects be based on their voluntary informed consent.

Let us assume that in a particular case participation as a research subject involves some rather significant risks. Accordingly, the researcher finds that potential subjects are reluctant to volunteer. At this point, if an unscrupulous researcher is willing to resort to the immoral using of other people (to achieve his or her own ends), two manifest options are available—deception and coercion. By way of deception, the researcher might choose to lie about the risks involved. For example, potential subjects could be explicitly told that there are no significant risks associated with research participation. On the other hand, the researcher could simply withhold a full disclosure of risks. Whether pumped full of false information or simply deprived of relevant information, the potential subject is intentionally deceived in such a way as to be led to a decision that furthers the researcher's ends. In manipulating the decision-making process of the potential subject in this way, the researcher is guilty of immorally using another person.

To explain how an unscrupulous researcher might immorally use another person via coercion, it is helpful to distinguish two basic forms of coercion.[1] "Occurrent" coercion involves the use of physical force. "Dispositional" coercion involves the threat of harm. If I am forcibly thrown out of my office by an intruder, I am the victim of occurrent coercion. If, on the other hand, I leave my office because an intruder has threatened to shoot me if I do not leave,

I am the victim of dispositional coercion. The victim of occurrent coercion literally has no choice in what happens. The victim of dispositional coercion, in contrast, does intentionally choose a certain course of action. However, one's choice, in the face of the threat of harm, is less than fully voluntary.

It is perhaps unlikely that even an unscrupulous researcher would resort to any very explicit measure of coercion. Deception, it seems, is less risky. Still, it is well known that Nazi medical experimenters ruthlessly employed coercion. By way of occurrent coercion, the Nazis literally forced great numbers of concentration camp victims to participate in experiments that entailed their own death or dismemberment. And if some concentration camp victims "volunteered" to participate in Nazi research to avoid even more unspeakable horrors, clearly we must consider them victims of dispositional coercion. The Nazi researchers, employing coercion, immorally used other human beings with a vengeance.

II. DECEPTION AND SEXUAL MORALITY

To this point, I have been concerned to identify and explicate the morally significant sense of "using another person." On the view proposed, A immorally uses B if and only if A intentionally acts in a way that violates the requirement that B's involvement with A's ends be based on B's voluntary informed consent. I will now apply this account to the area of human sexual interaction and explore its implications. For economy of expression in what follows, "using" (and its cognates) is to be understood as referring only to the morally significant sense.

If we presume a state of affairs in which A desires some form of sexual interaction with B, we can say that this desired form of sexual interaction with B is A's end. Thus A sexually *uses* B if and only if A intentionally acts in a way that violates the requirement that B's sexual interaction with A be based on B's voluntary informed consent. It seems clear then that A may sexually use B in at least two distinctive ways,

(1) via coercion and (2) via deception. However, before proceeding to discuss deception and then the more problematic case of coercion, one important point must be made. In emphasizing the centrality of coercion and deception as mechanisms for the sexual using of another person, I have in mind sexual interaction with a fully competent adult partner. We should also want to say, I think, that sexual interaction with a child inescapably involves the sexual using of another person. Even if a child "consents" to sexual interaction, he or she is, strictly speaking, incapable of *informed* consent. It's a matter of being *incompetent* to give consent. Similarly, to the extent that a mentally retarded person is rightly considered incompetent, sexual interaction with such a person amounts to the sexual using of that person, unless someone empowered to give "proxy consent" has done so. (In certain circumstances, sexual involvement might be in the best interests of a mentally retarded person.) We can also visualize the case of an otherwise fully competent adult temporarily disordered by drugs or alcohol. To the extent that such a person is rightly regarded as temporarily incompetent, winning his or her "consent" to sexual interaction could culminate in the sexual using of that person.

There are a host of clear cases in which one person sexually uses another precisely because the former employs deception in a way that undermines the informed character of the latter's consent to sexual interaction. Consider this example. One person, A, has decided, as a matter of personal prudence based on past experience, not to become sexually involved outside the confines of a loving relationship. Another person, B, strongly desires a sexual relationship with A but does not love A. B, aware of A's unwillingness to engage in sex without love, professes love for A, thereby hoping to win A's consent to a sexual relationship. B's ploy is successful; A consents. When the smoke clears and A becomes aware of B's deception, it would be both appropriate and natural for A to complain, "I've been used."

In the same vein, here are some other examples. (1) Mr. A is aware that Ms. B will consent to sexual involvement only on the understanding that in time the two will be married. Mr. A has no intention of marrying Ms. B but says that he will. (2) Ms. C has herpes and is well aware that Mr. D will never consent to sex if he knows of her condition. When asked by Mr. D, Ms. C denies that she has herpes. (3) Mr. E knows that Ms. F will not consent to sexual intercourse in the absence of responsible birth control measures. Mr. E tells Ms. F that he has had a vasectomy, which is not the case. (4) Ms. G knows that Mr. H would not consent to sexual involvement with a married woman. Ms. G is married but tells Mr. H that she is single. (5) Ms. I is well aware that Ms. J is interested in a stable lesbian relationship and will not consent to become sexually involved with someone who is bisexual. Ms. I tells Ms. J that she is exclusively homosexual, whereas the truth is that she is bisexual.

If one person's consent to sex is predicated on false beliefs that have been intentionally and deceptively inculcated by one's sexual partner in an effort to win the former's consent, the resulting sexual interaction involves one person sexually using another. In each of the above cases, one person explicitly *lies* to another. False information is intentionally conveyed to win consent to sexual interaction, and the end result is the sexual using of another person.

As noted earlier, however, lying is not the only form of deception. Under certain circumstances, the simple withholding of information can be considered a form of deception. Accordingly, it is possible to sexually use another person not only by (deceptively) lying about relevant facts but also by (deceptively) not disclosing relevant facts. If A has good reason to believe that B would refuse to consent to sexual interaction should B become aware of certain factual information, and if A withholds disclosure of this information in order to enhance the possibility of gaining B's consent, then, if B does consent, A sexually uses B via deception. One example will suffice. Suppose that Mr. A meets Ms. B in a singles bar. Mr. A realizes immediately that Ms. B is the sister of Ms. C, a woman that Mr. A has been sexually involved with for a long time. Mr. A, knowing that it is very unlikely that Ms. B will consent to sexual interaction if she becomes aware of Mr. A's involvement with her sister, decides not to disclose this information. If Ms. B eventually consents to sexual interaction, since her consent is the product of Mr. A's deception, it is rightly thought that she has been sexually used by him.

III. COERCION AND SEXUAL MORALITY

We have considered the case of deception. The present task is to consider the more difficult case of coercion. Whereas deception functions to undermine the *informed* character of voluntary consent (to sexual interaction), coercion either obliterates consent entirely (the case of occurrent coercion) or undermines the voluntariness of consent (the case of dispositional coercion).

Forcible rape is the most conspicuous, and most brutal, way of sexually using another person via coercion.[2] Forcible rape may involve either occurrent coercion or dispositional coercion. A man who rapes a woman by the employment of sheer physical force, by simply overpowering her, employs occurrent coercion. There is literally no sexual *interaction* in such a case; only the rapist performs an action. In no sense does the woman consent to or participate in sexual activity. She has no choice in what takes place, or rather, physical force results in her choice being simply beside the point. The employment of occurent coercion for the purpose of rape "objectifies" the victim in the strongest sense of that term. She is treated like a physical object. One does not interact with physical objects; one acts upon them. In a perfectly ordinary (not the morally significant) sense of the term, we "use" physical objects. But when the victim of rape is treated as if she were a physical object, there we have one of the most vivid examples of the immoral using of another person.

Frequently, forcible rape involves not occurrent coercion (or not *only* occurrent coercion) but dispositional coercion.[3] In dispositional coercion, the relevant factor is not physical force but the threat of harm. The rapist threatens his victim with immediate and serious bodily harm. For example, a man threatens to kill or beat a woman if she resists his sexual demands. She "consents," that is, she submits to his demands. He may demand only passive participation (simply not struggling against him) or he may demand some measure of active participation. Rape that employs dispositional coercion is surely just as wrong as rape that employs occurrent coercion, but there is a notable difference in the mechanism by which the rapist uses his victim in the two cases. With occurrent coercion, the victim's consent is entirely bypassed. With dispositional coercion, the victim's consent is not bypassed. It is coerced. Dispositional coercion undermines the *voluntariness* of consent. The rapist, by employing the threat of immediate and serious bodily harm, may succeed in bending the victim's will. He may gain the victim's "consent." But he uses another person precisely because consent is coerced.

The relevance of occurrent coercion is limited to the case of forcible rape. Dispositional coercion, a notion that also plays an indispensable role in an overall account of forcible rape, now becomes our central concern. Although the threat of immediate and serious bodily harm stands out as the most brutal way of coercing consent to sexual interaction, we must not neglect the employment of other kinds of threats to this same end. There are numerous ways in which one person can effectively harm, and thus effectively threaten, another. Accordingly, for example, consent to sexual interaction might be coerced by threatening to damage someone's reputation. If a person consents to sexual interaction to avoid a threatened harm, then that person has been sexually used (via dispositional coercion). In the face of a threat, of course, it remains possible that a person will refuse to comply with another's sexual demands. It is probably best to describe this sort of situation as a case not of coercion, which entails the *successful* use of threats to gain compliance, but of *attempted* coercion. Of course, the moral fault of an individual emerges with the *attempt* to coerce. A person who attempts murder is morally blameworthy even if the attempt fails. The same is true for someone who fails in an effort to coerce consent to sexual interaction.

Consider now each of the following cases:

Case 1

Mr. Supervisor makes a series of increasingly less subtle sexual overtures to Ms. Employee. These advances are consistently and firmly rejected by Ms. Employee. Eventually, Mr. Supervisor makes it clear that the granting of "sexual favors" is a condition of her continued employment.

Case 2

Ms. Debtor borrowed a substantial sum of money from Mr. Creditor, on the understanding that she would pay it back within one year. In the meantime, Ms. Debtor has become sexually attracted to Mr. Creditor, but he does not share her interest. At the end of the one-year period, Mr. Creditor asks Ms. Debtor to return the money. She says she will be happy to return the money so long as he consents to sexual interaction with her.

Case 3

Mr. Theatergoer has two tickets to the most talked-about play of the season. He is introduced to a woman whom he finds sexually attractive and who shares his interest in the theater. In the course of their conversation, she expresses disappointment that the play everyone is talking about is sold out; she would love to see it. At this point, Mr. Theatergoer suggests that she be his guest at the theater. "Oh, by the way," he says, "I always expect sex from my dates."

Case 4

Ms. Jetsetter is planning a trip to Europe. She has been trying for some time to develop a sexual relationship with a man who has shown little interest in her. She knows, however, that he has always wanted to go to Europe and that it is only lack of money that has deterred him. Ms. Jetsetter proposes that he come along as her traveling companion, all expenses paid, on the express understanding that sex is part of the arrangement.

Cases 1 and 2 involve attempts to sexually use another person whereas cases 3 and 4 do not. To see why this is so, it is essential to introduce a distinction between two kinds of proposals, viz., the distinction between *threats* and *offers*.[4] The logical form of a threat differs from the logical form of an offer in the following way. Threat: "If you *do not* do what I am proposing you do, I will bring about an *undesirable consequence* for you." Offer: "If you *do* what I am proposing you do, I will bring about a *desirable consequence* for you." The person who makes a threat attempts to gain compliance by attaching an undesirable consequence to the alternative of non-compliance. This person attempts to *coerce* consent. The person who makes an offer attempts to gain compliance by attaching a desirable consequence to the alternative of compliance. This person attempts not to coerce but to *induce* consent.

Since threats are morally problematic in a way that offers are not, it is not uncommon for threats to be advanced in the language of offers. Threats are represented as if they were offers. An armed assailant might say, "I'm going to make you an *offer*. If you give me your money, I will allow you to go on living." Though this proposal on the surface has the logical form of an offer, it is in reality a threat. The underlying sense of the proposal is this: "If you do not give me your money, I will kill you." If, in a given case, it is initially unclear whether a certain proposal is to count as a threat or an offer, ask the following question. Does the proposal in question have the effect of making a person *worse off upon noncompliance?* The recipient of an offer, upon noncompliance, *is not worse off* than he or she was before the offer. In contrast, the recipient of a threat, upon noncompliance, *is worse off* than he or she was before the threat. Since the "offer" of our armed assailant has the effect, upon noncompliance, of rendering its recipient worse off (relative to the preproposal situation of the recipient), the recipient is faced with a threat, not an offer.

The most obvious way for a coercer to attach an undesirable consequence to the path of noncompliance is by threatening to render the victim of coercion materially worse off than he or she has heretofore been. Thus a person is threatened with loss of life, bodily injury, damage to property, damage to reputation, etc. It is important to realize, however, that a person can also be effectively coerced by being threatened with the withholding of something (in some cases, what we would call a "benefit") to which the person is entitled. Suppose that A is mired in quicksand and is slowly but surely approaching death. When B happens along, A cries out to B for assistance. All B need do is throw A a rope. B is quite willing to accommodate A, "provided you pay me $100,000 over the next ten years." Is B making A an offer? Hardly! B, we must presume, stands under a moral obligation to come to the aid of a person in serious distress, at least when such

assistance entails no significant risk, sacrifice of time, etc. A is entitled to B's assistance. Thus, in reality, B attaches an undesirable consequence to A's noncompliance with the proposal that A pay B $100,000. A is undoubtedly better off that B has happened along, but A is not rendered better off *by B's proposal*. Before B's proposal, A legitimately expected assistance from B, "no strings attached." In attaching a very unwelcome string, B's proposal effectively renders A worse off. What B proposes, then, is not an offer of assistance. Rather, B threatens A with the withholding of something (assistance) that A is entitled to have from B. . . .

With the distinction between threats and offers clearly in view, it now becomes clear why cases 1 and 2 do indeed involve attempts to sexually use another person whereas cases 3 and 4 do not. Cases 1 and 2 embody threats, whereas cases 3 and 4 embody offers. In case 1, Mr. Supervisor proposes sexual interaction with Ms. Employee and, in an effort to gain compliance, threatens her with the loss of her job. Mr. Supervisor thereby attaches an undesirable consequence to one of Ms. Employee's alternatives, the path of noncompliance. Typical of the threat situation, Mr. Supervisor's proposal has the effect of rendering Ms. Employee worse off upon noncompliance. Mr. Supervisor is attempting via (dispositional) coercion to sexually use Ms. Employee. The situation in case 2 is similar. Ms. Debtor, as *she* might be inclined to say, "offers" to pay Mr. Creditor the money she owes him *if* he consents to sexual interaction with her. In reality, Ms. Debtor is threatening Mr. Creditor, attempting to coerce his consent to sexual interaction, attempting to sexually use him. Though Mr. Creditor is not now in possession of the money Ms. Debtor owes him, he is *entitled* to receive it from her at this time. She threatens to deprive him of something to which he is entitled. Clearly, her proposal has the effect of rendering him worse off upon noncompliance. Before her proposal, he had the legitimate expectation, "no strings attached," of receiving the money in question.

Cases 3 and 4 embody offers; neither involves an attempt to sexually use another person. Mr. Theatergoer simply provides an inducement for the woman he has just met to accept his proposal of sexual interaction. He offers her the opportunity to see the play that everyone is talking about. In attaching a desirable consequence to the alternative of compliance, Mr. Theatergoer in no way threatens or attempts to coerce his potential companion. Typical of the offer situation, his proposal does not have the effect of rendering her worse off upon noncompliance. She now has a new opportunity; if she chooses to forgo this opportunity, she is no worse off. The situation in case 4 is similar. Ms. Jetsetter provides an inducement for a man that she is interested in to accept her proposal of sexual involvement. She offers him the opportunity to see Europe, without expense, as her traveling companion. Before Ms. Jetsetter's proposal, he had no prospect of a European trip. If he chooses to reject her proposal, he is no worse off than he has heretofore been. Ms. Jetsetter's proposal embodies an offer, not a threat. She cannot be accused of attempting to sexually use her potential traveling companion.

Consider now two further cases, 5 and 6, each of which develops in the following way. Professor Highstatus, a man of high academic accomplishment, is sexually attracted to a student in one of his classes. He is very anxious to secure her consent to sexual interaction. Ms. Student, confused and unsettled by his sexual advances, has begun to practice "avoidance behavior." To the extent that it is possible, she goes out of her way to avoid him.

Case 5

Professor Highstatus tells Ms. Student that, though her work is such as to entitle her to a grade of B in the class, she will be assigned a D unless she consents to sexual interaction.

Case 6

Professor Highstatus tells Ms. Student that, though her work is such as to entitle her to a grade of B, she will be assigned an A if she consents to sexual interaction.

It is clear that case 5 involves an attempt to sexually use another person. Case 6, however, at least at face value, does not. In case 5, Professor Highstatus

threatens to deprive Ms. Student of the grade she deserves. In case 6, he *offers* to assign her a grade that is higher than she deserves. In case 5, Ms. Student would be worse off upon noncompliance with Professor Highstatus's proposal. In case 6, she would not be worse off upon noncompliance with his proposal. In saying that case 6 does not involve an attempt to sexually use another person, it is not being asserted that Professor Highstatus is acting in a morally legitimate fashion. In offering a student a higher grade than she deserves, he is guilty of abusing his institutional authority. He is under an obligation to assign the grades that students earn, as defined by the relevant course standards. In case 6, Professor Highstatus is undoubtedly acting in a morally reprehensible way, but in contrast to case 5, where it is fair to say that he both abuses his institutional authority *and* attempts to sexually use another person, we can plausibly say that in case 6 his moral failure is limited to abuse of his institutional authority.

There remains, however, a suspicion that case 6 might after all embody an attempt to sexually use another person. There is no question that the literal content of what Professor Highstatus conveys to Ms. Student has the logical form of an offer and not a threat. Still, is it not the case that Ms. Student may very well feel threatened? Professor Highstatus, in an effort to secure consent to sexual interaction, has announced that he will assign Ms. Student a higher grade than she deserves. Can she really turn him down without substantial risk? Is he not likely to retaliate? If she spurns him, will he not lower her grade or otherwise make it harder for her to succeed in her academic program? He does, after all, have power over her. Will he use it to her detriment? Surely he is not above abusing his institutional authority to achieve his ends; this much is abundantly clear from his willingness to assign a grade higher than a student deserves.

Is Professor Highstatus naive to the threat that Ms. Student may find implicit in the situation? Perhaps. In such a case, if Ms. Student reluctantly consents to sexual interaction, we may be inclined to say that he has *unwittingly* used her. More likely, Professor Highstatus is well aware of the way in which Ms. Student will perceive his proposal. He knows that threats need not be verbally expressed. Indeed, it may even be the case that he consciously exploits his underground reputation. "Everyone knows what happens to the women who reject Professor Highstatus's little offers." To the extent, then, that Professor Highstatus intends to convey a threat in case 6, he is attempting via coercion to sexually use another person. . . .

IV. THE IDEA OF A COERCIVE OFFER

In section III, I have sketched an overall account of sexually using another person *via coercion*. In this section, I will consider the need for modifications or extensions of the suggested account. As before, certain case studies will serve as points of departure.

Case 7

Ms. Starlet, a glamorous, wealthy, and highly successful model, wants nothing more than to become a movie superstar. Mr. Moviemogul, a famous producer, is very taken with Ms. Starlet's beauty. He invites her to come to his office for a screen test. After the screen test, Mr. Moviemogul tells Ms. Starlet that he is prepared to make her a star, on the condition that she agree to sexual involvement with him. Ms. Starlet finds Mr. Moviemogul personally repugnant; she is not at all sexually attracted to him. With great reluctance, she agrees to his proposal.

Has Mr. Moviemogul sexually used Ms. Starlet? No. He has made her an offer that she has accepted, however reluctantly. The situation would be quite different if it were plausible to believe that she was, before acceptance of his proposal, *entitled* to his efforts to make her a star. Then we could read case 7 as amounting to his threatening to deprive her of something to which she was entitled. But what conceivable grounds could be found for the claim that Mr. Moviemogul, before Ms. Starlet's acceptance of his proposal, is under an obligation to make her a star? He does not threaten her; he makes her an offer. Even if there are other good grounds for morally condemning his action, it is a mistake to think that he is guilty of coercing consent.

But some would assert that Mr. Moviemogul's offer, on the grounds that it confronts Ms. Starlet with an overwhelming inducement, is simply an example of a *coercive offer*. The more general claim at issue is that offers are coercive precisely inasmuch as they are extremely enticing or seductive. Though there is an important reality associated with the notion of a coercive offer, a reality that must shortly be confronted, we ought not embrace the view that an offer is coercive merely because it is extremely enticing or seductive. Virginia Held is a leading proponent of the view under attack here. She writes:

> A person unable to spurn an offer may act as unwillingly as a person unable to resist a threat. Consider the distinction between rape and seduction. In one case constraint and threat are operative, in the other inducement and offer. If the degree of inducement is set high enough in the case of seduction, there may seem to be little difference in the extent of coercion involved. In both cases, persons may act against their own wills.[5]

Certainly a rape victim who acquiesces at knife point is forced to act *against her will*. Does Ms. Starlet, however, act against her will? We have said that she consents "with great reluctance" to sexual involvement, but she does not act against her will. She *wants* very much to be a movie star. I might want very much to be thin. She regrets having to become sexually involved with Mr. Moviemogul as a means of achieving what she wants. I might regret very much having to go on a diet to lose weight. If we say that Ms. Starlet acts against her will in case 7, then we must say that I am acting against my will in embracing "with great reluctance" the diet I despise.

A more important line of argument against Held's view can be advanced on the basis of the widely accepted notion that there is a moral presumption against coercion. Held herself embraces this notion and very effectively clarifies it:

> . . . [A]lthough coercion is not *always* wrong (quite obviously: one coerces the small child not to run across the highway, or the murderer to drop his weapon), there is a presumption against it. . . . This has the standing of a fundamental moral principle. . . .
>
> What can be concluded at the moral level is that we have a prima facie obligation not to employ coercion.[6] [all italics hers]

But it would seem that acceptance of the moral presumption against coercion is not compatible with the view that offers become coercive precisely inasmuch as they become extremely enticing or seductive. Suppose you are my neighbor and regularly spend your Saturday afternoon on the golf course. Suppose also that you are a skilled gardener. I am anxious to convince you to do some gardening work for me and it must be done this Saturday. I offer you $100, $200, $300, . . . in an effort to make it worth your while to sacrifice your recreation and undertake my gardening. At some point, my proposal becomes very enticing. Yet, at the same time in no sense is my proposal becoming morally problematic. If my proposal were becoming coercive, surely our moral sense would be aroused.

Though it is surely not true that the extremely enticing character of an offer is sufficient to make it coercive, we need not reach the conclusion that no sense can be made out of the notion of a coercive offer. Indeed, there is an important social reality that the notion of a coercive offer appears to capture, and insight into this reality can be gained by simply taking note of the sort of case that most draws us to the language of "coercive offer." Is it not a case in which the recipient of an offer is in circumstances of genuine need, and acceptance of the offer seems to present the only realistic possibility for alleviating the need? Assuming that this sort of case is the heart of the matter, it seems that we cannot avoid introducing some sort of distinction between *genuine needs* and *mere wants*. Though the philosophical difficulties involved in drawing this distinction are not insignificant, I nevertheless claim that we will not achieve any clarity about the notion of a coercive offer, at least in this context, except in reference to it. Whatever puzzlement we may feel with regard to the host of borderline cases that can be advanced, it is nevertheless true, for example, that I *genuinely need* food and that I *merely want* a backyard tennis court. In the same spirit, I think it can be acknowledged by all that Ms. Starlet, though she *wants* very much to be a star, does not in any relevant sense *need* to be a star. Accordingly, there is little plausibility in thinking that Mr. Moviemogul makes her a coercive offer. The following case, in contrast, can more plausibly be thought to embody a coercive offer.

Case 8

Mr. Troubled is a young widower who is raising his three children. He lives in a small town and believes that it is important for him to stay there so that his children continue to have the emotional support of other family members. But economic times are tough. Mr. Troubled has been laid off from his job and has not been able to find another. His unemployment benefits have ceased and his relatives are in no position to help him financially. If he is unable to come up with the money for his mortgage payments, he will lose his rather modest house. Ms. Opportunistic lives in the same town. Since shortly after the death of Mr. Troubled's wife, she has consistently made sexual overtures in his direction. Mr. Troubled, for his part, does not care for Ms. Opportunistic and has made it clear to her that he is not interested in sexual involvement with her. She, however, is well aware of his present difficulties. To win his consent to a sexual affair, Ms. Opportunistic offers to make mortgage payments for Mr. Troubled on a continuing basis.

Is Ms. Opportunistic attempting to sexually use Mr. Troubled? The correct answer is yes, even though we must first accept the conclusion that her proposal embodies an offer and not a threat. If Ms. Opportunistic were threatening Mr. Troubled, her proposal would have the effect of rendering him worse off upon noncompliance. But this is not the case. If he rejects her proposal, his situation will not worsen; he will simply remain, as before, in circumstances of extreme need. It might be objected at this point that Ms. Opportunistic does in fact threaten Mr. Troubled. She threatens to deprive him of something to which he is entitled, namely, the alleviation of a genuine need. But this approach is defensible only if, before acceptance of her proposal, he is entitled to have his needs alleviated *by her.* And whatever Mr. Troubled and his children are entitled to from their society as a whole—they are perhaps slipping through the "social safety net"—it cannot be plausibly maintained that Mr. Troubled is entitled to have his mortgage payments made *by Ms. Opportunistic.*

Yet, though she does not threaten him, she is attempting to sexually use him. How can this conclusion be reconciled with our overall account of sexually using another person? First of all, I want to suggest that nothing hangs on whether or not we decide to call Ms. Opportunistic's offer "coercive." More important than the label "coercive offer" is an appreciation of the social reality that inclines us to consider the label appropriate. The label most forcefully asserts itself when we reflect on what Mr. Troubled is likely to say after accepting the offer. "I really had no choice." "I didn't want to accept her offer but what could I do? I have my children to think about." Both Mr. Troubled and Ms. Starlet (in our previous case) *reluctantly* consented to sexual interaction, but I think it can be agreed that Ms. Starlet had a choice in a way that Mr. Troubled did not. Mr. Troubled's choice was *severely constrained by his needs,* whereas Ms. Starlet's was not. As for Ms. Opportunistic, it seems that we might describe her approach as in some sense exploiting or taking advantage of Mr. Troubled's desperate situation. It is not so much, as we would say in the case of threats, that she coerces him or his consent, but rather that she achieves her aim of winning consent by taking advantage of the fact that he is already "under coercion," that is, his choice is severely constrained by his need. If we choose to describe what has taken place as a "coercive offer," we should remember that Mr. Troubled is "coerced" (constrained) by his own need or perhaps by preexisting factors in his situation rather than by Ms. Opportunistic or her offer.

Since it is not quite right to say that Ms. Opportunistic is attempting to coerce Mr. Troubled, even if we are prepared to embrace the label "coercive offer," we cannot simply say, as we would say in the case of threats, that she is attempting to sexually use him *via coercion.* The proper account of the way in which Ms. Opportunistic attempts to sexually use Mr. Troubled is somewhat different. Let us say simply that she attempts to sexually use him *by taking advantage of his desperate situation.* The sense behind this distinctive way of sexually using someone is that a person's choice situation can sometimes be subject to such severe prior constraints that the possibility of *voluntary* consent to sexual interaction is precluded. A advances an offer calculated to gain B's reluctant consent to sexual interaction by confronting B, who has no apparent way of alleviating a genuine need, with an opportunity to do so, but makes this opportunity

contingent upon consent to sexual interaction. In such a case, should we not say simply that B's need, when coupled with a lack of viable alternatives, results in B being incapable of *voluntarily* accepting A's offer? Thus A, in making an offer which B "cannot refuse," although not coercing B, nevertheless does intentionally act in a way that violates the requirement that B's sexual interaction with A be based upon B's voluntary informed consent. Thus A sexually uses B.

The central claim of this paper is that A sexually uses B if and only if A intentionally acts in a way that violates the requirement that B's sexual interaction with A be based on B's voluntary informed consent. Clearly, deception and coercion are important mechanisms whereby sexual using takes place. But consideration of case 8 has led us to the identification of yet another mechanism. In summary, then, limiting attention to cases of sexual interaction with a fully competent adult partner, A can sexually use B not only (1) by deceiving B or (2) by coercing B but also (3) by taking advantage of B's desperate situation.

NOTES

1. I follow here an account of coercion developed by Michael D. Bayles in "A Concept of Coercion," in J. Roland Pennock and John W. Chapman, eds., *Coercion: Nomos XIV* (Chicago: Aldine-Atherton, 1972), pp. 16–29.

2. Statutory rape, sexual relations with a person under the legal age of consent, can also be construed as the sexual using of another person. In contrast to forcible rape, however, statutory rape need not involve coercion. The victim of statutory rape may freely "consent" to sexual interaction but, at least in the eyes of the law, is deemed incompetent to consent.

3. A man wrestles a woman to the ground. She is the victim of occurrent coercion. He threatens to beat her unless she submits to his sexual demands. Now she becomes the victim of dispositional coercion.

4. My account of this distinction largely derives from Robert Nozick, "Coercion," in Sidney Morgenbesser, Patrick Suppes, and Morton White, eds., *Philosophy, Science, and Method* (New York: St. Martin's Press, 1969), pp. 440–472, and from Michael D. Bayles, "Coercive Offers and Public Benefits," *The Personalist* 55, no. 2 (Spring 1974), 139–144.

5. Virginia Held, "Coercion and Coercive Offers," in *Coercion: Nomos XIV,* p. 58.

6. Ibid., pp. 61, 62.

READING QUESTIONS

1. What is the morally significant sense of using another person according to Mappes?
2. Explain the difference between coercion and deception. What is the distinction between occurrent and dispositional coercion? Give examples of each.
3. How does Mappes distinguish between threats and offers?
4. What is a coercive offer? Why does Mappes find this idea problematic?

DISCUSSION QUESTIONS

1. Mappes describes several situations which are supposed to illustrate cases in which a person either is or is not being used by another. Should we accept the evaluations he makes about each of these cases? Are there any reasons why we might think that people are being used in the cases where Mappes claims they are not? Consider the situations Mappes suggests as cases of threats and offers as well.
2. How plausible is the idea of a coercive offer? How is taking advantage of someone similar to or different from a case of deception or coercion?

RAJA HALWANI

Virtue Ethics and Adultery

Halwani begins with a brief overview of virtue ethics, explaining some of its advantages over consequentialist and Kantian (deontological) "modern" moral theories. Although these modern moral theories take the concept of right action to be logically prior to the concept of virtue, virtue ethics, by contrast, understands right action in terms of virtue. Halwani then considers the moral issue of sexual fidelity in marriage and romantic commitments generally from a virtue ethics perspective. His central claim is that the goods of love, trust, and affection are central to these sorts of committed relationships—relationships which for many people partly constitute a flourishing life. A virtuous person, then, in protecting these goods would be a person who (with success) strives toward the ideal or virtue of fidelity. It follows on the virtue ethical conception of wrongness that adulterous actions are (at least typically) morally wrong because the person engaged in them fails to live up to this ideal.

From Raja Halwani, "Virtue Ethics and Adultery," *Journal of Social Philosophy* 29 (1998). Reprinted by permission of *Journal of Social Philosophy*.

Halwani concludes by considering possible cases in which it would not be wrong to engage in adultery, even though doing so may be a kind of moral failure.

Recommended Reading: virtue ethics, chap. 1, sec. 2E. Also relevant are consequentialism, chap. 1, sec. 2A, and Kantian moral theory, chap. 1, sec. 2C.

. . . I would like to take a look at adultery from the standpoint of an ethics of virtue, the reason being that such an ethics allows better for the complexities surrounding the topic.

In the first section, I list and briefly explain some of the most important misgivings that the friends of virtue ethics have with Kantian theory (and consequentialism). I also briefly explain the salient features of an ethics of virtue, some of its salient problems, and some possible replies to these problems. In the second section, . . . I discuss what an ethics of virtue has to say on adultery.

1. VIRTUE ETHICS

Recently, there has been some dissatisfaction with modern moral philosophy, that is, Kantian ethics, consequentialism, and their offshoots, such as social contract ethics and rights theory. Elizabeth Anscombe, Philippa Foot, Alasdair MacIntyre, and Bernard Williams are among the first philosophers to inveigh against modern moral philosophy, and their views have prompted the search for an alternative ethical theory. . . .

Most philosophers who have attacked modern moral philosophy have gathered around an ethics of virtue, an ethics which is still in its infancy insofar as its theoretical articulation is concerned. The core idea in an ethics of virtue is that the basic judgments in ethics are not judgments about acts but about character. According to Gregory Trianosky, "a pure ethics of virtue makes two claims. First it claims that at least some judgments about virtue can be validated independently of any appeal to judgments about the rightness of actions. Second . . . it is this antecedent goodness of traits which ultimately makes any right act right."[1] Under deontological and utilitarian conceptions, the notion of right behavior or acts is

logically prior to that of virtues. An ethics of virtue flips such a conception around: it is right behavior which is justified in terms of the virtues.

The question now of course is from what do the virtues themselves derive their justification. The answer usually given is that the virtues derive their justification from the notion of well-being or human flourishing. The virtues can then be thought of as being either *necessary* for well-being or as *constitutive* of it. However, and according to Statman, the linkage between the virtues and well-being is not essential to an ethics of virtue. What is essential is the claim that judgments about character are prior to judgments about the rightness or wrongness of behavior.[2] Such a claim can be a moderate one—that although most judgments are judgments of character, still, some actions can be evaluated independently of character—or it can be an extreme one. Under an extreme formulation, we can hold either a reductionist view or a replacement one. The former states that deontic concepts such as rightness and duty are useful, but that they are nevertheless derived from concepts of character. The latter, which is the most extreme formulation, states that deontic notions should be entirely discarded by an ethics of virtue and be replaced by other concepts, such as those of courage, benevolence, and generosity—the "thick concepts" of Bernard Williams.[3]

A good person is someone who is good because of the virtues he or she possesses. So not only are acts justified in terms of the virtues, but also whether a person is good or not will depend on the virtues, or lack thereof, that she has. This raises the question of what kind of an account of the virtues can be given. Typically, the understanding of the virtues has been dispositional: to have a certain virtue is to be disposed to act in certain ways given certain conditions. Such an understanding has been attacked by Mary Ella Savarino on the grounds that virtues do not turn out to be fundamental: "the focus is not on the virtue itself (courage), but on the person's behavior."[4] Savarino herself favors an account of virtues which takes them to be first actualities in the Aristotelian sense. In any case, the issue is still open: an adequate account of the virtues is needed.

It is obvious that virtue ethics has a number of advantages. For example, it makes room for the idea that it is not the case that for any moral problem there is only one right answer. Two virtuous people may act differently from one another when faced with the same situation, and yet both their actions can be right. A mother in poor health who has to work in the fields, who has five children, and who has an abortion upon her sixth pregnancy is not to be described as self-indulgent. Another mother in a similar situation might decide to go ahead with the pregnancy, and she is surely heroic. Both the actions are right despite the fact that the mothers acted differently. Second, virtue ethics is not in tension with the phenomenon of moral luck. As Statman put it, "According to Virtue Ethics, judgments of character, such as, 'Barbara is a friendly woman,' 'Tom is unbearably arrogant,' are not touched by the discovery that these traits are the result of genes, education, and circumstances, over which the agent had very limited control."[5]

Another important advantage of an ethics of virtue is its rejection of the distinction between the moral and the nonmoral. For if virtue ethics is concerned with the evaluation of character, then other nonmoral traits would be important, especially if the notion of well-being is taken to be primary. What enters into the well-being or flourishing of a person is not only what has been traditionally dubbed as "moral," but also a host of other "nonmoral" considerations, such as love, marriage, and sexual relations. . . .

2. ADULTERY AND VIRTUE ETHICS

In *Having Love Affairs,*[6] Richard Taylor gives us an interesting case of a married couple, the upshot of which is that whereas it is the wife who commits adultery, she is not the one to be described as unfaithful. The husband has been married to the same woman for a long time, and he has never been sexually unfaithful to her. He believes that sexual fidelity is of utmost importance, and he frowns upon any act of adultery committed by others. However, it is not in his nature, so to speak, to be sexually active. As a matter of fact, "[h]is intimacy with his own wife is perfunctory, infrequent, dutiful, and quite devoid of joy for himself or his spouse" (pp. 59–60). Moreover, it appears to others that the couple are of moderate financial means but hard-working. However, the husband, in complete secrecy from his wife and others, has a number of savings accounts which collectively contain a huge sum of money accumulated over the years. The wife, on the other hand, gets sick with cancer and undergoes a mastectomy, "[w]hereupon whatever small affection her husband ever had for her evaporates completely" (p. 60). The husband neglects her to the point of being "dimly aware" of her presence. In addition, the wife has always been an ardent writer of good poetry, and she meets a man who appreciates her talents. The man is oblivious to her physical scars, and loves her for who she is. Although Taylor does not explicitly say it, it seems that the wife has an affair with this man. The question that Taylor poses is, "Who has been faithless to whom?" (p. 60). The answer, of course, is, "The husband."[7]

I have gone into the details of this story because it gives us a good starting point as to how an ethics of virtue would deal with the issue of adultery. The picture we get from Taylor's story is that of a man (the husband) who lies, deceives, and is not to be commended for his sexual fidelity. He is the kind of person who is calculative, cold, selfish, and emotionally distant. Moreover, the fact that he did not commit adultery has nothing to do with his amazing ability to withstand sexual temptations, and has everything to do with the facts that he has never been tempted and that he is of a sexually passive nature. The wife, out of sheer bad luck, gets sick with cancer, suffers from its effects, and suffers from her husband's increased neglect. That she has an affair with another man is not only understandable, but even recommended, given her need for affirmation and love.

Under a Kantian picture, we are at a loss as to how to deal with Taylor's case. Did the wife violate her promise of sexual fidelity? Yes. Was her violation permissible in this case, that is, did she have a duty that can override her duty to keep her promise to her husband? If yes, what duty would that be? The duty to be happy? That would surely be a very strange duty, for under a Kantian scheme we do not have a duty to promote our own happiness. Does the fact that the husband violated his duty to love his wife justify her violation of the promise to sexual fidelity? Surely not, for if her violation is wrong, then, as the saying goes, two wrongs do not make a right, and if her violation is permissible, surely it is not because her husband violated his own promise. Perhaps a good way to think of this would be the following: had the husband done what he did, without having made any promises, he would still be a despicable person. The wife might very well have broken her promise of sexual fidelity and so violated a right that her husband has against her. But as Rosalind Hursthouse suggests in her paper on abortion and virtue ethics, "in exercising a moral right I can do something cruel, or callous, or selfish, light-minded, self-righteous, stupid, inconsiderate, disloyal, dishonest,—that is, act viciously."[8] Similarly but oppositely, in violating a right one might sometimes do what is morally correct. Violation of promises is not what is at stake here.

Does virtue ethics have any general picture to give us about adultery? Yes, and the answer can be approached from two perspectives: the nature of love and the nature of the virtuous person.

The wrongness of adultery stems from the fact that adultery occurs in the context of marriage or a love relationship, the basis of which is an emotional commitment. Although it is perhaps meaningful to speak of adultery when it occurs in the context of a purely sexual relationship between two people, the act of the adulterer does not appear to be so horrific in such a case. What seems to be horrible about adultery is that it indicates a more fundamental betrayal, namely, that of love. As Bonnie Steinbock puts it, "[s]exual infidelity has significance as a sign of a deeper betrayal—falling in love with someone else."[9] Logically speaking, of course, there is no necessary connection between sex and love, as gay male orgy rooms aptly demonstrate. Indeed, one can argue that given that it is possible for love and sex to be disconnected, the

permissibility of adultery follows. An argument that tries to show the immorality of adultery by arguing that since sex is connected with love, then sexual betrayal is tantamount to emotional betrayal, and hence adultery is wrong, is an invalid one, because there is no necessary connection between love and sex. This kind of reasoning[10] is correct but naive. It is true that sex is a pleasurable activity in and of itself, but sex is also typically an intimate activity. It requires a substantial amount of trust, it involves a good amount of self-exposure, and it is accompanied by the exchange of affection. We do not typically have sex in ways that are depicted in pornography movies, in which the partners have sex purely for sex's sake. Moreover, sex is connected to love precisely because it is a pleasurable activity: "People naturally have feelings of affection for those who make them happy, and sex is a very good way of making someone extraordinarily happy" (Steinbock, p. 190).

The fact that sex is intimately connected with love indicates the wrongness of adultery in two important ways. On the part of the adulterous spouse, the spouse, upon committing adultery, puts himself in a position in which emotional betrayal might be involved, and in which there is the possibility of increased affection between himself and the person he is having sex with. On the part of the nonadulterous spouse, the amount of pain and hurt upon the discovery is bad in itself, and it could lead to the destruction of the marriage. It could destroy the trust and affection that have been built over the years, and it could leave either party, if not both, emotionally and mentally damaged. I then endorse Steinbock's conclusion that sexual fidelity is an ideal in a marriage or in a romantic commitment.

If fidelity is an ideal in marriage, then a virtuous person would strive to stick to this ideal in a relationship. Moreover, a virtuous spouse would strive to maintain and foster the love, trust, and affection that exist between him and his spouse. These are healthy emotions and are an important part, surely, of any conception of a virtuous and flourishing person. To this end, adultery is to be avoided. This is a difficult endeavor, for it seems that we are not by nature sexually monogamous: we find people other than our spouses to be also sexually desirable, and we sometimes fantasize about them. Moreover, it is a fact that with time, the novelty of sex with one person wears out, and the temptation to seek sexual encounters with new partners increases. These facts warn us that sometimes failure to conform to the ideal is understandable. Be this as it may, it is crucial to strive for the ideal of fidelity. If the person is in love with someone, and if the person wants to be with that person for an indefinite period of time, then it is essential to strive for fidelity, given that adultery can damage the relationship and the persons involved. But to maintain the ideal of fidelity requires one to be a certain kind of person, a sexually faithful person, not because being sexually faithful guarantees the flourishing of the relationship and the people involved, but because in most cases it is pre-required by such flourishing.

A virtuous person is one who is to a large extent wise, courageous, fair, honest, moderate, caring, compassionate, benevolent, loving. Some of these virtues go a long way in helping to maintain the ideal of fidelity: the wisdom not to put oneself in tempting situations and in situations in which one cannot easily resist temptation (e.g., drunkenness), the wisdom to know when one is ready for a commitment, the wisdom to know whether one is the kind of person who is capable of being in a committed relationship, the courage to resist temptation, the compassion, care, and love for one's spouse that would form one's basis for refusing to commit adultery, and the honesty to one's spouse in the case of committing adultery. Other virtues do not seem to have room with respect to adultery. Adultery does not, for example, admit of moderation.[11]

But perhaps the important question is what virtue ethics tells us about the failure to conform to the ideal.[12] If in a drunken moment a spouse goes ahead and commits adultery, this would be a sorry and sad situation, but it would not be a tragedy, for the chances of emotional betrayal here are minimal, and to throw away a marriage, especially if it is good, because of what one spouse did in a moment of drunkenness is uncalled for. The fact that one might commit adultery in a drunken moment does not indicate that the marriage was going sour (the question, "Why else would one commit adultery?" often embodies this mistaken reasoning). As I mentioned, it does not seem to be in our nature to be sexually monogamous, and being

drunk can often unleash our inhibited desires. But this is no good reason to throw away a good marriage.

If a woman is abused by her spouse, treated as an object, neglected, or all of these, she cannot be described as self-indulgent if she has an affair with another person. Her self-worth and happiness are at stake, and an affair can go a long way in healing her scars. To argue that the wife should first get a divorce before she has an affair with another man is simplistic. Often there are important factors at play that block such a way out. The wife might have no independent economic means by which she can sustain herself. There might be children involved, and sometimes the wife reasons that it is not in their best interests if a divorce occurs. Also, the wife might wish to stay in the marriage in the hope that it will get better, even if she does not envision a clear way of how this would happen.

In communities, such as those of Renaissance Florence and some Middle Eastern countries, in which marriage is often not based on love, the risk that there is a mismatch between the two married people is high, and often in such communities dissolving the marriage is not an easy matter, given that much rests on the continuation of the marriage, such as family honor, money, and political alliances. If one of, or both, the spouses commits adultery, this would be understandable, and perhaps even encouraged. Being stuck with a person that one does not want to be with is not a trivial matter, and having an extramarital affair can make the situation a bit more bearable.

Furthermore, sometimes the decision to commit adultery is the right one, although it might still be a case of moral failing. A husband who thinks that his wife is not treating him well, who feels that his marital life falls short of what it should be, who is as a result miserable, but who fails to be honest about his thoughts and feelings because he is too cowardly to talk to his wife, or because he lacks the perception to realize that his wife is simply unaware of the results of her actions, might very well make the right decision in having an affair with someone who satisfies his psychological and emotional needs. But the husband has also failed by allowing the situation to reach the point where he feels the need for an affair. He lacked the requisite courage and honesty to deal with these problems with his wife.

A person who knows from experience that his sexual drive is very strong, and who feels unable to be sexually monogamous simply because he loves sex too much, and yet who desires to be in a relationship with some specific individual, should be quite honest about what the sexual expectations of such a relationship would be. A sexually open relationship might be the most desirable form. Many gay couples, for example, have such relationships. Yet the form of extramarital sex that they allow themselves to have is highly impersonal so as to avoid the possibility of emotional intimacy with the new sexual partner. Hence, they resort to cruising in parks, they resort to dark rooms in gay bars and discos, and these are places in which there is minimal or no verbal and emotional communication.

One last issue I would like to discuss briefly is the question of why utilitarianism cannot account, as successfully as virtue ethics, for the wrongness of adultery. After all, a utilitarian might advise married couples not to commit adultery because the consequences might be bad: loss of love between the spouses, possible anguish for the children, and so forth.[13]

As far as act utilitarianism goes, I find it unsuccessful to deal with this issue for two major reasons. The first is that act utilitarianism has certain undesirable consequences, and hence is in itself a bad theory *in general.* Act utilitarianism could justify acts of murder, of punishing the innocent, and of trampling on the rights of others if such acts proved to have a net effect of good consequences (typically, happiness) over bad ones. The second reason is that act utilitarianism, insofar as it is a utilitarian theory— which it is—is not concerned only with the effects that adultery has on the family in question. Insofar as it is a utilitarian theory, it is concerned with the effects it has on everyone. Hence, and at least in principle, act utilitarianism could justify an act of adultery by appealing to the overall consequences. For example, suppose that John is married to Judith, that they have no children because Judith cannot have them, and that they both refuse to adopt. Suppose further that on one dark night John finally succumbs to lust and has an affair with his secretary Jezebel. They fall in love with each other, and they get married after John and Judith get a divorce. John and Jezebel proceed to have three children, one who grows up to be a physicist and who ends up solving the problems of quantum mechanics, one who grows up to be a doctor and who finds a decisive cure for AIDS, and the third who grows up to be a famed economist, who solves the problem of the incompatibility of price inflation and high employment. It would seem, then, that act utilitarianism could justify wrong acts of adultery.

Rule utilitarianism, which states that certain kinds of acts are wrong because they violate certain rules, and which justifies these rules by appealing to the principle of utility, suffers from its own defects. In general, when certain rules conflict, a rule utilitarian, being a utilitarian, must resort to solving the problem by appealing to the consequences of each act. Hence, in cases when there is a conflict of rules, rule utilitarianism becomes act utilitarianism. Furthermore, when it comes to adultery, rule utilitarianism is not as well equipped as virtue ethics is to handle this problem. Rule utilitarianism becomes similar to Kantian ethics in telling us that adultery is wrong because it violates a certain rule (adultery is wrong; do not commit adultery). By not appealing to character traits, the history of the agents involved, and the circumstances at hand (because these are not part and parcel of this doctrine), rule utilitarianism is as ineffective as Kantian ethics. We have seen, however, that virtue ethics is equipped to give us good explanations and justifications for certain cases of adultery precisely because it is a theory which takes certain factors into account, factors that have hitherto been left out by deontological and consequentialist theories of ethics.[14]

There is no one single answer to the question, "Would a virtuous person refrain from committing adultery?" Part of what it is to be a virtuous person is to be sensitive to the details of the situation and to be sensitive to the fact that one is a member of a certain kind of community or culture. Virtue ethics does not lapse into a vicious form of relativism or particularism. It tells us that a virtuous spouse should strive to maintain the ideal of fidelity, difficult though this may be. But virtue ethics does not give us one formula for treating the issue, and this, I believe, is a positive aspect of virtue ethics. As Aristotle remarked, we should not demand exactness from a subject that is not exact.

NOTES

1. Gregory Trianosky, "What is Virtue Ethics All About?" *American Philosophical Quarterly,* vol. 27, 1990, p. 336.

2. Daniel Statman, *Virtue Ethics: A Critical Reader* (Washington, D.C.: Georgetown University Press, 1997).

3. Ibid., p. 9. Michael Slote, *From Morality to Virtue,* advocates the moderate view. Anscombe advocates the replacement view. Williams seems to hold the reductionist view. See also Philip Montague, "Virtue Ethics: A Qualified Success Story," *American Philosophical Quarterly,* vol. 29, no. 1, January 1992.

4. Mary Ella Savarino, "Toward an Ontology of Virtue Ethics," *Journal of Philosophical Research,* vol. 18, 1993, p. 245.

5. Statman, p. 17.

6. Buffalo: Prometheus Books, 1982. Page references in my paper are to this book.

7. Perhaps adultery is permissible because the wife had a duty that overrides her promise of sexual fidelity to her husband. From Michael Wreen's perspective, my guess is that he would not allow it. The case he gives is of a couple who experience sexual dysfunction, such that the only way to save their marriage is for one of them (the relevant party) to commit adultery. Crucial to this case is the goal (duty?) to save the marriage, a goal which is not operative in the case given by Taylor. Michael Wreen, "What's Really Wrong with Adultery? *International Journal of Applied Philosophy* 3, 1986, pp. 45–9.

8. "Virtue Theory and Abortion," *Philosophy and Public Affairs,* vol. 20, no. 3, 1991, p. 235.

9. "Adultery," in *Philosophy of Sex,* p. 192. Page references in my paper are to this anthology.

10. This reasoning is used by Richard Wasserstrom, "Is Adultery Immoral?" in *Philosophy and Sex,* R. Barker and F. Elliston, eds. (Buffalo: Prometheus Books, 1984).

11. Except in some special cases. A couple in an open relationship might want to be moderate in their extramarital sexual activities perhaps to avoid the higher risk of contracting diseases, especially the potentially fatal HIV. A person who is allowed by his or her spouse (for some reason or another) to engage in extramarital sex might still want to be moderate in what they do during their sexual escapades and in the frequency of such escapades.

12. In what follows, I owe much to Steinbock's "Adultery" and Hursthouse's "Virtue Theory and Abortion."

13. This suggestion was given by a reader from *The Journal of Social Philosophy.*

14. The reader from the journal also mentioned character utilitarianism, and why such a view cannot explain the wrongness of adultery as well as virtue ethics. I have never been entirely clear on what character utilitarianism exactly amounts to. As far as I understand it, it is the view that we should strive to have good characters. Stated in this way, it would seem to be a species of virtue ethics, and so, on my view, benign. But I still need to find a more articulate and coherent formulation of the view.

READING QUESTIONS

1. What are the advantages of virtue ethics according to Halwani?

2. Explain the case of adultery that Halwani uses as his main illustration. How does the virtue ethical response to such a case differ from the Kantian and consequentialist responses?

3. What is the ideal toward which the virtuous person should strive in a relationship according to Halwani? What virtues should the virtuous person acquire in order to attain this ideal? Explain how each of these virtues could play a role in achieving an ideal relationship.

4. What reasons does Halwani give for rejecting both act and rule utilitarianism?

DISCUSSION QUESTIONS

1. Is a virtue ethical approach the best one to take with respect to the situation of adultery? Why or why not? Discuss whether certain aspects of the virtue ethical approach could be incorporated into either Kantian or utilitarian approaches to these sorts of problems.

2. One of Halwani's objections to act utilitarianism is that it is concerned with the effect an action has on everyone involved. Are there any reasons to think that a virtue ethical approach might have the same problem?

ADDITIONAL RESOURCES

Web Resources

Pickett, Brent, "Homosexuality," <http://plato.stanford.edu/entries/homosexuality/>. Includes discussion of the history of same-sex attraction, natural law objections, and queer theory.

Authored Books

Halwani, Raja, *Philosophy of Love, Sex, and Marriage: An Introduction* (London: Routledge, 2010). The author explores the nature and ethics of love, sex, and marriage.

Edited Collections

Baker, Robert B., Kathleen J. Wininger, and Frederick A. Elliston (eds.), *Philosophy and Sex*, 3rd ed. (Amherst, NY: Prometheus Books, 1998). This anthology of forty-four essays is divided into three parts: (1) Love, Marriage, and Reproduction, (2) Gender, Sexuality, and Perversion, and (3) Desire, Pornography, and Rape.

Corvino, John (ed.), *Same Sex: Debating the Ethics, Science, and Culture of Homosexuality* (Lanham, MD: Rowman & Littlefield, 1997). This anthology includes twenty-one articles divided into four parts: Morality and Religion, Science and Identity, Identity and History, and Public Policy.

Power, N., R. Halwani, and A. Soble (eds.) *The Philosophy of Sex,* 6th ed. (Lanham, MD: Rowman & Littlefield, 2013). This recent anthology is probably the best of its kind. It has twenty-nine articles organized into the following four parts: (1) analysis and perversion, (2) queer issues, (3) objectification and consent—the theory, (4) objectification and consent—applied topics. It also includes an extensive bibliography on these and other topics.

Trevas, Robert, Arthur Zucker, and Donald Borchert (eds.), *Philosophy of Sex and Love*, 3rd ed. (Upper Saddle River, NJ: Prentice Hall, 1997). A wide-ranging collection of essays covering historical, religious, and philosophical perspectives on sex, love, and their relationship. Marriage, adultery, prostitution, pornography, homosexuality, sexual harassment, and perversion are among the topics of contemporary interest that are discussed.

4 } Pornography, Hate Speech, and Censorship

The Internet has made access to pornography relatively easy, while proliferation in the use of computers, tablets, and smartphones has made access to this material widespread. One often discusses the censorship concerns associated with limiting access to pornography by minors; but there are others, including, for example, censorship of pornographic materials that are judged to be violent or that involve such acts as bestiality.

Social media, including Twitter, Facebook, Snapchat, Instagram, and YouTube, provide a global platform for the communication of information and ideas. For instance, an anti-Islamic video ridiculing prophet Muhammad, posted on YouTube (owned by Google), created a storm of controversy for allegedly having provoked violence in the Muslim world in September 2012. The video is widely believed to have led to rioting and was also linked to the killing of a U.S. ambassador to Libya and three other American diplomatic personnel. In response to the controversy, Google restricted access to the video in Egypt and Libya, as well as in five other countries in which the content of the video violated local laws, a claim that under the company's own guidelines the video was not hate speech notwithstanding.

Pornography and hate speech raise difficult legal questions over whether such forms of expression ought to be censored or access to such materials in some way restricted. But one can also raise moral questions about the production, distribution, and consumption of those modes of expression. Concerning pornography and censorship, here are the basic questions of concern:

- Is either the production or consumption of pornography morally wrong?
- For any such activities that are wrong, what explains why they are wrong?
- Would it be morally acceptable for a government to pass laws that make the production and consumption of pornography illegal?

Similar questions can be asked about hate speech, but let us first consider disputes concerning pornography and then turn to disputes about hate speech.

1. WHAT IS PORNOGRAPHY?

According to most dictionary definitions, **pornography** is "the depiction of erotic behavior (as in pictures or writing) intended to cause sexual excitement."[1] But for purposes of moral and legal discussion, it is important to notice that within the category of pornography, there are importantly different species. The 1986 Attorney General's Commission on Pornography (included as one of our readings) distinguishes four categories of pornography: (1) violent pornography, (2) nonviolent but degrading pornography, (3) nonviolent, nondegrading pornography, and (4) the special category of child pornography. In discussing the issue of pornography, then, it is important to be clear about which species of pornography is in question. If I announce that pornography ought not to be censored and you respond by saying that it ought to be censored, then we will be talking past one another if I am thinking exclusively about nonviolent, nondegrading pornography and you are thinking exclusively about pornography that is either violent or degrading.

Here is a related point. When one looks to recent literature on pornography, one often finds the term "pornography" being used for a certain restrictive class of sexually explicit material. For instance, Helen E. Longino distinguishes pornography from what she calls **erotica.** She defines pornography as "verbal or pictorial material which represents or describes sexual behavior that is degrading or abusive to one or more of the participants in such a way as to endorse the degradation."[2] On this definition, what makes something pornography is not just its sexual content or the fact that it is intended to cause sexual excitement, but (in addition) its degradation of one or more of those being depicted *and* its endorsement of that degradation. Erotica is then characterized as including sexually explicit material that either is not degrading to one or more of the participants or does not endorse such degradation. Notice that the class of items picked out by Longino's definition of "pornography" coincides with the Attorney General's Commission's first two categories—violent and nonviolent but degrading pornography— whereas "erotica" coincides with the commission's category of nonviolent, nondegrading pornography. So, again, in thinking about the morality and legality of pornography, it is important to be clear about what is being referred to by the term.[3]

Cyberpornography is pornography available on the Internet. An article, "Naked Capitalism," published in *The Economist* (September 26, 2015) reports that "With most porn on the Internet now free and easy to find, the number of adult sites, and traffic to them, have exploded. The web boasts an estimated 700m–800m individual porn pages, three-fifths in America." One may well wonder how the free and easy availability of Internet pornography affects those who regularly consume it. This is the question addressed by Susan Dwyer in her selection below.

So-called revenge porn has been a subject of recent discussion and some regulation. The term, "revenge porn," taken literally, refers to the circulation by one party of sexually explicit images of another out of revenge or other hostile feelings toward the victim and without their consent. However, this is only one species of a broader phenomenon that is appropriately called "**nonconsensual pornography**," referring simply to the distribution of sexually explicit images of others without their consent. As of 2016, twenty-six U.S. states have made such distribution illegal.

2. LIBERTY-LIMITING PRINCIPLES

In order to provide a framework for thinking about censorship, it will help to introduce various principles—**liberty-limiting principles**—that figure prominently in debates over censorship. A "liberty-limiting" principle *purports* to specify considerations that may morally justify a government in passing laws that would interfere with the liberty of mentally competent adults (henceforth, "individuals"). Traditionally, the following four such principles have played an important role in moral and political philosophy.

The Harm Principle

According to the **harm principle**, a government may justifiably pass laws that interfere with the liberty of individuals in order to *prohibit individuals from causing harm to other individuals or to society.* To clarify this principle, we need to address the following three issues.

First, and mostly obviously, in applying the harm principle, we must determine what is going to count as harm (at least for purposes of justifying government interference). Certainly, physical harms such as killing, maiming, or inflicting physical pain on someone are to count, and we should also include psychological harms to one's mental health. Other harms include economic harms as well as harms to one's career and reputation. So, in applying the harm principle, we need to keep in mind the range of harms that might result from some activity.

Second, harms can vary in their seriousness. So, in applying the harm principle, we must also consider how serious would be the harm caused by some activity. Arguably, in order for the harm principle to justify government-backed prohibition of some activity, it must be the case that very serious harms would result from allowing citizens to engage in that activity.

Third, the harm principle can be viewed as an essentially consequentialist moral principle,[4] and therefore in applying it we must balance the likely good effects of passing and enforcing a law that prohibits some harmful behavior with the likely negative effects of not doing so. If the negative social consequences of enforcing a law against some activity would produce a greater level of harm than is produced by allowing the activity, then the harm principle cannot justify government legislation prohibiting the activity. With these points in mind, it is clear that laws against murder, maiming, severe physical injury, and theft are justified by appeal to the harm principle. But as we shall see, there is a good deal of controversy over whether this principle can justify government censorship of pornography.

The Offense Principle

According to the **offense principle**, a government may justifiably pass laws that interfere with individual liberty in order to *prohibit individuals from offending others,* where offensive behavior includes causing others shame, embarrassment, or discomfort. To distinguish this principle from the harm principle, we must distinguish psychological harms—harms to one's mental health—from unpleasant psychological states that do not constitute harms. Consider an example. Laws prohibiting public nudity seem to receive justification from the offense principle. Someone who appears naked in full public view may cause onlookers uneasiness and embarrassment, but normally such negative feelings do not constitute *harm* to those who have them. Notice that this principle is not meant to cover cases in which someone's mere knowledge of the behavior of others is offensive to that person. Rather, the principle is meant to apply to cases in which (1) "normal" or "average" persons would find the behavior deeply offensive—the *standard of universality,* and (2) encountering the offensive behavior cannot be reasonably avoided—the *standard of reasonable avoidability.* Obscene remarks over a loudspeaker, walking nude through a downtown, billboards and signage with obscene sexually explicit content are all examples of cases that fail the standard of reasonable avoidability.[5]

The Principle of Legal Paternalism

According to the principle of **legal paternalism,** a government may justifiably pass laws in order to *protect individuals from harming themselves.* Thus, for example, seat belt laws and motorcycle helmet laws might be defended on the basis of the principle of paternalism, as well as laws that prohibit the use of certain drugs—a subject discussed in the next chapter.

Principle of Legal Moralism

The principle of **legal moralism** states that a government may justifiably pass laws that interfere with individual liberty in order to *protect common moral standards, independently of whether the activities in question are harmful to others or to oneself.* Of course, murder, rape, and theft are immoral; but because they are also harmful, laws against such actions can be sufficiently justified by the harm principle. Appeals to the principle of legal moralism typically arise in attempts to justify laws against certain so-called victimless violations of common morality. Sodomy laws are perhaps an example.

There are four points about these liberty-limiting principles that should be kept in mind. First, it is here assumed that an individual's liberty (freedom of choice and action) is of great value, and thus interference with one's liberty requires some *moral* justification.[6] These principles, then, are intended to state conditions under which a government may be *morally* justified in restricting individual liberty through law. Second, each of these principles states considerations (harm to others, offense to others, harm to oneself, and immoral behavior) that *may* justify a government in passing laws against some activity. The emphasis on "may" was implicit in our discussion of the harm principle. Whether a government *is* justified in passing laws against some form of behavior based on the harm principle requires not only that the behavior really be harmful, but also that the harms would be serious and that the enforcement of laws against the behavior in question would not result in even greater harm than does the behavior itself.

Third, these principles are not mutually exclusive; one might accept more than one of them. Indeed, one might accept all four. Fourth, and finally, in claiming that these principles *purport* to specify considerations that may justify government interference with individual liberty, we leave open the question about which of them *ought* to serve as principles that morally justify such interference. Debate over the justification of these principles is a subject for social and political philosophy and hence beyond the scope of our present concerns. But a few brief remarks are in order here.

The most uncontroversial of the principles is the harm principle—certainly if a government is ever morally justified in using its coercive power to interfere with individual liberty, it is to protect individuals and society generally from being harmed by others. John Stuart Mill, in his influential classic *On Liberty* (1859), ardently defends the idea that the harm principle is the *only* legitimate liberty-limiting principle:

> [T]he only purpose for which power can be rightfully exercised over any member of a civilized community, against his will, is to prevent harm to others. His own good, either physical or moral, is not a sufficient warrant. He cannot rightfully be compelled to do or forbear because it will be better for him to do so, because it will make him happier, because, in the opinion of others, to do so would be wise or even right. These are good reasons for remonstrating with him, or reasoning with him, or persuading him, or entreating him, but not for compelling him or visiting him with any evil in case he do otherwise. To justify that, the conduct from which it is desired to deter him, must be calculated to produce evil to

someone else. The only part of the conduct of any one for which he is amenable to society, is that which concerns others. In the part which merely concerns himself, his independence is, of right, absolute.[7]

In this passage, Mill is clearly rejecting the principle of paternalism. Moreover, his remark about being compelled to forbear from some action because "in the opinion of others, to do so would be wise or even right," indicates his rejection of the principle of legal moralism.

Mill's position is representative of Liberalism. **Liberalism,** understood as a political ideology,[8] is associated with the idea of safeguarding individual liberties against government interference through a structure of equal rights. Of course, saying this does not distinguish Liberalism from all competing nonliberal ideologies. Ronald Dworkin has argued that the distinguishing idea of Liberalism is a certain conception of the equal treatment of citizens by a government as a fundamental moral ideal—a conception requiring that in order for a government to treat its citizens as equals, it must remain as neutral as possible on the question of the good life for human beings.[9] By contrast, nonliberal views, including versions of **Conservatism,** reject this particular conception of equal treatment, insisting that in treating their citizens equally, governments may (and perhaps must) make decisions based partly on some particular conception of what a truly good life for human beings requires.[10] On the basis of their conception of equality (as requiring government neutrality over the good life), liberals tend to be staunch defenders of a certain array of basic liberties, including those providing strong protection of speech, and a sphere of privacy to lead one's own life as one sees fit. Thus, liberal thinkers following in the tradition of Mill defend the harm principle (as well as the offense principle)[11] but tend to reject the principles of paternalism and legal moralism, since these principles (arguably) involve government interference based on a particular conception of the good life for human beings. Conservatives, by contrast, tend to accept the principles of paternalism and legal moralism, and so, for example, are not opposed to government interference on behalf of upholding standards of moral decency.

3. PORNOGRAPHY AND CENSORSHIP

Now that we have a rudimentary understanding of the various liberty-limiting principles, how might any of them serve as a basis for justifiably censoring at least some forms of pornography? In order for any of these principles to provide a good moral justification for censorship, two conditions must be met. First, the principle in question must be a *defensible* liberty-limiting principle. Second, it would have to be shown that pornography (its production or its consumption) has the characteristic mentioned in the principle. For example, to apply the harm principle, it would have to be shown that pornography causes serious harm to society. So let us briefly return to the liberty-limiting principles with these two questions in mind, taking each principle in turn.

Most disputes over pornography and censorship take place against the background of the right to freedom of speech. For example, this is the full text of the First Amendment of the U.S. Constitution:

> *Congress shall pass no law respecting an establishment of religion, or prohibiting the free exercise thereof; or abridging the freedom of speech, or of the press; or the right of people to peaceably assemble, and to petition the Government for a redress of its grievances.*

The first point to note about the First Amendment is that although it has sometimes been interpreted as placing an *absolute prohibition* on laws restricting free speech, more often it has been interpreted as placing a *very strong presumption* against laws that would restrict free speech. This is where the harm principle comes into play. The classic example here is falsely yelling "Fire!" in a crowded theater. Since such speech puts others at immediate risk of serious harm, and since the harm principle is widely recognized as a defensible liberty-limiting principle (by Liberals and nonliberals alike), this kind of speech is legitimately prohibited by law.

With respect to disputes about pornography and censorship in relation to the U.S. Constitution, the main things to keep in mind are these. First, because the harm principle is relatively uncontroversial as a liberty-limiting principle, much of the debate over pornography in close to forty years has focused on the question of its harmful effects on society. Second, since there is a strong presumption in favor of freedom of speech and expression, there is a strong burden of proof on those who are pro-censorship to show that pornography (at least certain forms of it) causes serious harm to society—serious enough to justify passing laws against its production and consumption.

The offense principle is perhaps more controversial than the harm principle (although it is widely accepted), and its role in pro-censorship arguments is primarily relevant in connection with, for example, public displays that are found offensive by nonconsenting individuals. Were a pornographic film to be shown outdoors at a public place where passersby might unavoidably see it, then the offense principle (assuming it is acceptable) might justify laws against such showings. Disputes over pornography have mainly to do with its production and use by *consenting* individuals, rather than cases in which nonconsenting individuals are subjected to it, and so the offense principle has not played as large a role in such disputes as has the harm principle.

As noted earlier, the principle of paternalism is controversial, and so appealing to it to justify antipornography laws is problematic; many people do not think the government ought to interfere in the liberty of its citizens for their own good. However, ignoring questions about its justification, if one were to use this principle in connection with censorship, one would have to show that producing or consuming pornography tends to seriously harm those who produce it, or those who participate in it, or those who consume it. One might claim that these individuals harm their own character by producing, participating in, or consuming pornography. But again, this claim would need to be shown, and even if it could be shown, one would also have to show that the principle of paternalism is an acceptable liberty-limiting principle.

Finally, the principle of legal moralism has played an important role in Conservative pro-censorship arguments. For example, some claim that pornographic magazines and films involve images and depictions of morally disgusting and "dirty" sexual activities and that to consume such images and depictions for purposes of sexual stimulation is immoral. One problem with this kind of argument is that there are questions about which moral standards should be imposed in applying the principle of legal moralism. But more importantly, the principle itself is highly disputed. As we saw earlier, many, following Mill, argue against it by claiming that it is not the proper role of government to get involved in the nonharmful personal lives of individuals.

These remarks help explain why, at least in debates having to do with U.S. First Amendment rights, claims about the harmfulness of pornography have been at the center of controversy over its censorship: the harm principle is uncontroversial, whereas the other principles are either not as relevant to the debate (offense) or are questionable (paternalism and legal moralism).

4. HATE SPEECH

In 1990, Robert A. Viktora was convicted under the St. Paul, Minnesota, city ordinance that prohibited forms of speech or expression that were likely to provoke "anger, alarm, or resentment in others on the basis of race, color, creed, religion, or gender." Viktora, together with several white teenagers, burned a cross on the lawn of a black family that had recently moved into a predominantly white neighborhood in St. Paul. Viktora challenged the conviction, arguing that it violated his freedom of speech. In the 1992 *R.A.V. v. St. Paul* decision, the U.S. Supreme Court struck down the St. Paul ordinance, arguing that while fighting words were not protected by the First Amendment, the sort of hateful expression engaged in by Viktora is protected, and that to outlaw such expression would amount to discrimination against speech on the basis of its content. The Court's ruling raises a battery of moral and legal issues that parallel the ones raised in connection with pornography.

But there is an important conceptual question as well: How is hate speech to be defined? This chapter began with the posting on YouTube of an anti-Islamic video in 2012, an event that sparked debate about Internet censorship. Google denied that the video constitutes hate speech, though it is reported that millions across the Muslim world took it be one of the most inflammatory (because hateful as well as mocking) items of content on the Internet. Commenting on fundamental questions raised by hate speech, Stanley Fish in his *New York Times* (November. 12, 2012) book review of *The Content and Context of Hate Speech* (see this chapter's "Additional Resources") wrote the following:

> What you learn in the course of reading this book is that there is no generally accepted account of (1) what hate speech is, (2) what it does (what its effects are) and (3) what, if anything, should be done about it. To be sure, everyone agrees that it is hate speech when words are used to directly incite violence against a specific person or group of persons. But as Arthur Jacobson and Bernhard Schlink point out in their contribution to the volume, on such occasions the words are instrumental "to an incipient assault," and it is the assault, not the words, that the state criminalizes . . . . There need be no debate about what to do in the face of that kind of speech because it is already being done by extant laws.

Fish goes on to describe what would be hard cases including, for example, a pamphlet that "explains how Muslim Americans plan to impose Shariah law and subvert the traditions of this country"—a piece of writing that may stir hatred for Muslims among some readers. Should this item be considered hate speech? Many other cases (real and imagined) raise the same question.

Keeping in mind the contentious nature of the very concept of hate speech—what does and does not count as such speech and thus how to define it—let us (at least provisionally) characterize **hate speech** as *language (oral or written) that expresses strong hatred, contempt, or intolerance for some social group, particularly social groups classified according to race, ethnicity, gender, sexual orientation, religion, disability, or nationality.*[12] Some characterizations also make explicit reference to the intentions of the speaker by adding that the aim of such speech is to degrade, dehumanize, intimidate, or incite violence against members of the group being targeted.

We can now raise a set of moral questions that parallel the ones raised earlier about pornography:

- Is hate speech morally wrong?
- If it is, what is the best explanation of why it is wrong?
- Furthermore, would it be morally permissible for a government to pass laws that would make hate speech illegal?

Now that we have some background for studying the topics of pornography, hate speech, and censorship, let us turn to the various moral arguments that we find represented in recent literature on these topics.

5. THEORY MEETS PRACTICE

Because much of the controversy over the censorship of pornography and hate speech focuses on the overall effects of such activities, let us begin with consequentialism.

Consequentialism

As we have seen, the claim that pornography causes substantial harm appeals to the alleged bad consequences of such expression as a basis for censorship. We may think of the harm principle as a specification of the general consequentialist theory of morality for use in connection with evaluating the morality of government interference with individual liberty.[13] And, as with all consequentialist approaches, it is important to consider the *overall* consequences of various alternative courses of action in determining which course is morally permissible. When it comes to the issue of censoring pornography, we have already noted the strong burden of proof on pro-censorship advocates to provide clear evidence of serious harm to society. Suppose that the evidence were very clear that pornography does cause substantial harm to society. This alone, however, would not be enough to justify censorship. We also noted that in applying the harm principle, one must consider the costs and benefits of passing and enforcing censorship laws against the costs and benefits of not doing so. Would passing and enforcing censorship laws have what is called a "chilling effect" on other forms of speech (e.g., political speech) that ought to be protected? That is, would passing laws against pornography make people more wary of other forms of unpopular speech and expression and discourage them from expressing themselves?[14] Another worry has to do with sliding down a slippery slope (a topic that is discussed more fully in the introduction to chapter 8). If we allow censorship of pornography, do we risk opening the door to the censorship of materials with sexual content that is merely unpopular or controversial from, say, certain religious perspectives? And if that happens, what about materials that are not sexual in content but unpopular?

The 1986 Meese Commission, whose report is included in our readings, cites what it takes to be evidence that certain forms of pornography cause harm, particularly to women. Moreover, some feminist writers have argued that pornography violates the basic civil rights of women, constituting harm to their interests, and is therefore subject to censorship.[15] However, Nadine Strossen, in a selection included in this chapter, attempts to rebut the Meese Commission's conclusions about pornography and harm, and she argues that censorship would likely result in more harm than good to women. Susan Owyer considers the harm to one's character that may be unique to the consumption of cyber pornography.

Turning briefly to hate speech, questions about its negative effects are central in the articles by John Arthur and Andrew Altman. Arthur argues that hate speech is protected and criticizes pro-censorship arguments based on the harm and offense principles. Appealing to the idea of expressive harm, Altman defends hate speech codes.

Kantian Ethics

We do find Kantian, nonconsequentialist arguments for the claim that pornography is morally wrong. Given the Kantian principle that we ought never to treat persons merely as means and always as ends in themselves, it follows from this analysis that pornography (its production and consumption) is morally wrong. Since hate speech expresses disrespect for members of some group, it seems to follow from Kant's principle that such speech is morally wrong. Notice that these Kantian arguments concern only the morality of the practices in question and don't *directly* have implications for questions about censorship (unless one accepts the principle of legal moralism). Nevertheless, if, as some feminists have argued, the production and consumption of pornography is degrading to women, then because this representation is likely to have negative effects on how women are perceived and treated in society, perhaps a case can be made in favor of censorship on the basis of the harm principle.

NOTES

1. From the *Merriam-Webster Online Dictionary.* Etymologically, the word *pornography* derives from the Greek word *pornographos,* which taken literally means "writing about the activities of prostitutes."

2. Helen E. Longino, "Pornography, Oppression, and Freedom: A Closer Look," in *Take Back the Night: Women on Pornography* (New York: Morrow, 1980).

3. The notion of obscenity is often used in characterizing pornography, but the ordinary concepts of the obscene and the pornographic are distinct. While pornography concerns forms of expression that have sexual content and are intended to arouse sexual excitement, obscenity (what is obscene) refers more generally to things that are morally repugnant. However, in U.S. law, the prevailing *legal* definition of "obscene" is to be found in *Miller v. California,* 413 U.S. 15, which involves a three-pronged test: material is obscene only if: "(a) the average person, applying contemporary community standards would find that the work, taken as a whole, appeals to the prurient interest, (b) . . . the work depicts or describes, in a patently offensive way, sexual conduct specifically defined by the applicable state law; and (c) . . . the work, taken as a whole, lacks serious literary, artistic, political, or scientific value" (25).

4. See chapter 1, section 2A, for a discussion of consequentialism.

5. These examples and general discussion of the offense principle are inspired by Joel Feinberg's discussion in his *Social Philosophy* (Englewood Cliffs, NJ: Prentice-Hall, 1973), 41–45.

6. This presumption of the value of liberty requires defense—a central topic in social and political philosophy.

7. J. S. Mill, *On Liberty*, ed., Elizabeth Rapaport, (Indianapolis, IN: Hackett Publishing Company, Inc., 1978, originally published in 1859), 9.

8. In the introduction to the previous chapter on sexual morality, I introduced the labels "conservative," "liberal," and "moderate" to classify general types of views one might take on some particular moral issue, where the difference between these views has to do with how restrictive they are about the morality of the issue in question. According to this usage, a conservative view is comparatively restrictive in what it considers to be morally permissible regarding the issue in question, a liberal view is comparatively unrestrictive, and a moderate view falls in between. But being a liberal or a conservative about some moral issue should not be confused with accepting the ideology of Liberalism or Conservatism, respectively. For instance, someone who holds a liberal view (small *l*) on some particular moral issue (abortion, for example) might be a political Conservative, maintaining that in general it is within the proper moral authority of a government to pass laws to protect morality. In addition to the essays by Ronald Dworkin cited in note 9, I recommend the essays "Liberalism" and "Conservatism" by Robert Eccleshall in his anthology *Political Ideologies: An Introduction,* 2nd ed. (London: Routledge, 1994), for a more thorough discussion of Liberalism and Conservatism.

9. See Ronald Dworkin's essays "Liberalism," "Why Liberals Should Care about Equality," and "What Justice Isn't," reprinted in his *A Matter of Principle* (Cambridge, MA: Harvard University Press, 1985).

10. Conservatism, as the label suggests, is often associated with preserving traditions (moral, religious, political) and being opposed to radical social change. Eccleshall, in his essay "Conservatism" (cited in note 8), argues that this conception is inaccurate. He claims that a "vindication of inequality" is the distinguishing feature of this ideology.

11. The offense principle is often recognized by liberals as a necessary supplement to the harm principle. On this point, see Feinberg, *Social Philosophy,* 41–45.

12. The term "hate speech" does not (yet) appear, for instance, in the *Merriam-Webster Online Dictionary,* but a Google search query for a definition turns up a number of sites that define the term in roughly the same way.

13. Strictly speaking, one need not embrace a consequentialist moral theory in order to accept the harm principle. For instance, one might hold that certain matters of personal morality are governed by such nonconsequentialist principles as Kant's Humanity version of the categorical imperative, while also claiming that matters of public policy ought to be decided on consequentialist grounds.

14. For a discussion of the chilling effect on speech brought about by recent actions of the FCC and U.S. Congress, see Katherine A. Fallow, "The Big Chill? Congress and the FCC Crack Down on Indecency," *Communications Lawyer* 22 (2004): 24–32.

15. See, for example, Catharine A. MacKinnon, "Francis Biddle's Sister: Pornography, Civil Rights, and Speech," in Catharine A. MacKinnon, *Feminism Unmodified: Discourses on Life and Law* (Cambridge, MA: Harvard University Press, 1987), 178.

THE ATTORNEY GENERAL'S COMMISSION ON PORNOGRAPHY

Pornography and Harm

In 1985, U.S. President Ronald Reagan appointed Attorney General Edwin Meese III to head an eleven-member commission whose purpose was to investigate the problem of pornography in the United States and, in particular, any role it might play in causing harm. In 1986 the Meese Commission made its report in which it distinguishes four types of pornography: (1) violent, (2) nonviolent but degrading, (3) nonviolent and nondegrading, and (4) child pornography. After reviewing the available evidence about the causal effects of pornography, the commission concluded that there is sufficient evidence linking both violent and nonviolent but degrading pornography to violence against women. However, its members could not reach sufficient agreement about whether exposure to nonviolent and nondegrading pornography is linked to harm. Finally, the commission explains the "special horror" of child pornography, which by definition involves the sexual exploitation of children.

Recommended Reading: consequentialism, chap. 1, sec. 2A.

Reprinted from *Final Report,* Washington, DC: United States Department of Justice, July 1986.

MATTERS OF METHOD

... The analysis of the hypothesis that pornography causes harm must start with the identification of hypothesized harms, proceed to the determination of whether those hypothesized harms are indeed harmful, and then conclude with the examination of whether a causal link exists between the material and the harm. When the consequences of exposure to sexually explicit material are not harmful, or when there is no causal relationship between exposure to sexually explicit material and some harmful consequence, then we cannot say that the sexually explicit material is harmful. But if sexually explicit material of some variety is causally related to, or increases the incidence of, some behavior that *is* harmful, then it is safe to conclude that the material is harmful. ...

The Problem of Multiple Causation

The world is complex, and most consequences are "caused" by numerous factors. Are highway deaths caused by failure to wear seat belts, failure of the automobile companies to install airbags, failure of the government to require automobile companies to install airbags, alcohol, judicial leniency towards drunk drivers, speeding, and so on and on? Is heart disease caused by cigarette smoking, obesity, stress, or excess animal fat in our diets? As with most other questions of this type, the answers can only be "all of the above," and so too with the problem of pornography. We have concluded, for example, that some forms of sexually explicit material bear a causal relationship both to sexual violence and to sex discrimination, but we are hardly so naive as to suppose that were these forms of pornography to disappear the problems of sex discrimination and sexual violence would come to an end.

If this is so, then what does it mean to identify a causal relationship? It means that the evidence supports the conclusion that if there were none of the material being tested, then the incidence of the consequences would be less. We live in a world of multiple causation, and to identify a factor as a *cause* in such a world means only that if this factor were eliminated while everything else stayed the same then the problem would at least be lessened. In most cases it is impossible to say any more than this, although to say this is to say quite a great deal. But when we identify something as a cause, we do not deny that there are other causes, and we do not deny that some of these other causes might bear an even *greater* causal connection than does some form of pornography. That is, it may be, for example, and there is some evidence that points in this direction, that certain magazines focusing on guns, martial arts, and related topics bear a closer causal relationship to sexual violence than do some magazines that are, in a term we will explain shortly, "degrading." If this is true, then the amount of sexual violence would be reduced more by eliminating the weaponry magazines and keeping the degrading magazines than it would be reduced by eliminating the degrading magazines and keeping the weaponry magazines. ...

OUR CONCLUSIONS ABOUT HARM

We present in the following sections our conclusions regarding the harms we have investigated with respect to the various subdividing categories we have found most useful. ...

Sexually Violent Material

The category of material on which most of the evidence has focused is the category of material featuring actual or unmistakably simulated or unmistakably threatened violence presented in sexually explicit fashion with a predominant focus on the sexually explicit violence. Increasingly, the most prevalent forms of pornography, as well as an increasingly prevalent body of less sexually explicit material, fit this description. Some of this material involves sado-masochistic themes, with the standard accoutrements of the genre, including whips, chains, devices of torture, and so on. But another theme of some of this material is not sado-masochistic, but involves instead the recurrent theme of a man making some sort of sexual advance to a woman, being rebuffed, and then raping the woman or in some other way violently forcing himself on the woman. In almost all of this material, whether in magazine or motion picture form, the woman eventually becomes aroused and ecstatic about the initially forced sexual activity, and usually is portrayed as begging for more. There is also a large body of material, more "mainstream" in its availability, that portrays sexual activity or sexually suggestive nudity coupled with extreme violence, such as disfigurement or murder. The so-called "slasher" films fit this description, as does some material, both in films and in magazines, that is less or more sexually explicit than the prototypical "slasher" film. . . .

When clinical and experimental research has focused particularly on sexually violent material, the conclusions have been virtually unanimous. In both clinical and experimental settings, exposure to sexually violent materials has indicated an increase in the likelihood of aggression. More specifically, the research, which is described in much detail later in this Report, shows a causal relationship between exposure to material of this type and aggressive behavior towards women.

Finding a link between aggressive behavior towards women and sexual violence, whether lawful or unlawful, requires assumptions not found exclusively in the experimental evidence. We see no reason, however, not to make these assumptions. The assumption that increased aggressive behavior towards women is causally related, for an aggregate population, to increased sexual violence is significantly supported by the clinical evidence, as well as by much of the less scientific evidence. They are also to all of us assumptions that are plainly justified by our own common sense. This is not to say that all people with heightened levels of aggression will commit acts of sexual violence. But it is to say that over a sufficiently large number of cases we are confident in asserting that an increase in aggressive behavior directed at women will cause an increase in the level of sexual violence directed at women.

Thus we reach our conclusions by combining the results of the research with highly justifiable assumptions about the generalizability of more limited research results. Since the clinical and experimental evidence supports the conclusion that there is a causal relationship between exposure to sexually violent materials and an increase in aggressive behavior directed towards women, and since we believe that an increase in aggressive behavior towards women will in a population increase the incidence of sexual violence in that population, we have reached the conclusion, unanimously and confidently, that the available evidence strongly supports the hypothesis that substantial exposure to sexually violent materials as described here bears a causal relationship to antisocial acts of sexual violence and, for some subgroups, possibly to unlawful acts of sexual violence.

Although we rely for this conclusion on significant scientific empirical evidence, we feel it worthwhile to note the underlying logic of the conclusion. The evidence says simply that the images that people are exposed to bear a causal relationship to their behavior. This is hardly surprising. What would be surprising would be to find otherwise, and we have not so found. We have not, of course, found that the images people are exposed to are a greater cause of sexual violence than all or even many other possible causes the investigation of which has been beyond our mandate. Nevertheless, it would be strange indeed if graphic representations of a form of behavior, especially in a form that almost exclusively portrays such behavior as desirable, did not have at least some effect on patterns of behavior.

Sexual violence is not the only negative effect reported in the research to result from substantial exposure to sexually violent materials. The evidence is also strongly supportive of significant attitudinal changes on the part of those with substantial exposure to violent pornography. These attitudinal changes are numerous. Victims of rape and other forms of sexual violence are likely to be perceived by people so exposed as more responsible for the assault, as having suffered less injury, and as having been less degraded as a result of the experience. Similarly, people with a substantial exposure to violent pornography are likely to see the rapist or other sexual offender as less responsible for the act and as deserving of less stringent punishment.

These attitudinal changes have been shown experimentally to include a larger range of attitudes than those just discussed. The evidence also strongly supports the conclusion that substantial exposure to violent sexually explicit material leads to a greater acceptance of the "rape myth" in its broader sense— that women enjoy being coerced into sexual activity, that they enjoy being physically hurt in sexual context, and that as a result a man who forces himself on a woman sexually is in fact merely acceding to the "real" wishes of the woman, regardless of the extent to which she seems to be resisting. The myth is that a woman who says "no" really means "yes," and that men are justified in acting on the assumption that the "no" answer is indeed the "yes" answer. We have little trouble concluding that this attitude is both pervasive and profoundly harmful, and that any stimulus reinforcing or increasing the incidence of this attitude is for that reason alone properly designated as harmful.

. . . All of the harms discussed here, including acceptance of the legitimacy of sexual violence against women but not limited to it, are more pronounced when the sexually violent materials depict the woman as experiencing arousal, orgasm, or other form of enjoyment as the ultimate result of the sexual assault. This theme, unfortunately very common in the materials we have examined, is likely to be the major, albeit not the only, component of what it is in the materials in this category that causes the consequences that have been identified. . . .

Nonviolent Materials Depicting Degradation, Domination, Subordination, or Humiliation

. . . It appears that effects similar to, although not as extensive as that involved with violent material, can be identified with respect to . . . degrading material, but that these effects are likely absent when neither degradation nor violence is present.

An enormous amount of the most sexually explicit material available, as well as much of the material that is somewhat less sexually explicit, is material that we would characterize as "degrading," the term we use to encompass the undeniably linked characteristics of degradation, domination, subordination, and humiliation. The degradation we refer to is degradation of people, most often women, and here we

are referring to material that, although not violent, depicts people, usually women, as existing solely for the sexual satisfaction of others, usually men, or that depicts people, usually women, in decidedly subordinate roles in their sexual relations with others, or that depicts people engaged in sexual practices that would to most people be considered humiliating. Indeed, forms of degradation represent the largely predominant proportion of commercially available pornography.

With respect to material of this variety, our conclusions are substantially similar to those with respect to violent material, although we make them with somewhat less assumption than was the case with respect to violent material. The evidence, scientific and otherwise, is more tentative, but supports the conclusion that the material we describe as degrading bears some causal relationship to the attitudinal changes we have previously identified. That is, substantial exposure to material of this variety is likely to increase the extent to which those exposed will view rape or other forms of sexual violence as less serious than they otherwise would have, will view the victims of rape and other forms of sexual violence as significantly more responsible, and will view the offenders as significantly less responsible. We also conclude that the evidence supports the conclusion that substantial exposure to material of this type will increase acceptance of the proposition that women like to be forced into sexual practices, and, once again, that the woman who says "no" really means "yes."

. . . We believe we are justified in drawing the following conclusions: Over a large enough sample of population that believes that many women like to be raped, that believes that sexual violence or sexual coercion is often desired or appropriate, and that believes that sex offenders are less responsible for their acts, [this population] will commit more acts of sexual violence or sexual coercion than would a population holding these beliefs to a lesser extent.

. . . Thus, we conclude that substantial exposure to materials of this type bears some causal relationship to the level of sexual violence, sexual coercion, or unwanted sexual aggression in the population so exposed.

We need mention as well that our focus on these more violent or more coercive forms of actual subordination of women should not diminish what we take to be a necessarily incorporated conclusion: Substantial exposure to materials of this type bears some causal relationship to the incidence of various nonviolent forms of discrimination against or subordination of women in our society. To the extent that these materials create or reinforce the view that women's function is disproportionately to satisfy the sexual needs of men, then the materials will have pervasive effects on the treatment of women in society far beyond the incidence of identifiable acts of rape or other sexual violence. . . .

Non-Violent and Non-Degrading Materials

Our most controversial category has been the category of sexually explicit materials that are not violent and are not degrading as we have used that term. They are materials in which the participants appear to be fully willing participants occupying substantially equal roles in a setting devoid of actual or apparent violence or pain. This category is in fact quite small in terms of currently available materials. There is some, to be sure, and the amount may increase as the division between the degrading and the non-degrading becomes more accepted, but we are convinced that only a small amount of currently available highly sexually explicit material is neither violent nor degrading. We thus talk about a small category, but one that should not be ignored.

We have disagreed substantially about the effects of such materials, and that should come as no surprise. We are dealing in this category with "pure" sex, as to which there are widely divergent views in this society. That we have disagreed among ourselves does little more than reflect the extent to which we are representative of the population as a whole. In light of that disagreement, it is perhaps more appropriate to explain the various views rather than indicate a unanimity that does not exist, within this Commission or within society, or attempt the preposterous task of saying that some fundamental view about the role of sexuality and portrayals of sexuality was accepted or defeated by such-and-such vote. We do not wish to give easy answers to hard questions, and thus feel better with describing the diversity of opinion rather than suppressing part of it.

In examining the material in this category, we have not had the benefit of extensive evidence. Research has only recently begun to distinguish the non-violent but degrading from material that is neither violent nor degrading, and we have all relied on a combination of interpretation of existing studies that may not have drawn the same divisions, studies that did draw these distinctions, clinical evidence, interpretation of victim testimony, and our own perceptions of the effect of images on human behavior. Although the social science evidence is far from conclusive, we are, on the current state of the evidence, persuaded that material of this type does not bear a causal relationship to rape and other acts of sexual violence. . . .

That there does not appear from the social science evidence to be a causal link with sexual violence, however, does not answer the question of whether such materials might not themselves simply for some other reason constitute a harm in themselves, or bear a causal link to consequences other than sexual violence but still taken to be harmful. And it is here that we and society at large have the greatest differences in opinion.

One issue relates to materials that, although undoubtedly consensual and equal, depict sexual practices frequently condemned in this and other societies. In addition, level of societal condemnation varies for different activities; some activities are condemned by some people, but not by others. We have discovered that to some significant extent the assessment of the harmfulness of materials depicting such activities correlates directly with the assessment of the harmfulness of the activities themselves. Intuitively and not experimentally, we can hypothesize that materials portraying such an activity will either help to legitimize or will bear some causal relationship to that activity itself. With respect to these materials, therefore, it appears that a conclusion about the harmfulness of these materials turns on a conclusion about the harmfulness of the activity itself. As to this, we are unable to agree with respect to many of these activities. Our differences reflect differences now extant in society at large, and actively debated, and we can hardly resolve them here.

A larger issue is the very question of promiscuity. Even to the extent that the behavior depicted is not inherently condemned by some or any of us, the manner of presentation almost necessarily suggests that the activities are taking place outside of the context of marriage, love, commitment, or even affection. Again, it is far from implausible to hypothesize that materials depicting sexual activity without marriage, love, commitment, or affection bear some causal relationship to sexual activity without marriage, love, commitment, or affection. There are undoubtedly many causes for what used to be called the "sexual revolution," but it is absurd to suppose that depictions or descriptions of uncommitted sexuality were not among them. Thus, once again our disagreements reflect disagreements in society at large, although not to as great an extent. Although there are many members of this society who can and have made affirmative cases for uncommitted sexuality, none of us believes it to be a good thing. A number of us, however, believe that the level of commitment in sexuality is a matter of choice among those who voluntarily engage in the activity. Others of us believe that uncommitted sexual activity is wrong for the individuals involved and harmful to society to the extent of its prevalence. Our view of the ultimate harmfulness of much of this material, therefore, is reflective of our individual views about the extent to whether sexual commitment is purely a matter of individual choice. . . .

THE SPECIAL HORROR OF CHILD PORNOGRAPHY

What is commonly referred to as "child pornography" is not so much a form of pornography as it is a form of sexual exploitation of children. The distinguishing characteristic of child pornography, as generally understood, is that actual children are photographed while engaged in some form of sexual activity, either with adults or with other children. To understand the very idea of child pornography requires understanding the way in which real children, whether actually identified or not, are photographed, and understanding the way in which the use of real children in photographs creates a special harm largely independent of the kinds of concerns often expressed with respect to sexually explicit materials involving only adults.

Thus, the necessary focus of an inquiry into child pornography must be on the process by which children, from as young as one week up to the age of majority, are induced to engage in sexual activity of one sort or another, and the process by which children are photographed while engaging in that activity. The inevitably permanent record of that sexual activity created by a photograph is rather plainly a harm to the children photographed. But even if the photograph were never again seen, the very activity involved in creating the photograph is itself an act of sexual exploitation of children, and thus the issues related to the sexual abuse of children and those related to child pornography are inextricably linked. Child pornography necessarily includes the sexual abuse of a real child, and there can be no understanding of the special problem of child pornography until there is understanding of the special way in which child pornography *is* child abuse. . . .

READING QUESTIONS

1. Explain the problem of multiple causation when it comes to identifying harms.
2. What are the four types of pornography that the commission describes in its report? What conclusion do the members reach regarding the harm caused by each of these types?
3. Why is child pornography considered a "special horror" by the commission? In what ways does it differ from the other types of pornography investigated?

DISCUSSION QUESTIONS

1. How useful is it to differentiate between various types of pornography in the way the commission does? Discuss whether there is any overlap between the various types.
2. Was the attorney general right to suggest that child pornography is a particularly horrible instance of pornography? Why or why not? Consider whether there are instances of adult pornography that are worse than child pornography.

NADINE STROSSEN

Why Censoring Pornography Would Not Reduce Discrimination or Violence against Women

Strossen is critical of the 1986 Meese Commission's report about the alleged negative effects of pornography on the interests of women. In rebutting the claims of the commission, she considers four types of evidence alleging a causal link: (1) laboratory research, (2) correlational data, (3) anecdotal data, and (4) studies of sex offenders, arguing that none of this work shows clearly that pornography is a cause of harm to women. She concludes that even if there were a causal link between pornography and harm to women, the negative effects of censorship would outweigh whatever positive benefits censorship would produce. In her view, "censoring pornography would do women more harm than good."

Recommended Reading: consequentialism, chap. 1, sec. 2A.

The only thing pornography is known to cause directly is the solitary act of masturbation. As for corruption, the only immediate victim is English prose.

—*Gore Vidal, writer*[1]

Even . . . [if] we could neutralize its negative side effects, would censorship "cure"—or at least reduce—the discrimination and violence against women allegedly caused by pornography? That is the assumption that underlies the feminist procensorship position, fueling the argument that we should trade in our free speech rights to promote women's safety and equality rights. In fact, though, the hoped-for benefits of censorship are as hypothetical as our exercise in wishing away the evils of censorship. I will show this by examining the largely unexamined assumption that censorship would reduce sexism and violence against women. This assumption rests, in turn, on three others:

• that exposure to sexist, violent imagery leads to sexist, violent behavior;

• that the effective suppression of pornography would significantly reduce exposure to sexist, violent imagery; and

• that censorship would effectively suppress pornography.

To justify censoring pornography on the rationale that it would reduce violence or discrimination against women, one would have to provide actual support for all three of these assumptions. Each presupposes the others. Yet the only one of them that has received substantial attention is the first—that exposure to sexist, violent imagery leads to sexist, violent behavior—and, as I show later in this chapter, there is no credible evidence to bear it out. Even feminist advocates of censoring pornography have acknowledged that this asserted causal connection cannot be proven, and therefore fall back on the argument that it should be accepted "on faith." Catharine MacKinnon has well captured this fallback position through her defensive double negative: "There is no evidence that pornography does no harm."

From Nadine Strossen, *Defending Pornography. Free Speech, Sex, and the Fight for Women's Rights* (New York: Anchor Books, 1995).

Of course, given the impossibility of proving that there is *no* evidence of *no* harm, we would have no free speech, and indeed no freedom of any kind, were such a burden of proof actually to be imposed on those seeking to enjoy their liberties. To appreciate this, just substitute for the word "pornography" in MacKinnon's pronouncement any other type of expression or any other human right. We would have to acknowledge that "there is no evidence" that television does no harm, or that editorials criticizing government officials do no harm, or that religious sermons do no harm, and so forth. There certainly is no evidence that feminist writing in general, or MacKinnon's in particular, does no harm.

In its 1992 *Butler* decision, accepting the antipornography feminist position, the Canadian Supreme Court also accepted this dangerous intuitive approach to limiting sexual expression, stating:

> It might be suggested that proof of actual harm should be required . . . [I]t is sufficient . . . for Parliament to have a reasonable basis for concluding that harm will result and this requirement does not demand actual proof of harm.[2]

Even if we were willing to follow the Canadian Supreme Court and procensorship feminists in believing, without evidence, that exposure to sexist, violent imagery does lead to sexist, violent behavior, we still should not accept their calls for censorship. Even if we assumed that *seeing* pornography leads to committing sexist and violent actions, it still would not follow that *censoring* pornography would reduce sexism or violence, due to flaws in the remaining two assumptions: we still would have to prove that pornography has a corner on the sexism and violence market, and that pornography is in fact entirely suppressible.

Even if pornography could be completely suppressed, the sexist, violent imagery that pervades the mainstream media would remain untouched. Therefore, if exposure to such materials caused violence and sexism, these problems would still remain with us. But no censorship regime could completely suppress pornography. It would continue to exist underground. . . .

Let's now examine in more detail the fallacies in each of the three assumptions underlying the feminist procensorship stance. And let's start with the single assumption that has been the focus of discussion—the alleged causal relationship between exposure to sexist, violent imagery and sexist, violent behavior.

MONKEY SEE, MONKEY DO?

Aside from the mere fear that sexual expression might cause discrimination or violence against women, advocates of censorship attempt to rely on four types of evidence concerning this alleged causal link: laboratory research data concerning the attitudinal effects of showing various types of sexually explicit materials to volunteer subjects, who are usually male college students; correlational data concerning availability of sexually oriented materials and anti-female discrimination or violence; anecdotal data consisting of accounts by sex offenders and their victims concerning any role that pornography may have played in the offenses; and studies of sex offenders, assessing factors that may have led to their crimes.

As even some leading procensorship feminists have acknowledged, along with the Canadian Supreme Court in *Butler,* none of these types of "evidence" prove that pornography harms women. Rather than retracing the previous works that have reviewed this evidence and reaffirmed its failure to substantiate the alleged causal connection, I will simply summarize their conclusions.

Laboratory Experiments

The most comprehensive recent review of the social science data is contained in Marcia Pally's 1994 book *Sex and Sensibility: Reflections on Forbidden Mirrors and the Will to Censor.*[3] It exhaustively canvasses laboratory studies that have evaluated the impact of exposing experimental subjects to sexually explicit expression of many varieties, and concludes that no credible evidence substantiates a clear causal connection between any type of sexually explicit material and any sexist or violent behavior. The book also draws the same conclusion from its thorough review of field and correlational studies, as well as sociological surveys, in the U.S., Canada, Europe, and Asia.

Numerous academic and governmental surveys of the social science studies have similarly rejected the purported link between sexual expression and aggression. The National Research Council's Panel on Understanding and Preventing Violence concluded, in 1993: "Demonstrated empirical links between pornography and sex crimes in general are weak or absent."[4]

Given the overwhelming consensus that laboratory studies do not demonstrate a causal tie between exposure to sexually explicit imagery and violent behavior, the Meese Pornography Commission Report's contrary conclusion, not surprisingly, has been the subject of heated criticism, including criticism by dissenting commissioners and by the very social scientists on whose research the report purportedly relied.

The many grounds on which the Commission's report was widely repudiated include that: six of the Commission's eleven members already were committed antipornography crusaders when they were appointed to it; the Commission was poorly funded and undertook no research; its hearings were slanted toward preconceived antipornography conclusions in terms of the witnesses invited to testify and the questions they were asked; and, in assessing the alleged harmful effects of pornography, the Commission's report relied essentially upon morality, expressly noting at several points that its conclusions were based on "common sense," "personal insight," and "intuition."

Two of the Meese Commission's harshest critics were, interestingly, two female members of that very Commission, Judith Becker and Ellen Levine. Becker is a psychiatrist and psychologist whose entire extensive career has been devoted to studying sexual violence and abuse, from both research and clinical perspectives. Levine is a journalist who has focused on women's issues, and who edits a popular women's magazine. In their formal dissent from the Commission's report, they concluded:

[T]he social science research has not been designed to evaluate the relationship between exposure to pornography and the commission of sexual crimes; therefore efforts to tease the current data into proof of a casual [sic] link between these acts simply cannot be accepted.[5]

Three of the foremost researchers concerned with the alleged causal relationship between sexually explicit materials and sexual violence, Edward Donnerstein, Daniel Linz, and Steven Penrod, also have sharply disputed the Meese Commission's findings about a purported causal relationship.[6]

Since the feminist censorship proposals aim at sexually explicit material that allegedly is "degrading" to women, it is especially noteworthy that research data show no link between exposure to "degrading" sexually explicit material and sexual aggression.

Even two research literature surveys that were conducted for the Meese Commission, one by University of Calgary professor Edna Einseidel and the other by then–Surgeon General C. Everett Koop, also failed to find any link between "degrading" pornography and sex crimes or aggression. Surgeon General Koop's survey concluded that only two reliable generalizations could be made about the impact of exposure to "degrading" sexual material on its viewers: it caused them to think that a variety of sexual practices were more common than they had previously believed, and it caused them to more accurately estimate the prevalence of varied sexual practices.[7]

Experiments also fail to establish any link between women's exposure to such materials and their development of negative self-images. Carol Krafka found that, in comparison with other women, women who were exposed to sexually "degrading" materials did not engage in more sex-role stereotyping; nor did they experience lower self-esteem, have less satisfaction with their body image, accept more anti-woman myths about rape, or show greater acceptance of violence against women.[8] Similar conclusions have been reached by Donnerstein, Linz, and Penrod.[9]

Correlational Data

Both the Meese Commission and procensorship feminists have attempted to rely on studies that allegedly show a correlation between the availability of sexually explicit materials and sexual offense rates. Of course, though, a positive correlation between two phenomena does not prove that one causes the other. Accordingly, even if the studies did consistently show a positive correlation between the prevalence of sexual materials and sexual offenses—which they do not—they still would not establish that exposure to the materials *caused* the rise in offenses. The same correlation could also reflect the opposite causal chain—if, for example, rapists relived their violent acts by purchasing sexually violent magazines or videotapes.

Any correlation between the availability of sexual materials and the rate of sex offenses could also reflect an independent factor that causes increases in both. Cynthia Gentry's correlational studies have identified just such an independent variable in geographical areas that have high rates of both the circulation of sexually explicit magazines and sexual violence: namely, a high population of men between the ages of eighteen and thirty-four.[10] Similarly, Larry Baron and Murray Straus have noted that areas where both sexual materials and sexual aggression are prevalent are characterized by a "hypermasculated or macho culture pattern," which may well be the underlying causal agent.[11] Accordingly, Joseph Scott and Loretta Schwalm found that communities with higher rape rates experienced stronger sales not only of porn magazines, but also of *all* male-oriented magazines, including *Field and Stream*.[12]

Even more damning to the attempt to rest the "porn-causes-rape-or-discrimination" theory on alleged correlations is that there simply are no consistent correlations. While the asserted correlation would not be *sufficient* to prove the claimed causal connection, it is *necessary* to prove that connection. Therefore, the existence of the alleged causal relationship is conclusively refuted by the fact that levels of violence and discrimination against women are often *inversely* related to the availability of sexually explicit materials, including violent sexually explicit materials. This inverse relationship appears in various kinds of comparisons: between different states within the United States; between different countries; and between different periods within the same country.

Within the United States, the Baron and Straus research has shown no consistent pattern between the availability of sexual materials and the number of rapes from state to state. Utah is the lowest-ranking state in the availability of sexual materials but twenty-fifth in the number of rapes, whereas New Hampshire ranks ninth highest in the availability of sexual materials but only forty-fourth in the number of rapes.

The lack of a consistent correlation between pornography consumption and violence against women is underscored by one claim of the procensorship feminists themselves: they maintain that the availability and consumption of pornography, including violent pornography, have been increasing throughout the United States. At the same time, though, the rates of sex crimes have been decreasing or remaining steady. The Bureau of Justice Statistics reports that between 1973 and 1987, the national rape rate remained steady and the attempted rape rate decreased. Since these data were gathered from household surveys rather than from police records, they are considered to be the most accurate measures of the incidence of crimes. These data also cover the period during which feminists helped to create a social, political, and legal climate that should have encouraged higher percentages of rape victims to report their assaults. Thus, the fact that rapes reported to the Bureau of Justice Statistics have not increased provokes serious questions about the procensorship feminists' theories of pornography-induced harm.[13] Similar questions are raised by data showing a decrease in wife battery between 1975 and 1985, again despite changes that should have encouraged the increased reporting of this chronically underreported crime.[14]

Noting that "[t]he mass-market pornography . . . industr[y] took off after World War II," Marcia Pally has commented:

> In the decades since the 1950s, with the marketing of sexual material . . . , the country has seen the greatest advances in sensitivity to violence against women and children. Before the . . . mass publication of sexual images, no rape or incest hot lines and battered women's shelters existed; date and marital rape were not yet phrases in the language. Should one conclude that the

presence of pornography . . . has inspired public outrage at sexual crimes?[15]

Pally's rhetorical question underscores the illogicality of presuming that just because two phenomena happen to coexist, they therefore are causally linked. I have already shown that any correlation that might exist between the increased availability of pornography and *increased* misogynistic discrimination or violence could well be explained by other factors. The same is true for any correlation that might exist between the increased availability of pornography and *decreased* misogynistic discrimination or violence.

In a comparative state-by-state analysis, Larry Baron and Murray Straus have found a positive correlation between the circulation of pornographic magazines and the state's "index of gender equality," a composite of twenty-four indicators of economic, political, and legal equality.[16] As the researchers have observed, these findings may suggest that both sexually explicit material and gender equality flourish in tolerant climates with fewer restrictions on speech.

The absence of any consistent correlation between the availability of sexual materials and sexual violence is also clear in international comparisons. On the one hand, violence and discrimination against women are common in countries where sexually oriented material is almost completely unavailable, including Saudi Arabia, Iran, and China (where the sale and distribution of erotica is now a capital offense). On the other hand, violence against women is uncommon in countries where such material is readily available, including Denmark, Germany, and Japan.

Furthermore, patterns in other countries over time show no correlation between the increased availability of sexually explicit materials and increased violence against women. The 1991 analysis by University of Copenhagen professor Berl Kutchinsky revealed that, while nonsexual violent crime had increased up to 300 percent in Denmark, Sweden, and West Germany from 1964 to 1984, all three countries' rape rates either declined or remained constant during this same period, despite their lifting of restrictions on sexual materials.

Kutchinsky's studies further show that sex crimes against girls dropped from 30 per 100,000 to 5 per 100,000 between 1965, when Denmark liberalized its obscenity laws, and 1982.

In the decade 1964–1974, there was a much greater increase in rape rates in Singapore, which tightly restricts sexually oriented expression, than in Sweden, which had liberalized its obscenity laws during that period. In Japan, where sexually explicit materials are easily accessible and stress themes of bondage, rape, and violence, rape rates decreased 45 percent during the same decade. Moreover, Japan reports a rape rate of 2.4 per 100,000 people, compared with 34.5 in the United States, although violent erotica is more prevalent in Japan.[17]

Anecdotes and Suspicions

As Seventh Circuit Court of Appeals judge Richard Posner observed about MacKinnon's book *Only Words:*

> MacKinnon's treatment of the central issue of pornography as she herself poses it—the harm that pornography does to women—is shockingly casual. Much of her evidence is anecdotal, and in a nation of 260 million people, anecdotes are a weak form of evidence.[18]

Many procensorship advocates attempt to rest their case on self-serving "porn-made-me-do-it" claims by sexual offenders, as well as on statements by victims or police officers that sexual offenders had sexually explicit materials in their possession at the time they committed their crimes.

The logical fallacy of relying on anecdotes to establish a general causal connection between exposure to sexual materials and violence against women was aptly noted by journalist Ellen Willis: "Anti-porn activists cite cases of sexual killers who were also users of pornography, but this is no more logical than arguing that marriage causes rape because some rapists are married."[19]

Even assuming that sexual materials really were the triggering factors behind some specific crimes, that could not justify restrictions on such materials. As former Supreme Court justice William O. Douglas wrote: "The First Amendment demands more than a horrible example or two of the perpetrator of a crime of sexual violence, in whose pocket is found a pornographic book, before it allows the Nation to be saddled with a regime of censorship."[20] If we attempted to ban all words or images that had ever been blamed for inspiring or instigating particular crimes by some aberrant or antisocial individual, we would end up with little left to read or view. Throughout history and around the world, criminals have regularly blamed their conduct on a sweeping array of words and images in books, movies, and television.

As noted by the 1979 report of the British Committee on Obscenity and Film Censorship, "For those who are susceptible to them, the stimuli to aggressive behavior are all around us."[21] To illustrate the innumerable crimes that have been incited by words or images, the Committee cited a young man who attempted to kill his parents with a meat cleaver after watching a dramatized version of Dostoyevsky's *The Brothers Karamazov,* and a Jamaican man of African descent in London who raped a white woman, saying that the televised showing of Alex Haley's *Roots* had "inspired" him to treat her as white men had treated black women. Additional examples cited by Ohio State University law professor Earl Finbar Murphy underscore that word blaming and image blaming extend to many religious works, too:

> Heinrich Pommerenke, who was a rapist, abuser, and mass slayer of women in Germany, was prompted to his series of ghastly deeds by Cecil B. DeMille's *The Ten Commandments.* During the scene of the Jewish women dancing about the Golden Calf, all the doubts of his life became clear: Women were the source of the world's troubles and it was his mission to both punish them for this and to execute them. Leaving the theater, he slew the first victim in a park nearby. John George Haigh, the British vampire who sucked his victims' blood through soda straws and dissolved their drained bodies in acid baths, first had his murder-inciting dreams and vampire longings from watching the "voluptuous" procedure of—an Anglican High Church Service.[22]

Were we to ban words or images on the grounds that they had incited some susceptible individuals to commit crimes, the Bible would be in great jeopardy. No other work has more often been blamed for more heinous crimes by the perpetrators of such crimes. The Bible has been named as the instigating or justifying factor for many individual and mass crimes, ranging from the religious wars, inquisitions, witch burnings, and pogroms of earlier eras to systematic child abuse and ritual murders today.

Marcia Pally's *Sex and Sensibility* contains a lengthy litany of some of the multitudinous, horrific bad acts that have been blamed on the "Good Book." She also cites some of the many passages depicting the "graphic, sexually explicit subordination of women" that would allow the entire Bible to be banned under the procensorship feminists' antipornography law. Pally writes:

> [T]he Bible has unbeatable worldwide sales and includes detailed justification of child abuse, wife battery, rape, and the daily humiliation of women. Short stories running through the text serve as models for sexual assault and the mauling of children. The entire set of books is available to children, who are encouraged or required to read it. It is printed and distributed by some of the world's most powerful organizations. . . .
>
> With refreshing frankness, the Bible tells men it is their rightful place to rule women. . . . [It] specifies exactly how many shekels less than men women are worth. Genesis 19:1–8 tells one of many tales about fathers setting up their daughters to be gang raped. Even more prevalent are . . . glamorized war stories in which the fruits of victory are the local girls. . . . [P]erhaps most gruesome is the snuff story about the guy who set his maid up to be gang raped and, after her death from the assault, cut her body up into little pieces. . . . Unlike movies and television programs, these tales are generally taken to be true, not simulated, accounts.[23]

In 1992, Gene Kasmar petitioned the Brooklyn Center, Minnesota, school board to ban the Bible from school classrooms and libraries on the ground that it is lewd, indecent, obscene, offensive, violent, and dangerous to women and children. He specifically complained about biblical references to concubines, explicit sex, child abuse, incest, nakedness, and mistreatment of women—all subjects, significantly, that would trigger the feminist-style antipornography laws.

In response, the chief counsel of Pat Robertson's American Center for Law and Justice in Virginia, Jay Sekulow, flew to Minnesota and argued that the Bible "is worthy of study for its literary and historic qualities."[24] While the Brooklyn Center School Board apparently agreed with this assessment, voting unanimously to reject Kasmar's petition, it must be recalled that Sekulow's argument would be unavailing under Dworkin-MacKinnon–type antipornography laws. Under the MacDworkin model law, any work could be banned on the basis of even one isolated passage that meets the definition of pornography, and the work could not be saved by any serious literary, historic, or other value it might offer. Consequently, the feminist antipornography law could be used by Kasmar and others to ban the Bible not only from public schools, but also from public libraries, bookstores, and all other venues.

The countless expressive works that have been blamed for crimes include many that convey profeminist messages. Therefore, an anecdotal, image-blaming rationale for censorship would condemn many feminist works. For example, the television movie *The Burning Bed,* which told the true story of a battered wife who set fire to her sleeping husband, was blamed for some "copycat" crimes, as well as for some acts of violence by men against women. The argument that such incidents would justify suppression would mark the end of any films or other works depicting—and deploring—the real violence that plagues the lives of too many actual women.

Under a censorship regime that permits anecdotal, book-blaming "evidence," all other feminist materials would be equally endangered, not "just" works that depict the violence that has been inflicted on women. That is because, as feminist writings themselves have observed, some sexual assaults are committed by men who feel threatened by the women's movement. Should feminist works therefore be banned on the theory that they might well motivate a man to act out his misogynistic aggression?

Studies of Sex Offenders

The scientists who have investigated the impact of exposure to sexual materials in real life have not found that either sexual materials or attitudes toward women play any significant role in prompting actual violence. In general, these studies show that sex offenders had less exposure to sexually explicit materials than most men, that they first saw such materials at a later age than nonoffenders, that they were overwhelmingly more likely to have been punished for looking at them as teenagers, and that they often find sexual images more distressing than arousing.[25]

While no evidence substantiates that viewing pornography leads to violence and discrimination against women, some evidence indicates that, if anything, there may well be an inverse causal relationship between exposure to sexually explicit materials and misogynistic violence or discrimination. One of the leading researchers in this area, Edward Donnerstein of the University of California at Santa Barbara, has written: "A good amount of research strongly supports the position that exposure to erotica can reduce aggressive responses in people who are predisposed to aggress."[26] Similarly, John Money, of Johns Hopkins Medical School, a leading expert on sexual violence, has noted that most people with criminal sexualities were raised with strict, antisexual, repressive attitudes. He predicts that the "current repressive attitudes toward sex will breed an ever-widening epidemic of aberrant sexual behavior."[27]

In one 1989 experiment, males who had been exposed to pornography were more willing to come to the aid of a female subject who appeared to be hurt than were men who had been exposed to other stimuli.[28] Laboratory studies further indicate that there may well be an inverse causal relationship between exposure to violent sexually explicit material and sexual arousal. For example, in 1991, Howard Barbaree and William Marshall, of Queen's College in Ontario, found:

> For most men, hearing a description of an encounter where the man is forcing the woman to have sex, and the woman is in distress or pain, dampens the arousal by about 50 percent compared to arousal levels using a scene of consenting lovemaking. . . . Ordinarily violence inhibits sexual arousal in men. A blood flow loss of 50 percent means a man would not be able to penetrate a woman.[29]

The foregoing research findings are certainly more consistent with what many feminist scholars have been writing about rape than is the procensorship feminists' pornocentric analysis: namely, rape is not a crime about sex, but rather, about violence.[30]

SEE NO PORNOGRAPHY, SEE NO SEXIST AND VIOLENT IMAGERY?

Pornography constitutes only a small subset of the sexist or violent imagery that pervades our culture and media. New York Law School professor Carlin Meyer recently conducted a comprehensive survey of the views of women's sexuality, status, and gender roles that are purveyed in nonpornographic media:

> Today, mainstream television, film, advertising, music, art, and popular (including religious) literature are the primary propagators of Western views of sexuality and sex roles. Not only do we read, see and experience their language and imagery more often and at earlier ages than we do most explicit sexual representation, but precisely because mainstream imagery is ordinary and everyday, it more powerfully convinces us that it depicts the world as it is or ought to be.[31]

Other cultural and media analysts have likewise concluded that more-damaging sexist imagery is more broadly purveyed through mainstream, nonsexual representations. Thelma McCormack, director of York University's Feminist Studies Centre, has concluded that "the enemy of women's equality is our mainstream culture with its images of women as family-centered," rather than imagery of women as sexual. According to McCormack:

> Surveys and public opinion studies confirm the connection between gender-role traditionalism and an acceptance or belief in the normality of a stratified social system. The more traditional a person's views are about women, the more likely he or she is to accept inequality as inevitable, functional, natural, desirable and immutable. In short, if any image of woman can be said to influence our thinking about gender equality, it is the domestic woman not the Dionysian one.[32]

Social science researchers have found that acceptance of the rape myth and other misogynistic attitudes concerning women and violence are just as likely to result from exposure to many types of mass media—from soap operas to popular commercial films—as from even intense exposure to violent, misogynistic sexually explicit materials.[33] Accordingly, if we really wanted to purge all sexist, violent representations from our culture, we would have to cast the net far beyond pornography, notwithstanding how comprehensive and elastic that category is. Would even procensorship feminists want to deal such a deathblow to First Amendment freedoms?

CENSOR PORNOGRAPHY, SEE NO PORNOGRAPHY?

Procensorship feminists themselves have acknowledged that censorship would probably just drive pornography underground. Indeed, as recently as 1987, Catharine MacKinnon recognized that "pornography cannot be reformed or suppressed or banned."[34]

The assumption that censorship would substantially reduce the availability or impact of pornography also overlooks evidence that censorship makes some viewers more desirous of pornography and more receptive to its imagery. This "forbidden fruits" effect has been corroborated by historical experience and social science research. All recent studies of the suppression of sexual expression, including Walter Kendrick's 1987 book *The Secret Museum: Pornography in Modern Culture* and Edward de Grazia's 1992 book *Girls Lean Back Everywhere: The Law of Obscenity and the Assault on Genius,* demonstrate that any censorship effort simply increases the attention that a targeted work receives. Social scientific studies that were included in the report of the 1970 President's Commission on Obscenity and Pornography suggested that censorship of sexually explicit materials may increase their desirability and impact, and also that a viewer's awareness that sexually oriented parts of a film have been censored may lead to frustration and subsequent aggressive behavior.[35]

The foregoing data about the impact of censoring pornography are consistent with broader research findings: the evidence suggests that censorship of *any* material increases an audience's desire to obtain the material and disposes the audience to be more receptive to it.[36] Critical viewing skills, and the ability to regard media images skeptically and analytically, atrophy under a censorial regime. A public that learns to question everything it sees or hears is better equipped to reject culturally propagated values than is one that assumes the media have been purged of all "incorrect" perspectives.

Even assuming for the sake of argument that there were a causal link between pornography and anti-female discrimination and violence, the insignificant contribution that censorship might make to reducing them would not outweigh the substantial damage that censorship would do to feminist goals. From the lack of actual evidence to substantiate the alleged causal link, the conclusion follows even more inescapably: Censoring pornography would do women more harm than good.

NOTES

1. Quoted in David Futrelle, "The Politics of Porn, Shameful Pleasures," *In These Times,* 7 March 1994, pp. 14–17.

2. *Butler v. the Queen* 1 SCR 452 (199), p. 505.

3. Marcia Pally, *Sex and Sensibility: Reflections on Forbidden Mirrors and the Will to Censor* (Hopewell, N.J.: Ecco Press, 1994).

4. Albert J. Reiss, Jr. and Jeffrey A. Roth, eds., *Understanding and Preventing Violence* (Washington, D.C.: National Academy Press, 1993), p. 111. (A project of the National Research Council.)

5. Judith Becker and Ellen Levine, paper presented to a meeting of the National Coalition Against Censorship, New York, N.Y., 17 June 1986.

6. Daniel Linz, Steven D. Penrod, and Edward Donnerstein, "The Attorney General's Commission on Pornography: The Gaps between 'Findings' and Facts," *American Bar Foundation Research Journal* 4 (Fall 1987): 713–36, at 723.

7. Edward Mulvey and Jeffrey Haugaard, *Surgeon General's Workshop on Pornography and Public Health* (Arlington, Virginia: U.S. Department of Health and Human Services, 1986).

8. Carol Krafka, "Sexually Explicit, Sexually Violent, and Violent Media: Effects of Multiple Naturalistic Exposures and Debriefing on Female Viewers" (Ph.D. dissertation, University of Wisconsin, 1985), p. 29.

9. Daniel Linz, Edward Donnerstein, and Steven Penrod, "The Effects of Long-Term Exposure to Violent and Sexually Degrading Depictions of Women," *Journal of Personality and Social Psychology* 55 (1988): 758–68.

10. Cynthia Gentry, "Pornography and Rape: An Empirical Analysis," *Deviant Behavior: An Interdisciplinary Journal* 12 (1991): 277–88, at 284.

11. Larry Baron and Murray Straus, "Four Theories of Rape: A Macro-Sociological Analysis," *Social Problems* 34, no. 5 (1987): 467–89.

12. Joseph Scott and Loretta Schwalm, "Pornography and Rape: An Examination of Adult Theater Rates and Rape Rates by State," in J. E. Scott and T. Hirchi (eds.), *Controversial Issues in Crime and Justice* (Beverly Hills: Sage, 1988).

13. Bureau of Justice Statistics, *Criminal Victimization in the United States* (Washington, D.C.: Government Printing Office, 1990); Pally, *Sex and Sensibility,* p. 22.

14. Richard J. Gelles and Murray Straus, *Intimate Violence: The Causes and Consequences of Abuse in the American Family* (New York: Touchstone, 1989), p. 112.

15. Pally, *Sex and Sensibility,* pp. 21, 23.

16. Baron and Straus, "Four Theories of Rape."

17. Pally, *Sex and Sensibility,* pp. 57–61.

18. Richard Posner, "Obsession," review of *Only Words* by Catharine MacKinnon, *New Republic,* 18 October 1993, pp. 31–36, at p. 34.

19. Ellen Willis, "An Unholy Alliance," *New York Newsday,* 25 February 1992, p. 78.

20. *Memoirs v. Massachusetts,* 383 U.S. 413, 432 (1966) (concurring).

21. Williams Committee, *The British Inquiry into Obscenity and Film Censorship* (London, England: Home Office Research and Planning Unit, 1979).

22. Earl Finbar Murphy, "The Value of Pornography," *Wayne Law Review* 10 (1964): 655–80, at 668.

23. Pally, *Sex and Sensibility,* pp. 99–100.

24. Associated Press, "Atheist Loses Fight to Ban Bible at School," *Chicago Tribune,* 11 November 1992.

25. Pally, *Sex and Sensibility,* pp. 25–61.

26. Edward Donnerstein, "Erotica and Human Aggression," in *Aggression: Theoretical and Empirical Reviews,* ed. Richard Green and Edward Donnerstein (New York: Academic Press, 1983), pp. 127–28.

27. Quoted in Jane Brody, "Scientists Trace Aberrant Sexuality," *New York Times,* 23 January 1990.

28. Pally, *Sex and Sensibility,* p. 50.

29. Howard Barbaree and William Marshall, "The Role

of Male Sexual Arousal in Rape: Six Models," *Journal of Consulting and Clinical Psychology* 59, no. 5 (1991): 621–30; Pally, *Sex and Sensibility*, pp. 44–45.

30. Susan Brownmiller, *Against Our Will: Men, Women, and Rape* (New York: Simon & Schuster, 1975); Susan Estrich, *Real Rape* (Boston: Harvard University Press, 1987).

31. Carlin Meyer, "Sex, Censorship, and Women's Liberation" (unpublished), pp. 42–43. [A revised version of this manuscript was published in *Texas Law Review* 72 (1994): 1097–1201.]

32. Thelma McCormack, "If Pornography Is the Theory, Is Inequality the Practice?" (presented at public forum, *Refusing Censorship: Feminists and Activists Fight Back,* York, Canada, 12 November 1992), p. 12.

33. Edward Donnerstein, Daniel Linz, and Steven Penrod, *The Question of Pornography: Research Findings and Policy Implications* (New York: Free Press, 1987), p. 107.

34. Catharine MacKinnon, "Not a Moral Issue," *Yale Law & Policy Review* 2 (1984): 321–45, at 325.

35. Percy H. Tannenbaum, "Emotional Arousal as a Mediator of Communication Effects," *Technical Report of the U.S. Commission on Obscenity and Pornography* 8 (1971), p. 353.

36. Timothy C. Brock, "Erotic Materials: A Commodity Theory Analysis of Availability and Desirability," *Technical Report of the U.S. Commission on Obscenity and Pornography* 6 (1971), pp. 131–37.

READING QUESTIONS

1. What are the three assumptions on which the claim that censorship would reduce sexism and violence against women rests according to Strossen?
2. What are the four types of evidence that are used to justify the assumptions about the effects of pornography? Why does Strossen believe that none of these types of evidence proves that pornography harms women?
3. Explain Strossen's reasons for thinking that the mainstream media is just as damaging (if not more damaging) to women as is pornographic material.
4. How does Strossen argue for the view that censoring pornography would not reduce its availability or impact?

DISCUSSION QUESTIONS

1. What kinds of evidence should we rely on when trying to answer questions about whether pornography is harmful to women? Should we reject anecdotal evidence and common sense intuitions as Strossen suggests? Why or why not?
2. Suppose that Strossen is right to claim that none of the evidence commonly presented proves that pornography harms women. Consider and discuss whether there are any other reasons to censor pornographic materials.

SUSAN DWYER

Enter Here—At Your Own Risk:
The Moral Dangers of Cyberporn

Taking an Aristotelian virtue ethics approach to pornography, Susan Dwyer argues that certain types of sexual fantasizing are morally risky. Pornography, she argues, "concretizes" such fantasies and thereby encourages one who consumes it to engage in "unbounded" sexual fantasies, to the possible detriment to one's moral character. Moreover, as Dwyer argues, the experience of consuming cyberpornography poses unique threats to one's character. First, it tends to keep consumers engaged in sexual fantasizing for long periods of time; one site often bumps one to a site with more "extreme" pornography of a problematic nature. Second, the cyberporn experience can also be quite passive, creating the illusion in the mind of consumers that one's agency is not engaged, when it is. Dwyer concludes that in both of these unique ways, cyberpornography poses a threat to one's character that goes beyond the dangers of consuming traditional forms of pornography.

Recommended Reading: virtue ethics, chap. 1. sec. 2E.

Cyberpornography is one of the few reliably profitable online businesses. In 1997, there were 10,000 sex industry sites, the biggest of them generating about $1 million a month. By 1998, there were at least three sites returning more than $100 million a year. In 2000, one or more of 60,000 sex sites was visited by one in four Internet users at least once a month.[1]

None of this should come as a surprise: sex sells. However, we must not be misled into thinking that the Internet is awash with smut or saturated with pornography, as some panicky critics would have us believe. Cyberpornography accounts for only one-fifth of the total annual pornography business in the United States, variously put between $10 and $14 billion. Hence, it might be doubted that there

is anything to say about cyberpornography that has not already been said about more traditional types of pornography. What, if any, new moral questions does cyberpornography raise?

Bracketing off the fact that many children can access cyberpornography more easily than they can access video and print pornography, cyberporn presents us with fundamentally the same sorts of moral issues as its technologically less sophisticated cousins. Nevertheless, in a somewhat surprising twist, the experience of consuming pornography on the Internet helps to illuminate a moral critique of pornography that is yet to receive the attention it deserves. The twist is surprising because the moral critique I have in mind appears rather old-fashioned. Indeed, the

From Susan Dwyer, "Enter Here — At Your Own Risk: The Moral Dangers of Cyberporn," in Robert J. Cavalier, ed. *The Impact of the Internet on Our Moral Lives* (2005), 69–94. Notes have been renumbered and edited.

critique has ancient precedent in Aristotle's account of the virtuous agent.

Put bluntly, the idea is that some pornography is morally problematic because it provides the raw material for and helps to nurture a class of morally bad actions—namely, sexual fantasizing about a variety of harms to oneself and/or to others. And, because of the unique phenomenology of consuming pornography certain kinds of cyberpornography are particularly effective in this regard. As I will argue, sexual fantasizing is something we deliberately and consciously *do*. We construct fantasies that please us and return to them over the course of our lives. Sexual fantasies are remarkably persistent; indeed, the empirical evidence suggests that they are among the most enduring elements of our respective psychologies. However, it is morally dangerous persistently and deliberately to engage in an activity that yokes sexual pleasure and satisfaction to conscious thoughts of degradation, humiliation, and violence. To do so is to run a serious risk of compromising one's moral character. If I am right about the unique experience of consuming cyberpornography, then cyberpornography might be quite risky indeed.

This controversial thesis is apt to meet with significance resistance from a number of sources. . . . However, one such source can be dealt with quickly. My concern here is with the *moral evaluation* of pornography (more precisely, with the moral evaluation of consuming pornography). I make no claims about what, if anything, the state should do about pornography, its producers and distributors, or its consumers. Nor are any particular policy recommendations implied by the critique I offer.[2] Debates about the moral status of pornography need not and should not be construed exclusively as debates about free speech and censorship. . . .

THE MORAL STATUS OF PORNOGRAPHY: SOME EARLIER ACCOUNTS

Few of us are wholly indifferent to pornography, unless perhaps we have never seen any. Many people clearly like it a lot, while others hate it all. However, I suspect that any reasonably reflective and honest person will concede that there is *something* problematic about Web sites devoted to representations of sexual torture, or, to cite a more prosaic example, about the fact that a nontrivial number of our fellow citizens invest considerable resources to return over and over to images of women being ejaculated on. But what is the source of this unease, and is it justified?

Since pornography became an object of systematic study, three main lines of criticism have emerged. In historical order, theorists have argued for the moral problematicity of pornography on the grounds of (1) its sexual content, (2) its alleged harmful effects on women, and (3) its role in the social construction of sexuality and gender. Each new critique was prompted by the revealed inadequacies of the one(s) that preceded it. I think all three approaches are flawed. However, for current purposes I will discuss only the first two.

Employing the most value-neutral characterization of pornography—namely, explicit pictorial or verbal representations of human sexual activity designed to produce sexual arousal—some people have condemned pornography just on the basis of its sexual content. In particular, they believe that the sort of sexual behavior portrayed in pornography perverts some 'true' purpose of sex, claiming, for example, that sex ought always aim at procreation or that it should always involve a profound connection between two persons.

There is no denying that pornographic sex is, literally, sterile. While some women may have conceived as a result of intercourse had in font of the cameras, making babies is not what pornography is about. Moreover, a good deal of pornographic sex happens between persons of the same sex, penetrations are oral and anal as well as vaginal, and, more often than not, a typical heterosexual pornographic scene ends with the ejaculation of semen onto a woman's face or body. Neither can we deny that pornographic sex is largely impersonal. Some pornography has narrative structure, but for the most part it cuts straight to the sex, focusing intensively on genitalia. And while actors obviously interact in quite intimate ways, their pleasure (real or simulated) seems quite solipsistic: any penis, any vagina, any mouth, any anus will do.

Still, it is hard to *see* what is *morally* wrong about sex without procreative intent or with sex that is not at the same time an instance of profound interpersonal communication. Indeed, it was surely one result of the so-called sexual revolution of the 1960s that these sorts of worries about pornography began to seem quaint. Nevertheless, as feminists started to think about pornography, a new critique emerged. The focus of feminist concerns turned to the alleged connection between pornography, especially violent pornography, and violence against women. Robin Morgan's remark "Pornography is the theory, rape is the practice" captured a feminist perspective on pornography that was extremely influential for over a decade.[3] This perspective had a powerful strategic advantage. If pornography does cause demonstrable harm to women, then it is obviously morally bad. More important, the substantiated harms of pornography would justify its censorship. For the Supreme Court has long conceded that speech that constitutes a clear and present danger can be restricted consistent with the First Amendment.[4]

There are two main reasons why this approach fails. First, the empirical claim that pornography causes harm to women, say, by making men rape and commit sexual assault, has not been established. A vast amount of social science research has produced conflicting results, and the research itself is plagued by familiar problems of bias and selective interpretation.[5] The second reason we should abandon this particular critique of pornography is deeper. As Laura Kipnis puts it, "The argument that pornography causes violent behavior in male consumers relies on a theory of the pornography consumer as devoid of rationality, contemplation, or intelligence, prone instead to witless brainwashing, to monkey see/monkey do re-enactment of the pornographic scene.[6]

. . . The central point is this: humans are not simple stimulus-response machines. Merely seeing some representation cannot by itself cause action. Viewing or reading pornography usually does cause sexual arousal, even in people who find pornography morally troubling. But an erection is not an action. . . .

To reiterate: the proposition I want to consider is that some pornography is morally problematic insofar as it plays a role (perhaps a pivotal one) in morally

dangerous sexual fantasizing. I suspect that the default position of many Americans is that a moral critique of sexual fantasizing is simply a non starter. But precisely because this is the prevailing view, the assumptions on which it rests need to be scrutinized.

FANTASIZING AS INNER

A common view is that fantasizing is essentially 'inner.' Killing a rival is morally wrong; merely fantasizing about killing her is not. There is little reason to think that fantasizing about X-ing makes actual X-ing more likely. And, one might think that if fantasizing does 'spill over' into overt behavior, then the fantasizing can be criticized, but only derivatively, in terms of the badness of the behavior to which it led.

Fantasizing *is* inner, in some sense of that term that also describes thinking in general. It is one among many ways in which we exercise our imaginations. And we engage in it in the privacy of our consciousness. . . . Fantasizing is not something that merely *happens* to us. It may be distinguished from having fleeting thoughts, daydreaming, or being subject to unbidden or intrusive images (the analogues in imagination of finger drumming). Rather, fantasizing is typically something we deliberately and consciously *do*. Undoubtedly, there are cases of compulsive fantasizing, just are there cases of compulsive hand washing. However, in the usual case, a person fantasizes for a reason: in order to distract, please, or motivate herself. Hence, despite its location inside our heads, fantasizing is properly described as a type of action and is therefore open to moral scrutiny. Of course, the grounds on which a person may be praised or blamed for fantasizing remain to be articulated.

As I noted, it might be conceded that some fantasizing can be morally criticized, but only if that fantasizing leads to harmful overt behavior. About a man with sadistic sexual fantasies we might say "They're all in his head. He is not hurting anyone. And maybe his fantasizing in this way is what keeps him from actually doing such things." But this is just beside the point, once we recognize that fantasizing is a type of action. For the purpose of moral evaluation, it does not matter whether a particular instance of fantasizing is associated with *another* action. My stabbing you is morally wrong irrespective of whether, having enjoyed it so much, I go on to stab someone else, or whether, filled with new sense of your own mortality, you go on to be a great philanthropist. Similarly, we can make sense of the idea that you act wrongly when you break your promise to take me to a baseball game, even though our not going makes it possible for me to do more work on my book. Hence, an instance of fantasizing need not lead to some other bad action in order to be morally bad itself.

It will be clear at this point that I reject a thoroughgoing consequentialism that holds that the moral status of an action is determined exclusively and exhaustively by its actual consequences. Some actions, like those previously described, may be judged on the basis of their intrinsic features alone. The consequences of our actions are not morally irrelevant. However, they are not *all* that is morally relevant. If we focus exclusively on the consequences of our actions, we ignore a large part of what constitutes our moral lives. We respond not only to the results of one another's overt behavior but also to one another's beliefs, desires, intentions, and characters—in short, to each other's moral *agency*. If this is right, then it is at least arguable that a person's fantasizing can be morally bad whether or not the person acts out the fantasy.

SEXUAL FANTASIZING IS DIFFERENT

An objector might grant that, insofar as fantasizing is a type of action, it is open to moral evaluation, and yet balk at the idea that *sexual* fantasizing is ever morally wrong, or that a person can ever be blameworthy for engaging in sexual fantasizing. (Indeed, consider the apparent oddity of *praising* someone for sexual fantasizing.) I believe this reluctance stems from the understandable worry that the moral evaluation of sexual fantasizing puts us at the beginning of an unpleasant slippery slope. When it comes to making judgments about people's sexual lives, the track record is not

good. For example, the erroneous judgment that homosexual sexual desire is morally perverse continues to play a significant role in the unjust treatment of homosexuals. Put this way, the objection is not that sexually fantasizing is always morally neutral or morally good, but rather that it would be better if we did not engage in the evaluation of sexual fantasies or desires period.

I take this concern seriously. However, it bears repeating that moral evaluation does not by itself warrant any particular state action. If we assume otherwise, if we forswear the moral evaluation of some human practices simply because we worry about what use might be made of those evaluations, then we effectively hold ourselves hostage to the irrationality and ill will of others. More important, as I will try to make clearer, when an agent engages in moral evaluation and moral judgment, he need not limit himself to evaluation of and judgment about the actions of *others*. Being a moral agent essentially involves turning those critical faculties on *oneself*, at least every now and then. This chapter, then, should not be read as invitation to point fingers at others whose sexual fantasizing one may find distasteful, but as an attempt to make space in the complex discussion of pornography for genuine first-personal—that is, self-assessment.

Nonetheless, there are deeper sources of resistance to the idea that sexual fantasizing can sometimes he morally bad, which are not always made explicit, in part, I think, because they are quite difficult to articulate. Since the thesis under consideration is so controversial, these assumptions are worth unpacking.

It will help to begin by considering some of the reasons a person might fantasize. First, fantasizing about an event can help us prepare for that event. Think of the teenager who fantasizes about losing both his parents, not because he wants them to die, but rather because doing so helps prepare him for loss. Second, fantasizing can motivate us. Think of the athlete who fantasizes about running in the Olympics. Third, we fantasize to entertain, please, or gratify ourselves. Quite often these reasons operate together; for example, the athlete might derive considerable pleasure by fantasizing about her Olympic performance. But, for present purposes, let us focus on the self-gratifying nature of fantasizing.

The gratification a person achieves by fantasizing may have several different explanations. First and most obviously, a person may simply have a desire to fantasize, which is then trivially satisfied when he does. Second, there are the familiar instances of fantasizing about something because one cannot, for practical reasons, bring it about; for example, I may fantasize about killing my noisy neighbor and derive a certain degree of satisfaction from doing so. And, within this class of cases we might draw a further distinction: I may actually have the full-blown desire that my neighbor die, such that I would kill her if I could dispense with the practical obstacles; or, I might have some merely prima facie desire that she die, such that even without any obstacles, I would never kill her. In the former, the satisfaction I achieve by fantasizing is the best I can get, given the circumstances. In the latter, the satisfaction I achieve by fantasizing is all the satisfaction I need. Lastly, there seem to be cases of fantasizing that are themselves about having certain desires that are satisfied in the fantasy. Examples here might involve desires that are radically at odds with desires the fantast has in either the full-blown or prima facie senses previously described, and which she positively doesn't want satisfied in any other way. To be sure, even in these kinds of cases, the fantast derives some pleasure from her fantasizing, but it is a pleasure she can experience *only* in the realm of fantasy. . . .

Whatever else it may be, fantasizing cannot be said to be off limits to moral evaluation just by dint of its being inner, private, or about sex. Neither is it the case that the moral status of fantasizing (sexual and nonsexual) depends on the probability of its issuing in overt behavior. Still, to argue that sexual fantasizing is morally evaluable is not yet to give an account of what makes sexual fantasizing morally bad when it is. It is to that issue that I now turn.

MORALLY PROBLEMATIC SEXUAL FANTASIZING: AN EXAMPLE

Dennis fantasizes about the following: he moves to a foreign city where he takes up residence in an abandoned building. He meets young man in a club and brings him hack to his place. For a sum of money, the young man agrees to allow Dennis to perform a sex act on him. After a while, Dennis kills him. This is just the first of several killings, some of which Dennis participates in with two other men. The killings all occur in a sexual context; Dennis and his collaborators either have sex with their victims or masturbate while one or the other of them beat or torture their victim.[7] Dennis becomes aroused when he engages in this fantasy and he deliberately calls it to mind when he masturbates. Sometimes he focuses on it when he has sex with a partner.

Now imagine two worlds, World A and World B, in all respects like the actual world, except that in World A, many people sexually fantasize about the sorts of things Dennis does, and in World B no one does. Take it as given that the Dennis's of World A never act out what they fantasize about. Which is the morally preferable world?

Many people would like to be able to say "Neither." Given the option of living in World A or World B, many would like to be able to say that it wouldn't matter. But if we are reflective and honest, I don't think we will find it is a matter of indifference that people around us engage in such fantasizing. Now, arguably, World A is the actual world, and so we do not have the option of living apart from such fantasizers. If the fantasies and their authors bother us, then the best we can do is not think about them. This is another piece of the explanation for the reluctance to entertain the possibility that sexual fantasizing is open to moral evaluation: evaluation requires paying attention to its objects—to fantasizers and the content of their fantasies. . . .

And Dennis fantasizes about what pleases him. He consciously and deliberately conjures up his favorite scenario of sexual debasement and torture, and he concentrates on it to have an orgasm. To say that the content of a fantasy pleases the fantast is to say that the fantast takes a pro-attitude toward that content. Sexual arousal on the basis of fantasizing would hardly be possible if we did not adopt such an attitude, if only for the duration of the fantasizing episode itself. The particular pro-attitude that a person takes to the content of his sexual fantasies can be usefully described by the term "eroticization," where, as John Corvino suggests, to eroticize an activity is to "actively is to "activity regard . . . the activity with sexual desire." Hence . . . , the fantast does adopt a pro-attitude toward the activity he fantasizes.

It is easy to be repelled by the content of Dennis's fantasy. But that repulsion by itself is not sufficient to warrant moral judgments about Dennis's fantasizing. Rather, it is the fact that Dennis's sexual fantasizing—an activity he deliberately engages in to experience intense pleasure—has that content that grounds the judgment that what Dennis does is morally problematic.

But why? This critique appears to be little more than a thinly veiled, nose-wrinkling disgust at the thought of what turns other people on—especially since the idea that fantasizing is morally bad (when it is) just in case either the fantasizing goes proxy for a harmful overt action or significantly raises the probability that the fantast will 'act out' his imaginings have been rejected. The view under consideration, recall, holds that some fantasizing is morally bad even if the fantast does not, in some sense of 'want,' want to do what he fantasizes doing, and even if his fantasizing does not make him more likely to carry out his fantasies. But how else can the moral badness of fantasizing be cashed out if not in terms of its causal or probabilistic consequences?

ACTIONS AND CHARACTER

As I mentioned earlier, at least on reflection, few of us believe that consequences are all that matter morally. We judge lying and the breaking of promises morally wrong, whether or not those actions have bad consequences. But an appeal to the violation of moral principles or duties of the sort that underpin our judgments about lying and promise-breaking will not help here. For it is not really plausible to say that I transgress a specific moral principle or that I violate a particular duty when I engage in certain kinds of fantasizing. But, more to the point, it is hard to see how one could specify the relevant principles or obligations in a nonquestion-begging way. We cannot

explain the moral badness of certain sorts of fantasizing by saying that those activities violate the principle, "It is morally wrong to fantasize about harming others." For the truth of such a principle is precisely what is in question.

A more promising approach emerges if we think about the relations between action, character, and moral agency. Moral agency refers to set of abilities or capacities: the ability to deliberate between options for action, taking into account not only one's own well-being, but the well-being of others; the capacity to recognize when a situation demands a moral response of some kind, for example, rendering assistance to strangers, not serving prime rib at a dinner for vegetarian friends; a sensitivity to the moods, emotions, and commitments of others; the ability to persevere when the going gets tough and resist distractions to important projects; the disposition to seek coherence among one's commitments, expectations, and efforts (integrity).

. . . Talk of a person's character is usefully construed as shorthand for whatever grounds and enables these practical competencies, where we can think of these grounds as the maxims—the regulative ideals— to which she holds herself and to which she believes she ought to hold herself. It is crucial to recognize that a person's character is not simply a laundry list of beliefs. First, because it is not only the *content* of a person's moral beliefs that matter but also her *attitudes* toward those beliefs. Central to the notion of character is the idea that a person endorses—at the very least, accepts—certain principles of right action. Second, in order to ground moral competencies across a life, the regulative ideals to which a person is committed (i.e., which she endorses) must be ordered in some way; they might, for example, be hierarchically ordered from most general to most specific, or lexically ordered according to some other principle. A mere concatenation of practical principles will not deliver the kind of stability over time that is a hallmark of character. Moreover, where there is no ordering of practical principles, inconsistencies are more likely; the kind of stability required for the exercise of moral agency is absent.

But this does not mean that character is static. Indeed, precisely the opposite is true. Although the experience of living a life as a reflective rational being will have the effect of reinforcing some elements of our characters, each of us is always a work in progress. New challenges can reveal aspects of our character we had been unaware of; we might embrace these elements, or, finding them to be inconsistent with other more familiar and more important elements, we might seek to eliminate them. Even though human beings (as rational beings) arc self-reflective, we are not utterly transparent to ourselves. In part, having a character involves the ongoing activity of self-scrutiny, self-discovery, and self-adjustment.

The dynamic nature of character indicates three ways in which actions and character are related. First and most obviously, a person's overt actions are evidence of the nature of his or her character. It is through observing the actions a person typically performs that we attribute to that individual a certain type of character. Less obviously, perhaps, a person's non-overt actions are evidence at least for *him* about the direction his character is taking. Second, some actions—actions for which the agent has a settled disposition, actions he reliably performs—are not merely evidence of his character; they express, in the sense of being constitutive elements of, that character. Finally, a person can attempt to perform a certain type of action because he wants eventually to acquire a settled disposition to perform that action. He wants, that is, for the maxim or practical principle determining that type of action to be an element of his character. We cannot construct a character out of nothing, and we committed to some practical principles simply by virtue of being the kinds of creatures we are.[8] But, beyond the basics, we have considerable latitude in fine-tuning our characters, making certain traits part of who we are.

An example will help tie these claims about moral agency, character, and action together. Imagine that George, a man who has never paid much attention to the ways in which gender makes a difference in the world, develops a friendship with a feminist theorist whom he respects. She talks to him about the many subtle ways in which gender structures the social world, often to the advantage of men and the disadvantage of women. George believes that men and women are equal and that if women arc badly

treated just on account of being women, this is a very bad thing. George worries that he has been oblivious to the effects of gender hierarchy; he doesn't want to be a person who discriminates unfairly, offends, and so on. So George decides that he needs to pay to more attention to gender, and as a practical exercise to keep gender before his consciousness, he decides always to use the feminine pronoun in his writing, except for instances when to do so would be a blatant absurdity (e.g., he cannot refer to his brother as she.) Over time, the action of using the feminine pronoun makes George more sensitive to gender. He notices things he had not noticed before, and he formulates practical principles that constrain the way he acts in situations in which gender is relevant. Through habitually acting in a certain way, he improves his moral agency. He is now more sensitive to morally significant facts around him.

George's story is, we might say, a success story. But the interplay between action, character, and moral agency that allows for human flourishing also allows for corruption. Habitually performing bad actions, or actions that desensitize one to morally salient facts, can seriously hinder the project of character development. Endorsing the wrong kinds of practical principles is corrosive of character. Consider again our sexual fantast Dennis. Here is a man who appears to endorse actions that might seriously undermine his character and thus his moral agency. He takes deep pleasure in fantasizing about harming others and he does so habitually. One ought not be the sort of person who takes sexual pleasure in the debasement of others. And one ought not act in ways that constitute being that sort of person.

These remarks hold outside the domain of sexual fantasizing. Consider other kinds of inner going-on, like emotions. Being overjoyed at and privately gloating about another's misfortune, irrespective of whether one actually laughs in the face of the other, are evil states of mind. Voluntary gloating is morally bad action. One ought not be the kind the kind of person who performs such actions.

The last sentence bears emphasis, if only to forestall the misunderstanding that, after explicitly rejecting consequentialism, I am now relying on precisely such a moral approach in speaking of the ways in which a person's actions affect his or her character. Of course our actions affect our characters. But to stress the moral significance of this truism is not to commit oneself to consequentialism. For the relation between a person's actions and that person's character is a constitutive relation. In this sense, it might be better to say that a person's actions *effect* part of that person's character.

So far I have been considering the proposal that certain types of sexual fantasizing are morally risky on account of the ways in which they constitute the undermining of moral agency and the corruption of character. But precisely how does this bear on pornography?

PORNOGRAPHY AND SEXUAL FANTASIZING

As enjoyable as sexual excitement is, pornography's popularity would be surprising if all it did was provide the color and sound for our inner black-and-white silent movies. Undoubtedly, pornography supplies its consumers with novel elements for their sexual fantasies as well as new ideas for their flesh and blood sexual encounters. More significantly, pornography concretizes existing sexual fantasies, providing enduring and substantive representations of what might otherwise exist 'just' in people's heads.

The implications of the publication and distribution of representations of sexual fantasies must not be underestimated. Like many other cultural discourses, pornography provides us with language and concepts, a framework within which to ground and organize our sexual experience. In this way, pornography and sexual fantasizing are mutually legitimating. The very existence of an industry devoted to producing sexual arousal—even though some people persist in thinking that pornography is marginal—tells us that it is okay to derive sexual pleasure from fantasizing in certain ways. Moreover, when a person sees the major elements of their favorite sexual fantasy acted out with real people, he can rest assured that he is not deviant; he can infer that others are turned on in similar ways. . . .

By supplying us with a constant supply of new and old sexual ideas, pornography permits and encourages us to engage in unbounded sexual fantasizing. This is precisely why some theorists defend pornography, seeing it as a tool of liberation. No doubt that it can be. But some pornography—like Dennis Cooper's described earlier—facilitates and helps to legitimize sexual fantasizing that is morally risky. . . .

CYBERPORNOGRAPHY

Cyberpornography may be more effective in facilitating and legitimizing sexual fantasizing than traditional forms of print and video pornography. This is not just because cyberporn is more accessible than other forms of pornography, though that is a factor. Rather, the very form of cyberporn determines a unique experience of consumption. Accessing and enjoying cyberporn implicates the consumer's agency in interesting ways.

Cyberporn is far more accessible than other types of pornography in at least two senses. First, it is easier to get at the material; opening Netscape Navigator takes less time than driving to the local video store or sex shop. Second, cyberporn can be delivered directly and privately to one's home. Hence, one traditional barrier to getting hold of pornography—embarrassment—is removed. But while these facts might prompt more people to try pornography and others to try more pornography, they do not yet suggest that cyberporn is morally more risky than print and video pornography.

Some critics have argued otherwise, claiming that the ready availability of porn online gives rise to addiction. The research and literature on Internet addiction—of a sexual and nonsexual kind—are highly controversial. But, in any case, it is beside the point for the argument under consideration here. If cyberporn is addictive, that would be unfortunate; but only in the sense that any addiction is a bad thing. Addiction compromises a person's agency, and distracts or prevents the person from engaging in a full range of valuable life projects. The present thesis is narrower, having to do with morally risky sexual fantasizing. Moreover, as I have been at pains to point out, the sexual fantast is *responsible* for his fantasizing and for the actions that support that fantasizing. He is not helpless in the face of an addiction that his 'agential self' cannot penetrate. (I will return to this point briefly.)

It is trivial to note that the Internet has changed and continues to alter the ways in which many people obtain information and communicate with one another. However, what has gone relatively unexplored are the ways in which individual use of the technology changes the *user*. It is, therefore, worth thinking about the phenomenology of computer-mediated communications and other human-Internet interactions. In what remains, I will offer some speculative remarks about two features of consuming cyberporn that, I believe, serve to buttress the claim that cyberporn is more morally dangerous than traditional print and video pornography.

First, consider the experience of browsing the World Wide Web. The ease of browsing (for *anything*) online, the speed at which vast quantities of information can be procured, might lead us to think that the Web is the ultimate desire-satisfaction machine. Want something? Open your favorite search engine or database, and what you desire is only a click or two away. This is certainly true when the desire in question is quite specific, for example, when I want to know the business hours of my local IKEA store or the directions to a restaurant. Such a desire is easily satisfied and, once it is, I have little motivation to continue browsing.

However, typically, we browse the Web precisely because we do not quite know what we want. Either we have no specific question for which we seek an answer, or we do not know what is 'out there' about a particular topic. Consider finding out about alternative treatments for some recently diagnosed medical condition. The experience of this type of browsing is quite different. When I don't have a particular question in mind, I have to work harder to get useful information. And, in some cases, what counts as useful information is constructed as I browse, somewhat after the fashion of the game Twenty Questions. When I browse, I am continually offered new links to different sites.

My desire, inchoate to begin with, is tweaked, refined, heightened; each link promises that the next site will be what I am looking for. In this way, my motivation for staying online is continuously energized.

The genius of Web browsing is that it feeds off desires, many of which the activity of browsing itself helps to create and to amplify, and some of which, by design, will never be satisfied. Purveyors of cyberporn exploit this aspect of the technology quite effectively. Go to the Web with a general curiosity about sexually explicit material (search engine keyword: "XXX") or with a specific sexual interest (search engine keyword: "BBW" or "BCT") and you will be provided with more sites than you know what to do with. More important, cyberpornographers have deliberately built their sites in ways that make it very difficult for a consumer to leave them. Open a pornography site and try to close the browser window. The chances are that you will be bumped to another (pornography) site. Soon you will have dozens of browser windows open on your desktop. And the escalation of unsatiated desire continues.

Browsing cyberporn is rarely just like browsing racks of print pornography or watching a lot of videos. To be sure, it has two similar effects—namely, it provides content for many new and different fantasies and, by its very existence, serves to legitimize the fantasies of its consumers. However, cyberporn also has the effect of keeping consumers engaged in the business of sexual fantasizing longer. First, the ways in which cyberporn is delivered to consumers helps to construct desires that are in turn prevented from being satisfied; one is always encouraged to go to another and then another site. Such 'movement' is relatively effortless, and the chain of new sites to which consumers are bumped is often characterized by increasingly 'extreme' content. (The term is the industry's own.) Furthermore, this rapid delivery of images keeps alive fantasies that the consumer might otherwise have ceased having for want of imagination or because they strike him as 'too bizarre.' Because of the unique nature of consuming pornography on line, consumers' sexual fantasizing is facilitated in previously unimaginable ways.

A potential objection at this point helps to highlight a second relevant aspect of the experience of consuming cyberporn. Someone might say that consumers of cyberporn can hardly be held responsible for the sexual fantasizing in which they engage while online or as a result of viewing cyberporn. For haven't I just suggested that the medium itself compromises agency? Cyberpon consumers are deliberately manipulated. As a result of being 'trapped' in Web sites, certain fantasies are forced on them. In other words, precisely how is the account I offer here different from an addiction account?

It must be conceded that users of technology are changed in more or less significant ways by their experience. But even cyborgs—those who see their machines as literal sexual prostheses—do not for that reason cease to be responsible agents. Nonetheless, I think that the cyberporn consumer's *sense* of his own agency is compromised. The genuine and deliberate activities of opening the first site, consciously following links, downloading images, and repeating the exercise can feel quite passive. The material is delivered to one's desktop. Most of the time, one doesn't have to do anything (except stay online) to find out about new sites. And opening a site requires just a click of the mouse. Moreover, the intense privacy of consuming porn online can make it seem as if one is not actively engaged in any way. Rather it appears that one's fantasizing and online pornography have serendipitously converged. In this way, the consumer is positively discouraged by the medium itself from keeping his own agency and responsibility for fantasizing in focus. It is not as if a consumer of online pornography is rendered helpless with respect to his actions. It is just that the experience itself serves to create the *illusion* that his agency is not engaged. In this way, we can say that the character of the consumer of cyberpornography-with-morally-problematic-content is *doubly* compromised. First, his actions threaten to make him a person of less desirable sort; second, the experience of consuming cyberpornography tends to render the very question of his own complicity otiose to *him*.

To summarize these speculations: consuming cyberporn, by its very nature, facilitates sexual fantasizing, often, of a morally problematic sort (when consumers are bumped to more extreme sites) and it simultaneously masks from the consumer his own agency in the act of consumption. The consumer's character is thus doubly threatened: morally risky sexually fantasizing is facilitated in quite aggressive ways, and the fantast's agency, his own complicity in such actions, is rendered obscure.

CONCLUSION

The overall agenda of this chapter has been to make room for a particular kind of moral critique of pornography, one that pays close attention to the moral effects pornography can have on its consumers. At the heart of that critique is the idea that it is morally risky to engage in certain kinds of sexual fantasizing on the grounds that to habitually link sexual pleasure and satisfaction with thoughts of degradation, abuse, and humiliation can undermine the development and maintenance of a sound moral character. Any pornography that encourages and facilitates such fantasizing—and it is plausible that cyberpornography is particularly efficacious in this regard—can thus be morally criticized. It bears emphasis yet again that this line of argument does not by itself imply restrictive public policies concerning pornography either on or offline. If anything, this particular moral critique of pornography would seem to make the prospects of state intervention quite poor. For we are and should be skeptical of *state*-imposed limitations on our freedom directed at the goal of making us better moral agents. That said, the present discussion is not without practical relevance. Each of us has a responsibility to make judgments about *our own* actions and attitudes. This is the sense in which morality is as much self-regarding as it is other-regarding. For the moral status of any social activity, like the consumption of pornography, may be analyzed in terms of its effects on its practitioners as well as on others.[9]

NOTES

1. Timothy Egan, "Technology Sent Wall Street into Market for Pornography," *The New York Times*, Monday, October 2000, AI, A20.

2. For the record, I am somewhat of a free speech absolutist. See my "Free Speech. A Plea to Ignore the Consequences," *Computer-Mediated Communication*, vol. 3, no. 1 (www.december.com/CMC/mag/1996/jan/toc.html), and my "Free Speech" *Sats: The Nordic Journal of Philosophy* 2 (2001): 80-97.

3. Robin Morgan, *Going Too Far; The Personal Chronicle of a Feminist* (New York: Random House, 1977), p. 169.

4. The so-called clear and present danger test as a tool in evaluating First Amendment challenges has its roots in *Schenck v. United States*, 249 U.S. 47 (1919), in which Justice Holmes wrote: "The question in every case is whether the words used are used in such circumstances and are of such a nature that they will bring about the substantive evils that Congress has a right to prevent" (p. 52).

5. See, e.g., Ferrell M. Christensen, "Cultural and Ideological Bias in Pornography Research," Philosophy of the Social Sciences 20 (1990): 351–375; Alison King, "Mystery and Imagination: The Case of Pornography Effect Studies," in *Bad Girls and Dirty Pictures*, eds. Alison Assister and Avedon Carol (London: Pluto Press, 1993), pp. 57–87; and Daniel G. Linz, Edward Donnerstein, and Steven Penrod, "The Findings and Recommendations of the Attorney General's Commission on Pornography: Do the Psychological 'Facts' Fit the Political Fury?" *American Psychologist* 42 (1987): 946–953.

6. Laura Kipnis, Bound and Gagged: *Pornography and the Politics of Fantasy in America* (New York: Grove Press, 1996), p. 175

7. The content of this fantasy is drawn from an except of Dennis Cooper's story "Numb," originally published in his *Frisk* (New York: Grove/Adantic, 1991) and reprinted in *Forbidden Passages: Writings Banned in Canada*, introductions by Pat Califia and Janine Fuller (Pittsburgh: Cleis Press, 1995), pp. 151–160. I do not know whether this srory describes the content of a sexual fantasy Mr. Cooper himself has. However, the story is intended as a piece of gay erotica, and it might be someone's fantasy.

8. The idea that humans have some native moral endowment is an ancient though controversial one. For a defense see my "Moral Selves and Moral Parameters," *Becoming Persons*, ed., Robert N. Fisher (Oxford: Applied Theology Press, 1995), pp. 471–500, and "Moral Competence," *Philosophy and Linguistics*, eds., Kumiko Murasugi and Robert Stainton (Boulder CO: Westview Press, 1999), pp. 169-190. And see Sissela Bok, "What Basis for Morality A Minimalist Approach," *The Monist* 76 (1993): 348–359 for a nonnativist account of a universal morality.

9. Many thanks to the following for useful discussion and provocative questions: Robert Cavalier, Felman Davis, Christine Koggel and her students at Bryn Mawr College, Alex London, Patrick McCroskery, Eduardo Mendieta, Paul Pietroski, Mandy Simons, Sarah Stroud, and Carol Voeller.

READING QUESTIONS

1. How does Dwyer criticize moral objections to pornography based on its alleged harmful effects on women?
2. At the end of the section entitled "Actions and Character," Dwyer claims that she has not argued that certain kinds of sexual fantasizing are wrong because of the *effects* on one's character, but because of how it can become part of what *constitutes* one's character. Try clarifying this distinction between being an *effect of something* versus *constituting that thing* by considering this question: Is happiness an *effect of* pleasure? Or is happiness partly *constituted by* pleasure?
3. Why does Dwyer think that sexual fantasizing can be detrimental to one's character?

DISCUSSION QUESTIONS

1. How plausible is Dwyer's claim that sexual fantasizing can be detrimental to one's character?
2. Are there any types of sexual fantasizing that can be good for one's character?

JOHN ARTHUR

Sticks and Stones

Arthur first explains the basis for protecting freedom of speech and then, after reviewing the interpretation of the First Amendment by the U.S. Supreme Court, explains why the Court has been rightly reluctant to treat hate speech as unprotected. In defending hate speech as a protected form of speech, Arthur distinguishes between wrongs and harms. You are wronged but not harmed if someone breaks into your car, takes nothing, and does no damage. He then argues that hate speech, despite wronging its victims, has not been shown (at least by itself) to cause various sorts of harms, including harm to one's self-esteem and physical harm. But even supposing that there is a causal link between hate speech and harm, Arthur argues that on balance there is compelling reason for such speech to receive First Amendment protection. He reaches a similar conclusion regarding pro-censorship arguments that appeal to the offense principle.

Recommended Reading: consequentialism, chap. 1, sec. 2A.

Proponents of limiting hate speech on college campuses and elsewhere have generally taken one of two approaches. One is to pass a "speech code" that identifies which words or ideas are banned, the punishment that may be imposed, and (as at the University of Michigan) an interpretive "Guide" meant to explain how the rules will be applied. The other approach has been to treat hate speech as a form of harassment. Here the censorship is justified on anti-discrimination grounds: hate speech, it is argued, subjects its victims to a "hostile" work environment, which courts have held constitutes job discrimination (*Meritor Savings Bank v. Vinson,* 1986).

. . . Rather than censoring all expressions of hatred, advocates of banning hate speech use the term narrowly, to refer to speech directed at people *in virtue of their membership in a (usually historically disadvantaged) racial, religious, ethnic, sexual or other group.*

Such a conception can be criticized, of course, on the ground that it arbitrarily narrows the field to one form of hate speech. Perhaps, however, there is

reason to focus on a limited problem: if it turns out, for example, that hate speech directed against such groups is especially harmful, then it may seem reasonable to have created this special usage of the term. In this paper I consider some of the important issues surrounding hate speech and its regulation: the political and legal importance of free speech; the types of harm that might be attributed to it; and whether, even if no harm results, causing emotional distress and offense is by itself sufficient to warrant censorship.

WHY PROTECT FREEDOM OF SPEECH?

Respecting freedom of speech is important for a variety of reasons. First, as J. S. Mill argued long ago, free and unfettered debate is vital for the pursuit of truth. If knowledge is to grow, people must be free

From John Arthur, "Sticks and Stones," in *Ethics in Practice: An Anthology,* ed., H. LaFollette, Blackwell, 1997. Reprinted by permission of the author.

to put forth ideas and theories they deem worthy of consideration, and others must be left equally free to criticize them. Even false ideas should be protected, Mill argued, so that the truth will not become mere dogma, unchallenged and little understood. "However true [an opinion] may be," he wrote, "if it is not fully, frequently, and fearlessly discussed, it will be held as a dead dogma, not a living truth" (Mill, 1978, p. 34). . . .

Free speech is also an essential feature of democratic, efficient and just government. Fair, democratic elections cannot occur unless candidates are free to debate and criticize each other's policies, nor can government be run efficiently unless corruption and other abuses can be exposed by a free press. . . .

A third value, individual autonomy, is also served by free speech. In chapter III of *On Liberty,* "Of Individuality, as One of the Elements of Well Being," Mill writes that "He who lets the world, or his own portion of it, choose his plan of life for him, has no need of any other faculty than the ape-like one of imitation. . . . Among the works of man, which human life is rightly employed in perfecting and beautifying, the first in importance surely is man himself" (Mill, 1978, p. 56). Mill's suggestion is that the best life does not result from being forced to live a certain way, but instead is freely chosen without coercion from outside. But if Mill is right, then freedom of speech as well as action are important to achieve a worthwhile life. Free and open discussion helps people exercise their capacities of reasoning and judgment, capacities that are essential for autonomous and informed choices.

Besides these important social advantages of respecting free speech, . . . freedom of expression is important for its own sake, because it is a basic human right. Not only does free speech *promote* autonomy, as Mill argued, but it is also a *reflection* of individual autonomy and of human equality. Censorship denigrates our status as equal, autonomous persons by saying, in effect, that some people simply cannot be trusted to make up their own minds about what is right or true. Because of the ideas they hold or the subjects they find interesting, they need not be treated with the same respect as other citizens with whom they disagree; only we, not they, are free to believe as we wish. . . .

Because it serves important social goals, and also must be respected in the name of equal citizenship, the right to speak and write freely is perhaps the most important of all rights. But beyond that, two further points also need to be stressed. Free speech is fragile, in two respects. The first is the chilling effect that censorship poses. Language banning hate speech will inevitably be vague and indeterminate, at least to some extent: words like "hate" and "denigrate" and "victimize," which often occur in such rules, are not self-defining. When such bans bring strict penalties, as they sometimes do, they risk sweeping too broadly, capturing valuable speech in their net along with the speech they seek to prohibit. Criminal or civil penalties therefore pose a threat to speech generally, and the values underlying it, as people consider the potential risks of expressing their opinions while threatened by legal sanctions. Censorship risks having a chilling effect.

The second danger of censorship, often referred to as the "slippery slope," begins with the historical observation that unpopular minorities and controversial ideas are always vulnerable to political repression, whether by authoritarian regimes hoping to remain in power, or elected officials desiring to secure reelection by attacking unpopular groups or silencing political opponents. For that reason, it is important to create a high wall of constitutional protection securing the right to speak against attempts to limit it. Without strong, politically resistant constraints on governmental efforts to restrict speech, there is constant risk—demonstrated by historical experience—that what begins as a minor breach in the wall can be turned by governmental officials and intolerant majorities into a large, destructive exception. . . .

FREE SPEECH AND THE CONSTITUTION

The Supreme Court has not always interpreted the First Amendment's free speech and press clauses in a manner consistent with speech's importance. Early in the twentieth century people were often jailed, and their convictions upheld, for expressing unpopular political views, including distributing pamphlets critical of American military intervention in the Russian revolution (*Abrams* v. *United States,* 1919). Then, in the McCarthy era of the 1950s, government prosecuted over a hundred people for what was in effect either teaching Marxism or belonging to the Communist Party (*Dennis* v. *United States,* 1951). Beginning in the 1960s, however, the US Supreme Court changed direction, interpreting the Constitution's command that government not restrict freedom of speech as imposing strict limits on governmental power to censor speech and punish speakers.

Pursuing this goal, the [Court] first defined "speech" broadly, to include not just words but other forms of expression as well. Free speech protection now extends to people who wear arm bands, burn the flag, and peaceably march. The Court has also made a critically important distinction, between governmental regulations aimed at the *content* or *ideas* a person wishes to convey and content-neutral restrictions on the *time, place, and manner* in which the speech occurs. Thus, government is given fairly wide latitude to curtail speakers who use bull-horns at night, spray-paint their ideas on public buildings, or invade private property in order to get their messages across. But when governmental censors object not to how or where the speech occurs, but instead to the content itself, the Constitution is far more restrictive. Here, the Supreme Court has held, we are at the very heart of the First Amendment and the values it protects. Indeed, said the Court, there is "no such thing as a false idea" under the US Constitution (*Gertz* v. *Robert Welch, Inc.,* 1974).

Wary of the chilling effect and the slippery slope, the Supreme Court has therefore held that government cannot regulate the content of speech unless it falls within certain narrowly defined categories. These constitutionally "unprotected categories" include libel (but criticisms of public officials must not only be false but uttered "maliciously" to be libelous), incitement to lawlessness (if the incitement is "immanent," such as yelling "Let's kill the capitalist!" in front of an angry mob), obscenity (assuming that the speech also lacks substantial social value), and "fighting words" (like "fascist pig" that are uttered in a face-to-face context likely to injure or provoke

immediate, hostile reaction). In that way, each of these unprotected categories is precisely defined so as not to endanger free expression in general. . . .

Applying these principles, the Supreme Court held in 1989 that a "flag desecration is constitutionally protected" (*Texas* v. *Johnson,* 1989). Texas's statute had defined "desecration" in terms of the tendency to "offend" someone who was likely to know of the act. But, said the Court in striking down the statute, not only does flag burning involve ideas, the statute is not viewpoint neutral. Because it singled out one side of a debate—those who are critical of government—the law must serve an especially clear and important purpose. Mere "offense," the justices concluded, was insufficiently important to warrant intrusion into free expression.

In light of this constitutional history, it is not surprising that attempts to ban hate speech have fared poorly in American courts. Responding to various acts of racist speech on its campus, the University of Michigan passed one of the most far-reaching speech codes ever attempted at an American university; it prohibited "stigmatizing or victimizing" either individuals or groups on the basis of "race, ethnicity, religion, sex, sexual orientation, creed, national origin, ancestry, age, marital status, handicap or Vietnam-era veteran status." According to a "Guide" published by the University to help explain the code's meaning, conduct that violates the code would include a male student who "makes remarks in class like 'Women just aren't as good in this field as men,' thus creating a hostile learning atmosphere for female classmates." Also punishable under the code were "derogatory" comments about a person's or group's "physical appearance or sexual orientation, or their cultural origins, or religious beliefs" (*Doe* v. *University of Michigan,* 1989, pp. 857–8). To almost nobody's surprise, the Michigan Code was rejected as unconstitutional, on grounds that it violated rights both to free speech and to due process of law. The case was brought by a psychology instructor who feared that his course in developmental psychology, which discussed biological differences between males and females, might be taken by some to be "stigmatizing and victimizing." The Court agreed with the professor, holding that the Michigan code was both "overbroad" and "unconstitutionally vague." A second code at the University of Wisconsin soon met a similar fate, even though it banned only slurs and epithets (*UMV Post* v. *Board of Regents of the University of Wisconsin,* 1991).

Confirming these lower court decisions, the Supreme Court in 1992 ruled unconstitutional a city ordinance making it a misdemeanor to place on public or private property any "symbol, object, appellation, characterization or graffiti" that the person knows or has reasonable grounds for knowing will arouse "anger, alarm or resentment" on the basis of race, color, creed, religion or gender (*R.A.V.* v. *City of St. Paul,* 1992, p. 2541). In overturning a juvenile's conviction for placing a burning cross on a black family's lawn, the majority held that even if the statute were understood very narrowly, to limit only "fighting words," it was nonetheless unconstitutional because it punished only some fighting words and not others. In so doing, argued one justice, the law violated the important principle of content neutrality: it censored some uses of fighting words, namely those focusing on race, color, creed, religion or gender, but not others. It prescribed political orthodoxy. Other justices emphasized that no serious harm had been identified that could warrant restrictions on speech. The law, wrote Justice White, criminalizes conduct that "causes only hurt feelings, offense, or resentment, and is protected by the First Amendment" (*R.A.V.* v. *City of St. Paul,* 1992, p. 2559).

Perhaps, however, the Court has gone too far in protecting hate speech. Advocates of banning hate speech commonly claim it harms its victims. "There is a great difference," writes Charles Lawrence, "between the offensiveness of words that you would rather not hear because they are labelled dirty, impolite, or personally demeaning and the injury [of hate speech]" (Lawrence, 1990, p. 74). Elsewhere he describes hate speech as "aimed at an entire group with the effect of causing significant *harm* to individual group members" (Lawrence, 1990, p. 57, emphasis added). Richard Delgado similarly claims that it would be rare for a white who is called a "dumb honkey" to be in a position to claim legal redress since, unlike a member of an historically oppressed group, it would be unlikely that a white person would "suffer *harm* from such an insult" (Delgado, 1982, p. 110, emphasis added).

But are these writers correct that various forms of hate speech cross the boundary from the distressing and offensive to the genuinely harmful?

HARM AND OFFENSE

To claim that someone has been harmed is different from claiming she has been wronged. I can break into your house undetected, do no damage, and leave. While I have wronged you, I might not have harmed you, especially if you didn't know about it and I didn't take anything.

What then must be the case for wronging somebody to also constitute a harm? First, to be harmed is not merely to experience a minor irritation or hurt, nor is it simply to undergo an unwanted experience. Though unwanted, the screech of chalk on the blackboard, an unpleasant smell, a pinch or slap, a brief but frightening experience, and a revolting sight are not harms. Harms are significant events. Following Joel Feinberg, I will assume that harms occur not when we are merely hurt or offended, but when our "interests" are frustrated, defeated or set back (Feinberg, 1984, pp. 31–51). By interests he means something in which we have a stake—just as we may have a "stake" in a company. So while many of our interests are obviously tied to our wants and desires, a mere want does not constitute an interest. A minor disappointment is not a frustration of interests in the relevant sense. Feinberg thus emphasizes the "directional" nature of interests that are "set back" when one is harmed, pointing out that the interests are "ongoing concerns" rather than temporary wants. Genuine harms thus impede or thwart people's future objectives or options, which explains why the unpleasant memory or smell and the bite's itch are not harms while loss of a limb, of freedom, and of health are. Harms can therefore come from virtually any source: falling trees, disease, economic or romantic competitors, and muggers are only a few examples. . . .

We now turn to the question of whether hate speech causes harm. In discussing this, we will consider various types of harm that might result, as well as making important distinctions . . . between cumulative and individual harm and between direct and indirect harm.

CUMULATIVE VERSUS INDIVIDUAL HARM

. . . [W]e must first distinguish between harms flowing from *individual* actions and *cumulative* harms. Often what is a singly harmless act can be damaging when added to other similar acts. One person walking across a lawn does little damage, but constant walking will destroy the lawn. Indeed the single act might be entirely without negative effect. Pollution, for instance, is often harmful only cumulatively, not singly. Though one car battery's lead may do no harm to those who drink the water downstream, when added to the pollution of many others the cumulative harm can be disastrous.

Further, the fact that it was singly harmless is no justification for performing the act. The complete response to a person who insists that he had a right to pollute since his action did no damage is that if everyone behaved that way great harm would follow: once a legal scheme protecting the environment is in place, criminal law is rightly invoked even against individually harmless acts on grounds of cumulative harm.

It might then be argued that even if individual hate speech acts do not cause harm, it should still be banned because of its cumulatively harmful effects. What might that harm consist in? Defending hate speech codes, Mari J. Matsuda writes that "As much as one may try to resist a piece of hate propaganda, the effect on one's self-esteem and sense of personal security is devastating. To be hated, despised, and alone is the ultimate fear of all human beings. . . . [R]acial inferiority is planted in our minds as an idea that may hold some truth" (Matsuda, 1989, p. 25). Besides the distress caused by the hate speech, Matsuda is suggesting, hate speech victims may also be harmed in either of two ways: reduced self-esteem or increased risk of violence and discrimination. I will begin with

self-esteem, turning to questions of violence and discrimination in the next section.

CUMULATIVE HARM TO SELF-ESTEEM

What then is self-esteem? Following Rawls, let us assume that by "self-esteem" or "self-respect" we mean the sense both that one's goals and life-plan are worthwhile and that one has talents and other characteristics sufficient to make their accomplishment possible (Rawls, 1971, pp. 440–6). Loss of self-esteem might therefore constitute harm because it reduces motivation and willingness to put forth effort. If hate-speech victims believe they have little or no chance of success, their future options will be reduced. . . .

Assuming loss of self-esteem is a harm, how plausible is Matsuda's suggestion that hate speech has the (cumulative) effect of reducing it? Many factors can reduce self-esteem. Demeaning portrayals of one's group in the media, widespread anti-social behavior of others in the group, family break-down, poor performance in school and on the job, drugs, and even well intended affirmative-action programs all may lessen self-esteem. Indeed, I suggest that, absent those other factors, simply being subject to hate speech would not significantly reduce self-esteem. An otherwise secure and confident person might be made angry (or fearful) by racial or other attacks, feeling the speaker is ignorant, rude, or stupid. But without many other factors it is hard to see that hate speech by itself would have much impact on self-esteem. . . .

But even assuming hate speech does reduce self-esteem to some degree, notice how far the argument has strayed from the original, robust claim that hate speech should be banned because it causes harm. First each individual act must be added to other acts of hate speech, but then it must also be added to the many other, more important factors that together reduce self-esteem. Given the importance of protecting speech I discussed earlier, and the presumption it creates against censorship, Matsuda's argument that it reduces self-esteem seems far too speculative and indirect to warrant criminalizing otherwise protected speech.

DISCRIMINATION AND VIOLENCE AS INDIRECT HARMS

But surely, it may be objected, the real issue is simply this: hate speech should be banned because it increases racial or other forms of hatred, which in turn leads to increased violence and discrimination—both of which are obviously harmful. That is a serious claim, and must be taken seriously. Notice first, however, that this effect of hate speech, if it exists, is only indirect; hate speech is harmful only because of its impact on others who are then led in turn to commit acts of violence or discrimination.

There are important problems with this as an argument for banning hate speech. One epistemological problem is whether we really know that the link exists between hate speech, increased hatred, and illegal acts. Suppose we discovered a close correlation between reading hate speech and committing acts of violence—what have we proved? Not, as might be thought, that hate speech causes violence. Rather, we would only know that *either* (A) reading such material increases hatred and violence, *or* (B) those who commit hate crimes also tend to like reading hate speech. The situation with respect to hate speech mirrors arguments about violence and pornography: the observation that rapists subscribe in greater proportion to pornographic magazines than do non-rapists does not show we can reduce rape by banning pornography. Maybe people who rape just tend also to like pornography. Similarly, reduction in hate speech might, or might not, reduce hate-related crime, even assuming that those who commit hate crimes are avid readers of hate literature.

. . . [W]e have on hand two different ways of dealing with acts of violence and discrimination motivated by hatred: by using government censorship in an effort at thought control, trying to eliminate hatred and prejudice, or by insisting that whether people like somebody or not they cannot assault them or discriminate against them. My suggestion is that passing and vigorously enforcing laws against violence and discrimination themselves is a better method of preventing indirect harm than curtailing speech. . . .

OFFENSIVE EXPRESSION AND EPITHETS

I have argued that hate speech should not be banned on the ground of preventing harm. But government often restricts behavior that is not strictly speaking harmful: it prevents littering, for instance, and limits how high we build our buildings, the drugs we take and the training our doctors receive, to mention only a few examples. Some of these restrictions are controversial, of course, especially ones that seem designed only to keep us from harming ourselves. But others, for example limiting alterations of historic buildings and preventing littering, are rarely disputed. Government also limits various forms of public behavior that are grossly offensive, revolting or shocking. An assault on the sense of smell and hearing, unusual or even common sexual activities in public, extreme provocations of anger, or threats that generate great anxiety or fear, are generally regarded as examples of behavior that can be restricted although they do not cause genuine harm.

Charles Lawrence suggests that this argument also applies to hate speech. The experience of being called "nigger," "spic," "Jap," or "kike," he writes, "is like receiving a slap in the face. The injury is instantaneous" (Lawrence, 1990, pp. 68–9). He describes the experience of a student who was called a "faggot" on a subway: "He found himself in a state of semi-shock, nauseous, dizzy, unable to muster the witty, sarcastic, articulate rejoinder he was accustomed to making" (Lawrence, 1990, p. 70).

. . . [B]ecause of speech's critical importance and government's tendency to regulate and limit political discussion to suit its own ends, I have argued, it is important to limit governmental censorship to narrowly and precisely defined unprotected categories. . . . Assuming that we might wish to keep this unprotected-categories approach, how might offensive hate speech be regulated? One possibility is to allow government to ban speech that "causes substantial distress and offense" to those who hear it. Were we to adopt such a principle, however, we would effectively gut the First Amendment. All kinds of political speech, including much that we would all think must be protected, is offensive to somebody somewhere. . . .

Nor would it work to limit the unprotected category to all speech that is distressing and offensive to members of historically stigmatized groups, for that too would sweep far too broadly. Speech critical of peoples, nations, and religious institutions and practices often offends group members, as do discussions of differences between the races and sexes. Social and biological scientists sometimes find themselves confronted by people who have been deeply wounded by their words, as the instructor who got in trouble at the University of Michigan over his comments about sex-linked abilities illustrates. Or what about psychologists who wish to do research into group IQ differences? Should only those who reach conclusions that are not offensive be allowed to publish?

Others, however, have suggested another, less sweeping approach: why not at least ban racial or other *epithets* since they are a unique form of "speech act" that does not deserve protection. Unlike other forms of protected speech, it is claimed that epithets and name calling are constitutionally useless; they constitute acts of "subordination" that treat others as "moral inferiors" (Altmann, 1993). Racial, religious and ethnic epithets are therefore a distinct type of speech act in which the speaker is subordinating rather than claiming, asserting, requesting, or any of the other array of actions we accomplish with language. So (it is concluded) while all the other types of speech acts deserve protection, mere epithets and slurs do not.

The problem with this argument, however, is that epithets are *not* simply acts of subordination, devoid of social and political significance or meaning, any more than burning a flag is simply an act of heating cloth. Besides "subordinating" another, epithets can also express emotion (anger or hatred, for example) or defiance of authority. And like burning or refusing to salute the flag (both protected acts), epithets also can be seen to express a political message, such as that another person or group is less worthy of moral consideration or is receiving undeserved preferences. That means, then, that however objectionable the content of such epithets is they go well beyond mere acts of "subordination" and therefore must be protected.

It is worth emphasizing, however, that although people have a political and constitutional *right* to use such language, it does not follow that they *should* use it or that they are behaving decently or morally when they exercise the right. A wrong remains a wrong, even if government may for good reason choose not to punish it. I am therefore in no way defending on moral grounds those who utter hate speech—an impossible task, in my view. . . .

But how, then, should others respond to those, on a university campus or off, who are offended and distressed when others exercise their right to speak? When children call each other names and cruelly tease each other, the standard adult response is to work on both sides of the problem. Teasers are encouraged to be more sensitive to others' feelings, and victims are encouraged to ignore the remarks. "Sticks and stones can break my bones, but names can never hurt me" was commonplace on the playground when I was a child. . . .

Like the sexual freedoms of homosexuals, freedom of speech is often the source of great distress to others. I have argued, however, that because of the risks and costs of censorship there is no alternative to accepting those costs, or more precisely to imposing the costs on those who find themselves distressed and offended by the speech. Like people who are offended by homosexuality or inter-racial couples, targets of hate speech can ask why they should have to suffer distress. The answer is the same in each case: nobody has the right to demand that government protect them against distress when doing so would violate others' rights. Many of us believe that racists would be better people and lead more worthwhile lives if they didn't harbor hatred, but that belief does not justify restricting their speech, any more than the Puritans' desire to save souls would warrant religious intolerance, or Catholics' moral disapproval of homosexuality justify banning homosexual literature.

REFERENCES

Abrams v. *United States,* 250 US 616 (1919).

Altmann, A.: "Liberalism and Campus Hate Speech," *Ethics,* 103 (1993).

Delgado, R.: "Words that Wound: A Tort Action for Racial Insults, Epithets, and Name Calling," 17, *Harvard Civil Rights—Civil Liberties Law Review,* 133 (1982); reprinted in Matsuda et al. (1993).

Dennis v. *United States,* 341 US 494 (1951).

Doe v. *University of Michigan,* 721 F. Supp. 852 (E. D. Mich. 1989).

Feinberg, J.: *The Moral Limits of the Criminal Law,* Volume I: *Harm to Others* (New York: Oxford University Press, 1984).

———:*The Moral Limits of the Criminal Law,* Volume II: *Offense to Others* (New York: Oxford University Press, 1985).

Gertz v. *Robert Welch, Inc.,* 418 US 323, 339 (1974).

Lawrence, C.: "If He Hollers Let Him Go: Regulating Racist Speech on Campus," *Duke Law Journal,* 431 (1990); reprinted in Matsuda et al. (1993).

Matsuda, M.: "Public Response to Racist Speech: Considering the Victim's Story," *Michigan Law Review,* 87 (1989); reprinted in Matsuda et al. (1993).

Matsuda, M., Lawrence, C. R., Delgado, R., and Crenshaw, K. W.: *Words that Wound: Critical Race Theory, Assaultive Speech, and the First Amendment* (Boulder, CO: Westview Press, 1993).

Meritor Savings Bank v. *Vinson,* 477 US 57 (1986).

Mill, J. S.: *On Liberty* (Indianapolis, IN: Hackett, 1978).

Rawls, J.: *A Theory of Justice* (Cambridge, MA: Harvard University Press, 1971).

Texas v. *Johnson,* 491 US 397 (1989).

UMV Post v. *Board of Regents of the University of Wisconsin,* 774 F. Supp. 1163 (1991).

READING QUESTIONS

1. How does Arthur define "hate speech"? What is the objection that he considers to this definition and how does he reply?
2. Explain the four different reasons offered by Arthur for why freedom of speech should be protected. Why does he think that freedom of speech is fragile? What are the four cases in which the government is permitted to regulate speech?
3. When is wronging someone harming them according to Arthur? How does he distinguish between cumulative and individual harm?
4. How does Arthur reply to those who advocate banning certain types of hate speech? How does he suggest we handle situations in which hate speech offends individuals?

DISCUSSION QUESTIONS

1. Discuss how the potential harmful aspects of hate speech compare to other forms of harm that individuals inflict and suffer. Should we accept Arthur's view that offensive speech is not always harmful? Why or why not?
2. Arthur suggests that overcoming the offensive nature of hate speech will require working with both the victims and the speakers. Does this suggestion offer a plausible solution to the problem? Why or why not? Consider and discuss some practical ways in which this sort of project could be carried out.

ANDREW ALTMAN

Speech Codes and Expressive Harm

Regarding the effects of speech, Andrew Altman distinguishes causal harm from expressive harm. Some have argued that hate speech causes psychological harm to those individuals and groups targeted by such speech. If so, then by the harm principle, university and college campus codes that prohibit such speech are legitimate exceptions to the First Amendment of the U.S. Constitution. After pointing to difficulties in defending a pro-censorship position based on claims of causal harm, Altman goes on to explain how hate speech involves *expressive harm*. Expressive harm results from expressing denigrating attitudes about some target, and it is on this basis that Altman argues that campus bans on hate speech can be justified.

Recommended Reading: Kantian moral theory, chap. 1, sec. 2C. Altman does not explicitly appeal to any one moral theory in defending his position. However, the Humanity formulation of Kant's categorical imperative with its appeal to *dignity* could be applied to the case of hate speech codes and the idea of expressive harm.

I INTRODUCTION

During the 1980s and early 1990s, many American colleges and universities adopted rules prohibiting speech that denigrates individuals on the basis of race, gender, ethnicity, religion, sexual orientation and similar categories of social identity. An apparent rash of racist and sexist incidents on campuses across the nation had led to the adoption of these 'speech codes'.[1] For example, at the University of Michigan, someone had written on a blackboard "A mind is a terrible thing to waste—especially on a nigger." (Lawrence, 1993, p. 55). The bigotry exhibited in such incidents was widely condemned. Yet, the codes designed to respond to this bigotry generated considerable controversy.

Critics argued that the codes violated the principle of free speech. They did not claim that all rules regulating speech on campus would be objectionable. Rules against rallies or demonstrations in the library would be unobjectionable. The aim of such rules would simply be to allow all students to use the library facilities without disruption, and no particular political beliefs or social attitudes would be singled out for suppression. But speech codes were entirely different, as the critics saw it: the codes aimed to suppress the expression of certain beliefs and attitudes. And such an aim, the critics argued, was incompatible with any adequate understanding of free speech.

Advocates of the codes pointed to the harm caused to those targeted by 'hate speech': generalized psychic distress, feelings of anger and alienation, a sense of physical insecurity, and the various academic and social difficulties that naturally flow from such psychological disturbances. Treating the interests of all students with equal consideration, argued the advocates, required rules punishing hate speech. Code advocates also argued that restrictions on campus hate speech could help combat bigoted attitudes and practices in society at large.

From Andrew Altman, "Speech Codes and Expressive Harm," in Hugh La Follette, ed., *Ethics in Practice*, 3rd ed. (Oxford: Blackwell Publishing Ltd., 2007) Blackwell. By permission of the author.

American courts have uniformly sided with the critics of campus speech codes (Shiell, 1998, pp. 73–97). In a series of cases, courts struck down a variety of codes as unconstitutional. It might seem that these legal rulings would have put the controversy to rest. But that has not happened. Discussion and debate over the legitimacy of speech codes continues.

Because the US Supreme Court has not taken up a speech code case, there is some room to argue that the legal door has not been shut entirely on the question of the constitutionality of the codes. But the continuation of the controversy does not depend on expectations about future court action. It continues because the codes raise crucial ethical and political questions in a society committed both to freedom of speech and to equality under the law. What is the best way to understand the principle of free speech? Are there special aspects of the university context that must be taken into account by that understanding? Are there special aspects of American history and society that make a difference to the speech code debate? Legal cases can help shed light on such questions, but no court ruling can decisively settle them.[2]

In my view, it is difficult to justify speech codes solely on the basis of the harmful causal effects of hate speech. But I think that there is another type of harm to consider, what has been called "expressive harm" (Pildes and Niemi, 1993; Anderson and Pildes, 2000). Expressive harm is not a causal consequence of hate speech. Rather, it is a harm that derives from the kind of attitude expressed in the very act of hate speech, and it is independent of the causal effects of such a speech act.

In the next section, I explain why the causally harmful results of hate speech provide an insufficient basis on which to justify speech codes. Section III then gives an account of the nature of expressive harm, focusing on how symbolic speech by public officials can do expressive harm to an individual's right to be treated by government with equal respect and consideration. Section IV compares and contrasts private individuals with public officials when it comes to speech that does expressive harm. That section also formulates two main obstacles to justifying speech codes. In Sections V and VI, I seek to surmount those obstacles and present the case for speech codes. Section VII examines several campus speech policies, arguing for the superiority of a certain type of speech code.

II CAUSAL HARM

In an influential essay, Mari Matsuda writes: "When racist propaganda appears on campus, target-group students experience debilitated access to the full university experience. This is so even when it is directed at groups rather than at individuals" (1993, p. 45). And to those speech-code skeptics inclined to dismiss the harm of hate speech as merely psychological, Charles Lawrence points out: "Psychic injury is no less an injury than being struck in the face, and it often is far more severe. Racial epithets and harassment often cause deep emotional scarring and feelings of anxiety and fear that pervade every aspect of a victim's life" (1993, p. 74).

There is little doubt that hate speech can have psychologically debilitating effects and those effects in turn can interfere with a student's opportunities to enjoy the educational and social benefits of campus life. Black students who walk into a classroom in which the blackboard has written on it a vicious racial epithet directed against them will likely—and reasonably—respond with anger and even rage. Moreover, additional psychological injury is certainly possible: the students may come to think that they are unwelcome and even unsafe on campus. As Matsuda notes, hate speech often uses symbols, such as a burning crosses and swastikas, which are associated with violence against minorities.

Advocates of speech codes also argue that hate speech reinforces and perpetuates bigoted attitudes and practices in society at large. Thus Lawrence writes that "racist speech. . . distorts the marketplace of ideas by muting or devaluing the speech of Blacks and other despised minorities" (1993, p. 78). He contends that racist speech defames Blacks as a group: it causes a reputational injury to all Blacks, not simply to the immediate targets. Delgado and Stefancic also point to the general social effects of hate speech: "the racist insult remains one of the most pervasive channels through which discriminatory attitudes are imparted" (1997, p. 4).

The harms cited by the advocates of speech codes are real and serious. Undoubtedly, the members of society have a moral obligation to combat those harms. The issue is whether university speech codes are a justifiable way to proceed.

Some critics of speech codes argue that other means of combating the harms of hate speech should be pursued. Such means include 'counterspeech', i.e., speaking out against the bigoted attitudes of hate speakers. Also included are educational programs aimed at promoting equality and highlighting the harm caused by bigotry. Thomas Simon doubts that speech codes or educational programs make any significant impact on racism but suggests that universities can exert some substantial leverage in society's fight for racial equality by "carefully examining their employment practices, investment decisions, and community service" (1994, p. 186).

Advocates of speech codes claim that the remedies suggested by Simon and others should be pursued in addition to speech codes, not in place of them. But that claim is persuasive only if speech codes are a justifiable way to regulate speech. The prima facie plausibility of the claim that the codes seek to suppress the expression of certain viewpoints places a substantial burden of argument on those who contend that they are justifiable. That burden is only increased by the availability of other ways of combating the causal harms of hate speech.

The arguments that we have canvassed thus far have little chance of meeting that burden because they appear to license restrictions on speech that sweep too broadly. The arguments would not only license speech codes banning the use of racial epithets and slurs. Philosophical, literary, religious, and scientific works conveying racist, sexist or heterosexist ideas would be subject to prohibition. As Martin Golding says in his critique of speech codes, racist and anti-Semitic beliefs that are 'sanitized' and presented in the form of scholarly work is potentially more harmful than the slurs and epithets that students may hurl at one another (2000, p. 54). Such sanitized bigotry, e.g., the notorious anti-Semitic tract, "Protocols of the Elders of Zion," has the appearance of a work of scholarship and so may well have a greater psychological and reputational impact on the group it targets than the vulgar racist rant of a student.

Yet, a university is precisely where any work that purports to have objective validity should be available for critical assessment. As Golding has argued, the university is "a form of institutionalized rationality" that subjects knowledge-claims to the test of "critical examination. . . by competent inquirers" (2000, pp. 18, 22). The function of the university requires "communal discussion" and "the organized pursuit of knowledge," and it would be seriously compromised by the prohibition of works that convey bigoted ideas and views (Golding, 2000, pp. 17-18).

Moreover, there is a body of literature that is not the fraudulent work of vicious bigots but is regarded as racist by many and would be subject to prohibition under the arguments of Lawrence and Matsuda. Consider the work on race of the psychologist J. P. Rushton, who summarizes it this way:

> In new studies and reviews of the world literature, I consistently find that East Asians and their descendants average a larger brain size, greater intelligence, more sexual restraint, slower rates of maturation, and greater law abidingness and social organization than do Europeans and their descendants who average higher scores on these dimensions than do Africans and their descendants. I proposed a gene-based evolutionary origin for this pattern. (2000)

Rushton's views have the potential to cause much more reputational damage to Blacks than an undergraduate's drunken utterance of a racial slur. Moreover, regardless of Rushton's intent, it is reasonable to think that his views would reinforce the bigoted attitudes of those inclined to treat Blacks as moral inferiors. And the views would obviously provoke anger among Black students.

Yet, Rushton's work may not be legitimately banned from libraries, classrooms, and other campus forums by a speech code. The institutional rationality of the university demands that the work be available for the critical analysis of scholarly experts and for the study of interested students.

The university's role as a testing ground for claims to knowledge makes it difficult for advocates of speech codes to meet their burden of justification solely by pointing to the harmful causal consequences of hate speech. But this does not necessarily doom all efforts to justify the codes. There is another form of harm associated with hate speech—expressive harm. A justification that takes account of both causal and expressive harm has better prospects for success. Let us turn to some examples to illustrate the existence and nature of expressive harm.

III EXPRESSIVE HARM: PUBLIC ACTORS

In the recent past, there was considerable controversy sparked by southern states that flew the Confederate flag over their capitols. On July 1, 2000, South Carolina became the last state to remove the flag from its site over the seat of the state government. Blacks and many others take the flag to be a symbol of slavery and racism, and they construed the display of the flag to be an expression of racist attitudes. Some southern whites rejected that interpretation and argued that the flag was a legitimate expression of reverence for the valor of their ancestors who suffered and died during the Civil War. But in the wake of protests, state legislators voted to take the flag down.

What was the harm of flying the flag over state capitols? In *NAACP* v. *Hunt* (1990), a federal appeals court rejected the claim that Alabama was violating the Equal Protection Clause of the Fourteenth Amendment by flying the confederate flag over its capitol. The court reasoned that the only harm done by the flying of the flag was the emotional distress of the plaintiffs and that such harm did not amount to a violation of the constitutional principle of equality.

However, the court's reasoning was flawed by its failure to see that there is another form of harm done by the flying of the flag, which did violate the equality principle. The flying of the flag did expressive harm to Blacks: aside from its causal consequences, the act of flying the flag was the expression of a racist attitude hostile, or at least grossly indifferent, to the interests of Blacks (Forman, 1991, p. 508). The official expression of such an attitude constituted a violation of the right to be treated by government with equal respect and consideration.

There are undoubtedly well-meaning individuals who take pride in the display of the Confederate flag. But they fail to realize that the nation is not sufficiently removed from its history of racial oppression for the flag to be a benign cultural symbol. The debilitating effects of past racism still severely hamper the life chances of Blacks, and current racism aggravates the wounds left by this history (Bobo, 1997). The meaning of the flag is still freighted with the history and legacy of racial oppression.

In such a context, flying the flag over the seat of government is, at best, an expression of a callous indifference toward the state's racial minorities and counts as an expressive harm to them. As Anderson and Pildes explain it, "a person suffers expressive harm when she is treated according to principles that express negative or inappropriate attitudes toward her" (2000, p. 1528). And Alabama was treating its Black citizens in exactly that way.

Another example of expressive harm is found in Amar's hypothetical variation of the Hunt case: suppose that Alabama adopted as its official motto the slogan "The White Supremacy State" (1998, 254). It would be strained to argue that non-White plaintiffs seeking a ruling that the state had violated the Equal Protection Clause would need to prove that the adoption of the motto had causal effects harmful to racial equality. Indeed, under certain scenarios, the motto might produce political backlash promoting equality. The fact is that the very adoption of the motto, apart from its causal consequences, is a harm to racial minorities. It is an expressive harm.

IV EXPRESSIVE HARM: PRIVATE ACTORS

In the Confederate flag and state motto cases, public officials were the ones whose actions did expressive harm. Their status as officials made the harms ascribable to the state and so—the circuit court's ruling notwithstanding—a constitutional violation. But the expressive harm they did was independent of their official status. State officials can typically exert much more causal power in the world than private citizens. And what they express through their acts might well have much more widespread causal effects than the expressive activities of a private individual. Those causal effects may result in harms that most private individuals simply do not have the causal capacity to produce, for example, widespread loss of employment opportunities. But the private individual is capable of doing expressive harm. Just as a state official can express callous indifference or hostility to racial minorities, so can a private citizen. And expression of such an attitude can amount to a harm in both sorts of cases.

On the other hand, there is a big difference between the expressive harm to racial equality committed by a state official and the same sort of harm done by a private individual. When the expressive harm is done by the communicative act of a private individual, it is protected by free speech principles. It is unjustifiable for the law to allow state officials to fly the Confederate Flag above their capitols, but the law should protect private individuals who wish to display the flag outside their homes or on their car antennas. Such private actions can express indifference or hostility to racial equality, but it should be not subject to legal sanction.

Private hate speakers thus have a free-speech shield that protects them from liability for the expressive harm they may do, just as that same shield usually protects them from liability for the harmful causal effects of their speech. So it may seem that we have not really advanced the argument for speech codes. Moreover, one can claim that the argument has been made even more difficult by the difference between official and private speech.

When a university punishes a student for a speech code violation, it seems to be committing an expressive harm against him. Aside from any bad causal effects the punishment may have on the student, it is an expression of the emphatic moral condemnation of his social attitudes. And critics of restrictions on hate speech might contend that such condemnation by government violates the rights of hate speakers to equal consideration. Everyone should be permitted to express their views, without discrimination on the basis of what those views are (Dworkin, 1995, pp. 200–1). Accordingly, we appear to have two strong reasons against speech codes. The campus hate speaker may do expressive harm, but that form of harm is no less protected by free speech principles that the causal harm he may do. And the university's punitive response to the hate speaker is a form of official moral condemnation that expressively harms the speaker. The challenge of justifying speech codes depends upon a cogent response to these two reasons. The next two sections seek to develop such a response.

MORAL CONTEMPT

The expressive harm of hate speech plays two related roles in the justification of speech codes. First, it helps explain why certain forms of hate speech should be regarded as "low value" speech in the university context. Second, it serves to distinguish those forms of hate speech that ought to be subject to official restriction from those that ought to be protected against such restriction. Let us begin with a look at how the meaning and use of racial epithets can be understood in terms of the idea of expressive harm.

Racial epithets and similar terms of abuse are communicative tools for expressing an extreme form of moral contempt.[3] Such contempt involves the attitude that the person targeted by the epithet belongs to a group whose members have a lower moral status than those in the group to which the speaker belongs. For those who think in such terms, it is appropriate to express such contempt when members of the morally subordinate groups seek to be treated as equals. The expression of extreme contempt is thought to be fitting because those who are moral inferiors are trying to act as equals: they are impostors who need to be treated as such. Racial epithets and similar terms of abuse are words whose use is to treat someone in a morally degrading way by expressing a certain form of moral contempt toward them. Racist or sexist speech in the form of scientific or philosophical discourse might also convey contempt, but that is not the principal purpose of those forms of discourse. Rather, the vocabulary of such discourse is for formulating and expressing ideas that claim to have objective validity. Any such validity-claim is subject to critical scrutiny and challenge by anyone who can raise such a challenge, even by those persons whom the claim might assert to be moral inferiors to the speaker. "Scientific racism" might explicitly assert that a certain racial group is inherently less intelligent or more prone to crime than other racial groups, but in making such claims it implicitly invites anyone to produce arguments and evidence to refute them.

It is true that the use of epithets can be part of assertions that claim objective validity. Anti-Semites can say "Kikes are all thieves." But hate speech couched in scientific or philosophical discourse does not employ such epithets because the discourse is meant to convey objective claims unadorned by the subjective feelings of the speaker. In contrast, the point of epithets is precisely to express the feelings of the speaker.

The contrast explains why hate speech couched in the discourse of science, philosophy, theology or other scholarly vocabularies should be protected. The claims that such speech makes are subject to the scrutiny, challenge and refutation of those operating within the institutional rationality of the university. As Golding has stressed, that rationality requires protection even for speech that claims or suggests some groups of humans are inherently inferior to others.

In contrast, speech using racist epithets and similarly abusive terms is "low value" speech in the university context because it contributes virtually nothing to the operation of the institutional rationality of the university at the same time that it is used to degrade members of the university community. The exercise of that rationality involves the critical assessment of claims to objective validity. It is difficult to see what role is played in that process by the use of epithets to express contempt for and degrade persons who are members of the university community on the basis of their race, gender, and other categories of social identity.

My argument might be rejected on the basis of the reasoning in the case of *Cohen* v. *California*. Writing for the Court, Justice Harlan said that the words on the jacket Cohen wore into a courthouse, "Fuck the Draft," conveyed a message in which the emotional and cognitive elements were inseparable. Protecting Cohen's message against the Vietnam War draft meant protecting the expletive in terms of which the message was expressed. And the Court held that the message must be protected as the expression of Cohen's political viewpoint.

It may be argued that Harlan's reasoning applies to the use of racist or sexist epithets. Such epithets convey a message in which emotional and cognitive elements are mixed and the message must be protected as the expression of certain viewpoint. However, there is an important difference between campus hate-speech cases and Cohen's case: the campus cases—but not Cohen's—are closely analogous to cases of verbal racial harassment in the workplace. And restrictions on such harassment at work are unobjectionable.

Cohen was not acting in an employment context but rather as a member of the general public,

expressing his views in a building open to the public. And he caused no disturbance in courthouse operations. But imagine that he were an employee at a business with Black employees and that he wore a jacket in the workplace saying "Fuck niggers." Such expression could be justifiably prohibited on grounds of equal employment opportunity.

Campus speech cases are more like such an employment case than they are like the actual Cohen case. Students are not employees. But they do have a defined role within the university, and they should not be materially disadvantaged in their role on account of their race, gender, or sexual orientation. The use of racial epithets and similar terms of abuse in the campus context is reasonably thought to interfere with equal educational opportunity, just as the use of such terms can interfere with equal employment opportunity in the workplace.

It is also true that the principle of equal educational opportunity must be construed in a way that is responsive to the special role of the university in critically examining all ideas claiming objective validity. Hate speech in the mode of scientific or philosophical discourse can cause psychological distress sufficient to interfere with a student's ability to enjoy the opportunities of campus life. But in that case, it is the ideas expressed that are the grounds for the distress. And, unlike other institutions, the role of the university in critically assessing ideas requires that distress caused by the assertion of ideas be excluded as a reason for adopting a speech policy. However, that role does not require the university to ignore the causal effects of racist epithets on the student.

Sadurski has claimed that "insensitivity to many psychic harms is the price of a broadened scope for individual autonomy" (1999, 224). It is also true that a certain degree of such insensitivity is the price of a university's commitment to the free expression and critical testing of ideas claiming objective validity. But the causal harm of racial epithets is not the result of putting forth propositions that claim objective validity. Rather, the causal harm is the product of the extreme moral contempt that the epithets express. Thus, a university speech policy that takes account of the causal harms of such epithets is not subject to the same objection as a policy that takes account of the causal harm of statements that claim objective validity.

VI OFFICIAL CONDEMNATION

Let us now turn to the matter of whether a speech code treats hate speakers with less than equal consideration. After all, such a code makes them liable to punitive measures for the expression of their social and political attitudes, and "the significance of punishment is moral condemnation" (Kahan, 1996, p. 598). There is no circumventing the fact that a speech policy that employs punishment to express such condemnation seeks to suppress speech for the viewpoint it expresses. And in so doing, the policy violates the equal expressive rights of those who hold the disfavored viewpoints.

Any viewpoint-biased speech restriction should be troubling to those who value strong protections for freedom of speech. But it is important to place the speech code debate in its broader social and historical context in order to understand how a limited departure from viewpoint neutrality can be justifiable.

Consider again the Confederate flag dispute. Blacks and many others reasonably took the flag as symbolic of the state's indifference, or even antagonism, to racial equality. Removal of the flag was reasonably construed as an expressive affirmation of that value. The removal was hardly viewpoint-neutral and could not have been in the situation. But the expressive affirmation of racial equality was justifiable, and even mandatory, under the circumstances.

The flag was reasonably construed as standing for a set of values associated with the Confederacy, including white supremacy. In theory, the flag can stand for such virtues as courage and honor without the taint of the white supremacist regime those virtues in fact served. But in contemporary American society the display of the flag cannot be purified of such a taint. There is no way for a state to display the flag over its capitol without it being reasonably interpreted as callous indifference to interests of its black citizens.

Many advocates of speech codes appear to see the code controversy in similar terms: adopting a speech code is a way of symbolically affirming the value of racial equality but not adopting one amounts to the expressive repudiation of that value (Shiffrin, 1999, pp. 78–80). But the analogy is not quite right. The failure to have a code is not analogous to displaying a symbol whose meaning is still inextricably intertwined with racism. For that reason,

it is wrong to think that it is morally, even if not legally, mandatory for any university to have a speech code. But having such a code still may be a justifiable option.

A speech code is an expressive affirmation of racial equality. So are other aspects of university life, such as the observance of the Martin Luther King holiday. Hate speakers may object to the holiday as a departure from viewpoint neutrality and a denigration of their right to equality. They don't get to have an official holiday for their favorite opponent of the civil rights movement. But the nation's commitment to racial equality means that hate speakers and advocates of racial equality simply are not treated in an absolutely evenhanded way, nor should they be. The history of racial injustice is so egregious, and its lingering effects still so troublesome, that some tilt away from strict expressive neutrality and in the direction of racial equality is entirely justifiable. The question is the degree and nature of the tilt.

Critics of speech codes may concede that symbolically affirming racial equality and condemning bigotry through official holidays is fine but then argue that it is an entirely different matter when it comes to using punitive measures for strictly symbolic purposes. But speech codes can be reasonably understood as more than a strictly symbolic gesture. Their condemnation of bigotry sends a strong educational message to the university community and arguably deters forms of verbal degradation that interfere with a student's opportunity to enjoy benefits of campus life.

It may be true that speech codes are not indispensable for providing equal educational opportunity: counterspeech that condemns instances of campus bigotry and other alternatives might work. But it is not unreasonable for a school to judge that a speech code would be of sufficient value to warrant its adoption. The question is how to formulate a code that serves equal opportunity while respecting the centrality of free expression to the role of the university.

VII SPEECH CODES

Some advocates of speech codes defend bans on hate speech that sweep more broadly than the use of epithets (Matsuda, 1993, pp. 44–5; Lawrence, 1993, p. 70). Such broad codes would prohibit hate speech formulated in scientific, philosophical, or theological terms. It should be clear that my analysis rejects codes of that kind as inconsistent with the central place that free speech must play in the life of the university. A speech code must be narrowly drawn in order to be justifiable (Weinstein, 1999, pp. 52, 127; Cohen, 1996, pp. 212–14).

A typical version of a narrow code prohibits hate speech only when (a) it uses racial epithets or analogously abusive terms based on sex, sexual orientation, and similar categories of social identity, (b) the speaker intends to degrade persons through his use of such terms, and (c) the terms are addressed directly to a specific person or small group of persons.

In criticizing narrow speech codes, some legal theorists have suggested that general rules against verbal harassment would be preferable to codes formulated in terms of race, gender, and so on (Golding, 2000, p. 60). Such general rules would not select out particular categories of verbal harassment, but would rather prohibit any verbal abuse that materially interfered with a (reasonable) student's ability to learn and enjoy the other benefits of campus life and that was intended to cause such interference. General harassment rules certainly have much to be said for them as an alternative to narrow speech codes. A student's opportunities to take advantage of the benefits of the university should not be materially interfered with by any form of verbal harassment. And if the speech policy of a university were restricted to racial epithets and the like, then students who were harassed for other reasons, e.g., their political affiliation, could rightly complain that the university was not adequately protecting their interest in equal educational opportunity. Accordingly, it is reasonable to think that general rules against all forms of verbal harassment would be preferable to a speech code limited to categories such as race and gender. Nonetheless, it is possible to give due recognition to the special expressive and causal harm of racial epithets within a set of general rules prohibiting any verbal harassment that interferes with a student's equal educational opportunity.

The capacity of racial epithets to express extreme moral contempt gives them an unusual power to interfere with a student's efforts to take advantage of her educational opportunities. General rules against verbal harassment can be interpreted and applied in a way that takes account of that fact. For instance, the use of anti-Semitic epithets could be judged a violation of the rules even in the case of just a single incident, while other forms of abusive speech, e.g., those targeting a person's political affiliation, would need to involve repeated episodes before they would rise to the level of a violation. Or the use of a racist epithet might be judged a violation when it is reasonably foreseeable that an individual in the targeted group would be exposed to the abusive term, even if the epithet were not specifically directed at her.[4] For other forms of verbal harassment, directly addressing the targeted individual might be required.

The basic standard for a violation would be the same in all cases of verbal harassment: Did the abusive speech materially interfere with a student's opportunity to take advantage of the benefits of campus life?[5] But in the interpretation and application of that standard, the distinctive expressive power of racist epithets and similar terms of abuse would be taken into account.[6]

A campus speech policy that took account of that special expressive power could do a better job of protecting equal opportunity than general rules against verbal harassment that failed to be responsive to expressive harm of hate speech. And the policy could also do a better job than speech codes limited to the prohibition of verbal abuse based on race, gender, sexual orientation, and similar categories of social identity. Taking account of the expressive power of racial epithets and analogous terms of abuse involves some departure from the principle that restrictions on speech should be viewpoint-neutral. But the departure is relatively minor and the value served—equal educational opportunity in our institutions of higher education—is an important one.

REFERENCES

Amar, Akhil (1998). *The Bill of Rights*. New Haven, CT: Yale University Press.

Anderson, Elizabeth and Richard Pildes (2000). "Expressive Theories of Law: A General Restatement," *University of Pennsylvania Law Review* 148: 1503–75.

Bobo, Lawrence (1997). "Laissez-Faire Racism: The Crystallization of a Kinder, Gentler, Antiblack Ideology." In Steven Tuch and Jack Martin (eds.), *Racial Attitudes in the 1990s*. Westport: Praeger.

Cohen v. *California*. 1971. 403 U.S. 15.

Cohen, Joshua (1996). "Freedom of Expression." In David Heyd (ed.), *Toleration*. Princeton, NJ: Princeton University Press, pp. 173–225.

Delgado, Richard and Jean Stefancic (1997). *Must We Defend Nazis?* New York: New York University Press.

Dworkin, Ronald (1995). *Freedom's Lam.* Cambridge, MA: Harvard University Press.

Forman, James (1991). "Driving Dixie Down: Removing the Confederate Flag from Southern State Capitols," *Yale Law Journal* 101: 505–26.

Golding, Martin (2000). *Free Speech on Campus.* Lanham, MD: Rowman and Littlefield.

Kahan, Daniel, (1996) "What Do Alternative Sanctions Mean?" *University of Chicago Law Review* 62: 591–653.

Lawrence, Charles (1993). "If He Hollers Let Him Go: Regulating Racist Speech on Campus." In Mari Masuda et al. (eds.), *Words that Wound.* Boulder, CO: Westview, pp. 53–88.

Matsuda, Mari (1993). "Public Response to Hate Speech: Considering The Victim's Story." In Mari Matsuda et al. (eds.), *Words that Wound.* Boulder, CO: Westview, pp. 17–51.

NAACP v. *Hunt.* 1990. 891 F.2d 1555 (11th Cir).

Pildes, Richard and Richard Niemi (1993). "Expressive Harms, 'Bizarre Districts' and Voting Rights," *Michigan Law Review* 92: 483–587.

Rushton, J. P. (2000). *http://www.sscl.uwo.ca/ psychology/faculty/rushton.html.*

Sadurski, Wojcieck (1999). *Freedom of Expression and Its Limits.* Dordrecht: Kluwer.

Shiell, Timothy (1998). *Campus Hate Speech on Trial.* Lawrence: University Press of Kansas.

Shiffrin, Steven (1999). *Dissent, Injustice, and the Meanings of America.* Princeton NJ: Princeton University Press.

Simon, Thomas (1994) "Fighting Racism: Hate Speech Detours." In M. N. S. Sellers (ed.), *An Ethical Education.* Providence, RI: Berg, pp. 171–86.

Weinstein, James (1999) *Hate Speech, Pornography, and the Radical Attack on Free Speech Doctrine.* Boulder, CO: Westview.

Wisconsin v. *Mitchell.* 1993. 113 S.Ct. 2194.

NOTES

1. In this essay, I use the term 'speech code' to refer to rules that punish individuals for speech that degrades or demeans others on the basis of race or the other listed features.

2. Under US constitutional law, there is an important distinction between state and private universities: the former, but not the latter, are subject to the free speech clause of the Constitution. For this essay, I will assume that most, if not all, private institutions of higher education place a high value on free speech and desire to respect free-speech principles.

3. My analysis of epithets is meant to capture a standard use of such terms. There are other uses.

4. Consider the case from the University of Michigan, cited in section I.

5. There should also be requirements that the speech intentionally interfere with the student's opportunities and that the response of the affected student be reasonable.

6. Delgado and Stefancic (1997) propose general rules against verbal harassment combined with provisions for extra punishment in cases where the harassment is based on race, gender, and the like. They point out that their proposal appears to be consistent with the Supreme Court ruling in *Wisconsin* v. *Mitchell* (1993), which permitted a state to enhance criminal penalties for crimes committed from racially discriminatory motives. It is unclear, though, whether the Court would extend that ruling to cases where the underlying "crime" is a speech offense. My proposal is not that extra punishment be given for hate speech, but rather that the expressive harm of such speech be factored into the question of whether an incident rises to the level of an offense. The two proposals are not incompatible, although I think that, aside from truly egregious cases, a university's punitive response to hate speech episodes should be relatively mild and mainly symbolic.

READING QUESTIONS

1. According to Altman, what is the burden that advocates of speech codes face in trying to defend such codes on the basis of causal harm?

2. According to Altman, what is the expressive harm resulting from hate speech?

3. How does Altman defend the claim that so-called scientific racism should not be banned by hate speech codes?

DISCUSSION QUESTIONS

1. Should we agree with Altman that racial epithets motivated by hate so interfere with educational opportunities of blacks and other targeted groups that speech codes are justified by appeal to considerations of racial equality?
2. How might John Arthur, the author of the preceding article, respond to Altman's claim that speech codes on campus, while not morally mandatory, are justified?

ADDITIONAL RESOURCES

Web Resources

American Civil Liberties Union, <www.aclu.org>. Organization devoted to protecting rights, among them, First Amendment rights to freedom of speech, association and assembly, press, and religion.

Feminists against Censorship (FAC), <http://www.fiawol.demon.co.uk/FAC/facfaq.htm>. Organization established in 1989 to fight censorship.

West, Caroline. "Pornography and Censorship," *The Stanford Encyclopedia of Philosophy,* 2012, Edward N. Zalta (ed.), <http://plato.stanford.edu/entries/pornography-censorship/>. An overview of the topic, including an extensive bibliography.

Authored Books

MacKinnon, Catharine, A. *Just Words* (Cambridge, MA: Harvard University Press, 1996). Feminist legal scholar MacKinnon advocates limiting freedom of speech to exclude hate speech and pornography based on considerations of equality.

Maitra, Ishani and Mary Kate McGowan (eds.), *Speech and Harm: Controversies Over Free Speech* (New York: Oxford University Press, 2012). Eight essays by various authors, drawing from work in philosophy, sociology, legal theory, feminist theory, and political science, discussing the issue of censoring hate speech against the background of modern liberal democracies committed to free speech.

Paul, Pamela, *Pornified: How Pornography Is Damaging Our Lives, Our Relationships and Our Families* (New York: The Holt Company, 2006). As the title indicates, Paul explores the damaging effects of pornography.

Waldron, Jeremy, *The Harm in Hate Speech* (Cambridge, MA: Harvard University Press, 2012). Waldron argues in favor of censoring hate speech, rejecting the view of constitutionalists that it is protected by the First Amendment, maintaining, instead, that such censorship is part of a commitment to human dignity.

Edited Collections

Baird, Robert M. and Stuart E Rosenbaum (eds.), *Pornography: Public Right or Public Menace?* (Amherst, NY: Prometheus Books, 1998). A collection of 25 essays (including an excerpt from the 1997 Supreme Court case: *Reno v. American Civil Liberties Union*), divided into five sections:

(1) The Communications Decency Act, (2) Feminist Perspectives, (3) Libertarian Perspectives, (4) Religious Perspectives, and (5) The Causal Issue.

Cornell, Drucilla (ed.), *Feminism and Pornography* (Oxford: Oxford University Press, 2000). A wide-ranging collection of essays organized into five parts: I, "Anti-Pornography Feminism," II, "Questioning Moralism," III, "An Historical and Cultural Analysis of Sexuality, Imperialism, and Modernity," IV, "Breaking Open the Ground of Sex and Gender," and V, "Erotic Hope, Feminine Sexuality, and the Beginnings of Sexual Freedom."

Dwyer, Susan (ed.), *The Problem of Pornography* (Belmont, CA: Wadsworth, 1995). An anthology of fourteen essays by various authors divided into four parts: (1) Characterizing Pornography, (2) Rights, Equality, and Free Speech, (3) Pornography, Sexuality, and Politics, and (4) Pornography and Speech Acts. Dwyer's introductory essay, legal appendix, and bibliography are very useful.

Herz, Michael and Peter Molnar (eds.), *The Content and Context of Hate Speech: Rethinking Regulation and Responses* (Cambridge: Cambridge University Press, 2012). A collection of twenty-three essays on the topic of hate speech by leading figures in law, philosophy, and social science.

Whisnant, Rebecca and Christine, Stark (eds.), *Not for Sale: Feminists Resisting Prostitution and Pornography* (North Melbourne, Australia: Spinifex Press, 2005). A collection of essays exploring connections among pornography, prostitution, and such evils as racism, poverty, and militarism.

5 } Drugs and Addiction

In 1973 President Richard M. Nixon appointed Myles Ambrose to head up a new federal agency—the Drug Enforcement Administration (DEA)—which announced a war on drugs. How successful this "war" has been in its forty-year history is a matter of dispute. According to various sources, international trade in illegal drugs is a thriving business with yearly profits in the billions. The war on drugs, which most recently has focused on the availability and use of prescription painkillers and heroin, has brought to public attention various moral and legal questions about drug use, among them the following:

- Is it morally permissible to take drugs?
- In those cases (if any) in which taking drugs is morally wrong, what explains its wrongness?
- Is it morally acceptable for a government to pass laws that make the production and consumption of some drugs illegal?

Our questions refer simply to drugs, but there are all sorts of drugs that can be easily obtained over the counter (aspirin, cold medications, and so on) as well as drugs one can legally obtain by prescription. Moral disputes about drugs have pertained only to certain kinds of drugs. So let us begin by clarifying the sorts of drugs that are at issue.

1. DRUGS

Speaking most generally, a **drug** is any chemical substance that affects the functioning of living things (including the organisms that inhabit living things). *Medical uses* of drugs are for the purposes of prevention and treatment of disease, whereas *nonmedical uses* include uses for religious, aesthetic, political, and recreational purposes.[1] What is often called *drug use* refers to the nonmedical use of so-called **psychotropic drugs** that produce changes in mood, feeling, and perception. Psychotropic drugs (at least those that are the subject of moral and legal scrutiny) are often classified into these groups: opiates, hallucinogens, stimulants, cannabis, and depressants. Figure 5.1 is a chart describing each of these types.

In moral and legal discussions of drugs, drug abuse, and drug addiction, the term "drug" is meant to refer to the kinds of psychotropic drugs listed in Figure 5.1.[2] Because there are

OPIATES	Include opium, heroin, and morphine. Opium, obtained from the seedpods of the poppy plant, has as one of its main constituents morphine, from which heroin was developed. These drugs (also referred to as *narcotics*) are highly effective in reducing or eliminating pain and inducing sleep, but they are also highly addictive and strongly associated with drug abuse.
HALLUCINOGENS	Often referred to as "psychedelics" and include: LSD, mescaline (the active ingredient in peyote cactus), and psilocybin and psilocin, which come from Mexican mushrooms. One effect of these drugs (for which they are sought) is their capacity to alter perception by inducing illusions and hallucinations.
STIMULANTS	Include cocaine (derived from coca plants), crack (a concentrated form of cocaine), caffeine, nicotine, amphetamines, methamphetamine, and diet pills. When taken in small doses, these stimulants typically produce a sense of well-being, increased mental alertness, and physical strength, but large doses may produce increased excitement and mental confusion.
CANNABIS DRUGS	Derived from a hemp plant (*Cannabis sativa*), include marijuana, hashish, and other related drugs. The effects of this drug vary in strength depending on the preparation, and compare to those associated with hallucinogens.
DEPRESSANTS	Include sedatives, barbiturates, and alcohol, which produce drowsiness and sedation.

FIGURE 5.1   Types of Psychotropic Drugs.

many types of (psychotropic) drugs, it is important to be aware of their differences, which may be important for sorting out the morality and legality of drug use. Heroin, LSD, and cocaine differ in some ways from one another, and as a group they all differ markedly from nicotine. But like the "harder" drugs, nicotine is addictive. So, if one argues for the legal prohibition of hard drugs based on their alleged addictive powers, what about smoking? Should it be illegal too? Before getting to these questions, let us briefly consider the nature of addiction.

2. ADDICTION

Addiction is most closely associated with drug use, but the term is often used very broadly to refer to a type of compulsive behavior involving dependence on some substance or activity which, for whatever reason, is undesirable. Thus, we hear of sexual addiction and gambling addiction, as well as drug addiction. If we concentrate on drug addiction, it is common to distinguish *physical addiction* from *psychological addiction*. Addiction of both sorts involves a dependence on a drug despite its ill effects on one's health, work, activities, and general well-being. Physical addiction is indicated by physical withdrawal symptoms that occur when an individual ceases to use the drug—symptoms that include body aches, constant movement, and fitful sleeping. Psychological dependence involves a strong desire or perceived need to take the drug for its psychological effects (e.g., a sense of well-being), where withdrawal does not produce the physical effects characteristic of physical dependence. As mentioned earlier, opiates are highly physically addictive, whereas marijuana is psychologically addictive.

What is called **drug abuse** is the excessive nonmedical use of a drug that may cause harm to oneself or to others, including, for instance, abuse of alcohol by drinking too much on some one occasion. Here, we are focused on addiction. There are disputes about the nature of drug addiction. On what Daniel Shapiro calls a "standard view," addiction is caused by the pharmacological effects of the drug—the drug itself is the source of the addiction. On a nonstandard view defended by Shapiro, addiction results from the interplay of the drug, a user's personality, and social circumstances.

The dangers of drug addiction are often cited in disputes over the morality of government interference in the use of drugs for nonmedical reasons. So let us turn to questions about drugs and the law.

3. LIBERTY-LIMITING PRINCIPLES

In discussions of the morality of the legal restriction and prohibition of drugs for nonmedical uses, the same liberty-limiting principles that we discussed in the previous chapter on censorship are relevant here. Here, then, is a brief summary of the previous discussion of these principles. (For more detail, see section 2 of the introduction to pornography, hate speech, and censorship.)

A **liberty-limiting principle** purports to set forth conditions under which a government may be morally justified in passing laws that limit the liberty of its citizens. There are four such principles.

The Harm Principle

According to the **harm principle**, a government may justifiably pass laws that interfere with the liberty of individuals in order to *prohibit individuals from causing harm to other individuals or to society.* The harms in question include both serious physical harms (e.g., maiming, killing, inflicting injury) as well as serious psychological and economic harms.

The Offense Principle

According to the **offense principle**, a government may justifiably pass laws that interfere with individual liberty in order to *prohibit individuals from offending others,* where offensive behavior includes causing others shame, embarrassment, or discomfort. Laws against public nudity are often defended by appealing to this principle.

The Principle of Legal Paternalism

According to the principle of **legal paternalism**, a government is morally justified in passing laws in order to *protect individuals from harming themselves.* Motorcycle helmet laws and seat belt laws are often defended on the basis of this principle.

The Principle of Legal Moralism

The principle of **legal moralism** states that a government may justifiably pass laws that interfere with individual liberty in order to *protect common moral standards, independently of whether the activities in question are harmful to others or to oneself.* This principle is often used in the attempt to justify laws against so-called victimless violations of moral standards—violations that are (arguably) harmful neither to self or others and, because they are not done in public, are not offensive to the viewing public.

There are two points about the use of these principles worth noting. First, in order for a government to appeal to one of these principles in an attempt to morally justify laws that interfere with individual liberty of its citizens, two conditions must be met. First, the principle in question must be a correct liberty-limiting principle—it must correctly state a condition under which a government can (really) morally justify limiting the liberty of its citizens. Second, the activity or practice in question must satisfy the condition set forth in the principle. If, for instance, one appeals to the harm principle to prohibit the production and consumption of a type of drug, then one must show that the use of the drug in question does cause harm to other individuals or to society generally. (Additionally, one must show that the level of harm that would be caused by use of the drug under conditions where it is not prohibited by law would be higher than the level of harm that would result from passing and enforcing laws against its use.)

The second general point is that some of these principles are relatively uncontroversial, but others are not. The harm principle is relatively uncontroversial. And perhaps the same can be said of the offense principle. However, the principles of paternalism and legal moralism are quite controversial, particularly in liberal democratic countries such as the United States. In such countries that strongly value individual liberty of choice, it is widely believed that the proper role of government is limited to preventing harm (and perhaps offense) to others.

4. DRUGS, LIBERTY, AND THE LAW

Here it is important to distinguish the issue of **drug prohibition** versus **legalization** from the issue of **drug criminalization** versus **decriminalization**. Peter de Marneffe, in his selection included in this chapter, defines drug prohibition as referring to legal penalties for the manufacture, sale, and distribution of large quantities of drugs. Drug legalization refers to having no such penalties. By contrast, drug criminalization refers to criminal penalties for using drugs and possessing small quantities of drugs, while drug decriminalization refers to the opposite of criminalization. The importance of distinguishing prohibition from criminalization is that it is possible to defend the former but reject the latter (as we shall see in our readings).

In debates over the legalization and the decriminalization of nonmedical uses of drugs, the principles of harm, paternalism, and legal moralism are all relevant. To appeal to the harm principle requires demonstration of harm to others or to society generally caused by the use of the drug in question. It is widely believed that many of the drugs mentioned earlier are addictive and thereby lead to the commission of crimes that cause harm to others and society.

However, as we shall see when we read the article by Daniel Shapiro, there is disagreement about whether drug use is the cause of crimes that are committed owing to addiction. Furthermore, in order to justify a law by the harm principle, one must show that the level of harm that would likely result from not having a law prohibiting use outweighs the level of harm that would likely result from having a law. Again, those in favor of the legalization of drugs often argue that given the crimes that are committed as a result of a black market in the production, distribution, and sale of drugs, existing drug laws ought to be repealed. David Boaz defends this view in the first selection, while Peter de Marneffe opposes legalization of the sale, manufacture and distribution of drugs, though he also argues that it ought not to be against the law for individuals to use drugs or possess small quantities of drugs.

It is interesting to note that since 2009, public attitudes toward drugs, particularly marijuana, have shifted significantly. In the U.S. November 2016 elections, at least twenty states will have marijuana legalization measures put before voters. According to a Pew Center report from 2014, "67% of Americans say that the government should focus on providing treatment for those who use illegal drugs such as heroin and cocaine, compared to just 26% who think the government's focus should be on prosecuting users of such drugs. More than six-in-ten (63%) now say that states moving away from mandatory prison sentences for non-violent drug offenders is a good thing, versus 32% who think it a bad thing" (http://www.people-press.org/2014/04/02/americas-new-drug-policy-landscape/). This is compared to public opinion in 1990, which found 73 percent of Americans favored a mandatory death penalty for major drug traffickers.

Nicotine is an addictive drug, and so the legality of smoking has recently received some attention from philosophers. In the United States, laws prohibit smoking in certain public places including airports and shopping malls. And some states have laws that prohibit smoking in restaurants. All of these laws can be justified by the harm principle. However, in his article, Robert E. Goodin takes a more radical approach to smoking and the law: he advocates a principle of legal paternalism and explores the implications of this liberty-limiting principle for the activity of smoking.

5. THEORY MEETS PRACTICE

We have already considered arguments regarding the moral permissibility of passing laws that would interfere with an individual's liberty to obtain and use drugs. So let us turn to issues of personal morality and consider the kinds of moral arguments that are grounded in some of the major moral theories.

Consequentialism

For the consequentialist, the morality of an action (or practice) depends on how much overall intrinsic value (or disvalue) it would bring about compared to alternative actions (including the alternative of simply refraining from the action under scrutiny). So this view implies that whether taking a drug is wrong depends on its effects—where we consider the effects both on the individual performing the action and on anyone else affected. Presumably for the consequentialist, the morality of some instance of taking a drug will vary from person to person depending on how much overall value would be brought about.[3] Applying the theory with any degree of accuracy will require some reliable information about one's own personality and circumstances—how taking a drug will likely affect you and others—and so will be no easy task.

Kantian Moral Theory

According to the Humanity formulation of Kant's categorical imperative, an action is morally right if and only if in performing it one does not treat persons merely as means to an end but as ends in themselves. What does this principle imply about the morality of drug use? Again, this will depend on the drug in question as well as the quantity used and the frequency of use. Of course, drug use that harms others constitutes a failure to treat those others as ends in themselves, as would any gratuitous harm. But perhaps the more interesting question from a Kantian perspective is whether drug use represents a violation of one's duty to self. Arguably, if drug use would hinder the development of those important physical, moral, aesthetic, or intellectual capacities that are part of a balanced human existence, then such activities would be wrong—a violation of one's duty to oneself.

Virtue Ethics

Enjoying oneself is certainly part of a flourishing human life, and as long as drug use does not interfere with (or threaten to interfere with) those ingredients of a good life, there is nothing wrong with it and perhaps some reason to use drugs, at least on occasion. If temperance in food and drink and other pleasures is a virtue and intemperance a vice, then the virtuous agent will avoid engaging in any form of drug use that would express intemperance. So if we accept a virtue account of right action according to which an action is morally right or permissible if and only if a virtuous agent (one who has the virtues) may choose to engage in the action, then whether or not the use of some particular drug on some occasion is right will depend on facts about the exercise of temperance by that person on that occasion.

NOTES

1. In 2012 Colorado and Washington became the first U.S. states to legalize the possession and sale of marijuana for recreational use, contrary to federal law. However, in 2009 the government issued new guidelines stating that patients and suppliers in states that legally allow the use of marijuana for medical purposes are not to be prosecuted under federal law for using or supplying this drug. As of 2016, thirty-five states and the District of Columbia permit the use of marijuana for medicinal purposes.

2. There are also moral and legal issues about performance-enhancing drugs (anabolic and androgenetic steroids) as well as inhalants and solvents that are often used for nonmedical purposes.

3. This holds for an *act* consequentialist. A *rule* consequentialist (as explained in chap. 1, sec. 2A) will compare the likely effects of a rule prohibiting the use of certain drugs with the likely effects of not having a prohibitive rule as a basis for arriving at a conclusion about the morality of particular acts of drug use.

DAVID BOAZ

Drug-Free America or Free America?

David Boaz favors the legalization of marijuana, heroin, and cocaine, arguing that individuals have a natural right to live as they choose so long as they do not violate the equal rights of others. Against those who argue that the right to take drugs is justifiably restricted in order to protect society from certain social harms, Boaz argues that drug prohibition has been a failure, creating greater social ills than would result from legalization.
Recommended Reading: rights-based moral theory, chap. 1, sec. 2D.

INTRODUCTION:
THE DRUG PROBLEM

Human beings have used mind-altering substances throughout recorded history. Why? . . . Perhaps because we fail to love one another as we should. Perhaps because of the social pressure for success. Perhaps because—and this is what really irks the prohibitionists—we enjoy drugs' mind-altering effects.

Though the reasons for drug use are numerous, the governmental response has been singular: almost as long as humans have used drugs, governments have tried to stop them. In the sixteenth century the Egyptian government banned coffee. In the seventeenth century the Czar of Russia and the Sultan of the Ottoman Empire executed tobacco smokers. In the eighteenth century England tried to halt gin consumption and China penalized opium sellers with strangulation.

The drug prohibition experiment most familiar to Americans is the prohibition of alcohol in the 1920s. The period has become notorious for the widespread illegal consumption of alcohol and the resultant crime. Movies such as *Some Like It Hot* typify the popular legend of the era. The failure of Prohibition, however, is not just legendary. Consumption of alcohol probably fell slightly at the beginning of Prohibition but then rose steadily throughout the period. Alcohol became more potent, and there were reportedly more illegal speakeasies than there had been legal saloons. More serious for nondrinkers, the per capita murder rate and the assault-by-firearm rate both rose throughout Prohibition.

Most of the same phenomena are occurring with today's prohibition of marijuana, cocaine, and heroin. Use of these drugs has risen and fallen during the seventy-seven years since Congress passed the Harrison Narcotics Act [designed to curb opium trafficking], with little relationship to the level of enforcement. In the past decade, the decade of the "War on Drugs," use of these drugs seems to have declined, but no faster than the decline in the use of the legal drugs, alcohol and tobacco. In the 1980s Americans became more health- and fitness-conscious, and use of all drugs seems to have correspondingly decreased. Drug prohibition, however, has not stopped thirty million people from trying cocaine and sixty million people from trying marijuana. Prohibition also has not stopped the number of heroin users from increasing by one hundred fifty percent and the number of cocaine users from increasing by ten thousand percent.

Moreover, prohibition has not kept drugs out of the hands of children: in 1988 fifty-four percent of high school seniors admitted to having tried illicit drugs; eighty-eight percent said it was fairly easy or very easy to obtain marijuana; and fifty-four percent said the same about cocaine.

Although drug prohibition has not curtailed drug use, it has severely limited some fundamental American liberties. Programs such as "Zero Tolerance," which advocates seizing a car or boat on the mere allegation of a law enforcement official that the vehicle contains drugs, ignore the constitutional principle that a person is innocent until proven guilty.

In attempting to fashion a solution to "the drug problem," one first needs to define the problem society is trying to solve. If the problem is the age-old human instinct to use mind-altering substances, then the solution might be God, or evolution, or stronger families, or Alcoholics Anonymous. History suggests, however, that the solution is unlikely to be found in the halls of Congress. If, on the other hand, the problem is the soaring murder rate, the destruction of inner-city communities, the creation of a criminal subculture, and the fear millions of Americans experience on their own streets, then a solution may well be found in Congress—not in the creation of laws but in their repeal.

This article proposes that the repeal of certain laws will force individuals to take responsibility for their actions; the repeal of other laws will provide individuals the right to make important decisions in their lives free from outside interference. Together these changes will create the society in which drugs can, and must, be legalized. Legalization of drugs, in turn, will end the need for the government to make the intrusions into our fundamental rights as it does so often in its War on Drugs.

THE FUTILITY OF PROHIBITION

A. The War on Drugs

Prohibition of drugs is not the solution to the drug problem. [Since 1981] the United States has waged a "War on Drugs." The goals of this War were simple: prohibit the cultivation or manufacture of drugs, prohibit the import of drugs, and prohibit the use of drugs. As the aforementioned statistics demonstrate, the War has not achieved its goals.

Prohibitionists, however, sometimes claim that the United States has not yet "really fought a drug war." The prohibitionists argue that a "true drug war" would sharply lower drug use. They feel that the government has not fully committed itself to winning this battle. One need only look at the War on Drugs record, however, to see the commitment.

- Congress passed stricter anti-drug laws in 1984, 1986, and 1988. Congress and state legislators steadily increased penalties for drug law violations, mandating jail time even for first offenders, imposing large civil fines, seizing property, denying federal benefits to drug law violators, and evicting tenants from public housing.
- Federal drug war outlays tripled between 1980 and 1988, and the federal government spent more than $20 billion on anti-drug activities during the decade. Adjusted for inflation, the federal government spends ten times as much on drug-law enforcement every year as it spent on Prohibition enforcement throughout the Roaring Twenties.
- Police officers made more than one million drug-law arrests in 1989, more than two-thirds of them for drug possession.
- The number of drug busts tripled during the 1980s, and the number of convictions doubled.
- America's prison population more than doubled between 1981 and 1990, from 344,283 to 755,425. Prisons in thirty-five states and the District of Columbia are under court orders because of overcrowding or poor conditions. An increasing percentage of these prisoners are in jail for nonviolent drug law violations.
- The armed services, Coast Guard, and Civil Air Patrol became more active in the drug fight, providing search and pursuit planes, helicopters, ocean interdiction, and radar. Defense Department spending on the War on Drugs rose from $200 million in 1988 to $800 million in 1990.

- The Central Intelligence Agency (CIA) and National Security Agency began using spy satellites and communications listening technology as part of the drug war. The CIA also designed a special Counter Narcotics Center.
- The federal government forced drug testing upon public employees and required contractors to establish "drug-free" workplaces. Drug testing has also expanded among private companies.
- Seizures of cocaine rose from 2,000 kilograms in 1981 to 57,000 kilograms in 1988.

Despite this enormous effort, drugs are more readily available than ever before. The War on Drugs has failed to achieve its primary goal of diminishing the availability and use of drugs.

B. Prohibition Creates Financial Incentives

One reason for the failure of the War on Drugs is that it ignores the fact that prohibition sets up tremendous financial incentives for drug dealers to supply the demand. Prohibition, at least initially, reduces the supply of the prohibited substance and thus raises the price. In addition, a large risk premium is added onto the price. One has to pay a painter more to paint the Golden Gate Bridge than to paint a house because of the added danger. Similarly, drug dealers demand more money to sell cocaine than to sell alcohol. Those who are willing to accept the risk of arrest or murder will be handsomely—sometimes unbelievably—rewarded.

Drug dealers, therefore, whatever one may think of them morally, are actually profit-seeking entrepreneurs. Drug researcher James Ostrowski points out that "[t]he public has the false impression that drug enforcers are highly innovative, continually devising new schemes to catch drug dealers. Actually, the reverse is true. The dealers, like successful businessmen, are usually one step ahead of the 'competition.'"[1]

New examples of the drug dealers' entrepreneurial skills appear every day. For example, partly because the Supreme Court upheld surveillance flights over private property to look for marijuana fields, marijuana growers have been moving indoors and underground. The Drug Enforcement Administration seized about 130 indoor marijuana gardens in California in 1989; by November the figure for 1990 was 259.

Overseas exporters have also been showing off their entrepreneurial skills. Some have been sending drugs into the United States in the luggage of children traveling alone, on the assumption that authorities will not suspect children and will go easy on them if they are caught. Others have concealed drugs in anchovy cans, bean-sprout washing machines, fuel tanks, and T-shirts. At least one man surgically implanted a pound of cocaine in his thighs. Some smugglers swallow drugs before getting on international flights. Professor Ethan Nadelmann has explained the spread of overseas exporters as the "push-down/pop-up factor": push down drug production in one country, and it will pop up in another.[2] For example, Nadelmann notes that "Colombian marijuana growers rapidly expanded production following successful eradication efforts in Mexico during the mid-1970s. Today, Mexican growers are rapidly taking advantage of recent Colombian government successes in eradicating marijuana."

Prohibition of drugs creates tremendous profit incentives. In turn, the profit incentives induce drug manufacturers and dealers to creatively stay one step ahead of the drug enforcement officials. The profit incentives show the futility of eradication, interdiction, and enforcement and make one question whether prohibition will ever be successful. . . .

INDIVIDUAL RIGHTS

Many of the drug enforcement ideas the prohibitionists suggest trample upon numerous constitutional and natural rights. In any discussion of government policies, it is necessary to examine the effect on natural rights for one simple reason: Individuals have rights that governments may not violate. In the Declaration of Independence, Thomas Jefferson defined these rights as life, liberty, and the pursuit of happiness. I argue that these inviolable rights can actually be classified as one fundamental right: Individuals have the right to live their lives in any way they choose so long as they do not violate the equal rights of others. To put this idea in the drug context, what right could be more basic, more inherent in human nature, than the right to choose what substances to put in one's own body? Whether it is alcohol, tobacco, laetrile, AZT, saturated fat, or cocaine, this is a decision that the individual should make, not the government. This point seems so obvious to me that it is, to borrow Jefferson's words, self-evident.

The prohibitionists, however, fail to recognize this fundamental freedom. They advance several arguments in an effort to rebut the presumption in favor of liberty. First, they argue, drug users are responsible for the violence of the drug trade and the resulting damage to innocent people. The erstwhile Drug Czar, William Bennett, when asked how his nicotine addiction differed from a drug addiction, responded, "I didn't do any drive-by shootings."[3] Similarly former First Lady Nancy Reagan said, "The casual user may think when he takes a line of cocaine or smokes a joint in the privacy of his nice condo, listening to his expensive stereo, that he's somehow not bothering anyone. But there is a trail of death and destruction that leads directly to his door. I'm saying that if you're a casual drug user, you are an accomplice to murder."[4]

The comments of both Mr. Bennett and Mrs. Reagan, however, display a remarkable ignorance about the illegal-drug business. Drug use does not cause violence. Alcohol did not cause the violence of the 1920s, Prohibition did. Similarly drugs do not cause today's soaring murder rates, drug prohibition does. The chain of events is obvious: drug laws reduce the supply and raise the price of drugs. The high price causes addicts to commit crimes to pay for a habit that would be easily affordable if obtaining drugs was legal. The illegality of the business means that business disputes—between customers and suppliers or between rival suppliers—can be settled only through violence, not through the courts. The violence of the business then draws in those who have a propensity—or what economists call a comparative advantage—for violence. When Congress repealed Prohibition, the violence went out of the liquor business. Similarly, when Congress repeals drug prohibition, the heroin and cocaine trade will cease to be

violent. As columnist Stephen Chapman put it, "the real accomplices to murder" are those responsible for the laws that make the drug business violent.[5]

Another prohibitionist argument against the right to take drugs is that drug use affects others, such as automobile accident victims and crack babies. With regard to the former, certainly good reasons exist to strictly penalize driving (as well as flying or operating machinery) while under the influence of drugs. It hardly seems appropriate, however, to penalize those who use drugs safely in an attempt to stop the unsafe usage. As for harm to babies, this is a heart-rending problem (though perhaps not as large a problem as is sometimes believed). Again, however, it seems unnecessary and unfair to ban a recreational drug just because it should not be used during pregnancy. Moreover, drug-affected babies have one point in common with driving under the influence: misuse of legal drugs (alcohol, tobacco, codeine, caffeine) as well as illegal drugs, contribute to both problems. Thus, if society wants to ban cocaine and marijuana because of these drugs' potential for misuse, society should logically also ban alcohol, tobacco, and similar legal drugs.

The question of an individual right to use drugs comes down to this: If the government can tell us what we can put into our own bodies, what can it not tell us? What limits on government action are there? We would do well to remember Jefferson's advice: "Was the government to prescribe to us our medicine and diet, our bodies would be in such keeping as our souls are now."[6]

THE SOLUTION: RE-ESTABLISH INDIVIDUAL RESPONSIBILITY

For the past several decades a flight from individual responsibility has taken place in the United States. Intellectuals, often government funded, have concocted a whole array of explanations as to why nothing that happens to us is our own fault. These intellectuals tell us that the poor are not responsible for their poverty, the fat are not responsible for their overeating, the alcoholic are not responsible for their drinking. Any attempt to suggest that people are sometimes responsible for their own failures is denounced as "blaming the victim."

These nonresponsibility attitudes are particularly common in discussions of alcohol, tobacco, and other drugs. Development of these attitudes probably began in the 1930s with the formulation of the classic disease theory of alcoholism. The disease theory holds that alcoholism is a disease that the alcoholic cannot control. People have found it easy to apply the theory of addiction to tobacco, cocaine, heroin, even marijuana. In each case, according to the theory, people get "hooked" and simply cannot control their use. Author Herbert Fingarette, however, stated that "*no* leading research authorities accept the classic disease concept [for alcoholism]."[7] Many scientists, though, believe it is appropriate to mislead the public about the nature of alcoholism in order to induce what they see as the right behavior with regard to alcohol.

In the popular press the addiction theory has spread rapidly. Popular magazines declare everything from sex to shopping to video games an addiction that the addicted person has no power to control. As William Wilbanks said, the phrase "I can't help myself" has become the all-purpose excuse of our time.[8]

The addiction theory has also gained prominence in discussions of illegal drugs. Both prohibitionists and legalizers tend to be enamored of the classic notion of addiction. Prohibitionists say that because people cannot help themselves with respect to addictive drugs, society must threaten them with criminal sanctions to protect them from their own failings. Legalizers offer instead a "medical model": treat drug use as a disease, not a crime. The legalizers urge that the billions of dollars currently spent on drug enforcement be transferred to treatment programs so that government can supply "treatment on demand" for drug addicts.

Despite the popular affection for the addiction theory, numerous commentators denounce the theory. For example, addiction researcher Stanton Peele deplores the effects of telling people that addictive behavior is uncontrollable:

> [O]ne of the best antidotes to addiction is to teach chil-
> dren responsibility and respect for others and to insist

on ethical standards for everyone—children, adults, addicts. Crosscultural data indicate, for instance, that when an experience is defined as uncontrollable, many people experience such loss of control and use it to justify their transgressions against society. For example, studies find that the "uncontrollable" consequences of alcohol consumption vary from one society to another, depending upon cultural expectations.[9]

. . . The United States requires . . . more reforms—in addition to drug legalization—to create the kind of society in which people accept responsibility for their actions. . . .

Americans might take . . . steps to restore traditional notions of individual responsibility. Laws regarding drugs should only punish persons who violate the rights of others; private actions should go unpunished. Thus, laws should strictly punish those who drive while under the influence of alcohol or other drugs. Intoxication, moreover, should not be a legal defense against charges of theft, violence, or other rights violations, nor should a claim of "shopping addiction" excuse people from having to pay their debts. Physicians, intellectuals, and religious leaders should recognize that the denial of responsibility has gone too far, and they should begin to stress the moral value of individual responsibility, the self-respect such responsibility brings, and the utilitarian benefits of living in a society in which all persons are held responsible for the consequences of their actions.

CONCLUSION

Society cannot really make war on drugs, which are just chemical substances. Society can only wage wars against people, in this case people who use and sell drugs. Before America continues a war that has cost many billions of dollars and many thousands of lives—more than eight thousand lives per year even before the skyrocketing murder rates of the past few years—Americans should be sure that the benefits exceed the costs. Remarkably, all of the high-ranking officers in the Reagan administration's drug war reported in 1988 that they knew of no studies showing that the benefits of prohibition exceeded the costs.

There is a good reason for the lack of such a study. Prohibition is futile. We cannot win the War on Drugs. We cannot even keep drugs out of our prisons. Thus, we could turn the United States into a police state, and we still would not win the War on Drugs. The costs of prohibition, however, are very real: tens of billions of dollars a year, corruption of law enforcement officials, civil liberties abuses, the destruction of inner-city communities, black-market murders, murders incident to street crime by addicts seeking to pay for their habit, and the growing sense that our major cities are places of uncontrollable violence.

Hundreds, perhaps thousands, of years of history teach us that we will never make our society drug-free. In the futile attempt to do so, however, we may well make our society unfree.

NOTES

1. Ostrowski, *Thinking About Drug Legalization*, 121 Pol'y Analysis, May 25, 1989, at 34. . . .

2. Nadelmann, *The Case for Legalization*, 92 Pub. Interest 3, 9 (1988). . . .

3. Isikoff, *Bennett Rebuts Drug Legalization Ideas*, Washington Post, Dec. 12, 1989, at A10, col. 1.

4. Chapman, *Nancy Reagan and the Real Villains in the Drug War*, Chicago Tribune, Mar. 6, 1988, § 4, at 3, col. 1. . . .

5. Chapman, supra note 4.

6. T. Jefferson, *Notes on Virginia*, in The Life and Selected Writings of Thomas Jefferson 187, 275 (1944).

7. H. Fingarette, Heavy Drinking at 3 (1988) (emphasis in original). . . .

8. Wilbanks, *The New Obscenity*, 54 Vital Speeches of the Day 658, 658–59 (1988).

9. See generally S. Peele, *Control Yourself*, Reason, Feb. 1990, at 25.

READING QUESTIONS

1. What reasons does Boaz give for thinking that prohibition of drugs like cocaine and marijuana has restricted liberty?

2. What are the three goals of the war on drugs? How has the government shown its commitment to fighting this war?

3. Why has the war on drugs failed according to Boaz? How, specifically, has the prohibition of certain drugs created financial incentives for dealers of illegal drugs?

4. In what ways does prohibition violate our natural and constitutional rights?

5. Explain Boaz's reasons for saying that drug use does not cause violence in the way suggested by supporters of prohibition and the war on drugs.

6. How does Boaz incorporate the notion of increased responsibility into a possible solution to the problems caused by the sale and use of illegal drugs?

DISCUSSION QUESTIONS

1. Boaz denies the claim that the benefits of the war on drugs has outweighed the costs. Is he right to deny this claim? If so, can you think of any changes to the way the war on drugs is waged that might make it more beneficial?

2. Should drug users be blamed for any of the violence that occurs as a result of their drug use? Try to come up with some examples of cases in which violence is caused by drug users that are either under the influence of a particular drug or otherwise impaired as a result of their involvement with drugs.

PETER DE MARNEFFE

Decriminalize, Don't Legalize

Peter de Marneffe defends the *decriminalization* of drugs but argues that this position is consistent with being against the *legalization* of such drugs. He bases his case for decriminalization largely on an appeal to respect for the autonomy of individuals. He bases his case for the legal prohibition of the manufacture and sale of large quantities of drugs on the claim that legalization would likely dramatically increase the incidence of drug abuse, thus bringing about an increase in harm to drug users and society generally. In defending his view, de Marneffe argues that drug prohibition does not violate individual rights, that it does not represent an unacceptable form of paternalism, and that it does not imply that alcohol, fatty foods, or tobacco ought also to be prohibited.

Recommended Reading: Section 3 of this chapter's introduction to liberty-limiting principles. Also relevant are Kantian moral theory, chap. 1, sec. 2C, and consequentialism, chap. 1, sec. 2A.

Drugs should be decriminalized, but not legalized. There should be no criminal penalties for using drugs or for possessing small quantities for personal use, but there should be criminal penalties for the manufacture and sale of drugs and for the possession of large quantities. Isn't this inconsistent? If it is legal to use drugs, shouldn't it also be legal to make and sell them? Here I explain why not.

First, some terminology. Drug prohibition refers to criminal penalties for the manufacture, sale, and possession of large quantities of drugs. Its opposite is drug legalization. Drug criminalization refers to criminal penalties for using drugs and for possessing small quantities of drugs. Its opposite is drug decriminalization. Here I defend drug prohibition, not drug criminalization.

THE BASIC ARGUMENT

The basic argument for drug prohibition is that if drugs are legalized, there will be more drug abuse.

People use drugs because they enjoy them; they find them fun and relaxing. If it is easier, safer, and less expensive to do something fun and relaxing, more people will do it and do it more often. If drugs are legalized, they will be easier to get, safer to use, and less expensive to buy. They will be easier to get because they will be sold at the local drug or liquor store. They will be safer to use because they will be sold in standard doses and will come with safety precautions. They will be less expensive because the supply will increase and the risk of making, transporting, and selling drugs will decrease. So if drugs are legalized, there will be more drug use and consequently more drug abuse.

Evidence comes from the study of drinking. Alcohol abuse declines with alcohol use, which declines with decreased availability and higher prices (Cook 2007). For example, alcohol abuse declined substantially during the early years of Prohibition, when alcohol became less easily available and more expensive (Miron and Zwiebel 1991). Evidence for this is that during Prohibition deaths from cirrhosis of the liver declined by about 50%, and admissions to state hospitals for alcoholic psychosis declined substantially as well (Warburton 1932). The study of alcohol regulation since Prohibition further supports the conclusion that alcohol abuse declines with an increase in price—resulting from excise taxes, for example—and that alcohol abuse also declines with availability—when, for example, the law restricts the times when alcohol can be legally sold and when it prohibits those under twenty-one from purchasing alcohol (Cook 2007). Another commonly cited piece of evidence that drug use declines with availability is that heroin use was much higher among army personnel in Vietnam where it was easily available than it was among veterans who returned to the U.S., where it was much less available (Robins, Davis, and Goodwin 1974). Another piece of evidence is that the percentage of physicians who use psychoactive drugs is much higher than the general population, which can be attributed to the fact that drugs are more available to doctors (Vaillant, Brighton, and McArthur 1970).

Critics of drug prohibition commonly argue that it does no good because there is still so much drug use even though drugs are illegal. This is a bad argument. It is true there is a lot of drug use in the U.S., but this is no reason to conclude that drug laws do no good or that drugs should be legalized. There is also a lot of theft in the U.S. and it doesn't follow that laws against larceny do no good or that theft should be decriminalized. This is because, although many things are now stolen, it is likely that many more things would be stolen if theft were decriminalized.

In fact almost everyone who studies the question agrees that drug abuse will probably increase if drugs are legalized. Where there is disagreement is on how much it will increase. Those who defend drug legalization believe that although drug abuse will probably increase with legalization, it will not increase by very much, and a moderate increase is justified by the benefits of drug legalization. What are these benefits? If drugs are legalized, the argument goes, there will no longer be a black market for drugs, and so the associated violence and police corruption will cease. There will be fewer drug overdoses because drugs will be safer, because they will be sold in standard, regulated doses. Drugs will also be cheaper, so drug addicts will not need to steal to support their habits. Finally,

if drugs are legalized the government can tax drugs the way it taxes alcohol and tobacco and thereby raise needed revenue. These benefits are so great, the defender of drug legalization maintains, that they justify the cost of a moderate increase in drug abuse that will probably accompany drug legalization.

The defender of drug prohibition has a different view. He believes that if drugs are legalized there will be a dramatic increase in drug abuse. He then argues that the risks of violence to innocent bystanders caused by the illegal drug trade can be reduced to acceptable levels by adequate community policing; that police corruption can be adequately controlled by proper police training, monitoring, and compensation; that there will not be significantly fewer overdoses with legalization because drug abuse will increase dramatically as a result and because heavy drug use is inherently dangerous and often reckless; that although drugs will be cheaper with legalization, there will be more drug addicts as a result, some of whom will stop working to concentrate on drug use, and so who will steal to support their habits; and that the social cost of a dramatic increase in drug abuse is much greater than anything that could be paid for by taxing legalized drugs. The probable costs of legalizing drugs therefore outweigh any probable benefit, the argument for prohibition goes, and the costs of prohibiting drugs can be reduced by wise policies of enforcement, by enough so that drug prohibition can be justified by its benefit in reducing drug abuse.

Who is right? No one is justified in feeling certain, but here I assume that the defenders of prohibition are right, partly because this is what I believe, but mostly because I want to explain how, on this assumption, it makes sense to support drug prohibition and not drug criminalization. Some people think that drug criminalization is wrong because it violates our rights to liberty. From this they naturally conclude that drugs should be legalized. This, however, is a non sequitur, because it makes perfect sense to hold that although drug criminalization violates our rights, drug prohibition does not, as I now explain.

The basic argument for drug prohibition is that drug abuse will increase substantially if drugs are legalized. By *drug abuse* I mean drug use that harms the user or others or that creates a significant risk of harm. The term "drug abuse" is sometimes used more broadly than this, to include the recreational use of any illegal drug. Since the drug is illegal, its use is abuse. This characterization is misleading, however, because recreational drug use, in itself, is not harmful, and does not always create a significant risk of harm. Usually nothing bad occurs when someone smokes marijuana, or snorts cocaine, or ingests a tablet of LSD. Only very rarely is the user harmed by a moderate dose of these drugs, and others are harmed even less often. Heavy drug use, in contrast, can have lasting negative effects on a person's life and on the lives of those who depend on him. If, for example, a young person uses heroin heavily, he is less likely to do his school work and finish high school. If a parent uses heroin heavily, he is more likely to neglect his children, and less likely to take care of his health and to meet other important obligations, such as showing up for work. When a child's parents neglect him due to heavy drug use or when a young person neglects his own education and career, this can have lasting bad consequences on his life. So it makes sense to want there to be less drug abuse of this kind.

It is natural to think that if this argument justifies drug prohibition, it also justifies drug criminalization. After all, if drug use is decriminalized, surely the amount of drug abuse will also increase. Isn't it inconsistent, then, to hold that drugs should be prohibited but not criminalized? No, because there are important differences between prohibition and criminalization.

One important difference is that whereas drug criminalization prohibits individuals from having certain experiences that are enjoyable and illuminating, drug prohibition does not do this. Drug prohibition is similar to alcohol prohibition of the 1920s, which prohibited the manufacture, sale, and transportation of alcohol for commercial purposes, but did not prohibit drinking or the making of alcoholic beverages for personal use. Likewise, drug prohibition prohibits the manufacture, sale and possession of large quantities, but it does not prohibit drug use or making drugs for personal use. Drug criminalization, in contrast, does prohibit this. It thus prohibits people from using their own minds and their own bodies for certain kinds of pleasure and adventure. It prohibits people from regulating their moods in certain ways.

This seems overly intrusive. As adults we are entitled to determine what happens in our minds and to our bodies, unless our decisions pose a serious risk of harm to others or to ourselves. Because drug use in itself does not pose a serious risk of harm to anyone, respect for persons, as independent beings who are properly sovereign over their own minds and bodies, seems incompatible with drug criminalization.

Drug prohibition, in contrast, is compatible with respect for persons. Drug prohibition makes it illegal to operate a certain kind of business; but it does not prohibit anyone from experimenting with drugs or from regulating their moods in the ways that illegal drugs provide. It does not deprive anyone of control over their own minds and bodies. Where will people get drugs if others are not permitted to manufacture and sell them? In some cases they can safely make them on their own. In other cases they can receive them as a gift from friends who are good at chemistry, and, of course, people can still buy drugs illegally even if they are prohibited. What's the point of drug prohibition if people still buy drugs anyway? Well, what's the point of murder laws if people are still murdered? Presumably murder laws reduce the number of murders by enough to justify the costs of enforcement and the risks of wrongful conviction. If drug prohibition significantly reduces the amount of drugs that are made and sold and thereby reduces drug abuse, it can likewise be justified as *reducing* drug abuse even if it does not *eliminate* it.

To the self-sovereignty argument against criminalization, we should add that adults have important interests in the freedom necessary to lead a life that seems worthwhile to them, a life that makes sense to them as the right sort of life for them to lead, provided that in doing so they do not seriously harm others or themselves or pose a serious risk of harm. Each of us has one earthly life to lead, and it is important that we determine how we lead this life, what experiences we have, what goals we pursue, what kinds of relationships we have, and what kinds of people we become. For some, drug use is an important part of the kind of life that makes most sense to them. This is true not only of those who use drugs in religious ceremonies. It is also true of those who orient their lives around certain kinds of social and aesthetic experiences. "Dead heads" used to orient their lives around attending Grateful Dead concerts, smoking marijuana, and sharing this experience with others. Assuming the use of marijuana does not pose a serious risk of harm to the user or others, the fact that marijuana played a central role in this kind of life is a strong argument against criminalizing its use.

It is not, however, a strong argument for *legalizing* marijuana. After all, a person who wants to orient his life in this way can do this perfectly well even if it is illegal to manufacture and sell marijuana for profit. He can grow his own or share with friends. No doubt some will want to live the life of a drug dealer; this is the kind of life they want to lead. What is distinctive, however, about the life of a drug dealer is a function of its illegality. Hence this career aspiration does not provide a compelling argument for legalization. If anything, it is a reason to prohibit drugs, because if drugs are legalized, those who value dealing drugs as part of an outlaw lifestyle will no longer have the opportunity to lead an outlaw life in this way. Nor is the loss of the opportunity to sell drugs legally a serious loss, because under drug prohibition similar job opportunities will continue to exist, such as the opportunity to legally sell pharmaceuticals and alcoholic beverages. (If you are tempted to argue that the opportunity to sell alcoholic beverages and pharmaceuticals is not in fact available to most of those who sell drugs now, you should understand that this counts in favor of drug prohibition, not legalization, since only prohibition offers this kind of business opportunity to those who otherwise have little chance of entering the corporate world.)

Drug criminalization threatens personal autonomy in a way that drug prohibition does not. This is the main point so far. The claim, however, that drug criminalization threatens autonomy might be jarring. Aren't some drugs highly addictive, and isn't drug addiction inconsistent with autonomy? Doesn't concern for autonomy therefore warrant the criminalization of drugs? No. For one thing, laws that criminalize drugs deprive people of the legal discretion to use drugs, whether for good reasons or bad, and so deprive them of a kind of personal authority, which is a form of personal autonomy. For another, only a small proportion of those who use drugs are addicts.

This is true even of those who use heroin, cocaine, and methamphetamine (Goode 1999). For this reason, respect for the autonomy of the vast majority of drug users provides a strong reason against criminalization. Furthermore, the claim that drug addiction is incompatible with autonomy is based on a misunderstanding of what addiction is. In the imagination of some philosophers, an addict is like a zombie who has lost the capacity to choose or to act in accordance with his own judgment of what is best. This is not an accurate picture of any real drug addict. We call people drug addicts for one or more of the following reasons. (1) They use a drug to relieve a craving. (2) They use a drug even though they obviously shouldn't, because of the harm their drug use is likely to do them or others. (3) Although they believe they should use this drug at the moment they choose to use it, at other times when their judgment is more reliable and less distorted by temptation, they sincerely believe they should not use this drug any more. Even when all these things are true of a person, it is an error to characterize him as a zombie who has lost his power of choice. The addict is still someone who chooses, and chooses on the basis of his own judgment of what is best, just like the rest of us. If the drug addict were someone whose real self has decided not to use drugs, but who is then attacked by an alien desire that takes over his body and forces him to use drugs against his will, and if a person is less likely to be attacked in this way if drugs are criminalized, there might be a sense in which drug criminalization promotes the autonomy of addicts. But drug addiction is nothing like this. The addict's desire to use drugs is just as much a part of his real self as any desire he might have to stop. It's not an alien desire that forces him to do something against his will. It arises from his own sincere belief that the pleasure or relief of using this drug is a good reason to use it. So it is a mistake to suppose that drug use, even heavy drug use, is not autonomous.

Autonomy means different things and one thing it means is independence. In this sense a person might be less autonomous due to drug abuse. If a person drops out of high school due to drug abuse, he may be less intellectually and emotionally mature as a result and less capable of supporting himself. A person who abuses drugs may also be less capable of holding a job. So a person who abuses drugs may be less intellectually, emotionally, and financially independent as a result. If drug laws reduce this kind of drug abuse, there is therefore a sense in which they promote autonomy. This is not because drug abuse itself is not autonomous or because addicts are zombies who have lost the capacity for choice. It is because drug abuse is often infantilizing.

In evaluating drug laws, we must therefore consider whether the way in which they promote autonomy justifies the way in which they limit it. Because most drug users are not addicts and because even addicts use drugs as a matter of choice, respect for autonomy seems incompatible with a blanket prohibition of drug use. But drug prohibition does not threaten personal autonomy in the same way. To this we should add that those at risk of being harmed by drug abuse have a stronger complaint against those who manufacture and sell drugs than they do against those who use them privately or make them for their own use. When a person grows marijuana and smokes it by himself or with friends, he does little to significantly increase anyone else's risk of harm. In contrast, when a businessman sets up a lab to make heroin and then distributes this product to retailers who sell it to any willing buyer, this businessman increases others' risk of harm significantly. Others therefore have a stronger complaint against his activities. Because those at risk of harm from drug abuse have a stronger complaint against drug manufacturers and dealers than they have against private users, and because there are weighty reasons of personal autonomy against drug criminalization, but not against drug prohibition, it makes sense to make a distinction between these policies, and *to* support one and not the other.

DOES DRUG PROHIBITION VIOLATE INDIVIDUAL RIGHTS?

Even so, prohibition might violate our rights. I have suggested that if the benefits of prohibition outweigh the costs, then this policy is justifiable. But a policy can violate a person's rights even if its aggregated benefits outweigh its aggregated costs. "Each person," writes John Rawls, "possesses an inviolability founded on justice that even the welfare of society as a whole cannot override" (Rawls 1971, 3). Utilitarianism, which Rawls rejects, directs the government to adopt whatever policies will result in the most happiness, summed over individuals, and this principle may warrant policies that violate our moral rights. Because it is wrong for a government to sacrifice the individual in this way, a defender of drug prohibition must therefore explain why this policy violates no one's rights.

Part of the explanation has already been given: unlike drug criminalization, drug prohibition does not pose a serious threat to personal autonomy. Recognizing the value of autonomy, however, is not all there is to taking rights seriously. Taking rights seriously also involves commitment to *individualism*, according to which we may not evaluate government policies solely by subtracting aggregated costs from aggregated benefits, but must also make one-to-one comparisons of the burdens that individuals bear under these policies. In this way we take seriously the separateness of persons. It is possible, although unlikely, that a system of slavery could be justified by utilitarian reasoning, because, although a few are harmed by this system, so many benefit from it. To understand what would be wrong with this, we must make one-to-one comparisons and recognize that the worst burden imposed on the individual slave is substantially worse than the worst burden anyone would bear if this system were rejected or abolished.

Sometimes, however, it is permissible for the government to limit the liberty of the few for the benefit of the many. It is permissible, for example, for the government to imprison some people to protect society as a whole. To apply individualism to the assessment of government policies, we must therefore find a way of evaluating whether a government policy objectionably sacrifices an individual for the benefit of society. I offer the following hypothesis: the government *objectionably* sacrifices a person in limiting her liberty if and only if it violates the *burdens principle*. This principle is that the government may not limit a person's liberty in ways that impose a burden on her that is substantially worse than the worst burden anyone would bear in the absence of this policy. When the government violates this principle in adopting policies for the good of society, it objectionably sacrifices someone for the benefit of society; it fails to respect her inviolability; it violates her rights. To illustrate, even if a system of slavery maximizes economic productivity, it imposes a burden on the individual slave that is substantially worse than the worst burden anyone would bear if the government were not to maintain this system. So the government violates the burdens principle in maintaining this system, and consequently violates the rights of those enslaved.

Does the burdens principle prove too much? Consider the following objection. Surely it is worse to be in jail than to have something stolen from a store one owns, works at, or shops at. Don't laws prohibiting shoplifting therefore violate the burdens principle? Doesn't this show that this principle is invalid? This challenge can be addressed once we understand how burdens are to be compared. The relative weight of burdens is to be assessed by the relative weight of reasons that individuals have to want or want not to be in the relevant situations. The reasons there are for us to want to be free to take whatever we want from a store without paying are not very weighty. Consequently, our reasons are not very weighty to want to avoid a situation in which we must either pay for what we take or risk criminal penalties. On the other hand, there are good reasons for each of us to want the government to enforce a rule prohibiting shoplifting, grounded partly in the fact that without this policy the availability of retail goods will decline sharply over time. A law that prohibits shoplifting therefore does not violate the burdens principle, provided this law is administered fairly, harsh penalties are avoided, and necessity is accepted as an excuse.

I now assume that the burdens principle provides the correct basis for assessing whether the government in limiting a person's liberty objectionably sacrifices her for the benefit of society as a whole. If so, a defender of drug prohibition should be able to explain why this policy does not violate this principle. Suppose, then, that if drugs are legalized, drug abuse by young people and parents will increase

dramatically. Suppose, too, that drug abuse by young people commonly damages their future prospects, because it results in a failure to perform important tasks, such as finishing school, and to develop important habits, such as being a reliable employee, and that these failures early on have a lasting negative impact on a person's life. Suppose, too, that drug abuse by parents commonly damages the future prospects of their children because it results in serious forms of child neglect. On these assumptions, there are good reasons for some people to prefer their situations when drugs are less easily available. Some people will therefore bear a significant burden as a result of drug legalization: those who will be at a substantially higher risk of harm from drug abuse if drugs are legalized. These burdens appear to be at least as great as the burden that drug prohibition imposes on businessmen in prohibiting them from manufacturing and selling drugs. The burden on businessmen is equivalent to the choice of not going into the drug business or risking legal penalties. This is not a heavy burden because there are alternative business opportunities under drug prohibition that are similar to those that would exist in the drug trade if drugs were legalized. Hence drug prohibition does not objectionably sacrifice the liberty of businessmen for the benefit of society as a whole, and so does not violate their rights.

If the burdens principle is valid as a constraint on government policies that limit individual liberty, then someone who defends drug prohibition but not drug criminalization must defend one of the following positions: (1) Although drug criminalization violates the burdens principle, drug prohibition does not. (2) Although neither drug criminalization nor drug prohibition violates the burdens principle, drug prohibition can be justified by a cost–benefit analysis whereas drug criminalization cannot. Note here that although the burdens principle imposes an individualistic constraint on the justification of liberty-limiting government policies, it allows a policy to be justified by a cost–benefit analysis provided that this policy does not violate the burdens principle. If the worst burden that a policy imposes on someone is not substantially worse than the worst burden someone would bear in the absence of this policy, then this policy does not violate the burdens principle, and it can be justified provided that its benefits outweigh its costs, however this is properly determined.

Given the important differences between drug criminalization and drug prohibition identified above, it makes sense to argue that whereas drug criminalization violates the burdens principle, drug prohibition does not. But even if drug criminalization does not violate the burdens principle, it makes sense to defend drug prohibition and not drug criminalization. Suppose for the sake of argument that the burden that drug criminalization imposes on drug users, although significant, is not substantially worse than the worst burden someone would bear as the result of drug decriminalization. Perhaps some young people will be at a significantly higher risk of self-destructive drug abuse or drug-induced parental neglect if drugs are decriminalized than they are when drugs are criminalized. Perhaps this burden is comparable to the burden that drug users bear when drugs are criminalized. (Bear in mind that drug criminalization might be justified even if harsh penalties for drug possession are not.) It is still arguable that whereas the costs of criminalization outweigh the benefits, this is not true of drug prohibition. Perhaps the aggregate costs in restricting personal autonomy and in prohibiting a form of adventure and mood control outweigh the aggregate costs of increased risk of drug abuse that would result from decriminalization, even though the aggregated costs of increased drug abuse that would result from drug legalization outweigh its aggregated costs.

COMMON OBJECTIONS

1. Paternalism

Sometimes the government violates a person's rights even when it does not sacrifice him for the benefit of society as a whole. Sometimes it violates a person's rights when it limits his liberty for his own benefit. A common objection to drug laws is that they are paternalistic: they limit people's liberty for their own good.

Because drug prohibition does not prohibit anyone from buying drugs for personal use, it does not limit the liberty of drug users in this way for their own good. Assuming, though, that this policy is effective, it does limit a drug user's opportunity to buy drugs. So if this policy is justified by the assumption that it is bad for some people to have these opportunities, there is arguably a sense in which this policy is paternalistic.

This kind of paternalism, however, is not the kind that defenders of individual liberty have found most objectionable. The most objectionable forms of paternalism are those that satisfy the following description: the policy prohibits a mature adult from doing what he sincerely and consistently believes it is best for him to do; this person is mentally competent and adequately informed about the possible negative consequences; this policy limits an important liberty of this person, such as religious or sexual freedom; this policy limits this liberty by imposing criminal penalties; this policy cannot be justified except as benefitting this person, by deterring him from doing something presumed by others to be unwise. Policies that satisfy this description seem to involve an unjustifiable restriction of personal autonomy. Drug prohibition, however, does not satisfy this description. For one thing, drug prohibition limits the liberty of businessmen for the benefit of others—those who would otherwise be at a higher risk of being harmed by drug abuse. It does not limit the liberty of businessmen for *their* own good. Furthermore, the primary intended beneficiaries of drug prohibition are young people—those who would otherwise be at a higher risk of self-destructive drug abuse and parental neglect—and not mature adults who enjoy using drugs and so would like to have a legal supply. Moreover, drug prohibition does not prohibit anyone from using drugs. So even granting, what might be questioned, that the freedom to use drugs is an important liberty, like religious and sexual freedom, drug prohibition does not restrict this liberty, since it does not prohibit anyone from using drugs. Finally, drug prohibition does not impose criminal penalties on anyone for drug use. One can therefore agree that any policy that satisfies the above description is objectionably paternalistic, and yet consistently defend drug prohibition, since this policy does not involve this kind of paternalism.

2. Prohibition and Harsh Penalties

Another common objection to drug laws is that it is terrible that so many people are in prison on drug offenses. This is terrible. It is important, however, to distinguish the question of drug prohibition from the question of penalties. It is possible that, although some drugs should be prohibited, our current penalties for drug dealing are too harsh. A defender of prohibition can hold that although there should be penalties of some sort for the manufacture and sale of drugs, the penalties for first offenses should be mild, and should increase only gradually, with stiffer penalties only for repeat offenses. Moreover, a defender of drug prohibition can consistently oppose any penalties for simple drug possession, which are the penalties most strongly protested by critics of U.S. drug laws. Observe, too, that someone who opposes the legalization of all drugs might nonetheless support the legalization of some. For example, someone who supports the prohibition of heroin, cocaine, and methamphetamine might nonetheless consistently support the legalization of marijuana and some hallucinogenic drugs, such as LSD, mescaline, peyote, and MDMA (Ecstasy). This makes sense because some drugs are more harmful than others.

3. Alcohol Prohibition?

Another common objection to drug laws is that it makes no sense to defend drug prohibition and not alcohol prohibition. After all, alcohol abuse is much more harmful than drug abuse, much more highly associated with violence, property crime, accidental injury and death. So if the government is justified in prohibiting drugs, it must also be justified in prohibiting the manufacture and sale of alcohol. Assuming that alcohol prohibition is unjustifiable, drug prohibition must be unjustifiable too.

One possible response is to hold, contrary to popular belief, that alcohol prohibition is justifiable.

In fact, general opposition to alcohol prohibition is based on false beliefs about its effects, such as that it does nothing to reduce alcohol abuse and that it necessarily results in a huge increase in crime and corruption (Moore 1989). But it is not necessary to endorse alcohol prohibition in order to defend drug prohibition. One can argue instead that, although drinking is more harmful than drug use, the costs of now instituting alcohol prohibition would outweigh the benefits, whereas this is not true of continuing the policy of drug prohibition. A policy that reduces the availability of a socially stigmatized drug is likely to do more to reduce its abuse than a policy that reduces the availability of a socially accepted drug. Drinking is socially accepted and fully integrated into normal social life. This is not true of heroin, cocaine, and methamphetamine, which are widely regarded as evil. For this reason drug prohibition might be much more effective at reducing drug abuse than alcohol prohibition would now be at reducing alcohol abuse. It is also true that if alcohol prohibition is adopted now, many people who have built their livelihood around manufacturing, selling, and serving alcohol would be adversely affected. These are people who made certain decisions, for example, to open a restaurant, based on the assumption that it will be legal to sell alcohol. This is not true of continuing the policy of drug prohibition. Taking these and other considerations into account, it is arguable that whereas the benefits of continuing drug prohibition outweigh the costs, the costs of now instituting alcohol prohibition outweigh the benefits, even though alcohol abuse is generally more destructive than the abuse of other drugs.

4. Fatty Foods and Tobacco Prohibition?

A related objection is that the consumption of other goods is at least as harmful as drug use and we do not think that these other goods should be prohibited. For example, obesity and smoking cause far more deaths than drug use does, and we don't think that the manufacture and sale of fatty foods or cigarettes should be prohibited. Isn't this inconsistent? No, because one can reasonably argue that whereas the benefits of continuing to prohibit the manufacture and sale of drugs outweigh the costs, this is not true of now prohibiting these other products. Food production and the food service industry is a large sector of our economy, and the production, sale, and preparation of fatty foods is a large part of this sector. If the government were now to prohibit the manufacture and sale of all fatty foods this would have a huge negative impact on our economy, our way of life, and our habits of socializing. The same cannot be said for continuing (and properly modifying) drug prohibition. Tobacco prohibition is a harder case, but even here there are important differences between the case for drug prohibition and for laws prohibiting the manufacture and sale of cigarettes. A central concern in defending drug laws is the damage that drug abuse does to young people in limiting their future prospects, by causing the loss of important opportunities that will be difficult to recover. If a young person neglects his schoolwork and employment as a result of drug abuse, this is likely to have a lasting negative impact on his life. If a child is neglected by her parents due to drug abuse, this will increase her risk of serious injury and may have a lasting negative impact on her emotional and intellectual development. The availability of cigarettes does not have this same kind of negative impact. When a young person smokes, she increases her risk of certain serious diseases as an adult. Smoking, however, does not interfere with a person's intellectual and emotional development in the way that drug abuse and parental neglect do. Furthermore, the risks created by smoking as teenager can be effectively reduced later in life, by quitting as an adult. A similar point may be made about obesity. Finally, although cigarette smoking and obesity may be more likely to shorten a person's life, the kind of drug abuse that results in parental neglect or dropping out of school may have a greater negative impact on the overall quality of a person's life. The risk to a young person of being in an environment where drugs are easily available is thus different, and in some ways significantly worse, than being in an environment where cigarettes or fatty foods are easily available. Consequently there is no inconsistency in accepting this argument for drug prohibition and rejecting corresponding arguments for prohibiting cigarettes and fatty foods.

CONCLUSION

To conclude, support for drug prohibition is consistent with opposing drug criminalization; it is consistent with respect for personal autonomy; it is consistent with the principle that each person possesses an inviolability founded on justice that even the welfare of society as a whole cannot override; it is consistent with opposing the kind of paternalism that defenders of individual liberty have found most appalling; it is consistent with not supporting alcohol prohibition; it is consistent with not supporting cigarette and fatty food prohibition.

It remains an open question whether the benefits of drug prohibition really justify its costs. One cost I haven't considered is the negative impact that drug prohibition has on the political cultures of drug producing countries, such as Mexico, Colombia and Afghanistan. Because drugs are illegal in Europe and North America, drug wholesalers in drug producing countries can make huge profits by selling drugs to drug retailers in rich countries, which the drug wholesalers then use to bribe and intimidate local police, judges, and politicians, fostering government corruption. It is also true that because drugs are illegal in these countries those in the drug trade must settle their disputes with violence and intimidation, and that innocent bystanders in these countries are sometimes harmed as a result. So it is arguable that drug prohibition harms the citizens of drug producing countries too much to be justified by the goal of reducing drug abuse in rich countries, even granting that drug abuse in rich countries would soar if drugs were legalized there.

This is a serious objection. Whether it is decisive depends on how much less corrupt the governments of drug producing nations would be and how much safer their citizens would be without drug prohibition. It depends, too, on how much drug abuse would increase in drug producing countries if drugs were legalized there. One of the most serious worries about legalizing drugs is the expected increase in drug abuse by relatively disadvantaged youth who already lack good educational and employment opportunities, and the expected increase in drug abuse by their parents. If there is reason to worry about the impact of drug legalization on the disadvantaged youth of rich countries, there is also reason to worry about the impact of drug legalization on the disadvantaged youth of drug producing nations, which are relatively poorer. When we consider the negative impact of drug prohibition on these countries, we must therefore also consider the likely negative impact of drug legalization. If drug abuse among young people and their parents in drug producing countries would increase dramatically with drug legalization, and if drug prohibition is not the primary cause of government corruption in these countries, and is not a major cause of violence to innocent bystanders, then it makes sense to believe that the overall benefits of drug prohibition to everyone outweigh the costs, and so to oppose drug legalization on this ground.

REFERENCES

Cook, Philip J. *Paying the Tab*. (Princeton, NJ: Princeton University Press, 2007).

Goode, Erich. *Drugs in American Society*, 5th ed. (New York: McGraw–Hill, 1999).

Miron, Jeffrey A. and Jeffrey Zwicbel. "Alcohol Consumption During Prohibition." *American Economic Review* 81 (1991): 242–47.

Moore, Mark. "Actually, Prohibition Was a Success." *New York Times*, October 16 (1989): A21.

Rawls, John. *A Theory of Justice*. (Cambridge, MA: Harvard University Press, 1971).

Robins, Lee N., Darlene H. Davis, and Donald Goodwin. "Drug Use by U.S. Army Enlisted Men in Vietnam: A Follow-Up on Their Return Home." *American Journal of Epidemiology* 99 (1974): 235–49.

Vaillant, George E., Jane R. Brighton, and Charles McArthur. "Physicians' Use of Mood-Altering Drugs." *The New England Journal of Medicine* 282 (1970): 365–70.

Warburton, Clark. *The Economic Results of Prohibition.* (New York: Columbia University Press, 1932).

READING QUESTIONS

1. According to de Marneffe, drug criminalization is incompatible with personal autonomy, but drug prohibition is not. How does de Marneffe argue for these claims?
2. In discussing drug prohibition and individual rights, de Marneffe invokes what he calls the "burdens principle." What is this principle and how does de Marneffe use it in defending his claim that drug prohibition is consistent with respecting individual rights?
3. What reasons does de Marneffe give for claiming that his position on drug prohibition does not automatically imply that prohibitions on alcohol, fatty foods and tobacco would be justified?

DISCUSSION QUESTIONS

1. Do you agree with de Marneffe that the legalization of drugs will result in a dramatic increase in serious and harmful drug abuse? Why or why not?
2. In the concluding section of his article, de Marneffe raises a potential objection to his view on drug prohibition, namely, that the benefits of prohibition are outweighed by the costs. What costs does de Marneffe mention? Do you think the costs in question are enough to outweigh the benefits of prohibition? (In thinking about this question, readers are advised to consult Web resources to gather information about drug-related violence and drug abuse.)

ROBERT E. GOODIN

Permissible Paternalism:
Saving Smokers from Themselves

Contrary to the widely shared assumption that legal paternalism is at odds with the proper practices of liberal democracies, Robert E. Goodin argues that some forms of control and interference may be morally justified on paternalist grounds. In defending legal paternalism, Goodin focuses on smoking, arguing that there may be good reasons, consistent with liberal democracy, for public officials to pass laws that would interfere with this activity. Goodin does recognize a presumption against paternalistic interference by government, and claims that public officials should refrain from paternalistic intervention in the lives of its citizens regarding any type of activity when they are convinced that persons engaging in that activity are acting on preferences that are *relevant, settled, preferred*, and perhaps *their own*. Using the case of Rose Cipollone (a smoker who successfully won a court case against a tobacco company) as an example, Goodin explains how the "manifest preferences" of smokers are often not relevant, not settled, not preferred, and not their own. Goodin concludes by considering the kinds of governmental regulation of smoking that might be paternalistically justified.

Recommended Reading: Section 3 of this chapter's introduction to liberty-limiting principles. Also relevant, chap. 1, sec. 2D, on rights.

Paternalism is desperately out of fashion. Nowadays notions of "children's rights" severely limit what even parents may do to their own offspring, in their children's interests but against their will. What public officials may properly do to adult citizens, in their interests but against their will, is presumably even more tightly circumscribed. So the project I have set for myself—carving out a substantial sphere of morally permissible paternalism—might seem simply preposterous in present political and philosophical circumstances.

Here I shall say no more about the paternalism of parents toward their own children. My focus will instead be upon ways in which certain public policies designed to promote people's interests might be morally justifiable even if those people were themselves opposed to such policies.

Neither shall I say much more about notions of rights. But in focusing upon people's interests rather than their rights, I shall arguably be sticking closely to the sorts of concerns that motivate rights theorists. Of course, what it is to have a right is itself philosophically disputed; and on at least one account (the so-called "interest theory") to have a right is nothing more than to have a legally protected interest. But on the rival account (the so-called "choice theory") the whole point of rights is to have a legally protected choice. There, the point of having a right is that your choice in the matter will be respected, even if that choice actually runs contrary to your own best interests.

From Robert E. Goodin, "Permissible Paternalism: Saving Smokers from Themselves," in William H. Shaw, ed., *Social and Personal Ethics*, 3rd edition, Wadsworth, 1999. Reprinted by permission of the author.

It is that understanding of rights which leads us to suppose that paternalism and rights are necessarily at odds, and there are strict limits in the extent to which we might reconcile the two positions. Still, there is some substantial scope for compromise between the two positions.

Those theorists who see rights as protecting people's choices rather than promoting their interests would be most at odds with paternalists who were proposing to impose upon people what is judged to be *objectively* good for them. That is to say, they would be most at odds if paternalists were proposing to impose upon people outcomes which are judged to be good for those people, whether or not there were any grounds for that conclusion in those people's own subjective judgments of their own good.

Rights theorists and paternalists would still be at odds, but less at odds, if paternalists refrained from talking about interests in so starkly objective a way. Then, just as rights command respect for people's choices, so too would paternalists be insisting that we respect choices that people themselves have or would have made. The two are not quite the same, to be sure, but they are much more nearly the same than the ordinary contrast between paternalists and rights theorists would seem to suggest.

That is precisely the sort of conciliatory gesture that I shall here be proposing. In paternalistically justifying some course of action on the grounds that it is in someone's interests, I shall always be searching for some warrant in that person's own value judgments for saying that it is in that person's interests.

"Some warrant" is a loose constraint, to be sure. Occasionally will we find genuine cases of what philosophers call "weakness of will": people being possessed of a powerful, conscious present desire to do something that they nonetheless just cannot bring themselves to do. Then public policy forcing them to realize their own desire, though arguably paternalistic, is transparently justifiable even in terms of people's own subjective values. More often, though, the subjective value to which we are appealing is one which is present only in an inchoate form, or will only arise later, or can be appreciated only in retrospect.

Paternalism is clearly paternalistic in imposing those more weakly-held subjective values upon people in preference to their more strongly held ones. But, equally clearly, it is less offensively paternalistic thanks to this crucial fact: at least it deals strictly in terms of values that are or will be subjectively present, at some point or another and to some extent or another, in the person concerned.

I. THE SCOPE OF PATERNALISM

When we are talking about public policies (and maybe even when we are talking of private, familial relations), paternalism surely can only be justified for the "big decisions" in people's lives. No one, except possibly parents and perhaps not even they, would propose to stop you from buying candy bars on a whim, under the influence of seductive advertising and at some marginal cost to your dental health.

So far as public policy is concerned, certainly, to be a fitting subject for public paternalism a decision must first of all involve high stakes. Life-and-death issues most conspicuously qualify. But so do those that substantially shape your subsequent life prospects. Decisions to drop out of school or to begin taking drugs involve high stakes of roughly that sort. If the decision is also substantially irreversible—returning to school is unlikely, the drug is addictive—then that further bolsters the case for paternalistic intervention.

The point in both cases is that people would not have a chance to benefit by learning from their mistakes. If the stakes are so high that losing the gamble once will kill you, then there is no opportunity for subsequent learning. Similarly, if the decision is irreversible, you might know better next time but be unable to benefit from your new wisdom.

II. EVALUATING PREFERENCES

The case for paternalism, as I have cast it, is that the public officials might better respect your own preferences than you would have done through your own actions. That is to say that public officials are engaged in evaluating your (surface) preferences, judging them according to some standard of your own (deeper) preferences. Public officials should refrain from paternalistic interference, and allow you to act without state interference, only if they are convinced that you are acting on:

- *relevant* preferences;
- *settled* preferences;
- *preferred* preferences; and, perhaps,
- *your own* preferences.

In what follows, I shall consider each of those requirements in turn. My running example will be the problem of smoking and policies to control it. Nothing turns on the peculiarities of that example, though. There are many others like it in relevant respects.

It often helps, in arguments like this, to apply generalities to particular cases. So, in what follows, I shall further focus in on the case of one particular smoker, Rose Cipollone. Her situation is nowise unique—in all the respects that matter here, she might be considered the prototypical smoker. All that makes her case special is that she (or more precisely her heir) was the first to win a court case against the tobacco companies whose products killed her.

In summarizing the evidence presented at that trial, the judge described the facts of the case as follows.

> Rose...Cipollone...began to smoke at age 16,...while she was still in high school. She testified that she began to smoke because she saw people smoking in the movies, in advertisements, and looked upon it as something "cool, glamorous and grown-up" to do. She began smoking Chesterfields...primarily because of advertising of "pretty girls and movie stars," and because Chesterfields were described as "mild."...
>
> Mrs. Cipollone attempted to quit smoking while pregnant with her first child..., but even then she would sneak cigarettes. While she was in labor she smoked an entire pack of cigarettes, provided to her at her request by her doctor, and after the birth...she resumed smoking. She smoked a minimum of a pack a day and as much as two packs a day.
>
> In 1955, she switched...to L&M cigarettes... because...she believed that the filter would trap whatever was "bad" for her in cigarette smoking. She relied upon advertisements which supported that contention.

> She...switched to Virginia Slims...because the cigarettes were glamorous and long, and were associated with beautiful women—and the liberated woman....
>
> Because she developed a smoker's cough and heard reports that smoking caused cancer, she tried to cut down her smoking. These attempts were unsuccessful....
>
> Mrs. Cipollone switched to lower tar and nicotine cigarettes based upon advertising from which she concluded that those cigarettes were safe or safer...[and] upon the recommendation of her family physician. In 1981 her cancer was diagnosed, and even though her doctors advised her to stop she was unable to do so. She even told her doctors and her husband that she had quit when she had not, and she continued to smoke until June of 1982 when her lung was removed. Even thereafter she smoked occasionally—in hiding. She stopped smoking in 1983 when her cancer had metastasized and she was diagnosed as fatally ill.

This sad history contains many of the features that I shall be arguing make paternalism most permissible.

Relevant Preferences

The case against paternalism consists in the simple proposition that, morally, we ought to respect people's own choices in matters that affect themselves and by-and-large only themselves. But there are many questions we first might legitimately ask about those preferences, without in any way questioning this fundamental principle of respecting people's autonomy.

One is simply whether the preferences in play are genuinely *relevant* to the decision at hand. Often they are not. Laymen often make purely factual mistakes in their means-ends reasoning. They think—or indeed, as in the case of Rose Cipollone, are led by false advertising to suppose—that an activity is safe when it is not. They think that an activity like smoking is glamorous, when the true facts of the matter are that smoking may well cause circulatory problems requiring the distinctly unglamorous amputation of an arm or leg.

When people make purely factual mistakes like that, we might legitimately override their surface preferences (the preference to smoke) in the name of their own deeper preferences (to stay alive and bodily intact). Public policies designed to prevent youngsters from taking up smoking when they want to, or to make it harder (more expensive or inconvenient) for existing smokers to continue smoking when they want to, may be paternalistic in the sense of running contrary to people's own manifest choices in the matter. But this overriding of their choices is grounded in their own deeper preferences, so such paternalism would be minimally offensive from a moral point of view.

Settled Preferences

We might ask, further, whether the preferences being manifested are "settled" preferences or whether they are merely transitory phases people are going through. It may be morally permissible to let people commit euthanasia voluntarily, if we are sure they really want to die. But if we think that they may subsequently change their minds, then we have good grounds for supposing that we should stop them.

The same may well be true with smoking policy. While Rose Cipollone herself thought smoking was both glamorous and safe, youngsters beginning to smoke today typically know better. But many of them still say that they would prefer a shorter but more glamorous life, and that they are therefore more than happy to accept the risks that smoking entails. Say what they may at age sixteen, though, we cannot help supposing that they will think differently when pigeons eventually come home to roost. The risk-courting preferences of youth are a characteristic product of a peculiarly dare-devil phase that virtually all of them will, like their predecessors, certainly grow out of.

Insofar as people's preferences are not settled—insofar as they choose one option now, yet at some later time may wish that they had chosen another—we have another ground for permissible paternalism. Policy-makers dedicated to respecting people's own choices have, in effect, two of the person's own choices to choose between. How such conflicts should be settled is hard to say. We might weigh the strength or duration of the preferences, how well they fit with the person's other preferences, and so on.

Whatever else we do, though, we clearly ought not privilege one preference over another just because it

got there first. Morally, it is permissible for policy-makers to ignore one of a person's present preferences (to smoke, for example) in deference to another that is virtually certain later to emerge (as was Rose Cipollone's wish to live, once she had cancer).

Preferred Preferences

A third case for permissible paternalism turns on the observation that people have not only multiple and conflicting preferences but also preferences for preferences. Rose Cipollone wanted to smoke. But, judging from her frequent (albeit failed) attempts to quit, she also wanted *not to want* to smoke.

In this respect, it might be said, Rose Cipollone's history is representative of smokers more generally. The US Surgeon General reports that some 90 percent of regular smokers have tried and failed to quit. That recidivism rate has led the World Health Organization to rank nicotine as an addictive substance on a par with heroin itself.

That classification is richly confirmed by the stories that smokers themselves tell about their failed attempts to quit. Rose Cipollone tried to quit while pregnant, only to end up smoking an entire pack in the delivery room. She tried to quit once her cancer was diagnosed, and once again after her lung was taken out, even then only to end up sneaking an occasional smoke.

In cases like this—where people want to stop some activity, try to stop it but find that they cannot stop—public policy that helps them do so can hardly be said to be paternalistic in any morally offensive respect. It overrides people's preferences, to be sure. But the preferences which it overrides are ones which people themselves wish they did not have.

The preferences which it respects—the preferences to stop smoking (like preferences of reformed alcoholics to stay off drink, or of the obese to lose weight)—are, in contrast, preferences that the people concerned themselves prefer. They would themselves rank those preferences above their own occasional inclinations to backslide. In helping them to implement their own preferred preferences, we are only respecting people's own priorities.

Your Own Preferences

Finally, before automatically respecting people's choices, we ought to make sure that they are really their *own* choices. We respect people's choices because in that way we manifest respect for them as persons. But if the choices in question were literally someone else's—the results of a post-hypnotic suggestion, for example—then clearly there that logic would provide no reason for our respecting those preferences.

Some people say that the effects of advertising are rather like that. No doubt there is a certain informational content to advertising. But that is not all there is in it. When Rose Cipollone read the tar and nicotine content in advertisements, what she was getting was information. What she was getting when looking at the accompanying pictures of movie stars and glamorous, liberated women was something else altogether.

Using the power of subliminal suggestion, advertising implants preferences in people in a way that largely or wholly bypasses their judgment. Insofar as it does so, the resulting preferences are not authentically that person's own. And those implanted preferences are not entitled to the respect that is rightly reserved for a person's authentic preferences, in consequence.

Such thoughts might lead some to say that we should therefore ignore altogether advertising-induced preferences in framing our public policy. I demur. There is just too much force in the rejoinder that, "Wherever those preferences came from in the first instance, they are mine now." If we want our policies to respect people by (among other things) respecting their preferences, then we will have to respect all of those preferences with which people now associate themselves.

Even admitting the force of that rejoinder, though, there is much that still might be done to curb the preference-shaping activities of, for example, the tobacco industry. Even those who say "they're my preferences now" would presumably have preferred, ahead of time, to make up their own minds in the matter. So there we have a case, couched in terms of people's own (past) preferences, for severely restricting the advertising and promotion of products—especially ones which people will later regret having grown to like, but which they will later be unable to resist.

III. CONCLUSIONS

What, in practical policy terms, follows from all that? Well, in the case of smoking, which has served as my running example, we might ban the sale of tobacco altogether or turn it into a drug available only on prescription to registered users. Or, less dramatically, we might make cigarettes difficult and expensive to obtain—especially for youngsters, whose purchases are particularly price-sensitive. We might ban all promotional advertising of tobacco products, designed as it is to attract new users. We might prohibit smoking in all offices, restaurants, and other public places, thus making it harder for smokers to find a place to partake and providing a further inducement for them to quit.

All of those policies would be good for smokers themselves. They would enjoy a longer life expectancy and a higher quality of life if they stopped smoking. But that is to talk the language of interests rather than of rights and choices. In those latter terms, all those policies clearly go against smokers' manifest preferences, in one sense or another. Smokers want to keep smoking. They do not want to pay more or drive further to get their cigarettes. They want to be able to take comfort in advertisements constantly telling them how glamorous their smoking is.

In other more important senses, though, such policies can be justified even in terms of the preferences of smokers themselves. They do not want to die, as a quarter of them eventually will (and ten to fifteen years before their time) of smoking-related diseases; it is only false beliefs or wishful thinking that make smokers think that continued smoking is consistent with that desire not to avoid a premature death. At the moment they may think that the benefits of smoking outweigh the costs, but they will almost certainly revise that view once those costs are eventually sheeted home. The vast majority of smokers would like to stop smoking but, being addicted, find it very hard now to do so.

Like Rose Cipollone, certainly in her dying days and intermittently even from her early adulthood, most smokers themselves would say that they would have been better off never starting. Many even agree that they would welcome anything (like a workplace ban on smoking) that might now make them stop. Given the internally conflicting preferences here in play, smokers also harbor at one and the same time preferences pointing in the opposite direction; that is what might make helping them to stop seem unacceptably paternalistic. But in terms of other of their preferences—and ones that deserve clear precedence, at that—doing so is perfectly well warranted.

Smoking is unusual, perhaps, in presenting a case for permissible paternalism on all four of the fronts here canvassed. Most activities might qualify under only one or two of the headings. However, that may well be enough. My point here is not that paternalism is always permissible but merely that it may always be.

In the discourse of liberal democracies, the charge of paternalism is typically taken to be a knock-down objection to any policy. If I am right, that knee-jerk response is wrong. When confronted with the charge of paternalism, it should always be open to us to say, "Sure, this proposal is paternalistic—but is the paternalism in view permissible or impermissible, good or bad?" More often than not, I think we will find, paternalism might prove perfectly defensible along the lines sketched here.

READING QUESTIONS

1. What should the scope of paternalism be according to Goodin?
2. When should public officials refrain from paternalistic interference according to Goodin?
3. Explain the case of Rose Cipollone and the differences among relevant, settled, preferred, and one's own preferences.
4. What are some of the public policies that Goodin thinks might be justified in the light of his considerations about the interests and preferences of smokers?

DISCUSSION QUESTION

1. Kant and many other philosophers hold that one has duties to oneself, including a duty to refrain from harmful activities. Can there be duties that one owes to oneself? If not, why not? If so, is refraining from smoking one of them?

DANIEL SHAPIRO

Addiction and Drug Policy

According to the "standard view" of addiction, certain drugs are highly addictive largely because of their pharmacological effects—effects on the brain owing to the chemical constitution of the drug. This kind of pharmacological explanation plays a significant role in some arguments in favor of legal bans on certain drugs, especially "hard drugs." Daniel Shapiro challenges the standard view, arguing that factors such as an individual's mind-set as well as an individual's social and cultural setting importantly contribute to drug addiction. According to Shapiro, then, cravings, increased drug tolerance, and withdrawal symptoms cannot explain drug addiction. He bolsters his case against the standard view by examining nicotine addiction.

Most people think that illegal drugs, such as cocaine and heroin, are highly addictive. Usually their addictiveness is explained by pharmacology: their chemical composition and its effects on the brain are such that, after a while, it's hard to stop using them. This view of drug addiction—I call it the standard view—underlies most opposition to legalizing cocaine and heroin. James Wilson's (1990) arguments are typical: legalization increases access, and increased access to addictive drugs increases addiction. The standard view also underlies the increasingly popular opinion, given a philosophical defense by Robert Goodin (1989), that cigarette smokers are addicts in the grip of a powerful drug.

However, the standard view is false: pharmacology, I shall argue, does not by itself do much to explain drug addiction. I will offer a different explanation of drug addiction and discuss its implications for the debate about drug legalization.

PROBLEMS WITH THE STANDARD VIEW

We label someone as a drug addict because of his behavior. A drug addict uses drugs repeatedly, compulsively, and wants to stop or cut back on his use but finds it's difficult to do so; at its worst, drug addiction dominates or crowds out other activities and concerns. The standard view attempts to explain this compulsive behavior by the drug's effects on the brain. Repeated use of an addictive drug induces cravings and the user comes to need a substantial amount to get the effect she wants, i.e., develops tolerance. If the user tries to stop, she then suffers very disagreeable effects, called withdrawal symptoms. (For more detail on the standard view, see American Psychiatric Association 1994, 176–81.)

Cravings, tolerance, and withdrawal symptoms: do these explain drug addiction? A craving or strong desire to do something doesn't *make* one do something: one can act on a desire or ignore it *or* attempt to extinguish it. Tolerance explains why the user increases her intake to get the effect she wants, but that doesn't explain why she would find it difficult to *stop wanting* this effect. Thus, the key idea in the standard view is really withdrawal symptoms, because that is needed to explain the difficulty in extinguishing the desire to take the drug or to stop wanting the effects the drug produces. However, for this explanation to work, these symptoms have to be really bad, for if they aren't, why not just put up with them as a small price to pay for getting free of the drug? However, withdrawal symptoms aren't *that* bad. Heroin is considered terribly addictive, yet pharmacologists describe its withdrawal symptoms as like having a bad flu for about a week: typical withdrawal symptoms include fever, diarrhea, sneezing, muscle cramps, and vomiting (Kaplan 1983, 15, 19, 35). While a bad flu is quite unpleasant, it's not so bad that one has little choice but to take heroin rather than experience it. Indeed, most withdrawal symptoms for any drug cease within a few weeks, yet most heavy users who relapse do so after that period and few drug addicts report withdrawal symptoms as the reason for their relapse (Peele 1985, 19–20, 67; Schacter 1982, 436–44; Waldorf, Reinarman, and Murphy 1991, 241).

Thus, cravings, tolerance, and withdrawal symptoms cannot explain addiction. An additional problem for the standard view is that most drug users, whether they use legal or illegal drugs, do not become addicts, and few addicts remain so permanently. (Cigarette smokers are a partial exception, which I discuss later.) Anonymous surveys of drug users by the Substance Abuse and Mental Health Services Administration (2002) indicate that less than 10 percent of those who have tried powder cocaine use it monthly (National Household Survey of Drug Abuse 2001, tables H1 and H2). Furthermore, most monthly users are not addicts; a survey of young adults, for example (Johnston, O'Malley, and Bachman for the National Institute on Drug Abuse 1996, 84–5), found that less

than 10 percent of monthly cocaine users used it daily. (Even a daily user need not be an addict; someone who drinks daily is not thereby an alcoholic.) The figures are not appreciably different for crack cocaine (Erickson, Smart, and Murray 1994, 167–74, 231–32; Morgan and Zimmer 1997, 142–44) and only slightly higher for heroin (Husak 1992, 125; Sullum 2003, 228). These surveys have been confirmed by longitudinal studies—studies of a set of users over time—which indicate that moderate and/or controlled use of these drugs is the norm, not the exception, and that even heavy users do not inevitably march to addiction, let alone remain permanent addicts (Waldorf, Reinarman, and Murphy 1991; Erickson, Smart, and Murray 1994; Zinberg 1984, 111–34, 152–71). The standard view has to explain the preeminence of controlled use by arguing that drug laws reduce access to illegal drugs. However, I argue below that even with easy access to drugs most people use them responsibly, and so something other than the law and pharmacology must explain patterns of drug use.

AN ALTERNATIVE VIEW

I will defend a view of addiction summed up by Norman Zinberg's book, *Drug, Set, and Setting* (1984). "Drug" means pharmacology; "set" means the individual's mindset, his personality, values, and expectations; and "setting" means the cultural or social surroundings of drug use. This should sound like common sense. Humans are interpretative animals, and so what results from drug use depends not just on the experience or effects produced by the drug but *also* on the interpretation of that experience or effects. And how one interprets or understands the experience depends on one's individuality and the cultural or social setting. I begin with setting. Hospital patients that get continuous and massive doses of narcotics rarely get addicted or crave the drugs after release from the hospital (Peele 1985, 17; Falk 1996, 9). The quantity and duration of their drug use pales in significance compared with the setting of their drug consumption: subsequent ill effects from the drug are rarely interpreted in terms of addiction. A study of Vietnam veterans, the largest study of untreated heroin users ever conducted, provides more dramatic evidence of the role of setting. Three-quarters of Vietnam vets who used heroin in Vietnam became addicted, but after coming home, only half of heroin users in Vietnam continued to use, and of those only 12 percent were addicts (Robins, Heltzer, Hesselbrock, and Wish 1980). Wilson also mentions this study and says that the change was because heroin is illegal in the U.S. (1990, 22), and while this undoubtedly played a role, so did the difference in social setting: Vietnam, with its absence of work and family, as well as loneliness and fear of death, helped to promote acceptance of heavy drug use.

Along the same lines, consider the effects of alcohol in different cultures. In Finland, for example, violence and alcohol are linked, for sometimes heavy drinkers end up in fights; in Greece, Italy, and other Mediterranean countries, however, where almost all drinking is moderate and controlled, there is no violence-alcohol link (Peele 1985, 25). Why the differences? Humans are social or cultural animals, not just products of their biochemistry, and this means, in part, that social norms or rules play a significant role in influencing behavior. In cultures where potentially intoxicating drugs such as alcohol are viewed as supplements or accompaniments to life, moderate and controlled use will be the norm—hence, even though Mediterranean cultures typically consume large amounts of alcohol, there is little alcoholism—while in cultures where alcohol is also viewed as a way of escaping one's problems, alcoholism will be more prevalent, which may explain the problem in Finland and some other Scandinavian cultures. In addition to cultural influences, most people learn to use alcohol responsibly by observing their parents. They see their parents drink at a ball game or to celebrate special occasions or with food at a meal, but rarely on an empty stomach; they learn it's wrong to be drunk at work, to drink and drive; they learn that uncontrolled behavior with alcohol is generally frowned upon; they absorb certain norms and values such as "know your limit," "don't drink alone," "don't drink

in the morning," and so forth. They learn about rituals which reinforce moderation, such as the phrase "let's have a drink." These informal rules and rituals teach most people how to use alchohol responsibly (Zinberg 1987, 258–62).

While social controls are harder to develop with illicit drugs—accurate information is pretty scarce, and parents feel uncomfortable teaching their children about controlled use—even here sanctions and rituals promoting moderate use exist. For example, in a study of an eleven-year follow-up of an informal network of middle-class cocaine users largely connected through ties of friendship, most of whom were moderate users, the authors concluded that:

> Rather than cocaine overpowering user concerns with family, health, and career, we found that the high value most of our users placed upon family, health, and career achievement . . . mitigated against abuse and addiction. Such group norms and the informal social controls that seemed to stem from them (e.g., expressions of concern, warning about risks, the use of pejorative names like "coke hog," refusal to share with abusers) mediated the force of pharmacological, physiological, and psychological factors which can lead to addiction (Murphy et al. 1989: 435).

Even many heavy cocaine users are able to prevent their use from becoming out of control (or out of control for significant periods of time) by regulating the time and circumstances of use (not using during work, never using too late at night, limiting use on weekdays), using with friends rather than alone, employing fixed rules (paying bills before spending money on cocaine), etc. (Waldorf, Reinarman, and Murphy 1991). Unsurprisingly, these studies of controlled cocaine use generally focus on middle-class users: their income and the psychological support of friends and family put them at less of a risk of ruining their lives by drug use than those with little income or hope (Peele 1991, 159–60).

I now examine the effects of set on drug use, that is, the effect of expectations, personality, and values. Expectations are important because drug use occurs in a pattern of ongoing activity, and one's interpretation of the drug's effects depends upon expectations of how those effects will fit into or alter those activities. Expectations explain the well-known placebo effect: if people consume something they mistakenly believe will stop or alleviate their pain, it often does. Along the same lines, in experiments with American college-age men, aggression and sexual arousal increased when these men were told they were drinking liquor, even though they were drinking 0 proof, while when drinking liquor and told they were not, they acted normally (Peele 1985, 17). The role of expectations also explains why many users of heroin, cocaine, and other psychoactive drugs do not like or even recognize the effects when they first take it and have to be taught to or learn how to appreciate the effects (Peele 1985, 13–14; Waldorf, Reinarman, and Murphy 1991, 264; Zinberg 1984, 117). The importance of expectations means that those users who view the drug as overpowering them will tend to find their lives dominated by the drug, while those who view it as an enhancement or a complement to certain experiences or activities will tend not to let drugs dominate or overpower their other interests (Peele 1991, 156–58, 169–70).

As for the individual's personality and values, the predictions of common sense are pretty much accurate. Psychologically healthy people are likely to engage in controlled, moderate drug use, or if they find themselves progressing to uncontrolled use, they tend to cut back. On other hand, drug addicts of all kinds tend to have more psychological problems before they started using illicit drugs (Peele 1991, 153–54, 157; Zinberg 1984, 74–76). People who are motivated to control their own lives will tend to make drug use an accompaniment or an ingredient in their lives, not the dominant factor. Those who place a high value on responsibility, work, family, productivity, etc., will tend to fit drug use into their lives rather than letting it run their lives (Waldorf, Reinarman, and Murphy 1991, 267; Peele 1991, 160–66). That's why drug use of all kinds, licit or illicit, tends to taper off with age: keeping a job, raising a family, and so forth leave limited time or motivation for uncontrolled or near continuous drug use (Peele 1985, 15). And it's why it's not uncommon for addicts to explain their addiction by saying that they drifted into the addict's life; with little to compete with their drug use, or lacking motivation to substitute other activities or interests, drug use comes to dominate their lives (DeGrandpre

and White 1996, 44–46). Those with richer lives, or who are motivated on an individual and/or cultural level to get richer lives, are less likely to succumb to addiction. To summarize: even with easy access to intoxicating drugs, most drug users don't become addicts, or if they do, don't remain addicts for that long, because most people have and are motivated to find better things to do with their lives. These better things result from their individual personality and values and their social or cultural setting.

CIGARETTE SMOKING AND THE ROLE OF PHARMACOLOGY

I've discussed how set and setting influence drug use, but where does pharmacology fit in? Its role is revealed by examining why it is much harder to stop smoking cigarettes—only half of smokers that try to stop smoking succeed in quitting—than to stop using other substances. (For more detail in what follows, see Shapiro 1994 and the references cited therein.)

Smokers smoke to relax; to concentrate; to handle anxiety, stress, and difficult interpersonal situations; as a way of taking a break during the day; as a social lubricant; as a means of oral gratification—and this is a partial list. Since smoking is a means to or part of so many activities, situations, and moods, stopping smoking is a major life change and major life changes do not come easily. Part of the reason smoking is so integrated into people's lives is pharmacological. Nicotine's effects on the brain are mild and subtle: it doesn't disrupt your life. While addicts or heavy users of other drugs such as cocaine, heroin, or alcohol *also* use their drugs as a means to or part of a variety of activities, situations, and moods, most users of these drugs are not lifelong addicts or heavy users, because these drugs are not so mild and heavy use has a stronger tendency over time to disrupt people's lives.

The pharmacology of smoking, however, cannot be separated from its social setting. Smoking doesn't disrupt people's lives in part because it is legal. Even with increasing regulations, smokers still can smoke in a variety of situations (driving, walking on public streets, etc.), while one cannot use illegal drugs except in a furtive and secretive manner. Furthermore, the mild effects of nicotine are due to its mild potency—smokers can carefully control their nicotine intake, getting small doses throughout the day—and its mild potency is due partly to smoking being legal. Legal drugs tend to have milder potencies than illegal ones for two reasons. First, illegal markets create incentives for stronger potencies, as sellers will favor concentrated forms of a drug that can be easily concealed and give a big bang for the buck. Second, in legal markets different potencies of the same drug openly compete, and over time the weaker ones come to be preferred—consider the popularity of low tar/nicotine cigarettes and wine and beer over hard liquor.

Thus, pharmacology and setting interact: smoking is well integrated into people's lives because the nicotine in cigarettes has mild pharmacological effects and because smoking is legal, and nicotine has those mild effects in part because smoking is legal. Pharmacology also interacts with what I've been calling set. The harms of smoking are slow to occur, are cumulative, and largely affect one's health, not one's ability to perform normal activities (at least prior to getting seriously ill). Furthermore, to eliminate these harms requires complete smoking cessation; cutting back rarely suffices (even light smokers increase their chances of getting lung cancer, emphysema, and heart disease). Thus, quitting smoking requires strong motivation, since its bad effects are not immediate and it does not disrupt one's life. Add to this what I noted earlier, that stopping smoking means changing one's life, and it's unsurprising that many find it difficult to stop.

Thus, it is a mistake to argue, as Goodin did, that the difficulty in quitting is mainly explicable by the effects of nicotine. Smokers are addicted to smoking, an *activity*, and their being addicted to it is not reducible to their being addicted to a *drug*. If my explanation of the relative difficulty of quitting smoking is correct, then the standard view of an addictive drug is quite suspect. That view suggests that knowledge of a drug's pharmacology provides a basis for making reasonable predictions about a drug's addictiveness. However, understanding nicotine's effects upon the brain (which is what Goodin

stressed in his explanation of smokers' addiction) does not tell us that it's hard to stop smoking; we only know that once we add information about set and setting. Generalizing from the case of smoking, all we can say is:

> The milder the effects upon the brain, the easier for adults to purchase, the more easily integrated into one's life, and the more the bad effects are cumulative, slow-acting and only reversible upon complete cessation, the more addictive the drug. (Goodin 1989)

Besides being a mouthful, this understanding of drug addiction requires introducing the *interaction* of set and setting with pharmacology to explain the addictiveness potential of various drugs. It is simpler and less misleading to say that people tend to *addict themselves* to various substances (and activities), this tendency varying with various cultural and individual influences.

CONCLUSION

My argument undercuts the worry that legalizing cocaine and heroin will produce an explosion of addiction because people will have access to inherently and powerfully addictive drugs. The standard view that cocaine and heroin are *inherently* addictive is false, because no drug is inherently addictive. The desire of most people to lead responsible and productive lives in a social setting that rewards such desires is what controls and limits most drug use. Ironically, if cocaine and heroin in a legal market would be as disruptive as many drug prohibitionists fear, then that is an excellent reason why addiction would not explode under legalization—drug use that tends to thrive is drug use that is woven into, rather than disrupts, responsible people's lives.

ADDENDUM

After I wrote this article, some of my students raised the following objection. I argue that drug addiction that disrupts people's lives would not thrive under legalization because most people's desire and ability to lead responsible lives would break or prevent such addiction. However, suppose that legalization of cocaine and heroin makes the use of those drugs similar to the use of cigarettes—small, mild doses throughout the day which are well integrated into people's lives. If legalization brings it about that those who addict themselves to these drugs are like those who addict themselves to smoking—their addiction does not disrupt their lives, but is integrated into it—wouldn't that mean that addiction to these drugs would become as prevalent as cigarette addiction?

It is possible that legalizing heroin and cocaine would make its use similar to the current use of cigarettes. However, if this happened, the main worry about heroin and cocaine addiction would be gone. We would not have a problem of a large increase in the number of people throwing away or messing up their lives. At worst, if legalizing cocaine and heroin produced as bad health effects as cigarette smoking does (which is dubious—see Carnwath and Smith 2002, 137–39; Morgan and Zimmer 1997, 131, 136, 141), then we would have a new health problem. Of course, someone might argue that one should not legalize a drug which could worsen the health of a significant percentage of its users, even if that use does not mess up most of its users' lives. It is beyond the scope of this paper to evaluate such arguments (however, see Shapiro 1994), but notice that the implications of my essay cut against the claim that these health risks were not voluntarily incurred. Since one's drug use partly depends on one's values and personality, then to the extent that one can be said to be responsible for the choices influenced by one's values and personality, then to that extent those who addict themselves to a certain drug can be said to have voluntarily incurred the risks involved in that drug use.

REFERENCES

American Psychiatric Association. 1994. *Diagnostic and Statistical Manual of Mental Disorders.* 4th ed. Washington, D.C.: American Psychiatric Association.

Carnwath, T., and I. Smith. 2002. *Heroin Century.* London: Routledge.

DeGrandpre, R., and E. White. 1996. "Drugs: In Care of the Self." *Common Knowledge* 3: 27–48.

Erickson, P., E. Edward, R. Smart, and G. Murray. 1994. *The Steel Drug: Crack and Cocaine in Perspective.* 2nd ed. New York: MacMillan.

Falk, J. 1996. "Environmental Factors in the Instigation and Maintenance of Drug Abuse." In W. Bickel and R. DeGrandpre, eds., *Drug Policy and Human Nature.* New York: Plenum Press.

Goodin, R. 1989. "The Ethics of Smoking." *Ethics* 99: 574–624.

Husak, D. 1992. *Drugs and Rights.* New York: Cambridge University Press.

Johnston, L. D., P. M. O'Malley, and J. G. Bachman. 1996. *Monitoring the Future Study, 1975–1994: National Survey Results on Drug Use.* Volume II: *College Students and Young Adults.* Rockville, Md.: National Institute on Drug Abuse.

Kaplan, J. 1983. *The Hardest Drug: Heroin and Public Policy.* Chicago: University of Chicago Press.

Morgan, J., and L. Zimmer. 1997. "The Social Pharmacology of Smokeable Cocaine: Not All It's Cracked Up to Be." In C. Reinarman and H. Levine, eds., *Crack in America: Demon Drugs and Social Justice.* Berkeley: University of California Press.

Murphy, S., C. Reinarman, and D. Waldorf. 1989. "An 11 Year Follow-Up of a Network of Cocaine Users." *British Journal of Addiction* 84: 427–36.

Peele, S. 1985. *The Meaning of Addiction: Compulsive Experience and Its Interpretation.* Lexington, Mass.: D.C. Heath and Company.

Peele, S. 1991. *The Diseasing of America: Addiction Treatment Out of Control.* Boston: Houghton Mifflin Company.

Robins, L., J. Helzer, M. Hesselbrock, and E. Wish. 1980. "Vietnam Veterans Three Years After Vietnam: How Our Study Changed Our View of Heroin." In L. Brill and C. Winick, eds., *The Yearbook of Substance Use and Abuse.* Vol. 2. New York: Human Sciences Press.

Schacter, S. 1982. "Recidivism and Self-Cure of Smoking and Obesity." *American Psychologist* 37: 436–44.

Shapiro, D. 1994. "Smoking Tobacco: Irrationality, Addiction and Paternalism." *Public Affairs Quarterly* 8: 187–203.

Substance Abuse and Mental Health Services Administration. 2002. *Tables from the 2001 National Household Survey on Drug Abuse,* Department of Health and Human Services, available online at http://www.sam-hsa.gov/oas/NHSDA/2klNHSDA/vol2/appendixh_1.htm.

Sullum, J. 2003. *Saying Yes*: *In Defense of Drug Use*. New York: Tarcher/Putnam.

Waldorf, D., C. Reinarman, and S. Murphy. 1991. *Cocaine Changes: The Experience of Using and Quitting*. Philadelphia: Temple University Press.

Wilson, J. 1990. "Against the Legalization of Drugs." *Commentary* 89: 21–28.

Zinberg, N. 1984. *Drug, Set, and Setting*. New Haven, Conn.: Yale University Press.

Zinberg, N. 1987. "The Use and Misuse of Intoxicants." In R. Hamowy, ed., *Dealing with Drugs*. Lexington, Mass.: D. C. Heath and Company.

READING QUESTIONS

1. How does Shapiro characterize the "standard view" of addiction as it relates to drugs like heroin and cocaine?
2. Explain the problems with the standard view according to Shapiro.
3. What is the alternative view of addiction suggested by Shapiro? What is meant by the terms "drug," "set," and "setting" in the context of this view?
4. How does Shapiro contrast the case of cigarette smoking with the cases of addiction predicted by the standard view?

DISCUSSION QUESTIONS

1. Are there any remaining merits of the standard view of addiction rejected by Shapiro?
2. Do you think that Shapiro overestimates the positive influences of social and individual controls on the use of illicit drugs like heroin and cocaine?
3. Are there any downsides to the legalization of illicit drugs that Shapiro fails to consider?

ADDITIONAL RESOURCES

Web Resources

U.S. Drug Enforcement Administration (DEA), <www.usdoj.gov/dea>. Provides information on drugs, drug laws, as well as prevention of drug abuse.

National Institute on Drug Abuse (NIDA), <www.nida.gov>. NIDA's main objective is to bring to bear on drug abuse the results of scientific inquiry. The agency also provides detailed information about specific drugs and about prevention of drug abuse.

National Organization for the Reform of Marijuana Laws (NORML), <www.norml.org>. A site with information about marijuana and dedicated to its legalization.

Authored Books and Articles

Butler, Keith, "The Moral Status of Smoking," *Social Theory and Practice* 19 (1993): 1–26. Argues that smoking routinely violates the harm principle.

de Marneffe, Peter, "Do We Have a Right to Use Drugs?" *Public Affairs Quarterly* 10 (1996): 229–47. De Marneffe argues that democratic countries are justified in passing some laws against the sale and use of certain drugs.

Husak, Douglas N., *Drugs and Rights* (New York: Cambridge University Press, 1992). Husak argues that the "war on drugs" violates basic human rights to take drugs for recreational purposes.

Husak, Douglas and Peter De Marneffe, *The Legalization of Drugs: For and Against* (Cambridge: Cambridge University Press, 2005). Husak defends the "for" position while de Marneffe defends the "against" position in this very readable and highly recommended book.

Miron, Jeffrey A. and Jeffrey Zwiebel, "The Economic Case Against Drug Prohibition," *Journal of Economic Perspectives* 9 (1995): 175–192. Authors argue that a free market in drugs is preferable to the current policy of drug prohibition.

Shapiro, Daniel, "Smoking Tobacco," *Public Affairs Quarterly* 8 (1994): 187–203. Critical of Goodin's case in favor of paternalistic laws aimed at regulating smoking.

Slone, Frank A., J. Ostermann, G. Picone, C. Conover, and D. H. Taylor Jr., *The Price of Smoking* (Boston: The MIT Press, 2006). Discussion of the social effects of smoking.

Wilson, James Q., "Against the Legalization of Drugs," *Commentary* 89 (1990): 21–28. Wilson presents arguments against legalization that appeal to both the harm principle and the principle of legal moralism.

Edited Collections

Belenko, Steven R. (ed.), *Drugs and Drug Policy in America* (Westport, CT: Greenwood Press, 2000). A collection of over 250 primary documents including court cases, speeches, laws, and opinion pieces that usefully trace the history of drugs and drug policy in America from the nineteenth century to the present.

Schaler, Jeffrey A. (ed.), *Shall We Legalize, Decriminalize, or Regulate?* (Buffalo, NY: Prometheus Books, 1998). Twenty-nine essays divided into eight parts: 1. Those Who Cannot Remember the Past, 2. A War on Drugs or a War on People? 3. Just Say 'No' to Drug Legalization, 4. Medical Marijuana: What Counts as Medicine? 5. Drug War Metaphors and Additions: Drugs are Property, 6. Addiction Is a Behavior: The Myth of Loss of Control, 7. Do Drugs Cause Crime? 8. State-Supported and Court-Ordered Treatment for Addiction Is Unconstitutional.

6 ⟩ Sexism, Racism, and Reparation

In 1865, the 13th Amendment to the U.S. Constitution was ratified by Congress, abolishing slavery in the United States. According to the text of the Amendment:

> Neither slavery nor involuntary servitude, except as a punishment for crime whereof the party shall have been duly convicted, shall exist within the United States, or any place subject to their jurisdiction. Congress shall have power to enforce this article by appropriate legislation.

Despite the abolishment of slavery so many years ago, incidents of racial prejudice, some of them outrageous, continue to occur.

Since 1880 there have been roughly five thousand reported incidents in the United States of lynchings, most of them perpetrated against African Americans. On June 15, 2005, the U.S. Senate issued a formal apology for its history of not having passed any one of approximately two hundred bills that would have made lynching a federal crime, the first of which was proposed over one hundred years ago. Blockage in the Senate of antilynching laws was mainly due to opposition from senators from the U.S. South. This one-hundred-year failure to make what was a terrible racially biased practice a federal crime is but one manifestation of deeply racist attitudes that mar the history of the United States. Many people believe that the history of racism in the United States morally demands some form of reparation (and not just apology) be made to those citizens who have either directly or indirectly suffered or been disadvantaged by racist practices.[1]

As we shall see in this chapter, moral questions about sexism and racism are not concerned with whether such discriminatory actions and practices are wrong—calling some action or practice racist or sexist is often taken to entail that the action or practice in question is at least presumptively morally wrong. There are, however, important questions about the scope of racist and sexist actions and practices, and there are moral questions about what (if anything) is owed to victims of gender-based and race-based discrimination. Here, then, are some of the main moral questions about sexism and racism:

- What best explains why sexism and racism are morally wrong?
- Given a history of racism and/or sexism in a country, is some sort of reparation or compensation owed to members of the victimized group?
- Supposing that some form of reparation or compensation is owed, what form should it take? For example, are affirmative action policies that we find in universities and other organizations morally justified?

In order to set the stage for understanding these questions and the moral controversies they involve, let us begin with some remarks about the concepts of sexism and racism.

1. SEXISM AND RACISM

The *Merriam-Webster Online Dictionary* defines these terms in the following way:

Sexism

1: prejudice or discrimination based on sex; *especially*: discrimination against women
2: behavior, conditions, or attitudes that foster stereotypes of social roles based on sex.

Racism

1: a belief that race is the primary determinant of human traits and capacities and that racial differences produce an inherent superiority of a particular race
2: racial prejudice or discrimination.

Both definitions mention prejudice and discrimination as part of the common meaning of these terms, so let us work with these notions, keeping in mind the differences between sexism and racism revealed in these definitions.[2]

First, let us distinguish between someone being a sexist or a racist and someone engaging in sexist or racist activities. To be a sexist is to have negative beliefs or attitudes about some individual because she or he is of a particular sex. To be a racist is to have negative beliefs or attitudes about some individual because that individual belongs to some ethnic group. These definitions of being a sexist or racist only require that one have a certain prejudice toward members of some group even if one never acts in a discriminatory way toward its members. If, for example, someone believes that someone else is inferior in some way because the latter person is, say, black (about whom the person has negative beliefs or attitudes), then the person in question has racist attitudes and counts as a racist. Similarly for someone being a sexist. To have sexist or racist beliefs or attitudes is to have a *prejudice* against the members of some group.

While being a sexist or a racist is a matter of being prejudiced, actions and practices directed against individuals belonging to a sex or ethnic group are *discriminatory.* For an action or activity to be sexist or racist is for it to be directed against some individual because one believes (whether truly or not) that the individual belongs to a sex or an ethnic group. An act of sexism or racism may be intentional—as when a person's hatred for members of a certain sex or race motivates the person to knowingly engage in the sexist or racist activity. But there can be cases of unintentional sexist or racist acts as when someone does not intend to act in a racist way, but unwittingly says something or does something that is prejudicial toward a member of some ethnic group that results from the person's prejudicial beliefs about the group in question. For instance, someone might tell a joke and not intend for it to be harmful or prejudicial toward members of some ethnic group, even though in fact the joke is racist.

My characterizations of sexism and racism have focused on the beliefs, attitudes, and actions of individuals that constitute what we may call *interpersonal* sexism and racism. But institutions, legal systems, economic systems, and cultures can be sexist or racist if those institutions, systems, and cultures are partly constituted by rules, laws, regulations, and expectations that serve to promote sexist or racist beliefs, attitudes, and actions. These are cases of *institutional* sexism and racism, and they are discussed in the selections by Ann E. Cudd and Leslie E. Jones and by J. L. A. Garcia.

As indicated, one of the main questions about sexism and racism is, "What best explains *why* these prejudices are wrong?" In my brief characterizations of these concepts I have spoken indifferently about a racist or a sexist having negative beliefs or attitudes about some individual or group because of her or his race or sex. But one may ask whether sexism and racism are fundamentally matters of holding certain negative *beliefs* about members of some race or sex or whether racism is most fundamentally a matter of having certain negative attitudes. In "The Heart of Racism" (included in our chapter), J. L. A. Garcia argues for what he calls a "volitional" explanation of the wrongness of racism, which he explains as follows:

> My proposal is that we conceive of racism as fundamentally a vicious kind of racially based disregard for the welfare of certain people. In its central and most vicious form, it is a hatred, ill-will, directed against a person or persons on account of their assigned race. . . . Racism, then, is something that essentially involves not our beliefs and their rationality or irrationality, but our wants, intentions, likes, and dislikes and their distance from moral virtues. (p. 228)

Following Garcia, one might argue that sexism, too, is a matter of the heart rather than belief. However, Garcia's proposal is challenged by Tommie Shelby in his "Is Racism in the 'Heart'?" also included among our chapter selections.

2. REPARATION

One of the main moral issues dealt with in some of the selections in this chapter is reparation for past wrongs against members of a sex or ethnic group. Roughly speaking, **reparation** involves making up for some past wrong. Often the wrongs in question were done to people who are now deceased, and so to them is not literally possible. Moreover, in some cases it is not possible to make up the past wrong to the descendants of the wronged victims. In such cases, we may engage in *reparative compensation,* which attempts to rectify past wrongs by providing to those wronged or their descendants some form of compensation in the form of money, tax breaks, property, or other goods that is in proportion to the degree of evil that resulted from the wrong. While some sort of financial compensation may be called for as a response to sexism and racism, affirmative action policies that have to do with a person's opportunities may also be a fitting response to such discriminatory practices.

In 2008, the U.S. House of Representatives voted to issue an apology to African Americans for the institution of slavery that was outlawed in 1865 by the 13th Amendment to the U.S. Constitution. In 2009, the Senate followed the House in passing a resolution to apologize. However, as of April 2016, neither resolution had been presented to President Obama for his signature because neither chamber agreed on language that would exempt the United States from future claims of reparation by black Americans as a result of slavery.

3. THEORY MEETS PRACTICE

Let us conclude by considering how the following four moral theories address the moral questions we have raised about sexism and racism.

Consequentialism

A consequentialist will explain the wrongness of sexism and racism in terms of the purported (overall) negative consequences of such actions and practices. Slavery and ethnic cleansing are but two clear cases of racist practices that have resulted in the maiming, murdering, and marginalization of members of various ethnic groups. It is very doubtful according to the consequentialist that the net value of the consequences of such activities is anything but extremely negative.

As for reparation generally and affirmative action policies in particular, the consequentialist will claim that such practices are morally required if they are more likely to have a greater net value for everyone affected than the value that would result from not engaging in these activities. These are matters that may divide consequentialists, since there may be doubts about the overall net value of at least certain forms of reparation and certain affirmative action policies.

Kantian Moral Theory

For a Kantian, all persons regardless of ethnicity and sex are deserving of equal respect in the sense that it is not permissible to treat anyone in a discriminatory manner, since doing so fails to treat them as ends in themselves. (This is an application of Kant's Humanity formulation of the categorical imperative presented in chapter 1, section 2C.) Moreover, a Kantian can claim that sexist and racist beliefs and attitudes are wrong (regardless of whether they result in the racist ever acting on his prejudicial beliefs or attitudes) because having them constitutes a failure to have a proper regard for the equal moral status of persons regardless of their sex or ethnicity.

If one uses Kant's Universal Law formulation of the categorical imperative, then whether a Kantian will claim that reparation or affirmative action policies are morally permissible (and perhaps morally required) will depend on whether the reparation or policies in question can be universalized. Can one consistently conceive and will that such practices be adopted by all? If so, then they are morally permissible. Can one consistently will that no such practices be adopted by all? If not, then not having such practices is morally wrong. Interestingly, Louis P. Pojman, in an article included in this chapter, argues that Kant's Humanity formulation can be used to argue against affirmative action policies. Kant's Universal Law and Humanity formulations of the categorical imperative are supposed to agree in their moral implications. If the Universal Law formulation conflicts in its verdict about affirmative action with the verdict reached by the Humanity formulation, this would reveal a deep incoherence in Kant's own moral theory. Whether these principles really do yield opposing verdicts about the morality of affirmative action is controversial and cannot be settled here.

Ethics of Prima Facie Duties

On W. D. Ross's moral theory (presented in chapter 1, section 2F), we have a prima facie duty of nonmaleficence—a prima facie duty not to harm others. This duty is not absolute—it can be overridden—however, it is clear that gross instances of sexism and racism are cases of maleficence that are not overridden by any other prima facie duty on Ross's list of seven such duties. Does Ross's view address sexist and racist prejudice even when having such beliefs and attitudes does not result in discriminatory actions? Ross's theory of prima facie duties may not clearly deal with this kind of case, since all of his prima facie duties have to do with actions and omissions. Robert Audi's version of an ethic of prima facie duties includes a duty of respectfulness: "We should, in the manner of our relations with other people, treat them respectfully."[3] But Audi's formulation of the duty of respectfulness does not address the morality of a person's attitudes; rather it concerns how we treat others. But we can easily revise Audi's principle so that it does make reference to one's beliefs and attitudes: we should, in the manner of our relations with other people *and in our attitudes toward them,* treat them and regard them respectfully. In having sexist or racist attitudes, one fails to have a proper respect for members of some sex or some ethnic group.

Both Ross and Audi recognize a prima facie duty of reparation: "We should make amends for our wrong-doing."[4] This principle, as stated, most directly applies to cases in which an individual has engaged in wrongdoing—she ought to make amends to the person(s) she has wronged. But what about cases in which the main perpetrators are our ancestors and the individuals directly wronged are now dead? Arguably, this is the case in contemporary North America in relation to the practice of slavery. Nevertheless, one can understand the "we" and "our" in the stated principle of reparation as the historical "we" and "our." If we are beneficiaries of past sexism or racism, then it may be morally incumbent on us to make reparations for past wrongs to those individuals of oppressed groups who (as a group) are less well off than they would be had their group not been a historical target of sexism or racism.

Virtue Ethics

One might approach moral questions about racism by first asking what sort of character traits are best to have and which are best to avoid—the virtues and the vices, respectively—and then asking whether racist activities (and being a racist) are expressions of some vice. If so, then such activities and attitudes are wrong. And here it seems that the virtue ethicist is going to be able to argue that this kind of moral theory does provide a basis for the moral condemnation of racist actions *and* racist attitudes. The kinds of motives from which racism and racist acts arise—for example, hatred and fear—are characteristic of the vices of hatred and arrogance, respectively. With regard to reparations and affirmative action policies, again, the virtue ethicist will want to evaluate the morality of particular policies by considering whether such policies are those that a virtuous agent would advocate.

One way to understand Thomas E. Hill Jr.'s defense of affirmative action is through the lens of the virtue approach to moral deliberation. Hill is critical of consequentialist ("forward-looking") approaches and also critical of essentially "backward-looking" approaches that would appeal to a prima facie duty of reparation. Instead, Hill argues that there are certain ideals (we might say virtues) that we ought to aspire to achieve, including mutual respect and trust.

NOTES

1. Contemporary discussion of reparation for black Americans was sparked by Ta-Nehisi Coates in his essay, "The Case for Reparations," *The Atlantic*, June 2014.

2. It should be noted that although there are important similarities between sexism and racism, particularly with respect to the psychological and social mechanisms that make them possible, there are also important differences. For instance, Ann Cudd and Leslie E. Jones in their article "Sexism" point out that racism "is based on dubious theories about the differences between races, while sexual difference can hardly be denied" (219).

3. Robert Audi, *The Good in the Right* (Princeton, NJ: Princeton University Press, 2004), 195.

4. Audi, *The Good in the Right,* 191.

ANN E. CUDD AND LESLIE E. JONES

Sexism

In their essay, Ann Cudd and Leslie Jones begin by initially defining sexism as "a historically and globally pervasive form of oppression against women," which they then proceed
to elucidate. They distinguish three forms of sexism—institutional, interpersonal, and
unconscious—and after explaining two types of feminist philosophy, they address a number
of objections to feminist struggles against sexism.

It is a pervasive, long-standing, and deeply disturbing fact that, by many ways of measuring well-being,
women around the globe live lesser lives than men.
In much of the world they are less well nourished,
less healthy, and less well educated (UNIFEM 2000).
Everywhere they are vulnerable to violence and
abuse by men. It has been estimated that as a result
of these facts, and because in many places girl babies
are disproportionately aborted or killed, there are
one hundred million missing women (Dreze and Sen
1989). Many more women in the world lack access
to education and many more are illiterate. Jobs that
are high paying are much less likely to be held by
women. Tedious and menial work is much more likely
to be done by women. Women in the workforce are
paid less than their male counterparts, are more often
harassed and intimidated in work, and are far more
often responsible for childcare and housework "after
work." Independently of their participation in the paying workforce, women suffer from domestic violence
at much greater rates, bear primary responsibility
for childrearing and housework, and are much more
likely to be sick and poor in their old age. In much
of the world women do not have access to safe abortion, or sometimes even to contraception, further putting women's health and well-being at risk. Women
everywhere bear almost the full burden of unplanned

pregnancies. Women in many nations of the world
lack full formal equality under the law. Where they
have it, they are less likely to be able to access the
judicial system, and so still lack substantive equality. And almost nowhere in the world do women hold
high government offices at anywhere near the rates
of men. In short, when we compare the life prospects
of women and men, we find that a woman is far more
likely to be poor, unhealthy, abused, and politically
disenfranchised, even while she works longer hours
and is largely responsible for the primary care of
future generations.

Two general explanations could account for this
remarkable disparity in life prospects: (I) women
are by nature inferior to men, and so less worthy of
concern or less able to benefit from equal concern,
or (2) women are systematically disadvantaged by
society. Under the first we include explanations based
on psychology, biology, sociobiology, and so on that
maintain that natural differences between men and
women are sufficient to justify the comparatively
sadder life prospects of women. As we will discuss
below in "Objections," we suspect that many such
claims depend on truant evidence (Fausto-Sterling
1985), and deny that any immediate normative implications follow from whatever differences might exist
between men and women.

From Ann E. Cudd and Leslie E. Jones, "Sexism," in R. G. Frey and C. H. Wellman, eds., *A Companion to Applied Ethics* (Oxford:
Blackwell 2003), 102–17. Reprinted by permission of Blackwell Publishing Ltd.

In what follows we proceed on the assumption that the more plausible course is to take some version of the second as true. To follow this line in investigating the ways in which women are systematically disadvantaged is to investigate sexism. We begin with a characterization of sexism. We then offer a brief history of its social recognition. We turn then to the levels at which sexism conditions human social life, and discuss some paradigm examples of sexism. We then set out the two principal types of feminist theories of sexism, and conclude with a brief discussion of three objections to struggles against sexism.

WHAT IS SEXISM?

It is important to note at the outset that sexism is a highly complex notion. It is thus much easier to define conceptually, though this is no small task, than to concretely and unequivocally identify. Though there are certainly patent cases of sexism, on many definitions sexism is often only identifiable by its symptoms or consequences. We can quite readily explain that, if some distribution of opportunities systematically deprives women of what is offered to men, and there is no apparent overriding reason which justifies such a distribution, then we have a clear prima facie case of sexism. As a general claim this seems to us both undeniable and unassailable. The idea that sexism involves systematic inequality is, in short, a commonly recognized working definition. Yet those who deny that there is (much) sexism in the world, or in a particular case, often demand clear, ostensible evidence. Objective, operational criteria would be helpful here, and helpful for doing research or making policy as well. The task of finding such criteria is often quite difficult and comes from a wide array of theories covering the gamut of the social and psychological world. For sexism happens not only in explicitly institutionally structured settings, such as, for example, the denial of equal opportunity for jobs, but also in the daily and presumably much more spontaneous interactions between persons. As these latter interactions involve a wide variety of motives

and causes, they may appear to be idiosyncratic and individualized rather than socially constructed. In such cases the charge of sexism might then appear less apt because less than obvious. Thus, conceptual work of clarifying the nature of sexism is a far easier task than the practical work of showing that some particular concrete instance involving the mistreatment of women is the result of sexism or an instance of sexism. It is for this reason that much feminist work focuses on conceptual clarification and the organization of women's experience.

In its widest sense the term "sexism" can be used to refer to anything that creates, constitutes, promotes, sustains, or exploits an unjustifiable distinction between the sexes (Frye 1983: 18). In this wide sense the term "sexism" (and its nominative "sexist") can be used to refer to any purported though mistaken difference between the sexes. This neutral descriptive use of the term however, is deeply unsatisfactory. First, because the history of the term (brief as it is) shows it to have been intentionally modeled on "racism." As "racism" does not merely describe attempts to differentiate between races, but instead refers to pernicious distinctions between races, the term "sexism" is better understood as referring to pernicious distinctions between the sexes. Second, a natural use of the term implicitly denies its conceptual role in binding together and illuminating the various faces of women's social difference, and the ways in which these differences are harmful. Again just as racism is most accurately used to refer to various forms of oppression against non-Caucasians (at least in Western societies), in the more accurate and more specific sense with which we will be concerned here, "sexism" refers to a historically and globally pervasive form of oppression against women. It is this more specific and explicitly normative sense of sexism that is the subject of feminist inquiry.

One catalyst for the identification of sexism was women's participation in struggles against racism. In fact, the first wave of the women's movement began with the participation of a number of thoughtful women in the abolition movement of the nineteenth century (Stanton and Anthony 1981), and the "second wave" can likewise trace its resurgence to the women of the civil rights movement in the twentieth century

(Evans 1979). When contemplating a name for "the problem that has no name," as Betty Friedan (1983: Ch. 1) put it, there is little doubt that for many feminists the parallels with racism made the term "sexism" appealing. In some ways it might seem that this was an unfortunate start, for the differences between racism and sexism are sometimes obscured by the easy way in which they form lists of social wrongs. Perhaps the most important difference is that racism is based on dubious theories about the differences between the races, while sexual difference can hardly be denied. Racism seems often to be motivated by a hatred or fear of the other from which the conclusion comes that other "races" than one's own are inferior, a kind of racism that Kwame Anthony Appiah has called "intrinsic racism." Sexism, by contrast, is typically akin to what he calls "extrinsic racism," where the judgment that the other is inferior derives from the judgment that aspects or abilities of the other are inferior (Appiah 1990). Thus, many sexist men when so-charged can truly object that "I am not sexist; l love women," but this only means, at best, that they are not intrinsic sexists. However, there are many parallels between racism and sexism. For one thing, both are pervasive and have a high human cost. But, more importantly, the psychological mechanisms that make sexism and racism possible and desirable are similar: namely, our penchant for categorizing by social group, and making invidious distinctions between in-group and out-group members (Cudd 1998). Furthermore, the social mechanisms that maintain sexism and racism are similar. Both sexism and racism are maintained through systematic violence and economic disadvantage. Both are difficult to pinpoint, but can be statistically documented and are much more readily perceived by the victims than by the respective dominant social groups. Both sexism and racism can have devastating psychological effects on individuals. And both inspire enormously powerful backlash when they are publicly challenged. Considerable work remains to be done, however, on the relationship between the concepts of sexism and racism (Alcoff l998).

If one holds, as we do, that sexism is pervasive, both historically and globally, then it will be no surprise that its ground will be both wide and deep.

Institutions that are sexist will be both causes and effects of sexism. When regarded as a result of past sexism, such institutions will then carry on a tradition of, say, excluding women from available high-paying work. Managers and others who carry on this tradition may, of course, overtly maintain extrinsic sexism. They may sincerely, but falsely, believe women to be incapable of carrying on this work. This *intentional extrinsic sexism* should be distinguished from what might be called *individuated extrinsic sexism*, which maintains that while women (as a group) are capable of carrying on this work, no individual woman is. In either case it will be extremely difficult to persuasively establish such trenchant attitudes as sexist. In the latter case though women in general are held to be able to do this work, the technique of holding that each one now applying cannot do the job will effectively, if unintentionally, maintain the sexist tradition. Within that tradition such judgments are considered to be matters of keeping high standards, not sexism. As this practice requires an increasingly high degree of dubious judgment the longer it continues, over time it becomes correspondingly less reasonable to attribute to managers and others the sincere belief that women (as a group) are equally capable. In the case of intentional extrinsic sexism the fact that there are currently no or few women in the field contributes to the view that women cannot or do not want to do the work. The tradition of excluding women is, in this case, *intentional*, but is labeled by those who practice it "realism," not "sexism."

One important effect of the practice of excluding women in these ways is, of course, that women are made more dependent on others, usually men. By reducing the opportunities women have available to them, women are less able to clearly establish, both to themselves and to others, their general ability to accomplish high-paying (or high-status) tasks. Where these patterns are left unchallenged there is thus little to counter the claim that women are, by nature, more dependent. Moreover, these effects of sexist hiring practices are reinforced in a number of ways. They are reinforced by patterns of language which mark and delimit appropriate activities and attitudes on the basis of sex, and relegate the activities and attitudes of women to a lower status (i.e.

sexist language). And they are reinforced by systems of education and enculturation which support, if not create and coerce, discrete proclivities for girls and boys, and relegate the proclivities of girls to a lower status. These social aspects of sexism are further mirrored in psychological dispositions, desires, and self-concepts. Accepting the activities, attitudes, and proclivities which are typically associated with men as "normal" or "standard" for human beings (i.e. the man standard) would render the activities, attitudes, and proclivities which are typically associated with women, when different, abnormal or substandard. For instance, women will appear "highly emotional" or "hysterical" when they display more emotion and concern than men, or "brooding" and "moody" when less. More pertinently, recognition of the man standard enables us to make as much sense as one can of the characterization of pregnancy as a form of illness or a temporary disability.

We stated earlier that sexism involves systematic inequality. Our discussion to this point has attempted to elucidate this notion. On our view sexism is a systematic, pervasive, but often subtle, force that maintains the oppression of women, and that is at work through institutional structures, in interpersonal interactions and the attitudes that are expressed in them, and in the cognitive, linguistic, and emotional processes of individual minds. In short, sexism structures our very experience of the world, and makes that world on the whole worse for women than for men. . . .

LEVELS OF SEXISM

Sexism can be seen as a force responding to and molding human interactions. As a force, it can be seen, roughly, to operate at three levels: institutional sexism, which works on and through the level of social institutions; interpersonal sexism, which works on and through interactions among individuals who are not explicitly mediated by institutional structures; and unconscious sexism, which works at the personal level of the cognitive and affective processes of individuals. It is helpful to sort out these levels in order

to explain why some charges of sexism are relatively uncontroversial, while others are difficult to see or evidence conclusively.

Institutional sexism

Institutional sexism refers to invidious sexual inequalities in the explicit rules and implicit norms governing and structuring social institutions. Religious institutions provide a useful example of how explicit rules and implicit norms structure institutions. In the Catholic Church, for instance, it is an explicit rule that all priests are men and all nuns an women. Only priests can run the church hierarchy, and priests outrank nuns in most decision-making situations. While it is clear how explicit rules can govern and structure institutions, this example can also help us to see that implicit norms also structure Catholic experience and create sexual inequality. While it is no longer widely accepted as an explicit rule that in heterosexual marriage the man is the head of the household and the woman is the helpmeet, it is implied by the relative rank of priests and nuns in the church and by its sacred writings. This implicit norm positions men above women in marriage (as in all other social institutions in which both sexes are present), clearly an invidious sexual inequality. In addition to the more explicitly rule-governed institutions of government, religion, family, health care, and education, there are crucially important informally or implicitly structured institutions prime among them being language, and the sites of cultural and artistic production. To say that sexism is a systematic social injustice based on one's sex (Radcliff Richards 1980), or a discriminatory sex-role differentiation (Bartky 1990), is to speak of institutional sexism. Sexism, then, must be understood as a part of the social order, similar to the economic order of capitalism or the political order of liberalism.

Interpersonal sexism

Whereas institutional sexism involves the explicit rules and their implicit norms that sustain oppressive social institutions, interpersonal sexism involves interactions between persons that are not governed by explicit rules. Interpersonal sexism comprises actions and other expressions between persons that create, constitute, promote, sustain, and/or exploit invidious sexual inequalities.

The person who is acting in a sexist way or making a sexist expression need not intend sexism; there are intentional and unintentional forms of interpersonal sexism. Here are some examples from our experiences:

- As a child, the girl is not allowed the free play of her brothers; she is prevented by her parents and teachers from engaging in rough-and-tumble play, not included in activities involving building, transportation, etc., not encouraged to try or expected to succeed at sports, mathematics, or leadership activities, and required, unlike her brothers, to do domestic chores.
- In school the teachers require her to speak less and restrain her behavior more than boys. Teachers reward her with better grades for her passivity, but boys exclude her from their games and begin to take the superior attitudes of their fathers.
- In sports she sees males and manhood extolled, females and womanhood ridiculed. Coaches and team-mates insult male athletes by calling them "woman" or "girl," and praise them with the term "man."
- When a man and a woman negotiate a car loan or a home loan, or buy an expensive machine, the salesperson speaks only to the man. Supermarket ads are aimed, meanwhile, at women as housewives.
- In conversations between colleagues men are routinely deferred to while women's remarks are ignored. When a male colleague repeats what a female has said, he is complimented for his good idea.

Sexism is a key motif that unifies this otherwise seemingly disparate set of personal experiences. This list could, of course, be greatly expanded, and much feminist work has been devoted to increasing our stock of example experiences. This work is important because sexism is such an integral but unspoken part of the everyday world that both men and women have a difficult time recognizing it. For society's ground of legitimacy seems to require that injustice be recognized and socially opposed. Yet the injustice of sexism is built into the very fabric of everyone's everyday experiences from infancy on.

Unconscious sexism

"Unconscious sexism" refers to the psychological mechanisms and tacit beliefs, emotions, and attitudes that create, constitute, promote, sustain, and/or exploit invidious sexual inequalities. This category will be denied by many as vague, unprovable, or too easily invoked. But there are both conceptual and empirical arguments in favor of its existence. The conceptual argument is that the statistical evidence concerning the lesser lives that women live would be completely puzzling given the legal guarantees of equality for men and women in many countries were it not for the possibility of such unconscious sexism. Institutional and interpersonal sexism cannot alone account for all the data. That implies that there are unconscious attitudes and beliefs that allow persons in positions of power unconsciously to prefer men to women when social rewards are distributed, and yet not to see themselves or be seen as applying sexist standards.

The empirical argument is widely diffused, but accessible. It consists first of all in evidence for the existence of unconscious motivations, which is vast in the psychological literature. Second, there is evidence that when the same work is attributed to a woman it is judged of less value than when attributed to a man (Valian 1998). Third, there is evidence that women find it more painful to think of themselves as oppressed, and men find it more painful to think of themselves as the privileged gender. Thus, there is motivation for neither women nor men to think of women as oppressed and men as dominant (Branscombe 1998). Fourth, there is a great deal of evidence from social cognitive psychology to suggest that persons make invidious distinctions among salient social categories, that we tend to amplify them well beyond the real differences between individuals in those categories, and that sex is one of those categories (Tajfel 1981). Now since it surely cannot be argued that men get the worse end of this deal, this fact constitutes evidence for the claim that such cognitive processes tend to create unconscious sexist attitudes and beliefs. There is, no doubt, a great deal more evidence that could be cited, but this much should be sufficient to make the point that unconscious sexism is a real, documented, psychological phenomenon.

Having demonstrated its reality, however, some discussion and examples will be helpful to see how unconscious sexism is manifested and how one might go about discovering it. The key to recognizing unconscious motivations, especially unsavory ones that persons are reluctant to acknowledge in themselves, is to look for decisions or actions that could not be justified by a reasonable assessment of the available evidence. What counts as "reasonable" and "available" are crucial issues here, of course. By "reasonable" we mean consistent with one's other explicitly held beliefs and widely shared, non-sexist, knowledge in the community. We insist on explicit beliefs here because, of course, if one has tacit sexist beliefs the action could be reasonable but sexist, and yet not counted as unconscious. By "available evidence" we are referring to reports that would be made by a member of the community who does not have sexist beliefs or attitudes, or whose sexist beliefs played no role in the reports, or to widely shared, non-sexist, knowledge in the community. Of course, there may be no non-sexist members of any community. The practices of sexism affect one's self-conception. Internal critique may not be enough to free oneself from identification with those practices. But we must begin to identify sexist practices somewhere. Granting that it is possible that we will not recognize all unconscious (or, indeed, all conscious) sexism, we can still begin by finding the more obvious cases. Consider the following examples:

• A philosophy department is looking to hire a new faculty member. One-third of the applicants are women. One-third of the interview list is made up of women. In the interviews the women are judged as doing worse than the men.

The comments afterwards are that they don't seem "as polished" or "professional" as the men. The fact is that the women do not meet the interviewers' expectations of what a philosopher or a faculty member is supposed to look like, a stereotype that includes being a man.

• A department is considering how to advise a female colleague and a male colleague concerning their chances for tenure. They have equal but modest publishing records, and roughly equal but modest teaching records. However, the female colleague has far more service. Both colleagues have been active participants in the departmental politics and have voiced strong opinions in departmental meetings. The male is judged to be an excellent colleague, while the female is judged to be uncollegial. They give the male colleague a very positive report for his tenure prospects, and the female is warned that she must publish more and improve her teaching to get tenure. In fact, the department has judged her to be worse because they feel uncomfortable with a strong, active woman, while the man is judged to have leadership qualities.

• A drug is being tested for its effectiveness in preventing heart disease. All the research subjects are men. When asked to account for this the research team leader responds that women's hormones would interfere with the study. While it is surely true that the drug could affect women differently from men as a result of female hormones, it is equally true that it could affect men differently from women as a result of male hormones. This symmetry is lost on the research team, who, like most of us, tend to think of women as the ones with the "interfering" or abnormal hormones.

Unconscious sexism often seems to be innocent, in the sense that the beliefs or feelings that make it up are never voiced, and often based on widely shared stereotypes. Whether or not it is innocent surely depends on the degree to which the individual has access to information that counters the unconscious sexist beliefs and attitudes, a condition that depends on larger social factors. Although we do believe that "sexism" names not only a mistake but a prima facie wrong, there are cases where one can commit this wrong and yet not be culpable.

These levels of sexism are, of course, interrelated. Understood as institutional discrimination, sexism concerns the interactions between men and women only as symptoms of a more pervasive problem. Social institutions guide, and on some accounts cause, our interpersonal attitudes. Our self-conceptions and our conception of others are at least partially a product of the social structures through which we interact with one another. How they are interrelated is a central question within feminism, feminist philosophy, and feminist social science. Different ways of understanding the inter-relations between these levels result in different, and sometimes quite divergent, accounts. Two types of account are prominent in the feminist literature. In the next section we discuss these two types.

TWO FEMINIST VIEWS OF SEXISM

Though feminists agree that sexism structures our very experience of the world, feminist theories of sexism vary considerably. None the less, they can be very roughly divided into two categories. First, what can be labeled "equality feminism" maintains that social institutions are the primary medium of sexism. Men and women do not differ markedly in their potential capacities, interests, and abilities. Given similar training, men and women would develop fairly similar talents, at least as similar as those between men or between women. Thus if we are to transform society it will require that we resist and undermine those institutions that enforce sex differences and disproportionately deprive women of opportunities to develop highly valued social skills. Equality feminists need not accept what we have above called "the man standard." Rather, most contemporary equality feminists employ measures of social value such as utility, respect for human rights, or hypothetical agreement in order to develop gender-neutral standards by which to judge the opportunities, activities, and proclivities of men and women.

Alternatively, "difference feminists" maintain that unconscious desires are the primary medium of sexism. Accordingly, social institutions are the result, rather than the cause, of sexism. Recently a variety of feminists holding this view have attempted to both articulate the differences between men and women and re-evaluate equality feminism. Some, like Carol Gilligan (1982), Nel Noddings (1984), and Sara Ruddick (1989), have argued that women's "different voice" involves a greater emphasis on responsiveness, caring, and the maintenance of particular, concrete relationships. This voice is undervalued in society, they argue, because of the dominance of "responsibility"—a notion which involves a strict adherence to principle and which, they argue, typifies the male point of view. Others skeptical of gender neutrality are also skeptical of the idea that caring and relationship maintenance best characterize women's difference. They thus seek to identify a different difference. Catherine MacKinnon (1987: 39) writes: "women value care because men have valued us according to the care we give them, and we could probably use some." In her view, since women's subordinate position in society informs their experience of the world, and so requires concrete critical evaluation, it can also give them a unique, and privileged, position from which to criticize our social traditions. Somewhat similarly, Luce Irigaray argues that the critical revaluation of women should neither reassert what has traditionally been taken to be women's nature, nor strive for equality with men. She maintains that the law has a duty to "offer justice to *two genders that differ* in their needs, their desires, their properties" (Irigaray 1993: 4).

Both views aim to transform institutional sexism, interpersonal sexism, and unconscious sexism. They differ, however, over just what form such a transformation would take. For equality feminists the notion that there is a significant difference between men and women, a difference that makes a difference, seems more likely to sustain the global disparity existing between men and women since this disparity has been built on the basis of sex differentiation. For difference feminists, on the other hand, the notion that there is no significant difference between men and women, seems likely to undermine women's emancipation. Since women have been defined and have defined themselves in relation to men, as subordinate to dominant, women's independence depends on discovering, or perhaps imaginatively inventing, a different identity. Importantly, both equality feminists and difference feminists have the same worry. For both, the idea that an attempted transformation of society will result in a mere modification of sexism rather than its elimination is, given its evident though under-acknowledged depth and pervasiveness, a predominant, reasonable, and clearly practical concern.

OBJECTIONS

Three kinds of objections have been raised to feminist struggles against sexism, which we shall call the objections from *essentialism, skepticism*, and *defeatism*. The objection from *essentialism* maintains that there are essential biological or psychological differences between men and women such that true equality or even equal evaluation of men and women will ultimately be impossible or will too greatly restrain our liberty. Such objections to feminist efforts to remedy the ravages of sexism have a long history, from Aristotle's view of woman as partial man through biological theories of inferiority propagated in the nineteenth and twentieth centuries to Freudian psychoanalytic theories of femininity. A recent and currently influential version of this objection appeals to evolutionary psychology to explain the differences between the status of men and women. According to evolutionary psychology, there are distinct male and female psychologies because of the different reproductive strategies that each sex pursues, and the resulting psychologies make males more competitive, independent, and aggressive, while females are more nurturing and concerned about interpersonal relations. In addition, at least one proponent of evolutionary psychology has claimed that male psychology makes it inevitable that men will "run to extremes—or, in other words, that men are disproportionately represented in the top and bottom of many measurements" (Guyot 2001: B15). Thus, the best lawyers, artists, politicians, businessmen, and so

on must be men. So, Guyot argues, it would be inefficient and morally wrong to bring about parity in gender representation of these fields.

To this objection we have three responses. First, specifically regarding evolutionary psychology, it is a highly theorized but largely untested hypothesis at this point. Given its genealogy as another in a string of allegedly scientific proofs of women's inferiority, it is important to be skeptical until and unless it scores empirical successes. Second, and this response applies to any scientific theory about sexual difference, normative implications of difference are never directly implied by any descriptive differences. That is, it is fallacious to infer from the fact of sexual difference that women should therefore not have equal chances for social success. Finally, the ideals of liberal individualism and equality require each individual to be treated as a unique person, deserving of praise or social rewards based on his or her actual individual merit, and not based on the average merits of her class, caste, race, or gender. So even if it were true that women on average are less well suited to be lawyers, or whatever, it does not follow that there should be no safeguards in place to ensure that women are not discriminated against because of their sex. In fact, if women are on average less well suited to various occupations it raises the likelihood that employers will unfairly judge individual women by their sex rather than their individual merits.

The objection from *skepticism* maintains that sexism is admittedly a serious problem in some other countries, but, though in has been a problem in our society in the past, sexism has largely been overcome. Women are not prevented from gaining an education, entering the workforce, or asserting their equal right to vote, to own property, or to divorce. In some cases women are treated preferentially and sometimes even outperform men. Therefore, there is no reason to pursue any remedies to sexism—it is already gone. This sort of objection has been leveled by Christina Hoff Sommers (2000). However, this objection overlooks a wealth of statistical information that proves that women's well-being is still compromised in contemporary American society. The gender wage gap hovers around 75 percent (Institute for Women's Policy Research 1997b)—up considerably from the 59 percent of the late 1970s, but still hardly something to be satisfied with. According to the Joint Center for Poverty Research, although the overall rate of poverty in the United States in 1997 was 13.3 percent, the rate for women was 24 percent. Women suffer from domestic violence at roughly four times the rate of men (US Department of Justice 2000). In 2001, 73 women served in the US Congress (13.6 percent): thirteen in the Senate, and 60 in the House, both all-time highs. Of course, no woman has ever been US President, and only two women are now and have ever been Justices of the Supreme Court. Women in state legislatures compose only 22.4 percent even of those bodies (Center for American Women in Politics 2001). Women own businesses at approximately half the rate of men, and of the top one hundred wealthiest people in *Forbes Magazine's* list for 2001, only ten were women. And this is only a partial list of the great inequalities suffered by women in contemporary US society. Finally, it is also important to point out to the skeptic that the fact that women are suffering from sexism in much of the world is itself harmful to all women. Women form a social group— a non-voluntary social group. They thereby share each other's fate to an extent. If women are harassed on the streets of Kabul then American women who travel there will be harassed. If women are subjected to humiliating or violent treatment in East Asia, then American women who travel there will be as well. If women are not taken seriously in a country, then how can a woman diplomat from America hope to do her job there? The skeptic thus underestimates both the degree to which sexism still exists in Western society and the effects that sexism worldwide has on all women.

The *defeatist* argues that there is nothing that he or anyone personally can do to fight sexism. Defeatists often continue by arguing that since they are not themselves mistreating women, do not dislike women or hold them to be inferior, they should not therefore be required to do anything to combat sexism; nor do they think that anything constructive can be done to eliminate it. Defeatists overlook the existence of institutional and unconscious sexism. They fail to recognize that they can participate in sexism even without oven, conscious sexist attitudes. If they take seriously the problem of sexism, then they should examine their behaviors, choices, and preferences for what those express to the world. Perhaps they will find

underneath a dislike of a certain co-worker, say, a prejudice against assertive women that they do not harbor against assertive men. This would be an example of unconscious sexism (made conscious). They should also examine how they respond to other people's overt interpersonal sexism. Do they laugh at wife jokes? Look the other way from sexual harassment in the office? Such behaviors support sexism, and thus injustice. Finally, the defeatist who acknowledges institutional sexism has the obligation not to support it: not to vote for it, not to buy from it, not to encourage it. The defeatist has no real defense, in other words, as long as he admits that there may be unconscious sexism, interpersonal sexism among others, or institutional sexism.

In conclusion, sexism is alive and well in contemporary Western society, and to an even greater degree in much of the rest of the world. Sexism is a serious form of oppression, and, as such, it is incumbent on decent people to oppose it, though the form that opposition should take remains a serious matter for theorists and activists alike.

REFERENCES

Alcoff, I. M. (1998) Racism. In *A Companion to Feminist Philosophy*. Malden, MA: Blackwell.

Appiah, A. (1990) Racisms. In D. T. Goldberg (ed.), *Anatomy of Racism*. Minneapolis: University of Minnesota Press.

Bartky, S.L. (1990). *Femininity and Domination*. New York: Routledge.

Branscombe, N. (1998) Thinking about one's gender group's privileges or disadvantages: consequences for Well-being in women and men. *British Journal of Social Psychology*, 37: 167-84.

Center for American Women in Politics (2001) www.rci.rutgers.edu/-cawp/ facis/cawpts.html.

Cudd, A. E. (1998) Psychological explanations of oppression. In C. Willen (ed.). *Theorizing Multiculturalism*. Malden, MA: Blackwell.

Dreze, J. and Sen, A (1989) *Hunger and Public Action*. Oxford: Clarendon Press.

Evans, S. (1979) *Personal Polities: The Roots of Women's Liberation in the Civil Right Movement and the New Left*. New York: Vintage Books.

Fausto-Sterling, A. (1985) *Myths of Gender: Biological Theories about Women and Men*. New York: Basic Books.

Friedan, B. (1983) *The Feminine Mystique*, 20th Anniv. edn New York: Dell.

Frye, M. (1983) *The Politics of Reality.* Trumansburg, New York: The Crossing Press.

Gilligan, C. (1982) *In a Different Voice: Psychological Theory and Woman's Development.* Cambridge, MA: HHarvard University Press.

Guyot, J. F. (2001) The defining moment for gender equity. *The Chronicle of Higher Education.* April 20

———. (1997b) *The Wage Gap: Men's and Women's Earnings.* Briefing Paper. Washington, DC.

Irigaray, L., (1993) *Sexes and Genealogies*, trans. Gillian Gill. New York: Columbia University Press.

MacKinnon, C., (1987) *Feminism Unmodified: Discourses on Life and Law.* Cambridge, MA: Harvard University Press.

Noddings, N. (1984) *Caring: A Feminine Approach to Ethics and Moral Education.* Berkeley, CA: University of California Press.

Radcliffe Richards, J. (1980) *The Skeptical Feminist.* London: Routledge & Kegan Paul.

Ruddiek, S. (1989) *Maternal Thinking: Toward a Politics of Peace.* New York: Basic Books.

Sommers, C. H. (2000) *The War Against Boys: How Misguided Feminism is Harming our Young Men.* New York: Simon and Schuster.

Stanton, E. C. and Anthony, S. B. (1981) *Correspondence Writing, Speeches*, ed. E. C. DuBois. New York: Schocken Books.

Tajfel. H. (1981) *Human Groups and Social Categories.* Cambridge: Cambridge University Press.

UNIFEM (2000) *Progess of the World's Woman 2000.* New York: United Nations.

US Department of Justice. Office of Justice Programs (2000) *Extent, Nature, and Consequences of Intimate Partner Violence: Findings from the National Violence against Women Survey.* Washington, DC.

Valian, V. (1998) *Why So Slow? The Advancement of Woman.* Cambridge, MA; MTT Press.

READING QUESTIONS

1. How do the authors characterize the three levels of sexism they discuss—institutional, interpersonal, and unconscious?
2. What are the two feminist views of sexism? How do they differ?
3. What are the three objections to attempts to eradicate sexism that Cudd and Jones raise, and how do they answer them?

DISCUSSION QUESTIONS

1. Consider whether classifying an individual as either male or female is morally wrong. How might the oppression of women in society be overcome without having to avoid gender division?
2. Consider unconscious sexism. How might this form of sexism in an individual be recognized and eliminated?

J. L. A. GARCIA

The Heart of Racism

Some conceptions of racism are belief-based in the sense that they take the holding of racist beliefs to be necessary and perhaps sufficient for an individual to be a racist. J. L. A. Garcia opposes this view, arguing that racism is best understood as a matter of attitudes of hatred, disregard, or in some cases lack of proper regard for members of a certain race because of their race. After explaining this "volitional" conception of racism, Garcia proceeds to explore various implications and advantages of this view, and to consider some cases that might appear to be problematic for his conception.

Recommended Reading: virtue ethics, chap. 1, sec. 2E.

The phenomenon of racism having plagued us for many centuries now, it is somewhat surprising to learn that the concept is so young. The second edition of *The Oxford English Dictionary* (1989) dates the earliest appearances of the term 'racism' only to the 1930s.[1] During that decade, as the shadow of Nazism lengthened across Europe, social thinkers coined the term to describe the ideas and theories of racial biology and anthropology to which the Nazi movement's intellectual defenders appealed in justifying its political program. . . .

These origins are reflected in the definition that the *O.E.D.* still offers: "The theory that distinctive human characteristics and abilities are determined by race."[2] Textbook definitions also echo this origin: "Racism—a doctrine that one race is superior" (Schaefer, 1990: p. 27). Recently, however, some have argued that these definitions no longer capture what people mean when they talk of racism in the moral and political discourse that has become the term's primary context. Some on the political left argue that definitions reducing racism to people's beliefs do not do justice to racism as a sociopolitical reality. Robert Miles records the transition in the thought of Ambalvaner Sivanandan, director of Britain's

Institute of Race Relations, who abandoned his earlier account of racism (1973) as "an explicit and systematic ideology of racial superiority" because later (1983) he came to think that "racism is about power not prejudice." Eventually (1985), he saw racism as "structures and institutions with power to discriminate" (1985). (Quoted at Miles, 1989: p. 54.)[3] From the right, the philosopher Antony Flew has suggested that, to identify racism with "negative beliefs" about "actual or alleged matters of fact" is a "sinister and potentially dangerous thing"—it "is to demand, irrespective of any evidence which might be turned up to the contrary, that everyone must renounce certain disapproved propositions." Flew worries that this poses a serious threat to intellectual freedom, and proposes a behavioral understanding of 'racism' as "meaning the advantaging or disadvantaging of individuals for no better reason than that they happen to be members of this racial group rather than that."

I agree with these critics that in contemporary moral and political discourse and thought, what we have in mind when we talk of racism is no longer simply a matter of beliefs However, I think their proposed reconceptions are themselves inadequate. In this paper, I present an account of racism that, I

From "The Heart of Racism," *Journal of Social Philosophy* 27 (1996): pp. 5–22 and 34.

think, better reflects contemporary usage of the term, especially its primary employment as both descriptive and evaluative, and I sketch some of this view's implications for the morality of race-sensitive discrimination in private and public life. I will also briefly point out some of this account's advantages over various other ways of thinking about racism that we have already mentioned—racism as a doctrine, as a socioeconomic system of oppression, or as a form of action. One notable feature of my argument is that it begins to bring to bear on this topic in social philosophy points made in recent criticisms of modernist moral theory offered by those who call for increased emphasis on the virtues. (This voice has hitherto largely been silent in controversies within practical social philosophy.)

A VOLITIONAL CONCEPTION OF RACISM

Kwame Anthony Appiah rightly complains that, although people frequently voice their abhorrence of racism, "rarely does anyone stop to say what it is, or what is wrong with it" (Appiah, 1990:3). This way of stating the program of inquiry we need is promising, because, although racism is not essentially "a moral doctrine," *pace* Appiah, it is always a moral evil (Appiah, 1990: 13). No account of what racism is can be adequate unless it at the same time makes clear what is wrong with it. How should we conceive racism, then, if we follow Appiah's advice "to take our ordinary ways of thinking about race and racism and point up some of their presuppositions"? (Appiah, 1990: 4). My proposal is that we conceive of racism as fundamentally a vicious kind of racially based disregard for the welfare of certain people. In its central and most vicious form, it is a hatred, ill-will, directed against a person or persons on account of their assigned race. In a derivative form, one is a racist when one either does not care at all or does not care enough (i.e., as much as morality requires) or does not care in the right ways about people assigned to a certain racial group, where this disregard is based

on racial classification. Racism, then, is something that essentially involves not our beliefs and their rationality or irrationality, but our wants, intentions, likes, and dislikes and their distance from the moral virtues. Such a view helps explain racism's conceptual ties to various forms of *hatred* and contempt. (Note that 'contempt' derives from 'to contemn'—not to care (about someone's needs and rights)).

It might be objected that there can be no such thing as racism because, as many now affirm, "there are no races." This objection fails. First, that 'race' is partially a social construction does not entail that there are no races. One might even maintain, though I would not, that race-terms, like 'person,' preference,' 'choice,' 'welfare,' etc., and, more controversially, such terms as 'reason for action,' 'immoral,' 'morally obligatory,' etc. may be terms that, while neither included within nor translatable into, the language of physics, nevertheless arise in such a way and at such a fundamental level of social or anthropological discourse that they should be counted as real, at least, for purposes of political and ethical theory. Second, as many racial anti-realists concede, even if it were true that race is unreal, what we call racism could still be real (Appiah, 1992: p. 45). What my account of racism requires is not that there be races, but that people make distinctions in their hearts, whether consciously or not on the basis of their (or others') racial classifications. That implies nothing about the truth of those classifications.

Lawrence Blum raises a puzzling question about this. We can properly classify a person S as a racist even if *we* do not believe in races. But what if S herself does not believe in them? Suppose S is a White person who hates Black people, but picks them out by African origin, attachment to African cultures, residence or rearing in certain U.S. neighborhoods, and so on. Should we call S racist if she does not hate Black people *as* such (i.e., on the basis of her assigning them to a Black race), but hates all people she thinks have been corrupted by their internalizing undesirable cultural elements from Harlem or Watts, or from Nairobi, or the Bunyoro? I think the case underdescribed. Surely, a person can disapprove of a culture or a family of cultures without being racist. However, cultural criticism can be a mask for a deeper (even unconscious) dislike that is defined by racial classifications. If the person transfers her disapproval of the group's culture to contempt or disregard for those designated as the group's members, then she is already doing something morally vicious. When she assigns all the groups disliked to the same racial classification, then we are entitled to suspect racism, because we have good grounds to suspect that her disavowals of underlying racial classifications are false. If S hates the cultures of various Black groups for having a certain feature, but does not extend that disapproval to other cultures with similar features, then that strongly indicates racism.

Even if she is more consistent, there may still be racism, but of a different sort. Adrian Piper suggests that, in the phenomenon she calls 'higher order discrimination,' a person may claim to dislike members of a group because she thinks they have a certain feature, but really disapprove of the feature because she associates it with the despised group. This 'higher order discrimination' would, of course, still count as racist in my account, because the subject's distaste for the cultural element derives from and is morally infected by race-based disregard.

We should also consider an additional possibility. A person may falsely attribute an undesirable feature to people she assigns to a racial group because of her disregard for those in the group. This will often take the forms of exaggeration, seeing another in the worst light, and withholding from someone the benefit of the doubt. So, an anti-Semite may interpret a Jew's reasonable frugality as greed; a White racist may see indolence in a Black person's legitimate resistance to unfair expectations of her, and so on.

Thinking of racism as thus rooted in the heart fits common sense and ordinary usage in a number of ways. It is instructive that contemptuous White racists have sometimes called certain of their enemies 'Nigger-lovers.' When we seek to uncover the implied contrast-term for this epithet, it surely suggests that enemies of those who "love" Black people, as manifested in their efforts to combat segregation, and so forth, are those who hate Black people or who have little or no human feelings toward us at all. This is surely born out by the behavior and rhetoric of paradigmatic White racists. . . .

On my account, racism retains its strong ties to intolerance. This tie is uncontroversial. Marable, for example, writes of "racism, and other types of intolerance, such as anti-Semitism . . . [and] homophobia . . ." (Marable, 1992: 3, 10). Intolerant behavior is to be expected if racism is hatred. How, after all, can one tolerate those whom one wants to injure, and why ought one to trouble oneself to tolerate those whom one disregards?

Such an account of racism as I propose can both retain and explain the link between the two "senses of" racism found in some dictionaries: (i) belief in superiority of R1s to R2s, and (ii) inter-racial 'antagonism'.[4] I suggest that we think of these as two elements within most common forms of racism. In real racists, I think, (ii) is normally a ground of (i) (though sometimes the reverse is true), and (i) is usually a rationalization of (ii). What is more important is that (i) may not be logically *necessary* for racism. (In some people, it may nonetheless be a psychological necessity.) However, even when (ii) is a result of (i), it is (ii) and not (i), that makes a person a racist. (Logically, not causally.)

My view helps explain why racism is always immoral. . . . Its immorality stems from its being opposed to the virtues of benevolence and justice. Racism is a form of morally insufficient (i.e., vicious) concern or respect for some others. It infects actions in which one (a) tries to injure people assigned to a racial group because of their XXXXX, or (b) objectionably fails to take care *not* to injure them (where the agent accepts harm to R1s because she disregards the interests and needs of R1s because they are R1s). We can also allow that an action is racist in a derivative and weaker sense when it is less directly connected to racist disregard, for example, when someone (c) does something that (regardless of its intended, probable, or actual effects) stems in significant part from a belief or apprehension about other people, that one has (in significant part) because of one's disaffection toward them because of (what one thinks to be their) race. Racism, thus, will often offend against justice, not just against benevolence, because one sort of injury to another is withholding from her the respect she is owed and the deference and trust that properly express that respect. Certain forms of paternalism, while benevolent in some of their goals, may be vicious in the means employed. The paternalist may deliberately choose to deprive another of some goods, such as those of (licit) freedom and (limited) self-determination in order to obtain other goods for her. Here, as elsewhere, the good end need not justify the unjust means. Extreme paternalism constitutes an instrumentally malevolent benevolence: one harms A to help her. I return to this below in my discussion of 'Kiplingesque' racism.

If, as I maintain, racism is essentially a form of racially focused ill-will or disregard (including disrespect), then that explains why "Racism' is inescapably a morally loaded term. . . .

My account of racism suggests a new understanding of racist behavior and of its immorality. This view allows for the existence of both individual racism and institutional racism. Moreover, it makes clear the connection between the two, and enables us better to understand racism's nature and limits. Miles challenges those who insist on talking only of 'racisms' in the plural to "specify what the many different racisms have in common" (Miles, 1989: p. 65). This may go too far. Some philosophers have offered respected accounts of common terms that seem not to require that every time A is an F and B is an F, then A and B must have some feature in common (other than that of being-an-F, if that *is* a feature). Nominalism and Wittgenstein's "family resemblance" view are two examples. However, if we are not dealing with two unrelated concepts the English terms for which merely happen to have the same spelling and pronunciation (like the 'bank' of a river and the 'bank' that offers loans), then we should be able to explain how the one notion develops out of the other.

Some think that institutions, etc. are racist when they are structures of racial domination, and that individual beliefs, etc. are racist when they express, support, or justify racial superiority. Both, of course, involve denying or violating the equal dignity and worth of all human beings independent of race. This sort of approach contains some insight. However, it leaves unclear how the two levels or types of racism are related, if they are related at all. Thus, such views leave us rather in the dark about what it is in virtue of which each is a form of racism. Some say that institutional racism is what is of central importance; individual racism, then, matters only inasmuch as it perpetuates institutional racism. I think that claim reverses the order of moral importance, and I shall maintain that the individual level has more explanatory importance.

At the individual level, it is in desires, wishes, intentions, and the like that racism fundamentally lies, not in actions or beliefs. Actions and beliefs are racist in virtue of their *coming from* racism in the desires, wishes, and intentions of individuals, not in virtue of their *leading to* these or other undesirable effects. Racism is, for this reason, an interesting case study in what we might call 'infection' (or 'input-centered' or backward-looking) models of wrongdoing, in contrast to the more familiar consequentialist and other result-driven approaches. Infection models of wrongdoing—according to which an action is wrong because of the moral disvalue of what goes into it rather than the nonmoral value of what comes out of it—seem the best approach within virtues-based ethics. In such ethical systems, actions are immoral insofar as they are greedy, arrogant, uncaring, lustful, contemptuous, or otherwise corrupted in their motivational sources. Finally, desires, wishes, and intentions *are* racist when they either are, or in certain ways reflect, attitudes that withhold from people, on the basis of their being assigned to a particular race, levels or forms of good-will, caring, and well-wishing that moral virtue demands. At its core, then, racism consists in vicious attitudes toward people based on their assigned race. From there, it extends to corrupt the people, individual actions, institutional behavior, and systemic operations it infects. Some, however, seem not to think of racism in this way, as something that, like cruelty or stupidity, can escalate from its primary occurrence in individual people to infect collective thought and decision-making of organizations and, from there, to contaminate the behavior of institutions as well. So to think of it is to see the term as not merely descriptive and evaluative, but also as having some explanatory force.

How is institutional racism connected to racism within the individual? Let us contrast two pictures. On the first, institutional racism is of prime moral and explanatory importance. Individual racism, then, matters (and, perhaps, occurs) only insofar as it contributes to the institutional racism which subjugates a racial group. On the second, opposed view, racism within individual persons is of prime moral and explanatory import, and institutional racism occurs and matters because racist attitudes (desires, aims, hopes, fears, plans) infect the reasoning, decision-making, and action of individuals not only in their private behavior, but also when they make and execute the policies of those institutions in which they operate. I take the second view. Institutional racism, in the central sense of the term, occurs when institutional behavior stems from (a) or (b) above or, in an extended sense, when it stems from (c). Obvious examples would be the infamous Jim Crow laws that originated in the former Confederacy after Reconstruction. Personal racism exists when and insofar as a person is racist in her desires, plans, aims, etc., most notably when this racism informs her conduct. In the same way, institutional racism exists when and insofar as an institution is racist in the aims, plans, etc., that people give it, especially when their racism informs its behavior. Institutional racism begins when racism extends from the hearts of individual people to become institutionalized. What matters is that racist attitudes contaminate the operation of the institution; it is irrelevant what its original point may have been, what its designers meant it to do. If it does not operate from those motives (at time T1), then it does not embody institutional racism (at T1). On this view, some phenomena sometimes described as institutionally racist will turn out not to be properly so describable, but others not normally considered to be institutionally racist will fit the description. . . .

Not only is individual racism of greater explanatory import, I think it also more important morally. Those of us who see morality primarily as a matter of suitably responding to other people and to the opportunities they present for us to pursue value will understand racism as an offense against the virtues of benevolence and justice in that it is an undue restriction on the respect and goodwill owed people. (Ourselves as well as others; racism, we must remember, can take the form of self-hate.) Indeed, as follows from what I have elsewhere argued, it is hard to render coherent the view that racist hate is bad mainly for its bad effects. The sense in which an action's effects are bad is that they are undesirable. But that it is to say that these effects are evil things to want and thus things the desire for which is evil, vicious. Thus, any claim that racial disadvantage is a bad thing presupposes a more basic claim that race-hatred is vicious. What is more basic morally is also morally more important in at least one sense of that term.[5] Of course, we should bear in mind that morality is not the same as politics. What is morally most important may not be the problem whose rectification is of greatest political urgency.

IMPLICATIONS AND ADVANTAGES

There are some noteworthy implications and advantages of the proposed way of conceiving of racism.

First, it suggests that prejudice, in its strict sense of 'pre-judgment,' is not essential to racism, and that some racial prejudice may not be racist, strictly speaking. Racism is not, on this view, primarily a cognitive matter, and so it is not in its essence a matter of how or when one makes one's judgments. Of course, we can still properly call prejudiced-based beliefs racist in that they *characteristically* either are rooted in prior racial disregard, which they rationalize, or they foster such disregard. Whether having such a belief is immoral in a given case will depend in large part on whether it is a rationalization for racial disaffection. It may depend on *why* the individual is so quick to think the worst of people assigned to the other racial group. Of course, even when the order is reversed and the prejudice does not whitewash a prior and independent racial disaffection, but causes a subsequent one, the person will still be racist because of that disaffection, even if she is not racist in holding that belief, that is, even if she does not hold it for what we might call 'racist reasons.' My guess is that, in most people who have been racists for some expanse of time, the belief and the disregard will reinforce each other.

A person may hold prejudices about people assigned to a race without herself being racist and without it being racist of her to hold those prejudices.[6] The beliefs themselves can be called 'racist' in an extended sense because they are characteristically racist. However, just as one may make a wise move without acting wisely (as when one makes a sound investment for stupid reasons), so one may hold a racist belief without holding it for racist reasons. One holds such a belief for racist reasons when it is duly connected to racial disregard: when it is held in order to rationalize that disaffection or when contempt inclines one to attribute undesirable features to people assigned to a racial group. One whose racist beliefs have no such connection to any racial disregard in her heart does not hold them in a racist way and if she has no such disregard, she is not herself a racist, irrespective of her prejudices.

Second, when racism is so conceived, the person with racist feelings, desires, hopes, fears, and dispositions is racist even if she never acts on these attitudes in such a way as to harm people designated as members of the hated race. (This is not true when racism is conceived as consisting in a system of social oppression.) It is important to know that racism can exist in (and even pervade) societies in which there is no systematic oppression, if only because the attempts to oppress fail. Even those who think racism important primarily because of its effects should find this possibility of inactive racism worrisome for, so long as this latent racism persists, there is constant threat of oppressive behavior.

Third, on this view, race-based preference (favoritism) need not be racist. *Preferential* treatment in affirmative action, while race-based, is not normally based on any racial disregard. This is a crucial difference between James Meredith's complaint against the University of Mississippi and Allan Bakke's complaint against the University of California at Davis Medical School (see Appiah, 1990: p. 15). Appiah says that what he calls "Extrinsic racism has usually been the basis [1] for treating people worse than we otherwise might, [2] for giving them less than their humanity entitles them to" (Appiah, 1992:18). What is important to note here is that (1) and (2) are not at all morally equivalent. Giving someone less than her humanity entitles her to is morally wrong. To give someone less than we could give her, and even to give

her less than we would if she (or we, or things) were different is to treat her "worse [in the sense of 'less well'] than we otherwise might." However, the latter is not normally morally objectionable. Of course, we may not deny people even gratuitous favors out of hatred or contempt, whether or not race-based, but that does not entail that we may not licitly choose to bestow favors instead on those to whom we feel more warmly. That I feel closer to A than I do to B does not mean that I feel hatred or callousness toward B. I may give A more than A has a claim to get from me and more than I give B, while nevertheless giving B everything to which she is entitled (and even more). Thus, race-based favoritism does not have to involve (2) and need not violate morality.

Appiah recognizes this fact, saying that 'intrinsic racism,' because of its ties to solidarity, fraternity, and even "family feeling," is often merely "the basis for acts of supererogation, the treatment of others better than we otherwise might, better than moral duty demands of us" (Appiah, 1990: 11). However, he warns ominously, "This is a contingent fact. There is no logical impossibility in the idea of racialists whose moral beliefs lead them to feelings of hatred for other races while leaving them no room for love for members of their own" (Appiah, 1990: 12). But why should the fact that this remains a logical possibility incline us to condemn racial preference? When the possibility is actualized, and someone feels, not special regard for those who share assignment to her own racial group (along with adequate affection for people assigned to other groups), but hatred for those allocated to other groups (whether or not there is affection for people allocated to her own), then we have illicit antipathy not licit favoritism. When this ugly possibility is not actualized, however, then we need some independent argument against favoritism. Appiah invokes Kant for this purpose (Appiah, 1992: 18; 1990: 14, 15). However, the invocation is insufficient. There is no obvious inconsistency in willing that a moderate form of race preference, like other moderate forms of kinship preference, should be a universal law of nature, as Kant's own principal test of universalization requires.[7]

Discrimination *on the basis of* race, then, need not be immoral. It is discrimination *against* people because of their racial assignment that cannot but be immoral. Christopher Jencks says "we need formal discrimination in favor of blacks to offset the effects of persistent informal discrimination against them."[8] Suppose Jencks' claim about our need for discrimination is true. Can racial favoritism ever be justified? It will help to remind ourselves that discriminating *in favor of* R1s need not entail discriminating *against* R2s. The latter consists in acting either (i) with intention of harming R2s, or (ii) with hard-hearted racist indifference to the action's foreseeable ill effects on R2s,[9] or (iii) from racist beliefs held because of racist disaffection. Similarly, racial self-segregation need not be immoral. It may be especially suspect when White people do it, because we have good historical reason to be suspicious that what is presented as merely greater-than-morally-required concern for fellow White people really involves less-than-morally-required concern for Black people. It may also be ill-advised even when it is Black people who do it. However, in neither case must it be immoral. In neither case must it be racist.

According to this conception of racism, *de jure racial segregation* violates political morality primarily because (and, therefore, when) it expresses a majority's (or minority's) racial indifference, contempt, or ill-will. It is therein vicious, offending against the virtues of both benevolence and justice. However, it need not have such origin, a fact illustrated by recent suggestions to establish separate academies to deal with the educational challenges confronting young Black males, and by efforts to control the racial demography of public housing projects in order to avoid problems that have sometimes arisen when such projects became virtually all-Black or virtually all-White. Whatever the social merit of such proposals, in cases like these, even if the segregation in the end proves immoral, this is not intrinsic. There must be some special additional factor present that makes it immoral. De facto racial segregation (mere separation or disproportional representation) need not be morally problematic at all when it happens to result from decently and responsibly motivated individual or social actions.[10] However, it will be immoral if its bad effects on, say, R1s are accepted out of racist hardheartedness, that is, out of racist indifference to the harm done R1s. This will sometimes, but not always, be the case when harms are disproportionally distributed across the various racial groupings to which people are assigned.

Fourth, on this view of racism, racist discrimination need not always be conscious. The real reason why person P1 does not rent person P2 a room may be that P1 views P2 as a member of a racial group R2, to whose members P1 has an aversion. That may be what it is about P2 that turns P1 off, even if P1 convinces herself it was for some other reason that she did not rent. As racist discrimination need not always be conscious, so it need not always be intended to harm. Some of what is called 'environmental racism,' especially the location of waste dumps so as disproportionally to burden Black people, is normally not intended to harm anyone at all. Nevertheless, it is racist if, for example, the dumpers regard it as less important if it is 'only,' say, Black people who suffer. However, it will usually be the case that intentional discrimination based on racist attitudes will be more objectionable morally, and harder to justify, than is unintentional, unconscious racist discrimination. *Racial* discrimination is not always racist discrimination. The latter is always immoral, because racism is inherently vicious and it corrupts any differentiation that it infects. The former—racial discrimination—is not inherently immoral. Its moral status will depend on the usual factors—intent, knowledge, motive, and so on—to which we turn to determine what is vicious.

This understanding of racism also offers a new perspective on the controversy over efforts to restrict racist "hate speech." Unlike racially *offensive* speech, which is defined by its (actual or probable) effects, racist *hate* speech is defined by its origins, i.e., by whether it expresses (and is thus an act of) racially directed hate. So we cannot classify a remark as racist hate speech simply on the basis of *what* was said, we need to look to *why* the speaker said it. Speech laden with racial slurs and epithets is presumptively hateful, of course, but merely voicing an opinion that members of R1 are inferior (in some germane way) will count as racist (in any of the term's chief senses, at least) only if, for example, it expresses an opinion held from the operation of some predisposition to believe bad things about R1s, which predisposition itself stems in part from racial disregard.[11]

This understanding of racist hate speech should allay the fears of those who think that racial oversensitivity and the fear of offending the oversensitive will stifle the discussion of delicate and important matters beneath a blanket of what is called 'political correctness.' Racist hate speech is defined by its motive forces and, given a fair presumption of innocence, it will be difficult to give convincing evidence of ugly motive behind controversial opinions whose statement is free of racial insults.

SOME DIFFICULTIES

It may seem that my view fails to meet the test of accommodating clear cases of racism from history. Consider some members of the southern White aristocracy in the antebellum or Jim Crow periods of American history—people who would never permit racial epithets to escape their lips, and who were solicitous and even protective of those they considered 'their Negroes' (especially Black servants and their kin), but who not only acquiesced in, but actively and strongly supported the social system of racial separatism, hierarchy, and oppression. These people strongly opposed Black equality in the social, economic, and political realms, but they appear to have been free of any vehement racial hatred. It appears that we should call such people racists. The question is: Does the account offered here allow them to be so classified?

This presents a nice difficulty, I think, and one it will be illuminating to grapple with. There is, plainly, a kind of hatred that consists in opposition to a person's (or group's) welfare. Hatred is the opposite of love and, as to love someone is to wish her well (i.e., to want and will that she enjoy life and its benefits), so one kind of hatred for her is to wish her ill (i.e., to want and will that she not enjoy them). It is important to remember, however, that not all hatred is wishing another ill for its own sake. When I take revenge, for example, I act from hate, but I also want to do my enemy ill for a purpose (to get even). So too when I act from envy. (I want to deprive the other of goods in order to keep her from being better off than I, or from being better off than I wish her to be.) I have sometimes talked here about racial "antipathy" ("animosity," "aversion," "hostility," etc.), but I do not mean that the attitude in question has to be especially negative or passionate. Nor need it be notably ill-mannered or crude in its expression. What is essential is that it consists in either opposition to the well-being of people classified as members of the targeted racial group or in a racially based callousness to the needs and interests of such people.

This, I think, gives us what we need in order to see part of what makes our patricians racists, for all their well-bred dispassion and good manners. They stand against the advancement of Black people (as a group, even if they make an exception for 'their Negroes'). They are averse to it as such, not merely doing things that have the *side* effect of setting back the interests of Black people. Rather, they *mean* to retard those interests, to keep Black people "in their place" relative to White people. They may adopt this stance of active, conscious, and deliberate hostility to Black welfare either simply to benefit themselves at the expense of Black people or out of the contemptuous belief that, because they are Black, they merit no better. In any event, these aristocrats and their behavior can properly be classified as racist.

Recall, too, that even if the central case of racism is racial hatred (malevolence), the racial disaffection that constitutes racism also extends to racial callousness, heartlessness, coldness, or uncaring. (We might group these as the vice of nonbenevolence). These too are racism, for it is surely vicious morally to be so disposed toward people classified as belonging to a certain racial group that one does not care whether they prosper or suffer, and is thus indifferent to the way in which the side effects of one's action disadvantage them. Indeed, I think that, as described, our genteel, oppressive members of the gentry go beyond this to manifest a kind of practical hostility: they consciously and actively act to suppress Black people. However, even those who do not go that far are still racist. (Dr. King famously reminded us that to the extent that the good are silent in the face of evil, they are not (being) good). Morally, much will depend on what these agents mean to do. Do they seek to deprive Black people of various positions and opportunities precisely because they wish Black people not to have these things because the things are good? If so, this is a still deeper type of race malice.

It may not be clear how the understanding of racism offered here accommodates the common-sense view that the attitudes, rhetoric, behavior, and representatives of the mindset we might characterize as the 'white man's burden'-view count as racist.[12] One who holds such a Kiplingesque view (let's call her K) thinks non-Whites ignorant, backward, undisciplined, and generally in need of a tough dose of European 'civilizing' in important aspects of their lives. This training in civilization may sometimes be harsh, but it is supposed to be for the good of the 'primitive' people. Moreover, it is important, for our purposes, to remember that K may think that, for all their ignorance, lack of discipline, and other intellectual and moral failings, individuals within the purportedly primitive people may in certain respects, and even on the whole, be moral superiors to certain of their European 'civilizers.' Thus, Kipling's notorious coda to "Gunga Din."[13]

The matter is a complex one, of course, but I think that, at least in extreme instances, such an approach can be seen to fit the model of racism whose adoption I have urged. What is needed is to attend to and apply our earlier remarks about breaches of respect and the vice of injustice. An important part of respect is recognizing the other as a human like oneself, including treating her like one. There can be extremes of condescension so inordinate they constitute degradation. In such cases, a subject goes beyond more familiar forms of paternalism to demean the other, treating her as utterly irresponsible. Plainly, those who take it upon themselves to conscript mature, responsible, healthy, socialized (and innocent) adults into a regimen of education designed to strip them of all authority over their own lives and make them into 'civilized' folk condescend in just this way.[14] This abusive paternalism borders on contempt and it can violate the rights of the subjugated people by denying them the respect and deference to which their status entitles them. By willfully depriving the oppressed people of the goods of freedom, even as part of an ultimately well-meant project of 'improving' them, the colonizers act with the kind of instrumentally malevolent benevolence we discussed above. The colonizers stunt and maim in order to help, and therein plainly will certain evils to the victims they think of as beneficiaries. Thus, their conduct counts as a kind of malevolence insofar as we take the term literally to mean willing evils.[15]

Of course, the Kiplingesque agent will not think of herself as depriving responsible, socialized people of their rights over their lives; she does not see them that way and thinks them too immature to have such rights. However, we need to ask why she regards Third World peoples as she does. Here, I suspect, the answer is likely to be that her view of them is influenced, quite possibly without her being conscious of it, by her interest in maintaining the social and economic advantages of having her group wield control over its subjects. If so, her beliefs are relevantly motivated and affected by (instrumental) ill-will, her desire to gain by harming others. When this is so, then her beliefs are racist not just in the weak sense that their content is the sort that characteristically is tied to racial disaffection, but in the stronger and morally more important sense that her own acceptance of these beliefs is partially motivated by racial disaffection. She is *being* racist in thinking as she does. I conclude that the account of racism offered here can allow that, and help explain why, many people who hold the 'white man's burden'-mentality are racist, indeed, why they maybe racist in several different (but connected) ways.

Having said all this about some who are what I have called Kiplingesque racists and about some 'well-meaning' southern aristocrats, I must admit that my account suggests that some people in these situations, some involved in racially oppressive social systems, will not themselves be racist in their attitudes, in their behavior, or even in their beliefs (at least, in the stronger sense of being racist in holding her beliefs). I do not shrink from this result, and think it should temper our reliance on the concept of collective responsibility. There are real cases where people share in both wrongdoing and blameworthiness, but collective responsibility for racism is philosophically problematic (in ways I cannot here pursue) and, I think, it is neither so common nor so important morally as some maintain (see May, 1992).

SOME CASES

John Cottingham asks us to imagine that "walking down the street, I come across two beggars, both equally in need of assistance, and I have only a single banknote, so that I cannot assist both." If, moreover, "one of the mendicants is white and the other black, may not a black passerby legitimately choose to give his banknote to the latter for no other reason than 'he's one of my race'?" (Cottingham, 1986: pp. 359, 362). He also asks us to imagine ourselves in a position heroically to rescue only one of two people trapped in a burning building. If they are of different races, may I legitimately direct my supererogatory efforts to saving the one who is of my own race?[16]

The view of racism suggested here can help us see how to think about such cases. It indicates, at least, that its being done from nonmalicious racial partiality need not tend to render an action wrong. For a Black person, or a White one, to give to the Black mendicant out of racial preference seems to me unobjectionable, so long as the gift is not likely to mean the difference between life and death. Giving preferentially to the White mendicant is more suspicious, but there is no more vicious ('wrong-making,' as some say) tendency *inherent* in this preference than there is in the other. (I see little or none in the other.) However, if 'Because he's Black [like me or like the ones I prefer]' states a morally acceptable answer to the question why someone gave to the Black beggar when she acts from the pro-Black preference, then do we not have to say that 'Because he's Black' (or 'Because he isn't White [as I am and as are the ones I prefer]') is a legitimate answer to the question why one did not give to the Black beggar when she acts from a different preference? And mustn't we avoid being committed to this, and admit that the latter answer is clearly racist and illegitimate? Well, no; we do not have to admit that. To explain a failure to help someone by saying 'Because he's Black' sounds ugly because, given the history of anti-Black attitudes and behavior in this society, it sounds as if the agent were acting in order to deprive Black people of certain goods. This is likely racist. In our case, however, this answer is merely a misleading way of saying that

this person lost out, not on his rights, but on special favors, and not because of ill-will toward Black people but because of extra good will toward some other group. Once the explanation 'Because he's Black' is itself explained, I think, some of our initial suspicion of racism evaporates. (Of course, we might still deem the conduct undesirable and insensitive.)

What of the rescues from the burning building? Even here, I suspect, appeals to race are not as such immoral. They may, however, be inappropriate to the gravity of what is at stake. Surely, it would be objectionable to make the two trapped people play a game, or pick a number, to decide who gets saved. For similar reasons, it would be improper to subject them to a questionnaire and then save the one whose answers were "correct" in matching one's own trivial preferences. No one should lose her life even in part because her favorite color, or football team, or musical performer is different from mine. That is not because there is anything wrong with my having such preferences or, normally, with acting from them. It is because it mocks the seriousness of what is at stake and demeans the persons involved to bring such frivolous matters into these deliberations. By the same token, it may be that strictly racial preference, though innocent in itself, remains too trifling a basis for choice to be made the crux in so weighty a matter. Exactly what seems objectionable about these procedures is hard to specify, but surely it centers on the contrast between the comparative insignificance of the decisive factor (race) and the gravity of what is to be decided (life and death). It makes it more difficult to attend to the importance and solemnity of the end when we must deal with means we have properly trained ourselves to take none too seriously. Race, of course, is a more serious matter in our society than are sports or color preferences, primarily because of its historical over-emphasis in programs of oppression and their rationalization. In itself, and more properly, it forms no deep part of one's identity, I think; but, like rooting for the sports teams of one's neighborhood or hometown or school, it may be associated psychologically with interpersonal connections of a more serious nature.

Nonetheless, while perhaps racial classification as such cannot bear the moral weight of life and death choices, the notions of race and of shared race may be masking work done by more serious features and affinities: e. g., heightened compassion for those with a history of shared or comparable suffering, a sense of kinship, shared community (not of race but) of social/political connection, and so on. In any case, within a properly virtues-based ethical theory, the important question is not (i) what has B done that legitimizes A's abandoning her? but (ii) in what way is A vicious toward B (cruel? unjust? callous?) if A prefers to help C even when that precludes her also helping B? It is not at all clear that or how attending to affinities connected with the admittedly crude notion of race must always suffice to render A's choice vicious.

Consider the related problem of disfavoritism.[17] Suppose Persons D and E both have more regard for people assigned to every race than morality requires of them. D plays favorites, however, loving (people she considers to be) members of Rl more than she loves those of any other racial group. E plays disfavorites (as we might say), specially reserving (people she considers to be) members of Rl for *less* concern than she has for others. Is what E does/feels racism? Is it morally permissible?

It seems to me that what E does is not racism, because her so-called "disfavoritism" is only a special case of favoritism. She picks out all (people she considers to be) *non* members of R1 for preferential good treatment. (I. e., better than that she accords R1s.) This is likely to be more dangerous socially than are standard cases of favoritism, because it threatens more easily to degenerate into insufficient regard for R1s (or even into antipathy toward them). It is thus a dangerous business, but it lacks the moral ugliness of true racism.

Perhaps it would be a better world without any such racial favoritism. The more important human interconnections, after all, are those founded on joint projects, shared understandings, and common commitments. In short, they are ones that help more fully to humanize us, that bind us one to another in binding us to what is greater than ourselves. All that is a separate matter, however, and one that has no direct bearing on our question of whether acting from such favoritism is permissible.

CONCLUSION

These reflections suggest that an improved understanding of racism and its immorality calls for a comprehensive rethinking of racial discrimination, of the preferential treatment programs sometimes disparaged as 'reverse discrimination,' and of institutional conduct as well. They also indicate the direction such a rethinking should take, and its dependence on the virtues and other concepts from moral psychology. That may require a significant change in the way social philosophers have recently treated these and related topics.[18]

NOTES

1. The same dictionary dates the cognate 'racist', as both adjective and noun, to the same period, but places the first appearances of 'racialism' and 'racialist' three decades earlier.

2. Merriam-Webster's *Ninth New Collegiate Dictionary* offers a secondary definition: "racial prejudice or discrimination."

3. For a negative appraisal of Sivanandan's thought, see David Dale, "Racial Mischief: The Case of Dr. Sivanandan," in ed. Frank Palmer, *Anti-Racism* (London: Sherwood, 1986), pp. 82–94.

4. I shall use such terms as 'R1' and 'R2' to refer to racial groups, and such expressions as 'R1s' and 'R2s' to refer to people assigned to such groups. This usage holds potential for some confusion, since the plural term 'R1s' is not the plural of the singular term 'R1', but I think the context will always disambiguate each instance of this usage.

5. See Garcia, 1986, and Garcia, 1987.

6. See Appiah, 1992.

7. Note that action from maxims that pass Kant's universalizability test is therein permissible, not necessarily obligatory.

8. Quoted in Hacker, "The New Civil War," p. 30.

9. I say 'foreseeable' effects rather than 'foreseen' because S's racist contempt may be the reason she does not bother to find out, and thus does not foresee some of the bad effects of her behavior.

10. See Carter, 1991.

11. For a helpful discussion of the controversy surrounding efforts to identify and regulate hate speech, and of the different grounds offered for these restrictions, see Simon, 1994.

12. Philip Kitcher directed my attention to this topic.

13. "Though I've belted you and flayed you, By the livin' Gawd that made you, You're a better man than I am, Gunga Din." Rudyard Kipling, "Gunga Din," in *Kipling: a Selection of his Stories and Poems* (Garden City: Doubleday, n.d.).

14. It is in the form of Kiplingesque, "white man's burden'-racism that racism most nearly approaches the structure of sexism. Sexism is, of course, a form of social bias to which many assume racism is structurally similar, and those who introduced the notion of sexism as a concept of social explanation explicitly modeled it on (their understanding of) racism. In general, however, I think the similarity is not great. Sexism appears *normally* to be a form of condescension, wherein males deprive women of authority and power in order to protect them from the consequences of their supposed immaturity and weakness. This sort of disrespect can violate the virtue of justice in just the ways I have been describing. However, noticing that racism in certain peripheral forms can resemble what sexism seems to be in its most central forms helps reveal a significant dissimilarity between these two social vices. (For a sophisticated comparative account of racism and sexism, see Thomas, 1980.)

15. See Garcia, 1987.

16. I follow him in assuming that the prospective agent stands in no special personal relationship to either of the trapped people (e.g., son) and occupies no role that specially calls for impartiality (e.g., paid village fire-fighter).

17. Robert Audi raised this problem with me in conversation.

18. I am grateful to many people who discussed these matters with me. Henry Richardson, Martha Minow, David Wilkins, David Wong, Anthony Appiah, Susan Wolf, Dennis Thompson, Glenn Loury, and Judith Lichtenberg offered thoughtful comments on earlier drafts of some of this material. Discussions with Russell Hittinger, Ken Taylor, and others also profited me greatly. I am especially indebted to Lawrence Blum for repeated acts of encouragement and assistance, including reading and discussing my manuscripts and letting me read from his unpublished work, and I thank him and an audience at Rutgers' 1994 conference on philosophy and race, for making suggestions and raising forceful objections.

My work was made possible by generous sabbatical support from Georgetown University, by research assistance from Rutgers University, and by grants from the National Endowment for the Humanities and from Harvard's Program in Ethics and the Professions. This paper would not have been written without the stimulation and the opportunity for reflection afforded me at the annual Ford Foundation Fellows conferences. To all these institutions I am indebted.

REFERENCES

Appiah, Anthony. "Racisms." In *Anatomy of Racism*, ed. D. T. Goldberg. Minneapolis: University of Minnesota Press, 1990, pp. 3–17.

_____. *In My Father's House: Africa in the Philosophy of Culture.* Oxford: Oxford University Press, 1992.

Carter, Stephen. *Reflections of an Affirmative Action Baby.* New York: Basic Books, 1991.

Cottingham, John. "Partiality, Favouritism and Morality." *Philosophical Quarterly* 36 (1986), pp. 357–73.

Garcia, J. L. A. "The Tunsollen, the Siensollen, and the Soseinsollen." *American Philosophical Quarterly* 23 (1986), pp. 267–76.

_____. "Goods and Evils." *Philosophy and Phenomenological Research* 47 (1987), pp. 385–412.

Hacker, Andrew. "The New Civil War." *New York Review of Books.* April 23, 1992, pp. 30–33.

Flew, Antony. "Clarifying the Concepts." In *Anti-Racism: An Assault on Education and Value*, ed. Frank Palmer. London: Sherwood, 1986.

Marable, Manning. *Black America: Multicultural Democracy in the Age of Clarence Thomas and David Duke.* Open Magazine Pamphlet Series, #16. Westfield, NJ, 1992.

May, Larry, ed. *Collective Responsibility.* Lanham, MD: Rowman & Littlefield, 1992.

Miles, Robert. *Racism.* London: Routledge, 1989.

Piper, Adrian M. "Higher Order Discrimination." In *Identity, Character, & Morality*, ed. O. Flanagan and A. Rorty. Cambridge, MA: MIT Press.

Schaefer, Richard. *Racial and Ethnic Groups.* 4th ed. Glenview, IL: Scott, Foresman, 1990.

Simon, Thomas. "Fighting Racism: Hate Speech Detours." In *An Ethical Education: Community and Morality in the Multicriltural University,* ed. Mortimer Sellers. Oxford: Berg, 1994.

Thomas, Laurence. "Racism and Sexism: Some Conceptual Differences." *Ethics* 90 (1980), pp. 239–50.

READING QUESTIONS

1. Garcia claims that his volitional conception of racism can explain its immorality. What explanation does his view offer?
2. What is the difference between personal racism and institutional racism? Which of the two types does Garcia think is basic and why?
3. What is Garcia's position on race-based preferences including various affirmative action policies?
4. Garcia claims that his volitional conception of racism offers a new perspective on hate speech? How so?
5. In the section entitled "Some Difficulties," Garcia considers historical cases of racism that might present a problem for his volitional conception. What are those cases, why might they present a problem for Garcia's volitional conception, and how does he respond to the various apparently problematic cases?
6. In the section entitled "Some Cases," Garcia considers the case of someone in a position to rescue either a white or a black person from a burning building. What is Garcia's view about saving someone of one's own race (assuming the rescuer is either white or black)?

DISCUSSION QUESTIONS

1. What would Garcia likely say about someone who simply *believes* that members of a certain race (other than his or her own) are inferior because of belonging to the race in question, but does not have hostile feelings toward members of that race? Do you think his likely response is plausible?
2. Is it possible for someone to hate members of a racial group because of their race without having racist beliefs about those individuals?
3. Can someone harbor racist attitudes and thus be a racist without being aware that the attitudes are racist?

Tommie Shelby

Is Racism in the "Heart"?

Tommie Shelby's article is a response to Garcia's volitional conception of racism. Contrary to Garcia's analysis of racism as essentially a matter of attitudes (other than beliefs), Shelby argues that racist beliefs are both necessary and sufficient for racism to exist. Appealing to concrete examples, he supports his position that racism is fundamentally a type of ideology, which he characterizes as "widely accepted illusory systems of belief that function to establish and reinforce structures of social oppression."

In a series of thought-provoking articles and in his forthcoming book, Jorge Garcia has defended what he calls a *volitional* conception of racism.[1] On this account, racism is rooted, not in the content or irrationality of certain beliefs about so-called races, as is commonly supposed, but in certain noncognitive attitudes, motives, and feelings. Garcia suggests that we view racism as "a vicious kind of racially based disregard for the welfare of certain people."[2] This way of approaching racism sees it as essentially involving the "heart" of the racist—that is, his or her wants, intentions, hopes, fears, predilections, aversions, and so on. According to Garcia, this connection to human sentiments and attitudes is what explains why racism is always wrong. For as he maintains, "its immorality stems from its being opposed to the virtues of benevolence and justice."[3] Racism, on Garcia's account, is fundamentally a type of individual moral vice, the expression of a bad character. Building on the idea of racism's being "rooted in the heart," he goes on to develop what he calls an "infection model" of racism. According to this model, an *act* is racist insofar as a racist *heart* infects the conduct of the racist; and an *institution* is racist insofar as it is rooted in the racist attitudes and the resulting racist-infected actions of its founders and/or current functionaries.

I want to critically examine Garcia's analysis of racism. While it is highly sophisticated and vigorously argued for, it suffers, I believe, from a number of significant defects. A careful examination of these defects will reveal how we might develop a more adequate conception of racism.

METHODOLOGICAL CONSIDERATIONS

Garcia, like many people these days, thinks that racism is necessarily wrong. And he maintains that "no account of what racism is can be adequate unless it at the same time makes clear what is wrong with it."[4] However, Garcia offers little argument for this claim, despite the fact that it is far from obvious. Clearly, a *sociological* or *historical* account of racism need not make clear what is wrong with it; it would be sufficient if such accounts explained the nature and origins of racism—surely a demanding enough task. So, assuming Garcia would not disagree with this, I take it that he means to apply this methodological

From Tommie Shelby, "Is Racism in the 'Heart'?" *Journal of Social Philosophy* 33 (2002): 411–20.

requirement to only *moral-philosophical* analyses of racism. However, I would like to suggest that even here the requirement is unreasonable.

One type of philosophical investigation Garcia might be engaged in here assumes the usefulness of the commonsense thick concept "racism" and goes on to clarify why racism is necessarily evil and perhaps to tighten up our often slipshod usage of the notion.[5] This approach simply seeks to provide a rigorous philosophical reconstruction that preserves the descriptive core and condemnatory force of the concept. The strategy seems to work best when our pretheoretic understanding of the relevant phenomenon is sufficiently clear and complete to justify the generalization that all manifestations of it are morally problematic. When this condition is met, the task of the moral philosopher is to make explicit precisely what makes it wrong. So, for example, if we were analyzing "murder"—the malicious killing of one human being by another—we would want to explain why this type of homicide is always immoral (e.g., that it is incompatible with autonomy and natural right, that it prematurely and gratuitously ends a life of value, that it causes unnecessary pain and suffering, or whatever). But this approach will be much less successful when (1) the relevant phenomenon is not clearly wrong, or (2) ordinary use of the relevant concept is so vague or inconsistent that moral appraisal lacks a distinct and steady target. The concept "fornication" is an example of the first obstacle to this type of philosophical analysis. Its descriptive content is clear enough—voluntary sexual relations between two or more persons who are not married to each other—but its inherent wrongness is widely (and rightly) disputed. Thus, any moral analysis of "fornication" that aims to preserve its ordinary descriptive and normative content will have to convince us *that* it is wrong in the process of explaining precisely what makes it wrong. However, I take it that "racism" does not present us with this particular problem; instead, it illustrates the second obstacle to thick conceptual analysis. Nowadays, as Garcia himself correctly points out, the term "racism" is so haphazardly thrown about that it is no longer clear that we all mean, even roughly, the same thing by it.[6] Some even complain that the term is fast becoming

(or has long since become) a mere epithet, with strong emotive force but little or no clear content. This doesn't mean the concept is no longer useful, but it does suggest that we need to clearly specify its referent before we can determine whether the relevant phenomenon is always morally problematic. This will require some philosophical reconstruction, which may diverge, even radically, from ordinary usage. Until such a reconstructive project is completed, though, we should remain agnostic about whether every instance of "racism" is immoral, for our best reconstruction may show that many of our pretheoretic moral convictions are unfounded or inconsistent. Thus, if Garcia is engaged in thick conceptual analysis, he cannot lay down as a condition of adequacy that any analysis of racism must show it to be always morally wrong. The claim that racism is necessarily immoral must be a *conclusion* of such an analysis, not a theoretical presupposition.

A second approach to the moral analysis of racism simply *stipulates* that racism is always immoral. According to it, the term "racism" functions within the relevant theoretical discourse as a term of condemnation, and the role of the moral philosopher is to define it so that it (1) picks out only those attitudes, behaviors, and practices that are moral evils and (2) retains as much of its ordinary descriptive content as is compatible with analytical clarity. But this approach would make Garcia's methodological "requirement"—that any account of racism show why it is necessarily wrong—a presupposition of his particular theoretical project. This leaves it entirely open for another social theorist or philosopher to take a nonmoralized approach to racism without running afoul of logic, clarity, or good sense, provided the resulting analysis is an illuminating one.

I want to suggest an alternative to both the "thick concept" and "stipulative" approaches, one that takes place in two distinct parts. In the first, we make use of the behavioral sciences (including psychology and history) to define the concept of racism in a morally neutral way. Our reconstruction of the concept should illuminate the history, structure, psychological mechanisms, and social consequences of the phenomenon. Once we have properly identified its referent, we can then offer our moral evaluation, *but without antecedently assuming that everything that is properly called "racism" on our theoretical account will turn out to be immoral.* Now of course as philosophers engaged in moral-philosophical analysis, our investigation should have some moral import. But we can satisfy this desideratum without requiring that every philosophical inquiry into the nature of racism show it to be inherently evil. It is enough if we require that any such inquiry have *moral significance*: it must seek to reveal what is and what isn't morally troublesome about the phenomenon under investigation.

Garcia would likely reject this proposal, for he thinks that the ordinary concept of racism is so morally loaded and uncomplimentary that it is "counterintuitive" to use it in a morally neutral way. As he says, "the term is used almost entirely as a dyslogistic one today. Virtually no one is willing to accept the label 'racist' for herself or himself, nor do we bestow it on others without a sense of impugning them."[7] But ordinary usage, no matter how broad or entrenched, is not morally infallible. There are many condemnatory thick concepts that have dubious moral content (e.g., "fornication," "slut," "shack up," "fag," even "nigger"). Even if we want to hold on to such a term, as we might want to do with "racism," it simply is not reasonable to allow ordinary usage to determine substantive moral questions. Now Garcia might say at this point that, given its thorough moralization in ordinary discourse, using the term "racism" in a morally neutral manner would be just too misleading. But this practical worry can be dealt with simply by being explicit about our theoretical reconstruction and moral-political aims. As we know, philosophical projects can sometimes be esoteric and misunderstood and yet may nevertheless reveal something important.

THE ROLE OF RACIST BELIEFS

We can better appreciate the relevance of the above discussion once we consider the role of racist *beliefs* in an adequate account of racism. According to Garcia, racist beliefs are a secondary and an inessential feature of racism.[8] Race-based noncognitive attitudes are the key ingredient, and it is the possession of these attitudes that makes an individual a racist and, thus, morally vicious. Garcia maintains that in the typical racist, race-based animosity or contempt is the root cause of the racist's belief in the superiority of his own "racial group" and in the inferiority of another, and that this belief is just a convenient rationalization for his vicious attitude toward the other "race" or some member of it. While Garcia admits that racist beliefs may be *psychologically* necessary for some racists—given our deep need to justify our actions to others, ourselves, and perhaps God—he insists that it is not *logically* necessary for the existence of racism. And in those (presumably rare) cases where racist beliefs lead (causally) to racist attitudes, rather than the other way around, Garcia maintains that it is the attitudes, not the beliefs, that make the person a racist.

Now, I would agree that racist beliefs are typically rationalizations for racist attitudes, actions, and institutions; however, contrary to what Garcia maintains, I contend that such beliefs are essential to and even sufficient for racism. For one thing, we cannot even identify a person's intention as a racist one without positing that he or she holds some racist belief. If all we know, say, is that Stephen (a white person) dislikes Andre (a black person), then we don't yet know whether Stephen's dislike for Andre is racist. To settle that, we also need to know *why* he dislikes him. If it is simply because Andre is having a love affair with the woman Stephen loves (who, let us say, happens to be white), then this is not racist, provided Andre's "race" is not an aggravating factor. In order for his dislike to be racist, it would have to be based at least in part on the fact that Andre is a member of the "black race," where Andre's "blackness" (at least partially) grounds Stephen's dislike. Thus, if Stephen's dislike of Andre is racist, this has to be (at least in part) because of Stephen's beliefs about the racial characteristics of black people and the role that these beliefs play in his motivation, speech, and conduct.

In response to this, Garcia might say, as he sometimes does, that it is enough for Stephen to be a racist if his dislike is "racially based," that is, if he dislikes Andre because of Andre's racial designation. On this view, in order for Stephen's dislike of Andre to be racist, Stephen need not dislike him because of any beliefs he (Stephen) holds about "races" in general or about black people in particular, provided he makes a racial distinction "in his heart."[9] But is this correct? Let's suppose that Peter X, a white but problack radical, has contempt for Andre because Peter believes that no self-respecting black man committed to the black freedom struggle would be involved romantically with a white woman. Peter's contempt is directed at Andre because of Andre's "race," but in being contemptuous of him for this reason Peter would be simply echoing the sentiment of many blacks who believe that the cause of black liberation requires observing the rule of racial endogamy. Peter's contempt for Andre may be unjustified, but surely it is not racist, despite its being "racially based." Thus, the fact that a vicious attitude has a "racial basis" is not sufficient to ground the charge of racism; the exact nature of the corresponding racial beliefs will also be relevant. (It is perhaps also worth pointing out that Garcia's talk of making distinctions "within one's heart" is quite misleading, for surely our ability to discriminate on "racial" grounds is a cognitive capacity, and not a purely volitional one.)

Now one response to this objection is to say that the relevant vicious motive or intention must be based *simply* on the fact that the targeted person(s) is (are) of one "race" rather than another, and for no better reason. The more complicated story involving Peter's commitment to black nationalism would obviously not meet this criterion. However, I think this approach would leave the motives of the racist largely opaque, mysterious, even unintelligible. What would it mean for a racist to hate someone *simply* because he or she is black? Does the racist hate blacks because they have dark skin and kinky hair? Surely "blackness" has deeper meaning for the racist than that—unless he or she is psychotic. Unpacking this "meaning" is a matter of uncovering and making explicit the beliefs of the racist that "make sense," from a hermeneutic standpoint, of his or her attitudes and actions. Fully comprehending the attitudes and actions of a (possible) racist, especially when our ultimate aim is

moral appraisal, must involve appreciating his or her particular beliefs about so-called races.

Now, there are some people who have a visceral dislike for the members of certain "races" but are unable to adequately explain why they have this strange aversion. Perhaps Garcia is simply trying to make room for these people within the class of racists when he denies that racist beliefs are essential for racism. But I think we can accommodate this group while still allowing that racist beliefs are necessary. Leaving aside the (implausible) view that racism is a "natural" disposition to favor one's "kin," the best explanation for their visceral dislike of blacks is that they have been socialized into a racist culture, where racist beliefs and attitudes are widespread, taken for granted, reinforced through a variety of media, and often tacitly transmitted from generation to generation. In such a culture, like our own, the existence of pervasive racist ideas, often unspoken and implicit, explains the attitudes of the "visceral" racist, attitudes which would otherwise be quite puzzling. So, even here, racist beliefs are central to the analysis of racism.

Rather than focus on the mental states of individuals without regard to their sociohistorical context, which can often lead us astray, I would suggest that we view racism as fundamentally a type of *ideology*. Put briefly and somewhat crudely, "ideologies" are widely accepted illusory systems of belief that function to establish or reinforce structures of social oppression. We should also note that these social illusions, like the belief that blacks are an inferior "race," are often, even typically, accepted because of the unacknowledged desires or fears of those who embrace them (e.g., some white workers have embraced racist beliefs and attitudes when they were anxious about the entrance of lower-paid blacks into a tight labor market.[10] Racial ideologies emerged with the African slave trade and European imperialist domination of "darker" peoples. These peoples were "racialized" in an effort to legitimize their subjugation and exploitation: the idea of biological "race," the linchpin of the ideology, was used to impute an inherent and unchangeable set of physically based characteristics to the subordinate Other, an "essential nature" which supposedly set them apart from and explained why they were appropriately exploited by the dominant group. This ideology served (and still serves) to legitimize the subordination and economic exploitation of non-white people. Even after slavery was abolished and decolonization was well under way, the ideology continued to have an impact on social relations, as it functioned to legitimize segregation, uneven socioeconomic development, a racially segmented labor market, and the social neglect of the urban poor. The ideology is so powerful and devious that oppressors from all over the world have found it to be an effective tool of domination. Indeed, even some members of oppressed groups have been seduced by it, though often remolding or reinterpreting its discursive content for their own purposes. While racist ideology has far fewer explicit adherents or proud defenders in the United States today than it once did, it continues to exert an influence on the culture, politics, race relations, and economic conditions of the United States.[11]

Given his theoretical and moral concerns, this way of thinking about racism has several virtues of which Garcia should approve. First, viewing racism as an ideology passes the test of moral significance, for ideologies function to enable and sustain *oppression.* Though ideologies, being belief systems, are not in themselves immoral, they do perpetuate social injustice; and thus they are the proper objects of our moral concern. Second, we can retain the pejorative force of "racism" if we treat it as referring to an ideology, since ideologies, especially racist ones, are epistemically unsound, are irrationally held (given their dependence on self-deception), and serve as vehicles for domination and exploitation. This is not the same as saying that racism, qua ideology, is itself immoral; however, it does suggest that where racist ideology exists, immorality and injustice are probably not far behind. Finally, the ideology approach is compatible with Garcia's "infection model" of racism. Like vicious racist attitudes, racist *beliefs,* especially when sustained through false consciousness, can also "infect" the behavior of an individual, leading a person (consciously or not) to racially discriminate against others or to act on the basis of false assumptions or stereotypes about members of other "races." And when a racist ideology influences the decision making of those acting in official capacities, this can "infect" the basic institutions of social life (e.g., consider the impact of widely accepted racial stereotypes on the operation of the criminal justice system).

So why, then, is Garcia so adamant about rejecting belief-centered accounts of racism? I think part of the explanation is to be found in his commitment to the immorality requirement discussed above. His reasoning is something like the following. If racism must always be morally wrong, and racism is primarily a matter of having certain beliefs, then it must be possible to be held morally blameworthy for holding some viewpoints. This conclusion, however, seems problematic on at least two grounds. First, it would appear to commit a category mistake. Beliefs aren't the kinds of things that can be immoral; they can be true or false, warranted or unwarranted, rational or irrational, but certainly not virtuous or evil, just or unjust, at least not in themselves. Second, a belief-centered conception of racism seems to be incompatible with freedom of thought and expression. It would be intolerant and illiberal of us to morally condemn people for sincerely holding certain beliefs, however wrongheaded or unsound we may think they are. Racist beliefs are no exception. It is only when such beliefs lead to race-based hatred, racist actions, or racist institutions, that we rightly condemn those who hold them; and even then, we should condemn them not for holding the beliefs, but for the vicious attitudes and the actions and institutions that these attitudes bring into being.

This all seems quite compelling, but only if we assume that racism is *necessarily* wrong and, thus, that the racist is always morally vicious and his or her racist actions are always immoral. Indeed, much of Garcia's case against the necessity and sufficiency of racist beliefs for racism rests on this assumption. But as I argued earlier, we need not accept this methodological constraint as a condition of adequacy for an account of racism. Given our weaker methodological constraint—that an account of racism must have moral significance—a belief-centered conception of racism does not commit a category mistake, and it is no threat to intellectual freedom. In treating racism as an ideology, we are not claiming that ideological beliefs are in themselves immoral; nor are we suggesting that people should be (legally or otherwise) prevented from expressing their racist opinions.

But Garcia sometimes employs a different argumentative strategy against the claim that racist beliefs are essential to racism. The basic move is to take some specific racist belief (e.g., that whites are superior to blacks in some important respect), and then show that a person need not hold it in order to be a racist, provided he or she has racist motives and sentiments.[12] This maneuver will be convincing, however, only if a person can be a racist without holding *any* racist belief. But as I've argued above, we cannot identify an intention, action, or institution as racist without knowing that it is rooted in racist beliefs. The mere fact that the victim of a vicious attitude, action, or institution is a member of some despised "race," or that the perpetrator(s) is (are) of a different "race," is inconclusive. Moreover, while the belief in the racial superiority of one's own "race" is a paradigmatic racist belief, racist views are part of a complex and dynamic system of ideological belief. These beliefs have greater specificity and variety than the belief in a hierarchy of "races"; they often shift and are reformulated given specific political contingencies, economic circumstances, and sociohistorical context. And, with the possible exception of the belief in the reality of "races," no one belief is essential to the legitimating function of the belief system: during the period of American slavery, black slaves were commonly thought to be docile, superstitious, easily satisfied, and obsequious, but in the present postindustrial phase of capitalist development, blacks are more often viewed as socially parasitic, full of (unjustified) anger, irresponsible, and dangerous. So, there is no one belief (again, with the possible exception of the belief that there are "races"), or even a set of beliefs, that definitively constitutes racist ideology. But this doesn't show that racism is not a matter of people holding certain beliefs.

IS A RACIST HEART ESSENTIAL?

Now that we have established that racist beliefs are essential to racism, we need to ask whether vicious racist attitudes, intentions, or motives (i.e., what

Garcia calls a "racist heart") are also necessary. According to Garcia, the most fundamental conative states of mind that are relevant to the charge of racism are hatred, animosity, hostility, dislike, contempt, ill will, hard-hearted indifference, and disregard for the welfare of others.[13] There is no doubt that racists often have these attitudes toward other "races," but I think it would be a mistake to hold that racism exists only when such attitudes are present.

Consider the case where racist ideology is advanced to justify economic exploitation, as was the case with American slavery. Here, as many historians of New World slavery would maintain, the motive is financial profit, not hatred—as the historian Barbara Fields argues, the primary goal of American slavery was not the production of "white supremacy" but the production of cotton, sugar, rice, and tobacco.[14] This exploitative practice is racist because racist ideology is invoked to conceal the injustice, particularly from the exploiters themselves. Now Garcia might say that, though he doesn't necessarily hate them, the racist exploiter doesn't care enough or in the right sort of way about the racial Others he is exploiting.[15] I would certainly agree, but the exploiter's lack of concern for the welfare of his victims need not be because of their "race"; he might just as well have exploited those of his own "racial kind" had this been a more expedient and cost-effective option. Perhaps he exploits members of another "race" because he would receive less resistance that way and because he and others like him can convince themselves (with perhaps more than a bit of self-deception) of a silly theory about their own racial superiority in order to legitimize their oppressive conduct at a time when liberty and equality are supposed to be the foundation of their social life. I think it is clear that this type of conduct is still racist, even paradigmatically so. What could be more "counter-intuitive" than to deny this? But even if economic exploiters do hate those they exploit, they need not hate them because of their racial classification. They may hate them because the subordinate Other reminds them of their own injustice; or perhaps the conditions of servitude and degradation naturally breed contempt (which would also explain so-called racial self-hate), as Tocqueville suggests.[16]

Consider a different type of racist. She has no ill will toward blacks but learned as a child to believe that they are "naturally" disposed to be violent, irresponsible, and indolent, and now that she is an adult, she uncritically continues to hold on to this belief, much as she does certain of her religious beliefs and many of her social values. She is what Appiah would call a "sincere extrinsic racist."[17] Now Garcia is forced to say that she is not "really" a racist, since her racist beliefs are not rooted in racist motives. But is this plausible? What if she relies on this belief while acting as a juror in a criminal case involving a black defendant; or what if this belief leads her to discriminate against blacks in hiring, renting property, or approving loans? I can't see how these acts fail to be racist just because the perpetrator has a "pure" heart. And if I'm right, then the following claim must be false: "One whose racist beliefs have no such connection to any racial disregard in her heart does not hold them in a racist way and if she has no such disregard, she is not herself a racist, irrespective of her prejudices."[18]

This last example suggests that a fundamental problem with a volitional conception of racism—and indeed with many overly moralized analyses of racism—is that it can blind us to the ways in which seemingly "innocent" people can often be unwittingly complicitous in racial oppression. Thus, in order to avoid this defect, perhaps we might extend Garcia's "infection" metaphor: racist ideology is a virus that people can catch and spread through no fault of their own and without (fully) knowing that they are contaminated by it. If this is acknowledged, we must recognize that the "heart" does not have to be involved in order for an action or institution to be racist, and unjust *because* racist. It is sufficient for the existence of racism that individuals with racist beliefs act on those beliefs in their private lives, the marketplace, or the public sphere. Such actions lead to and perpetuate oppression—an unnecessary, systemic, and undeserved burden that is imposed on one group as a result of the actions of another—and they have this result whether or not they are performed with a racist heart. Racist ideology enables and sustains the oppression of subordinate "racial" groups, and this gives racist beliefs great moral significance, regardless of whether these beliefs are accompanied by racially based vicious intentions.[19]

NOTES

1. J. L. A. Garcia, "The Heart of Racism," *Journal of Social Philosophy* 27 (1996): 5–45; "Current Conceptions of Racism," *Journal of Social Philosophy* 28 (1997): 5–42; and "Philosophical Analysis and the Moral Concept of Racism," *Philosophy & Social Criticism* 25 (1999): 1–32.

2. Garcia, "The Heart of Racism," 6.

3. Garcia, "The Heart of Racism," 9.

4. Garcia, "The Heart of Racism," 6. See also Garcia, "Current Conceptions of Racism," 6; and "Philosophical Analysis and the Moral Concept of Racism," 7.

5. "Thick concepts," to use Bernard Williams's characterization, are concepts whose application is simultaneously "world-guided and action-guiding"; that is, they have both descriptive and evaluative content. Bernard Williams, *Ethics and the Limits of Philosophy* (Cambridge: Harvard University Press, 1985), 141.

6. Garcia, "Current Conceptions of Racism," 5.

7. Garcia, "Philosophical Analysis and the Moral Concept of Racism," 5.

8. Garcia, "The Heart of Racism," 9.

9. Garcia, "The Heart of Racism," 6–7.

10. See Edna Bonacich, "Advanced Capitalism and Black/White Race Relations in the United States: A Split Labor Market Interpretation," *American Sociological Review* 41 (1976): 34–51. Also see David R. Roediger, *The Wages of Whiteness: Race and the Making of the American Working Class* (London: Verso, 1991).

11. See e.g., David O. Sears, "Symbolic Racism," in *Eliminating Racism: Profiles in Controversy,* ed. Phyllis A. Katz and Dalmas A. Taylor (New York: Plenum Press, 1988), 53–84; Andrew Hacker, *Two Nations: Black and White, Separate, Hostile, Unequal* (New York: Ballantine Books, 1992); Douglas S. Massey and Nancy A. Denton, *American Apartheid: Segregation and the Making of the Underclass* (Cambridge: Harvard University Press, 1993); Howard Schuman, Charlotte Steeh, Lawrence Bobo, and Maria Krysan, *Racial Attitudes in America: Trends and Interpretations* (Cambridge: Harvard University Press, 1997); and Robert M. Entman and Andrew Rojecki, *The Black Image in the White Mind: Media and Race in America* (Chicago: University of Chicago Press, 2000).

12. Garcia, "Philosophical Analysis and the Moral Concept of Racism," 4.

13. Garcia, "The Heart of Racism," 6–15.

14. Barbara J. Fields, "Slavery, Race and Ideology in the United States of America," *New Left Review* (1990): 99.

15. Garcia, "The Heart of Racism," 6.

16. Alexis de Tocqueville, *Democracy in America,* ed. J. P. Mayer and trans. George Lawrence (New York: HarperPerennial, 1969), 341.

17. Kwame Anthony Appiah, "Racism," in *Anatomy of Racism,* ed. David Theo Goldberg (Minneapolis: University of Minnesota Press, 1990), 5.

18. Garcia, "The Heart of Racism," 13.

19. For helpful comments on earlier drafts of this essay, I would like to thank Anthony Appiah, Lawrence Blum, Jorge Garcia, David Kim, David Lyons, Howard McGary, and Kathleen Schmidt. A version of the paper was presented at the 2001 Pacific Division APA Meeting.

READING QUESTIONS

1. In the first section of his article, Shelby distinguishes two types of philosophical investigation into the concept of racism that he rejects. What are they, and why does Shelby find them problematic? What is Shelby's positive proposal for investigating the nature of racism?
2. How does Shelby argue that, from the fact that a person's dislike of another has a racial basis, it does not follow that the person's attitude is racist?
3. According to Shelby, what assumption leads Garcia to reject belief-based accounts of the nature of racism?
4. How does Shelby argue, contrary to Garcia, that racist attitudes are not necessary for racism to exist?

DISCUSSION QUESTIONS

1. In comparing the competing conceptions of racism that we find in Garcia and Shelby, which of them (if either one) do you find more compelling? Why?
2. How might Garcia reply to Shelby's criticisms of his account of racism?

Louis P. Pojman

Why Affirmative Action Is Immoral

Louis Pojman critically evaluates two common pro–affirmative action arguments: the forward-looking "level playing field" argument and the backward-looking "compensation" argument. He concludes that neither of them succeeds in morally justifying what he calls "preferential affirmative action." He further argues that affirmative action policies are immoral because they involve unjust discrimination against innocent white males.

The underlying moral principle guiding Pojman's position is the Kantian principle that respect for persons requires that we treat each person as an end in him- or herself and never merely as a means to social purposes.

Recommended Reading: Kantian moral theory, chap. 1, sec. 2C.

The state shall not discriminate against, or grant preferential treatment to, any individual or group on the basis of race, sex, color, ethnicity, or national origin in the operation of public employment, public education, or public contracting
—(California Civil Rights Initiative, *Proposition 209*).

When affirmative action was first proposed in the early 1960s, as a civil rights activist and member of CORE, I supported it. The shackled runner metaphor, set forth by President Lyndon Johnson in his 1965 Howard University speech, seemed to make moral sense. An opportunity gap existed between White and Black societies which greatly handicapped Blacks. This was my *forward-looking* reason for supporting affirmative action. But I had a *backward-looking* argument, as well. America owed compensation to Blacks who had been hideously oppressed in our society. The reasons that caused me to change my mind on this issue will be discussed in this paper, in which I will argue that *preferential* affirmative action is immoral. I have given comprehensive critiques of affirmative action (henceforth AA) elsewhere, and space prevents a repetition of that

material.[1] In this short paper I limit my arguments to AA regarding race, since if any group deserves AA it is African-Americans. Also I concentrate on university admittance and hiring, since these are the areas with which I am most familiar.

First some definitional preliminaries: By *Affirmative Action* I refer to preferential treatment based on race, gender or ethnicity. We might call this *Preferential Affirmative Action* as opposed to *Procedural Affirmative Action,* which requires that special attention be given to insure that everything reasonable is done to recruit and support equally qualified minorities and women. I support *Procedural Affirmative Action* even to the point of allowing the properties in question to function as tie-breakers. In my experience, however, *Procedural Affirmative Action* tends to slip into *Preferential Affirmative Action*. Bureaucracies in general cannot be trusted to abide by the rules, hence the present need to eliminate AA altogether. Recall how race-norming procedures and AA admittance policies were kept secret for years. In the early 1990s, the University of Delaware withdrew Linda Gottfriedson's fellowship because she exposed the practice of race-norming. If and when

From Louis P. Pojman, "Why Affirmative Action Is Immoral," in L. Hinman, ed., *Contemporary Moral Issues: Diversity and Consensus*, 2nd ed. (Upper Saddle River, NJ: Prentice Hall, 2000).

we are committed to fair evaluations, *Procedural Affirmative Action* will be morally acceptable.

Let me turn to the two arguments that once persuaded me of the soundness of *Preferential Affirmative Action,* which I now believe to be unsound.

THE LEVEL PLAYING FIELD ARGUMENT

This is a version of President Johnson's Howard University "Shackled Runner" speech. Here is how Mylan Engel puts the argument:

> Consider a race, say a hundred yard dash. Mr. White starts at the 50 yard mark, while Mr. Black starts at the 0 yard mark. The gun goes off and sure enough Mr. White wins. Now very few people would think that sort of race was fair. . . . They certainly wouldn't think that Mr. White deserved significant economic gain for beating Mr. Black in such a race. Now, it seems to me that a similar sort of argument can be made in defense of strong AA. One need not appeal to compensation for past injustices, etc. The fact is that many white males have an unfair head start in the education and employment game. Consider a statistic reported on NPR today: 27% of Blacks and Latinos currently are living below the poverty line (the poverty line is now $16,400 for a family of four), whereas only 11% of (non-Asian) whites are living below the poverty line. And at each level above the poverty line, there is a disproportionate number of whites. The economic advantage experienced by whites is that more whites can afford to send their children to exclusive college preparatory private schools, and even those whites who can't afford to send their children to private schools, still have a better chance of living in a wealthy school district with better public schools. So, by the time the Young Mr. Whites and the Young Mr. Blacks are ready to start the university application process, more often than not, the young Mr. Whites already have the equivalent of a 50 or at least a 25-yard head start in the college application game.[2]

First of all, more should be done for poor families and poor neighborhoods, as well as poor schools. Economic disparities between the rich and the poor should be reduced. Programs, such as the East German youth program and President Clinton's Youth Corps, which has unfortunately foundered, in which every American youth gives 2 years to national service, either in the military or in community service, . . . [should] be geared toward improving the lot of the economically and educationally disadvantaged. The reward would be free college or grad school tuition or job/career training.

Secondly, I gradually came to see that the Level Playing Field Argument could best support a class-based approach to AA, rather than a race-based one. On current poverty statistics, 74 percent of Blacks and Hispanics are not living in poverty and 11 percent of Whites are, so this kind of AA would cut across racial and gender lines. I am sympathetic to class-based AA. The question is: what kind of help should be given?

Financial assistance would seem to be the best kind. Candidates would be accepted into universities on the basis of their qualifications, but would then be assisted according to need.[3] There is nothing new about this kind of program, it has traditionally been used (Pell Grants, etc.). Tie breakers could be used too. If Mr. Poor and Mr. Rich both had similar scores, it would be reasonable to take the disadvantage into consideration and award a place to Mr. Poor.

Engel points out, as an objection to this argument, that AA actually harms the very people it seeks to help, especially by stigmatizing them with the label "AA admittee" = "inferior student." But isn't the point that AA admittees are often not equipped to handle the rigors of the top schools? So we are doubly harming them. Even Bok and Bowen's new book *The Shape of the River,* which advocates AA in college admittance, concedes that blacks with identical SAT scores as whites get (on average) lower grades. The Center for Civil Rights has shown that in every state university examined (Michigan, North Carolina, Washington, etc.), Black admittance rates are based on much lower SAT scores and their failure and drop out rates are usually more than double those of whites. So AA actually is counterproductive, contributing to harming those it would help. Moreover, some schools have had to lower their standards to accommodate less qualified Blacks. While I was teaching at the University of Mississippi, a strong AA program was implemented. The Math Department had to switch to a high school algebra text in order to teach that course. The Affirmative Action handbook stated that any qualified minority (and female) candidate had a presumptive claim on any open academic position in the university. Sidney Hook relates an incident where a Religious Studies Department was instructed by an accrediting association to drop the requirements of Hebrew and Greek, since it was discouraging members of minority groups to major in that discipline.

It gradually dawned on me that affirmative action was guilty of enacting the Peter Principle, which states that we should promote people to positions beyond their present abilities, where they will very likely fail. So Black students with SATs of 1150 are admitted to Harvard or Berkeley, from which they drop out or fail, whereas they would have done very well at a first rate state university or less prestigious small college.

My own experience is that of a poor teen-ager who started off at mediocre Morton High and Morton Jr. College in Cicero, Illinois, and who worked his way up to Columbia University and Union Seminary, then fellowships to the University of Copenhagen, and finally to Oxford University. I didn't get into Oxford until my 30s and would have failed had I gone right out of high school or junior college. I saw my community college, not as a stigma, but as an opportunity to improve myself so that I might be worthy of a more rigorous challenge.

Furthermore, it isn't Mr. Rich who is likely to be affected by AA. It's Mr. Poor-but-talented-White who is likely to be harmed. Mr. Rich has had such support, coaching and early advantages that he's on his way to success. Neither Mr. Poor Black nor Mr. Poor White is normally helped by AA. Mr. and Miss Middle Class Black is the main beneficiary.

There is another problem with the Level Playing Field Argument. It supposes that if everything were just, we'd have equal results in every area of life. But why should we expect this? Anyone who is familiar with Irish, Italian and Jewish ethnic patterns in New York City can attest to the fact that people from different ethnic communities (with the same economic status) turn out very differently: the Irish and Italian tended to go into the fire department and police force;

the Jews into academics, science and technology. There is evidence that Ashkanazy Jews have on average higher intelligence (measured in terms of academic ability, at least) than other ethnic groups. Both genetically and culturally differences exist between people and may exist between groups. This point may be uncomfortable to egalitarians, but, as philosophers, we should be concerned with the evidence, which, at least, gives us no reason to think that every group has the same average abilities.[4]

There is one other argument that caused me to give up the Leveling Argument. It can function as a disincentive to responsible parenting. If you and I both have the same economic opportunities but you save your money and dedicate your life to producing two excellent children with the best advantages, whereas I gamble, drink, spend enormous amounts of money on expensive cars, and neglect my 10 children, why should your two better qualified children be denied admission to Yale simply because my children are more needy (or are Black)? This seems to me to be a disincentive to good parenting as well as a denial of the merit attained by the better qualified. AA programs aren't fine grained enough to sort out these nuances.[5]

In conclusion, while many Middle Class Blacks and other minorities may be helped by AA policies, these policies do little to help the truly disadvantaged. The Leveling Argument is unsound. But even if it were sound, since it is basically a utilitarian argument, other considerations of justice could still override it. I turn to the second argument that once led me to support AA.

THE COMPENSATION ARGUMENT FOR PREFERENTIAL AFFIRMATIVE ACTION

The argument goes like this: historically Blacks have been wronged and severely harmed by Whites. Therefore white society should compensate Blacks for the injury caused them. Reverse discrimination in terms of preferential hiring, contracts, and scholarships seemed a fitting way to compensate for the past wrongs.[6] I was a member of Riverside Church in New York City when at a Sunday service in May of 1969, James Foreman pushed aside the minister and issued the Black Manifesto, demanding $500 million from the American religious establishment for reparations to Blacks. Foreman's disruption caused me to reassess my support of this argument, and gradually I began to realize that it involves a distorted notion of compensation.

Normally, we think of compensation as owed by a specific person A to another person B whom A has wronged in a specific way C. For example, if I have stolen your car and used it for a period of time to make business profits that would have gone to you, it is not enough that I return your car. I must pay you an amount reflecting your loss and my ability to pay. If I have made $5,000 and only have $10,000 in assets, it would not be possible for you to collect $20,000 in damages—even though that is the amount of loss you have incurred.

Sometimes compensation is extended to groups of people who have been unjustly harmed by the greater society. For example, the United States government has compensated the Japanese-Americans who were interred during the Second World War, and the West German government has paid reparations to the survivors of Nazi concentration camps. But here specific individuals have been identified who were wronged in an identifiable way by the government of the nation in question.

On the face of it, demands by Blacks for compensation do not fit the usual pattern. Southern states with Jim Crow laws could be accused of unjustly harming blacks, but it is hard to see that the United States government was involved in doing so. Much of the harm done to Blacks was the result of private discrimination, rather than state action. So the Germany/US analogy doesn't hold. Furthermore, it is not clear that all blacks were harmed in the same way or whether some were *unjustly* harmed or harmed more than poor Whites and others (e.g., Jews, Poles, short people). Finally, even if identifiable blacks were harmed by identifiable social practices, it is not clear that most forms of Affirmative Action are appropriate to restore the situation. The usual practice of a financial payment, as I noted earlier, seems more appropriate than giving a high level job to someone unqualified or only minimally qualified, who, speculatively, might have been better qualified had he not been subject to racial discrimination. If John is the star tailback of our college team with a promising professional future, and I accidentally (but culpably) drive my pick-up truck over his legs, and so cripple him, John may be due compensation, but he is not due the tailback spot on the football team.

Still, there may be something intuitively compelling about compensating members of an oppressed group who are minimally qualified. Suppose that the Hatfields and the McCoys are enemy clans and some youths from the Hatfields go over and steal diamonds and gold from the McCoys, distributing it within the Hatfield economy. Even though we do not know which Hatfield youths did the stealing, we would want to restore the wealth, as far as possible, to the McCoys. One way might be to tax the Hatfields, but another might be to give preferential treatment in terms of scholarships and training programs and hiring to the McCoys.

This is perhaps the strongest argument for Affirmative Action, and it may well justify some weaker versions of AA, but it is doubtful whether it is sufficient to justify strong versions with quotas and goals and time tables in skilled positions. There are at least three reasons for this. First, we have no way of knowing how many people of any given group would have achieved some given level of competence had the world been different. Secondly, the normal criterion of competence is a strong prima facie consideration when the most important positions are at stake. There are three reasons for this: (1) treating people according to their merits respects them as persons, as ends in themselves, rather than as means to social ends (if we believe that individuals possess a dignity which deserves to be respected, then we ought to treat that individual on the basis of his or her merits, not as a mere instrument for social policy); (2) society has given people expectations that if they attain certain levels of excellence they will be rewarded appropriately;

and (3) filling the most important positions with the best qualified is the best way to ensure efficiency in job-related areas and in society in general. These reasons are not absolutes. They can be overridden.[7] But there is a strong presumption in their favor, so that a burden of proof rests with those who would override them.

The third reason against using affirmative action to compensate has to do with the arbitrariness of using preferential treatment in a market-driven process. Take the hiring of professors according to affirmative action guidelines. Should we hire (or admit into professional schools) minimally qualified AA candidates over better qualified candidates because they have suffered injustice as *individuals* or because they belong to a *group* that has suffered? If it is because they have suffered injustice, then it is irrelevant that they are members of minority groups. We should treat them as individuals and compensate them accordingly. So race and gender are really irrelevant. What counts is the injustice done to them. But if we reward them because they are members of an oppressed group, then we may do injustice by not rewarding individuals of other groups who have suffered injustice. Poor coal miners of West Virginia, railroad workers who worked under oppressive conditions to build the transcontinental railroads, short people, ugly people, people from abusive homes, and so forth all deserve some compensation from a society that has dealt them a raw deal. But hiring or admitting to special professional schools is arbitrary compensation in that it compensates only a few of the oppressed, and, generally, not the worst off. It compensates the best off Blacks and women, many who come from relatively wealthy families, leaving the truly disadvantaged, impoverished Blacks and Whites, males and females, in the same situation they already were in.[8]

At this point we face the objection that "innocent" White males have enormously profited from racism and sexism, so that while some of the above has merit, it doesn't acquit White males altogether. Preferential treatment to previously oppressed people may still be justified, all things considered. We turn to this argument.

THE ARGUMENT FOR COMPENSATION FROM THOSE WHO INNOCENTLY BENEFITED FROM PAST INJUSTICE

Young White males as innocent beneficiaries of unjust discrimination against blacks and women have no grounds for complaint when society seeks to level the tilted field. They may be innocent of oppressing blacks, other minorities, and women, but they have unjustly benefited from that oppression or discrimination. So it is perfectly proper that less qualified women and blacks be hired before them.

The operative principle is: He who knowingly and willingly benefits from a wrong must help pay for the wrong. Judith Jarvis Thomson puts it this way: "Many [white males] have been direct beneficiaries of policies which have down-graded blacks and women . . . and even those who did not directly benefit . . . had, at any rate, the advantage in the competition which comes of the confidence in one's full membership [in the community], and of one's right being recognized as a matter of course."[9] That is, white males obtain advantages in self-respect and self-confidence deriving from a racist/sexist system which denies these to blacks and women.

Here is my response to this argument: As I noted in the previous section, compensation is normally individual and specific. If A harms B regarding X, B has a right to compensation from A in regards to X. If A steals B's car and wrecks it, A has an obligation to compensate B for the stolen car, but A's son has no obligation to compensate B. Suppose A is unable to compensate B himself but he could steal C's car (roughly similar to B's). A has no right to steal C's car to compensate A. Furthermore, if A dies or disappears, B has no moral right to claim that society compensate him for the stolen car, though if he has insurance, he can make such a claim to the insurance company. Sometimes a wrong cannot be compensated, and we just have to make the best of an imperfect world.

Recently (mid-September, 1998), an umpire called what would have been Mark McGwire's

66th home run of the season a ground-rule double on the grounds that a fan caught the ball before it made it to the stands. A replay showed that the ball had already cleared the stands, so that it was a home run. The commissioner of baseball refused to over-rule the umpire's decision. Two days later Sammy Sosa hit two home runs, thus tying McGwire for the home run lead. McGwire was the victim of an unintended injustice (if the fact that it was an hon-est mistake bothers you, suppose the umpire did it on purpose). Should Sosa give up one of his home runs in order to rectify the injustice to McGwire? Morally, McGwire deserves to hold the record for home runs, but according to the rules, he has a right only to a tie at this point.

Suppose my parents, divining that I would grow up to have an unsurpassable desire to be a basket-ball player, bought an expensive growth hormone for me. Unfortunately, a neighbor stole it and gave it to little Michael, who gained the extra 13 inches—my 13 inches—and shot up to an enviable 6 feet 6 inches. Michael, better known as Michael Jordan, would have been a runt like me but for his luck. As it is he profited from the injustice, and excelled in basket-ball, as I would have done had I had my proper dose.

Do I have a right to the millions of dollars that Jordan made as a professional basketball player—the unjustly accused innocent beneficiary of my growth hormone? I have a right to something from the neigh-bor who stole the hormone, and it might be kind of Jordan to give me free tickets to the Bulls basketball games, and remember me in his will. As far as I can see, however, he does not owe me anything, either legally or morally.

Suppose further that Michael Jordan and I are in high school together and we are both qualified to play basketball, only he is far better than I. Do I deserve to start in his position because I would have been as good as he is had someone not cheated me as a child? Again, I think not. But if being the lucky ben-eficiary of wrongdoing does not entail that Jordan (or the coach) owes me anything in regard to basketball, why should it be a reason to engage in preferential hiring in academic positions or highly coveted jobs? If minimal qualifications are not adequate to override excellence in basketball, even when the minimality

is a consequence of wrongdoing, why should they be adequate in other areas?

AFFIRMATIVE ACTION REQUIRES DISCRIMINATION AGAINST A DIFFERENT GROUP

Here is the third reason why I changed my mind on AA. Weak or procedural AA weakly discriminates against new minorities, mostly innocent young White males, and strong or preferential Affirmative Action strongly discriminates against these new minorities. As I argued earlier, this discrimination is unwar-ranted, since, even if some compensation to Blacks were indicated, it would be unfair to make innocent white males bear the whole brunt of the payments. Recently I had this experience. I knew a brilliant young philosopher, with outstanding publications in first level journals, who was having difficulty get-ting a tenure-track position. For the first time in my life I offered to make a phone call on his behalf to a university to which he had applied. When I reached the Chair of the Search Committee, he offered that the committee was under instructions from the Administration to hire a woman or a Black. They had one of each on their short-list, so they weren't even considering the applications of White males. At my urging he retrieved my friend's file, and said, "This fellow looks far superior to the two candidates we're interviewing, but there's nothing I can do about it." Cases like this come to my attention regularly. In fact, it is poor White youth who become the new pariahs on the job market. The children of the wealthy have little trouble getting into the best private grammar schools and, on the basis of superior early education, into the best universities, graduate schools, manage-rial and professional positions. Affirmative Action simply shifts injustice, setting Blacks, Hispanics, Native Americans, Asians and women against young White males, especially ethnic and poor white males. It makes no more sense to discriminate in favor of a rich Black or female who had the opportunity of the best family and education available against a poor White, than it does to discriminate in favor of White males against Blacks or women. It does little to rectify the goal of providing equal opportunity to all.

At the end of his essay supporting Affirmative Action, Albert Mosley points out that other groups besides Blacks have been benefited by AA, "women, the disabled, the elderly."[10] He's correct in including the elderly, for through powerful lobbies, such as the AARP, they do get special benefits, including Medicare, and may sue on the grounds of being discriminated against due to *Ageism,* prejudice against older people. Might this not be a reason to reconsider Affirmative Action? Consider the sheer rough percentages of those who qualify for some type of AA programs.

Group	Percentage in Population
1. Women	52
2. Blacks	12
3. Hispanics	9
4. Native Americans	2
5. Asian-Americans	4
6. Physically and Mentally Disabled	10
7. Welfare Recipients	6
8. The Elderly	25 (est. Adults over 60)
9. Italians (in New York City)	3
Total	123

The Office of Federal Contract Compliance (OFCC) includes as protected categories not only Blacks but "all persons of Mexican, Puerto Rican, Cuban or Spanish origin or ancestry." The Small Business Administration adds Eskimos and Aleuts. Federal contracting programs include the following groups as meriting preferential treatment: People from Burma, Thailand, Malaysia, Indonesia, Singapore, Brunei, Japan, China, Taiwan, Laos, Cambodia, Vietnam, Korea, the Philippines, U.S. Trust Territory of the Pacific Islands, Republic of the Marshall Islands, Federated States of Micronesia, the Commonwealth of the Northern Mariana Islands, Guam, Samoa, Macao, Hong Kong, Fiji, Tonga, Kiribati, Tuvalu, Mauru, India, Pakistan, Bangladesh,

Sri Lanka, Bhutan, the Maldives Islands, and Nepal.[11] Recent immigrants from these countries sometimes are awarded contracts in preference to lower bids by White male owned firms. Recently, it has been proposed that homosexuals be included in oppressed groups deserving Affirmative Action.[12] At Northeastern University in 1996 the faculty governing body voted to grant homosexuals Affirmative Action status at this university. How many more percentage points would this add? Several authors have advocated putting all poor people on the list.[13] And if we took handicaps seriously, would we not add ugly people, obese people, people who stammer, color-blind people, people with genetic liabilities, and, especially, short people, for which there is ample evidence of discrimination? How about left-handed people (about 9% of the population), they can't play short-stop or third base and have to put up with a right-handedly biased world. The only group not on the list is that of White males. Are they, especially healthy, middle-class young White males, becoming the new "oppressed class"? Should we add them to our list?

Respect for persons entails that we treat each person as an end in himself or herself, not simply as a means to be used for social purposes. What is wrong about discrimination against Blacks is that it fails to treat Black people as individuals, judging them instead by their skin color not their merit. What is wrong about discrimination against women is that it fails to treat them as individuals, judging them by their gender, not their merit. What is equally wrong about *Affirmative Action* is that it fails to treat White males with dignity as individuals, judging them by *both their race and gender,* instead of their merit. *Current Strong Affirmative Action is both racist and sexist.*

CONCLUSION

Let me sum up my discussion. The goal of the Civil Rights movement and of moral people everywhere has been justice for all, for a color-blind society, where people will not be judged by their race or gender but by their moral character and abilities. The question is: How best to get there? Civil rights legislation removed the unjust legal barriers, opening the way towards equal opportunity, but it did not tackle other factors, causes that result in unjust discrimination. Procedural Affirmative Action aims at encouraging minorities and women to strive for excellence in all areas of life, without unduly jeopardizing the rights of other groups, such as White males and Asians. The problem of Procedural Affirmative Action is that it easily slides into Preferential Affirmative Action where quotas, "goals and time-tables," "equal results,"—in a word, *reverse discrimination*—prevail and are forced onto groups, thus promoting mediocrity, inefficiency, and resentment. My argument has been that, if we are serious about attaining a color-blind society, with a large amount of opportunity for all, we should shape our lives and our institutions in ways that make that more likely. AA vitiates that goal by setting up a new class of pariah, young White males, depriving them of the opportunities that they merit. Furthermore, AA frequently aims at the higher levels of society—universities and skilled jobs, but, if we want to improve our society, the best way to do it is to concentrate on families, children, early education, and the like, so that all are prepared to avail themselves of opportunity. Affirmative Action, on the one hand, is arbitrary, compensating a few of the better-off members of AA groups, and doing nothing for the truly disadvantaged, and on the other hand, is doubly arbitrary in exacting a penalty from unlucky talented young white males, who themselves may have been victims of oppression, while leaving better-off members of society untouched by its policies.

In addition to the arguments I have offered, Affirmative Action, rather than unite people of good will in the common cause of justice, tends to balkanize us into segregation-thinking. Professor Derrick Bell of Harvard Law School recently said that the African-American Supreme Court judge Clarence Thomas, in his opposition to Affirmative Action, "doesn't think black."[14] Does Bell really claim that there is a standard and proper "Black" (and presumably a White) way of thinking? Ideologues like Bell, whether radical Blacks like himself, or Nazis who advocate "think

Aryan," both represent the same thing: cynicism about rational debate, the very antithesis of the quest for impartial truth and justice. People of good will, who believe in reason to resolve our differences will oppose this kind of balkanization of ethnic groups.

Martin Luther said that humanity is like a man mounting a horse who always tends to fall off on the other side of the horse. This seems to be the case with Affirmative Action. Attempting to redress the discriminatory iniquities of our history, our well-intentioned social engineers now engage in new forms of discriminatory iniquity and thereby think that they have successfully mounted the horse of racial harmony. They have only fallen off on the other side of the issue.[15]

NOTES

1. See "The Moral Status of Affirmative Action" in *Public Affairs Quarterly,* vol. 6:2 (1992) and "The Case against Strong Affirmative Action" in *International Journal for Applied Philosophy,* vol. 12 (1998).

2. Mylan Engel, Correspondence, September 24, 1998.

3. Objective measures, such as SAT and ACT scores, along with high school grade point average, have considerable validity. The charge of being prejudicial has been adequately refuted. Actually, they predict better for Blacks than for Whites. Wherever possible recommendations and personal interviews should be used to supplement these measures.

4. Also, many Haitians and Latinos are recent immigrants to the USA (sometimes illegally so). Why should they be given preference over young white males? Why should the university be made to carry the heavy burden of leveling society when people come to our land voluntarily? Note too that poor Blacks and Hispanics typically have larger families than Whites and middle-class Blacks. If the poor are to be given special benefits, don't procreative responsibilities go along with them?

5. Many people think that it is somehow unjust if one community (or family) spends more money or resources on its children's education than another. A few years ago the New Jersey legislature passed a bill prohibiting communities from spending more than the average amount of money on its children's public education, lest inequalities emerge. But, if we believe that parents should have considerable freedom on how they use their resources, why is disparity unjust? Suppose you choose to have only 2 children

and make enormous sacrifices for their education and upbringing (say 40 units on each child) and I (with similar resources) have 10 children and spend less total resources to all 10 (averaging 5 units on each child). Why, should society have to make up the difference between what is spent on the 10 children. Surely, such supplementary aid, beyond a certain minimal limit, is a disincentive to be a responsible parent. Yet we don't want the children to suffer either. This may be a prima facie reason to require licenses for parenting (which has its own serious problems).

6. For a good discussion of this argument see B. Boxill, "The Morality of Reparation" in *Social Theory and Practice* 2:1 (1972) and Albert G. Mosley in his and Nicholas Capaldi, *Affirmative Action; Social Justice or Unfair Preference?* (Totowa, NJ: Rowman and Littlefield, 1996), pp. 23–27.

7. Merit sometimes may be justifiably overridden by need, as when parents choose to spend extra earnings on special education for their disabled child rather than for their gifted child. Sometimes we may override merit for utilitarian purposes. For example, suppose you are the best shortstop on a baseball team but are also the best catcher. You'd rather play shortstop, but the manager decides to put you at catcher because, while your friend can do an adequate job at short, no one else is adequate at catcher. It's permissible for you to be assigned the job of catcher. Probably, some expression of appreciation would be due you.

8. I am indebted to Robert Simon's "Preferential Hiring" *Philosophy and Public Affairs* 3 (1974) for helping me to formulate this argument.

9. Judith Jarvis Thomson, "Preferential Hiring" in Marshall Cohen, Thomas Nagel, and Thomas Scanlon, eds., *Equality and Preferential Treatment* (Princeton: Princeton University Press, 1977).

10. Albert Mosley, op. cit., p. 53.

11. For a discussion of these figures, see Terry Eastland, *Ending Affirmative Action* (New York: Basic Books, 1996), p. 5Sf and 140f.

12. J. Sartorelli, "The Nature of Affirmative Action, Anti-Gay Oppression, and the Alleviation of Enduring Harm" *International Journal of Applied Philosophy* (vol. 11. No. 2, 1997).

13. For example, Iddo Landau, "Are You Entitled to Affirmative Action?" *International Journal of Applied Philosophy* (vol. 11. No. 2, 1997) and Richard Kahlenberg "Class Not Race" (*The New Republic* April 3, 1995).

14. See L. Gordon Crovitz, "Borking Begins, but Mudballs Bounce Off Judge Thomas," *The Wall Street Journal,* July 17, 1991. Have you noticed the irony in this mudslinging at Judge Thomas? The same blacks and whites who oppose Judge Thomas, as not the best person for the job, are themselves the strongest proponents of Affirmative Action, which embraces the tenet that minimally qualified Blacks and women should get jobs over White males.

15. Some of the material in this essay appeared in "The Moral Status of Affirmative Action" *Public Affairs Quarterly,* vol. 6:2 (1992). I have not had space to consider all the objections to my position or discuss the issue of freedom of association which, I think, should be given much scope in private but not in public institutions. Barbara Bergmann (*In Defense of Affirmative Action* (New York: Basic Books, 1996, pp. 122–125)) and others argue that we already offering preferential treatment for athletes and veterans, especially in university admissions, so, being consistent, we should provide it for women and minorities. My answer is that I am against giving athletic scholarships, and I regard scholarships to veterans as a part of a contractual relationship, a reward for service to one's country. But I distinguish entrance programs from actual employment. I don't think that veterans should be afforded special privilege in hiring practices, unless it be as a tie breaker.

I should also mention that my arguments from merit and respect apply more specifically to public institutions than private ones, where issues of property rights and freedom of association carry more weight.

READING QUESTIONS

1. Explain the "level playing field" and "compensation" arguments in favor of affirmative action. What objections does Pojman raise for each of these arguments?
2. How does Pojman distinguish between preferential and procedural affirmative action?
3. Why does Pojman think that affirmative action encourages discrimination against different groups? What group in particular does he think affirmative action discriminates against?
4. Explain Pojman's reasons for thinking that affirmative action policies fail to show respect for persons and to treat them with dignity.

DISCUSSION QUESTIONS

1. Is Pojman's worry that preferential affirmative action would slide into procedural affirmative action justified? Why or why not?
2. Should we accept Pojman's claim that affirmative action discriminates against innocent white males? Why or why not? Suppose that affirmative action does discriminate against innocent white males in the way Pojman describes. Consider and discuss whether discrimination against one group of people is any more or less wrong than discrimination against another.

THOMAS E. HILL JR.

The Message of Affirmative Action

Thomas Hill is critical of "forward-looking" consequentialist attempts to justify affirmative action policies, and he is also critical of standard "backward-looking" attempts that would appeal, for example, to Ross's principle of reparation to justify such policies. Both approaches, argues Hill, convey the wrong message about the nature of racism and sexism and affirmative actions policies. In order to properly address the morality of affirmative action, Hill sketches a "narrative" framework for thinking about racism and sexism that emphasizes one's historical and cultural context and, in particular, the idea that many of our values are "cross-time wholes, with past, present, and future parts united in certain ways." Emphasizing the cross-time ideals or virtues of mutual respect and trust and the value of equal opportunity, Hill explains how affirmative action policies such as we find in many universities can be morally justified.

Recommended Reading: virtue ethics, chap. 1, sec. 2E. Also relevant are consequentialism, chap. 1, sec. 2A, and the ethics of prima facie duty, chap. 1, sec. 2F.

Affirmative Action Programs remain controversial, I suspect, partly because the familiar arguments for and against them start from significantly different moral perspectives. Thus I want to step back for a while from the details of debate about particular programs and give attention to the moral viewpoints presupposed in different *types* of argument. My aim, more specifically, is to compare the "messages" expressed when affirmative action is defended from different moral perspectives. Exclusively forward-looking (for example, utilitarian) arguments, I suggest, tend to express the wrong message, but this is also true of exclusively backward-looking (for example, reparation-based) arguments. However, a moral outlook that focuses on cross-temporal narrative values (such as mutually respectful social relations) suggests a more appropriate account of what affirmative action should try to express. Assessment of the message, admittedly, is only one aspect of a complex issue, but it is a relatively neglected one. My discussion takes for granted some common-sense ideas about the communicative function of action, and so I begin with these.

Actions, as the saying goes, often *speak* louder than words. There are times, too, when only actions can effectively communicate the message we want to convey and times when giving a message is a central part of the purpose of action. What our actions say to others depends largely, though not entirely, upon our avowed reasons for acting; and this is a matter for reflective decision, not something we discover later by looking back at what we did and its effects. The decision is important because "the same act" can have very different consequences, depending upon how we choose to justify it. In a sense, acts done for different reasons are not "the same act" even if they are otherwise similar, and so not merely the consequences but also the moral nature of our acts depends in part on our decisions about the reasons for doing them.

Unfortunately, the message actually conveyed by our actions does not depend only on our intentions and reasons, for our acts may have a meaning for others quite at odds with what we hoped to express. Others may misunderstand our intentions, doubt our sincerity, or discern a subtext that undermines the primary message. Even if sincere, well-intended, and successfully conveyed, the message of an act or policy does not by itself justify the means by which it is conveyed; it is almost always a relevant factor, however, in the moral assessment of an act or policy. . . .

I shall focus attention for a while upon this relatively neglected issue of the message of affirmative action. In particular, I want to consider what messages we *should try* to give with affirmative action programs and what messages we should try to avoid.

What is the best way to convey the intended message, and indeed whether it is likely to be heard, are empirical questions that I cannot settle; but the question I propose to consider is nonetheless important, and it is a *prior* question. What do we want to say with our affirmative action programs, and why? Since the message that is received and its consequences are likely to depend to some extent on what we decide, in all sincerity, to be the rationale for such programs, it would be premature and foolish to try to infer or predict these outcomes without adequate reflection on what the message and rationale should be. Also, for those who accept the historical/narrative perspective described in [this essay], there is additional reason to focus first on the desired message; for that perspective treats the message of affirmative action not merely as a minor side effect to be weighed in, for or against, but rather as an important part of the legitimate purpose of affirmative action.

Much useful discussion has been devoted to the constitutionality of affirmative action programs, to the relative moral rights involved, and to the advantages and disadvantages of specific types of programs. By deemphasizing these matters here, I do not mean to suggest that they are unimportant. Even more, my remarks are not meant to convey the message, "It doesn't matter what we do or achieve, all that matters is what we *say*." To the contrary, I believe that mere gestures are insufficient and that universities cannot even communicate what they should by affirmative action policies unless these are sincerely designed to result in increased opportunities for those disadvantaged and insulted by racism and sexism. . . .

STRATEGIES OF JUSTIFICATION: CONSEQUENCES AND REPARATIONS

Some arguments for affirmative action look exclusively to its future benefits. The idea is that what has happened in the past is not in itself relevant to what we should do; at most, it provides clues as to what acts and policies are likely to bring about the best future. The philosophical tradition associated with this approach is utilitarianism, which declares that the morally right act is whatever produces the best consequences. Traditionally, utilitarianism evaluated consequences in terms of happiness and unhappiness, but the anticipated consequences of affirmative action are often described more specifically. For example, some argue that affirmative action will ease racial tensions, prevent riots, improve services in minority neighborhoods, reduce unemployment, remove inequities in income distribution, eliminate racial and sexual prejudice, and enhance the self-esteem of blacks and women. Some have called attention to the fact that women and minorities provide alternative perspectives on history, literature, philosophy, and politics, and that this has beneficial effects for both education and research.

These are important considerations, not irrelevant to the larger responsibilities of universities. For several reasons, however, I think it is a mistake for advocates of affirmative action to rest their case exclusively on such forward-looking arguments. First, critics raise reasonable doubts about whether affirmative action is necessary to achieve these admirable results. The economist Thomas Sowell argues that a free-market economy can achieve the same results more efficiently; his view is therefore that even if affirmative action has beneficial results (which he denies), it is not necessary for the purpose.[1] Though Sowell's position can be contested, the controversy itself tends to weaken confidence in the entirely forward-looking defense of affirmative action.

An even more obvious reason why affirmative action advocates should explore other avenues for its defense is that the exclusively forward-looking approach must give equal consideration to possible negative consequences of affirmative action. It may be, for example, that affirmative action will temporarily increase racial tensions, especially if its message is misunderstood. Even legitimate use of race and sex categories may encourage others to abuse the categories for unjust purposes. If applied without sensitive regard to the educational and research purposes of the university, affirmative action might severely undermine its efforts to fulfill these primary responsibilities. If affirmative action programs were to lower academic standards for blacks and women, they would run the risk of damaging the respect that highly qualified blacks and women have earned by leading others to suspect that these highly qualified people lack the merits of white males in the same positions. This could also be damaging to the self-respect of those who accept affirmative action positions. Even programs that disavow "lower standards" unfortunately arouse the suspicion that they don't really do so, and this by itself can cause problems. Although I believe that well-designed affirmative action programs can minimize these negative effects, the fact that they are a risk is a reason for not resting the case for affirmative action on a delicate balance of costs and benefits.

Reflection on the *message* of affirmative action also leads me to move beyond entirely forward-looking arguments. For if the sole purpose is to bring about a brighter future, then we give the wrong message to both the white males who are rejected and to the women and blacks who are benefited. To the latter what we say, in effect, is this: "Never mind how you have been treated. Forget about the fact that your race or sex has in the past been actively excluded and discouraged, and that you yourself may have had handicaps due to prejudice. Our sole concern is to bring about certain good results in the future, and giving you a break happens to be a useful means for doing this. Don't think this is a recognition of your rights as an individual or your disadvantages as a member of a group. Nor does it mean that we have confidence in your abilities. We would do the same for those who are privileged and academically inferior if it would have the same socially beneficial results."

To the white male who would have had a university position but for affirmative action, the exclusively forward-looking approach says: "We deny you the place you otherwise would have had simply as a means to produce certain socially desirable outcomes. We have not judged that others are more deserving, or have a right, to the place we are giving them instead of you. Past racism and sexism are irrelevant. The point is just that the sacrifice of your concerns is a useful means to the larger end of the future welfare of others."

This, I think, is the wrong message to give. It is also unnecessary. The proper alternative, however, is not to ignore the possible future benefits of affirmative action but rather to take them into account as a part of a larger picture.

A radically different strategy for justifying affirmative action is to rely on backward-looking arguments. Such arguments call our attention to certain events in the past and assert that *because* these past events occurred, we have certain duties now. The modern philosopher who most influentially endorsed such arguments was W. D. Ross.[2] He argued that there are duties of fidelity, justice, gratitude, and reparation that have a moral force independent of any tendency these may have to promote good consequences. The fact that you have made a promise, for example, gives you a strong moral reason to do what you promised, whether or not doing so will on balance have more beneficial consequences. The Rossian principle that is often invoked in affirmative action debates is a principle of reparation. This says that those who wrongfully injure others have a (prima facie) duty to apologize and make restitution. Those who have wronged others owe reparation. . . .

There are, however, serious problems in trying to justify affirmative action by this backward-looking argument, especially if it is treated as the exclusive or central argument. Degrees of being advantaged and disadvantaged are notoriously hard to measure. New immigrants have not shared our history of past injustices, and so the argument may not apply to them in any straightforward way. The argument appeals to controversial ideas about property rights, inheritance, and group responsibilities. Some argue that affirmative action tends to benefit the least disadvantaged blacks and women; though this does not mean that they are owed nothing, their claims would seem to have lower priority than the needs of the most disadvantaged. Some highly qualified blacks and women object that affirmative action is damaging to their reputations and self-esteem, whereas the reparation argument seems to assume that it is a welcome benefit to all blacks and women.

If we focus on the message that the backward-looking argument sends, there are also some potential problems. Though rightly acknowledging past injustice, the argument (by itself) seems to convey the message that racial and sexual oppression consisted primarily in the loss of tangible goods, or the deprivation of specific rights and opportunities, that can be "paid back" in kind. The background idea, which goes back at least to Aristotle, is that persons wrongfully deprived of their "due" can justly demand an "equivalent" to what they have lost.[3] But, while specific deprivations were an important part of our racist and sexist past, they are far from the whole story. Among the worst wrongs then, as now, were humiliations and contemptuous treatment of a type that cannot, strictly, be "paid back." The problem was, and is, not just that specific rights and advantages were denied, but that prejudicial attitudes damaged self-esteem, undermined motivations, limited realistic options, and made even "officially open" opportunities seem undesirable. Racism and sexism were (and are) *insults*, not merely tangible *injuries*.[4] These are not the sort of thing that can be adequately measured and repaid with equivalents. The trouble with treating insulting racist and sexist practices on a pure reparation model is not merely the practical difficulty of identifying the offenders, determining the degree of guilt, assessing the amount of payment due, etc. It is also that penalty payments and compensation for lost benefits are not the only, or primary, moral responses that are called for. When affirmative action is defended exclusively by analogy with reparation, it tends to express the misleading message that the evils of racism and sexism are all tangible losses that can be "paid off;" by being silent on the insulting nature of racism and sexism, it tends to add insult to insult.

The message suggested by the reparation argument, by itself, also seems objectionable because it conveys the idea that higher education, teaching, and doing research are mainly benefits awarded in response to self-centered demands. The underlying picture too easily suggested is that applicants are a group of self-interested, bickering people, each grasping for limited "goodies" and insisting on a right to them. When a university grants an opportunity through affirmative action, its message would seem to be this. "We concede that you have a valid claim to this benefit and we yield to your demand, though this is not to suggest that we have confidence in your abilities or any desire to have you here." This invitation seems too concessive, the atmosphere too adversarial, and the emphasis too much on the benefits rather than the responsibilities of being a part of the university.

PHILOSOPHICAL INTERLUDE: AN ALTERNATIVE PERSPECTIVE

Here I want to digress from the explicit consideration of affirmative action in order to consider more abstract philosophical questions about the ways we evaluate acts and policies. At the risk of oversimplifying, I want to contrast some assumptions that have, until recently, been dominant in ethical theory with alternatives suggested by contemporary philosophers who emphasize historical context, narrative unity, and community values.[5] Although these alternatives, in my opinion, have not yet been adequately developed, there seem to be at least four distinguishable themes worth considering.

First, when we reflect on what we deeply value, we find that we care not merely about the present moment and each future moment in isolation but also about how our past, present, and future cohere or fit together into a life and a piece of history. Some of our values, we might say, are cross-time wholes, with past, present, and future parts united in certain ways. Thus, for example, the commitments I have made, the projects I have begun, what I have shared with those I love, the injuries I have caused, and the hopes I have encouraged importantly affect both whether I am satisfied with my present and how I want the future to go.

Second, in reflecting on stretches of our lives and histories, we frequently use evaluative concepts drawn more from narrative literature than from accounting. Thus, for example, we think of our lives as having significant beginnings, crises, turning points, dramatic tension, character development, climaxes, resolutions, comic interludes, tragic disruptions, and eventually fitting (or unfitting) endings. The value of any moment often depends on what came before and what we anticipate to follow. And since our lives are intertwined with others in a common history, we also care about how our moments cohere with others' life stories. The past is seen as more than a time of accumulated debts and assets, and the future is valued as more than an opportunity for reinvesting and cashing in assets.

Third, evaluation must take into account one's particular historical context, including one's cultural, national, and ethnic traditions, and the actual individuals in one's life. Sometimes this point is exaggerated, I think, to suggest a dubious cultural relativism or "particularism" in ethics: for example, the thesis that what is valuable for a person is defined by the person's culture or that evaluations imply no general reasons beyond particular judgments, such as "That's *our* way" and "John is *my* son." But, construed modestly as a practical or epistemological point, it seems obvious enough, on reflection, that we should take into account the historical context of our acts and that we are often in a better position to judge what is appropriate in particular cases than we are to articulate universally valid premises supporting the judgment. . . .

Fourth, when we evaluate particular acts and policies as parts of lives and histories, what is often most important is the value of the whole, which cannot always be determined by "summing up" the values of the parts. Lives, histories, and interpersonal relations over time are what G. E. Moore called "organic unities"—that is, wholes the value of which is not necessarily the sum of the values of the parts.[6] The point here is not merely the obvious practical limitation that we cannot measure and quantify values in this area. More fundamentally, the idea is that it would be a mistake even to try to evaluate certain unities by assessing different parts in isolation from one another, then adding up all their values. Suppose, for example, a woman with terminal cancer considered two quite different ways of spending her last days. One way, perhaps taking a world cruise, might seem best when evaluated in terms of the quality of each future moment, in isolation from her past and her present ties; but another way, perhaps seeking closure in projects and with estranged family members, might seem more valuable when seen as a part of her whole life.

Taken together, these ideas cast doubt on both the exclusively forward-looking method of assessment and the standard backward-looking alternative. Consequentialism, or the exclusively forward-looking method, attempts to determine what ought to be done at present by fixing attention entirely on future results. To be sure, any sensible consequentialist will consult the past for lessons and clues helpful in predicting future outcomes: for example, recalling that you offended someone yesterday may enable you to predict that the person will be cool to you tomorrow unless you apologize. But beyond this, consequentialists have no concern with the past, for their "bottom line" is always "what happens from now on," evaluated independently of the earlier chapters of our lives and histories. For the consequentialist, assessing a life or history from a narrative perspective becomes impossible or at least bizarre, as what must be evaluated at each shifting moment is "the story from now on" independently of what has already been written.[7]

The standard Rossian alternative to this exclusively forward-looking perspective is to introduce certain, (prima facie) *duties* to respond to certain past events in specified ways—for example, pay debts, keep promises, pay reparation for injuries. These duties are supposed to be self-evident and universal (though they are prima facie), and they do not hold because they tend to promote anything good or valuable. Apart from aspects of the acts mentioned in the principles (for example, fulfilling a promise, returning favors, not injuring, etc.), details of historical and personal context are considered irrelevant.

By contrast, the narrative perspective sketched above considers the past as an integral part of the valued unities that we aim to bring about, not merely as a source of duties. If one has negligently wronged another, Ross regards this past event as generating a duty to pay reparations even if doing so will result in nothing good. But from the narrative perspective, the past becomes relevant in a further way. One may say, for example, that the *whole* consisting of your life and your relationship with that person from the time of the injury into the future will be a better thing if you acknowledge the wrong and make efforts to restore what you have damaged. For Ross, the duty is

generated by the past and unrelated to bringing about anything good; from the narrative perspective, however, the requirement is just what is required to bring about a valuable connected whole with past, present, and future parts—the best way to complete a chapter, so to speak, in two intersecting lifestories.

So far, neither the Rossian nor the narrative account has told us much about the ultimate reasons for their evaluations, but they reveal ways to consider the matter. The Rossian asks us to judge particular cases in the light of "self-evident" general principles asserting that certain past events tend to generate present (or future) duties. The alternative perspective calls for examining lives and relationships, over time, in context, as organic unities evaluated (partly) in narrative terms.

To illustrate, consider two persons, John and Mary. John values having Mary's trust and respect, and conversely, Mary values having John's; moreover, John values the fact that Mary values being trusted and respected by him, and conversely Mary values the same about John.

Now suppose that other people have been abusive and insulting to Mary, and that John is worried that Mary may take things he had said and done as similarly insulting, even though he does not think that he consciously meant them this way. Though he is worried, Mary does not seem to suspect him; he fears that he may only make matters worse if he raises the issue, creating suspicions she did not have or focusing on doubts that he cannot allay. Perhaps, he thinks, their future relationship would be better served if he just remained silent, hoping that the trouble, if any, will fade in time. If so, consequentialist thinking would recommend silence. Acknowledging this, he might nonetheless feel that duties of friendship and fidelity demand that he raise the issue, regardless of whether or not the result will be worse. Then he would be thinking as a Rossian.

But, instead, he might look at the problem from an alternative perspective, asking himself what response best affirms and contributes to the sort of ongoing relationship he has and wants to continue with Mary. Given their history together, it is important to him to do his part towards restoring the relationship if it indeed has been marred by perceived insults or suspicions.

To be sure, he wants *future* relations of mutual trust and respect, but not at any price and not by just any means. Their history together is not irrelevant, for what he values is not merely a future of a certain kind, but that their relationship over time be of the sort he values. He values an ongoing history of mutual trust and respect that *calls for* an explicit response in this current situation, not merely as a means to a brighter future but as a present affirmation of what they value together. Even if unsure which course will be best for the future, he may be reasonably confident that the act that best expresses his respect and trust (and his valuing hers, etc.) is to confront the problem, express his regrets, reaffirm his respect, ask for her trust, be patient with her doubts, and welcome an open dialogue. If the insults were deep and it is not entirely clear whether or not he really associated himself with them, then mere words may not be enough to convey the message or even to assure himself of his own sincerity. Positive efforts, even at considerable cost, may be needed to express appropriately and convincingly what needs to be said. How the next chapter unfolds is not entirely up to him, and he would not be respectful if he presumed otherwise by trying to manipulate the best future unilaterally.

The example concerns only two persons and their personal values, but it illustrates a perspective that one can also take regarding moral problems involving many persons.

MUTUAL RESPECT, FAIR OPPORTUNITY, AND AFFIRMATIVE ACTION

Turning back to our main subject, I suggest that some of the values that give affirmative action its point are best seen as cross-time values that fall outside the exclusively forward-looking and backward-looking perspectives. They include having a history of racial and gender relations governed, so far as possible, by the ideals of mutual respect, trust, and fair opportunity for all.

Our national history provides a context of increasing recognition and broader interpretation of the democratic ideal of the equal dignity of all human beings—an ideal that has been flagrantly abused from the outset, partially affirmed in the bloody Civil War, and increasingly extended in the civil rights movement, but is still far from being fully respected. More specifically, blacks and women were systematically treated in an unfair and demeaning way by public institutions, including universities, until quite recently, and few could confidently claim to have rooted out racism and sexism even now.[8] The historical context is not what grounds or legitimates democratic values, but it is the background of the current problem, the sometimes admirable and often ugly way the chapters up until now have been written.

Consider the social ideal of mutual respect and trust among citizens. The problem of implementing this in the current context is different from the problem in the two-person example discussed above, for the history of our racial and gender relations is obviously not an idyllic story of mutual respect and trust momentarily interrupted by a crisis. Even so, the question to ask is not merely, "What will promote respectful and trusting racial and gender relations in future generations?", but rather, "Given our checkered past, how can we appropriately express the social value of mutual respect and trust that we want, so far as possible, to characterize our history?" We cannot change our racist and sexist past, but we also cannot express full respect for those present individuals who live in its aftermath if we ignore it. What is called for is not merely repayment of tangible debts incurred by past injuries, but also a message to counter the deep insult inherent in racism and sexism. . . .

CONCLUSION

The message is called for not just as a means to future good relations or a dutiful payment of a debt incurred by our past. It is called for by the ideal of being related to other human beings over time, so that our histories and biographies reflect the responses of those who deeply care about fair opportunity, mutual trust, and respect for all.

If so, what should public universities try to say to those offered opportunities through affirmative action? Perhaps something like this: "Whether we individually are among the guilty or not, we acknowledge that you have been wronged—if not by specific injuries which could be named and repaid, at least by the humiliating and debilitating attitudes prevalent in our country and our institutions. We deplore and denounce these attitudes and the wrongs that spring from them. We acknowledge that, so far, most of you have had your opportunities in life diminished by the effects of these attitudes, and we want no one's prospects to be diminished by injustice. We recognize your understandable grounds for suspicion and mistrust when we express these high-minded sentiments, and we want not only to ask respectfully for your trust but also to give concrete evidence of our sincerity. We welcome you respectfully into the university community and ask you to take a full share of the responsibilities as well as the benefits. By creating special opportunities, we recognize the disadvantages you have probably suffered; we show our respect for your talents and our commitment to the ideals of the university however, by not faking grades and honors for you. Given current attitudes about affirmative action, accepting this position will probably have drawbacks as well as advantages. It is an opportunity and a responsibility offered neither as charity nor as entitlement, but rather as part of a special effort to welcome and encourage minorities and women to participate more fully in the university at all levels. We believe that this program affirms some of the best ideals implicit in our history without violating the rights of any applicants. We hope that you will choose to accept the position in this spirit as well as for your own benefit."

The appropriate message is no doubt harder to communicate to those who stand to lose some traditional advantages under a legitimate affirmative action program. But if we set aside practical difficulties and suppose that the proper message could be sincerely given and accepted as such, what would it say? Ideally, it would convey an understanding of the moral reasoning for the program; perhaps, in conclusion, it would say something like the following.

"These are the concerns that we felt made necessary the policy under which the university is temporarily giving special attention to women and minorities. We respect your rights to formal justice and to a policy guided by the university's education and research mission as well as its social responsibilities. Our policy in no way implies the view that your opportunities are less important than others', but we estimate (roughly, as we must) that as a white male you have probably had advantages and encouragement that for a long time have been systematically, unfairly, insultingly unavailable to most women and minorities. We deplore invidious race and gender distinctions; we hope that no misunderstanding of our program will prolong them. Unfortunately, nearly all blacks and women have been disadvantaged to some degree by bias against their groups, and it is impractical for universities to undertake the detailed investigations that would be needed to assess how much particular individuals have suffered or gained from racism and sexism. We appeal to you to share the historical values of fair opportunity and mutual respect that underlie this policy; we hope that, even though its effects may be personally disappointing, you can see the policy as an appropriate response to the current situation."

Unfortunately, as interests conflict and tempers rise, it is difficult to convey this idea without giving an unintended message as well. White males unhappy about the immediate effects of affirmative action may read the policy as saying that "justice" is the official word for giving preferential treatment to whatever group one happens to favor. Some may see a subtext insinuating that blacks and women are naturally inferior and "cannot make it on their own." Such cynical readings reveal either misunderstanding or the willful refusal to take the moral reasoning underlying affirmative action seriously. They pose serious obstacles to the success of affirmative action—practical problems that may be more intractable than respectful moral disagreement and counter-argument. But some types of affirmative action invite misunderstanding and suspicion more than others. For this reason, anyone who accepts the general case for affirmative action suggested here would do well to reexamine in detail the means by which they hope to communicate its message.[9]

NOTES

1. Thomas Sowell, *Race and Economics* (New York: David McKay Co., 1975), ch. 6; *Markets and Minorities* (New York: Basic Books, Inc., 1981), pp. 114–15.

2. W. D. Ross, *The Right and the Good* (Oxford: Clarendon Press, 1930).

3. Aristotle, *Nicomachean Ethics,* tr. A. K. Thomson (Baltimore: Penguin Books, Inc., 1955), bk. V, esp. pp. 143–55.

4. See Boxill, *Blacks and Social Justice* (Totowa: Rowman & Allenheld, 1984), pp. 132ff., and Ronald Dworkin, "Reverse Discrimination," in *Taking Rights Seriously* (Cambridge: Harvard University Press, 1978), pp. 231ff.

5. See, for example, Alasdair MacIntyre, *After Virtue* (Notre Dame: Notre Dame University Press, 1981). Similar themes are found in Carol Gilligan's *In A Different Voice* (Cambridge: Harvard University Press, 1982) and in Lawrence Blum, *Friendship, Altruism, and Morality* (Boston: Routledge and Kegan Paul, 1980).

6. G. E. Moore, *Principia Ethica* (Cambridge University Press, 1912), pp. 27ff.

7. That is, the evaluation is independent of the past in the sense that the past makes no intrinsic difference to the final judgment and the future is not evaluated as a part of a temporal whole including the past. As noted, however, consequentialists will still look to the past for lessons and clues about how to bring about the best future.

8. Racism and sexism present significantly different problems, but I shall not try to analyze the differences here. For the most part my primary focus is on racism, but the relevance of the general type of moral thinking considered here to the problems of sexism should nonetheless be evident.

9. Although my aim in this essay has been to survey general types of arguments for thinking that some sort of affirmative action is needed, rather than to argue for any particular program, one cannot reasonably implement the general idea without considering many contextual factors that I have set aside here. Thus, the need for more detailed discussion is obvious.

READING QUESTIONS

1. Explain the backward- and forward-looking perspectives on affirmative action. What are some of the objections that Hill raises for each of these views? Consider in particular his problems with the messages they send.
2. Explain Hill's cross-temporal narrative value perspective. Focus on the four themes he lays out concerning the assumptions dominant in ethical theory. How does this view offer an advantage over the two views he rejects?
3. What sort of message does Hill believe ought to be sent by a successful affirmative action policy? What is one of the potential problems facing this message?

DISCUSSION QUESTIONS

1. To what extent should we be concerned with the message sent by policies and perspectives on affirmative action? How important should considerations such as motivations and results be in the affirmative action debate?
2. Suppose that Hill is correct about the importance of sending the right kind of message with an affirmative action policy. Reread his suggestion for an affirmative action statement that could be issued by a university and consider what messages it sends and whether those messages are in accord with the one he thinks is appropriate. What message should an affirmative action policy send?

ADDITIONAL RESOURCES

Web Resources

Civilrights.org, <http://www.civilrights.org/>. A civil rights advocacy organization involving the Leadership Conference on Civil Rights and the Leadership Conference on Civil Rights Education Fund.

Fullinwider, Robert, "Affirmative Action," <http://plato.stanford.edu/entries/affirmative-action/>. An overview of the legal and social controversy regarding affirmative action.

James, Michael, "Race," <http://plato.stanford.edu/entries/race/>. Includes discussion of the history of the concept of race, race as a social construction, and moral, legal, and social dimensions of the concept.

Haslanger, Sally and Tuana, Nancy, "Topics in Feminism," <http://plato.stanford.edu/entries/feminism-topics/>. An overview of feminist understandings of sexism and how properly to address it. This article also includes an extensive list of Internet resources on feminism and related topics.

National Organization of Women, <http://www.now.org/>. An organization of feminists whose chief goal is to bring about equality for all women.

Race, Gender and Affirmative Action, <http://www-personal.umich.edu./~eandersn/biblio.htm.>. A very useful annotated bibliography for teachers and students on the topics featured in this chapter.

Race Project, <http://www.understandingrace.org/home.html>. A project of the American Anthropological Association providing information about the nature of race.

Racism Review, <http://www.racismreview.com/>. A site aimed primarily at educators and researchers. It describes itself as "intended to provide a credible and reliable source of information for journalists, students and members of the general public who are seeking solid evidence-based research and analysis of race, racism, ethnicity, and immigration issues."

Southern Poverty Law Center, <http://www.splcenter.org/>. This center, founded in 1971, engages in legal and educational activities to combat intolerance and hate crimes.

Authored Books and Articles

Blum, Lawrence, *I'm not a racist, but…* (Ithaca and London: Cornell University Press, 2002). A critical examination of the concepts of race and racism as they have affected our ways of looking at things, including our moral interactions with others.

Corlett, J. Angelo, *Race, Racism, and Reparations* (Ithaca and London: Cornell University Press, 2003). A careful analysis of race, ethnic identity, and related matters of public policy.

Glasgow, Joshua, "Racism as Disrespect," *Ethics* 120 (2009): 64–93. A defense of the claim that racism should be understood in terms of disrespect.

Lippert-Rasmussen, Kasper, "The Badness of Discrimination," *Ethical Theory and Moral Practice* 9 (2006): 167–85. Argues that the badness of discrimination is explained by its harmfulness. Critical of accounts that would explain the badness by appeal to disrespect-based views, according to which the badness is owing to the disrespect that discrimination expresses regardless of its harmful effects.

Zack, Naomi, *The Ethics and Mores of Race: Equality after the History of Philosophy* (Lanham, MD: Rowman & Littlefield, 2011). The author addresses the question of how to develop an "ethics of race" in light of the history of Western moral philosophy.

Edited Collections

Anderson, Jami L. (ed.), *Race, Gender, and Sexuality* (Upper Saddle River, NJ: Prentice Hall, 2003). An extensive collection of essays organized into chapters on Sex and Gender, Sex and Sexuality, Race and Ethnicity, Racism, Sexism, Heterosexism and Homophobia, Equality and Preferential Treatment, Discriminatory Harassment, Identity Speech and Political Speech, Sexual Speech, and Sexual Assault.

Crosby, Faye J. and Cheryl Van DeVeer, (eds.) *Sex, Race, and Merit: Debating Affirmative Action in Education and Employment* (Ann Arbor: University of Michigan Press, 2000). A wide-ranging collection of articles from newspapers, essays by scholars from various academic fields, and important legal and political documents that have shaped debate and policy over affirmative action.

Zack, Naomi (ed.), *Race/Sex: Their Sameness, Difference, and Interplay* (London and New York: Routledge, 1997). A collection of 16 essays by different authors exploring the analysis, comparison, phenomenology, and issues of performance regarding sex and race.

7 The Ethics of Immigration

Debate in the United States over immigration has a long history dating back to the early 1600s.[1] In 2014 there were an estimated 11.3 million unauthorized immigrants living in the United States. As of 2012 there were roughly 8 million unauthorized immigrants in the U.S. workforce.[2] Attempts by Congress to reform national immigration policy have not been successful.[3] In recent years public debate in the United States over immigration has intensified, at a time when the U.S. economy endured a recession (2007–2009) followed by a slow recovery.

Frustrated with the failure of the federal government to pass immigration legislation, many U.S. states have enacted their own laws designed to curb immigration. For instance, in April 2010 then Arizona governor Jan Brewer signed into law a restrictive immigration bill (SB 1070). The law included four main provisions that:

- make it unlawful for immigrants to fail to register with the federal government,
- make it a crime for undocumented immigrants to work or look for a job,
- allow police to arrest individuals without a warrant if they have reason to think the individuals have done things that would make them deportable under federal law, and
- require police to question anyone who is stopped for a traffic violation or who is arrested, in order to determine his or her immigration status, if the officer "reasonably suspects" that the person is undocumented. (Critics have referred to this as the "show me your papers" provision.)

This law met opposition in the courts and eventually a case was heard by the U.S. Supreme Court. In May 2011, in a 5–3 decision, the Court upheld the fourth provision, striking down the other three, which were said to interfere with the federal government's role in setting immigration policy. In the meantime other U.S. states have followed Arizona in passing laws designed to discourage unauthorized immigrants from residing or working in those states.

On July 15, 2012, President Barack Obama issued an executive order, effective immediately, that may have affected as many as 700,000 immigrants who were brought to this country as children and face deportation. The Associated Press described the implications of the president's order as follows:

> Under the administration plan, illegal immigrants will be immune from deportation if they were brought to the United States before they turned 16 and are younger than 30, have been in the country for at least five continuous years, have no criminal history, graduated from a U.S. high school or earned a GED or served in the military. They can also apply for a work permit that will be good for two years with no limits on how many times it can be renewed.[4]

In 2014, Obama expanded his 2012 program to include an additional 3.9 million unauthorized immigrants. Under this expanded program, included are parents who have lived in the United States since 2010 and have children who were either born in the United States or are legal permanent residents. In response, Texas and twenty-five other states have filed lawsuits to block these executive actions.

Related to legal issues about immigration legislation are ethical issues about whether nation-states have a moral obligation to open their borders to would-be immigrants, or whether they have a moral right to enforce a policy of closed borders. More than a million migrants and refugees crossed into Europe in 2015. This has resulted in division among the countries in the European Union over how best to deal with resettling these people. According to a March 4, 2016, BBC news report, "The conflict in Syria continues to be by far the biggest driver of migration. But the ongoing violence in Afghanistan and Iraq, abuses in Eritrea, as well as poverty in Kosovo, are also leading people to look for new lives elsewhere." The resulting ethical debate is often framed in terms of what wealthy nations are obligated to do to help alleviate the plight of the world's poor and oppressed individuals. Among the most fundamental moral questions about immigration policy are these (a list not intended to be exhaustive):

- Do wealthy nation-states have an obligation to adopt an open immigration policy that allows noncitizens to immigrate to those states, particularly in light of the plight of the world's poor and oppressed?
- If not, what explains why a right exists to embrace a closed immigration policy?
- If such countries as the United States have a non-overridden right to adopt a closed immigration policy, how (if) does this impact its obligations to help alleviate worldwide poverty and oppression?
- Even if a wealthy country is not obligated to allow foreigners to immigrate in order to improve their standard of living, is such a country nevertheless obligated to allow political refugees and persons who are stateless to migrate to that country and be allowed to seek citizenship?
- More generally, which criteria of selection are morally justified in determining who may and who may not immigrate to a country?

These are among the questions that are addressed in the readings in this chapter. Answers to these questions often depend on a host of complex empirical issues that figure in the debate over immigration, so in what follows we briefly sample these issue before turning to some main philosophical approaches to the ethics of immigration.

1. EMPIRICAL ISSUES: A SAMPLING

Most of the empirical questions can be sorted into the following categories.

Economic Issues

What impact will immigrants have on job competition and job wages in the host country? What groups are most likely to be affected negatively by such competition? Will consumers benefit by lower costs for, say, farm products? Will immigrant workers as consumers and tax payers benefit a nation's economic well-being? How would one or another immigration policy affect the global economy?

Issues Regarding the Distribution of Benefits

The United States, Canada, Sweden, and many other countries provide benefits and services to citizens, including health care, education, and welfare payments. How would immigration affect such benefit programs? Would it impose a severe burden on these programs and have the effect of eroding their support by the public?

Cultural Issues

A nation's citizens have an interest in preserving its distinctive public culture. How, if at all, would an influx of immigrants affect the culture of the host nation? Would immigration erode a shared cultural tradition that citizens have an interest in preserving, or would newcomers assimilate to their new environment? Is it true that a nation's citizens have a shared public culture? And isn't a nation's culture constantly in flux regardless of immigration?

Security Issues

States have an obligation to protect their citizens, particularly from terrorist threats. How, if at all, would restricting immigration increase a nation's security, particularly against those plotting terrorist attacks on that nation? Would a closed immigration policy simply result in those with terrorist intent traveling to countries as tourists or as visiting students?

Political Stability Issues

Do outsiders who might immigrate pose a threat to the functioning of a liberal democratic society with its commitment to freedom of speech, freedom of association, freedom of religion, and other freedoms?

Concerns about these issues are often the basis for anti-immigration arguments that appeal to the likely negative effects of open immigration on these matters of concern to a nation's citizens. But because these issues are complex, critics of such empirically based anti-immigration arguments often challenge the empirical claims. Those who confidently argue, for example, that an open immigration policy poses a danger to the nation's economic well-being are in the position of having to defend such claims. Of course, so is someone who suggests that an open immigration policy would have no appreciable effect on a nation's economy or would positively benefit it. A similar point applies to the other empirical issues: answers to the questions just posed require good empirical evidence if they are to be used responsibly in addressing the effects of immigration.

Before turning to philosophical approaches to the ethics of immigration, it is worth noting that I have been speaking loosely about the debate over immigration as between those who favor "open" borders and those who favor "closed" borders. But the last of the bulleted questions listed earlier (the one about criteria of selection) clearly indicates that the ethical debate is one over *how open* a nation-state's borders ought to be versus *how closed* a nation-state's borders may be in a given period in history. The desirability of preventing known terrorists who plot against one's country from entering one's country is not in dispute; certainly *some* limits on immigration are morally justified. One main question, then, is over the extent to which a nation-state may curtail immigration at any particular time in its history.

2. Theory Meets Practice

The debate over immigration is an issue at the intersection of moral and political philosophy, though it is often framed in terms of positions commonly discussed in political philosophy. So it will be useful to briefly characterize those positions that figure in the immigration debate as it is conducted in our selections.

Cosmopolitanism

In the *Stanford Encyclopedia of Philosophy*, Pauline Kleingeld and Eric Brown characterize **cosmopolitanism** and its significance as follows:

> The nebulous core shared by all cosmopolitan views is the idea that all human beings, regardless of their political affiliation, do (or at least can) belong to a single community, and that this community should be cultivated . . . The philosophical interest in cosmopolitanism lies in its challenge to commonly recognized attachments to fellow-citizens, the local state, parochially shared cultures, and the like.[5]

As Kleingeld and Brown point out, there are various forms of cosmopolitanism: *moral, political, cultural, and economic*. The most common form (and the form most relevant for this chapter) is moral cosmopolitanism, according which those in a position to do so have an obligation to assist those in need owing to poverty and to promote basic human rights regardless of the citizenship of those with such needs. In its standard form, the basic cosmopolitan commitment is that the obligation to provide aid and promote basic human rights neither outweighs nor is outweighed by obligations to provide assistance to one's fellow citizens. Generally speaking, this position favors greater openness of borders to allow foreigners to immigrate.

It is worth noting that moral cosmopolitanism may be grounded in most any variety of moral theory. Thus, some moral philosophers defend moral cosmopolitanism on consequentialist grounds, others on Kantian grounds, still others from the perspective of virtue ethics. Furthermore, within political philosophy, one finds a variety of cosmopolitan approaches to immigration, including egalitarian and libertarian approaches. Both deserve brief comment.

Egalitarian Cosmopolitanism

Joseph H. Carens, in his essay included in this chapter, defends the cosmopolitan position from the standpoint of liberal egalitarianism, a position that he characterizes as morally committed to the idea that individuals should be free to pursue their own projects as long as these plans do not interfere with the rights of others, to equal opportunity to pursue social positions regardless of, for example, one's class, race, or sex, and to the idea that economic, social, and political inequalities ought to be minimized "partly as a means of realizing equal freedom and equal opportunity and partly as a desirable end in itself." Freedom of movement, including immigration is taken by Carens as essential to the liberal egalitarian's commitments. Again, the liberal egalitarian's commitment to freedom and equality can be grounded in any of the moral theories presented in the Moral Theory Primer.

Libertarian Cosmopolitanism

Another cosmopolitan approach to immigration can be found in libertarian political thought. Peter Vallentyne characterizes libertarianism as "the moral view that agents initially fully own themselves and have certain moral powers to acquire property rights in external things."[6] In the context of the debate over immigration, cosmopolitans who take a libertarian approach typically argue in two ways. First, focusing on an individual's property rights, they assert that limiting immigration violates one's right to invite foreigners to visit one's property. Second, the libertarian's strong commitment to acquire property rights in external things stresses the importance of freedom of movement (including immigration) in order to exercise such rights. A closed immigration policy obviously interferes with these freedoms.

Again, it is worth noting the relation between libertarianism and the moral theories featured throughout much of this anthology. Vallentyne further writes:

> Libertarianism can be understood as a basic moral principle or as a derivative one. It might, for example, be advocated as a basic natural rights doctrine. Alternatively, it might be defended on the basis of rule consequentialism or teleology . . . or rule contractarianism . . .

And one can add Kantian ethics, virtue ethics, and the ethics of prima facie duty to this list of views on the basis of which a libertarian position might be defended.

Anticosmopolitanism

If the moral cosmopolitan position on the ethics of immigration favors open borders, then the opposing position deserves the label "**anticosmopolitanism**," though it should be kept in mind that one can be an anticosmopolitan about immigration, but still favor a cosmopolitan approach to other moral, political, cultural, and economic matters. In our readings, the "anti-" position is defended by Stephen Macedo and by Christopher Heath Wellman. Both authors agree that nation-states have obligations to the world's poor and oppressed but contend that strong moral reasons justify (without requiring) a more or less closed border policy. Macedo sees the debate over U.S. immigration policy as reflecting the difficulty of reconciling obligations to help the world's poor and oppressed and the country's special obligation to its own citizens which, given the likely impact of an open borders policy, would conflict with meeting the special obligation.

Wellman appeals to freedom of association, which includes the prima facie right to decide with whom one does *not* want to associate, in arguing for the presumptive right of the United States and other wealthy countries to adopt a (more or less) closed border policy. He considers this right to be deontologically based and thus at home in the moral philosophies of Immanuel Kant and W. D. Ross. He expresses his position in Rossian terms: freedom of association is the basis of a prima facie right to adopt a closed borders policy. So, in defending his view, he considers counterarguments by egalitarians and libertarians and argues that the considerations such counterarguments bring to bear on the issue of immigration do not override the prima facie right of countries to adopt a closed borders policy he claims to have established. The strength of Wellman's freedom of association argument is challenged by Sarah Fine in the final selection of this chapter.

NOTES

1 For a concise historical timeline of legal and illegal immigration to the U.S., see "Illegal Immigration" at <http://ProCon.org>.

2 See "Five Facts about Illegal Immigration in the U.S., Nov. 2015" at <http://pewreserach.org>.

3. For instance, in 2006 the Senate passed legislation crafted by the late Democratic Senator Edward Kennedy of Massachusetts and Arizona Republican Senator John McCain that offered a path to citizenship and created a guest worker program. But the bill failed in the House of Representatives. Again, in 2007, President George W. Bush initiated an immigration reform effort that proposed a route to citizenship for undocumented immigrants and a guest worker program, but was met with much opposition by groups condemning the bill as giving amnesty to individuals who had broken the law by being undocumented residents, either illegally entering or illegally remaining in the United States.

4. "New Obama Policy Will Spare Some Deportation," Associated Press, July 15, 2012. <http://bigstory.ap.org/article/new-obama-policy-will-spare-some-deportation>.

5. Kleingeld, Pauline, and Brown, Eric, "Cosmopolitanism," *The Stanford Encyclopedia of Philosophy* (Spring 2011 Edition), Edward N. Zalta (ed.), <http://plato.stanford.edu/archives/spr2011/entries/cosmopolitanism/>.

6. Vallentyne, Peter, "Libertarianism," *Stanford Encyclopedia of Philosophy* (Spring 2012 Edition), Edward N. Zalta (ed.), URL = <http://plato.stanford.edu/archives/spr2012/entries/libertarianism/>.

7. Ibid.

STEPHEN MACEDO

The Moral Dilemma of U.S. Immigration Policy: Open Borders versus Social Justice?

Stephen Macedo approaches the ethical issue of immigration from the perspective of distributive justice. The dilemma over immigration policy as he sees it concerns on one hand a state's apparently special obligations to care for its own citizens and, on the other hand, the obligation of economically well-off countries like the United States to be equally concerned with the welfare of noncitizens who would benefit by immigrating. Cosmopolitan egalitarians argue that distributive justice is primarily an obligation that holds irrespective of citizenship; states in a position to do so ought to be concerned about the plight of human beings generally and not give special weight to their own citizens. This view favors more or less an open immigration policy. Macedo argues that although states do have obligations to help alleviate the plight of the world's disadvantaged, they have special obligations to their own poorest citizens that generally outweigh obligations to noncitizens. In defending his "civic view" position on immigration, Macedo explains what he takes to be the moral basis of a country's special obligations to its poor and considers how the United States and other comparatively wealthy countries should handle their obligations to the world's poor.

Recommended Reading: social contract theory, chap. 1 sec. 2G, in particular the discussion of Rawls's principles of distributive justice.

IMMIGRATION POLICY AS A MORAL DILEMMA

How should we think about U.S. Immigration policy from the standpoint of basic justice, especially distributive justice, which encompasses our obligations to the less well-off? Does a justifiable immigration policy take its bearings (in part) from the acknowledgment that we have special obligations to "our own" poor, our least well-off fellow citizens? Or, on the other hand, do our moral duties simply argue for attending to the interests of the least well-off persons in the world, giving no special weight to the interests of the least well-off Americans?

. . .[T]here are reasons to believe that recent American immigration policy has had a deleterious impact on the distribution of income among American citizens. According to influential arguments—associated with George Borjas and others—by admitting large numbers of relatively poorly educated and low-skilled workers, we have increased competition for low-skilled jobs, lowering the wages of the poor and increasing the gap between rich and poor Americans. The high proportion of noncitizens among the poor may also lessen political support for social welfare policies.

How should we think about the apparent ethical conflict between, on the one hand, the cosmopolitan humanitarian impulse to admit less well-off persons from abroad who wish to immigrate to the United States and, on the other hand, the special obligations we have to less well-off Americans, including or especially African Americans? Those with liberal sensibilities need to consider whether all the things that they might favor—humanitarian concern for the world's poor, an openness to an ever-widening social diversity, and concern for distributive justice within our political community—necessarily go together.

These are vexing questions not only in politics but in contemporary political theory and moral philosophy, and what I say will be controversial, though the perspective I defend is shared by some others. I argue that if high levels of immigration have a detrimental impact on our least well-off fellow citizens, that is a reason to limit immigration, even if those who seek admission seem to be poorer than our own poor whose condition is worsened by their entry. Citizens have special obligations to one another: we have special reasons to be concerned with the distribution of wealth and opportunities among citizens. The comparative standing of citizens matters in some ways that the comparative standing of citizens and noncitizens does not. Of course, distributive justice is only one consideration bearing on immigration policy, though a weighty one.

I argue against what is sometimes characterized as a "cosmopolitan" position with respect to distributive justice and defend the idea that distributive justice is an obligation that holds among citizens, a position that has also been defended by Michael Walzer, John Rawls, and David Miller, among others.[1] What is the basis of these special obligations among citizens? I argue that it is as members or co-participants in self-governing political communities that we have special obligations to our fellow members.

Do we conclude, therefore, that the borders should be closed and immigration by the poor restricted? That conclusion would be far too hasty. For one thing, we do have significant moral obligations to poor people abroad, although these are different from what we owe to fellow citizens. In addition, measures designed to "tighten up" the borders may do more harm than good. On balance, we should perhaps accept ongoing high levels of movement back and forth across the U.S.-Mexico border. . . . But we also need to consider whether high levels of immigration by low-skilled workers make it less likely that we will fulfill our moral obligations to the poorest Americans. The distributive impact of immigration policy is important.

This chapter proceeds as follows. The first part describes why it is reasonable to think that we face a dilemma in shaping U.S. immigration policy. I feature the sorts of claims advanced by George Borjas not because I am sure he is right but because he raises important moral questions. In the next section, I consider the debate between "cosmopolitans"— who argue against the moral significance of shared

From Stephen Macedo, "The Moral Dilemma of U.S. Immigration Policy: Open Borders versus Social Justice?" in Carol M. Swain, ed., *Debating Immigration*, Cambridge: Cambridge University Press, 2007.

citizenship and in favor of universal obligations of distributive justice—and those who argue for the existence of special obligations of justice among citizens. I seek to clarify the moral grounds for regarding shared membership in a political community as morally significant but also emphasize that we do have significant cosmopolitan duties. In the final section, I return to the moral dilemma of U.S. immigration policy and offer some reflections on policy choices.

One point is worth making before moving on. The perspective adopted and defended here is politically liberal. John Rawls and Michael Walzer . . . . are philosophers of the Left in American politics. It might be thought that this limits the relevance of my argument, but this may not be so. For one thing, the vast majority of Americans profess a belief in some liberal principles, such as equality of opportunity. While Americans are less supportive than Europeans of measures designed directly to reduce income disparities between the wealthy and the poor, they overwhelmingly affirm that institutions such as public education should ensure that every child has a good start in life, irrespective of accidents of birth. The question of whether we have special obligations to our fellow citizens is important independently of the details of one's convictions about what justice requires among citizens. Even those who believe that "equality of opportunity" mandates only a modest level of educational and other social services may still think that the mandate holds among fellow citizens and not all of humanity. The general thrust of my argument should therefore be of relevance to those who do not accept the specific prescriptions of Rawls and Walzer.

THE CONTOURS OF THE IMMIGRATION DILEMMA

Over the last 40 years, American immigration policies and practices have become, in some respects, more accommodating to the less well-off abroad. Some argue that this "generosity" has exacted a significant cost in terms of social justice at home.

The basic facts are striking. Whereas in 1970, 5 percent of the general population was composed of immigrants, that figure is now 12 percent, the highest in nearly 80 years. By 2002, there were 56 million immigrants and first-generation Americans (children of immigrants), comprising 20 percent of the U.S. population in 2000, the highest overall number in U.S. history according to the Census Bureau, though not the highest percentage.[2]

The composition of the growing immigrant pool has changed markedly in recent decades, with the skill level and earnings of immigrants declining relative to that of the native U.S. population. Whereas in 1960 the average immigrant man living in the United States earned 4 percent more than the average native-born American, by 1998 the average immigrant earned 23 percent less. Most of the growth in immigration since 1960 has been among people entering at the bottom 20 percent of the income scale. This is partly because, as George Borjas observes, "[s]ince the immigration reforms of 1965, U.S. immigration law has encouraged family reunification and discouraged the arrival of skilled immigrants."[3] At the same time, the ethnic makeup of immigration has also changed, with the percentage arriving from Europe and Canada falling sharply and the percentage from Latin America and Asia rising.[4]

In Borjas's influential if controversial analysis, recent decades of immigration have worsened income disparities in the United States. Immigration from 1980 to 1995 increased the pool of high school dropouts in the United States by 21 percent while increasing the pool of college graduates by only 4 percent, and this, argues Borjas, has contributed to a substantial decline in the wages of high school dropouts. He argues that immigration between 1980 and 2000 had the effect of lowering wages overall by about 4 percent while lowering wages among those without a high school diploma (roughly the bottom 10 percent of wage earners) by 7.4 percent. To put it another way, it is widely agreed that in the United States in the 1980s and early 1990s there was a substantial widening of the wage gap between more and less well-educated workers. Borjas argues that nearly half of this widening wage gap between high school dropouts and others may be due to the increase in the low-skilled labor pool caused by immigration.

Steven A. Camarota . . . associates recent immigration with employment losses among Americans: from 2000 to 2004, unemployment among native-born Americans increased by more than two million, while more than two million immigrants entered the labor force (half of them illegally).[5] A study funded by the Congressional Black Caucus Foundation argues that labor force participation among African American males with low levels of education has fallen especially steeply, with immigration being one possible contributing factor.

Of course, all Americans have benefited from cheaper fruits and vegetables and other products that immigrants (including undocumented workers) help produce. But wealthier Americans have also benefited from increased access to cheap menial labor—such as service work performed by nannies, gardeners, and others. Firms have also benefited from cheap labor. However, Borjas argues that native-born African American and Hispanic workers have suffered disproportionately because they have disproportionately lower skills and education, own few firms, and often compete directly with low-skilled immigrants for jobs.[6]

Let me add one other element to this admittedly controversial account before moving on. Nations with notably more progressive domestic policies often have immigration laws that are quite different from those of the United States. American immigration policy emphasizes family reunification (including children, spouses, parents, and adult siblings), with a very small percentage of immigrants—around 5 percent in recent decades—receiving visas based on the possession of desirable skills. Canada, by contrast, has a quota system that gives greater weight to educational background, occupation, and English-language proficiency of applicants for admission. Canada's policy favors better-educated and higher-skilled workers, and this seems likely to have distributive effects that are the opposite of U.S. policy. By increasing the pool of skilled workers relative to the unskilled, Canadian policy tends to lower the wages of the better-off and to raise the relative wage levels of the worse-off.[7]

Finally, recent patterns of immigration to the United States may also tend to lower public support for social welfare and redistributive programs. Economic inequality in the United States has increased sharply since 1970, but this has not led to increased pressure for redistribution. If anything, the reverse would seem to be the case: the real value of the minimum wage has fallen, and taxes paid by the better-off have been cut, including top marginal tax rates and the estate and capital gains taxes. Congress restricted alien access to many federally funded welfare benefits in 1996; nevertheless, immigrants to the United States receive various forms of public assistance at a higher rate than native-born Americans.

Nolan McCarty, Keith T. Poole, and Howard Rosenthal argue that recent patterns of immigration help explain why increasing inequality has come about without an increase in political pressure toward redistribution. Since 1972, the percentage of noncitizens has risen and their incomes relative to those of other Americans have fallen. According to McCarty, et al., "From 1972 to 2000, the median family income of non-citizens fell from 82% of the median income of voters to 65% while the fraction of the population that is non-citizen rose from 2.6% to 7.7%."[8] Over this time, the incomes of the median voters—the voters likely to be the "swing voters" who decide close elections—have not fallen. Increasing economic inequality has left these median voters no worse off in terms of relative income. Meanwhile, the income of the median family living in the United States (including voters and nonvoters) has fallen on account of the sharp decline in the incomes of non-citizens. According to this analysis, immigration to the United States has made the median voter better off relative to the population as a whole (including voters and nonvoters), decreasing the median voter's likelihood of supporting redistribution.

There are yet other ways in which immigration might have an impact on distributive justice. I have not considered the argument that welfare states benefit from the presence of a shared culture, a position ably defended by David Miller.[9] There is evidence suggesting that cultural diversity leads to lower trust among groups and declining support for the provision of public goods.[10] We have enough on the table to raise some relevant ethical questions, though I should also emphasize that all of these empirical questions cry out for additional investigation.

The questions before us include the following: if U.S. immigration policies appear to be liberal and generous to the less well-off abroad (or at least some of them), does this generosity involve injustice toward poorer native-born Americans, including—or perhaps especially—African Americans? If we have special obligations to our poorer fellow citizens—obligations that are sufficiently urgent and weighty—then U.S. immigration policy may be hard or impossible to defend from the standpoint of justice.

Of course, the question of how we should respond to this—if it is true—is not straightforward. It does not follow that greater justice argues for more restrictive immigration policies. It may be that justice requires us to change the laws and policies that allow the immigration of low-skilled workers and thus generate adverse effects on the native-born poor. The inegalitarian distributive effects of immigration could be offset via a higher minimum wage or improved education and training for the unemployed along with other social benefits for all of the less well-off. And yet we have seen that high levels of low-skilled immigration may also lower public support for social welfare. This sharpens the dilemma.

COSMOPOLITAN VERSUS CIVIC OBLIGATIONS?

If the better-off have moral obligations to help the least well-off, why shouldn't those obligations focus on the least well-off of the world? Can we justify special obligations to our own poor, even if they are less poor than many others in the world?

Consider two ways in which we might care about the condition of the poor and seek to do something about it. We might care only about their absolute level of poverty or deprivation, or we might care about relative deprivation: the gap between the lives of the poorest and those of the richest. In response to the first concern, we would engage in *humanitarian assistance* and seek to establish a floor of material well-being: a standard of decency below which no

one should fall. In response to the latter concern, we would articulate and enforce principles of social or *distributive justice*: standards to regulate the major institutions of taxation, inheritance, social provision, wage policies, education, and so forth that help determine over time the relative levels of income, wealth, and opportunity available to different groups.

Most people seem to accept that wealthy societies owe the first sort of concern to human beings generally. Via humanitarian assistance, wealthier societies should pool their efforts and seek to lift poorer countries at least up to a level of basic decency; exactly what level is adequate or morally required is an important question. This sort of cosmopolitan moral concern has been likened to the duty we all have to be "Good Samaritans."

The latter species of concern—social or distributive justice—requires the establishment of institutions to regulate market inequalities: systems of progressive taxation, inheritance taxes, and the provision of social services. As noted, most Americans profess a belief that every child born in the United States should have a fair chance to attain a good job—to compete based on his or her talents and effort—and this requires that governments raise taxes in order to provide good schools for all. Virtually everyone accepts some degree of progressiveness in the tax structure, so efforts to promote fair equality of opportunity are typically redistributive and constitute part of a system of distributive justice. Opportunity is one of the things we "redistribute" by building public institutions—including tax-supported schools—alongside market institutions. As we have seen, immigration policies may also have an impact on the distribution of opportunities and rewards in society.

Do we have special moral obligations to our fellow citizens, especially obligations falling under the rubric of distributive justice? The question is whether, and if so, how, national borders matter with respect to our fundamental moral obligations to one another.

There are, roughly speaking, two opposing lines of thought. One emphasizes the moral arbitrariness of borders and the universality of our obligations to the less well-off. The other argues that borders are morally significant, that we have special obligations to poorer fellow citizens, and that obligations of distributive justice in particular apply only among citizens. The first position is often referred to as a form of moral "cosmopolitanism"; the latter position—for which I argue—goes under various names, and I will refer to it as the "civic view."

I want to join those who argue that we have special obligations of mutual justification to our fellow citizens and that distributive justice often has special force among fellow citizens. With respect to people in the rest of the world, our duties are different, though still quite important: fair dealing—including curbs on the exploitative potential of our corporations and doing our fair share to address common problems (e.g., environmental dangers such as global warming); more specific projects of historical rectification and redress in response to particular past acts of injustice; and humanitarian assistance to help lift other societies (insofar as we can) out of poverty.

Michael Walzer strikingly asserts that, "Distributive justice begins with membership; it must vindicate at one and the same time the limited right of closure, without which there could be no communities at all, and the political inclusiveness of existing communities."[11] It seems to me that Walzer is on the right track here, though he is not very clear about the moral grounds for his claims. He has a distinctive approach to the practice of justifying moral claims in politics to one another, and this helps explain why he argues that obligations of distributive justice apply within political communities only. Walzer famously argues that moral arguments in politics should avoid philosophical system building and abstraction; arguments of political morality should take the form of interpreting "shared social meanings." We should, he says, think about principles of justice in light of "the particularism of history, culture, and membership." Social goods should be distributed according to criteria internal to their social meanings, and these shared social meanings are located within particular political communities.[12]

Given this account of the nature of moral argument and distributive justice, it is not surprising that Walzer should argue that distributive justice applies within ongoing political communities that are the natural homes of shared meanings. For Walzer, the rejection of cosmopolitan obligations of distributive justice goes hand in hand with the claim that common understandings of values are shared within particular political communities but not across them.

Walzer's argument may contain part of the truth, but it is also puzzling. Achieving shared meanings with respect to justice is a worthy aspiration. But while shared meanings are an important goal of public argument, an achievement to be worked toward, the extent of shared meanings is not the proper ground for circumscribing claims of social justice. Publicly justified "common meanings" seem more like a goal of public argument and deliberation rather than the basis (or the presupposition) of political obligations.

Shared social meanings—common understandings, shared assumptions of various sorts—are important for sustaining a political system based on discussion and mutual justification, but they would seem not to be the central criterion for demarcating the range of those to whom we owe justice. The range of those with whom we should seek to establish common and publicly justified principles of justice consists of those with whom we share a system of binding laws.

Walzer sometimes lays too much emphasis on consensus and shared meanings in another way as well: what we should want is a justified consensus that is the result of criticism and testing. Critical argumentation (which I would characterize as philosophical) is essential to this project of public justification because what we should work toward are common understandings that are sound, and their soundness is essential to their authoritativeness. The mere fact of agreement, the mere existence of conventions, is not enough.

David Miller has argued eloquently for the advantages to political communities of a shared national culture and a common language because these can help support a collective identity and bonds of mutual sympathy and understanding: "Social justice will always be easier to achieve in states with strong national identities and without internal communal divisions.[13] Social scientists are only beginning to explore systematically the relationship between heterogeneity, social capital, and social justice.

Particular political societies—at least when they are well ordered rather than tyrannical, oppressive, or desperately poor—will tend to generate common understandings among members, including standards for how disputes and disagreements should be resolved. They may generate a plethora of disagreements and conflicts, but these will be manageable if the society has set standards and practices for how disagreements should be dealt with and a reserve of rough agreement on other matters sufficient to sustain a common willingness to continue to share a political order.

In his *The Law of Peoples,* Rawls cites and endorses Walzer's discussion of the moral significance of membership and borders. He argues that the political community—or "people"—is the appropriate site of distributive justice: there are no obligations of distributive justice simply among human beings. We have humanitarian duties to relieve those in distress—as mentioned earlier—but both Walzer and Rawls agree that we have no obligations across borders to regulate the relative well-being of better- and worse-off people (or to create institutions capable of doing so).

Why does Rawls embrace Walzer's view of the limited scope of distributive justice? Rawls does not as a general matter share Walzer's emphasis on the authority of shared social meanings. Moreover, Rawls's general method seems designed to encourage us to transcend the limited perspective of morally arbitrary accidents of birth, so there is a puzzle here.

When Rawls argues about domestic justice, the guiding thought is that when we consider principles of justice to regulate the "basic structure" of a polity, we should regard each other as free and equal persons and put aside moral claims based on morally arbitrary differences and accidents of fate. We put aside claims to unequal rewards based on advantages flowing from accidents of birth, including the good fortune of being born into a well-off family or with a superior genetic endowment. We do this by imagining ourselves in an "original position" behind a "veil of ignorance": we ask which principles of social justice we would choose if we did not know the social position we would occupy.[14] This helps us consider which principles of justice for regulating the design of the basic structure are fair to all and so capable of being freely accepted by reasonable

people regardless of the position they occupy in society. To affirm mutually justified principles to regulate basic social institutions is to affirm that we regard one another as moral equals.

The upshot of Rawls's thought experiment is his argument that two basic principles of justice would be chosen by citizens of modern pluralistic democracies:

1. Each person has an equal claim to a fully adequate scheme of equal basic rights and liberties, which scheme is compatible with the same scheme for all; and in this scheme the equal political liberties, and only those liberties, are to be guaranteed their fair value.
2. Social and economic inequalities are to satisfy two conditions: (a) They are to be attached to positions and offices open to all under conditions of fair equality of opportunity; and, (b) they are to be to the greatest benefit of the least advantaged members of society.[15]

Principle 2 (b) is also known as the "difference principle."

What is the relevance of all this to obligations across borders? If being born into a well-off family or with especially advantageous genes is to be regarded as morally arbitrary when thinking about justice, surely it seems equally arbitrary whether one is born in New Mexico or Mexico. One's place of birth with respect to nationality or political community seems quintessentially arbitrary. And yet Rawls follows Walzer in arguing that obligations of distributive justice (such as the difference principle and the principle of fair equality of opportunity) apply only within the borders of a political community and only among co-participants in a shared political order. What can justify this?

Like Walzer, Rawls mentions the fact of greater diversity on the international scale, the fact that reasonable pluralism "is more evident within a society of well-ordered peoples than it is within one society alone."[16] Some have supposed that this invocation of diversity signals a retreat in Rawls's later writings with respect to his ambitions regarding justice. Suffice it for these purposes to say that I think this interpretation is wrong, and in any event we should seek a better one if we can find it.

The diversity-based argument for limiting obligations of distributive justice to particular political communities would appear to be a nonmoral account of why justice's sails need trimming, a matter of bowing before unfortunate necessities, a pragmatic or prudential concession rather than a full moral justification. I believe there is a moral justification for confining obligations of distributive justice to co-participants in particular political communities. But what might it be?

THE MORAL SIGNIFICANCE OF COLLECTIVE SELF-GOVERNANCE

Borders are morally significant because they bound systems of collective self-governance.[17] . . . Co-participation in governance is an important moral relation. As members of a political community, we are joined in a collective enterprise across generations through which we construct and sustain a comprehensive system of laws and institutions that regulate and shape free-riding, including environmental problems such as global warming, disaster relief, and humanitarian assistance.

Second, societies have specific obligations to other countries or groups growing out of particular relations of exploitation, oppression, or domination, which give rise to specific obligations of *rectification and redress*; that is, if we have exploited or oppressed poorer and weaker societies, or if we have allowed our corporations to do so, then we have debts to these other societies that require some sort of recompense.

I should emphasize that these first two categories almost certainly generate strong demands for serious reform of the ways in which countries such as the United States conduct themselves in international affairs.

Finally, it seems right to say that well-off societies have general *humanitarian duties* to relieve those in destitution or distress and to respond to gross and systematic violations of human rights. Our duty is to do what we can to relieve distress, to end suffering, to stop gross violations of human rights, and to get a society on its feet so that it can look after its own affairs. These duties may involve substantial resource commitments, and they certainly require rich countries such as the United States to spend more than they currently do on assistance. It is crucial to specify the target: the proper target of aid could be such that all members of a given society are capable of leading good lives; while Americans and other consumerists might disagree, Aristotle was right to note long ago that the good life does not require vast amounts of wealth.

Crucially, members of wealthier societies do not owe to all the people of the world precisely the same consideration that they owe to fellow citizens. The reason is that fellow citizens stand in a special moral relation with one another: they share extensive institutional relations of shared governance.

U.S. IMMIGRATION POLICY AND DISTRIBUTIVE JUSTICE

As we have seen, it is not implausible to think that U.S. immigration policy of the last 40 years has been bad for distributive justice within the United States. It may have worsened income inequalities by admitting large numbers of poor people. Those poor immigrants are better off for having been allowed to immigrate, but the burdens of funding some social welfare programs are increased, and those programs may be less politically popular as a consequence. What, from an egalitarian perspective at least, could possibly be wrong in making the United States more like Canada by reducing overall levels of immigration and giving greater priority to immigration by the better-educated and higher-skilled? . . .

I have argued, however, that there are good reasons for believing that we have special obligations for our fellow citizens, obligations arising from membership in a self-governing community. In shaping immigration policies, concerns about distributive justice are relevant and urgent, and these concerns are inward-looking rather than cosmopolitan, emphasizing the special obligations we have toward our poorer fellow citizens. If the United States were to move toward a more Canadian-style immigration policy, this could improve the lot of less-well-off American workers. Considerations of distributive justice—taken in the abstract—argue for the superiority of the Canadian system: this would mean limiting immigration based on family reunification (perhaps limiting that preference to spouses and minor children), placing greater weight on priorities for education and other skills, and curbing undocumented or illegal immigration.

However, sound policy recommendations in this vexing area of policy need to take into account a great deal more of the relevant context, including geography and the heavy residue of historical patterns and practice. The United States is not Canada, and the costs of pursuing a Canadian-style immigration policy in the United States could be prohibitive. Empirical description, and careful analysis and prediction, must be combined with moral judgment. I can only sketch a few of the relevant considerations here.

The United States shares a 2,500-mile border with Mexico, and that border represents vast differences in development, income, and wealth. For more than 60 years, there have been high levels of migration from Mexico to the United States, and the United States has periodically welcomed massive influxes of migrant workers. In the period 1965–1986, 1.3 million Mexicans entered the United States legally along with 46,000 contract workers, but 28 million entered as undocumented migrants. The vast majority subsequently returned to Mexico, yielding a net migration to the United States of around five million during this time.[18] These patterns of immigration and return are self-reinforcing: migration prepares the way for more migration as language and labor market skills are acquired, along with personal contacts, including Mexicans who remain in the United States.[19] In 2000, there were eight million American citizens who were born in Mexico. Estimates of the number of undocumented persons working in the United States illegally vary widely. Stephen Camarota puts the total number of illegals at 9.1 million as of March 2004, with about 5.5 million illegal workers. In addition, 3.4 million Mexicans enter the United States yearly on nonimmigrant visas, and there are 213 million

short-term border crossings. The United States and Mexico (along with other Western Hemisphere nations) are committed to policies of open markets and free trade.[20] The costs of trying to close the border would be quite high.

What is the most ethically defensible way of responding to concerns about immigration, including concerns stemming from social justice within the United States? The answer is far from simple. We must, however, consider the humanitarian costs of attempts to massively alter long-standing patterns of movement across a long and long-porous border.

One approach is to try to limit legal migration and stop illegal immigration by more vigorously controlling the southern border, by constructing a security fence, and by other means.[21] Would this be effective? It could just lead to a surge in illegal migration by tunnel, sea, and air. It is far from obvious that a fence by itself would accomplish anything useful.

A more feasible way of curtailing illegal migration by poor workers would focus on stemming the demand for migrant workers in the United States. We might institute a national identification card, increase penalties for forging identification papers, and vigorously punish employers who hire undocumented people. None of these proposals are new, and some have been tried before. Obviously, if such policies were implemented effectively, the cost of low-skilled labor would increase considerably in many areas, especially in agriculture, but that would appear to be good insofar as wages rise at the bottom of the income scale. It is often said that illegal migrants do work that Americans are unwilling to do, but of course the reality is Americans are unwilling to do the same work at the prevailing low wage, and that is just the problem from the standpoint of distributive justice.

An alternative approach would be to accept and regularize the flow of migrant labor, as Douglas Massey, Jorge Durand, and Nolan J. Malone recommend. Their proposals include increasing the annual quota of legal entry visas from Mexico from 20,000 (the same as for the Dominican Republic) to 60,000 and instituting a temporary two-year work visa, which would be renewable once for each Mexican worker. They propose making available 300,000 such visas per year. This would regularize the flow of migrant workers and rechannel the flow of illegal migrants into a legal flow. The work visas would be awarded to workers, not employers, so that workers are free to quit. Fees for these visas plus savings in the Immigration and Naturalization Service budget could generate hundreds of millions of dollars a year that could be passed along to states and localities with high concentrations of migrants to offset the costs of some local services. Finally, Massey and his colleagues would curtail the priorities that are now provided to family members of those who become naturalized Americans: they would eliminate the priority given to adult siblings of naturalized citizens, and they recommend making it easier for Mexican relatives of U.S. citizens to get tourist visas so they can visit and return home more easily.[22]

One advantage of this approach is that it seems to deal directly with the underlying force generating migration to the United States from Mexico: poverty in Mexico. Massey and his colleagues emphasize that immigration is part of the development process and is temporary. The poorest nations do not send out migrants—witness sub-Saharan Africa. Developing countries typically send out immigrants for eight or nine decades until growth at home relieves the pressures to leave. Facilitating short-term migration and return would help promote growth in Mexico, and it is consistent with the general emphasis of the North American Free Trade Agreement on the integration of North American markets.

One moral problem with this approach is that it regularizes a system that would seem to impose downward pressure on low-wage jobs in the United States. It takes seriously the interests of poor people in a neighboring country—with whom we have long-standing ties and very likely unpaid historical debts—and it benefits American employers, American consumers, and better-off Americans, but it does not address the special obligations we have to our poorest fellow citizens. The distributive justice problem could be dealt with by explicitly coupling these reforms with measures designed to improve the condition of poor Americans; that would be appropriate and overdue in any case. But as we have seen, high levels of immigration by low-income people may make transfer payments less politically popular and, if so, that is a liability of the proposal, perhaps

one that can be partially addressed by excluding guestworkers from many public benefits.

Another possible problem with this policy is the intrinsic status of guestworkers. Adequate protections must be built into any guestworker program so that workers are not exploited and oppressed. The fact is that wages and work conditions among agricultural workers in the United States are currently awful, and a regulated guestworker program ought to be coupled with measures to require decent wages and work conditions, basic health care, protection from poisoning by pesticides, and so on. However, if a guestworker in the United States becomes seriously ill, the program might be designed so that he or she is entitled to a trip to the emergency room and then a one-way ticket home. Such provisions seem likely to be part of the price of getting Americans to accept a guestworker program, and they seem legitimate so long as work conditions, wages, and protections are such that we can regard the conditions of work as humane and reasonable. (If such provisions led workers to conceal and postpone treatment of serious illnesses, then we would need to rethink the acceptability of the provision.)[23]

CONCLUSION

There is reason to believe that current patterns of immigration do raise serious issues from the standpoint of social justice: high levels of immigration by poor and low-skilled workers from Mexico and elsewhere in Central America and the Caribbean may worsen the standing of poorer American citizens. Furthermore, such immigration may lessen political support for redistributive programs. Nevertheless, as we have also seen, the costs of "tightening up" the border could be extremely high: border security efforts have imposed great hardships and expense on migrant workers without stemming the tide of immigration. Employer sanctions could be a more humane enforcement mechanism, though it remains to be seen whether Americans have the political will to impose such measures. In addition, it is not clear how many poor Americans would be interested in doing the agricultural work done by many migrants, though independent of all other considerations, work conditions and wages for migrant agricultural work should be improved.

I have argued that U.S. immigration policy presents us with the necessity of grappling with the tension between two important moral demands: justice to our fellow citizens and humanitarian concern with the plight of poor persons abroad. I have argued that we do indeed have urgent reasons to shape major public policies and institutions with an eye toward the distributive impact. Justice demands that we craft policies that are justifiable not simply from the standpoint of aggregate welfare—or the greatest good of the greatest number. We must consider the justifiability of policies from the standpoint of the least well-off among our fellow citizens. John Rawls's theory of justice stands for the proposition that the political equality of citizens requires this sort of "distributive" justification among citizens: it is not reasonable to expect our less-well-off fellow citizens to accede to a policy on the grounds that it makes those with the luck of superior endowment by nature and birth even better off. Immigration policy—as part of the basic structure of social institutions—ought to be answerable to the interests of the poorest Americans. An immigration policy cannot be considered morally acceptable in justice unless its distributive impact is defensible from the standpoint of disadvantaged Americans.

And yet, we must also consider the collateral costs of border security measures given the long border and long-standing patterns of migration from Mexico. It is possible that the best combination of policies would be something like the Massey proposals involving guestworkers, coupled with more generous aid to poorer Americans. But we also need to consider whether immigration policies themselves significantly affect the political saleability of aid to the poor; they may well do so. Of course, it is possible that under current conditions the prospects of doing anything serious for poorer Americans are dim, and given that, we should simply do good where we can and for whom we can. The proposals by Massey and his colleagues hold out the prospect of doing some real good for hundreds of thousands of migrant workers and for Mexicans and Americans as a whole.[24]

NOTES

1. Walzer and Rawls are discussed later in the chapter. See also Thomas Nagel, "The Problem of Global Justice," *Philosophy and Public Affairs* 33 (2005): 113–147; and David Miller, *On Nationality* (Oxford: Oxford University Press, 1975).

2. Nearly all data are from George J. Borjas, *Heaven's Door: Immigration Policy and the American Economy* (Princeton, NJ: Princeton University Press, 1999), 8–11. The final statistic, on first-generation newcomers, is from the U.S. Census Bureau, Profile of the Foreign Born Population in the United States: 2000. Current Population Reports, Special Studies. U.S. Census Bureau (document P23–206) (Washington, DC: U.S. Government Printing Office, December 2001).

3. George J. Borjas, "The U.S. Takes the Wrong Immigrants," *Wall Street Journal,* April 5, 1990, A18. The quotation continues, "75% of legal immigrants in 1987 were granted entry because they were related to an American citizen or resident, while only 4% were admitted because they possessed useful skills."

4. The basic statistics here are from Borjas.

5. Steven A. Camarota, "Immigration and Future Population Change in America," in Carol M. Swain, ed., *Debating Immigration* (Cambridge: Cambridge University Press, 2007), Chap. 10.

6. Borjas, *Heaven's Gate,* 11, and 22–38, 82–86, 103–104. For an update, see George Borjas, "The Labor Demand Curve Is Downward Sloping: Reexamining the Impact of Immigration on the Labor Market," *Quarterly Journal of Economics* 118, No. 4 (2003): 1335–1374.

7. Borjas, *Heaven's Gate,* 176–177.

8. Nolan McCarty, Keith T. Poole, and Howard Rosenthal, *Polarized America: The Dance of Ideology and Unequal Riches* (Walras-Pareto Lectures) (Cambridge, MA: MIT Press, 2006), Chapter 4.

9. See Miller, *On Nationality.*

10. See A. Alesina, R. Baquir, and W. Easterley, "Public Goods and Ethnic Divisions," *Quarterly Journal of Economics* 114 (1999): 1243–1284.

11. Michael Walzer, *Spheres of Justice: A Defense of Pluralism and Equality* (New York: Basic Books, 1983); see Chapter 2, "Membership."

12. Walzer has developed this argument in a number of places, perhaps most pointedly in his "Philosophy and Democracy," *Political Theory* 9 (1981): 379–399; this essay complements the approach of his *Spheres of Justice.*

13. Miller, *On Nationality,* 96.

14. I paraphrase here the general approach of John Rawls, *A Theory of Justice* (Cambridge, MA: Harvard, 1971).

15. John Rawls, *Political Liberalism* (New York: Columbia University Press, 1993), 5–6. See also Rawls, *Theory of Justice.*

16. John Rawls, *The Law of Peoples* (Cambridge, MA: Harvard University Press, 1999), 18. Rawls also emphasizes that principles of justice among peoples should take seriously an international duty of toleration.

17. The account that follows draws on my "What Self-Governing Peoples Owe to One Another: Universalism, Diversity, and The Law of Peoples," *Fordham Law Review* 72 (2004): 1721–1738.

18. D. S. Massey, J. Durand, and N. J. Malone, *Beyond Smoke and Mirrors*: *Immigration Policy and Global Economic Integration* (New York; Russell Sage Foundation, 2002): 41–45.

19. Ibid., 54–70.

20. Ibid., 158; *1999 Statistical Yearbook of the Immigration and Naturalization Service* (Washington, DC: U.S. Government Printing Office, 2000).

21. See http://www.house.gov/hunter/TRUE.security. html.

22. Massey et al., *Beyond Smoke and Mirrors,* 157–163.

23. I am grateful to Ronald Dworkin for raising this question and also for supplying part of the answer.

24. I am also grateful for very helpful comments on versions of this chapter from Michael Blake, Rainer Forst, Matt Lister, Douglas Massey, Jamie Mayerfield, Philip Pettit, Walter Sinnott-Armstrong, and Leif Wenar. I also thank the participants in the Fellows seminar of the University Center for Human Values, Princeton University, in May 2005, especially Nir Eyal and Sanjay Reddy, for their extended comments. I am grateful to the discussants at workshops of the Program in Law and Public Affairs at Princeton and the Philosophy Department of the University of Utah in September 2005, and at the New York University Legal Theory Colloquium in December 2005, for which special thanks are given to Ronald Dworkin and Thomas Nagel, who raised a number of points that led to corrections and improvements to this chapter.

READING QUESTIONS

1. Macedo distinguishes two possible ways, which he labels "humanitarian assistance" and "distributive justice," of seeking to improve the condition of the poor. Explain these two approaches to assisting the poor.
2. Why does Macedo claim that cosmopolitan distributive justice "makes no sense"?
3. Macedo mentions three categories of obligations that societies have to one another. What are they?
4. One approach to concerns about immigration discussed by Macedo is put forth by Massey, Durand, and Malone. What is their approach, and what problems does Macedo raise for it?

DISCUSSION QUESTIONS

1. Explain why you agree or disagree with Macedo's claim that the comparative standing of citizens matters in ways that the comparative standing of citizens and noncitizens does not.
2. Discuss the pros and cons of the various proposals for a U.S. immigration policy based on Macedo's discussion of the proposal by Massey, Durand, and Malone.

JOSEPH H. CARENS

Migration and Morality:
A Liberal Egalitarian Perspective

Joseph Carens examines the liberal egalitarian case for freedom of movement across borders. Then, after presenting a case that creates a presumption in favor of such movement, he considers arguments that might trump that presumption. Finally, having evaluated various objections as to force, Carens concludes that liberal egalitarians should favor more open immigration policies.

Recommended Reading: social contract theory, chap. 1, sec. 2G, in particular the discussion of Rawls's principles of distributive justice.

What must we do to treat all human beings as free and equal moral persons? That is the question that liberal egalitarianism demands we ask of all institutions and social practices, including those affecting citizenship, borders and migration.

Like any tradition of moral discourse, liberal egalitarianism is filled with conflicting arguments. The issue of movement across borders has only recently received any sustained attention, but already one can find major splits among liberal egalitarians. Some claim there should be no restrictions on freedom of movement, or almost none; others say that states are morally entitled to admit or exclude whomever they want with only a few qualifications; still others adopt some position in between.[1] In this chapter, therefore, I will not claim to represent the consensus of the tradition. Instead I will offer my current view of what anyone committed to liberal egalitarianism ought to think about migration, noting along the way the major points of disagreement within the tradition and indicating the places where I feel least certain about my own argument.

Overall, my position is this. Liberal egalitarianism entails a deep commitment to freedom of movement as both an important liberty in itself and a prerequisite for other freedoms. Thus the presumption is for free migration and anyone who would defend restrictions faces a heavy burden of proof. Nevertheless, restrictions may sometimes be justified because they will promote liberty and equality in the long run or because they are necessary to preserve a distinct culture or way of life.

I

Like all those in the liberal tradition, liberal egalitarians care about human freedoms.[2] People should be free to pursue their own projects and to make their own choices about how they live their lives so long as this does not interfere with the legitimate claims of other individuals to do likewise. In addition, liberal egalitarians are committed to equal opportunity. Access to social positions should be determined by an individual's actual talents and capacities, not

From Joseph H. Carens, "Migration and Morality: A Liberal Egalitarian Perspective," in B. Barry and R. E. Goodin, eds., *Free Movement: Ethical Issues in the Transnational Migration of People and of Money* (Hertfordshire: Harvester Wheatsheaf, 1992).

limited on the basis of arbitrary native characteristics (such as class, race, or sex). Finally, liberal egalitarians want to keep actual economic, social and political inequalities as small as possible, partly as a means of realizing equal freedom and equal opportunity and partly as a desirable end in itself.[3]

Freedom of movement is closely connected to each of these three concerns. First, the right to go where you want to go is itself an important freedom. It is precisely this freedom, and all that this freedom makes possible, that is taken away by imprisonment. Second, freedom of movement is essential for equality of opportunity. You have to be able to move to where the opportunities are in order to take advantage of them. Third, freedom of movement would contribute to a reduction of political, social and economic inequalities. There are millions of people in the Third World today who long for the freedom and economic opportunity they could find in affluent First World countries. Many of them take great risks to come: Haitians setting off in leaky boats, Salvadorians being smuggled across the border in hot, airless trucks, Tamils paying to be set adrift off the coast of Newfoundland. If the borders were open, millions more would move. The exclusion of so many poor and desperate people seems hard to justify from a perspective that takes seriously the claims of all individuals as free and equal moral persons.

Consider the case for freedom of movement in light of the liberal critique of feudal practices that determined a person's life chances on the basis of his or her birth. Citizenship in the modern world is a lot like feudal status in the medieval world. It is assigned at birth; for the most part it is not subject to change by the individual's will and efforts; and it has a major impact upon that person's life chances. To be born a citizen of an affluent country like Canada is like being born into the nobility (even though many belong to the lesser nobility). To be born a citizen of a poor country like Bangladesh is (for most) like being born into the peasantry in the Middle Ages. In this context, limiting entry to countries like Canada is a way of protecting a birthright privilege. Liberals objected to the way feudalism restricted freedom, including the freedom of individuals to move from one place to another in search of a better life. But

modern practices of citizenship and state control over borders tie people to the land of their birth almost as effectively. If the feudal practices were wrong, what justifies the modern ones?

Some would respond to this challenge by drawing a distinction between freedom of exit and freedom of entry and arguing that the two are asymmetrical.[4] The former, the right to leave one's own state ought to be virtually absolute, precisely because restrictions resemble the objectionable feudal practices. But that does not imply a right to enter any particular place. From a liberal egalitarian perspective this answer is clearly unsatisfactory if entry is so restricted in most states that most people who want to leave have no place to go. That is certainly the case in the modern world. The liberal egalitarian branch of liberalism is sympathetic to the charge that liberal freedoms can be empty formalities under some circumstances. Liberal egalitarians want to pay attention to the conditions (material and other) that make formal freedoms meaningful and effective. So, a right of exit that does not carry with it some reasonable guarantee of entry will not seem adequate.

The initial allocation of citizenship on the basis of birthplace, parentage, or some combination thereof is not objectionable from a liberal egalitarian perspective. Indeed it is morally required because children are born into a community with ties to others that should be acknowledged. In principle, however, individuals should be free to change their membership at will.

Finally, compare freedom of movement *within* the state to freedom of movement across state borders. Like every freedom involving human action, freedom of movement is not unlimited, but because it is an important liberty limitations have to be justified in a way that gives equal weight to the claims of all. Some restrictions on movement are easy to justify, e.g. traffic regulations or a right to exclude others from one's home (assuming everyone has a home or a reasonable opportunity to obtain one). But imagine an attempt by officials in one city or county to keep out people from another. That sort of restriction is seen as fundamentally incompatible with a commitment to free and equal citizenship. Cities and provinces have borders but not ones that can be used to keep people in or out against their will. Indeed freedom of movement *within* the nation-state is widely acknowledged as a basic human right, and states are criticized for restricting internal movement even by those who accept the conventional view of state sovereignty. People *are* generally free to change their membership in sub-national political communities at will.

If it is so important for people to have the right to move freely within a state, is it not equally important for them to have the right to move across state borders? Every reason why one might want to move within a state may also be a reason for moving between states. One might want a job; one might fall in love with someone from another country; one might belong to a religion that has few adherents in one's native state and many in another; one might wish to pursue cultural opportunities that are only available in another land. The radical disjuncture that treats freedom of movement within the state as a moral imperative and freedom of movement across state borders as merely a matter of political discretion makes no sense from a perspective that takes seriously the freedom and equality of all individuals.

II

The arguments in the preceding section create at least a presumption for freedom of movement from a liberal egalitarian perspective. Can this presumption ever be overriden? One possible approach is to argue that restrictions on free movement are necessary in order to promote freedom and equality in the long run. On this view, free movement is an aspect of the liberal egalitarian ideal which we should ultimately try to achieve but to adopt the practice of open borders now would jeopardize those liberal egalitarian institutions and practices that currently exist and slow their development elsewhere.[5]

This argument takes several related forms, most of them focusing on the need to protect existing liberal egalitarian cultures and institutions (however imperfectly realized). First, there is the question of national security. Presumably an invading army is not entitled to unopposed entry on the grounds of free movement.

But that does not entail any real modification because the principle of free movement does not entitle citizens to organize their own armies to challenge the authority of the state either. What about subversives? Again, if it is against the law for citizens to try to overthrow the state, that kind of activity would presumably justify refusal of entry to outsiders. So, people who pose a serious threat to national security can legitimately be excluded.

A related argument concerns the danger to a liberal egalitarian regime posed by a large influx of people who come from non-liberal societies, even if they do not come with any subversive intent. To put it another way, are people committed to treating all individuals as free and equal moral persons obliged to admit people who are not so committed? This is close to the familiar question of the toleration of the intolerant in liberal regimes. One conventional answer (which I accept) is that liberal regimes are obliged to tolerate the intolerant and respect their liberties so long as they do not pose an actual threat to the maintenance of liberal institutions. When they do pose a threat, however, their liberties may be curtailed in order to preserve the regime.[6] Here that answer would imply that restrictions on non-liberal entrants would be justified only if one had good reason to believe that they would threaten the liberal character of the regime if admitted. This entails the conclusion that it could be legitimate to exclude people for holding beliefs and values that are also held by people who are already members but only because of the presumed cumulative effect of their presence.

Would it be justifiable to expel non-liberal members because of their beliefs and values if their numbers grew large enough to constitute a threat? No. I argued above that the radical disjuncture between freedom of entry and freedom of exit in conventional morality is not justified. Nevertheless, there is something to the claim of asymmetry. Under many circumstances, the right to leave is much more important than the right to enter any particular place. It is only in the limiting case where there is nowhere to go that the two become equivalent, although as I noted above that limiting case is closely approximated in the real world for many people. Similarly, under many, perhaps most circumstances the right to remain in a country where one is already a member is much more fundamental than the right to get in. All of the ties that one creates in the course of living in a place mean that one normally (though not always) has a much more vital interest in being able to stay where one is than in being able to get in somewhere new. This is not a denigration of the importance of the freedom to move, but rather a claim that the freedom to remain is even more important. Thus, expulsions of members are almost never justified from a liberal egalitarian perspective.

Although it is a distraction from the threat to liberalism argument, it is worth pausing here to explore the implications of this point about expulsions for the issue of migrant workers and their families.[7] In the preceding paragraph, I deliberately used the term 'members' rather than 'citizens' because being a member of a society and having the moral claims of a member is not dependent upon having the formal status of a citizen. Indeed, one of the ways states may act unjustly is by denying citizenship to people who are members. When a state admits people to live and work in the territory it governs, it admits them to membership so long as they stay any significant period of time. It cannot do otherwise and still treat them as free and equal moral persons. Thus it is obliged to admit their immediate families as well and to open the doors to citizenship to them and their families. Even if they do not become citizens, they have a right to stay for all of the reasons discussed in the preceding paragraph. So, the state cannot rightly expel them even if circumstances have changed and it is no longer advantageous to have them. And again in parallel with the preceding paragraph, it is much worse to deport people who have already come and settled than to refuse entry to new workers.

These claims about membership and the right to remain are not altered even if the migrant workers were admitted under terms that explicitly provided for their return should circumstances change. Liberal egalitarianism places limits on freedom of contract, rendering void any agreements that are incompatible with equal respect for persons. And unlike most of the claims I make in this chapter about what liberal egalitarianism requires with respect to migration, these claims about migrant workers are generally reflected in the practices of contemporary liberal democratic societies.

To return to the threat to liberalism argument, another variant focuses not on beliefs and values but on sheer numbers. Given the size of the potential demand, if a rich country like Canada or the United States were to open its borders, the number of those coming might overwhelm the capacity of the society to cope, leading to chaos and a breakdown of public order. The risk would be especially great if only one or two of the rich countries were to open their borders. One cannot assume that the potential immigrants would see the danger and refrain from coming because of the time lag between cause and effect, because of collective action problems, and so on. Call this the public order problem. Note that the 'public order' is not equivalent to the welfare state or whatever public policies are currently in place. It is a minimalist standard, referring only to the maintenance of law and order. A threat to public order could be used to justify restrictions on immigration on grounds that are compatible with respecting every individual as a free and equal moral person, because the breakdown of public order makes everyone worse off in terms of both liberty and welfare. In some ways, this is reminiscent of Garrett Hardin's famous lifeboat ethics argument.[8] It does no one any good to take so many people into the boat that it is swamped and everyone drowns.

Even if one accepts all of the arguments above as sources of possible constraint on entry, the basic commitment to free movement as the fundamental goal and underlying principle remains intact. Just as those in a lifeboat are positively obliged to take in as many as they can without jeopardizing the safety of the boat as a whole (a point that those fond of this analogy often neglect), the state is obliged to admit as many of those seeking entry as it can without jeopardizing national security, public order and the maintenance of liberal institutions.

One obvious danger, however, is that an expansive interpretation of the criteria in the preceding arguments will open the door to a flood of restrictions. For example, the United States has used the national security justification to deny entry (even for temporary visits) to people identified as homosexuals, as well as to all sorts of people whose views do not conform to the reigning American ideology. And if national security is linked to the state's economic performance (as it often is), any economic costs connected with immigration can be seen as threatening national security. Exclusionists in the nineteenth century in the United States cited the dangers of immigration from non-liberal societies as grounds for keeping out Catholics and Jews from Europe and all Asians and Africans. Canada and Australia had comparable restrictions on similar grounds. (Today Islamic fundamentalism seems to be the main target of those worried about non-liberal values.) And, of course, some people see a threat to public order in any new demand placed on a social system. They want a safety margin of fifty empty places in a lifeboat built for sixty.

Despite these sad examples, one should not exclude proper concerns, at least at the level of theory, because they are subject to exaggeration and abuse in practice. The task is to distinguish between reasonable and unreasonable uses of these sorts of arguments. As Rawls puts it in acknowledging that liberties may sometimes be restricted for the sake of public order and security, the hypothetical possibility of a threat is not enough. Rather there must be a 'reasonable expectation' that damage will occur in the absence of restrictions and the expectation has to be based on 'evidence and ways of reasoning acceptable to all'.[9] The same strictures apply to all attempts to justify restrictions on immigration along the lines sketched above, and none of the examples cited is really justified as a reasonable use of restrictive criteria.

A variation of the preceding arguments that is based on real concerns but is much more problematic from a liberal egalitarian perspective is what might be called the backlash argument. On this view, the commitment to liberal egalitarian principles is not very secure even in liberal societies. Current citizens might object to the ethnic and cultural characteristics of new immigrants, fear them as competitors in the workplace, and perceive them as economic burdens placing excessive demands upon the social welfare system. At the least, this reaction might erode the sense of mutuality and community identification that makes egalitarian and redistributive programmes

politically possible. At the worse, it might threaten the basic liberal democratic framework. A glance at current European politics makes it clear that this threat is all too real. In several countries, extreme right-wing parties, using veiled and not so veiled racist and neo-fascist appeals, have gained ground, primarily, it seems, by making opposition to current immigrants and future immigration a key element in their platforms. In this context, to open the borders more now might well provoke a political reaction that would quickly slam the doors shut and damage other liberal egalitarian institutions and policies as well.

Would this justify restrictions on immigration from a liberal egalitarian perspective? The answer must be 'no' at the level of principle and 'perhaps' at the level of practice. I am assuming here that the claims to exclude do not rest on some as yet unspecified valid argument. By hypothesis then we are dealing with a case in which restrictions on immigration would not be justified if one took a perspective in which all were regarded as free and equal moral persons. Those advocating exclusion are either putting forward claims that are intrinsically unjust (e.g. racist claims) or ones that are legitimate concerns (e.g. their economic interests) but outweighed by the claims of the potential immigrants (both in terms of their right to free movement and in terms of their own economic interests). The 'justification' for restrictions is simply that if no concessions are made to the exclusionists they may make things even worse. Put that way it is clearly no justification at all at the level of principle though one cannot say that such concessions are never prudent in practice.

Compare this issue to such questions as whether slaveowners should have been compensated for the loss of their property when slavery was abolished, whether holders of feudal privilege should have been compensated when those privileges were abolished and whether segregation should have been ended gradually (with 'all deliberate speed') rather than all at once. All of these questions were live issues once in political contexts where defenders of the old ways still had sufficient political power to resist change and perhaps even reverse it if pressed too hard. In none of these cases, it seems to me, were concessions required as a matter of principle, but in any of them they may have been defensible in practice as the best that could be achieved under the circumstances. The latter seems an appropriate moral guide to political action assuming a definition of the good that takes into account independent ethical constraints upon action. And so the backlash argument, too, may provide grounds of this limited sort for restrictions in some cases.

Finally, there are arguments for restriction that focus not on the protection of liberal egalitarian institutions and practices in states that currently have them but on their development elsewhere and on the reduction of global inequalities. According to the 'brain drain' hypothesis, the movement of people from the Third World to the First World actually increases global inequalities because the best educated and most talented are among the most likely to move in order to take advantage of the greater professional and economic opportunities in affluent societies. Even among the poor, it is the most energetic and ambitious who move, and usually people from the lower middle classes rather than the worst off because the latter do not have the resources needed for migration. Thus migration actually involves a transfer of human resources from poor countries to rich ones. This often involves the loss of actual, economic investments in the form of scarce and costly expenditures on education and training, but the greatest cost is the loss of people with the capacity to contribute to the transformation of their country's condition. Freer movement would only make the situation worse, making development in the Third World and a reduction of global inequalities even more unlikely than it is now.

A variant of this argument stresses politics rather than economics, drawing attention to the way in which easy exit may act as a safety valve for a repressive regime. It may be easier to silence domestic opposition by sending it abroad than by suppressing it internally. And if exit is an easy option, those living under a repressive regime may devote their energies to getting out rather than to transforming the system under which they live.

On the whole, I think these are the sorts of arguments that have given utilitarianism a bad name in some quarters, although, as is often the case, I do not think a clear thinking utilitarian would support them.

What is particularly objectionable is the way they propose to extract benefits for some people by, in effect, imprisoning others. As is so often the case in discussing migration, it is helpful to compare internal migration with migration across state borders. Many states suffer from severe regional inequalities and it is often suggested that these inequalities are made worse by the movement of the brightest, best-trained people from poor regions to rich ones – an internal brain drain. But what would we think if Canada tried to cope with its regional disparities by prohibiting people from moving from Newfoundland to Ontario, or if Italy limited migration from Naples to Milan? The regional differences are a serious problem that states have a duty to address, but they would be wrong to try to solve this problem by limiting the basic freedoms of their citizens.

So, too, with the international brain drain. International inequality is a serious moral problem, but restricting movement is not a morally permissible tactic for dealing with it. And that assumes that it would be a useful tactic. In fact, the benefits themselves are extremely problematic. Emigrants contribute in various ways to their communities of origin (often through direct financial remittances), and it is far from clear that making them stay home would lead to the desired economic and political transformation. On the other hand, the cost to those denied permission to leave is clear and direct. Limitations of important freedoms should never be undertaken lightly. In the face of great uncertainty about their effects they should not be undertaken at all.

What about financial compensation for the costs of education and training? Here it is important to distinguish between basic education and advanced education or training. For the former no compensation is due. Everyone is entitled to basic education, and children cannot enter into binding contracts. Whatever investments a society makes in its young, it cannot rightly require direct repayment. Advanced training is somewhat different both because it is provided only to a few and because those receiving it are normally old enough to assume responsibility for their choices. If it is subsidized by the state, especially a state with comparatively few resources, it may be reasonable to expect the recipients to commit themselves to a few years of service in the country or to repay the costs of the training. But these sorts of expectations must be limited and reasonable. Liberal egalitarianism is incompatible with any form of indentured servitude.

In arguing that the state may not normally limit migration as a way of enforcing a claim to the services of its citizens, I am not saying that people have no obligations to their communities of origin. It is a familiar feature of most liberal theories that the state should not enforce many sorts of moral duties or obligations not just on the prudential grounds that enforcement will be costly or ineffective but on the principle that individuals must have considerable scope to define their own lives and identities, including the moral worlds that they inhabit. This does not mean that all moral commitments are a matter of choice. From the individual's perspective, the moral ties may be experienced as given, a product of unchosen relationships with members of one's family, ethnic group, religious faith, or even political community. Take a black doctor in the United States. He or she might or might not feel a special obligation to work in the black community. If he or she does, he or she might or might not think that other black doctors have a comparable obligation. Liberal egalitarianism has nothing to say about these matters. It does not try to fill the whole moral world. It does not deny the existence of such obligations or imply that they are purely subjective and not subject to rational discussion. The only limit that liberal egalitarianism places on such moral views and moral commitments is that they must not conflict with the rights and duties that liberal egaliteranism itself prescribes.

People from poor countries may feel a special obligation to use their talents at home, and they may think that their compatriots have the same obligation. Liberal egalitarianism does not deny or affirm this view. It only denies the moral propriety of enforcing it through restrictions on movement.

My arguments about the brain drain have focused on the countries of origin. What about the countries of destination? It would be both paternalistic and hypocritical for rich countries to say that they were closing their borders to help the poor ones out. Moreover, given my arguments above about the relationship between the right of exit and the right of entry, it would be wrong to do so with the goal of denying potential emigrants any place to go.

III

One objection to the line of argument I have been developing so far is that the whole problem of freedom of movement is essentially epiphenomenal. Other things being equal, one could expect that most people would not want to leave the land where they were born and raised, a place whose language, customs and ways of life are familiar. But other things are not equal. There are vast economic inequalities among states, and some states deny basic liberties to their own citizens. These are the circumstances that create such a vast potential for movement across borders and that make the issue of migration seem like an urgent moral problem. But from a liberal egalitarian perspective, these circumstances are at least as morally objectionable as restrictions on freedom of movement. States have an obligation to respect their citizens' basic liberties, and rich states have an obligation to transfer resources and adopt other measures to reduce drastically the prevailing international economic inequalities. If they fulfilled these obligations, migration would no longer be a serious moral problem, because relatively few people would want to move and those who did could and would be accommodated somewhere.

If one replies that states will not meet these obligations, the response is that we gain nothing by focusing on another obligation which they are equally unlikely to fulfil. Most of the same practical and self-interested considerations that will prevent rich states from transferring significant resources to poor states, will keep them from opening their borders wide to poor immigrants. In struggling against injustice, it is a bad strategy to make the admission of new immigrants to rich countries a priority, because restrictions are a symptom, not a cause, of the real problems, because immigration can never be a solution for more than a relatively small number, no matter how open the borders, and because this focus on people who want to move from the Third World to the First World may perpetuate neo-colonial assumptions about the superiority of the First World.

I think there is something to be said for this objection. International inequalities and political oppression are certainly more important moral and political problems than restrictions on migration. The sense that the latter is an urgent problem derives in large part from the size of the potential demand and that in turn derives from international inequalities and other forms of injustice that free movement will do little to cure. Nevertheless, we cannot entirely ignore the question of immigration. In the long run, the transformation of the international politico-economic order might reduce the demand for international migration and the resistance to it, but, as Keynes said, in the long run we are all dead. We have to consider the moral claims of those whom we confront here and now (as well as the claims of future generations). For example, refugees who have no reasonable prospect of a return to their homes in the near term need a place to settle if they are to have any chance of a decent life. Moreover, we lack knowledge as well as will when it comes to radically reducing international inequalities, as is illustrated by the failures of most attempts to eliminate regional inequalities *within* states. In terms of politics, it is not clear that increasing aid and increasing immigration are really incompatible. In general, the same political actors support or oppose both.

But the objection that the demand for free movement is essentially epiphenomenal poses a theoretical challenge as well as a practical one. To what extent does my earlier claim about the liberal egalitarian commitment to free movement rest upon the current realities of international inequalities and political oppression? Would people have the right to move freely in a world without the deep injustices of the one we live in, or might there be legitimate grounds for restricting free movement, say, for the sake of a certain kind of community? In other words, is free movement epiphenomenal at the theoretical level, not derived directly from fundamental principles but rather from the application of those principles to the circumstances in which we find ourselves?

To explore this question, I propose to focus in the next two sections on the question of movement across borders when the states in question enjoy comparable levels of affluence and comparable liberal democratic political institutions.

IV

The epiphenomenon argument raises questions about the consequences of focusing on possible changes in migration policies in abstraction from other issues, but it does not directly challenge the principle that free movement is good from a liberal egalitarian perspective. Are there any elements in the liberal egalitarian tradition that would give pause to this general embrace of openness?

One possible source is the liberal egalitarian commitment to pluralism, and the consequent respect for difference and diversity. Consider first the case of Japan. Should Japan's immigration policy be the same as that of the United States or Canada? A commitment to free movement seems to require a positive response to this question, except that the public order constraint might kick in sooner because of the high population density in Japan. But to answer that question positively seems counter-intuitive, and not just because we assume that all states have the right to control their borders. Rather a positive response seems to imply that all states have a moral obligation to become like us—multicultural countries with large numbers of immigrants (or at least to open themselves to that possibility). (This sounds like a form of North American moral imperialism; our way is the only right way.)

Now that does not prove that the claim is wrong. Appeals to diversity and pluralism carry no weight when it comes to the violation of basic human rights. From a liberal egalitarian perspective all states are obliged to respect such rights regardless of their history, culture or traditions. As we have seen, it is possible to claim that freedom of movement is a basic human right from a liberal egalitarian perspective. But perhaps that claim does not pay sufficient attention to the costs that freedom of movement can impose.

To return to the Japanese case, Japan is a country with a highly homogeneous population. It is not completely homogeneous. There are religious differences and ethnic minorities in Japan as there are in every country. But most people in Japan share a common culture, tradition and history to a much greater extent than people do in countries like Canada and the United States. It seems reasonable to suppose that many Japanese cherish their distinctive way of life, that they want to preserve it and pass it on to their children because they find that it gives meaning and depth to their lives. They cannot pass it on unchanged, to be sure, because no way of life remains entirely unchanged, but they can hope to do so in a form that retains both its vitality and its continuity with the past. In these ways many Japanese may have a vital interest in the preservation of a distinctive Japanese culture; they may regard it as crucial to their life projects. From a liberal egalitarian perspective this concern for preserving Japanese culture counts as a legitimate interest, assuming (as I do) that this culture is compatible with respect for all human beings as free and equal moral persons.

It also seems reasonable to suppose that this distinctive culture and way of life would be profoundly transformed if a significant number of immigrants came to live in Japan. A multicultural Japan would be a very different place. So, limits on new entrants would be necessary to preserve the culture if any significant number of people wanted to immigrate.

Would the limits be justified? That depends, I think, on why the people wanted to come. We have to weigh the claims of those trying to get in equally with the claims of those who are already inside, but to do that we have to know something about the nature of those claims. For example, suppose some non-Japanese person had married a Japanese citizen. It would clearly be wrong to exclude the non-Japanese spouse, even if mixed marriages were seen as subversive of Japanese culture. Here the fundamental right of individuals to marry whom they want and to live together, along with the fundamental right of the Japanese citizen not to be expelled from his or her home, should trump any communal concerns for the preservation of culture. (And, as far as I know, Japan does indeed admit spouses.)

Suppose, however, that people wanted to come to live and work in Japan as a way of pursuing economic opportunity. Should that trump the concern of the Japanese to preserve their culture? The answer might depend in part on the nature of the alternatives the potential immigrants face if Japan is closed. Recall that we have temporarily put to one side, by hypothesis, the problems of deep international inequalities and refugee-generating forms of oppression. Presumably, then, the potential immigrants have reasonable economic opportunities elsewhere, even if ones that are not quite as good. I do not see why an interest in marginally better economic opportunities should count more than an interest in preserving a culture.

One obvious rejoinder is that restricting immigration limits individual freedom, while cultural changes that develop as a by-product of uncoordinated individual actions do not violate any legitimate claims of individuals. The problem with this sort of response (which clearly does fit with some strains in the liberal tradition and even with some forms of liberal egalitarianism) is that it uses too narrow a definition of freedom. It excludes by fiat any concern for the cumulative, if unintended, consequences of individual actions. A richer concept of freedom will pay attention to the context of choice, to the extent to which background conditions make it possible for people to realize their most important goals and pursue their most important life projects. That is precisely the sort of approach that permits us to see the ways in which particular cultures can provide valuable resources for people and the costs associated with the loss of a culture, while still permitting a critical assessment of the consequences of the culture both for those who participate in it and for those who do not.

But if we say that exclusion may be justified to preserve Japanese culture, does that not open the door to any other state that wants to exclude others, or certain kinds of others, to preserve its culture and its way of life? Doesn't it legitimate racist immigration policies? What about the White Australia policy, for example? That was defended as an attempt to preserve a particular culture and way of life, as were similar racial and ethnic policies in Canada and the United States.[10]

From some viewpoints every form of exclusion that draws distinctions based on race, ethnicity, or cultural heritage is morally objectionable. I think, however, that one cannot make such a blanket judgement. Difference does not always entail domination. One has to consider what a particular case of exclusion means, taking the historical, social and political context into account.[11] For example, the White Australia policy cannot be separated from British imperialism and European racism. That is why it was never a defensible form of exclusion.

Japan's exclusionary policy seems quite different. First it is universal, i.e. it applies to all non-Japanese. It is not aimed at some particular racial or ethnic group that is presumed to be inferior, and it is not tied to a history of domination of the excluded. Japan has a centuries-old tradition of exclusion based partly on fears of the consequences of European penetration. Of course, there is also the Japanese imperialism of the twentieth century, but that developed only after the West had forced Japan to end its isolation. Moreover, it was only during its period of imperialist expansion that Japan adopted a non-exclusionary policy, declaring all the subjects of the Japanese Empire to be Japanese citizens and bringing thousands of Koreans into Japan as workers. Both before and after this period, Japan strictly limited new entrants. Unlike much of Western Europe, for example, Japan rejected proposals for guest worker programmes to solve labour shortages in the 1960s and 1970s. I trust that it is clear that I am in no way defending or excusing Japanese imperialism. On the contrary, my point is that the Japanese policy of exclusion was not a product of, and was in important ways antagonistic to, Japanese imperialism. In that respect, at least, exclusion was not linked to domination.

But does not a policy of exclusion always imply that the culture and the people being protected through exclusion are superior to the ones being excluded? Not necessarily. It may simply reflect an attachment to what is one's own. Presumably it does entail the view that this way of life is worth preserving, that it is better than whatever would replace it under conditions of openness. But that is not necessarily objectionable in itself. Besides, having relatively open borders may also generate a sense of cultural superiority, as the American case reveals.

I do not pretend to have established the legitimacy of Japanese exclusion. That would require a much more detailed and careful examination than I can provide here. What I do hope to have established is that such an examination would be worthwhile, that exclusion for the sake of preserving Japanese culture is not self-evidently wrong, at least in a context where we have temporarily assumed away the most urgent concerns (desperate poverty and fear of oppression) that motivate so many of those who actually want to move and that make their claims so powerful.

What if we let those concerns back in and at the same time assumed that the positive case for the preservation of a distinctive Japanese culture could be sustained? One possibility is that we would conclude that not all of the rich states should have precisely the same responsibilities regarding admission of new members and assistance to poor states. Perhaps it would be appropriate for Japan to meet most of its responsibilities through aid rather than through admissions. (I express these thoughts tentatively because I feel unsure about them.)

Even if one did follow this line of thought, however, Japan would face certain responsibilities regarding the admission and integration of 'outsiders'. For example, Japan should admit some reasonable number of refugees on a permanent basis. Their needs cannot be met by aid and Japan cannot rightly expect others to assume all the burdens of resettlement. Perhaps it would be acceptable to select among the refugees on the basis of their adaptability to or compatability with Japanese culture.

Even more important, Japan has a responsibility to treat its Korean minority differently. Most of the Koreans in Japan are people who were brought over to work in Japan during World War II or their descendants. They have lived in Japan for many years. Most of the children have never lived anywhere else, and many do not even speak any other language than Japanese. Japan has an obligation to treat these people as full members of society, to grant them citizenship easily if they wish it and to make their position as permanent residents more secure and more equitable if they prefer to retain their Korean citizenship. In short, Japan's desire to protect its cultural cohesiveness is outweighed in some cases by the legitimate claims of others to entry and integration.

The discussion of Japan makes a preliminary case for exclusion for the sake of preserving a cultural tradition and a way of life. In Japan this cultural tradition and way of life are closely associated with the political boundaries of a sovereign state. But this does not establish anything about the moral status of the state as such nor does it rule out the possibility that there may be other communities with cultures and ways of life worth preserving that do not exist as states. Take, for example, the case of native communities in North America who are trying to preserve a traditional way of life within some defined land area. Most of what has been said about the Japanese case could also be said about them: they are trying to maintain a distinctive culture and way of life that gives meaning to those who inhabit it and which they regard as highly preferable to the way of life that would be entailed if they mixed with others, they cannot maintain this culture if any significant number of outsiders come to settle on their land and the reasons the outsiders have for coming (e.g. to use the land for recreational purposes) generally seem far less compelling than the reasons the natives have for keeping them out.

I accept these general claims. Indeed the control that native peoples exercise over their land provides a striking exception to the general right of free mobility within the modern state, and one that is entirely justified from a liberal egalitarian perspective in my view. So, it is not the state as such that gives rise to a claim to exclude, but rather the existence of a community with a distinctive and valuable way of life that would be threatened by immigration.

V

Can a parallel argument be developed on behalf of the state as such, perhaps on the grounds that each (legitimate) state has a distinct political culture worthy of preservation and protection? By 'political culture' I mean the collective self-understanding, the way citizens think of themselves and of their relationship with one another as this is reflected in their political

institutions, policies and practices. One reason people have for wanting to restrict entry is their desire to protect the democratic autonomy of the community in which they live. This view presupposes that there is some significant space between what is morally required of all and morally prohibited to all so that different communities can legitimately make different choices about goals, institutions and policies, or, more broadly, about the ways they lead their collective lives. Call this the zone of the morally permissible. One need not think of this as a realm of mere preferences, however. The moral arguments that belong here (and are most apt to be used in real political debates) are ones about the history and character of the community rather than about universal rights and duties. Most forms of liberal egalitarianism do not pretend to settle all moral questions. So, different communities will make different decisions, adopt different policies and develop different characters. But these differences may be threatened by open borders.

Let me offer a concrete example from a comparison between Canada and the United States.[12] (I write as someone born and raised in the United States who has lived in Canada for the past four years.) Canada has a national health insurance plan that pays for the medical care of all citizens and permanent residents. The United States does not. According to some estimates, 30 per cent of the American population has no health insurance, and many more are underinsured. Should Americans with serious health problems be able to move to Canada to take advantage of its health care system? Take those with AIDS as an example. This is an illness that requires a lot of expensive medical care over a long period, care that may simply be unavailable in the United States if one has no insurance. People with AIDS and without insurance might well choose to move to Canada if they could do so. But Canada's population as a whole is only 10 per cent of that of the United States. If even a small proportion of the Americans with AIDS moved, it would put a severe strain on the Canadian health care system. At present, Canadian immigration requirements keep out potential immigrants with medical problems that seem likely to put an unusually high financial burden on the health care system. Is that an unjust restriction on potential American immigrants?

Canada's health care system is only one example of a pervasive difference between Canada and the United States in social welfare policy. In one area after another Canada provides greater benefits to those in need, and, of course, Canadians pay much higher taxes than Americans to fund these programmes. If the borders were open and if many of the needy moved across, both the capacity and the willingness to support the programmes would be in jeopardy. The capacity would be threatened by the relative size of the Canadian and American populations, the willingness by the sense that Americans were taking advantage of Canadians (not so much the needy Americans, who would probably arouse both sympathy and resentment, as the greedy ones who refused to bear the costs of caring for their own and tried to shift these costs onto others). Restrictions on immigration from the United States therefore may help to make it possible for Canadians to take a different and more generous path from Americans when it comes to social policy. Does liberal egalitarianism require them to open the borders anyway?

If the questions in the last two paragraphs sound rhetorical, it is only because the presumption that states have the right to control entry is so deeply rooted in our thinking. One has only to shift the focus to intra-state movement to see why the questions are real and important. In the United States as in many federal systems, sub-units bear much of the responsibility for social policy and they differ greatly in the ways they carry out these responsibilities. For example, Wisconsin's welfare policies are much more generous (or much less stingy) than those of the neighbouring state of Illinois. Some Wisconsin officials claim that people are moving from Illinois to Wisconsin for the sake of these benefits. These officials propose to discourage the influx by reducing benefits for new residents during a temporary waiting period – a strategy that may or may not pass legislative and judicial scrutiny. But not even the most ardent advocates of exclusion think that they can prohibit people from moving to Wisconsin from Illinois or keep them from gaining access to all of the state's social programmes after a waiting period. This is not just a quirk of the US constitutional system. As we have seen, freedom of movement within the nation-state is widely regarded as a basic human right, and if this freedom is to be more than a mere formality, it necessarily entails that new arrivals have access to the rights and privileges that current residents enjoy, at least after the satisfaction of a modest residency requirement and, in some cases, immediately. But this freedom of movement has the same effect of eroding or at least limiting the democratic autonomy of Wisconsin as it would that of Canada.

Is that bad? Should Wisconsin have the right to keep out people from Illinois after all? Or should Canada be obliged to admit people from the United States? If the two cases are different, how and why are they different? I find these questions genuinely puzzling, but in the end I cannot see that sovereignty makes that much difference from a liberal egalitarian perspective. Despite my attachment to Canada's social welfare policies, I do not think they justify restrictions on movement. On the other hand, I do think that this commitment to free movement is compatible with shortterm residency requirements so that one must live somewhere for a few months before becoming eligible for social programmes, and that such requirements would do a great deal to protect against the erosion of social programmes. Living in Canada, one cannot help but be aware of the importance some people (especially in Quebec) attach to maintaining the distinct culture and way of life of their province. It turns out to be possible to do so even within a context of free migration within the state and considerable immigration from outside. Despite its occasional effects on social policies, it is easy to exaggerate the impact of free movement within the state and also to ignore its importance to those who do take advantage of it. The same is true of movement across borders. Perhaps even the Japanese ought in principle to begin with a policy of open doors, closing them only if a substantial demand actually appears. Given the difficulties of fitting into Japanese society as an outsider, how many would actually want to settle there if they had reasonable opportunities elsewhere?

So, I return to the theme with which I began. Liberal egalitarianism entails a deep and powerful commitment to freedom of movement which can be overridden at the level of principle only with great difficulty. . . .

VII

I will conclude with a few remarks on criteria of inclusion and exclusion. Assuming that there will be some restrictions on entry, either for legitimate reasons like the public order constraint or for illegitimate ones like a desire to protect economic privilege, are there some criteria of inclusion and exclusion that are more (or less) objectionable than others from a liberal egalitarian perspective? Certainly need should be one important criterion for admission, and refugees seeking permanent resettlement rank very high on this score since they literally need a place to live. The claims of immediate family members (spouse, minor children) rank very highly as well. No one should be denied the right to live with his or her family. Other relatives also have some claim but not as strong a one.

To return to the criterion of need, if one accepts the brain drain hypothesis, it would seem appropriate to give priority to the least skilled and most needy among potential immigrants as this would have the least negative impact on the countries of origin. On the other hand, if one admits people with skills and education, it may reduce the backlash problem (which appears to be a real or potential problem in every country that accepts immigrants, especially refugees).

Are criteria that serve the interests of the receiving country always morally problematic in this way, defensible only on prudential grounds? Not necessarily. Taking linguistic and cultural compatibility into account does not seem objectionable if it is not a disguised form of racial or ethnic prejudice and if the cumulative effects of such policies by different countries do not leave out some groups altogether.

Criteria of selection that discriminate against potential immigrants on the basis of race, ethnicity, religion, sex, or sexual orientation are particularly objectionable from a liberal egalitarian perspective. Can these criteria ever be used legitimately to give priority to some? Again, one crucial question is whether they constitute *de facto* forms of discrimination. Consider four recent or current policies with these sorts of factors (I oversimplify a bit, but I think I describe the main lines accurately):

1. Britain removed citizenship from holders of overseas passports and citizens of commonwealth countries, except for those whose grandfather was born in Great Britain.
2. Ireland grants an automatic right to citizenship to anyone with a grandparent born in Ireland, provided that the person comes to Ireland to live.
3. Germany grants citizenship (upon application in Germany) to anyone of ethnic German descent, no matter how long since the person's ancestors lived in Germany.
4. Israel grants automatic citizenship to any Jew who comes to live in Israel.

Of these, the British law is the most objectionable from a liberal egalitarian perspective and the Irish law the least, despite their formal similarity. The British law is a thinly disguised form of racism. It was designed to preserve the citizenship rights of as many descendants of white settlers as possible while depriving as many Asians and Africans as possible of theirs. The Irish grandfather clause, by contrast, has no hidden exclusionary goal. It is merely an attempt to lure back the descendants of some of those who left. The German law is troubling for two related reasons. First, the explicit link between ethnicity and citizenship raises questions about whether those German citizens who are not ethnic Germans are really regarded as equal citizens. Second, the easy grant of citizenship to people who have never lived in Germany before and some of whom do not even speak the language contrasts sharply with the reluctance to grant citizenship automatically to the children of Turkish 'guest workers' even when the children were born and brought up in Germany (and sometimes speak no other language). Finally, the Israeli 'Law of Return' raises questions about whether the Arab citizens of Israel whose friends and relatives do not have comparably easy access to citizenship are really regarded as equal citizens. On the other hand, the Israeli law is tied both to national security concerns and to the historic purpose of Israel as a homeland for Jews.

VIII

Liberal egalitarians are committed to an idea of free movement, with only modest qualifications. That idea is not politically feasible today and so it mainly serves to provide a critical standard by which to assess existing restrictive practices and policies. While almost all forms of restriction on movement are wrong from a liberal egalitarian perspective, some practices and policies are worse than others. Expulsion is worse than a refusal to admit. Racism and other forms of discriminatory exclusion are worse than policies that exclude but do not distinguish in objectionable ways among those excluded. Ideals do not always translate directly into prescriptions for practice because of the second-best problems familiar from economic theory which have their analogue in moral theory. In theory this might seem to make it difficult to identify the policy implications of liberal egalitarianism with regard to free movement. One can doubtless imagine cases where the sudden opening of the borders of one country (with all the other circumstances of the modern world remaining unchanged) would do more harm than good from a liberal egalitarian perspective. In practice, however, we can usually ignore this concern because, in every polity, domestic political considerations will confine feasible policy options to a relatively narrow range, excluding alternatives that would entail major costs to current citizens. Given these political realities, liberal egalitarians should almost always press for more openness towards immigrants and refugees.

NOTES

1. For a defence of few or no restrictions, see Joseph H. Carens, "Aliens and Citizens: The Case for Open Borders," *The Review of Politics,* 49 (Spring 1987), 251–73; Bruce Ackerman, *Social Justice in the Liberal State* (New Haven, Conn.: Yale University Press, 1980), pp. 89–95; Judith Lichtenberg, "National Boundaries and Moral Boundaries: A Cosmopolitan View," *Boundaries: National Autonomy and Its Limits,* ed. Peter Brown and Henry Shue (Totowa, N.J.: Rowman & Littlefield, 1981), pp. 79–100; and Roger Nett, "The Civil Right We Are Not Yet Ready For: The Right of Free Movement of People on the Face of the Earth," *Ethics,* 81 (1971), 212–27. For the state's right to control entry, see Michael Walzer, *Spheres of Justice* (New York: Basic Books, 1983), pp. 31–63. For the middle position, see Frederick Whelan, "Citizenship and Freedom of Movement: An Open Admission Policy" in *Open Borders? Closed Societies?: The Ethical and Political Issues,* ed. Mark Gibney (Westport, Conn.: Greenwood Press, 1988), pp. 3–39.

2. The arguments in this section draw upon Carens, "Aliens and Citizens" and Whelan, "Citizenship and Freedom of Movement."

3. This brief sketch necessarily covers over deep disagreements among liberal egalitarians with regard to many issues such as how much inequality is compatible with or required by the commitment to freedom, whether affirmative action for groups historically subject to discrimination is a violation of, or a means of realizing, liberal egalitarian principles, what are the foundations (if any) of liberal egalitarian commitments, and so on.

4. See Walzer, *Spheres of Justice.* For a detailed discussion of the right of exit see Frederick Whelan, "Citizenship and the Right to Leave," *American Political Science Review,* 75 (1981), 636–53.

5. I have discussed these sorts of arguments previously in "Aliens and Citizens."

6. Here I follow John Rawls, *A Theory of Justice* (Cambridge, Mass.: Harvard University Press, 1971), pp. 216–21.

7. I develop the claims in the next two paragraphs at greater length in "Membership and Morality: Admission to Citizenship in Liberal Democratic States," *Immigration and the Politics of Citizenship in Europe and North America,* ed. William Rogers Brubaker (Lanham, Md.: German Marshall. Fund of America and University Press of America, 1989), pp. 31–49.

8. Garrett Hardin, "Living on a Lifeboat," *Bioscience* (October 1974).

9. Rawls, *A Theory of Justice,* p. 213.

10. For a fuller discussion of the White Australia policy, see Joseph H. Carens, "Nationalism and the Exclusion of Immigrants: Lessons from Australian Immigration Policy," *Open Borders? Closed Societies?: The Ethical and Political Issues,* ed. Mark Gibney (Westport, Conn.: Greenwood Press, 1988), pp. 41–60.

11. For a fuller defence of this approach see Joseph H. Carens, "Difference and Domination: Reflections on the Relation between Pluralism and Equality," *Majorities and Minorities: NOMOS XXXII,* ed. John Chapman and Alan

Wertheimer (New York: New York University Press, 1990), pp. 226–50.

12. I explore the relevance of differences in social welfare policy between Canada and the United States in a similar way in "Immigration and the Welfare State," *Democracy and the Welfare State,* ed. Amy Gutmann (Princeton, N.J.: Princeton University Press, 1988), pp. 207–30.

READING QUESTIONS

1. Which liberal egalitarian concerns does Carens present as importantly related to freedom of movement? How does freedom of movement bear on these concerns?
2. Carens discusses what he calls the "backlash argument," one of the objections to his view. What is this argument, and how does Carens reply to it?
3. In section III, Carens considers the objection that from a liberal egalitarian perspective, rich nations have an obligation to "transfer resources and adopt other measures to reduce drastically the prevailing international economic inequalities" and so if such nations fulfilled these obligations, migration would cease to be a serious moral problem. How does Carens reply to this objection?
4. The interest in preserving one's culture is sometimes used as a reason for limiting immigration. Carens discusses this objection, using Japanese culture as an example. How does he respond to the "culture preservation" objection?

DISCUSSION QUESTIONS

1. Which of the various objections to Carens's position on immigration do you think makes the strongest case for limiting immigration? Explain why you think Carens's reply is either effective or ineffective in responding to the objection in question.
2. Does the "preservation of culture" argument for limiting immigration provide a strong reason for the United States to adopt a restrictive immigration policy? Why or why not?

CHRISTOPHER HEATH WELLMAN

Immigration and Freedom of Association

Granting that wealthy countries have obligations of global distributive justice to help the world's poor and oppressed, Christopher Heath Wellman defends the position, based on freedom of association, that nation-states have a presumptive right to close their borders to all potential immigrants. After arguing for his position in section I, Wellman proceeds in sections II and III to examine and critically assess egalitarian and libertarian arguments for open borders. He concludes that the various considerations featured in such arguments are not strong enough to override the prima facie right of states to close their borders to immigrants. In section IV, Wellman considers questions about using considerations of race, religion, and ethnicity as a basis for denying immigration to individuals.

In this article I appeal to freedom of association to defend a state's right to control immigration over its territorial borders. Without denying that those of us in wealthy societies may have extremely demanding duties of global distributive justice, I ultimately reach the stark conclusion that every legitimate state has the right to close its doors to all potential immigrants, even refugees desperately seeking asylum from incompetent or corrupt political regimes that are either unable or unwilling to protect their citizens' basic moral rights.

This article is divided into four sections. First, I argue for a presumptive case in favor of a state's right to limit immigration as an instance of its more general right to freedom of association. In the second and third sections, I respond to egalitarian and libertarian cases for open borders. Finally, in the fourth section, I consider the permissibility of screening immigrants based upon their race, ethnicity or religion.

I. THE CASE FOR THE RIGHT TO CLOSED BORDERS

To appreciate the presumptive case in favor of a state's right to control its borders that can be built upon the right to freedom of association, notice both that (1) freedom of association is widely thought to be important and that (2) it includes the right not to associate and even, in many cases, the right to disassociate.

That freedom of association is highly valued is evident from our views on marriage and religion. In the past, it was thought appropriate for one's father to select one's marital partner or for one's state to determine the religion one practiced, but, thankfully, those times have (largely) passed. Today, virtually everyone agrees that we are entitled to marital and religious freedom of association; we take it for granted that each individual has a right to choose his or her marital partner and the associates with whom he or she practices his or her religion. Put plainly, among our most firmly settled convictions is the belief that each of us enjoys a morally privileged position of dominion over our self-regarding affairs, a position which entitles us to freedom of association in the marital and religious realms.

Second, notice that freedom of association includes a right to reject a potential association and (often) a right to disassociate. As Stuart White explains: "Freedom of association is widely seen as one of those basic freedoms which is fundamental to a genuinely free society. With the freedom to associate, however, there comes the freedom to refuse association. When a group of people get together to form an association of some kind (e.g., a religious association, a trade union, a sports club), they will frequently wish to exclude some people from joining their association. What makes it *their* association, serving their purposes, is that they can exercise this 'right to exclude.'"[1]

In the case of matrimony, for instance, this freedom involves more than merely having the right to get married. One fully enjoys freedom of association only if one may choose whether or not to marry a second party who would have one as a partner. Thus, one must not only be permitted to marry a willing partner whom one accepts; one must also have the discretion to reject the proposal of any given suitor and even to remain single indefinitely if one so chooses. As David

Gauthier puts it, "I may have the right to choose the woman of my choice who also chooses me, but not the woman of my choice who rejects me."[2] We understand religious self-determination similarly: whether, how, and with whom I attend to my humanity is up to me as an individual. If I elect to explore my religious nature in community with others, I have no duty to do so with anyone in particular, and I have no right to force others to allow me to join them in worship.

In light of our views on marriage and religious self-determination, the case for a state's right to control immigration might seem straightforward: just as an individual has a right to determine whom (if anyone) he or she would like to marry, a group of fellow-citizens has a right to determine whom (if anyone) it would like to invite into its political community. And just as an individual's freedom of association entitles one to remain single, a state's freedom of association entitles it to exclude all foreigners from its political community. There are at least two reasons that this inference from an individual's to a state's right to freedom of association might strike some as problematic, however. First, presumably there are morally relevant differences between individuals and groups, and these differences might explain why only individuals can have a right to self-determination. Second, even if it is possible for groups to have rights, presumably the interests a group of citizens might have in controlling immigration are nowhere near as important as an individual's interest in having a decisive say regarding whom he or she marries. Let us consider these two issues in turn.

In response to concerns about the differences between individuals and groups, let me begin by highlighting some commonly held convictions which illustrate that we typically posit at least a presumptive group right to freedom of association. Think, for instance, of the controversy that has surrounded groups like the Boy Scouts of America or the Augusta National Golf Club, both of which have faced considerable public pressure and even legal challenges regarding their rights to freedom of association. In particular, some have contested the Boy Scouts' right to exclude homosexuals and atheists, while others have criticized Augusta National's exclusion of women.[3] These cases raise a number of thorny issues. We need not adjudicate either of these conflicts here,

however, because the requisite point for our purposes is a minimal one. Specifically, notice that even those who insist that the Boy Scouts should be legally forced to include gays and atheists or that Augusta National cannot justify their continued exclusion of women typically concede that there are weighty reasons in favor of allowing these groups to determine their own membership. That is, even activists lobbying for intervention usually acknowledge that there are reasons to respect these groups' rights to autonomy; the activists claim only that the prima facie case in favor of group self-determination is liable to be outweighed in sufficiently compelling instances (e.g., when society as a whole discriminates against women or privileges theism and heterosexuality over atheism and homosexuality). The key point, of course, is that questioning Augusta National's group right to determine its own membership does not require one to deny that groups have a presumptive right to freedom of association because one could simply assert that this presumptive right is vulnerable to being overridden. And because I seek at this stage to defend only a presumptive case in favor of a state's right to control its own borders, it is enough to note how uncontroversial it is to posit a group's right to freedom of association.

There is still room to question my slide from an individual's to a state's right to freedom of association, however, because, unlike the Boy Scouts and the Augusta National Golf Club, political states do not owe their membership to the autonomous choices of their constituents. The nonvoluntary nature of political states can raise complex problems for those who would defend a state's right to political self-determination (problems I address at length elsewhere), but here I would like merely to highlight some of the unpalatable implications that follow from denying a country's right to freedom of association.[4] In particular, consider the moral dynamics of regional associations like the North American Free Trade Agreement (NAFTA) or the European Union (EU). If legitimate states did not enjoy a right to freedom of association—a right which entitles them to decline invitations to associate with others—then they would not be in a position to either accept or reject the terms of these regional associations. Think of Canada's choice to join NAFTA, or Slovenia's decision to enter the EU, for instance.

No one believes that it would be permissible to force Canada into NAFTA or to coerce Slovenia to join the EU. (Of course, nor may Canada or Slovenia unilaterally insert themselves into these associations!) And the reason it is wrong to forcibly include these countries is because Canada's and Slovenia's rights to self-determination entitle them to associate (or not) with other countries as they see fit. Put plainly, if one denies that legitimate states like Canada and Slovenia have a right to freedom of association, one could not explain why they would be righteously aggrieved at being forced into these mergers.

Indeed, there would be even more awkward implications because, without positing a right to freedom of association, we could not satisfactorily explain what is wrong with one country forcibly annexing another. Imagine, for instance, that a series of plebiscites revealed both that an overwhelming majority of Americans wanted to merge with Canada and that an equally high proportion of Canadians preferred to maintain their independence. Would it be permissible for the United States to forcibly annex Canada? I assume without argument that, even if the United States could execute this unilateral merger without disrupting the peace or violating the individual rights of any Canadians, this hostile takeover would be impermissible. The crucial point for our purposes is that one cannot explain the wrongness of unilateral annexations like this unless one supposes that countries like Canada enjoy a right to autonomy, a right which accords Canadians the freedom to associate with others as they see fit.[5]

If the analysis to this point has been sound, then there is no reason to doubt that groups, even political states, can have rights to autonomy analogous to those enjoyed by individuals. Even if one agrees that legitimate states can have rights to self-determination, though, one might still question the argument sketched above on the grounds that the intimacy of marriage makes freedom of association immeasurably more important in the marital context than in the political realm. After all, in the vast majority of cases, fellow citizens will never even meet one another. On this point, consider Stuart White's contention that "if the formation of a specific association is essential to the individual's ability to exercise properly his/her liberties of conscience and expression, *or to his/her ability to form and enjoy intimate attachments,* then exclusion rules which are genuinely necessary to protect the association's primary purposes have an especially strong presumption of legitimacy."[6] Transposing White's reasoning, one might insist that, since there is no intimacy among compatriots, it is not at all clear why we need to respect freedom of association for groups of citizens.[7]

I concede that freedom of association is much more important for individuals in the marital context than for groups of citizens in the political realm, but my argument does not rely upon these two types of freedom of association being equally important. Notice, for instance, that being able to choose the associates with whom one worships is also less important than having discretion over one's marital partner, but no one concludes from this that we need not respect freedom of association in the religious realm. It is important to recognize that I seek at this stage to establish only that there is a prima facie case in favor of each legitimate state's right to control immigration (it will be the burden of the remainder of this article to show that competing considerations are not as weighty as one might think). Nonetheless, let me say a bit more about this presumptive case.

In my view, autonomous individuals and legitimate states both have rights to autonomy. This means that they occupy morally privileged positions of dominion over their self-regarding affairs. Such a position can be outweighed by sufficiently compelling considerations, of course, but in general people and states have a right to order their own affairs as they please. Freedom of association is not something that requires an elaborate justification, then, since it is simply one component of the self-determination which is owed to all autonomous individuals and legitimate states. As a consequence, I think that there is a very natural and straightforward case to be made in favor of freedom of association in all realms. Just as one need not explain how playing golf is inextricably related to the development of one's moral personality, say, in order to justify one's right to play golf, neither must one show that one's membership in a golf club is crucial to one's basic interests to establish the club members' right to freedom of association. And if no one doubts that golf clubs have a presumptive right to exclude others, then there seems no reason to suspect that a group of citizens cannot also have the right to freedom of association, even if control over membership in a country is not nearly as significant as control regarding one's potential spouse.

What is more, for several reasons it seems clear that control over membership in one's state is extremely important. To see this, think about why people might care about the membership rules for their golf club. It is tempting to think that club members would be irrational to care about who else are (or could become) members; after all, they are not forced to actually play golf with those members they dislike. But this perspective misses something important. Members of golf clubs typically care about the membership rules because they care about how the club is organized and the new members have a say in how the club is organized. Some members might want to dramatically increase the number of members, for instance, because the increased numbers will mean that each individual is required to pay less. Other members might oppose expanding the membership because of concerns about the difficulty of securing desirable tee times, the wear and tear on the course, and the increased time it takes to play a round if there are more people on the course at any given time.

And if there is nothing mysterious about people caring about who are (or could become) members of their golf clubs, there is certainly nothing irrational about people being heavily invested in their country's immigration policy. Again, to note the lack of intimacy among compatriots is to miss an important part of the story. It is no good to tell citizens that they need not personally (let alone intimately) associate with any fellow citizens they happen to dislike because fellow citizens nonetheless remain political associates; the country's course will be charted by the members of this civic association. The point is that people rightly care very deeply about their countries, and, as a consequence, they rightly care about those policies which will affect how these political communities evolve. And since a country's immigration policy affects who will share in controlling the country's future, it is a matter of considerable importance.

These examples of the golf club and the political state point toward a more general lesson that is worth

emphasizing: because the members of a group can change, an important part of group self-determination is having control over what the "self" is. In other words, unlike individual self-determination, a significant component of group self-determination is having control over the group which in turn gets to be self-determining. It stands to reason, then, that if there is any group whose self-determination we care about, we should be concerned about its rules for membership. This explains why freedom of association is such an integral part of the self-determination to which some groups (including legitimate states) are entitled. If so, then anyone who denies that we should care about the freedom of association of nonintimate groups would seem to be committed to the more sweeping claim that we should not care about the self-determination of any nonintimate groups. But, unless one implausibly believes that we should care only about intimate groups, then why should we suppose that only the self-determination of intimate groups matters? Thus, people rightly care deeply about their political states, despite these states being large, anonymous, and multicultural, and, as a consequence, people rightly care about the rules for gaining membership in these states. Or, put another way, the very same reasoning which understandably leads people to jealously guard their state's sovereignty also motivates them to keep an eye on who can gain membership in this sovereign state.

A second, less obvious, reason to care about immigration policy has to do with one's duties of distributive justice. As I will argue in the next section, it seems reasonable to think that we have special distributive responsibilities to our fellow citizens. If this is right, then in the same way that one might be reluctant to form intimate relationships because of the moral freight attached, one might want to limit the number of people with whom one shares a morally significant political relationship. Thus, just as golf club members can disagree about the costs and benefits of adding new members, some citizens might want to open the doors to new immigrants (e.g., in order to expand the labor force), while others would much rather forgo these advantages than incur special obligations to a greater number of people.

Finally, rather than continue to list reasons why citizens ought to care about issues of political membership, let me merely point out that citizens today obviously do care passionately about immigration. I do not insist that the current fervor over political membership is entirely rational, but it is worth noting that anyone who submits that freedom of association in this context is of no real importance is committed to labeling all those who care about this issue as patently irrational. Thus, even though the relationship among citizens does not involve the morally relevant intimacy of that between marital partners, the considerations quickly canvassed above, as well as the behavior of actual citizens, indicate that we need not conclude that control over immigration is therefore of negligible significance, If so, then neither the observation that (1) individual persons are importantly disanalogous to political states nor the fact that (2) freedom of association is much more important for individuals in the marital context than for groups of citizens in the political realm should lead us to abandon our initial comparison between marriage and immigration. As a consequence, we have no reason to abandon the claim that, like autonomous individuals, legitimate political regimes are entitled to a degree of self-determination, one important component of which is freedom of association. In sum, the conclusion initially offered only tentatively can now be endorsed with greater conviction: just as an individual has a right to determine whom (if anyone) he or she would like to marry, a group of fellow-citizens has a right to determine whom (if anyone) it would like to invite into its political community. And just as an individual's freedom of association entitles him or her to remain single, a state's freedom of association entitles it to exclude all foreigners from its political community.

Before turning to the case against political freedom of association, I would like to highlight two features of the view I am advancing here: (1) I defend a deontological right to limit immigration rather than a consequential account of what would be best, and (2) my view might be dubbed "universalist" rather than "particularist" insofar as it neither suggests nor implies that only distinct nations, cultures, or other "communities of character" are entitled to limit immigration. Consider each of these points in turn.

First, let me stress that I seek to defend a deontological conclusion about how legitimate states are entitled to act, not a consequential prescription for how to maximize happiness or a practical recipe for how states might best promote their own interests. I understand that groups can have weighty reasons to limit immigration in certain circumstances, but what the best policy would be for any given state's constituents (and or for those foreigners affected) will presumably depend upon a variety of empirical matters, matters about which others are more knowledgeable. Thus, I doubt that any one-size-fits-all immigration policy exists, and I, qua philosopher, have no special qualification to comment on the empirical information that would be relevant to fashioning the best policy for any given state. However, if anything, I am personally inclined toward more open borders. My parents were born and raised in different countries, so I would not even be here to write this article if people were not free to cross political borders. What is more, my family and I have profited enormously from having lived and worked in several different countries, so it should come as no surprise that I believe that, just as few individuals flourish in personal isolation, open borders are typically (and within limits) best for political communities and their constituents. Still, just as one might defend the right to divorce without believing that many couples should in fact separate, I defend a legitimate state's right to control its borders without suggesting that strict limits on immigration would necessarily maximize the interests of either the state's constituents or humanity as a whole. My aim is merely to show that whatever deontological reasons there are to respect freedom of association count in favor of allowing political communities to set their own immigration policy.

I hasten to emphasize, however, that, while I conceive of freedom of association in deontological terms, I do not thereby suppose that it is necessarily absolute. I consider freedom of association a deontological matter because it is something to which a party can be entitled (it is something to which people can have a moral right), and I do not believe that matters of entitlement can be adequately cashed out in exclusively consequential terms. In saying this, however, I do not thereby commit myself to the view that such a right must be perfectly general and absolute. A right can be independent of, and largely immune from, consequential calculus without being entirely invulnerable to being outweighed by all competing considerations. (Prince William has a right to marry anyone who will have him, for instance. And while this right gives him the discretion to marry any number of people, presumably it would be defeated if his marrying a particular person would set off a chain of events leading to World War III.) In this regard, my views tend to resemble those of W. D. Ross more than those of Immanuel Kant. Moreover, like Ross, I know of no algorithm for determining in advance when and under what circumstances a party's right to freedom of association would be defeated. In the end, then, I see nothing contradictory about conceiving of freedom of association as a deontological consideration (and thus of speaking of a right to choose one's associates) and simultaneously conceding that the case in favor of freedom of association is merely presumptive.

The second aspect of my account worth highlighting is that my defense of freedom of association makes no mention of a political community's distinctive character or culture. I emphasize this to distinguish myself from those who argue that ethnic, cultural, or national groups have a right to limit immigration in order to preserve their distinctive characters. In particular, the most compelling treatments of the morality of immigration with which I am familiar are Michael Walzer's seminal discussion of membership in *Spheres of Justice* and David Miller's recent article, "Immigration: The Case for Limits."[8] Other ways in which my account diverges from theirs will become apparent in due course; for now, notice that Walzer and Miller both emphasize the importance of preserving culture. As Walzer puts it: "Admission and exclusion are at the core of communal independence. They suggest the deepest meaning of self-determination. Without them, there could not be *communities of character,* historically stable, ongoing associations of men and women with some special commitment to one another and some special sense of their common life."[9]

In a similar vein, Miller suggests that "the public culture of their country is something that people have an interest in controlling: they want to be able to shape the way that their nation develops, including the values that are contained in the public culture."[10] He is especially interested in political groups being able to preserve their distinctive identities because he believes

that states must maintain a decent level of social solidarity in order to secure social justice. Unless compatriots sufficiently identify with one another, Miller argues, it is unlikely that the political climate will engender mutual trust or fellow feeling, elements liberal democratic states need if they are to inspire their constituents to make the sacrifices necessary to sustain a healthy democracy and an equitable welfare state.

In contrast to authors like Walzer and Miller, my account emphasizes that anyone is entitled to freedom of association. Thus, just as few would suggest that individuals have a right to marry only people of their own ethnicity, culture, nationality, or character, I do not believe that a group's right to limit immigration depends upon its members sharing any distinctive ethnic/cultural/national characteristics.

Now, I could certainly see why distinct cultural groups might in certain circumstances be more interested in or more inclined to exclude others, but I deny that they alone have the right to do so, since I believe that everyone—not just members of distinct nations—is entitled to freedom of association. To see why, think again of groups like the Boy Scouts or the Augusta National Golf Club. I presume that no one would suggest that the Boy Scouts are entitled to freedom of association only because they are all heterosexual theists or that Augusta National's claim to group autonomy depends upon their membership being all male. Indeed, if anything, it is just the opposite: the group autonomy of the Boy Scouts and Augusta National is challenged precisely because the former explicitly exclude gays and atheists and the latter has no female members. And since more diverse groups of scouts or golf club members would be at least equally entitled to freedom of association, there seems no reason to believe that only groups whose members share a distinctive characteristic are entitled to freedom of association. If so, then we need not suppose that only populations with distinct characters are entitled to limit immigration into their territories. To reiterate: even if it is true that countries whose populations understand themselves to be importantly distinct from (most) foreigners exhibit the greatest interest in excluding nonnatives, we should not infer from this that only these groups are entitled to control their territorial borders.

In sum, the commonly prized value of freedom of association provides the basic normative building blocks for a presumptive case in favor of each legitimate state's right to exclude others from its territory. But, while freedom of association provides a weighty consideration in favor of a state's right to limit immigration, it is obviously not the only value of importance. Thus, even if my reasoning to this point has been sound, the case in favor of a state's dominion is only presumptive and may be outweighed by competing considerations. With this in mind, let us now review the arguments in favor of open borders to see if they defeat a state's right to limit immigration.

II. THE EGALITARIAN CASE FOR OPEN BORDERS

Egalitarians survey the vast inequalities among states and then allege that it is horribly unjust that people should have such dramatically different life prospects simply because they are born in different countries. The force of this view is not difficult to appreciate. Given that one's country of birth is a function of brute luck, it seems grossly unfair that one's place of birth would so profoundly affect one's life prospects. Some believe that the solution is clear: political borders must be opened, so that no one is denied access to the benefits of wealthy societies. Although he couches his argument in terms of a principle of humanity rather than equality, Chandran Kukathas makes this point particularly forcefully: "A principle of humanity suggests that very good reasons must be offered to justify turning the disadvantaged away. It would be bad enough to meet such people with indifference and to deny them positive assistance. It would be even worse to deny them the opportunity to help themselves. To go to the length of denying one's fellow citizens the right to help those who are badly off, whether by employing them or by simply taking them in, seems even more difficult to justify—if, indeed, it is not entirely perverse."[11]

For several reasons, this case for open borders presents an especially imposing obstacle to the prima facie case for the right to restrict immigration outlined above. For starters, both its moral and empirical premises appear unexceptionable. How could one plausibly deny either that all humans are in some fundamental sense equally deserving of moral consideration or that the staggering inequalities across the globe dramatically affect people's prospects for living a decent life? Indeed, looked at from this perspective, sorting humans according to the countries in which they were born appears tantamount to a geographical caste system. As Joseph Carens famously argues: "Citizenship in Western liberal democracies is the modern equivalent to feudal privilege—an inherited status that greatly enhances one's life chances. Like feudal birthright privileges, restrictive citizenship is hard to justify when one thinks about it closely."[12] What is more, notice that advocating this position does not require one to deny the importance of freedom of association: an egalitarian who presses this objection can agree that we should generally be free to choose our associates, as long as the resulting associations do not lead to unjust arrangements. Thus, allowing states to limit immigration is regarded as problematic on this view only because countries cannot enjoy this form of freedom of association without people's life prospects being seriously affected by morally irrelevant matters, that is, factors entirely beyond their control.

Despite the intuitive appeal of this line of reasoning, I will counter this objection with two arguments. First, I suggest that the most compelling understanding of equality does not require us to guarantee that no one's life prospects are affected by matters of luck; more minimally, equality demands that we address those inequalities that render people vulnerable to oppressive relationships. If this is correct, then the particular theory of equality required to motivate the egalitarian case for open borders is suspect and should be rejected in favor of a theory of relational equality. Second, even if luck egalitarianism is the best theory of equality, it would not generate a duty to leave borders open, because a wealthy state's redistributive responsibilities can be discharged without including the recipients in the union. Consider each of these responses in turn.

I should begin by acknowledging the obvious appeal of luck egalitarianism. After all, it does seem unfair that some people's life prospects are dramatically worse than others when neither the poorly off nor the well off did anything to deserve their initial starting points. And it is hard to deny that the world would be better if everyone enjoyed roughly equal prospects for a rewarding life. It is important to recognize, though, that luck egalitarianism is not the only game in town. In *Political Philosophy,* for instance, Jean Hampton recommends an approach she ascribes to Aristotle: "We want, he says, a society in which people treat each other as equals (no one should be allowed to be the master of another or the slave of another) and in which these equals treat each other as partners—or 'civic friends.' The way to get that is to pursue not exact equality of resources but sufficient equality to ensure that no one is able to use his greater wealth to gain political advantage over others in a way that damages their partnership."[13]

Now, one might be struck by Hampton's suggestion that we need not pursue "exact" equality, but I want to call attention to another, related feature of her view: its relational nature. As Hampton emphasizes, Aristotle is concerned with equality because he sees it as necessary to sustain the desired relationships among fellow citizens. We need not concern ourselves with securing exact equality, then, because (political) relationships are not undermined by slight disparities in wealth; clearly, compatriots can interact as political equals even if some have more than others, regardless of whether or not their unequal resources are deserved.

Others share Hampton's preference for relational theories of equality, but no one, to my knowledge, has better motivated this approach than Elizabeth Anderson.[14] Key to Anderson's defense of relational equality is the question: "What is the point of equality?" In her view, answering this question reveals most clearly why relational theories are preferable to those which fixate on luck. The crucial point is that we should care about inequality principally to the extent that subordinates are dominated in oppressive relationships. For this reason, Anderson insists that we should be "fundamentally concerned with the relationships within which the goods are distributed, not only the distribution of goods themselves."[15]

To appreciate the force of this point, compare two possible inequalities. The first exists between two societies, A and B. Assume that everyone in A is equally well off; everyone in B is doing equally poorly; and no one in either A or B knows anything of the other society's existence, since they are on opposite sides of the earth and have never had any contact. The second inequality mirrors the disparity between the As and Bs, except that it exists within a single society C. And because the Cs share a single political community, not only are they aware that others are faring considerably better/worse but also their relationships are affected by these inequalities. I take it as uncontroversial that the inequality among the Cs is much more worrisome than the same inequality between the As and Bs. In other words, whether or not we should care about the inequality between the As and Bs, clearly we should be much more concerned to eliminate the inequality among the Cs. Based in part upon reasoning like this, Anderson concludes: "Negatively, people are entitled to whatever capabilities are necessary to enable them to avoid or escape entanglement in oppressive relationships. Positively, they are entitled to the capabilities necessary for functioning as an equal citizen in a democratic state."[16]

Arguments like Anderson's convince me that we should be keenly aware of the relationships within which the goods are distributed, but I stop short of concluding that relational equality is the one correct theory of equality. In my view, luck equality matters, but it matters considerably less than relational equality. In other words, although I would not hesitate to eliminate the inequality between the As and Bs if I could do so by waving a magic wand, this inequality is not sufficiently worrisome that I would necessarily interfere in the internal affairs of the As in order to eliminate the inequality between them and the Bs. However, because I am much more concerned about the inequality among the Cs, I would be correspondingly less reluctant to demand that the wealthy Cs take measures to ensure that the less well off Cs are not entangled in oppressive relationships.

As a consequence, while I do not think that there is nothing of moral consequence to be gained from realizing luck equality, I do accept a more modest claim: even if achieving relational equality is important enough to trump other values like freedom of association, realizing luck equality is not important enough to deny people their rights to self-determination. And this more modest conclusion has important implications for the morality of immigration. Most obviously, even if we would prefer a world with no inequality between the As and the Bs, eliminating this inequality is not important enough to justify limiting the As' right to freedom of association. In short, given that the moral importance of any particular inequality is a function of the relationship in which the goods are distributed, the lack of a robust relationship between the constituents of a wealthy state and the citizens of a poorer country implies that this admittedly lamentable inequality does not generate sufficient moral reasons to obligate the wealthy state to open its borders, even if nothing but luck explains why those living outside of the territorial borders have dramatically worse prospects of living a rewarding life.

Here two potential objections present themselves. First, although it is not false to say that the citizens of some countries are relatively well off while the constituents of others are relatively poorly off (as I do in my example of the As and Bs), this cryptic description is nonetheless misleading insofar as it fails to capture that, in the real world, those in the developed countries are staggeringly wealthy in comparison to the masses who are imperiled (when not outright killed) by eviscerating poverty. In short, given the radical inequality and objective plight that make Carens's reference to "feudal privilege" apt, it is not so easy to dismiss global inequality merely because it does not exist between compatriots. Second, because of the history of colonization, as well as the current levels of international trade (among other things), it is simply not the case that the world's wealthy and poor are unconnected and unaware of each other (as I stipulate in my example of the As and Bs). On the contrary, one consequence of the emerging global basic structure is that virtually all of the world's people now share some type of relationship, so presumably even relational egalitarians cannot dismiss the moral significance of global inequality. I think there are important truths in both of these objections, so I will consider each in turn.

To begin, the twin facts that the world's poor are so desperately needy and the world's wealthy are so spectacularly well off that they could effectively help the impoverished without sacrificing anything of real consequence is unquestionably morally significant, but in my mind these facts indicate that the real issue is not about equality. Rather than being exercised merely because some are relatively worse off through no fault of their own, we are (or at least should be) concerned simply because others are suffering in objectively horrible circumstances.[17] What is more, the reason that we may have a duty to help is not because mere luck explains why we are doing better than they (presumably we would be obligated to relieve their suffering even if our relative standing was fully attributable to morally relevant factors like our hard work). Instead, our duty to help stems most straightforwardly from samaritanism: one has a natural duty to assist others when they are sufficiently imperiled and one can help them at no unreasonable cost to oneself. As a result, I am inclined to respond to the first objection in disjunctive fashion: if the less well off Bs are not doing terribly badly in objective terms, then the inequality between the As and Bs does not generate a duty on the part of the As to help the Bs. If the Bs are clearly suffering in absolute poverty, on the other hand, then the As may indeed have stringent duties to help, but these duties spring from a samaritan source rather than from the mere fact that the As are (for morally arbitrary reasons) doing better than the Bs. If this is right, then even the previously unfathomable inequalities we now see in the real world do not sufficiently buttress the luck egalitarian's case for open borders.

Regarding the second objection, I am inclined to agree that the emerging global infrastructure entails that virtually all of us have increasingly substantial relationships with people all over the world. And as a relational egalitarian, it seems to follow that the more robust these relationships become, the more concerned we should be about the inequalities within them. But I can concede all of this without jettisoning my response to the egalitarian case for open borders because my account has never relied upon the claim that being fellow citizens of a country is the only morally relevant relationship. On the contrary, my account requires only that the less ambitious (and more plausible) claim that the relationship among compatriots is one relationship with morally relevant implications for inequality. To see the significance of this point, notice what I would say about inequalities within a particular state. Even though I think that the relationship shared among compatriots is relevant when assessing the inequalities among two people, I would never allege that no relationships within a state are morally relevant. Because familial relations are particularly liable to oppression, for instance, we might worry about the inequalities between wife and husband, between the parents and children, or among the children in a way that we would not among compatriots who are not members of the same family. For example, we would likely be less comfortable with a scenario in which a family paid for the sons but not the daughters to go to college than one in which one set of parents paid for the children's college expenses and another set of parents did not. Thus, there is nothing about my insistence on the moral relevance of the relationship among compatriots that forces me to deny the possibility of other relationships within the states which are significant for the purposes of inequality. And if I can acknowledge important relationships within a state, there seems no reason why I cannot accept that citizens of separate states can stand in relationships which matter from the point of equality. Most important, notice that conceding this last point does not undermine my response to the egalitarian case for open borders, because I can still insist that (whatever other relationships there are which matter from the standpoint of equality) the relationship between fellow citizens is one particularly important relationship which explains why we need not necessarily restrict the liberty of the better-off citizens in one country merely because nothing but luck explains why they are faring so much better than the citizens of a foreign state.

Finally, a persistent critic might counter that, even if the case based on luck egalitarianism fails, both samaritanism and the morally relevant relationships among foreigners explain why we have duties to those outside of our borders. In response, I suggest that these duties, even if stringent, can be fully satisfied without necessarily allowing those to whom we are duty bound entry to our country. That this is so will become apparent shortly when I explain why, even if luck egalitarianism is correct, it cannot shoulder the argumentative burden required of it by the case for open borders.

Before turning to this argument, though, it is worth noting that, while he does not use the luck/relational equality terminology, Walzer implicitly endorses the position on equality for which I am lobbying here. This occurs most clearly in his important discussion of Germany's bringing in "guest workers" from countries like Turkey. Here Walzer argues that, while Germans are not morally obligated to admit these workers, they nonetheless may not bring the workers in as political subordinates. He writes: "Democratic citizens, then, have a choice: if they want to bring in new workers, they must be prepared to enlarge their own membership; if they are unwilling to accept new members, they must find ways within the limits of the domestic labor market to get socially necessary work done. And those are their only choices."[18]

Now at first glance Walzer's position seems curious. After all, if prospective immigrants have no right to entry, how can they have a conditional right to equality if admitted? (By comparison, if Miriam has no right that Patrick sell her his gently used copy of *Spheres of Justice,* presumably Miriam would thereby also lack the conditional right to a cheap price if Patrick chose to sell it to her.) One would think that the right to equal treatment either gives the prospective workers a right to equal citizenship within Germany or it does not, but it could not generate a conditional right which depends upon the choice of the Germans. Reflecting upon the distinction between luck and relational theories of equality shows why this is not so, however. Walzer's positing a conditional right to equality-if-admitted makes perfect sense if he is implicitly presuming a relational theory of equality (as I believe he is), because such a theory implies that the same inequalities which would clearly be pernicious among compatriots might well be benign when present between foreigners. Thus, there is nothing inconsistent about Walzer's voicing no objection to an inequality between Germans and Turks, on the one hand, and objecting to this same inequality when it exists between two people (whatever their nationality) subject to the same political community within Germany, on the other hand.

In light of Walzer's analysis, we are now in a position to conclude the first prong of our critique of the egalitarian case for open borders with two points.

First, this case depends upon a particular theory of equality, luck egalitarianism, which leading theorists have rejected on grounds that have nothing to do with immigration. Second, without explicitly weighing in on this topic, one of the most prominent and sophisticated discussions of immigration implicitly endorses relational equality by staking out positions which presuppose that the moral importance of any inequality is a function not only of its magnitude but also of the relationship in which the goods are distributed. For the sake of argument, however, let us assume that I am wrong to criticize luck egalitarianism. Suppose that luck egalitarianism is the best theory of equality, or that securing luck equality is as least as important as securing relational equality, or at the very least that realizing luck equality is sufficiently important to justify restricting people's rights to freedom of association. Even if we grant one of these assumptions, it would still not follow that legitimate states are therefore not entitled to freedom of association. To see why, consider how marital freedom of association is typically combined with the demands of domestic distributive justice.

Even the most zealous critics of inequality typically recommend neither that we must abolish marriage nor that wealthy couples must literally open up their marriages to the less well off. Instead, it is standard to keep separate our rights to freedom of association and our duties of distributive justice, so that wealthy people are able to marry whomever they choose and then are required to transfer a portion of their wealth to others no matter whom (or even whether) they marry. Admittedly, history includes radical movements like the Khmer Rouge, who abolished marriage because it was thought to be inconsistent with their quest for complete equality, but most egalitarians rightly shy away from this degree of fanaticism. Indeed, consider this: despite the enormous disagreement about what type of responsibilities the likes of Bill Gates and Warren Buffet have in virtue of their staggering wealth, no one alleges that, unlike the rest of us, these billionaires are required to marry poor spouses. And just as our domestic redistribution of wealth among individuals has not led us to prohibit marriage, global redistribution does not require us to open all political borders. Instead, even if we presume that wealthy societies have extensive distributive duties, these duties are distinct and can be kept separate from the societies' rights to freedom of association. To reiterate: if wealthy couples need not open up their marriages to those less well off, why think that wealthy countries must open their borders to less fortunate immigrants? Just as relatively wealthy families are required merely to transfer some of their wealth to others, why cannot wealthy countries fully discharge their global distributive duties without including the recipients in their political union, simply by transferring the required level of funds abroad?

Thus, no matter how substantial their duties of distributive justice, wealthier countries need not open their borders. At most, affluent societies are duty bound to choose between allowing needy foreigners to enter their society or sending some of their wealth to those less fortunate. . . .

Even if legitimate states have no duty to open their borders to the world's poor, however, surely it would be unconscionable for a state to slam its doors on people desperately fleeing unjust regimes. After all, even authors like Walzer, who are in general prepared to defend a state's right to control its membership, make an exception for refugees.[19] The core idea behind this exception is that, unlike those who merely lack exportable resources, some asylum seekers are actively threatened by their states, and thus they cannot be helped by an international transfer of goods; their only escape from peril is to be granted asylum.

As implausible as it might initially seem, I suggest that, even in cases of asylum seekers desperately in need of a political safe haven, a state is not required to take them in. I adopt this stance not because I am unmoved by the plight of asylum seekers but because I am not convinced that the only way to help victims of political injustice is by sheltering them in one's political territory. In my view, these people might also be helped in something like the fashion in which wealthy societies could choose to assist impoverished foreigners: by, as it were, exporting justice. Admittedly, one cannot ship justice in a box, but one can intervene, militarily if necessary, in an unjust political environment to ensure that those currently vulnerable to the state are made safe in their homelands. Let me be clear: I am not suggesting that this is always easy or even advisable, nor do I assert that states are necessarily obligated to take this course of action. I claim instead that where asylum seekers are genuinely left vulnerable because their government is either unable or unwilling to protect their basic rights, then their government is illegitimate, it has no claim to political self-determination, and thus it stands in no position to protest if a third party were to intervene on behalf of (some of) its constituents. Think, for instance, of the Kurds in Iraq. One way to help them is to allow them to emigrate en masse. Another option, though, is to use military force to create a safe haven and nofly zone in Northern Iraq. And since the Iraqi government was the party threatening the Kurds, it had no right to object to this interference with its sovereignty. I suspect that Walzer stops short of this conclusion only because he wrongly, I think, respects the political self-determination of virtually all states, even those persecuting asylum seekers.

Walzer and I diverge on this point, then, not because I am less impressed than he by the plight of asylum seekers but because he is more impressed than I by the claims to political self-determination of failed and rogue states, those regimes either unable or unwilling to secure their citizens' basic moral rights. Thus, I once again conclude that affluent societies have a duty to help but that it is a disjunctive duty: just as global poverty requires wealthy states to either export aid or import unfortunate people, the presence of those desperately seeking political asylum renders those of us in just political communities duty bound either to grant asylum or to ensure that these refugees no longer need fear their domestic regimes. Miller seems to me to get it just right when he suggests: "The lesson for other states, confronted with people whose lives are less than decent, is that they have a choice: they must either ensure that the basic rights of such people are protected in the places where they live—by aid, by intervention, or by some other means—or they must help them to move to other communities where their lives will go better. Simply shutting one's borders and doing nothing else is not a morally defensible option here."[20]

Before turning to what might be called the "libertarian" case for open borders, I would like to emphasize that nothing in the preceding critique of the egalitarian

case for open borders is intended as a rejection of egalitarianism or as a defense of the status quo. On the contrary, I believe that most of us in affluent societies have pressing restitutive, samaritan, and egalitarian duties to do considerably more to help the masses of people in the world tragically imperiled by poverty, and I even think that one good way to provide this assistance is to allow more immigrants from poorer countries. If sound, the arguments of this section establish merely that egalitarian considerations do not by themselves generate a moral duty which requires wealthy countries to open their borders, in part because the egalitarian case for open borders depends upon a suspect theory of equality, but also because wealthy countries have the discretion to discharge their distributive responsibilities in other manners.

III. THE LIBERTARIAN CASE FOR OPEN BORDERS

To motivate the libertarian case for open borders, Carens imagines the following scenario. "Suppose a farmer from the United States wanted to hire workers from Mexico. The government would have no right to prohibit him from doing this. To prevent the Mexicans from coming would violate the rights of both the American farmer and the Mexican workers to engage in voluntary transactions.[21] As this example illustrates, libertarian arguments against restricting immigration can take either of two forms, depending upon whether they focus on property rights or rights to free movement. The former emphasizes the rights of those within the state and contends that limiting immigration violates individual property owners' rights to invite foreigners to visit their private property. The latter stresses the rights of foreigners, claiming that closing territorial borders wrongly restricts an individual's right to freedom of movement.

According to the first type of argument, states may not limit immigration because doing so wrongly restricts their constituents' rights to private property. The appeal of this idea is apparent: if a farmer owns a piece of property, then she occupies a position of moral dominion over that land which gives her the discretion to determine who may and who may not enter that land. If the farmer's government denies foreigners access to its political territory, however, then it thereby effectively denies the farmer the right to invite foreigners onto her land. Thus, since a state cannot limit immigration to its territory without also limiting its constituents' property rights, political communities clearly are not morally entitled to control who crosses their borders.

It is worth noting that this argument is not skeptical of the moral importance of freedom of association; it merely questions why the state should get to enjoy this right when its doing so necessarily limits the ability of its individual constituents to do so. In a conflict between an individual's right versus a state's right, a libertarian will typically argue that the individual's right should take precedence. When the state as a whole gets to limit immigration, however, its doing so effectively curtails the rights of its citizens to unilaterally invite foreigners onto their land. And because inviting others to join one on one's privately owned land is one type of freedom of association, it is impossible to grant a state the right to control its borders without stripping property owners of their rights to freedom of association. So if either party should have priority in claiming the right to freedom of association, it is the individual, not the state.

In response, I concede that there is a conflict between a state's sovereignty over its territory and an individual property owner's dominion over her land, but in this case I am inclined to favor the claims of a (duly limited) state. I am a staunch defender of individual self-determination, but the crucial point here is that one cannot consistently insist that property rights are totally unlimited without committing oneself to anarchism. This is because political states are functionally incompatible with extending unlimited dominion to their constituents. States must be sufficiently territorially contiguous in order to perform their requisite functions, and achieving contiguity requires them to nonconsensually coerce all those within their territorial borders. Thus, while it is perfectly intelligible to claim that individual dominion should always take precedence over state sovereignty,

one cannot maintain this position without implicitly endorsing anarchism. To reiterate, effective political society would not be possible unless some crucial decisions were made by the group as a whole, and (as this example of the conflict between a state's controlling its territory and an individual controlling her land indicates) all areas of group sovereignty imply a corresponding lack of individual dominion. In light of this, I suggest that, in the choice between unlimited property rights and the anarchy it entails versus limited property rights and the statism is allows, one should favor the latter.

Of course, one might eschew anarchism and still suggest that individual property rights take precedence over a state's right to control its borders, but this position would require an additional argument designed specifically to show why the individual should take precedence over the group in matters of freedom of association. We should not presume in advance that such an argument could not be furnished, but there are several reasons to be skeptical of this approach.

To begin, notice that, in matters unrelated to immigration, we take it for granted that the group as a whole has a right to freedom of association. Consider again, for instance, Canada's participation in NAFTA or Slovenia's membership in the European Union. In these cases, everyone acknowledges that Canadians as a whole must determine whether they would like to join NAFTA and that Slovenians as a group should decide whether or not Slovenia will enter the EU. If each individual's right to freedom of association must always take precedence over the group's, on the other hand, then it follows that every single Canadian had the right to veto Canada's involvement in NAFTA or a single Slovenian citizen would be entitled unilaterally to block Slovenia's membership in the EU. I presume without argument that this position is untenable. And if no one thinks that individuals have the right to veto their county's entrance into associations like NAFTA or the EU, then we seem similarly committed to denying that individuals have the right to veto their country's immigration policy.

At this point one might answer that a country's limiting immigration is in principle distinct from joining NAFTA, the EU, or even the merger between East and West Germany because the latter three are all acts of association, whereas restricting immigration is a refusal to associate. The idea is that, of course an individual may not appeal to the value of freedom of association to criticize any of these mergers because each expands her possibilities for association. But this carries no implications for whether an individual might rightfully object to her state's restricting immigration, which limits the people with whom one may associate.

The distinction between expanding and limiting association is a real one, but I nonetheless doubt that it will do the necessary work. To see why, consider an uncontested secession like Norway's break from Sweden in 1905. In this case, more than 99 percent of the Norwegians voted in favor of political divorce and Sweden as a country did not resist the separation.[22] Whatever one thinks about the justifiability of statebreaking, this seems like a paradigmatic case of permissible secession. If each individual's right to freedom of association trumps the state's right to self-determination in those cases in which the group as a whole seeks to disassociate from others, however, then Norway's secession was unjustified; it was impermissible because every last Norwegian (if not also each Swede) had the right unilaterally to veto the political divorce and the plebiscite in favor of separation did not garner unanimous consent. Again, I presume without argument that this position is implausible. And if an individual's claim to freedom of association does not trump her state's right in the case of secession, there seems good reason to believe that an individual's right would be equally impotent in the realm of immigration.

A second reason to doubt that an individual's dominion over her private property takes precedence over the state's control of its territorial borders stems from the twin facts that (1) an inability to invite foreigners onto one's land is typically not an onerous imposition and (2) bringing outsiders into the political community has real consequences for one's compatriots. I will explain below why being unable to invite foreigners onto one's land is in most cases not a huge limitation of one's dominion over one's property. To appreciate why inviting foreigners to live permanently on one's property has consequences for others, one need only reflect upon the implications of the relational theory of equality outlined above. In particular, recall Walzer's conclusion that affluent societies have no obligation to invite guest workers into their territory but that they are obligated to treat as political equals all those they do admit. The idea here is that once an individual enters the territory and becomes subject to the dictates of the state, she becomes more vulnerable than outsiders to political oppression. Thus, Walzer rightly concludes that all those who enter the territory for an indefinite period must be welcomed as equal members of the political community. If so, however, this explains why a person's inviting foreigners onto her land has important moral implications for all of the state's citizens. This invitation does not merely entitle the invitee to stay on one's land; it morally requires all of one's fellow citizens to share the benefits of equal political standing with this new member of the political community. And because the costs of extending the benefits of political membership can be substantial, it makes sense that each individual should not have the right unilaterally to invite in as many foreigners as she would like. It is only appropriate that the group as a whole should decide with whom the benefits of membership should be shared.[23]

Although I think the preceding considerations show why the libertarian is wrong to assume that the state's right to freedom of association must give way to individual property rights, I do think there is room for an intermediate position that accommodates in a principled way both associational and property rights, giving each right its due. And this is important because a state should not restrict individual dominion any more than is necessary. In particular, while I am skeptical that an individual has the right to invite foreigners to live on her land indefinitely, I do not see why property owners may not invite outsiders to visit for limited periods. In fact, one need not even object to a guest worker arrangement, as long as the worker does not stay too long. Indeed, this strikes me as an appealing compromise, because allowing for these sponsored visits gives property owners greater dominion over their land than the status quo without creating any additional imposition upon their compatriots (since citizens are not obligated to extend the benefits of political membership to those foreigners visiting for a limited amount of time). What is more, this solution enables us to avoid the standard practical problem of foreigners entering the country on a limited visa and then staying indefinitely, because the state could require the property owner to be responsible (putting up collateral, perhaps) for all those she invites to visit. In the end, then, I am inclined to conclude that a property owner's dominion over her land might well entitle her to invite foreigners to visit her land but that it would not justify a more sweeping curtailment of a state's right to control immigration into its territory. And once we make room for this additional right for property owners, one gets a better sense of why the remaining restrictions upon their dominion over their property is rarely terribly onerous.

At this stage a libertarian might concede all that I have argued so far and still insist that states may not restrict immigration, not because doing so unjustifiably limits the property rights of its citizens but because it violates foreigners' rights to freedom of movement. Surely each of us has a right to migrate as we please; if not, then states would be justified prohibiting emigration or even free migration within the country. And just as our rights to freedom of movement allow us to leave or travel within our country, they entitle us to enter other countries as well. As Carens emphasizes: "No liberal state restricts internal mobility. Those states that do restrict internal mobility are criticized for denying basic human freedoms. If freedom of movement within the state is so basic that it overrides the claims of local political communities, on what grounds can we restrict freedom of movement across states?"[24] Thus, unless one is prepared to accept a state's right to deny either emigration or internal migration, consistency appears to demand that states not limit immigration either.

My response to this second prong of the libertarian case for open borders is analogous to my arguments above: I concede that there is a right to freedom of movement, and I certainly believe that states must take great care not to violate the individual rights of either constituents or foreigners, but I do not think that the right to free movement is perfectly general and absolute. My right to freedom of movement does not entitle me to enter your house without your permission, for instance, so why think that this right

gives me a valid claim to enter a foreign country without that country's permission? Some might counter that this response essentially denies the right in question, but this is not so. No one says that I am denied my right to marriage merely because I cannot unilaterally choose to marry you against your will. So, just as my freedom of association in the marital realm remains intact despite your right to not associate with me, there seems no reason why my right to freedom of movement does not similarly remain intact despite foreign states' retaining the right to exclude me. . . .

I am no more impressed by the second prong of the libertarian case for open borders than by the first. In both instances, the libertarian gestures toward an important right, but the existence of this right could defeat the presumptive case for a state's claim to control its borders only if the right is wrongly presumed to be perfectly general and absolute. In the end, then, neither the egalitarian nor the libertarian case for open borders undermines the case that can be made on behalf of a legitimate state's right to restrict immigration.

IV. A QUESTION OF CRITERIA

In *Who Are We?* Samuel Huntington worries not only about the raw number of immigrants entering the United States but is especially concerned that so many are from Mexico.[25] He views the United States as defined not just in terms of its distinctive American creed but also by its Anglo-Protestant culture. Thus, unless it more stringently limits the flow of Mexican immigrants, America will forever lose its distinctive—and distinctly valuable—character. This provocative proposal raises a difficult and important question. . . . Assuming that states have the right to control who, if anyone, may enter their territories, does it follow that a country may adopt a policy that explicitly excludes people based upon their race, religion or ethnicity? What if a country wanted to admit only whites, for instance? This question is especially difficult, I think, because, if the state is genuinely at liberty to exclude everyone, how could an applicant righteously complain about not being admitted?

On the other hand, most take it for granted that, even if a business is not required to hire anyone, it may not adopt a policy to hire only whites. And if a company cannot select employees in this way, presumably a state may not screen potential immigrants according to this type of criterion. . . .

I would like to suggest an . . . explanation as to why states may not limit immigration according to racist criteria.[26] In doing so, I will focus upon the rights of those already within the political community rather than the rights of those who might want to enter. I shift the emphasis from foreign immigrants to citizens of the state whose policy is in question because, given the relational theory of equality detailed above, it makes sense to presume that we may have responsibilities to our compatriots that we do not equally owe to foreigners. In particular, we have a special duty to respect our fellow citizens as equal partners in the political cooperative. With this in mind, I suggest that a country may not institute an immigration policy which excludes entry to members of a given race because such a policy would wrongly disrespect those citizens in the dispreferred category.

Even if we assume that there is a special responsibility not to treat one's compatriots as less than equal partners, someone might still question how an immigration policy (which cannot evict any current citizens) could possibly affect any of a state's constituents. To see how such a policy might disrespect existing citizens, consider the analogous situation from the familial context. Rather than focusing upon racists who are unwilling to marry outside of their race, imagine a family of two white parents with two children, one white and another black. (For the purposes of this thought-experiment, imagine that white parents sometimes gave birth to black children, and vice versa.) Now, imagine the parents announcing that, as much as they would love to have a third child, they have decided against it for fear that she might be black. I take it as obvious how hurtful this announcement could be to the existing black child, even though the decision not to have any additional children obviously does not threaten his or her chances of coming into existence. In light of this analogy, it is not difficult to see how [a] black . . . , for instance, might feel disrespected by

an immigration policy banning entry to nonwhites. Even though this policy in and of itself in no way threatens blacks with expulsion, it sends a clear message that, qua blacks, they are not equally valued as partners in the political union. . . .

A possible exception to this rule might be a religious state like Israel. When a country is designed as a state for Jews, it might be thought entirely appropriate to deny non-Jews entry. I am not so sure about this conclusion, however, because I do not see why a state's being designed to cater especially to a specific group should license it to disrespect those subjects not in the favored group. Thus, assuming that I am right that barring all but Jewish immigrants would treat the current non-Jewish citizens as less than equal members of the political community, only a state that was completely Jewish could permissibly adopt such an anti-non-Semitic immigration policy.

Of course, in the case of Israel, the moral horror of the holocaust makes it tempting to accept an immigration policy that excludes non-Semites. After all, as Hannah Arendt famously emphasized, an early but crucial step toward rendering the Jews vulnerable to inhumane treatment was stripping them of their citizenship. Against the backdrop of this tragic history, the idea of a state prepared to act as a safe haven for all and only Jews might seem unobjectionable. In my view, however, while this type of consideration could well justify Israel's controversial Law of Return (which automatically grants admission to all Jews), it would not justify Israel's admitting all and only Jews. An immigration policy that summarily rejected all non-Jews might be acceptable for a state which included no non-Jewish subjects, but because roughly 20 percent of Israel's population is not Jewish, it may not adopt such an immigration policy. Even a wrong that follows on the heels of the utterly horrific wrong of the holocaust (like all second wrongs) does not make a right. To emphasize: whether or not we are sympathetic to the idea of a state designed especially to serve a specific racial, ethnic, or religious constituency, such a state is not exempt from the requirement to treat all of its subjects as equal citizens. So if I am right that restricting immigration according to racial, ethnic, or religious criteria wrongs the current subjects in the banned groups, then only a state completely devoid of people in the banned category could permissibly institute this type of immigration policy. . . .

V. CONCLUSION

In this article I have tried first to construct a presumptive case in favor of a state's right to set its own immigration policy and then to defend this prima facie case against the formidable arguments that have been made on behalf of open borders. If my arguments are sound, then we should conclude that, even if egalitarians are right that those of us in wealthy societies have demanding duties of global distributive justice and even if libertarians are correct that individuals have rights both to freedom of movement and to control their private property, legitimate states are entitled to reject all potential immigrants, even those desperately seeking asylum from corrupt governments.[27]

NOTES

1. Stuart White, "Freedom of Association and the Right to Exclude," *Journal of Political Philosophy* 5 (1997): 373–91, 373.

2. David Gauthier, "Breaking Up: An Essay on Secession," *Canadian Journal of Philosophy* 24 (1994): 357–92, 360–61.

3. Some also object to the Boy Scouts' refusal to admit girls.

4. For an extended discussion of some of the issues associated with group autonomy, see chap. 3 of my book *A Theory of Secession* (New York: Cambridge University Press, 2005).

5. Here one might be tempted to object that Canada's right to independence is more straightforwardly accounted for in terms of its right to self-determination. But, as I shall argue below, it is misleading to contrast freedom of association with self-determination because freedom of association is actually a central component of the more general right to self-determination. In the case of political states, for instance, a state cannot fully enjoy the right to political self-determination unless its rights to freedom of association are respected.

6. White, "Freedom of Association and the Right to Exclude," 381 (emphasis added).

7. It should be noted White is not necessarily committed to this line of argument because his analysis is explicitly restricted to "secondary" groups (which I take to be groups within states) which adopt "categorical" exclusion (i.e., exclusion based upon an individual's race, gender, sexuality, or religion).

8. See Michael Walzer, *Spheres of Justice* (New York: Basic, 1983), 31–63; and David Miller, "Immigration: The Case for Limits," in *Contemporary Debates in Applied Ethics,* ed. Andrew I. Cohen and Christopher Heath Wellman (Malden, MA: Blackwell, 2005), 193–206. In *Toward a Theory of Immigration* (New York: Palgrave, 2001), the only monograph I know of which defends a state's right to craft its own immigration policy, Peter Meilander takes a similar tack, arguing that legitimate national identities have a right to defend themselves against the threat posed by immigration.

9. Walzer, *Spheres of Justice,* 62.

10. Miller, "Immigration: The Case for Limits," 200. Miller also stresses the role that limiting immigration can play in curbing population growth, but his flagship argument features the importance of preserving culture.

11. Chandran Kukathas, "The Case for Open Immigration," in Cohen and Wellman, *Contemporary Debates in Applied Ethics,* 207–20, 211.

12. Joseph H. Carens, "Aliens and Citizens: The Case for Open Borders," *Review of Politics* 49 (1987): 251–73, 252.

13. Jean Hampton, *Political Philosophy* (Boulder, CO: Westview, 1996), 158.

14. Other prominent defenses include David Miller, "What Kind of Equality Should the Left Pursue?" in *Equality,* ed. Jane Franklin (London: Institute for Public Policy Research, 1997), 83–99; Jonathan Wolff, "Fairness, Respect, and the Egalitarian Ethos," *Philosophy & Public Affairs* 27 (1998): 97–122; Andrew Mason, "Equality, Personal Responsibility, and Gender Socialisation," *Proceedings of Aristotelian Society* 100 (1999–2000): 227–46; and Samuel Scheffler, "What Is Egalitarianism?" *Philosophy & Public Affairs* 31 (2003): 5–39.

15. Elizabeth S. Anderson, "What Is the Point of Equality?" *Ethics* 109 (1999):287–337, 314.

16. Ibid., 316.

17. Harry Frankfurt makes a similar point in "Equality as a Moral Ideal," *Ethics* 98 (1987): 21–43.

18. Walzer, *Spheres of Justice,* 61.

19. It is important to note, though, that those who make an exception for refugees (as defined by international law) apparently cannot do so on principled grounds. As theorists like Andrew Shacknove and Michael Dummett have pointed out, restricting the status of refugees to those who have crossed an international border because of a wellfounded fear of persecution is morally arbitrary. See Andrew Shacknove, "Who Is a Refugee?" *Ethics* 95 (1985): 274–84; and Michael Dummett, *On Immigration and Refugees* (New York: Routledge, 2001).

20. Miller, "Immigration: The Case for Limits," 198.

21. Carens, "Aliens and Citizens: The Case for Open Borders," 253.

22. In a referendum in August of 1905, 368,392 Norwegians voted in favor of political divorce and only 184 voted against.

23. One might object that this argument presumes a relational theory of equality, which a libertarian might reject. I do not worry about this argument's reliance upon the relational theory of equality, however, both because those drawn to libertarianism are likely to be much less uncomfortable with relational egalitarianism than with luck egalitarianism and because one cannot summarily dismiss all concerns regarding inequality on the grounds that they require some type of positive rights unless one is willing to embrace anarchism (since statism also requires the existence of positive rights).

24. Carens, "Aliens and Citizens: The Case for Open Borders," 267.

25. Samuel Huntington, *Who Are We?* (New York: Simon & Schuster, 2004).

26. The view I advance here is similar to that which Michael Blake develops in "Immigration," in *A Companion to Applied Ethics,* ed. R. G. Frey and Christopher Heath Wellman (Malden, MA: Blackwell, 2003), 224–37.

27. I am extremely grateful for the constructive criticism I received from two anonymous reviewers and the editors of this journal. In addition to audiences at Washington University, University of Missouri, and Australian National University, I am indebted to Andrew Altman, Michael Blake, Joseph Carens, Thomas Christiano, Andrew I. Cohen, Robert Goodin, John Kleinig, Chandran Kukathas, David Lefkowitz, Matt Lister, Larry May, David Miller, Mathias Risse, Alex Sager, Fernando Teson, Andrew Valls, and Carl Wellman for their written comments on earlier drafts of this essay. Above all, I would like to thank the Earhart Foundation for generously supporting my work on this project.

READING QUESTIONS

1. What is the right of association as Wellman explains it? How does he defend this right?
2. What reasons does Wellman give for rejecting the idea that the preservation of one's culture is a firm basis for a policy of closed borders?
3. In his discussion of egalitarian reasons for open immigration, Wellman distinguishes two notions of equality: luck equality and relational equality. What is the difference between these two notions?
4. Why does Wellman think that egalitarian considerations—whether based on luck equality or relational equality—fail to create an *obligation* for wealthy states to open their borders to immigration?
5. One libertarian argument in favor of open borders focuses on property rights of individuals. Explain this argument and Wellman's response to it.
6. Another libertarian argument focuses on an individual's freedom of movement which, according to this line of argument, gives foreigners a right to migrate. How does Wellman respond to this argument?
7. What reasons does Wellman offer for rejecting racial considerations as a basis for denying immigration to members of one or another race?

DISCUSSION QUESTIONS

1. Wellman uses the examples of families, golf clubs, and other such associations, which arguably have a right to exclude individuals from joining these associations, to make a case for a similar right of nation-states to adopt a policy of closed borders. Are there significant differences between the associations in question and nation-states that weaken Wellman's argument?
2. Explain why you agree or disagree with Wellman that nation-states have a right to exclude refugees from migrating and seeking citizenship in those states.
3. Do the basic rights of human beings include a right to immigrate to a nation-state of their choice? If not, why not? If so, how would this affect Wellman's position on immigration?

SARAH FINE

Freedom of Association Is Not the Answer

As the title indicates, Sarah Fine's article is a direct response to Wellman's. After outlining Wellman's case for a state's right to close its borders, Fine raises of number of objections to Wellman's view. One of her objections concerns the harm to foreigners that may result from a policy of exclusion. She believes that this harm is so substantial that it may trump a state's right to close its borders, contrary to Wellman. She also points out that the compelling case for freedom of association when it comes to marriage and religion, which figure importantly in Wellman's argument, are intimate or expressive associations, hence arguably protected from admitting outsiders. But, she argues, it is very doubtful that the aggregate of a nation's citizens constitutes either an intimate or an expressive association. Fine also contends that absent an argument for the claim that states have territorial rights over what they claim for themselves, Wellman's argument from association cannot alone establish a right for a state to close it borders to would-be immigrants.

Cosmopolitan liberals have long argued that, contrary to prevailing practices and assumptions, there is a tension between liberal principles, on the one hand, and the coercively enforced borders and exclusive membership practices that are familiar features of nation states, on the other hand.[1] In that vein, it has become common to emphasize the liberal commitments to universalism and moral equality and to highlight the moral arbitrariness of birth place in order to question the relevance of borders in relation to a person's rights and opportunities. It is notable, too, that liberal principles are often regarded as the universalist antidote to the more particularist or exclusionary tendencies of the other features (sovereignty, nationality, democracy) that make up the modern state.

This is one of the reasons why Christopher Heath Wellman's article "Immigration and Freedom of Association" is so novel and interesting: Wellman puts forward what appears to be a distinctly liberal case for the state's right to exclude would-be immigrants.[2] As Wellman points out, we must not overlook the potentially exclusionary implications of the liberal commitment to freedom of association. There is a widespread and apparently uncontroversial view of the relationship between freedom of association and exclusion: few would argue with Amy Gutmann's statement that "the freedom to associate . . . entails the freedom to exclude."[3] Thus, if Wellman can establish that states—like individuals—should enjoy the freedom to associate and that this includes a right to exclude prospective members, then we would have clear foundations at least for the state's prima facie right to exclude.

In fact, Wellman's position appears to be doubly contentious; not only does he make a liberal case for a right to exclude voluntary immigrants, but he also maintains that states actually have the right to "close [their] doors to all potential immigrants, even refugees desperately seeking asylum from incompetent

From Sarah Fine, "Freedom of Association Is Not the Answer," *Ethics* 120 (2010): 338–356.

or corrupt political regimes that are either unable or unwilling to protect their citizens' basic moral rights" (300). In this respect he seems to go further than other progressive political philosophers who have offered more qualified defenses of immigration restrictions.[4] In short, this is a bold argument, which makes a significant contribution to a most topical debate.

I outline the key points of Wellman's two-stage argument in Section I. In Sections II and III, I develop an internal critique of Wellman's position. The main target of my response is his central claim that "the commonly prized value of freedom of association provides the basic normative building blocks for a presumptive case in favor of each legitimate state's right to exclude others from its territory" (306). I highlight the way in which exclusion has the potential to harm the interests of would-be immigrants, and I point out some crucial distinctions between the state and associations in civil society.[5] In Section IV, I contend that, beyond the issues of external harm and the distinctiveness of the state, a successful defense of the state's right to exclude others from its territory could not rest on the appeal to freedom of association alone: it also would require a justification of the state's territorial rights, something that is conspicuous by its absence from Wellman's argument. The search for the normative foundations of the state's purported right to exclude would-be immigrants continues: freedom of association is not the answer.

I

There are two main steps on Wellman's path to the conclusion that states have the right to exclude all prospective immigrants. First, he seeks to establish that there is a prima facie case for the state's right to exclude; second, he aims to illustrate that the presumption in favor of a right to exclude is not outweighed by potentially competing "egalitarian" and "libertarian" considerations.

Wellman's case for a presumptive right to exclude is quite straightforward. He begins with the claim that everybody seems to think freedom of association is

important. Taking marriage and religion as his central examples, Wellman draws attention to the widespread agreement that people should be free to choose their own (willing) marital partners and their own (willing) religious associates. This, he suggests, is indicative of a common conviction "that each of us enjoys a morally privileged position of dominion over our self-regarding affairs," or, in short, a commitment to individual self-determination (300). The freedom to associate is part of what it means to be self-determining.

And what does a commitment to freedom of association imply? Wellman contends that it includes "the right not to associate and even, in many cases, the right to disassociate" (300). Freedom of marital association, for example, comprises a right to marry a willing partner but also the right not to marry a given suitor and even not to marry anyone. Freedom of religious association similarly means a right to associate with consenting others for religious purposes, as well as the right not to associate with anyone in particular or indeed anyone at all. Neither marital nor religious associational freedom includes a right to associate with nonconsenting others (300–01).

From these apparently uncontroversial liberal premises, Wellman reaches the following somewhat more controversial conclusion: "Just as an individual has a right to determine whom (if anyone) he or she would like to marry, a group of fellow-citizens has a right to determine whom (if anyone) it would like to invite into its political community. And just as an individual's freedom of association entitles one to remain single, a state's freedom of association entitles it to exclude all foreigners from its political community" (304).

Wellman then responds to a number of potential objections to his move from premises to conclusion. None of these objections deters him from confidently contending that he has established at least a prima facie case for a state's right to exclude all would-be immigrants (316). If the first part of Wellman's argument is correct, then, all other things being equal, we should favor states' rights to exclude over would-be immigrants' claims to be admitted.

The prima facie case, he acknowledges, could be outweighed by competing claims. First, the presumption in favor of a state's right to restrict immigration might be trumped by what Wellman calls "the egalitarian case for open borders." Wellman accepts that individuals and states have significant duties to outsiders living in abject poverty, and, in line with his relational view of equality, he maintains that, as relationships between insiders and outsiders become more "robust," the inequalities between them are a greater cause for concern (306–11). He argues, however, that states may choose to "export justice" rather than open their borders to immigrants. Export options include, in Wellman's view, the transfer of aid to poor countries in place of admitting immigrants who are fleeing poverty, and, rather more contentiously, military intervention to protect those whose governments are "unable or unwilling to secure their . . . basic moral rights" instead of admitting refugees of corrupt or inept regimes (311).

Next, Wellman critically appraises "the libertarian case for open borders." Opponents might contend that the state's right to exclude illegitimately restricts the citizens' freedom to invite outsiders onto their property and/or the would-be immigrants' freedom of movement. Wellman argues that the state's "sovereignty over its territory" must take precedence over the individual citizen's right to invite others onto her property and, anyway, inviting people into the state for indefinite periods of time actually has far-reaching, costly consequences for one's fellow-citizens, which means that this sort of decision should not be made unilaterally. Furthermore, the right to freedom of movement is not absolute: I have no right to enter your house without permission, so why should I have a right to enter another country without its consent (311–14)? Yet he claims that states should not interfere with self-determining individuals "any more than is necessary" (313). Hence, states can have no reasonable objection to individuals inviting outsiders onto their property or to foreigners entering the territory provided that these visits are for "duly limited" periods. [Wellman's position on "duly limited" periods does not appear in this volume, but can be found on pages 136–37 of the source given on page 300].

Despite these apparent concessions, Wellman does not shy away from his stark conclusion that "even if egalitarians are right that those of us in wealthy societies have stringent duties of global distributive justice, and even if libertarians are correct that individuals have rights both to freedom of movement and to control their private property, legitimate states are entitled to reject all potential immigrants, even those desperately seeking asylum from corrupt governments" (316).

Wellman's defense of the state's right to exclude rests on two debatable claims. The first is that the state has a right to freedom of association, which is a component of its right to self-determination. All liberals are familiar with the claim that individuals have associational rights, and many would accept that groups formed by consenting individuals also can have associational rights. However, Wellman does not elaborate on the precise sense in which the state has a right to freedom of association. He does not explain whether we should understand the state as the right-holder or whether the state exercises the right on behalf of its citizens. At times he refers to "the citizens' right," at others he refers to the "state's right." If the state acts on behalf of its citizens as a collective body, then presumably the state has no right to exclude those with whom the citizens collectively choose to associate. He also does not reveal exactly how this purported collective right relates to the individual right to freedom of association. The citizens' (or the state's) right to freedom of association does not emerge from the citizens exercising their individual rights and choosing to associate together as a group in the first place; as Wellman acknowledges, ordinarily membership of the political community is nonvoluntary (301). Moreover, as he points out, the citizens' collective right to refuse to associate with outsiders may conflict with the associative rights of those individual citizens who wish to associate with the excluded outsiders (312). In lieu of a response to these questions about the nature of the state's right to freedom of association, Wellman simply suggests that there are some unpalatable consequences of denying that states have such a right. For example, without positing that right, he argues, we would be unable to identify the wrong that occurs when one state forcibly annexes another state (302). Despite the lack of clarification, let us accept for the sake of argument that the state may have a right to freedom of association.

The second controversial claim is that the state's freedom to associate includes a right to exclude would-be immigrants. In order to understand the basis of that claim, it is useful to distinguish between a state's right to exclude outsiders from its territory (from simply crossing its borders), its right to exclude them from settling within that territory, and its right to exclude them from membership of the political community (from acquiring citizenship status). Although Wellman obscures these distinctions by writing, interchangeably, of a state's right to "control immigration over its territorial borders," "close its doors," and "set its own immigration policy," it transpires that the central focus of his freedom of association position is actually the state's right to exclude would-be immigrants from obtaining citizenship status. Wellman's argument is that the citizens together ought to enjoy a collective right to determine the membership rules for their political community, and so it is the freedom of the citizens, as a group, to choose their fellow political associates that is at stake. Access to citizenship matters because "the country's course will be charted by the members of this civic association"—that is how Wellman connects the citizens' collective right to self-determination and their right to freedom of association (303–04). . . .

How does Wellman move from the contention that the state should have control of its civic boundaries to the argument that the state should have control of its "territorial" boundaries? . . . At first it might appear as though the attempt to defend the state's right to exclude would-be immigrants from its territory by appeal to freedom of association is something of a nonstarter. David Miller, for example, swiftly dismisses this line of argument. According to him, it depends on the notion that "we have a deep interest in not being forced into association with others against our wishes," a notion that has little force in the context of the modern liberal state since it is implausible to claim that the "mere presence" of immigrants within the state's territory harms the (associational) interests of the citizens.[6] In that respect, Miller must be correct. The mere presence of immigrants within the state's borders cannot be a serious problem with regard to the associational rights of individual citizens—it is certainly compatible with their individual rights to associate freely within civil society, where they remain free to choose to associate, or not to associate, with newcomers and with other citizens in their private lives. In addition, it seems to be compatible with the collective right of citizens, as a group, to associate or not to associate with others in their political community.

The issue of movement across territorial borders and subsequent settlement (as opposed to full membership) only enters Wellman's argument insofar as he agrees with Michael Walzer that all long-term residents of a state should have the option of acquiring equal rights of membership to protect them against political oppression. For states to function effectively, Wellman contends, they must "nonconsensually coerce all those within their territorial borders" (312). The state, then, is both a nonvoluntary, coercive, territorial institution and the site (and representative?) of a self-determining political community. The requirement to offer citizenship status to long-term residents is a democratic one; in the absence of that guarantee, resident noncitizens are subject to the state's coercive authority without any say over the state's actions and they are comparable to "live-in servants," governed by a "band of citizen tyrants."[7] In other words, a democratic state is not entitled permanently to withhold citizenship status from those residing (for indefinite periods) within its territory. The citizens' collective freedom to associate (and to refuse association) does not extend to excluding long-term residents of the state from the political community.

Thus, while Wellman cannot defend the right to exclude outsiders from the state's territory by direct appeal to the citizens' individual or collective rights to freedom of association, because their mere presence within the state's territorial boundaries is not a problem from that perspective, the democratic state's right to exclude would-be immigrants from settling indefinitely in the territory indirectly becomes a necessary extension of the right to exclude them from full membership of the political community. The citizens' collective freedom to choose their political associates (their fellow citizens) relies on their freedom to exclude would-be long-term residents at the territorial borders. Wellman's defense of a right to exclude would-be immigrants by appeal to freedom of association therefore depends both on the assumption that states have a right to freedom of association and on the validity of the claim that all long-term residents must be offered the option of acquiring the complete rights of full membership; if the latter claim is without substance, then Wellman's argument would fail because the citizens could control access to membership of the political community and enjoy the collective right to freedom of association without controlling access to the state's territory. Furthermore, the citizens' collective claim to freedom of association must be weighty enough to override not only the would-be immigrants' claims to become members of the political community but also their claims to settle in the state's territory.

Even if we do not challenge these two foundations of Wellman's position, the argument that the state has a right to exclude would-be immigrants by virtue of its right to freedom of association still fails on its own terms. In what follows, I raise three objections, focusing on harm to others, the distinctiveness of the state, and the absence of a justification for the state's territorial rights.

II

The first central problem emerges on closer inspection of Wellman's conception of self-determination. As indicated in Section I, Wellman describes the individual right to self-determination in the following terms: "Each of us enjoys a morally privileged position of dominion over our self-regarding affairs," and this is a position "which entitles us to freedom of association" (300). Although he does not elaborate on the idea of self-determination in the immigration discussion, in a previous article he notes that "it is not always clear when any given action is purely self-regarding," but "many people believe that we should be allowed to choose freely when our behavior is not harmful to others."[8] Behavior that is harmful to others wrongly causes them to be worse off than they

would be otherwise (where "worse off" means that their interests are set back or thwarted).[9] Wellman's omission of the harm clause in the immigration piece is significant because, as I will show, the potential to cause harm to others obstructs his path to the conclusion that the state enjoys a right to exclude.

To explain, there is no denying that Wellman's claim about the importance of individual self-determination has a good liberal pedigree. We are familiar with this as an argument in favor of allowing people the freedom "to be the authors of their own lives."[10] It is a "let them be" position and one that makes perfect sense with reference to the beliefs or actions of an individual. "You do not like the way that Ali chooses to live her life? If she is not harming anyone then you have no say in the matter. Let her be!" In Wellman's words, "it is *her* life."[11] The presumptive case lies with Ali.

From Wellman's conception of individual self-determination, we might extrapolate a comparable notion of group self-determination: groups enjoy a morally privileged position of dominion over their self-regarding affairs and should be allowed to choose freely when their behavior is not harmful to others. Matters become more complicated here because of the clear potential for groups illegitimately to restrict the autonomy of their own members. One common liberal response is to "let groups be" on the condition that the members of the group enjoy a right of exit.[12] The individual right of exit represents a form of safeguard against the group's potential to abuse its power.[13]

Yet the actions of groups affect not only the autonomy of their members; just like the actions of individuals, they may (directly or indirectly) affect third parties as well. When a private club in a residential area regularly arranges noisy late-night gatherings, the group's actions have spill-over effects for the local residents. In that way, while seemingly going about its own business, the private club has the potential to harm the interests of nonmembers. And, whereas a right of exit might go some way toward protecting the individual autonomy of the members, outsiders often are unwillingly exposed to the effects of a group's decisions. In such instances, where the nonmembers do not seek to interfere in the affairs of others for paternalist reasons, "let them be" is not an appropriate response to their appeals. Clearly, it is not the case that every action with potentially harmful effects ought to be prohibited, but, once the potential for harm to others enters the picture, the presumption in favor of the group members' freedom to do as they please is called into question, as is implied by Wellman's claim that "we should be allowed to choose freely *when our behavior is not harmful to others.*"[14] In fact, the potential for harm represents a good, if not a conclusive, reason for intervening in the group's affairs in order to prevent the harm.

There is also another way in which the actions of groups, unlike those of individuals, necessarily affect and even potentially harm third parties. As Wellman explains, "an important part of group self-determination is having control of what the 'self' is," and this is why he is so concerned with the citizens' freedom to select their political associates (303). Having control of that "self" means choosing "who is in and who is out," which, in turn, means including some people and excluding others.[15] The very act of excluding people may thwart their interests, either making them worse off than they are at present, or making them worse off than they would be otherwise, if they were left to act on their own plans and the group did not act to exclude them. For example, when a patch of green land, open to the general public, is purchased by a private group which plans to reserve the land for the use of members only, then current users of the land who are excluded from the group are made worse off. In another case, if a necessary condition of securing work in the teaching profession is membership of a national teachers' trade union, then qualified teachers excluded from the union are made worse off than they would be otherwise—exclusion bars them from pursuing their chosen career. Again, though not every action with potentially harmful effects can or should be prohibited, sometimes the interests in question are so substantial, and thwarting them is so detrimental to the well-being of the excluded, that exclusion itself becomes a cause for concern.

The potential to cause harm to others has important implications for Wellman's argument regarding the state's right to exclude. Would-be immigrants seek to leave one state and to enter another for a variety of reasons. Some effectively have no choice but to leave their state of origin, while others elect to move. Here we might distinguish between those who are unable to live a minimally decent life in their present country and those whose basic needs are currently met but who wish to settle elsewhere in order to further their (various) interests. We know that emigration is generally accompanied by significant costs, including separation from family and friends, from a wider community, and from familiar surroundings, and often involves moving to somewhere unfamiliar, somewhere in which one is a stranger. It seems reasonable to assume, therefore, that those who are willing (or are forced) to incur such costs have substantial interests in living in another state and that thwarting their pursuit of those interests may be detrimental to the well-being of the excluded. This is particularly true if, as Wellman contends, in order to control access to membership of the political community, states must also enjoy a right to exclude outsiders from settling indefinitely within their territorial borders, because it means that those who are excluded from membership of the political community are unable to further any of their interests in long-term residence within the state (just as teachers who are excluded from the teaching union are unable to further their career interests).

Those who cannot live a minimally decent life in their country have an interest in meeting their basic needs. Wellman maintains that states must not ignore that interest but are free to "export justice" to them instead of granting them access to the state's territory and political community. Even if this were a plausible and legitimate option, it could not fully resolve the question of harm to would-be immigrants. In a world where all the adverse political and economic (and, we might add, ecological and social) causes of forced migration had been eliminated, as Joseph Carens has emphasized, "people might have powerful reasons to want to migrate from one state to another."[16] Most importantly for our purposes, the interests in living in state *A* are not always interchangeable with the interests in living in state *B* or state *C*. Prohibiting outsiders from settling in and becoming members of a particular state hinders or prevents their pursuit of all the many familial, social, religious, cultural, political, or economic interests tied to residence and citizenship in that state, despite the fact that some, if not all, of their basic needs could be met elsewhere. Once more, this potential for harm to others represents a good, though not conclusive, reason against permitting the group to exclude some or all would-be members.

Therefore, while we may grant that there is a strong presumption in favor of individuals enjoying "dominion over their self-regarding affairs," group rights to self-determination are, by definition, always more troublesome, because groups consist of individuals who may be harmed by their group's actions and because the very act determining the group "self" is necessarily exclusionary, possibly at significant cost, even harm, to the excluded would-be members. Wellman thinks he establishes that there is a presumption in favor of the state's right to exclude prospective immigrants because he does not pause to consider the possibility that the act of exclusion is potentially harmful to them insofar as it thwarts the interests that they have in long-term settlement or in acquiring membership. And, as I have sought to illustrate, when the acts of a self-determining group are accompanied by potential harm to others, there does not appear to be a clear presumption on the group's side—the potential for harm represents a parallel reason to interfere with the group's actions.

III

In response, Wellman might wish to invoke the examples of marriage and religion again to illustrate that the refusal of a marriage proposal or exclusion from a religious group both may "damage the interests of others" and cause "pain or loss" in some sense, and yet everyone appears to assume that there is a clear presumption in favor of the refuser and the excluder in those cases.[17] However, this only serves to highlight why Wellman's inference from the examples of marriage and religion to the example of a state is problematic in the first place. While liberals are likely to accept that the presumption lies with the excluder in

the marriage and religion cases despite the potential for causing "pain or loss" to the excluded, for many of them this is because there is something special about certain forms of association, which gives them a privileged status. They might argue, in line with Amy Gutmann and Stuart White, for example, that there is a particularly compelling case for freedom of association, and by extension exclusion, in intimate or expressive contexts.[18] According to White's view, as quoted by Wellman himself, "if the formation of a specific association is essential to the individual's ability to exercise properly his/her liberties of conscience and expression, or to his/her ability to form and enjoy intimate attachments, then exclusion rules which are genuinely necessary to protect the association's primary purposes have an especially strong presumption of legitimacy."[19] The idea is that it would be objectionable to compel individuals to form or maintain intimate attachments against their will or to betray their own consciences. Does the modern liberal state enjoy a privileged status on a similar basis?

Although the liberal state obviously cannot be viewed as an intimate association, perhaps it has more of a claim to be viewed primarily as an expressive association, certainly not in the sense that it subscribes to a particular religious doctrine but at least insofar as it is (supposedly) committed to a set of principles that represent its liberal character. While there is a great deal of debate between liberals about how comprehensive or perfectionist those principles may be, and liberals of various stripes will disagree about the basic list and ranking, it is uncontroversial to claim that a liberal state is committed, in some way, to toleration, equality before the law, and individual liberty, for example. However, the liberal state's adherence to a basic set of common principles is not sufficient to suggest that it constitutes an expressive association. The label 'expressive association' implies, as Gutmann notes, "that the primary purpose of an association is expression of a point of view."[20] The members of liberal states are a diverse bunch, many of whom do not see themselves as making any sort of principled statement by remaining resident within the borders of a particular state. Citizens in a liberal state may endorse a variety of liberal principles, or may be indifferent to them, or may reject them altogether. Freedom of association within a liberal state is supposed to facilitate the citizens' freedom to express various points of view, including views antithetical to liberalism. When governments mistake the state itself for something akin to an expressive association with a single, comprehensive point of view, the result is often distinctly and disturbingly illiberal, as in the case of the American government's clampdown on communist views in the McCarthy era or the suppression of political opposition in the former Soviet Union. Hence, since the liberal state cannot claim to be primarily an intimate or expressive association, the initial case for exclusion then must be weaker than in the examples of marriage and religion.

Wellman acknowledges that freedom of association is "much more important for individuals" in the examples of marriage and religion, but he denies that this imperils his position regarding a presumptive right to exclude because he believes that "there is a very natural and straightforward case to be made in favor of freedom of association in all realms" (302). He points out that freedom of association for members of a golf club is obviously not as important as marital and religious freedom of association, and yet, "if no one doubts that golf clubs have a presumptive right to exclude others, then there seems no reason to suspect that a group of citizens cannot also have the right to freedom of association, even if control over membership in a country is not nearly as significant as control regarding one's potential spouse" (302–03).

The freedom of association principle, Wellman maintains, applies collectively to citizens of a state, just as it applies to members of a golf club. This argument by analogy is awkward again, though, because one might be reluctant to accept that a state has a presumptive right to exclude precisely because of the ways in which a state differs dramatically from a golf club. As a number of theorists have emphasized over the years, states are not like clubs. For one thing, it is not possible today for would-be immigrants to get together and set up a state of their own. Moreover, it is generally fair to assume that exclusion from a golf club is unlikely to have a devastating impact on the life of the would-be member, whereas exclusion

from a particular state—as the bearer of an enormous range of resources and options, many of which are not interchangeable with those on offer in other states and are not accessible to nonresidents and noncitizens—may have exactly that effect.

This suggests that there might well be a presumption in favor of a group's right to exclude would-be members in two quite different cases. The first case, as in the examples of marital and religious freedom of association, is when the associational freedom and accompanying exclusion are intricately connected to intimate attachments or expressive purposes. The second case, as in the golf club example, is when associations are not intimate or expressive but exclusion is generally fairly innocuous. Although Wellman invokes both sorts of case in his attempt to support the state's presumptive right to exclude, neither is relevantly comparable to that of the state, and so the examples do very little to help his cause. Interestingly enough, however, when particular clubs or associations start to look a bit more like states in the sense that outsiders have significant interests in becoming members and exclusion brings with it high costs to the nonmembers without serving clear expressive or intimate purposes, the argument in favor of exclusion seems weaker. That certainly appears to have been the view of the U.S. Supreme Court in the case of *Roberts v. United States,* 1984. The Court ruled that it was not unconstitutional to deny the U.S. Junior Chamber (Jaycees)—a nonintimate, nonexpressive, and formerly all-male association, which was understood to have clear career-enhancing advantages for its members—a right to exclude its regional chapters that chose to admit women as full members.[21] . . .

In summary, then, without denying that citizens have an interest in setting the rules of membership for their political community in order to maintain some control over the policy direction of their state, I have illustrated that, contra Wellman, the appeal to self-determination and freedom of association does not deliver a presumptive case in favor of a state's right to exclude would-be immigrants from settling within its borders and obtaining citizenship status. Excluding would-be immigrants from a state clearly has the potential to harm their interests to a significant degree, and this potential for harm also represents a good reason for challenging the citizens' right to exclude them. Groups may enjoy a presumptive right to exclude outsiders when the associations in question are intimate or primarily expressive or when exclusion is ordinarily reasonably "harmless," but the state does not meet the criteria necessary to qualify for that presumption.

Furthermore, once it becomes clear that the potential for harming the would-be immigrants' interests negates the case for the state's presumptive right to exclude based on the citizens' collective right to freedom of association, it is also apparent that Wellman's response to the "egalitarian" objection to the state's right to exclude is insufficient. Even if the state is able and willing to fulfill its duties to outsiders living in poverty or the victims of incompetent or brutal regimes by "exporting justice" abroad, excluding people who wish to pursue interests specific to that particular state is still potentially harmful, and that potential for harm remains an important challenge to Wellman's position.

Wellman might argue that he does directly confront that potential for harm to outsiders since he considers whether the citizens' right to exclude, grounded in their collective right to freedom of association, conflicts with the would-be immigrants' right to freedom of movement. In a sense, this is something of a red herring; as I emphasized at the outset, the citizens' collective right to freedom of association could not support a right to prevent outsiders crossing the state's borders anyway because their mere presence has no bearing on the citizens' individual or collective associational freedoms. Thus, it is not a surprise when Wellman concludes that the right to exclude is compatible with the rights of outsiders to enter the state's territory, provided that their visits are temporary. As the state is under no obligation to extend the full rights of membership to temporary visitors, their presence within the state does not pose a problem for the citizens' collective right to self-determination and freedom of association. . . . Nevertheless, again, this response does not serve to mitigate the harms that may accompany exclusion from permanent residence and citizenship. People who are not free to settle within a state are not at liberty to form or maintain long-term intimate relationships with citizens; to take advantage of the political, religious, and social options in that state; or, generally, to make a stable life for themselves there. . . .

IV

Wellman does not deliver a conclusive case in favor of the citizens' position—that would require him to explain why the citizens' claim to self-determination is sufficiently strong to outweigh the harm to would-be immigrants. I will add that the argument in favor of preventing harm to the would-be immigrants seems more appealing once we recognize that we are not being asked to make a stark choice between self-determination and the interests of outsiders: while "having control of what the 'self' is" may be one element of group self-determination, it is not the only, or even a necessary, component. In the absence of full control over access to membership, a group still can be self-determining to the extent that it is free to set its own internal policy agenda without external interference. That freedom might be limited by the lack of control over membership rules, but liberal and democratic principles already constrain the extent of the citizens' discretion to control the membership of their political community. Wellman accepts the democratic requirement that long-term residents are offered citizenship rights, and presumably that same requirement extends to prohibiting the arbitrary expulsion of existing members. Moreover, as Walzer argues, in theory, states also could control membership by regulating birth rates and selectively awarding the right to give birth, choosing between different ethnic groups, or setting "class or intelligence quotas." This, he contends, "would require very high, and surely unacceptable, levels of coercion: the dominance of political power over kinship and love."[22] Therefore, since denying a group full control over membership rules is not an automatic denial of its right to self-determination, the citizens are not forced to sacrifice all control over their common life in order to prevent significant harm to others.

Nonetheless, aside from the issue that Wellman's argument about controlling the rules of membership is inconclusive, there is an additional difficulty for Wellman's defense of the right to exclude based on a commitment to freedom of association. As Wellman contends that citizens must enjoy not only a right to exclude would-be members from the political community but also would-be residents from the state's territory, his position calls for a further justification of the state's purported rights over that particular territory. To see why the freedom of association argument is insufficient here, consider the example of a private club. The club members might enjoy the right to exclude outsiders from membership and from using the club's property and resources, provided that they have rights of ownership over the premises. However, while a yoga group that meets in Central Park might be free to reject prospective members, it is not entitled to bar them from making use of Central Park itself because the park is not the members' property. In other words, Wellman's position begs the question whether citizens and/or their states have the relevant rights over the territory from which they wish to exclude others and thus whether they are within their rights not just to control the rules of membership but also to control settlement within that territory. . . .

V

Wellman maintains that it is possible to defend a state's presumptive right to exclude would-be immigrants by appeal to the liberal commitment to freedom of association. He draws attention to the widespread conviction that individuals "should be allowed to choose freely when [their] behavior is not harmful to others," but I have argued that there is no clear presumption in favor of the state's position based upon the freedom to associate since exclusion from the state obviously has the potential to harm the interests of others—interests that would not disappear even if wealthy liberal states did, to use Wellman's words, "export justice" and thereby fulfill some of their duties to outsiders (310). The potential for exclusion to result in harm must be

taken seriously, in line with Wellman's own argument, and more must be said about why the freedom of citizens takes precedence over the interests of the would-be immigrants, especially since states are neither intimate nor expressive associations. Moreover, freedom of association alone cannot deliver a right to exclude would-be immigrants from entering and settling within a state: absent a further argument in support of states' rights over the territory they claim for themselves, we are left wondering whether states are entitled to control access to their territory at all.[23]

NOTES

1. See, e.g., Joseph H. Carens, "Aliens and Citizens: The Case for Open Borders," *Review of Politics* 49 (1987): 251–73; and Phillip Cole, *Philosophies of Exclusion: Liberal Political Theory and Immigration* (Edinburgh: Edinburgh University Press, 2000).

2. Christopher Heath Wellman, "Immigration and Freedom of Association," *Ethics* 119 (2008): 109–41 [Page numbers in the main text refer to Wellman's article reprinted in this text—ed.]

3. Amy Gutmann, "Freedom of Association: An Introductory Essay," in *Freedom of Association,* ed. Amy Gutmann (Princeton, NJ: Princeton University Press, 1998), 3–32, 11.

4. See, e.g., Michael Walzer, *Spheres of Justice: A Defense of Pluralism and Equality* (New York: Basic Books, 1983), chap. 2; and David Miller, "Immigration: The Case for Limits," in *Contemporary Debates in Applied Ethics,* ed. Andrew I. Cohen and Christopher Heath Wellman (Oxford: Blackwell, 2004), 193–206.

5. This is an internal critique insofar as it seeks to illustrate that Wellman's freedom of association argument in defense of a right to exclude does not succeed on its own terms. . . .

6. David Miller, *National Responsibility and Global Justice* (Oxford: Oxford University Press, 2008), 210–11.

7. See Walzer, *Spheres of Justice,* chap. 2.

8. Christopher Heath Wellman, "The Paradox of Group Autonomy," *Social Policy and Philosophy* 20 (2003): 265–85, 265.

9. Christopher Heath Wellman, *A Theory of Secession: The Case for Political Self-Determination* (New York: Cambridge University Press, 2005), 11 n. 7, 12 n. 9. Wellman is following Joel Feinberg's analysis of the

harm principle. For a full discussion, see Joel Feinberg, *The Moral Limits of Criminal Law,* vol. 1, *Harm to Others* (New York: Oxford University Press, 1987).

10. Wellman, *A Theory of Secession,* 2.

11. Wellman, "The Paradox of Group Autonomy," 266, author's emphasis.

12. See, e.g., John Stuart Mill, "On Liberty," in *On Liberty and Other Writings,* ed. Stefan Collini (Cambridge: Cambridge University Press, 1989), 91–92, where Mill considers the example of Mormons; and Chandran Kukathas, *Liberal Archipelago: A Theory of Diversity and Freedom* (Oxford: Oxford University Press, 2003), 95–96. It worth noting that this response is not considered sufficient by many (liberals and nonliberals alike), owing, e.g., to the possibility of crippling costs imposed on leavers—as in the case of "shunning."

13. Wellman is alert to the possibility that groups might illegitimately restrict the autonomy of their members; on that basis, he has argued that liberal principles point to a presumption (though not a conclusive case) against the sort of group rights that grant groups control over their own members. See Christopher Heath Wellman, "Liberalism, Communitarianism and Group Rights," *Law and Philosophy* 18 (1999): 13–40, esp. 33. . . .

14. Wellman, "The Paradox of Group Autonomy," 265, emphasis added.

15. Michael Walzer, "Exclusion, Injustice, and the Democratic State," *Dissent* 40 (1993): 55–64, 55.

16. Carens, "Aliens and Citizens," 258.

17. Mill, "On Liberty," 94–95.

18. See Gutmann, "Freedom of Association," 7–13; Stuart White, "Freedom of Association and the Right to Exclude," *Journal of Political Philosophy* 5 (1997): 373–91.

19. White, "Freedom of Association and the Right to Exclude," 381, cited in Wellman, "Immigration and Freedom of Association," 113.

20. Gutmann, "Freedom of Association," 11.

21. For further discussion, see Gutmann, "Freedom of Association," esp. 8–9.

22. Walzer, *Spheres of Justice,* 34–35.

23. I am very grateful to Duncan Bell, Noam Gur, Robert Jubb, David Miller, Kieran Oberman, Andrea Sangiovanni, Ben Saunders, Julia Skorupska, and Bas van der Vossen for extremely valuable comments and discussions. I would also like to thank two anonymous reviewers, as well as Henry Richardson and Catherine Galko Campbell at *Ethics.* Special thanks to David Miller and Christopher Heath Wellman.

READING QUESTIONS

1. In section I, Fine identifies as questionable two assumptions of Wellman's case for the right to exclusion. What are these assumptions?
2. What are the substantial harms that Fine believes foreigners might suffer as a result of closed borders in countries to which they would like to immigrate?
3. Fine asserts that a state's citizens as a collective do not count as an expressive association. Why not?

DISCUSSION QUESTION

1. Consider the various objections Fine raises against Wellman's view and how Wellman might reply to them.

ADDITIONAL RESOURCES

Web Resources

The Pew Forum on Religion & Public Life, <http://pewforum.org/docs/>. This is an excellent nonpartisan site for learning about the debate over immigration.

"Illegal Immigration" at <ProCom.org>. An overview of the pros and cons of immigration.

Authored Books and Articles

Wellman, Christopher Heath, "Immigration," *The Stanford Encyclopedia of Philosophy (Summer 2010 Edition)*, Edward N. Zalta (ed.), <http://plato.stanford.edu/archives/sum2010/entries/immigration/>. Excellent overview of the debate, including an extensive bibliography.

Wellman, Christopher Heath and Phillip Cole, *Debating the Ethics of Immigration* (Oxford: Oxford University Press, 2011). An extended defense of the right to exclude immigrants espoused by Wellman (a moral, fully developed defense of the position he takes in the article included in this chapter) and an extended defense of open borders by Cole.

Edited Collections

Barry, Brian and Robert E. Goodin (eds.), *Free Movement: Ethical Issues in the Transnational Migration of People and of Money* (Hertfordshire: Harvester Whaeatsheaf, 1992). A collection of essay by various authors organized according to the perspectives of liberal egalitarians (including the essays by Carens appearing in this chapter), libertarians, Marxists, proponents of natural law, and political realists.

Swain, Carol M. (ed.), *Debating Immigration* (Cambridge: Cambridge University Press, 2007). Eighteen essays by various authors organized according to the following perspectives: Philosophy and Religion; Law and Policy; Alien Rights, Citizen Rights, and the Politics of Restriction; Economics and Demographics; Race; and Cosmopolitanism.

8 Euthanasia and Physician-Assisted Suicide

The sad case of Terri Schiavo was intermittently in the news for a number of years. Schiavo suffered severe brain damage in 1990 owing to cardiac arrest. She was diagnosed by many physicians as being in a "persistent vegetative state," in which the individual is arguably not consciously experiencing anything, but unlike being in a coma, the individual undergoes periods of wakefulness. Schiavo's case was the subject of an intense public debate after her feeding tube was removed on March 18, 2005, at the request of her husband and after many legal battles with the parents of Schiavo. On March 21, 2005, Congress passed special legislation that would allow the parents of Schiavo to seek a review of their case in federal court to have a feeding tube reinserted, legislation that was signed that same day by President George W. Bush. Various federal courts turned down the appeal from Schiavo's parents to have the case reviewed further. Terri Schiavo died from dehydration on March 31, 2005.

As we shall see shortly, the decision to remove Schiavo's feeding tube, thus allowing her to die of dehydration, is a case of passive euthanasia. A number of legal and constitutional issues are raised by the Schiavo case, but no doubt what stirred such intense public interest in this case are the moral issues concerning euthanasia and suicide. Some of the most basic questions are these:

- Is euthanasia or suicide ever morally permissible?
- In those cases in which either of these activities is wrong, what best explains their wrongness?

Here, as with the issue of abortion, we (unfortunately) find parties to the debate being labeled as pro-life or pro-choice, which, of course, frames the issue as though one must (or should) respond to the first question with a simple yes or a simple no. But, as with most all controversial moral issues, there is a range of possible views, including moderate views which, in the case of euthanasia (and suicide), would reject simple answers and insist that details of specific cases do matter morally. In order to make progress in our understanding of the moral disputes over euthanasia and suicide, let us first explain what practices and types of action are the subject of these disputes, and then we will be prepared to understand how various ethical theories approach the moral questions just mentioned.

1. EUTHANASIA

Euthanasia is typically defined as the act or practice of killing or allowing someone to die on grounds of mercy. Because this definition covers a number of importantly different types of activity that may differ in their moral status, let us begin by calling attention to these types. There are two dimensions, so to speak, to be considered. First there is what we may call the "mode of death" dimension, which has to do with whether the death results from actively intervening to bring about the death of the patient or whether the death results from (or is hastened by) withholding some form of treatment which, had it been administered, would likely have prolonged the life of the patient. The former type of case is one of **active euthanasia,** whereas the latter type is often called **passive euthanasia.**

The other dimension has to do with matters concerning the consent or nonconsent of the patient. And here we need to distinguish three importantly different cases. Cases of **voluntary euthanasia** are those in which the patient has consented to the active bringing about of her death or to some means of passively allowing her to die. There are various ways in which a patient might consent, including the making of a living will in which the person specifies how he is to be treated under conditions in which his consent in that situation is not possible. Cases of **nonvoluntary euthanasia** are those in which the patient has not given his consent to be subject to euthanasia because the patient has not expressed a view about what others may do in case, for example, he goes into a persistent vegetative state. Cases of **involuntary euthanasia** are those in which the patient expresses (or may be presumed to have) a desire not to be the subject of euthanasia.

Although these distinctions are commonly made in the literature on euthanasia, the active/passive distinction, as I've explained it, seems to leave out, or at least does not clearly include, cases like that of Terri Schiavo in which treatment (the feeding tube) is withdrawn. On one hand, withdrawing treatment is doing something active, but on the other hand, in withdrawing treatment one is allowing nature to take its course, and so rather than actively bringing about the death, one is passively allowing it to come about. Because space does not allow us to pursue this matter in any detail, I propose that because there does seem to be an important moral difference between clear cases of actively bringing about the death of a patient (e.g., by way of lethal injection) on one hand, and cases of withholding and withdrawing treatment on the other, we ought to classify cases of withdrawing treatment as a type of passive euthanasia, making sure that within that category we recognize the two cases in question.

If we now combine the various modes of death with the various modes bearing on consent, we have nine distinct types of euthanasia. On the next page, is a visual aid that charts the types of cases just explained (Fig. 8.1).

In light of this taxonomy, we can now formulate moral questions about euthanasia more precisely by asking, for each type of euthanasia (e.g., nonvoluntary passive withholding), whether it is ever morally permissible and if so under what conditions. Clearly, whether or not someone has given their consent to be a subject of euthanasia has an important bearing on the morality of euthanasia.

But what about the distinction between active and passive euthanasia: Does this distinction mark a morally relevant difference? One might suppose that it does because it

Mode of Death

		Active	Passive	
			Withdrawing	Withholding
Mode of Consent	Voluntary	Lethal injection with patient's consent	Disconnecting patient from life support with patient's	Refraining from administering a life-extending drug with patient's consent
	Nonvoluntary	Lethal injection without patient's consent	Disconnecting patient from life support without patient's consent	Refraining from administering a life-extending drug without patient's consent
	Involuntary	Lethal injection against patient's consent	Disconnecting patient from life support against patient's consent	Refraining from administering a life-extending drug against patient's consent

FIGURE 8.1   Types of Euthanasia

might seem that *all else equal,* actively killing someone is morally worse than allowing someone to die. This supposition is challenged by James Rachels in his contribution to this chapter, while Philippa Foot in her reply to Rachels defends the moral relevance of the distinction between actively killing and allowing someone to die. So, one interesting theoretical question in ethics entails the moral relevance of the killing/letting die distinction, and thus over the moral relevance of the active/passive distinction in connection with euthanasia.

2. SUICIDE

Whereas euthanasia, by definition, involves the termination of someone's life by someone else, **suicide** involves intentionally and thus voluntarily ending one's own life. This definition, then, rules out the possibility of there being nonvoluntary or involuntary cases of suicide. But this definition does not rule out the possibility of passive suicide—suicide in which one either withdraws some means of life support or refrains from intervening to save oneself from death. However, most discussion of the morality of suicide is focused on cases of active suicide.

Assisted suicides are those cases in which another person is involved to some degree in assisting an individual to commit suicide. Much recent discussion on this topic has focused on the role of physicians in helping a patient to commit suicide. Of particular interest is the dispute in the United States over Death with Dignity laws.

3. DEATH WITH DIGNITY LAWS

In 1997 the Death with Dignity Act took effect in the state of Oregon; this legislation allows residents of that state who are diagnosed as terminally ill to request medication that will end their lives.[1] "Terminal illness" is defined in the act as "an incurable and irreversible disease that has been medically confirmed and will, within reasonable medical judgment, produce death within six months." Various safeguards are part of the act, including (1) the patient must make two written requests of his or her attending physician fifteen days apart, (2) the patient must sign a consent form in front of two witnesses, at least one of whom is not related to the patient, and (3) the attending physician's diagnosis of the patient must be confirmed by a second physician.

In 2015, Governor Jerry Brown of California signed into law a bill that legalized assisted suicide for terminally ill patients. This was in part prompted by the high-profile case of twenty-nine-year-old Brittany Maynard who in 2014 became a symbol in the debate over the moral and legal right to control the time and manner of one's own death. Maynard, a California resident, was diagnosed in early 2014 with an aggressive and lethal form of brain cancer and was told she had six months to live. She announced that she would take her life on November 1, 2014, which she did. Because at the time assisted suicide was not legal in California, she and her husband moved to Oregon to take advantage of the death with dignity act, where she ended her life.

To date, five U.S. states have passed "aid-in-dying" laws that allow assisted suicide, while public support for such laws has grown quickly from 51 percent in 2013 to 68 percent in 2015. Again in 2015, a Gallup poll found that 56 percent of U.S. citizens think that doctor-assisted suicide is morally permissible, up from 45 percent in 2013.

It is notable that the American Medical Association opposes the Death with Dignity Act, citing the AMA Code of Medical Ethics, which states: "Physician-assisted suicide is fundamentally incompatible with the physician's role as a healer." Whether physician-assisted suicide is truly incompatible with the role of physicians is contentious. Michael B. Gill discusses this question in his article about the Oregon law, included here.

4. THEORY MEETS PRACTICE

Let us turn to four theoretical approaches to the topics of euthanasia and suicide: Kantian moral theory, consequentialism, natural law theory, and the ethics of prima facie duty, some of them featured in this chapter's selections.

Kantian Moral Theory

Kant argued that suicide is morally wrong because it violates the dignity of the human being who commits it. The problem with his argument is that he assumes that suicide in all (or most) cases represents a violation of human dignity, but this assumption needs defense—more than Kant provides. If my life is close to an end and I am in excruciating pain about which physicians can do nothing, is it a violation of my dignity if I end my life rather than pointlessly live on for a month or two? Perhaps so, but the case needs to be argued. The same general point holds in any attempt to apply Kant's Humanity formulation of the categorical imperative to cases of euthanasia: whether any such case fails to treat the patient as an end in herself requires supporting argument.

Consequentialism

Many discussions of euthanasia and suicide focus exclusively on the likely consequences of these practices, thus appealing, at least implicitly, to consequentialist moral theory. And here, as with many other issues featured in this book, worries about slippery slopes are raised. A slippery slope argument may take various forms, but behind all such arguments is the idea that if we allow some action or practice *P*, then we will open the door to other similar actions and practices that will eventually lead us down a slope to disastrous results. So, the argument concludes, *P* should not be permitted. Any such argument, in order to be good, must meet two requirements. First, it must be true that the envisioned results really are bad. But second, the central idea of the argument—that allowing one action or practice will likely lead us down a path to disaster—must be plausible. If either of these conditions is not met, the argument is said to commit the "slippery slope *fallacy*."

Used in connection with euthanasia and assisted suicide, one common slippery slope worry is that if we allow voluntary euthanasia, we will put ourselves on the road to permitting (or encouraging) *in*voluntary euthanasia—cases of murder. This particular slippery slope argument apparently meets the first condition of any good slippery slope argument, but does it meet the second? And if so, will the same worries apply to assisted suicide? These are difficult questions because to answer them, we must rely on predictions about the likely effects (within a culture over a particular span of time) of engaging in, say, voluntary euthanasia. And for predictions to be reliable (and not just a prejudice based on one's antecedent views about the morality of these practices), we need solid empirical evidence—evidence that we probably lack at this time. Many opponents of euthanasia will, at this point, appeal to what we may call the "moral safety" argument, according to which when we are in doubt about such matters, it is better to play it safe and not start out on a road that *may* lead to disaster. What about the consequences of just having an institutional right to die? In his selection in our chapter, David Velleman argues that just having the right, even if one does not exercise it, can have the unwanted consequence of having to justify one's existence.

As with any consequentialist approach to moral issues, the crucial factor in determining the rightness or wrongness of some action or practice depends on how much net intrinsic value the action or practice will likely bring about compared to alternative actions and practices. Consequentialist defenders of euthanasia (and/or assisted suicide) will stress the great benefits of such practices in relation to relieving great human suffering. And, of course, consequentialists might be opposed to some forms of euthanasia but in favor of some forms of assisted suicide.

Natural Law Theory

Part of the traditional natural law approach to matters of life and death rests on the distinction between intentionally bringing about the death of someone and unintentionally but foresee-ably doing so. (This distinction is central in the doctrine of double effect explained in chapter 1, section 2B.) According to the natural law theory, intentionally taking innocent human life is always wrong; if certain conditions are met, however, one may be justified in foreseeably bringing about the death of an innocent person unintentionally, where, roughly, this means that the person's death is not one's aim in action, nor is it a means to achieving some further end. Thus, according to natural law thinking, any form of euthanasia that involves intentionally bringing about the death of a patient, even for reasons of mercy, is morally forbidden. A critical evaluation of the use of the doctrine of double effect by those who oppose physician-assisted suicide is to be found in Michael B. Gill's selection included in this chapter.

Ethics of Prima Facie Duty

Finally, one might approach the moral issues of euthanasia and suicide from the perspective of an ethic of prima facie duties. Both W. D. Ross and Robert Audi, defenders of this sort of moral theory, hold that we have a prima facie duty to avoid harming ourselves and others, and they both recognize a prima facie duty of self-improvement, which, as formulated by Audi, involves the prima facie duty to sustain, as well as develop, our distinctively human capacities.[2] If euthanasia and suicide count as harms, then one has a prima facie obligation to not engage in such actions. Additionally, since being alive is a necessary condition for sustaining our distinctively human capacities, one may conclude we have a prima facie duty of self-improvement to not participate in euthanasia or commit suicide. From these two basic prima facie duties we may derive a further prima facie duty—the prima facie duty to not engage in euthanasia or in suicide.

But as we learned in the moral theory primer, the very idea of prima facie duty allows that in a particular case it can be overridden by some other, more stringent prima facie duty that also applies to the case. So the fundamental moral question for this theoretical approach to these topics is whether there are cases in which the prima facie duty prohibiting euthanasia and suicide is overridden. If we recognize that we have a prima facie duty to relieve horrible suffering in the world, then we have a basis for arguing that there may be morally permissible cases of euthanasia and suicide. One might do so by arguing that the only way of relieving the horrible suffering of certain patients—perhaps patients who are terminally ill—is to bring about their death mercifully. If one adds that we also have a prima facie duty to respect the autonomy of patients, we can build a case for the claim that some cases of voluntary euthanasia are morally permissible because the duty of relieving suffering outweighs the prima facie duty prohibiting euthanasia and suicide. But the validity of appealing to autonomy to support euthanasia and suicide is controversial and a topic of dispute that is debated in the selections by Daniel Callahan and Michael B. Gill.

NOTES

1. In 1997, the state of Oregon enacted the Death with Dignity Act, the first physician-assisted suicide law in the United States. In 2001, U.S. attorney general John D. Ashcroft issued a directive that stated that the use of controlled substances to assist suicides violates the Federal Controlled Substances Act. One aim of Ashcroft's directive was to allow the federal government to try as criminals physicians in Oregon who assisted in suicides. After legal battles between Ashcroft and lower courts, the case made it all the way to the U.S. Supreme Court. In 2006, in the case *Gonzales v. State of Oregon* (No. 04-623), the Court upheld Oregon's law allowing physician-assisted suicide.

2. See Robert Audi, *The Good in the Right* (Princeton, NJ: Princeton University Press, 2004), 193–94.

James Rachels

Active and Passive Euthanasia

James Rachels is critical of the 1973 American Medical Association (AMA) policy regarding euthanasia, which he understands as forbidding all mercy killing but permitting some cases of allowing a patient to die. Rachels argues that this policy would force physicians to sometimes engage in the inhumane treatment of patients and that it would allow life-and-death decisions to be made on morally irrelevant grounds. He then proceeds to argue that the policy is based on the false assumption that killing is intrinsically morally worse than letting someone die.

Recommended Reading: natural law theory, esp. doctrine of double effect, chap. 1, sec. 2B. Rachels does not mention this doctrine, but it is relevant for thinking about the AMA's policy that he criticizes.

The distinction between active and passive euthanasia is thought to be crucial for medical ethics. The idea is that it is permissible, at least in some cases, to withhold treatment and allow a patient to die, but it is never permissible to take any direct action designed to kill the patient. This doctrine seems to be accepted by most doctors, and it is endorsed in a statement adopted by the House of Delegates of the American Medical Association on December 4, 1973:

> The intentional termination of the life of one human being by another—mercy killing—is contrary to that for which the medical profession stands and is contrary to the policy of the American Medical Association.
>
> The cessation of the employment of extraordinary means to prolong the life of the body when there is irrefutable evidence that biological death is imminent is the decision of the patient and/or his immediate family. The advice and judgment of the physician should be freely available to the patient and/or his immediate family.

However, a strong case can be made against this doctrine. In what follows, I will set out some of the relevant arguments, and urge doctors to reconsider their views on this matter.

To begin with a familiar type of situation, a patient who is dying of incurable cancer of the throat is in terrible pain, which can no longer be satisfactorily alleviated. He is certain to die within a few days, even if present treatment is continued, but he does not want to go on living for those days since the pain is unbearable. So he asks the doctor for an end to it, and his family joins in the request.

Suppose the doctor agrees to withhold treatment, as the conventional doctrine says he may. The justification for his doing so is that the patient is in terrible agony, and since he is going to die anyway, it would be wrong to prolong his suffering needlessly. But now notice this. If one simply withholds treatment, it may take the patient longer to die, and so he may suffer more than he would if more direct action were taken and a lethal injection given. This fact provides strong reason for thinking that, once the initial decision not to prolong his agony has been made, active euthanasia is actually preferable to passive euthanasia, rather than the reverse. To say otherwise is to endorse the option that leads to more suffering rather than less, and is contrary to the humanitarian impulse

From James Rachels, "Active and Passive Euthanasia," *New England Journal of Medicine* 292 (1975): 78–80.

that prompts the decision not to prolong his life in the first place.

Part of my point is that the process of being "allowed to die" can be relatively slow and painful, whereas being given a lethal injection is relatively quick and painless. Let me give a different sort of example. In the United States about one in 600 babies is born with Down's syndrome. Most of these babies are otherwise healthy—that is, with only the usual pediatric care, they will proceed to an otherwise normal infancy. Some, however, are born with congenital defects such as intestinal obstructions that require operations if they are to live. Sometimes, the parents and the doctor will decide not to operate, and let the infant die. Anthony Shaw describes what happens then:

> . . . When surgery is denied [the doctor] must try to keep the infant from suffering while natural forces sap the baby's life away. As a surgeon whose natural inclination is to use the scalpel to fight off death, standing by and watching a salvageable baby die is the most emotionally exhausting experience I know. It is easy at a conference, in a theoretical discussion, to decide that such infants should be allowed to die. It is altogether different to stand by in the nursery and watch as dehydration and infection wither a tiny being over hours and days. This is a terrible ordeal for me and the hospital staff—much more so than for the parents who never set foot in the nursery.[1]

I can understand why some people are opposed to all euthanasia, and insist that such infants must be allowed to live. I think I can also understand why other people favor destroying these babies quickly and painlessly. But why should anyone favor letting "dehydration and infection wither a tiny being over hours and days"? The doctrine that says that a baby may be allowed to dehydrate and wither, but may not be given an injection that would end its life without suffering, seems so patently cruel as to require no further refutation. The strong language is not intended to offend, but only to put the point in the clearest possible way.

My second argument is that the conventional doctrine leads to decisions concerning life and death made on irrelevant grounds.

Consider again the case of the infants with Down's syndrome who need operations for congenital defects unrelated to the syndrome to live. Sometimes, there is no operation, and the baby dies, but when there is no such defect, the baby lives on. Now, an operation such as that to remove an intestinal obstruction is not prohibitively difficult. The reason why such operations are not performed in these cases is, clearly, that the child has Down's syndrome and the parents and doctor judge that because of that fact it is better for the child to die.

But notice that this situation is absurd, no matter what view one takes of the lives and potentials of such babies. If the life of such an infant is worth preserving, what does it matter if it needs a simple operation? Or, if one thinks it better that such a baby should not live on, what difference does it make that it happens to have an unobstructed intestinal tract? In either case, the matter of life and death is being decided on irrelevant grounds. It is the Down's syndrome, and not the intestines, that is the issue. The matter should be decided, if at all, on that basis, and not be allowed to depend on the essentially irrelevant question of whether the intestinal tract is blocked.

What makes this situation possible, of course, is the idea that when there is an intestinal blockage, one can "let the baby die," but when there is no such defect there is nothing that can be done, for one must not "kill" it. The fact that this idea leads to such results as deciding life or death on irrelevant grounds is another good reason why the doctrine should be rejected.

One reason why so many people think that there is an important moral difference between active and passive euthanasia is that they think killing someone is morally worse than letting someone die. But is it? Is killing, in itself, worse than letting die? To investigate this issue, two cases may be considered that are exactly alike except that one involves killing whereas the other involves letting someone die. Then, it can be asked whether this difference makes any difference to the moral assessments. It is important that the cases be exactly alike, except for this one difference, since otherwise one cannot be confident that it is this difference and not some other that accounts for any variation in the assessments of the two cases. So, let us consider this pair of cases:

In the first, Smith stands to gain a large inheritance if anything should happen to his six-year-old cousin. One evening while the child is taking his bath, Smith sneaks into the bathroom and drowns the child, and then arranges things so that it will look like an accident.

In the second, Jones also stands to gain if anything should happen to his six-year-old cousin. Like Smith, Jones sneaks in planning to drown the child in his bath. However, just as he enters the bathroom Jones sees the child slip and hit his head, and fall face down in the water. Jones is delighted; he stands by, ready to push the child's head back under if it is necessary, but it is not necessary. With only a little thrashing about the child drowns all by himself, "accidentally," as Jones watches and does nothing.

Now Smith killed the child, whereas Jones "merely" let the child die. That is the only difference between them. Did either man behave better, from a moral point of view? If the difference between killing and letting die were in itself a morally important matter, one should say that Jones's behavior was less reprehensible than Smith's. But does one really want to say that? I think not. In the first place, both men acted from the same motive, personal gain, and both had exactly the same end in view when they acted. It may be inferred from Smith's conduct that he is a bad man, although that judgment may be withdrawn or modified if certain further facts are learned about him—for example, that he is mentally deranged. But would not the very same thing be inferred about Jones from his conduct? And would not the same further considerations also be relevant to any modification of this judgment? Moreover, suppose Jones pleaded, in his own defense, "After all, I didn't do anything except just stand there and watch the child drown. I didn't kill him; I only let him die." Again, if letting die were in itself less bad than killing, this defense should have at least some weight. But it does not. Such a "defense" can only be regarded as a grotesque perversion of moral reasoning. Morally speaking, it is no defense at all.

Now, it may be pointed out, quite properly, that the cases of euthanasia with which doctors are concerned are not like this at all. They do not involve personal gain or the destruction of normally healthy children. Doctors are concerned only with cases in which the patient's life is of no further use to him, or

in which the patient's life has become or will soon become a terrible burden. However, the point is the same in these cases: the bare difference between killing and letting die does not, in itself, make a moral difference. If a doctor lets a patient die, for humane reasons, he is in the same moral position as if he had given the patient a lethal injection for humane reasons. If his decision was wrong—if, for example, the patient's illness was in fact curable—the decision would be equally regrettable no matter which method was used to carry it out. And if the doctor's decision was the right one, the method used is not in itself important.

The AMA policy statement isolates the crucial issue very well; the crucial issue is "the intentional termination of the life of one human being by another." But after identifying this issue, and forbidding "mercy killing," the statement goes on to deny that the cessation of treatment is the intentional termination of a life. This is where the mistake comes in, for what is the cessation of treatment, in these circumstances, if it is not "the intentional termination of the life of one human being by another?" Of course, it is exactly that, and if it were not, there would be no point to it.

Many people will find this judgment hard to accept. One reason, I think, is that it is very easy to conflate the question of whether killing is, in itself, worse than letting die, with the very different question of whether most actual cases of killing are more reprehensible than most actual cases of letting die. Most actual cases of killing are clearly terrible (think, for example, of all the murders reported in the newspapers), and one hears of such cases every day. On the other hand, one hardly ever hears of a case of letting die, except for the actions of doctors who are motivated by humanitarian reasons. So one learns to think of killing in a much worse light than of letting die. But this does not mean that there is something about killing that makes it in itself worse than letting die, for it is not the bare difference between killing and letting die that makes the difference in these cases. Rather, the other factors—the murderer's motive of personal gain, for example, contrasted with the doctor's humanitarian motivation—account for different reactions to the different cases.

I have argued that killing is not in itself any worse than letting die; if my contention is right, it follows that active euthanasia is not any worse than passive euthanasia. What arguments can be given on the other side? The most common, I believe, is the following:

"The important difference between active and passive euthanasia is that, in passive euthanasia, the doctor does not do anything to bring about the patient's death. The doctor does nothing, and the patient dies of whatever ills already afflict him. In active euthanasia, however, the doctor does something to bring about the patient's death: he kills him. The doctor who gives the patient with cancer a lethal injection has himself caused his patient's death; whereas if he merely ceases treatment, the cancer is the cause of the death."

A number of points need to be made here. The first is that it is not exactly correct to say that in passive euthanasia the doctor does nothing, for he does do one thing that is very important: he lets the patient die. "Letting someone die" is certainly different, in some respects, from other types of action—mainly in that it is a kind of action that one may perform by way of not performing certain other actions. For example, one may let a patient die by way of not giving medication, just as one may insult someone by way of not shaking his hand. But for any purpose of moral assessment, it is a type of action nonetheless. The decision to let a patient die is subject to moral appraisal in the same way that a decision to kill him would be subject to moral appraisal: it may be assessed as wise or unwise, compassionate or sadistic, right or wrong. If a doctor deliberately let a patient die who was suffering from a routinely curable illness, the doctor would certainly be to blame for what he had done, just as he would be to blame if he had needlessly killed the patient. Charges against him would then be appropriate. If so, it would be no defense at all for him to insist that he didn't "do anything." He would have done something very serious indeed, for he let his patient die.

Fixing the cause of death may be very important from a legal point of view, for it may determine whether criminal charges are brought against the doctor. But I do not think that this notion can be used to show a moral difference between active and passive euthanasia. The reason why it is considered bad to be the cause of someone's death is that death is regarded as a great evil—and so it is. However, if it has been decided that euthanasia—even passive euthanasia—is desirable in a given case, it has also been decided that in this instance death is no greater an evil than the patient's continued existence. And if this is true, the usual reason for not wanting to be the cause of someone's death simply does not apply.

Finally, doctors may think that all of this is only of academic interest—the sort of thing that philosophers may worry about but that has no practical bearing on their own work. After all, doctors must be concerned about the legal consequences of what they do, and active euthanasia is clearly forbidden by the law. But even so, doctors should also be concerned with the fact that the law is forcing upon them a moral doctrine that may well be indefensible, and has a considerable effect on their practices. Of course, most doctors are not now in the position of being coerced in this matter, for they do not regard themselves as merely going along with what the law requires. Rather, in statements such as the AMA policy statement that I have quoted, they are endorsing this doctrine as a central point of medical ethics. In that statement, active euthanasia is condemned not merely as illegal but as "contrary to that for which the medical profession stands," whereas passive euthanasia is approved. However, the preceding considerations suggest that there is really no moral difference between the two, considered in themselves (there may be important moral differences in some cases in their *consequences,* but, as I pointed out, these differences may make active euthanasia, and not passive euthanasia, the morally preferable option). So, whereas doctors may have to discriminate between active and passive euthanasia to satisfy the law, they should not do any more than that. In particular, they should not give the distinction any added authority and weight by writing it into official statements of medical ethics.

NOTE

1. A. Shaw: "Doctor, Do We Have a Choice?" *The New York Times Magazine,* Jan. 30, 1972, p. 54.

READING QUESTIONS

1. What is the AMA's 1973 policy regarding euthanasia? What are some of the differences between passive and active forms of euthanasia according to Rachels? Describe some cases of allowing a patient to die and killing a patient directly.
2. What is Rachels's main concern with allowing a patient to die? How does direct action by a doctor differ from cases where treatment is withheld from a patient?
3. Explain Rachels's argument for the claim that decisions to let patients die are made on morally irrelevant grounds. What objections are raised against this view, and how does Rachels respond?
4. Why does Rachels think that doctors accepted the AMA's policy? How does he think that doctors should act with respect to policy and the law?

DISCUSSION QUESTIONS

1. Rachels presents hypothetical cases of individuals drowning to illustrate the difference between killing and letting die. Are there any reasons to think that an individual who allows another to drown while looking on is not like the case of a doctor who allows a patient to die by withholding treatment? Consider the morally relevant features of such situations which incline us to make the evaluations that we do.
2. What are the morally relevant differences between allowing someone to die and killing someone directly? Is allowing someone to die always a slow and painful process as Rachels suggests? Is taking direct action in order to kill someone always quick and painless?

PHILIPPA FOOT

Killing and Letting Die

Philippa Foot's essay is a reply to Rachels's claim that there is no morally relevant difference per se between killing someone and letting the person die. Foot makes her case in two steps. First, she provides examples (Rescue I and Rescue II) in which she thinks readers will agree that there is a morally relevant difference between killing and letting die—cases in which one holds fixed the motives of the agent and the outcomes of the two rescue cases. The essential element in cases of killing that distinguished them from cases of letting die is one's agency

From Philippa Foot, "Killing and Letting Die," in J. L. Garfield and P. Hennessy, *Abortion: Moral and Legal Perspectives*. Amherst: The University of Massachusetts Press, 1984. Reprinted with permission of the University of Massachusetts Press.

in initiating the death. Second, she proposes an explanation of *why* this distinction is at least sometimes morally relevant. Her explanation is in terms of two classes of rights: rights to noninterference and rights to goods and services.

Recommended Reading: rights-focused approach to moral issues, chap. 1, sec. 2D.

Is there a morally relevant distinction between killing and allowing to die? Many philosophers say that there is not, and further insist that there is no other closely related difference, as for instance that which divides act from omission, whichever plays a part in determining the moral character of an action. James Rachels has argued this case in his well-known article on active and passive euthanasia, Michael Tooley has argued it in his writings on abortion, and Jonathan Bennett argued it in the Tanner Lectures given in Oxford in 1980.[1] I believe that these people re mistaken, and this is what I shall try to show in this essay. . . .

The question with which we are concerned has been dramatically posed by asking whether we are as equally to blame for allowing people in Third World countries to starve to death as we would be for killing them by sending poisoned food? In each case it is true that if we acted differently—by sending good food or by not sending poisoned food—those who are going to die because we do not send the good food or do send the poisoned food would not die after all. Our agency plays a part in what happens whichever way they die. Philosophers such as Rachels, Tooley, and Bennett consider this to be all that matters in determining our guilt or innocence. Or rather they say that although related things are morally relevant, such as our reasons for acting as we do and the cost of acting otherwise, these are only contingently related to the distinction between doing and allowing. If we hold *them* steady and vary only the way in which our agency enters into the matter, no moral differences will be found. It is of no significance, they say, whether we kill others or let them die, or whether they die by our act or our omission. Whereas these latter differences may at first seem to affect the morality of action, we shall always find on further enquiry that some other difference—such as a difference of motive or cost—has crept in.

Now this, on the face of it, is extremely implausible. We are not inclined to think that it would be no worse to murder to get money for some comfort such as a nice winter coat than it is to keep the money back before sending a donation to Oxfam or Care. We do not think that we might just as well be called murderers for one as for the other. And there are a host of other examples which seem to make the same point. We may have to allow one person to die if saving him would mean that we could not save five others, as for instance when a drug is in short supply and he needs five times as much as each of them, but that does not mean that we could carve up one patient to get "spare parts" for five.

These moral intuitions stand clearly before us, but I do not think it would be right to conclude from the fact that these examples all seem to hang on the contrast between killing and allowing to die that this is precisely the distinction that is important from the moral point of view. For example, having someone killed is not strictly *killing* him, but seems just the same morally speaking; and on the other hand, turning off a respirator might be called killing, although it seems morally indistinguishable from allowing to die. Nor does it seem that the difference between 'act' and 'omission' is quite what we want, in that a respirator that had to be turned on each morning would not change the moral problems that arise with the ones we have now. Perhaps there is no locution in the language which exactly serves our purposes and we should therefore invent our own vocabulary. Let us mark the distinction we are after by saying that one person may or may not be 'the agent' of harm that befalls someone else.

When is one person 'the agent' in this special sense of someone else's death, or of some harm other than death that befalls him? This idea can easily be described in a general way. If there are difficulties when it comes to detail, some of these ideas may be best left unsolved, for there may be an area of indefiniteness reflecting the uncertainty that belongs to our moral judgments in some complex and perhaps infrequently encountered situations. The idea of agency, in the sense that we want, seems to be composed of two subsidiary ideas. First, we think of particular effects as the result of particular sequences, as when a certain fatal sequence leads to someone's death. This idea is implied in coroners' verdicts telling us what someone died of, and this concept is not made suspect by the fact that it is sometimes impossible to pick out a single fatal sequence—as in the lawyers' example of the man journeying into the desert who had two enemies, one of whom bored a hole in his water barrel while another filled it with brine. Suppose such complications absent. Then we can pick out the fatal sequence and go on to ask who initiated it. If the subject died by poisoning and it was I who put the poison into his drink, then I am the agent of his death; likewise if I shot him and he died of a bullet wound. Of course there are problems about fatal sequences which would have been harmless but for special circumstances, and those which although threatening would have run out harmlessly but for something that somebody did. But we can easily understand the idea that a death comes about through our agency if we send someone poisoned food or cut him up for spare parts, but not (ordinarily) if we fail to save him when he is threatened by accident or disease. Our examples are not problem cases from *this* point of view.

Nor is it difficult to find more examples to drive our original point home, and show that it is sometimes permissible to allow a certain harm to befall someone, although it would have been wrong to bring this harm on him by one's own agency, i.e., by originating or sustaining the sequence which brings the harm. Let us consider, for instance, a pair of cases which I shall call Rescue I and Rescue II. In the first Rescue story we are hurrying in our jeep to save some people—let there be five of them— who are imminently threatened by the ocean tide. We have not a moment to spare, so when we hear of a single person who also needs rescuing from some other disaster we say regretfully that we cannot rescue him, but must leave him to die. To most of us this seems clear, and I shall take it as clear. . . . This is

Rescue I and with it I contrast Rescue II. In this second story we are again hurrying to the place where the tide is coming in in order to rescue the party of people, but this time it is relevant that the road is narrow and rocky. In this version the lone individual is trapped (do not ask me how) on the path. If we are to rescue the five we would have to drive over him. But can we do so? If we stop he will be all right eventually: he is in no danger unless from us. But of course all five of the others will be drowned. As in the first story our choice is between a course of action which will leave one man dead and five alive at the end of the day and a course of action which will have the opposite result. And yet we surely feel that in one case we can rescue the five men and in the other we cannot. We can allow someone to die of whatever disaster threatens him if the cost of saving him is failing to save five; we cannot, however, drive over *him* in order to get to *them.* We cannot originate a fatal sequence, although we can allow one to run its course. Similarly, in the pair of examples mentioned earlier, we find a contrast between on the one hand refusing to give to one man the whole supply of a scarce drug, because we can use portions of it to save five, and on the other, cutting him up for spare parts. And we notice that we may not originate a fatal sequence even if the resulting death is in no sense our object. We could not knowingly subject one person to deadly fumes in the process of manufacturing some substance that would save many, even if the poisoning were a mere side effect of the process that saves lives.

Considering these examples, it is hard to resist the conclusion that it makes all the difference whether those who are going to die if we act a certain way will die as a result of a sequence that we originate or of one that we allow to continue, it being of course something that did not *start* by our agency. So let us ask how this could be? If the distinction—which is roughly that between killing and allowing to die— *is* morally relevant, because it sometimes makes the difference between what is right and what is wrong, how does this work? After all, it cannot be a magical difference, and it does not satisfy anyone to hear that what we have is just an ultimate moral fact. Moreover, those who deny the relevance can point to cases in which it seems to make no difference to the goodness or badness of an action having a certain result, as, for example, that some innocent person dies, whether due to a sequence we originate or because of one we merely allow. And if the way the result comes about *sometimes* makes no difference, how can it ever do so? If it sometimes makes an action bad that harm came to someone else as a result of a sequence we *originated,* must this not always contribute some element of badness? How can a consideration be a reason for saying that an action is bad in one place without being at least a reason for saying the same elsewhere?

Let us address these questions. As to the route by which considerations of agency enter the process of moral judgment, it seems to be through its connection with different types of rights. For there are rights to noninterference, which form one class of rights; and there are also rights to goods or services, which are different. And corresponding to these two types of rights are, on the one hand, the duty not to interfere, called a 'negative duty,' and on the other the duty to provide the goods or services, called a 'positive duty.' These rights may in certain circumstances be overridden, and this can in principle happen to rights of either kind. So, for instance, in the matter of property rights, others have in ordinary circumstances a duty not to interfere with our property, though in exceptional circumstances the right is overridden, as in Elizabeth Anscombe's example of destroying someone's house to stop the spread of a fire.[2] And a right to goods or services depending, for example, on a promise will quite often be overridden in the same kind of case. There is, however, no guarantee that the special circumstances that allow one kind of right to be overridden will always allow the overriding of the other. Typically, it takes more to justify an interference than to justify the withholding of goods or services; and it is, of course, possible to think that nothing whatsoever will justify, for example, the infliction of torture or the deliberate killing of the innocent. It is not hard to find how all this connects with the morality of killing and allowing to die—and in general with harm which an agent allows to happen and harm coming about through his agency, in my special sense having to do with originating or sustaining harmful sequences. For the violation of a right to noninterference consists in interference, which implies breaking into an existing sequence and initiating a new one. It is not usually possible, for instance, to violate that right to noninterference, which is at least part of what is meant by 'the right to life' by failing to save someone from death. So if, in any circumstances, the right to noninterference is the only right that exists, or if it is the only right special circumstances have not overridden, then it may not be permissible to initiate a fatal sequence, but it *may* be permissible to withhold aid.

The question now is whether we ever find cases in which the right to noninterference exists and is not overridden, but where the right to goods or services either does not exist or *is* here overridden. The answer is, of course, that this is quite a common case. It often happens that whereas someone's rights stand in the way of our interference, we owe him no *service* in relation to that which he would lose if we interfered. We may not deprive him of his property, though we do not have to help him secure his hold on it, in spite of the fact that the balance of good and evil in the outcome (counting his loss or gain and the cost to us) will be the same regardless of how they come about. Similarly, where the issue is one of life and death, it is often impermissible to kill someone—although special circumstances having to do with the good of others make it permissible, or even required, that we do not spend the time or resources needed to save his life, as for instance, in the story of Rescue I, or in that of the scarce drug.

It seems clear, therefore, that there are circumstances in which it makes all the difference, morally speaking, whether a given balance of good and evil came about through our agency (in our sense), or whether it was rather something we had the ability to prevent but, for good reasons, did not prevent. Of course, we often have a strict duty to prevent harm to others, or to ameliorate their condition. And even where they do not, strictly speaking, have a *right* to our goods or services, we should often be failing (and sometimes grossly failing) in charity if we did not help them. But, to reiterate, it may be right to allow one person to die in order to save five, although it would not be right to kill him to bring the same good to them.

How is it, then, that anyone has ever denied this conclusion, so sympathetic to our everyday moral intuitions and apparently so well grounded in a very generally recognized distinction between different types of rights? We must now turn to an argument first *given,* by James Rachels, and more or less followed by others who think as he does. Rachels told a gruesome story of a child drowned in a bathtub in two different ways: in one case someone pushed the child's head under water, and in the other he found the child drowning and did not pull him out. Rachels says that we should judge one way of acting as bad as the other, so we have an example in which killing is as bad as allowing to die. But how, he asks, can the distinction ever be relevant if it is not relevant here?[3]

Based on what has been said earlier, the answer to Rachels should be obvious. The reason why it is, in ordinary circumstance, "no worse" to leave a child drowning in a bathtub than to push it under, is that both charity and the special duty of care that we owe to children give us a positive obligation to save them, and we have no particular reason to say that it is "less bad" to fail in this than it is to be in dereliction of the negative duty by being the agent of harm. The level of badness is, we may suppose, the same, but because a different kind of bad action has been done, there is no reason to suppose that the two ways of acting will always give this same result. In other circumstances one might be worse than the other, or only one might be bad. And this last result is exactly what we find in circumstances that allow a positive but not a negative duty to be overridden. Thus, it could be right to leave someone to die by the roadside in the story of Rescue I, though wrong to run over him in the story of Rescue II; and it could be right to act correspondingly in the cases of the scarce drug and the "spare parts."

Let me now consider an objection to the thesis I have been defending. It may be said that I shall have difficulty explaining a certain range of examples in which it seems permissible, and even obligatory, to make an intervention which jeopardizes people not already in danger in order to save others who are.

The following case has been discussed. Suppose a runaway trolley is heading toward a track on which five people are standing, and that there is someone who can possibly switch the points, thereby diverting the trolley onto a track on which there is only one person. It seems that he should do this, just as the pilot whose plane is going to crash has a duty to steer, if he can, toward a less crowded street than the one he sees below. But the railway man then puts the one man newly in danger, instead of allowing the five to be killed. Why does not the one man's right to noninterference stand in his way, as one person's right to noninterference impeded the manufacture of poisonous fumes when this was necessary to save five?

The answer seems to be that this is a special case, in that we have here the *diverting* of a fatal sequence and not the starting of a new one. So we could not start a flood to stop a fire, even when the fire would kill more than the flood, but we could divert a flood to an area in which fewer people would be drowned.

A second and much more important difficulty involves cases in which it seems that the distinction between agency and allowing is inexplicably irrelevant. Why, I shall be asked, is it not morally permissible to allow someone to die deliberately in order to use his body for a medical procedure that would save many lives? It might be suggested that the distinction between agency and allowing is relevant when what is allowed to happen is itself aimed at. Yet this is not quite right, because there are cases in which it does make a difference whether one originates a sequence or only allows it to continue, although the allowing is with deliberate intent. Thus, for instance, it may not be permissible to deprive someone of a possession which only harms him, but it may be reasonable to refuse to get it back for him if it is already slipping from his grasp.[4] And it is arguable that nonvoluntary passive euthanasia is sometimes justifiable although nonvoluntary active euthanasia is not. What these examples have in common is that *harm* is not in question, which suggests that the 'direct', i.e., deliberate, intention of *evil* is what makes it morally objectionable to allow the beggar to die. When this element is present it is impossible to justify an action by indicating that no *origination* of evil is involved. But this special case leaves no doubt about the relevance of distinguishing between originating an evil and allowing it to occur. It was never suggested that there will *always and everywhere* be a difference of permissibility between the two. . . .

NOTES

1. James Rachels, "Active and Passive Euthanasia," *New England Journal of Medicine* 292 (January 9, 1975): 78–80; Michael Tooley, "Abortion and Infanticide," *Philosophy and Public Affairs* 2, no. 1 (Fall 1972); Jonathan Bennett, "Morality and Consequences," in *The Tanner Lectures on Human Values,* vol. 2, ed. Sterling McMurrin (Cambridge: Cambridge University Press, 1981).

2. G. E. M. Anscombe, "Modern Moral Philosophy," *Philosophy* 33 (1958): 1–19.

3. Rachels, "Active and Passive Euthanasia."

4. Cf. Philippa Foot, "Killing, Letting Die, and Euthanasia: A Reply to Holly Smith Goldman," *Analysis* 41, no. 4 (June 1981).

READING QUESTIONS

1. Crucial to Foot's case is her account of a person who is "the agent" of someone's death. Explain her notion of being the agent in this special sense.
2. Describe Foot's two rescue cases. How does her special sense of being an agent figure in these examples to explain one's moral intuitions about the two cases?
3. What is Foot's example of a case in which a duty of noninterference can be legitimately overridden by a duty to provide goods or services?
4. What explanation does Foot give for why Rachels denies the moral significance of the distinction between killing and letting die?

DISCUSSION QUESTIONS

1. Suppose Foot is right in thinking that there are cases in which there is a morally relevant distinction between killing and letting die. What implications does this distinction have for cases of both active and passive euthanasia? (Keep in mind the distinctions between voluntary, involuntary, and nonvoluntary cases.)
2. In one of the many trolley examples that figure in discussions of killing and letting die, one is standing on a bridge that goes over the trolley tracks next to a large individual wearing a backpack. By pushing the large individual onto the tracks, one could stop the trolley before it ran over five trapped workers who otherwise would be run over and killed. Of course the backpacker will be killed if he is pushed onto the tracks and the trolley smashes into him. Would pushing the backpacker to his death be morally permissible on Foot's account? Why or why not?
3. Now consider a variant of the case described in question 2. The backpacker, in trying to walk across the tracks, trips, and one foot is caught in the tracks, he can't get the foot loose, and the trolley is fast approaching. You are nearby and can pull him to safety. Of course, if you do not intervene in the unfolding events, the backpacker will be killed, but the five trapped workers will be saved. What would Foot say about pulling the backpacker to safety? Are you obligated to intervene and save his life?

DANIEL CALLAHAN

A Case against Euthanasia

Daniel Callahan considers euthanasia to be a form of suicide. He begins by noting that suicide is comparatively rare among people who face debilitating pain or incapacitating diseases, and that it is common for people to look upon suicide with sadness and perhaps revulsion. These facts do not serve as an argument against the moral permissibility of suicide, but Callahan does think making sense of such reactions offers a perspective on human life that can reveal why euthanasia and suicide are morally problematic. After arguing that three prominent arguments in favor of suicide are flawed, he turns critical attention to the issue of legalization of euthanasia and physician-assisted suicide of the sort found in Dutch law and in the Oregon Death with Dignity Act. Here the focus is on the small minority who choose euthanasia (including physician-assisted suicide) and the potential abuse of such laws.

Consider what I take to be a mystery. Life presents all of us with many miseries, sick or well. Why is it then that so few people choose to end their own lives in response to them? Why is it that when someone does commit suicide—even for reasons that seem understandable—the common reaction (at least in my experience) is one of sorrow, a feeling of pity that someone was driven to such a desperate extreme, particularly when most others in a similar situation do not do likewise? I ask these questions because, behind the movement and arguments in favor of euthanasia or physician-assisted suicide (PAS)—and I consider euthanasia a form of suicide—lies an effort to make the deliberate ending of one's life something morally acceptable and justifiable; and which looks as well to the help of government and the medical profession to move that cause along.[1]

It goes against the grain, I believe, of reason, emotion, and tradition, and all at the same time. If not utterly irrational, it is at least unreasonable—that is, it is not a sensible way to deal with the tribulations of life, of which a poor death is only one of life's horrible possibilities. Suicide generally provokes a negative emotional response in people, even if they can grasp the motive behind it. That response does not prove it is wrong, but it is an important signal of a moral problem. As for tradition, the doctor is being asked by a patient to go against the deep historical convictions of his discipline, to use his or her skills to take life rather than to preserve it, and to lend to the practice of euthanasia the blessing of the medical profession. I understand all of this to be opening the door to new forms of killing in our society, not a good development.

There have been, in Western culture, only three generally accepted reasons for taking the life of another, which is what euthanasia amounts to: self-defense when one's life is threatened, warfare when the cause is serious and just, and capital punishment, the ultimate sanction against the worst crimes. The movement to empower physicians legally to take the life of a patient, or help the patient take his own life,

From "A Case Against Euthanasia" by Daniel Callahan, in *Contemporary Debates in Applied Ethics*, edited by Andrew I. Cohen and Christopher Heath Wellman, Blackwell Publishing Co., 2005, pp. 179–190.

would then legitimate a form of suicide, but would also add still another reason by calling on medical skills to end a person's life.

SUICIDE: THE WAY (RARELY) TAKEN

Let me return to the first of my two questions. Why do comparatively few people turn to suicide as a way of dealing with awful lives? People die miserable deaths all the time, from a wide range of lethal diseases and other causes. While it may cross their minds from time to time, few seem to want euthanasia or physician-assisted suicide as a way out. Millions of people have been brutally treated in concentration camps, with many of them ultimately to die—and yet suicide has never been common in such camps. Many millions of others have undergone all kinds of personal tragedy—the death of children or a spouse, the end of marriage or a deep romance, failures in their work or profession—but most of them do not turn to suicide either. The disabled have been long known to have a lower suicide rate than able-bodied people.

Euthanasia is often presented as a "rational" choice for someone in great pain and whose prospects are hopeless. And yet rationality implies some predictability of behavior, that is, some reasonable certainty that people will act in a consistent and foreseeable way under certain familiar circumstances. Yet it is almost impossible, save for severe depression, to predict whether someone suffering from a lethal illness is likely to turn to suicide. It is far more predictable that, when faced with even the worst horrors of life, most people will *not* turn to suicide. It is no less predictable that, when gripped by pain and suffering, they will want relief, but not to the extent of ending their lives to get it.

We may of course say that people fear ending their own lives, lacking the nerve to do so, or that religious beliefs have made suicide a taboo, or that it has hitherto been difficult to find expert assistance in ending one's life. Those are possible explanations, but since some people do in fact commit suicide, we know that it is hardly impossible to overcome those deterrents.

Moreover, to say that most of the great religions and moral traditions of the world have condemned suicide does not in the end explain much at all. *Why* have they done so, even when at the same time they usually do not condemn laying down one's life to save another? In the same vein, why has the Western medical tradition for some 2,500 years, going back to Hippocrates, prohibited physicians from helping patients to commit suicide?

My guess is that the answer to the first of those two questions is that suicide is seen as a particularly bad way to handle misery and suffering, even when they are overwhelming—and the behavior of most people in turning away from suicide suggests they share that perception. It is bad because human life is better, even nobler, when we human beings put up with the pain and travail that come our way. Life is full of pain, stress, tragedy, and travail, and we ought not to want to tempt others to see suicide as a way of dealing with it. We would fail ourselves and, by our witness, our neighbor as well, who will know what we did and be led to do so themselves some day.

I began by asking at the outset why most suicides are treated as unhappy events, even when they obviously relieved someone's misery, which we would ordinarily consider valuable. Those readers who have been to the funerals of suicides will know how rarely those at such funerals feel relief that the misery of the life leading up to them has now been relieved. They almost always wish the life could have ended differently, that the suffering could have been borne. My surmise is that those of us who are bystanders or spectators to such deaths know that a fundamental kind of taboo of a rational kind has been broken, some deep commitment to life violated, and that no relief of pain and suffering can justify that. To say this is by no means to condemn those who do so. We can often well enough comprehend why they were driven to that extreme. Nor do I want to imply that they must have been clinically depressed. I am only saying that it is very hard to feel good about suicide or to rejoice that it was the way chosen to get out of a burdensome life.

I present these considerations about suicide as speculations only, not as some kind of decisive arguments against euthanasia. But I think it important to see what sense can be made of a common revulsion against suicide, and sadness when it happens, that has marked generations of people in most parts of the world. Moreover, as I will develop more fully below, it turns out that the experience with the Dutch euthanasia laws and practice, as well as with the Oregon experience with physician-assisted suicide, indicates that it is not misery, pain, and suffering in any ordinary sense that are the motivation for the desire to put an end to one's life. It is instead in great part a function of a certain kind of patient with a certain kind of personality and outlook upon the world.

It is, I believe, important that we try to make sense of these background experiences and reactions. They tell us something about ourselves, our traditions, and our human nature. They offer an enriched perspective when considering the most common arguments in favor of euthanasia. On the surface those arguments are meant to seem timely, in tune with our mainstream values, commonsensical and compassionate, and of no potential harm to our medical practice or our civic lives together. I would like to show that they are indeed in tune with many of our mainstream values, but that they are misapplied in this case, harmful to ourselves and others if we accept them.

THREE ARGUMENTS IN FAVOR OF EUTHANASIA

I want now to turn to the main arguments in favor of euthanasia, and to indicate why I think they are weak and unpersuasive. I will follow that with a discussion of the legal problem of euthanasia and physician-assisted suicide, and conclude with some comments on the experience with euthanasia and physician-assisted suicide in the Netherlands and the state of Oregon.

Three moral arguments have been most prominent in the national debate. One of them is that we ought, if we are competent, to have the right to control our body as we see fit and to end our life if we choose to do so. This is often called the right of self-determination.

Another is that we owe it to each other, in the name of beneficence or charity, to relieve suffering when we can do so. Still another is that there is no serious or logical difference between terminating the treatment of a dying patient, allowing the patient to die, and directly killing a patient by euthanasia. I will look at each of these arguments in turn.

If there is any fundamental American value, it is that of freedom and particularly the freedom to live our own lives in light of our own values. The only limit to that value is that, in the name of freedom, we may not do harm to others. At least a hundred years ago the value of freedom was extended to the inviolability of our bodies – that is, our right not to have our bodies invaded, abused, or used without our consent. Even to put our hands on another without their permission can lead to our being charged with assault and battery. That principle was extended to participation in medical research and the notion of informed consent: no individual can use your body for medical research without your specific informed consent granting them permission to do so. In later years, many construed earlier bans on abortion as an interference with the right of a woman to make her own choices about her body and the continuance of a pregnancy.

It seemed, then, only a small and logical step to extend the concept of freedom and self-determination to the end of our life. If you believe that your pain and suffering are insupportable, and if there is no hope that medicine can cure you of a fatal disease, why should you not have the right to ask a physician directly to end your life (euthanasia) or to provide you with the means of doing so (physician-assisted suicide)? After all, it is your body, your suffering, and if there is no reason to believe others will be harmed by your desire to see your life come to an end, what grounds are there for denying you that final act of self-determination? As I suggested above, it is precisely because the claim of self-determination in this context seems so much in tune with our traditional value of liberty that it seems hard to find a reason to reject it.

But we should reject it, and for a variety of considerations, three of which seem most important. The first is that euthanasia is mistakenly understood as a personal and private matter only of self-determination. Suicide, once a punishable crime, was removed from the law some decades ago in this country. But it is one thing not to prosecute a person for attempting suicide and quite another to think that euthanasia is a private act, impacting on no other lives. On the contrary, with euthanasia as its means, it becomes a social act by virtue of calling upon the physician to take part in it. Legalizing it would also provide an important social sanction and legitimation of those practices. They would require regulation and legal oversight.

Most critically, it would add to the acceptable range of killing in our society, noted above, one more occasion for the taking of life. To do so would be to reverse the long-developing trend to limit the occasions of socially sanctioned killing, too often marked by abuse. Euthanasia would also reinstate what I would call "private killing," by which I mean a situation where the agreement of one person to kill another is ratified in private by the individuals themselves, not by public authorities (even if it is made legal and supposed safeguards put in place). Dueling as a way of settling differences was once accepted, a form of private killing, something between the duelists only. But it was finally rejected as socially harmful and is nowhere now accepted in civilized society. The contention that it was *their* bodies at stake, *their* private lives, was rejected as a good moral reason to legally accept dueling.

EUTHANASIA AS A SOCIAL, NOT PRIVATE, ACT

A closely related objection is that what makes euthanasia and physician-assisted suicide social, and not individual, matters is that, by definition, they require the assistance of a physician. Two points are worth considering here. The first is whether we want to sanction the private killing that is euthanasia by allowing physicians to be one of the parties to euthanasia agreements. Since the doctor-patient relationship is protected by the long-standing principle of confidentiality—what goes on between doctor and patient may not be legally revealed to any third party—that gives doctors enormous power over patients.

Whatever the law might be, there will be no way of knowing whether doctors are obeying regulations allowing for euthanasia or physician-assisted suicide, no way of knowing whether they are influencing patient decisions in wrongful ways, no way of knowing whether they are acting with professional integrity. As Sir Charles Allbutt, a British physician, nicely put the problem a century ago:

> If all professions have their safeguards they also have their temptations, and ours is no exception. . . . Unfortunately the game of medicine is played with the cards under the table . . . who is there to note the significant glance, the shrug, the hardly expressed innuendo of our brethren. . . . Thus we work not in the light of public opinion but in the secrecy of the chamber. (Cited in Scarlett, 1991: 24–5)

To give physicians the power to kill patients, or assist in their suicide, when their actions are clothed in confidentiality is to run a considerable risk, one hard to spot and one hard to act upon. As will be noted below, the Dutch experience with euthanasia makes clear how easy it was for doctors to violate the court-established rules for euthanasia and to do so with impunity. There is just no way, in the end, for outsiders to know exactly what doctors do behind the veil of confidentiality; that in itself is a threat.

The second consideration is that the tradition of medicine has, for centuries, opposed the use of medical knowledge and skill to end life. Every important Western medical code of ethics has rejected euthanasia—and rejected it even in those eras when there were many fewer ways of relieving pain than are now available. That could hardly have been because earlier generations of doctors knew less about, or were more indifferent to, pain and suffering. Their relief was at the very heart of the doctor's professional obligation.

There was surely another reason. The medical tradition knew something of great importance: doctors are all too skilled in knowing how to kill to be entrusted with the power to deliberately use that skill. This is not to say that physicians are corrupt, prone to misuse their power; not at all. It is only to say, on the one hand, that the very nature of their profession is to save and protect life, not end it; and that they also, on the other hand, become inured much more than the rest of us to death. Ordinary prudence suggests that the temptation to take life should be kept from them as far as possible. To move in any other direction is to risk the corruption of medicine and to threaten the doctor-patient relationship.

But what of the duty to relieve suffering, to act out of compassion for another? Did the moral strictures against euthanasia and physician-assisted suicide in effect simply forget about, or ignore, that duty? Not at all, but the duty to relieve suffering has never been an absolute duty, overriding all moral objections. No country now allows, or has ever allowed, euthanasia without patient consent even if the patient is incompetent and obviously suffering. Nor are patients' families authorized to request euthanasia under those circumstances. Moreover, as time has gone on, the ability of physicians to relieve patients of just about all pain and suffering through good palliative care has shown that most suffering can be relieved without the ultimate solution of killing the patient. In any event, any alleged duty to relieve suffering has historically always given way to the considerations, noted above, about the nature of medicine as a profession whose principal duty is construed as the saving not the taking of life, and not even when the life cannot medically be saved.

The third argument against euthanasia I want to consider is based on the belief that there is no inherent moral difference between killing a patient directly by euthanasia and allowing a patient to die by deliberately terminating a patient's life-supporting treatment (by turning off a ventilator, for example). Since physicians are allowed to do the latter, it is said that they should be allowed to do the former as well— and indeed that it may be more merciful to carry out euthanasia than to stop treatment, perhaps increasing and prolonging the suffering before the patient actually dies. In effect, the argument goes, terminating treatment will foreseeably end the life of the patient, a death hastened by the physician's act; and that is no different, in its logic or outcome, from killing the patient directly by euthanasia (Rachels, 1975).

There are some mistakes in this argument. One of them is a failure to remember that patients with truly lethal, fatal diseases cannot be saved in the long run. The most that can be accomplished is, by aggressive

treatment, to delay their death. At some point, typically, a physician will legitimately decide that treatment cannot bring the patient back to good health and cannot reverse the downhill course of the illness. The disease is in control at that point and, when the physician stops treatment, the disease takes over and kills the patient. It has been long accepted that, in cases of that kind, the cause of death is the disease, not the physician's action.

Moreover, how can it be said that a physician has "hastened" a patient's death by ending life-saving treatment? After all, but for the doctor's action in keeping the patient alive in the first place and then continuing the life-sustaining treatment, the patient would have died much earlier. Put another way, the doctor saves the patient's life at one point in time, sustains the patient's life through a passage of time, and then allows the patient to die at still another time. Since no physician has the power to stay indefinitely the hand of death, at some point or other, in any case, the physician's patient will be irreversibly on the way to death; that is, at some point, life-sustaining treatment will be futile. To think that doctors "kill" patients by terminating treatment is tantamount at that point to saying that doctors have abolished lethal disease and that they now die only because of a physician's actions. It would be lovely if doctors have achieved that kind of power over nature, with death solely in their hands. It has not happened, and is not likely ever to happen. To say this is not to deny that physicians can misuse their power to terminate treatment wrongly: they can stop treatment when it could still do some good, or when a competent patient wants it continued. In that case, however, the physician is blameworthy. It is still the underlying disease that does the killing, but the physician is culpable for allowing that to happen when it ought not to have happened.

EUTHANASIA AND THE LAW

I have provided some reasons why, ethically speaking, euthanasia and physician-assisted suicide cannot be well defended. But what of the law? If we claim to live in a free country, and believe in pluralism, should not the law leave it up to us as individuals to decide how our lives should end? Many people will reject my arguments against euthanasia, and public opinion polls have consistently shown a majority of Americans to be in favor of it. A law that simply allowed those practices, but coerces no one to embrace them, would seem the most reasonable position.

Not necessarily. I noted earlier that the moral acceptance of euthanasia would have the effect of legitimating the role of the physician as someone now empowered to end life. It would also bring an enormous change in the role of the physician, changing the very notion of what it means to be one (Kass, 2002). Seen in that light, a law permitting euthanasia would have social implications far beyond simply giving patients the right to choose how their lives end. As in so many other matters, what on the surface looks like a narrowly private decision turns out, with legalization, to send much wider ripples through society in general and the practice of medicine in particular. It has been said that, in addition to its regulatory functions, the law is a teacher, providing a picture of the way we think people should live together. Legalized euthanasia would teach the wrong kind of lesson.

The actual enforcement of a law on euthanasia would be enormously difficult to carry out. The privacy of the doctor-patient relationship means that there is an area that the law cannot enter. Whatever conditions the law might set for legal euthanasia, there is in the end no good way to know whether it is being obeyed. Short of having a policeman sitting in on every encounter between a doctor and a patient, what they agree to will remain unavailable to the rest of us. All laws are subject to abuse, particularly when they are controversial in the first place. Not everyone will agree with the law as written, and we can be sure that some will bend it or ignore it if they can get away with it. But in most cases it is possible to detect the violation. We know when our goods have been stolen, just as we can know when someone has been brutally beaten.

It would be far more difficult to detect abuses with euthanasia. For one thing, two of the main reasons offered in favor of euthanasia—self-determination and the relief of suffering—do not readily lend themselves to the limits of law. Why should a right of self-determination be limited to those in a terminal state, which is what is commonly proposed and is required in Holland and Belgium? The Dutch law, which does not require a terminal illness, but only unbearable suffering, is in that respect much more perceptive about the logical and legal implications of the usual moral arguments in favor of euthanasia, which is why it rejected a terminal illness requirement.

The Dutch realized that the open-ended logic of the moral reasons behind euthanasia do not lend themselves well to artificial, legal barriers. Impending death is not the only horrible thing in life and, if an individual's body is her own, why should any interference with her choice be tolerated? The requirement of an impending death seems arbitrary in the extreme. As for the relief of suffering, why should someone have to be competent and able to give consent, as if the suffering of those lacking such capacities counts for less? In short, the main reasons given for the legalization of euthanasia seem, logically, to resist the kinds of limit built into the Oregon and Belgian laws. That reality opens the way to abuse of the law. All it requires is a physician who finds the law too narrow, the deed too easy, and a desperate patient all too eager to die.

THE DUTCH EXPERIENCE

This is not speculation. The Netherlands offers a case study of how it happens. For many decades, until a formal change in the law only recently, the Dutch courts had permitted euthanasia if certain conditions were met: a free choice, a considered and persistent request, unacceptable suffering, consultation with another physician, and accurate reporting on the cause of death. Throughout the 1970s and 1980s euthanasia (and occasionally physician-assisted suicide) was carried out, with many assurances that the conditions were being met. But, curious to find out about the actual practice, the Dutch government established a Commission on Euthanasia in 1990 to carry out an anonymous survey of Dutch physicians (Van der Maas, 1992).

The survey encompassed a sample of 406 physicians, and two other studies, which, taken together, were eye-opening. The official results showed that, based on their sample, out of a total of 129,000 deaths there were some 2,300 cases of voluntary ("free choice") euthanasia and 400 cases of assisted suicide. In addition, most strikingly, there were some 1,000 cases of intentional termination of life without explicit request, what the Dutch called "non-voluntary euthanasia." In sum, out of 3,300 euthanasia deaths, nearly one-third were non-voluntary. Less than 50 percent of the euthanasia cases were reported as euthanasia: another violation of the court rules. Worst of all, some 10 percent of the non-voluntary cases were instances of euthanasia with competent patients who were not asked for their consent.

None of that was supposed to be happening—a clear abuse of the court-established rules. A number of doctors had obviously taken it upon themselves to unilaterally end the lives of many patients. If that could happen there, it could happen here. Since that time, the Dutch have officially established a legal right to euthanasia (replacing the early court-established guidelines), but the government there has recently found that only 50 percent of the physicians who carry it out report doing so, and that there continue to be 400 cases a year of voluntary euthanasia (Sheldon, 2003).

The American state of Oregon, which legalized physician-assisted suicide in 1994, but whose actual implementation was delayed until 1997 by a number of court challenges, offers a variety of further insights into the practice. To the surprise of many, the actual number of people to take advantage of the new law has been small. The number of prescriptions for physician-assisted suicide, written for the first four years, beginning in 1998, has been 24 (1998), 33 (1999), 39 (2000) and 44 (2001)—and the thing seems to depend on individual differences in values, not in bodily responses to pain or impending death. In reporting on the first year of the Oregon law, the state Oregon Health Commission noted that a majority of the 16 reported cases involved people

with a particular fear of a "loss of control or the fear of loss of general control, and a loss of bodily function" (Chin et al., 1999: 580, 582). It was not the unbearable and unrelievable physical pain so often and luridly emphasized in the efforts to legalize PAS, or a fear of abandonment, or dependency on others (though some mentioned that), or a feeling of meaninglessness in suffering.

Worry about such a loss represents a particular set of personal (and idiosyncratic) values, by no means a widely distributed set. This was well brought out in the official state report. What the state officials did was to match those who received PAS (called the "case" group) with a group (called the "control" group) of patients with "similar underlying illnesses," and matched as well for age and date of death (Chin et al., 1999: 578). Their findings were striking: the PAS group was much more concerned about autonomy and control than the other group. Even more provocative was the fact that the PAS group was far more able to function physically than the control group: "21 percent of the case patients, as compared with 84 percent of the control patients . . . were completely disabled" (Chin et al., 1999: 580). In other words, the PAS group was far better off physically than the control group. It was their personal values that led them in one direction rather than another, not the objective intensity of their incapacities. Or to put it in terms we used earlier, PAS represents a legitimation of suicide for those who have a particular conception of the optimum life and its management, one of complete control.

CATERING TO A SMALL MINORITY

If it turns out, then, that PAS heavily attracts a particular kind of person, one very different from most terminally ill people, then much of the public policy argument on its behalf fails. It is not a general problem requiring drastic changes in law, tradition, and medical practice. Just as suicide in general, whatever the level of misery, is not the way most people seek to deal with it, so also are euthanasia and PAS the desire of a tiny minority. These results, it should be added, are much the same as those found in the Netherlands. At a 1991 conference there with the leaders of the Dutch euthanasia movement, I asked the physicians how it was possible reliably to diagnose "unbearable" or "untreatable" suffering as a medical condition and thus suitable for their euthanasia or PAS ministrations. They conceded that there is no reliable medical diagnosis, no way of really knowing what was going on within the mind and emotions of the patient, and—consistent with the findings of the Oregon state study—no correlation *whatever* between a patient's actual medical condition and the reported suffering.

Perhaps euthanasia is not, as many would like to put it, simply a logical extension of the physician's duty to relieve pain and suffering, an old obligation in a new garment. Perhaps it is just part of the drift toward the medicalization of the woes of life, particularly that version of life that regards the loss of control as the greatest of human indignities. Not only that, but even the fear of a loss of control is for many tantamount to its actual loss. I wonder if the voters of Oregon, and all of those who believe euthanasia a needed progressive move, mean to empower unto death that special, and small, subclass of patients uncommonly bent on the control of their lives and eager to have the help of doctors to do so. Somehow I doubt it, but it looks as if that may be what they got.

Underlying much of what I have written here are two assumptions, which need some defense. One of them is that good palliative care, a rapidly growing medical specialty, can relieve most pain and suffering. Some cases, I readily concede, may not be helped, or not enough, by even the best palliative care, but the overwhelming majority can be. My second assumption is this: it is bad public policy to abandon long-standing legal prohibitions, with important reasons and traditions behind them, for the sake of a very small minority, and particularly when the consequences open the way for abuse and a fundamental change in medical values. The fact, for so it seems, that the small minority reflects not some general human response to pain and suffering but a personal, and generally idiosyncratic, view of suffering is all

the more reason to hesitate before legally blessing euthanasia. Human beings, in their lives and in their deaths, have long been able to see their lives come to an end without feeling some special necessity to have it ended of them, directly by euthanasia or self-inflicted by physician-assisted suicide.

What about the notion of "death with dignity," a phrase much used by euthanasia supporters? It is a misleading, obfuscating phrase. Death is no indignity, even if accompanied by pain and a loss of control. Death is a fundamental fact of human biology, as fundamental as any other part of human life. If that human life has dignity as human life, it cannot be lost because death brings it to an end, even if in a disorderly, unpleasant fashion. It takes more than that to erase our dignity. Human beings in concentration camps did not lose their essential human value and dignity by being tortured, humiliated, and degraded. Euthanasia confers no dignity on the process of dying; it only creates the illusion of dignity for those who, mistakenly, believe a loss of control is not to be endured. It can be, and most human beings have endured it. No one would say that the newborn baby, unable to talk, incontinent, utterly unable to control her situation, and unable to interact with others, lacks dignity. Neither does the dying older person, even if displaying exactly the same traits. Dignity is not so easily taken from human beings. Nor can euthanasia confer it on someone.

NOTES

1. Unless there is a need to deal with the difference between euthanasia and physician-assisted suicide, I will hereafter refer only to euthanasia. By euthanasia I mean the direct killing of a patient by a doctor, ordinarily by means of a lethal injection. By physician-assisted suicide I mean the act of killing oneself by means of lethal drugs provided by a physician.

REFERENCES

Chin, Arthur E., Hedberg, Katrina, Higginson, Grant K., and Fleming, David W. (1999). "Legalized physician-assisted suicide in Oregon—the first year's experience." *The New England Journal of Medicine,* 340: 577–83.

Kass, Leon Richard (2002). "'I will give no deadly drugs': why doctors must not kill." In K. Foley and H.

Hendin (eds.), *The Case against Assisted Suicide: For the Right to End-of-life Care.* Baltimore, MD: Johns Hopkins University Press.

Oregon Death with Dignity Legal Defense and Education Center (2000). *Oregon Death with Dignity.* Portland, OR: Oregon Death with Dignity Legal Defense and Education Center.

Rachels, James (1975). "Active and passive euthanasia." *The New England Journal of Medicine,* 292: 78–80.

Scarlett, Earle (1991). "What is a profession?" In B. R. Reynolds and J. Stone (eds.), *On Doctoring: Stories, Poems, Essays* (pp. 124–5). New York: Simon & Schuster.

Sheldon, Tony (2003). "Only half of Dutch doctors report euthanasia." *British Medical Journal,* 326: 1164.

Van der Maas, Paul J. (1992). *Euthanasia and other Decisions at the End of Life.* Amsterdam: Elsevier.

READING QUESTIONS

1. What reasons does Callahan give for asserting that relief of pain and suffering cannot justify suicide? Does he think this is a position based merely on tradition and religion, or are there reasons based in rationality alone?
2. How does Callahan describe "private killing"? Why would euthanasia be a form of private killing, and what, according to Callahan, is wrong with it as such?
3. Explain the argument given by Callahan's opponents that there is no moral difference between killing a patient directly and allowing a patient to die by withholding or withdrawing treatment. Include an explanation of the causal difference between the two, according to Callahan.
4. Why does Callahan think that legalized euthanasia would teach the wrong kind of lesson to society?
5. What difference does Callahan note between the Dutch laws surrounding euthanasia and the Oregon Death with Dignity Act?

DISCUSSION QUESTIONS

1. Do you agree with Callahan that a negative emotional response to suicide is an important signal of a moral problem with PAS?
2. Callahan worries that legalized PAS gives physicians too much power to kill patients, including influencing patient decisions in wrongful ways. What reasons can you think of that a physician might have for doing this? Do you think it is plausible that this could be a widespread concern?
3. Discuss the tension created by having both a duty to relieve suffering and a duty to save life, given that the two are incompatible in some cases. How would you respond if you were a physician in such cases?
4. Callahan argues that in the case of withdrawing treatment from a dying patient, the disease causes death, unlike cases of euthanasia whereby the physician causes the death. Do you agree that there is a causal difference, and if so, do you think it matters morally? Why or why not?
5. Do you agree with Callahan that fear of losing control and autonomy over one's own life is not a reason to hasten death, since this is an eventuality faced by most of us anyway? Is relief of pain and suffering a stronger reason? Why or why not?

MICHAEL B. GILL

A Moral Defense of Oregon's Physician-Assisted Suicide Law

Michael Gill considers two main lines of moral argument against Oregon's physician-assisted suicide law: (1) that for reasons grounded in a person's autonomy, suicide is intrinsically wrong and (2) that given the moral foundations of the medical profession, it is wrong for a physician to assist in a patient's suicide. The second of these arguments leads Gill to a critical discussion of the principle of double effect, which is sometimes invoked in objecting to physician-assisted suicide.

Recommended Reading: natural law theory, especially the principle of double effect, chap. 1, Sec. 2B.

INTRODUCTION

Since 1998, physician-assisted suicide (PAS) has been legal in the state of Oregon. If an Oregon resident has less than six months to live and is mentally competent, she can request that a physician prescribe her drugs that will cause a quick and painless death.

Most of the objections to the Oregon law fall into one of three categories. In the first category is the claim that it is intrinsically wrong for someone to kill herself. In the second category is the claim that it is intrinsically wrong for physicians to assist someone in killing herself. In the third category is the claim that legalizing PAS will lead to very bad consequences for the sick, the elderly and other vulnerable elements of our population.

In this article, I address the first and second categories of objections. In the first part of the article, I try to show that it is not intrinsically wrong for someone with a terminal disease to kill herself. In

the second part, I try to show that it is not intrinsically wrong for physicians to assist someone with a terminal disease who has reasonable grounds for wanting to kill herself.

I do not discuss the consequentialist arguments that occupy the third category of objections to the Oregon law. These consequentialist arguments are important, and they need to be addressed. But they fall outside my current purview.

Let me also mention another important aspect of my position. I do not argue that anyone has a constitutionally protected *right* to assisted suicide. Laws prohibiting PAS and laws allowing PAS may both be equally consistent with the US Constitution. I try to give reasons for thinking that we ought to support the Oregon law, but I do not try to show that the Constitution demands that we make PAS available. I try to show that there may be good moral reasons for implementing a law allowing PAS, even if there is no basis for anyone to claim that she has a constitutionally protected right to assistance in suicide.

From "A Moral Defense of Oregon's Physician-Assisted Suicide Law" by Michael B. Gill, *Mortality*, Feb. 2005; 10 (2), pp. 53–67. Reproduced with permission.

WHY IT IS NOT INTRINSICALLY WRONG FOR A TERMINAL PATIENT TO COMMIT SUICIDE

Arguments against the Autonomy-Based Justification for Allowing Suicide

Leon Kass has provided one of the most influential statements of the belief that someone using the Oregon law to kill herself is doing something intrinsically wrong. Kass uses the concept of tragedy to frame his opposition. Something is tragic, Kass tells us, if it is necessarily self-contradictory. "In tragedy the failure is imbedded in the hero's success, the defeats in his victories, the miseries in his glory" (Kass, 2002a: 48). Kass claims that many of the recent developments in health care are tragic in the way that he defines it, or necessarily self-contradictory. PAS under the Oregon law is one of his prime examples. PAS, Kass argues, inevitably destroys the thing of value that it is intended to promote.

The value the Oregon law is intended to promote is the autonomy of human beings. In the following, I say more about how we ought to conceive of what is valuable about autonomy, but for now we can think of it simply as a person's ability to make decisions for herself, to decide for herself what will happen to her own body. According to its proponents, the Oregon law promotes autonomy because it expands the range of decisions a person can make. When PAS is legal, a person has the choice of deciding whether or not to end her life by taking a pill. But when PAS is illegal, a person does not have that choice. And a state of affairs that gives a person more choices is, from the standpoint of trying to promote autonomy, better than a state of affairs that offers a person fewer choices.

According to Kass, however, this way of thinking is tragically simplistic, shallow and short-sighted. For in fact the legalization of PAS does not promote autonomy but encourages its destruction. Far from giving people more choices, PAS brings about a state of affairs in which a person has lost the ability to make choices altogether. For the person who engages in PAS will, obviously, be dead, and someone who is dead can no longer exercise her autonomy. It is thus *self-contradictory* to argue for PAS by claiming that it promotes autonomy, as PAS destroys a person's ability to make decisions. As Kass puts it, there can be "no ground at all" for claiming that "autonomy licenses an act that puts our autonomy permanently out of business" (Kass, 2002a: 217–218).

Opponents of PAS often color in this charge of self-contradiction by contending that the autonomy-based justification of PAS leads to obvious absurdities (Callahan, 2002: 61–63). One such absurdity is the legalization of a certain kind of slavery. It is illegal to sell yourself into slavery. Even if you want to contract with someone to become her slave, you are not allowed to do so. The contract would be null and void. According to PAS opponents, however, the autonomy-based justification of PAS implies that forbidding someone from selling herself into slavery restricts her range of self-determining choices, and that as a result we should give everyone the option of deciding whether or not to become a slave. So the autonomy-based justification of PAS implies that we should legalize self-slavery contracts. But the idea of legalizing slavery of any kind is absurd. And so, PAS opponents conclude, the autonomy-based justification of PAS is fundamentally flawed.

Another absurdity PAS opponents try to foist on the attempted justification of the Oregon law is the legalization of PAS for people who are healthy and non-terminal. Oregon's law allows PAS only for people who have six months or less to live. But the autonomy-based justification of PAS implies that we ought to expand the range of self-regarding decisions every competent individual can make. The autonomy-based justification implies, then, that we should give even healthy and non-terminal people the option of deciding whether or not to commit suicide. But, opponents of PAS argue, the idea of legalizing PAS for healthy and non-terminal people is absurd. So we have, once again, a clear reason to reject the autonomy-based justification for PAS.

Defense of the Oregon Law's Autonomy-Based Justification for Allowing Suicide

Proponents of PAS can respond to these criticisms of their autonomy-based justification in one of two ways. First, they can take the hard-line libertarian route, which consists of biting the bullet and embracing the implications that PAS opponents say are absurd. Hard-line libertarian supporters of PAS will agree that their justification of PAS implies that we should legalize self-slavery and assisted suicide for healthy, non-terminal individuals, but then go on to argue that people *should* be allowed to sell themselves into slavery if they freely choose to do so, and that healthy, non-terminal individuals should be allowed to seek assisted suicide. According to this hard-line libertarian approach, everyone really should be given the legal option to make whatever self-regarding decisions she wants. Whether we think a decision is moral or immoral is legally irrelevant. As long as no one else is harmed, the moral status of a person's justificatory principles is none of the law's business. So even if we come to believe that there is some kind of "self-contradiction" involved in a person's choosing to undertake some course of action, that would not justify using the law to prevent a person from undertaking that course of action, so long as no other person is hurt. This hard-line libertarian position has an internal consistency that shields it from any quick and simple refutation. A full treatment of this position would, however, involve us in a large-scale critique of the American legal system, and would thus take us far afield from the Oregon law, which is in fact in conflict with the hard-line libertarian position. I think, consequently, that we would do best to leave to one side the libertarian defense of assisted suicide. It's a topic for a different discussion.

The reason the Oregon law conflicts with the hard-line libertarian position is that it does not allow healthy, non-terminal individuals to choose PAS. And this feature of the Oregon law points towards the second way in which one can try to defend the autonomy-based justification of PAS against the charge of self-contradiction. Those proposing this second kind of defense will agree that self-slavery and assisted suicide for healthy, non-terminal individuals ought to remain illegal, but then go on to argue that their autonomy-based justification of the Oregon law does not imply that those other things ought to be legal. They will argue, rather, that there is a clear and morally significant difference between what the Oregon law provides for, on the one hand, and self-slavery and assisted suicide for healthy, non-terminal individuals, on the other. So while it would be wrong to legalize self-slavery and assisted suicide for healthy, non-terminal individuals, the autonomy-based defense of the Oregon law does not commit one to holding that those other things should be legal. The self-contradiction that afflicts those other things does not afflict the kind of assisted suicide that the Oregon law allows.

The Oregon law has provisions to ensure that the people who engage in PAS are competent, and that their decision to commit suicide is a result of autonomous decision making. But, crucially, it also has provisions to ensure that the people who engage in PAS have terminal illnesses. Specifically, the Oregon law allows a person to receive lethal drugs only if two doctors have verified that she has six months or less to live. And what defenders of the Oregon law can argue is that the suicide of a person who is about to die does not violate the value of autonomy because the person's decision-making ability is going to disappear whether she commits suicide or not. The person with a terminal disease who decides to commit suicide is not changing the universe from a place in which she would have been able to exercise her autonomy in the future into a place in which she will not be able to exercise her autonomy in the future. For she will not be able to exercise her autonomy in the future no matter what she does. Hers is not a decision to prevent herself from being able to make future decisions, because future decisions will not be hers to make regardless. The ending of her decision-making ability is a foregone conclusion. She is simply choosing that it end in one way rather than another. The person who commits suicide under the Oregon law should be compared to someone who blows out a candle that has used up all its wax and is now nothing but a sputtering wick that is just about to go out on its own. She should not be compared to someone who snuffs out the bright, strong flame of a new candle.

This autonomy-based defense of the Oregon law gains strength through a consideration of how the final stages of a terminal disease can corrode a person's autonomous nature. Progressive bodily deterioration can limit and ultimately eliminate one's ability to undertake physical action, and mental deterioration can limit and ultimately eliminate one's ability to make any kind of decision at all. In the end, one may be barely conscious and maintained by machines, bereft of the autonomous nature that gives human beings dignity and inestimable moral worth. It is this lingering half-life that persons who use the Oregon law may seek to prevent. And such a decision does not necessarily contradict the value of autonomy because during such a half-life autonomy does not exist anyway. Indeed, defenders of the Oregon law can argue that the decision to commit suicide in the final stages of a terminal illness can proceed from a great respect for autonomy, as such a decision can reveal that what a person values about herself is not simply her physical existence but the ability to decide what happens to her.

The fact that the Oregon law allows only terminal patients to commit suicide also gives PAS proponents the conceptual resources for repelling the absurd consequences PAS opponents try to foist on them. Opponents, recall, claimed that the autonomy-based justification of PAS implied that we should legalize self-slavery and assisted suicide for healthy, non-terminal individuals. But PAS proponents can point to a clear moral difference between the suicides allowed under the Oregon law, on the one hand, and self-slavery and the assisted suicide of healthy, non-terminal individuals, on the other. Someone who makes herself into a slave or commits suicide while healthy is throwing away the capacity for self-determination. If she does not make herself a slave or commit suicide, she will be able to make her own decisions for years to come; but if she does either of those things, she will not be able to make her own future decisions. But a person who is about to die is not going to be able to make decisions for years to come, whether she commits suicide or not. She is not throwing away her ability to determine her future because

that ability no longer exists. So the autonomy-based justification of assisted suicide for terminal individuals is completely compatible with the prohibitions on self-slavery and assisted suicide for healthy, non-terminal individuals. PAS proponents can consistently condemn actions that destroy the ability to make future decisions, because the suicide of a terminal individual is not a case of such destruction.

Opponents of PAS will respond, however, by claiming that the suicide of a person with a terminal disease *is* a case of the destruction of the ability to make future decisions. For a person who has six months to live has, after all, six months to live. And while she may be unconscious and unable to make her own decisions for part of that time, she will be conscious and able to make her own decisions for the other part. It might be true that her ability to make decisions will persist for only a few weeks or months. But, according to this way of criticizing the Oregon law, that ability is still of ultimate value, even if its temporal reach is relatively short. Earlier, I compared a terminal individual who commits suicide to someone who blows out a dying candle. There is a difference, however, between extinguishing a candle that is almost burned out but still providing light, and letting the candle burn itself out. A person who blows out a candle, even one that is almost finished, is undertaking a course of action that extinguishes light. As a result of her action, darkness comes sooner than it otherwise would have. Similarly, allowing a person to kill herself is allowing her to destroy the ability to make decisions, and that remains true even if the person would die of natural causes in a few months time anyway.

Opponents of PAS could try to put the point of the previous paragraph in terms of a nasty dilemma for proponents. If proponents of PAS really do base their position on the value of autonomy, opponents might argue, then they must be opposed both to the killing of a person who is incompetent to make her own decisions (which the Oregon law does in fact prohibit) and to the suicide of someone who will be able to make her own decisions in the future (no matter how short that future may be). But everyone falls into one of those two categories. Everyone is either incompetent to make her own decisions or will be able to make her own decisions in the (immediate) future. So the value of autonomy implies the moral legitimacy of the suicide of no one.

Autonomy as the Ability to Make "Big Decisions"

Does this criticism defeat the autonomy-based justification of PAS? Does the fact that even a terminal patient still possesses decision-making ability show that the value of autonomy cannot be used to support the Oregon law? I don't think so. I think, rather, that the goal of promoting autonomy is consistent with PAS in general and the Oregon law in particular, and that the criticism described in the previous two paragraphs is mistaken. In order to explain what is wrong with the criticism, however, we need to say a bit more about the value of autonomy.

Many ethical discussions that invoke the value of autonomy equate autonomy with the ability to make one's own decisions. To this point, I too have accepted this equation. But if we want to be clear about what the value of autonomy in end-of-life issues really involves, we need to draw a distinction between the kinds of decisions a person may make. The distinction I want to draw is between what I will call "big decisions" and "little decisions."

Big decisions are decisions that shape your destiny and determine the course of your life. Big decisions call on you to make a choice in light of things that matter most to you, in light of the things that give your life whatever meaning it has. Big decisions proceed from your deepest values. Little decisions, by contrast, concern matters that are momentary or insignificant. They do not proceed from your deepest values, but draw only on preferences that rest on the surface of your character. Big decisions are momentous, in that making one big decision rather than another will change in some non-negligible way the course of your life. But little decisions don't matter that much. Regardless of whether you make one little decision or another, your life will continue in much the same way. Little decisions don't shape your destiny. So an example of a big decision would be deciding to get married, while an example of a

little decision would be deciding to eat the blue jello instead of the red jello.[1]

I maintain that to respect autonomy is, first and foremost, to respect a person's ability to make big decisions. It is to respect a person's ability to determine her own fate, to shape her own life. The capacity to make little decisions matters less. That's not to say that the freedom to make little decisions doesn't matter at all. We should let people make as many of the little decisions that affect them as is possible. But it is the ability to make big decisions that is of inestimable value. That is where the great moral weight of the value of autonomy lies.

A person who meets the Oregon law's criteria of competence and terminality will probably have the capacity to make little decisions for weeks or months to come. She will, that is, probably be able to continue to make decisions about many of the details of her daily routine. But she may very well not have the same ability to make big decisions. Her ability to determine her own destiny, to shape her own life, may be all but gone. There are two reasons for this. First, the limited amount of time a person with a terminal disease has left to live eliminates many of the options that constitute big decision making. Long-range planning of a life is impossible when the life will end in a few months. Second, the nature of many terminal diseases can preclude big decision making in a manner that is distinct even from the amount of time a person has left to live. Terminal diseases can consume the mind as well as the body. And all too often, the only decisions a person ends up making at the end-stage are those that concern pain management and the most basic of bodily functions. The kinds of concerns that involve big decision making, the kind that call on one's deepest values and create the opportunity to shape a life, are crowded out by the immediacy of disease.

There is, however, one big decision a person who meets Oregon's criteria will still be able to make, one choice about her destiny that will still be open to her. She can still decide how and when to die. She can still choose the shape of the end of her life, the concluding words of her final chapter. This may, in fact, be the only big decision that her limited time left affords her. Thus, giving a person with a terminal disease the option of PAS can promote the thing of value that we have in mind when we talk of respect of autonomy. For the option of PAS can enhance such a person's ability to make a big decision for herself. When, by contrast, we make it more difficult for a person with a terminal disease to commit suicide, we restrict her ability to make a big decision. And this restriction cannot be justified by claiming that we are respecting her autonomy, unless what we mean by autonomy is simply the capacity to make little decisions for a few more weeks or months. For besides the choice of how she wants her life to end, ever littler decisions may be all that such a person has any prospect of making.

Once again, then, we can see the clear difference between PAS for people with terminal diseases, on the one hand, and the suicide of healthy people, on the other. A typical healthy person possesses the ability to make big decisions in the future. Such a person, typically, can control her own destiny and shape her own life for years to come. So by killing herself, a healthy person does violate what is most important about autonomy: she has before her the choice between a future in which she can make big decisions and a future in which she cannot make big decisions, and she opts for the latter. But a person with a terminal disease may not be able to make big decisions in the future, no matter what decision she makes now. So it is not necessarily the case that a person with a terminal disease will be choosing between a future in which she can make big decisions and a future in which she cannot make big decisions. It may be the case, rather, that such a person's ability to make big decisions will be nonexistent in all the futures between which she must choose.

The difference between PAS for people with diseases and self-slavery is even more clear and instructive. A slave may very well be able to make numerous little decisions throughout her life. She may be in control of the details of fulfilling her basic bodily needs, and she could have some degree of choice about how to go about completing her assigned tasks. But even if a slave possesses the capacity to make little decisions, we will still believe that her slavery violates autonomy in a fundamental way. And that is because the slave lacks the ability to make big decisions. She lacks the ability to control her own destiny, to shape

her own life. It is the ability to make big decisions that is of profound moral importance. The fact that the slave may be able to make little decisions is, by comparison, morally insignificant. It is the ability to make big decisions that ought not to be tossed away. But a person with a terminal disease who chooses PAS will not necessarily be tossing away her ability to make big decisions; she may, rather, be exercising it in the only way she can. For the ability of such a person to make big decisions may already be all but gone, the only big decision left to her being that of deciding how her life will end. Now it is true that a person with a terminal disease who chooses PAS will be tossing away a few weeks or months of little decision making. But as the case of the slave illustrates, the ability to make little decisions is relatively unimportant.

Opponents of PAS may object that I have underestimated the extent to which a person with a terminal disease can be able to make big decisions. They may argue that even a person whose physical abilities are severely limited and who will die within a few months may still be able to do many things to affect the shape of her life. Such a person may, for instance, use the time she has left to change her will or to make vital arrangements for the care of her loved ones. She may reconcile with people from whom she has long been estranged. Through the experience of suffering and dying, she may learn profound truths about herself and the human condition. She may forge a new relationship with God. All of these things are of the utmost importance to the shape of a life. None of them is little or insignificant. But by availing herself of PAS, a person destroys her ability to do any of these things.

In response to this objection, let me say first of all that it is true that *some* people may have profound, life-changing experiences at the very end of life. The very end of life may be the time when *some* people achieve a new awareness or forge new relationships that cast all their previous years in an entirely different light. What is crucial to realize, however, is that this may not be true for *all* people. There may also be people who have settled all their worldly and spiritual affairs a month or two before they are expected to die. Some people may have no need to make financial arrangements or pursue any sort of interpersonal reconciliation in the final months of life because they may already have done all the work on their wills and their relationships that they believe they need to do. Some people may not need to experience any more suffering and dying because they may believe that they have learned all the lessons about themselves and the human condition that they are ever going to learn. Some people may have already achieved exactly the relationship with God to which they aspire. So while PAS may be the wrong thing for *some* people, it is not necessarily the wrong thing for *all* people. Proponents of the Oregon law do not claim, of course, that everyone with a terminal disease should commit suicide. They claim, rather, that because suicide may be right for some people, it should be an option. It should be available to all people who are terminal and competent to make their own decisions.

Opponents of PAS seem to believe, however, that it is wrong for *anyone* with a terminal disease to commit suicide. They seem to believe that there are morally significant reasons against suicide in every situation, that everyone should live for as long as she can so that she can learn for herself, and teach others, profound lessons about the meaning of life. Thus, Kass maintains that "what humanity needs most" are people who "continue to live and work and love as much as they can for as long as they can," and that such people are worthy of admiration in a way that suicides are not (Kass, 2002b: 39). And Callahan implies that people who live for as long as they can in the face of suffering and a lack of control are more "noble and heroic" than those who choose suicide (Callahan, 2002: 57), that the former fulfill the "duty to bear suffering as a form of mutual human support" in a way that the latter do not (Callahan, 2002: 66).

But some people may believe that the very end of their lives will *not* produce any profound and meaningful insights, for them or anyone else, into "the point or purpose or end of human existence" (Callahan, 2002: 58). And this belief of theirs may follow from their own fundamental values. It may proceed from their own deepest views of what is profound and meaningful about life. To respect autonomy is to promote their ability to act on these fundamental values. Suicide may be an unreasonable end to the lives of some people with terminal diseases. But it may not be an unreasonable end for the lives of others. And everyone should be allowed to decide for herself whether she is the first sort of person or the second. It is a big decision, deciding what sort of ending is for you the fundamentally right one, maybe one of the biggest decisions of all. That is why everyone whose end is imminent should be allowed to make it for herself.

WHY IT IS NOT INTRINSICALLY WRONG FOR A PHYSICIAN TO PARTICIPATE IN PAS

Physicians and the Decision of Whether Life Is Worth Living

Let us now turn to the second objection to PAS as it occurs under the Oregon law. This objection is based on the role of a physician. Even if it is in some cases morally acceptable for a person to commit suicide, PAS opponents maintain, it still will always be wrong for a physician to assist her. Those who defend PAS "misunderstand the moral foundations of medical practice," failing to appreciate that medicine "is intrinsically a moral profession, with *its own* immanent principles and standards of conduct that set limits on what physicians may properly do" (Kass, 2002b: 19).

Now it is worth noting, first, that even if physicians' special moral position makes it wrong for them to assist in suicide, that does not mean that it is wrong for *anyone* to assist in suicide.[2] Perhaps we should allow members of some other profession—such as lawyers—to provide lethal drugs to competent people with terminal diseases (see Sade & Marshall, 1996). Indeed, the more the argument against PAS depends upon principles that are special to the medical profession, the less applicable it will be to other professions' assistance in suicide.

But of course the Oregon law does allow physicians to prescribe lethal drugs. So in the interests of defending the Oregon law, let me now address the charge that assisting in suicide violates the essential moral duty of the medical profession.

Opponents of the Oregon law contend that, in requesting PAS, a person is asking her physician to make a decision that is inappropriate for a physician to make. This is because a physician who must decide whether to assist in a person's suicide is forced to make a judgment about moral and spiritual matters that have nothing to do with medicine. Thus Kass contends that to comply with a request for PAS, "the physician must, willy-nilly, play the part of judge, and his judgments will be decidedly nonmedical and nonprofessional, based on personal standards" (Kass, 2002b: 29–30). And Pellegrino maintains that in prescribing a lethal dose a physician is making the nonmedical judgment that her patient's "life is unworthy of living" (Pellegrino, 2002: 51). Callahan makes the same point when he writes, "The purpose of medicine is not to relieve all the problems of human mortality, the most central and difficult of which is why we have to die at all or die in ways that seem pointless to us . . . This is not the role of medicine because it has no competence to manage the meaning of life and death, only the physical and psychological manifestations of those problems. Medicine's role must be limited to what it can appropriately do, and it has neither the expertise nor the wisdom necessary to respond to the deepest and oldest human questions" (Callahan, 2002: 59).

This criticism seems to me to miss entirely the provisions of the Oregon law. For the Oregon law makes very clear the role physicians are to play in requests for PAS. It says that physicians are to determine if the patient requesting PAS has a terminal disease and if the patient is competent. These are both medical judgments. In order to make them, a physician does not need to make any judgments about "fundamental philosophical and religious matters" pertaining to the meaning of life. The physician is not asked to decide for the patient whether or not life is worth living. The patient makes that decision for herself. Indeed, it is Kass, Pellegrino and Callahan who would take the decision about whether life is worth living out of the hands of the patient. For they are the ones who contend that suicide is always the morally inferior option. It is their view that passes a substantive "philosophical and religious" judgment on how one should cope with terminal disease. The Oregon law, by contrast, asks physicians to make two medical judgments, and then (if the patient meets the relevant criteria) to assist the patient in doing whatever the patient herself has decided about how best to cope with suffering and loss of control at the end of life.[3]

Of course, there may be some physicians who are personally morally opposed to all forms of suicide (just as there are some physicians who are personally morally opposed to abortion), and such physicians should have the option of refusing to participate in any requests for PAS. But there may also be some physicians who believe that an individual should be allowed to make up her own mind about how she wants her life to end, and those physicians' participation in requests for PAS will consist entirely of their making medical judgments about individuals' mental competence and life expectancy, and then facilitating the patient's own decision.

The Duty to Promote Health and the Duty to Reduce Suffering

Kass, Pellegrino and Callahan go on to argue, however, that so long as the physician is knowingly involved in a process that leads to suicide, she is doing something wrong. For, according to Kass, Pellegrino and Callahan, to participate in such a process is to violate the essential moral duty of the medical profession: it is to violate the medical duty to promote health (Callahan, 2002: 58; Kass, 2002b: 20–21).

Kass, Pellegrino and Callahan are certainly correct in saying that physicians have a moral duty to promote health. But there is an obvious problem with claiming that trying to make patients healthy is a physician's *only* moral duty. The problem is that people with terminal diseases cannot be made healthy. A physician cannot heal someone whose disease is lethal and untreatable. So if trying to make patients healthy were their *only* duty, physicians would have no role to play in the care of dying patients. It is clear, however, that physicians do have a role to play in the care of the dying. No one advocates that physicians are obligated by their professional ethic to abandon their patients upon making a terminal diagnosis. On the contrary, it is well recognized that physicians have especially pressing obligations to such patients' care.

In caring for dying patients, one of a physician's principal roles is to reduce suffering. When healing is no longer possible, the reduction of suffering takes center stage.

This duty to reduce the suffering of dying patients is limited in at least one crucial respect. If the dying patient is competent, then physicians should reduce her suffering only in ways to which the patient consents. This limitation on the duty to reduce suffering also applies to the physician's duty to promote health. It is just as wrong for a physician to try to cure a competent patient by undertaking a course of action to which the patient does not agree as it is for a physician to try to reduce the suffering of a competent patient by undertaking a course of action to which the patient does not agree.

Kass, Pellegrino and Callahan acknowledge this role of the physician. They agree that a physician has a moral duty to help to reduce the suffering of a patient with a terminal disease. I presume they would also agree with the limitation on the duty to reduce pain that I have described—that is, that they would agree that physicians should undertake courses of action to reduce the suffering of competent patients with terminal diseases only if the patients have consented to those courses of action. But Kass, Pellegrino and Callahan place another limitation on this duty as well. They argue that a physician's duty to reduce the suffering of patients with terminal diseases can never include assistance in suicide.

So while the Oregon law implies that a physician's duty to reduce the pain of competent patients with terminal diseases should be limited by the patient's own wishes, Kass, Pellegrino and Callahan believe that this duty should also be limited by a prohibition on assisting in suicide. But why do they believe the additional limitation is warranted? Why do they believe that if a patient is competent and dying, her physician should not be allowed to help her reduce her suffering by suicide, if that is what she requests?

Kass argues that the second limitation on the duty to reduce suffering is warranted because it is impossible to benefit a patient by helping to bring about her death. Thus, the idea that we can make a patient better off by helping to kill must be morally incoherent. As Kass puts it, " 'Better off dead' is logical nonsense—unless, of course, death is not death indeed but instead a gateway to a new and better life beyond. Despite loose talk to the contrary, it is in fact impossible to compare the goodness or badness of one's existence with the goodness or badness of one's 'nonexistence,' because it nonsensically requires treating 'nonexistence' as a condition one is nonetheless able to experience and enjoy . . . [T]o intend and to act for someone's good requires that person's continued existence for the benefit to be received . . . This must be the starting point in discussing all medical benefits: no benefit without a beneficiary" (Kass, 2002b: 34).

Kass claims, then, that it is logically impossible and morally incoherent to try to justify assisted suicide by saying that a person may be better off dead than alive. And perhaps there is some peculiarly literal reading of the words "person" and "better off" that makes Kass's claim true. But there is nothing at all incoherent about a person's preferring a state of affairs in which she is dead to a state of affairs in which she is alive. Throughout human history, many people have believed death is preferable to life under intolerable conditions. And some of the people who have acted on those preferences—people who have sacrificed their lives—have been deemed morally heroic. Even if we refrain from saying that these people are "better off" dead, we can still make perfect sense of the idea that they had morally impeccable reasons for their actions. But what of others who assisted those who sacrificed their lives? What should we say about those who have helped another person undertake a course of action that leads to her death? Again, we might refrain from saying that these others made the person who sacrificed her life "better off." But that does not mean that what those others did is morally incoherent. If a person has morally impeccable reasons to sacrifice her life, then a person who helps her may have reasons that are equally morally impeccable. Just as assisting someone in carrying out the ultimate sacrifice can be morally coherent, so too may helping a dying patient carry out suicide be morally coherent. There is no logical barrier to justifying these courses of action in terms of the wishes and suffering of the person who will die as a result of them. A person who is dying may reasonably prefer to be dead rather than alive. Helping that person take a course of action that leads to her death can accord with the duty to respect the person's autonomy and to reduce her suffering. The fact that the person will not be able to "experience and enjoy" the results of this course of action does not vitiate any attempted justification to help her. Indeed, Kass's own attitude towards certain kinds of care at the end of life reveals that he himself believes that it may be right to help someone undertake a course of action even if she will not able to "experience and enjoy" the results of it. For Kass believes that a physician may be right to undertake courses of action that will increase the likelihood of death (Kass, 2002b: 22 and 37).

But perhaps what Kass means to argue is that participating in PAS violates physicians' first duty of promoting health. It is not clear, however, that that duty *can* be violated when a patient has an incurable, terminal disease. If it is impossible to heal someone, it is difficult to see how the duty to heal her even applies. Physicians have the duty to try to heal patients who can be healed (and who want to be healed). But when a patient cannot be healed, the duty to reduce suffering (in concert with the patient's wishes) takes center stage. The duty to heal no longer seems to be in the picture.

The Principle of Double Effect

Kass, Pellegrino and Callahan would probably object at this point that my conception of the duty to heal is illegitimately attenuated and isolated. That duty, Kass, Pellegrino and Callahan might say, stems from an even more fundamental duty—the duty to life itself. It is life itself to which physicians must always remain devoted. And this devotion must

take precedence over all other considerations, even the attempt to reduce pain or accede to patients' requests.

The idea that physicians must always place morally conclusive value on life itself fits well with Kass, Pellegrino and Callahan's suggestion that all people ought "to live. . . . for as long as they can." But this devotion to life seems *not* to fit with a practice that is common to the medical profession today—the practice of participating in the withdrawal of life-sustaining treatment, including food and water, which Kass, Pellegrino and Callahan all explicitly endorse (Kass, 2002b: 22; Pellegrino, 2002: 50–51; Callahan, 2002: 54). A physician who participates in the withdrawal of life-sustaining treatment undertakes a course of action that does not promote life itself. Such a physician is participating in a course of action that will lead to less life rather than more. So how do Kass, Pellegrino and Callahan justify physician participation in the withdrawal of life-sustaining treatment without committing themselves to the justifiability of assisted suicide? How do they fit the withdrawal of life-sustaining treatment into their conception of the moral role of physicians while at the same time keeping PAS out? They do so by deploying the principle of double effect. As Kass explains, "The well-established rule of medical ethics that governs this practice is known as the principle of double effect. . . . It is morally licit to embrace a course of action that intends and serves a worthy goal (like relieving suffering), employing means that may have, as an unintended and undesired consequences, some harm or evil for the patient. Such cases are distinguished from the morally illicit efforts that indirectly 'relieve suffering' by deliberately providing a lethal dose of a drug and thus eliminating the sufferer" (Kass, 2002b: 37).

So the argument that the Oregon law conflicts with physicians' moral duty presupposes the principle of double effect. Indeed, the principle of double effect seems to be doing more work in this argument than the duty to heal or promote life. For Kass, Pellegrino and Callahan's endorsement of the withdrawal of life-sustaining treatment shows that they accept physician participation in courses of action that are intended neither to heal nor to promote life, which seems to imply (in contrast to some of their other comments) that they do not take the duty to heal or promote life to be always applicable to medical practice.

Now the principle of double effect is a general moral principle. It is not unique to the world of medical ethics. This is worth noting because opponents of the Oregon law sometimes contend that their arguments against PAS are based on the special moral status of physicians. Callahan, for instance, often relies on claims about the "purpose of medicine" or "medicine's role" (Callahan, 2002: 59) and Kass maintains that his "argument rests on understanding the special moral character of the medical profession and the ethical obligations it entails" (Kass, 2002b: 17). If a person really understands the intrinsic moral character of medicine, opponents of the Oregon law suggest, she will never accept PAS. We now find, however, that their arguments against PAS depend on the principle of double effect. And a defense of that principle cannot be grounded in the "special moral character of the medical profession." The anti-PAS position is based, in other words, not on the unique moral role of medicine but on a contentious non-medical moral principle.

This raises the question of whether there are in fact decisive grounds for accepting the principle of double effect. I myself think that the principle is extremely problematic. It relies on the drawing of a very sharp distinction between, on the one hand, the intentions and goals of all the physicians who engage in terminal sedation or withdraw food and water and, on the other hand, the intentions and goals of all the physicians who would prescribe a lethal dose of drugs. It seems to me, however, that there is no principled way of distinguishing the morally relevant features of the intentions and goals of these two groups of physicians, no non-question-begging reason to think that there is some feature of the actions of all those who would prescribe lethal doses that is inconsistent with the practice of medicine but is also absent from the actions of all those who engage in terminal sedation or withdraw food and water. Unfortunately, an extensive treatment of the principle of double effect is beyond the scope of this article. Note, however, that even if the principle is generally defensible, that on its own will not vindicate Kass, Pellegrino and Callahan's argument against the Oregon law. For not

all defensible moral principles ought to be enforced by law. Some moral questions are so difficult, profound or personal that the law rightly allows each person the opportunity to answer them for herself. If reasonable people can disagree about the soundness of a moral principle, the best public policy might be one that is neutral between a person's living in accord with it or not. And it seems that the principle of double effect is something with which reasonable people can disagree. Indeed, the traditionally most influential defenses of the principle are based on religio-theological commitments. But such religio-theological commitments are not shared by every reasonable person, and they are not typically thought of as the basis for public policy in a secular society. At the very least, the opponents of PAS must give us reasons for believing not merely that the principle of double effect is philosophically defensible but also that it ought to shape our legislation concerning end-of-life decisions.

Kass's claim that the principle of double effect is a "well-established rule of medical ethics" does not help to make the case. For not all medical ethicists or physicians agree that the essential moral duty of physicians implies that the principle of double effect should be used to forbid PAS. Miller, Brody and Quill, for instance, have argued that assisting in suicide can be entirely consistent with the integrity of the medical profession (see Quill, 1991; Miller & Brody, 1995; Quill *et al.,* 1997).

Moreover, when the principle of double effect is invoked in medical ethics, it is usually done so in the context of explaining the prohibition on PAS. To say that the principle of double effect is a "well-established rule of medical ethics" is to say little more than that physicians have traditionally been prohibited from assisting in suicide. But the pressing question is whether physicians *should* be prohibited from assisting in suicide. The fact that PAS has been prohibited in the past does not constitute an argument for continuing to prohibit it in the future.

But the greatest weakness of the attempt to use the principle of double effect to defeat the Oregon law is that the principle will imply the wrongness of PAS only on the assumption that it is bad that a person with a terminal disease die sooner rather than later. The only business the principle of double effect is in is telling us when it is permissible to perform an action that has foreseeable bad consequences and when it is impermissible. If an action's consequences are not bad, the principle is completely inapplicable. Now the opponents of PAS believe that it is bad if a terminal patient dies sooner rather than later, and it is on the basis of the badness of such a death that they deploy the principle of double effect. But many proponents of PAS disagree, holding that in certain circumstances it is not bad if a terminal patient dies sooner rather than later. Of course, there is a great deal of dispute about which side is correct—about whether it is necessarily bad that a terminal patient dies sooner rather than later (this was one of the topics of the first part of this article). But unless that issue is resolved in their favor, opponents of PAS cannot use the principle of double effect to argue against the Oregon law. Even if the principle is generally philosophically defensible, and even if it should be enshrined in law (two big ifs), we still will not have reason to prohibit PAS unless there are also independent grounds for thinking that it is always bad for a terminal, competent patient to die sooner rather than later. The principle of double effect is downstream of the central justificatory question of whether it is bad that a terminal, competent patient commits suicide.

The final point I want to make about the principle of double effect is that it cannot be used to bolster another significant criticism of PAS that Kass, Pellegrino and Callahan present. This other criticism is that although it may seem as though the Oregon law leaves the decision of whether or not to request PAS entirely up to the patient, in fact the law leads her physician to make that decision for her. In theory, the Oregon law restricts the physician's role simply to medical judgments. But in practice (according to Kass, Pellegrino and Callahan's criticism), the physician's own values will pressure the patient into whatever decision finally gets made. The patient's thinking will be "easily and subtly manipulated" by the physician (Kass, 2002b: 24). The physician will exercise "subtle coercion" that will undermine "the patient autonomy that assisted suicide and euthanasia presume to protect" (Pellegrino, 2002: 48).

Now in claiming that the legalization of PAS will increase the chance of manipulation and coercion,

Kass, Pellegrino and Callahan are making an essentially consequentialist argument.[4] They are contending not that PAS is intrinsically morally wrong but that it will lead to morally unacceptable consequences. This consequentialist argument against PAS has to be taken very seriously. If it turns out that the Oregon law increases manipulation and coercion, then there will be at least one consequentialist but still extremely important reason to reject the law.

It seems to me, however, that the fact that physicians can ethically participate in the withdrawal of life-sustaining treatment gives us at least some reason for doubting that the legalization of PAS will necessarily lead to increased manipulation and coercion. For if allowing physicians to participate in the withdrawal of food and water does not necessarily increase manipulation and coercion, why think that allowing physicians to participate in PAS will do so? If it is possible for the option of withdrawing life-sustaining treatment to exist without an increase in manipulation and coercion, why should it not also be possible for the option of PAS to exist with an increase in manipulation and coercion?

We have seen, of course, that opponents of the Oregon law believe that there is an intrinsic moral difference between assisting in suicide and withdrawing life-support, a difference explained by the principle of double effect. But they cannot rely on that putative intrinsic difference when they are making the consequentialist argument that the Oregon law will lead physicians to manipulate and coerce patients into choosing PAS. For this consequentialist argument is based on claims about the real-world effects of the Oregon law. And we cannot determine what those effects will be simply through an examination of the morally contentious principle of double effect.

CONCLUSION

I have presented reasons for thinking that there is nothing intrinsically morally wrong with PAS as it is currently practiced in Oregon. In the first part of this article, I have tried to show that there are morally reasonable grounds to restrict PAS to individuals who are competent and have less than six months to live. In the second part, I have tried to show that participation in PAS does not necessarily violate physicians' professional integrity. The value of autonomy and physicians' duty to reduce the suffering of dying patients together imply that PAS can sometimes be a morally acceptable option.

NOTES

1. Of course this distinction is far from sharp. For one thing, the combination of all of your little decisions does affect in a non-negligible way the shape of your overall life. For another thing, there are many decisions that fall somewhere between the big and the little, decisions that are not as momentous as deciding to get married but are nonetheless more important than deciding to eat the blue jello. There is a continuum between big decisions and little ones, not an absolute cut-off. Still, some decisions are clearly closer to one end of the continuum rather than the other, and we often find it natural and easy enough to draw such a distinction.

2. Showing that it might be morally acceptable for a person to commit suicide does not on its own show that it might be morally acceptable for someone else to assist in the suicide. There can be goals that are morally acceptable for me to pursue but that nonetheless it would morally unacceptable for others to help me pursue. It is, for instance, morally acceptable for me to try to win a competitive sporting event but it is morally unacceptable for a referee to try to help me win. I believe, however, that the burden of proof lies with those who would argue that assistance is morally unacceptable. If a course of action is morally acceptable for me to pursue, then generally there will be no absolute moral reasons forbidding anyone else from helping me to pursue it (which is not to say that I necessarily have the *right* to demand assistance in the pursuit of my morally acceptable goal). Those who contend that it is morally unacceptable to assist someone in performing a morally acceptable act will need to explain the added moral feature that makes assistance unacceptable in that particular circumstance. In the case of a competitive sporting event, it is morally unacceptable for a referee to try to help me win because (as competitive sporting events are zero-sum games) it is unfair to the side against which I am competing.

3. So I disagree with Callahan in that I hold that allowing PAS is "socially neutral" on the question of whether "some suffering is meaningless and unnecessary" (Callahan, 2002: 57). A society that allows PAS, it seems to me, does not take a position on whether it is better or worse for a dying, competent person to commit suicide; such a society facilitates each person's making that decision for herself. Callahan, in contrast, bases his opposition to society's allowing PAS on a non-neutral view of the positive value of suffering (Callahan, 2002: 58–59).

4. Perhaps Kass, Pellegrino and Callahan would argue that it is misleading to say that worries about physician manipulation and coercion are entirely "consequentialist." For they may contend that the role physicians play in patient decision making would make it impossible for them *not* to exert undue pressure on patients for whom PAS is an option. But the claim that it would be impossible for physicians not to exert undue pressure depends upon a certain view of what is essential to the role of physicians, a view others might not share (see, for example, Miller & Brody, 1995). That claim also seems to me to be contradicted by the fact that the possibility of the withdrawal of life-sustaining treatment does not necessarily produce undue pressure on patients.

REFERENCES

Callahan, D. (2002). Reason, self-determination, and physician-assisted suicide. In K. Foley & H. Hendin (Eds), *The case against assisted suicide.* Baltimore and London: Johns Hopkins University Press.

Kass, L. (2002a). *Life, liberty and the defense of dignity.* San Francisco: Encounter Books.

Kass, L. (2002b). 'I will give no deadly drug': Why doctors must not kill. In K. Foley & H. Hendin (Eds), *The case against assisted suicide.* Baltimore and London: Johns Hopkins University Press.

Miller, F. G., & Brody, H. (1995). Professional integrity and physician-assisted death. *Hastings Center Report, 25,* 8–17.

Pellegrino, E. (2002). Compassion is not enough. In K. Foley & H. Hendin (Eds), *The case against assisted suicide.* Baltimore and London: Johns Hopkins University Press.

Quill, T. E. (1991). Death and dignity: A case of individualized decision making. *New England Journal of Medicine, 324,* 691–694.

Quill, T. E., Dresser, R., & Brock, D. W. (1997). The rule of double effect—A critique of its role in end-of-life decision making. *The New England Journal of Medicine, 337,* 1768–1771.

Sade, R. M., & Marshall, M. F. (1996). Legistrothanatry: a new specialty for assisting in death. *Perspectives in Biology and Medicine, 39,* 222–224.

READING QUESTIONS

1. Gill first suggests that we can think of the value of autonomy as simply a person's ability to make decisions for herself. But Kass—a PAS opponent—thinks PAS is tragically self-contradictory with regard to autonomy. What does Kass mean by this?

2. Explain the hardline libertarian response to opponents of PAS who claim it leads to absurd permissible outcomes such as selling oneself into slavery or electing PAS when fully healthy.

3. How does Gill argue for the claim that PAS of a terminal individual is not a case of destroying the ability to make future decisions? How do his opponents respond?

4. Gill argues that terminally ill patients have few opportunities left to make big decisions. How does Gill reply to the objection that a terminally ill patient may, in fact, have profoundly important decisions yet to make?

5. How does Gill describe the role of the physician under the Oregon law, and how is this different from the view taken by PAS opponents?

6. Gill claims that opponents of PAS must rely on the general principle of double effect to support their position, rather than an appeal to the "special moral character of the medical profession" to promote life. What reasons does he give for this claim?

7. Why does Gill maintain that we must first determine whether it is bad that a terminal patient dies sooner rather than later before we can use the principle of double effect to argue against the Oregon law?

DISCUSSION QUESTIONS

1. Should we agree with Gill's candle analogy? What is his point, and what are the morally significant differences, if any, between the dying candle and the dying patient?

2. Gill gives his "big decisions" argument to refute the claim by PAS opponents that the value of autonomy cannot be used to support Oregon law. Discuss the big decision argument and the extent to which it succeeds in meeting the PAS opponents' claim.

3. Discuss the logical point made by some opponents of PAS that it is impossible to be better off dead than alive. Even if the logical argument were sound, are there other reasons to claim that suicide for a terminally ill patient is morally justified?

4. Do you agree with Gill that the general principle of double effect is extremely problematic? Identify his reasons for this claim and discuss to what extent you think his argument succeeds or not. How does this argument support Gill's view that public policy ought to remain neutral with respect to PAS?

DAVID VELLEMAN

Against the Right to Die

David Velleman argues against an *institutional* right to die—a right requiring caregivers to honor a patient's request to be helped to die. Velleman approaches this issue from a consequentialist perspective. But his argument is not based on the claim that a patient might mistakenly exercise a right to die when in fact he or she would be better off living. Rather, it is that increasing patients' medical options can be a harm, regardless of whether they choose to exercise the option. The idea is that having the option of choosing death means that the default of staying alive is replaced by the option of staying alive or choosing death. However, Velleman argues that given various features of contemporary culture, the option of choosing death also brings the likely felt burden of justifying to others one's continued existence, an unwelcome burden for many which constitutes the harm in question.

Recommended Reading: consequentialism, chap. 1, sec. 2A.

In this paper I offer an argument against establishing an institutional right to die, but I do not consider how my argument fares against countervailing considerations, and so I do not draw any final conclusion on the subject. The argument laid out in this paper has certainly inhibited me from favoring a right to die, and it has also led me to recoil from many of the arguments offered for such a right. But I am very far from an all-things-considered judgment.

My argument is addressed to a question of public policy—namely, whether the law or the canons of medical practice should include a rule requiring, under specified circumstances, that caregivers honor a patient's request to be allowed or perhaps even helped to die. This question is distinct from the question whether anyone is ever morally entitled to be allowed or helped to die. I believe that the answer to the latter question is yes, but I doubt whether our moral obligation to facilitate some people's deaths is best discharged through the establishment of an institutional right to die.

Although I believe in our obligation to facilitate some deaths, I want to dissociate myself from some of the arguments that are frequently offered for such an

obligation. These arguments, like many arguments in medical ethics, rely on terms borrowed from Kantian moral theory—terms such as "dignity" and "autonomy." Various kinds of life-preserving treatment are said to violate a patient's dignity or to detain him in an undignified state; and the patient's right of autonomy is said to require that we respect his competent and considered wishes, including a wish to die. There may or may not be some truth in each of these claims. Yet when we evaluate such claims, we must take care not to assume that terms like "dignity" and "autonomy" always express the same concepts, or carry the same normative force, as they do in a particular moral theory.

When Kant speaks, for example, of the dignity that belongs to persons by virtue of their rational nature, and that places them beyond all price (Kant, 1964, p. 102), he is not invoking anything that requires the ability to walk unaided, to feed oneself, or to control one's bowels. Hence the dignity invoked in discussions of medical ethics—a status supposedly threatened by physical deterioration and dependency—cannot be the status whose claim on our moral concern is so fundamental to Kantian thought. We must therefore ask

Published with permission of the author.

whether this other sort of dignity, whatever it may be, embodies a value that's equally worthy of protection.

My worry, in particular, is that the word "dignity" is sometimes used to dignify, so to speak, our culture's obsession with independence, physical strength, and youth. To my mind, the dignity defined by these values—a dignity that is ultimately incompatible with *being cared for* at all—is a, dignity not worth having.[1]

I have similar worries about the values expressed by the phrase "patient autonomy"; for there are two very different senses in which a person's autonomy can become a value for us. On the one hand, we can obey the categorical imperative, by declining to act for reasons that we could not rationally propose as valid for all rational beings, including those who are affected by our action, such as the patient. What we value in that case is the patent's *capacity* for self-determination, and we value it in a particular way—namely, by according it *respect*. We respect the patient's autonomy by regarding the necessity of sharing our reasons with him, among others, as a constraint on what decisions we permit ourselves to reach.

On the other hand, we can value the patient's autonomy by making it our goal to maximize his effective options. What we value, in that case, is not the patient's capacity but his *opportunities* for self-determination—his having choices to make and the means with which to implement them; and we value these opportunities for self-determination by regarding them as *goods*—as objects of desire and pursuit rather than respect.

These two ways of valuing autonomy are fundamentally different. Respecting people's autonomy, in the Kantian sense, is not just a matter of giving them effective options. To make our own decisions only for reasons that we could rationally share with others is not necessarily to give *them* decisions to make, nor is it to give them the means to implement their actual decisions.[2]

As with the term "dignity," then, we must not assume that the term "autonomy" is always being used in the sense made familiar by Kantian moral theory; and we must therefore ask ourselves what sort of autonomy is being invoked, and whether it is indeed something worthy of our moral concern. I believe that, as with the term "dignity," the answer to the latter question may be no in some cases, including the case of the right to die.

Despite my qualms about the use of Kantian language to justify euthanasia, I do believe that euthanasia can be justified, and on Kantian grounds. In particular, I believe that respect for a person's dignity, properly conceived, can require us to facilitate his death when that dignity is being irremediably compromised. I also believe, however, that a person's dignity can be so compromised only by circumstances that are likely to compromise his capacity for fully rational and autonomous decision making. So although I do not favor euthanizing people against their wills, of course, neither do I favor a policy of euthanizing people for the sake of deferring to their wills, since I think that people's wills are usually impaired in the circumstances required to make euthanasia permissible. The sense in which I oppose a right to die, then, is that I oppose treating euthanasia as a protected option for the patient.

One reason for my opposition is the associated belief (also Kantian) that so long as patients would be fully competent to exercise an option of being euthanized, their doing so would be immoral, in the majority of cases, because their dignity as persons would still be intact. I discuss this argument elsewhere, but I do not return to it in the present paper.[3] In this paper I discuss a second reason for opposing euthanasia as a protected option for the patient. This reason, unlike the first, is consequentialist.

What consequentialist arguments could there be against giving the option of euthanasia to patients?

One argument, of course, would be that giving this option to patients, even under carefully defined conditions, would entail providing euthanasia to some patients for whom it would be a harm rather than a benefit (Kamisar, 1970). But the argument that interests me does not depend on this strategy. My consequentialist worry about the right to die is not that some patients might mistakenly choose to die when they would be better off living.

In order to demonstrate that I am not primarily worried about mistaken request to die, I shall assume, from this point forward, that patients are infallible, and that euthanasia would therefore be chosen only by those for whom it would be a benefit. Even so, I believe, the establishment of a right to die would harm many patients, by increasing their autonomy in a sense that is not only un-Kantian but also very undesirable.

This belief is sometimes expressed in public debate, although it is rarely developed in any detail. Here, for example, is Yale Kamisar's argument against "Euthanasia Legislation":

> Is this the kind of choice. . . . that we want to offer a gravely ill person? Will we not sweep up, in the process, some who are not really tired of life, but think others are tired of them; some who do not really want to die, but who feel they should not live on, because to do so when there looms the legal alternative of euthanasia is to do a selfish or a cowardly act? Will not some feel an obligation to have themselves "eliminated". . . ? (Kamisar, 1970)

Note that these considerations do not, strictly speaking, militate against euthanasia itself. Rather, they militate against a particular decision procedure for euthanasia—namely, the procedure of placing the choice of euthanasia in the patient's hands. What Kamisar is questioning in this particular passage is, not the practice of helping some patients to die, but rather the practice of asking them to choose whether to die. The feature of legalized euthanasia that troubles him is precisely its being an option offered to patients—the very feature for which it's touted, by its proponents, as an enhancement of the patients' autonomy. Kamisar's remarks thus betray the suspicion that this particular enhancement of one's autonomy is not to be welcomed.

But what exactly is the point of Kamisar's rhetorical questions? The whole purpose of giving people choices, surely, is to allow those choices to be determined by their reasons and preferences rather than ours. Kamisar may think that finding one's life tiresome is a good reason for dying whereas thinking that others find one tiresome is not. But if others honestly think otherwise, why should we stand in their way? Whose life is it anyway?

A theoretical framework for addressing this question can be found in Thomas Schelling's book *The Strategy of Conflict* (1960), and in Gerald Dworkin's paper "Is More Choice Better Than Less?" (1982). These authors have shown that our intuitions about the value of options are often mistaken, and their

work can help us to understand the point of arguments like Kamisar's.

We are inclined to think that, unless we are likely to make mistakes about whether to exercise an option (as I am assuming we are not), the value of having the option is as high as the value of exercising it and no lower than zero. Exercising an option can of course be worse than nothing, if it causes harm. But if we are not prone to mistakes, then we will not exercise a harmful option; and we tend to think that simply *having* the unexercised option cannot be harmful. And insofar as exercising an option would make us better off than we are, having the option must have made us better off than we were before we had it—or so we tend to think.

What Schelling showed, however, is that having an option can be harmful even if we do not exercise it and—more surprisingly—even if we exercise it and gain by doing so. Schelling's examples of this phenomenon were drawn primarily from the world of negotiation, where the only way to induce one's opponent to settle for less may be by proving that one doesn't have the option of giving him more. Schelling pointed out that in such circumstances, a lack of options can be an advantage. The union leader who cannot persuade his membership to approve a pay-cut, or the ambassador who cannot contact his head-of-state for a change of brief, negotiates from a position of strength; whereas the negotiator for whom all concessions are possible deals from weakness. If the rank-and-file give their leader the option of offering a pay-cut, then management may not settle for anything less, whereas they might have settled for less if he hadn't had the option of making the offer. The union leader will then have to decide whether to take the option and reach an agreement or to leave the option and call a strike. But no matter which of these outcomes would make him better off, choosing it will still leave him worse off than he would have been if he had never had the option at all.

Dworkin has expanded on Schelling's point by exploring other respects in which options can be undesirable. Just as options can subject one to pressure from an opponent in negotiation, for example, they can subject one to pressure from other sources as well. The night cashier in a convenience store doesn't want the option of opening the safe—and not because he fears that he'd make mistakes about when to open it. It is precisely because the cashier would know when he'd better open the safe that his having the option would make him an attractive target for robbers; and it's because having the option would make him a target for robbers that he'd be better off without it. The cashier who finds himself opening the safe at gunpoint can consistently think that he's doing what's best while wishing that he'd never been given the option of doing it.

Options can be undesirable, then, because they subject one to various kinds of pressure; but they can be undesirable for other reasons, too. Offering someone an alternative to the status quo makes two outcomes possible for him, but neither of them is the outcome that was possible before. He can now choose the status quo or choose the alternative, but he can no longer *have* the status quo without *choosing* it. And having the status quo by default may have been what was best for him, even though choosing the status quo is now worst. If I invite you to a dinner party, I leave you the possibilities of choosing to come or choosing to stay away; but I deprive you of something that you otherwise would have had—namely, the possibility of being absent from my table by default, as you are on all other occasions. Surely, preferring to accept an invitation is consistent with wishing you had never received it. These attitudes are consistent because refusing to attend a party is a different outcome from *not* attending without having to refuse; and even if the former of these outcomes is worse than attending, the latter may still have been better. Having choices can thus deprive one of desirable outcomes whose desirability depends on their being unchosen.

The offer of an option can also be undesirable because of what it expresses. To offer a student the option of receiving remedial instruction after class is to imply that he is not keeping up. If the student needs help but doesn't know it, the offer may clue him in. But even if the student does not need any help, to begin with, the offer may so undermine his confidence that he will need help before long. In the latter case, the student may ultimately benefit from accepting the offer, even though he would have been better off not receiving it at all.

Note that in each of these cases, a person can be harmed by having a choice even if he chooses what's best for him. Once the option of offering a concession has undermined one's bargaining position, once the option of opening the safe has made one the target of a robbery, once the invitation to a party has eliminated the possibility of absence by default, once the offer of remedial instruction has implied that one needs it—in short, once one has been offered a problematic choice—one's situation has already been altered for the worse, and choosing what's best cannot remedy the harm that one has already suffered. Choosing what's best in these cases is simply a way of cutting one's losses.

Note, finally, that we cannot always avoid burdening people with options by offering them a second-order option as to which options they are to be offered. If issuing you an invitation to dinner would put you in an awkward position, then asking you whether you want to be invited would usually do so as well; if offering you the option of remedial instruction would send you a message, then so would asking you whether you'd like that option. In order to avoid doing harm, then, we are sometimes required, not only to withhold options, but also to take the initiative for withholding them.

Of course, the options that I have discussed can also be unproblematic for many people in many circumstances. Sometimes one has good reason to welcome a dinner invitation or an offer of remedial instruction. Similarly, some patients will welcome the option of euthanasia, and rightly so. The problem is how to offer the option only to those patients who will have reason to welcome it. Arguments like Kamisar's are best understood, I think, as warning that the option of euthanasia may unavoidably be offered to some who will be harmed simply by having the option, even if they go on to choose what is best.

I think that the option of euthanasia may harm some patients in all of the ways canvassed above; but I will focus my attention on only a few of those ways. The most important way in which the option of euthanasia may harm patients, I think, is that it will deny them the possibility of staying alive by default.

Now, the idea of surviving by default will be anathema to existentialists, who will insist that the choice between life and death is a choice that we have to make every day, perhaps every moment.[4] Yet even if there is a deep, philosophical sense in which we do continually choose to go on living, it is not reflected in our ordinary self-understanding. That is, we do not ordinarily think of ourselves or others as continually rejecting the option of suicide and staying alive by choice. Thus, even if the option of euthanasia won't alter a patient's existential situation, it will certainly alter the way in which his situation is generally perceived. And changes in the perception of a patient's situation will be sufficient to produce many of the problems that Schelling and Dworkin have described, since those problems are often created not just by *having* options but by *being seen* to have them.

Once a person is given the choice between life and death, he will rightly be perceived as the agent of his own survival. Whereas his existence is ordinarily viewed as a given for him—as a fixed condition with which he must cope—formally offering him the option of euthanasia will cause his existence thereafter to be viewed as his doing.

The problem with this perception is that if others regard you as choosing a state of affairs, they will hold you responsible for it; and if they hold you responsible for a state of affairs, they can ask you to justify it. Hence if people ever come to regard you as existing by choice, they may expect you to justify your continued existence. If your daily arrival in the office is interpreted as meaning that you have once again declined to kill yourself, you may feel obliged to arrive with an answer to the question "Why not?"

I think that our perception of one another's existence as a given is so deeply ingrained that we can hardly imagine what life would be like without it. When someone shows impatience or displeasure with us, we jokingly say, "Well, excuse me for living!" But imagine that it were no joke; imagine that living were something for which one might reasonably be thought to need an excuse. The burden of justifying one's existence might make existence unbearable—and hence unjustifiable. . . .

. . . Forcing a patient to take responsibility for his continued existence may therefore be tantamount to confronting him with the following prospect: unless he can explain, to the satisfaction of others, why he chooses to exist, his only remaining reasons for existence may vanish.

Unfortunately, our culture is extremely hostile to any attempt at justifying an existence of passivity and dependence. The burden of proof will lie heavily on the patient who thinks that his terminal illness or chronic disability is not a sufficient reason for dying.

What is worse, the people with whom a patient wants to maintain intercourse, and to whom he therefore wants to justify his choices, are often in a position to incur several financial and emotional costs from any prolongation of his life. Many of the reasons in favor of his death are therefore likely to be exquisitely salient in their minds. I believe that some of these people may actively pressure the patient to exercise the option of dying. (Students who hear me say this usually object that no one would ever do such a thing. My reply is that no one would ever do such a thing as abuse his own children or parents— except that many people do.)

In practice, however, friends and relatives of a patient will not have to utter a word of encouragement, much less exert any overt pressure, once the option of euthanasia is offered. For in the discussion of a subject so hedged by taboos and inhibitions, the patient will have to make some assumptions about what they think and how they feel, irrespective of what they say (see Schelling, 1984). And the rational assumption for him to make will be that they are especially sensible of the considerations in favor of his exercising the option.

Thus, even if a patient antecedently believes that his life is worth living, he may have good reason to assume that many of the people around him do not, and that his efforts to convince them will be frustrated by prevailing opinions about lives like his, or by the biases inherent in their perspective. Indeed, he can reasonably assume that the offer of euthanasia is itself an expression of attitudes that are likely to frustrate his efforts to justify declining it. He can therefore assume that his refusal to take the option of euthanasia will threaten his standing as a rational person in the eyes of friends and family, thereby threatening the very things that make his life worthwhile. This patient may rationally judge that he's better off taking the option of euthanasia, even though he would have been best off not having the option at all.

Establishing a right to die in our culture may thus be like establishing a right to duel in a culture obsessed with personal honor.[5] If someone defended the right to duel by arguing that a duel is a private transaction between consenting adults, he would have missed the point of laws against dueling. What makes it rational for someone to throw down or pick up a gauntlet may be the social costs of choosing not to, costs that result from failing to duel only if one fails to duel by choice. Such costs disappear if the choice of dueling can be removed. By eliminating the option of dueling (if we can), we eliminate the reasons that make it rational for people to duel in most cases. To restore the option of dueling would be to give people reasons for dueling that they didn't previously have. Similarly, I believe, to offer the option of dying may be to give people new reasons for dying.

Do not attempt to refute this argument against the right to die by labeling it paternalistic. The argument is not paternalistic—at least, not in any derogatory sense of the word. Paternalism, in the derogatory sense, is the policy of saving people from self-inflicted harms, by denying them options that they might exercise unwisely. Such a policy is distasteful because it expresses a lack of respect for others' ability to make their own decisions.

But my argument is not paternalistic in this sense. My reason for withholding the option of euthanasia is not that others cannot be trusted to exercise it wisely. On the contrary, I have assumed from the outset that patients will be infallible in their deliberations. What I have argued is—not that people to whom we offer the option of euthanasia might harm themselves—but rather that in offering them this option, *we* will do them harm. My argument is therefore based on a simple policy of non-malfeasance rather than on the policy of paternalism. I am arguing that we must not harm others by giving them choices, not that we must withhold the choices from them lest they harm themselves.

. . . As I have said, I favor euthanasia in some cases. And of course, I believe that euthanasia must not be administered on competent patients without their consent. To that extent, I think that the option of dying will have to be presented to some patients, so that they can receive the benefit of a good death.

On the basis of the foregoing arguments, however, I doubt whether policymakers can formulate a general definition that distinguishes the circumstances in which the option of dying would be beneficial from those in which it would be harmful. The factors that make an option problematic are too subtle and too various to be defined in a statute or regulation. How will the option of euthanasia be perceived by the patient and his loved ones? How will it affect the relations among them? Is he likely to fear being spurned for declining the option? Would he exercise the option merely as a favor to them? And are they genuinely willing to accept that favor? Sensitivity to these and related questions could never be incorporated into an institutional rule defining conditions under which the option must be offered.

Insofar as I am swayed by the foregoing arguments, then, I am inclined to think that society should at most permit, and never require, health professionals to offer the option of euthanasia or to grant patients' requests for it. We can probably define some conditions under which the option should never be offered; but we are not in a position to define conditions under which it should always be offered; and so we can at most define a legal permission rather than a legal requirement to offer it. The resulting rule would leave caregivers free to withhold the option whenever they see fit, even if it is explicitly and spontaneously requested. And so long as caregivers are permitted to withhold the option of euthanasia, patients will not have a right to die.

The foregoing arguments make me worry even about an explicitly formulated permission for the practice of euthanasia, since an explicit law or regulation to this effect would already invite patients, and hence potentially pressure them, to request that the permission be exercised in their case. I feel most comfortable with a policy of permitting euthanasia by default—that is, by a tacit failure to enforce the institutional rules that currently serve as barriers to justified euthanasia, or a gradual elimination of those rules without fanfare. The best public policy of euthanasia, I sometimes think, is no policy at all.

This suggestion will surely strike some readers as scandalous, because of the trust that it would place in the individual judgment of physicians and patients. But I suspect that to place one's life in the hands of another person, in the way that one does today when placing oneself in the care of a physician, may simply be to enter a relationship in which such trust is essential, because it cannot be replaced or even underwritten by institutional guarantees. Although I do not share the conventional view that advances in medical technology have outrun our moral understanding of how they should be applied, I am indeed tempted to think they have outrun the capacity of institutional rules to regulate their application. I am therefore tempted to think that public policy regulating the relation between physician and patient should be weak and vague by design; and that insofar as the aim of medical ethics is to strengthen or sharpen such policy, medical ethics itself is a bad idea.

Notes

This is a revised version of a paper that was originally published in *The Journal of Medicine and Philosophy* (1992). That paper began as a comment of a paper by Dan Brock, presented at the Central Division of the APA in 1991. See his "Voluntary Active Euthanasia" (Brock, 1992). I received help in writing that paper from: Dan Brock, Elizabeth Anderson, David Hills, Yale Kamisar, and Patricia White. [The version of the paper reprinted here is a revised version of the original --Ed.]

1. Here I echo some excellent remarks on the subject by Felicia Ackerman (Ackerman, 1990). I discuss the issue of "dying with dignity" in (Velleman, 1999a).

2. I discuss this issue further in (Velleman, 1999b), pp. 356–58, esp. nn. 69, 72.

3. See (Velleman, 1999a).

4. The *locus classicus* for this point is of course Camus's essay "The Myth of Sisyphus" (Camus, 1955).

5. For this analogy, see (Stell, 1979). Stell argues—implausibly, in my view—that one has the right to die for the same reason that one has a right to duel.

References

Ackerman, Felicia: 1990, "No, Thanks. I Don't Want to Die with Dignity," *Providence Journal-Bulletin*, April 19, 1990.

Camus, Albert: 1955, "The Myth of Sisyphus" in *The Myth of Sisyphus and Other Essays*, tr. Justin O'Brien, Vintage Books, New York.

Dworkin, Gerald: 1982, "Is More Choice Better Than Less?" *Midwest Studies in Philosophy* 7, pp. 47–61.

Kamisar, Yale: 1970, "Euthanasia Legislation: Some Non-Religious Objections," in A. B. Downing (ed.), *Euthanasia and the Right to Die*, Humanities Press, New York. pp. 85–133.

Kant, I.: 1964, *Groundwork of the Metaphysic of Morals*, trans. H. J. Paton, Harper and Row, New York.

Schelling, Thomas: 1960, *The Strategy of Conflict*, Harvard University Press, Cambridge, Massachusetts.

Schelling, Thomas: 1984, "Strategic Relationships in Dying," in *Choice and Consequence*, Harvard University Press, Cambridge, Massachusetts.

Stell, Lance K.: 1979, "Dueling and the Right to Life," *Ethics* 90, pp. 7–26.

Velleman, J. David: 1991, "Well-Being and Time," *Pacific Philosophical Quarterly* 72, pp. 48–77.

Velleman, J. David: 1999a, "A Right of Self-Termination?" *Ethics* 109, pp. 606–28.

Velleman, J. David: 1999b, "Love as a Moral Emotion," *Ethics* 109, pp. 338–74.

READING QUESTIONS

1. What worries does Velleman raise about appeals to dignity and autonomy in arguments over euthanasia?
2. What does Velleman identify as the most troubling aspect of having a legal right to die?
3. How does Velleman respond to the worry that his view is overly paternalistic?

DISCUSSION QUESTIONS

1. Is there a feasible way to formulate a legal right to die that avoids Velleman's worries?
2. Suppose there is no law that guarantees a right to die, but that there is no law that forbids choosing euthanasia? If there is no law against choosing euthanasia, do Velleman's worries about a legal right to die arise for individuals who may choose euthanasia?

ADDITIONAL RESOURCES

Web Resources

Pew Research Center, <http://pewresearch.org/>. A nonpartisan site that conducts public opinion polls on public policy issues. One can find numerous links from this site to articles about attitudes toward physician-assisted suicide.

Young, Robert, "Voluntary Euthanasia," <http://plato.stanford.edu/entries/voluntary-euthanasia/>. An overview of the debate over voluntary euthanasia.

Authored Books

Dworkin, Gerald, R. G. Frey, and Sissela Bok (eds.) *Euthanasia and Physician Assisted Suicide: For and Against* (Cambridge: Cambridge University Press, 1998). In this two-part book Dworkin and Frey defend the practices of euthanasia and physician-assisted suicide, and Bok argues against these practices.

Keown, John, *Euthanasia, Ethics and Public Policy: An Argument Against Legalisation* (Cambridge: Cambridge University Press, 2002). As the title indicates, Keown makes a case for not legalizing euthanasia and assisted suicide.

Orfali, Robert, *Death with Dignity: The Case for Legalizing Physician-Assisted Dying and Euthanasia* (Minneapolis, MN: Mill City Press, 2011). Employing recent data from Oregon and the Netherlands, Orfali defends the legalization of physician-assisted suicide, answering critics who oppose PAS by appealing to considerations of the integrity of medicine, the sanctity of life, and slippery slopes.

Edited Collections and Articles

Battin, Margaret P., Rosamond Rhodes, and Anita Silvers (eds.), *Physician Assisted Suicide: Expanding the Debate* (New York: Routledge, 1998). This collection features 23 essays, mostly by philosophers, debating the moral, social, and legal implications of physician-assisted suicide. The essays are organized into five parts: (1) Conceptual Issues, (2) Considering Those at Risk, (3) Considering the Practice of Medicine, (4) Considering the Impact of Legalization, and (5) Considering Religious Perspectives.

Birnbacher, Dieter and Edgar Dahl (eds.), *Giving Death a Helping Hand: Physician-Assisted Suicide and Public Policy: An International Perspective*. International Library of Ethics, Law, and the New Medicine. (New York: Springer, 2008). This anthology includes 13 essays by a broad array of authors, including academics and health care practitioners, and incorporates various international perspectives on physician-assisted suicide.

Foley, K. M. and H. Hendin (eds.), *The Case against Assisted Suicide: For the Right to End-of-Life Care* (Baltimore: Johns Hopkins University Press, 2002). Fourteen essays by professionals in law, medicine, and bioethics arguing against the legalization of physician-assisted suicide.

Hastings Center Report, vol. 22, March–April, 1992. This issue of HCR includes the entire version of Dan Brock's defense of voluntary active euthanasia. Brock's position is opposed in an essay by Daniel Callahan in that same issue.

Moreno, Jonathan D. (ed.), *Arguing Euthanasia: The Controversy Over Mercy Killing, Assisted Suicide, And The "Right To Die"* (New York: Touchstone, 1995). This collection features both outspoken advocates and critics debating the moral and social implications of euthanasia and assisted suicide.

9 } The Ethical Treatment of Animals

Nonhuman animals are used by humans as sources of food, clothing, entertainment, companionship, and experimentation. For example, in 2008 U.S. military researchers dressed pigs in armor and subjected them to various explosions in order to study the link between roadside bombs and brain damage. The point of the study, of course, was to help benefit U.S. soldiers fighting in Iraq and Afghanistan. Pigs were selected because their brains, hearts, and lungs are similar to those of humans. Are such experiments aimed at benefiting humans morally justified? Furthermore, what about the many other uses humans have for (nonhuman) animals, uses that do not necessarily inflict extreme pain on animals? Is there anything wrong with, say, painlessly killing and eating an animal for the taste of the meat? What about using animals for entertainment? On March 16, 2016, as a result of pressure by animal welfare advocates, SeaWorld announced that it would cease the practice of "orca breeding" at all of its marine parks and phase out its killer whale shows. Trophy hunting? When Walter Palmer, a wealthy dentist from Minnesota, killed Cecil the lion in Zimbabwe in 2015, news of this particular trophy hunt sparked international outrage by various groups and individuals. As a result of action by the Animal Legal Defense Fund, the Humane Society of the U.S., and public demand, American Airlines, Delta Airlines, and United Airlines announced bans on the transport of "trophies" (i.e., animal parts) from Africa's so-called big five species: the African lion, African elephant, Cape buffalo, African leopard, and white/black rhinoceros.

In order to properly focus the ethical dispute over the use of animals, let us consider these two questions:

- Do any animals have direct moral standing?
- If so, what does this imply about various practices such as eating meat and using animals as subjects for experimentation?

In order to introduce the readings in this chapter, let us first explain what is meant in the first question by talk of "direct moral standing."

1. DIRECT MORAL STANDING

For purposes of introducing the selections both in this chapter and in the next, let us distinguish between two types of moral standing: *direct* and *indirect*. Roughly, for something to have **direct moral standing** is for it, independently of its relation to other things or creatures, to possess features in virtue of which it deserves to be given moral consideration by agents who are capable of making moral choices. Different moral theories represent direct moral standing in different ways. To claim that a creature has rights is one way of explaining how it is that it has direct moral standing. So is the claim that something has intrinsic or inherent value. And to claim that we have duties *to* something and not just duties *with regard* to it is yet another way of representing the idea that the item in question has direct moral standing. Of course, if something has direct moral standing—whether because it has rights, intrinsic value, or is something toward which we have duties—there must be some features or properties of the item in question in virtue of which it has such standing. Just what those features are is what is most philosophically contentious in debates about the ethical treatment of animals. As we shall see in the next chapter, this same general issue arises in the controversy over abortion.

Direct moral standing contrasts with indirect moral standing. For something to have mere **indirect moral standing** is for it to deserve moral consideration only because it is related to something with direct moral standing. Such items, including most obviously one's material possessions, do not themselves have features that would make taking, changing, or destroying them a wrong that is done *to or against* them. Rather, whatever moral requirements we have *with regard to* our treatment of material possessions is dependent upon their relation to beings that have direct moral standing.

As mentioned at the outset of this chapter, most everyone agrees that animals ought not to be treated cruelly. But being against the cruel treatment of animals does not require one to think that they have direct moral standing. The real philosophical dispute, then, which is reflected in the first question listed earlier, is whether any of them have what we are calling direct moral standing. If they do, then presumably it will be possible to launch arguments against various forms of treatment including killing and eating them and using them for certain sorts of experimentation.[1] But do they?

2. SPECIESISM?

Racism and sexism are familiar forms of morally unjustified prejudice. These practices involve the systematic discrimination against the interests of members of some racial groups because of their race in the case of racism and against the members of one sex because of their sex in the case of sexism, respectively. Because people of all races and both men and women have direct moral standing, the sort of discrimination characteristic of racism and sexism is morally unjustified. These types of discrimination are the subject of chapter 6.

The basic idea of systematic discrimination against the interests of members of some group has been extended by some philosophers to the treatment of animals. **Speciesism**, then, refers to the systematic discrimination against the members of some species by the members of another species. And certainly such discrimination goes on today. But whether such discrimination is morally wrong depends upon such questions as whether any of the nonhuman animals who are the victims of discrimination have direct moral standing. The articles included in this chapter are focused on this central issue.

3. THEORY MEETS PRACTICE

In our chapter's readings, we find appeals to consequentialism, rights, the ethics of prima facie duty, and virtue ethics prominent in debates about the ethical treatment of animals. Let us briefly consider each of these approaches.

Consequentialism

Utilitarianism is the most familiar form of consequentialism that has played an important role in arguments over the ethical treatment of animals. According to one standard version of the principle of utility, an action is wrong just in case (and because) performing it will likely fail to maximize happiness impartially considered. Moreover, for traditional utilitarians, happiness (and unhappiness) over a period of time in a creature's life is a matter of its experiences of pleasure and experiences of displeasure or pain. Further, since many nonhuman animals can experience pleasure and pain, these utilitarians conclude that they have direct moral standing and must be factored into our decision making. Utilitarian arguments, of course, depend heavily on factual claims about the overall comparative effects of contemplated courses of action. Peter Singer argues on utilitarian grounds that when we estimate overall net happiness for all sentient creatures, we ought to conclude that many of our present practices involving the use of animals are morally wrong. Critics of this line of argument, whether or not they share a commitment to utilitarianism, challenge the utility calculation. And, of course, there are those who reject a strictly utilitarian approach to moral issues. Alastair Norcross agrees with Singer's position on the wrongness of meat-eating. However, instead of appealing to moral theory in defense of his position, Norcross argues by analogy.

Rights Approaches

According to a rights-focused approach that would accord animals direct moral standing, the nonhuman animals in question possess the relevant characteristics that qualify them for having rights, including a right to life, to some kinds of liberty, and perhaps to whatever kind of life would allow them some measure of happiness. This approach is famously defended by Tom Regan, but its plausibility requires a defense of the nature of rights, their content, and their relative strengths—topics that are controversial. In a selection included below, Carl Cohen argues that Regan's defense fails and that moral rights remain exclusively within the human realm.

Social Contract Moral Theory

According to versions of social contract moral theory (also referred to as "contractualism"), what is right or wrong is determined by agreement among ideally situated human beings who are motivated to find principles and rules to govern their behavior toward one another. In our selection from Peter Carruthers, he argues, based on contractualism, that nonhuman animals lack direct moral standing and hence lack rights. He goes on to explain why, even so, human beings do have duties with regard to nonhuman animals.

Virtue Ethics

Although none of the readings in this chapter appeal to a virtue-based moral theory and its application to the ethical treatment of animals, the article by Thomas E. Hill Jr. in the final chapter, on the environment, does take a virtue approach to environmental issues. His approach, which appeals specifically to vices that represent a lack of the virtue of humility, could easily be extended to the case of animals.

NOTE

1. Although, even if some animals do have direct moral standing, it does not automatically follow that using them for such things as food and experimentation is wrong. For instance, direct moral standing may come in degrees so that the members of some species only have it to some small degree, in which case perhaps their use by humans under certain circumstances is not, all things considered, morally wrong.

PETER SINGER

All Animals Are Equal

Singer approaches moral issues from a utilitarian perspective, which implies a principle of equality: the interests of all beings should be given equal consideration. Singer argues that nonhuman animals, because they can suffer, have interests, and so their interests should be taken into account. An implication of this line of thinking is that meat-eating and much animal experimentation are wrong; such practices involve a kind of discrimination that Singer compares to racism and sexism.

Recommended Reading: consequentialism, chap. 1, sec. 2A.

"Animal Liberation" may sound more like a parody of other liberation movements than a serious objective. The idea of "The Rights of Animals" actually was once used to parody the case for women's rights. When Mary Wollstonecraft, a forerunner of today's feminists, published her *Vindication of the Rights of Women* in 1792, her views were widely regarded as absurd, and before long an anonymous publication appeared entitled *A Vindication of the Rights of Brutes*. The author of this satirical work (now known to have been Thomas Taylor, a distinguished Cambridge philosopher) tried to refute Mary Wollstonecraft's arguments by showing that they could be carried one stage further. If the argument for equality was sound when applied to women, why should it not be applied to dogs, cats, and horses? The reasoning seemed to hold for these "brutes" too, yet to hold that brutes had rights was manifestly absurd; therefore the reasoning

From Peter Singer, "All Animals Are Equal," from *Animal Liberation*, (New York: New York Review of Books 1975): pp. 1–22. By permission of the author.

by which this conclusion had been reached must be unsound, and if unsound when applied to brutes, it must also be unsound when applied to women, since the very same arguments had been used in each case.

In order to explain the basis of the case for the equality of animals, it will be helpful to start with an examination of the case for the equality of women. Let us assume that we wish to defend the case for women's rights against the attack by Thomas Taylor. How should we reply?

One way in which we might reply is by saying that the case for equality between men and women cannot validly be extended to nonhuman animals. Women have a right to vote, for instance, because they are just as capable of making rational decisions about the future as men are; dogs, on the other hand, are incapable of understanding the significance of voting, so they cannot have the right to vote. There are many other obvious ways in which men and women resemble each other closely, while humans and animals differ greatly. So, it might be said, men and women are similar beings and should have similar rights, while humans and nonhumans are different and should not have equal rights.

The reasoning behind this reply to Taylor's analogy is correct up to a point, but it does not go far enough. There *are* important differences between humans and other animals, and these differences must give rise to *some* differences in the rights that each have. Recognizing this obvious fact, however, is no barrier to the case for extending the basic principle of equality to nonhuman animals. The differences that exist between men and women are equally undeniable, and the supporters of Women's Liberation are aware that these differences may give rise to different rights. Many feminists hold that women have the right to an abortion on request. It does not follow that since these same feminists are campaigning for equality between men and women they must support the right of men to have abortions too. Since a man cannot have an abortion, it is meaningless to talk of his right to have one. Since a dog can't vote, it is meaningless to talk of its right to vote. There is no reason why either Women's Liberation or Animal Liberation should get involved in such nonsense. The extension of the basic principle of equality from one group to another does

not imply that we must treat both groups in exactly the same way, or grant exactly the same rights to both groups. Whether we should do so will depend on the nature of the members of the two groups. The basic principle of equality does not require equal or identical *treatment;* it requires equal *consideration.* Equal consideration for different beings may lead to different treatment and different rights.

So there is a different way of replying to Taylor's attempt to parody the case for women's rights, a way that does not deny the obvious differences between humans and nonhumans but goes more deeply into the question of equality and concludes by finding nothing absurd in the idea that the basic principle of equality applies to so-called brutes. At this point such a conclusion may appear odd; but if we examine more deeply the basis on which our opposition to discrimination on grounds of race or sex ultimately rests, we will see that we would be on shaky ground if we were to demand equality for blacks, women, and other groups of oppressed humans while denying equal consideration to nonhumans. To make this clear we need to see first, exactly why racism and sexism are wrong.

When we say that all human beings, whatever their race, creed, or sex, are equal, what is it that we are asserting? Those who wish to defend hierarchical, inegalitarian societies have often pointed out that by whatever test we choose it simply is not true that all humans are equal. Like it or not we must face the fact that humans come in different shapes and sizes; they come with different moral capacities, different intellectual abilities, different amounts of benevolent feeling and sensitivity to the needs of others, different abilities to communicate effectively, and different capacities to experience pleasure and pain. In short, if the demand for equality were based on the actual equality of all human beings, we would have to stop demanding equality.

Still, one might cling to the view that the demand for equality among human beings is based on the actual equality of the different races and sexes. Although, it may be said, humans differ as individuals there are no differences between the races and sexes *as such.* From the mere fact that a person is black or a woman we cannot infer anything about that person's intellectual or moral capacities. This, it may be said, is why racism and sexism are wrong. The white racist claims that whites are superior to blacks, but this is false—although there are differences among individuals, some blacks are superior to some whites in all of the capacities and abilities that could conceivably be relevant. The opponent of sexism would say the same: a person's sex is no guide to his or her abilities, and this is why it is unjustifiable to discriminate on the basis of sex.

The existence of individual variations that cut across the lines of race or sex, however, provides us with no defense at all against a more sophisticated opponent of equality, one who proposes that, say, the interests of all those with IQ scores below 100 be given less consideration than the interests of those with ratings over 100. Perhaps those scoring below the mark, would, in this society, be made the slaves of those scoring higher. Would a hierarchical society of this sort really be so much better than one based on race or sex? I think not. But if we tie the moral principle of equality to the factual equality of the different races or sexes, taken as a whole, our opposition to racism and sexism does not provide us with any basis for objecting to this kind of inegalitarianism.

There is a second important reason why we ought not to base our opposition to racism and sexism on any kind of actual equality, even the limited kind that asserts that variations in capacities and abilities are spread evenly between the different races and sexes: we can have no absolute guarantee that these capacities and abilities really are distributed evenly, without regard to race or sex, among human beings. So far as actual abilities are concerned there do seem to be certain measurable differences between both races and sexes. These differences do not, of course, appear in each case, but only when averages are taken. More important still, we do not yet know how much of these differences is really due to the different genetic endowments of the different races and sexes, and how much is due to poor schools, poor housing, and other factors that are the result of past and continuing discrimination. Perhaps all of the important differences will eventually prove to be environmental rather than genetic. Anyone

opposed to racism and sexism will certainly hope that this will be so, for it will make the task of ending discrimination a lot easier; nevertheless it would be dangerous to rest the case against racism and sexism on the belief that all significant differences are environmental in origin. The opponent of, say, racism who takes this line will be unable to avoid conceding that *if* differences in ability do after all prove to have some genetic connection with race, racism would in some way be defensible.

Fortunately there is no need to pin the case for equality to one particular outcome of a scientific investigation. The appropriate response to those who claim to have found evidence of genetically based differences in ability between the races or sexes is not to stick to the belief that the genetic explanation must be wrong, whatever evidence to the contrary may turn up: instead we should make it quite clear that the claim to equality does not depend on intelligence, moral capacity, physical strength, or similar matters of fact. Equality is a moral idea, not an assertion of fact. There is no logiically compelling reason for assuming that a factual difference in ability between two people justifies any difference in the amount of consideration we give to their needs and interests. *The principle of the equality of human beings is not a description of an alleged actual equality among humans; it is a prescription of how we should treat humans.*

Jeremy Bentham, the founder of the reforming utilitarian school of moral philosophy, incorporated the essential basis of moral equality into his system of ethics by means of the formula: "Each to count for one and none for more than one." In other words, the interests of every being affected by an action are to be taken into account and given the same weight as the like interests of any other being. A later utilitarian, Henry Sidgwick, put the point in this way: "The good of any one individual is of no more importance, from the point of view (if I may say so) of the Universe, than the good of any other." More recently the leading figures in contemporary moral philosophy have shown a great deal of agreement in specifying as a fundamental presupposition of their moral theories some similar requirement that operates so as to give everyone's interests equal consideration—although these writers generally cannot agree on how this requirement is best formulated.[1]

It is an implication of this principle of equality that our concern for others and our readiness to consider their interests ought not to depend on what they are like or on what abilities they may possess. Precisely what this concern or consideration requires us to do may vary according to the characteristics of those affected by what we do: concern for the well-being of a child growing up in America would require that we teach him to read; concern for the well-being of a pig may require no more than that we leave him alone with other pigs in a place where there is adequate food and room to run freely. But the basic element—the taking into account of the interests of the being, whatever those interests may be—must, according to the principle of equality, be extended to all beings, black or white, masculine or feminine, human or nonhuman.

Thomas Jefferson, who was responsible for writing the principle of the equality of men into the American Declaration of Independence, saw this point. It led him to oppose slavery even though he was unable to free himself from his slaveholding background. He wrote in a letter to the author of a book that emphasized the notable intellectual achievements of Negroes in order to refute the then common view that they had limited intellectual capacities:

> Be assured that no person living wishes more sincerely than I do, to see a complete refutation of the doubts I have myself entertained and expressed on the grade of understanding allotted to them by nature, and to find that they are on a par with ourselves . . . but whatever be their degree of talent it is no measure of their rights. Because Sir Isaac Newton was superior to others in understanding, he was not therefore lord of the property or person of others.[2]

Similarly when in the 1850s the call for women's rights was raised in the United States a remarkable black feminist named Sojourner Truth made the same point in more robust terms at a feminist convention:

> . . . they talk about this thing in the head; what do they call it? ["Intellect," whispered someone near by.] That's it. What's that got to do with women's rights or Negroes' rights? If my cup won't hold but a pint and

yours holds a quart, wouldn't you be mean not to let me have my little half-measure full?[3]

It is on this basis that the case against racism and the case against sexism must both ultimately rest; and it is in accordance with this principle that the attitude that we may call "speciesism," by analogy with racism, must also be condemned. Speciesism—the word is not an attractive one, but I can think of no better term—is a prejudice or attitude of bias toward the interests of members of one's own species and against those members of other species. It should be obvious that the fundamental objections to racism and sexism made by Thomas Jefferson and Sojourner Truth apply equally to speciesism. If possessing a higher degree of intelligence does not entitle one human to use another for his own ends, how can it entitle humans to exploit nonhumans for the same purpose?[4]

Many philosophers and other writers have proposed the principle of equal consideration of interests, in some form or other, as a basic moral principle, but not many of them have recognized that this principle applies to members of other species as well as to our own. Jeremy Bentham was one of the few who did realize this. In a forward-looking passage written at a time when black slaves had been freed by the French but the British dominions were still being treated in the way we now treat animals, Bentham wrote:

> The day may come when the rest of the animal creation may acquire those rights which never could have been withholden from them but by the hand of tyranny. The French have already discovered that the blackness of the skin is no reason why a human being should be abandoned without redress to the caprice of a tormentor. It may one day come to be recognized that the number of the legs, the villosity of the skin, or the termination of the *os sacrum,* are reasons equally insufficient for abandoning a sensitive being to the same fate. What else is it that should trace the insuperable line? Is it the faculty of reason, or perhaps the faculty of discourse? But a full-grown horse or dog is beyond comparison a more rational, as well as a more conversable animal, than an infant of a day or a week or even a month old. But suppose they were otherwise, what would it avail? The question is not, Can they reason? nor Can they talk? but, Can they suffer?[5]

In this passage Bentham points to the capacity for suffering as the vital characteristic that gives a being the right to equal consideration. The capacity for suffering—or more strictly, for suffering and/or enjoyment or happiness—is not just another characteristic like the capacity for language or higher mathematics. Bentham is not saying that those who try to mark "the insuperable line" that determines whether the interests of a being should be considered happen to have chosen the wrong characteristic. By saying that we must consider the interests of all beings with the capacity for suffering or enjoyment Bentham does not arbitrarily exclude from consideration any interests at all—as those who draw the line with reference to the possession of reason or language do. The capacity for suffering and enjoyment is *a prerequisite for having interests at all,* a condition that must be satisfied before we can speak of interests in a meaningful way. It would be nonsense to say that it was not in the interests of a stone to be kicked along the road by a schoolboy. A stone does not have interests because it cannot suffer. Nothing that we can do to it could possibly make any difference to its welfare. A mouse, on the other hand, does have an interest in not being kicked along the road, because it will suffer if it is.

If a being suffers there can be no moral justification for refusing to take that suffering into consideration. No matter what the nature of the being, the principle of equality requires that its suffering be counted equally with the like suffering—in so far as rough comparisons can be made—of any other being. If a being is not capable of suffering, or of experiencing enjoyment or happiness, there is nothing to be taken into account. So the limit of sentience (using the term as a convenient if not strictly accurate shorthand for the capacity to suffer and/or experience enjoyment) is the only defensible boundary of concern for the interests of others. To mark this boundary by some other characteristic like intelligence or rationality would be to mark it in an arbitrary manner. Why not choose some other characteristic, like skin color?

The racist violates the principle of equality by giving greater weight to the interests of members of his own race when there is a clash between their interests and the interests of those of another race. The sexist violates the principle of equality by favoring the interests of his own sex. Similarly the speciesist allows the interests of his own species to override the greater interests of members of other species. The pattern is identical in each case.

Most human beings are speciesists. Ordinary human beings—not a few exceptionally cruel or heartless humans, but the overwhelming majority of humans—take an active part in, acquiesce in, and allow their taxes to pay for practices that require the sacrifice of the most important interests of members of other species in order to promote the most trivial interests of our own species. . . .

Animals can feel pain. As we saw earlier, there can be no moral justification for regarding the pain (or pleasure) that animals feel as less important than the same amount of pain (or pleasure) felt by humans. But what exactly does this mean, in practical terms? To prevent misunderstanding I shall spell out what I mean a little more fully.

If I give a horse a hard slap across its rump with my open hand, the horse may start, but it presumably feels little pain. Its skin is thick enough to protect it against a mere slap. If I slap a baby in the same way, however, the baby will cry and presumably does feel pain, for its skin is more sensitive. So it is worse to slap a baby than a horse, if both slaps are administered with equal force. But there must be some kind of blow—I don't know exactly what it would be, but perhaps a blow with a heavy stick—that would cause the horse as much pain as we cause a baby by slapping it with our hand. That is what I mean by "the same amount of pain" and if we consider it wrong to inflict that much pain on a baby for no good reason then we must, unless we are speciesists, consider it equally wrong to inflict the same amount of pain on a horse for no good reason.

There are other differences between humans and animals that cause other complications. Normal adult human beings have mental capacities which will, in certain circumstances, lead them to suffer more than animals would in the same circumstances. If, for instance, we decided to perform extremely painful or lethal scientific experiments on normal adult humans, kidnapped at random from public parks for this purpose, every adult who entered a park would become fearful that he would be kidnapped. The resultant terror would be a form of suffering additional to the pain of the experiment. The same experiments performed on nonhuman animals would cause less suffering since the animals would not have the anticipatory dread of being kidnapped and experimented upon. This does not mean, of course, that it would be right to perform the experiment on animals, but only that there is a reason, which is *not* speciesist, for preferring to use animals rather than normal adult humans, if the experiment is to be done at all. It should be noted, however, that this same argument gives us a reason for preferring to use human infants—orphans perhaps—or retarded humans for experiments, rather than adults, since infants and retarded humans would also have no idea of what was going to happen to them. So far as this argument is concerned nonhuman animals and infants and retarded humans are in the same category; and if we use this argument to justify experiments on nonhuman animals we have to ask ourselves whether we are also prepared to allow experiments on humans, on what basis can we do it, other than a barefaced—and morally indefensible—preference for members of our own species?

There are many areas in which the superior mental powers of normal adult humans make a difference: anticipation, more detailed memory, greater knowledge of what is happening, and so on. Yet these differences do not all point to greater suffering on the part of the normal human being. Sometimes an animal may suffer more because of his more limited understanding. If, for instance, we are taking prisoners in wartime we can explain to them that while they must submit to capture, search, and confinement they will not otherwise be harmed and will be set free at the conclusion of hostilities. If we capture a wild animal, however, we cannot explain that we are not threatening its life. A wild animal cannot distinguish an attempt to overpower and confine from an attempt to kill; the one causes as much terror as the other.

It may be objected that comparisons of the sufferings of different species are impossible to make, and that for this reason when the interests of animals and humans clash the principle of equality gives no guidance. It is probably true that comparisons of suffering between members of different species cannot be made precisely, but precision is not essential. Even if we were to prevent the infliction of suffering on animals only when it is quite certain that the interests of humans will not be affected to anything like the extent that animals are affected, we would be forced to make radical changes in our treatment of animals that would involve our diet, the farming methods we use, experimental procedures in many fields of science, our approach to wildlife and to hunting, trapping and the wearing of furs, and areas of entertainment like circuses, rodeos, and zoos. As a result, a vast amount of suffering would be avoided.

So far I have said a lot about the infliction of suffering on animals, but nothing about killing them. This omission has been deliberate. The application of the principle of equality to the infliction of suffering is, in theory at least, fairly straightforward. Pain and suffering are bad and should be prevented or minimized, irrespective of the race, sex, or species of the being that suffers. How bad a pain is depends on how intense it is and how long it lasts, but pains of the same intensity and duration are equally bad, whether felt by humans or animals.

The wrongness of killing a being is more complicated. I have kept, and shall continue to keep, the question of killing in the background because in the present state of human tyranny over other species the more simple, straightforward principle of equal consideration of pain or pleasure is a sufficient basis for identifying and protesting against all the major abuses of animals that humans practice. Nevertheless, it is necessary to say something about killing.

Just as most humans are speciesists in their readiness to cause pain to animals when they would not cause a similar pain to humans for the same reason, so most humans are speciesists in their readiness to kill other animals when they would not kill humans. We need to proceed more cautiously here, however, because people hold widely differing views about when it is legitimate to kill humans, as the continuing debates over abortion and euthanasia attest. Nor have moral philosophers been able to agree on exactly what it is that makes it wrong to kill humans, and under what circumstances killing a human being may be justifiable.

Let us consider first the view that it is always wrong to take an innocent human life. We may call this the "sanctity of life" view. People who take this view oppose abortion and euthanasia. They do not usually, however, oppose the killing of nonhumans—so perhaps it would be more accurate to describe this view as the "sanctity of *human* life" view.

The belief that human life, and only human life, is sacrosanct is a form of speciesism. To see this, consider the following example.

Assume that, as sometimes happens, an infant has been born with massive and irreparable brain damage. The damage is so severe that the infant can never be any more than a "human vegetable," unable to talk, recognize other people, act independently of others, or develop a sense of selfawareness. The parents of the infant, realizing that they cannot hope for any improvement in their child's condition and being in any case unwilling to spend, or ask the state to spend, the thousands of dollars that would be needed annually for proper care of the infant, ask the doctor to kill the infant painlessly.

Should the doctor do what the parents ask? Legally, he should not, and in this respect the law reflects the sanctity of life view. The life of every human being is sacred. Yet people who would say this about the infant do not object to the killing of nonhuman animals. How can they justify their different judgments? Adult chimpanzees, dogs, pigs, and many other species far surpass the brain-damaged infant in their ability to relate to others, act independently, be self-aware, and any other capacity that could reasonably be said to give value to life. With the most intensive care possible, there are retarded infants who can never achieve the intelligence level of a dog. Nor can we appeal to the concern of the infant's parents, since they themselves, in this imaginary example (and in some actual cases) do not want the infant kept alive.

The only thing that distinguishes the infant from the animal, in the eyes of those who claim it has a "right to life," is that it is, biologically, a member of the species Homo sapiens, whereas chimpanzees, dogs, and pigs are not. But to use *this* difference as

the basis for granting a right to life to the infant and not to the other animals is, of course, pure speciesism.[6] It is exactly the kind of arbitrary difference that the most crude and overt kind of racist uses in attempting to justify racial discrimination.

This does not mean that to avoid speciesism we must hold that it is as wrong to kill a dog as it is to kill a normal human being. The only position that is irredeemably speciesist is the one that tries to make the boundary of the right to life run exactly parallel to the boundary of our own species. Those who hold the sanctity of life view do this because while distinguishing sharply between humans and other animals they allow no distinctions to be made within our own species, objecting to the killing of the severely retarded and the hopelessly senile as strongly as they object to the killing of normal adults.

To avoid speciesism we must allow that beings which are similar in all relevant respects have similar right to life—and mere membership in our own biological species cannot be a morally relevant criterion for this right. Within these limits we could still hold that, for instance, it is worse to kill a normal adult human, with a capacity for self-awareness, and the ability to plan for the future and have meaningful relations with others, than it is to kill a mouse, which presumably does not share all of these characteristics; or we might appeal to the close family and other personal ties which humans have but mice do not have to the same degree; or we might think that it is the consequences for other humans, who will be put in fear of their own lives, that makes the crucial difference; or we might think it is some combination of these factors, or other factors altogether.

Whatever criteria we choose, however, we will have to admit that they do not follow precisely the boundary of our own species. We may legitimately hold that there are some features of certain beings which make their lives more valuable than those of other beings; but there will surely be some nonhuman animals whose lives, by any standards, are more valuable than the lives of some humans. A chimpanzee, dog, or pig, for instance, will have a higher degree of self-awareness and a greater capacity for meaningful relations with others than a severely retarded infant or someone in a state of advanced senility. So if we base the right to life on these characteristics we must grant these animals a right to life as good as, or better than, such retarded or senile humans.

Now this argument cuts both ways. It could be taken as showing that chimpanzees, dogs, and pigs, along with some other species, have a right to life and we commit a grave moral offense whenever we kill them, even when they are old and suffering and our intention is to put them out of their misery. Alternatively one could take the argument as showing that the severely retarded and hopelessly senile have no right to life and may be killed for quite trivial reasons, as we now kill animals.

Since the focus here is on ethical questions concerning animals and not on the morality of euthanasia I shall not attempt to settle this issue finally. I think it is reasonably clear, though, that while both of the positions just described avoid speciesism, neither is entirely satisfactory. What we need is some middle position that would avoid speciesism but would not make the lives of the retarded and senile as cheap as the lives of pigs and dogs now are, nor make the lives of pigs and dogs so sacrosanct that we think it wrong to put them out of hopeless misery. What we must do is bring nonhuman animals within our sphere of moral concern and cease to treat their lives as expendable for whatever trivial purposes we may have. At the same time, once we realize that the fact that a being is a member of our own species is not in itself enough to make it always wrong to kill that being, we may come to reconsider our policy of preserving human lives at all costs, even when there is no prospect of a meaningful life or of existence without terrible pain.

I conclude, then, that a rejection of speciesism does not imply that all lives are of equal worth. While self-awareness, intelligence, the capacity for meaningful relations with others, and so on are not relevant to the question of inflicting pain—since pain is pain, whatever other capacities, beyond the capacity to feel pain, the being may have—these capacities may be relevant to the question of taking life. It is not arbitrary to hold that the life of a self-aware being, capable of abstract thought, of planning for the future, of complex acts of communication, and so on, is more valuable than the life of a being without these capacities. To see the difference between the issues of inflicting pain and taking life, consider how we would choose within our own species. If we had to choose to save the life of a normal human or a mentally defective human, we would probably choose to save the life of the normal human; but if we had to choose between preventing pain in the normal human or the mental defective—imagine that both have received painful but superficial injuries, and we only have enough painkiller for one of them—it is not nearly so clear how we ought to choose. The same is true when we consider other species. The evil of pain is, in itself, unaffected by the other characteristics of the being that feels the pain; the value of life is affected by these other characteristics.

Normally this will mean that if we have to choose between the life of a human being and the life of another animal we would choose to save the life of the human, but there may be special cases in which the reverse holds true, because the human being in question does not have the capacities of a normal human being. So this view is not speciesist, although it may appear to be at first glance. The preference, in normal cases, for saving a human life over the life of an animal when a choice *has* to be made is a preference based on the characteristics that normal humans have, and not on the mere fact that they are members of our own species. This is why when we consider members of our own species who lack the characteristics of normal humans we can no longer say that their lives are always to be preferred to those of other animals. In general, the question of when it is wrong to kill (painlessly) an animal is one to which we need give no precise answer. As long as we remember that we should give the same respect to the lives of animals as we give to the lives of those humans at a similar mental level, we shall not go far wrong.

In any case, the conclusions that are argued for here flow from the principle of minimizing suffering alone. The idea that it is also wrong to kill animals painlessly gives some of these conclusions additional support which is welcome, but strictly unnecessary. Interestingly enough, this is true even of the conclusion that we ought to become vegetarians, a conclusion that in the popular mind is generally based on some kind of absolute prohibition on killing.

NOTES

1 For Bentham's moral philosophy, see his *Introduction to the Principles of Morals and Legislation,* and for Sidgwick's see *The Methods of Ethics* (the passage quoted is form the seventh edition, p. 382).

2 Letter to Henri Gregoire, February 25, 1809.

3 Reminiscences by Francis D. Gage, from Susan B. Anthony, *The History of Woman Suffrage,* vol. l; the passage is to be found in the extract in Leslie Tanner, ed., *Voices from Women's Liberation* (New York: Signet, 1970).

4 I owe the term "speciesism" to Richard Ryder.

5 *Introduction to the Principles of Morals and Legislation,* chapter 17.

6 I am here putting aside religious views, for example the doctrine that all and only humans have immortal souls, or are made in the image of God. Historically these views have been very important, and no doubt are partly responsible for the idea that human life has a special sanctity. Logically, however, these religious views are unsatisfactory, since a reasoned explanation of why it should be that all humans and no nonhumans have immortal souls is not offered. This belief too, therefore, comes under suspicion as a form of speciesism. In any case, defenders of the "sanctity of life" view are generally reluctant to base their position on purely religious doctrines, since these doctrines are no longer as widely accepted as they once were.

READING QUESTIONS

1. What does Singer mean by "speciesism"?
2. How does Singer argue against views that would attempt to draw a morally significant line between humans and nonhuman animals on the basis of differences in rationality?
3. Why does Singer think that appeals to the sanctity of human life in arguing that only human interests count are really forms of speciesism?

DISCUSSION QUESTIONS

1. Is what Singer calls "speciesism" really a form of discrimination on a par with sexism and racism?
2. Suppose one grants Singer's position on nonhuman animals, namely, that it is wrong to kill them for "trivial" reasons. What sorts of nontrivial reasons might nevertheless justify killing nonhuman animals for food?

CARL COHEN

Do Animals Have Rights?

Cohen's negative answer to his title question involves two parts. First, he explains why non-human animals lack moral rights, even though humans have moral obligations with regard to them. Second, he critically evaluates Tom Regan's argument (from his 1983 book, *The Case for Animal Rights*) for the claim that nonhuman animals have rights. Regan's argument depends crucially on the claim that nonhuman animals, like human beings, have inherent value, and that therefore they have moral rights. Cohen argues that Regan's argument commits the fallacy of equivocation owing to multiple meanings of the term "inherent value."

Recommended Reading: rights-focused approaches, chap. 1, sec. 2D.

Whether animals have rights is a question of great importance because if they do, those rights must be respected, even at the cost of great burdens for human beings. A right (unlike an interest) is a valid claim, or potential claim, made by a moral agent, under principles that govern both the claimant and the target of the claim. Rights are precious; they are dispositive; they count.

You have a right to the return of money you lent me; we both understand that. It may be very convenient for me to keep the money, and you may have no need of it whatever; but my convenience and your needs are not to the point. You have a *right* to it, and we have courts of law partly to ensure that such rights will be respected.

If you make me a promise, I have a moral right to its fulfillment—even though there may be no law to enforce my right. It may be very much in your interest to break that promise, but your great interests and the silence of the law cut no mustard when your solemn promise—which we both well understood—had been given. Likewise, those holding power may have a great and benevolent interest in denying my rights to travel or to speak freely—but their interests are overridden by my rights.

A great deal was learned about hypothermia by some Nazi doctors who advanced their learning by soaking Jews in cold water and putting them in refrigerators to learn how hypothermia proceeds. We have no difficulty in seeing that they may not advance medicine in that way; the subjects of those atrocious experiments had rights that demanded respect. For those who ignored their rights we have nothing but moral loathing.

Some persons believe that animals have rights as surely as those Jews had rights, and they therefore look on the uses of animals in medical investigations just as we look at the Nazi use of the Jews, with moral loathing. They are consistent in doing so. If animals have rights they certainly have the right not to be killed, even to advance our important interests.

Some may say, "Well, they have rights, but we have rights too, and our rights override theirs." That may be true in some cases, but it will not solve the problem because, although we may have a weighty *interest* in learning, say, how to vaccinate against polio or other diseases, we do not have a *right* to learn such things. Nor could we honestly claim that we kill research animals in self-defense; they did not attack us. If animals have rights, they certainly have

Reprinted from *Ethics and Behavior*, 1997, vol. 7, no. 2, pp. 91–102.

the right not to be killed to advance the interests of others, whatever rights those others may have.

In 1952 there were about 58,000 cases of polio reported in the United States, and 3,000 polio deaths; my parents, parents everywhere, trembled in fear for their children at camp or away from home. Polio vaccination became routine in 1955, and cases dropped to about a dozen a year; today polio has been eradicated completely from the Western Hemisphere. The vaccine that achieved this, partly developed and tested only blocks from where I live in Ann Arbor, could have been developed *only* with the substantial use of animals. Polio vaccines had been tried many times earlier, but from those earlier vaccines children had contracted the disease; investigators had become, understandably, exceedingly cautious.

The killer disease for which a vaccine now is needed most desperately is malaria, which kills about 2 million people each year, most of them children. Many vaccines have been tried—not on children, thank God—and have failed. But very recently, after decades of effort, we learned how to make a vaccine that does, with complete success, inoculate mice against malaria. A safe vaccine for humans we do not yet have—but soon we will have it, thanks to the use of those mice, many of whom will have died in the process. To test that vaccine first on children would be an outrage, as it would have been an outrage to do so with the Salk and Sabin polio vaccines years ago. We use mice or monkeys *because there is no other way*. And there never will be another way because untested vaccines are very dangerous; their first use on a living organism is inescapably experimental; there is and will be no way to determine the reliability and safety of new vaccines without repeated tests on live organisms. Therefore, because we certainly may not use human children to test them, we will use mice (or as we develop an AIDS vaccine, primates) *or we will never have such vaccines*.

But if those animals we use in such tests have rights as human children do, what we did and are doing to them is as profoundly wrong as what the Nazis did to those Jews not long ago. Defenders of animal rights need not hold that medical scientists are vicious; they simply believe that what medical investigators are doing with animals is morally wrong.

Most biomedical investigations involving animal subjects use rodents: mice and rats. The rat is the animal appropriately considered (and used by the critic) as the exemplar whose moral stature is in dispute here. Tom Regan is a leading defender of the view that rats do have such rights, and may not be used in biomedical investigations. He is an honest man. He sees the consequences of his view and accepts them forthrightly. In *The Case for Animal Rights* (Regan, 1983) he wrote,

> The harms others might face as a result of the dissolution of [some] practice or institution is no defense of allowing it to continue. . . . No one has a right to be protected against being harmed if the protection in question involves violating the rights of others. . . . No one has a right to be protected by the continuation of an unjust practice, one that violates the rights of others. . . . Justice *must* be done, though the. . . . heavens fall. (pp. 346–347)

That last line echoes Kant, who borrowed it from an older tradition. Believing that rats have rights as humans do, Regan (1983) was convinced that killing them in medical research was morally intolerable. He wrote,

> On the rights view, [he means, of course, the Regan rights view] we cannot justify harming a single rat *merely* by aggregating "the many human and humane benefits" that flow from doing it. . . .Not even a single rat is to be treated as if that animal's value were reducible to his *possible utility* relative to the interests of others. (p. 384)

If there are some things that we cannot learn because animals have rights, well, as Regan (1983) put it, so be it.

This is the conclusion to which one certainly is driven if one holds that animals have rights. If Regan is correct about the moral standing of rats, we humans can have no right, ever, to kill them—unless perchance a rat attacks a person or a human baby, as rats sometimes do; then our right of self-defense may enter, I suppose. But medical investigations cannot honestly be described as self-defense, and medical investigations commonly require that many mice and rats be killed. Therefore, all medical investigations relying on them, or any other animal subjects—which includes most studies and all the most important studies of certain kinds—will have to stop. Bear in mind that the replacement of animal subjects by computer simulations, or tissue samples, and so on, is in most research a phantasm, a fantasy. Biomedical investigations using animal subjects (and of course all uses of animals as food) will have to stop.

This extraordinary consequence has no argumentative force for Regan and his followers; they are not consequentialists. For Regan the interests of humans, their desire to be freed of disease or relieved of pain, simply cannot outweigh the rights of a single rat. For him the issue is one of justice, and the use of animals in medical experiments (he believes) is simply not just. But the consequences of his view will give most of us, I submit, good reason to weigh very carefully the arguments he offers to support such far-reaching claims. Do you believe that the work of Drs. Salk and Sabin was morally right? Would you support it now, or support work just like it saving tens of thousands of human children from diphtheria, hepatitis, measles, rabies, rubella, and tetanus (all of which relied essentially on animal subjects)—as well as, now, AIDS, Lyme disease, and malaria? I surely do. If you would join me in this support we must conclude that the defense of animal rights is a gigantic mistake. I next aim to explain why animals cannot possess rights.

WHY ANIMALS DO NOT HAVE RIGHTS

Many obligations are owed by humans to animals; few will deny that. But it certainly does not follow from this that animals have rights because it is certainly not true that every obligation of ours arises from the rights of another. Not at all. We need to be clear and careful here. Rights entail obligations. If you have a right to the return of the money I borrowed, I have an obligation to repay it. No issue. If we have the right to speak freely on public policy matters, the community has the obligation to respect our right to do so. But the proposition *all rights entail obligations* does not convert simply, as the logicians say. From the true proposition that all trees are plants, it does not follow that all plants are trees. Similarly, not all obligations are entailed by rights. Some obligations, like mine to repay the money I borrowed from you, do arise out of rights. But many obligations are owed to persons or other beings who have no rights whatever in the matter.

Obligations may arise from commitments freely made: As a college professor I accept the obligation to comment at length on the papers my students submit, and I do so; but they have not the right to *demand* that I do so. Civil servants and elected officials surely ought to be courteous to members of the public, but that obligation certainly is not grounded in citizens' rights.

Special relations often give rise to obligations: Hosts have the obligation to be cordial to their guests, but the guest has not the right to demand cordiality. Shepherds have obligations to their dogs, and cowboys to their horses, which do not flow from the rights of those dogs or horses. My son, now 5, may someday wish to study veterinary medicine as my father did; I will then have the obligation to help him as I can, and with pride I shall—but he has not the authority to demand such help as a matter of right. My dog has no right to daily exercise and veterinary care, but I do have the obligation to provide those things for her.

One may be obliged to another for a special act of kindness done; one may be obliged to put an animal out of its misery in view of its condition—but neither the beneficiary of that kindness nor that dying animal may have had a claim of right.

Beauchamp and Childress (1994) addressed what they called the "correlativity of rights and obligations" and wrote that they would defend an "untidy" (pp. 73–75) variety of that principle. It would be very untidy indeed. Some of our most important obligations—to members of our family, to the needy, to neighbors, and to sentient creatures of every sort—have no foundation in rights at all. Correlativity appears critical from the perspective of one who holds a right; your right correlates with my obligation to respect it. But the claim that rights and obligations are reciprocals, that every obligation flows from another's right, is false, plainly inconsistent with our general understanding of the differences between what we think we ought to do, and what others can justly *demand* that we do.

I emphasize this because, although animals have no rights, it surely does not follow from this that one is free to treat them with callous disregard. Animals are not stones; they feel. A rat may suffer; surely we have the obligation not to torture it gratuitously, even though it be true that the concept of a right could not possibly apply to it. We humans are obliged to act humanely, that is, being aware of their sentience, to apply to animals the moral principles that govern us regarding the gratuitous imposition of pain and suffering; which is not, of course, to treat animals as the possessors of rights.

Animals cannot be the bearers of rights because the concept of rights is essentially *human*; it is rooted in, and has force within, a human moral world. Humans must deal with rats—all too frequently in some parts of the world—and must be moral in their dealing with them; but a rat can no more be said to have rights than a table can be said to have ambition. To say of a rat that it has rights is to confuse categories, to apply to its world a moral category that has content only in the human moral world.

Try this thought experiment. Imagine, on the Serengeti Plain in East Africa, a lioness hunting for her cubs. A baby zebra, momentarily left unattended by its mother, is the prey; the lioness snatches it, rips open its throat, tears out chunks of its flesh, and departs. The mother zebra is driven nearly out of her wits when she cannot locate her baby; finding its carcass she will not even leave the remains for days. The scene may be thought unpleasant, but it is entirely natural, of course, and extremely common. If the zebra has a right to live, if the prey is just but the predator unjust, we ought to intervene, if we can, on behalf of right. But we do not intervene, of course—as we surely would intervene if we saw the lioness about to attack an unprotected human baby or you. What accounts for the moral difference? We justify different responses to humans and to zebras on the ground (implicit or explicit) that their moral stature is very different. The human has a right not

to be eaten alive; it is, after all, a human being. Do you believe the baby zebra has the right not to be slaughtered by that lioness? That the lioness has the *right* to kill that baby zebra for her cubs? If you are inclined to say, confronted by such natural rapacity—duplicated with untold variety millions of times each day on planet earth—that neither is right or wrong, that neither has a *right* against the other, I am on your side. Rights are of the highest moral consequence, yes; but zebras and lions and rats are totally amoral; there is no morality for them; they do no wrong, ever. In their world there are no rights.

A contemporary philosopher who has thought a good deal about animals, referring to them as "moral patients," put it this way:

> A moral patient lacks the ability to formulate, let alone bring to bear, moral principles in deliberating about which one among a number of possible acts it would be right or proper to perform. Moral patients, in a word, cannot do what is right, nor can they do what is wrong. . . . Even when a moral patient causes significant harm to another, the moral patient has not done what is wrong. Only moral agents can do what is wrong. (Regan, 1983, pp. 152–153)

Just so. The concepts of wrong and right are totally foreign to animals, not conceivably within their ken or applicable to them, as the author of that passage clearly understands.

When using animals in our research, therefore, we ought indeed be humane—but we can never violate the rights of those animals because, to be blunt, they have none. Rights do not *apply* to them.

But humans do have rights. Where do our rights come from? Why are we not crudely natural creatures like rats and zebras? This question philosophers have struggled to answer from earliest times. A definitive account of the human moral condition I cannot here present, of course. But reflect for a moment on the kinds of answers that have been widely given:

- Some think our moral understanding, with its attendant duties, to be a divine gift. So St. Thomas said: The moral law is binding, and humans have the power, given by God, to grasp its binding character, and must therefore respect the rights that other humans possess. God makes us (Saint Augustine said before him) in his own image, and therefore with a will that is free, and gives us the power to recognize that, and therefore, unlike other creatures, we must choose between good and evil, between right and wrong.

- Many philosophers, distrusting theological justifications of rights and duties, sought the ground of human morality in the membership, by all humans, in a moral community. The English idealist, Bradley, called it an organic moral community; the German idealist, Hegel, called it an objective ethical order. These and like accounts commonly center on human interrelations, on a moral *fabric* within which human agents always act, and within which animals never act and never can possibly act.

- The highly abstract reasoning from which such views emerge has dissatisfied many; you may find more nearly true the convictions of ethical intuitionists and realists who said, as H. A. Prichard, Sir David Ross, and my friend and teacher C. D. Broad, of happy memory, used to say, that there is a direct, underivative, intuitive cognition of rights as possessed by other humans, but not by animals.

- Or perhaps in the end we will return to Kant, and say with him that critical reason reveals at the core of human action a uniquely moral will, and the unique ability to grasp and to lay down moral laws for oneself and for others—an ability that is not conceivably within the capacity of any nonhuman animal whatever.

To be a moral agent (on this view) is to be able to grasp the generality of moral restrictions on our will. Humans understand that some things, which may be in our interest, *must not be willed*; we lay down moral laws for ourselves, and thus exhibit, as no other animal can exhibit, moral autonomy. My dog knows that there are certain things she must not do—but she knows this only as the outcome of her learning about her interests, the pains she may suffer if she does what had been taught forbidden. She does not know, cannot know (as Regan agrees) that any conduct is wrong. The proposition *It would be highly advantageous to act in such-and-such a way, but I may not because it would be wrong* is one that no dog or mouse or rabbit, however sweet and endearing, however loyal or attentive to its young, can ever entertain, or intend, or begin to grasp. Right is not in their world. But right and wrong are the very stuff of human moral life, the ever-present awareness of human beings who can do wrong, and who by seeking (often) to avoid wrong conduct prove themselves members of a moral community in which rights may be exercised and must be respected.

Some respond by saying, "This can't be correct, for human infants (and the comatose and senile, etc.) surely have rights, but they make no moral claims or judgments and can make none—and any view entailing that children can have no rights must be absurd." Objections of this kind miss the point badly. It is not individual persons who qualify (or are disqualified) for the possession of rights because of the presence or absence in them of some special capacity, thus resulting in the award of rights to some but not to others. Rights are universally human; they arise in a *human moral world*, in a moral *sphere*. In the human world moral judgments are pervasive; it is the fact that all humans including infants and the senile are members of that moral community—not the fact that as individuals they have or do not have certain special capacities, or merits—that makes humans bearers of rights. Therefore, it is beside the point to insist that animals have remarkable capacities, that they really have a consciousness of self, or of the future, or make plans, and so on. And the tired response that because infants plainly cannot make moral claims they must have no rights at all, or rats must have them too, we ought forever put aside. Responses like these arise out of a misconception of right itself. They mistakenly suppose that rights are tied to some identifiable individual abilities or sensibilities, and they fail to see that rights arise only in a community of moral beings, and that therefore there are spheres in which rights do apply and spheres in which they do not.

Rationality is not at issue; the capacity to communicate is not at issue. My dog can reason, if rather weakly, and she certainly can communicate. Cognitive criteria for the possession of rights, ... are morally perilous. Indeed they are. Nor is the capacity to suffer here at issue. And, if *autonomy* be understood only as the capacity to choose this course rather than that, autonomy is not to the point either. But *moral autonomy*—that is, *moral self-legislation*—is to the point, because moral autonomy is uniquely human and is for animals out of the question, as we have seen, and as Regan and I agree. In talking about autonomy, therefore, we must be careful and precise.

Because humans do have rights, and these rights can be violated by other humans, we say that some humans commit *crimes*. But whether a crime has been committed depends utterly on the moral state of mind of the actor. If I take your coat, or your book, honestly thinking it was mine, I do not steal it. The *actus reus* (the guilty deed) must be accompanied, in a genuine crime, by a guilty mind, a *mens rea*. That recognition, not just of possible punishment for an act, but of moral duties that govern us, no rat or cow ever can possess. In primitive times humans did sometimes bring cows and horses to the bar of human justice. We chuckle at that practice now, realizing that accusing cows of crimes marks the primitive moral view as inane. Animals never can be criminals because they have no moral state of mind. . . .

WHY ANIMALS ARE MISTAKENLY BELIEVED TO HAVE RIGHTS

From the foregoing discussion it follows that, if some philosophers believe that they have proved that animals have rights, they must have erred in the alleged proof. Regan is a leader among those who claim to *argue* in defense of the rights of rats; he contends that the best arguments are on his side. I aim next to show how he and others with like views go astray. . . .

[Regan's] case is built entirely on the principle that allegedly *carries over* almost everything earlier claimed about human rights to rats and other animals. What principle is that? It is the principle, put in italics but given no name, that equates moral agents with moral patients:

The validity of the claim to respectful treatment, and thus the case for the recognition of the right to such treatment, cannot be any stronger or weaker in the case of moral patients than it is in the case of moral agents. (Regan, p. 279)

But hold on. Why in the world should anyone think this principle to be true? Back [on page 392], where Regan first recounted his view of moral patients, he allowed that some of them are, although capable of experiencing pleasure and pain, lacking in other capacities. But he is interested, he told us there, in those moral patients—those animals—that are like humans in having *inherent value*. This is the key to the argument for animal rights, the possession of inherent value. How that concept functions in the argument becomes absolutely critical. I will say first briefly what will be shown more carefully later: *Inherent value* is an expression used by Regan (and many like him) with two very different senses—in one of which it is reasonable to conclude that those who have inherent value have rights, and in another sense in which that inference is wholly unwarranted. But the phrase, *inherent value* has some plausibility in both contexts, and thus by sliding from one sense of inherent value to the other Regan appears to succeed, in two pages, in making the case for animal rights.

The concept of inherent value first entered the discussion in the seventh chapter of Regan's (1983) book, at which point his principal object is to fault and defeat utilitarian arguments. It is not (he argued there) the pleasures or pains that go "into the cup" of humanity that give value, but the "cups" themselves; humans are equal in value because they are humans, having inherent value. So we are, all of us, equal—equal in being moral agents who have this inherent value. This approach to the moral stature of humans is likely to be found quite plausible. Regan called it the "postulate of inherent value"; all humans, "The lonely, forsaken, unwanted, and unloved are no more nor less inherently valuable than those who enjoy a more hospitable relationship with others" (p. 237). And Regan went on to argue for the proposition that all moral agents are "equal in inherent value." Holding some such views we are likely to say, with Kant, that all humans are beyond price. Their inherent value gives them moral dignity, a unique role in the moral world, as agents having the capacity to act morally and make moral judgments. This is inherent value in Sense 1.

The expression *inherent value* has another sense, however, also common and also plausible. My dog has inherent value, and so does every wild animal, every lion and zebra, which is why the senseless killing of animals is so repugnant. Each animal is unique, not replaceable in itself by another animal or by any rocks or clay. Animals, like humans, are not just things; they live, and as unique living creatures they have inherent value. This is an important point, and again likely to be thought plausible; but here, in Sense 2, the phrase *inherent value* means something quite distinct from what was meant in its earlier uses.

Inherent value in Sense 1, possessed by all humans but not by all animals, which warrants the claim of human rights, is very different from inherent value in Sense 2, which warrants no such claim. The uniqueness of animals, their intrinsic worthiness as individual living things, does not ground the possession of rights, has nothing to do with the moral condition in which rights arise. Regan's argument reached its critical objective with almost magical speed because, having argued that beings with inherent value (Sense 1) have rights that must be respected, he quickly asserted (putting it in italics lest the reader be inclined to express doubt) that rats and rabbits also have rights because they, too, have inherent value (Sense 2).

This is an egregious example of the fallacy of equivocation: the informal fallacy in which two or more meanings of the same word or phrase have been confused in the several premises of an argument (Cohen & Copi, 1994, pp. 143–144). Why is this slippage not seen at once? Partly because we know the phrase inherent value often is used loosely, so the reader is not prone to quibble about its introduction; partly because the two uses of the phrase relied on are both common, so neither signals danger; partly because inherent value in Sense 2 is indeed shared by those who have it in Sense 1; and partly because the phrase *inherent value* is woven into accounts of what Regan (1983) elsewhere called the *subject-of-a-life criterion*, a phrase

of his own devising for which he can stipulate any meaning he pleases, of course, and which also slides back and forth between the sphere of genuine moral agency and the sphere of animal experience. But perhaps the chief reason the equivocation between these two uses of the phrase *inherent value* is obscured (from the author, I believe, as well as from the reader) is the fact that the assertion that animals have rights appears only indirectly, as the outcome of the application of the principle that moral patients are entitled to the same respect as moral agents—a principle introduced at a point in the book long after the important moral differences between moral patients and moral agents have been recognized, with a good deal of tangled philosophical argument having been injected in between. . . .

Animals do not have rights. Right does not apply in their world. We do have many obligations to animals, of course, and I honor Regan's appreciation of their sensitivities. I also honor his seriousness of purpose, and his always civil and always rational spirit. But he is, I submit, profoundly mistaken. I conclude with the observation that, had his mistaken views about the rights of animals long been accepted, most successful medical therapies recently devised—antibiotics, vaccines, prosthetic devices, and other compounds and instruments on which we now rely for saving and improving human lives and for the protection of our children—could not have been developed; and were his views to become general now (an outcome that is unlikely but possible) the consequences for medical science and for human well-being in the years ahead would be nothing less than catastrophic.

Advances in medicine absolutely require experiments, many of which are dangerous. Dangerous experiments absolutely require living organisms as subjects. Those living organisms (we now agree) certainly may not be human beings. Therefore, most advances in medicine will continue to rely on the use of nonhuman animals, or they will stop. Regan is free to say in response, as he does, "so be it." The rest of us must ask if the argument he presents is so compelling as to force us to accept that dreadful result.

REFERENCES

Beauchamp, T. L., & Childress, J. F. (1994). *Principles of biomedical ethics* (4th ed.). New York: Oxford University Press.

Cohen, C., & Copi, I. M. (1994). *Introduction to logic* (9th ed.). New York: Macmillan.

Regan, T. (1983). *The case for animal rights*. Berkeley: University of California Press.

READING QUESTIONS

1. Explain Cohen's distinction between interests and rights, giving examples of each.
2. Cohen claims that although rights entail obligations, the converse obligations entail rights is not true. Give your own example to support Cohen's negative claim.
3. What are the ways in which obligations arise according to Cohen?
4. Describe the four different views about where human rights come from according to Cohen.
5. What is Cohen's response to those who argue that humans such as infants have rights but can't make moral judgments?
6. What reasons does Cohen give for claiming that nonhuman animals lack moral rights?
7. Explain the particular fallacy of equivocation that Cohen claims Regan's argument for animal rights commits.

DISCUSSION QUESTIONS

1. Suppose that Cohen is correct in claiming that Regan's argument commits the fallacy of equivocation. Can you think of another argument for the claim that nonhuman animals have rights?
2. Suppose nonhuman animals do have some rights. How do they compare in content and strength to the basic rights of typical human beings?
3. Cohen admits that human beings do have obligations toward nonhuman animals even if those animals do not have rights. What sorts of obligations do we have toward nonhuman animals? Do these obligations differ in any significant ways from the obligations we have toward other human beings?
4. Cohen argues that human beings are the only kind of thing for which morality is an issue and that nonhuman animals are essentially amoral. What evidence do we have, if any, that nonhuman animals understand the difference between right and wrong? Is their understanding any different from our own?

PETER CARRUTHERS

Against the Moral Standing of Animals

Peter Carruthers approaches questions about the moral standing of nonhuman animals from the perspective of social contract moral theory (contractualism). In his essay he employs two versions of contractualism as a basis for arguing the all human beings, including infants and the senile, have direct moral standing and thus rights, while nonhuman animals do not. However, Carruthers goes on to argue that nonhuman animals may be accorded indirect moral standing from the contractualist perspective. The idea is that although nonhuman animals lack moral rights, humans can have duties *with regard to* such animals not to engage in acts of cruelty toward them. Carruthers defends this claim by explaining how contractualism accords special importance to considerations of character.

Recommended Reading: social contract theory, ch. 1, sec. G.

I shall argue in this essay that the lives and suffering of nonhuman animals (hereafter "animals") make no direct moral claims on us. At the same time I shall argue that the lives and sufferings of human infants and senile old people *do* make such claims on us. In short: I shall argue that no animals possess *moral standing,* while arguing all human beings possess such standing. I shall allow, however, that some of the things that one might do (or fail to do) to an animal might attract justified moral criticism. But this will be criticism of an indirect (and perhaps culturally local) sort, not deriving from any violations of the rights that the animal might possess. On the contrary, because animals lack standing, they have no rights.

ASSUMPTIONS

In this section I shall lay out two sets of assumptions that form the background to my argument. One is about the mental lives and cognitive capacities of

animals; the other is about the correct framework for moral theory. While I shall make no attempt to defend these assumptions here, they are quite widely shared, and each is, I believe, fully defensible.

Animal Minds

I shall assume that most animals have minds much like our own. They have beliefs and desires, and engage in practical reasoning in the light of their beliefs and desires. (This is true even of some invertebrates, including bees and jumping spiders, I believe.) Many animals feel pain and fear, and (in some cases) an emotion much like grief. (For discussion of the evidence supporting these claims, see Carruthers, 2006, ch.2.) In short: most animals can *suffer.* Stronger still, I shall assume for these purposes that most animals undergo experiences and feelings that are *conscious,* having the same kind of rich phenomenology and inner "feel" as do our own conscious mental states.

I shall also assume, however, that animals don't count as *rational agents* in the following (quite demanding) sense: A rational agent is a creature that is capable of governing its behavior in accordance with universal rules (such as "Don't tell lies") and that is capable of thinking about the costs and benefits of the general adoption of a given rule, to be obeyed by most members of a community that includes other rational agents. This assumption is quite obviously true in connection with most animals. I believe that it is also true (although this is slightly more controversial) in connection with members of other species of great ape, such as chimpanzees and gorillas. (If it should turn out that the members of some species of animal *do* count as rational agents in this sense, then those creatures will be accorded full moral standing, on the approach taken here.) Why the absence of rational agency should matter will emerge in the sections that follow.

Moral Theory

I shall assume that some or other version of contractualist moral theory is correct. (The problems with utilitarian theories are notorious, and well known. Forms of virtue theory are best pursued and accounted for within the framework of contractualism, I believe.) All contractualists agree that moral truths are, in a certain sense, human constructions, emerging out of some or other variety of hypothetical rational agreement concerning the basic rules to govern our behavior.

In one version of contractualism, moral rules are those that would be agreed upon by rational agents choosing, on broadly self-interested grounds, from behind a "veil of ignorance" (Rawls, 1972). On this account, we are to picture rational agents as attempting to agree on a set of rules to govern their conduct for their mutual benefit in full knowledge of all facts of human psychology, sociology, economics, and so forth, but in ignorance of any particulars about themselves—their own strengths, weaknesses, tastes, life plans, or position in society. All they are allowed to assume as goals when making their choice are the things that they will want *whatever* particular desires and plans they happen to have—namely, wealth, happiness, power, and self-respect. Moral

rules are then the rules that would be agreed upon in this situation, provided that the agreement is made on rational grounds. The governing intuition behind this approach is that justice is fairness: Since the situation behind the veil of ignorance is fair (all rational agents are equivalently placed), the resulting agreement must also be fair.

In another version of contractualism, moral rules are those that no rational agent could reasonably reject who shared (as their highest priority) the aim of reaching free and unforced general agreement on the rules that are to govern their behavior (Scanlon, 1982, 1998). On this account, we start from agents who are allowed full knowledge of their particular qualities and circumstances (as well as of general truths of psychology and so forth). But we imagine that they are guided, above all, by the goal of reaching free and unforced agreement on the set of rules that are to govern everyone's behavior. Here each individual agent can be thought of as having a veto over the proposed rules. But it is a veto that will only be exercised if it doesn't derail the agreement process, making it impossible to find any set of rules that no one can reasonably reject.

It should be stressed that within a contractualist approach, as I shall understand it, rational agents aren't allowed to appeal to any moral beliefs as part of the idealized contract process: Since moral truths are to be the output of the contract process, they cannot be appealed to at the start. Put differently: Since morality is to be constructed through the agreement of rational agents, it cannot be supposed to exist in advance of that agreement. It is also worth pointing out that on each of the previously mentioned approaches, some moral rules will be mere local conventions. This will happen whenever the contract process entails that there should be *some* moral rule governing a behavior or set of circumstances, but where there are no compelling grounds for selecting one candidate rule over the others.

In what follows I shall often consider arguments from the perspective of *both* of these forms of contractualism. In that way we can increase our confidence that the conclusions are entailed by contractualist approaches as such, rather than by the specifics of some or other particular variety.

ALL HUMANS HAVE STANDING

In the present section I shall argue that all human beings have moral standing, irrespective of their status as rational agents. I shall argue first that all rational agents have standing, and will then show that the same basic sort of standing should be accorded to human infants and senile (or otherwise mentally delective) adult humans.[1] Since these arguments don't extend to animals (as we will see [on pages 400–01]), they constitute a reply to Singer's (1979) challenge. For Singer claims that contractualism can't consistently deny moral standing to animals without *also* withholding it from infants and mentally defective humans. This section and the one following will demonstrate that he is mistaken.

The Basic Case: Rational Agents Have Standing

The contractualist framework plainly entails that all rational agents should have the same moral standing. For moral rules are here conceived to be constructed *by* rational agents *for* rational agents. It is obvious that rational agents behind a veil of ignorance would opt to accord the same basic rights, duties, and protections to themselves (that is to say: to all rational agents, since they are choosing in ignorance of their particular identities). And likewise within Scanlon's framework: It is obvious that any proposed rule that would withhold moral standing from some subset of rational agents could reasonably be rejected by the members of that subset.

It should be stressed that contractualism accords the same basic moral standing to all rational agents as such, and not merely to the members of some actual group or society. On Rawls's approach, contracting agents don't even know which group or society they will turn out to be members of once the veil is drawn aside. And on Scanlon's account, although we are to picture rational agents seeking to agree on a framework of rules in full knowledge of who they are and the groups to which they belong, those rules can be vetoed by *any* rational agent, irrespective of group membership. It follows that if Mars should turn out to be populated by a species of rational agent, then contractualism will accord the members of that species full moral standing.

Nonrational Humans: The Argument from Social Stability

It seems that rational contractors wouldn't automatically cede moral standing to those human beings who are *not* rational agents (e.g., infants and senile old people), in the way that they must cede standing to each other. But there are considerations that should induce them to do so, nevertheless. The main one is this.[2] Notice that the basic goal of the contract process is to achieve a set of moral rules that will provide social stability and preserve the peace. This means that moral rules will have to be *psychologically supportable*, in the following sense: They have to be such that rational agents can, in general, bring themselves to abide by them without brainwashing. (Arguably, no rational agent would consent to the loss of autonomy involved in any form of the latter practice.) But now the contractors just have to reflect that, if anything counts as part of "human nature" (and certainly much does; see Pinker, 2002), then people's deep attachment to their infants and aged relatives surely belongs within it. In general, people care as deeply about their immediate relatives as they care about anything (morality included), irrespective of their relatives' status as rational agents. In which case contracting agents should accord moral standing to all human beings, and not just to those human beings who happen to be rational agents.

Consider what a society would be like that denied moral standing to infants and/or senile old people. The members of these groups would, at most, be given the same type of protection that gets accorded to items of private property, deriving from the legitimate concerns of the rational agents who care about them. But that would leave the state or its agents free to destroy or cause suffering to the members of these groups whenever it might be in the public interest to do so, provided that their relatives receive financial compensation. (For example, senile old people might be killed so that their organs can be harvested, or it might be particularly beneficial to use human infants in certain painful medical experiments.) We can see in advance that these arrangements would be highly unstable. Those whose loved ones were at risk would surely resist with violence, and would band together with others to so resist. Foreseeing this, contracting rational agents should agree that all human beings be accorded moral standing.[3]

CONCLUSION: ALL HUMANS HAVE STANDING

We can conclude the following. If, as I claim, contractualism is the correct framework for moral theorizing, then it follows that all human beings— whether infant, child, adult, old, or senile—should be accorded the same basic structure of rights and protections. In [the next] section I shall show, in contrast, that contractualism leaves all animals beyond the moral pale, withholding moral standing from them.

Before completing this section it is worth noting that infants and senile old people aren't by any means accorded "second-class moral citizenship" by contractualism. Although it is only rational agents who get to grant moral standing through the contract process, and although the considerations that should lead them to grant moral standing to humans who aren't rational agents are indirect ones (not emerging directly out of the structure of the contract process, as does the moral standing of rational agents themselves), this has no impact on the product. Although the considerations that demonstrate the moral standing of rational agents and of nonrational humans may differ from one another, the result is the same: Both groups have moral standing, and both should have similar basic rights and protections.

NO ANIMALS HAVE STANDING

In this section I shall maintain, first, that the argument just given for according moral standing to all human beings doesn't extend to animals. Then, second, I shall consider two further attempts to secure moral standing for animals within contractualism, showing that they fail. The upshot can be captured in the slogan: "Humans in, animals out."

Social Stability Revisited

The argument of [the last] section was that nonrational humans should be accorded moral standing in order to preserve social stability, since people's attachments to their infants and aged relatives are generally about as deep as it is possible to go. Someone might try presenting a similar argument to show that animals, too, should be accorded moral standing, citing the violence that has *actually* occurred in Western societies when groups of people (like members of the Animal Liberation Front) have acted in defense of the interests of animals. Such an argument fails, however, because members of these groups are acting, not out of attachments that are a normal product of human emotional mechanisms, but out of (what they take to be justified) moral beliefs.

Recall that rational agents engaging in the contract process are forbidden from appealing to any antecedent moral beliefs—whether their own or other people's. (This is because moral truth is to be the outcome of the contract, and shouldn't be presupposed at the outset.) So contracting rational agents should *not* reason that animals ought to be accorded moral standing on the grounds that some people have a moral belief in such standing, and may be prepared to kill or engage in other forms of violence in pursuit of their principles. The proper response is that such people aren't entitled to their belief in the moral standing of animals unless they can show that rational agents in the appropriate sort of contract situation would agree to it.

Many people come to care quite a bit about their pets, of course, and this is something that rational contractors might be expected to know. Could this give rise to a social-stability argument for moral standing? The answer is "no," for at least two distinct reasons. One is that it is far from clear that the phenomenon of pet-keeping and attachment to pets is a human universal (in contrast with attachment to infants and aged relatives). It may be rather a product of local cultural forces operating in some societies but not others. And if the latter is the case, then such attachments aren't a "fixed point" of human nature, which should constrain rational contractors in their deliberations. They might appropriately decide, instead, that society should be arranged in such a way that people don't develop attachments that are apt to interfere with correct moral decision making.

A second problem with the suggestion is that attachment to pets is rarely so deep as attachments to relatives, in any case. Hence people should have little difficulty in coming to accept that pets can only be accorded the sorts of protections granted to other items of private property. Most of us would think that it would be foolish (indeed, reprehensible) to continue to keep a pet that threatens the life of a child (e.g., through severe allergic reactions). And when the state declares that the public interest requires that someone's dog be put down (e.g., because it is dangerous), it would surely be unreasonable to take up arms to defend the life of the animal, just as it would be unreasonable to kill to preserve a house that had been condemned for demolition.

Representing the Interests of Animals

While the argument from social stability doesn't show that animals should be accorded moral standing, other arguments could still be successful. One suggestion would be that some rational agents behind the veil of ignorance should be assigned to represent the interests of animals, much as a lawyer might be assigned to represent the interests of a pet in a court of law in a case involving a disputed will. If it was the job of those representatives to look out for the interests of animals in the formulation of the basic moral contract, then they might be expected to insist upon animals being granted moral standing.

This suggestion, however, is plainly at odds with the guiding idea of contractualism. For what possible motive could there be for assigning some agents to represent the interests of animals in the contract process, unless it were believed that animals *deserve* to

have their interests protected? But that would be to assume a moral truth at the outset: the belief, namely, that animals deserve to be protected. We noted earlier, in contrast, that contractualism assumes that the contracting parties should come to the contract situation either without any moral beliefs at all, or setting aside (taking care not to rely upon) such moral beliefs as they do have.

The point is even easier to see in Scanlon's version of contractualism. Real individual agents with knowledge of their own particulars, but who either lack moral beliefs or have set aside their moral beliefs while trying to agree to rules that no one could reasonably reject, could have no reason to assign some of their number to represent the interests of animals. For to do so would be tantamount to insisting at the outset that animals should be accorded moral standing, preempting and usurping the constructive contract process. . . .

Conclusion: No Animals Have Standing

I conclude that while the moral standing of all humans (including infants and senile old people) is entailed by contractualism, by the same token such standing should be denied to animals. Even if this position is theoretically impeccable, however it faces a serious challenge. This is that most people believe very strongly indeed that it is possible to act wrongly in one's dealings with animals. And most people believe, too, that it is something about what is happening *to the animal* that warrants the moral criticism. These are intuitions that need to be explained, or explained away. This will form topic of [the next two] sections.

FORMS OF INDIRECT MORAL SIGNIFICANCE FOR ANIMALS

Imagine that while walking in a city one evening you turn a corner to confront a group of teenagers who have caught a cat, doused it in kerosene, and are about to set it alight. Of course you would be horrified. You would think that the teenagers were doing something very wrong; and the vast majority of people would agree with you. It would be a serious black mark against contractualist moral theories in general, and against the line that I am pursuing in this essay in particular, if this intuition couldn't be accommodated.

Offense to Animal Lovers

One suggestion would be that we have *indirect* duties toward animals. These fail to have any corresponding rights on the part of the animal, but rather derive from a direct duty not to cause unnecessary offense to the feelings of animal lovers or animal owners. Compare the scenario just mentioned with this one: While walking through a city you come across a pair of young people, stark naked, making love on a park bench in broad daylight. Here, too, you would be horrified, and you would think that what they were doing was wrong. But the wrongness isn't, as it were, intrinsic to the activity. It is rather that the lovemaking is being conducted in a way that might be disturbing or distressing to other people: namely, in public. Likewise, it might be said, in the case of the teenagers setting light to the cat: What they are doing is wrong because it is likely to be disturbing or distressing to other people.

On the face of it this proposal isn't very promising. For while it can explain why the teenagers are wrong to set light to a cat in the street (since there is a danger that they might be observed), it can't so easily explain our intuition that it would be wrong of them to set light to the cat in the privacy of their own garage. Admittedly, there is some wiggle room here if one wanted to defend the proposal. For animals, having minds of their own, are apt to render public a suffering that was intended to remain private. The burning cat might escape from the garage, for example, or might emit such ear piercing screams that the neighbors feel called upon to investigate. But we can demonstrate the inadequacy of this whole approach through an example where such factors are decisively controlled for. This is the example of Astrid the astronaut.

You are to imagine that Astrid is an extremely rich woman who has become tired of life on Earth, and

who purchases a space rocket for herself so that she can escape that life permanently. She blasts off on a trajectory that will eventually take her out of the solar system, and she doesn't even carry with her a radio or other means of communication. We can therefore know that she will never again have any contact with another human being. Now suppose that Astrid has taken with her a cat for company, but that at a certain point in the journey, out of boredom, she starts to use the cat for a dartboard, or does something else that would cause the cat unspeakable pain. Don't we think that what Astrid does is very wrong? But of course the ground of its wrongness can't be the danger that animal lovers will discover what she has done and be upset. For we know from the description of the case that there is no such danger.

Judging Acts by Character

Another approach, which I shall spend most of the remainder of this essay developing and defending, would be to claim that the action of torturing a cat is wrong because of what it shows about the moral character of the actor, not because it infringes any rights or is likely to cause distress to other people. Specifically, what the teenagers do in the street and what Astrid does on her space rocket show them to be *cruel*. And this would be our ground for saying that the actions themselves are wrong. In order for this account to work, however, it needs to be shown more generally that we sometimes judge actions by the qualities of moral character that they evince, irrespective of any morally significant harm that they cause, or of any rights that they infringe. I shall argue as much here, before briefly providing a contractualist rationale in [the next] section.

Return to the example of Astrid the astronaut. But now suppose that, in addition to a cat, she has taken with her another person. In one version of the story, this might be her beloved grandfather. In another version of the story (to avoid contaminating our intuitions with beliefs about family duties) it might be an employee whom she hires to work for her as a lifetime servant. Now at a certain point in the journey this other person dies. Astrid's response is to cut up the corpse into small pieces, thereafter storing them in the refrigerator and feeding them one by one to the cat.

Surely what Astrid does is wrong. But why? It causes no direct harm of a morally relevant sort. (Her companion, after all, is dead, and can't know or be upset.) And nor can any harm be caused indirectly to others. For in the nature of the case, no one else can ever know and be offended. Nor are any rights infringed. For even if one thinks that the dead have rights (which is doubtful), Astrid might know that her companion was an atheist who took not the slightest interest in ceremonies for the dead. Indeed, he might once have said to her, "Once I am dead I don't care what happens to my corpse; you can do what you like with it," thus waiving any rights that he might have in the matter. But still what Astrid does is very wrong.

Why is what Astrid does wrong? Surely this is because of what it shows about *her.* Just as her treatment of her cat shows her to be cruel, so her treatment of her dead companion displays a kind of disrespectful, inhuman, attitude toward humanity in general, and her companion in particular. (Note that practices for honoring the dead, and for treating corpses with respect, are a human universal. They are common to all cultures across all times.) And in each case we judge the action to be wrong because of the flaw that it evinces (both manifesting and further encouraging and developing) in her moral character.

Consider a different sort of example. Suppose that Lazy Jane is a doctor who is attending a conference of other medical professionals at a large hotel. She is relaxing in the bar during the evening, sitting alone with her drink in a cubicle. The bar is so arranged that there are many separate cubicles surrounding it, from each of which the bar itself is plainly visible, but the insides of which are invisible to each other. Jane is idly watching someone walk alone toward the bar when he collapses to the floor with all the signs of having undergone a serious heart attack. Jane feels no impose to assist him, and continues calmly sipping her martini.

Plainly what Jane does (or in this case, doesn't do) is wrong. But why? For we can suppose that no harm is caused. Since the man collapses in plain view of dozens of medical personnel, expert help is swift in arriving; and she had every reason to believe that this would be so in the circumstances. And no rights are infringed. For even if there is such a thing as a general right to medical assistance when sick (which is doubtful), the man had no claim on *her* help in particular. If he had still been able to speak, he could have said, and (perhaps) said truly, "Someone should help me." But he certainly wouldn't have been correct if he had said, "Jane, in particular, should help me." Since our belief in the wrongness of Jane's inactivity survives these points, the explanation must be the one that we offered in connection with Astrid: It is wrong because of what it reveals about *her.* Specifically, it shows her to be callous and indifferent to the suffering of other people; or at least it shows that she lacks the sort of spontaneous, emotional, noncalculative concern for others that we think a good person should have.

My suggestion, then, is that our duties toward animals are indirect in the following way. They derive from the good or bad qualities of moral character that the actions in question would display and encourage; where those qualities *are* good or bad in virtue of the role that they play in the agent's interactions with other human beings. On this account, the most basic kind of wrongdoing toward animals is *cruelty.* A cruel action is wrong because it evinces a cruel chararter. But what makes a cruel character bad is that it is likely to express itself in cruelty toward *people,* which would involve direct violations of the rights of those who are caused to suffer.[4] Our intuition that the teenagers and Astrid all act wrongly is thereby explained, but explained in a way that is consistent with the claim that animals lack moral standing.

CONTRACTUALISM, VIRTUE ETHICS, AND ANIMALS

How, in general, do qualities of character acquire their significance within a contractualist moral framework? This question needs to be answered before the position sketched previously can be considered acceptable. And we need to investigate, too, in what ways cruelty to animals and cruelty to humans are linked to one another.

Contractualism and Character

Contracting rational agents should know in advance that human beings aren't calculating machines. We have limited time, limited memory, limited attention, and limited intellectual powers. In consequence, in everyday life we frequently have to rely on a suite of "quick and dirty" heuristics for decision making, rather than reasoning our way slowly and laboriously to the optimal solution (Gigerenzer et al., 1999). Contracting rational agents should realize, too, the vital role that motivational states and emotional reactions play in human decision making (Damasio, 1994). Hence they should do far more than agree on a framework of rules to govern their behavior. They should also agree to foster certain long-term dispositions of motivation and emotion that will make right action much more likely (especially when action is spontaneous, or undertaken under severe time constraints). That is to say: Contracting agents should agree on a duty to foster certain qualities of character, or *virtues*.

For example, contracting agents should agree on a duty to develop the virtue of *beneficence*. This is because they should foresee that more than merely rules of justice (which are for the most part negative in form: "don't steal, don't kidnap, don't kill, etc.") are necessary for human beings to flourish. People also need to develop positive attachments to the welfare of others, fostering a disposition and willingness to help others when they can do so at no important cost to themselves. For there are many ways in which people will inevitably, at some point in their lives, need the assistance of others if they are to succeed with their plans and projects, ranging from needing the kindness of a neighbor to jump-start one's car on a frosty morning, to needing someone on the river bank to throw one a life buoy or a rope when one is drowning.

Rational contractors should also agree that people's actions can be judged (that is, praised or blamed) for the qualities of character they evince, independently of the harm caused, and independently of violations of right. This is because people *should possess,* or should develop, the required good qualities. Although these good qualities *are* good, in general, because of their effects on the welfare and rights of other people, their display on a given occasion can

be independent of such effects. Hence we can, and should, evaluate the action in light of the qualities of character that it displays, independently of other considerations.

Cruelty to Animals and Cruelty to Humans

If the account given of the reasons that it is wrong for the teenagers to set light to a cat is to be successful, then cruelty to animals must be psychologically and behaviorally linked to cruelty to humans. To a first approximation, it must be the case that there is a single virtue of kindness, and a single vice of cruelty, that can be displayed toward either group. How plausible is this?

Certainly it would appear that attitudes toward the sufferings of animals and of humans are quite deeply linked in Western culture. For many of us have pets whom we treat as honorary family members, toward whom we feel filial obligations. And our practices of child-rearing make central use of animal subjects in moral education. Indeed, a child's first introduction to moral principles will frequently involve ones that are focused upon animals. A parent says, "Don't be cruel—you mustn't pull the whiskers out of the cat," "You must make sure that your pet gerbil has plenty of water," and so on and so forth. It would not be surprising, then, if attitudes toward the sufferings and welfare of animals and humans should thereafter be pretty tightly linked. This will warrant us in saying that the teenagers who are setting light to a cat are doing something wrong, not because the cat has moral standing, but because they are evincing attitudes that are likely to manifest themselves in their dealings with human beings (who do have moral standing, of course).

It seems possible, however, that the linkages that exist between attitudes to animal and to human suffering depend upon local cultural factors. For it seems implausible that these linkages should reflect properties of a universal human nature. In cultures where pets aren't kept, where people's interactions with animals are entirely pragmatic (e.g., through farming), and where animals aren't used as exemplars in moral education, it is possible that these attitudes are pretty cleanly separable. In which case, someone in such a culture who hangs a dog in a noose, strangling it to death slowly (perhaps because this is believed to make the meat taste better), won't be displaying cruelty, although someone in our culture who behaved likewise would be.

It may therefore be that our Western moral attitudes toward animals form part of the *conventional* content of our morality. If there is nothing in our human nature that links cruelty to animals with cruelty to humans, then contracting rational agents would have no reason to insist upon a rule forbidding cruelty to animals, or a rule mandating a virtue of kindness that extends to animals. But contracting agents have to settle upon some or other way of bringing up their children, and cultural practices (such as pet-keeping) may be adopted for reasons having nothing to do with the moral contract itself, but which nevertheless have an impact upon morals. Given such facts, we can become obliged not to be cruel to animals.

Acting for the Sake of the Animal

Notice that in our culture, someone with the right sort of kindly character who acts to prevent suffering to an animal will do so *for the sake of the animal.* For this is what having the right sort of sympathetic attitude consists in. It involves a spontaneous upwelling of sympathy at the sight or sound of suffering. Likewise it is something about the animal itself (its pain) that forms the immediate object of the emotion, and of the subsequent response. Certainly someone acting to ease the suffering of an animal won't be doing it to try to make himself into a better person! Nevertheless, the reason why this attitude is a virtue at all can be because of the way in which it is likely to manifest itself in the person's dealings with other human beings.

We can therefore *explain away* the commonsense intuition that when we are morally required to act to prevent the suffering of an animal, we are required to do so *for the sake of the animal,* where this is understood to mean that the animal itself has moral standing. As a theoretical claim about what grounds our duties toward animals, this is false, since animals lack standing. But as a psychological claim about the state of mind and motivations of the actor, who has acquired the right sort of kindly attitude, it is true. While agents should act as they do for the animal's sake (with the animal's interests in mind), the reason that they are required to do so doesn't advert to facts about the animal (which would require animals to have standing), but rather to wider effects on human beings.

CONCLUSION

I have argued in this essay that moral standing is possessed by all and only human beings (together with other rational agents, if there are any), who thus make direct moral claims upon us. Animals, in contrast, lack standing and make no direct claims upon us. Nevertheless, I have shown how there can be justified moral criticism for things that we do, or don't do, to an animal. This derives from the good or bad qualities of character that our actions evince. But these criticisms may have a conventional and culturally local quality, deriving from contingent facts about contemporary Western cultures. They aren't criticisms that are warranted by rules that no rational agents could reasonably reject (whatever their culture) when guided by facts about human nature.

ACKNOWLEDGMENTS

The ideas in this essay develop and modify the position that I defended at much greater length in Carruthers (1992). I am grateful to many generations of skeptical students for helping me to think more clearly about these issues, and to Christopher Morris for his comments on an earlier draft of the essay.

NOTES

1. It is an interesting question what this and related arguments show about the moral status of abortion. I believe (although I shall not argue here) that they would show early (e.g., first trimester) abortions to be permissible, while ruling out most later forms of abortion.

2. For other arguments for the same conclusion, see Carruthers (1992), chapter 5.

3. This doesn't mean that all humans are accorded the same rights, however. While normal human adults might be given a right to autonomy, for example, it will make little sense to accord such a right to a human who isn't an autonomous agent.

4. The United Kingdom's Royal Society for the Prevenstion of Cruelty to Animals claims on its Web site to have amassed voluminous evidence that people who are cruel to animals are also likely to engage in cruelty that involves human beings, and that the society's prosecutions for cruelty to animals are almost always built upon this premise. The ASPCA in the United States makes similar claims on its "information for professionals" Web site, citing a number of empirical studies.

REFERENCES

Carruthers, P. (1992). *The Animals Issue.* Cambridge University Press.

Carruthers, P. (2000). *Phenomenal Consciousness.* Cambridge University Press.

Carruthers, P. (2005). *Consciousness.* Oxford University Press.

Carruthers, P. (2006). *The Architecture of the Mind.* Oxford University Press.

Damasio, A. (1994). *Descartes' Error.* Papermac.

Gigerenzer, G., Todd, P., and the ABC Research Group. (1999). *Simple Heuristics That Make Us Smart.* Oxford University Press.

Pinker, S. (2002). *The Blank Slate.* Viking Press.

Rawls, J. (1972). *A Theory of Justice.* Oxford University Press.

Regan, T. (1984). *The Case for Animal Rights.* Routledge.

Scanlon, T. (1982). Contractualism and Utilitarianism. In A. Sen and B. Williams (eds.), *Utilitarianism and Beyond.* Cambridge University Press.

Scanlon, T. (1998). *What We Owe to Each Other.* Harvard University Press.

Singer, P. (1979) *Practical Ethics.* Cambridge University Press.

READING QUESTIONS

1. What are the forms of contractualism Carruthers deploys in defending his position on the ethical treatment of animals?

2. How does Carruthers defend the claim that nonrational human beings, including infants and the senile, enjoy direct moral standing according to contractualist moral theory?

3. Carruthers claims that humans can have an "indirect duty" to avoid cruel treatment of animals. What makes such duties "indirect"? What rationale does Carruthers give for his claim that humans can have such duties?

DISCUSSION QUESTIONS

1. According to contractualist moral theory, what *makes* torturing animals morally wrong is that such treatment expresses the negative character trait of cruelty on the part of torturer. Do you agree that this is the correct explanation of the wrongness of such treatment?

2. Discuss Carruthers's claim in the section "Acting for the Sake of the Animal" that the morality of the treatment of nonhuman animals may be culturally relative.

ALASTAIR NORCROSS

Puppies, Pigs, and People: Eating Meat and Marginal Cases

Alastair Norcross argues that eating meat, whether or not it comes from factory farming, is morally wrong. In the first part of his essay, Norcross appeals to the reader's moral intuitions featuring the hypothetical case of Fred, who engages in the practice of torturing puppies for (as it turns out) his own gustatory pleasure. Norcross argues that there is no morally relevant difference between the clearly wrongful behavior of Fred and those who knowingly eat meat produced through factory farming. Thus, if Fred's behavior is morally wrong, so is eating factory-farmed meat. Putting aside the issue of factory farming, a defender of meat-eating might argue that because human beings have a higher moral status than do nonhuman animals, this justifies meat-eating. In the second part of his essay, Norcross responds with the "challenge of marginal cases." The marginal cases in question feature infants, the senile, and other humans who lack whatever property (e.g., rationality) that is supposed to elevate all other humans over nonhumans and justify using them for food and experimentation. Norcross argues that attempts to answer this challenge all fail. He concludes with a diagnosis of what he takes to be the central confusion in the position of his opponents concerning the status of agents and patients.

Recommended Reading: consequentialism, chap. 1, sec. A and sec. B on the doctrine of double effect.

FRED'S BASEMENT

Consider the story of Fred, who receives a visit from the police one day. They have been summoned by Fred's neighbors, who have been disturbed by strange sounds emanating from Fred's basement. When they enter the basement they are confronted by the following scene: Twenty-six small wire cages, each containing a puppy, some whining, some whimpering, some howling. The puppies range in age from newborn to about six months. Many of them show signs of mutilation. Urine and feces cover the bottoms of the cages and the basement floor. Fred explains that he keeps the puppies for twenty-six weeks, and then butchers them while holding them upside-down. During their lives he performs a series of mutilations on them, such as slicing off their noses and their paws with a hot knife, all without any form of anesthesia. Except for the mutilations, the puppies are never allowed out of the cages, which are barely big enough to hold them at twenty-six weeks. The police are horrified, and promptly charge Fred with animal abuse. As details of the case are publicized, the public is outraged. Newspapers are flooded with letters demanding that Fred be severely punished. There are calls for more severe penalties for animal abuse. Fred is denounced as a vile sadist.

From Alastair Norcross, "Puppies, Pigs, and People: Eating Meat and Marginal Cases," *Philosophical Perspectives* 18 (2004): 229–45. Reprinted by permission of Blackwell Publishing. Notes have been renumbered and edited.

Finally, at his trial, Fred explains his behavior, and argues that he is blameless and therefore deserves no punishment. He is, he explains, a great lover of chocolate. A couple of years ago, he was involved in a car accident, which resulted in some head trauma. Upon his release from hospital, having apparently suffered no lasting ill effects, he visited his favorite restaurant and ordered their famous rich dark chocolate mousse. Imagine his dismay when he discovered that his experience of the mousse was a pale shadow of its former self. The mousse tasted bland, slightly pleasant, but with none of the intense chocolaty flavor he remembered so well. The waiter assured him that the recipe was unchanged from the last time he had tasted it, just the day before his accident. In some consternation, Fred rushed out to buy a bar of his favorite Belgian chocolate. Again, he was dismayed to discover that his experience of the chocolate was barely even pleasurable. Extensive investigation revealed that his experience of other foods remained unaffected, but chocolate, in all its forms, now tasted bland and insipid. Desperate for a solution to his problem, Fred visited a renowned gustatory neurologist, Dr. T. Bud. Extensive tests revealed that the accident had irreparably damaged the godiva gland, which secretes cocoamone, the hormone responsible for the experience of chocolate. Fred urgently requested hormone replacement therapy. Dr. Bud informed him that, until recently, there had been no known source of cocoamone, other than the human godiva gland, and that it was impossible to collect cocoamone from one person to be used by another. However, a chance discovery had altered the situation. A forensic veterinary surgeon, performing an autopsy on a severely abused puppy, had discovered high concentrations of cocoamone in the puppy's brain. It turned out that puppies, who don't normally produce cocoamone, could be stimulated to do so by extended periods of severe stress and suffering. The research, which led to this discovery, while gaining tenure for its authors, had not been widely publicized, for fear of antagonizing animal welfare groups. Although this research clearly gave Fred the hope of tasting chocolate again, there were no commercially available sources of puppy-derived cocoamone. Lack of demand, combined with fear of bad publicity, had deterred drug

companies from getting into the puppy torturing business. Fred appeals to the court to imagine his anguish, on discovering that a solution to his severe deprivation was possible, but not readily available. But he wasn't inclined to sit around bemoaning his cruel fate. He did what any chocolate lover would do. He read the research, and set up his own cocoamone collection lab in his basement. Six months of intense puppy suffering, followed by a brutal death, produced enough cocoamone to last him a week, hence the twenty-six cages. He isn't a sadist or an animal abuser, he explains. If there were a method of collecting cocoamone without torturing puppies, he would gladly employ it. He derives no pleasure from the suffering of the puppies itself. He sympathizes with those who are horrified by the pain and misery of the animals, but the court must realize that human pleasure is at stake. The puppies, while undeniably cute, are mere animals. He admits that he would be just as healthy without chocolate, if not more so. But this isn't a matter of survival or health. His life would be unacceptably impoverished without the experience of chocolate.

End of story. Clearly, we are horrified by Fred's behavior, and unconvinced by his attempted justification. It is, of course, unfortunate for Fred that he can no longer enjoy the taste of chocolate, but that in no way excuses the imposition of severe suffering on the puppies. I expect near universal agreement with this claim (the exceptions being those who are either inhumanly callous or thinking ahead, and wish to avoid the following conclusion, to which such agreement commits them). No decent person would even contemplate torturing puppies merely to enhance a gustatory experience. However, billions of animals endure intense suffering every year for precisely this end. Most of the chicken, veal, beef, and pork consumed in the US comes from intensive confinement facilities, in which the animals live cramped, stress-filled lives and endure unanaesthetized mutilations.[1] The vast majority of people would suffer no ill health from the elimination of meat from their diets. Quite the reverse. The supposed benefits from this system of factory farming, apart from the profits accruing to agribusiness, are increased levels of gustatory pleasure for those who claim that they couldn't enjoy a meat-free diet as much as their current meat-filled diets. If we are prepared to condemn Fred for torturing puppies merely to enhance his gustatory experiences, shouldn't we similarly condemn the millions who purchase and consume factory-raised meat? Are there any morally significant differences between Fred's behavior and their behavior?

FRED'S BEHAVIOR COMPARED WITH OUR BEHAVIOR

The first difference that might seem to be relevant is that Fred tortures the puppies himself, whereas most Americans consume meat that comes from animals that have been tortured by others. But is this really relevant? What if Fred had been squeamish and had employed someone else to torture the puppies and extract the cocoamone? Would we have thought any better of Fred? Of course not.

Another difference between Fred and many consumers of factory-raised meat is that many, perhaps most, such consumers are unaware of the treatment of the animals, before they appear in neatly wrapped packages on supermarket shelves. Perhaps I should moderate my challenge, then. If we are prepared to condemn Fred for torturing puppies merely to enhance his gustatory experiences, shouldn't we similarly condemn those who purchase and consume factory-raised meat, in full, or even partial, awareness of the suffering endured by the animals? While many consumers are still blissfully ignorant of the appalling treatment meted out to meat, that number is rapidly dwindling, thanks to vigorous publicity campaigns waged by animal welfare groups. Furthermore, any meat-eating readers of this article are now deprived of the excuse of ignorance.

Perhaps a consumer of factory-raised animals could argue as follows: While I agree that Fred's behavior is abominable, mine is crucially different. If Fred did not consume his chocolate, he would not raise and torture puppies (or pay someone else to do so). Therefore Fred could prevent the suffering of the puppies. However, if I did not buy and consume factory-raised meat, no animals would be spared lives of misery. Agribusiness is much too large to respond to the behavior of one consumer. Therefore I cannot prevent the suffering of any animals. I may well regret the suffering inflicted on animals for the sake of human enjoyment. I may even agree that the human enjoyment doesn't justify the suffering. However, since the animals will suffer no matter what I do, I may as well enjoy the taste of their flesh.

There are at least two lines of response to this attempted defense. First, consider an analogous case. You visit a friend in an exotic location, say Alabama. Your friend takes you out to eat at the finest restaurant in Tuscaloosa. For dessert you select the house specialty, "Chocolate Mousse à la Bama," served with a small cup of coffee, which you are instructed to drink before eating the mousse. The mousse is quite simply the most delicious dessert you have ever tasted. Never before has chocolate tasted so rich and satisfying. Tempted to order a second, you ask your friend what makes this mousse so delicious. He informs you that the mousse itself is ordinary, but the coffee contains a concentrated dose of cocoamone, the newly discovered chocolate-enhancing hormone. Researchers at Auburn University have perfected a technique for extracting cocoamone from the brains of freshly slaughtered puppies, who have been subjected to lives of pain and frustration. Each puppy's brain yields four doses, each of which is effective for about fifteen minutes, just long enough to enjoy one serving of mousse. You are, naturally, horrified and disgusted. You will certainly not order another serving, you tell your friend. In fact, you are shocked that your friend, who had always seemed to be a morally decent person, could have both recommended the dessert to you and eaten one himself, in full awareness of the loathsome process necessary for the experience. He agrees that the suffering of the puppies is outrageous, and that the gain in human pleasure in no way justifies the appalling treatment they have to endure. However, neither he nor you can save any puppies by refraining from consuming cocoamone. Cocoamone production is now Alabama's leading industry, so it is much too large to respond to the behavior of one or two consumers. Since the puppies will suffer no matter what either of you does, you may as well enjoy the mousse.

If it is as obvious as it seems that a morally decent person, who is aware of the details of cocoamone production, couldn't order Chocolate Mousse à la Bama, it should be equally obvious that a morally decent person, who is aware of the details of factory farming, can't purchase and consume factory-raised meat. If the attempted excuse of causal impotence is compelling in the latter case, it should be compelling in the former case. But it isn't.

The second response to the claim of causal impotence is to deny it. Consider the case of chickens, the most cruelly treated of all animals raised for human consumption, with the possible exception of veal calves. In 1998, almost 8 billion chickens were slaughtered in the US,[2] almost all of them raised on factory farms. Suppose that there are 250 million chicken eaters in the US, and that each one consumes, on average, 25 chickens per year (this leaves a fair number of chickens slaughtered for non-human consumption, or for export). Clearly, if only one of those chicken eaters gave up eating chicken, the industry would not respond. Equally clearly, if they all gave up eating chicken, billions of chickens (approximately 6.25 billion per year) would not be bred, tortured, and killed. But there must also be some number of consumers, far short of 250 million, whose renunciation of chicken would cause the industry to reduce the number of chickens bred in factory farms. The industry may not be able to respond to each individual's behavior, but it must respond to the behavior of fairly large numbers. Suppose that the industry is sensitive to a reduction in demand for chicken equivalent to 10,000 people becoming vegetarians. (This seems like a reasonable guess, but I have no idea what the actual numbers are, nor is it important.) For each group of 10,000 who give up chicken, a quarter of a million fewer chickens are bred per year. It appears, then, that if you give up eating chicken, you have only a one in ten thousand chance of making any difference to the lives of chickens, unless it is certain that fewer than 10,000 people will ever give up eating chicken, in which case you have no chance. Isn't a one in ten thousand chance small enough to render your continued consumption

of chicken blameless? Not at all. While the chance that your behavior is harmful may be small, the harm that is risked is enormous. The larger the numbers needed to make a difference to chicken production, the larger the difference such numbers would make. A one in ten thousand chance of saving 250,000 chickens per year from excruciating lives is morally and mathematically equivalent to the certainty of saving 25 chickens per year. We commonly accept that even small risks of great harms are unacceptable. That is why we disapprove of parents who fail to secure their children in car seats or with seat belts, who leave their small children unattended at home, or who drink or smoke heavily during pregnancy. Or consider commercial aircraft safety measures. The chances that the oxygen masks, the lifejackets, or the emergency exits on any given plane will be called on to save any lives in a given week, are far smaller than one in ten thousand. And yet we would be outraged to discover that an airline had knowingly allowed a plane to fly for a week with nonfunctioning emergency exits, oxygen masks, and lifejackets. So, even if it is true that your giving up factory raised chicken has only a tiny chance of preventing suffering, given that the amount of suffering that would be prevented is in inverse proportion to your chance of preventing it, your continued consumption is not thereby excused.

But perhaps it is not even true that your giving up chicken has only a tiny chance of making any difference. Suppose again that the poultry industry only reduces production when a threshold of 10,000 fresh vegetarians is reached. Suppose also, as is almost certainly true, that vegetarianism is growing in popularity in the US (and elsewhere). Then, even if you are not the one, newly converted vegetarian, to reach the next threshold of 10,000, your conversion will reduce the time required before the next threshold is reached. The sooner the threshold is reached, the sooner production, and therefore animal suffering, is reduced. Your behavior, therefore, does make a difference. Furthermore, many people who become vegetarians influence others to become vegetarian, who in turn influence others, and so on. It appears, then, that the claim of causal impotence is mere wishful thinking, on the part of those meat lovers who are morally sensitive enough to realize that human gustatory pleasure does not justify inflicting extreme suffering on animals.

Perhaps there is a further difference between the treatment of Fred's puppies and the treatment of animals on factory farms. The suffering of the puppies is a necessary means to the production of gustatory pleasure, whereas the suffering of animals on factory farms is simply a by-product of the conditions dictated by economic considerations. Therefore, it might be argued, the suffering of the puppies is *intended as a means* to Fred's pleasure, whereas the suffering of factory raised animals is merely *foreseen* as a side-effect of a system that is a means to the gustatory pleasures of millions. The distinction between what is intended, either as a means or as an end in itself, and what is "merely" foreseen is central to the Doctrine of Double Effect. Supporters of this doctrine claim that it is sometimes permissible to bring about an effect that is merely foreseen, even though the very same effect could not permissibly be brought about if intended. (Other conditions have to be met in order for the Doctrine of Double Effect to judge an action permissible, most notably that there be an outweighing good effect.) Fred acts impermissibly, according to this line of argument, because he intends the suffering of the puppies as a means to his pleasure. Most meat eaters, on the other hand, even if aware of the suffering of the animals, do not intend the suffering.

In response to this line of argument, I could remind the reader that Samuel Johnson said, or should have said, that the Doctrine of Double Effect is the last refuge of a scoundrel.[3] I won't do that, however, since neither the doctrine itself, nor the alleged moral distinction between intending and foreseeing can justify the consumption of factory-raised meat. The Doctrine of Double Effect requires not merely that a bad effect be foreseen and not intended, but also that there be an outweighing good effect. In the case of the suffering of factory-raised animals, whatever good could plausibly be claimed to come out of the system clearly doesn't outweigh the bad. Furthermore, it would be easy to modify the story of Fred to render the puppies' suffering "merely" foreseen. For example, suppose that the cocoamone is produced by a chemical reaction that can only occur when large quantities of drain-cleaner are forced down the throat of a conscious, unanaesthetized puppy. The consequent appalling suffering, while not itself a means to the production of cocoamone, is nonetheless an unavoidable side-effect of the means. In this variation of the story, Fred's behavior is no less abominable than in the original.

One last difference between the behavior of Fred and the behavior of the consumers of factory-raised meat is worth discussing, if only because it is so frequently cited in response to the arguments of this paper. Fred's behavior is abominable, according to this line of thinking, because it involves the suffering of *puppies*. The behavior of meat-eaters, on the other hand, "merely" involves the suffering of chickens, pigs, cows, calves, sheep, and the like. Puppies (and probably dogs and cats in general) are morally different from the other animals. Puppies *count* (morally, that is), whereas the other animals don't, or at least not nearly as much.

So, what gives puppies a higher moral status than the animals we eat? Presumably there is some morally relevant property or properties possessed by puppies but not by farm animals. Perhaps puppies have a greater degree of rationality than farm animals, or a more finely developed moral sense, or at least a sense of loyalty and devotion. The problems with this kind of approach are obvious. It's highly unlikely that any property that has even an outside chance of being ethically relevant is both possessed by puppies and not possessed by any farm animals. For example, it's probably true that most puppies have a greater degree of rationality (whatever that means) than most chickens, but the comparison with pigs is far more dubious. Besides, if Fred were to inform the jury that he had taken pains to acquire particularly stupid, morally obtuse, disloyal and undevoted puppies, would they (or we) have declared his behavior to be morally acceptable? Clearly not. This is, of course, simply the puppy version of the problem of marginal cases (which I will discuss later). The human version is no less relevant. If their lack of certain degrees of rationality, moral sensibility, loyalty, devotion, and the like makes it permissible to torture farm animals for our gustatory pleasure, it should be permissible to do the same to those unfortunate humans who also lack those properties. Since the latter behavior isn't permissible, the lack of such properties doesn't justify the former behavior.

Perhaps, though, there *is* something that separates puppies, even marginal puppies (and marginal humans) from farm animals—our sympathy. Puppies count more than other animals, because we care more about them. We are outraged to hear of puppies abused in scientific experiments, but unconcerned at the treatment of laboratory rats or animals on factory farms. Before the 2002 World Cup, several members of the England team sent a letter to the government of South Korea protesting the treatment of dogs and cats raised for food in that country. The same players have not protested the treatment of animals on factory farms in England. This example, while clearly illustrating the difference in attitudes towards cats and dogs on the one hand, and farm animals on the other, also reveals one of the problems with this approach to the question of moral status. Although the English footballers, and the English (and US) public in general, clearly care far more about the treatment of cats and dogs than of farm animals, the South Koreans, just as clearly, do not. Are we to conclude that Fred's behavior would not be abominable were he living in South Korea, where dogs and cats are routinely abused for the sake of gustatory pleasure? Such relativism is, to put it mildly, hard to swallow. Perhaps, though, we can maintain the view that human feelings determine the moral status of animals, without condoning the treatment of dogs and cats in South Korea (and other countries). Not all human feelings count. Only the feelings of those who have achieved exactly the right degree of moral sensibility. That just so happens to be those in countries like the US and Britain who care deeply for the welfare of dogs and cats, but not particularly for the welfare of cows, chickens, pigs, and other factory-raised animals. Dog and cat eaters in South Korea are insufficiently sensitive, and humane farming advocates in Britain and the US are overly so. But, of course, it won't do simply to insist that this is the right degree of moral sensibility. We need an explanation of why this is the right degree of sensibility. Moral sensibility consists, at least in part, in reacting differently to different features of situations, actions, agents, and patients. If the right degree of moral sensibility requires reacting differently to puppies and to farm animals, there must be a morally relevant difference between puppies and farm animals. Such a difference can't simply consist in the fact that (some) people do react differently to them. The appeal to differential human sympathy illustrates a purely descriptive psychological difference between the behavior of Fred and that of someone who knowingly consumes factory-raised meat. It can do no serious moral work.

I have been unable to discover any morally relevant differences between the behavior of Fred, the puppy torturer, and the behavior of the millions of people who purchase and consume factory-raised meat, at least those who do so in the knowledge that the animals live lives of suffering and deprivation. If morality demands that we not torture puppies merely to enhance our own eating pleasure, morality also demands that we not support factory farming by purchasing factory-raised meat. . . .

HUMANS' VERSUS ANIMALS' ETHICAL STATUS—THE RATIONALITY GAMBIT

For the purposes of this discussion, to claim that humans have a superior ethical status to animals is to claim that it is morally right to give the interests of humans greater weight than those of animals in deciding how to behave. Such claims will often be couched in terms of rights, such as the rights to life, liberty or respect, but nothing turns on this terminological matter. One may claim that it is generally wrong to kill humans, but not animals, because humans are rational, and animals are not. Or one may claim that the suffering of animals counts less than the suffering of humans (if at all), because humans are rational, and animals are not. These claims may proceed through the intermediate claim that the rights of humans are more extensive and stronger than those (if any) of animals. Alternatively, one may directly ground the judgment about the moral status of certain types of behavior in claims about the alleged natural properties of the individuals involved. . . .

What could ground the claim of superior moral status for humans? Just as the defender of a higher moral status for puppies than for farm animals needs to find some property or properties possessed by puppies but not by farm animals, so the defender of a higher moral status for humans needs to find some property or properties possessed by humans but not by other animals. The traditional view, dating back at least to Aristotle, is that rationality is what separates humans, both morally and metaphysically, from other animals. With a greater understanding of the cognitive powers of some animals, recent philosophers have often refined the claim to stress the kind and level of rationality required for moral reasoning. Let's start with a representative sample of three. Consider first these claims of Bonnie Steinbock:

> While we are not compelled to discriminate among people because of different capacities, if we can find a significant difference in capacities between human and non-human animals, this could serve to justify regarding human interests as primary. It is not arbitrary or smug, I think, to maintain that human beings have a different moral status from members of other species because of certain capacities which are characteristic of being human. We may not all be equal in these capacities, but all human beings possess them to some measure, and non-human animals do not. For example, human beings are normally held to be responsible for what they do. . . . Secondly, human beings can be expected to reciprocate in a way that non-human animals cannot. Thirdly. . . . there is the "desire for self-respect."[4]

Similarly, Mary Anne Warren argues that "the rights of persons are generally stronger than those of sentient beings which are not persons." Her main premise to support this conclusion is the following:

> [T]here is one difference [between human and nonhuman nature] which has a clear moral relevance: people are at least sometimes capable of being moved to action or inaction by the force of reasoned argument.[5]

Carl Cohen, one of the most vehement modern defenders of what Peter Singer calls "speciesism" states his position as follows:

> Between species of animate life, however—between (for example) humans on the one hand and cats or rats on the other—the morally relevant differences are enormous, and almost universally appreciated. Humans engage in moral reflection; humans are morally autonomous; humans are members of moral communities, recognizing just claims against their own interest. Human beings do have rights, theirs is a moral status very different from that of cats or rats.[6]

So, the claim is that human interests and/or rights are stronger or more important than those of animals, because humans possess a kind and level of rationality not possessed by animals. How much of our current behavior towards animals this justifies depends on just how much consideration should be given to animal interests, and on what rights, if any, they possess. Both Steinbock and Warren stress that animal interests need to be taken seriously into account. Warren claims that animals have important rights, but not as important as human rights. Cohen, on the other hand, argues that we should actually *increase* our use of animals.

THE CHALLENGE OF MARGINAL CASES

One of the most serious challenges to this defense of the traditional view involves a consideration of what philosophers refer to as "marginal cases." Whatever kind and level of rationality is selected as justifying the attribution of superior moral status to humans will either be lacking in some humans or present in some animals. To take one of the most commonly-suggested features, many humans are incapable of engaging in moral reflection. For some, this incapacity is temporary, as is the case with infants, or the temporarily cognitively disabled. Others who once had the capacity may have permanently lost it, as is the case with the severely senile or the irreversibly comatose. Still others never had and never will have the capacity, as is the case with the severely mentally disabled. If we base our claims for the moral superiority of humans over animals on the attribution of such capacities, won't we have to exclude many humans? Won't we then be forced to the claim that there is at least as much moral reason to use cognitively deficient humans in experiments and for food as to use animals? Perhaps we could exclude the only temporarily disabled, on the grounds of potentiality, though that move has its own problems. Nonetheless, the other two categories would be vulnerable to this objection.

I will consider two lines of response to the argument from marginal cases. The first denies that we have to attribute different moral status to marginal humans, but maintains that we are, nonetheless, justified in attributing different moral status to animals who are just as cognitively sophisticated as marginal humans, if not more so. The second admits that, strictly speaking, marginal humans are morally inferior to other humans, but proceeds to claim pragmatic reasons for treating them, at least usually, *as if* they had equal status.

As representatives of the first line of defense. I will consider arguments from three philosophers, Carl Cohen, Alan White, and David Schmidtz. First, Cohen:

> [the argument from marginal cases] fails; it mistakenly treats an essential feature of humanity as though it were a screen for sorting humans. The capacity for moral judgment that distinguishes humans from animals is not a test to be administered to human beings one by one. Persons who are unable, because of some disability, to perform the full moral functions natural to human beings are certainly not for that reason ejected from the moral community. The issue is one of kind.... What humans retain when disabled, animals have never had.[7]

Alan White argues that animals don't have rights, on the grounds that they cannot intelligibly be spoken of in the full language of a right. By this he means that they cannot, for example, claim, demand, assert, insist on, secure, waive, or surrender a right. This is what he has to say in response to the argument from marginal cases:

> Nor does this, as some contend, exclude infants, children, the feeble-minded, the comatose, the dead, or generations yet unborn. Any of these may be for various reasons empirically unable to fulfill the full role of right-holder. But . . . they are logically possible subjects of rights to whom the full language of rights can significantly, however falsely, be used. It is a misfortune, not a tautology, that these persons cannot exercise or enjoy, claim, or waive, their rights or do their duty or fulfil their obligations.[8]

David Schmidtz defends the appeal to typical characteristics of species, such as mice, chimpanzees, and humans, in making decisions on the use of different species in experiments. He also considers the argument from marginal cases:

> Of course, some chimpanzees lack the characteristic features in virtue of which chimpanzees command respect as a species, just as some humans lack the characteristic features in virtue of which humans command respect as a species. It is equally obvious that some chimpanzees have cognitive capacities (for example) that are superior to the cognitive capacities of some humans. But whether every human being is superior to every chimpanzee is beside the point. The point is that we can, we do, and we should make decisions on the basis of our recognition that mice, chimpanzees, and humans are relevantly different *types*. We can have it both ways after all. Or so a speciesist could argue.[9]

There is something deeply troublesome about the line of argument that runs through all three of these responses to the argument from marginal cases. A particular feature, or set of features is claimed to have so much moral significance that its presence or lack can make the difference to whether a piece of behavior is morally justified or morally outrageous. But then it is claimed that the presence or lack of the feature in any *particular* case is not important. The relevant question is whether the presence or lack of the feature is *normal*. Such an argument would seem perfectly preposterous in most other cases. Suppose, for example, that ten famous people are on trial in the afterlife for crimes against humanity. On the basis of conclusive evidence, five are found guilty and five are found not guilty. Four of the guilty are sentenced to an eternity of torment, and one is granted an eternity of bliss. Four of the innocent are granted an eternity of bliss, and one is sentenced to an eternity of torment. The one innocent who is sentenced to torment asks why he, and not the fifth guilty person, must go to hell. Saint Peter replies, "Isn't it obvious Mr. Ghandi? You are male. The other four men—Adolf Hitler, Joseph Stalin, George W. Bush, and Richard Nixon—are all guilty. Therefore the normal condition for a male defendant in this trial is guilt. The fact that you happen to be innocent is irrelevant. Likewise, of the five female defendants in this trial, only one was guilty. Therefore the normal condition for female defendants in this trial is innocence. That is why Margaret Thatcher gets to go to heaven instead of you."

As I said, such an argument is preposterous. Is the reply to the argument from marginal cases any better? Perhaps it will be claimed that a biological category such as a species is more "natural," whatever that means, than a category like "all the male (or female) defendants in this trial." Even setting aside the not inconsiderable worries about the conventionality of biological categories, it is not at all clear why this distinction should be morally relevant. What if it turned out that there were statistically relevant differences in the mental abilities of men and women? Suppose that men were, on average, more skilled at manipulating numbers than women, and that women were, on average, more empathetic than men. Would such differences in what was "normal" for men and women justify us in preferring an innumerate man to a female math genius for a job as an accountant, or an insensitive woman to an ultra-sympathetic man for a job as a counselor? I take it that the biological distinction between male and female is just as real as that between human and chimpanzee.

A second response to the argument from marginal cases is to concede that cognitively deficient humans really do have an inferior moral status to normal humans. Can we, then, use such humans as we do animals? I know of no-one who takes the further step of advocating the use of marginal humans for food (though R. G. Frey has made some suggestive remarks concerning experimentation). How can we advocate this second response while blocking the further step? Warren suggests that "there are powerful practical and emotional reasons for protecting non-rational human beings, reasons which are absent in the case of most non-human animals.[10] It would clearly outrage common human sensibilities, if we were to raise retarded children for food or medical experiments.[11] . . .

This line of response clearly won't satisfy those who think that marginal humans really do deserve equal moral consideration with other humans. It is also a very shaky basis on which to justify our current practices. What outrages human sensibilities is a very fragile thing. Human history is littered with examples of widespread acceptance of the systematic mistreatment of some groups who didn't generate any sympathetic response from others. That we do feel a kind of sympathy for retarded humans that we don't feel for dogs is, if true, a contingent matter. To see just how shaky a basis this is for protecting retarded humans, imagine that a new kind of birth defect (perhaps associated with beef from cows treated with bovine growth hormone) produces severe mental retardation, green skin, and a complete lack of emotional bond between parents and child. Furthermore, suppose that the mental retardation is of the same kind and severity as that caused by other birth defects that don't have the other two effects. It seems likely that denying moral status to such defective humans would not run the same risks of outraging human sensibilities as would the denial of moral status to other, less easily distinguished and more loved defective humans. Would these contingent empirical differences between our reactions to different sources of mental retardation justify us in ascribing different direct moral status to their subjects? The only difference between them is skin color and whether they are loved by others. Any theory that could ascribe moral relevance to differences such as these doesn't deserve[10] to be taken seriously.

Finally, perhaps we could claim that the practice of giving greater weight to the interests of all humans than of animals is justified on evolutionary grounds. Perhaps such differential concern has survival value for the species. Something like this may well be true, but it is hard to see the moral relevance. We can hardly justify the privileging of human interests over animal interests on the grounds that such privileging serves human interests!

AGENT AND PATIENT—THE SPECIESIST'S CENTRAL CONFUSION

Although the argument from marginal cases certainly poses a formidable challenge to any proposed criterion of full moral standing that excludes animals, it doesn't, in my view, constitute the most serious flaw in such attempts to justify the status quo. The proposed criteria are all variations on the Aristotelian criterion of rationality. But what is the moral relevance of rationality? Why should we think that the possession of a certain level or kind of rationality renders the possessor's interests of greater moral significance than those of a merely sentient being? In Bentham's famous words "The question is not, Can they reason? nor Can they talk? But, Can they suffer?"[12]

What do defenders of the alleged superiority of human interests say in response to Bentham's challenge? Some, such as Carl Cohen, simply reiterate the differences between humans and animals that they claim to carry moral significance. Animals are not members of moral communities, they don't engage in moral reflection, they can't be moved by moral reasons, *therefore* (?) their interests don't count as much as ours. Others, such as Steinbock and Warren, attempt to go further. Here is Warren on the subject:

> Why is rationality morally relevant? It does not make us "better" than other animals or more "perfect." . . . . But it is morally relevant insofar as it provides greater possibilities for cooperation and for the nonviolent resolution of problems.[13]

Warren is certainly correct in claiming that a certain level and kind of rationality is morally relevant. Where she, and others who give similar arguments, go wrong is in specifying what the moral relevance amounts to. If a being is incapable of moral reasoning, at even the most basic level, if it is incapable of being moved by moral reasons, claims, or arguments, then it cannot be a moral agent. It cannot be subject to moral obligations, to moral praise or blame. Punishing a dog for doing something "wrong" is no more than an attempt to alter its future behavior. So long as we are undeceived about the

dog's cognitive capacities, we are not, except metaphorically, expressing any moral judgment about the dog's behavior. (We may, of course, be expressing a moral judgment about the behavior of the dog's owner, who didn't train it very well.) All this is well and good, but what is the significance for the question of what weight to give to animal interests? That animals can't be moral *agents* doesn't seem to be relevant to their status as moral *patients*. Many, perhaps most, humans are both moral agents and patients. Most, perhaps all, animals are only moral patients. Why would the lack of moral agency give them diminished status as moral patients? Full status as a moral patient is not some kind of reward for moral agency. I have heard students complain in this regard that it is *unfair* that humans bear the burdens of moral responsibility, and don't get enhanced consideration of their interests in return. This is a very strange claim. Humans are subject to moral obligations, because they are the kind of creatures who *can* be. What grounds moral agency is simply different from what grounds moral standing as a patient. It is no more unfair that humans and not animals are moral agents, than it is unfair that real animals and not stuffed toys are moral patients.

One other attempt to justify the selection of rationality as the criterion of full moral standing is worth considering. Recall the suggestion that rationality is important insofar as it facilitates cooperation. If we view the essence of morality as reciprocity, the significance of rationality is obvious. A certain twisted, but all-too-common, interpretation of the Golden Rule is that we should "do unto others in order to get them to do unto us." There's no point, according to this approach, in giving much, if any, consideration to the interests of animals, because they are simply incapable of giving like consideration to our interests. In discussing the morality of eating meat, I have, many times, heard students claim that we are justified in eating meat, because "the animals would eat us, if given half a chance." (That they say this in regard to our practice of eating cows and chickens is depressing testimony to their knowledge of the animals they gobble up with such gusto.) Inasmuch as there is a consistent view being expressed here at all, it concerns self-interest, as opposed to morality. Whether it serves my interests to give the same weight to the interests of animals as to those of humans is an interesting question, but it is not the same question as whether it is *right* to give animals' interests equal weight. The same point, of course, applies to the question of whether to give equal weight to my interests, or those of my family, race, sex, religion, etc. as to those of other people.

Perhaps it will be objected that I am being unfair to the suggestion that the essence of morality is reciprocity. Reciprocity is important, not because it serves *my* interests, but because it serves the interests of all. Reciprocity facilitates cooperation, which in turn produces benefits for all. What we should say about this depends on the scope of "all." If it includes all sentient beings, then the significance of animals' inability to reciprocate is in what it tells us about *how* to give their interests equal consideration. It certainly can't tell us that we should give less, or no, consideration to their interests. If, on the other hand, we claim that rationality is important for reciprocity, which is important for cooperation, which is important for benefiting humans, which is the ultimate goal of morality, we have clearly begged the question against giving equal consideration to the interests of animals.

It seems that any attempt to justify the claim that humans have a higher moral status than other animals by appealing to some version of rationality as the morally relevant difference between humans and animals will fail on at least two counts. It will fail to give an adequate answer to the argument from marginal cases, and, more importantly, it will fail to make the case that such a difference is morally relevant to the status of animals as moral patients as opposed to their status as moral agents.

I conclude that our intuitions that Fred's behavior is morally impermissible are accurate. Furthermore, given that the behavior of those who knowingly support factory farming is morally indistinguishable, it follows that their behavior is also morally impermissible.[14]

NOTES

1. For information on factory farms, see, for example, Jim Mason and Peter Singer, *Animal Factories,* 2nd ed. (New York: Harmony Books, 1990), Karen Davis, *Prisoned Chickens, Poisoned Eggs: An Inside Look at the Modern Poultry Industry* (Summertown, TN: Book Publishing Co., 1996), John Robbins, *Diet for a New America* (Walpole, NH: Stillpoint, 1987).

2. *Livestock Slaughter 1998 Summary,* NASS, USDA (Washington, D.C.: March 1999), 2; and *Poultry Slaughter,* NASS, USDA (Washington, D.C.; February 2, 1999), 1f.

3. For a fine critique of the Doctrine of Double Effect, see Jonathan Bennett, *The Act Itself* (Oxford 1995), ch. 11.

4. Bonnie Steinbock, "Speciesism and the Idea of Equality," *Philosophy* 53, no. 204 (April 1978). Reprinted in *Contemporary Moral Problems,* 5th edition, James E. White (ed.) (West, 1997) 467–468.

5. Mary Anne Warren, "Difficulties with the Strong Animal Rights Position," *Between the Species* 2, no. 4, 1987. Reprinted in *Contemporary Moral Problems,* 5th edition, James E. White (ed.) (West, 1997), 482.

6. Carl Cohen. "The Case for the Use of Animals in Biomedical Research," *New England Journal of Medicine* 315 (1986). Reprinted in *Social Ethics,* 4th edition, Thomas A. Mappes and Jane S. Zembaty (eds.) (New York: McGraw-Hill, 1992), 463.

7. Cohen, op. cit. 461.

8. Alan White, *Rights* (OUP 1984). Reprinted in *Animal Rights and Human Obligations,* 2nd edition, Tom Regan and Peter Singer (eds.) (Prentice Hall, 1989), 120.

9. David Schmidtz, "Are All Species Equal?" *Journal of Applied Philosophy* 15, no. 1 (1998), 61, my emphasis.

10. Warren, op. cit. 483.

11. For a similar argument, see Peter Carruthers, *The Animals Issue: Moral Theory in Practice* (Cambridge University Press, 1992).

12. Jeremy Bentham, *Introduction to the Principles of Morals and Legislation,* (Various) chapter 17.

13. Warren, op. cit. 482.

14. This paper, in various forms, has been presented in more places than I can remember, and has benefited from the comments of more people than I can shake a stick at. I particularly wish to thank, for their helpful comments, Doug Ehring, Mylan Engel, Mark Heller, and Steve Sverdlik.

READING QUESTIONS

1. What are the alleged differences between the behavior of Fred and consumers of factory-raised meat that Norcross discusses in the section "Fred's Behavior Compared with Our Behavior"?
2. How does Norcross argue that the differences in question do not justify consuming factory-raised meat?
3. What is the "argument from marginal cases"? What are the two lines of response to this argument, and how does Norcross respond to them?
4. According to Norcross, what is the significance of distinguishing between being a moral agent and being a moral patient in the debate over the morality of meat-eating?

DISCUSSION QUESTIONS

1. Norcross reports that he has "been unable to discover any morally relevant differences between the behavior of Fred, the puppy torturer, and the behavior of millions of people who purchase and consume factory-raised meat." Has Norcross overlooked some further morally relevant difference that may explain why Fred's behavior is morally wrong but meat-eating is not?
2. Do you agree with Norcross that attempts to rebut the argument from marginal cases all fail? Why or why not?

ADDITIONAL RESOURCES

Web Resources

Gruen, Lori, "The Moral Status of Animals," <http://plato.stanford.edu/entries/moral-animal/>. An overview of the debate over the moral standing of nonhuman animals.
People for the Ethical Treatment of Animals, <http://www.peta.org/>. Site of one of the most prominent animal advocacy organizations.

Authored Books

Francione, Gary L. and Robert Garner, *The Animal Rights Debate: Abolition or Regulation?* (New York: Columbia University Press, 2010). The authors engage in a lively debate over different approaches to the protection of nonhuman animals.
Gruen, Lori, *Ethics and Animals: An Introduction* (Cambridge: Cambridge University Press, 2011). A clear, concise, and balanced overview of the major issues regarding the ethical treatment of animals.
Regan, Tom, *The Case for Animal Rights*, 2nd ed. (Berkeley: University of California Press, 2004). An elaboration and defense of the view presented in his article in this chapter.
Singer, Peter, *Animal Liberation*, 2nd ed. (New York: Harper Perennial, 2002). Citing a wealth of empirical information, Singer's classic book (first published in 1975) defends the equal treatment of all sentient creatures.

Scully, Matthew, *Dominion*: *The Power of Man, the Suffering of Animals, and the Call to Mercy* (New York: St. Martin's Griffin, 2003). Journalist and former speechwriter for President George W. Bush, Scully argues against affording rights to animals and instead holds that the same goals of those who advocate animal rights can be obtained by appealing to the proper respect we ought to have toward animals.

Edited Collections

Armstrong, Susan J. and Richard G. Botzler (eds.), *The Animal Ethics Reader* (London: Routledge, 2003). An encyclopedic anthology covering all facets of the ethical treatment of animals, including for example, articles on animal experimentation, animals and entertainment, and animals and biotechnology.

Baird, Robert M. and Stuart E. Rosenbaum (eds.), *Animal Experimentation*: *The Moral Issues* (Amherst, NY: Prometheus Books, 1991). A collection of sixteen essays including articles about the utilitarian and rights approaches to the issues.

Singer, Peter, (ed.), *In Defense of Animals: The Second Wave* (Oxford: Blackwell, 2006). A collection of eighteen essays, most of them appearing here for the first time, representing the most recent wave of thinking about the ethical treatment of animals.

Sunstein, Cass R. and Martha C. Nussbaum (eds.), *Animal Rights: Current Debates and New Directions* (Oxford: Oxford University Press, 2004). A collection of essays addressing ethical questions about ownership, protection against unjustified suffering, and the ability of animals to make their own choices free from human control.

10 }Abortion

Perhaps the most hotly disputed of the moral questions represented in this book is the one over abortion. Here, unfortunately, is one topic where, in much of the public debate, passions run high while reason often goes on holiday. Some of the ongoing moral and legal controversy over abortion has focused on second-trimester abortions that involve a particular medical procedure known as *intact dilation and extraction* (I-D&E) and is referred to by its opponents as "partial-birth abortion."[1] In 2003, U.S. president George W. Bush signed into law the "Partial-Birth Abortion Ban Act," which makes I-D&E abortions illegal. This ban does not provide an exception to protect a woman's health. While this particular legal and moral controversy is over a particular method of terminating a woman's pregnancy in the middle stages of pregnancy, there are controversies over first-trimester abortions including nonsurgical abortions that make use of the so-called abortion pill.[2]

As a start, we can raise the moral question of abortion in a simple way with this question:

- Is abortion ever morally permissible?

In order to clarify disputed issues concerning abortion, let us consider some basic matters of biology, after which we will be in a better position to understand the abortion controversy. (Later in this introduction, I will suggest a more precise way of raising the central moral question over abortion.)

1. SOME BASICS ABOUT FETAL DEVELOPMENT

Certainly having some basic information about the biological facts of fetal development is important for coming to have a justified view about the morality of abortion. Figure 10.1 is a chart that summarizes what seem to be the most important biological facts that are often discussed in the literature on the morality of abortion.

The terminology in the chart (**zygote, embryo,** and **fetus**) reflects strict medical usage, and so a fetus is not present until (roughly) the eighth week of pregnancy. But this medical use of the term is almost always ignored in ethical discussions of abortion where the term "fetus" is used also to refer to both the zygote and the embryo. My label for the chart reflects this broader usage, and henceforth I will be using the term in this way.

Stage	Time	Terminology	Comments
Fertilization/conception	Beginning of pregnancy	"Zygote" (fertilized ovum). Also called a "conceptus."	Sperm unites with fertile ovum (egg) in the fallopian tube; 23 chromosomes of the female nucleus combine with 23 chromosomes contributed by the male nucleus resulting in a one-cell zygote with a human genetic code.
Cell division	Roughly every 22 hours		The process continues in the fallopian tube for about 72 hours until the zygote reaches the uterus.
Implantation	Day 5 or 6	Sixty-cell berrylike cluster called a "morula." (*Morum* is Latin for "mulberry.") The morula develops into what is called the "blastocyst" consisting of two types of cells: the inner cell mass and the outer, enveloping layer of cells.	At implantation, the outer layer of cells ("trophoblast") connects with the maternal uterus, thus stimulating the formation of the placenta. The placenta transfers nutrients through the umbilical cord from the woman to the developing conceptus.
Embryonic stage	Weeks 2–4	Referred to as the "embryo" until week 8.	During this period, the embryo undergoes cell differentiation into three cell types: the ectoderm (producing skin and nervous system); the mesoderm (producing connective tissues, muscles, circulatory system, and bones); and the endoderm (producing the digestive system, lungs, and urinary system). The embryo divides into head and trunk and the internal organs (heart, brain) begin to develop. Limb buds begin to appear.

FIGURE 10.1   Stages of Fetal Development

Embryonic stage, continued	Weeks 4–8		Continuation of development
Fetal stage	Week 8–birth	Name changed to "fetus" (also spelled "foetus").	Used in a strict biological sense, a fetus is an unborn vertebrate animal that has developed to the point of having the basic structure that is characteristic of its kind. This stage is characterized by growth and full development of its organs.
	Week 21 (roughly)	"Viability" refers to the stage in fetal development wherein it is possible for the fetus to survive outside the uterus.	
	Weeks 24–28		Developed capacity to feel pain (**sentience**).

FIGURE 10.1   Stages of Fetal Development (*continued*)

Having covered some of the biology of fetal development, let us proceed to clarify the dispute over abortion, beginning with a definition of what it is.

2. WHAT IS ABORTION?

Unfortunately, the term **abortion** is defined in importantly different ways. On some definitions, abortion refers to the *termination of a pregnancy before viability.*[3] Notice that although this definition does not explicitly refer to the death of the fetus, its death is implied given the definition of **viability** as the stage wherein it is possible for the fetus to survive outside the uterus. Notice also that this definition allows us to distinguish between spontaneous abortions and induced abortion. Spontaneous abortions (also called "miscarriages") result from "natural causes" and without the aid of deliberate interference. It is estimated that around 40 percent of pregnancies end in spontaneous abortion, many of them occurring very early in pregnancy and often mistaken for a delayed menstrual period. Induced abortions, then, are those that are brought about as a result of deliberate intervention.

But, then, if abortion is defined as the termination of a pre-viable fetus, what should we call the termination of a pregnancy after viability has been reached? Some post-viable terminations are due to premature birth. However, others are medically induced where the aim is to preserve the life of the fetus, as in cases of caesarean sections. Such cases are normally not a matter of moral dispute. The problematic cases are so-called partial birth abortions, which are defined as abortions in the second or third trimester of pregnancy in which the death of the fetus is induced after it has passed partway through the birth canal. Since viability occurs roughly in the middle of the second trimester, the definition of abortion with which we began would not classify many such cases as those of abortion. So, in order to recognize all cases that are of concern in the controversy over abortion, let us broaden the definition of "abortion" and use the term to refer to all cases in which *a pregnancy is intentionally interrupted and involves (as part of the process or aim of interruption) the intentional killing of the fetus.* This definition rules out so-called spontaneous abortions as being abortions, which we may instead refer to as miscarriages.

3. THE FETUS AND MORAL STANDING

Now that we have before us some information about fetal development and a working definition of abortion, let us focus for a moment on questions about the moral standing of the fetus.

Roughly, to say that something has moral standing is to say that it counts morally, that it needs to be taken into account in moral decision making. This idea is sometimes expressed by claiming that the thing or creature in question has rights, or that it has intrinsic value, or that we have duties *to* it and not just duties *with regard to* it. In order to clarify this idea a bit more, we can distinguish between something's having **direct moral standing** and something's having merely **indirect moral standing**. (This distinction was introduced in the previous chapter on the ethical treatment of animals.) Something possesses direct moral standing when it possesses properties in virtue of which it has moral standing. The rough idea here is that there is something inherent in the item in question that grounds its standing. By contrast, something has mere indirect moral standing when its standing depends entirely on its being related to something else that has direct moral standing. One might hold, for instance, that to have direct moral standing, a creature must be capable of rational, deliberate action and that (at least on Earth) only human beings and perhaps some higher primates have this property. It would then follow that all other creatures and nonliving things that have any moral standing will have it only because of how their existence bears on the lives of beings with direct moral standing.

Does a human fetus, at least at some stage of development, have direct moral standing? If we assume that direct moral standing can come in degrees, does it ever come to have strong direct moral standing—moral standing strong enough to make abortion seriously wrong? Answers to these questions require that one explain what it is about the fetus in virtue of which it has moral standing and in what degree: we need to specify some "marks" of direct moral standing. And much of the literature on abortion concerns the plausibility of various proposed criteria. Among the criteria that are often mentioned, we find having an immortal soul, having a human genetic code, having personhood, sentience, readable brain activity, being a potential person, having a future like that of an adult human being, viability, and birth. As we shall see, many of these criteria will be considered in the read-ings in this chapter.

In thinking clearly about the various proposed criteria of direct moral standing, it is useful to be aware of the distinction between necessary and sufficient conditions. To say that something X is a necessary condition for Y is to say that Y will not occur (exist or come to be) unless X is present. A necessary condition for someone's committing suicide is that they die. But clearly dying is not sufficient for having committed suicide. To say that X is a sufficient condition for Y is to say that if X occurs, its occurrence is enough for (sufficient for) Y's occurring. Dying is necessary but not sufficient for suicide. Jumping from a fifty-story building under normal conditions and landing on the pavement below is sufficient for committing suicide, but not necessary; there are many other ways to com-mit suicide.

Return now to questions about the moral standing of the fetus. Those who defend a con-servative view (see section 5) about the morality of abortion often argue that in early preg-nancy, the fetus possesses certain features that are *sufficient* for having strong direct moral standing. Nonconservatives often cite features that fetuses lack (either early on or perhaps throughout the entire pregnancy) that they take to be *necessary* for having strong direct moral standing, and thereby arrive at moderate or liberal positions on abortion. In thinking about what people say and write about the moral standing of the fetus, it is always a good idea to be clear about what claim is being made: Is the claim that such and so feature is sufficient for having direct moral standing? If so, then in order to test the proposal, you try to think of something that clearly has the feature in question but that does not have moral standing. Is the claim that such-and-so feature is necessary for having direct moral standing? If so, then to test the proposal, you try to think of something that has moral standing but lacks the feature in question.

4. REASONS FOR SEEKING AN ABORTION

Besides questions about the moral status of the fetus, there are questions about the reasons someone might propose for having an abortion. Often such reasons fall into one of the fol-lowing categories (the list is not meant to be exhaustive):

- *Therapeutic* reasons: reasons relating to the life and health of the pregnant woman.
- *Eugenic* reasons: reasons relating to fetal abnormality.
- *Humanitarian* reasons: reasons that deal with a pregnancy due to incest or rape.
- *Socioeconomic* reasons: reasons relating, for example, to poverty, social stigma, or family size.
- *Personal* reasons: these include reasons other than any of the ones just mentioned that relate to a woman's preferences and projects. Two such reasons would be the desire to devote time to a professional career and just not wanting to be inconvenienced by the pregnancy.

The obvious point to be made here is that in thinking carefully about the morality of abortion, it is important to consider what reasons someone might propose for having an abortion and whether the reason in question is a genuinely good reason. Considerations of self-defense where a woman's life is endangered by her pregnancy presumably justify her having an abortion, and many conservative positions on abortion recognize this. What is controversial is whether any of the other kinds of considerations on the prior list can justify having an abortion. (And notice that putting the issue in this way—whether such and so reason can justify abortion—already seems to assume that at some stage of its development, the fetus has some moral standing.)

5. A RANGE OF VIEWS ON THE MORALITY OF ABORTION

In light of the preceding discussion, we can make our leading question about the morality of abortion more precise by restating it as follows:

- At what stage in fetal development (if any) and for what reasons (if any) is abortion ever morally permissible?

This way of posing the issue calls attention to the two main areas of moral dispute just described. First, there is dispute over the moral standing of the fetus at various stages in fetal development. One might hold, for instance, that at conception a human fetus (technically, a zygote) has no moral standing, and thus aborting the fetus very early in pregnancy is not morally wrong, although later in pregnancy (because of changes in the developing fetus), it does have moral standing and therefore later-stage abortions are wrong. The second area of dispute is over what sorts of reasons for having an abortion (if any) would morally justify such a procedure. One might hold, for instance, that the fact that the pregnant woman will die unless she aborts her fetus would justify having an abortion but that, say, economic reasons would not. And, of course, it is possible to hold the view that as the fetus develops its moral standing becomes stronger, and thus the reasons that would justify having an abortion must be correspondingly strong.

The labels "pro-life" and "conservative" are often used to refer to those who morally oppose abortion, whereas the terms "pro-choice" and "liberal" are often used to characterize those who do not. But such labels grossly oversimplify the complexity of the abortion issue and thereby falsely suggest that there are only two positions one might take on the issue. Given the way in which the main ethical question about abortion was formulated earlier, together with the discussion of the moral standing of the fetus and reasons for seeking an abortion, it should be clear that there is a range of views that one might hold about the morality of abortion. We can distinguish three broad categories of views: liberal, moderate, and conservative, so long as we keep in mind that each of these categories allows for a "more or less" version. Referring to our central moral question about abortion, an extreme liberal view would be one according to which abortion is morally permissible at any stage of moral development for any reason, whereas an extreme conservative view would hold that abortions are morally wrong at any stage of fetal development and for any reason. But, of course, there are liberal and conservative views that are not this extreme. And many people hold views that are most appropriately seen as moderate: some abortions are wrong and some aren't depending on the stage of fetal development and kind of reason one might have for having an abortion. So rather than think of the abortion dispute as between pro-life (conservative) and pro-choice (liberal), we should rather think in terms of a spectrum of possible views one might hold about the morality of abortion, as indicated by the following visual aid.[4]

| Liberal | Moderate | Conservative |

6. THE LEGALITY OF ABORTION

The 1973 U.S. Supreme Court decision in *Roe v. Wade* made many abortions legal.[5] In that case, a Texas resident, under the fictitious name of Jane Roe, challenged the then Texas law that made abortion illegal except in cases in which the woman's life was threatened by her pregnancy. Although the Court recognized a woman's right to privacy, including a right to decide to terminate her pregnancy, it also recognized a state's legitimate interest in protecting the life and health of the pregnant woman as well as a legitimate interest in protecting prenatal life. The decision in the case of *Roe* represented an attempt by the Court to balance these interests and resulted in striking down the Texas law. The ruling in effect gave a woman a constitutionally guaranteed right to an abortion throughout the first two-thirds of pregnancy, allowing some restrictions on the methods and circumstances of abortion for medical reasons. The *Roe* decision continues to be a source of heated moral and legal debate in the United States. In 1992 in the case *Planned Parenthood of Southeastern Pennsylvania v. Casey*,[6] the Court upheld the basic right to abortion established in *Roe*, but overturned the trimester formula of *Roe*, replacing it with viability as the stage of pregnancy at which a state's interest in prenatal life may override a pregnant woman's right to choose abortion. As noted above, in 2003 the Partial-Birth Abortion Ban Act was signed into law that prohibits partial-birth abortions (defined in note 1). In 2007 this act was upheld as constitutional by the U.S. Supreme Court in *Gonzales, Attorney General v. Carhart et al.*[7] by a 5-to-4 vote.

In 2013, the Texas legislature enacted a law whose effect would dramatically decrease the number of clinics offering abortion in that state. Texas officials claim that the rationale for the law is to protect women's health. However, the law was challenged by serval Texas clinics and doctors, arguing that it imposes expensive restrictions on clinics and is a ruse simply intended to put many clinics out business. In 2016, the Supreme Court, in a 5-3 decision, ruled that the Texas law was unconstitutional.

7. THEORY MEETS PRACTICE

The various readings in this chapter reflect arguments about abortion from the perspectives of natural law theory, rights approaches, and virtue ethics. Although none of the authors in this chapter approach the issue from a utilitarian or consequentialist perspective, let us begin with this perspective and then briefly consider how representatives of the other moral theories approach abortion.

Consequentialism

The consequentialist will approach the morality of abortion by considering the overall intrinsic value of the consequences of abortions. An *act* consequentialist will claim that whether a particular act of abortion is morally right will depend on the overall intrinsic value of that act's consequences compared to the overall intrinsic value that would result were the abortion not performed. And, of course, in some cases the consequences of having an abortion will be better than not having one, while in others it will be the other way around. For the *rule* consequentialist, whether an abortion is morally permissible will depend on which rule, from among the various rules a society might adopt governing abortions, would have the highest **acceptance value**. For instance, a rule consequentialist might argue that a rule permitting abortions for therapeutic reasons only would have a higher acceptance value than a rule prohibiting all abortions without exception. And perhaps a rule that allows abortions for both therapeutic and humanitarian reasons would have a greater acceptance value than either of the other two just mentioned. Given the various reasons for having an abortion and the potential significance of the different stages of fetal development, there are many competing rules that might be crafted, and so the rule consequentialist is in the position of having to estimate the likely acceptance values of the various rules as a basis for judging the morality of particular abortions.

Natural Law Theory

Although the article by Patrick Lee and Robert P. George does not explicitly mention natural law theory, the idea that from conception a fetus is an undeveloped human being with the same moral status as fully developed human beings is often presented as an implication of natural law thinking. Lee and George do discuss attempts to defend at least some abortion on the basis of the doctrine of double effect—one of the elements of traditional natural law theory.

Rights Approaches

The abortion dispute is often cast as a battle of rights: the (alleged) rights of the fetus versus the rights of the pregnant woman. Such disputes involve an inquiry into the basis of rights and a determination of the strengths of various rights of the woman compared to any rights a fetus may have. The articles by Mary Anne Warren, Judith Jarvis Thomson, and Patrick Lee and Robert P. George are concerned with such issues and their implications for the morality of abortion.

Virtue Ethics

Rosalind Hursthouse approaches the abortion issue from the perspective of virtue ethics, according to which rightness and wrongness depend on considerations of virtue and vice. This approach makes questions about a person's motives and questions of overall character salient in thinking about the morality of abortion. Such questions as whether having an abortion would be callous or self-centered, or rather whether, in some cases, it would be an expression of humility or modesty, are central in a virtue ethics approach for deciding whether some case of abortion would be morally right or wrong.

NOTES

1. Intact dilation and extraction involves removing or partially removing the fetus from the woman's cervix, after which the fetus is killed. It is defined as follows: "An abortion in which the person performing the abortion (A) deliberately and intentionally vaginally delivers a living fetus until, in the case of the head-first presentation, the entire fetal head is outside the body of the mother, or, in the case of breech presentation, any part of the fetal trunk past the navel is outside the body of the mother, for the purpose of performing an overt act that the person knows will kill the partially delivered living fetus; and (B) performs the overt act, other than completion of the delivery, that kills the partially delivered living fetus." This method of D&E is distinguished from "standard D&E" in which the fetus is torn apart and thus dies before its body parts are extracted. The Partial-Birth Abortion Ban Act does not prohibit standard D&E abortions.

2. Nonsurgical abortions, which may be performed in the first 63 days of pregnancy, involve the use of RU-486 (the generic name for mifepristone), which is taken either in pill form or by injection (methotrexate).

3. See, for example, the *Merriam-Webster Online Dictionary* entry.

4. See the introduction to chapter 3 on sexual morality (section 1) for a related discussion of the spectrum of views one might hold about the morality of sexual behavior. Readers should be aware that taking a conservative moral position on some issue does not commit one to the political ideology of Conservatism, nor does taking a liberal view on some issue commit one to the ideology of Liberalism. For more on these ideologies, see chapter 4 on pornography, hate speech, and censorship, section 1.

5. 410 U.S. 113 (1973).

6. 505 U.S. 833.

7. 550 U.S. 124.

MARY ANNE WARREN

On the Moral and Legal Status of Abortion

Warren first argues that the so-called genetic code argument—the argument that attempts to establish the moral standing of the fetus by appealing to biological facts—is fallacious. She then goes on to consider the issue of whether the fetus (at some stage of development) is a person by developing an account of the nature of personhood. According to Warren's analysis, a fetus is not a person at any stage in its development, and from this she concludes that abortion is not morally wrong. In arguing for her view, she considers and rejects opposing arguments that appeal to facts about fetal development, potentiality, and infanticide.

Recommended Reading: rights-focused approach to moral issues, chap. 1, sec. 2D.

The question which we must answer in order to produce a satisfactory solution to the problem of the moral status of abortion is this: How are we to define the moral community, the set of beings with full and equal moral rights, such that we can decide whether a human fetus is a member of this community or not? What sort of entity, exactly, has the inalienable rights to life, liberty, and the pursuit of happiness? Jefferson attributed these rights to all *men,* and it may or may not be fair to suggest that he intended to attribute them *only* to men. Perhaps he ought to have attributed them to all human beings. If so, then we arrive, first, at [John] Noonan's problem of defining what makes a being human, and, second, at the equally vital question which Noonan does not consider, namely, What reason is there for identifying the moral community with the set of all human beings, in whatever way we have chosen to define that term?

1. ON THE DEFINITION OF "HUMAN"

One reason why this vital second question is so frequently overlooked in the debate over the moral status of abortion is that the term "human" has two distinct, but not often distinguished, senses. This fact results in a slide of meaning, which serves to conceal the fallaciousness of the traditional argument that since (1) it is wrong to kill innocent human beings, and (2) fetuses are innocent human beings, then (3) it is wrong to kill fetuses. For if "human" is used in the same sense in both (1) and (2) then, whichever of the two senses is meant, one of these premises is question-begging. And if it is used in two different senses then of course the conclusion doesn't follow.

Thus, (1) is a self-evident moral truth,[1] and avoids begging the question about abortion, only if "human being" is used to mean something like "a full-fledged member of the moral community." (It may or may not also be meant to refer exclusively to members of the species *Homo sapiens.*) We may call this the *moral* sense of "human." It is not to be confused with what

we will call the *genetic* sense, i.e., the sense in which *any* member of the species is a human being, and no member of any other species could be. If (1) is acceptable only if the moral sense is intended, (2) is non-question-begging only if what is intended is the genetic sense.

In "Deciding Who Is Human," Noonan argues for the classification of fetuses with human beings by pointing to the presence of the full genetic code, and the potential capacity for rational thought.[2] It is clear that what he needs to show, for his version of the traditional argument to be valid, is that fetuses are human in the moral sense, the sense in which it is analytically true that all human beings have full moral rights. But, in the absence of any argument showing that whatever is genetically human is also morally human, and he gives none, nothing more than genetic humanity can be demonstrated by the presence of the human genetic code. And, as we will see, the *potential* capacity for rational thought can at most show that an entity has the potential for *becoming* human in the moral sense.

2. DEFINING THE MORAL COMMUNITY

Can it be established that genetic humanity is sufficient for moral humanity? I think that there are very good reasons for not defining the moral community in this way. I would like to suggest an alternative way of defining the moral community, which I will argue for only to the extent of explaining why it is, or should be, self-evident. The suggestion is simply that the moral community consists of all and only *people,* rather than all and only human beings;[3] and probably the best way of demonstrating its self-evidence is by considering the concept of personhood, to see what sorts of entity are and are not persons, and what the decision that a being is or is not a person implies about its moral rights.

What characteristics entitle an entity to be considered a person? This is obviously not the place to attempt a complete analysis of the concept of personhood, but we do not need such a fully adequate analysis just to determine whether and why a fetus is or isn't a person. All we need is a rough and approximate list of the most basic criteria of personhood, and some idea of which, or how many, of these an entity must satisfy in order to properly be considered a person.

In searching for such criteria, it is useful to look beyond the set of people with whom we are acquainted, and ask how we would decide whether a totally alien being was a person or not. (For we have no right to assume that genetic humanity is necessary for personhood.) Imagine a space traveler who lands on an unknown planet and encounters a race of beings utterly unlike any he has ever seen or heard of. If he wants to be sure of behaving morally toward these beings, he has to somehow decide whether they are people, and hence have full moral rights, or whether they are the sort of thing which he need not feel guilty about treating as, for example, a source of food.

How should he go about making this decision? If he has some anthropological background, he might look for such things as religion, art, and the manufacturing of tools, weapons, or shelters, since these factors have been used to distinguish our human from our prehuman ancestors, in what seems to be closer to the moral than the genetic sense of "human." And no doubt he would be right to consider the presence of such factors as good evidence that the alien beings were people, and morally human. It would, however, be overly anthropocentric of him to take the absence of these things as adequate evidence that they were not, since we can imagine people who have progressed beyond, or evolved without ever developing, these cultural characteristics.

I suggest that the traits which are most central to the concept of personhood, or humanity in the moral sense, are, very roughly, the following:

1. consciousness (of objects and events external and/or internal to the being), and in particular the capacity to feel pain;
2. reasoning (the *developed* capacity to solve new and relatively complex problems);
3. self-motivated activity (activity which is relatively independent of either genetic or direct external control);
4. the capacity to communicate, by whatever means, messages of an indefinite variety of types, that is, not just with an indefinite number of possible contents, but on indefinitely many possible topics;
5. the presence of self-concepts, and self-awareness, either individual or racial, or both.

Admittedly, there are apt to be a great many problems involved in formulating precise definitions of these criteria, let alone in developing universally valid behavioral criteria for deciding when they apply. But I will assume that both we and our explorer know approximately what (1)–(5) mean, and that he is also able to determine whether or not they apply. How, then, should he use his findings to decide whether or not the alien beings are people? We needn't suppose that an entity must have *all* of these attributes to be properly considered a person; (1) and (2) alone may well be sufficient for personhood, and quite probably (1)–(3) are sufficient. Neither do we need to insist that any one of these criteria is *necessary* for personhood, although once again (1) and (2) look like fairly good candidates for necessary conditions, as does (3), if "activity" is construed so as to include the activity of reasoning.

All we need to claim, to demonstrate that a fetus is not a person, is that any being which satisfies *none* of (1)–(5) is certainly not a person. I consider this claim to be so obvious that I think anyone who denied it, and claimed that a being which satisfied none of (1)–(5) was a person all the same, would thereby demonstrate that he had no notion at all of what a person is—perhaps because he had confused the concept of a person with that of genetic humanity. If the opponents of abortion were to deny the appropriateness of these five criteria, I do not know what further arguments would convince them. We would probably have to admit that our conceptual schemes were indeed irreconcilably different, and that our dispute could not be settled objectively.

I do not expect this to happen, however, since I think that the concept of a person is one which is very nearly universal (to people), and that it is common to both proabortionists and antiabortionists, even though neither group has fully realized the relevance of this concept to the resolution of their dispute. Furthermore, I think that on reflection even the antiabortionists ought to agree not only that (1)–(5) are central to the concept of personhood, but also that it is a part of this concept that all and only people have full moral rights. The concept of a person is in part a moral concept; once we have admitted that *x* is a person we have recognized, even if we have not agreed to respect, *x*'s right to be treated as a member of the moral community. It is true that the claim that *x is a human being* is more commonly voiced as part of an appeal to treat *x* decently than is the claim that *x* is a person, but this is either because "human being" is here used in the sense which implies personhood, or because the genetic and moral senses of "human" have been confused.

Now if (1)–(5) are indeed the primary criteria of personhood, then it is clear that genetic humanity is neither necessary nor sufficient for establishing that an entity is a person. Some human beings are not people, and there may well be people who are not human beings. A man or woman whose consciousness has been permanently obliterated but who remains alive is a human being which is no longer a person; defective human beings, with no appreciable mental capacity, are not and presumably never will be people; and a fetus is a human being which is not yet a person, and which therefore cannot coherently be said to have full moral rights. Citizens of the next century should be prepared to recognize highly advanced, self-aware robots or computers, should such be developed, and intelligent inhabitants of other worlds, should such be found, as people in the fullest sense, and to respect their moral rights. But to ascribe full moral rights to an entity which is not a person is as absurd as to ascribe moral obligations and responsibilities to such an entity.

3. FETAL DEVELOPMENT AND THE RIGHT TO LIFE

Two problems arise in the application of these suggestions for the definition of the moral community to the determination of the precise moral status of a human fetus. Given that the paradigm example of a person is a normal adult human being, then (1) How like this paradigm, in particular how far advanced since conception, does a human being need to be before it begins to have a right to life by virtue, not of being fully a person as of yet, but of being *like* a person? and (2) To what extent, if any, does the fact that a fetus has the *potential* for becoming a person endow it with some of the same rights? Each of these questions requires some comment.

In answering the first question, we need not attempt a detailed consideration of the moral rights of organisms which are not developed enough, aware enough, intelligent enough, etc., to be considered people, but which resemble people in some respects. It does seem reasonable to suggest that the more like a person, in the relevant respects, a being is, the stronger is the case for regarding it as having a right to life, and indeed the stronger its right to life is. Thus we ought to take seriously the suggestion that, insofar as "the human individual develops biologically in a continuous fashion. . . . the rights of a human person might develop in the same way."[4] But we must keep in mind that the attributes which are relevant in determining whether or not an entity is enough like a person to be regarded as having some of the same moral rights are no different from those which are relevant to determining whether or not it is fully a person—i.e., are no different from (1)–(5)—and that being genetically human, or having recognizably human facial and other physical features, or detectable brain activity, or the capacity to survive outside the uterus, are simply not among these relevant attributes.

Thus it is clear that even though a seven- or eight-month fetus has features which make it apt to arouse in us almost the same powerful protective instinct as is commonly aroused by a small infant, nevertheless it is not significantly more personlike than is a very small embryo. It is *somewhat* more personlike; it can apparently feel and respond to pain, and it may even have a rudimentary form of consciousness, insofar as its brain is quite active. Nevertheless, it seems safe to say that it is not fully conscious, in the way that an infant of a few months is, and that it cannot reason, or communicate messages of indefinitely many sorts, does not engage in self-motivated activity, and has no self-awareness. Thus, in the *relevant* respects, a fetus, even a fully developed one, is considerably less personlike than is the average mature mammal, indeed the average fish. And I think that a rational person must conclude that if the right to life of a fetus is to be based upon its resemblance to a person, then it cannot be said to have any more right to life than, let us say, a newborn guppy (which also seems to be capable of feeling pain), and that a right of that magnitude could never override a woman's right to obtain an abortion, at any stage of her pregnancy.

There may, of course, be other arguments in favor of placing legal limits upon the stage of pregnancy in which an abortion may be performed. Given the relative safety of the new techniques of artificially inducing labor during the third trimester, the danger to the woman's life or health is no longer such an argument. Neither is the fact that people tend to respond to the thought of abortion in the later stages of pregnancy with emotional repulsion, since mere emotional responses cannot take the place of moral reasoning in determining what ought to be permitted. Nor, finally, is the frequently heard argument that legalizing abortion, especially late in the pregnancy, may erode the level of respect for human life, leading, perhaps, to an increase in unjustified euthanasia and other crimes. For this threat, if it is a threat, can be better met by educating people to the kinds of moral distinctions which we are making here than by limiting access to abortion (which limitation may, in its disregard for the rights of women, be just as damaging to the level of respect for human rights).

Thus, since the fact that even a fully developed fetus is not personlike enough to have any significant right to life on the basis of its personlikeness shows that no legal restrictions upon the stage of pregnancy in which an abortion may be performed can be justified on the grounds that we should protect the rights of the older fetus, and since there is no other apparent justification for such restrictions, we may conclude that they are entirely unjustified. Whether or not it would be *indecent* (whatever that means) for a woman in her seventh month to obtain an abortion just to avoid having to postpone a trip to Europe, it would not, in itself, be *immoral*, and therefore it ought to be permitted.

4. POTENTIAL PERSONHOOD AND THE RIGHT TO LIFE

We have seen that a fetus does not resemble a person in any way which can support the claim that it has even some of the same rights. But what about its *potential,* the fact that if nurtured and allowed to develop naturally it will very probably become a person? Doesn't that alone give it at least some right to life? It is hard to deny that the fact that an entity is a potential person is a strong prima facie reason for not destroying it; but we need not conclude from this that a potential person has a right to life, by virtue of that potential. It may be that our feeling that it is better, other things being equal, not to destroy a potential person is better explained by the fact that potential people are still (felt to be) an invaluable resource, not to be lightly squandered. Surely, if every speck of dust were a potential person, we would be much less apt to conclude that every potential person has a right to become actual.

Still, we do not need to insist that a potential person has no right to life whatever. There may well be something immoral, and not just imprudent, about wantonly destroying potential people, when doing so isn't necessary to protect anyone's rights. But even if a potential person does have some prima facie right to life, such a right could not possibly outweigh the right of a woman to obtain an abortion, since the rights of any actual person invariably outweigh those of any potential person, whenever the two conflict. Since this may not be immediately obvious in the case of a human fetus, let us look at another case.

Suppose that our space explorer falls into the hands of an alien culture, whose scientists decide to create a few hundred thousand or more human beings, by breaking his body into its component cells, and using these to create fully developed human beings, with, of course, his genetic code. We may imagine that each of these newly created men will have all of the original man's abilities, skills, knowledge, and so on, and also have an individual self-concept, in short that each of them will be a bona fide (though hardly unique) person. Imagine that the whole project will take only seconds, and that its chances of success are extremely high, and that our explorer knows all of this, and also knows that these people will be treated fairly. I maintain that in such a situation he would have every right to escape if he could, and thus to deprive all of these potential people of their potential lives; for his right to life outweighs all of theirs together, in spite of the fact that they are all genetically human, all innocent, and all have a very high probability of becoming people very soon, if only he refrains from acting.

Indeed, I think he would have a right to escape even if it were not his life which the alien scientists planned to take, but only a year of his freedom, or, indeed, only a day. Nor would he be obligated to stay if he had gotten captured (thus bringing all these people-potentials into existence) because of his own carelessness, or even if he had done so deliberately, knowing the consequences. Regardless of how he got captured, he is not morally obligated to remain in captivity for *any* period of time for the sake of permitting any number of potential people to come into actuality, so great is the margin by which one actual person's right to liberty outweighs whatever right to life even a hundred thousand potential people have. And it seems reasonable to conclude that the rights of a woman will outweigh by a similar margin whatever right to life a fetus may have by virtue of its potential personhood.

Thus, neither a fetus's resemblance to a person, nor its potential for becoming a person provides any basis whatever for the claim that it has any significant right to life. Consequently, a woman's right to protect her health, happiness, freedom, and even her life,[5] by terminating an unwanted pregnancy, will always override whatever right to life it may be appropriate to ascribe to a fetus, even a fully developed one. And thus, in the absence of any overwhelming social need for every possible child, the laws which restrict the right to obtain an abortion, or limit the period of pregnancy during which an abortion may be performed, are a wholly unjustified violation of a woman's most basic moral and constitutional rights.[6]

POSTSCRIPT ON INFANTICIDE

Since the publication of this article, many people have written to point out that my argument appears to justify not only abortion, but infanticide as well. For a newborn infant is not significantly more personlike than an advanced fetus, and consequently it would seem that if the destruction of the latter is permissible so too must be that of the former. Inasmuch as most people, regardless of how they feel about the morality of abortion, consider infanticide a form of murder, this might appear to represent a serious flaw in my argument.

Now, if I am right in holding that it is only people who have a full-fledged right to life, and who can be murdered, and if the criteria of personhood are as I have described them, then it obviously follows that killing a newborn infant isn't murder. It does *not* follow, however, that infanticide is permissible, for two reasons. In the first place, it would be wrong, at least in this country and in this period of history, and other things being equal, to kill a newborn infant, because even if its parents do not want it and would not suffer from its destruction, there are other people who would like to have it, and would, in all probability, be deprived of a great deal of pleasure by its destruction. Thus, infanticide is wrong for reasons analogous to those which make it wrong to wantonly destroy natural resources, or great works of art.

Secondly, most people, at least in this country, value infants and would much prefer that they be preserved, even if foster parents are not immediately available. Most of us would rather be taxed to support orphanages than allow unwanted infants to be destroyed. So long as there are people who want an infant preserved, and who are willing and able to provide the means of caring for it, under reasonably humane conditions, it is ceteris paribus, wrong to destroy it.

But, it might be replied, if this argument shows that infanticide is wrong, at least at this time and in this country, doesn't it also show that abortion is wrong? After all, many people value fetuses, are disturbed by their destruction, and would much prefer that they be preserved, even at some cost to themselves. Furthermore, as a potential source of pleasure to some foster family, a fetus is just as valuable as an infant. There is, however, a crucial difference between the two cases: so long as the fetus is unborn, its preservation, contrary to the wishes of the pregnant woman, violates her rights to freedom, happiness, and self-determination. Her rights override the rights of those who would like the fetus preserved, just as if someone's life or limb is threatened by a wild animal, his right to protect himself by destroying the animal overrides the rights of those who would prefer that the animal not be harmed.

The minute the infant is born, however, its preservation no longer violates any of its mother's rights, even if she wants it destroyed, because she is free to put it up for adoption. Consequently, while the moment of birth does not mark any sharp discontinuity in the degree to which an infant possesses the right to life, it does mark the end of its mother's right to determine its fate. Indeed, if abortion could be performed without killing the fetus, she would never possess the right to have the fetus destroyed, for the same reasons that she has no right to have an infant destroyed.

On the other hand, it follows from my argument that when an unwanted or defective infant is born into a society which cannot afford and/or is not willing to care for it, then its destruction is permissible. This conclusion will, no doubt, strike many people as heartless and immoral; but remember that the very existence of people who feel this way, and who are willing and able to provide care for unwanted infants, is reason enough to conclude that they should be preserved.

NOTES

1. Of course, the principle that it is (always) wrong to kill innocent human beings is in need of many other modifications, e.g., that it may be permissible to do so to save a greater number of other innocent human beings, but we may safely ignore these complications here.

2. John Noonan, "Deciding Who Is Human," *Natural Law Forum,* 13 (1968), 135.

3. From here on, we will use "human" to mean genetically human, since the moral sense seems closely connected to, and perhaps derived from, the assumption that genetic humanity is sufficient for membership in the moral community.

4. Thomas L. Hayes, "A Biological View," *Commonweal,* 85 (March 17, 1967), 677–78; quoted by Daniel Callahan, in *Abortion: Law, Choice and Morality* (London: Macmillan & Co., 1970).

5. That is, insofar as the death rate, for the woman, is higher for childbirth than for early abortion.

6. My thanks to the following people, who were kind enough to read and criticize an earlier version of this paper: Herbert Gold, Gene Glass, Anne Lauterbach, Judith Thomson, Mary Mothersill, and Timothy Binkley.

READING QUESTIONS

1. How does Warren criticize what she refers to as the "traditional argument" against abortion?
2. Warren claims that being genetically human is not sufficient for moral humanity (personhood). How does she defend this claim?
3. Warren also claims that being genetically human is not necessary for moral humanity. How does she defend this claim?
4. What argument does Warren give for claiming that being a potential person cannot be used to defend an antiabortion position?
5. What reasons does Warren give for claiming that the gradualist approach to moral standing fails to show that even middle- to late-stage abortions are wrong?
6. How does Warren attempt to show that infanticide is morally wrong?

DISCUSSION QUESTIONS

1. Should we find Warren's account of personhood plausible? If not, why not?
2. Should we find Warren's explanation of the wrongness of infanticide convincing? Why or why not?

JUDITH JARVIS THOMSON

A Defense of Abortion

In what is perhaps the most famous of philosophical articles on abortion, Thomson argues for the claim that even if a fetus is a person from conception (and hence has a full right to life), a pregnant woman still has a right to have an abortion. If her argument is cogent, then those who think that the abortion issue can be settled by determining at what stage (if any) the fetus is a person are mistaken. Nevertheless, as Thomson explains, even if a pregnant woman has a right to an abortion, it does not follow that there would be nothing morally problematic about her choosing to act on this right. She claims that in some cases, depending on the circumstances, choosing an abortion would be callous or self-centered, and thus in such cases a woman ought not to choose abortion even if she has a right to.

Thomson's appeal to the vices of callousness and self-centeredness is a major theme in the virtue approach to abortion defended in the article by Rosalind Hursthouse.

Recommended Reading: rights-focused approach to moral issues, chap. 1, sec. 2D. Also relevant is virtue ethics, chap. 1, sec. 2E.

Most opposition to abortion relies on the premise that the fetus is a human being, a person, from the moment of conception. The premise is argued for, but, as I think, not well. Take, for example, the most common argument. We are asked to notice that the development of a human being from conception through birth into childhood is continuous; then it is said that to draw a line, to choose a point in this development and say "before this point the thing is not a person, after this point it is a person" is to make an arbitrary choice, a choice for which in the nature of things no good reason can be given. It is concluded that the fetus is, or anyway that we had better say it is, a person from the moment of conception. But this conclusion does not follow. Similar things might be said about the development of an acorn into an oak tree, and it does not follow that acorns are oak trees, or that we had better say they

are. Arguments of this form are sometimes called "slippery slope arguments"—the phrase is perhaps self-explanatory—and it is dismaying that opponents of abortion rely on them so heavily and uncritically.

I am inclined to agree, however, that the prospects for "drawing a line" in the development of the fetus look dim. I am inclined to think also that we shall probably have to agree that the fetus has already become a human person well before birth. Indeed, it comes as a surprise when one first learns how early in its life it begins to acquire human characteristics. By the tenth week, for example, it already has a face, arms and legs, fingers and toes; it has internal organs, and brain activity is detectable.[1] On the other hand, I think that the premise is false, that the fetus is not a person from the moment of conception. A newly fertilized ovum, a newly implanted clump of cells, is no more a person than an acorn is an oak tree. But I

From Judith Jarvis Thomson, "A Defense of Abortion," *Philosophy and Public Affairs* 1 (1971). Reprinted by permission of Princeton University Press.

shall not discuss any of this. For it seems to me to be of great interest to ask what happens if, for the sake of argument, we allow the premise. How, precisely, are we supposed to get from there to the conclusion that abortion is morally impermissible? Opponents of abortion commonly spend most of their time establishing that the fetus is a person, and hardly any time explaining the step from there to the impermissibility of abortion. Perhaps they think the step too simple and obvious to require much comment. Or perhaps instead they are simply being economical in argument. Many of those who defend abortion rely on the premise that the fetus is not a person, but only a bit of tissue that will become a person at birth; and why pay out more arguments than you have to? Whatever the explanation, I suggest that the step they take is neither easy nor obvious, that it calls for closer examination than it is commonly given, and that when we do give it this closer examination we shall feel inclined to reject it.

I propose, then, that we grant that the fetus is a person from the moment of conception. How does the argument go from here? Something like this, I take it. Every person has a right to life. So the fetus has a right to life. No doubt the mother has a right to decide what shall happen in and to her body; everyone would grant that. But surely a person's right to life is stronger and more stringent than the mother's right to decide what happens in and to her body, and so outweighs it. So the fetus may not be killed; an abortion may not be performed.

It sounds plausible. But now let me ask you to imagine this. You wake up in the morning and find yourself back to back in bed with an unconscious violinist. A famous unconscious violinist. He has been found to have a fatal kidney ailment, and the Society of Music Lovers has canvassed all the available medical records and found that you alone have the right blood type to help. They have therefore kidnapped you, and last night the violinist's circulatory system was plugged into yours, so that your kidneys can be used to extract poisons from his blood as well as your own. The director of the hospital now tells you, "Look, we're sorry the Society of Music Lovers did this to you—we would never have permitted it if we had known. But

still, they did it, and the violinist now is plugged into you. To unplug you would be to kill him. But never mind, it's only for nine months. By then he will have recovered from his ailment, and can safely be unplugged from you." Is it morally incumbent on you to accede to this situation? No doubt it would be very nice of you if you did, a great kindness. But do you *have* to accede to it? What if it were not nine months, but nine years? Or longer still? What if the director of the hospital says, "Tough luck, I agree, but you've now got to stay in bed, with the violinist plugged into you, for the rest of your life. Because remember this. All persons have a right to life, and violinists are persons. Granted you have a right to decide what happens in and to your body, but a person's right to life outweighs your right to decide what happens in and to your body. So you cannot ever be unplugged from him." I imagine you would regard this as outrageous, which suggests that something really is wrong with that plausible-sounding argument I mentioned a moment ago.

In this case, of course, you were kidnapped; you didn't volunteer for the operation that plugged the violinist into your kidneys. Can those who oppose abortion on the ground I mentioned make an exception for a pregnancy due to rape? Certainly. They can say that persons have a right to life only if they didn't come into existence because of rape; or they can say that all persons have a right to life, but that some have less of a right to life than others, in particular, that those who came into existence because of rape have less. But these statements have a rather unpleasant sound. Surely the question of whether you have a right to life at all, or how much of it you have, shouldn't turn on the question of whether or not you are the product of a rape. And in fact the people who oppose abortion on the ground I mentioned do not make this distinction, and hence do not make an exception in case of rape.

Nor do they make an exception for a case in which the mother has to spend the nine months of her pregnancy in bed. They would agree that would be a great pity, and hard on the mother; but all the same, all persons have a right to life, the fetus is a person, and so on. I suspect, in fact, that they would not make an exception for a case in which, miraculously enough, the pregnancy went on for nine years, or even the rest of the mother's life.

Some won't even make an exception for a case in which continuation of the pregnancy is likely to shorten the mother's life; they regard abortion as impermissible even to save the mother's life. Such cases are nowadays very rare, and many opponents of abortion do not accept this extreme view. . . .

Where the mother's life is not at stake, the argument I mentioned at the outset seems to have a much stronger pull. "Everyone has a right to life, so the unborn person has a right to life." And isn't the child's right to life weightier than anything other than the mother's own right to life, which she might put forward as ground for an abortion?

This argument treats the right to life as if it were unproblematic. It is not, and this seems to me to be precisely the source of the mistake.

For we should now, at long last, ask what it comes to, to have a right to life. In some views having a right to life includes having a right to be given at least the bare minimum one needs for continued life. But suppose that what in fact *is* the bare minimum a man needs for continued life is something he has no right at all to be given? If I am sick unto death, and the only thing that will save my life is the touch of Henry Fonda's cool hand on my fevered brow, then all the same, I have no right to be given the touch of Henry Fonda's cool hand on my fevered brow. It would be frightfully nice of him to fly in from the West Coast to provide it. It would be less nice, though no doubt well meant, if my friends flew out to the West Coast and carried Henry Fonda back with them. But I have no right at all against anybody that he should do this for me. Or again, to return to the story I told earlier, the fact that for continued life that violinist needs the continued use of your kidneys does not establish that he has a right to be given the continued use of your kidneys. He certainly has no right against you that *you* should give him continued use of your kidneys. For nobody has any right to use your kidneys unless you give him such a right; and nobody has the right against you that you shall give him this right—if you do allow him to go on using your kidneys, this is a kindness on your part, and not something he can claim from

you as his due. Nor has he any right against anybody else that *they* should give him continued use of your kidneys. Certainly he had no right against the Society of Music Lovers that they should plug him into you in the first place. And if you now start to unplug yourself, having learned that you will otherwise have to spend nine years in bed with him, there is nobody in the world who must try to prevent you, in order to see to it that he is given something he has a right to be given.

Some people are rather stricter about the right to life. In their view, it does not include the right to be given anything, but amounts to, and only to, the right not to be killed by anybody. But here a related difficulty arises. If everybody is to refrain from killing that violinist, then everybody must refrain from doing a great many different sorts of things. Everybody must refrain from slitting his throat, everybody must refrain from shooting him—and everybody must refrain from unplugging you from him. But does he have a right against everybody that they shall refrain from unplugging you from him? To refrain from doing this is to allow him to continue to use your kidneys. It could be argued that he has a right against us that *we* should allow him to continue to use your kidneys. That is, while he had no right against us that we should give him the use of your kidneys, it might be argued that he anyway has a right against us that we shall not now intervene and deprive him of the use of your kidneys. I shall come back to third-party interventions later. But certainly the violinist has no right against you that *you* shall allow him to continue to use your kidneys. As I said, if you do allow him to use them, it is a kindness on your part, and not something you owe him.

The difficulty I point to here is not peculiar to the right to life. It reappears in connection with all the other natural rights; and it is something which an adequate account of rights must deal with. For present purposes it is enough just to draw attention to it. But I would stress that I am not arguing that people do not have a right to life—quite to the contrary, it seems to me that the primary control we must place on the acceptability of an account of rights is that it should turn out in that account to be a truth that all persons have a right to life. I am arguing only that having a right to life does not guarantee having either a right to be given the use of or a right to be allowed continued use of another person's body—even if one needs it for life itself. So the right to life will not serve the opponents of abortion in the very simple and clear way in which they seem to have thought it would.

There is another way to bring out the difficulty. In the most ordinary sort of case, to deprive someone of what he has a right to is to treat him unjustly. Suppose a boy and his small brother are jointly given a box of chocolates for Christmas. If the older boy takes the box and refuses to give his brother any of the chocolates, he is unjust to him, for the brother has been given a right to half of them. But suppose that, having learned that otherwise it means nine years in bed with that violinist, you unplug yourself from him. You surely are not being unjust to him, for you gave him no right to use your kidneys, and no one else can have given him any such right. But we have to notice that in unplugging yourself, you are killing him; and violinists, like everybody else, have a right to life, and thus in the view we were considering just now, the right not to be killed. So here you do what he supposedly has a right you shall not do, but you do not act unjustly to him in doing it.

The emendation which may be made at this point is this: the right to life consists not in the right not to be killed, but rather in the right not to be killed unjustly. This runs a risk of circularity, but never mind: it would enable us to square the fact that the violinist has a right to life with the fact that you do not act unjustly toward him in unplugging yourself, thereby killing him. For if you do not kill him unjustly, you do not violate his right to life, and so it is no wonder you do him no injustice.

But if this emendation is accepted, the gap in the argument against abortion stares us plainly in the face: it is by no means enough to show that the fetus is a person, and to remind us that all persons have a right to life—we need to be shown also that killing the fetus violates its right to life, i.e., that abortion is unjust killing. And is it?

I suppose we may take it as a datum that in a case of pregnancy due to rape the mother has not given the unborn person a right to the use of her body for food and shelter. Indeed, in what pregnancy could it be supposed that the mother has given the unborn person such a right? It is not as if there were unborn persons drifting about the world, to whom a woman who wants a child says "I invite you in."

But it might be argued that there are other ways one can have acquired a right to the use of another person's body than by having been invited to use it by that person. Suppose a woman voluntarily indulges in intercourse, knowing of the chance it will issue in pregnancy, and then she does become pregnant; is she not in part responsible for the presence, in fact the very existence, of the unborn person inside her? No doubt she did not invite it in. But doesn't her partial responsibility for its being there itself give it a right to the use of her body? If so, then her aborting it would be more like the boy's taking away the chocolates, and less like your unplugging yourself from the violinist—doing so would be depriving it of what it does have a right to, and thus would be doing it an injustice.

And then, too, it might be asked whether or not she can kill it even to save her own life: If she voluntarily called it into existence, how can she now kill it, even in self-defense?

The first thing to be said about this is that it is something new. Opponents of abortion have been so concerned to make out the independence of the fetus, in order to establish that it has a right to life, just as its mother does, that they have tended to overlook the possible support they might gain from making out that the fetus is *dependent* on the mother, in order to establish that she has a special kind of responsibility for it, a responsibility that gives it rights against her which are not possessed by any independent person—such as an ailing violinist who is a stranger to her.

On the other hand, this argument would give the unborn person a right to its mother's body only if her pregnancy resulted from a voluntary act, undertaken in full knowledge of the chance a pregnancy might result from it. It would leave out entirely the unborn person whose existence is due to rape. Pending the availability of some further argument, then, we would be left with the conclusion that unborn persons whose existence is due to rape have no right to the use of their mothers' bodies, and thus that aborting them is not depriving them of anything they have a right to and hence is not unjust killing.

And we should also notice that it is not at all plain that this argument really does go even as far as it purports to. For there are cases and cases, and the details make a difference. If the room is stuffy, and I therefore open a window to air it, and a burglar climbs in, it would be absurd to say, "Ah, now he can stay, she's given him a right to the use of her house—for she is partially responsible for his presence there, having voluntarily done what enabled him to get in, in full knowledge that there are such things as burglars, and that burglars burgle." It would be still more absurd to say this if I had had bars installed outside my windows, precisely to prevent burglars from getting in, and a burglar got in only because of a defect in the bars. It remains equally absurd if we imagine it is not a burglar who climbs in, but an innocent person who blunders or falls in. Again, suppose it were like this: people-seeds drift about in the air like pollen, and if you open your windows, one may drift in and take root in your carpets or upholstery. You don't want children, so you fix up your windows with fine mesh screens, the very best you can buy. As can happen, however, and on very, very rare occasions does happen, one of the screens is defective; and a seed drifts in and takes root. Does the person-plant who now develops have a right to the use of your house? Surely not— despite the fact that you voluntarily opened your windows, you knowingly kept carpets and upholstered furniture, and you knew that screens were sometimes defective. Someone may argue that you are responsible for its rooting, that it does have a right to your house, because after all you *could* have lived out your life with bare floors and furniture, or with sealed windows and doors. But this won't do— for by the same token anyone can avoid a pregnancy due to rape by having a hysterectomy, or anyway by never leaving home without a (reliable!) army.

It seems to me that the argument we are looking at can establish at most that there are *some* cases in which the unborn person has a right to the use of its mother's body, and therefore *some* cases in which abortion is unjust killing. There is room for much

discussion and argument as to precisely which, if any. But I think we should side-step this issue and leave it open, for at any rate the argument certainly does not establish that all abortion is unjust killing.

There is room for yet another argument here, however. We surely must all grant that there may be cases in which it would be morally indecent to detach a person from your body at the cost of his life. Suppose you learn that what the violinist needs is not nine years of your life, but only one hour: all you need do to save his life is to spend one hour in that bed with him. Suppose also that letting him use your kidneys for that one hour would not affect your health in the slightest. Admittedly you were kidnapped. Admittedly you did not give anyone permission to plug him into you. Nevertheless it seems to me plain you *ought* to allow him to use your kidneys for that hour—it would be indecent to refuse.

Again, suppose pregnancy lasted only an hour, and constituted no threat to life or health. And suppose that a woman becomes pregnant as a result of rape. Admittedly she did not voluntarily do anything to bring about the existence of a child. Admittedly she did nothing at all which would give the unborn person a right to the use of her body. All the same it might well be said, as in the newly emended violinist story, that she *ought* to allow it to remain for that hour—that it would be indecent of her to refuse.

Now some people are inclined to use the term "right" in such a way that it follows from the fact that you ought to allow a person to use your body for the hour he needs, that he has a right to use your body for the hour he needs, even though he has not been given that right by any person or act. They may say that it follows also that if you refuse, you act unjustly toward him. This use of the term is perhaps so common that it cannot be called wrong; nevertheless it seems to me to be an unfortunate loosening of what we would do better to keep a tight rein on. Suppose that box of chocolates I mentioned earlier had not been given to both boys jointly, but was given only to the older boy. There he sits, stolidly eating his way through the box, his small brother watching enviously. Here we are likely to say "You ought not to be so mean. You ought to give your brother some of those chocolates." My own view is that it just does not follow from the truth of this that the brother has any right to any of the chocolates. If the boy refuses to give his brother any, he is greedy, stingy, callous—but not unjust. I suppose that the people I have in mind will say it does follow that the brother has a right to some of the chocolates, and thus that the boy does act unjustly if he refuses to give his brother any. But the effect of saying this is to obscure what we should keep distinct, namely the difference between the boy's refusal in this case and the boy's refusal in the earlier case, in which the box was given to both boys jointly, and in which the small brother thus had what was from any point of view clear title to half.

A further objection to so using the term "right" that from the fact that A ought to do a thing for B, it follows that B has a right against A that A do it for him, is that it is going to make the question of whether or not a man has a right to a thing turn on how easy it is to provide him with it; and this seems not merely unfortunate, but morally unacceptable. Take the case of Henry Fonda again. I said earlier that I had no right to the touch of his cool hand on my fevered brow, even though I needed it to save my life. I said it would be frightfully nice of him to fly in from the West Coast to provide me with it, but that I had no right against him that he should do so. But suppose he isn't on the West Coast. Suppose he has only to walk across the room, place a hand briefly on my brow—and lo, my life is saved. Then surely he ought to do it, it would be indecent to refuse. Is it to be said "Ah, well, it follows that in this case she has a right to the touch of his hand on her brow, and so it would be an injustice in him to refuse"? So that I have a right to it when it is easy for him to provide it, though no right when it's hard? It's rather a shocking idea that anyone's rights should fade away and disappear as it gets harder and harder to accord them to him.

So my own view is that even though you ought to let the violinist use your kidneys for the one hour he needs, we should not conclude that he has a right to do so—we should say that if you refuse, you are, like the boy who owns all the chocolates and will give none away, self-centered and callous, indecent in fact, but not unjust. And similarly, that even

supposing a case in which a woman pregnant due to rape ought to allow the unborn person to use her body for the hour he needs, we should not conclude that he has a right to do so; we should conclude that she is self-centered, callous, indecent, but not unjust, if she refuses. The complaints are no less grave; they are just different. However, there is no need to insist on this point. If anyone does wish to deduce "he has a right" from "you ought," then all the same he must surely grant that there are cases in which it is not morally required of you that you allow that violinist to use your kidneys, and in which he does not have a right to use them, and in which you do not do him an injustice if you refuse. And so also for mother and unborn child. Except in such cases as the unborn person has a right to demand it—and we were leaving open the possibility that there may be such cases—nobody is morally *required* to make large sacrifices, of health, of all other interests and concerns, of all other duties and commitments, for nine years, or even for nine months, in order to keep another person alive.

We have in fact to distinguish between two kinds of Samaritan: the Good Samaritan and what we might call the Minimally Decent Samaritan. The story of the Good Samaritan, you will remember, goes like this:

> A certain man went down from Jerusalem to Jericho, and fell among thieves, which stripped him of his raiment, and wounded him, and departed, leaving him half dead.
>
> And by chance there came down a certain priest that way; and when he saw him, he passed by on the other side.
>
> And likewise a Levite, when he was at the place, came and looked on him, and passed by on the other side.
>
> But a certain Samaritan, as he journeyed, came where he was; and when he saw him he had compassion on him.
>
> And went to him, and bound up his wounds, pouring in oil and wine, and set him on his own beast, and brought him to an inn, and took care of him.
>
> And on the morrow, when he departed, he took out two pence, and gave them to the host, and said unto him, "Take care of him; and whatsoever thou spendest more, when I come again, I will repay thee."
>
> (Luke 10:30–35)

The Good Samaritan went out of his way, at some cost to himself, to help one in need of it. We are not told what the options were, that is, whether or not the priest and the Levite could have helped by doing less than the Good Samaritan did, but assuming they could have, then the fact they did nothing at all shows they were not even Minimally Decent Samaritans, not because they were not Samaritans, but because they were not even minimally decent.

These things are a matter of degree, of course, but there is a difference, and it comes out perhaps most clearly in the story of Kitty Genovese, who, as you will remember, was murdered while thirty-eight people watched or listened, and did nothing at all to help her. A Good Samaritan would have rushed out to give direct assistance against the murderer. Or perhaps we had better allow that it would have been a Splendid Samaritan who did this, on the ground that it would have involved a risk of death for himself. But the thirty-eight not only did not do this, they did not even trouble to pick up a phone to call the police. Minimally Decent Samaritanism would call for doing at least that, and their not having done it was monstrous.

After telling the story of the Good Samaritan, Jesus said "Go, and do thou likewise." Perhaps he meant that we are morally required to act as the Good Samaritan did. Perhaps he was urging people to do more than is morally required of them. At all events it seems plain that it was not morally required of any of the thirty-eight that he rush out to give direct assistance at the risk of his own life, and that it is not morally required of anyone that he give long stretches of his life—nine years or nine months—to sustaining the life of a person who has no special right (we were leaving open the possibility of this) to demand it.

Indeed, with one rather striking class of exceptions, no one in any country in the world is *legally* required to do anywhere near as much as this for anyone else. The class of exceptions is obvious. My main concern here is not the state of the law in respect to abortion, but it is worth drawing attention to the fact that in no state in this country is any man compelled by law to be even a Minimally Decent Samaritan to any person; there is no law under which charges could be brought against the thirty-eight who stood by while Kitty Genovese died. By contrast, in most states in this country women are compelled by law to be not merely Minimally Decent Samaritans, but Good Samaritans to unborn persons inside them. This doesn't by itself settle anything one way or the other, because it may well be argued that there should be laws in this country—as there are in many European countries—compelling at least Minimally Decent Samaritanism.[2] But it does show that there is a gross injustice in the existing state of the law. And it shows also that the groups currently working against liberalization of abortion laws, in fact working toward having it declared unconstitutional for a state to permit abortion, had better start working for the adoption of Good Samaritan laws generally, or earn the charge that they are acting in bad faith.

I should think, myself, that Minimally Decent Samaritan laws would be one thing, Good Samaritan laws quite another, and in fact highly improper. But we are not here concerned with the law. What we should ask is not whether anybody should be compelled by law to be a Good Samaritan, but whether we must accede to a situation in which somebody is being compelled—by nature, perhaps—to be a Good Samaritan. We have, in other words, to look now at third-party interventions. I have been arguing that no person is morally required to make large sacrifices to sustain the life of another who has no right to demand them, and this even where the sacrifices do not include life itself; we are not morally required to be Good Samaritans or anyway Very Good Samaritans to one another. But what if a man cannot extricate himself from such a situation? What if he appeals to us to extricate him? It seems to me plain that there are cases in which we can, cases in which a Good Samaritan would extricate him. There you are, you were kidnapped, and nine years in bed with that violinist lie ahead of you. You have your own life to lead. You are sorry, but you simply cannot see giving up so much of your life to the sustaining of his. You cannot extricate yourself, and ask us to do so. I should have thought that—in light of his having no right to the use of your body—it was obvious that we do not have to accede to your being forced to give up so much. We can do what you ask. There is no injustice to the violinist in our doing so.

Following the lead of the opponents of abortion, I have throughout been speaking of the fetus merely as a person, and what I have been asking is whether or not the argument we began with, which proceeds only from the fetus' being a person, really does establish its conclusion. I have argued that it does not.

But of course there are arguments and arguments, and it may be said that I have simply fastened on the wrong one. It may be said that what is important is not merely the fact that the fetus is a person, but that it is a person for whom the woman has a special kind of responsibility issuing from the fact that she is its mother. And it might be argued that all my analogies are therefore irrelevant—for you do not have that special kind of responsibility for that violinist, Henry Fonda does not have that special kind of responsibility for me. And our attention might be drawn to the fact that men and women both *are* compelled by law to provide support for their children.

I have in effect dealt (briefly) with this argument above; but a (still briefer) recapitulation now may be in order. Surely we do not have any such "special responsibility" for a person unless we have assumed it, explicitly or implicitly. If a set of parents do not try to prevent pregnancy, do not obtain an abortion, and then at the time of birth of the child do not put it out for adoption, but rather take it home with them, then they have assumed responsibility for it, they have given it rights, and they cannot *now* withdraw support from it at the cost of its life because they now find it difficult to go on providing for it. But if they have taken all reasonable precautions against having a child, they do not simply by virtue of their biological relationship to the child who comes into existence have a special responsibility for it. They may wish to assume responsibility for it, or they may not wish to. And I am suggesting that if assuming responsibility for it would require large sacrifices, then they may refuse. A Good Samaritan would not refuse—or anyway, a Splendid Samaritan, if the sacrifices that had to be made were enormous. But then so would a Good Samaritan assume responsibility for that violinist; so would Henry Fonda, if he is a Good Samaritan, fly in from the West Coast and assume responsibility for me.

My argument will be found unsatisfactory on two counts by many of those who want to regard abortion as morally permissible. First, while I do argue that abortion is not impermissible, I do not argue that it is always permissible. There may well be cases in which carrying the child to term requires only Minimally Decent Samaritanism of the mother, and this is a standard we must not fall below. I am inclined to think it a merit of my account precisely that it does *not* give a general yes or a general no. It allows for and supports our sense that, for example, a sick and desperately frightened fourteen-year-old schoolgirl, pregnant due to rape, may of *course* choose abortion, and that any law which rules this out is an insane law. And it also allows for and supports our sense that in other cases resort to abortion is even positively indecent. It would be indecent in the woman to request an abortion, and indecent in a doctor to perform it, if she is in her seventh month, and wants the abortion just to avoid the nuisance of postponing a trip abroad. The very fact that the arguments I have been drawing attention to treat all cases of abortion, or even all cases of abortion in which the mother's life is not at stake, as morally on a par ought to have made them suspect at the outset.

Secondly, while I am arguing for the permissibility of abortion in some cases, I am not arguing for the right to secure the death of the unborn child. It is easy to confuse these two things in that up to a certain point in the life of the fetus it is not able to survive outside the mother's body; hence removing it from her body guarantees its death. But they are importantly different. I have argued that you are not morally required to spend nine months in bed, sustaining the life of that violinist; but to say this is by no means to say that if, when you unplug yourself, there is a miracle and he survives, you then have a right to turn round and slit his throat. You may detach yourself even if this costs him his life; you have no right to be guaranteed his death, by some other means, if unplugging yourself does not kill him. There are some people who will feel dissatisfied by this feature of my argument. A woman may be utterly devastated by the thought of a child, a bit of herself, put out for adoption and never seen or heard of again. She may therefore want not merely that the child be detached from her, but more, that it die. Some opponents of abortion are inclined to regard this as beneath contempt—thereby showing insensitivity to what is surely a powerful source of despair. All the same, I agree that the desire for the child's death is not one which anybody may gratify, should it turn out to be possible to detach the child alive.

At this place, however, it should be remembered that we have only been pretending throughout that the fetus is a human being from the moment of conception. A very early abortion is surely not the killing of a person, and so is not dealt with by anything I have said here.

NOTES

I am very much indebted to James Thomson for discussion, criticism, and many helpful suggestions.

1. Daniel Callahan, *Abortion: Law, Choice and Morality* (New York, 1970), p. 373. This book gives a fascinating survey of the available information on abortion. The Jewish tradition is surveyed in David M. Feldman, *Birth Control in Jewish Law* (New York, 1968), Part 5, the Catholic tradition in John T. Noonan, Jr., "An Almost Absolute Value in History," in *The Morality of Abortion,* ed. John T. Noonan, Jr. (Cambridge, Mass., 1970).

2. For a discussion of the difficulties involved, and a survey of the European experience with such laws, see *The Good Samaritan and the Law,* ed. James M. Ratcliffe (New York, 1966).

READING QUESTIONS

1. What is the main point Thomson makes with her "famous violinist" example?
2. How does Thomson propose to understand the right to life?
3. What is Thomson's response to the following argument? If a woman engages in voluntarily sexual intercourse with the knowledge that she might become pregnant as a result, then if she does become pregnant, she has in effect given over the use of her body to the fetus and so the fetus has a right to the use of her body. But since (in such circumstances) the fetus has a right to the use of her body in order to survive, having an abortion would be morally wrong.
4. Consider this claim: If you ought to give another person something A, then that other person has a right against you that you give him or her A. How would Thomson respond to this claim? (Focus on what Thomson says about the box of chocolates and the Henry Fonda examples.)
5. In cases of pregnancy, what (according to Thomson) would constitute being a Good Samaritan? What would constitute being a Minimally Decent Samaritan?

DISCUSSION QUESTION

1. How (if at all) does Thomson's view address cases in which a woman becomes pregnant despite the fact that although she used reliable birth control methods, they failed to prevent her pregnancy through no fault of hers?

PATRICK LEE AND ROBERT P. GEORGE

The Wrong of Abortion

Patrick Lee and Robert George argue that at all stages of pregnancy (from conception on) one should view the developing fetus as a human being with a right to life (a person) even though, during gestation, it is in its early stages of development. After defending their view in the first section of the article, the authors go on to consider various objections, including arguments that deny that the fetus is a person. Other counterarguments, which appeal to the doctrine of double effect, are based on the assertion that some abortions are foreseen but are morally permissible because the killings are non-intentional.

Recommended Reading: the discussion of the doctrine of double effect in chap. 1, sec. 2B, which is relevant to the authors' discussion of arguments concerning abortion as justified non-intentional killing.

Much of the public debate about abortion concerns the question whether deliberate feticide ought to be unlawful, at least in most circumstances. We will lay that question aside here in order to focus first on the question: is the choice to have, to perform, or to help procure an abortion morally wrong?

We shall argue that the choice of abortion is objectively immoral. By "objectively" we indicate that we are discussing the choice itself, not the (subjective) guilt or innocence of someone who carries out the choice: someone may act from an erroneous conscience, and if he is not at fault for his error, then he remains subjectively innocent, even if his choice is objectively wrongful.

The first important question to consider is: what is killed in an abortion? It is obvious that some living entity is killed in an abortion. And no one doubts that the moral status of the entity killed is a central (though not the only) question in the abortion debate. We shall approach the issue step by step, first setting forth some (though not all) of the evidence that demonstrates that what is killed in abortion—a human embryo—is indeed a human being, then examining the ethical significance of that point.

HUMAN EMBRYOS AND FETUSES ARE COMPLETE (THOUGH IMMATURE) HUMAN BEINGS

It will be useful to begin by considering some of the facts of sexual reproduction. The standard embryology texts indicate that in the case of ordinary sexual reproduction the life of an individual human being begins with complete fertilization, which yields a genetically and functionally distinct organism, possessing the resources and active disposition for internally directed development toward human maturity.[1] In normal conception, a sex cell of the father, a sperm, unites with a sex cell of the mother, an ovum. Within the chromosomes of these sex cells are the

From Patrick Lee and Robert P. George, "The Wrong of Abortion," in Andrew I. Cohen and Christopher Heath Wellman (eds.), *Contemporary Debates in Applied Ethics* (Blackwell Publishing Co., 2005).

DNA molecules which constitute the information that guides the development of the new individual brought into being when the sperm and ovum fuse. When fertilization occurs, the 23 chromosomes of the sperm unite with the 23 chromosomes of the ovum. At the end of this process there is produced an entirely new and distinct organism, originally a single cell. This organism, the human embryo, begins to grow by the normal process of cell division—it divides into 2 cells, then 4, 8, 16, and so on (the divisions are not simultaneous, so there is a 3-cell stage, and so on). This embryo gradually develops all of the organs and organ systems necessary for the full functioning of a mature human being. His or her development (sex is determined from the beginning) is very rapid in the first few weeks. For example, as early as eight or ten weeks of gestation, the fetus has a fully formed, beating heart, a complete brain (although not all of its synaptic connections are complete—nor will they be until sometime *after* the child is born), a recognizably human form, and the fetus feels pain, cries, and even sucks his or her thumb.

There are three important points we wish to make about this human embryo. First, it is from the start *distinct* from any cell of the mother or of the father. This is clear because it is growing in its own distinct direction. Its growth is internally directed to its own survival and maturation. Second, the embryo is *human:* it has the genetic makeup characteristic of human beings. Third, and most importantly, the embryo is a *complete* or *whole* organism, though immature. The human embryo, from conception onward, is fully programmed actively to develop himself or herself to the mature stage of a human being, and, *unless prevented by disease or violence, will actually do so, despite possibly significant variation in environment* (in the mother's womb). None of the changes that occur to the embryo after fertilization, for as long as he or she survives, generates a new direction of growth. Rather, *all* of the changes (for example, those involving nutrition and environment) either facilitate or retard the internally directed growth of this persisting individual.

Sometimes it is objected that if we say human embryos are human beings, on the grounds that they have the potential to become mature humans, the same will have to be said of sperm and ova. This objection is untenable. The human embryo is radically unlike the sperm and ova, the sex cells. The sex cells are manifestly not *whole* or *complete* organisms. They are not only genetically but also functionally identifiable as parts of the male or female potential parents. They clearly are destined either to combine with an ovum or sperm or die. Even when they succeed in causing fertilization, they do not survive; rather, their genetic material enters into the composition of a distinct, new organism.

Nor are human embryos comparable to somatic cells (such as skin cells or muscle cells), though some have tried to argue that they are. Like sex cells, a somatic cell is functionally only a part of a larger organism. The human embryo, by contrast, possesses from the beginning the internal resources and active disposition to develop himself or herself to full maturity; all he or she needs is a suitable environment and nutrition. The direction of his or her growth *is not extrinsically determined,* but the embryo is internally directing his or her growth toward full maturity.

So, a human embryo (or fetus) is not something distinct from a human being; he or she is not an individual of any non-human or intermediate species. Rather, an embryo (and fetus) is a human being at a certain (early) stage of development—the embryonic (or fetal) stage. In abortion, what is killed is a human being, a whole living member of the species *Homo sapiens,* the same *kind* of entity as you or I, only at an earlier stage of development.

NO-PERSON ARGUMENTS: THE DUALIST VERSION

Defenders of abortion may adopt different strategies to respond to these points. Most will grant that human embryos or fetuses are human beings. However, they then distinguish "human being" from "person" and claim that embryonic human beings are not (yet) *persons.* They hold that while it is wrong to kill persons, it is not always wrong to kill human beings who are not persons.

Sometimes it is argued that human beings in the embryonic stage are not persons because embryonic human beings do not exercise higher mental capacities or functions. Certain defenders of abortion (and infanticide) have argued that in order to be a person, an entity must be self-aware (Singer, 1993; Tooley, 1983; Warren, 1984). They then claim that, because human embryos and fetuses (and infants) have not yet developed self-awareness, they are not persons.

These defenders of abortion raise the question: Where does one draw the line between those who are subjects of rights and those that are not? A long tradition says that the line should be drawn at *persons*. But what is a person, if not an entity that has self-awareness, rationality, etc.?

This argument is based on a false premise. It implicitly identifies the human person with a consciousness which inhabits (or is somehow associated with) and uses a body; the truth, however, is that we human persons are particular kinds of physical organisms. The argument here under review grants that the human organism comes to be at conception, but claims nevertheless that you or I, the human person, comes to be only much later, say, when self-awareness develops. But if this human organism came to be at one time, but *I* came to be at a later time, it follows that I am one thing and this human organism with which *I* am associated is another thing.

But this is false. We are not consciousnesses that *possess or inhabit* bodies. Rather, we *are* living bodily entities. We can see this by examining the kinds of action that we perform. If a living thing performs bodily actions, then it is a physical organism. Now, those who wish to deny that we are physical organisms think of *themselves,* what each of them refers to as *"I,"* as the subject of self-conscious acts of conceptual thought and willing (what many philosophers, ourselves included, would say are nonphysical acts). But one can show that this "I" is identical to the subject of physical, bodily actions, and so is a living, bodily being (an organism). Sensation is a bodily action. The act of seeing, for example, is an act that an animal performs with his eyeballs and his optic nerve, just as the act of walking is an act that he

performs with his legs. But it is clear in the case of human individuals that it must be the same entity, the same single subject of actions, that performs the act of sensing and that performs the act of understanding. When I know, for example, that "That is a tree," it is by my understanding, or a self-conscious intellectual act, that I apprehend what is meant by "tree," apprehending what it is (at least in a general way). But the subject of that proposition, what I refer to by the word "That," is apprehended by sensation or perception. Clearly, it must be the same thing—the same I—which apprehends the predicate and the subject of a unitary judgment.

So, it is the same substantial entity, the same agent, which understands and which senses or perceives. And so what all agree is referred to by the word "I" (namely, the subject of conscious, intellectual acts) is identical with the physical organism which is the subject of bodily actions such as sensing or perceiving. Hence the entity that I am, and the entity that you are—what you and I refer to by the personal pronouns "you" and "I"—is in each case a human, physical organism (but also with nonphysical capacities). Therefore, since you and I are *essentially* physical organisms, *we* came to be when these physical organisms came to be. But, as shown above, the human organism comes to be at conception.[2] Thus you and I came to be at conception; we once were embryos, then fetuses, then infants, just as we were once toddlers, preadolescent children, adolescents, and young adults.

So, how should we use the word "person"? Are human embryos persons or not? People may stipulate different meanings for the word "person," but we think it is clear that what we normally mean by the word "person" is that substantial entity that is referred to by personal pronouns—"I," "you," "she," etc. It follows, we submit, that a person is a distinct subject with the natural capacity to reason and make free choices. That subject, in the case of human beings, is identical with the human organism, and therefore that subject comes to be when the human organism comes to be, even though it will take him or her months and even years to actualize the natural capacities to reason and make free choices, natural capacities which are already present (albeit in radical, i.e. root, form) from the beginning. So it makes no sense to say that the human organism came to be at one point but the person—you or I—came to be at some later point. To have destroyed the human organism that you are or I am even at an early stage of our lives would have been to have killed you or me.

NO-PERSON ARGUMENTS: THE EVALUATIVE VERSION

Let us now consider a different argument by which some defenders of abortion seek to deny that human beings in the embryonic and fetal stages are "persons" and, as such, ought not to be killed. Unlike the argument criticized in the previous section, this argument grants that the being who is you or I came to be at conception, but contends that you and I became valuable and bearers of rights only much later, when, for example, we developed the proximate, or immediately exercisable, capacity for self-consciousness. Inasmuch as those who advance this argument concede that you and I once were human embryos, they do not identify the self or the person with a non-physical phenomenon, such as consciousness. They claim, however, that being a person is an accidental attribute. It is an accidental attribute in the way that someone's being a musician or basketball player is an accidental attribute. Just as you come to be at one time, but become a musician or basketball player only much later, so, they say, you and I came to be when the physical organisms we are came to be, but we became persons (beings with a certain type of special value and bearers of basic rights) only at some time later (Dworkin, 1993; Thomson, 1995). Those defenders of abortion whose view we discussed in the previous section disagree with the pro-life position on an ontological issue, that is, on what *kind of entity* the human embryo or fetus is. Those who advance the argument now under review, by contrast, disagree with the pro-life position on an evaluative question.

Judith Thomson argued for this position by comparing the right to life with the right to vote: "If children are allowed to develop normally they will have a right to vote; that does not show that they now have a right to vote" (1995). According to this position, it is true that we once were embryos and fetuses, but in the embryonic and fetal stages of our lives we were not yet valuable in the special way that would qualify us as having a right to life. We acquired that special kind of value and the right to life that comes with it at some point after we came into existence.

We can begin to see the error in this view by considering Thomson's comparison of the right to life with the right to vote. Thomson fails to advert to the fact that some rights vary with respect to place, circumstances, maturity, ability, and other factors, while other rights do not. We recognize that one's right to life does not vary with place, as does one's right to vote. One may have the right to vote in Switzerland, but not in Mexico. Moreover, some rights and entitlements accrue to individuals only at certain times, or in certain places or situations, and others do not. But to have the right to life is to have *moral status at all*; to have the right to life, in other words, is to be the sort of entity that can have rights or entitlements to begin with. And so it is to be expected that *this* right would differ in some fundamental ways from other rights, such as a right to vote.

In particular, it is reasonable to suppose (and we give reasons for this in the next few paragraphs) that having moral status at all, as opposed to having a right to perform a specific action in a specific situation, follows from an entity's being the *type of thing* (or substantial entity) it is. And so, just as one's right to life does not come and go with one's location or situation, so it does not accrue to someone in virtue of an acquired (i.e., accidental) property, capacity, skill, or disposition. Rather, this right belongs to a human being at all times that he or she exists, not just during certain stages of his or her existence, or in certain circumstances, or in virtue of additional, accidental attributes.

Our position is that we human beings have the special kind of value that makes us subjects of rights in virtue of *what* we are, not in virtue of some attribute that we acquire some time after we have come to be. Obviously, defenders of abortion cannot maintain that the accidental attribute required to have the special kind of value we ascribe to "persons" (additional to being a human individual) is an *actual* behavior. They of course do not wish to exclude from personhood people who are asleep or in reversible comas. So, the additional attribute will have to be a capacity or potentiality of some sort.[3] Thus, they will have to concede that sleeping or reversibly comatose human beings will be persons because they have the potentiality or capacity for higher mental functions.

But human embryos and fetuses also possess, albeit in radical form, a capacity or potentiality for such mental functions; human beings possess this radical capacity in virtue of the kind of entity they are, and possess it by coming into being as that kind of entity (viz., a being with a rational nature). Human embryos and fetuses cannot of course *immediately* exercise these capacities. Still, they are related to these capacities differently from, say, how a canine or feline embryo is. They are the kind of being—a natural kind, members of a biological species—which, if not prevented by extrinsic causes, in due course develops by active self-development to the point at which capacities initially possessed in root form become immediately exercisable. (Of course, the capacities in question become immediately exercisable only some months or years after the child's birth.) Each human being comes into existence possessing the internal resources and active disposition to develop the immediately exercisable capacity for higher mental functions. Only the adverse effects on them of other causes will prevent this development.

So, we must distinguish two sorts of capacity or potentiality for higher mental functions that a substantial entity might possess: first, an immediately (or nearly immediately) exercisable capacity to engage in higher mental functions; second, a basic, natural capacity to develop oneself to the point where one does perform such actions. But on what basis can one require the first sort of potentiality – as do proponents of the position under review in this section – which is an accidental attribute, and not just the second? There are three decisive reasons against supposing that the first sort of potentiality is required to qualify an entity as a bearer of the right to life.

First, the developing human being does not reach a level of maturity at which he or she performs a type of mental act that other animals do not perform—even animals such as dogs and cats—until at least several months after birth. A six-week-old baby lacks the immediately (or nearly immediately) exercisable capacity to perform characteristically human mental functions. So, if full moral respect were due only to those who possess a nearly immediately exercisable capacity for characteristically human mental functions, it would follow that six-week-old infants do not deserve full moral respect. If abortion were morally acceptable on the grounds that the human embryo or fetus lacks such a capacity for characteristically human mental functions, then one would be logically committed to the view that, subject to parental approval, human infants could be disposed of as well.

Second, the difference between these two types of capacity is merely a difference between stages along a continuum. The proximate or nearly immediately exercisable capacity for mental functions is only the development of an underlying potentiality that the human being possesses simply by virtue of the kind of entity it is. The capacities for reasoning, deliberating, and making choices are gradually developed, or brought towards maturation, through gestation, childhood, adolescence, and so on. But the difference between a being that deserves full moral respect and a being that does not (and can therefore legitimately be disposed of as a means of benefiting others) cannot consist only in the fact that, while both have some feature, one has more of it than the other. A mere *quantitative* difference (having more or less of the same feature, such as *the development* of a basic natural capacity) cannot by itself be a justificatory basis for treating different entities in *radically* different ways. Between the ovum and the approaching thousands of sperm, on the one hand, and the embryonic human being, on the other hand, there *is* a clear difference in kind. But between the embryonic human being and that same human being at any later stage of its maturation, there is only a difference in degree.

Note that there *is* a fundamental difference (as we showed above) between the gametes (the sperm and the ovum), on the one hand, and the human embryo and fetus, on the other. When a human being comes to be, a substantial entity that is identical with the entity that will later reason, make free choices, and so on, begins to exist. So, those who propose an accidental characteristic as qualifying an entity as a bearer of the right to life (or as a "person" or being with "moral worth") are *ignoring* a radical difference among groups of beings, and instead fastening onto a mere quantitative difference as the basis for treating different groups in radically different ways. In other words, there are beings a, b, c, d, e, etc. And between a's and b's on the one hand and c's, d's and e's on the other hand, there is a *fundamental difference,* a difference in kind not just in degree. But proponents of the position that being a person is an accidental characteristic ignore that difference and pick out a mere difference in degree between, say, d's and e's, and make that the basis for radically different types of treatment. That violates the most basic canons of justice.

Third, being a whole human being (whether immature or not) is an either/or matter – a thing either is or is not a whole human being. But the acquired qualities that could be proposed as criteria for personhood come in varying and continuous degrees: there is an infinite number of degrees of the *development of* the basic natural capacities for self-consciousness, intelligence, or rationality. So, if human beings were worthy of full moral respect (as subjects of rights) only because of such qualities, and not in virtue of the kind of being they are, then, since such qualities come in varying degrees, no account could be given of why basic rights are not possessed by human beings in varying degrees. The proposition that all human beings are created equal would be relegated to the status of a superstition. For example, if developed self-consciousness bestowed rights, then, since some people are more self-conscious than others (that is, have developed that capacity to a greater extent than others), some people would be greater in dignity than others, and the rights of the superiors would trump those of the inferiors where the interests of the superiors could be advanced at the cost of the inferiors. This conclusion would follow no matter which of the acquired qualities generally proposed as qualifying some human beings (or human beings at some stages) for full respect were selected. Clearly, developed self-consciousness, or desires, or so on,

are arbitrarily selected degrees of development of capacities that all human beings possess in (at least) radical form from the coming into existence of the human being until his or her death. So, it cannot be the case that some human beings and not others possess the special kind of value that qualifies an entity as having a basic right to life, by virtue of a certain degree of development. Rather, human beings possess that kind of value, and therefore that right, in virtue of what (i.e., the kind of being) they are; and *all* human beings—not just some, and certainly not just those who have advanced sufficiently along the developmental path as to be able immediately (or almost immediately) to exercise their capacities for characteristically human mental functions—possess that kind of value and that right.[4]

Since human beings are valuable in the way that qualifies them as having a right to life in virtue of what they are, it follows that they have that right, whatever it entails, from the point at which they come into being—and that point (as shown in our first section) is at conception.

In sum, human beings are valuable (as subjects of rights) in virtue of what they are. But what they are are human physical organisms. Human physical organisms come to be at conception. Therefore, what is intrinsically valuable (as a subject of rights) comes to be at conception.

THE ARGUMENT THAT ABORTION IS JUSTIFIED AS NON-INTENTIONAL KILLING

Some "pro-choice" philosophers have attempted to justify abortion by denying that all abortions are intentional killing. They have granted (at least for the sake of argument) that an unborn human being has a right to life but have then argued that this right does not entail that the child *in utero* is morally entitled to the use of the mother's body for life support. In effect, their argument is that, at least in many cases, abortion is not a case of intentionally killing the child, but a choice not to provide the child with assistance, that is, a choice to expel (or "evict") the child from the womb, despite the likelihood or certainty that expulsion (or "eviction") will result in his or her death (Little, 1999; McDonagh, 1996; Thomson, 1971).

Various analogies have been proposed by people making this argument. The mother's gestating a child has been compared to allowing someone the use of one's kidneys or even to donating an organ. We are not *required* (morally or as a matter of law) to allow someone to use our kidneys, or to donate organs to others, even when they would die without this assistance (and we could survive in good health despite rendering it). Analogously, the argument continues, a woman is not morally required to allow the fetus the use of her body. We shall call this "the bodily rights argument."

It may be objected that a woman has a special responsibility to the child she is carrying, whereas in the cases of withholding assistance to which abortion is compared there is no such special responsibility. Proponents of the bodily rights argument have replied, however, that the mother has not voluntarily assumed responsibility for the child, or a personal relationship with the child, and we have strong responsibilities to others only if we have voluntarily assumed such responsibilities (Thomson, 1971) or have consented to a personal relationship which generates such responsibilities (Little, 1999). True, the mother may have voluntarily performed an act which she knew may result in a child's conception, but that is distinct from consenting to gestate the child if a child is conceived. And so (according to this position) it is not until the woman consents to pregnancy, or perhaps not until the parents consent to care for the child by taking the baby home from the hospital or birthing center, that the full duties of parenthood accrue to the mother (and perhaps the father).

In reply to this argument we wish to make several points. We grant that in some few cases abortion is not intentional killing, but a choice to expel the child, the child's death being an unintended, albeit foreseen and (rightly or wrongly) accepted, side effect. However, these constitute a small minority of abortions. In the vast majority of cases, the death of the child *in utero* is precisely the object of the abortion.

In most cases the end sought is to avoid being a parent; but abortion brings that about only by bringing it about that the child dies. Indeed, the attempted abortion would be considered by the woman requesting it and the abortionist performing it to have been *unsuccessful* if the child survives. In most cases abortion *is* intentional killing. Thus, even if the bodily rights argument succeeded, it would justify only a small percentage of abortions.

Still, in some few cases abortion is chosen as a means precisely toward ending the condition of pregnancy, and the woman requesting the termination of her pregnancy would not object if somehow the child survived. A pregnant woman may have less or more serious reasons for seeking the termination of this condition, but if that is her objective, then the child's death resulting from his or her expulsion will be a side effect, rather than the means chosen. For example, an actress may wish not to be pregnant because the pregnancy will change her figure during a time in which she is filming scenes in which having a slender appearance is important; or a woman may dread the discomforts, pains, and difficulties involved in pregnancy. (Of course, in many abortions there may be mixed motives: the parties making the choice may intend both ending the condition of pregnancy and the death of the child.)

Nevertheless, while it is true that in some cases abortion is not intentional killing, it remains misleading to describe it simply as choosing not to provide bodily life support. Rather, it is actively expelling the human embryo or fetus from the womb. There is a significant moral difference between *not doing* something that would assist someone, and *doing* something that causes someone harm, even if that harm is an unintended (but foreseen) side effect. It is more difficult morally to justify the latter than it is the former. Abortion is the *act* of extracting the unborn human being from the womb—an extraction that usually rips him or her to pieces or does him or her violence in some other way.

It is true that in some cases causing death as a side effect is morally permissible. For example, in some cases it is morally right to use force to stop a potentially lethal attack on one's family or country, even if one foresees that the force used will also result in the assailant's death. Similarly, there are instances in which it is permissible to perform an act that one knows or believes will, as a side effect, cause the death of a child *in utero*. For example, if a pregnant woman is discovered to have a cancerous uterus, and this is a proximate danger to the mother's life, it can be morally right to remove the cancerous uterus with the baby in it, even if the child will die as a result. A similar situation can occur in ectopic pregnancies. But in such cases, not only is the child's death a side effect, but the mother's life is in proximate danger. It is worth noting also that in these cases *what is done* (the means) is the correction of a pathology (such as a cancerous uterus, or a ruptured uterine tube). Thus, in such cases, not only the child's death, but also the ending of the pregnancy, are side effects. So, such acts are what traditional casuistry referred to as *indirect* or *non-intentional,* abortions.

But it is also clear that not every case of causing death as a side effect is morally right. For example, if a man's daughter has a serious respiratory disease and the father is told that his continued smoking in her presence will cause her death, it would obviously be immoral for him to continue the smoking. Similarly, if a man works for a steel company in a city with significant levels of air pollution, and his child has a serious respiratory problem making the air pollution a danger to her life, certainly he should move to another city. He should move, we would say, even if that meant he had to resign a prestigious position or make a significant career change.

In both examples, (a) the parent has a special responsibility to his child, but (b) the act that would cause the child's death would avoid a harm to the parent but cause a significantly worse harm to his child. And so, although the harm done would be a side effect, in both cases the act that caused the death would be an *unjust* act, and morally wrongful *as such*. The special responsibility of parents to their children requires that they *at least* refrain from performing acts that cause terrible harms to their children in order to avoid significantly lesser harms to themselves.

But (a) and (b) also obtain in intentional abortions (that is, those in which the removal of the child is directly sought, rather than the correction of a life-threatening pathology) even though they are not, strictly speaking, intentional killing. First, the mother has a special responsibility to her child, in virtue of being her biological mother (as does the father in virtue of his paternal relationship). The parental relationship itself—not just the voluntary acceptance of that relationship—gives rise to a special responsibility to a child.

Proponents of the bodily rights argument deny this point. Many claim that one has full parental responsibilities only if one has voluntarily assumed them. And so the child, on this view, has a right to care from his or her mother (including gestation) only if the mother has accepted her pregnancy, or perhaps only if the mother (and/or the father?) has in some way voluntarily begun a deep personal relationship with the child (Little, 1999).

But suppose a mother takes her baby home after giving birth, but the only reason she did not get an abortion was that she could not afford one. Or suppose she lives in a society where abortion is not available (perhaps very few physicians are willing to do the grisly deed). She and her husband take the child home only because they had no alternative. Moreover, suppose that in their society people are not waiting in line to adopt a newborn baby. And so the baby is several days old before anything can be done. If they abandon the baby and the baby is found, she will simply be returned to them. In such a case the parents have not voluntarily assumed responsibility; nor have they consented to a personal relationship with the child. But it would surely be wrong for these parents to abandon their baby in the woods (perhaps the only feasible way of ensuring she is not returned), even though the baby's death would be only a side effect. Clearly, we recognize that parents do have a responsibility to make sacrifices for their children, even if they have not voluntary assumed such responsibilities, or given their consent to the personal relationship with the child.

The bodily rights argument implicitly supposes that we have a primordial right to construct a life simply as we please, and that others have claims on us only very minimally or through our (at least tacit) consent to a certain sort of relationship with them. On the contrary, we are by nature members of communities. Our moral goodness or character consists to a large extent (though not solely) in contributing to the communities of which we are members. We ought to act for our genuine good or flourishing (we take that as a basic ethical principle), but our flourishing involves being in communion with others. And communion with others of itself—even if we find ourselves united with others because of a physical or social relationship which precedes our consent—entails duties or responsibilities. Moreover, the contribution we are morally required to make to others will likely bring each of us some discomfort and pain. This is not to say that we should simply ignore our own good, for the sake of others. Rather, since what (and who) I am is in part constituted by various relationships with others, not all of which are initiated by my will, my genuine good includes the contributions I make to the relationships in which I participate. Thus, the life we constitute by our free choices should be in large part a life of mutual reciprocity with others.

For example, I may wish to cultivate my talent to write and so I may want to spend hours each day reading and writing. Or I may wish to develop my athletic abilities and so I may want to spend hours every day on the baseball field. But if I am a father of minor children, and have an adequate paying job working (say) in a coal mine, then my clear duty is to keep that job. Similarly, if one's girlfriend finds she is pregnant and one is the father, then one might also be morally required to continue one's work in the mine (or mill, factory, warehouse, etc.).

In other words, I have a duty to do something with my life that contributes to the good of the human community, but that general duty becomes specified by my particular situation. It becomes specified by the connection or closeness to me of those who are in need. We acquire special responsibilities toward people, not only by *consenting* to contracts or relationships with them, but also by having various types of union with them. So, we have special responsibilities to those people with whom we are closely united. For example, we have special responsibilities to our parents, and brothers and sisters, even though we did not choose them.

The physical unity or continuity of children to their parents is unique. The child is brought into being out of the bodily unity and bodies of the mother and the father. The mother and the father are in a certain

sense prolonged or continued in their off-spring. So, there is a natural unity of the mother with her child, and a natural unity of the father with his child. Since we have special responsibilities to those with whom we are closely united, it follows that we in fact do have a special responsibility to our children anterior to our having voluntarily assumed such responsibility or consented to the relationship.[5]

The second point is this: in the types of case we are considering, the harm caused (death) is much worse than the harms avoided (the difficulties in pregnancy). Pregnancy can involve severe impositions, but it is not nearly as bad as death—which is total and irreversible. One needn't make light of the burdens of pregnancy to acknowledge that the harm that is death is in a different category altogether.

The burdens of pregnancy include physical difficulties and the pain of labor, and can include significant financial costs, psychological burdens, and interference with autonomy and the pursuit of other important goals (McDonagh, 1996: ch. 5). These costs are not inconsiderable. Partly for that reason, we owe our mothers gratitude for carrying and giving birth to us. However, where pregnancy does not place a woman's life in jeopardy or threaten grave and lasting damage to her physical health, the harm done to other goods is not total. Moreover, most of the harms involved in pregnancy are not irreversible: pregnancy is a nine-month task—if the woman and man are not in a good position to raise the child, adoption is a possibility. So the difficulties of pregnancy, considered together, are in a different and lesser category than death. Death is not just worse in degree than the difficulties involved in pregnancy; it is worse in kind.

It has been argued, however, that pregnancy can involve a unique type of burden. It has been argued that the *intimacy* involved in pregnancy is such that if the woman must remain pregnant without her consent then there is inflicted on her a unique and serious harm. Just as sex with consent can be a desired experience but sex without consent is a violation of bodily integrity, so (the argument continues) pregnancy involves such a close physical intertwinement with the fetus that not to allow abortion is analogous to rape—it involves an enforced intimacy (Boonin, 2003: 84; Little, 1999: 300–3).

However, this argument is based on a false analogy. Where the pregnancy is unwanted, the baby's "occupying" the mother's womb may involve a harm; but the child is committing no injustice against her. The baby is not forcing himself or herself on the woman, but is simply growing and developing in a way quite natural to him or her. The baby is not performing any action that could in any way be construed as aimed at violating the mother.[6]

It is true that the fulfillment of the duty of a mother to her child (during gestation) is unique and in many cases does involve a great sacrifice. The argument we have presented, however, is that being a mother *does* generate a special responsibility, and that the sacrifice morally required of the mother is less burdensome than the harm that would be done to the child by expelling the child, causing his or her death, to escape that responsibility. Our argument equally entails responsibilities for the father of the child. His duty does not involve as direct a bodily relationship with the child as the mother's, but it may be equally or even more burdensome. In certain circumstances, his obligation to care for the child (and the child's mother), and especially his obligation to provide financial support, may severely limit his freedom and even require months or, indeed, years of extremely burdensome physical labor. Historically, many men have rightly seen that their basic responsibility to their family (and country) has entailed risking, and in many cases, losing, their lives. Different people in different circumstances, with different talents, will have different responsibilities. It is no argument against any of these responsibilities to point out their distinctness.

So, the burden of carrying the baby, for all its distinctness, is significantly less than the harm the baby would suffer by being killed; the mother and father have a special responsibility to the child; it follows that intentional abortion (even in the few cases where the baby's death is an unintended but foreseen side effect) is unjust and therefore objectively immoral.

NOTES

1. See, for example: Carlson (1994: chs. 2–4); Gilbert (2003: 183–220, 363–90); Larson (2001: chs. 1–2); Moore and Persaud (2003: chs. 1–6); Muller (1997: chs. 1–2); O'Rahilly and Mueller (2000: chs. 3–4).

2. For a discussion of the issues raised by twinning and cloning, see George and Lobo (2002).

3. Some defenders of abortion have seen the damaging implications of this point for their position (Stretton, 2004), and have struggled to find a way around it. There are two leading proposals. The first is to suggest a mean between a capacity and an actual behavior, such as a disposition. But a disposition is just the development or specification of a capacity and so raises the unanswerable question of why just that much development, and not more or less, should be required. The second proposal is to assert that the historical fact of someone having exercised a capacity (say, for conceptual thought) confers on her a right to life even if she does not now have the immediately exercisable capacity. But suppose we have baby Susan who has developed a brain and gained sufficient experience to the point that just now she has the immediately exercisable capacity for conceptual thought, but she has not yet exercised it. Why should she be in a wholly different category than say, baby Mary, who is just like Susan except she did actually have a conceptual thought? Neither proposal can bear the moral weight assigned to it. Both offer criteria that are wholly arbitrary.

4. In arguing against an article by Lee, Dean Stretton claims that the basic natural capacity of rationality also comes in degrees, and that therefore the argument we are presenting against the position that moral worth is based on having some accidental characteristic would apply to our position also (Stretton, 2004). But this is to miss the important distinction between having a basic natural capacity (of which there are no degrees, since one either has it or one doesn't), and the *development of that capacity* (of which there are infinite degrees).

5. David Boonin claims, in reply to this argument – in an earlier and less developed form, presented by Lee (1996: 122)—that it is not clear that it is impermissible for a woman to destroy what is a part of, or a continuation of, herself. He then says that to the extent the unborn human being is united to her in that way, "it would if anything seem that her act is *easier* to justify than if this claim were not true" (2003: 230). But Boonin fails to grasp the point of the argument (perhaps understandably since it was not expressed very clearly in the earlier work he is discussing). The unity of the child to the mother is the basis for this child being related to the woman in a different way from how other children are. We ought to pursue our own good *and the good of others with whom we are united in various ways*. If that is so, then the closer someone is united to us, the deeper and more extensive our responsibility to the person will be.

6. In some sense being bodily "occupied" when one does not wish to be *is* a harm; however, just as the child

does not (as explained in the text), neither does the state inflict this harm on the woman, in circumstances in which the state prohibits abortion. By prohibiting abortion the state would only prevent the woman from performing an act (forcibly detaching the child from her) that would unjustly kill this developing child, who is an innocent party.

REFERENCES

Boonin, David (2003). *A Defense of Abortion.* New York: Cambridge University Press.

Carlson, Bruce (1994). *Human Embryology and Developmental Biology.* St. Louis, MO: Mosby.

Dworkin, Ronald (1993). *Life's Dominion: An Argument about Abortion, Euthanasia, and Individual Freedom.* New York: Random House.

Feinberg, Joel (ed.) (1984). *The Problem of Abortion,* 2nd edn. Belmont, CA: Wadsworth, 1984.

George, Robert (2001). "We should not kill human embryos—for any reason." In *The Clash of Orthodoxies: Law, Religion, and Morality in Crisis* (pp. 317–23). Wilmington, DE: ISI Books.

George, Robert and Lobo, Gòmez (2002). "Personal statement." In *The President's Council on Bioethics* (2002, pp. 294–306).

Gilbert, Scott (2003). *Developmental Biology,* 7th edn. Sunderland, MA: Sinnauer Associates.

Larson, William J. (2001). *Human Embryology,* 3rd edn. New York: Churchill Livingstone.

Lee, Patrick (1996). *Abortion and Unborn Human Life.* Washington, DC: Catholic University of America Press.

Little, Margaret Olivia (1999). "Abortion, intimacy, and the duty to gestate." *Ethical Theory and Moral Practice,* 2: 295–312.

McDonagh, Eileen (1996). *Breaking the Abortion Deadlock: From Choice to Consent.* New York: Oxford University Press, 1996.

Moore, Keith and Persaud, T. V. N. (2003). *The Developing Human, Clinically Oriented Embryology,* 7th edn. New York: W. B. Saunders.

Muller, Werner A. (1997). *Developmental Biology.* New York: Springer Verlag.

O'Rahilly, Ronan and Mueller, Fabiola (2000). *Human Embryology and Teratology,* 3rd edn. New York: John Wiley & Sons.

The President's Council on Bioethics (2002). *Human Cloning and Human Dignity: The Report of the President's Council on Bioethics.* New York: Public Affairs.

Singer, Peter (1993). *Practical Ethics,* 2nd edn. Cambridge: Cambridge University Press. Stretton, Dean (2004). "Essential properties and the right to life: a response to Lee." *Bioethics,* 18/3: 264–82.

Thomson, Judith Jarvis (1971). "A defense of abortion." *Philosophy and Public Affairs,* 1: 47–66; reprinted, among other places, in Feinberg (1984, pp. 173–87).

Thomson, Judith Jarvis (1995). "Abortion." *Boston Review.* Available at <www.bostonreview. mit.edu/BR20.3/ thomson.html>.

Tooley, Michael (1983). *Abortion and Infanticide.* New York: Oxford University Press.

Warren, Mary Ann (1984). "On the moral and legal status of abortion." In Feinberg (1984, pp. 102–19).

READING QUESTIONS

1. Lee and George insist that a human embryo is radically unlike sperm and ova. What are their reasons for this claim, and what is the significance of this distinction?
2. The authors reject the "dualist no-person argument" by objecting that it relies on a false implicit premise. What is this premise, and why do they allege that it is false?
3. Why do the authors think that Thomson's right-to-vote analogy fails?
4. What reasons do Lee and George give for the claim that a human being's degree of development cannot be the criterion for having a basic right to life? What, in their view, is required in order to be worthy of having rights?
5. With regard to intentional versus non-intentional killing of the fetus, Lee and George point out that an abortion would be "unsuccessful" if the fetus survives. This is a premise in an argument the authors are making for what conclusion?
6. Lee and George say that in most cases, abortion violates a provision of the doctrine of double effect. Which provision is it?

DISCUSSION QUESTIONS

1. Could someone agree with the authors' arguments for the wrongness of abortion but still allow that the procedure is permissible in cases of pregnancy by rape? If so, how? Which reasons can be given to justify this exception?
2. Lee and George claim that a fetus, as a human being, is an entity identical to the entity that will later reason, make free choices, and so on. Discuss whether and to what extent you think it is true that a fetus and a rational adult have an identity relation.
3. According to Lee and George, the "bodily rights argument" of their opponents includes an appeal to the doctrine of double effect according to which the death of the fetus is an unintended, albeit fore-seen, side effect of expelling the child for whom the mother has not voluntarily assumed responsibility. Lee and George object, giving several examples of both intentional and non-intentional killing of the fetus. Do you agree that the cases of non-intentional killing are very few? Why or why not?
4. Do you agree with the authors that parents have a special relationship to a child? Does this alone entail that some cases of non-intentional killing are also wrong?

ROSALIND HURSTHOUSE

Virtue Theory and Abortion

After laying out the basic structure of a version of virtue ethics, Hursthouse proceeds to explain how this kind of moral theory can be useful in guiding moral thought and decision making generally and how, in particular, it can be used to think about the morality of abortion. According to Hursthouse, thinking about the morality of abortion in terms of virtues and vices transforms the debate about abortion. This debate is typically cast in terms of the apparent and conflicting rights of the fetus and the pregnant woman. However, according to Hursthouse, approaching the issue from the perspective of virtue ethics makes appealing to rights largely irrelevant to the moral issue properly understood. By contrast, a virtue theoretic approach to abortion understands the morality of some act of abortion in terms of whether it would (in the circumstances) express certain character traits with regard to various goods and evils. In Hursthouse's view, some abortions are wrong because they express such vices as callousness, greediness, or selfishness, though other abortions are not wrong because they may express such virtues as humility or modesty.

Recommended Reading: virtue ethics, chap. 1, sec. 2E.

From Rosalind Hursthouse, "Virtue Theory and Abortion," *Philosophy and Public Affairs* 20 (1991).

The sort of ethical theory derived from Aristotle, variously described as virtue ethics, virtue-based ethics, or neo-Aristotelianism, is becoming better known, and is now quite widely recognized as at least a possible rival to deontological and utilitarian theories. With recognition has come criticism, of varying quality. In this article I shall discuss . . . criticisms that I have frequently encountered, most of which seem to me to betray an inadequate grasp either of the structure of virtue theory or of what would be involved in thinking about a real moral issue in its terms. In the first half I aim particularly to secure an understanding that will reveal that many of these criticisms are simply misplaced, and to articulate what I take to be the major criticism of virtue theory. I reject this criticism, but do not claim that it is necessarily misplaced. In the second half I aim to deepen that understanding and highlight the issues raised by the criticisms by illustrating what the theory looks like when it is applied to a particular issue, in this case, abortion.

VIRTUE THEORY

Now let us consider what a skeletal virtue theory looks like. It begins with a specification of right action:

> P.1. An action is right if it is what a virtuous agent would do in the circumstances.[1]

This . . . is a purely formal principle. . . that forges the conceptual link between *right action* and *virtuous agent*. . . . [I]t must, of course, go on to specify what the latter is. The first step toward this may appear quite trivial, but is needed to correct a prevailing tendency among many critics to define the virtuous agent as one who is disposed to act in accordance with a deontologist's moral rules.

> P.1a. A virtuous agent is one who acts virtuously, that is, one who has and exercises the virtues.

This subsidiary premise lays bare the fact that virtue theory aims to provide a nontrivial specification of the virtuous agent *via* a nontrivial specification of the virtues, which is given in its second premise:

> P.2. A virtue is a character trait a human being needs to flourish or live well.

This premise forges a conceptual link between *virtue* and *flourishing* (or *living well* or *eudaimonia*). . . . [V]irtue ethics, in theory, [then] goes on to argue that each favored character trait meets its [specification].

These are the bare bones of virtue theory. Following are five brief comments directed to some misconceived criticisms that should be cleared out of the way.

First, the theory does not have a peculiar weakness or problem in virtue of the fact that it involves the concept of *eudaimonia* (a standard criticism being that this concept is hopelessly obscure). Now no virtue theorist will pretend that the concept of human flourishing is an easy one to grasp. I will not even claim here (though I would elsewhere) that it is no more obscure than the concepts of *rationality* and *happiness,* since, if our vocabulary were more limited, we might, *faute de mieux,* call it (human) *rational happiness,* and thereby reveal that it has at least some of the difficulties of both. But virtue theory has never, so far as I know, been dismissed on the grounds of the *comparative* obscurity of this central concept; rather, the popular view is that it has a problem with this which deontology and utilitarianism in no way share. This, I think, is clearly false. Both *rationality* and *happiness*, as they figure in their respective theories, are rich and difficult concepts—hence all the disputes about the various tests for a rule's being an object of rational choice, and the disputes, dating back to Mill's introduction of the higher and lower pleasures, about what constitutes happiness.

Second, the theory is not trivially circular; it does not specify right action in terms of the virtuous agent and then immediately specify the virtuous agent in terms of right action. Rather, it specifies her in terms of the virtues, and then specifies these, not merely as dispositions to right action, but as the character traits (which are dispositions to feel and react as well as act in certain ways) required for *eudaimonia*.

Third, it does answer the question "What should I do?" as well as the question "What sort of person should I be?" (That is, it is not, as one of the catchphrases has it, concerned only with Being and not with Doing.)

Fourth, the theory does, to a certain extent, answer this question by coming up with rules or principles (contrary to the common claim that it does not come up with any rules or principles). Every virtue generates a positive instruction (act justly, kindly, courageously, honestly, etc.) and every vice a prohibition (do not act unjustly, cruelly, like a coward, dishonestly, etc.). So trying to decide what to do within the framework of virtue theory is not, as some people seem to imagine, necessarily a matter of taking one's favored candidate for a virtuous person and asking oneself, "What would they do in these circumstances?" (as if the raped fifteen-year-old girl might be supposed to say to herself, "Now would Socrates have an abortion if he were in my circumstances?" and as if someone who had never known or heard of anyone very virtuous were going to be left, according to the theory, with no way to decide what to do at all). The agent may instead ask herself, "If I were to do such and such now, would I be acting justly or unjustly (or neither), kindly or unkindly [and so on]?" I shall consider below the problem created by cases in which such a question apparently does not yield an answer to "What should I do?" (because, say, the alternatives are being unkind or being unjust); here my claim is only that it sometimes does—the agent may employ her concepts of the virtues and vices directly, rather than imagining what some hypothetical exemplar would do. . . .

Finally, I want to articulate, and reject, what I take to be the major criticism of virtue theory. Perhaps because it is *the* major criticism, the reflection of a very general sort of disquiet about the theory, it is hard to state clearly—especially for someone who does not accept it—but it goes something like this.[2] My interlocutor says:

> Virtue theory can't *get* us anywhere in real moral issues because it's bound to be all assertion and no argument. You admit that the best it can come up with in the way of action-guiding rules are the ones that rely on the virtue and vice concepts, such as "act charitably," "don't act cruelly," and so on; and, as if that weren't bad enough, you admit that these virtue concepts, such as charity, presuppose concepts such as the *good,* and the

worthwhile, and so on. But that means that any virtue theorist who writes about real moral issues must rely on her audience's agreeing with her application of all these concepts, and hence accepting all the premises in which those applications are enshrined. But some other virtue theorist might take different premises about these matters, and come up with very different conclusions, and, within the terms of the theory, there is no way to distinguish between the two. While there is agreement, virtue theory can repeat conventional wisdom, preserve the status quo, but it can't get us anywhere in the way that a normative ethical theory is supposed to, namely, by providing rational grounds for acceptance of its practical conclusions.

My strategy will be to split this criticism into two: one . . . addressed to the virtue theorist's employment of the virtue and vice concepts enshrined in her rules—act charitably, honestly, and so on—and the other . . . addressed to her employment of concepts such as that of the *worthwhile.* Each objection, I shall maintain, implicitly appeals to a certain *condition of adequacy* on a normative moral theory, and in each case, I shall claim, the condition of adequacy, once made explicit, is utterly implausible.

It is true that when she discusses real moral issues, the virtue theorist has to assert that certain actions are honest, dishonest, or neither; charitable, uncharitable, or neither. And it is true that this is often a very difficult matter to decide; her rules are not always easy to apply. But this counts as a criticism of the theory only if we assume, as a condition of adequacy, that any adequate action-guiding theory must make the difficult business of knowing what to do if one is to act well easy, that it must provide clear guidance about what ought and ought not to be done which any reasonably clever adolescent could follow if she chose. But such a condition of adequacy is implausible. Acting rightly *is* difficult, and *does* call for much moral wisdom, and the relevant condition of adequacy, which virtue theory meets, is that it should have built into it an explanation of a truth expressed by Aristotle,[3] namely, that moral knowledge—unlike mathematical knowledge—cannot be acquired merely by attending lectures and is not characteristically to be found in people too young to have had much experience of life. There are youthful mathematical geniuses, but rarely, if ever, youthful moral geniuses, and this tells us something significant about the sort of knowledge that moral knowledge is. Virtue ethics builds this in straight off precisely by couching its rules in terms whose application may indeed call for the most delicate and sensitive judgment. . . .

What about the virtue theorist's reliance on concepts such as that of the *worthwhile?* If such reliance is to count as a fault in the theory, what condition of adequacy is implicitly in play? It must be that any good normative theory should provide answers to questions about real moral issues whose truth is in no way determined by truths about what is worthwhile, or what really matters in human life. Now although people are initially inclined to reject out of hand the claim that the practical conclusions of a normative moral theory have to be based on premises about what is truly worthwhile, the alternative, once it is made explicit, may look even more unacceptable. Consider what the condition of adequacy entails. If truths about what is worthwhile (or truly good, or serious, or about what matters in human life) do *not* have to be appealed to in order to answer questions about real moral issues, then I might sensibly seek guidance about what I ought to do from someone who had declared in advance that she knew nothing about such matters, or from someone who said that, although she had opinions about them, these were quite likely to be wrong but that this did not matter, because they would play no determining role in the advice she gave me.

I should emphasize that we are talking about real moral issues and real guidance; I want to know whether I should have an abortion, take my mother off the life-support machine, leave academic life and become a doctor in the Third World, give up my job with the firm that is using animals in its experiments, tell my father he has cancer. Would I go to someone who says she has *no* views about what is worthwhile in life? Or to someone who says that, as a matter of fact, she tends to think that the only thing that matters is having a good time, but has a normative theory that is consistent both with this view and with my own rather more puritanical one, which will yield the guidance I need?

I take it as a premise that this is absurd. The relevant condition of adequacy should be that the practical conclusions of a good normative theory *must* be in part determined by premises about what is worthwhile, important, and so on. Thus I reject this "major criticism" of virtue theory, that it cannot get us anywhere in the way that a normative moral theory is supposed to. According to my response, a normative theory that any clever adolescent can apply, or that reaches practical conclusions that are in no way determined by premises about what is truly worthwhile, serious, and so on, is guaranteed to be an inadequate theory. . . .

As promised, I now turn to an illustration of such discussion, applying virtue theory to abortion. Before I embark on this tendentious business, I should remind the reader of the aim of this discussion. I am not, in this article, trying to solve the problem of abortion; I am illustrating how virtue theory directs one to think about it. . . .

ABORTION

As everyone knows, the morality of abortion is commonly discussed in relation to just two considerations: first, and predominantly, the status of the fetus and whether or not it is the sort of thing that may or may not be innocuously or justifiably killed; and second, and less predominantly (when, that is, the discussion concerns the *morality* of abortion rather than the question of permissible legislation in a just society), women's rights. If one thinks within this familiar framework, one may well be puzzled about what virtue theory, as such, could contribute. Some people assume the discussion will be conducted solely in terms of what the virtuous agent would or would not do (cf. the third, fourth, and fifth criticisms above). Others assume that only justice, or at most justice and charity, will be applied to the issue, generating a discussion very similar to Judith Jarvis Thomson's.[4]

Now if this is the way the virtue theorist's discussion of abortion is imagined to be, no wonder people think little of it. It seems obvious in advance that in any such discussion there must be either a great deal of extremely tendentious application of the virtue terms *just, charitable,* and so on or a lot of rhetorical appeal to "this is what only the virtuous agent knows." But these are caricatures; they fail to appreciate the way in which virtue theory quite transforms the discussion of abortion by dismissing the two familiar dominating considerations as, in a way, fundamentally irrelevant. In what way or ways, I hope to make both clear and plausible.

Let us first consider women's rights. Let me emphasize again that we are discussing the *morality* of abortion, not the rights and wrongs of laws prohibiting or permitting it. If we suppose that women do have a moral right to do as they choose with their own bodies, or, more particularly, to terminate their pregnancies, then it may well follow that a *law* forbidding abortion would be unjust. Indeed, even if they have no such right, such a law might be, as things stand at the moment, unjust, or impractical, or inhumane: on this issue I have nothing to say in this article. But, putting all questions about the justice or injustice of laws to one side, and supposing only that women have such a moral right, *nothing* follows from this supposition about the morality of abortion, according to virtue theory, once it is noted (quite generally, not with particular reference to abortion) that in exercising a moral right I can do something cruel, or callous, or selfish, light-minded, self-righteous, stupid, inconsiderate, disloyal, dishonest—that is, act viciously.[5] Love and friendship do not survive their parties' constantly insisting on their rights, nor do people live well when they think that getting what they have a right to is of preeminent importance; they harm others, and they harm themselves. So whether women have a moral right to terminate their pregnancies is irrelevant within virtue theory, for it is irrelevant to the question "In having an abortion in these circumstances, would the agent be acting virtuously or viciously or neither?"

What about the consideration of the status of the fetus—what can virtue theory say about that? One might say that this issue is not in the province of *any* moral theory; it is a metaphysical question, and an extremely difficult one at that. Must virtue theory then wait upon metaphysics to come up with the answer?

At first sight it might seem so. For virtue is said to involve knowledge, and part of this knowledge consists in having the *right* attitude to things. "Right" here does not just mean "morally right" or "proper" or "nice" in the modern sense; it means "accurate, true." One cannot have the right or correct attitude to something if the attitude is based on or involves false beliefs. And this suggests that if the status of the fetus is relevant to the rightness or wrongness of abortion, its status must be known, as a truth, to the fully wise and virtuous person.

But the sort of wisdom that the fully virtuous person has is not supposed to be recondite; it does not call for fancy philosophical sophistication, and it does not depend upon, let alone wait upon, the discoveries of academic philosophers. And this entails the following, rather startling, conclusion: that the status of the fetus—that issue over which so much ink has been spilt—is, according to virtue theory, simply not relevant to the rightness or wrongness of abortion (within, that is, a secular morality).

Or rather, since that is clearly too radical a conclusion, it is in a sense relevant, but only in the sense that the familiar biological facts are relevant. By "the familiar biological facts" I mean the facts that most human societies are and have been familiar with—that, standardly (but not invariably), pregnancy occurs as the result of sexual intercourse, that it lasts about nine months, during which time the fetus grows and develops, that standardly it terminates in the birth of a living baby, and that this is how we all come to be. . . .

Now if we are using virtue theory, our first question is not "What do the familiar biological facts show—what can be derived from them about the status of the fetus?" but "How do these facts figure in the practical reasoning, actions and passions, thoughts and reactions, of the virtuous and the nonvirtuous? What is the mark of having the right attitude to these facts and what manifests having the wrong attitude to them?" This immediately makes essentially relevant not only all the facts about human reproduction I mentioned above, but a whole range of facts about our emotions in relation to them as well. I mean such facts as that human parents, both male and female, tend to care passionately about their offspring, and that family relationships are among the deepest and strongest in our lives—and, significantly, among the longest-lasting.

These facts make it obvious that pregnancy is not just one among many other physical conditions; and hence that anyone who genuinely believes that an abortion is comparable to a haircut or an appendectomy is mistaken. The fact that the premature termination of a pregnancy is, in some sense, the cutting off of a new human life, and thereby, like the procreation of a new human life, connects with all our thoughts about human life and death, parenthood, and family relationships, must make it a serious matter. To disregard this fact about it, to think of abortion as nothing but the killing of something that does not matter, or as nothing but the exercise of some right or rights one has, or as the incidental means to some desirable state of affairs, is to do something callous and light-minded, the sort of thing that no virtuous and wise person would do. It is to have the wrong attitude not only to fetuses, but more generally to human life and death, parenthood, and family relationships.

Although I say that the facts make this obvious, I know that this is one of my tendentious points. In partial support of it I note that even the most dedicated proponents of the view that deliberate abortion is just like an appendectomy or haircut rarely hold the same view of spontaneous abortion, that is, miscarriage. It is not so tendentious of me to claim that to react to people's grief over miscarriage by saying, or even thinking, "What a fuss about nothing!" would be callous and light-minded, whereas to try to laugh someone out of grief over an appendectomy scar or a botched haircut would not be. . . .

To say that the cutting off of a human life is always a matter of some seriousness, at any stage, is not to deny the relevance of gradual fetal development. Notwithstanding the well-worn point that clear boundary lines cannot be drawn, our emotions and attitudes regarding the fetus do change as it develops, and again when it is born, and indeed further as the baby grows. Abortion for shallow reasons in the later stages is much more shocking than abortion for the same reasons in the early stages in a way that matches the fact that deep grief over miscarriage in the later stages is more appropriate than it is over miscarriage in the earlier stages (when, that is, the grief is solely about the loss of *this* child, not about, as might be the case, the loss of one's only hope of having a child or of having one's husband's child). Imagine (or recall) a woman who already has children; she had not intended to have more, but finds herself unexpectedly pregnant. Though contrary to her plans, the pregnancy, once established as a fact, is welcomed—and then she loses the embryo almost immediately. If this were bemoaned as a tragedy, it would, I think, be a misapplication of the concept of what is tragic. But it may still properly be mourned as a loss. The grief is expressed in such terms as "I shall always wonder how she or he would have turned out" or "When I look at the others, I shall think, 'How different their lives would have been if this other one had been part of them.'" It would, I take it, be callous and light-minded to say, or think, "Well, she has already *got* four children; what's the problem?"; it would be neither, nor arrogantly intrusive in the case of a close friend, to try to correct prolonged mourning by saying, "I know it's sad, but it's not a tragedy; rejoice in the ones you have." The application of *tragic* becomes more appropriate as the fetus grows, for the mere fact that one has lived with it for longer, conscious of its existence, makes a difference. To shrug off an early abortion is understandable just because it is very hard to be fully conscious of the fetus's existence in the early stages and hence hard to appreciate that an early abortion is the destruction of life. It is particularly hard for the young and inexperienced to appreciate this, because appreciation of it usually comes only with experience.

I do not mean "with the experience of having an abortion" (though that may be part of it) but, quite generally, "with the experience of life." Many women who have borne children contrast their later pregnancies with their first successful one, saying that in the later ones they were conscious of a new life growing in them from very early on. And, more generally, as one reaches the age at which the next generation is coming up close behind one, the counterfactuals "If I, or she, had had an abortion, Alice, or Bob, would not have been born" acquire a significant application, which casts a new light on the conditionals "If I or Alice have an abortion then some Caroline or Bill will not be born."

The fact that pregnancy is not just one among many physical conditions does not mean that one can never regard it in that light without manifesting a vice. When women are in very poor physical health, or worn out from childbearing, or forced to do very physically demanding jobs, then they cannot be described as self-indulgent, callous, irresponsible, or light-minded if they seek abortions mainly with a view to avoiding pregnancy as the physical condition that it is. To go through with a pregnancy when one is utterly exhausted, or when one's job consists of crawling along tunnels hauling coal, as many women in the nineteenth century were obliged to do, is perhaps heroic, but people who do not achieve heroism are not necessarily vicious. That they can view the pregnancy only as eight months of misery, followed by hours if not days of agony and exhaustion, and abortion only as the blessed escape from this prospect, is entirely understandable and does not manifest any lack of serious respect for human life or a shallow attitude to motherhood. What it does show is that something is terribly amiss in the conditions of their lives, which make it so hard to recognize pregnancy and childbearing as the good that they can be. . . .

The foregoing discussion, insofar as it emphasizes the right attitude to human life and death, parallels to a certain extent those standard discussions of abortion that concentrate on it solely as an issue of killing. But it does not, as those discussions do, gloss over the fact, emphasized by those who discuss the morality of abortion in terms of women's rights, that abortion, wildly unlike any other form of killing, is the termination of a pregnancy, which is a condition of a woman's body and results in *her* having a child if it is not aborted. This fact is given due recognition not by appeal to women's rights but by emphasizing the relevance of the familiar biological and psychological facts and their connection with having the right attitude to parenthood and family relationships. But it may well be thought that failing to bring in women's rights still leaves some important aspects of the problem of abortion untouched.

Speaking in terms of women's rights, people sometimes say things like, "Well, it's her life you're talking about too, you know; she's got a right to her own life, her own happiness." And the discussion stops there. But in the context of virtue theory, given

that we are particularly concerned with what constitutes a good human life, with what true happiness or *eudaimonia* is, this is no place to stop. We go on to ask, "And is this life of hers a good one? Is she living well?"

If we are to go on to talk about good human lives, in the context of abortion, we have to bring in our thoughts about the value of love and family life, and our proper emotional development through a natural life cycle. The familiar facts support the view that parenthood in general, and motherhood and childbearing in particular, are intrinsically worthwhile, are among the things that can be correctly thought to be partially constitutive of a flourishing human life.[6] If this is right, then a woman who opts for not being a mother (at all, or again, or now) by opting for abortion may thereby be manifesting a flawed grasp of what her life should be, and be about—a grasp that is childish, or grossly materialistic, or shortsighted, or shallow.

I said "*may* thereby": this *need* not be so. Consider, for instance, a woman who has already had several children and fears that to have another will seriously affect her capacity to be a good mother to the ones she has—she does not show a lack of appreciation of the intrinsic value of being a parent by opting for abortion. Nor does a woman who has been a good mother and is approaching the age at which she may be looking forward to being a good grandmother. Nor does a woman who discovers that her pregnancy may well kill her, and opts for abortion and adoption. Nor, necessarily, does a woman who has decided to lead a life centered around some other worthwhile activity or activities with which motherhood would compete.

People who are childless by choice are sometimes described as "irresponsible," or "selfish," or "refusing to grow up," or "not knowing what life is about." But one can hold that having children is intrinsically worthwhile without endorsing this, for we are, after all, in the happy position of there being more worthwhile things to do than can be fitted into one lifetime. Parenthood, and motherhood in particular, even if granted to be intrinsically worthwhile, undoubtedly take up a lot of one's adult life, leaving no room for some other worthwhile pursuits. But some women who choose abortion rather than have their first child, and some men who encourage their partners to choose abortion, are not avoiding parenthood for the sake of other worthwhile pursuits, but for the worthless one of "having a good time," or for the pursuit of some false vision of the ideals of freedom or self-realization. And some others who say "I am not ready for parenthood yet" are making some sort of mistake about the extent to which one can manipulate the circumstances of one's life so as to make it fulfill some dream that one has. Perhaps one's dream is to have two perfect children, a girl and a boy, within a perfect marriage, in financially secure circumstances, with an interesting job of one's own. But to care too much about that dream, to demand of life that it give it to one and act accordingly, may be both greedy and foolish, and is to run the risk of missing out on happiness entirely. Not only may fate make the dream impossible, or destroy it, but one's own attachment to it may make it impossible. Good marriages, and the most promising children, can be destroyed by just one adult's excessive demand for perfection.

Once again, this is not to deny that girls may quite properly say "I am not ready for motherhood yet," especially in our society, and, far from manifesting irresponsibility or light-mindedness, show an appropriate modesty or humility, or a fearfulness that does not amount to cowardice. However, even when the decision to have an abortion is the right decision—one that does not itself fall under a vice-related term and thereby one that the perfectly virtuous could recommend—it does not follow that there is no sense in which having the abortion is wrong, or guilt inappropriate. For, by virtue of the fact that a human life has been cut short, some evil has probably been brought about,[7] and that circumstances make the decision to bring about some evil the right decision will be a ground for guilt if getting into those circumstances in the first place itself manifested a flaw in character.

What "gets one into those circumstances" in the case of abortion is, except in the case of rape, one's sexual activity and one's choices, or the lack of them, about one's sexual partner and about contraception. The virtuous woman (which here of course does not mean simply "chaste woman" but "woman

with the virtues") has such character traits as strength, independence, resoluteness, decisiveness, self-confidence, responsibility, serious-mindedness, and self-determination—and no one, I think, could deny that many women become pregnant in circumstances in which they cannot welcome or cannot face the thought of having *this* child precisely because they lack one or some of these character traits. So even in the cases where the decision to have an abortion is the right one, it can still be the reflection of a moral failing—not because the decision itself is weak or cowardly or irresolute or irresponsible or light-minded, but because lack of the requisite opposite of these failings landed one in the circumstances in the first place. Hence the common universalized claim that guilt and remorse are never appropriate emotions about an abortion is denied. They may be appropriate, and appropriately inculcated, even when the decision was the right one.

Another motivation for bringing women's rights into the discussion may be to attempt to correct the implication, carried by the killing-centered approach, that insofar as abortion is wrong, it is a wrong that only women do, or at least (given the preponderance of male doctors) that only women instigate. I do not myself believe that we can thus escape the fact that nature bears harder on women than it does on men,[8] but virtue theory can certainly correct many of the injustices that the emphasis on women's rights is rightly concerned about. With very little amendment, everything that has been said above applies to boys and men too. Although the abortion decision is, in a natural sense, the woman's decision, proper to her, boys and men are often party to it, for well or ill, and even when they are not, they are bound to have been party to the circumstances that brought it up. No less than girls and women, boys and men can, in their actions, manifest self-centeredness, callousness, and light-mindedness about life and parenthood in relation to abortion. They can be self-centered or courageous about the possibility of disability in their offspring; they need to reflect on their sexual activity and their choices, or the lack of them, about their sexual partner and contraception; they need to grow up and take responsibility for their own actions and life in relation to fatherhood. If it is true, as I maintain, that insofar as motherhood is intrinsically worthwhile, being a mother is an important purpose in women's lives, being a father (rather than a mere generator) is an important purpose in men's lives as well, and it is adolescent of men to turn a blind eye to this and pretend that they have many more important things to do.

CONCLUSION

Much more might be said, but I shall end the actual discussion of the problem of abortion here, and conclude by highlighting what I take to be its significant features. These hark back to many of the criticisms of virtue theory discussed earlier.

The discussion does not proceed simply by our trying to answer the question "Would a perfectly virtuous agent ever have an abortion and, if so, when?"; virtue theory is not limited to considering "Would Socrates have had an abortion if he were a raped, pregnant fifteen-year-old?" nor automatically stumped when we are considering circumstances into which no virtuous agent would have got herself. Instead, much of the discussion proceeds in the virtue- and vice-related terms whose application, in several cases, yields practical conclusions (cf. the third and fourth criticisms above). These terms are difficult to apply correctly, and anyone might challenge my application of any one of them. So, for example, I have claimed that some abortions, done for certain reasons, would be callous or light-minded; that others might indicate an appropriate modesty or humility; that others would reflect a greedy and foolish attitude to what one could expect out of life. Any of these examples may be disputed, but what is at issue is, should these difficult terms be there, or should the discussion be couched in terms that all clever adolescents can apply correctly? (Cf. the first half of the "major objection" above.)

Proceeding as it does in the virtue- and vice-related terms, the discussion thereby, inevitably,

also contains claims about what is worthwhile, serious and important, good and evil, in our lives. So, for example, I claimed that parenthood is intrinsically worthwhile, and that having a good time was a worthless end (in life, not on individual occasions); that losing a fetus is always a serious matter (albeit not a tragedy in itself in the first trimester) whereas acquiring an appendectomy scar is a trivial one; that (human) death is an evil. Once again, these are difficult matters, and anyone might challenge any one of my claims. But what is at issue is, as before, should those difficult claims be there or can one reach practical conclusions about real moral issues that are in no way determined by premises about such matters? (Cf. the fifth criticism, and the second half of the "major criticism.")

The discussion also thereby, inevitably, contains claims about what life is like (e.g., my claim that love and friendship do not survive their parties' constantly insisting on their rights; or the claim that to demand perfection of life is to run the risk of missing out on happiness entirely). What is at issue is, should those disputable claims be there, or is our knowledge (or are our false opinions) about what life is like irrelevant to our understanding of real moral issues? (Cf. both halves of the "major criticism.")

Naturally, my own view is that all these concepts should be there in any discussion of real moral issues and that virtue theory, which uses all of them, is the right theory to apply to them. . . .

NOTES

Versions of this article have been read to philosophy societies at University College, London, Rutgers University, and the Universities of Dundee, Edinburgh, Oxford, Swansea, and California–San Diego; at a conference of the Polish and British Academies in Cracow in 1988 on "Life, Death and the Law," and as a symposium paper at the Pacific Division of the American Philosophical Association in 1989. I am grateful to the many people who contributed to the discussions of it on these occasions, and particularly to Philippa Foot and Anne Jaap Jacobson for private discussion.

1. It should be noted that this premise intentionally allows for the possibility that two virtuous agents, faced

with the same choice in the same circumstances, may act differently. For example, one might opt for taking her father off the life-support machine and the other for leaving her father on it. The theory requires that neither agent thinks that what the other does is wrong...but it explicitly allows that no action is uniquely right in such a case—both are right. It also intentionally allows for the possibility that in some circumstances—those into which no virtuous agent could have got herself—no action is right. I explore this premise at greater length in "Applying Virtue Ethics," [in *Virtue and Reason: Philippa Foot and Moral Theory,* R. Hursthouse, G. Lawrence, W. Quinn, eds. (Oxford: Clarendon Press, 1995)].

2. Intimations of this criticism constantly come up in discussion; the clearest statement of it I have found is by Onora O'Neill, in her review of Stephen Clark's *The Moral Status of Animals,* in *Journal of Philosophy* 77 (1980): 440–46. For a response I am much in sympathy with, see Cora Diamond, "Anything But Argument?" *Philosophical Investigations* 5 (1982): 23–41.

3. Aristotle, *Nicomachean Ethics* 1142a12–16.

4. Judith Jarvis Thomson, "A Defense of Abortion," *Philosophy & Public Affairs* 1, no. 1 (Fall 1971): 47–66. One could indeed regard this article as proto-virtue theory (no doubt to the surprise of the author) if the concepts of callousness and kindness were allowed more weight.

5. One possible qualification: if one ties the concept of justice very closely to rights, then if women do have a moral right to terminate their pregnancies it *may* follow that in doing so they do not act unjustly. (Cf. Thomson, "A Defense of Abortion.") But it is debatable whether even that much follows.

6. I take this as a premise here, but argue for it in some detail in my *Beginning Lives* (Oxford: Basil Blackwell, 1987). In this connection I also discuss adoption and the sense in which it may be regarded as "second best," and the difficult question of whether the good of parenthood may properly be sought, or indeed bought, by surrogacy.

7. I say "some evil has probably been brought about" on the ground that (human) life is (usually) a good and hence (human) death usually an evil. The exceptions would be (*a*) where death is actually a good or a benefit, because the baby that would come to be if the life were not cut short would be better off dead than alive, and (*b*) where death, though not a good, is not an evil either because the life that would be led (e.g., in a state of permanent coma) would not be a good.

8. I discuss this point at greater length in *Beginning Lives.*

READING QUESTIONS

1. Hursthouse claims that even if a woman has a moral right to an abortion, "*nothing* follows from this supposition." How does she defend this claim?
2. Hursthouse claims that questions about the status of the fetus are not relevant (or not especially relevant) according to virtue ethics in determining whether abortion is right or wrong. How does she defend this claim?
3. According to Hursthouse's view on abortion, how are facts about the gradual development of the fetus relevant to the morality of abortion?
4. What does Hursthouse say about those who would seek an abortion saying, "I am not ready for parenthood/motherhood yet"?
5. Explain why Hursthouse claims that even in cases where having an abortion is not morally wrong, having an abortion can still reflect a moral failing.

DISCUSSION QUESTIONS

1. Is Hursthouse's virtue ethics approach to abortion superior to Thomson's rights-focused approach? Why or why not?
2. Should we agree with Hursthouse that questions about the moral status of the fetus are not as relevant to the abortion issue as many have supposed?

DON MARQUIS

Why Abortion Is Immoral

Marquis's approach to the morality of abortion is to begin by asking what it is that makes killing a normal adult human being presumptively morally wrong. His proposal is that the wrongness of such killing is best explained by the fact that it deprives the individual of all future experiences and activities of value. He then argues that because a fetus has a "future like ours," killing it would be presumptively morally wrong for the same reason that it is wrong to kill a normal adult human being. He concludes by explaining why his argument does not entail that contraception is presumptively morally wrong.

Recommended Reading: ethics of prima facie duty, chap.1, sec. 2F.

The view that abortion is, with rare exceptions, seriously immoral has received little support in the recent philosophical literature. No doubt most philosophers affiliated with secular institutions of higher education believe that the anti-abortion position is either a symptom of irrational religious dogma or a conclusion generated by seriously confused philosophical argument. The purpose of this essay is to undermine this general belief. This essay sets out an argument that purports to show, as well as any argument in ethics can show, that abortion is, except possibly in rare cases, seriously immoral, that it is in the same moral category as killing an innocent adult human being.

This argument is based on a major assumption: If fetuses are in the same category as adult human beings with respect to the moral value of their lives, then the *presumption* that any particular abortion is immoral is exceedingly strong. Such a presumption could be overridden only by considerations more compelling than a woman's right to privacy. The defense of this assumption is beyond the scope of this essay.[1]

Furthermore, this essay will neglect a discussion of whether there are any such compelling considerations and what they are. Plainly there are strong candidates: abortion before implantation, abortion when the life of a woman is threatened by a pregnancy or abortion after rape. The casuistry of these hard cases will not be explored in this essay. The purpose of this essay is to develop a general argument for the claim that, subject to the assumption above, the overwhelming majority of deliberate abortions are seriously immoral....

... A necessary condition of resolving the abortion controversy is a ... theoretical account of the wrongness of killing. After all, if we merely believe, but do not understand, why killing adult human beings such as ourselves is wrong, how could we conceivably show that abortion is either immoral or permissible?...

In order to develop such an account, we can start from the following unproblematic assumption concerning our own case: it is wrong to kill *us*. Why is it wrong? Some answers can be easily eliminated. It might be said that what makes killing us wrong is that a killing brutalizes the one who kills. But the brutalization consists of being inured to the performance of an act that is hideously immoral; hence, the brutalization does not explain the immorality. It might be said that what makes killing us wrong is the great loss others would experience due to our absence. Although

From Don Marquis, "Why Abortion Is Immoral," *Journal of Philosophy* 86 (1989). Reprinted by permission of the author and the publisher.

such hubris is understandable, such an explanation does not account for the wrongness of killing hermits, or those whose lives are relatively independent and whose friends find it easy to make new friends.

A more obvious answer is better. What primarily makes killing wrong is neither its effect on the murderer nor its effect on the victim's friends and relatives, but its effect on the victim. The loss of one's life is one of the greatest losses one can suffer. The loss of one's life deprives one of all the experiences, activities, projects, and enjoyments that would otherwise have constituted one's future. Therefore, killing someone is wrong, primarily because the killing inflicts (one of) the greatest possible losses on the victim. To describe this as the loss of life can be misleading, however. The change in my biological state does not by itself make killing me wrong. The effect of the loss of my biological life is the loss to me of all those activities, projects, experiences, and enjoyments which would otherwise have constituted my future personal life. These activities, projects, experiences, and enjoyments are either valuable for their own sakes or are means to something else that is valuable for its own sake. Some parts of my future are not valued by me now, but will come to be valued by me as I grow older and as my values and capacities change. When I am killed, I am deprived both of what I now value which would have been part of my future personal life, but also what I would come to value. Therefore, when I die, I am deprived of all of the value of my future. Inflicting this loss on me is ultimately what makes killing me wrong. This being the case, it would seem that what makes killing *any* adult human being prima facie seriously wrong is the loss of his or her future.[2]

How should this rudimentary theory of the wrongness of killing be evaluated? It cannot be faulted for deriving an "ought" from an "is," for it does not. The analysis assumes that killing me (or you, reader) is prima facie seriously wrong. The point of the analysis is to establish which natural property ultimately explains the wrongness of the killing, given that it is wrong. A natural property will ultimately explain the wrongness of killing, only if (1) the explanation fits with our intuitions about the matter and (2) there is no other natural property that provides the basis for a better explanation of the wrongness of killing. This analysis rests on the intuition that what makes killing a particular human or animal wrong is what it does to that particular human or animal. What makes killing wrong is some natural effect or other of the killing. Some would deny this. For instance, a divine-command theorist in ethics would deny it. Surely this denial is, however, one of those features of divine-command theory which renders it so implausible.

The claim that what makes killing wrong is the loss of the victim's future is directly supported by two considerations. In the first place, this theory explains why we regard killing as one of the worst of crimes. Killing is especially wrong, because it deprives the victim of more than perhaps any other crime. In the second place, people with AIDS or cancer who know they are dying believe, of course, that dying is a very bad thing for them. They believe that the loss of a future to them that they would otherwise have experienced is what makes their premature death a very bad thing for them. A better theory of the wrongness of killing would require a different natural property associated with killing which better fits with the attitudes of the dying. What could it be?

The view that what makes killing wrong is the loss to the victim of the value of the victim's future gains additional support when some of its implications are examined. In the first place, it is incompatible with the view that it is wrong to kill only beings who are biologically human. It is possible that there exists a different species from another planet whose members have a future like ours. Since having a future like that is what makes killing someone wrong, this theory entails that it would be wrong to kill members of such a species. Hence, this theory is opposed to the claim that only life that is biologically human has great moral worth, a claim which many anti-abortionists have seemed to adopt. This opposition, which this theory has in common with personhood theories, seems to be a merit of the theory.

In the second place, the claim that the loss of one's future is the wrong-making feature of one's being killed entails the possibility that the futures of some actual non-human mammals on our own planet are sufficiently like ours that it is seriously wrong to kill them also. Whether some animals do have the same right to life as human beings depends on adding to the account of the wrongness of killing some additional account of just what it is about my future or the futures of other adult human beings which makes it wrong to kill us. No such additional account will be offered in this essay. Undoubtedly, the provision of such an account would be a very difficult matter. Undoubtedly, any such account would be quite controversial. Hence, it surely should not reflect badly on this sketch of an elementary theory of the wrongness of killing that it is indeterminate with respect to some very difficult issues regarding animal rights.

In the third place, the claim that the loss of one's future is the wrong-making feature of one's being killed does not entail, as sanctity of human life theories do, that active euthanasia is wrong. Persons who are severely and incurably ill, who face a future of pain and despair, and who wish to die will not have suffered a loss if they are killed. It is, strictly speaking, the value of a human's future which makes killing wrong in this theory. This being so, killing does not necessarily wrong some persons who are sick and dying. Of course, there may be other reasons for a prohibition of active euthanasia, but that is another matter. Sanctity-of-human-life theories seem to hold that active euthanasia is seriously wrong even in an individual case where there seems to be good reason for it independently of public policy considerations. This consequence is most implausible, and it is a plus for the claim that the loss of a future of value is what makes killing wrong that it does not share this consequence.

In the fourth place, the account of the wrongness of killing defended in this essay does straightforwardly entail that it is prima facie seriously wrong to kill children and infants, for we do presume that they have futures of value. Since we do believe that it is wrong to kill defenseless little babies, it is important that a theory of the wrongness of killing easily account for this. Personhood theories of the wrongness of killing, on the other hand, cannot straightforwardly account for the wrongness of killing infants and young children. Hence, such theories must add special ad hoc accounts of the wrongness of killing the young. The plausibility of such ad hoc theories seems to be a function of how desperately

one wants such theories to work. The claim that the primary wrong-making feature of a killing is the loss to the victim of the value of its future accounts for the wrongness of killing young children and infants directly; it makes the wrongness of such acts as obvious as we actually think it is. This is a further merit of this theory. Accordingly, it seems that this value of a future-like-ours theory of the wrongness of killing shares strengths of both sanctity-of-life and personhood accounts while avoiding weaknesses of both. In addition, it meshes with a central intuition concerning what makes killing wrong.

The claim that the primary wrong-making feature of a killing is the loss to the victim of the value of its future has obvious consequences for the ethics of abortion. The future of a standard fetus includes a set of experiences, projects, activities, and such which are identical with the futures of adult human beings and are identical with the futures of young children. Since the reason that is sufficient to explain why it is wrong to kill human beings after the time of birth is a reason that also applies to fetuses, it follows that abortion is prima facie seriously morally wrong.

This argument does not rely on the invalid inference that, since it is wrong to kill persons, it is wrong to kill potential persons also. The category that is morally central to this analysis is the category of having a valuable future like ours; it is not the category of personhood. The argument to the conclusion that abortion is prima facie seriously morally wrong proceeded independently of the notion of person or potential person or any equivalent. Someone may wish to start with this analysis in terms of the value of a human future, conclude that abortion is, except perhaps in rare circumstances, seriously morally wrong, infer that fetuses have the right to life, and then call fetuses "persons" as a result of their having the right to life. Clearly, in this case, the category of person is being used to state the *conclusion* of the analysis rather than to generate the *argument* of the analysis.

The structure of this anti-abortion argument can be both illuminated and defended by comparing it to what appears to be the best argument for the wrongness of the wanton infliction of pain on animals. This latter argument is based on the assumption that it is prima facie wrong to inflict pain on me (or you, reader). What is the natural property associated with the infliction of pain which makes such infliction wrong? The obvious answer seems to be that the infliction of pain causes suffering and that suffering is a misfortune. The suffering caused by the infliction of pain is what makes the wanton infliction of pain on me wrong. The wanton infliction of pain on other adult humans causes suffering. The wanton infliction of pain on animals causes suffering. Since causing suffering is what makes the wanton infliction of pain wrong and since the wanton infliction of pain on animals causes suffering, it follows that the wanton infliction of pain on animals is wrong.

This argument for the wrongness of the wanton infliction of pain on animals shares a number of structural features with the argument for the serious prima facie wrongness of abortion. Both arguments start with an obvious assumption concerning what it is wrong to do to me (or you, reader). Both then look for the characteristic or the consequence of the wrong action which makes the action wrong. Both recognize that the wrong-making feature of these immoral actions is a property of actions sometimes directed at individuals other than postnatal human beings. If the structure of the argument for the wrongness of the wanton infliction of pain on animals is sound, then the structure of the argument for the prima facie serious wrongness of abortion is also sound, for the structure of the two arguments is the same. The structure common to both is the key to the explanation of how the wrongness of abortion can be demonstrated without recourse to the category of person. In neither argument is that category crucial. . . .

Of course, this value of a future-like-ours argument, if sound, shows only that abortion is prima facie wrong, not that it is wrong in any and all circumstances. Since the loss of the future to a standard fetus, if killed, is, however, at least as great a loss as the loss of the future to a standard adult human being who is killed, abortion, like ordinary killing, could be justified only by the most compelling reasons. The loss of one's life is almost the greatest misfortune that can happen to one. Presumably abortion could be justified in some circumstances, only if the loss consequent on failing to abort would be at least as great. Accordingly, morally permissible abortions will be rare indeed unless, perhaps, they occur so

early in pregnancy that a fetus is not yet definitely an individual. Hence, this argument should be taken as showing that abortion is presumptively very seriously wrong, where the presumption is very strong—as strong as the presumption that killing another adult human being is wrong. . . .

In this essay, it has been argued that the correct ethic of the wrongness of killing can be extended to fetal life and used to show that there is a strong presumption that any abortion is morally impermissible. If the ethic of killing adopted here entails, however, that contraception is also seriously immoral, then there would appear to be a difficulty with the analysis of this essay.

But this analysis does not entail that contraception is wrong. Of course, contraception prevents the actualization of a possible future of value. Hence, it follows from the claim that futures of value should be maximized that contraception is prima facie immoral. This obligation to maximize does not exist, however; furthermore, nothing in the ethics of killing in this paper entails that it does. The ethics of killing in this essay would entail that contraception is wrong only if something were denied a human future of value by contraception. Nothing at all is denied such a future by contraception, however.

Candidates for a subject of harm by contraception fall into four categories: (1) some sperm or other, (2) some ovum or other, (3) a sperm and an ovum separately, and (4) a sperm and an ovum together. Assigning the harm to some sperm is utterly arbitrary, for no reason can be given for making a sperm the subject of harm rather than an ovum. Assigning the harm to some ovum is utterly arbitrary, for no reason can be given for making an ovum the subject of harm rather than a sperm. One might attempt to avoid these problems by insisting that contraception deprives both the sperm and the ovum separately of a valuable future like ours. On this alternative, too many futures are lost. Contraception was supposed to be wrong, because it deprived us of one future of value, not two. One might attempt to avoid this problem by holding that contraception deprives the combination of sperm and ovum of a valuable future like ours. But here the definite article misleads. At the time of contraception, there are hundreds of millions of sperm, one (released) ovum and millions of possible combinations of all of these. There is no actual combination at all. Is the subject of the loss to be a merely possible combination? Which one? This alternative does not yield an actual subject of harm either. Accordingly, the immorality of contraception is not entailed by the loss of a future-like-ours argument simply because there is no non-arbitrarily identifiable subject of the loss in the case of contraception. . . .

The purpose of this essay has been to set out an argument for the serious presumptive wrongness of abortion subject to the assumption that the moral permissibility of abortion stands or falls on the moral status of the fetus. Since a fetus possesses a property, the possession of which in adult human beings is sufficient to make killing an adult human being wrong, abortion is wrong. This way of dealing with the problem of abortion seems superior to other approaches to the ethics of abortion, because it rests on an ethics of killing which is close to self-evident, because the crucial morally relevant property clearly applies to fetuses, and because the argument avoids the usual equivocations on "human life," "human being," or "person." The argument rests neither on religious claims nor on Papal dogma. It is not subject to the objection of "speciesism." Its soundness is compatible with the moral permissibility of euthanasia and contraception. It deals with our intuitions concerning young children.

Finally, this analysis can be viewed as resolving a standard problem—indeed, *the* standard problem—concerning the ethics of abortion. Clearly, it is wrong to kill adult human beings. Clearly, it is not wrong to end the life of some arbitrarily chosen single human cell. Fetuses seem to be like arbitrarily chosen human cells in some respects and like adult humans in other respects. The problem of the ethics of abortion is the problem of determining the fetal property that settles this moral controversy. The thesis of this essay is that the problem of the ethics of abortion, so understood, is solvable.

NOTES

1. Judith Jarvis Thomson has rejected this assumption in a famous essay, "A Defense of Abortion," *Philosophy and Public Affairs* 1, #1 (1971), 47–66.

2. I have been most influenced on this matter by Jonathan Glover, *Causing Death and Saving Lives* (New York: Penguin, 1977), ch. 3; and Robert Young, "What Is So Wrong with Killing People?" *Philosophy*, LIV, 210 (1979): 515–528.

READING QUESTIONS

1. According to Marquis, what is wrong with the claim that what explains why killing an innocent adult human being is wrong is that the death of the victim would be a great loss to his or her family and friends?
2. According to Marquis, there are two considerations that "directly" support his claim about what makes killing an innocent adult human being wrong. What are those considerations?
3. Marquis also claims that his view about the wrongness of killing gains additional support when its various implications are examined. What are the implications in question?
4. What reasons does Marquis give for claiming that his view on the morality of abortion does not imply that contraception is morally wrong?

DISCUSSION QUESTIONS

1. Should we find Marquis's claim that his view on the morality of abortion does not imply that contraception is wrong plausible? Explain why or why not.
2. How does Marquis's "future like ours" explanation of the wrongness of abortion differ from views that attempt to explain the wrongness of abortion by appealing to the idea that the fetus is a potential person?

L. W. SUMNER

A Moderate View

Sumner faults conservative and liberal views on abortion for assuming that the moral status of a fetus remains the same throughout pregnancy. Rejecting this assumption, claims Sumner, allows for the development of a moderate view, according to which early-stage abortions are generally less morally problematic than abortions in the later stages of pregnancy. To support his moderate position, he defends a criterion of moral standing which, when applied to the issue of abortion, yields an in-between, moderate view.

Recommended Reading: consequentialism, chap. 1, sec. 2A.

A complete view of abortion, one that answers the main moral questions posed by the practice of abortion, is an ordered compound of three elements: an account of the moral status of the fetus, which grounds an account of the moral status of abortion, which in turn grounds a defense of an abortion policy. It is not enough, however, that a view of abortion be complete—it must also be well grounded. If we explore what is required to support an account of the moral status of the fetus, we will discover what it means for a view of abortion to be well grounded. The main requirement at this level is a *criterion of moral standing* that will specify the (natural) characteristic(s) whose possession is both necessary and sufficient for the possession of moral standing. A criterion of moral standing will therefore have the following form: all and only beings with characteristic C have moral standing. (Characteristic C may be a single property or a conjunction or disjunction of such properties.) A criterion of moral standing thus determines, both exhaustively and exclusively, the membership of the class of beings with such standing. Such a criterion will define the proper scope of our moral concern, telling us for all moral contexts which beings must be accorded moral consideration in their own right. Thus it will determine, among other things, the moral status of inanimate natural objects, artifacts, nonhuman animals, body parts, superintelligent computers, androids, and extraterrestrials. It will also determine the moral status of (human) fetuses. An account of the moral status of the fetus is well grounded when it is derivable from an independently plausible criterion of moral standing. The independent plausibility of such a criterion is partly established by following out its implications for moral contexts other than abortion. But a criterion of moral standing can also be given a deeper justification by being grounded in a moral theory. The function of a moral theory is to identify those features of the world to which we should be morally sensitive and to guide that sensitivity. By providing us with a picture of the content and structure of morality, a moral theory will tell us, among other things, which beings merit moral consideration in their own right and what form this consideration should take. It will thereby generate and support a criterion of moral standing, thus serving as the last line of defense for a view of abortion.

From L. W. Sumner, "Abortion," in D. VanDeVeer & T. Regan, eds. *Health Care Ethics* (Philadelphia, PA: Temple University Press, 1987). Reprinted with permission of the author.

THE ESTABLISHED VIEWS

We are seeking a view of abortion that is both complete and well grounded. These requirements are not easily satisfied. The key elements remain an account of the moral status of the fetus and a supporting criterion of moral standing. Our search will be facilitated if we begin by examining the main contenders. The abortion debate in most of the Western democracies has been dominated by two positions that are so well entrenched that they may be called the established views. The liberal view supports what is popularly known as the "pro-choice" position on abortion.[1] At its heart is the contention that the fetus at every stage of pregnancy has no moral standing. From this premise it follows that although abortion kills the fetus it does not wrong it, since a being with no moral standing cannot be wronged. Abortion at all stages of pregnancy lacks a victim; circumstantial differences aside, it is the moral equivalent of contraception. The decision to seek an abortion, therefore, can properly be left to a woman's discretion. There is as little justification for legal regulation of abortion as there is for such regulation of contraception. The only defensible abortion policy is a permissive policy. The conservative view, however, supports what is popularly known as the "pro-life" position on abortion. At its heart is the contention that the fetus at every stage of pregnancy has full moral standing—the same status as an adult human being. From this premise it follows that because abortion kills the fetus it also wrongs it. Abortion at all stages of pregnancy has a victim; circumstantial differences aside, it is the moral equivalent of infanticide (and of other forms of homicide as well). The decision to seek an abortion, therefore, cannot properly be left to a woman's discretion. There is as much justification for legal regulation of abortion as there is for such regulation of infanticide. The only defensible abortion policy is a restrictive policy.

Before exploring these views separately, we should note an important feature that they share. On the substantive issue that is at the heart of the matter, liberals and conservatives occupy positions that are logical contraries, the latter holding that all fetuses have standing and the former that none do. Although contrary positions cannot both be true, they can both be false. From a logical point of view, it is open to someone to hold that some fetuses have standing while others do not. Thus while the established views occupy the opposite extremes along the spectrum of possible positions on this issue, there is a logical space between them. This logical space reflects the fact that each of the established views offers a uniform account of the moral status of the fetus—each, that is, holds that all fetuses have the same status, regardless of any respects in which they might differ. The most obvious respect in which fetuses can differ is in their gestational age and thus their level of development. During the normal course of pregnancy, a fetus gradually evolves from a tiny one-celled organism into a medium-sized and highly complex organism consisting of some six million differentiated cells. Both of the established views are committed to holding that all of the beings at all stages of this transition have precisely the same moral status. The gestational age of the fetus at the time of abortion is thus morally irrelevant on both views. So also is the reason for the abortion. This is irrelevant on the liberal view because no reason is necessary to justify abortion at any stage of pregnancy and equally irrelevant on the conservative view because no reason is sufficient to do so. The established views, therefore, despite their differences, agree on two very important matters: the moral irrelevance of both when and why an abortion is performed. . . .

A MODERATE VIEW

We can now catalogue the defects of the established views. The common source of these defects lies in their uniform accounts of the moral status of the fetus. These accounts yield three different sorts of awkward implications. First, they require that all abortions be accorded the same moral status regardless of the stage of pregnancy at which they are performed. Thus, liberals must hold that late abortions are as morally innocuous as early ones, and conservatives must hold that early abortions are as morally serious as late ones. Neither view is able to support the common conviction that late abortions are more serious than early ones. Second, these accounts require that all abortions be accorded the same moral status regardless of the reason for which they are performed. Thus, liberals must hold that all abortions are equally innocuous whatever their grounds, and conservatives must hold that all abortions are equally serious whatever their grounds. Neither view is able to support the common conviction that some grounds justify abortion more readily than others. Third, these accounts require that contraception, abortion, and infanticide all be accorded the same moral status. Thus, liberals must hold that all three practices are equally innocuous, while conservatives must hold that they are all equally serious. Neither view is able to support the common conviction that infanticide is more serious than abortion, which is in turn more serious than contraception.

Awkward results do not constitute a refutation. The constellation of moral issues concerning human reproduction and development is dark and mysterious. It may be that no internally coherent view of abortion will enable us to retain all of our common moral convictions in this landscape. If so, then perhaps the best we can manage is to embrace one of the established views and bring our attitudes (in whatever turns out to be the troublesome area) into line with it. However, results as awkward as these do provide a strong motive to seek an alternative to the established views and thus to explore the logical space between them.

There are various obstacles in the path of developing a moderate view of abortion. For one thing, any such view will lack the appealing simplicity of the established views. Both liberals and conservatives begin by adopting a simple account of the moral status of the fetus and end by supporting a simple abortion policy. A moderate account of the moral status of the fetus and a moderate abortion policy will inevitably be more complex. Further, a moderate account of the moral status of the fetus, whatever its precise shape, will draw a boundary between those fetuses that have moral standing and those that do not. It will then have to show that the location of this boundary is not arbitrary. Finally, a moderate view may seem nothing more than a compromise between the more

extreme positions that lacks any independent rationale of its own.

These obstacles may, however, be less formidable than they appear. Although the complexity of a moderate view may render it harder to sell in the marketplace of ideas, it may otherwise be its greatest asset. It should be obvious by now that the moral issues raised by the peculiar nature of the fetus, and its peculiar relationship with its mother, are not simple. It would be surprising therefore if a simple resolution of them were satisfactory. The richer resources of a complex view may enable it to avoid some of the less palatable implications of its simpler rivals. The problem of locating a nonarbitrary threshold is easier to deal with when we recognize that there can be no sharp breakpoint in the course of human development at which moral standing is suddenly acquired. The attempt to define such a breakpoint was the fatal mistake of the naive versions of the liberal and conservative views. If, as seems likely, an acceptable criterion of moral standing is built around some characteristic that is acquired gradually during the normal course of human development, then moral standing will also be acquired gradually during the normal course of human development. In that case, the boundary between those beings that have moral standing and those that do not will be soft and slow rather than hard and fast. The more sophisticated and credible versions of the established views also pick out stages of development rather than precise breakpoints as their thresholds of moral standing; the only innovation of a moderate view is to locate this stage somewhere during pregnancy. The real challenge to a moderate view, therefore, is to show that it can be well grounded, and thus that it is not simply a way of splitting the difference between two equally unattractive options.

Our critique of the established views has equipped us with specifications for the design of a moderate alternative to them. The fundamental flaw of the established views was their adoption of a uniform account of the moral status of the fetus. A moderate view of abortion must therefore be built on a *differential* account of the moral status of the fetus, awarding moral standing to some fetuses and withholding it from others. The further defects of the established views impose three constraints on the shape of such a differential account. It must explain the moral relevance of the gestational age of the fetus at the time of abortion and thus must correlate moral status with level of fetal development. It must also explain the moral relevance, at least at some stages of pregnancy, of the reason for which an abortion is performed. And finally it must preserve the distinction between the moral innocuousness of contraception and the the moral seriousness of infanticide. When we combine these specifications, we obtain the rough outline of a moderate view. Such a view will identify the stage of pregnancy during which the fetus gains moral standing. Before that threshold, abortion will be as morally innocuous as contraception and no grounds will be needed to justify it. After the threshold, abortion will be as morally serious as infanticide and some special grounds will be needed to justify it (if it can be justified at this stage at all).

A moderate view is well grounded when it is derivable from an independently plausible criterion of moral standing. It is not difficult to construct a criterion that will yield a threshold somewhere during pregnancy.[2] Let us say that a being is sentient when it has the capacity to experience pleasure and pain and thus the capacity for enjoyment and suffering. Beings that are self-conscious or rational are generally (though perhaps not necessarily) also sentient, but many sentient beings lack both self-consciousness and rationality. A sentience criterion of moral standing thus sets a lower standard than that shared by the established views. Such a criterion will accord moral standing to the mentally handicapped regardless of impairments of their cognitive capacities. It will also accord moral standing to many, perhaps most, non-human animals.

The plausibility of a sentience criterion would be partially established by tracing out its implications for moral contexts other than abortion. But it would be considerably enhanced if such a criterion could also be given a deeper grounding. Such a grounding can be supplied by what seems a reasonable conception of the nature of morality. The moral point of view is just one among many evaluative points of view. It appears to be distinguished

from the others in two respects: its special concern for the interest, welfare, or well-being of creatures and its requirement of impartiality. Adopting the moral point of view requires in one way or another according equal consideration to the interests of all beings. If this is so, then a being's having an interest to be considered is both necessary and sufficient for its having moral standing. While the notion of interest or welfare is far from transparent, its irreducible core appears to be the capacity for enjoyment and suffering: all and only beings with this capacity have an interest or welfare that the moral point of view requires us to respect. But then it follows easily that sentience is both necessary and sufficient for moral standing.

A criterion of moral standing is well grounded when it is derivable from some independently plausible moral theory. A sentience criterion can be grounded in any member of a class of theories that share the foregoing conception of the nature of morality. Because of the centrality of interest or welfare to that conception, let us call such theories welfare based. A sentience criterion of moral standing can be readily grounded in any welfare-based moral theory. The class of such theories is quite extensive, including everything from varieties of rights theory on the one hand to varieties of utilitarianism on the other. Whatever their conceptual and structural differences, a sentience criterion can be derived from any one of them. The diversity of theoretical resources available to support a sentience criterion is one of its greatest strengths. In addition, a weaker version of such a criterion is also derivable from more eclectic theories that treat the promotion and protection of welfare as one of the basic concerns of morality. Any such theory will yield the result that sentience is sufficient for moral standing, though it may also be necessary, thus providing partial support for a moderate view of abortion. Such a view is entirely unsupported only by moral theories that find no room whatever for the promotion of welfare among the concerns of morality.

When we apply a sentience criterion to the course of human development, it yields the result that the threshold of moral standing is the stage during which the capacity to experience pleasure and pain is first required. This capacity is clearly possessed by a newborn infant (and a full-term fetus) and is clearly not possessed by a pair of gametes (or a newly fertilized ovum). It is therefore acquired during the normal course of gestation. But when? A definite answer awaits a better understanding than we now possess of the development of the fetal nervous system and thus of fetal consciousness. We can, however, venture a provisional answer. It is standard practice to divide the normal course of gestation into three trimesters of thirteen weeks each. It is likely that a fetus is unable to feel pleasure or pain at the beginning of the second trimester and likely that it is able to do so at the end of that trimester. If this is so, then the threshold of sentience, and thus also the threshold of moral standing, occurs sometime during the second trimester.

We can now fill in our earlier sketch of a moderate view of abortion. A fetus acquires moral standing when it acquires sentience, that is to say at some stage in the second trimester of pregnancy. Before that threshold, when the fetus lacks moral standing, the decision to seek an abortion is morally equivalent to the decision to employ contraception; the effect in both cases is to prevent the existence of a being with moral standing. Such decisions are morally innocuous and should be left to the discretion of the parties involved. Thus, the liberal view of abortion, and a permissive abortion policy, are appropriate for early (prethreshold) abortions. After the threshold, when the fetus has moral standing, the decision to seek an abortion is morally equivalent to the decision to commit infanticide; the effect in both cases is to terminate the existence of a being with moral standing. Such decisions are morally serious and should not be left to the discretion of the parties involved (the fetus is now one of the parties involved).

It should follow that the conservative view of abortion and a restrictive abortion policy are appropriate for late (post-threshold) abortions. But this does not follow. Conservatives hold that abortion, because it is homicide, is unjustified on any grounds. This absolute position is indefensible even for post-threshold fetuses with moral standing. Of the four categories of grounds for abortion, neither humanitarian nor socioeconomic grounds will apply to post-threshold abortions, since a permissive policy for the period before the threshold will afford women the opportunity to decide freely whether they wish to continue their pregnancies. Therapeutic grounds will however apply, since serious risks to maternal life or health may materialize after the threshold. If they do, there is no justification for refusing an abortion. A pregnant woman is providing life support for another being that is housed within her body. If continuing to provide that life support will place her own life or health at serious risk, then she cannot justifiably be compelled to do so, even though the fetus has moral standing and will die if deprived of that life support. Seeking an abortion in such circumstances is a legitimate act of self-preservation.[3]

A moderate abortion policy must therefore include a therapeutic ground for post-threshold abortions. It must also include a eugenic ground. Given current technology, some tests for fetal abnormalities can be carried out only in the second trimester. In many cases, therefore, serious abnormalities will be detected only after the fetus has passed the threshold. Circumstantial differences aside, the status of a severely deformed post-threshold fetus is the same as the status of a severely deformed newborn infant. The moral issues concerning the treatment of such newborns are themselves complex, but there appears to be a good case for selective infanticide in some cases. If so, then there is an even better case for late abortion on eugenic grounds, since here we must also reckon in the terrible burden of carrying to term a child that a woman knows to be deformed.

A moderate abortion policy will therefore contain the following ingredients: a time limit that separates early from late abortions, a permissive policy for early abortions, and a policy for late abortions that incorporates both therapeutic and eugenic grounds. This blueprint leaves many smaller questions of design to be settled. The grounds for late abortions must be specified more carefully by determining what is to count as a serious risk to maternal life or health and what is to count as a serious fetal abnormality. While no general formulation of a policy can settle these matters in detail, guidelines can and should be supplied. A policy should also specify the procedure that is to be followed in deciding when a particular case has met these guidelines.

But most of all, a moderate policy must impose a defensible time limit. As we saw earlier, from the moral point of view there can be no question of a sharp breakpoint. Fetal development unfolds gradually and cumulatively, and sentience like all other capacities is acquired slowly and by degrees. Thus we have clear cases of presentient fetuses in the first trimester and clear cases of sentient fetuses in the third trimester. But we also have unclear cases, encompassing many (perhaps most) second-trimester fetuses. From the moral point of view, we can say only that in these cases the moral status of the fetus, and thus the moral status of abortion, is indeterminate. This sort of moral indeterminacy occurs also at later stages of human development, for instance when we are attempting to fix the age of consent or of competence to drink or drive. We do not pretend in these latter cases that the capacity in question is acquired overnight on one's sixteenth or eighteenth birthday, and yet for legal purposes we must draw a sharp and determinate line. Any such line will be somewhat arbitrary, but it is enough if it is drawn within the appropriate threshold stage. So also in the case of a time limit for abortion, it is sufficient if the line for legal purposes is located within the appropriate threshold stage. A time limit anywhere in the second trimester is therefore defensible, at least until we acquire the kind of information about fetal development that will enable us to narrow the threshold stage and thus to locate the time limit with more accuracy.

CONCLUSIONS

. . . .While both of the established views have obvious and serious defects, many people seem to feel that there is no coherent third alternative available to them. But a moderate view does appear to provide such an alternative. It does less violence than either of the established views to widely shared convictions about contraception, abortion, and infanticide, and it can be grounded upon a criterion of moral standing that seems to generate acceptable results in other moral contexts and is in turn derivable from a wide range of moral theories sharing a plausible conception of the nature of morality. Those who are dissatisfied with the established views need not therefore fear that in moving to the middle ground they are sacrificing reason for mere expediency.

NOTES

1. The terms 'liberal' and 'conservative,' as used in the chapter generally, refer respectively to those who think abortion permissible and those who believe it impermissible. Thus, 'liberal' here is not synonymous with 'political liberal' and 'conservative' is not synonymous with 'political conservative.'

2. The sentience criterion is defended in my *Abortion and Moral Theory* (Princeton, N.J.: Princeton University Press, 1981), 128–46.

3. This position is defended in Judith Jarvis Thomson, "A Defense of Abortion," in *The Rights and Wrongs of Abortion*, ed. Marshall Cohen et al. (Princeton, N.J.: Princeton University Press, 1974); for contrary views, see John Finnis, "The Rights and Wrongs of Abortion," in *The Rights and Wrongs of Abortion*, and Baruch Brody, *Abortion and the Sanctity of Human Life: A Philosophical View* (Cambridge, Mass.: MIT Press, 1975), Chapters 1 and 2.

READING QUESTIONS

1. According to Sumner, what important feature do the conservative and the liberal views on abortion share?
2. What are the so-called awkward implications of both conservative and liberal views on abortion, according to Sumner?
3. How does Sumner attempt to "ground" his sentience criterion of moral standing?
4. What sorts of considerations would justify a third-trimester abortion according to Sumner?

DISCUSSION QUESTION

1. Is sentience an acceptable criterion of moral standing? (To address this question, you should break it down into questions: Is sentience necessary for having moral standing? Is it sufficient?)

ADDITIONAL RESOURCES

Web Resources

The Centers for Disease Control and Prevention, <www.cdc.gov>. Includes information about health safety and abortion.

Emedicine Health, <http://www.emedicinehealth.com/abortion/article em.htm>. Features basic information on abortion including its legal status in the United States.

The National Right to Life Organization, <www.nrlc.org>. Advocates of the pro-life position.

NARAL Pro-Choice America, <www.prochoiceamerica.org>. Advocates of the pro-choice position.

Authored Books and Articles

Beckwith, Francis, J., *Politically Correct Death: Answering the Arguments for Abortion Rights* (Cedar Rapids, MI: Baker Book House, 1994). A defense of a conservative "pro-life" position with criticisms of what Beckwith takes to be the "pro-choice agenda."

Boonin, David, *A Defense of Abortion* (Cambridge: Cambridge University Press, 2003). A thorough and careful defense of the morality of abortion.

English, Jane, "Abortion and the Concept of a Person," *Canadian Journal of Philosophy* 5 (1975): 233–43. Argues that the concept of a person is not precise enough to determine whether the fetus is clearly a person or clearly not a person (considering all stages of fetal development). English also argues that a woman's right to self-defense justifies abortions even on the assumption that the fetus is a person.

Hare, R. M., "Abortion and the Golden Rule," *Philosophy and Public Affairs* 4 (1975): 210–22. An appeal to a version of the golden rule in defense of a moderate position on abortion.

Harman, Elizabeth, "The Potentiality Problem," *Philosophical Studies* 114 (2003): 173–98. Argues against the claim that potentiality confers moral standing on a fetus.

Kaczor, Christopher, *The Ethics of Abortion: Woman's Rights, Human Life, and the Question of Justice* (London: Routledge, 2010). A careful philosophical defense of an antiabortion position.

Lee, Patrick, *Abortion & Unborn Human Life* "Washington, DC: The Catholic University Press of America 2010). A defense of an antiabortion stance from a coauthor of "The Wrong of Abortion" included in this chapter.

Luker, Kristin, *Abortion and the Politics of Motherhood* (Berkeley, CA: University of California Press, 1984). Contains an illuminating discussion of the history and sociology of the debate over abortion that began in the 19th century.

Shrage, Laurie, *Abortion and Social Responsibility: Depolarizing the Debate* (New York: Oxford University Press, 2003). A critical examination of *Roe v. Wade*'s regulatory scheme with a proposed alternative scheme that aims to depolarize the debate, win broader public support, and thus make legal abortion services more accessible to women in the United States.

Sherwin, Susan, "Abortion through a Feminist Ethics Lens," *Dialogue* 30 (1990): 327–42. Defense of a woman's right to choose abortion grounded in the importance of sexual and reproductive freedom for women.

Sinnott-Armstrong, Walter, "You Can't Lose What You Ain't Never Had: A Reply to Marquis on Abortion," *Philosophical Studies* 96 (1997): 59–72. Argues that Marquis's argument for the claim that abortion is seriously morally wrong commits the fallacy of equivocation.

Steinbock, Bonnie, *Life Before Birth: The Moral and Legal Status of Embryos and Fetuses,* 2nd ed. (Oxford: Oxford University Press, 2011). In addition to abortion, the author treats a variety of bioethical issues grounded in an "interests-based" approach to moral standing.

Tooley, Michael, "Abortion and Infanticide," *Philosophy and Public Affairs* 2 (1972): 37–65. Defense of the moral permissibility of abortion and infanticide.

Tooley, Michael, Celia Wolf-Devine, Philip E. Devine, and Alison M. Jaggar, *Abortion: Three Perspectives* (New York: Oxford University Press, 2009). Four philosophers present three different positions concerning the moral permissibility of abortion, with point and counterpoint responses to one another.

Edited Anthologies

Beckwith, Francis J. and Louis P. Pojman (eds.), *The Abortion Controversy* (Belmont, CA: Wadsworth, 1988). Wide-ranging collection of articles debating abortion.

Baird, Robert M. and Stuart E. Rosenbaum (eds.), *The Ethics of Abortion: Pro-Life Vs. Pro-Choice*, 3rd ed. (New York: Prometheus Books, 2001). Twenty-two essays by various scholars organized into five parts: (1) The Issue, (2) Abortion and the Constitution, (3) Abortion and Feminism, (4) Abortion and Christianity, and (5) Abortion and Moral Philosophy.

Dwyer, Susan and Joel Feinberg (eds.), *The Problem of Abortion*, 3rd ed. (Belmont, CA: Wadsworth, 1996). A collection of essays, mostly by philosophers, representing a spectrum of views about the morality of abortion.

11 } Cloning and Genetic Enhancement

Reproductive technology has made significant advances in the past forty years. For instance, **in vitro** ("under glass") **fertilization** (IVF) through which a sperm fertilizes an egg in a petri dish and, after a few days of growth, is then implanted in a woman's uterus, is available to otherwise infertile couples. In 1978, Louise Brown, the first "test tube" baby, was born using in vitro fertilization, and since then over 5 million children have been born using this procedure. And just as this procedure was subject to intense moral scrutiny when it came on the scene, so also have cloning and the prospect of genetic enhancement, the subjects of this chapter. In order to gain a basic understanding of what is at stake in the moral controversy over these developments, let us focus first on the issue of cloning—what it is and the moral controversy it has caused—and then turn briefly to the ethics of genetic enhancement.

In 1997, a research team, led by Dr. Ian Wilmut of the Roslin Institute in Scotland, produced a cloned sheep named Dolly. The significance of Dolly is that she was the first mammal ever cloned, making it very probable that cloning other mammals, including humans, is possible. The apparently real prospect of cloning a human being—**reproductive cloning**—has generated much recent scientific and ethical debate. And so has **therapeutic cloning**, whose purpose is the production of embryos for use in medical research. If we turn our attention to *human* reproductive and therapeutic cloning, the central moral questions are the following:

- Is either type of human cloning (therapeutic or reproductive) ever morally permissible?
- If not, what best explains why such activities are morally wrong?

In order to appreciate the significance of these questions, we will need to review some very elementary scientific facts about the two types of cloning in question. After we understand what cloning is, we will proceed to recount recent attempts to ban this type of biotechnology and then return to the ethical issues just raised.

1. WHAT IS CLONING?

If we consider **cloning** an organism as an activity that we may choose to perform, then we can say that it involves the process of "asexually" producing a biological organism that is virtually genetically identical to another organism.[1] (The terms "asexual" and "sexual" have technical scientific meanings that are explained later.) The process in question involves **somatic cell**[2] **nuclear transfer** (SCNT for short), and the basic idea here is easy to understand. So, let us begin with what we are calling reproductive cloning and then turn to therapeutic cloning.

In sexual reproduction an unfertilized egg (called an **oocyte**, pronounced, oh-oh-site) is fertilized by a sperm resulting in what is called a **zygote**—a one-cell organism whose nucleus contains genetic information contributed by the individual who produced the egg and by the individual who produced the sperm. A one-cell zygote then undergoes cellular division, and many cells later we have what is commonly called an **embryo**. As the embryo develops, its cells begin to differentiate, forming cells with different functions—nerve cells, blood cells, fat cells, and so on. A complex organism is the eventual result.[3] Here is it important to notice that the process just described refers to cases in which reproduction takes place entirely in a woman's reproductive system *and* to cases in which fertilization is made to occur *in vitro*. Both count as "sexual" in the technical sense of the term, because both involve the genetic contribution from two individuals.

Cloning involves asexual reproduction in which (1) the nucleus of an unfertilized egg is removed and (2) the nucleus of another cell—the "donor" nucleus—is removed and then (3) inserted into the "hollow" unfertilized egg, (4) which is then implanted in a female's uterus. In this process, incidentally, the unfertilized egg and the donor nucleus may be contributed by different individuals, neither of whom may be the individual in whom the embryo is implanted. The resulting individual will be virtually genetically identical—will have nearly the same genetic makeup—as the individual from whom the donor nucleus was taken.[4] The crucial difference between sexual and asexual reproduction, then, is that in the former, the genetic makeup of the zygote and the resulting offspring are the direct result of the genetic contributions of two individuals—the produced offspring is not genetically identical to either of the other two individuals. However, individuals produced asexually by the process of nuclear transfer are virtually genetically identical to the nuclear donor. Let us call the offspring produced by what we are calling reproductive cloning **SCNT individuals**.

We now turn from reproductive cloning to therapeutic cloning. They differ mainly in the purposes for which the process of nuclear transfer is being used. But to understand the therapeutic use of cloning, we need to explain the nature and importance of **stem cells**. Stem cells are found throughout the body and are significant because they have the capability of developing into various kinds of cells or tissues in the body. Stem cells have three general properties: (1) Unlike muscle cells, blood cells, and nerve cells, stem cells have the capacity to renew themselves for long periods of time. (2) Stem cells are "undifferentiated" in that they do not have a specific function as do, for instance, red blood cells whose job is to carry oxygen through the bloodstream. (3) Stem cells can result in specialized cells through a process called differentiation. There are two main types of stem cells that we need to distinguish.

Adult stem cells are undifferentiated cells found among differentiated cells in a tissue or organ. Adult stem cells function to help maintain and repair damaged differentiated cells of the same organ or tissue type in which they are found. This would appear to limit their therapeutic use, since, for example, a heart adult stem cell could only be used to generate heart cells and thus not cells of any other type.[5]

Embryonic stem cells are found in embryos and are "pluripotent," that is, they can become any cell type found in the body. The use of embryonic stem cells, derived from human embryos created by *in vitro* fertilization, has generated moral controversy because extracting these pluripotent cells from embryos inevitably resulted in the destruction of the embryos. However, the use of embryonic stem cells, given that they can be manipulated to become a particular body cell type, makes them particularly valuable for treating disease and other medical conditions. Indeed, cloning makes it possible for a patient who, let us say, is suffering from heart disease, to have the nucleus of one of her body cells injected into an enucleated egg, which could then be induced to multiply, thereby producing an embryo. From the embryo, stem cells could be extracted and used for purposes of producing heart cells that would be used to treat one's heart disease. Because the embryonic stem cells produced in this way match your genetic makeup, there is reduced risk of tissue rejection and thus greater chance of success.

Until recently, use of embryonic stem cells for purposes of research required the destruction of the embryos from which these stem cells were derived. And the destruction of embryos has been a basis of moral objection to such research by those who consider the embryo to have direct moral standing. However, in 2006, scientists developed a technique for extracting embryonic stem cells without destroying the embryos. This breakthrough was greeted by some as removing any serious moral objections to the use of such cells in research.[6]

So, although both types of human cloning—reproductive and therapeutic—involve the process of nuclear transfer, the former has as its aim the bringing about of a child, while the latter aims only at producing a human embryo, stem cells from which might then be used for medical purposes. And, as we have just seen, although there have been moral objections to therapeutic cloning of the sort that involves the destruction of embryos, with new advances in the extraction of stem cells from human embryos that do not destroy the embryo, therapeutic cloning promises to become less morally problematic. In any case, it is the issue of reproductive cloning that has stirred most of the recent moral controversy over cloning and is the topic of concern in our selections dealing with cloning.

2. THE MOVE TO BAN CLONING

In the United States, one immediate response to the announcement of Dolly (the cloned sheep mentioned earlier) was the creation by President William Clinton of the National Bioethics Advisory Council (NBAC), whose task it was to investigate American public policy on the topic of cloning. After conducting hearings during which religious and secular moral arguments were presented and discussed, the NBAC called on Congress to pass laws that would make reproductive cloning a federal crime. To date, Congress has not been able to pass any such law.

On August 9, 2001, President George W. Bush announced that federal funding for stem cell research would be restricted to stem cell lines already in existence on the date of his announcement. This was generally seen as a compromise between factions that oppose therapeutic cloning and those in favor of it. On March 9, 2009, President Barack Obama issued an executive order ("Removing Barriers to Responsible Research Involving Human Stem Cells") that lifted the funding restrictions that President Bush's directive prohibited. Obama's order lifted the ban on the use of federal funding for research on stem cells created with private money, but did not address the ban on the use of federal funds to develop new stem cell lines.

As of 2015, eight U.S. states had passed laws to ban human cloning for any purpose.[7] According to the Center for Genetics and Society based in California, as of December of 2009, approximately fifty countries had passed laws banning reproductive cloning.

3. GENETIC ENHANCEMENT

Our developed capacity to manipulate human genetic material not only promises to provide ways to treat disease and other human maladies, but also may enable us to enhance our bodies and our minds. **Genetic enhancement** differs from cloning in that the latter is a form of asexual reproduction as explained earlier, whereas (human) genetic enhancement refers to manipulating genetic material in order to "improve" the talents and capacities of living humans or to produce offspring with certain desirable traits. For instance, the Genetics and IVF Institute in Fairfax, Virginia, already offers a process of sperm separation through which the sex of offspring can be selected. Creating "designer babies," as they are often called, is now an option for those who can afford it. There are further implications. For instance, **eugenics,** the project of "improving" humanity by bringing about genetic changes in future generations, is now very much a possibility.

A new technique for manipulating genes, called CRISPR, has gained worldwide attention. The technique allows scientists to cut away a piece of an organism's DNA responsible for hereditary diseases such as Huntington's chorea, sickle cell anemia, and muscular dystrophy. What differentiates CRISPR from other forms of gene therapy is that it can be used to modify genes on the human germ line and thus alter the human gene pool. While this technique can be used for therapeutic purposes, it potentially could be used for purposes of enhancement and to produce designer babies. So CRISPR raises many of the ethical and legal questions raised by therapeutic and reproductive cloning.

Let us suppose that therapeutic (medical) genetic manipulation is at least sometimes morally permissible. So the controversy that has generated much recent discussion concerns these questions:

- Is genetic manipulation *for purposes of enhancement* ever morally permissible?
- If they are not, why is such manipulation for such purposes morally impermissible?

4. THEORY MEETS PRACTICE

Let us now turn to some of the moral arguments about cloning and genetic enhancement that are grounded in various moral theories.

Natural Law Theory

One kind of natural law argument against reproductive cloning begins with the thought that cloning (and other forms of assisted reproduction such as in vitro fertilization), because they are asexual, break the natural connection between sex and reproduction—they represent "unnatural" activities. If one then thinks that "unnatural" activities are morally wrong, one will conclude that cloning is morally wrong.[8] (For a critical assessment of arguments that appeal to the idea of "unnaturalness," see the article in chapter 3 by John Corvino.)

But a natural law approach need not appeal to the alleged unnaturalness of actions. Instead, natural law theorists often take reproduction to be intrinsically good and thus something that we are morally obliged to preserve and protect. Our moral obligations regarding reproduction are also taken to include proper child rearing—child rearing that fully respects the dignity of the child. Worries about respecting the worth of the child are a basis for natural law objections to cloning. And here is one place where natural law theory and Kantian ethics coincide in their moral concern about cloning. Let us pursue this line of thought further by turning to the Kantian perspective on this issue.

Kantian moral theory

The idea that morality requires that we respect the humanity in both ourselves and others is a guiding idea of the Kantian approach to moral issues. One of the most commonly voiced arguments against reproductive cloning is that it violates the dignity of the SCNT individual—it involves treating the individual as a mere means to some end. The specific manner in which this form of argument is expressed may differ from author to author, but we find a representative example of it in the article from Leon R. Kass included in this chapter.

The plausibility of this line of argument depends on the crucial claim that cloning represents or necessarily involves treating someone merely as a means. But this claim is contested by those who otherwise accept a Kantian approach. For instance, one might argue that there is nothing about cloning that necessarily involves treating anyone merely as a means.[9] Rather, so the argument might continue, whether a child is treated merely as a means and is thus treated immorally depends on the details of how he or she is treated, regardless of how that child was produced.

Consequentialism

Consequentialist thinking about ethical issues is guided by judgments about the likely consequences of actions and practices. Those who oppose cloning point to what they think are likely negative consequences of cloning including, in particular, physical and psychological harms they think are likely be to be suffered by SCNT individuals.

One particular consequentialist argument is called the "slippery slope." A slippery slope argument may take various forms, but behind all such arguments is the idea that if we allow some action or practice *P*, then we will open the door to other similar actions and practices that will eventually lead us down a slope to disastrous results. So, the argument concludes, we morally ought not to allow *P*. Any such argument, in order to be good, must meet two requirements. First, it must be true that the envisioned results really are bad. But second, the central idea of the argument—that allowing one action or practice will be likely to lead us down a path to disaster—must be plausible. If either of these conditions is not met, the argument is said to commit the slippery slope *fallacy*.

With regard to cloning, the argument is that if we allow certain forms of reproductive cloning for what may seem like acceptable reasons, this will open the door to further and further cases of cloning, leading eventually to its abuse and thus to disaster.[10] Perhaps the most vivid portrayal of what might happen is to be found in Aldous Huxley's 1932 novel, *Brave New World,* in which cloning is the chief means of reproduction through which the majority of humans in that world are genetically engineered for various purposes. Huxley's novel portrays a world in which cloning plays a central role in the loss of human dignity and individuality. In light of the recent advances in biotechnology and the very real possibility of reproductive cloning, Francis Fukuyama writes that "Huxley was right, that the most significant threat posed by contemporary biotechnology is the possibility that it will alter human nature and thereby move us into a 'posthuman' stage in history."[11] Voicing similar worries, Leon R. Kass, in an article included in this chapter, explicitly raises the specter of *Brave New World* in his opposition to cloning.

How forceful are such consequentialist arguments? Their plausibility depends crucially on the estimates of the likely consequences of cloning. Gregory Pence, in one of the selections included in this chapter, attempts to rebut the claims of the anticloning consequentialists. Still, many people who oppose reproductive cloning seem to base their opposition at least partly on what they take to be its likely consequences. Notice that those whose opposition to cloning depends *entirely* on an appeal to consequences will have to retract their moral stance on this topic if we have good reason (now or in the future) to believe that the effects of cloning are no more disastrous than, say, IVF.

Peter Singer raises consequentialist concerns about the ethics of allowing a "genetic supermarket" in which prospective parents can pay to have an embryo genetically modified with the aim of producing a child whose abilities are likely to be superior to a child they would have otherwise had. Singer's "Parental Choice and Human Improvement" is the final selection in this chapter.

Rights Approaches

Approaching the moral issues of both therapeutic and reproductive cloning from the perspective of rights has led to various opposing conclusions about such practices. For instance, some argue that various forms of assisted reproduction are plausibly included within a general right to reproductive liberty.[12] On this basis, one might argue that cloning should be regarded as something we may choose and which is presumptively morally permissible, unless there are compelling reasons against exercising this form of reproductive liberty. Thus, unlike many writers on the ethics of cloning who think that the burden of moral justification rests with those who favor cloning, one might appeal to rights of reproduction and claim that the burden of moral justification rests with those who think that there is something morally wrong with the practice.

But rights are often center stage in arguments that oppose therapeutic as well as reproductive cloning. A main ethical objection to therapeutic cloning is based on the fact that extracting stem cells from a human embryo inevitably destroys the embryo. Those who think that a human embryo has a right to life are against therapeutic cloning for the same reason they are against abortion—such activities involve the killing of an innocent human being with a right to life. Of course, whether this argument is sound depends on the crucial moral claim that a human embryo has a right to life, an issue discussed in the chapter on abortion.

Virtue Ethics

The ethical issues that genetic enhancement raises are much like the ones implicated in the debate over cloning. Consequentialist worries about the likely negative effects of this practice, Kantian worries about whether it is somehow dehumanizing, and natural law questions about its "naturalness" are all represented in the literature on the ethics of enhancement. In addition, ethical concerns that focus on the dispositions and attitudes that would be expressed through engaging in or condoning genetic enhancement—concerns that focus on virtue, vice, and the morality of character—have been raised by some critics of the practice. Michael J. Sandel, whose essay is included here, is one such critic whose approach to the ethics of enhancement is perhaps best viewed as an example of applied virtue ethics. Sandel's position is subjected to critical scrutiny by Frances M. Kamm in her essay included in this chapter.

NOTES

1. Strictly speaking "cloning" refers very generally to the process of duplicating genetic material. There are different types of cloning: DNA cloning, reproductive cloning, and therapeutic cloning. The Human Genome Project has information on types of cloning. See Additional Resources for reference.

2. A **somatic cell** is any cell in the body other than an egg or sperm (gametes).

3. For more detail about human fetal development, see the introduction to the chapter on abortion.

4. The clone's chromosomal or nuclear DNA is the same as the donor's. Some of the clone's genetic material is contributed by the mitochondrial DNA in the cytoplasm of the enucleated egg, hence the claim that clones are "nearly" genetically identical to the cell donor.

5. Through a process of what is called "transdifferentiation" it may be possible for an adult stem cell to differentiate into a different cell type. For example, an adult brain stem cell might differentiate into a blood cell. However, whether this process does actually occur in humans is controversial.

6. Very recently scientists have been able to "reprogram" adult somatic cells so that they come to be like embryonic stem cells—cells that can become differentiated cells of most any type. Such genetically reprogrammed cells are called **induced pluripotent stem (iPS) cells**. If adult cells can be used for the same purposes as embryonic stem cells, then there is no need to engage in the process of cloning to produce an embryo from which embryonic stem cells are then extracted. For more information about iPS cells, consult "Stem Cell Information" to be found on the National Institutes of Health website mentioned in Additional Resources for this chapter.

7. This statistic is reported by the National Conference of State Legislatures (NCSL). See <http://www.ncsl.org/issuesresearch/health/humancloninglaws/tabid/14284/default.aspx>.

8. This form of argument can be found in Leon Kass's "The Wisdom of Repugnance," *The New Republic* 216: 22, June 1997. Notice that this argument, if sound, would also show that IVF is morally wrong, since sexual intercourse is not involved in the process. One might respond to this argument by pointing out that although there is a "natural" connection between eating and nutrition, breaking this connection by intravenous feeding would not be morally wrong. Thus, the mere breaking of a "natural" connection cannot make an action morally wrong. See also the Vatican declaration pertaining to bio-ethical issues mentioned in Additional Resources for this chapter under Congregation for the Doctrine of the Faith.

9. This argument is to be found in Philip Kitcher's *The Lives to Come* mentioned in Additional Resources for this chapter.

10. This same slippery slope argument is often used to oppose therapeutic cloning. What forms of cloning might be understood as at least initially acceptable? There is some dispute over whether there are such cases.

11. Francis Fukuyama, *Our Posthuman Future* (New York: Farrar, Straus and Giroux, 2002), 7.

12. See, for instance, John Robertson, "Liberty, Identity, and Human Cloning," *Texas Law Review* 1371, 1998.

Leon R. Kass

Preventing Brave New World

Kass has been a vocal and longtime opponent of cloning. In the selection that follows, he begins by describing the dystopian world envisioned in Aldous Huxley's 1932 *Brave New World* and then proceeds to raise four moral arguments against reproductive cloning. In addition to objections based on likely bad consequences of cloning, Kass argues that cloning is "unethical in itself" because in various ways it represents a degradation of our human nature and thus is not in accord with respect for humanity. Kass concludes by raising a slippery slope objection to defenders of cloning who, like John Robertson, base their defense on "reproductive liberty."

Recommended Reading: Kantian moral theory, chap. 1, sec. 2C, particularly the Humanity formulation of Kant's categorical imperative. Also relevant is natural law theory, chap. 1, sec. 2B.

I

The urgency of the great political struggles of the twentieth century, successfully waged against totalitarianisms first right and then left, seems to have blinded many people to a deeper and ultimately darker truth about the present age: all contemporary societies are travelling briskly in the same utopian direction. All are wedded to the modern technological project; all march eagerly to the drums of progress and fly proudly the banner of modern science; all sing loudly the Baconian anthem, "Conquer nature, relieve man's estate." Leading the triumphal procession is modern medicine, which is daily becoming ever more powerful in its battle against disease, decay, and death, thanks especially to astonishing achievements in biomedical science and technology—achievements for which we must surely be grateful.

Yet contemplating present and projected advances in genetic and reproductive technologies, in neuroscience and psychopharmacology, and in the development of artificial organs and computer-chip implants for human brains, we now clearly recognize new uses for biotechnical power that soar beyond the traditional medical goals of healing disease and relieving suffering. Human nature itself lies on the operating table, ready for alteration, for eugenic and psychic "enhancement," for wholesale re-design. In leading laboratories, academic and industrial, new creators are confidently amassing their powers and quietly honing their skills, while on the street their evangelists are zealously prophesying a post-human future. For anyone who cares about preserving our humanity, the time has come to pay attention.

Some transforming powers are already here. The Pill. In vitro fertilization. Bottled embryos. Surrogate wombs. Cloning. Genetic screening.

Genetic manipulation. Organ harvesting. Mechanical spare parts. Chimeras. Brain implants. Ritalin for the young, Viagra for the old, Prozac for everyone. And, to leave this vale of tears, a little extra morphine accompanied by Muzak.

Years ago Aldous Huxley saw it coming. In his charming but disturbing novel, *Brave New World* (it appeared in 1932 and is more powerful on each re-reading), he made its meaning strikingly visible for all to see. Unlike other frightening futuristic novels of the past century, such as Orwell's already dated *Nineteen Eighty-Four,* Huxley shows us a dystopia that goes with, rather than against, the human grain. Indeed, it is animated by our own most humane and progressive aspirations. Following those aspirations to their ultimate realization, Huxley enables us to recognize those less obvious but often more pernicious evils that are inextricably linked to the successful attainment of partial goods.

Huxley depicts human life seven centuries hence, living under the gentle hand of humanitarianism rendered fully competent by genetic manipulation, psychoactive drugs, hypnopaedia, and high-tech amusements. At long last, mankind has succeeded in eliminating disease, aggression, war, anxiety, suffering, guilt, envy, and grief. But this victory comes at the heavy price of homogenization, mediocrity, trivial pursuits, shallow attachments, debased tastes, spurious contentment, and souls without loves or longings. The Brave New World has achieved prosperity, community, stability and nigh-universal contentment, only to be peopled by creatures of human shape but stunted humanity. They consume, fornicate, take "soma," enjoy "centrifugal bumble-puppy," and operate the machinery that makes it all possible. They do not read, write, think, love, or govern themselves. Art and science, virtue and religion, family and friendship are all passé. What matters most is bodily health and immediate gratification: "Never put off till tomorrow the fun you can have today." Brave New Man is so dehumanized that he does not even recognize what has been lost.

Huxley's novel, of course, is science fiction. Prozac is not yet Huxley's "soma"; cloning by nuclear transfer or splitting embryos is not exactly "Bokanovskification"; MTV and virtual-reality parlors are not quite the "feelies"; and our current safe and consequenceless sexual practices are not universally as loveless or as empty as those in the novel. But the kinships are disquieting, all the more so since our technologies of bio-psycho-engineering are still in their infancy, and in ways that make all too clear what they might look like in their full maturity. Moreover, the cultural changes that technology has already wrought among us should make us even more worried than Huxley would have us be.

In Huxley's novel, everything proceeds under the direction of an omnipotent—albeit benevolent—world state. Yet the dehumanization that he portrays does not really require despotism or external control. To the contrary, precisely because the society of the future will deliver exactly what we most want—health, safety, comfort, plenty, pleasure, peace of mind and length of days—we can reach the same humanly debased condition solely on the basis of free human choice. No need for World Controllers. Just give us the technological imperative, liberal democratic society, compassionate humanitarianism, moral pluralism, and free markets, and we can take ourselves to a Brave New World all by ourselves—and without even deliberately deciding to go. In case you had not noticed, the train has already left the station and is gathering speed, but no one seems to be in charge.

Some among us are delighted, of course, by this state of affairs: some scientists and biotechnologists, their entrepreneurial backers, and a cheering claque of sci-fi enthusiasts, futurologists, and libertarians. There are dreams to be realized, powers to be exercised, honors to be won, and money—big money—to be made. But many of us are worried, and not, as the proponents of the revolution self-servingly claim, because we are either ignorant of science or afraid of the unknown. To the contrary, we can see all too clearly where the train is headed, and we do not like the destination. We can distinguish cleverness about means from wisdom about ends, and we are loath to entrust the future of the race to those who cannot tell the difference. No friend of humanity cheers for a post-human future.

Yet for all our disquiet, we have until now done nothing to prevent it. We hide our heads in the sand because we enjoy the blessings that medicine keeps supplying, or we rationalize our inaction by declaring that human engineering is inevitable and we can do nothing about it. In either case, we are complicit in preparing for our own degradation, in some respects more to blame than the bio-zealots who, however misguided, are putting their money where their mouth is. Denial and despair, unattractive outlooks in any situation, become morally reprehensible when circumstances summon us to keep the world safe for human flourishing. Our immediate ancestors, taking up the challenge of their time, rose to the occasion and rescued the human future from the cruel dehumanizations of Nazi and Soviet tyranny. It is our more difficult task to find ways to preserve it from the soft dehumanizations of well-meaning but hubristic biotechnical "re-creationism"—and to do it without undermining biomedical science or rejecting its genuine contributions to human welfare. . . .

Not the least of our difficulties in trying to exercise control over where biology is taking us is the fact that we do not get to decide, once and for all, for or against the destination of a post-human world. The scientific discoveries and the technical powers that will take us there come to us piecemeal, one at a time and seemingly independent from one another, each often attractively introduced as a measure that will "help [us] not to be sick." But sometimes we come to a clear fork in the road where decision is possible, and where we know that our decision will make a world of difference—indeed, it will make a permanently different world. Fortunately, we stand now at the point of such a momentous decision. Events have conspired to provide us with a perfect opportunity to seize the initiative and to gain some control of the biotechnical project. I refer to the prospect of human cloning, a practice absolutely central to Huxley's fictional world. Indeed, creating and manipulating life in the laboratory is the gateway to a Brave New World, not only in fiction but also in fact.

"To clone or not to clone a human being" is no longer a fanciful question. Success in cloning sheep, and also cows, mice, pigs, and goats, makes it perfectly clear that a fateful decision is now at hand: whether we should welcome or even tolerate the cloning of human beings. If recent newspaper reports are to be believed, reputable scientists and physicians have announced their intention to produce the first human clone in the coming year. Their efforts may already be under way. . . .

But we dare not be complacent about what is at issue, for the stakes are very high. Human cloning, though partly continuous with previous reproductive technologies, is also something radically new in itself and in its easily foreseeable consequences—especially when coupled with powers for genetic "enhancement" and germline genetic modification that may soon become available, owing to the recently completed Human Genome Project. I exaggerate somewhat, but in the direction of the truth: we are compelled to decide nothing less than whether human procreation is going to remain human, whether children are going to be made to order rather than begotten, and whether we wish to say yes in principle to the road that leads to the dehumanized hell of *Brave New World*.

[W]e have here a golden opportunity to exercise some control over where biology is taking us. The technology of cloning is discrete and well defined, and it requires considerable technical know-how and dexterity; we can therefore know by name many of the likely practitioners. The public demand for cloning is extremely low, and most people are decidedly against it. Nothing scientifically or medically important would be lost by banning clonal reproduction; alternative and non-objectionable means are available to obtain some of the most important medical benefits claimed for (nonreproductive) human cloning. The commercial interests in human cloning are, for now, quite limited; and the nations of the world are actively seeking to prevent it. Now may be as good a chance as we will ever have to get our hands on the wheel of the runaway train now headed for a post-human world and to steer it toward a more dignified human future.

II

What is cloning? Cloning, or asexual reproduction, is the production of individuals who are genetically identical to an already existing individual. The procedure's name is fancy—"somatic cell nuclear transfer"—but its concept is simple. Take a mature but unfertilized egg; remove or deactivate its nucleus; introduce a nucleus obtained from a specialized (somatic) cell of an adult organism. Once the egg begins to divide, transfer the little embryo to a woman's uterus to initiate a pregnancy. Since almost all the hereditary material of a cell is contained within its nucleus, the re-nucleated egg and the individual into which it develops are genetically identical to the organism that was the source of the transferred nucleus.

An unlimited number of genetically identical individuals—the group, as well as each of its members, is called "a clone"—could be produced by nuclear transfer. In principle, any person, male or female, newborn or adult, could be cloned, and in any quantity; and because stored cells can outlive their sources, one may even clone the dead. Since cloning requires no personal involvement on the part of the person whose genetic material is used, it could easily be used to reproduce living or deceased persons without their consent—a threat to reproductive freedom that has received relatively little attention.

Some possible misconceptions need to be avoided. Cloning is not Xeroxing: the clone of Bill Clinton, though his genetic double, would enter the world hairless, toothless, and peeing in his diapers, like any other human infant. But neither is cloning just like natural twinning: the cloned twin will be identical to an older, existing adult; and it will arise not by chance but by deliberate design; and its entire genetic makeup will be preselected by its parents and/or scientists. Moreover, the success rate of cloning, at least at first, will probably not be very high: the Scots transferred two hundred seventy-seven adult nuclei into sheep eggs, implanted twenty-nine clonal embryos, and achieved the birth of only one live lamb clone.

For this reason, among others, it is unlikely that, at least for now, the practice would be very popular; and there is little immediate worry of mass-scale production of multicopies. Still, for the tens of thousands of people who sustain more than three hundred assisted-reproduction clinics in the United States and already avail themselves of in vitro fertilization and other techniques, cloning would be an option with virtually no added fuss. Panos Zavos, the Kentucky reproduction specialist who has announced his plans to clone a child, claims that he has already received thousands of e-mailed requests from people eager to clone, despite the known risks of failure and damaged offspring. Should commercial interests develop in "nucleus-banking," as they have in sperm-banking and egg-harvesting; should famous athletes or other celebrities decide to market their DNA the way they now market their autographs and nearly everything else; should techniques of embryo and germline genetic testing and manipulation arrive as anticipated, increasing the use of laboratory assistance in order to obtain "better" babies—should all this come to pass, cloning, if it is permitted, could become more than a marginal practice simply on the basis of free reproductive choice.

What are we to think about this prospect? Nothing good. Indeed, most people are repelled by nearly all aspects of human cloning: the possibility of mass production of human beings, with large clones of look-alikes, compromised in their individuality; the idea of father-son or mother-daughter "twins"; the bizarre prospect of a woman bearing and rearing a genetic copy of herself, her spouse, or even her deceased father or mother; the grotesqueness of conceiving a child as an exact "replacement" for another who has died; the utilitarian creation of embryonic duplicates of oneself, to be frozen away or created when needed to provide homologous tissues or organs for transplantation; the narcissism of those who would clone themselves, and the arrogance of others who think they know who deserves to be cloned; the Frankensteinian hubris to create a human life and increasingly to control its destiny; men playing at being God. Almost no one finds any of the suggested reasons for human cloning compelling, and almost everyone anticipates its possible misuses and abuses. And the popular belief that human cloning cannot be prevented makes the prospect all the more revolting.

Revulsion is not an argument; and some of yesterday's repugnances are today calmly accepted—not always for the better. In some crucial cases, however, repugnance is the emotional expression of deep wisdom, beyond reason's power completely to articulate it. Can anyone really give an argument fully adequate to the horror that is father-daughter incest (even with consent), or bestiality, or the mutilation of a corpse, or the eating of human flesh, or the rape or murder of another human being? Would anybody's failure to give full rational justification for his revulsion at those practices make that revulsion ethically suspect?

I suggest that our repugnance at human cloning belongs in this category. We are repelled by the prospect of cloning human beings not because of the strangeness or the novelty of the undertaking, but because we intuit and we feel, immediately and without argument, the violation of things that we rightfully hold dear. We sense that cloning represents a profound defilement of our given nature as procreative beings, and of the social relations built on this natural ground. We also sense that cloning is a radical form of child abuse. In this age in which everything is held to be permissible so long as it is freely done, and in which our bodies are regarded as mere instruments of our autonomous rational will, repugnance may be the only voice left that speaks up to defend the central core of our humanity. Shallow are the souls that have forgotten how to shudder.

III

Yet repugnance need not stand naked before the bar of reason. The wisdom of our horror at human cloning can be at least partially articulated, even if this is finally one of those instances about which the heart has its reasons that reason cannot entirely know. I offer four objections to human cloning: that it constitutes unethical experimentation; that it threatens identity and individuality; that it turns procreation into manufacture (especially when understood as the harbinger of manipulations to come); and that it means despotism over children and perversion of parenthood. Please note: I speak only about so-called reproductive cloning, not about the creation of cloned embryos for research. The objections that may be raised against creating (or using) embryos for research are entirely independent of whether the research embryos are produced by cloning. What is radically distinct and radically new is reproductive cloning.

Any attempt to clone a human being would constitute an unethical experiment upon the resulting child-to-be. In all the animal experiments, fewer than two to three percent of all cloning attempts succeeded. Not only are there fetal deaths and stillborn infants, but many of the so-called "successes" are in fact failures. As has only recently become clear, there is a very high incidence of major disabilities and deformities in cloned animals that attain live birth. Cloned cows often have heart and lung problems; cloned mice later develop pathological obesity; other live-born cloned animals fail to reach normal developmental milestones.

The problem, scientists suggest, may lie in the fact that an egg with a new somatic nucleus must re-program itself in a matter of minutes or hours (whereas the nucleus of an unaltered egg has been prepared over months and years). There is thus a greatly increased likelihood of error in translating the genetic instructions, leading to developmental defects some of which will show themselves only much later. (Note also that these induced abnormalities may also affect the stem cells that scientists hope to harvest from cloned embryos. Lousy embryos, lousy stem cells.) Nearly all scientists now agree that attempts to clone human beings carry massive risks of producing unhealthy, abnormal, and malformed children. What are we to do with them? Shall we just discard the ones that fall short of expectations? Considered opinion is today nearly unanimous, even among scientists: attempts at human cloning are irresponsible and unethical. We cannot ethically even get to know whether or not human cloning is feasible.

If it were successful, cloning would create serious issues of identity and individuality. The clone may experience concerns about his distinctive identity not only because he will be, in genotype and in appearance, identical to another human being, but because he may also be twin to the person who is his "father" or his "mother"—if one can still call them that. Unaccountably, people treat as innocent the homey case of intra-familial cloning—the cloning of husband or wife (or single mother). They forget about the unique dangers of mixing the twin relation with the parent-child relation. (For this situation, the relation of contemporaneous twins is no precedent; yet even this less problematic situation teaches us how difficult it is to wrest independence from the being for whom one has the most powerful affinity.) Virtually no parent is going to be able to treat a clone of himself or herself as one treats a child generated by the lottery of sex. What will happen when the adolescent clone of Mommy becomes the spitting image of the woman with whom Daddy once fell in love? In case of divorce, will Mommy still love the clone of Daddy, even though she can no longer stand the sight of Daddy himself?

Most people think about cloning from the point of view of adults choosing to clone. Almost nobody thinks about what it would be like to be the cloned child. Surely his or her new life would constantly be scrutinized in relation to that of the older version. Even in the absence of unusual parental expectations for the clone—say, to live the same life, only without its errors—the child is likely to be ever a curiosity, ever a potential source of déjà vu. Unlike "normal" identical twins, a cloned individual—copied from whomever—will be saddled with a genotype that has already lived. He will not be fully a surprise to the world: people are likely always to compare his doings in life with those of his alter ego, especially if he is a clone of someone gifted or famous. True, his nurture and his circumstance will be different; genotype is not exactly destiny. But one must also expect parental efforts to shape this new life after the original—or at least to view the child with the original version always firmly in mind. For why else did they clone from the star basketball player, the mathematician, or the beauty queen—or even dear old Dad—in the first place?

Human cloning would also represent a giant step toward the transformation of begetting into making, of procreation into manufacture (literally, "handmade"), a process that has already begun with in vitro fertilization and genetic testing of embryos. With cloning, not only is the process in hand, but the total genetic blueprint of the cloned individual is selected and determined by the human artisans. To be sure, subsequent development is still according to natural processes; and the resulting children will be recognizably human. But we would be taking a major step into making man himself simply another one of the man-made things.

How does begetting differ from making? In natural procreation, human beings come together to give existence to another being that is formed exactly as we were, by what we are—living, hence perishable, hence aspiringly erotic, hence procreative human beings. But in clonal reproduction, and in the more advanced forms of manufacture to which it will lead, we give existence to a being not by what we are but by what we intend and design.

Let me be clear. The problem is not the mere intervention of technique, and the point is not that "nature knows best." The problem is that any child whose being, character, and capacities exist owing to human design does not stand on the same plane as its makers. As with any product of our making, no matter how excellent, the artificer stands above it, not as an equal but as a superior, transcending it by his will and creative prowess. In human cloning, scientists and prospective "parents" adopt a technocratic attitude toward human children: human children become their artifacts. Such an arrangement is profoundly dehumanizing, no matter how good the product.

Procreation dehumanized into manufacture is further degraded by commodification, a virtually inescapable result of allowing baby-making to proceed under the banner of commerce. Genetic and reproductive biotechnology companies are already growth industries, but they will soon go into commercial orbit now that the Human Genome Project has been completed. "Human eggs for sale" is already a big business, masquerading under the pretense of "donation." Newspaper advertisements on elite college campuses offer up to $50,000 for an egg "donor" tall enough to play women's basketball and with SAT scores high enough for admission to Stanford; and to nobody's surprise, at such prices there are many young coeds eager to help shoppers obtain the finest babies money can buy. (The egg and womb-renting entrepreneurs shamelessly proceed on the ancient, disgusting, misogynist premise that most women will give you access to their bodies, if the price is right.) Even before the capacity for human cloning is perfected, established companies will have invested in the harvesting of eggs from ovaries obtained at autopsy or through ovarian surgery, practiced embryonic genetic alteration, and initiated the stockpiling of prospective donor tissues. Through the rental of surrogate-womb services, and through the buying and selling of tissues and embryos priced according to the merit of the donor, the commodification of nascent human life will be unstoppable.

Finally, the practice of human cloning by nuclear transfer—like other anticipated forms of genetically engineering the next generation—would enshrine and aggravate a profound misunderstanding of the meaning of having children and of the parent-child relationship. When a couple normally chooses to procreate, the partners are saying yes to the emergence of new life in its novelty—are saying yes not only to having a child, but also to having whatever child this child turns out to be. In accepting our finitude, in opening ourselves to our replacement, we tacitly confess the limits of our control.

Embracing the future by procreating means precisely that we are relinquishing our grip in the very activity of taking up our own share in what we hope will be the immortality of human life and the human species. This means that our children are not our children: they are not our property, they are not our possessions. Neither are they supposed to live our lives for us, or to live anyone's life but their own. Their genetic distinctiveness and independence are the natural foreshadowing of the deep truth that they have their own, never-before-enacted life to live. Though sprung from a past, they take an uncharted course into the future.

Much mischief is already done by parents who try to live vicariously through their children. Children are sometimes compelled to fulfill the broken dreams of unhappy parents. But whereas most parents normally have hopes for their children, cloning parents will have expectations. In cloning, such overbearing parents will have taken at the start a decisive step that contradicts the entire meaning of the open and forward-looking nature of parent-child relations. The child is given a genotype that has already lived, with full expectation that this blueprint of a past life ought to be controlling the life that is to come. A wanted child now means a child who exists precisely to fulfill parental wants. Like all the more precise eugenic

manipulations that will follow in its wake, cloning is thus inherently despotic, for it seeks to make one's children after one's own image (or an image of one's choosing) and their future according to one's will.

Is this hyperbolic? Consider concretely the new realities of responsibility and guilt in the households of the cloned. No longer only the sins of the parents, but also the genetic choices of the parents, will be visited on the children—and beyond the third and fourth generation; and everyone will know who is responsible. No parent will be able to blame nature or the lottery of sex for an unhappy adolescent's big nose, dull wit, musical ineptitude, nervous disposition, or anything else that he hates about himself. Fairly or not, children will hold their cloners responsible for everything, for nature as well as for nurture. And parents, especially the better ones, will be limitlessly liable to guilt. Only the truly despotic souls will sleep the sleep of the innocent.

IV

The defenders of cloning are not wittingly friends of despotism. Quite the contrary. Deaf to most other considerations, they regard themselves mainly as friends of freedom: the freedom of individuals to reproduce, the freedom of scientists and inventors to discover and to devise and to foster "progress" in genetic knowledge and technique, the freedom of entrepreneurs to profit in the market. They want large-scale cloning only for animals, but they wish to preserve cloning as a human option for exercising our "right to reproduce"— our right to have children, and children with "desirable genes." As some point out, under our "right to reproduce" we already practice early forms of unnatural, artificial, and extra-marital reproduction, and we already practice early forms of eugenic choice. For that reason, they argue, cloning is no big deal.

We have here a perfect example of the logic of the slippery slope. The principle of reproductive freedom currently enunciated by the proponents of cloning logically embraces the ethical acceptability of sliding all the way down: to producing children wholly in the laboratory from sperm to term (should it become feasible), and to producing children whose entire genetic makeup will be the product of parental eugenic planning and choice. If reproductive freedom means the right to have a child of one's own choosing by whatever means, then reproductive freedom knows and accepts no limits.

Proponents want us to believe that there are legitimate uses of cloning that can be distinguished from illegitimate uses, but by their own principles no such limits can be found. (Nor could any such limits be enforced in practice: once cloning is permitted, no one ever need discover whom one is cloning and why.) Reproductive freedom, as they understand it, is governed solely by the subjective wishes of the parents-to-be. The sentimentally appealing case of the childless married couple is, on these grounds, indistinguishable from the case of an individual (married or not) who would like to clone someone famous or talented, living or dead. And the principle here endorsed justifies not only cloning but also all future artificial attempts to create (manufacture) "better" or "perfect" babies. . . .

If you think that such scenarios require outside coercion or governmental tyranny, you are mistaken. Once it becomes possible, with the aid of human genomics, to produce or to select for what some regard as "better babies"—smarter, prettier, healthier, more athletic—parents will leap at the opportunity to "improve" their offspring. Indeed, not to do so will be socially regarded as a form of child neglect. Those who would ordinarily be opposed to such tinkering will be under enormous pressure to compete on behalf of their as yet unborn children—just as some now plan almost from their children's birth how to get them into Harvard. Never mind that, lacking a standard of "good" or "better," no one can really know whether any such changes will truly be improvements.

Proponents of cloning urge us to forget about the science-fiction scenarios of laboratory manufacture or multiple-copy clones, and to focus only on the sympathetic cases of infertile couples exercising their reproductive rights. But why, if the single cases are so innocent, should multiplying their performance be so off-putting? (Similarly, why do others object to people's making money from that practice if the practice itself is perfectly acceptable?) The so-called science-fiction cases—say, Brave New World—make vivid the meaning of what looks to us, mistakenly, to be benign. They reveal that what looks like compassionate humanitarianism is, in the end, crushing dehumanization.

V

Whether or not they share my reasons, most people, I think, share my conclusion: that human cloning is unethical in itself and dangerous in its likely consequences, which include the precedent that it will establish for designing our children. Some reach this conclusion for their own good reasons, different from my own: concerns about distributive justice in access to eugenic cloning; worries about the genetic effects of asexual "in-breeding"; aversion to the implicit premise of genetic determinism; objections to the embryonic and fetal wastage that must necessarily accompany the efforts; religious opposition to "man playing God." But never mind why: the overwhelming majority of our fellow Americans remain firmly opposed to cloning human beings. . . .

READING QUESTIONS

1. According to Kass, What significance does a person's feeling of repugnance at the thought of reproductive cloning have for questions about the morality of this practice?
2. According to Kass, why would reproductive cloning involve unethical experimentation?
3. According to Kass, why would reproductive cloning "create serious issues for identity and individuality"?
4. Kass claims that reproductive cloning would represent "a giant step toward transformation of begetting into making." What does he mean in saying this? What reasons does he give in support of this claim?
5. According to Kass, why is reproductive cloning "inherently despotic"?

DISCUSSION QUESTIONS

1. Consider how a critic might respond to each of Kass's four objections to reproductive cloning.
2. How would Kass respond to Robertson's appeal to reproductive liberty in defense of reproductive cloning?

GREGORY E. PENCE

Will Cloning Harm People?

Many object to reproductive cloning on consequentialist grounds—they claim that this sort of cloning will have bad or even disastrous effects on the individuals who are cloned and on society generally. Pence argues that such objections are often a combination of ignorance about, and unwarranted fear of, the realities of cloning. Of particular interest here are the claims about predicted psychological harm to cloned children. For instance, some worry that reproductive cloning will severely limit the cloned individual's future, since in the process of cloning some decision is made about the clone's genotype. Wouldn't choosing a genotype limit a child's future, genetically determining her or his future life? Pence argues that this sort of reasoning is based on the false view of "genetic determinism" and thus fails to consider the fact that differences in gestation, parents, and environment importantly contribute to the personality, interests, and future prospects of any child. Pence's article thus represents a rebuttal of consequentialist arguments against reproductive cloning, including the various objections brought up in the previous article by Leon Kass.

Recommended Reading: consequentialism, chap. 1, sec. 2A.

The most important moral objection to originating a human by cloning is the claim that the resulting person may be unnecessarily harmed, either by something in the process of cloning or by the unique expectations placed upon the resulting child. This essay considers this kind of objection.

By now the word "cloning" has so many bad associations from science fiction and political demagoguery that there is no longer any good reason to continue to use it. A more neutral phrase, meaning the same thing, is "somatic cell nuclear transfer" (SCNT), which refers to the process by which the

From "Will Cloning Harm People?" Gregory E. Pence, *Flesh of My Flesh: The Ethics of Cloning Humans*, G. E. Pence (Lanham, MD: Rowman and Littlefield, 1998).

genotype of an adult, differentiated cell can be used to create a new human embryo by transferring its nucleus to an enucleated human egg. The resulting embryo can then be gestated to create a baby who will be a delayed twin of its genetic ancestor.

For purposes of clarity and focus, I will only discuss the simple case where a couple wants to originate a single child by SCNT and not the cases of multiple origination of the same genotype. I will also not discuss questions of who would regulate reproduction of genotypes and processes of getting consent to reproduce genotypes.

PARALLELS WITH IN VITRO FERTILIZATION: REPEATING HISTORY?

Any time a new method of human reproduction may occur, critics try to prevent it by citing possible harm to children. The implicit premise: before it is allowed, any new method must prove that only healthy children will be created. Without such proof, the new method amounts to "unconsented to" experimentation on the unborn. So argued the late conservative, Christian bioethicist Paul Ramsey in the early 1970s about in vitro fertilization (IVF).[1]

Of course, ordinary sexual reproduction does not guarantee healthy children every time. Nor can a person consent until he is born. Nor can he really consent until he is old enough to understand consent. The requirement of "consent to be born" is silly.

Jeremy Rifkin, another critic of IVF in the early 1970s, seemed to demand that new forms of human reproduction be risk-free.[2] Twenty years later, Rifkin predictably bolted out the gate to condemn human cloning, demanding its world-wide ban, with penalties for transgressions as severe as those for rape and murder: "It's a horrendous crime to make a Xerox of someone," he declared ominously. "You're putting a human into a genetic straitjacket. For the first time, we've taken the principles of industrial design— quality control, predictability—and applied them to a human being."[3]

Daniel Callahan, a philosopher who had worked in the Catholic tradition and who founded the Hastings Center for research in medical ethics, argued in 1978 that the first case of IVF was "probably unethical" because there was no possible guarantee that Louise Brown would be normal.[4] Callahan added that many medical breakthroughs are unethical because we cannot know (using the philosopher's strong sense of "know") that the first patient will not be harmed. Two decades later, he implied that human cloning would also be unethical: "We live in a culture that likes science and technology very much. If someone wants something, and the rest of us can't prove they are going to do devastating harm, they are going to do it."[5]

Leon Kass, a social conservative and biologist-turned-bioethicist, argued strenuously in 1971 that babies created by artificial fertilization might be deformed: "It doesn't matter how many times the baby is tested while in the mother's womb," he averred, "they will never be certain the baby won't be born without defect."[6]

What these critics overlooked is that no reasonable approach to life avoids all risks. Nothing in life is risk-free, including having children. Even if babies are born healthy, they do not always turn out as hoped. Taking such chances is part of becoming a parent.

Without some risk, there is no progress, no advance. Without risk, pioneers don't cross prairies, astronauts don't walk on the moon, and Freedom Riders don't take buses to integrate the South. The past critics of assisted reproduction demonstrated a psychologically normal but nevertheless unreasonable tendency to magnify the risk of a harmful but unlikely result. Such a result—even if very bad—still represents a very small risk. A baby born with a lethal genetic disease is an extremely bad but unlikely result; nevertheless, the risk shouldn't deter people from having children.

HUMANITY WILL NOT BE HARMED

Human SCNT is even more new and strange-sounding than in vitro fertilization (IVF). All that means is that it will take longer to get used to. Scaremongers have predicted terrible harm if children are born by SCNT, but in fact very little will change. Why is that?

First, to create a child by SCNT, a couple must use IVF, which is an expensive process, costing about $8,000 per attempt [in 1998]. Most American states do not require insurance companies to cover IVF, so IVF is mostly a cash-and-carry operation. Second, most IVF attempts are unsuccessful. The chances of any couple taking home a baby is quite low—only about 15%.

Only about 40,000 IVF babies have been born in America since the early 1980s. Suppose 50,000 such babies are born over the next decade. How many of these couples would want to originate a child by SCNT? Very few—at most, perhaps, a few hundred.

These figures are important because they tamp down many fears. As things now stand, originating humans by SCNT will never be common. Neither evolution nor old-fashioned human sex is in any way threatened. Nor is the family or human society. Most fears about human cloning stem from ignorance.

Similar fears linking cloning to dictatorship or the subjugation of women are equally ignorant. There are no artificial wombs (predictions, yes; realities, no—otherwise we could save premature babies born before 20 weeks). A healthy woman must agree to gestate any SCNT baby and such a woman will retain her right to abort. Women's rights to abortion are checks on evil uses of any new reproductive technology.

NEW THINGS MAKE US FEAR HARMS IRRATIONALLY

SCNT isn't really so new or different. Consider some cases on a continuum. In the first, the human embryo naturally splits in the process of twinning and produces two genetically-identical twins. Mothers have been conceiving and gestating human twins for all of human history. Call the children who result from this process Rebecca and Susan.

In the second case a technique is used where a human embryo is deliberately twinned in order to create more embryos for implantation in a woman who has been infertile with her mate. Instead of a random quirk in the uterus, now a physician and an infertile couple use a tiny electric current to split the embryo. Two identical embryos are created. All embryos are implanted and, as sometimes happens, rather than no embryo implanting successfully or only one, both embryos implant. Again, Rebecca and Susan are born.

In the third case, one of the twinned embryos is frozen (Susan) along with other embryos from the couple and the other embryo is implanted. In this case, although several embryos were implanted, only the one destined to be Rebecca is successful. Again, Rebecca is born.

Two years pass, and the couple desires another child. Some of their frozen embryos are thawed and implanted in the mother. The couple knows that one of the implanted embryos is the twin of Rebecca. In this second round of reproductive assistance, the embryo destined to be Susan successfully implants and a twin is born. Now Susan and Rebecca exist as twins, but born two years apart. Susan is the delayed twin of Rebecca. (Rumors abound that such births have already occurred in American infertility clinics.)

Suppose now that the "embryo that could become Susan" was twinned, and the "non-Susan" embryo is frozen. The rest of the details are then the same as the last scenario, but now two more years pass and the previously-frozen embryo is now implanted, gestated, and born. Susan and Rebecca now have another identical sister, Samantha. They would be identical triplets, born two and four years apart. In contrast to SCNT, where the mother's contribution of mitochondrial genes introduces small variations in nearly-identical genotypes, these embryos would have identical genomes.

Next, suppose that the embryo that could have been Rebecca miscarried and never became a child. The twinned embryo that could become Susan still exists. So the parents implant this embryo and Susan is born. Query to National Bioethics Advisory Commission: have the parents done something illegal? A child has been born who was originated by reproducing an embryo with a unique genotype. Remember, the embryo-that-could-become Rebecca existed first. So Susan only exists as a "clone" of the non-existent Rebecca.

Now, as bioethicist Leroy Walters emphasizes, let us consider an even thornier but more probable scenario.[7] Suppose we took the embryo-that-could-become Susan and transferred its nucleus to an enucleated egg of Susan's mother. Call the person who will emerge from this embryo "Suzette," because she is like Susan but different, because of her new mitochondrial DNA. Although the "Susan" embryo was created sexually, Suzette's origins are through somatic cell nuclear transfer. It is not clear that this process is illegal. The NBAC *Report* avoids taking a stand on this kind of case.[8]

Now compare all the above cases to originating Susan asexually by SCNT from the genotype of the adult Rebecca. Susan would again have a nearly-identical genome with Rebecca (identical except for mitochondrial DNA contributed by the gestating woman). Here we have nearly identical female genotypes, separated in time, created by choice. But how is this so different from choosing to have a delayed twin-child? Originating a child by SCNT is not a breakthrough in kind but a matter of degree along a continuum invoking twins and a special kind of reproductive choice.

COMPARING THE HARMS OF HUMAN REPRODUCTION

The question of multiple copies of one genome and its special issues of harm are ones that will not be discussed in this essay, but one asymmetry in our moral intuitions should be noticed.

The increasing use of fertility drugs has expanded many times the number of humans born who are twins, triplets, quadruplets, quintuplets, sextuplets, and even (in November of 1997 to the McCaugheys of Iowa) septuplets. If an entire country can rejoice about seven humans who are gestated in the same womb, raised by the same parents, and simultaneously created randomly from the same two sets of chromosomes, why should the same country fear deliberately originating copies of the same genome, either at once or over time? Our intuitions are even more skewed when we rejoice in the statistically-unlikely case of the seven

healthy McCaughey children and ignore the far more likely cases where several of the multiply-gestated fetuses are disabled or dead.

People exaggerate the fears of the unknown and downplay the very real dangers of the familiar. In a very important sense, driving a car each day is far more dangerous to children than the new form of human reproduction under discussion here. Many, many people are hurt and killed every day in automobile wrecks, yet few people consider not driving.

In SCNT, there are possible dangers of telomere shortening, inheritance of environmental effects on adult cells passed to embryonic cells, and possible unknown dangers. Mammalian animal studies must determine if such dangers will occur in human SCNT origination. Once such studies prove that there are no special dangers of SCNT, the crucial question will arise: how safe must we expect human SCNT to be before we allow it?

In answering this question, it is very important to ask about the baseline of comparison. How safe is ordinary, human sexual reproduction? How safe is assisted reproduction? Who or what counts as a subject of a safety calculation about SCNT?

At least 40% of human embryos fail to implant in normal sexual reproduction.[9] Although this fact is not widely known, it is important because some discussions tend to assume that every human embryo becomes a human baby unless some extraordinary event occurs such as abortion. But this is not true. Nature seems to have a genetic filter, such that malformed embryos do not implant. About 50% of the rejected embryos are chromosomally abnormal, meaning that if they were somehow brought to term, the resulting children would be mutants or suffer genetic dysfunction.

A widely-reported but misleading aspect of Ian Wilmut's work was that it took 277 embryos to produce one live lamb. In fact, Wilmut started with 277 eggs, fused nuclei with them to create embryos, and then allowed them to become the best 29 embryos, which were allowed to gestate further. He had three lambs almost live, with one true success, Dolly. Subsequent work may easily bring the efficiency rate to 25%. When the calves "Charlie" and "George" were born in 1998, four live-born calves were created from an initial batch of only 50 embryos.[10]

Wilmut's embryo-to-birth ratio only seems inefficient or unsafe because the real inefficiency fate of accepted forms of human assisted reproduction is so little known. In in vitro fertilization, a woman is given drugs to stimulate superovulation so that physicians can remove as many eggs as possible. At each cycle of attempted in vitro fertilization, three or four embryos are implanted. Most couples make several attempts, so as many as nine to twelve embryos are involved for each couple. As noted, only about 15–20% of couples undergoing such attempts ever take home a baby.

Consider what these numbers mean when writ large. Take a hundred couples attempting assisted reproduction, each undergoing (on average) three attempts. Suppose there are unusually good results and that 20% of these couples eventually take home a baby. Because more than one embryo may implant, assume that among these 20 couples, half have non-identical twins. But what is the efficiency rate here? Assuming a low number of three embryos implanted each time for the 300 attempts, it will take 900 embryos to produce 30 babies, for an efficiency rate of 1 in 30.

Nor is it true that all the loss of human potential occurred at the embryonic stage. Unfortunately, some of these pregnancies will end in miscarriages of fetuses, some well along in the second trimester.

Nevertheless, such loss of embryos and fetuses is almost universally accepted as morally permissible. Why is that? Because the infertile parents are trying to conceive their own children, because everyone thinks that is a good motive, and because few people object to the loss of embryos and fetuses *in this context of trying to conceive babies.* Seen in this light, what Wilmut did, starting out with a large number of embryos to get one successful lamb at birth, is not so novel or different from what now occurs in human assisted reproduction.

SUBJECTS AND NONSUBJECTS OF HARM

One premise that seems to figure in discussions of the safety of SCNT and other forms of assisted reproduction is that loss of human embryos morally matters. That premise should be rejected.

As the above discussion shows, loss of human embryos is a normal part of human conception and, without this process, humanity might suffer much more genetic disease. This process essentially involves the loss of human embryos as part of the natural state of things. Indeed, some researchers believe that for every human baby successfully born, there has been at least one human embryo lost along the way.

In vitro fertilization is widely-accepted as a great success in modern medicine. As said, over 40,000 American babies have been born this way. But calculations indicate that as many as a million human embryos may have been used in creating such successes.

Researchers often create embryos for subsequent cycles of implantation, only to learn that a pregnancy has been achieved and that such stored embryos are no longer needed. Thousands of such embryos can be stored indefinitely in liquid nitrogen. No one feels any great urgency about them and, indeed, many couples decline to pay fees to preserve their embryos.

The above considerations point to the obvious philosophical point that embryos are not persons with rights to life. Like an acorn, their value is all potential, little actual. Faced with a choice between paying a thousand dollars to keep two thousand embryos alive for a year in storage, or paying for an operation to keep a family pet alive for another year, no one will choose to pay for the embryos. How people actually act says much about their real values.

Thus an embryo cannot be harmed by being brought into existence and then being taken out of existence. An embryo is generally considered such until nine weeks after conception, when it is called a "fetus" (when it is born, it is called a "baby"). Embryos are not sentient and cannot experience pain. They are thus not the kind of subjects that can be harmed or benefitted.

As such, whether it takes one embryo to create a human baby or a hundred does not matter morally. It may matter aesthetically, financially, emotionally, or in time spent trying to reproduce, but it does not matter morally. As such, new forms of human reproduction such as IVF and SCNT that involve significant loss of embryos cannot be morally criticized on this charge.

Finally, because embryos don't count morally, they could be tested in various ways to eliminate defects in development or genetic mishaps. Certainly, if four or five SCNT embryos were implanted, only the healthiest one should be brought to term. As such, the risk of abnormal SCNT babies could be minimized.

SETTING THE STANDARD ABOUT THE RISK OF HARM

Animal tests have not yet shown that SCNT is safe enough to try in humans, and extensive animal testing should be done over the next few years. That means that, before we attempt SCNT in humans, we will need to be able to routinely produce healthy offspring by SCNT in lambs, cattle, and especially, nonhuman primates. After this testing is done, the time will come when a crucial question must be answered: how safe must human SCNT be before it is allowed? This is probably the most important, practical question before us now.

Should we have a very high standard, such that we take virtually no risk with a SCNT child? Daniel Callahan and Paul Ramsey, past critics of IVF, implied that unless a healthy baby could be guaranteed the first time, it was unethical to try to produce babies in a new way. At the other extreme, a low standard would allow great risks.

What is the appropriate standard? How high should be the bar over which scientists must be made to jump before they are allowed to try to originate a SCNT child? In my opinion, the standard of Callahan and Ramsey is too high. In reality, only God can meet that Olympian standard. It is also too high for those physicians trying to help infertile couples. If this high standard had been imposed on these people in the past, no form of assisted reproduction—including in vitro fertilization—would ever have been allowed.

On the other end of the scale, one could look at the very worst conditions for human gestation, where mothers are drug-dependent during pregnancy or exposed to dangerous chemicals. Such worst-case conditions include parents with a 50% chance of passing on a lethal genetic disease. The lowest standard of harm allows human reproduction even if there is such a high risk of harm ("harm" in the sense that the child would likely have a sub-normal future). One could argue that since society allows such mothers and couples to reproduce sexually, it could do no worse by allowing a child to be originated by SCNT.

I believe that the low standard is inappropriate to use with human SCNT. There is no reason to justify down to the very worst conditions under which society now tolerates humans being born. If the best we can do by SCNT is to produce children as good as those born with fetal-maternal alcohol syndrome, we shouldn't originate children this way.

Between these standards, there is the normal range of risk that is accepted by ordinary people in sexual reproduction. Human SCNT should be allowed when the predicted risk from animal studies falls within this range. "Ordinary people" refers to those who are neither alcoholic nor dependent on an illegal drug and where neither member of the couple knowingly passes on a high risk for a serious genetic disease.

This standard seems reasonable. It does not require a guarantee of a perfect baby, but it also rejects the "anything goes" view. For example, if the rate of serious deformities in normal human reproduction is 1%, and if the rate of chimpanzee SCNT reproduction were brought down to this rate, and if there were no reason to think that SCNT in human primates would he any higher, it should be permissible to attempt human SCNT. . . .

PSYCHOLOGICAL HARM TO THE CHILD

Another concern is about psychological harm to a child originated by SCNT. According to this objection, choosing to have a child is not like choosing a car or house. It is a moral decision because another being is affected. Having a child should be a careful, responsible choice and focused on what's best for the child. Having a child originated by SCNT is not morally permissible because it is not best for the child.

The problem with this argument is the last six words of the last sentence, which assumes bad motives on the part of parents. Unfortunately, SCNT is associated with bad motives in science fiction, but until we have evidence that it will be used this way, why assume the worst about people?

Certainly, if someone deliberately brought a child into the world with the intention of causing him harm, that would be immoral. Unfortunately, the concept of harm is a continuum and some people have very high standards, such that not providing a child a stay-at-home parent constitutes harming the child. But there is nothing about SCNT per se that is necessarily linked to bad motives. True, people would have certain expectations of a child created by SCNT, but parents-to-be already have certain expectations about children.

Too many parents are fatalistic and just accept whatever life throws at them. The very fact of being a parent for many people is something they must accept (because abortion was not a real option). Part of this acceptance is to just accept whatever genetic combination comes at birth from the random assortment of genes.

But why is such acceptance a good thing? It is a defeatist attitude in medicine against disease; it is a defeatist attitude toward survival when one's culture or country is under attack; and it is a defeatist attitude toward life in general. "The expectations of parents will be too high!" critics repeat. "Better to leave parents in ignorance and to leave their children as randomness decrees." The silliness of that view is apparent as soon as it is made explicit.

If we are thinking about harm to the child, an objection that comes up repeatedly might be called the argument for an open future. "In the case of cloning," it is objected, "the expectations are very specifically tied to the life of another person. So in a sense, the child's future is denied to him because he will be expected to be like his ancestor. But part of the wonder of having children is surprise at how they turn out. As such, some indeterminacy should remain a part of childhood. Human SCNT deprives a person of an open future because when we know how his previous twin lived, we will know how the new child will live."

It is true that the adults choosing this genotype rather than that one must have some expectations. There has to be some reason for choosing one genotype over another. But these expectations are only half based in fact. As we know, no person originated by SCNT will be identical to his ancestor because of mitochondrial DNA, because of his different gestation, because of his different parents, because of his different time in history, and perhaps, because of his different country and culture. Several famous pairs of conjoined twins, such as Eng and Chang, with both identical genotypes and identical uterine/childhood environments, have still had different personalities.[11] To assume that a SCNT child's future is not open is to assume genetic reductionism.

Moreover, insofar as parents have specific expectations about children created by SCNT, such expectations will likely be no better or worse than the normal expectations by parents of children created sexually. As said, there is nothing about SCNT per se that necessitates bad motives on the part of parents.

Notice that most of the expected harm to the child stems *from the predicted, prejudicial attitudes of other people to the SCNT child.* ("Would you want to be a cloned child? Can you imagine being called a freak and having only one genetic parent?") As such, it is important to remember that social expectations are *merely* social expectations. They are malleable and can change quickly. True, parents might initially have expectations that are too high and other people might regard such children with prejudice. But just as such inappropriate attitudes faded after the first cases of in vitro fertilization, they will fade here too.

Ron James, the Scottish millionaire who funded much of Ian Wilmut's research, points out that social attitudes change fast. Before the announcement of Dolly, polls showed that people thought that cloning animals and gene transfer to animals were "morally problematic," whereas germ-line gene therapy fell in the category of "just wrong." Two months after the announcement of Dolly, and after much discussion of human cloning, people's attitudes had shifted to accepting animal cloning and gene transfer to humans as "morally permissible," whereas germ-line gene therapy had shifted to being merely "morally problematic."[12]

James Watson, the co-discoverer of the double helix, once opposed in vitro fertilization by claiming that prejudicial attitudes of other people would harm children created this way. . . .[13] In that piece, the prejudice was really in Watson, because the way that he was stirring up fear was doing more to create the prejudice than any normal human reaction. Similarly, Leon Kass's recent long essay in *The New Republic . . .* where he calls human asexual reproduction "repugnant" and a "horror," creates exactly the kind of prejudiced reaction that he predicts.[14] Rather than make a priori, self-fulfilling prophecies, wouldn't it be better to be empirical about such matters? To be more optimistic about the reactions of ordinary parents?

Children created by SCNT would not *look* any different from other children. Nobody at age two looks like he does at age 45 and, except for his parents, nobody knows what the 45-year-old man looked liked at age two. And since ordinary children often look like their parents, no one would be able to tell a SCNT child from others until he had lived a decade.

Kass claims that a child originated by SCNT will have "a troubled psychic identity" because he or she will be "utterly" confused about his social, genetic, and kinship ties.[15] At worst, this child will be like a child of "incest" and may, if originated as a male from the father, have the same sexual feelings towards the wife as the father. An older male might in turn have strong sexual feelings toward a young female with his wife's genome.

Yet if this were so, any husband of any married twin might have an equally troubled psychic identity because he might have the same sexual feelings toward the twin as his wife. Instead, those in relationships with twins claim that the individuals are very different.

Much of the above line of criticism simply begs the question and assumes that humans created by SCNT will be greeted by stigma or experience confusion. It is hard to understand why, once one gets

beyond the novelty, because a child created asexually would know *exactly* who his ancestor was. No confusion there. True, prejudicial expectations could damage children, but why make public policy based on that?

Besides, isn't this kind of argument hypocritical in our present society? Where no one is making any serious effort to ban divorce, despite the overwhelming evidence that divorce seriously damages children, even teenage children. It is always far easier to concentrate on the dramatic, far-off harm than the ones close-at-hand. When we are really concerned about minimizing harm to children, we will pass laws requiring all parents wanting to divorce to go through counseling sessions or to wait a year. We will pass a federal law compelling child-support from fathers who flee to other states, and make it impossible to renew a professional license or get paid in a public institution in another state until all child-support is paid. After that is done, then we can non-hypocritically talk about how much our society cares about not harming children who may be originated in new ways.

In conclusion, the predicted harms of SCNT to humans are wildly exaggerated, lack a comparative baseline, stem from irrational fears of the unknown, overlook greater dangers of familiar things, and are often based on the armchair psychological speculation of amateurs. Once studies prove SCNT as safe as normal sexual reproduction in non-human mammals, the harm objection will disappear. Given other arguments that SCNT could substantially benefit many children, the argument that SCNT would harm children is a weak one that needs to be weighed against its many potential benefits.[16]

NOTES

1. Paul Ramsey, *Fabricated Man: The Ethics of Genetic Control* (New Haven, Conn.: Yale University Press, 1970).

2. "What are the psychological implications of growing up as a specimen, sheltered not by a warm womb but by steel and glass, belonging to no one but the lab technician who joined together sperm and egg? In a world already populated with people with identity crises, what's the personal identity of a test-tube baby?" J. Rifkin and

T. Howard, *Who Shall Play God?* (New York: Dell, 1977), 15.

3. Quoted in Ehsan Masood, "Cloning Technique 'Reveals Legal Loophole'," *Nature* 38, 27 February 1987.

4. *New York Times,* 27 July 1978, A16.

5. Knight-Ridder newspapers, 10 March 1997.

6. Leon Kass, "The New Biology: What Price Relieving Man's Estate?" *Journal of the American Medical Association,* vol. 174, 19 November 1971, 779–788.

7. Leroy Walters, "Biomedical Ethics and Their Role in Mammalian Cloning," Conference on Mammalian Cloning: Implications for Science and Society, 27 June 1997, Crystal City Marriott, Crystal City, Virginia.

8. National Bioethics Advisory Commission (NBAC), *Cloning Human Beings: Report and Recommendations of the National Bioethics Advisory Commission,* Rockville, Md., June 1997.

9. A. Wilcox et al., "Incidence of Early Loss of Pregnancy," *New England Journal of Medicine* 319, no. 4, 28 July 1988, 189–194. See also J. Grudzinskas and A. Nysenbaum, "Failure of Human Pregnancy after Implantation," *Annals of New York Academy of Sciences* 442, 1985, 39–44; J. Muller et al., "Fetal Loss after Implantation," *Lancet* 2, 1980, 554–556.

10. Rick Weiss, "Genetically Engineered Calves Cloned," 21 January 1998, *Washington Post,* A3.

11. David R. Collins, *Eng and Chang: The Original Siamese Twins* (New York: Dillon Press, 1994). Elaine Landau, *Joined at Birth: The Lives of Conjoined Twins* (New York: Grolier Publishing, 1997). See also Geoffrey A. Machin, "Conjoined Twins: Implications for Blastogenesis," *Birth Defects: Original Articles Series* 20, no. 1, 1993, March of Dimes Foundation, 142.

12. Ron James, Managing Director, PPL Therapeutics, "Industry Perspective: The Promise and Practical Applications," Conference on Mammalian Cloning: Implications for Science and Society, 27 June 1997, Crystal City Marriott, Crystal City, Virginia.

13. James D. Watson, "Moving Towards the Clonal Man," *Atlantic,* May 1971, 50–53.

14. Leon Kass, "The Wisdom of Repugnance," *The New Republic,* 2 June 1997.

15. Kass, "The Wisdom of Repugnance," 22–23.

16. Thanks to Mary Litch for comments on this essay.

READING QUESTIONS

1. What is the primary aim of Pence's article?
2. Why does Pence think that reproductive cloning will not harm humanity?
3. How does Pence defend the claim that an embryo cannot be the subject of harm?
4. One argument against reproductive cloning is that individuals who are brought about by this method will lack an "open future." Explain this argument. How does Pence criticize the argument?
5. How does Pence criticize Kass's "troubled psychic identity" objection to reproductive cloning?

DISCUSSION QUESTIONS

1. Pence claims that objections to reproductive cloning based on alleged psychological harms to cloned individuals are not good objections. Should we agree with him about this matter?
2. Given that infertile couples can try to have children by means of IVF (in vitro fertilization), can you think of any situations in which someone has good reason to prefer reproductive cloning to IVF as a method of assisted reproduction?

Michael J. Sandel

The Case against Perfection

Sandel's article is concerned with the ethics of genetic engineering and, in particular, with the prospect of enhancing human beings through such processes as sex selection; in short, it is concerned with the "ethics of enhancement," including eugenics. Sandel argues that such enhancement is morally questionable, not because of its likely consequences but because of the attitudes toward human beings that it expresses and promotes. As Sandel puts it, "The deepest moral objection to enhancement lies less in the perfection it seeks than in the human disposition it expresses and promotes." Enhancement, claims Sandel, devalues the moral significance of what he calls "giftedness," which "honors the cultivation and display of natural talents." From a religious perspective, enhancement devalues natural gifts because by allowing our talents and powers to be subject to human design, we "confuse our role with God's." From a secular perspective, if we come to see our talents as up to us, we damage the virtues of humility, responsibility, and solidarity. He explains why this is so in his discussion of eugenics.

Sandel's moral case against genetic engineering can be viewed as grounded in considerations of virtue and hence a virtue ethics approach to this issue. Here, it is important to recall from the moral theory primer that some consequentialists in ethics (perfectionists) make considerations of human perfection the basis of their theory of right conduct. Morally right actions are ones that best promote such human perfections as knowledge and achievement. This is not Sandel's approach to the ethics of enhancement. Rather, he stresses the kinds of dispositions of character and associated attitudes toward human life that loss of a sense of giftedness would bring in its wake.

Recommended Reading: virtue ethics, chap. 1, sec. 2E. Also relevant is consequentialism, chap. 1, sec. 2A.

Breakthroughs in genetics present us with a promise and a predicament. The promise is that we may soon be able to treat and prevent a host of debilitating diseases. The predicament is that our newfound genetic knowledge may also enable us to manipulate our own nature—to enhance our muscles, memories, and moods; to choose the sex, height, and other genetic traits of our children; to make ourselves "better than well." When science moves faster than moral understanding, as it does today, men and women struggle to articulate their unease. In liberal societies they reach first for the language of autonomy, fairness, and individual rights. But this part of our moral vocabulary is ill equipped to address the hardest questions posed by genetic engineering. The genomic revolution has induced a kind of moral vertigo.

Consider cloning. The birth of Dolly the cloned sheep, in 1997, brought a torrent of concern about

From Michael J. Sandel, "The Case Against Perfection: What's Wrong with Designer Children, Bionic Athletes, and Genetic Engineering?" *Atlantic Monthly*, April 2004.

the prospect of cloned human beings. There are good medical reasons to worry. Most scientists agree that cloning is unsafe, likely to produce offspring with serious abnormalities. (Dolly recently died a premature death.) But suppose technology improved to the point where clones were at no greater risk than naturally conceived offspring. Would human cloning still be objectionable? Should our hesitation be moral as well as medical? What, exactly, is wrong with creating a child who is a genetic twin of one parent, or of an older sibling who has tragically died—or, for that matter, of an admired scientist, sports star, or celebrity?

Some say cloning is wrong because it violates the right to autonomy: by choosing a child's genetic makeup in advance, parents deny the child's right to an open future. A similar objection can be raised against any form of bioengineering that allows parents to select or reject genetic characteristics. According to this argument, genetic enhancements for musical talent, say, or athletic prowess, would point children toward particular choices, and so designer children would never be fully free.

At first glance the autonomy argument seems to capture what is troubling about human cloning and other forms of genetic engineering. It is not persuasive, for two reasons. First, it wrongly implies that absent a designing parent, children are free to choose their characteristics for themselves. But none of us chooses his genetic inheritance. The alternative to a cloned or genetically enhanced child is not one whose future is unbound by particular talents but one at the mercy of the genetic lottery.

Second, even if a concern for autonomy explains some of our worries about made-to-order children, it cannot explain our moral hesitation about people who seek genetic remedies or enhancements for themselves. Gene therapy on somatic (that is, non-reproductive) cells, such as muscle cells and brain cells, repairs or replaces defective genes. The moral quandary arises when people use such therapy not to cure a disease but to reach beyond health, to enhance their physical or cognitive capacities, to lift themselves above the norm.

Like cosmetic surgery, genetic enhancement employs medical means for nonmedical ends—ends unrelated to curing or preventing disease or repairing injury. But unlike cosmetic surgery, genetic enhancement is more than skin-deep. If we are ambivalent about surgery or Botox injections for sagging chins and furrowed brows, we are all the more troubled by genetic engineering for stronger bodies, sharper memories, greater intelligence, and happier moods. The question is whether we are right to be troubled, and if so, on what grounds.

In order to grapple with the ethics of enhancement, we need to confront questions largely lost from view—questions about the moral status of nature, and about the proper stance of human beings toward the given world. Since these questions verge on theology, modern philosophers and political theorists tend to shrink from them. But our new powers of biotechnology make them unavoidable. To see why this is so, consider four examples already on the horizon: muscle enhancement, memory enhancement, growth-hormone treatment, and reproductive technologies that enable parents to choose the sex and some genetic traits of their children. In each case what began as an attempt to treat a disease or prevent a genetic disorder now beckons as an instrument of improvement and consumer choice.

Muscles

Everyone would welcome a gene therapy to alleviate muscular dystrophy and to reverse the debilitating muscle loss that comes with old age. But what if the same therapy were used to improve athletic performance? Researchers have developed a synthetic gene that, when injected into the muscle cells of mice, prevents and even reverses natural muscle deterioration. The gene not only repairs wasted or injured muscles but also strengthens healthy ones. This success bodes well for human applications. H. Lee Sweeney, of the University of Pennsylvania, who leads the research, hopes his discovery will cure the immobility that afflicts the elderly. But Sweeney's bulked-up mice have already attracted the attention of athletes seeking a competitive edge. Although the therapy is not yet approved for human use, the prospect of genetically enhanced weight lifters, home-run sluggers, linebackers, and sprinters is easy to imagine.

The widespread use of steroids and other perfor-mance-improving drugs in professional sports suggests that many athletes will be eager to avail themselves of genetic enhancement.

Suppose for the sake of argument that muscle-enhancing gene therapy, unlike steroids, turned out to be safe—or at least no riskier than a rigorous weight-training regimen. Would there be a reason to ban its use in sports? There is something unsettling about the image of genetically altered athletes lifting SUVs or hitting 650-foot home runs or running a three-minute mile. But what, exactly, is troubling about it? Is it simply that we find such superhuman spectacles too bizarre to contemplate? Or does our unease point to something of ethical significance?

It might be argued that a genetically enhanced athlete, like a drug-enhanced athlete, would have an unfair advantage over his unenhanced competitors. But the fairness argument against enhancement has a fatal flaw: it has always been the case that some athletes are better endowed genetically than others, and yet we do not consider this to undermine the fairness of competitive sports. From the standpoint of fairness, enhanced genetic differences would be no worse than natural ones, assuming they were safe and made available to all. If genetic enhancement in sports is morally objectionable, it must be for reasons other than fairness.

Memory

Genetic enhancement is possible for brains as well as brawn. In the mid-1990s scientists managed to manipulate a memory-linked gene in fruit flies, creating flies with photographic memories. More recently researchers have produced smart mice by inserting extra copies of a memory-related gene into mouse embryos. The altered mice learn more quickly and remember things longer than normal mice. The extra copies were programmed to remain active even in old age, and the improvement was passed on to offspring.

Human memory is more complicated, but biotech companies, including Memory Pharmaceuticals, are in hot pursuit of memory-enhancing drugs, or "cog-nition enhancers," for human beings. The obvious market for such drugs consists of those who suffer from Alzheimer's and other serious memory disor-ders. The companies also have their sights on a bigger market: the 81 million Americans over fifty, who are beginning to encounter the memory loss that comes naturally with age. A drug that reversed age-related memory loss would be a bonanza for the pharmaceu-tical industry: a Viagra for the brain. Such use would straddle the line between remedy and enhancement. Unlike a treatment for Alzheimer's, it would cure no disease; but insofar as it restored capacities a person once possessed, it would have a remedial aspect. It could also have purely nonmedical uses: for exam-ple, by a lawyer cramming to memorize facts for an upcoming trial, or by a business executive eager to learn Mandarin on the eve of his departure for Shanghai.

Some who worry about the ethics of cogni-tive enhancement point to the danger of creating two classes of human beings: those with access to enhancement technologies, and those who must make do with their natural capacities. And if the enhance-ments could be passed down the generations, the two classes might eventually become subspecies—the enhanced and the merely natural. But worry about access ignores the moral status of enhancement itself. Is the scenario troubling because the unenhanced poor would be denied the benefits of bioengineering, or because the enhanced affluent would somehow be dehumanized? As with muscles, so with memory: the fundamental question is not how to ensure equal access to enhancement but whether we should aspire to it in the first place.

Height

Pediatricians already struggle with the ethics of enhancement when confronted by parents who want to make their children taller. Since the 1980s human growth hormone has been approved for chil-dren with a hormone deficiency that makes them much shorter than average. But the treatment also increases the height of healthy children. Some par-ents of healthy children who are unhappy with their stature (typically boys) ask why it should make a difference whether a child is short because of a hormone deficiency or because his parents happen to be short. Whatever the cause, the social consequences are the same.

In the face of this argument some doctors began prescribing hormone treatments for children whose short stature was unrelated to any medical problem. By 1996 such "off-label" use accounted for 40 percent of human-growth-hormone prescriptions. Although it is legal to prescribe drugs for purposes not approved by the Food and Drug Administration, pharmaceutical companies cannot promote such use. Seeking to expand its market, Eli Lilly & Co. recently persuaded the FDA to approve its human growth hormone for healthy children whose projected adult height is in the bottom one percentile—under five feet three inches for boys and four feet eleven inches for girls. This concession raises a large question about the ethics of enhancement: If hormone treatments need not be limited to those with hormone deficiencies, why should they be available only to very short children? Why shouldn't all shorter-than-average children be able to seek treatment? And what about a child of average height who wants to be taller so that he can make the basketball team?

Some oppose height enhancement on the grounds that it is collectively self-defeating; as some become taller, others become shorter relative to the norm. Except in Lake Wobegon, not every child can be above average. As the unenhanced began to feel shorter, they, too, might seek treatment, leading to a hormonal arms race that left everyone worse off, especially those who couldn't afford to buy their way up from shortness.

But the arms-race objection is not decisive on its own. Like the fairness objection to bioengineered muscles and memory, it leaves unexamined the attitudes and dispositions that prompt the drive for enhancement. If we were bothered only by the injustice of adding shortness to the problems of the poor, we could remedy that unfairness by publicly subsidizing height enhancements. As for the relative height deprivation suffered by innocent bystanders, we could compensate them by taxing those who buy their way to greater height. The real question is whether we want to live in a society where parents feel compelled to spend a fortune to make perfectly healthy kids a few inches taller.

Sex Selection

Perhaps the most inevitable nonmedical use of bioengineering is sex selection. For centuries parents have been trying to choose the sex of their children. Today biotech succeeds where folk remedies failed.

One technique for sex selection arose with prenatal tests using amniocentesis and ultrasound. These medical technologies were developed to detect genetic abnormalities such as spina bifida and Down syndrome. But they can also reveal the sex of the fetus—allowing for the abortion of a fetus of an undesired sex. Even among those who favor abortion rights, few advocate abortion simply because the parents do not want a girl. Nevertheless, in traditional societies with a powerful cultural preference for boys, this practice has become widespread.

Sex selection need not involve abortion, however. For couples undergoing in vitro fertilization (IVF), it is possible to choose the sex of the child before the fertilized egg is implanted in the womb. One method makes use of preimplantation genetic diagnosis (PGD), a procedure developed to screen for genetic diseases. Several eggs are fertilized in a petri dish and grown to the eight-cell stage (about three days). At that point the embryos are tested to determine their sex. Those of the desired sex are implanted; the others are typically discarded. Although few couples are likely to undergo the difficulty and expense of IVF simply to choose the sex of their child, embryo screening is a highly reliable means of sex selection. And as our genetic knowledge increases, it may be possible to use PGD to cull embryos carrying undesired genes, such as those associated with obesity, height, and skin color. The science-fiction movie *Gattaca* depicts a future in which parents routinely screen embryos for sex, height, immunity to disease, and even IQ. There is something troubling about the *Gattaca* scenario, but it is not easy to identify what exactly is wrong with screening embryos to choose the sex of our children.

One line of objection draws on arguments familiar from the abortion debate. Those who believe that an embryo is a person reject embryo screening for the same reasons they reject abortion. If an eight-cell embryo growing in a petri dish is morally equivalent to a fully developed human being, then discarding it is no better than aborting a fetus, and both practices are equivalent to infanticide. Whatever its merits, however, this "pro-life" objection is not an argument against sex selection as such.

The latest technology poses the question of sex selection unclouded by the matter of an embryo's moral status. The Genetics & IVF Institute, a for-profit infertility clinic in Fairfax, Virginia, now offers a sperm-sorting technique that makes it possible to choose the sex of one's child before it is conceived. X-bearing sperm, which produce girls, carry more DNA than Y-bearing sperm, which produce boys; a device called a flow cytometer can separate them. The process, called MicroSort, has a high rate of success.

If sex selection by sperm sorting is objectionable, it must be for reasons that go beyond the debate about the moral status of the embryo. One such reason is that sex selection is an instrument of sex discrimination—typically against girls, as illustrated by the chilling sex ratios in India and China. Some speculate that societies with substantially more men than women will be less stable, more violent, and more prone to crime or war. These are legitimate worries—but the sperm-sorting company has a clever way of addressing them. It offers MicroSort only to couples who want to choose the sex of a child for purposes of "family balancing." Those with more sons than daughters may choose a girl, and vice versa. But customers may not use the technology to stock up on children of the same sex, or even to choose the sex of their firstborn child. (So far the majority of MicroSort clients have chosen girls.) Under restrictions of this kind, do any ethical issues remain that should give us pause?

The case of MicroSort helps us isolate the moral objections that would persist if muscle-enhancement, memory-enhancement, and height-enhancement technologies were safe and available to all.

It is commonly said that genetic enhancements undermine our humanity by threatening our capacity to act freely, to succeed by our own efforts, and to consider ourselves responsible—worthy of praise or blame—for the things we do and for the way we are. It is one thing to hit seventy home runs as the result of disciplined training and effort, and something else, something less, to hit them with the help of steroids or genetically enhanced muscles. Of course, the roles of effort and enhancement will be a matter of degree. But as the role of enhancement increases, our admiration for the achievement fades—or, rather, our admiration for the achievement shifts from the player to his pharmacist. This suggests that our moral response to enhancement is a response to the diminished agency of the person whose achievement is enhanced.

Though there is much to be said for this argument, I do not think the main problem with enhancement and genetic engineering is that they undermine effort and erode human agency. The deeper danger is that they represent a kind of hyperagency—a Promethean aspiration to remake nature, including human nature, to serve our purposes and satisfy our desires. The problem is not the drift to mechanism but the drive to mastery. And what the drive to mastery misses and may even destroy is an appreciation of the gifted character of human powers and achievements.

To acknowledge the giftedness of life is to recognize that our talents and powers are not wholly our own doing, despite the effort we expend to develop and to exercise them. It is also to recognize that not everything in the world is open to whatever use we may desire or devise. Appreciating the gifted quality of life constrains the Promethean project and conduces to a certain humility. It is in part a religious sensibility. But its resonance reaches beyond religion.

It is difficult to account for what we admire about human activity and achievement without drawing upon some version of this idea. Consider two types of athletic achievement. We appreciate players like Pete Rose, who are not blessed with great natural gifts but who manage, through striving, grit, and determination, to excel in their sport. But we also admire players like Joe DiMaggio, who display natural gifts with grace and effortlessness. Now, suppose we learned that both players took performance-enhancing drugs. Whose turn to drugs would we find more deeply disillusioning? Which aspect of the athletic ideal—effort or gift—would be more deeply offended?

Some might say effort: the problem with drugs is that they provide a shortcut, a way to win without striving. But striving is not the point of sports; excellence is. And excellence consists at least partly in the display of natural talents and gifts that are no doing of the athlete who possesses them. This is an uncomfortable fact for democratic societies. We want to believe that success, in sports and in life, is something we earn, not something we inherit. Natural gifts, and the admiration they inspire, embarrass the meritocratic faith; they cast doubt on the conviction that praise and rewards flow from effort alone. In the face of this embarrassment we inflate the moral significance of striving, and depreciate giftedness. This distortion can be seen, for example, in network-television coverage of the Olympics, which focuses less on the feats the athletes perform than on heartrending stories of the hardships they have overcome and the struggles they have waged to triumph over an injury or a difficult upbringing or political turmoil in their native land.

But effort isn't everything. No one believes that a mediocre basketball player who works and trains even harder than Michael Jordan deserves greater acclaim or a bigger contract. The real problem with genetically altered athletes is that they corrupt athletic competition as a human activity that honors the cultivation and display of natural talents. From this standpoint, enhancement can be seen as the ultimate expression of the ethic of effort and willfulness—a kind of high-tech striving. The ethic of willfulness and the biotechnological powers it now enlists are arrayed against the claims of giftedness.

The ethic of giftedness, under siege in sports, persists in the practice of parenting. But here, too, bio-engineering and genetic enhancement threaten to dislodge it. To appreciate children as gifts is to accept them as they come, not as objects of our design or products of our will or instruments of our ambition. Parental love is not contingent on the talents and attributes a child happens to have. We choose our friends and spouses at least partly on the basis of qualities we find attractive. But we do not choose our children. Their qualities are unpredictable, and even the most conscientious parents cannot be held wholly responsible for the kind of children they have. That is why parenthood, more than other human relationships, teaches what the theologian William F. May calls an "openness to the unbidden."

May's resonant phrase helps us see that the deepest moral objection to enhancement lies less in the perfection it seeks than in the human disposition it expresses and promotes. The problem is not that parents usurp the autonomy of a child they design. The problem lies in the hubris of the designing parents, in their drive to master the mystery of birth. Even if this disposition did not make parents tyrants to their children, it would disfigure the relation between parent and child, and deprive the parent of the humility and enlarged human sympathies that an openness to the unbidden can cultivate. . . .

The mandate to mold our children, to cultivate and improve them, complicates the case against enhancement. We usually admire parents who seek the best for their children, who spare no effort to help them achieve happiness and success. Some parents confer advantages on their children by enrolling them in expensive schools, hiring private tutors, sending them to tennis camp, providing them with piano lessons, ballet lessons, swimming lessons, SAT-prep courses, and so on. If it is permissible and even admirable for parents to help their children in these ways, why isn't it equally admirable for parents to use whatever genetic technologies may emerge (provided they are safe) to enhance their children's intelligence, musical ability, or athletic prowess?

The defenders of enhancement are right to this extent: improving children through genetic engineering is similar in spirit to the heavily managed, high-pressure child-rearing that is now common. But this similarity does not vindicate genetic enhancement. On the contrary, it highlights a problem with the trend toward hyperparenting. One conspicuous example of this trend is sports-crazed parents bent on making champions of their children. Another is the frenzied drive of overbearing parents to mold and manage their children's academic careers.

As the pressure for performance increases, so does the need to help distractible children concentrate on the task at hand. This may be why diagnoses of attention deficit and hyperactivity disorder have increased so sharply. Lawrence Diller, a pediatrician and the author of *Running on Ritalin*, estimates that five to six percent of American children under eighteen (a total of four to five million kids) are currently prescribed Ritalin,

Adderall, and other stimulants, the treatment of choice for ADHD. (Stimulants counteract hyperactivity by making it easier to focus and sustain attention.) The number of Ritalin prescriptions for children and adolescents has tripled over the past decade, but not all users suffer from attention disorders or hyperactivity. High school and college students have learned that prescription stimulants improve concentration for those with normal attention spans, and some buy or borrow their classmates' drugs to enhance their performance on the SAT or other exams. Since stimulants work for both medical and nonmedical purposes, they raise the same moral questions posed by other technologies of enhancement. . . .

This demand for performance and perfection animates the impulse to rail against the given. It is the deepest source of the moral trouble with enhancement.

Some see a clear line between genetic enhancement and other ways that people seek improvement in their children and themselves. Genetic manipulation seems somehow worse—more intrusive, more sinister—than other ways of enhancing performance and seeking success. But morally speaking, the difference is less significant than it seems. Bioengineering gives us reason to question the low-tech, high-pressure child-rearing practices we commonly accept. The hyperparenting familiar in our time represents an anxious excess of mastery and dominion that misses the sense of life as a gift. . . .

Why not shake off our unease about genetic enhancement as so much superstition? What would be lost if biotechnology dissolved our sense of giftedness?

From a religious standpoint the answer is clear: To believe that our talents and powers are wholly our own doing is to misunderstand our place in creation, to confuse our role with God's. Religion is not the only source of reasons to care about giftedness, however. The moral stakes can also be described in secular terms. If bioengineering made the myth of the "self-made man" come true, it would be difficult to view our talents as gifts for which we are indebted, rather than as achievements for which we are responsible. This would transform three key features of our moral landscape: humility, responsibility, and solidarity.

In a social world that prizes mastery and control, parenthood is a school for humility. That we care deeply about our children and yet cannot choose the kind we want teaches parents to be open to the unbidden. Such openness is a disposition worth affirming, not only within families but in the wider world as well. It invites us to abide the unexpected, to live with dissonance, to rein in the impulse to control. A *Gattaca*-like world in which parents became accustomed to specifying the sex and genetic traits of their children would be a world inhospitable to the unbidden, a gated community writ large. The awareness that our talents and abilities are not wholly our own doing restrains our tendency toward hubris.

Though some maintain that genetic enhancement erodes human agency by overriding effort, the real problem is the explosion, not the erosion, of responsibility. As humility gives way, responsibility expands to daunting proportions. We attribute less to chance and more to choice. Parents become responsible for choosing, or failing to choose, the right traits for their children. Athletes become responsible for acquiring, or failing to acquire, the talents that will help their teams win.

One of the blessings of seeing ourselves as creatures of nature, God, or fortune is that we are not wholly responsible for the way we are. The more we become masters of our genetic endowments, the greater the burden we bear for the talents we have and the way we perform. Today when a basketball player misses a rebound, his coach can blame him for being out of position. Tomorrow the coach may blame him for being too short. Even now the use of performance-enhancing drugs in professional sports is subtly transforming the expectations players have for one another; on some teams players who take the field free from amphetamines or other stimulants are criticized for "playing naked."

The more alive we are to the chanced nature of our lot, the more reason we have to share our fate with others. Consider insurance. Since people do not know whether or when various ills will befall them, they pool their risk by buying health insurance and life insurance. As life plays itself out, the healthy wind up subsidizing the unhealthy, and those who live to a ripe old age wind up subsidizing the families of those who die before their time. Even without a sense of mutual obligation, people pool their risks and resources and share one another's fate.

But insurance markets mimic solidarity only insofar as people do not know or control their own risk factors. Suppose genetic testing advanced to the point where it could reliably predict each person's medical future and life expectancy. Those confident of good health and long life would opt out of the pool, causing other people's premiums to skyrocket. The solidarity of insurance would disappear as those with good genes fled the actuarial company of those with bad ones.

The fear that insurance companies would use genetic data to assess risks and set premiums recently led the Senate to vote to prohibit genetic discrimination in health insurance. But the bigger danger, admittedly more speculative, is that genetic enhancement, if routinely practiced, would make it harder to foster the moral sentiments that social solidarity requires.

Why, after all, do the successful owe anything to the least-advantaged members of society? The best answer to this question leans heavily on the notion of giftedness. The natural talents that enable the successful to flourish are not their own doing but, rather, their good fortune—a result of the genetic lottery. If our genetic endowments are gifts, rather than achievements for which we can claim credit, it is a mistake and a conceit to assume that we are entitled to the full measure of the bounty they reap in a market economy. We therefore have an obligation to share this bounty with those who, through no fault of their own, lack comparable gifts.

A lively sense of the contingency of our gifts—a consciousness that none of us is wholly responsible for his or her success—saves a meritocratic society from sliding into the smug assumption that the rich are rich because they are more deserving than the poor. Without this, the successful would become even more likely than they are now to view themselves as self-made and self-sufficient, and hence wholly responsible for their success. Those at the bottom of society would be viewed not as disadvantaged, and thus worthy of a measure of compensation, but as simply unfit, and thus worthy of eugenic repair. The meritocracy, less chastened by chance, would become harder, less forgiving. As perfect genetic knowledge would end the simulacrum of solidarity in insurance markets, so perfect genetic control would erode the actual solidarity that arises when men and women reflect on the contingency of their talents and fortunes. . . .

It is often assumed that the powers of enhancement we now possess arose as an inadvertent by-product of biomedical progress—the genetic revolution came, so to speak, to cure disease, and stayed to tempt us with the prospect of enhancing our performance, designing our children, and perfecting our nature. That may have the story backwards. It is more plausible to view genetic engineering as the ultimate expression of our resolve to see ourselves astride the world, the masters of our nature. But that promise of mastery is flawed. It threatens to banish our appreciation of life as a gift, and to leave us with nothing to affirm or behold outside our own will.

READING QUESTIONS

1. Why does Sandel claim that the main ethical problem with genetic enhancement does not have to do with human autonomy?
2. In his discussion of various types of enhancement (muscles, memory, and height) Sandel asks readers to set aside questions about fairness and equal access to the means of such enhancements in reflecting on the morality of genetic enhancement. Why does he do this?
3. What is the difference between what Sandel calls the "ethic of giftedness" and the "ethic of willfulness"?
4. According to Sandel, what is the main moral objection to human genetic enhancement?

DISCUSSION QUESTIONS

1. Should we agree with Sandel that among the likely effects of human genetic enhancement will be a diminished sense of humility and solidarity?
2. Are there reasons, besides the ones that Sandel gives, for thinking that human genetic enhancement is morally wrong?

FRANCES M. KAMM

Is There a Problem with Enhancement?

This selection by Frances M. Kamm is a reply to the preceding essay by Michael Sandel. Her essay is divided into four sections and a conclusion. In section I she briefly summarizes Sandel's main objections to human enhancement, which include considerations having to do with (1) a designer's desire for mastery, (2) treatment versus enhancement, (3) parent-child relationships, and (4) social justice. In the three sections that follow, Kamm takes up (in order) these objections, arguing that they fail to be convincing. In her concluding section, Kamm briefly considers what she calls the "lack of imagination" objection to enhancement (not given by Sandel) which she takes seriously as a worry about some forms of enhancement.

Recommended Reading: Kantian moral theory; in particular, the discussion of the Humanity formulation of the categorical imperative, chap. 1, sec. 2C. Relevant to Kamm's discussion of enhancement and social justice is Rawls's social contract account of distributive justice, chap. 1, sec. 2G.

Should we enhance human performance? There are at least two types of enhancement. In the first, we increase above the norm so that more people are above the norm in ways that many people are already quite naturally. For example, we might increase intelligence so that people who would otherwise be only normally intelligent function as well as those few who are geniuses. In the second form of enhancement, we introduce improvements that no human being has yet evidenced—for example, living to be two hundred years old and healthy. The question of whether we should engage in either type of enhancement has arisen recently within the context of human genetics. Here one generation would probably modify the next. However, enhancement can also occur by way of drugs or intensive training and be done by a person to himself or to another.

Michael Sandel has recently argued that there is a moral problem with both types of enhancements

From Frances M. Kamm, "Is There a Problem with Enhancement?" *The American Journal of Bioethics* 5 (2005): 5–14.

regardless of the way in which they would be brought about, even if there were agreement (which there often is not) that the changes would be improvements, that they were safe, and they were fairly distributed among socioeconomic groups (Sandel 2004). Sandel's discussion is worth significant attention both because he is a member of the President's Council on Bioethics and because it expresses in compact form, readily available to the general public, some of the themes of the longer work on this subject produced by the President's Council. In this essay, I will present what seem to me to be the important components of Sandel's argument and then evaluate it.

I. SANDEL'S VIEWS

Sandel thinks that the deepest objection to enhancement is the desire for mastery that it expresses. He focuses especially (but not exclusively) on the attempt of parents to enhance their children, whether by genetic manipulation, drugs, or extensive training. He says:

> the deepest moral objection to enhancement lies less in the perfection it seeks than the human disposition it expresses and promotes. The problem is not that parents usurp the autonomy of a child they design. The problem is in the hubris of the designing parents, in their drive to master the mystery of birth . . . it would disfigure the relation between parent and child, and deprive the parent of the humility and enlarged human sympathies that an openness to the unbidden can cultivate. (Sandel 2004, 57)

And he thinks:

> . . . the promise of mastery is flawed. It threatens to banish our appreciation of life as a gift, and to leave us with nothing to affirm or behold outside our own will. (62)

However, he believes this objection is consistent with the permissibility and even the obligation to treat illnesses by genetic modification, drugs, or training. He is, therefore, arguing for a moral distinction between treatment and enhancement. He says,

(Sandel 2004, 57): "Medical intervention to cure or prevent illness or restore the injured to health does not desecrate nature but honors it." He also thinks parents must "shape and direct the development of their children . . . ," but he thinks there must be an equilibrium between "accepting love" and "transforming love."

Among the bad effects of mastery, he identifies the increasing responsibility that we must bear for the presence or absence of characteristics in ourselves and others and the effects this may have on human solidarity. The first point is concerned with the fact that we will no longer be able to say that our lacking a perfection is a matter of luck, something outside our control. We might be blamed for not improving ourselves or others. The second point is (supposedly) related to this. Sandel believes that the more our characteristics are a matter of chance rather than choice, "the more reason we have to share our fate with others" (Sandel 2004, 60). He goes on:

> Consider insurance. Since people do no know whether or when various ills will befall them, they pool their risk . . . insurance markets mimic solidarity only insofar as people do not know or control their own risk factors. . . . Why, after all, do the successful owe anything to the least-advantaged members of society? The best answer to this leans heavily on the idea of giftedness. . . . A lively sense . . . that none of us is wholly responsible for his or her success makes us willing to share the fruits of our talents with the less successful. (Sandel 2004, 60)

II. DESIRE FOR MASTERY

Let us clarify the nature of Sandel's objections to enhancement based on the desire for mastery over process. First, note that it implies that if (both types of) enhancements were occurring quire naturally, without our intervention, Sanddel's objection to enhancement would not be pertinent. Indeed, interfering with the natural enhancing changes would itself require mastery over life process, and so Sandel's objection might pertain to this. It is also important to keep in mind several distinctions. Actual mastery is different from the desire for it. We could achieve and exercise mastery over nature as a side effect of doing other things, without desiring it. This might be acceptable to Sandel. Suppose we did desire mastery, however. We could desire it as a means to some other end (e.g., achieving such good aims as health, beauty, virtue) or we could desire it as an end in itself. So long as we desire it as a means to other things considered good, it is clearly wrong for Sandel to conclude that desire for mastery will "leave us with nothing to affirm or behold outside our own will" (Sandel 2004, 62). Even if mastery were desired as an end in itself, this need not mean that it is our only end, and so we could still continue to affirm other good aims (such as virtue, health, etc.) as ends. I shall assume that if we desire mastery, it is as a means to good ends, as this seems most reasonable.

Such a desire for mastery is not inconsistent with an openness to the unbidden that Sandel emphasizes (Sandel 2004, 56), if the unbidden means just "those things that come without our deliberately calling for or causing them."[1] For if many good things were to come without our deliberately intervening to bring them about, presumably we would be happy to have them and not regret that they did not come about just because we deliberately brought them about. Such a form of openness to the unbidden does not, however, necessarily imply a willingness to accept whatever comes even if it is bad. Sometimes people are also unwilling to accept things that merely differ from their preferences, though the things are not necessarily bad. One or both of the latter forms of being closed to the unbidden may be what Sandel is concerned with, as he speaks of enlarged human sympathies resulting from an openness to the unbidden.

So far, I have been distinguishing various attitudes and states of mind that might be involved in a desire for mastery. Suppose some form of the desire for mastery and nonopenness to the unbidden is bad. The further question is whether there is any relation between having even a bad attitude and the impermissibility of enhancing conduct. As noted above, even Sandel supports the efforts to find certain treatments for illnesses. But seeking treatments for illnesses by manipulating the genome typically involves desiring mastery as a means, not being open to all things unbidden, and attempting to master the mystery of birth. Hence, Sandel may think that while there is something bad per se about desiring mastery even as a means, not being open to the unbidden, and attempting to master the mystery of birth, these bad aims can be outweighed by the good of curing diseases (if not by the pursuit of enhancements). Alternatively, he may believe that when the unbidden is very horrible—not a gift, even in disguise— not being open to the unbidden is not bad at all. If he believes these things, the question becomes why enhancements cannot outweigh or transform what Sandel believes are bads in the same way he thinks that treatments outweigh or transform them.[2]

There is a further, deeper problem about the relation between having bad dispositions and the impermissibility of conduct. For suppose that desiring mastery as one's sole end in life is a bad desire to have. Suppose a scientist who works on finding a cure for congenital blindness is motivated only by such a bad desire for mastery. Does this make his conduct impermissible? Presumably not. The good of treating diseases still justifies the work of the scientist even when his primary aim is not that there be no disease, but rather to achieve mastery. This is a case where there may be a duty to do the work. However, even when the act we would do would produce a good it is not our duty to produce, I think the act can be permissible independent of our intentions or disposition in doing it. So suppose several people could be saved only if you do an act that has a high probability of killing you. It is not typically your duty to do such an act, though it could be morally outstanding to do it. If the only reason you do it is to make those who care about you worry, this alone will not make saving the people impermissible. More generally, it has been argued, the intentions and attitudes of an agent reflect on the agent's character but not on the permissibility of his act (Scanlon 2002; Thomson 1990).[3]

Perhaps, however, this is not true. Sometimes we think an act is permissible only if it is satisfying a certain desire in an agent who does the act. For example, suppose we set aside scarce resources for a musical performance in order that those who desire pleasure from music shall have some. If someone's only aim in going to a concert is to mingle with other people, this is an indication he has no desire for music per se. Hence, it is an indication that an end which justified the use of scarce resources for musical performances will not be achieved. Hence, this agent should not go to the concert not because of his intention per se, but only because it is an indication that some justifying effect will not come about. Now, suppose someone has a bad aim (e.g., to show off) in doing something otherwise permissible, such as chewing gum. It might be appropriate for him to, in a sense, be punished for the bad aim with which he would chew the gum, by making it impermissible for him to chew the gum. This, of course, is not just any punishment. It specifically makes it the case that his bad aim is not efficacious. But if the achievement of an important good for others or the performance of a dutiful act (e.g., not harming someone) is at stake and this can justify the act, it would not be appropriate to require someone to forgo an act as a way of making his bad aim inefficacious. That would be to punish others for the agent's bad attitude.

It seems, then, that if Sandel is right and "the deepest moral problem with enhancement. . . ." is "the human disposition it expresses," then the deepest moral problem may provide no grounds at all for thinking that acts seeking enhancement are morally impermissible (Sandel 2004, 57). We will have to decide whether particular changes are permissible independently of the aims, attitudes, and dispositions of agents who act. Among the factors we might consider are the good ends to be brought about and the bad effects that might also occur. It is true that if the good outweighs the bad, then it is possible for a rational agent to have as his aim the pursuit of the good, rather than the (supposedly) bad aim of seeking mastery above all else. But it is the evaluation of objective goods and bads, rather than the agent's aims or desires that play a role in accounting for the permissibility of acting. If the only possible aim of a rational agent in seeking a particular change were to seek mastery as an end in itself, then presumably the good ends achieved in the change would not themselves be able to justify the act. But we need not be restricted to a consequentialist weighing of goods and bads in accounting for the permissibility of an act. Individual rights may be at stake. Furthermore, the causal role of bad effects (e.g., whether they are side effects or necessary means to good aims) can be crucial in a nonconsequentialist analysis of permissibility, even if agent's intention and disposition are not.

In connection with the effects of enhancing, there is a further point that Sandel makes, for he is concerned not only with the disposition that enhancement expresses but with "the human disposition it . . . . promotes." Promoting that disposition to seek mastery could be an effect of seeking enhancements, and we have said that the effects of acts can be relevant to their permissibility even if the attitudes of agents who perform the acts are not. Indeed, considering the disposition as an effect helps us understand that when Sandel says that "the deepest moral problem with enhancement is the human disposition it expresses," he is not so much giving an explanation of the wrongness of acts of enhancement, as simply focusing on the bad type of people we will be if we seek mastery.[4] But should we condemn a disposition even if it never leads to any impermissible acts and the disposition always leads people to act for the sake of the very properties that make the acts permissible because they make it permissible? (This is unlike the disposition of the scientist described above, yet it too is ruled out by Sandel's view). Is it inappropriate to be the sort of people who will be disposed to master nature as a means because the goods to be achieved outweigh the bads and no further nonconsequentialist objections are relevant?

Perhaps such a disposition could still be bad to have, if it leads us to focus on these types of acts to the exclusion of other worthwhile activities. Consider an artist who is always seeking to improve her paintings. She never rests content with just appreciating her own and other people's great works. Other people may have a better appreciation of great masters that she lacks. But it is not clear to me that her way of responding to value—by trying to create more of it—is inferior to the admittedly good alternative way of responding to value. And in some people these two approaches to value may be combined to one degree or another. Similarly for the dispositions to enhance and to appreciate goods already present.

III. TREATMENT VERSUS ENHANCEMENT

One conclusion so far is that we must look to such things as the properties of our acts and their effects, rights involved, and the required causal role of bad effects in producing the good, rather than to the dispositions of agents, to decide whether acts of enhancement are wrong. Hence, the disposition that Sandel identifies as a primary moral problem with enhancement has nothing to do with whether producing enhancements is right or wrong. However, one might rephrase an objection bearing on the permissibility of such acts. One might argue that the goods achievable by enhancement do not merit a causal role for the bads of people's uncovering mysteries of birth or mastering nature (whether they desire these or not), rather than letting nature give us whatever gifts it will.

There are two problems with rephrasing in this way. First, it may not be true that people's mastering nature, uncovering the secrets of life, and trying to improve what comes in life are bad in and of themselves. If they are not bad in themselves—but even good in themselves—then we do not have to show that there are great goods at stake that outweigh using the bads, in order to permissibly engage in these activities. Second, if they are bad, one would have to show not only that the good ends of enhancement are not as important as the goods of treatment but that they are not great enough to outweigh or transform the bads.

There are several possible routes to showing that the goods of enhancement are not as important as the goods of treatment. One is the idea of diminishing marginal utility, according to which the benefit someone gets out of a given improvement in his condition decreases the better off he is. Hence, we do more good if we help those who are worse off than if we help those who are already better off. A second route is the view that there is greater moral value in helping people the worse off they are in absolute terms, even if we produce a smaller benefit to them than we could to people who are better off. This is known as prioritarianism. A possible third route is to distinguish qualitatively between what some call harmed states and merely not being as well off as one might be but not badly off in

absolute terms (Shiffrin 1999). None of these routes to comparing the good ends of enhancement and treatment, however, shows that enhancements are not in themselves great enough goods to justify mastery as a means. They also do not rule out that providing enhancements might itself permissibly be a means to achieving the treatments. That is, suppose it is only if we are much smarter than we currently are that we will find a cure for terrible illnesses quickly. Then the importance of finding treatments could be transmitted to the enhancement of intelligence. (Of course, not all means are permitted to even justified ends. So if enhancements were sufficiently intrinsically objectionable, it might not be permissible to use the only available means to acquire treatments.)

At one point, Sandel tries to draw the distinction between treatment and enhancement by claiming that "medical intervention to cure or prevent illness . . . does not desecrate nature but honors it. Healing sickness or injury does not override a child's natural capacities but permits them to flourish" (Sandel 2004, 57). The assumption behind the first sentence is that nature is sacred and should be honored. But why should we believe this? Cancer cells, AIDS, tornadoes, and poisons are all parts of nature. Are they sacred and to be honored? The natural and the good are distinct conceptual categories and the two can diverge: the natural can fail to be good and the good can be unnatural (e.g., art, dams, etc.).[5] Suppose nature was sacred and to be honored. We would clearly be overriding its dictates by making people able to resist (by immunization) illnesses that they could not naturally resist. Is doing this impermissible because it does not honor nature? Surely not.

Sandel's view may better be expressed as the view that we may permissibly override and not honor nature when we get rid of the things in nature that interfere with the other parts of nature that are its gifts (i.e. good things). But if this is so, then Sandel's position does not rule out dramatically lengthening the human life span and preventing the interference of the aging process with the exercise of natural gifts that we have had all our lives. Most people would consider this a radical enhancement.

When Sandel claims that curing and preventing illness does not desecrate nature, he implies that enhancement is a problem because of the sort of relation we should have to nature. Emphasizing that healing allows a child's capacities to flourish, may seem to suggest that enhancement (but not treatment) is a problem because of its effects on our relations to other persons. But while Sandel does move on to the latter issue (and I will discuss his views on it below), he is here still focused on whether we are interfering with nature and the capacities (gifts) that nature has given someone when we enhance rather than cure. Hence, it is pertinent to ask, what if a child's natural capacities are those of a Down's Syndrome child and we seek to supplement these and provide greater gifts than nature provided by changing the child's genome? This would change or add to natural capacities, not merely permit them to flourish. Yet, presumably, Sandel would want to classify this with allowable treatment rather than enhancement. This form of treatment, which involves supplementing nature's gifts with new one's raises the more general question of why appreciation of nature's gifts requires limiting ourselves to them. We can appreciate what is given and yet supplement it with something new.

There are three primary conclusions of this section. First, Sandel's attempt to draw a distinction between treatment and enhancement does not seem successful. Second, given the way he draws the treatment/enhancement distinction, Sandel's objection to enhancement does not rule out maintaining natural gifts (that would otherwise wither) throughout a greatly extended human life span. Third, we would need much more argument to show that there is some duty owed to nature that we offend against when we change natural capacities, and that it is our relation to nature rather than to persons that should be a primary source of concern with enhancement.

IV. PARENTAL AND SOCIAL RELATIONS

In this section I will examine Sandel's views on how enhancement may negatively affect our relations to persons, ourselves or others.

A. One's Children

As noted above, Sandel paints with a broad brush in condemning enhancements due not only to genomic changes but to drugs and training. However, he also realizes that much of ordinary good parenting consists of what might ordinarily be called enhancement. Hence, he says the crucial point is to balance accepting love and transformative love. (Perhaps Sandel would want to apply this idea to changes adults seek to make to themselves as well.) He also seems to think of transformative love as concerned with helping natural gifts be fulfilled, framing and molding them so that they shine forth. (Similarly, in sport, he thinks that good running shoes help bring out a natural gift by comparison to drugs that would change a gift into something else.)

Let us first deal with the issue of balance. For all Sandel says, it remains possible that many more enhancements than he considers appropriate are ones that satisfy the balance between accepting and transformative love. This would most clearly be true if transformation were not merely a matter of molding nature's gifts, but of adding new ones. Furthermore, it is not clear what falls under "balancing." For example, suppose my child already has an IQ of 160. Might balancing the two types of love in her case imply that I may (if this will be good for her) increase her IQ another 10 but not 20 points, even though a parent whose child has an IQ of 80 should not change her child as much as to also give her a 170 IQ, for this would err on the side of too much transformation?

An alternative to such a balancing view might be called Sufficientarianism. It could imply that there is no need at all to increase the first child's IQ and that in the second child's case much more transformation (in the sense of adding to natural gifts) than acceptance is appropriate in order to reach a sufficient level. Sufficientarians are not interested in perfection, though they want enough mastery as a means to getting sufficient goods.

Let us now restrict ourselves to Sandel's sense of transformation—bringing out natural gifts—and consider the ways in which this may be done. To the extent to which Sandel allows training and appliances to be used to transform gifts, should he not also allow genetic manipulation that does exactly the same thing? So suppose that a certain amount of voice training is permitted to strengthen vocal chords. Would a drug or genetic manipulation that could strengthen vocal chords to the same degree also be permissible? If the argument Sandel gives does not rule out training, it alone will not rule out transformation by drugs or genetic means, because a gift is transformed to the same degree by each method. (If appliances such as running shoes are allowed, why not genetically transformed feet that function in the same way?) A different type of argument, based on the possible moral difference in using different means would be necessary to rule out the genetic means, but Sandel does not provide it. Rather, as we have noted, he treats training, drugs, and genetic manipulation on a par.

Hence, while he rightly condemns excessive pressure to transform oneself and one's children in a competitive, meritocratic society, especially if it is governed by shallow values, he does not condemn moderate training for worthwhile transformation.[6] Unless he emphasizes a difference in means used, he should then permit moderate, worthwhile genetic transformations, even if not excessive ones driven by competitive pressures and/or governed by shallow values.

Now consider one way in which Sandel may be wrong not to distinguish different ways of transforming or bringing about more radical enhancement. Perhaps we should separate how we treat changes that are made before a child exists (what I will call *ex ante changes*) from those that are made once a child exists (what I will call *ex post changes*). The former are primarily genetic, while the latter will include drugs and training. Love, it has been said, is for a particular. Consider love for an adult. Before we love someone, we may be interested in meeting a person who has various properties, such as kindness, intelligence, artistic ability, a good sense of humor, etc. When we meet such a person we may be interested in him rather than someone else because he has these properties. However, though it is through these properties that we may be led to love this particular person, it is the particular person that we wind

up loving, not his set of properties. For if another person appears with the same set of properties, that does not mean that we could as easily substitute him for the person we already love. Even if the person we love loses some of the properties through which we were originally led to love him (e.g., his beauty) and another person has more of the good properties that originally interested us, we would not necessarily stop loving the particular person we love (Nozick 1977).

It seems then that when we love a particular person, this involves much of what Sandel calls *accepting* love. If we do seek transformation in the properties of the person we love, this may be because of moral requirements or because we want what is good for him. By contrast, before a particular person whom we love exists (just as before we find someone to love), it is permissible to think more broadly in terms of the characteristics we would like to have in a person and that we think it is best for a person to have, at least so long as these characteristics would not be bad for the person who will have them and are consistent with respect for persons. (The latter constraint could conflict with merely doing what is best for someone. For example, suppose peace of mind and equanimity are goods for a person. Nevertheless, insuring their presence by modifying someone so that she is self-deceived about awful truths would be inconsistent with taking seriously that one is creating a person, an entity worthy of respect. Sandel says, "Not everything in the world is open to whatever use we may desire or devise" (Sandel 2004, 54). This is certainly true of persons, even when we desire their good.)

Before the existence of a person, there is no person yet with certain characteristics that we have to accept if we love him and do not want to impose undue burdens necessary for changes. Hence, not accepting whatever characteristics nature will bring but altering them ex ante does not show lack of love. Nor can it insult or psychologically pressure a person the way ex post changes might, as no conscious being yet exists. Importantly, it is (somewhat paradoxically) rational and acceptable to seek good characteristics in a new person, even though we know that when the child comes to be and we love him or her, many of these characteristics may come and go and we will continue to love the particular person. This is an instance of what I call the distinction between "caring to have" and "caring about." That is, one can know that one will care about someone just as much whether or not she has certain traits and yet care to have someone that has, rather than lacks, these traits (Kamm 2004).[7] Sandel says that "parental love is not contingent on talents and attributes a child happens to have" (Sandel 2004, 55). This is true. But I have tried to show this is consistent with seeking better attributes.

Applying what I have said to the issue of enhancement suggests that even if transformative and enhancing projects should be based primarily on what is best for the child, this is consistent with trying to achieve ex ante a child with traits that will be desirable per se, so long as they will not be bad for the child and are not inconsistent with respect for persons. Ex ante enhancement will primarily be through genetic alteration. By contrast ex post enhancement may have to be more constrained for it could involve psychological pressure on the child and lead to fear of rejection. (Altering a fetus or early infant will be somewhere in between.)

Drawing a distinction between the methods of ex ante and ex post "designing" does not, however, put to rest different sorts of objections to even ex ante transformations. First, Sandel thinks that people are not products to be designed. I agree that people are not products in the sense that they are not commodities, but rather beings worthy of concern and respect in their own right. But I do not think this implies that it is morally wrong to design them. Consider first if it would be acceptable to redesign oneself. We are accustomed to people having replacement parts, such as knees, hips, and transplants. Suppose when our parts wore out, we were offered alternatives among the new ones. For example, teeth of various colors, joints that were more or less flexible, limbs that were longer or shorter. It might well make sense to make selections that involved redesigning our bodies. Similarly, if we could replace brain cells, it might make sense to choose ones that gave us new abilities. This would be redesigning ourselves.

Now consider creating new people. We already have much greater control over the timing of pregnancy and, via artificial reproduction, over whether someone can conceive at all. Rather than humility, we have justifiable pride in these accomplishments. Now suppose we each had been designed in detail by other persons. Presumably, we would still be beings of worth and entitled to respect. In this sense, designing persons is not inconsistent with their personhood. But might it be that although a being retains its high status despite such an origin, it is inconsistent with respect for persons to choose such an origin for them? (Analogously, a person retains his status as a rights bearer even when his rights are violated, but it is not, therefore, appropriate to violate his rights.) But suppose that the natural way of reproducing required that properties be selected for offspring, otherwise they would be mere lumps of flesh. Surely selecting properties would be permissible. Would we be obligated, out of respect for persons, to search for a way to alter this (imagined) natural way for definite properties to come about when it is going well, so that they would happen by chance? I do not think so. Hence, I conclude, designing of persons is not per se inconsistent with respect for persons.[8]

A second objection asks, if someone wants to have a child, should they not focus only on the most basic goods, such as having a normal child to love? If so, then if they focus on achieving many superior qualities, does that not show they are interested in the wrong things in having a child? To answer this worry, consider an analogy. If the primary concern for a philosopher in getting a job should be that she be able to do philosophy, does that mean that it is wrong to choose between possible jobs equally satisfying that characteristic on the basis of other desirable properties such as higher salary or better location? If not, why is the search for properties other than the basic ones in a child wrong, when the basic ones are not thereby put in jeopardy? (Of course, in the case of the child-to-be, unlike the job, the enhanced properties are usually to be for its benefit, not only for those doing the selecting.)

Furthermore, searching for more than the basics does not by itself imply that if one could not achieve those enhancements, one would not still happily have a child who had only the basics. (And even while someone who would refuse to have a child without enhancements might thereby show that he did not care very much about the core reasons for having a child, this does not show he is unfit to be a parent. For he could still come to love the child if he actually has it, through attachment to it as a particular, as described above.)

A third concern is that in the relation of parent to child, a parent will simply have greater control over the child's nature, whether she seeks it or not. (This does not mean that the child has less control, for it is chance, not the child, that will determine things, if persons, such as parents, do not. Nor does it mean that the issues of "designing" children and parental control are not separable in principle. For if someone other than the parent designed the child, relative to the parent the child would still be part of the unbidden). But in numerous areas of life, persons now stand in relations of control over other people where once chance ruled. The important thing is that this be done justly, benevolently, and wisely. Furthermore, if we choose certain characteristics in offspring, the balance of control over the child's life may shift to the child rather than the parent. What I have in mind is that if we could ensure that a child has such enhancing traits as self control and good judgment, the child would be less, not more, likely to be subject to parental control after birth. This is most important.

A fourth concern is that if each parent individually tries to do what is best for its child, all parents will end up making the situation worse for all their children. To avoid this prisoner's dilemma situation, some rule that coordinates the choices of parents seems called for.[9]

B. Social Justice

Finally we come to Sandel's views on the connection between enhancement and the twin issues of the burdens of responsibility and distributive justice. If people are able to enhance themselves or others, can they not be held responsible in the sense of being blamed for not giving themselves or others desirable characteristics? Not necessarily, for one does not have a duty to do everything that could make oneself or someone else better, and if one has no duty, then one is not at fault in not enhancing and so not to be blamed. Even if one has certain duties, for example, to be the best doctor one can be, and taking certain drugs would help one to perform better, it is not necessarily one's duty to take the drugs. Hence, one need not even be at fault if one does not do what will help one perform one's duties better. But one could retain a right not to alter one's body in order to better fulfill one's duties as a physician, without making such alterations impermissible for anyone who wants them. Of course, if the characteristics one will have must be decided by others (for example, one's parents), then one could not be held morally accountable for causing or not causing certain traits, as one could not direct one's parents' behavior.

What about cases in which one can be blamed for a choice not to enhance? Thomas Scanlon has emphasized that one can hold someone responsible for an outcome in the sense of blaming him for it without thereby thinking that it is also his responsibility to bear the costs of his choice (Scanlon unpublished). These are conceptually two separate issues. For example, suppose someone is at fault for acting carelessly in using his hairdryer. If he suffers severe damage and will die without medical treatment, his being at fault in a minor way does not mean that he forfeits a claim on others he otherwise had to free medical care.

Sandel thinks the issue of responsibility for choosing to have or to lack certain characteristics is intimately related to how much of a claim we have against others for aid. However, he is not always clear in distinguishing the role of choice from the role of mere knowledge of one's characteristics. For example, in discussing why we have insurance schemes, he seems to imply that even if we had no control over our traits but only knew what they were (for example, via genetic testing), we would lose a claim against others to share our fate. For if they knew they were not at risk, people would not enter into insurance schemes that mimic solidarity. This is an argument against knowledge as well as against control. But those who urge us to use a veil of ignorance in deciding about what allocation of resources is just are, in effect, saying that even if we have knowledge of each other's traits, there are moral reasons for behaving as though we lack the knowledge.

Let us put aside the issue of blameworthiness for, and the effect of mere knowledge of, one's traits. How should the possibility of making choices that determine one's traits affect responsibility for bearing costs for the outcome of choices. Sandel seems to share with some philosophers (known as luck egalitarians) the view (roughly) that if we have not chosen to have traits but have them as a matter of luck (or other people's choices), the costs of having them should be shared. However, if we choose the traits (by act or by omitting to change them if we can), then even if we do not in any deep sense deserve to have made this choice, there is no reason for the costs of having the traits to be shared. (We may, however, choose to buy insurance that will protect us against bad choices.) Sandel says he cannot think of any better reason for the well-off to help those who are not well-off except that each is not fully responsible for his situation. (Many, however, do not find this a compelling reason for sharing with others. Robert Nozick, for example, argued that one could be entitled to what followed from the exercise of traits that one was not responsible for having[10]).

But it seems that often we want to give people new options without taking away from them help they would have gotten from others when they had no control over their fates. One example given above involved someone whose choice to use a hairdryer should not lead to his forfeiting aid to avert a major disaster. Similarly, if someone for reasons of conscience refuses to take advantage of the option to abort a difficult pregnancy, we do not think that she should forfeit medical care simply because she could have avoided the need for it. In many cases, arguments for the duty to aid others seem to have more to do with respect and concern for the value of other persons than with whether they have or have not gotten themselves into whatever situation they are in. Of course, in cases I have been considering, someone chooses in a way that leads to a bad outcome he does not per se choose. But recall that Kant thought we had a duty to help people pursue even the ends they themselves had deliberately chosen because people

matter in their own right, rather than because they could not be held responsible for their choices or because it was only the unwilled consequences of choices with which we were asked to help.

Finally, suppose it were true that to some degree as we increase the range of individual choice, we limit the claim of a person to the assistance of others. (For example, choosing to be paralyzed because one preferred that sort of life might be considered an "expensive taste," and public assistance for it might be denied). It is still true that, if having the option to enhance leads many people to improve themselves or others, there will be fewer instances of people who are badly off (because they lack good traits) and, hence, fewer who require the assistance of others. For example, rather than redistributing wealth that only the talented can produce in a certain environment, each person would have a talent and so have the opportunity to be more productive in that environment. Furthermore, each person would not only have the material benefits that can be redistributed from some to others. Each person could have the abilities and talents whose intrinsic rewards (that come just from their exercise) cannot be redistributed.

The primary conclusions of this section are that Sandel does not successfully show that we should limit options to enhance ourselves or others as a way of ensuring a right to social assistance. He also does not show that seeking to enhance children, especially ex ante, is inconsistent with a proper balance between accepting and transforming love.

V. CONCLUSION

Sandel focuses on the desire for mastery and the unwillingness to live with what we do not control as objections to enhancement. (He also focuses on the more contingent issue of the misuse of the ability to enhance ourselves and others that is likely to occur in a competitive environment, especially governed by shallow values.) I have argued that what is most troubling about enhancement is neither that there will be people who desire to have control over nature, offspring, and themselves, nor the unwillingness to accept what comes unbidden. However, I do think there are major problems with enhancement. Some are the ones Sandel puts to one side. Namely, could we really safely alter people, not making disastrous mistakes? And given our scarce resources, should enhancement be at the top of the list of things to which we should be attending?

A deeper issue, I think, is our lack of imagination as designers. That is, most people's conception of the varieties of goods is very limited, and if they designed people their improvements would likely conform to limited, predictable types. But we should know that we are constantly surprised at the great range of good traits in people, and even more the incredible range of combinations of traits that turn out to produce "flavors" in people that are, to our surprise, good. For example, could we predict that a very particular degree of irony combined with a certain degree of diffidence would constitute an interesting type of personality? In section IV A, I mentioned the view that potential parents should focus on having children with basic good properties rather than seek improvements beyond this. Oddly, the "lack of imagination" objection to enhancement I am now voicing is based on a concern that in seeking enhancements people will focus on too simple and basic a set of goods.

How does the lack of imagination objection relate to Sandel's view that an openness to the unbidden extends the range of our sympathies? One construal of his point is that if we have no control, we are forced to understand and care about people, as we should, even when they are difficult and nonideal. (Even if we have some control but lack complete control, we would, I think, have to cultivate such a virtue). By contrast, the lack of imagination objection emphasizes that when creatures of limited imagination do not design themselves and others, they are likely to extend the range of their appreciation of goods because the range of goods is likely to be larger. A parent who might have designed his child to have the good trait of composing classical music, could not have conceived that it would be good to have a child who turns out to be one of the Beatles. (To have conceived it, would have involved creating the style before the Beatles did.) The lack

of imagination objection is concerned that too much control will limit the number and combination of goods from what is possible. Hence, at least in those cases where enhancement—greater goods—is more likely to come about if chance rather than unimaginative choice is in control, the desire for enhancement will militate against control.

Finally, if the controlled selection of enhanced properties is a morally acceptable means, at least sometimes, what are the good ends to which it could safely be used? Presumably, it would be a safe end to enhance our capacities to recognize and fulfill our moral duties (or recognize when these are overridden). Recognizing and fulfilling moral duties (or recognizing when it is morally permissible for these to be overridden) is a side constraint on the exercise of any other capacities and the pursuit of any ends. There is no point in worrying about the risk that having such moral capacities will interfere with other unimagined goods. This is because if such moral capacities interfere with other goods, this just means that those other goods are not morally permissible options for us.

NOTES

1. Notice that not deliberately causing something is not the same as not causing it. For example, a parent may cause his child's IQ to move down from 160 to 140 by inadvertently eating improperly during pregnancy. This reduction is unbidden, though caused by the parent. It is in part because we might be causally responsible for making things worse than they could naturally be, that some may think that we have a duty to achieve at least the knowledge of life processes that prevents our interfering with naturally occurring goods.

2. I shall return to this point below.

3. Judith Thomson (1990, 1999) has argued that intention never matters to the permissibility of action. Thomas Scanlon (2000) makes a somewhat more limited claim.

4. As emphasized by Paul Litton and Larry Temkin.

5. Similarly, the human and the good are distinct conceptual categories. Human traits (such as arrogance) could be bad, and inhuman altruism could be good.

6. Hilary Bok emphasized this point.

7. I previously argued for this distinction when discussing the compatibility of (a) a disabled person caring about his life as much as non-disabled person cares about

his life and (b) a disabled person caring to have a non-disabled life rather than a disabled one.

8. Notice also that designing the gene pool so that only enhanced options are available is compatible with chance determination of any given individual.

9. Larry Temkin emphasized this point.

10. See his *Anarchy, State, and Utopia.*

REFERENCES

Kamm, F. 2004. Deciding whom to help, health-adjusted life years, and disabilities. In *Public health, ethics, and equity,* ed. S. Anand, F. Peters, and A. Sen, 225–242. Oxford, UK: Oxford University Press.

Nozick, R. 1977. *Anarchy, state and utopia.* New York: Basic Books.

Sandel, M. 2004. The case against perfection. *The Atlantic Monthly* 293(3): 51–62.

Scanlon, T. 2000. Intention and permissibility I. *Proceedings of the Aristotelian Society* Suppl. 74: 301–317.

Scanlon, T. *Blame.* Unpublished article.

Shiffrin, S. 1999. Wrongful life, procreative responsibility, and the significance of harm. *Legal Theory* 5(2): 117–148.

Thomson, J. J. 1990. *The realm of rights.* Cambridge, MA: Harvard University Press.

Thomson, J. J. 1999. Physician-assisted suicide: Two moral arguments. *Ethics* 109(3): 497–518.

READING QUESTIONS

1. Kamm offers an analysis of Sandel's notion of mastery. What is Kamm's distinction between actual mastery and desire for mastery? Why does she think that having a desire for mastery is not inconsistent with an "openness to the unbidden"?

2. What is Kamm's painter analogy—and the painter's way of responding to value—supposed to show with respect to enhancement?

3. Kamm does not think that we should determine whether acts of enhancement are wrong by looking to the disposition of agents. What sorts of things should we look to instead, according to Kamm?

4. What does Kamm suggest as the three possible routes for showing that the goods of enhancement are not as important as the goods of treatment? How does she respond to each?

5. What is Sandel's concept of the balance between "accepting love" and "transformative love"?

6. What does Kamm think the relation is between responsibility for one's choices and rights to social assistance? How does this bear on the issue of self-enhancement and genetic selection for one's children?

DISCUSSION QUESTIONS

1. Sandel does not distinguish between genetic manipulation, drugs, or extensive training as forms of enhancement. All are attempts at mastery, and as such, morally wrong. Do you agree? Why or why not?

2. Discuss the many different ways in which humans "interfere" with nature. Do you think a standard (or standards) can be established to determine which interventions are morally permissible and which are not? Are there some interventions that are morally obligatory? Give examples and reasons for your view.

3. Kamm worries that one of the bigger concerns of genetic enhancement (and what Sandel ignores) is our lack of imagination as designers, which could limit the number and combination of goods possible. How plausible is this idea? Can you think of other contexts in which imaginative enhancement is used to increase the number and combinations of goods? How does this differ, if at all, from the context of genetic enhancement?

PETER SINGER

Parental Choice and Human Improvement[1]

Peter Singer frames his discussion of genetic engineering by considering the idea of a genetic supermarket where prospective parents can pay to have a child that is likely genetically superior to a child they would have had without engineering. Singer's discussion explores the following three possible negative social consequences of a genetic supermarket and how they might be remedied: (1) possible loss of human diversity, (2) the possible negative effects of engineering children to have so-called positional goods, and (3) the possible negative effects on equality of opportunity. Singer argues that addressing such questions and, in particular, the second and third, raises important questions about what goods a society ought to promote and thus basic questions about value.

Recommended Reading: consequentialism, chap. 1, sec. 2A.

Consider . . . the issue of genetic engineering. Many biologists tend to think the problem is one of design, of specifying the best types of persons so that biologists can proceed to produce them. Thus they worry over what sort(s) of person there is to be and who will control this process. They do not tend to think, perhaps because it diminishes the importance of their role, of a system in which they run a "genetic supermarket," meeting the individual specifications (within certain moral limits) of prospective parents. . . . This supermarket system has the great virtue that it involves no centralized decision fixing the future of human type(s).

— *Robert Nozick,* Anarchy, State and Utopia
(New York: Basic Books) 1974, 315n.

BUYING YOURSELF A TALL, BRAINY CHILD

Advertisements in newspapers in some of America's most prestigious universities commonly offer sub-stantial sums to egg donors who are tall, athletic, and have scored extremely well in scholastic aptitude tests. The fees offered range up to $50,000. Actual sums paid are said to be closer to $10,000, but that is still substantial, and indicates the willingness of some couples to pay for the chance—and by this method it is only a chance—of having a child with above aver-age scholastic aptitude, height, and athletic ability.[2]

Our rapidly increasing knowledge of human genetics already makes it possible for some couples to have children who are genetically superior to the children they would be likely to produce if they left it to the random process of normal reproduction. At present, this is done by prenatal, and sometimes pre-implantation, diagnosis of embryos and fetuses. These techniques are becoming increasingly sophis-ticated and will in future be able to detect more and more genetically-influenced traits. Later, it will most likely be possible to insert new genetic material safely into the *in vitro* embryo. Both of these techniques will enable couples to have a child whose abilities are likely to be superior to those offered by the natural

From Peter Singer, "Parental Choice and Human Improvement" in Julian Savulescu and Nick Bostrom, eds., *Human Enhancement* (2009). By permission of Oxford University Press.

lottery but who will be "theirs" in the sense of having their genes, not the genes of only one of them (as in cloning), or the genes of a third person (as when an egg is purchased).

Many people say that they accept selection against serious diseases and disabilities, but not for enhancement beyond what is normal. There is, however, no bright line between selection against disabilities and selection for positive characteristics. From selecting against Huntington's Disease it is no great step to selecting against genes that carry a significantly elevated risk of breast or colon cancer, and from there it is easy to move to giving one's child a better than average genetic health profile.

In any case, even if it is possible to distinguish between selection for disabilities and selection for enhancement, it would need further argument to show that this distinction is morally significant. If, as surveys in most developed countries show, at least 85 per cent of couples are willing to abort a fetus that has Down's syndrome, most of them will also be willing to abort one with genes that indicate other intellectual limitations, for example genes that correlate with IQ scores below 80. But why stop at 80? Why not select for at least average IQ? Or, since genetics is only one factor in the determination of IQ, select for genes that make an above average IQ likely, just in case the environmental factors don't work out so well? The existing market in human eggs suggests that some people will also select for height, which in turn correlates to some extent with income. Nor will we spurn the opportunity to ensure that our children are beautiful, to the extent that that is under genetic control.

How should we react to these likely developments? Do they point to a nightmarish future in which children are made to order, and wanted for their specifications, not loved for themselves, however they may turn out? Or should we welcome the prospect of healthier, more intelligent, happier, and perhaps even more ethical children? Do the likely benefits outweigh the costs?

First we need to ask what exactly the costs are going to be. This is itself highly controversial. Is it a problem if, as Michael Sandel has suggested may happen, genetic enhancement will "banish our

appreciation of life as a gift, and to leave us with nothing to affirm or behold outside our own will."[3] I hope that human beings will continue to leave some natural ecosystems intact, so that we can always affirm and behold things that are outside our own will. Beyond that, I'm not sure that the idea of life as a "gift" makes much sense independently of belief in God. If there is no God, life can only be a gift from one's parents. And if that is the case, wouldn't we all prefer parents who try to make the gift as good as possible, rather than leaving everything to chance? Indeed, even Sandel does not think parents should leave everything to chance. He opposes "perfectionism", but not current practices of prenatal diagnosis that are aimed at eliminating serious genetic diseases and disabilities. The argument for taking life as a gift clearly has limits. If it is outweighed by the importance of avoiding children with serious diseases or disabilities, it may also be outweighed by the positive characteristics that genetic selection could bring.

Is this weighing of positive and negative aspects of genetic selection an issue for the legislature to resolve for all of us? Nozick's words cited at the head of this paper suggest a different approach: it is not up to government, he argued, to judge whether the outcome of this process will be better or worse. In a free society, all we can legitimately do is make sure that the process consists of freely chosen individual transactions. Let the genetic supermarket rule—and not only the market, but also altruistic individuals, or voluntary organizations, anyone who wishes, for whatever reason, to offer genetic services to anyone who wants them and is willing to accept them on the terms on which they are offered. Similarly, those who wish to preserve the idea that their child's life, with all his or her inherited characteristics, is a gift, may do so, and hence avoid genetic selection or enhancement. Others for whom that idea makes little sense, or is unimportant, may choose to make use of the technologies available to give their child a better chance of having the characteristics that they favor.

That the United States should allow a market in eggs and sperm which goes some way towards fulfilling Nozick's prophecy is no accident. In other countries a practice that threatens to turn the child of a marriage into an item of commerce would meet powerful opposition from both conservative "family values" politics and from left of center groups horrified at the idea of leaving to the market something as socially momentous as the way in which future generations are conceived. In the United States, however, that leftist attitude is restricted to groups on the margins of political life, and the conservatives who dominate Congress show their support for family values merely by preventing the use of federal funds for ends that they dislike; in other respects, they allow their belief that the market always knows best to override their support for traditional family values.

There are strong arguments against state interference in reproductive decisions, at least when those decisions are made by competent adults. If we follow Mill's principle that the state is justified in interfering with its citizens only to prevent harm to others, we could see such decisions as private ones, harming no one, and therefore properly left to the private realm.[4] For who is harmed by the genetic supermarket? The parents are not harmed by having the healthier, handsomer and more intelligent children that they want. Are the children harmed? In an article on the practice of buying eggs from women with specific desired characteristics like height and intelligence, George Annas has commented:

> What's troubling is this commodification, this treating kids like products. Ordering children to specification can't be good for the children. It may be good for adults in the short run, but it's not good for kids to be thought of that way.[5]

But to say that this is "not good" for these children forces us to ask the question: not good compared with *what*? The children for whom this is supposed not to be good could not have existed by any other means. If the egg had not been purchased, to be fertilized with the husband's sperm, that child would not have been alive. Is life going to be so bad for this child that he or she will wish never to have been born? That hardly seems likely. So on one reading of what the standard of comparison should be, it is clearly false that the purchase of these eggs is not good for the kids.[6]

Suppose that we read "not good for kids" as meaning "not the best thing for the next child of this couple". Then whether the purchase of the egg is or

is not good for the kid will depend on a comparison with other ways in which the couple could have had a child. Suppose, to make the comparison easier, they are not infertile—they bought an egg only in order to increase their chances of having a tall, athletic child who would get into a very good university. If they had not done so, they would have had a child in the normal way, who would have been their genetic child. Was it bad for their child to buy the egg? Their child may have a more difficult life because he or she was "made to order", and perhaps will disappoint his or her parents. But perhaps their own child would have disappointed them even more, by being less likely to be any of the things that they wanted their child to be. I don't see how we can know which of these outcomes is more likely. So I do not think we have grounds for concluding that a genetic supermarket would harm either those who choose to shop there, or those who are created from the materials they purchase.

If we switch from an individualist perspective to a broader social one, however, the negative aspects of a genetic supermarket become more serious. Even if we make the optimistic assumption that parents will select only genes that are of benefit to their children, there are at least three separate grounds for thinking that this may have adverse social consequences. The first is that a genetic supermarket would mean less diversity among human beings. Not all forms of diversity are good. Diversity in longevity is greater when there are more people with genes that doom them to an early death. The loss of this diversity is welcome. But what about the loss of the merely unusual, or eccentric? Antony Rao, a specialist in behavioral therapy in children, finds that many middle and upper class parents come to him when their children behave in unusual ways, wanting them to be medicated, because "they fear that any deviation from the norm may cripple their child's future."[7] If this is true of behavioral abnormalities that for many children are merely a passing phase, it is likely to be even more true of genetic abnormalities. It is easy to imagine genetic screening reports that indicate that the child's genes are unusual, although the significance of the abnormality is not well understood (usually medical shorthand for "We don't have a clue"). Would many parents decide to terminate the pregnancy in those circumstances, and if so, would there be a loss of diversity that would leave human society a less rich place?

I am more concerned about a second problem: many of the advantages people will seek to ensure for their children will be advantageous for them only in comparative, not absolute terms. Consider the difference between being tall, and living longer. Living longer than today's average lifespan today is something most of us would want, and the extent to which we want it is not, by and large, affected by whether everyone achieves this good, and so the average lifespan increases. For the purposes of this chapter, I'll call this kind of good an intrinsic good (ignoring the fact that most of us don't really think living longer is intrinsically good, since we would not want to live longer if we were in a coma for all of the additional years). Being taller than a specified height, however, is not something most of us would want for its own sake. True, being above average height correlates significantly with having above average income, and with being able to see over the heads of the crowd, but to gain these advantages we must be taller than the average in our society. To increase one's childrens' height, therefore, is beneficial only if it also moves them up relative to the height of others in their society. There would be no advantage in being 6′3″ if the average height is 6′6″. I will call this a positional good.

If everyone gains a positional good, no one is better off. They may all be worse off. In the case of height, arguably, it would be better if everyone were shorter, because we would require less food to sustain us, could live in smaller houses, drive smaller, less powerful cars, and reduce our impact on the environment. Thus being able to select for height— something couples are already doing, on a small scale, by offering more for the eggs of tall women— could start the human equivalent of the peacock's tail—an escalating "height race" in which the height that distinguishes "tall" people from those who are "normal" increases year by year, to no one's benefit, at considerable environmental cost, and perhaps eventually even at some health cost to the children themselves.[8] Genetic enhancement could lead to a collective action problem, in which the rational pursuit of individual self-interest makes us all worse off.

A third significant ground for objecting to a genetic supermarket is its threat to the ideal of equality of opportunity. It is, of course, something of a myth to believe that equality of opportunity prevails in the United States or anywhere else, because everywhere wealthy parents already give their children enormous advantages in the race for success. Nevertheless, a future in which the rich have beautiful, brainy, healthy children, while the poor, stuck with the old genetic lottery, fall further and further behind, is not a pleasing prospect. Inequalities of wealth will be turned into genetic inequalities, and the clock will be turned back on centuries of struggle to overcome the privileges of aristocracy. Instead the present generation of wealthy people will have the opportunity to embed their advantages in the genes of their offspring. These offspring will then have not only the abundant advantages that the rich already give their children, but also whatever additional advantages the latest development in genetics can bestow on them. They will most probably therefore continue to be wealthier, longer-lived and more successful than the children of the poor, and will in turn pass these advantages on to their children, who will take advantage of the ever more sophisticated genetic techniques available to them. Will this lead to a *Gattaca* society in which "Invalids" clean toilets while "Valids" run the show and get all the interesting jobs?[9] Lee Silver has pictured a USA a millenium hence in which the separation between "Gene-enriched" humans and "Naturals" has solidified into separate species.[10] That is too far in the future to speculate about, but Maxwell Mehlman and Jeffrey Botkin may well be right when they predict that a free market in genetic enhancement will widen the gap between the top and bottom strata of our society, undermine belief in equality of opportunity, and close the "safety valve" of upward mobility.[11]

How might we respond to these three problems? I think the solution to the first problem is easy. We would face a serious loss of genetic diversity only if the genetic supermarket was very widely used for a long time in a way that tended to focus on a small number of genotypes. Before this had had any real impact, we could observe what is happening, and stop the social experiment. I therefore do not see this as a decisive objection to opening the genetic supermarket.

The other two problems, of the pursuit of positional goods, and of making genetic inequality more rigidly structured than it is now, are more serious. What choices do we have? We might try to ban all uses of genetic selection and genetic engineering that go beyond the elimination of what are clearly defects. There are some obvious difficulties with this course of action:

1. Who will decide what is clearly a defect? Presumably, a government panel will be assigned the task of keeping abreast with relevant genetic techniques, and deciding which are lawful and which are not. This allows the government a role in reproductive decisions, which some may see as even more dangerous than the alternative of leaving them to the market.

2. There are serious questions about whether a ban on genetic selection and engineering for enhancement purposes could be made to work across the United States, given that matters regulating conception and birth are in the hands of the states, rather than the federal government. In the case of infertile couples seeking to pay a woman to bear a child for them, attempts by various U.S. states to make the practice illegal, or to declare surrogacy contracts void, have had little effect because a few states are more friendly to surrogacy. Couples seeking a surrogate to bear a child for them are prepared to travel to achieve what they want. As Lee Silver remarks: "What the brief history of surrogacy tells us is that Americans will not be hindered by ethical uncertainty, state-specific injunctions, or high costs in their drive to gain access to any technology that they feel will help them achieve their reproductive goals."[12]

3. Assume that one nation, for example the United States, decides that genetic selection is not a good thing, and Congress bans genetic selection and engineering when used for enhancement. Suppose also that this ban can be enforced effectively within the nation's boundaries. We would still have to deal with the fact that we now live in a global economy. An effective global ban seems very unlikely. A small nation might be tempted to allow enhancement genetics, thus setting up a niche industry serving wealthy couples from those nations that have banned enhancement. Moreover, in view of the competitive nature of the global economy, it may pay industrialized nations to encourage enhancement genetics, thus giving them an edge on those that do not. Singapore's former Prime Minister, Lee Kuan Yew, used to speak about the heritability of intelligence, and its importance for Singapore's future. His government introduced measures explicitly designed to encourage university graduates to have more children.[13] Had genetic enhancement been available to Lee Kuan Yew at the time, he might well have preferred it to the government-sponsored computer dating services and financial incentives on which he was then forced to rely. It might appeal to Singapore's present Prime Minister, who is, not coincidentally, Lee Kuan Yew's son.

If a ban in one country turns out to be unattainable, ineffective, or contrary to the vital interests of that country in a competitive global economy, and a global ban is not feasible, a bolder strategy could be tried. Assuming that the objective is to avoid a society divided in two along genetic lines, genetic enhancement services could be subsidized, so that everyone can afford them. But could society afford to provide everyone with the services that otherwise only the rich could afford? Mehlman and Botkin propose an ingenious solution: the state should run a lottery in which the prize is the same package of genetic services that the rich commonly buy for themselves. Tickets in the lottery would not be sold; instead every adult citizen would be given one. The number of prizes would relate to how many of these packages society could afford to pay for, and thus would vary with the costs of the genetic services, as well as with the resources available to provide them. To avoid placing a financial burden on the state, Mehlman and Botkin suggest, the use of genetic technologies could be taxed, with the revenue going to fund the lottery.[14] Clearly universal coverage would be preferable, but the use of a lottery would at least ensure that everyone has some hope that their children will join the ranks of the elite, and taxing those who are, by their use of genetic enhancement for their own children, changing the meaning of human reproduction seems a fair way to provide funds for it.

If we are serious about equality of opportunity then, instead of providing genetic enhancement for everyone, we could use our new techniques to provide genetic enhancement for those at the bottom, and restrict enhancement for those at the top.[15] That's a possible strategy, for those who consider equality of opportunity so important a value that it should override the benefits achieved by providing enhancement for those at the top. If, however, equality of opportunity is embraced for consequentialist reasons, rather than its intrinsic value, that is a dubious judgment. Unless we take a gloomy view of human nature, there seems a fair chance that enhancement for all, including those at the top, will eventually improve the situation of everyone, including the worst-off.

There is still a further problem that state provision of genetic enhancement to all citizens does not solve. If the rich nations were to act on this, it would still leave those living in poor countries without enhancement. So the divide that we feared would open up within a society would instead open up between societies. Unless we argue for an obligation for the rich nations to provide genetic enhancement for people living in countries unable to provide similar services, it is difficult to see any way of overcoming this problem.[16]

There is therefore a strong argument that the state should be directly involved in promoting genetic enhancement. But this takes us back to the question of which enhancement services the state should fund, and so we come back to the issue of positional goods. One proposal would be that the state should fund genetic enhancement that provides intrinsic goods, but not genetic enhancement that provides positional goods. For what would be the point of funding everyone to improve their positional goods? It would be as if the authorities dealt with drugs in sport by handing out equal doses of performance enhancing drugs to all athletes. If the drugs pose even small risks to athletes, no one could sensibly favor such a proposal. But now we need a government committee to decide which forms of genetic enhancement confer intrinsic goods, and which confer positional goods. Suppose, for example, that we can find genes that correlate with doing well on IQ tests and scholastic aptitude tests used as part of the admission process by elite universities. Doing well on university admission tests is obviously a positional good. If everyone does better, the scores needed to get in will rise. If the tests are well designed, however, a good score presumably indicates an ability to learn, or to solve problems, or to write clearly and well. That sounds more like an intrinsic good, and an important one.

Bizarre as it may seem, there are some who might deny that the ability to learn or solve problems is an intrinsic good. Suppose that it is shown that scores on scholastic aptitude tests correlate inversely with the belief that God has an important role to play in one's life—not a far-fetched hypothesis, since we know that educational level does correlate inversely with this belief.[17] Those who think that belief in God is necessary for personal salvation, and that nothing can be more important than salvation, might then deny that scholastic aptitude is good at all.

Recent research on voles—small mouse-like rodents—has suggested that a characteristic more likely to appeal to Christians may be influenced by genetic modification. There are different kinds of voles, and they show different forms of mating behavior. Prairie voles tend to be monogamous, whereas meadow voles are more promiscuous. Researchers noticed that variations in a single gene—the arginine vasopressin receptor gene, which determines the way the brain responds to the hormone vasopressin—correlate with this difference in mating behavior. By manipulating the gene, the behavior of the normally promiscuous meadow voles was altered, so that they became as monogamous as prairie voles. If something similar can be shown for human behavior, would parents who place a high value on sexual fidelity wish to select or modify their children so that they would be more likely to be faithful to their sexual partners? Instead of exchanging promises and rings will people want their potential partners to make a different kind of commitment. Will they ever say: "If you really loved me, you'd get your vasopressin receptors enhanced, so you wouldn't be tempted to stray!" Or is there, as Immanuel Kant might have held, greater moral worth in being faithful *despite* have a genetic tendency to stray?[18] Does making it easier for humans to be faithful somehow reduce the value of faithfulness? Is the only moral virtue worth having that which is achieved through an act of will, rather than with the assistance of genetic modification? But what if having strength of will is itself something that is subject to genetic influence?

CONCLUSION

As these examples show, judgments about what goods we ought to promote will raise fundamental value questions that will not be easy to resolve.

In addition to distinguishing intrinsic and positional goods, each nation will have to consider whether to promote forms of genetic enhancement that have social benefits. Just as societies now spend money on education, especially in science and technology, in the hope of gaining an economic edge by having better-educated people than other nations, so too some nations will seize on genetic enhancement as a way of achieving the same goal. We may therefore have no choice but to allow it, and indeed encourage it, if we want our economy to remain strong.

In the case of promoting scholastic aptitude, the interests of the nation, of the person who is selected for the enhanced characteristics, and of the parents, may all coincide. But that will not always be the case. Some advocates of genetic enhancement hold out the prospect of improving human nature by selecting for children who are less aggressive, or more altruistic. In this way, they suggest, we can hope one day to live in peace, free of war and violence. The regulated and subsidized form of parental choice that I am suggesting might not lead to that happy outcome. There is a collective action problem here, the reverse of that we found with positional goods. We would all be better off if we each selected children who will be less aggressive and more altruistic, but unless the culture changes significantly, our own children may be

better off—at least by conventional measures of what counts as "better off"—if we do not select them in this way. The only way we could get the desired outcome would be to use coercion. Moreover if the desired end is world peace, and not merely a better, more compassionate society in our own country, this coercion would have to be carried out globally, perhaps by each government agreeing to enforce it on its own citizens. Politically, for the foreseeable future, this is fantasy. Genetic enhancement may have benefits, but it doesn't look as if world peace will be one of them.

NOTES

1. This is a substantially revised version of an essay that previously appeared in John Rasko, Gabrielle O'Sullivan, and Rachel Ankeny (eds), *The Ethics of Inheritable Genetic Modification* (Cambridge: Cambridge University Press), 2006.

2. Gina Kolata, "$50,000 Offered to Tall, Smart Egg Donor," *The New York Times,* March 3, 1999, A10; the suggestion that the amount paid is usually significantly less comes from Gregory Stock, personal communication.

3. See Michael Sandel, "The Case Against Perfection," *Atlantic Monthly,* April 2004, 51–62.

4. J. S. Mill, *On Liberty,* first published 1859, available at www.utilitarianism.com/ol/one.html

5. Lisa Gerson, "Human Harvest," *Boston Magazine,* May 1999, www.bostonmagazine.com/highlights/human-harvest.shtml

6. On the difficult issue of whether we can benefit a child by bringing it into existence, see Derek Parfit, *Reasons and Persons* (Oxford: Clarendon Press), 1984, 367, and Peter Singer, *Practical Ethics* (Cambridge: University Press), 2nd edn., 1993, 123–5.

7. Jerome Groopman, "The Doubting Disease," *New Yorker,* April 10, 2000, 55.

8. Helena Cronin, *The Ant and the Peacock* (Cambridge: Cambridge University Press), 1991, ch. 5.

9. *Gattaca,* written and directed by Andrew Niccol, 1997.

10. Lee Silver, *Remaking Eden* (New York: Avon), 1998, 282.

11. Maxwell Mehlman and Jeffrey Botkin, *Access to the Genome: The Challenge to Equality* (Washington, DC: Georgetown University Press), 1998, ch. 6.

12. *Remaking Eden,* 177.

13. Chan Chee Khoon and Chee Heng Leng, "Singapore 1984: Breeding for Big Brother," in Chan Chee Khoon

and Chee Heng Leng, *Designer Genes: I.Q., Ideology and Biology,* Institute for Social Analysis (Insan), Selangor, Malaysia, 1984, 4–13.

14. Mehlman and Botkin, op. cit., 126–8.

15. Dan Brock made this point in discussion, although without endorsing the view that we should give this much weight to equality of opportunity.

16. I owe this point to Art Caplan.

17. Gallup International Millennium Survey, 1999. Available at http://www.gallup-international.com/ContentFiles/millennium15.asp

18. Immanuel Kant, *Groundwork of the Metaphysics of Morals,* trans. Mary Gregor (Cambridge: University Press), 1997.

READING QUESTIONS

1. How does Singer dismiss the "life as a gift" argument against genetic enhancement?
2. Why does Singer object to a completely free-market "genetic supermarket"?
3. Explain Singer's "collective action problem" claim that if everyone gains a positional good, no one is better off. How does this differ from gaining an intrinsic good?
4. What three difficulties does Singer foresee in connection with attempts to ban all uses of genetic selection and engineering that go beyond elimination of defects?
5. In what ways does Singer speculate about the relation of genetic enhancement to the national and global economy?
6. Explain Singer's proposal that the state should subsidize and regulate genetic enhancement.

DISCUSSION QUESTIONS

1. Singer does not agree with the claim that the genetic supermarket would be bad for the child who is a product of genetic selection. What reasons (other than the "disappointment" reason) can be given in support of the claim that it would be bad for the child?
2. Singer argues that not all forms of diversity are good. What examples does he give? Discuss forms of diversity that, by contrast, are good.
3. Singer's argument is clearly utilitarian, and he concludes that there are more benefits than harms to regulated genetic enhancement. But is there an opposing argument according to which genetic selection is morally wrong even if there are more benefits than harms?

ADDITIONAL RESOURCES

Web Resources

Note: the first three of the following Web resources were selected mainly for their information about genetics, cloning, and stem cell research.

Center for Genetics and Society, <www.geneticsandsociety.org>. A nonprofit organization that disseminates information about reproductive technologies. According to its site, "The Center supports benign and beneficent medical applications of the new human genetic and reproductive technologies, and opposes those applications that objectify and commodify human life and threaten to divide human society."

Genomics.Energy.Gov, <http://genomics.energy.gov>. Site of the genome programs of the U.S. Department of Energy Office of Science. Includes information about cloning.

The National Institutes of Health, <www.nih.gov>. Includes information about stem cells, stem cell research, ethical issues raised by such research, and information on U.S. policy regarding the use of stem cells in research.

Devolder, Katrien, "Cloning," <http://plato.stanford.edu/entries/cloning>. An overview of the ethical dispute over therapeutic and reproductive cloning, including some discussion of religious perspectives.

Siegel, Andrew, "The Ethics of Stem Cell Research," <http://plato.stanford.edu/entries/stem-cells>. An overview of the ethical controversy over use of stem cells for therapeutic and reproductive purposes.

Authored Books

Agar, Nicholas, *Liberal Eugenics: In Defense of Human Enhancement* (Oxford: Blackwell, 2004). As the title indicates, Agar defends the morality of human enhancement employing what he calls the "method of moral images" that appeals to the idea of treating like cases alike.

Congregation for the Doctrine of the Faith, *Instruction* Dignitas Personae *on Certain Bioethical Questions*, 2008. An update of the Vatican's stance on biomedical issues in which it condemns in vitro fertilization, human cloning, genetic testing on embryos, embryonic stem cell research (that involves destruction of the embryos), and use of the RU-486 pill.

Kass, Leon R., *Human Cloning and Human Dignity: The Report of the President's Council on Bioethics* (New York: PublicAffairs Reports, 2002). A report from President George W. Bush's bioethics council with Kass as its chairman in which the ethical issues raised by cloning and matters of public policy are discussed.

Kitcher, Philip, *The Lives to Come: The Genetic Revolution and Human Possibilities* (New York: Simon & Schuster, 1997). A guide to advances in biomedical research including discussion of important moral and political questions such research raises.

Mehlman, Maxwell J., *Transhumanist Dreams and Dystopian Nightmares: The Promise and Peril of Genetic Engineering.* (Baltimore, MD: The Johns Hopkins Press, 2012). The author explores scientific and ethical questions raised by the prospect of human genetic engineering.

Pence, Gregory E., *Flesh of My Flesh: The Ethics of Cloning Humans* (Lanham, MD: Rowman & Littlefield, 1998). An examination of the ethical arguments over cloning and a qualified defense of the practice.

Pence, Gregory E., *Cloning After Dolly: Who's Still Afraid?* (Lanham, MD: Rowman & Littlefield, 2005). A follow up to his 1998 book, extending his case in favor of cloning.

Stock, Gregory, *Redesigning Humans: Our Inevitable Genetic Future* (New York: Houghton Mifflin Co, 2002). Examines the emerging reproductive technologies for selection and alteration of human embryos. Stock argues that ethical objections to such selection and alteration are much like the objections formerly raised against in vitro fertilization.

Wilkinson, Stephen, *Choosing Tomorrow's Children* (New York: Oxford University Press, 2010). An examination of the moral issues raised by the prospects of selective reproduction.

Edited Collections

Klotzko, Arlene Judith (ed.), *The Cloning Sourcebook* (Oxford: Oxford University Press, 2001). Twenty-eight essays divided into four parts: (1) The Science of Cloning, (2) The Context of Cloning, (3) Cloning: The Ethical Issues, and (4) Cloning and Germ-Line Intervention: Policy Issues.

McGee, Glenn (ed.), *The Human Cloning Debate* (Berkeley, CA: Berkeley Hills Books, 2002). This anthology has nineteen selections debating the morality of cloning and includes five articles representing various religious (Jewish, Catholic, Protestant, Buddhist, and Islamic) perspectives on the issue.

Nussbaum, Martha C. and Cass R. Sunstein (eds.), *Clones and Clones: Facts and Fantasies about Human Cloning* (New York: W. W. Norton, 1998). A collection of twenty-four contributions organized into five sections: (1) Science, (2) Commentary, (3) Ethics and Religion, (4) Law and Public Policy, and (5) Fiction and Fantasy.

Rantala, M. L. and Arthur J Milgram (eds.), *Cloning: For and Against* (Chicago: Open Court, 1999). A wide-ranging collection of fifty-four essays by scientists, journalists, philosophers, religious leaders, and legal experts debating the ethical issues and matters of public policy regarding the prospect of cloning.

Ruse, Michael and Christopher A. Pynes (eds.), *The Stem Cell Controversy*, 2nd ed. (Amherst, NY: Prometheus Books, 2006). Twenty-eight essays organized into five parts: (1) The Science of Stem Cells, (2) Medical Cures and Promises, (3) Moral Issues, (4) Religious Issues, and (5) Policy Issues.

Savulescu, Julian and Nick Bostrom, (eds.), *Human Enhancement* (Oxford: Oxford University Press, 2009). Eighteen essays debating the general topic of human enhancement as well as specific applications including, for example, the issue of selection of children and the use of enhancements to improve athletic performance.

12) The Death Penalty

As of 2015, the death penalty was legal in thirty-one U.S. states. What is often called "the modern era" of the death penalty in the United States dates from 1976 when the 1972 moratorium on the death penalty was lifted by the U.S. Supreme Court. As of April 2016, 1,431 individuals have been executed in the United States.[1] Although traditionally there has been wide support among U.S. citizens for the death penalty, this support has been declining in recent years. A Gallup Poll conducted in 1988 indicated that 79 percent of U.S. citizens favored the death penalty for the crime of murder. A 2015 Gallup Poll indicated that 61 percent of U.S. citizens support the death penalty for the crime of murder, while 37 percent are opposed. Another Gallup Poll conducted in 2006 is perhaps more revealing. This poll indicated that when presented with the option of sentencing someone to life in prison *without parole* for the crime of murder or sentencing that person to die, only 47 percent favored the death penalty, 48 percent favored life without parole, and 5 percent had no opinion.[2] At least in the United States, the death penalty continues to be a source of moral controversy.[3]

This controversy was fueled in 2009 by the case of Cameron Todd Willingham, who in 2004 was executed in the state of Texas for setting fire to his house in 1991, an act that had killed his three children. Willingham denied setting the fire and refused to enter a plea of guilty in exchange for a life sentence. In 2004 and after a detailed arson report concluded that the evidence against Willingham was "flimsy and inconclusive," Texas governor Rick Perry nevertheless denied a reprieve and Willingham was executed. In 2009, the Forensic Fire Commission hired an arson expert to review the evidence in the Willingham case. The expert, Craig L. Beyler, reported that the evidence in the case did not support the claim that the fire was a case of arson. In October of 2009, Beyler was set to testify before the Texas Forensic Science Commission, but two days before the commission was to hear this testimony, Governor Perry replaced the head and two other members of the commission. The newly appointed head, John M. Bradley, then canceled the meeting. The matter is still under consideration by the commission. Many are convinced that Texas executed an innocent man, and in his article, "Trial by Fire," about the Willingham case published in the *The New Yorker*, David Grann notes that Texas may be the first state forced to acknowledge that it carried out the execution of an innocent person.[4] Perhaps the most forceful moral argument against the death penalty is based on the claim that some people innocent of the crimes for which they are sentenced to die (Willingham may have been such a person) have been and likely will continue to be wrongly put to death. In recent years the use of DNA testing has also played a large role in exonerating some death row convicts and thus calling into question the death penalty. According to the *Innocence Project*, 337 individuals convicted of crimes have been exonerated in the United States by the use of DNA testing, 20 of whom were at one time sentenced to death.[5]

In addition to questions about the morality of the death penalty, there are also questions about its legality. The Eighth Amendment to the U.S. Constitution forbids "cruel and unusual" punishment, and some argue that the death penalty, because it is cruel and unusual, is unconstitutional and hence ought to be made illegal. This question of the constitutionality of the death penalty is the leading *general* question about its legality; but there are also *specific* legal questions about its use. For instance, in March 2005, the U.S. Supreme Court ruled it unconstitutional to execute juveniles—those under the age of eighteen who commit murder—a decision[6] in which the Court stressed the importance of appealing to "the evolving standards of decency that mark the progress of a maturing society" in determining which punishments are cruel and unusual.

But our concern here is with the *morality* of the death penalty, and the main questions are these:

- Is the death penalty ever a morally permissible form of punishment?
- If it is ever morally permitted, what best explains why such killing is permissible?

Those who answer the first question negatively are often referred to as **abolitionists,** and those who think that the death penalty is (or could be) morally justified (or perhaps even required) are often referred to as **retentionists.**[7] Of course, a retentionist need not and typically will not think that use of the death penalty is morally justified under *all* conditions. And so anyone who answers the first question affirmatively must address the second question.

In the remainder of this introduction, we shall consider important theoretical background that one must understand to be in a position to follow the moral controversy over the death penalty. We begin with some remarks about the idea of legal punishment and then proceed to outline two general approaches to the morality of punishment that influence moral discussion and debate over the specific punishment of execution.

1. LEGAL PUNISHMENT

The focus of this chapter is **legal punishment**—punishment administered by a legal authority. So, it is important at the outset to begin with a working definition of legal punishment, which will enable us to clarify the moral issues connected with legal punishment generally and the death penalty in particular.

Obviously, legal punishment presupposes a legal system, involving a set of laws and some mechanism of enforcement of those laws. Here, then, is a list of requirements that serve to define the very idea of a legal punishment.[8]

1. It must involve pain or other consequences normally considered unpleasant;
2. It must be for an offense against legal rules;
3. It must be of an actual or supposed offender for his or her offense;
4. It must be intentionally administered by human beings other than the offender;
5. It must be imposed and administered by an authority constituted by a legal system against which the offense is committed.

Because there is a moral presumption against the intentional infliction of pain or other unpleasant consequences on human beings, the practice of legal punishment calls for a moral justification. This moral question is addressed by theories about the morality of punishment.

2. THEORY MEETS PRACTICE

Two theories about the morality of punishment inform much of the debate over the death penalty. One theory is the **retributive theory of punishment**, which is basically Kantian in flavor; the other is the **consequentialist theory of punishment**. These theories attempt to answer two basic questions about the morality of punishment:

- What (if anything) morally justifies the practice of punishment?
- How much and what kinds of punishment are morally justified for various legal offenses?

The retributive and consequentialist theories provide competing answers to these two questions.

The Retributive Theory

The retributive theory in effect looks to the deeds of wrongdoers—both the fact that such deeds break laws and the specific nature of the deeds performed—in order to answer the two questions. So, the retributivist answer to the first question is

R1   What morally justifies punishment of wrongdoers is that those who break the law (and are properly judged to have done so) *deserve* to be punished.

A sense of fairness or justice prevails here. Wrongdoers are viewed as attempting to take unfair advantage of others and law-governed society generally, and the idea behind R1 is simply that justice demands that in response to crime, the wrongdoer suffer some sort of deprivation.

The retributivist response to the second question is

R2   The punishment for a particular offense against the law should "fit" the crime.

The task for the retentionist who accepts the retributive theory is to show that the death penalty is either required by, or at least consistent with, these two basic retributive principles (properly interpreted); opponents of the death penalty who accept the retributive theory must show that there is something about the death penalty that violates one or both of these principles (properly interpreted).

It is clear that R1 is neutral with regard to the moral justification of the death penalty—both retentionists and abolitionists, who otherwise accept the retributivist theory, can agree that punishment in general is justified because the wrongdoer deserves it. So the main focus of the retentionist's strategy in arguing about the death penalty will be R2. And here we find a variety of interpretations of R2, owing to the fact that there is more than one way of understanding the idea of a punishment *fitting* the crime. I will briefly mention two of them.

According to the principle expressed by **lex talionis** (law of retribution), making the punishment fit the crime is a matter of doing to the wrongdoer the *same kind of action* that he or she did to his or her victim(s). This "eye for an eye" principle implies that the appropriate punishment for the crime of murder is the death penalty.

An alternative interpretation of what it means to make the punishment fit the crime is the **principle of proportionality**, according to which the appropriate moral measure of specific punishments requires that they be in "proportion" to the crime: that the severity of the punishment should "be commensurate" with the gravity of the offense.

Thus, the task of the retributivist who wants to defend the death penalty is to provide an interpretation of R2 that (1) represents a philosophically defensible principle of punishment *and* that (2) implies or at least is consistent with having the death penalty. This challenge is discussed by Stephen Nathanson in one of the readings in this chapter, and he argues that it cannot plausibly be met.

Although Kant famously defends the death penalty by appealing to retributivist ideas about the morality of punishment, some abolitionists appeal (rather ironically) to Kant's Humanity formulation of the categorical imperative: *an action is right if and only if (and because) it is consistent with treating human beings as ends in themselves—as beings with an inherent worth or dignity.* Nathanson, for instance, appeals to Kant's principle in arguing against the morality of the death penalty, claiming that execution fails to comport with what he calls "personal desert" grounded in one's innate dignity as a human being.

The Consequentialist Theory

The consequentialist theory of the morality of punishment follows fairly directly from the basic idea of the consequentialist moral theory of right conduct that was presented in chapter 1: *an action or practice is right if and only if (and because) the overall value of the consequences of the action or practice would be at least as great as the overall value of the consequences of alternative actions and practices.* If we now appeal to this basic principle in responding to the two questions about the morality of punishment, we have

C1 Punishment as a response to crime is morally justified if and only if this practice, compared to any other response to crime, will likely produce as much overall intrinsic value as would any other response.

C2 A specific punishment for a certain crime is morally justified if and only if it would likely produce at least as much overall intrinsic value as would any other alternative punishment.

Consequentialist thinking about the death penalty focuses on C2 and thus on an assessment of the values of the consequences that are likely to result from having the death penalty compared to the values of the consequences that are likely to result from eliminating the death penalty. (Again, in cases in which a society does not currently have the death penalty, the comparison will be between instituting this punishment and not instituting it.)

Three things should be kept in mind about consequentialism as it bears on the morality of the death penalty. First, those who accept the consequentialist approach to the morality of punishment may or may not be committed thereby to the claim that the death penalty is morally justified—it all depends on what the values of the likely consequences of having the death penalty are compared with not having it. Second, this issue about values of the likely consequences is partly a moral issue but also partly a complicated empirical issue. The moral issue is this. What sorts of states of affairs (that might be consequences of some action or practice) have positive value, and what sorts have negative value? As we noted in the general introduction to this book, some consequentialists are utilitarians who think that happiness (welfare) is what has positive intrinsic value. But other consequentialists are perfectionists who hold that in addition to human happiness, such items as knowledge and achievement are intrinsically good. However, all parties to the dispute over the death penalty can agree that preserving human life—at least innocent human life, because it is necessary for achieving anything of intrinsic value—has a very high value, that the loss of human life is intrinsically bad or evil. If we agree, then, to focus on the value of human life when it comes to assessing the rightness of the death penalty, there is still the complicated empirical issue of determining whether employing this form of punishment will produce overall good enough consequences for society. This is an issue that criminologists and social scientists have studied and that is still being disputed.[9]

The third observation is that for purposes of evaluating the morality of some action or practice in terms of the values of its likely consequences, it is important to keep in mind that in so doing, one must consider not only the possible positive effects of the death penalty but also any negative effects that are likely to occur in allowing the death penalty. The same point applies when considering the possibility of abolishing the death penalty. So if we are to compare having the death penalty with not having it on strictly consequentialist grounds, then we have to consider the pluses and minuses of both options before we can move to a moral verdict about the morality of the death penalty.

Among the possible positive effects of having the death penalty are the following:

- **Deterrence:** Someone is *deterred* from committing murder by the threat of the death penalty only if his recognition of the death penalty as a possible consequence of committing murder explains why he doesn't commit it. Those who defend the death penalty on deterrence grounds argue that this punishment is *uniquely* effective in its deterrence effects in that there are some people who would be (or are) deterred by the threat of the death penalty, but would not be (or are not) deterred by a lesser punishment such as life without parole.
- **Prevention:** Someone is *prevented* by execution from committing a murder only if *had he not been executed, he would have gone ahead and committed the murder.* The point to be made about prevention and the death penalty is that even though someone's death prevents him from any further activity, it does not follow that he has thereby been prevented from performing certain specific acts. If, had he lived on, he would not have performed some action (for example, running for a seat in Congress), then it is not strictly correct to say that his death prevented him from running for a seat in Congress.

Among the possible negative consequences of having the death penalty are the following:

- Executing the innocent: The risk of executing innocent individuals owing to errors in the legal process that lead to conviction and "capital" (death penalty) sentencing.

- Incitement effect: Some argue that the death penalty may actually incite murder.[10]
- Financial cost: Death penalty cases cost more than other cases, and imposing the death penalty generally costs more than a sentence of life imprisonment without parole.[11]

These considerations about the consequences of the death penalty are taken up in the articles by Ernest van den Haag, Jeffrey H. Reiman, and the authors of the report on the evidence of errors in capital sentencing. Van den Haag defends the retentionist position on both retributivist and consequentialist grounds. Reiman is critical of the so-called common sense argument for the claim that the death penalty is a crime deterrent, an argument advanced by van den Haag. The final selection in this chapter is a report of an empirical study which, according to the authors, provides evidence of a significant error rate in the sentencing in death penalty cases.

NOTES

1. In the 1972 landmark decision *Furman v. Georgia* (408 U.S. 238), the U.S. Supreme Court ruled that the death penalty was unconstitutional *as then administered* because state statutes failed to provide guidelines for its use that would guard against its being imposed in an arbitrary and capricious manner. As a result of the Court's 1972 decision, states wanting to impose the death penalty worked to devise standards for its use that would provide safeguards against arbitrariness. In the 1976 case *Gregg v. Georgia* (428 U.S. 153), the Court approved Georgia's revised statutes governing the death penalty, thus lifting the moratorium.

2. The statistics just cited are taken from the website Death Penalty Information Center, www.deathpenaltyinfo.org.

3. According to *Amnesty International* (http://web.amnesty.org/pages/deathpenalty-countries-eng), as of 2012 more than two-thirds of the world's countries have abolished the death penalty either by law or by practice.

4. Grann's article was published in the September 7, 2009, edition. It can be found online at http://www.newyorker.com.

5. The *Innocence Project*, established in 1992, is devoted to "exonerating wrongfully convicted people through DNA testing and reforming the criminal justice system to prevent future injustice" <innocenceproject.org>.

6. *Roper v. Simmons,* No. 03-633.

7. Of course, this terminology is apt only if we are considering the morality of the death penalty in a country or state that currently allows it. Otherwise, those who are pro–death penalty are in favor of instituting it where it does not exist, and those against it are against its being instituted.

8. This list is taken from H. L. A. Hart, "Prolegomenon to the Principles of Punishment," in *Punishment and Responsibility* (Oxford: Oxford University Press, 1968).

9. See, for example, Richard A. Berk, "New Claims about Executions and General Deterrence: Déjà Vu All Over Again?" *Journal of Empirical Legal Studies* (July 19, 2004). Available at http://preprints.stat.ucla.edu/396/JELS.pap.pdf.

10. See for example, Mark Costonzo, *Just Revenge* (New York: St. Martin's Press, 1997).

11. See Richard C. Dieter, "Millions Misspent," in *The Death Penalty in America,* ed. Hugo Adam Bedau (Oxford: Oxford University Press, 1997).

STEPHEN NATHANSON

An Eye for an Eye?

Stephen Nathanson is critical of attempts to defend the morality of the death penalty on retributivist grounds. Focusing on the retributivist idea that a morally justified punishment must "fit" the crime, he considers two versions of what he calls the "equality" interpretation of this idea. Against both versions of the equality interpretation Nathanson raises moral and practical objections. Nathanson then argues that the proportionality interpretation of "fit" also cannot be used to morally justify the death penalty. In the final section of his paper, Nathanson presents two arguments against the death penalty.

Recommended Reading: Kantian moral theory, chap. 1, sec. 2C.

AN EYE FOR AN EYE?

Suppose we . . . try to determine what people deserve from a strictly moral point of view. How shall we proceed?

The most usual suggestion is that we look at a person's actions because what someone deserves would appear to depend on what he or she does. A person's actions, it seems, provide not only a basis for a moral appraisal of the person but also a guide to how he should be treated. According to the *lex talionis* or principle of "an eye for an eye," we ought to treat people as they have treated others. What people deserve as recipients of rewards or punishments is determined by what they do as agents.

This is a powerful and attractive view, one that appears to be backed not only by moral common sense but also by tradition and philosophical thought. The most famous statement of philosophical support for this view comes from Immanuel Kant, who linked it directly with an argument for the death penalty. Discussing the problem of punishment, Kant writes,

> What kind and what degree of punishment does legal justice adopt as its principle and standard? None other than the principle of equality . . . the principle of not treating one side more favorably than the other. Accordingly, any undeserved evil that you inflict on someone else among the people is one that you do to yourself. If you vilify, you vilify yourself: if you steal from him, you steal from yourself; if you kill him, you kill yourself. Only the law of retribution (*jus talionis*) can determine exactly the kind and degree of punishment.[1]

Kant's view is attractive for a number of reasons. First, it accords with our belief that what a person deserves is related to what he does. Second, it appeals to a moral standard and does not seem to rely on any particular legal or political institutions. Third, it seems to provide a measure of appropriate punishment that can be used as a guide to creating laws and instituting punishments. It tells us that the punishment is to be identical with the crime. Whatever the criminal did to the victim is to be done in turn to the criminal.

From Stephen Nathanson, *An Eye for an Eye?* 2nd ed. (Lanham, MD: Rowman and Littlefield, 2001). Reprinted by permission.

In spite of the attractions of Kant's view, it is deeply flawed. When we see why, it will be clear that the whole "eye for an eye" perspective must be rejected.

PROBLEMS WITH THE EQUAL PUNISHMENT PRINCIPLE

There are two main problems with this view. First, appearances to the contrary, it does not actually provide a measure of moral desert. Second, it does not provide an adequate criterion for determining appropriate levels of punishment.

Let us begin with the second criticism, the claim that Kant's view fails to tell us how much punishment is appropriate for particular crimes. We can see this, first, by noting that for certain crimes, Kant's view recommends punishments that are not morally acceptable. Applied strictly, it would require that we rape rapists, torture torturers, and burn arsonists whose acts have led to deaths. In general, where a particular crime involves barbaric and inhuman treatment, Kant's principle tells us to act barbarically and inhumanly in return. So, in some cases, the principle generates unacceptable answers to the question of what constitutes appropriate punishment.

This is not its only defect. In many other cases, the principle tells us nothing at all about how to punish. While Kant thought it obvious how to apply his principle in the case of murder, his principle cannot serve as a general rule because it does not tell us how to punish many crimes. Using the Kantian version or the more common "eye for an eye" standard, what would we decide to do to embezzlers, spies, drunken drivers, airline hijackers, drug users, prostitutes, air polluters, or persons who practice medicine without a license? If one reflects on this question, it becomes clear that there is simply no answer to it. We could not in fact design a system of punishment simply on the basis of the "eye for an eye" principle.

In order to justify using the "eye for an eye" principle to answer our question about murder and the death penalty, we would first have to show that it worked for a whole range of cases, giving acceptable answers to questions about amounts of punishment. Then, having established it as a satisfactory general principle, we could apply it to the case of murder. It turns out, however, that when we try to apply the principle generally, we find that it either gives wrong answers or no answers at all. Indeed, I suspect that the principle of "an eye for an eye" is no longer even a principle. Instead, it is simply a metaphorical disguise for expressing belief in the death penalty. People who cite it do not take it seriously. They do not believe in a kidnapping for a kidnapping, a theft for a theft, and so on. Perhaps "an eye for an eye" once was a genuine principle, but now it is merely a slogan. Therefore, it gives us no guidance in deciding whether murderers deserve to die.

In reply to these objections, one might defend the principle by saying that it does not require that punishments be strictly identical with crimes. Rather, it requires only that a punishment produce an amount of suffering in the criminal which is equal to the amount suffered by the victim. Thus, we don't have to hijack airplanes belonging to airline hijackers, spy on spies, etc. We simply have to reproduce in them the harm done to others.

Unfortunately, this reply really does not solve the problem. It provides no answer to the first objection, since it would still require us to behave barbarically in our treatment of those who are guilty of barbaric crimes. Even if we do not reproduce their actions exactly, any action which caused equal suffering would itself be barbaric. Second, in trying to produce equal amounts of suffering, we run into many problems. Just how much suffering is produced by an airline hijacker or a spy? And how do we apply this principle to prostitutes or drug users, who may not produce any suffering at all? We have rough ideas about how serious various crimes are, but this may not correlate with any clear sense of just how much harm is done.

Furthermore, the same problem arises in determining how much suffering a particular punishment would produce for a particular criminal. People vary in their tolerance of pain and in the amount of unhappiness that a fine or a jail sentence would cause them. Recluses will be less disturbed by banishment than extroverts. Nature lovers will suffer more in prison than people who are indifferent to natural beauty. A literal application of the principle would require that we tailor punishments to individual sensitivities, yet this is at best impractical. To a large extent, the legal system must work with standardized and rather crude estimates of the negative impact that punishments have on people.

The move from calling for a punishment that is identical to the crime to favoring one that is equal in the harm done is no help to us or to the defense of the principle. "An eye for an eye" tells us neither what people deserve nor how we should treat them when they have done wrong.

PROPORTIONAL RETRIBUTIVISM

The view we have been considering can be called "equality retributivism," since it proposes that we repay criminals with punishments equal to their crimes. In the light of problems like those I have cited, some people have proposed a variation on this view, calling not for equal punishments but rather for punishments which are proportional to the crime. In defending such a view as a guide for setting criminal punishments, Andrew von Hirsch writes:

> If one asks how severely a wrongdoer deserves to be punished, a familiar principle comes to mind: Severity of punishment should be commensurate with the seriousness of the wrong. Only grave wrongs merit severe penalties; minor misdeeds deserve lenient punishments. Disproportionate penalties are undeserved—severe sanctions for minor wrongs or vice versa. This principle has variously been called a principle of "proportionality" or "just deserts"; we call it commensurate deserts.[2]

Like Kant, von Hirsch makes the punishment which a person deserves depend on that person's actions, but he departs from Kant in substituting proportionality for equality as the criterion for setting the amount of punishment.

In implementing a punishment system based on the proportionality view, one would first make a list of crimes, ranking them in order of seriousness. At one end would be quite trivial offenses like parking meter violations, while very serious crimes such as murder would occupy the other. In between, other crimes would be ranked according to their relative gravity. Then a corresponding scale of punishments would be constructed, and the two would be correlated. Punishments would be proportionate to crimes so long as we could say that the more serious the crime was, the higher on the punishment scale was the punishment administered.

This system does not have the defects of equality retributivism. It does not require that we treat those guilty of barbaric crimes barbarically. This is because we can set the upper limit of the punishment scale so as to exclude truly barbaric punishments. Second, unlike the equality principle, the proportionality view is genuinely general, providing a way of handling all crimes. Finally, it does justice to our ordinary belief that certain punishments are unjust because they are too severe or too lenient for the crime committed.

The proportionality principle does, I think, play a legitimate role in our thinking about punishments. Nonetheless, it is no help to death penalty advocates, because it does not require that murderers be executed. All that it requires is that if murder is the most serious crime, then murder should be punished by the most severe punishment on the scale. The principle does not tell us what this punishment should be, however, and it is quite compatible with the view that the most severe punishment should be a long prison term.

This failure of the theory to provide a basis for supporting the death penalty reveals an important gap in proportional retributivism. It shows that while the theory is general in scope, it does not yield any *specific* recommendations regarding punishment. It tells us, for example, that armed robbery should be punished more severely than embezzling and less severely than murder, but it does not tell us how much to punish any of these. This weakness is, in effect, conceded by von Hirsch, who admits that if we want to implement the "commensurate deserts" principle, we must supplement it with information about what level of punishment is needed to deter crimes.[3] In a later discussion of how to "anchor" the punishment system, he deals with this problem in more depth, but the factors he cites as relevant to making specific judgments (such as available prison space) have nothing to do with what people deserve. He also seems to suggest that a range of punishments may be appropriate for a particular crime. This runs counter to the death penalty supporter's sense that death alone is appropriate for some murderers.[4]

Neither of these retributive views, then, provides support for the death penalty. The equality principle fails because it is not in general true that the appropriate punishment for a crime is to do to the criminal what he has done to others. In some cases this is immoral, while in others it is impossible. The proportionality principle may be correct, but by itself it cannot determine specific punishments for specific crimes. Because of its flexibility and open-endedness, it is compatible with a great range of different punishments for murder.[5] . . .

THE SYMBOLISM OF ABOLISHING THE DEATH PENALTY

What is the symbolic message that we would convey by deciding to renounce the death penalty and to abolish its use?

I think that there are two primary messages. The first is the most frequently emphasized and is usually expressed in terms of the sanctity of human life, although I think we could better express it in terms of respect for human dignity. One way we express our respect for the dignity of human beings is by abstaining from depriving them of their lives, even if they have done terrible deeds. In defense of human well-being, we may punish people, for their crimes, but we ought not to deprive them of everything, which is what the death penalty does.

If we take the life of a criminal, we convey the idea that by his deeds he has made himself worthless and totally without human value. I do not believe that we are in a position to affirm that of anyone. We may hate such a person and feel the deepest anger against him, but when he no longer poses a threat to anyone, we ought not to take his life.

But, one might ask, hasn't the murderer forfeited whatever rights he might have had to our respect? Hasn't he, by his deeds, given up any rights that he had to decent treatment? Aren't we morally free to kill him if we wish?

These questions express important doubts about the obligation to accord any respect to those who have acted so deplorably, but I do not think that they prove that any such forfeiture has occurred. Certainly, when people murder or commit other crimes, they do forfeit some of the rights that are possessed by the law-abiding. They lose a certain right to be left alone. It becomes permissible to bring them to trial and, if they are convicted, to impose an appropriate—even a dreadful—punishment on them.

Nonetheless, they do not forfeit all their rights. It does not follow from the vileness of their actions that we can do anything whatsoever to them. This is part of the moral meaning of the constitutional ban on cruel and unusual punishments. No matter how terrible a person's deeds, we may not punish him in a cruel and unusual way. We may not torture him, for example. His right not to be tortured has not been forfeited. Why do these limits hold? Because this person remains a human being, and we think that there is something in him that we must continue to respect in spite of his terrible acts.

One way of seeing why those who murder still deserve some consideration and respect is by reflecting again on the idea of what it is to deserve something. In most contexts, we think that what people deserve depends on what they have done, intended, or tried to do. It depends on features that are qualities of individuals. The best person for the job deserves to be hired. The person who worked especially hard deserves our gratitude. We can call the concept that applies in these cases *personal* desert.

There is another kind of desert, however, that belongs to people by virtue of their humanity itself and does not depend on their individual efforts or achievements. I will call this impersonal kind of desert *human* desert. We appeal to this concept when we think that everyone deserves a certain level of treatment no matter what their individual qualities are. When the signers of the Declaration of Independence affirmed that people had inalienable rights to "life, liberty, and the pursuit of happiness," they were, appealing to such an idea. These rights do not have to be earned by people. They are possessed "naturally," and everyone is bound to respect them.

According to the view that I am defending, people do not lose all of their rights when they commit terrible crimes. They still deserve some level of decent treatment simply because they remain living, functioning human beings. This level of moral desert need not be earned, and it cannot be forfeited. This view may sound controversial, but in fact everyone who believes that cruel and unusual punishment should be forbidden implicitly agrees with it. That is, they agree that even after someone has committed a terrible crime, we do not have the right to do anything whatsoever to him.

What I am suggesting is that by renouncing the use of death as a punishment, we express and reaffirm our belief in the inalienable, unforfeitable core of human dignity.

Why is this a worthwhile message to convey? It is worth conveying because this belief is both important and precarious. Throughout history, people have found innumerable reasons to degrade the humanity of one another. They have found qualities in others that they hated or feared, and even when they were not threatened by these people, they have sought to harm them, deprive them of their liberty, or take their lives from them. They have often felt that they had good reasons to do these things, and they have invoked divine commands, racial purity, and state security to support their deeds.

These actions and attitudes are not relics of the past. They remain an awful feature of the contemporary world. By renouncing the death penalty, we show our determination to accord at least minimal respect even to those whom we believe to be personally vile or morally vicious. This is, perhaps, why we speak of the *sanctity* of human life rather than its value or worth. That which is sacred remains, in some sense, untouchable, and its value is not dependent on its worth or usefulness to us. Kant expressed this ideal of respect in the famous second version of the Categorical Imperative: "So act as to treat humanity, whether in thine own person or in that of any other, in every case as an end withal, never as a means only."[6] . . .

THE MORALITY OF RESTRAINT

I have argued that the first symbolic meaning conveyed by a renunciation of the death penalty is that human dignity must be respected in every person. To execute a person for murder is to treat that person as if he were nothing but a murderer and to deprive him of everything that he has. Therefore, if we want to convey the appropriate message about human dignity, we will renounce the death penalty.

One might object that, in making this point, I am contradicting the claim that killing in defense of oneself or others can be morally justified. If it is wrong to execute a person because this violates his dignity as a human being and deprives him of everything, it would seem to be equally wrong to kill this person as a means of defense. Defensive killing seems to violate these ideals in the same way that I claim punishing by death does. Isn't this inconsistent? Mustn't I either retreat to the absolute pacifist view or else allow that the death penalty is permissible?

. . . What I need to do now is to show that defensive killing is compatible with respect for human dignity. We can easily see that it is by recalling the central fact about killing to ward off an assault on one's own life. In this circumstance, someone will die. The only question open is whether it will be the attacker or the intended victim. We cannot act in any way that shows the very same respect and concern for both the attacker and the intended victim. Although we have no wish to harm the attacker, this is the only way to save the innocent person who is being attacked. In this situation, assuming that there are no alternative means of preventing the attack from succeeding, it is permissible to kill the attacker.

What is crucial here is that the choice is forced on us. If we do not act, then one person will be destroyed. There is no way of showing equal concern for both attacker and victim, so we give preference to the intended victim and accept the morality of killing the attacker.

The case of punishing by death is entirely different. If this punishment will neither save the life of the victim nor prevent the deaths of other potential victims, then the decision to kill the murderer is avoidable. We can restrain ourselves without sacrificing the life or well-being of other people who are equally deserving of respect and consideration. In this situation, the restrained reaction is the morally right one.

In addition to providing an answer to the objection, this point provides us with the second important message conveyed by the renunciation of punishing by death. When we restrain ourselves and do not take the lives of those who kill, we communicate the importance of minimizing killing and other acts of violence. We reinforce the idea that violence is morally legitimate only as a defensive measure and should be curbed whenever possible. . . .

When the state has a murderer in its power and could execute him but does not, this conveys the idea that even though this person has done wrong and even though we may be angry, outraged, and indignant with him, we will nonetheless control ourselves in a way that he did not. We will not kill him, even though we could do so and even though we are angry and indignant. We will exercise restraint, sanctioning killing only when it serves a protective function.

Why should we do this? Partly out of a respect for human dignity. But also because we want the state to set an example of proper behavior. We do not want to encourage people to resort to violence to settle conflicts when there are other ways available. We want to avoid the cycle of violence that can come from retaliation and counter-retaliation. Violence is a contagion that arouses hatred and anger, and if unchecked, it simply leads to still more violence.

The state can convey the message that the contagion must be stopped, and the most effective principle for stopping it is the idea that only defensive violence is justifiable. Since the death penalty is not an instance of defensive violence, it ought to be renounced.

We show our respect for life best by restraining ourselves and allowing murderers to live, rather than by following a policy of a life for a life. Respect for life and restraint of violence are aspects of the same ideal. The renunciation of the death penalty would symbolize our support of that ideal.

NOTES

1. Kant, *Metaphysical Elements of Justice,* translated by John Ladd (Indianapolis: Bobbs-Merrill, 1965), 101.

2. *Doing Justice* (New York: Hill & Wang, 1976), 66; reprinted in *Sentencing,* edited by H. Gross and A. von Hirsch (Oxford University Press, 1981), 243. For a more recent discussion and further defense by von Hirsch, see his *Past or Future Crimes* (New Brunswick, N.J.: Rutgers University Press, 1985).

3. von Hirsch, *Doing Justice,* 93–94. My criticisms of proportional retributivism are not novel. For helpful discussions of the view, see Hugo Bedau, "Concessions to Retribution in Punishment," in *Justice and Punishment,* edited by J. Cederblom and W. Blizek (Cambridge, Mass.: Bellinger, 1977), and M. Golding, *Philosophy of Law* (Englewood Cliffs, N.J.: Prentice Hall, 1975), 98–99.

4. See von Hirsch, *Past and Future Crimes,* ch. 8.

5. For more positive assessments of these theories, see Jeffrey Reiman, "Justice, Civilization, and the Death Penalty," *Philosophy and Public Affairs* 14 (1985): 115–48; and Michael Davis, "How to Make the Punishment Fit the Crime," *Ethics* 93 (1983).

6. *Fundamental Principles of the Metaphysics of Morals,* translated by T. Abbott (New York: Liberal Arts Press, 1949), 46.

READING QUESTIONS

1. Why is an eye for an eye an attractive view according to Nathanson? What are the two main problems he raises for this view, and what are the possible replies an advocate of such a view might make?

2. What is proportional retributivism and how does it differ from an eye for an eye?

3. What are the two messages that would be sent by abolishing the death penalty according to Nathanson? How does he reply to the objection that murderers forfeit their right to be respected as human beings?

4. How does Nathanson argue that killing in self defense is compatible with respect for the dignity of human life?

DISCUSSION QUESTIONS

1. Consider whether proportional retributivism is really an improvement on the view of an eye for an eye. How could an advocate of an eye for an eye respond to the claim that equality retributivism provides an adequate criterion for determining appropriate levels of punishment? Are there any other objections to the view that Nathanson fails to consider?
2. Would abolishing the death penalty send the messages that Nathanson suggests? What other messages, positive or negative, might the abolition of the death penalty send? What messages should be sent and how could we ensure that the right messages are sent?

ERNEST VAN DEN HAAG

A Defense of the Death Penalty

In response to various abolitionist arguments of the sort featured in the articles by Nathanson and Bedau, Ernest van den Haag defends the morality of the death penalty. In particular, he responds to these objections to the death penalty: (1) that it is unfairly administered, (2) that it is irreversible, (3) that it does not deter, (4) that its financial costs are prohibitive, (5) that it endorses and perhaps encourages unlawful killing, and (6) that it is degrading. Van den Haag then argues that the death penalty can be justified from both consequentialist and retributivist perspectives.

Recommended Reading: consequentialism, chap. 1, sec. 2A.

In an average year about 20,000 homicides occur in the United States. Fewer than 300 convicted murderers are sentenced to death. But because no more than 30 murderers have been executed in any recent year, most convicts sentenced to death are likely to die of old age. Nonetheless, the death penalty looms large in discussions: it raises important moral questions independent of the number of executions.

The death penalty is our harshest punishment. It is irrevocable: it ends the existence of those punished,

From Ernest van den Haag, "The Ultimate Punishment: A Defense," *Harvard Law Review* 99 (1986): 1662–69. Reprinted by permission of the author.

instead of temporarily imprisoning them. Further, although not intended to cause physical pain, execution is the only corporal punishment still applied to adults. These singular characteristics contribute to the perennial, impassioned controversy about capital punishment.

DISTRIBUTION

Consideration of the justice, morality, or usefulness, of capital punishment is often conflated with objections to its alleged discriminatory or capricious distribution among the guilty. Wrongly so. If capital punishment is immoral *in se*, no distribution among the guilty could make it moral. If capital punishment is moral, no distribution would make it immoral. Improper distribution cannot affect the quality of what is distributed, be it punishments or rewards. Discriminatory or capricious distribution thus could not justify abolition of the death penalty. Further, maldistribution inheres no more in capital punishment than in any other punishment.

Maldistribution between the guilty and the innocent is, by definition, unjust. But the injustice does not lie in the nature of the punishment. Because of the finality of the death penalty, the most grievous maldistribution occurs when it is imposed upon the innocent. However, the frequent allegations of discrimination and capriciousness refer to maldistribution among the guilty and not to the punishment of the innocent.

Maldistribution of any punishment among those who deserve it is irrelevant to its justice or morality. Even if poor or black convicts guilty of capital offenses suffer capital punishment, and other convicts equally guilty of the same crimes do not, a more equal distribution, however desirable, would merely be more equal. It would not be more just to the convicts under sentence of death.

Punishments are imposed on persons, not on racial or economic groups. Guilt is personal. The only relevant question is: does the person to be executed deserve the punishment? Whether or not others who deserved the same punishment, whatever their economic or racial group, have avoided execution is irrelevant. If

they have, the guilt of the executed convicts would not be diminished, nor would their punishment be less deserved. To put the issue starkly, if the death penalty were imposed on guilty blacks, but not on guilty whites, or, if it were imposed by a lottery among the guilty, this irrationally discriminatory or capricious distribution would neither make the penalty unjust, nor cause anyone to be unjustly punished, despite the undue impunity bestowed on others.

Equality, in short, seems morally less important than justice. And justice is independent of distributional inequalities. The ideal of equal justice demands that justice be equally distributed, not that it be replaced by equality. Justice requires that as many of the guilty as possible be punished, regardless of whether others have avoided punishment. To let these others escape the deserved punishment does not do justice to them, or to society. But it is not unjust to those who could not escape.

These moral considerations are not meant to deny that irrational discrimination, or capriciousness, would be inconsistent with constitutional requirements. But I am satisfied that the Supreme Court has in fact provided for adherence to the constitutional requirement of equality as much as is possible. Some inequality is indeed unavoidable as a practical matter in any system. But, *ultra posse nemo obligatur.* (Nobody is bound beyond ability.)

Recent data reveal little direct racial discrimination in the sentencing of those arrested and convicted of murder. The abrogation of the death penalty for rape has eliminated a major source of racial discrimination. Concededly, some discrimination based on the race of murder victims may exist; yet, this discrimination affects criminal victimizers in an unexpected way. Murderers of whites are thought more likely to be executed than murderers of blacks. Black victims, then, are less fully vindicated than white ones. However, because most black murderers kill blacks, black murderers are spared the death penalty more often than are white murderers. They fare better than most white murderers. The motivation behind unequal distribution of the death penalty may well have been to discriminate against blacks, but the result has favored them. Maldistribution is thus a straw man for empirical as well as analytical reasons.

MISCARRIAGES OF JUSTICE

In a recent survey Professors Hugo Adam Bedau and Michael Radelet found that 7,000 persons were executed in the United States between 1900 and 1985 and that 25 were innocent of capital crimes. Among the innocents they list Sacco and Vanzetti as well as Ethel and Julius Rosenberg. Although their data may be questionable, I do not doubt that, over a long enough period, miscarriages of justice will occur even in capital cases.

Despite precautions, nearly all human activities, such as trucking, lighting, or construction, cost the lives of some innocent bystanders. We do not give up these activities, because the advantages, moral or material, outweigh the unintended losses. Analogously, for those who think the death penalty just, miscarriages of justice are offset by the moral benefits and the usefulness of doing justice. For those who think the death penalty unjust even when it does not miscarry, miscarriages can hardly be decisive.

DETERRENCE

Despite much recent work, there has been no conclusive statistical demonstration that the death penalty is a better deterrent than are alternative punishments. However, deterrence is less than decisive for either side. Most abolitionists acknowledge that they would continue to favor abolition even if the death penalty were shown to deter more murders than alternatives could deter. Abolitionists appear to value the life of a convicted murderer or, at least, his non-execution, more highly than they value the lives of the innocent victims who might be spared by deterring prospective murderers.

Deterrence is not altogether decisive for me either. I would favor retention of the death penalty as retribution even if it were shown that the threat of execution could not deter prospective murderers not already deterred by the threat of imprisonment. Still, I believe the death penalty, because of its finality, is more feared than imprisonment, and deters some prospective murderers not deterred by the threat of imprisonment. Sparing the lives of even a few prospective victims by deterring their murderers is more important than preserving the lives of convicted murderers because of the possibility, or even the probability, that executing them would not deter others. Whereas the lives of the victims who might be saved are valuable, that of the murderer has only negative value, because of his crime. Surely the criminal law is meant to protect the lives of potential victims in preference to those of actual murderers.

Murder rates are determined by many factors; neither the severity nor the probability of the threatened sanction is always decisive. However, for the long run, I share the view of Sir James Fitzjames Stephen: "Some men, probably, abstain from murder because they fear that if they committed murder they would be hanged. Hundreds of thousands abstain from it because they regard it with horror. One great reason why they regard it with horror is that murderers are hanged." Penal sanctions are useful in the long run for the formation of the internal restraints so necessary to control crime. The severity and finality of the death penalty is appropriate to the seriousness and the finality of murder.

INCIDENTAL ISSUES: COST, RELATIVE SUFFERING, BRUTALIZATION

Many nondecisive issues are associated with capital punishment. Some believe that the monetary cost of appealing a capital sentence is excessive. Yet most comparisons of the cost of life imprisonment with the cost of execution, apart from their dubious relevance, are flawed at least by the implied assumption that life prisoners will generate no judicial costs during their imprisonment. At any rate, the actual monetary costs are trumped by the importance of doing justice.

Others insist that a person sentenced to death suffers more than his victim suffered, and that this (excess) suffering is undue according to the *lex talionis* (rule of retaliation). We cannot know whether the murderer on death row suffers more than his victim suffered; however, unlike the murderer, the victim deserved none of the suffering inflicted. Further, the limitations of the *lex talionis* were meant to restrain private vengeance, not the social retribution that has taken its place. Punishment—regardless of the motivation—is not intended to revenge, offset, or compensate for the victim's suffering, or to be measured by it. Punishment is to vindicate the law and the social order undermined by the crime. This is why a kidnapper's penal confinement is not limited to the period for which he imprisoned his victim; nor is a burglar's confinement meant merely to offset the suffering or the harm he caused his victim; nor is it meant only to offset the advantage he gained.

Another argument heard at least since Beccaria is that, by killing a murderer, we encourage, endorse, or legitimize unlawful killing. Yet, although all punishments are meant to be unpleasant, it is seldom argued that they legitimize the unlawful imposition of identical unpleasantness. Imprisonment is not thought to legitimize kidnapping; neither are fines thought to legitimize robbery. The difference between murder and execution, or between kidnapping and imprisonment, is that the first is unlawful and undeserved, the second a lawful and deserved punishment for an unlawful act. The physical similarities of the punishment to the crime are irrelevant. The relevant difference is not physical, but social.

JUSTICE, EXCESS, DEGRADATION

We threaten punishments in order to deter crime. We impose them not only to make the threats credible but also as retribution (justice) for the crimes that were not deterred. Threats and punishments are necessary to deter and deterrence is a sufficient practical justification for them. Retribution is an independent moral justification. Although penalties can be unwise, repulsive, or inappropriate, and those punished can be pitiable, in a sense the infliction of legal punishment on a guilty person cannot be unjust.

By committing the crime, the criminal volunteered to assume the risk of receiving a legal punishment that he could have avoided by not committing the crime. The punishment he suffers is the punishment he voluntarily risked suffering and, therefore, it is no more unjust to him than any other event for which one knowingly volunteers to assume the risk. Thus, the death penalty cannot be unjust to the guilty criminal.

There remain, however, two moral objections. The penalty may be regarded as always excessive as retribution and always morally degrading. To regard the death penalty as always excessive, one must believe that no crime—no matter how heinous—could possibly justify capital punishment. Such a belief can be neither corroborated nor refuted; it is an article of faith.

Alternatively, or concurrently, one may believe that everybody, the murderer no less than the victim, has an imprescriptible (natural?) right to life. The law therefore should not deprive anyone of life. I share Jeremy Bentham's view that any such "natural and imprescriptible rights" are "nonsense upon stilts."

Justice Brennan has insisted that the death penalty is "uncivilized," "inhuman," inconsistent with "human dignity" and with "the sanctity of life," that it "treats members of the human race as nonhumans, as objects to be toyed with and discarded," that it is "uniquely degrading to human dignity" and "by its very nature, [involves] a denial of the executed person's humanity." Justice Brennan does not say why he thinks execution "uncivilized." Hitherto most civilizations have had the death penalty, although it has been discarded in Western Europe, where it is currently unfashionable probably because of its abuse by totalitarian regimes.

By "degrading," Justice Brennan seems to mean that execution degrades the executed convicts. Yet philosophers, such as Immanuel Kant and G. W. F. Hegel, have insisted that, when deserved, execution, far from degrading the executed convict, affirms his humanity by affirming his rationality and his responsibility for his actions. They thought that execution, when deserved, is required for the sake of the convict's dignity. (Does not life imprisonment violate human dignity more than execution, by keeping alive a prisoner deprived of all autonomy?)

Common sense indicates that it cannot be death—our common fate—that is inhuman. Therefore, Justice Brennan must mean that death degrades when it comes not as a natural or accidental event, but as a deliberate social imposition. The murderer learns through his punishment that his fellow men have found him unworthy of living; that because he has murdered, he is being expelled from the community of the living. This degradation is self-inflicted. By murdering, the murderer has so dehumanized himself that he cannot remain among the living. The social recognition of his self-degradation is the punitive essence of execution. To believe, as Justice Brennan appears to, that the degradation is inflicted by the execution reverses the direction of causality.

Execution of those who have committed heinous murders may deter only one murder per year. If it does, it seems quite warranted. It is also the only fitting retribution for murder I can think of.

READING QUESTIONS

1. Why does van den Haag think that equality of distribution would not make the death penalty any more just to convicts?
2. What reasons does van den Haag give for thinking that miscarriages of justice are not enough to justify the claim that the death penalty is an unjust practice?
3. Why is deterrence not a decisive factor in the debate about the morality of the death penalty according to van den Haag?
4. How does van den Haag respond to the objections that the penalty of death is always excessive and always morally degrading?

DISCUSSION QUESTIONS

1. Should we agree with van den Haag's claims regarding the death penalty and miscarriages of justice? How many miscarriages of this kind do you believe would have to occur before they would fail to be offset by the moral benefit of the death penalty?
2. Van den Haag claims that "if execution deters only one murderer a year, it is still warranted." He also claims that the death penalty is the only fitting retribution for murder. Does he provide sufficient reasons to accept each of these claims? Why or why not? If not, consider cases in which the death penalty would be warranted or what might be a fitting retribution for murder instead of the death penalty.

JEFFREY H. REIMAN

Civilization, Safety, and Deterrence

Some defenders of the death penalty, including Ernest van den Haag, argue that even if we currently lack good scientific evidence that the death penalty is a uniquely effective deterrent, common sense tells us that this penalty is a crime deterrent. Against this common sense argument, Reiman raises four objections.

Recommended Reading: consequentialism, chap. 1, sec. 2A.

Were the death penalty clearly proven a better deterrent to the murder of innocent people than life in prison, we might have to admit that we had not yet reached a level of civilization at which we could protect ourselves without imposing this horrible fate on murderers, and thus we might have to grant the necessity of instituting the death penalty. But this is far from proven. The available research by no means clearly indicates that the death penalty reduces the incidence of homicide more than life imprisonment does. Even the econometric studies of Isaac Ehrlich, which purport to show that each execution saves seven or eight potential murder victims, have not changed this fact, as is testified to by the controversy and objections from equally respected statisticians that Ehrlich's work has provoked.[1]

Conceding that it has not been proven that the death penalty deters more murders than life imprisonment, van den Haag has argued that neither has it been proven that the death penalty does *not* deter more murders, and thus we must follow common sense which teaches that the higher the cost of something, the fewer people will choose it, and therefore at least some potential murderers who would not be deterred by life imprisonment will be deterred by the death penalty. Van den Haag writes:

> . . . .our experience shows that the greater the threatened penalty, the more it deters.

...Life in prison is still life, however unpleasant. In contrast, the death penalty does not just threaten to make life unpleasant—it threatens to take life altogether. This difference is perceived by those affected. We find that when they have the choice between life in prison and execution, 99% of all prisoners under sentence of death prefer life in prison. . . .

From this unquestioned fact a reasonable conclusion can be drawn in favor of the superior deterrent effect of the death penalty. Those who have the choice in practice. . . . fear death more than they fear life in prison. . . . If they do, it follows that the threat of the death penalty, all other things equal, is likely to deter more than the threat of life in prison. One is most deterred by what one fears most. From which it follows that whatever statistics fail, or do not fail, to show, the death penalty is likely to be more deterrent than any other.[2]

Those of us who recognize how common-sensical it was, and still is, to believe that the sun moves around the earth, will be less willing than Professor van den Haag to follow common sense here, especially when it comes to doing something awful to our fellows. Moreover, there are good reasons for doubting common sense on this matter. Here are four:

1. From the fact that one penalty is more feared than another, it does not follow that the more feared penalty will deter more than the less feared, unless we know that the less feared penalty is not fearful enough to deter everyone who can

From Jeffrey H. Reiman, "Justice, Civilization, and the Death Penalty: Answering van den Haag," *Philosophy and Public Affairs* 14 (1985), pp. 115–48.

be deterred—and this is just what we don't know with regard to the death penalty. Though I fear the death penalty more than life in prison, I can't think of any act that the death penalty would deter me from that an equal likelihood of spending my life in prison wouldn't deter me from as well. Since it seems to me that whoever would be deterred by a given likelihood of death would be deterred by an *equal* likelihood of life behind bars, I suspect that the common-sense argument only seems plausible because we evaluate it unconsciously assuming that potential criminals will face larger likelihoods of death sentences than of life sentences. If the likelihoods were equal, it seems to me that where life imprisonment was improbable enough to make it too distant a possibility to worry much about, a similar low probability of death would have the same effect. After all, we are undeterred by small likelihoods of death every time we walk the streets. And if life imprisonment were sufficiently probable to pose a real deterrent threat, it would pose as much of a deterrent threat as death. And this is just what most of the research we have on the comparative deterrent impact of execution versus life imprisonment suggests.

2. In light of the fact that roughly 500 to 700 suspected felons are killed by the police in the line of duty every year, and the fact that the number of privately owned guns in America is substantially larger than the number of households in America, it must be granted that anyone contemplating committing a crime *already* faces a substantial risk of ending up dead as a result.[3] It's hard to see why anyone *who is not already deterred by this* would be deterred by the addition of the more distant risk of death after apprehension, conviction, and appeal. Indeed, this suggests that people consider risks in a much cruder way than van den Haag's appeal to common sense suggests—which should be evident to anyone who contemplates how few people use seatbelts (14% of drivers, on some estimates), when it is widely known that wearing them can spell the difference between life (outside prison) and death.[4]

3. Van den Haag has maintained that deterrence doesn't work only by means of cost–benefit calculations made by potential criminals. It works also by the lesson about the wrongfulness of murder that is slowly learned in a society that subjects murderers to the ultimate punishment. But if I am correct in claiming that the refusal to execute even those who deserve it has a civilizing effect, then the refusal to execute also teaches a lesson about the wrongfulness of murder. My claim here is admittedly speculative, but no more so than van den Haag's to the contrary. And my view has the added virtue of accounting for the failure of research to show an increased deterrent effect from executions *without having to deny the plausibility of van den Haag's common-sense argument that at least some additional potential murderers will be deterred by the prospect of the death penalty.* If there is a deterrent effect from *not executing,* then it is understandable that while executions will deter some murderers, this effect will be balanced out by the weakening of the deterrent effect of not executing, such that no net reduction in murders will result.[5] And this, by the way, also disposes of van den Haag's argument that, in the absence of knowledge one way or the other on the deterrent effect of executions, we should execute murderers rather than risk the lives of innocent people whose murders might have been deterred if we had. If there is a deterrent effect of not executing, it follows that we risk innocent lives either way. And if this is so, it seems that the only reasonable course of action is to refrain from imposing what we know is a horrible fate.[6]

4. Those who still think that van den Haag's common-sense argument for executing murderers is valid will find that the argument proves more than they bargained for. Van den Haag maintains that, in the absence of conclusive evidence on the relative deterrent impact of the death penalty versus life imprisonment, we must follow common sense and assume that if one punishment is more fearful than another, it will deter some potential criminals not deterred by the less fearful punishment. Since people sentenced to death will almost universally try to get their sentences changed to life in prison, it follows that death is more fearful than life imprisonment, and thus that it will deter some additional murderers. Consequently, we should institute the

death penalty to save the lives these additional murderers would have taken. But, since people sentenced to be tortured to death would surely try to get their sentences changed to simple execution, the same argument proves that death-by-torture will deter still more potential murderers. Consequently, we should institute death-by-torture to save the lives these additional murderers would have taken. Anyone who accepts van den Haag's argument is then confronted with a dilemma: Until we have conclusive evidence that capital punishment is a greater deterrent to murder than life imprisonment, he must grant *either* that we should not follow common sense and not impose the death penalty; *or* we should follow common sense and torture murderers to death. In short, either we must abolish the electric chair or reinstitute the rack. Surely, this is the *reductio ad absurdum* of van den Haag's common-sense argument.

NOTES

1. Isaac Ehrlich, "The Deterrent Effect of Capital Punishment: A Question of Life or Death," *American Economic Review* 65 (June 1975):397–417. For reactions to Ehrlich's work, see Alfred Blumstein, Jacqueline Cohen, and Daniel Nagin, eds., *Deterrence and Incapacitation: Estimating the Effects of Criminal Sanctions on Crime Rates* (Washington, D.C.: National Academy of Sciences, 1978), esp. pp. 59–63 and 336–60; Brian E. Forst, "The Deterrent Effect on Capital Punishment: A Cross-State Analysis," *Minnesota Law Review 61* (May 1977):743–67, Deryck Beyleveld, "Ehrlich's Analysis of Deterrence," *British Journal of Criminology 22* (April 1982):101–23, and Isaac Ehrlich, "On Positive Methodology, Ethics and Polemics in Deterrence Research," *British Journal of Criminology 22* (April 1982):124–39.

2. Ernest van den Haag and John P. Conrad, *The Death Penalty: A Debate* (New York: Plenum Press, 1983), 68, 69.

3. On the number of people killed by the police, see Lawrence W. Sherman and Robert H. Langworthy, "Measuring Homicide by Police Officers," *Journal of Criminal Law and Criminology 70*, no. 4 (Winter 1979):546–60; on the number of privately owned guns, see Franklin Zimring, *Firearms and Violence in American Life* (Washington, D.C.: U.S. Government Printing Office, 1968), pp. 6–7.

4. *AAA World* (Potomac ed.) 4, no. 3 (May–June 1984), pp. 18c and 18i.

5. A related claim has been made by those who defend the so-called brutalization hypothesis by presenting evidence to show that murders *increase* following an execution. See, for example, William J. Bowers and Glenn L. Pierce, "Deterrence or Brutalization: What is the Effect of Executions?" *Crime & Delinquency 26*, no. 4 (October 1980):453–84. They conclude that each execution gives rise to two additional homicides in the month following, and that these are real additions, not just a change in timing of the homicides (ibid., p. 481). My claim, it should be noted, is not identical to this, since, as I indicate in the text, what I call "the deterrence effect of not executing" is not something whose impact is to be seen immediately following executions but over the long haul, and, further, my claim is compatible with finding no net increase in murders due to executions. Nonetheless, should the brutalization hypothesis be borne out by further studies, it would certainly lend support to the notion that there is a deterrent effect of not executing.

6. Van den Haag writes: "If we were quite ignorant about the marginal deterrent effects of execution, we would have to choose—like it or not—between the certainty of the convicted murderer's death by execution and the likelihood of the survival of future victims of other murderers on the one hand, and on the other his certain survival and the likelihood of the death of new victims. I'd rather execute a man convicted of having murdered others than put the lives of innocents at risk. I find it hard to understand the opposite choice" (p. 69). Conway was able to counter this argument earlier by pointing out that the research on the marginal deterrent effects of execution was not *inconclusive* in the sense of *tending to point both ways*, but rather in the sense of *giving us no reason to believe that capital punishment saves more lives than life imprisonment*. He could then answer van den Haag by saying that the choice is not between risking the lives of murderers and risking the lives of innocents, but between killing a murderer with no reason to believe lives will be saved, and sparing a murderer with no reason to believe lives will be lost (David A. Conway, "Capital Punishment and Deterrence: Some Considerations in Dialogue Form," *Philosophy & Public Affairs*, 3 (1974), pp. 442–43). This, of course, makes the choice to spare the murderer more understandable than van den Haag allows. Events, however, have overtaken Conway's argument. The advent of Ehrlich's research, contested though it may be, leaves us in fact with research that tends to point both ways.

READING QUESTIONS

1. How does Reiman characterize van den Haag's argument for the death penalty?
2. What are the four reasons Reiman offers for thinking that we should doubt some of our common sense intuitions about the nature of the death penalty as a deterrent?
3. Explain in detail why Reiman thinks that the refusal to execute has a civilizing effect and that it teaches the wrongfulness of murder. Explain also why he believes that van den Haag's argument proves more than it might seem to.

DISCUSSION QUESTIONS

1. Is Reiman right to claim that the refusal to execute individuals would have a civilizing effect? Why or why not? What reasons could we offer for thinking that refusing to execute murderers does not teach the wrongfulness of murder?
2. To what extent do you think criminals take the consequences of their actions into consideration, especially in the case of murder? Discuss how the answers to this question could affect the debate about the moral status of capital punishment.

JAMES S. LIEBMAN, JEFFREY FAGAN, VALERIE WEST, AND JONATHAN LLOYD

Capital Attrition: Error Rates in Capital Cases, 1973–1995

The authors of this report studied the error rate in U.S. cases from 1975 to 1995 involving "capital sentences" (cases in which the sentence was the death penalty). One of the central findings of this research is that in 68 percent of capital cases that underwent judicial review, the death sentences were overturned owing to various errors including incompetent legal representation of the accused and suppression by the prosecution of evidence. One implication that the authors draw from this research is that the public's awareness of such error rates would lower the public's confidence in the credibility of the death penalty.

Capital Attrition: Error Rates in Capital Cases, 1973–1995. Reprinted with permission from *Texas Law Review*, 1839 (2000).

I. INTRODUCTION

Americans seem to be of two minds about the death penalty. In the last several years, the overall number of executions has risen steeply, reaching a fifty-year high this year. Although two-thirds of the public support the penalty, this figure represents a sharp decline from the four-fifths of the population that endorsed the death penalty only six years ago, leaving support for capital punishment at a twenty-year low. When life without parole is offered as an alternative, support for the penalty drops even more—often below a majority. Grants of executive clemency reached a twenty-year high in 1999.

In 1999 and 2000, governors, attorneys general, and legislators in Alabama, Arizona, Florida, and Tennessee fought high-profile campaigns to increase the speed and number of executions. In the same period, however:

- The Republican Governor of Illinois, with support from a majority of the electorate, declared a moratorium on executions in that state.
- The Nebraska Legislature attempted to enact a similar moratorium. Although the Governor vetoed the legislation, the legislature appropriated money for a comprehensive study of the even-handedness of the state's exercise of capital punishment.
- Similar studies have been ordered in Illinois by the Chief Justice, task forces of both houses of the state legislature, and the governor. Indiana, Maryland, and the Attorney General of the United States have followed suit.
- Serious campaigns to abolish the death penalty are under way in New Hampshire and (with the support of the governor and a popular former Republican senator) in Oregon.
- The Florida Supreme Court and Mississippi Legislature recently acted to improve the quality of counsel in capital cases, and bills with bipartisan sponsorship aiming to do the same and to improve capital prisoners' access to DNA evidence have been introduced in both houses of the United States Congress.

Observers in the *Wall Street Journal, New York Times Magazine, Salon,* and on *ABC This Week*

see "a tectonic shift in the politics of the death penalty."

In April 2000 alone, George Will and Reverend Pat Robertson—both strong death penalty supporters—expressed doubts about the manner in which government officials carry out the penalty in the United States, and Robertson subsequently advocated a moratorium on *Meet the Press*. In response, Reverend Jerry Falwell called for continued—even swifter—execution of death sentences.

Fueling these competing initiatives are two beliefs about the death penalty: One is that death sentences move too slowly from imposition to execution, undermining deterrence and retribution, subjecting our criminal laws and courts to ridicule, and increasing the agony of victims. The other is that death sentences are fraught with error, causing justice too often to miscarry, and subjecting innocent and other undeserving defendants—mainly, racial minorities and the poor—to execution.

Some observers attribute these seemingly conflicting events and opinions to "America's own schizophrenia. . . . We believe in the death penalty, but shrink from it as applied." These views may not conflict, however, and Americans who hold *both* may not be irrational. It may be that capital sentences spend too much time under review *and* that they are fraught with disturbing amounts of error. Indeed, it may be that capital sentences spend so much time under judicial review precisely *because* they are persistently and systematically fraught with alarming amounts of error, and that the expanding production of death sentences may compound the production of error. We are led to this conclusion by a study of all 4,578 capital sentences that were finally reviewed by state direct appeal courts and all 599 capital sentences that were finally reviewed by federal habeas corpus courts between 1973 and 1995.

II. SUMMARY OF CENTRAL FINDINGS

In *Furman v. Georgia* in 1972, the Supreme Court reversed all existing capital statutes and death sentences. The modern death-sentencing era began the next year with the implementation of new capital statutes designed to satisfy *Furman.* In order to collect information about capital sentences imposed and reviewed after 1973 (no central repository exists), we conducted a painstaking search, beginning in 1995, of all published state and federal judicial opinions in the United States conducting direct and habeas review of capital judgments, and many of the available opinions conducting state post-conviction review of those judgments. We then (1) checked and catalogued all cases the opinions revealed, (2) collected hundreds of items of information about each case from the published decisions and the NAACP Legal Defense Fund's quarterly death row census, (3) tabulated the results, and (4) (still in progress) conducted multivariate statistical analyses to identify factors that may contribute to those results.

Six years in the making, our central findings thus far are these:

- Between 1973 and 1995, approximately 5,760 death sentences were imposed in the United States. Only 313 (5.4 percent; one in 19) of those resulted in an execution during the period.

- Of the 5,760 death sentences imposed in the study period, 4,578 (79 percent) were finally reviewed on "direct appeal" by a state high court. Of those, 1,885 (41 percent) were thrown out on the basis of "serious error" (error that substantially undermines the reliability of the outcome).

- Most of the remainder of the death sentences were then inspected by state post-conviction courts. Although incomplete, our data (reported in *A Broken System*[1]) reveal that state post-conviction review is an important source of review in some states, including Florida, Georgia, Indiana, Maryland, Mississippi, and North Carolina. In Maryland, for example, at least 52 percent of capital judgments reviewed in state post-conviction proceedings during the study period were overturned due to serious error; the same was true for at least 25 percent of the capital judgments that were similarly reviewed in Indiana, and at least 20 percent of those reviewed in Mississippi.

- Of the death sentences that survived state direct and post-conviction review, 599 were finally reviewed on a first habeas corpus petition during the 23-year study period. Of those 599, 237 (40 percent) were overturned due to serious error.

- The "overall success rate" of capital judgments undergoing judicial inspection, and its converse, the "overall error-rate," are crucial factors in assessing the efficiency of our capital punishment system. The "overall *success* rate" is the proportion of capital judgments that underwent, and *passed,* the three-stage judicial inspection process during the study period. The "overall *error* rate" is the frequency with which capital judgments that underwent full inspection were *overturned* at one of the three stages due to serious error. Nationally, over the entire 1973–1995 period, the overall error-rate in our capital punishment system was 68 percent.

- Because "serious error" is error that substantially undermines the reliability of the guilt finding or death sentence imposed at trial, each instance of that error warrants public concern. The most common errors found at the state post-conviction stage (where our data are most complete) are (1) egregiously incompetent defense lawyering (accounting for 37 percent of the state post-conviction reversals), and (2) prosecutorial suppression of evidence that the defendant is innocent or does not deserve the death penalty (accounting for another 16 percent—or 19 percent, when all forms of law enforcement misconduct are considered). These two violations count as "serious," and thus warrant reversal, *only* when there is a "reasonable probability" that, but for the responsible lawyer's miscues, the outcome of the trial would have been different.

The result of very high rates of serious, reversible error among capital convictions and sentences, and very low rates of capital reconviction and resentencing, is the severe attrition of capital judgments. Figure 12.1 illustrates the sources of attrition, and the eventual disposition of cases where death sentences were reversed.

For every 100 death sentences imposed and reviewed during the study period, 41 were turned

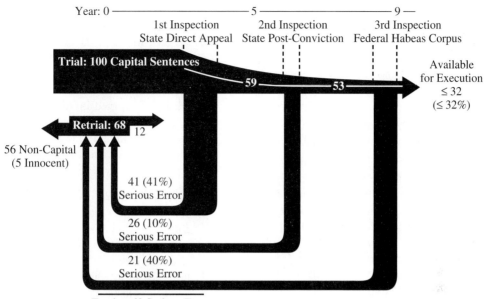

FIGURE 12.1   The Attrition of Capital Judgments

back at the state direct appeal phase because of serious error. Of the 59 that got through that phase to the second, state post-conviction stage, at least 10 percent—six more of the original 100—were turned back due to serious flaws. And, of the 53 that got through that stage to the third, federal habeas checkpoint, 40 percent—an additional 21 of the original 100—were turned back because of serious error. Overall, at least 68 of the original 100 were thrown out because of serious flaws, compared to only 32 (or less) that were found to have passed muster—after an average of nine to ten years had passed.

And for each such 68 individuals whose death sentences were overturned for serious error, 82 percent (56) were found on retrial *not* to have deserved the death penalty, including 7 percent (5) who were *cleared of the capital offense.*

• The seriousness of these errors is also revealed by what happens on retrial when the errors are supposed to be cured. In our state post-conviction sub-study where the post-reversal outcome is known, over four-fifths (56 out of 68) of the capital judgments that were reversed were replaced

on retrial with a sentence less than death, or no sentence at all. In the latter regard, fully 7 percent of the reversals for serious error resulted in a determination on retrial that the defendant was *not guilty* of the offense for which he previously was sentenced to die.

• High error rates pervade American capital-sentencing jurisdictions, and are geographically dispersed. Among the twenty-six death-sentencing jurisdictions in which at least one case has been reviewed in both the state and federal courts and in which information about all three judicial inspection stages is available:

1. 24 (92 percent) have overall error rates of 52 percent or higher;
2. 22 (85 percent) have overall error rates of 60 percent or higher;
3. 15 (61 percent) have overall error rates of 70 percent or higher;
4. Among other states, Georgia, Alabama, Mississippi, Indiana, Oklahoma, Wyoming, Montana, Arizona, and California have overall error rates of 75 percent or higher.

It is sometimes suggested that Illinois, whose governor declared a moratorium on executions in January 2000 because of the spate of death row exonerations there, generates less reliable death sentences than other states. Our data do not support this hypothesis: The overall rate of error found to infect Illinois capital sentences (66 percent) is slightly *lower* than the rate in capital-sentencing states as a whole (68 percent).

- High error rates have persisted for decades. More than 50 percent of all cases reviewed were found seriously flawed in twenty of the twenty-three study years, including in seventeen of the last nineteen years. In half of the years studied, the error rate was over 60 percent. Although error rates detected on state direct appeal and federal habeas corpus dropped modestly in the early 1990s, they went back up in 1995. The amount of error detected on state post-conviction has risen sharply throughout the 1990s.
- The 68 percent rate of *capital* error found by the three stage inspection process is much higher than the <15 percent rate of error those same three inspections evidently discover in *noncapital* criminal cases.
- Appointed federal judges are sometimes thought to be more likely to overturn capital sentences than elected state judges. In fact, state judges are the first and most important line of defense against erroneous death sentences. Elected state judges found serious error in and reversed 90 percent (2,133 of 2,370) of the capital sentences that were overturned during the study period.
- Under current state and federal law, capital prisoners have a legal right to one round of direct appellate, state post-conviction, and federal habeas corpus review. The high rates of error found at *each* stage, and at the *last* stage, and the persistence of high error rates over time and across the nation, confirm the need for multiple judicial inspections. Without compensating changes at the front-end of the process, the contrary policy of cutting back on judicial inspection would seem to make no more sense than responding to the impending insolvency of the Social Security System by forbidding it to be audited.

- Finding this much error takes time. Calculating the amount of time using information in published decisions is difficult. Only a small percentage of direct appeals decisions report the sentence date. By the end of the habeas stage, however, a much larger proportion of sentencing dates is reported in some decision in the case. It accordingly is possible to get an accurate sense of timing for the 599 cases that were finally reviewed on habeas corpus. Among those cases:

1. It took an average of 7.6 years after the defendant was sentenced to die to complete federal habeas corpus consideration in the 40 percent of habeas cases in which reversible error was found.
2. In the cases in which no error was detected at the third inspection stage and an execution occurred, the average time between sentence and execution was nine years.

As Figure 12.2 reveals, high rates of error frustrate the goals of the death penalty system. Figure 12.2 compares the overall rates of error detected during the state direct appeal and federal inspection process in the twenty-eight states with at least one capital judgment that has completed that process, to the percentage of death sentences imposed by each state that it has carried out by execution. In general, where the overall error rate reaches 55 percent or above (as is true for the vast majority of the states), the percentage of death sentences carried out drops below 7 percent.

Figure 12.2 illustrates another finding of interest: The pattern of capital outcomes for the State of Virginia is clearly an outlier—the State's high execution rate is nearly *double* that of the next nearest state and *five times* the national average, and its low rate of capital reversals is nearly *half* that of the next nearest state and less than *one-fourth* the national average. A sharp discrepancy between Virginia and other capital-sentencing jurisdictions characterizes most of our analyses. That discrepancy presents an important question for further study: Are Virginia capital judgments in fact half as prone to serious error as the next lowest state and four times less than the national average? Or, on the other hand, are its courts more

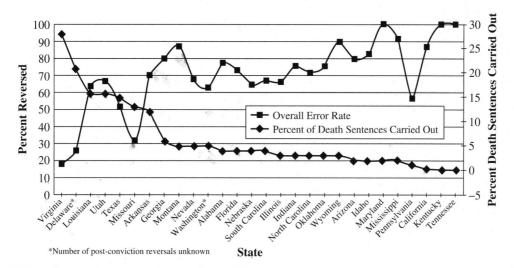

FIGURE 12.2   Overall Error Rate and Percent of Death Sentences Carried Out, 1973–1995

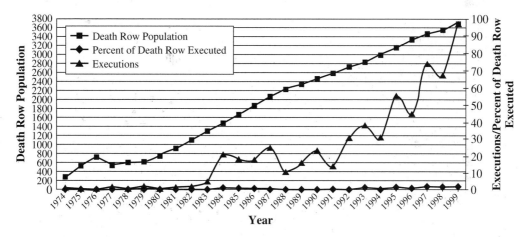

FIGURE 12.3   Persons on Death Row and Percent and Number Executed, 1976–1999

tolerant of serious error? Or, have Virginia's legislature and courts censored opportunities to inspect verdicts and detect error by procedurally constraining the definition of error and the time within which errors can be identified? We will address this issue below and in a subsequent report.

The rising number of executions nationally does not render these patterns obsolete. Instead of indicating improvement in the *quality* of death sentences under review, the rising number of executions may

simply reflect how many *more* sentences have piled up awaiting review. If the error-induced pile-up of cases on death row is the *cause* of rising executions, their rise provides no proof that a cure has been found for disturbingly high and persistent error rates. The rising execution rate and the persistent error rate increase the likelihood of an increase in the incidence of wrongful executions. To see why this is true, consider a factory that produced 100 toasters in a year, only 32 of which worked. The factory's production problem would not be deemed fixed if the company simply raised its production run to 200 the next year in order to double the number of working toasters to 66. Thus, the real question isn't the *number* of death sentences carried out each year, but the *proportion*.

Figure 12.3 shows that in contrast to the annual *number* of executions (the middle line in the chart), the *proportion* of death row inmates executed each year (the bottom line in the chart) has remained remarkably stable—and extremely low. Since post-*Furman* executions began in earnest in 1984, the nation has executed only an average of about 1.3 percent of its death row inmates each year; in no year has it carried out more than 2.6 percent—or one in thirty-nine—of death sentences exposed to full review.

Figure 12.3 suggests that the rising number of executions (the middle line) is *not* caused by any improvement in the quality of capital judgments, but instead by the inexorable pile-up of people on death row (the top line in the chart) as judges struggle to exercise a degree of quality control over decade upon decade of error-prone capital judgments.

III. CONFIRMATION FROM A PARALLEL STUDY

Results from a parallel study by the U.S. Department of Justice suggest that our 32 percent figure for valid death sentences actually overstates the chance of execution. The 1998 Justice Department study includes a report showing the outcome of the 263 death sentences imposed in 1989. A final disposition of only 103 of the 263 death sentences had been reached nine years later. Of those 103, 78 (76 percent) had been overturned by a state or federal court. Only thirteen death sentences had been carried out. So, for every one member of the death row class of 1989 whose case was finally reviewed and who was executed as of 1998, six members of the class had their cases overturned in the courts. Because of the intensive review needed to catch so much error, 160 (61 percent) of

the 263 death sentences imposed in 1989 were still under scrutiny nine years later.

The approximately 3,500 people on death row today have been waiting an average of 7.4 years for a final declaration that their capital verdict is error-free—or, far more probably, that it is the product of serious error. Of the 6,700 people sentenced to die between 1973 and 1999, only 598—less than one in eleven—were executed. About three times as many had their capital judgments overturned or gained clemency.

IV. IMPLICATIONS OF CENTRAL FINDINGS

To help appreciate these findings, consider a scenario that might unfold any of the nearly 300 times a year that a death sentence is imposed in the United States. Suppose the defendant, or a relative of the victim, asks a lawyer or the judge, "What now?" Based on almost a quarter century of experience in thousands of cases in twenty-eight death-sentencing states in the United States between 1973 and 1995, a responsible answer would be: "The capital conviction or sentence will probably be overturned due to serious error. It'll take about nine years to find out, given how many other capital cases being reviewed for likely error are lined up ahead of this one. If the judgment is overturned, a lesser conviction or sentence will probably be imposed."

As any person hearing this statement would likely conclude as a matter of common sense, these reversals due to serious error, and the time it takes to expose them, are costly. Capital trials and sentences cost more than noncapital ones. Each time they have to be done over—as happens 68 percent of the time—some or all of that difference is doubled. The error-detection system all this capital error requires is itself a huge expense—evidently *millions of dollars* per case.

When retrial demonstrates that nearly four-fifths of the capital judgments in which serious error is found are more appropriately handled as non-capital cases (and in a sizable number of instances, as non-murder or even *non-criminal* cases), it is hard to escape the conclusion that most of the resources the capital system currently consumes are not buying the public, or victims, the valid death sentences for egregious offenses that a majority support. Rather, those resources are being wasted on the trial and review of cases that for the most part are not capital and are seriously flawed.

Public faith in the courts and the criminal justice system is another casualty of high capital error rates. When the vast majority of capital sentencing jurisdictions carry out fewer than 6 percent of the death sentences they impose, and when the nation as a whole never executes more than 3 percent of its death population in a year, the retributive and deterrent credibility of the death penalty is low.

When condemned inmates turn out to be *innocent,* the error is different in its consequences, but *not* evidently different in its causes, from the other serious error discussed here. There is no accounting for this cost: to the wrongly convicted; to the family of the victim, whose search for justice and closure has been in vain; to later victims whose lives are threatened—and even taken—because the real killers remain at large; and to the wrongly *executed,* should justice miscarry at trial, and should reviewing judges, harried by the amount of capital error they are asked to catch, miss one.

If the issue was the fabrication of toasters (to return to our prior example), or the licensing of automobile drivers, or the conduct of any other private- or public-sector activity, neither the consuming public nor managers and investors would tolerate the error rates and attendant costs that dozens of states and the nation as a whole have tolerated in their capital punishment systems over the course of decades. Any system with this much error and expense would be halted immediately, examined, and either reformed or scrapped. We ask taxpayers, public managers, and policymakers whether that same response is warranted here, when the issue is not the content and quality of tomorrow's breakfast but whether society has a swift and sure response to murder and whether thousands of men and women condemned for that crime in fact deserve to die.

NOTE

1. For a fuller description of the findings presented in this article, see "A Broken System: The Persistent Patterns of Reversals of Death Sentences in the United States," by Andrew Gelman, James S. Liebman, Valerie West, and Alexander Kiss, *Journal of Empirical Legal Studies* 1 (July 2004), pp. 209–61.

READING QUESTIONS

1. How do the authors define overall success and failure rates? What were the overall success and error rates of convictions for capital murder? Cite some of the other relevant statistics mentioned by the authors regarding the error rates in capital cases.
2. What are the three stages of judicial review the cases in consideration can undergo? How do the authors define "serious error"? What are the two most common types of error found in capital murder cases?
3. Explain what the authors discovered about the average time involved in the review of capital cases. What effect does the length of the review process have on the criminal justice system?
4. What are some of the implications of these findings according to the authors? Why do the authors think that public faith in the courts is a casualty of these findings?

DISCUSSION QUESTIONS

1. Are the authors right to assume that knowledge of information regarding the overall success and failure rates of capital cases would undermine the public's faith in the court system? Why or why not? What other responses might the public have to this information?

2. What do the authors' findings suggest about the moral status of the death penalty? Consider and discuss whether the death penalty could be morally permissible even if there are serious errors made in capital cases.

ADDITIONAL RESOURCES

Web Resources

Amnesty International, <http://web.amnesty.org/pages/deathpenalty>. Pro-abolitionist site that reports data regarding the death penalty and its use worldwide.

Bedau, Hugo Adam, "Punishment," <http://plato.stanford.edu/entries/punishment>. An overview of theories about the ethical justification of punishment.

Death Penalty Information Center, <http://www.deathpenaltyinfo.org/>. Pro-abolitionist forum.

The Pew Forum on Religion & Public Life, <http://pewforum.org/docs/>. An excellent, non-partisan resource for learning about the history of the death penalty in the United States and the current debate over its moral status.

Pro-Death Penalty.Com, <http://www.prodeathpenalty.com/>. A retentionist forum.

Authored Books

Costanzo, Mark, *Just Revenge: Costs and Consequences of the Death Penalty* (New York: St. Martin's Press, 1997). An accessible, short book with emphasis on the social scientific research relevant to the death penalty.

Hanks, Gardner C., *Against the Death Penalty: Christian and Secular Arguments against the Death Penalty* (Scottdale, PA: Herald Press, 1997). A survey and defense of Christian and secular arguments against the death penalty.

Pojman, Louis and Jeffrey Reiman, *The Death Penalty* (Lanham, MD: Rowman & Littlefield, 1997). A debate between Pojman, a retentionist, and Rieman, an abolitionist.

Van den Haag, Ernest and John P. Conrad, *The Death Penalty: A Debate* (New York: Plenum Books, 1983). Van den Haag defends the retentionist view and Conrad defends the abolitionist position.

Edited Collections

Baird, Robert M. and Stuart E. Rosenbaum (eds.), *Death Penalty: Debating the Moral, Legal, and Political Issues* (Amherst, NY: Prometheus Books, 2010). A collection of essays by leading experts, including articles that address the impact of new advances in DNA technology on the moral, political, and legal questions about the death penalty.

Bedau, Hugo Adam (ed.), *The Death Penalty in America: Current Controversies* (Oxford: Oxford University Press, 1997). A comprehensive anthology with thirty-three articles ranging over issues about the constitutionality, racial bias, public support, and morality of the death penalty in the United States.

Bedau, Hugo Adam and Paul G. Cassell (eds.), *Debating the Death Penalty: Should America Have Capital Punishment? The Experts on Both Sides Make Their Case* (Oxford: Oxford University Press, 2005). A collection of seven essays by a range of experts—judges, lawyers, prosecutors, and philosophers—debating the death penalty.

13 } War, Terrorism, and Torture

The contemporary world is besieged by acts of war, terrorism, and torture. The 9/11 destruction of the World Trade Center in New York and the coordinated attack on the Pentagon, as well as the terrorist bombings in Madrid (2004), London (2005), Mumbai (2006, 2009), Boston (2013), Paris (2015), Brussels (2016), and Istanbul (2016) have ignited intense worldwide debate over the nature, causes, and morality of war and terrorism. This debate has been further intensified, particularly in the United States, as a result of the U.S. wars in Iraq and Afghanistan. Also, the deplorable abuse of prisoners by U.S. military personnel at the Abu Ghraib prison near the Iraqi capital of Baghdad, as well as so-called enhanced interrogation techniques including waterboarding, has sparked not only worldwide outrage, but also debate over the nature and morality of torture. Many people believe that at least some wars are, or could be, morally justifiable, even if many past and present wars are not justifiable. Terrorism and torture are widely condemned as morally wrong. The central moral questions these practices raise are these:

- Is (war), (terrorism), (torture) ever morally permissible?
- If any of these activities are ever morally permissible, what best explains why this is so?

I have inserted parentheses in the first question to indicate that for each of the three activities, we can raise the moral questions just mentioned, and so we should not just assume that their moral status—whether they are ever permissible and, if so, why—is the same. It may turn out, as some have argued, that, for instance, war is sometimes permissible but terrorism and torture never are.

In order to begin thinking about these moral issues, let us first consider questions and issues about the morality of war, and then turn to terrorism and torture in order.

1. WAR

As with all disputed moral issues, we must begin by specifying the subject of dispute—war. The *Merriam-Webster Online Dictionary* has this entry:

War

(1): a state of usually open and declared armed hostile conflict between states or nations; (2): a period of such armed conflict.[1]

There are also entries for both "hot" and "cold" wars. A **hot war** is defined as "a conflict involving actual fighting," whereas a **cold war** is described as "a conflict over ideological differences carried on by methods short of sustained overt military action and usually without breaking off diplomatic relations." The focus in this chapter is on so-called hot wars—which, in the twentieth century, include World Wars I and II, the Korean War, the Vietnam War, and the Gulf War—and are often the focus of contemporary moral discussions.

One particularly contentious moral question about war concerns the conditions under which a state is morally justified in going to war. Many would readily agree that if attacked first, a state has a right of self-defense to fight back. However, the U.S. initiation of the recent U.S–Iraq war continues to be a subject of dispute, both on moral and legal grounds, given that Iraq did not pose a clear imminent threat to the United States or her allies—the kind of the threat that might justify a preemptive strike, thus launching a **preemptive war**. Rather, the United States engaged in what is properly referred to as a **preventive war**, which David Rodin characterizes as "a first strike against a potential future aggressor who does not yet pose an imminent threat." (See the selection from Rodin from which this quote is taken.) Assuming that a preemptive war can sometimes be morally justified on grounds of self-defense (a controversial assumption): Could there be circumstances in which a preventive war is morally justified? This question is debated in our selections from Rodin and Walter Sinnott-Armstrong.

Preventive military strikes are also a topic of concern over the use of drones—remotely controlled aircraft that the United States has used extensively in recent years to target leaders of terrorist organizations. Moral and legal controversy over the use of drones has been cast in terms of the legitimacy of employing preventive strikes. Robert Shane, in a front-page story in *The New York Times* (Nov. 25, 2012) wrote the following:

> Facing the possibility that President Obama might not win a second term, his administration accelerated work in the weeks before the election to develop explicit rules for the targeted killing of terrorists by unmanned drones, so that a new president would inherit standards and procedures. . . . Mr. Obama and his advisors are still debating whether remote-control killing should be a measure of last resort against imminent threats to the United States, or a more flexible tool, available to help allied governments attack their enemies or to prevent militants from controlling territory.

Here, again, the contrast between using drones strictly as a preemptive measure ("of last resort against imminent threats") or more liberally as a preventive measure is the focus of attention.

2. TERRORISM

As with moral questions about war, a discussion of the morality of terrorism must begin with a working definition of terrorism. Here we immediately run into controversy, partly because some individuals make the moral wrongness of the violence associated with terrorism part of terrorism's very definition so that by definition terrorism is morally wrong. Such "question-begging" definitions—definitions that merely assume something controversial about what is being defined—are to be avoided here because for one thing, they inhibit asking legitimate moral questions about the sort of violent activity carried on in the name of some cause that we want to be able to ask. For another thing, merely defining terrorism as morally wrong will not solve any moral issues about this kind of violence. After all, those who might think that some forms of violence—for, say, political causes—are morally justified (or might be) can simply grant the morally loaded use of the term "terrorism" and call the kind of violence they might defend by some other name—"freedom fighting," for example. Again, mere verbal stipulation will not settle legitimate moral questions about various forms of violence carried out in the name of various causes.

One definition that avoids the sort of question-begging just mentioned and that seems to capture what most people mean when speaking of terrorism is offered by James P. Sterba:

> **Terrorism** is the use or threat of violence against innocent people to elicit terror in them, or in some other group of people, in order to further a political objective.[2]

There are three elements of this definition worth noting. First, terrorism on Sterba's definition is not confined to nonstate groups and individuals; rather, it allows that states can engage in terrorism. In this way, Sterba's definition is broader than the one embraced by the U.S. Department of State, which restricts terrorist activity to "subnational groups or clandestine agents." Second, Sterba's definition restricts the targets of terrorist activity to "innocent people," and similar definitions restrict targets to "noncombatants." But we find other definitions that are not as restrictive in this way. For instance, Tomis Kapitan defines terrorism as being directed upon "civilians," leaving open the matter of whether civilians are innocent.[3] Third, many, if not most definitions of terrorism, like Sterba's, mention *political* goals and objectives as part of what terrorism is. This seems to be entirely in keeping with how the term is typically used. However, we do find definitions that are not restrictive in this way. For instance, Haig Khatchadourian defines terrorism as involving "acts of coercion or of actual use of force, aiming at monetary gain (predatory terrorism), revenge (retaliatory terrorism), a political end (political terrorism), or a putative moral/religious end (moralistic/religious terrorism)."[4] One implication of this definition is that acts of bank robbery for monetary gain, for example, count as acts of terrorism, thus greatly widening the scope of what is to count as terrorism. In any case, the important point here is that in reading about terrorism one must keep an eye on how the term is being defined. Issues about the definition of terrorism are discussed by Andrew Valls in the selection included here, "Can Terrorism Be Justified?"

3. TORTURE

The main focus of discussion about the morality of torture is whether it is absolutely morally wrong or whether in certain "necessity" cases—often illustrated by "ticking bomb" scenarios—the use of torture to extract potentially life-saving information is morally permissible. Of course, we have to begin with the question "What is torture?"

According to article 1 of the 1984 United Nations Convention against Torture and Other Cruel, Inhuman or Degrading Treatment or Punishment:

> "**Torture**" means any act by which severe pain or suffering, whether physical or mental, is intentionally inflicted on a person for such purposes as [1] obtaining from him or a third person information or a confession, [2] punishing him for an act he or a third person has committed or is suspected of

having committed, or [3] intimidating or coercing him or a third person, or [4] for any reason based on discrimination of any kind, when such pain or suffering is inflicted by or at the instigation of or with the consent or acquiescence of a public official or other person acting in an official capacity.[5]

Three observations about this definition are worth making here. First, the bracketed numbers (which I have inserted) indicate the various purposes or aims of acts of torture. Taking note of these various possible purposes is important because if torture is ever morally permissible, its permissibility will certainly depend in large measure upon the purposes of the torturer. For instance, it is common to distinguish between **terrorist torture** (which would presumably include acts of torture motivated by the sorts of purposes mentioned in 2, 3, and 4 in the previous definition) and **interrogational torture,** done for the purpose (mentioned in 1) of obtaining information from the victim in order, for example, to prevent or avert some impending terrorist attack.

Second, the UN convention also distinguishes torture from what it refers to as "acts of cruel, inhuman, or degrading treatment or punishment which do not amount to torture as defined in article 1." This raises the obvious problem of distinguishing acts of torture from acts of cruel, inhumane, or degrading treatment. Here is not the place to delve into this difficult matter. Rather, for present purposes, it will suffice to list a few acts of what are widely taken to be torture: severe beatings, being made to stand for hours or days at a time, extended sleep deprivation, withholding food or water, being buried alive, electric shocks, having one's head forced underwater until nearly asphyxiated, rape, threatened rape, and threatened death. Such activities as slaps in the face that fall short of severe beatings, shouting obscenities at prisoners, and making prisoners engage in sexual acts are clearly instances of inhuman and degrading treatment, but they seem to fall short of torture.[6]

The third observation about the previous UN convention definition is that to count as torture, the act must be performed by, initiated by, or consented to by a public official or someone acting in an official capacity. This rules out cases that we might ordinarily consider as torture, as when an individual, acting alone and for reasons of personal revenge, kidnaps and inflicts severe pain and suffering on his victim over an extended period of time. But this restriction is perfectly reasonable, given that the aim of the convention was to establish international law.

With a basic understanding of the concepts of war, terrorism, and torture now before us, let us turn to moral issues.

4. THEORY MEETS PRACTICE

Let us begin by distinguishing two sorts of questions we may ask about the morality of war. First, when (if ever) is a state or nation morally justified in going to war against another state or nation? Second, which sorts of military activities are morally permissible within war? In relation to both questions, we find what we may nonprejudicially refer to as extreme positions: moral nihilism and moral pacifism. Let us consider each of these in order, after which we will proceed to consider other, less "extreme," moral perspectives on war.

In discussions about the morality of war, **moral nihilism** is the view that moral considerations do not apply to war, that questions of moral right and wrong, good and bad do not apply because war creates a context in which "anything goes." Thus, to the question "Is war

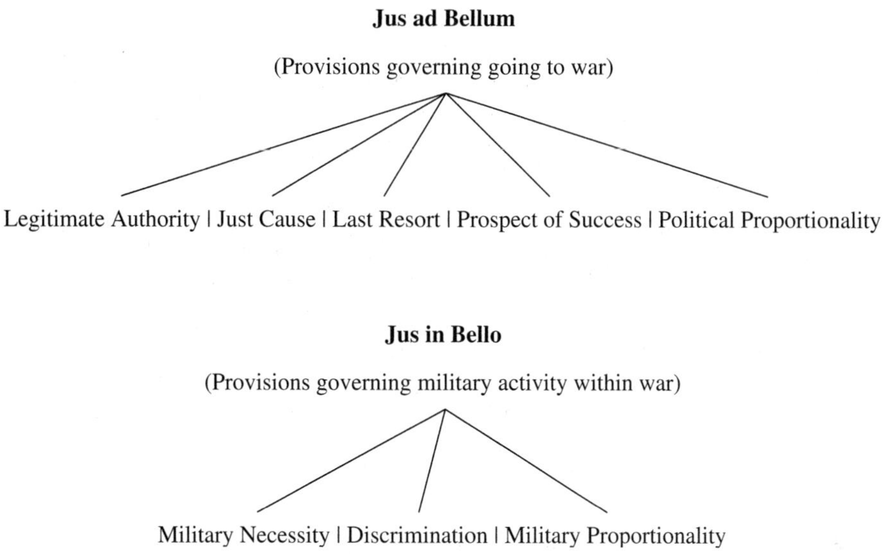

Jus ad Bellum

(Provisions governing going to war)

Legitimate Authority | Just Cause | Last Resort | Prospect of Success | Political Proportionality

Jus in Bello

(Provisions governing military activity within war)

Military Necessity | Discrimination | Military Proportionality

FIGURE 13.1   Just-War Theory

ever morally justified?" the nihilist in effect refuses to answer the question, claiming that questions about morality do not arise in connection with war. Of course, since there are two general sorts of questions about the morality of war—going to war and conduct within war—one might hold the view that although morality does apply to the decision to go to war and thus claim that some wars are morally justified and others are not, one might also hold that within war, anything goes morally speaking.

At the other end of the moral spectrum is **antiwar pacifism,** according to which wars are always (or at least nearly always) morally wrong.[7] One basis for such a view is the idea that all intentional killing of human beings is morally wrong. But many individuals, including many moral philosophers, hold that some cases of intentionally killing human beings are morally justified—cases of self-defense being the most widely accepted. In the context of war, this would mean that wars of self-defense might sometimes be justified. But there is far more to the moral positions of those who would defend the morality of at least some wars, and here we find that perhaps the most prominent moral approach to war (or at least the most widely discussed) is **just-war theory,** to which we now turn.

Natural Law and Just-War Theory

Just-war theory is perhaps best understood as an extension of natural law ethics applied to the issue of war. One need not embrace natural law theory in order to accept the moral provisions of just-war theory, but in outlining this approach to the morality of war (and terrorism), appealing to some ideas from natural law theory—particularly the doctrine of double effect—is useful.[8]

Just-war theory makes the common distinction between questions about the morality of going to war, **jus ad bellum,** and about the morality of activities within a war, **jus in bello.** Each of these two parts is made up of various moral provisions. Figure 13.1 offers a visual aid.

In what immediately follows, I will briefly state each of these provisions, at least as they are often understood.

Jus ad Bellum

Here, then, is a statement of the five principles composing this part of just-war theory:[9]

Legitimate authority: War must be declared by a legitimate authority—typically under-stood as the officials of a recognized government. This condition is often understood as a requirement for violence or force to be considered war. So, for instance, spontaneous uprisings that result in violence do not count as wars.

Just cause: There must be a just cause for going to war. A very restrictive interpretation of this provision would require that the war be one of self-defense, in which a govern-ment is responding to violent aggression or is attempting to prevent imminent violent aggression by another state. This restrictive interpretation rules out any "aggressive" war that would, for example, forcefully interfere with the internal affairs of some state for "humanitarian" purposes.

Last resort: All reasonable alternatives to going to war must be exhausted. What counts as a "reasonable alternative" is left open to interpretation. Certainly, nonviolent diplo-matic solutions are to be sought before going to war.

Prospect of success: In going to war, there must be a reasonable prospect of success. Again, what counts as reasonable is left open, as is the question of what counts as success. Clearly, winning a war counts as success, but in some cases a futile struggle to the death might be justified if the alternative is enslavement or extermination by a nation's opponent.

Political proportionality: The violence of war must be proportional to the wrong being resisted. Both here and in the provisions of jus in bello, considerations of consequences are relevant, though, unlike a pure consequentialist approach, this provision is but one requirement of the just-war approach to the morality of war.

Let us now turn to the provisions of jus in bello. Here my plan is to relate them to the **doctrine of double effect (DDE)**, which was presented in the moral theory primer (chapter 1) as part of natural law ethics. This doctrine is meant to address the question of whether it is ever morally permissible to knowingly bring about evil consequences in the pursuit of some good. According to DDE, in cases in which an action would produce (or likely produce) at least some good effects but at least one bad effect (where for present purposes we can restrict good and bad to the preservation and loss of human life respec-tively), the action in question is morally permitted only if all of the following conditions are met:

Intrinsic permissibility: The action, apart from its effects, must be morally permissible;

Necessity: The bad effect is unavoidable, and thus the action is necessary if the good effect is to be brought about;

Nonintentionality: The bad effect is not intended—it is neither one's end nor a means to one's end; and

Proportionality: The badness of the bad effect is not grossly out of proportion to the good-ness of the good effect being sought.

The latter three principles, reformulated so that they each address aggression in war, yield the following provisions that compose jus in bello:

Jus in Bello

Military necessity: The military activity in question (e.g., the bombing of a military installation) must be judged to be *necessary* in order to bring about some justifiable military end.

Discrimination: The deaths of innocent noncombatants must not be directly intended either as an end of the military action or as a means to some further military purpose. Talk of innocent noncombatants here is meant to refer in particular to citizens of a state who are not actively engaged in that state's war efforts. Clearly, an unarmed young child counts as an innocent noncombatant, whereas armed soldiers do not. Other individuals—for example, those forced to work in a munitions plant—present hard cases requiring that this provision be more finely interpreted.

Military proportionality: Whatever good end the military action in question is supposed to serve, the likely evil that results from that activity (e.g., deaths and loss of property) must not be grossly out of proportion to the intended good ends of that activity.

To understand these provisions, consider cases of "tactical bombing," in which the aim of the mission is to destroy an enemy military base; however, in so doing, it is predictable (given the base's location) that a number of innocent noncombatants will be killed by the bombing. If the conditions of necessity and proportionality are met in a particular case of tactical bombing, then because the deaths of innocent civilians is not intended (either as an end or as a means to the tactical mission), this kind of activity would be morally permitted by just-war theory. Readers can contrast such tactical cases with cases of "terrorist bombing," in which the immediate aim is to kill innocent civilians in an effort to weaken enemy morale.

Finally, it is worth emphasizing that these provisions, as I have indicated in my presentation, require a good deal of interpretation in applying them to concrete cases. But, of course, this is true of all general moral principles.

Turning for a moment to our readings, Michael Walzer begins with the premise that terrorism is always wrong and proceeds to examine various "excuses" that have been offered in defense of terrorist acts. He argues that none of them are morally legitimate. Andrew Valls argues that if the provisions of just-war theory can morally justify some wars, they can also morally justify some acts of terrorism. He thus opposes Walzer's claim that all instances of terrorism are, by definition, morally wrong. With regard to the moral justification for going to war, the "just cause" provision of just-war theory limits going to war to cases of self-defense which, as earlier presented, does not include preventive wars. But Walter Sinnott-Armstrong is critical of standard interpretations of the just-cause provision that are taken to rule out all preventive wars.

Rights Approaches

As explained in chapter 1, section 2D, a rights-based moral theory takes the notion of moral rights as basic in approaching moral issues. Different rights-based theories disagree over which rights are fundamental. David Rodin defends a rights-based theory of self-defense and argues that preventive wars cannot be morally justified on any plausible interpretation of this sort of theory.

Kantian Theory

None of the selections that follow take a Kantian approach to one or another of the chapter's various topics. But Kant's Humanity formulation of the categorical imperative, which requires that one treat others not merely as means to one's own ends but as ends in themselves, sometimes figures in discussions of the morality of war, terrorism, and torture. This principle is often used to evaluate acts of terrorist torture that involve harming individuals as a means of intimidating others—a reasonably clear case of using someone *merely* as a means.

Consequentialism

Consequentialist approaches to torture may take either an act or a rule form. You may recall from chapter 1, section 2A, that act consequentialism focuses on the specific, concrete action being morally evaluated and considers the net intrinsic value of the consequences that would likely be caused by the action and compares them to the net intrinsic value of the likely consequences of some alternative action open to the agent at the time. By contrast, rule consequentialism considers not the values of the likely consequences of the specific, concrete actions under scrutiny, but rather the values of the likely consequences of the general acceptance of various alternative rules under which the action and its alternatives fall. On this version of consequentialism, a concrete action is permitted in a certain set of circumstances if a rule permitting acts of that type in the circumstances in question has at least as high an **acceptance value** as any other alternative rule for those circumstances.[10] So a specific, concrete act of torture would be wrong from a rule consequentialist perspective if a rule prohibiting torture in those circumstances would, if widely accepted, result in a greater level of net intrinsic value than would a rule permitting torture in those circumstances.

Walter Sinnott-Armstrong approaches the issue of preventive war from an act consequentialist perspective, arguing (as one would expect) that whether such wars can be morally justified depends on the actual consequences of engaging in wars for preventive purposes. Alan M. Dershowitz in "Should the Ticking Bomb Terrorist Be Tortured?" also embraces an act consequentialist (he calls it a "case utilitarian") approach in addressing questions about the permissibility of torture. The case of the ticking bomb terrorist is often brought up as a reasonably clear case in which most will agree that torture would be morally permissible; the view defended by Dershowitz. However, such cases are hypothetical, and one might ask, as Marcia Baron does in her essay included here, whether this particular hypothetical case is unacceptably artificial in light of real-world circumstances. She argues that it is, and so should not be used to compromise an absolute prohibition on torture.

NOTES

1. As a third item, this dictionary includes "state of war," which is then linked to further definitions of this expression.

2. James P. Sterba, "Terrorism and International Justice," in, *Terrorism and International Justice,* ed. James P. Sterba (New York: Oxford University Press, 2003), 211.

3. Tomis Kapitan, "The Terrorism of 'Terrorism,'" in *Terrorism and International Justice*, 47.

4. Haig Khatchadourian, *The Morality of Terrorism* (New York: Peter Lang, 1998).

5. A full text of this convention is available online at www.hrweb.org/legal/cat.html. This document goes on to state that "no exceptional circumstances whatsoever, whether a state of war or a threat of war, internal political instability or any other public emergency" would justify the use of torture: torture, according to this declaration, is *absolutely* prohibited. See article 16. It also prohibits the practice of "rendition" (article 3), whereby one country sends its prisoners to another country—often to a country known for harsh treatment of its prisoners. In 1994, the United States ratified the UN convention, though in so doing it adopted a more restrictive definition of torture requiring that in order to be torture, the act "must be *specifically intended* to inflict *severe* physical or mental pain or suffering." For a useful discussion of the definition of torture generally as well as torture under U.S. law, see John T. Parry, "Escalation and Necessity: Defining Torture at Home and Abroad," in *Torture: A Collection,* ed. Sanford Levinson (New York: Oxford University Press, 2004), 145.

6. In the wake of the Abu Ghraib prison scandal, U.S. senator (and former Vietnam War POW) John McCain proposed an amendment (attached to a defense spending bill) that protects anyone in U.S. custody from "cruel, inhuman, or degrading treatment." On December 15, 2005, the President George W. Bush-led U.S. White House, under pressure from members of both Republican and Democratic parties, agreed to the language of McCain's amendment.

7. There are other more restrictive forms of pacifism, including, for example, nonviolent pacifism, which maintains that any form of violence against human beings is wrong.

8. For instance, Michael Walzer in *Just and Unjust Wars,* 2nd ed. (New York: Basic Books, 1992) defends a version of just-war approach to the morality of war, but he is not a natural law theorist.

9. In presenting the provisions of jus ad bellum, I am following C. A. J. Coady's presentation of it in his "War and Terrorism," in *A Companion to Applied Ethics,* ed. R. G. Frey and Christopher Heath Wellman (Oxford: Blackwell Publishing, 2003), 254.

10. The "acceptance value" of rule (in relation to some group) is defined as the net intrinsic value that would result were the rule accepted by a significant proportion of the members of the group in question.

DAVID RODIN

The Problem with Prevention[1]

After distinguishing preventive from preemptive wars, Rodin argues that consequentialist attempts to address the issue of preventive war are unacceptable because, lacking relevant empirical knowledge about likely outcomes of such wars, they are useless in practice. He then considers arguments that appeal to the right of self-defense in attempting to justify preventive wars and finds that on any plausible interpretation of this right, such arguments fail.

Recommended Reading: consequentialism, chap. 1, sec. 2A; rights theory, chap. 1, sec. 2D.

In September 2002, one year after the terrorist attacks on Washington and New York, the Bush administration released its 'National Security Strategy of the United States of America', the blueprint for the development of US military and security policy. This document contained a radical innovation in the grounds for waging war. It proclaimed a readiness to fight preventive wars against 'emerging threats before they are fully formed'.[2] Just over a year later, the United States, together with Britain and a number of other allies, put the policy of preventive war to dramatic effect by invading, defeating, and occupying Iraq in a matter of weeks.[3] The doctrine of preventive war and its implementation in Iraq caused consternation among many long-standing American allies, particularly in Europe. For its critics, the policy is a dangerous and misguided challenge to the legal and moral international order. For its advocates, the policy is a morally and strategically justified response to new forms of security threat.

In this chapter, I argue that there are profound moral problems with the doctrine of preventive war. The argument is structured in two parts. In the first part, I examine consequentialist approaches to preventive war. The case both for and against preventive war is often made in consequentialist terms. This seems to me a mistake. Consequentialism suffers from debilitating epistemological problems that renders it effectively useless as a moral theory of war. Consequentialism would require historical judgments about the long term overall effects of war that are intrinsically indeterminate and unknowable. Moreover rule-consequentialist assessment of the laws of war suffers from what I call the impasse problem: the persistent presence of equally plausible rule-consequentialist arguments for countervailing conclusions. Much of this part of the discussion uses as its foil a recent and significant contribution to the debate on prevention by David Luban, which provides a vigorous defense of the consequentialist approach to war.[4]

In the second part of the chapter, I examine whether preventive action can be viewed as a legitimate component of the right of self-defense. I argue that it cannot. The right of self-defense has historically been grounded in a number of different theoretical justifications including those that invoke a conception of psychological necessity and those that invoke human rights. On neither of these theories, however, can preventive self-defense be justified. . . .

From David Rodin, "The Problem of Preventive War," in *Preemption: Military Action and Moral Justification*, H. Shue and D. Rodin, eds. Oxford: Oxford University Press, pp. 143–153; 160–166.

PREVENTION AND PREEMPTION

First, however, I want to address an important issue of terminology. In the National Security Strategy and in the speeches of the Bush and Blair administrations, the policy that is to be our concern is referred to as 'preemptive' rather 'preventive' war. But this is a rhetorical sleight of hand. According to well-established legal usage, preemption consists in a first strike against an enemy who has not yet attacked but whose attack is clearly imminent. It involves 'anticipating' an aggressor who is literally poised to attack. Prevention, on the other hand, involves a first strike against a potential future aggressor who does not yet pose an imminent threat. In Michael Walzer's words it is ' . . . an attack that responds to a distant danger, a matter of foresight and free choice'.[5]

It is sometimes said that a right of preemptive self-defense is clearly and uncontroversialy recognized under international law.[6] This is simply not true. Many scholars believe that even a limited right of preemption against imminent attack is ruled out under international law. The UN Charter is very clear that the right of self-defense can only be invoked 'if an armed attacks occurs' (UN Charter, Article 51). Under traditional means of treaty interpretation this has been taken to unequivocally rule out a right to preemption. On the other hand there does exist older customary law, in the form of the famous Caroline doctrine (of which more later), which encompasses a limited right to engage in preemptive strikes against an imminent attack. Those who support a right of preemptive self-defense must argue that Article 51 does not replace, but merely supplements, this older customary law right. But this customary law argument is undermined by the fact that states have tended to avoid invoking a right of preemptive defense even in circumstances that might justify it (e.g. the right was not invoked by Israel to justify its first strike against Egypt in the Six Day War, which is often regarded as the *locus classicus* of justified preemptive action by the doctrine's supporters). Thus, while it is possible to argue that there exists a right of preemptive self-defense in international law, it is by no means a settled question.

On the other hand, there is no uncertainty as to the legality of undertaking unilateral military action against 'emerging threats before they are fully formed'. Such action against a nonimminent threat is properly referred to as 'prevention' rather than 'preemption', and it clearly contravenes international law as it currently stands.[7] The 'Bush doctrine' articulated in the National Security Strategy, while not historically unprecedented, does represent a genuine innovation in the grounds for war, one which would transform the moral and legal framework on the international use of force.

THE DISUTILITY OF CONSEQUENTIALISM

It is not difficult to construct a consequentialist argument for preventive war, particularly in light of the much-discussed potential nexus between international terrorism and WMD. *If* undertaking a particular preventive war is an effective way of averting a significant terrorist attack or act of future aggression from a hostile state, and *if* the war does not itself cause more harm than it prevents, and *if* there is no less costly way of achieving the same good, and *if* the opportunity costs of the expended blood and treasure do not outweigh the projected goods, then the war would be prima facie justified on consequentialist grounds.

These are all big ifs, and much of the plausibility of the consequentialist argument rests on its ability to fulfill the evidentiary burdens they impose. I argue that the consequentialist approach to war quite generally suffers from two traditional vulnerabilities of consequentialist theory. The first is its tendency to generate counterintuitive ethical conclusions and assessments. The second, and far more serious, is a severe epistemological weakness resulting from the radical indeterminacy of the historical judgments required to yield a meaningful consequentialist conclusion about the justification of war. This criticism is not new, it was made by Walzer in *Just and Unjust Wars*,[8] but I believe that the full force of the objection has not been fully appreciated by consequentialist writers on war.

Of course, we may expect the case of preventive war to generate special difficulties for any ethical theory. Let us begin, therefore, with what should be an easy case: the Allies' war against Nazi Germany, which many feel is the clearest modern example of a justified war. The first problem is that it is not clear that a consequentialist analysis supports this judgment. The Nazi regime was brutal and aggressive: it systematically murdered approximately six million innocent people, and subjected many millions more to a regime of extraordinary moral repugnance. But the costs of the war against Germany were in many ways more horrific still. Those who lost their lives to the war outnumber the victims of German murder and genocide, by approximately ten to one. This does not yet include the suffering of the approximately forty million persons displaced or made homeless by the war and the incalculable destruction to the world's cultural and material wealth. This was a horrific price to pay for stopping Nazi Germany. Even allowing for the expanded genocide that would certainly have taken place if the war had not been fought, it is not obvious that *on strict consequentialist grounds* it was a price worth paying.[9]

What is most striking about the assessment of war from a consequentialist perspective, however, is not that particular wars fail or pass the test in a counterintuitive way, but rather the near impossibility of accurately determining the long-term balance of consequences of engaging in war. To return to World War II, there is a very real sense in which we still do not know the long-term balance of consequences of this war six decades after its end. This is the case for a number of reasons. First, we do not, even now, know the actual casualty figures of the war with any degree of precision. Estimates of the Soviet War casualties alone have ranged from seven to forty million persons.[10] That is a margin of error of 470 per cent—an almost incomprehensible thirty three million human lives!

Chairman Zhou En-lai famously responded that 'its too early to tell' when asked about the impact of the French Revolution. In a similar way, it may be literally true that it is too early to tell what the ultimate balance sheet of World War II's costs and benefits is, because the war continues to have a profound and ongoing impact on the world today. This is true both on the macro and on the micro level. The war and its aftermath continue to shape patterns of political alliance and economic exchange within Europe and around the world (e.g. it continues to play a significant role in the development of the European Union). On a micro level the war continues to affect the lives and well-being of countless individuals in both subtle and profound ways. To take but one example, the trauma of experiencing the war has left legacies of mental illness and emotional abuse that continue to ripple down through the generations of many families.

Secondly and most damagingly, because consequentialist assessment requires a comparative judgment between the consequences of fighting and not fighting a given war, it always depends upon questions of counterfactual history that are intrinsically unknowable. For example, if the Allies had not chosen to fight Nazi Germany we can assume that it would have continued to expand its genocidal and aggressive policies—but by how much? Would the Nazi state have collapsed under the weight of its own inefficiency and inequity as the Soviet Union did 45 years later? Would National Socialism have survived the death or assassination of Hitler? There is simply no reliable way to answer these and countless other relevant counterfactual questions like them.

These profound epistemological difficulties arise even when conducting a retrospective analysis, with the benefit of hindsight and decades of painstaking academic research. But if consequentialism is to function as a guide to action for policymakers rather than simply as a form of backward-looking moral assessment, then it is necessary to undertake an immeasurably more difficult task still. That is an accurate prospective analysis of the likely long-term consequences of engaging in war before the conflict has even begun. To return to World War II, it is almost impossible to believe that any of the leaders in 1939 could have reliably foreseen the long-term consequences of the war that was about to begin. . . .

Moreover, World War II commenced with clear and unambiguous acts of aggression on the part of Germany. But the case of preventive war generates further difficulties still for consequentialism. This is because the feared act of aggression lies sometime in the future and indeed may never eventuate. In such a case, the problems of indeterminacy and the dependence on unknowable counterfactual judgments, present in all war, are magnified many times over.

Now, I certainly do not want to claim that we can never make an accurate and well-founded determination of whether the balance of consequences favors war or not. In fact it is often very easy to make this determination *in the negative*. Because initiating a war always has very significant moral costs, it is obvious that going to war to prevent a minor infringement or slight injury will not lead to better over all consequences.[11] This points to an important asymmetry in our ability to assess the consequences of war. In general, it is easier to fulfill the evidentiary burdens of the negative judgment that engaging in war will *not* lead to better overall consequences than it is to fulfill the burdens of the positive judgment that fighting *will* lead to better consequences.

There is a structural factor inherent to war that explains why a positive assessment of the likely consequences of war will always be more problematic and less reliable than the purely negative assessment. As Clausewitz observed, war is subject to an inherent tendency to escalate to levels of violence beyond those that combatants would rationally have chosen or indeed predicted at the outset: 'If one side uses force without compunction, undeterred by the bloodshed it involves, while the other side refrains, the first will gain the upper hand. That side will force the other to follow suit . . . '. 'Each side, therefore, compels its opponent to follow suit; a reciprocal action is started which must lead in theory to extremes'.[12]

Clausewitz's structural observation about the logic of escalation in war is, moreover, backed up by empirical evidence which shows that historically most war leaders have assumed, prior to conflict, that the war on which they were about to embark would be short and relatively easy. Sometimes they are correct. More often they are not, and the war proves to be more protracted, difficult and costly than generally expected. If this is correct, this points to a general and persistent tendency for leaders and war planners to underestimate the costs and overestimate the benefits of war.

Act-consequentialism appears to offer an obvious strategy for justifying preventive wars (or wars more generally). But the appearance is illusory. There are many straightforward cases in which a decision to go to war would unambiguously lead to morally worse consequences than other policy alternatives. But it is exceptionally difficult to meet the epistemological burdens for demonstrating that going to war would lead to *better* consequences than alternatives. Wars are events of enormous historical magnitude, and extreme unpredictability. Action in war is subject to a pervasive tendency toward escalation, that can make even the most careful and good-faith assessments of its projected costs wildly inaccurate. Consequentialist analysis necessarily involves issues of counterfactual history that are quite literally unknowable. In the case of preventive war, the relevant counterfactual questions include whether the feared attack would even have taken place without war—in other words whether a preventive war has 'prevented' anything at all.[13] For governments and citizens seeking to justify a preventive war, act-consequentialism has almost no use.[14]

Rule Consequentialism and the Impasse Problem

When philosophers talk of a consequentialist approach to war, they are often thinking about rule-consequentialism. Unfortunately, rule-consequentialism faces even greater difficulties than act-consequentialism as an ethical theory of war. This should not surprise us. Rule-consequentialism requires assessing the long-term consequences of iterated patterns of behavior, and hence it amplifies further the epistemological weaknesses inherent in act-consequentialism. I argue that rule-consequentialism suffers from two forms of epistemological weakness. First, we have no sufficient empirical data for assessing the truth of rule-consequentialist judgments. Second the rule-consequentialist arguments invoked by philosophers and International Relations theorists to support their conclusions persistently generate what I call the impasse problem: the existence of equally plausible rule-consequentialist arguments for countervailing conclusions.

The rule-consequentialist argument for preventive war is very old. It dates back at least to Cicero who argued in favor of preventive war against the internal threat of Marcus Antonius by observing that 'every evil is easily crushed at its birth; become inveterate it as a rule gathers strength.'[15] Alberico Gentili, the Oxford jurist of the sixteenth century echoed these sentiments: 'it is better to provide that men should not acquire too great power, than to be obliged to seek remedy later, when they have already become too powerful.'[16] Michael Walzer takes as the starting point for his discussion of prevention the argument of Edmond Burke, which develops this theme by invoking the notion of balance of power. According to Burke an effective balance of power between the main states of Europe preserves European liberty by preventing any one state from becoming too dominant, and secondly that fighting early, before the balance has become unstable, is less costly than waiting till the threat becomes imminent.[17]

As David Luban points out, the Bush doctrine as spelled out in the National Security Strategy turns this argument on its head, by claiming that the *imbalance* of power (i.e. US dominance) is worth preserving because it is necessary to protect *American* liberty. But Luban suggests that both variants of the argument can be assimilated to a more general argumentative scheme:

1. that some state of affairs X (balance of power, U.S. dominance, whatever) preserves some important value V (European liberty, U.S. liberty, whatever) and is therefore worth defending even at some cost; and
2. that to fight early, before X begins to unravel, greatly reduces the cost of the defense, while waiting doesn't mean avoiding war (unless one gives up V) but only fighting on a larger scale and at worse odds.[18]

This rule-consequentialist argument seems plausible. However as both Walzer and Luban point out, there is a rule-consequentialist rejoinder that is at least as plausible. The rejoinder is that even if (1) and (2) are true, it would be better on consequentialist grounds for states not to accept them because doing so would expand the grounds for going to war and thereby lead (in Burke's words) to 'innumerable and fruitless wars.' The ultimate consequences of a general rule permitting preventive war would therefore be worse than one that prohibited it.[19] What we are faced with

is what I call the impasse problem: two competing and apparently equally plausible rule-consequentialist interpretations of the preventive-war norm. One interpretation claims that a rule permitting preventive war would lead to better overall consequences because wars fought early would have less human cost, and would protect valuable goods such as national or international liberties. The other interpretation claims that a rule prohibiting preventive war would lead to better overall consequences because a more permissive doctrine would multiply the number of wars fought.

Which interpretation is correct? Luban has three rule-consequentialist arguments for why a general norm permitting preventive war should be rejected. I suggest that each can be matched by an equally plausible rule-consequentialist interpretation for the opposite conclusion, hence the impasse problem is not avoided. I want to stress that my intention is not to endorse these counterarguments as the correct rule-consequentialist assessment of prevention. Rather by showing the ease with which rule-consequentialist arguments can be matched by apparently equally plausible counterargument I wish to draw attention to the spurious character of these arguments' apparent plausibility.

Luban's first argument is that a general right of prevention would make war more likely because it would broaden the category of permissible war. In particular it would justify first strikes by both sides in all the world's most dangerous hotspots. For example, it would justify a first strike by both India and Pakistan, North Korea and Japan, Israel and Syria, and most frighteningly during the Cold War it would have justified preventive strikes by both the United States and the Soviet Union given a favorable opportunity.[20]

But the counterinterpretation of these cases runs as follows: the existence of such hotspots itself imposes substantial moral cost because of the risk and instability they bring to international affairs, and the way they impede valuable economic and cultural exchange. Over the long term, a rule permitting prevention would have positive consequences, by transforming the strategic environment itself in ways that make such dangerous strategic standoffs less likely. Thus, if a norm of prevention had permitted dominant states to hit early and hit hard when a potential rival emerged, many of the hotspots referred to by Luban might never have developed. For example, had the United States used its nuclear monopoly at the end of World War II to act preventively against the Soviet Union, there might never have been a Cold War with the associated risks of global nuclear annihilation. Similarly, one may argue, the other hotspots only pose a danger to the world because the emerging standoff was not nipped in the bud by early preventive action.

Luban's second argument is that a general doctrine of prevention introduces too much ambiguity into the rules of war, which will in turn make war more likely. The reason the doctrine introduces ambiguity is that the judgment as to whether a state constitutes a sufficient threat to justify preventive action necessarily involves what Rawls calls *burdens of judgment* [the inevitability that different (reasonable) people's judgment will diverge] and *infirmities of judgment* (the fact that people's judgment about matters of great moment and high risk is seldom rational).

But it is not clear that increased ambiguity in the rules of war would increase the incidence of war. Michael Byers has argued that ambiguous laws increase the latitude of action for strong states while having little effect on the ability of weak states to engage in military action. This is because ambiguity 'allow[s] power and influence to play a greater role in the application of the law to particular situations.'[21] Strong states can bring to bear various forms of political, economic, and military pressure to influence the assessments pertaining to the application of the law, while still retaining the law as a diplomatic tool to be deployed against weaker states. If this assessment is correct, then one can see how an ambiguous law could increase the overall stability of the international system, especially when (as is now the case) the international system is dominated by one powerful state. By freeing the hand of the strong state to take decisive measures against potential rivals and disruptive smaller states, the rule could have a strong deterrent effect that would mean fewer wars in the long run. Moreover, because the strong will disproportionately influence how the ambiguous criteria for the rule are applied, there is little risk of a general increase in violence among weaker states. Luban's

third argument is linked to the first two. The doctrine of prevention 'actually *makes* rival states into potential threats to each other by permitting preventive invasion of potential adversaries based on risk calculations whose indeterminacy makes them inherently unpredictable by the adversary—and then it licenses attacks by both of them, because now they are potential threats to each other.'[22]

But here we need to know much more about the specific incentive structures in play and how they would cash out in real strategic negotiations. According to standard assumptions of International Relations theory, the primary interest of states is to maintain their own security. Typically states will seek to achieve this through building up their military capability and developing alliances to deter neighbors or rivals from attacking them. This deterrence strategy can result in reasonably long periods of stability and security. But the strategy is not cost free. It can also contribute to the initiation of disastrous conflicts that diminish the security of all states involved, as for example the armament and alliance strategies of the major European powers did in the lead up to World War I.

Luban's argument suggests that a general doctrine of prevention would radically increase the costs of the deterrence strategy by making it much more difficult to develop and maintain a stable relationship of military deterrence. This conclusion contradicts the arguments I have just given which suggest that stabilizing deterrence effects could indeed be increased by recognizing a general doctrine of prevention. But suppose Luban's conclusion is correct. In this case, the effects of a doctrine of prevention could play out in other ways.

In essence, if Luban is correct then the deterrence strategy of military armament and alliance formation would cease to function as a rational strategy for states to maintain their security under a general doctrine of prevention. Given this, states would have to look to alternative strategies to maintain their security. Plausible alternatives would include strategies of mutual assurance and disarmament, for example through the implementation of strong nonaggression treaties and mutual disarmament initiatives backed up by independent inspections and monitoring. It is moreover plausible that the mutual assurance and disarmament strategy would result in less cost overall than the deterrence strategy. Therefore by changing the incentive structures so as to make the current deterrence and armament strategy untenable (if indeed this was the effect), a general doctrine of prevention could still lead to better overall consequences.

Once again we are faced with an impasse between differing and opposed rule-consequentialist interpretations of the doctrine of prevention. As I have said, I certainly do not want to claim that my counterarguments should be accepted as the correct and authoritative rule-consequentialist interpretation of prevention. Nor, indeed, do I need to establish this for my argument to succeed. I simply need to show that they are as plausible as the countervailing interpretations given available information. The relevant question is of course: is there a conclusive empirical basis for ruling out one set of rule-consequentialist arguments or interpretations in favor of those that support their contradictory?

What is most striking in the rule-consequentialist literature on war is the general absence of reference to empirical evidence that could answer these questions.[23] On reflection, it seems obvious why this is. There does not seem to be any empirical evidence capable of verifying rule-consequentialist interpretations of the rules of war. It is certainly possible to subject the historical record of war to statistical analysis (although it is interesting how little interest most rule-consequentialist philosophers show in sustained analysis of the historical record). But at best this can tell us what the incidence of war *was* during periods when the rules of war were interpreted differently. It cannot tell us what the incidence of war *would have been,* had the rules of war been different. For we have no way to control for the effects that differing social, economic, technological, climatic, administrative, and institutional conditions have on the incidence of war. Not only do we not have the required empirical evidence to settle such rule-consequentialist questions, it is unclear even what could count as empirical evidence.

In light of this absence of empirical evidence, rule-consequentialists are compelled to resort to general arguments of the form Luban offers. It is not that these arguments seem implausible. On the contrary they seem very plausible. It is just that there are rule consequentialist arguments for the countervailing position that are equally plausible. Once we recognize this, we can see that the apparent plausibility of these rule-consequentialist arguments is spurious. The arguments are a kind of armchair conjecture, conducted without empirical data or even a clear conception of what would count as empirical data.

Rule-consequentialist arguments, like their act-consequentialist counterparts, can provide no useful justification of preventive war. There is no empirical evidence that could settle the question of which interpretation of the laws of war will lead to the best overall consequences, and the arguments that philosophers and legal theorists use to defend their preferred consequentialist interpretation of the rules of war can be matched, point for point, with equally plausible arguments for the exact opposite conclusion. . . .

PREVENTIVE WAR AND SELF-DEFENSE

I believe that the best way of investigating the justice of preventive war, is to look at the question of whether preventive war can be justified as an act of legitimate self-defense. The notion of self-defense is fundamental to the way we think about the ethics of war, and the National Security Strategy itself casts the issue of prevention as one of self-defense. The right of self-defense is normally taken to require that three conditions be met.

1. Necessity: defensive action must be necessary in the sense that there is no less harmful way to avert the harm or attack.
2. Proportionality: harm inflicted in the course of defensive action must be proportionate to (or not disproportionately greater than) the harm or attack one is seeking to avert.
3. Imminence: the harm or attack one is defending against cannot be a distant or remote one, but must be truly imminent.

The National Security Strategy addresses, at least implicitly, each of these conditions. The condition of imminence is explicitly acknowledged, but it is argued that 'we must adapt the concept of imminent threat to the capabilities and objectives of today's adversaries.'[24] This adapted conception of imminence is clearly meant to include more than the 'visible mobilization of armies, navies, and air forces preparing for attack'[25] and would permit action against 'emerging threats before they are fully formed'[26] and 'even if uncertainty remains as to the time and place of the enemies, attack'.[27]

But this talk of 'adapting' the concept of imminence is, once again, mere rhetoric. Any doctrine which allows the use of force against potential threats that have not yet fully formed and where it is unclear when, or even if, an attack will occur has not adapted the traditional condition of imminence, but has abandoned it. The real challenge of the Bush doctrine, therefore, is not whether the concept of imminence needs reform but whether it needs to be abandoned entirely. To put the question another way: can we can make sense of the right of national self-defense, without the traditional condition of imminence? It is this question I propose to discuss and I hope to show that the notion of imminence lies very deep in the idea of self-defense. Correspondingly, it is very difficult to understand preventive war as a legitimate part of self-defense.

I used to believe otherwise: that the concept of imminence is not fundamental to the right of self-defense. I previously argued that the condition of imminence is subsidiary to the condition of necessity.[28] Imminence, I argued, is derived from necessity because of epistemic constraints on human action. The point is that one cannot *know* that defensive action is necessary, unless the attack one is defending against is really imminent. If on the other hand, one had superhuman knowledge and could foresee that the only way to prevent some future wrongful harm or attack was to engage in defensive measures, then one would not be required to wait till the attack was imminent: necessity would be enough.

If such an interpretation were correct, then it would open a way to allowing prevention as a legitimate form of self-defense. The view would certainly place an enormous, and probably unsustainable, burden on the intelligence used as a basis for going to war, for one would have to be certain that the defensive measures were really necessary to prevent the harm in question. But the idea of a preventive war of

self-defense against a nonimminent threat would not be ruled out at the level of moral theory.

I now think that this view is wrong, and that the condition of imminence is much more fundamental to the right of self-defense. To see this we must look into the theoretical underpinnings of the right of self-defense. The right of self-defense as we currently have it in law and moral theory, has been influenced by at least three distinct traditions of thought. The first is the consequentialist tradition. The second tradition views self-defense as action conditioned by a kind of psychological necessity. The third tradition views the aggressor as morally liable to harm by an act of legitimate self-defense and explains this liability on the basis of his fault or culpability for initiating the attack. As I have discussed consequentialism above, I will say no more about it here. But I do intend to examine the role played by imminence in the other two traditions, both of which have been influential on modern ideas of legitimate self-defense.

Self-Defense as Necessity

The connection between self-defense and necessity is an old and deep one. In fact, in some jurisdictions self-defense is referred to simply as 'necessary defense'. Necessity in this context is close to the legal concept of duress. It is a form of excuse stemming from the fact that a wrongful action is viewed as psychologically necessary or unavoidable in situations of extreme danger or pressure.[29] . . .

What underlies this necessity approach is a compassionate stance towards the frailty of human nature. Given the kinds of creature we are, there are some things (such as abstaining from taking action sufficient to save our own life) that we simply cannot be expected to do. As Aristotle says they 'strain human nature to breaking-point and no one would endure.'[30] If it is to be just and humane, the law must take account of this, and not hold us responsible for actions taken under the enormous psychological pressures of the shadow of death. This psychological necessity view of self-defense was reflected in the medieval law of *se defendendo*. According to this law one was not to be punished for killing in the course of a fight, if one quite literally 'had one's back against the wall', and taking the opponent's life was the only way of saving one's own.

Now one might think that such a conception of self-defense can have little connection with the laws of war, for states are not psychological entities that feel fear in the way that individual persons do. But it is precisely this account which is suggested by the most famous legal text on the right of national self-defense: the Caroline doctrine. This text states that a nation's right of self-defense is based on a' . . . . necessity of self-defense, instant, overwhelming, leaving no choice of means, and no moment for deliberation'.[31] Although states do not experience the psychological fear of a real person, perhaps they can experience something analogous.

Viewing self-defense in this way, does however, have a number of significant and somewhat unpalatable consequences. The first is that contrary to modern legal theory, self-defense is viewed not as a justification but merely as an excuse. An act is justified if it is the right or permissible thing to do in the circumstances. An act is excused if it was the wrong thing to do, but the agent ought not in the circumstances be held fully responsible for the act. . . .

The second consequence is that self-defense on this view takes a form which is rather peculiar to the modern eye. The modern right of self-defense encompasses, in most jurisdictions, the defense of others including strangers. But because on the psychological necessity view self-defense is grounded in the idea of action under extreme fear or pressure, the excuse is only available for defending certain kinds of person. The medieval claim of *se defendendo* was only available if one was defending one's own life or that of close friends or family. Only then were the psychological pressures considered sufficiently grave to provide an excuse for murder.

Thirdly, the necessity view makes no discriminations based on fault as to who can claim the excuse of self-defense. The excuse is available to anyone facing the extinction of their life, be they innocent victim or culpable aggressor of the original attack.

What is clear, however, is that the psychological necessity view of self-defense is quite incompatible with the idea of a preventive war. For on this view it is precisely the imminence of the potentially fatal attack and the extreme psychological pressure this imposes that makes defensive acts excusable. When the attack is remote and merely potential there is no psychological necessity of this form. What is required on the necessity view is precisely suggested by the language of the Caroline doctrine: '. . . necessity of self-defense, instant, overwhelming, leaving no choice of means, and no moment for deliberation'.[32] In contrast (and almost in contradiction) to this the National Security Strategy explicitly states: 'We will always proceed deliberately, weighing the consequences of our actions.'[33] This brings out an important feature of preventive wars; they are wars of choice. Their function, strategically, is to engage the enemy at a time and on terms of one's own choosing. As such they are antithetical to the tradition of thought on self-defense which views that right as grounded in the overwhelming psychological necessity of facing an imminent lethal attacker.

If a doctrine of preventive war is to be integrated into self-defense then it must be on the basis of a very different theory of self-defense to that of psychological necessity. In fact, the most plausible theory of self-defense *is* very different to the necessity view. It is a theory which views self-defense as a justification grounded in a conception of human rights and concomitant notions of liability to harm.

Self-Defense and Rights

Here I do no more than sketch out the rights-based theory of self-defense which I have defended in detail elsewhere.[34] One starts with the observation that human beings have rights. Paramount among these is the right not to be killed or subject to significant bodily harm. But killing and harming another human is precisely what is done in acts of self-defense including the fighting of a defensive war. This raises a simple but profound question for the theory of self-defense: what is it that makes the person against whom one is using defensive force liable to be harmed in this way? Some part of our theory of self-defense must account for the fact that an aggressor has lost or forfeited or fails to possess the right to life when he is killed in defense.

The best way to account for this moral liability to harm on the part of aggressors is to point to the fact that they commit wrong by engaging in an act of aggression. One way to understand this is to observe that many rights are implicitly reciprocal in their nature. Thus on a plausible understanding of rights, one only has the right to life so long as one respects the right to life of others. At the moment one wrongfully attacks the life of another, one becomes morally vulnerable or liable to being killed in self-defense. This explains why we believe that it is permissible to kill an aggressor in self-defense but not to kill an innocent bystander even if this were the only way to save one's life. For an innocent bystander has done us no wrong and therefore has the right not to be killed by us, even if this were the only way to save our life.

If one accepts that the permission to kill in self-defense is tied to some wrongdoing on the part of the aggressor, then it is easy to see why there is a problem with preventive acts of self-defense. In a preventive war, one attacks and kills those who have not yet committed an act of wrongful aggression against you. Without the presence of active aggression it is difficult to see how there can exist the liability to harm which seems to be such a crucial part of the classic model of self-defense.

Against this, it might be objected that in cases of preventive self-defense one has good reason to believe that the persons one is using force against are *about to* engage in wrongful aggression. Is not this sufficient to establish their liability to be harmed? If you have good reason to believe that they will act aggressively, why must one wait till they actually engage in aggression before using defensive force?

To answer this question, we may consider an analogy with liability for punishment in criminal law. The analogy is not perfect because self-defense is not itself a form of punishment. Nonetheless there are sufficient similarities in the grounds of liability for punishment and self-defense to make the comparison instructive. In order for there to exist liability for punishment one must establish both a criminal intent and the existence of a criminal act—both *mens rea* and *actus reus*. Without criminal intent and the existence of a criminal act a person may not be punished even if we have good reason to think that he will commit a certain crime in the future.

In the movie 'Minority Report', magical clairvoyants have the ability to see infallibly into the future. Law enforcement agencies are able to use these predictions to arrest and punish those whom the clairvoyants had predicted will commit murder, before they ever have the chance to commit the crime. This procedure is viewed as efficient law enforcement in this imaginary future world. But most of us feel a deep moral repugnance toward such an idea (this indeed is the point of the movie), and this stems from the fact that it is unjust to punish someone who has not yet *done anything* to merit punishment (even if we grant some supernaturally reliable prediction that they *will* do it).

On the rights-based theory of self-defense a similar problem arises with preventive self-defense. A Minority Report style supernatural example is not required to see this. Imagine that I know you have a violently jealous nature and that if you ever discovered that I have been sleeping with your wife, you would almost certainly take your revenge by killing me. Suppose now that I see you reading through my private papers and that among those papers is a letter proving my infidelity. As soon as you read that letter you are almost certain to form and act upon a murderous intent. But it seems clear in this case that I would be justified in using defensive force only after this had happened. Until such time, there is nothing you have done that makes you liable to my defensive force. Preventive self-defense is therefore ruled out, because you retain your full rights not to be attacked or harmed.

Examples like these show us that the conditions of self-defense (necessity, proportionality, and imminence) function in a fundamentally different way within a forfeiture-of-right theory of self-defense than they do within a consequentialist theory of self-defense. Within a consequentialist theory, the conditions of self-defense are interpreted so as to ensure that the balance of harms in a self-defense situation is maximally conducive to overall welfare. It is therefore appropriate to construe the conditions in a way that is probabilistic. For example, a highly harmful potential attack with a low probability of occurring might yield the same defensive justification as a less harmful attack with a high probability of occurring. But within a forfeit of right account of self-defense, the function of the self-defense conditions is quite different. Although on this account the necessity, proportionality, and imminence conditions often function to reduce harm, they are not intended to reliably minimize overall harm, as on the consequentialist model (e.g. one is entitled to kill virtually any number of culpable aggressors if this is necessary to save one's own life). Instead their central function is to ensure that the person or persons against whom defensive force is used *are really morally liable* to the infliction of force, and that the level of harm inflicted on each aggressor is proportionate to his or her individual moral liability.

The imminence requirement, then, does more than simply bolster the necessity requirement in conditions of imperfect knowledge or ensure that the outcome of conflict situations are welfare maximizing. By requiring that self-defense cannot be undertaken until an unjust attack is imminent, the condition guarantees that those who are subject to defensive force are morally liable to it because they are currently engaged in an unjust aggressive attack. It would seem then, that the condition of imminence has an essential not derivative role in the theory of self-defense and that preventive self-defense is thereby ruled out at the level of moral theory.

NOTES

1. I am indebted to many people for careful and helpful criticism and comments particularly Henry Shue, Jeff McMahan, Alan Buchanan, Bob Goodin, members of the Princeton Center for Human Values research seminar especially Charles Beitz, Michael Smith, Stephen Macedo, Philip Pettit, and most especially all the other participants of the Changing Character of War workshop including the fellow contributors to this volume.

2. National Security Strategy of the United States of America, September 2002, p. 2.

3. The doctrine of preventive war was not the stated legal justification for the war, which instead invoked rights granted under earlier Security Council resolutions dating from the termination of the first Gulf War. Nonetheless, the doctrine of prevention and the reasoning behind it figured strongly in the debate over the war and its public justification.

4. David Luban, 'Preventive War', *Philosophy and Public Affairs,* vol. 32, no. 3, 2004, 207–48.

5. Michael Walzer, *Just and Unjust Wars,* Basic Books, 3rd edn, 2000, p. 75.

6. See, e.g. David Luban, 'Preventive War', *Philosophy and Public Affairs,* vol. 32, no. 3, 2004, 207–48, pp. 212–14.

7. Unilateral preventive action in this context refers to the use of force by a state or group of states without Security Council authorization. The Security Council is mandated to authorize preventive force in order to maintain international peace and security under Chapter VII of the UN Charter.

8. Michael Walzer, *Just and Unjust Wars,* Basic Books, 1977, p. 77.

9. Of course a sophisticated form of consequentialism will consider a range of morally relevant consequences beyond the crude metric of lives lost or saved. It would consider, for example, the moral disvalue of the potential subjection of many millions of people to a regime as deeply unjust as Nazism. It may also be the case that genocide is morally worse than the murder of an equivalent number of unrelated people. But even on a sophisticated form of consequentialism it is very difficult to see how a consequentialist could justify World War II given the magnitude of its actual moral costs. Consider how one of the ultimate consequences of the war was to usher in the Soviet Union's brutal half-century dominion over the states of Eastern Europe.

10. See Eric Hobsbawn, *The Age of Extremes,* Michael Joseph, London, 1994, pp. 43–4.

11. My argument concerns a consequentialist assessment of *war.* I make no claims about international use of force that falls below the threshold of war.

12. Clausewitz, Carl Von, *On War,* Michael Howard and Peter Paret (eds), Princeton University Press, Princeton, 1976, b. 1, ch. 1, §3 pp. 75–6 and 77.

13. As Walter Sinnott-Armstrong points out in this volume if the effects of war are as indeterminate and unpredictable as I have suggested, this raises the difficult question of how *any* rational military or political planning is possible. What precisely are planners doing when they assess that going to war would be, for instance, in the national interest? I think that much military planning is subject to similar difficulties, and many policymakers, if they are honest will say as much. But it is also important to note that the criteria according to which most policymakers assess military decisions are substantially narrower in scope than those proposed by consequentialism. For example, judging what is in the national interest is a much narrower (and hence easier) question than judging what will generate best overall long-term consequences (consider: what is in the national interest need not be in the interest of all or even the majority of the members of the nation). Often the consequences that matter to policymakers are more narrow still—the consequences of a given military action for their own political party, department, or career.

14. An alternative way of interpreting this argument is to view it not as a critique of consequentialism per se, but as a strong rule-consequentialist argument for pacifism, or at least a moral presumption against war close to pacifism. Walter Sinnott-Armstrong considers this possibility in his chapter in

[*Preemption*, Shue and Rodin, eds., p. 211], and I think that if the epistemological difficulties of consequentialism could be overcome, this would indeed be its likely conclusion.

15. Cicero, *Works,* XIV, Loeb Classical Library, London and Cambridge, MA, 1979, 16–17 (*Pro Milone,* 10–11).

16. Quoted in Richard Tuck, *The Rights of War and Peace: Political Thought and the International Order From Grotius to Kant,* Oxford University Press, Oxford, 1999, p. 18.

17. Michael Walzer, *Just and Unjust Wars,* Basic Books, 3rd edn, 2000, pp. 76–7.

18. David Luban, 'Preventive War', *Philosophy and Public Affairs,* vol. 32, no. 3, 2004, 207–48, p. 220.

19. Michael Walzer, *Just and Unjust Wars,* p. 77; David Luban, 'Preventive War', *Philosophy and Public Affairs,* vol. 32, no. 3, 2004, 207–48, pp. 223ff.

20. David Luban, 'Preventive War', *Philosophy and Public Affairs,* vol. 32, no. 3, 2004, 207–48, p. 226–7.

21. Michael Byers, 'Preemptive Self-Defense: Hegemony, Equality and Strategies of Legal Change', *The Journal of Political Philosophy,* vol. 11, no. 2, 2003, 171–90, p. 182.

22. David Luban, 'Preventive War', *Philosophy and Public Affairs,* vol. 32, no. 3, 2004, 207–48, p. 227.

23. Luban does gesture at one point to what 'experience has taught us', without explaining either which experience he has in mind or how he supposes that it has taught us.

(David Luban, 'Preventive War', *Philosophy and Public Affairs,* vol. 32, no. 3, 2004, 207–48, p. 225.)

24. National Security Strategy of the United States of America, September 2002, p. 15

25. Ibid.

26. Ibid., v.

27. Ibid., 15.

28. See David Rodin, *War and Self-Defense,* Oxford University Press, Oxford, 2001, p. 41.

29. The term 'necessity' can have two meanings in moral and legal theory. The first is the excuse under discussion here. The second is the condition found *inter alia* within just war theory and the law of self-defense which requires that an action may only be undertaken if there is no less costly or harmful way of achieving the same result.

30. Aristotle, *Nicomachean Ethics,* Crisp, R. (tr.), Cambridge: Cambridge University Press, 2000, 1110*a*.

31. Quoted in Yoram Dinstein, *War, Aggression and Self-Defense,* 4th edn, Cambridge University Press, Cambridge, 1988, p. 249.

32. Quoted in Yoram Dinstein, *War, Aggression and Self-Defense,* p. 249.

33. National Security Strategy of the United States of America, September 2002, p. 16.

34. David Rodin, *War and Self-Defense,* Oxford, Oxford University Press, 2002, ch. 4.

READING QUESTIONS

1. How does Rodin argue that act consequentialist defenses of preventive war fail?
2. Explain the "impasse" problem that Rodin uses in criticizing rule consequentialist attempts to address the moral justification of preventive war.
3. Rodin claims that he used to hold that the concept of imminence is fundamental to the right of self-defense. Why does he now reject this view?
4. What objections does Rodin raise against self-defense understood as a psychological necessity as a basis for justifying preventive wars?
5. Why does Rodin think that rights-based defenses of preventive war are problematic?

DISCUSSION QUESTIONS

1. Discuss how might one respond to Rodin's epistemological objection to the act consequentialist approach to preventive war.
2. Rodin argues that appeal to the right of self-defense cannot be used to justify preventive wars. He bases his argument on claims about the conditions under which one is liable for criminal punishment. Discuss whether there are important disanalogies between conditions applying to the justification of criminal punishment and conditions under which (for reasons of self-defense) a preventive war would be morally justified.

WALTER SINNOTT-ARMSTRONG

Preventive War—What Is It Good For?

Approaching the issue of the moral justification from an act consequentialist perspective, Walter Sinnott-Armstrong defends this approach to preventive war against Rodin's charge of "uselessness" presented in the preceding selection. Sinnott-Armstrong then proceeds to critically consider the just war approach to preventive war, in particular, the "just cause" provision of *jus ad bellum* concerning the moral justification of going to war. He also critically evaluates appeals to imminence, which is used to distinguish preemptive from preventive wars, and argues that meeting this condition is not necessary for an anticipatory war to be morally justified. He concludes by considering the implications of consequentialism regarding preventive war.

Recommended Reading: consequentialism, chap. 1, sec. 2A, and the presentation of just-war theory in this chapter's introduction.

After the horrific terrorist attack on September 11, 2001, US President George W. Bush announced a policy of preventive war. True to his word, Bush soon implemented his policy.[1]

The first war occurred in Afghanistan. This war was aimed partly at punishing al-Qaeda terrorists and partly at helping the people of Afghanistan by liberating them from the Taliban and creating a democracy with greater freedom and prosperity. Hence, this war was not purely preventive. Still, one of its goals was to prevent attacks on the United States and its allies by terrorists from training camps in Afghanistan, and Bush admitted that no attacks by Afghanistan were imminent. To that extent the war in Afghanistan was preventive.[2]

Bush's next war was in Iraq. The Iraq War had several announced aims, including the enforcement of UN resolutions and international law as well as helping the people in Iraq partly by removing Saddam Hussein and introducing democracy. Of course, critics charged that Bush's real aims were to control Iraq's oil, to help his cronies make money, and to avenge or surpass his father, who had failed to subdue Iraq in 1991. In any case, both sides agreed that one of the main announced goals of the Iraq War was to prevent or reduce distant future terrorist attacks on the United States and its allies, especially attacks with WMD. If this announced goal really was Bush's goal, which has been questioned, then to that extent the Iraq War was a preventive war. That is how I will view the Iraq War here.[3]

Many opponents of the Iraq War responded by denying that any preventive war is ever justified. This reaction goes too far in my opinion. Bush's preventive war in Iraq is morally wrong, and his policy is too broad, but some exceptional preventive wars can still be morally justified.

To see which and why, we need to explore the general moral theories behind these opposing stances. Most of Bush's arguments for his policy and the Iraq War are about consequences. Bush usually emphasized consequences for the United

From Walter Sinnott-Armstrong, "Preventive War—What Is It Good For?" in *Preemption: Military Action and Moral Justification*, H. Shue and D. Rodin, eds. Oxford: Oxford University Press, pp. 202–221.

States, but sometimes he adds consequences for others, including allies in the coalition and Iraqis and others in the Middle East. Either way, Bush dwells on consequences. As his National Security Strategy announces, 'We will always proceed deliberately, weighing the consequences of our actions.'[4] In contrast, Bush's critics often argue that the Iraq War violates absolute rules against certain general kinds of acts that are defined independently of consequences. The most often-cited rule is a prohibition on preventive war. In their view, preventive wars are always morally wrong by their very nature, regardless of their consequences.

This practical debate mirrors a deep divide in philosophical moral theory. Consequentialists hold that what we morally ought to do depends on consequences alone. Nothing else counts, except insofar as it affects consequences. Deontologists claim that what we morally ought to do also depends on other factors (such as the agent's intention or the kind of action) that are independent of consequences. Some deontologists allow consequences to matter as well, but they still think that other factors sometimes make something morally wrong even when it has better consequences.

Although Bush's arguments recall the consequentialist approach, Bush is not a consistent consequentialist. He freely cites deontological rules against some actions he opposes, such as abortion and stem cell research. Even in the case of war, Bush alludes to a right to national defense, which can conflict with consequentialism. Nonetheless, it might seem that consequentialists would support Bush's war and policy if they agreed with him about the consequences of his war and policy, whereas deontologists could still oppose the war and policy on non-consequentialist grounds.

This appearance might lead Bush's critics away from consequentialism so that they would have something left to say against Bush if they reached an impasse in arguing about the consequences of the Iraq War. That retreat would be a mistake. The strongest arguments against Bush's war and policy are consequentialist, not deontological. To show why, I shall develop and defend a version of consequentialism about war. Then I shall criticize the relevant part

of the most common deontological alternative, just war theory. Finally, I shall apply all of this theory to preventive war in general and Bush's war and policy in particular.

DEEP MORALITY *VERSUS* PUBLIC RULES

My argument will hinge on a certain characterization of the issue. I will assume that both consequentialist and deontological theories are about objective moral wrongness. The question they address is whether certain wars really are morally wrong, not whether people think that they are morally wrong or even whether it is reasonable to think that they are morally wrong. Moreover, these competing theories concern what McMahan calls the deep morality of war.[5] These theories try to specify conditions that must be met for war not to be morally wrong. They do not claim that their conditions should be written directly into public laws of war that are or should be accepted by international groups or enforced by international courts.

Such public laws might need to be formulated differently from deep morality in order to be useful in practice. For example, as McMahan argues, many combatants are innocent and nonthreatening, whereas many noncombatants are guilty and threatening, so the deep morality of war should not distinguish combatants from noncombatants. It still might be too difficult in practice to tell who is innocent or threatening, so the public laws of war might need to forbid attacks on noncombatants but not combatants. In such ways, practical public laws of war can come apart from the deep morality of war. I will then be concerned mainly with the deep morality of war.[6]

A consequentialist theory of the deep morality of war can admit that public rules of war should be formulated in deontological terms. Such public rules might have better consequences because actual agents would make too many mistakes in applying public rules formulated directly in terms of consequences. Even if so, the deep morality of war still might be consequentialist because the public rules are justified only by their consequences. Thus, theorists who claim only that deontological rules should be publicly accepted and enforced do not deny what is claimed by a consequentialist theory of the deep morality of war. To disagree with consequentialism on that topic, deontologists need to argue that some factor independent of consequences determines which wars are really morally wrong.

Some just war theorists might not make any such claim. They might talk only about public rules and not consider deep morality at all. If so, consequentialists have no quarrel with them. That kind of just war theory is simply beside the point here. However, many other just war theorists and deontologists do claim that their rules determine which wars are morally wrong, and they deny that consequences alone determine moral wrongness. Those are the just war theorists whom consequentialists oppose and whom I will discuss here. . . .

CONSEQUENTIALIST MORAL THEORY

My consequentialist theory of the deep morality of war is an application of a more general approach to morality.[7] Consequentialism as a general moral theory claims that the moral status of an act depends only on consequences. I favor act-consequentialism which claims that an agent morally ought not to do an act if and only if that act has significantly worse consequences than any available alternative. Consequences are worse when they contain more death, pain, disability (including lack of freedom), and possibly injustice and rights violations, considering everyone equally.

This act-consequentialism contrasts with the rule-consequentialism adopted by other[s] . . . including David Luban.[8] Rule-consequentialism is the claim that whether a particular act is morally wrong depends on whether that act violates a general rule that is justified by its own consequences. Rule consequentialism is indirect in the sense that the moral status of

one thing (an act) depends on the consequences of a different thing (a rule). In contrast, act consequentialism is direct insofar as it morally judges one thing by the consequences of that thing itself.

The first problem for rule utilitarianism is its indirectness. Why should the moral status of one thing depend on the consequences of something else? More specifically, since a rule as an abstract entity cannot have consequences, what are called the consequences of the rule are really consequences of most or all people in a certain group endorsing, teaching, following, and/or enforcing that rule. Rule consequentialism, thus, makes the moral status of one particular act by one particular agent in one particular set of circumstances depend on consequences of separate acts by separate agents in separate circumstances. I see no adequate reason for such indirection.

Moreover, any particular act falls under many general rules. A war, for example, might violate a rule against preventive war while also being the only way to avoid violating another rule that requires protecting citizens. I see no non-arbitrary way to determine which rules are the ones whose consequences matter for judging an act that is distinct from all of those rules.

Rules are also used in many ways in many contexts. Rules might be used to teach children or to award damages in international courts. Different rules might be justified in different circumstances, often because of varying dangers of misuse. Act consequentialists can recognize this variety and say that it is morally right to use one rule for teaching children and a different rule for international courts. Rule consequentialists, however, need to pick one role for rules as the one and only central role that determines whether a particular act is or is not morally wrong. I see no good reason why one role would be decisive for all moral judgments, so rule consequentialists again cannot avoid arbitrariness.

Admittedly, moral theorists must allow some roles for rules, but act consequentialists can do so. Just as they assess acts directly by consequences of those acts, so they assess rules directly by consequences of using those rules. Act consequentialists can (and usually do) also admit that people normally ought to decide what to do not by calculating consequences but, instead, by consulting rules. This move does not turn act consequentialism into rule consequentialism, because act consequentialists can still insist that an act is morally wrong even when its agent used the best rules as a guide or decision procedure if the particular act fails their standard or criterion of the right, because it causes more harm than some alternative.

PROBLEMS FOR CONSEQUENTIALISM

Critics propose a slew of counterexamples to act consequentialism. A popular case involves transplanting organs from one healthy person to save five other people. This and most other alleged counterexamples, however, depend on secrecy. It would not make the world better if people knew it was going on. Thus, such counterexamples do not apply to consequentialism about war, since wars are hard to keep secret.[9]

Other critics of consequentialism cite common-sense principles that are supposed to be obvious and exceptionless, such as the claim that it is always morally wrong to intentionally kill an innocent person. However, wars are filled with emergencies that create exceptions. In the Vietnam War, the Vietcong sometimes tied explosives to the back of a young child and told the child that a certain group of American soldiers had candy. The child ran to the soldiers to get the candy. The soldiers sometimes had no way to save their lives except to shoot the child before the child got too close. They were killing (or at least harming) the child as a means to save their own and others' lives, even though they knew the child was totally innocent. Soldiers usually felt horrible about such acts, and their feelings are understandable, but their acts were not morally wrong. Thus, the commonsense principle is not exceptionless after all, and it cannot be used to refute consequentialism about war.

More generally, such principles and counterexamples depend on moral intuitions. Moral intuitions in contexts of war are particularly unreliable, because

they are notoriously subject to disagreement as well as distortion by partiality, culture, and strong emotions, such as fear.[10] Our moral intuitions evolved to fit situations in everyday life that are very different from war. Hence, any objections that depend on such moral intuitions lose their force when applied to consequentialism about war.

Critics might respond that our moral intuitions are reliable and run counter to consequentialism outside war. I would be happy to defend consequentialism in general on another occasion. For now it is enough if consequentialism can be defended as a criterion of what is right in war.

The most serious remaining objection to consequentialism about war is epistemological. This objection arises elsewhere, but it is particularly pressing in war, because wars are so unpredictable.[11] It is hard to predict in advance how many people will die on either side of a war. This problem would not be serious if the point were only that we often cannot be sure that a war is justified on consequentialist terms. Everyone should agree that there are many cases where we do not know what is morally right.

Rodin thinks the point goes deeper, because consequentialism is 'useless' even in 'clear' cases. The Allies' war against Nazi Germany is often presented as the clearest example of a justified war. Rodin argues, however, that it is not clear whether even that war minimized bad consequences:

> The Nazi regime was brutal and aggressive: it systematically murdered approximately 6 million innocent people, and subjected many millions more to a regime of extraordinary moral repugnance. But the war itself cost somewhere in the region of 55 million lives. In addition it made 40 million persons homeless, caused incalculable destruction to the world's cultural and material wealth, and had the after-effect of initiating the Soviet Union's brutal half-century dominion over Eastern Europe. This was a horrific price to pay for stopping Nazi Germany. It is certainly not obvious on strict consequentialist grounds it was a price worth paying.[12]

The challenge seems simple: The war against the Nazis is clearly morally justified, but it would not be clearly morally justified if consequentialism were correct, so consequentialism is not correct.

Consequentialists can respond in several ways. One possibility is to deny that the war against the Nazis is 'an easy case'. Any act that causes so much death and destruction is at least questionable. Indeed, it was questioned by many opponents of US entry into the war and by many pacifists during World War II. And even if it does seem easy to assess this war, consequentialism might show us that it is not as easy as it seems. The fact that consequentialism raises serious doubts about cases that previously seemed easy might show how illuminating consequentialism is. That is a virtue, not a vice, of consequentialism.[13]

Consequentialists can add that, compared to other wars, it is relatively clear that war against the Nazis minimized bad consequences. The Nazis did not merely kill six million Jews. They also killed millions of non-Jews. They had aggressive plans to continue occupying more and more territory. Resistance was inevitable and would lead to more killing. If the Nazis took over Europe, then there would also be loss not only of life but also of freedom and other values. Europeans would have lived in constant fear of arbitrary execution or imprisonment. Their 'regime of extraordinary moral repugnance' would have continued for much longer than the war.[14] Moreover, if the Nazis had been allowed to rule Europe without opposition, they could have built up strength and continued their expansion. The larger wave of fascism that accompanied the rise of the Nazis would most likely have spread elsewhere, leading to more wars. When all these bad consequences are considered together, it seems relatively clear (or at least reasonable to conclude) that refusing to fight the Nazis would probably have cost far more than fifty-five million lives over the long run.

Consider also the perspective of a single country. The United States, for example, did not have a choice between war and no war. There was going to be a war as soon as Hitler invaded his neighbors. The only options for the United States were (a) a war between the Nazis and the Allies without the United States or (b) a war between the Nazis and the Allies with the United States. Option (a) had a higher probability of Hitler taking over Europe, including Britain, and then continuing to expand

the Third Reich. Option (b) reduced that probability even though it increased the chances of US losses. I see little reason to doubt that option (b) has less bad consequences overall than option (a). That comparison is all that is needed for consequentialists to conclude that the United States was morally justified in entering the war. Similar comparisons for other countries could show why each of the Allies was justified in joining up.

We also need to ask why the costs of the war against the Nazis were so high. Many historians argue that part of the reason is that the United States took too long to get involved. If so, consequentialists can say that for the United States to join the war in 1941 was better than not joining the war ever or until later, but joining the war in 1941 was also not as good as joining the war sooner. This example might then suggest consequentialist reasons for preventive war, contrary to any blanket deontological prohibition.

Of course, we cannot be certain about any of this. It is possible that the war against the Nazis did more harm than good. However, that is unlikely, and we have to live with probabilities here as elsewhere. Consequentialists need to admit that they are often unsure about the right thing to do, especially with regard to war. Is this a problem? No, because we often are and should be unsure whether to enter into war.

This admission is not enough, according to Rodin, because it is unclear even what could count as empirical evidence for any conclusion that a war minimizes bad consequences.[15] However, the evidence is clear. Every bit of pain, death, and disability in a war is a bit of evidence for the moral wrongness of that war. Of course, every bit of pain, death, and disability that is prevented by a war is a bit of evidence against the moral wrongness of the war. The problem is not in finding evidence but in weighing all of the evidence together. It is not clear how to do that, but many people seem to focus on one or a small number of reasons that strike them as more likely and important, to discount possibilities that are unlikely or balanced by opposite possibilities, and to remain open to new considerations. The process is hardly mechanical, but it is still based on evidence. Anyway, however they do it, many people do somehow succeed in making decisions by weighing together many and varied long-term consequences (or, at least, by using defeasible heuristics). Military planners do it. So do everyday people who choose careers, get married, or decide to have children. Since we make such choices reasonably in everyday life, it is not clear why we cannot also make such choices reasonably in war.

Admittedly, as Rodin says, 'Consequentialism is frequently a deeply disappointing guide.'[16] Still, this does not make consequentialism 'useless'. Even if we could not weigh the consequences of any war as costly as the war against the Nazis, we still might be justified in believing that other less costly wars are not morally wrong. And even if we were never justified in believing that any war has good consequences overall, we still might be justified in believing that certain wars *are* morally wrong. We can know, for example, that it was morally wrong for Nazi Germany to invade Poland. Such negative judgments provide guidance insofar as they tell us what not to do. These suppositions might lead to the conclusion that we are never justified in believing that any war is morally right, but we can still be justified in believing that some wars are morally wrong. If so, consequentialism leads to an epistemic variation on pacifism. That conclusion is not obviously implausible, if the suppositions are granted.

Still, I am not as pessimistic about our epistemic abilities as Rodin is. It strikes me as reasonable to believe that the war against the Nazis prevented more harm than it caused. I admit uncertainty, but that need not force me to give up my belief or even my meta-belief that my belief is reasonable and justified. Admittedly, consequentialists still need some way to make decisions in the face of uncertainty. . . . I wish I could be more definitive, but I can only admit that I, along with all other moral philosophers (deontologists as well as consequentialists), need to develop better ways of dealing with the crucial and pervasive issue of uncertainty. Luckily, since my act consequentialism provides a criterion of the right instead of a decision procedure, I can set this issue of uncertainty aside for now.

Other consequentialists might try to avoid problems of uncertainty by claiming that moral wrongness depends not on actual consequences but, instead, on foreseen or reasonably foreseeable consequences. If so, consequentialists do not have to argue that the war against the Nazis actually did minimize bad consequences. All they have to claim is that the Allies believed or had reason to believe that this war would prevent more harm than it would cause. If they could not have expected, for example, the Soviet domination of Eastern Europe after World War II, then those bad consequences could not show that the war was morally wrong on their view.

However, consequentialists who count only expected or expectable consequences run into problems of their own. Such consequentialists have trouble answering, 'Foreseen or foreseeable *by whom?*' If an observer foresees horrific consequences that the agent cannot foresee, the observer should not say that the agent ought to do the act with horrific consequences.[17] Moreover, in a collective action, such as a war, different people would be able to foresee different consequences. Hence, if moral wrongness depended on foreseeable consequences, it would make no sense to ask whether the war was morally wrong without qualification. Finally, it is hard to understand why the true moral status of an act would depend on its agent's false beliefs, even if reasonable. When an act has overall bad consequences that its agent could not have reasonably foreseen, the agent should not be blamed or criticized morally as an agent, but the act itself can still be morally wrong. Every moral theory needs to distinguish agents and acts, and the most natural way to recognize this distinction is to let foreseeable consequences determine whether the agent is blameworthy and actual consequences determine whether the act ought to be done.

For such reasons, I am inclined to think that the moral rightness of wars depends on their actual consequences, including counterfactual consequences or what would have happened if a different act had been actual. However, if I had to give up that position and count foreseeable consequences instead, I would not be terribly upset. What is important is that the moral status of a war depends only on consequences of that war rather than on any rule or factor that is independent of consequences.

JUST WAR THEORY

Despite its virtues, consequentialism is not as popular as its main rival, just war theory. It is difficult to discuss just war theory as a whole because it contains so many parts and comes in so many versions. . . .

Some just war theories propose only public rules of war. These versions might seem to conflict with consequentialism, because their public rules refer to deontological factors other than consequences. However, as I said, consequentialists can accept such public rules and even justify them by their consequences. Hence, just war theories that are only about public rules do not conflict with consequentialism. I am interested in versions of just war theory that challenge consequentialism. Thus, although just war theories about public rules might be correct and important, they are simply not my topic here.

Just war theories conflict with consequentialism only when they make claims about the deep morality of war. Just war theories of deep morality specify conditions that must be met for a war to be not merely just but morally justified overall. These conditions are normally divided into three parts: *jus ad bellum, jus in bello,* and *jus post bellum.*[18] What concerns us here is *jus ad bellum*—when it is or is not morally wrong to go to war. Within that subdivision, the condition that is most relevant to preventive war is just cause.

Just Cause

The condition of just cause says that it is morally wrong for anyone to wage war without a just cause. But that cannot be all there is to it. Even consequentialists grant that wars need some just cause in order to be morally justified, since wars have bad consequences, so they cannot make the world better overall unless they have compensating benefits. Consequentialists and just war theorists also agree that the just cause must be important enough to overcome the strong presumption against war. The conflict between consequentialism and just war theory arises only when just war theorists specify exactly which causes can justify war.

Which causes are just causes? Wars have been fought for many reasons: defense of self or allies or others against external attack, enforcement of international law or punishment for past aggression, to stop internal atrocities or defend human rights, to spread a religion or form of government, for economic gain or glory, out of hatred of the enemy or love of battle, and so on. Just war theorists need to specify which of these candidates are just causes and, hence, adequate to justify war given the other conditions in their theory. They also need to say why these candidates are just causes and why the others are not. This task will not be easy. Many of these candidates are controversial. Emotions, partiality, and culture are likely to distort intuitions. And just war theorists cannot specify just causes by reference to consequences without, in effect, giving in to consequentialism. So it is not clear how just war theorists can justify their claims.

Some just war theorists might think that they can avoid these problems by limiting their claims to the clearest case: self-defense.[19] However, even if everyone agreed that self-defense is sufficient to justify war given other conditions, its sufficiency would not show that it is necessary. Other causes might also be sufficient. Hence, just war theorists who talk only about self-defense cannot argue that any war lacks a just cause or that consequentialism justifies wars without just causes. To reach such a negative conclusion, just war theorists need to explain why self-defense is the only just cause and nothing else on the above list is a just cause. It is hard to imagine any good argument for that claim.

Some just war theorists . . . seem to suggest an argument like this: Until you have been wronged, you have no good enough reason to use force. However, the reason for a preventive war is to prevent harmful attacks. That sure looks like a good reason. It simply begs the question to assume that this good reason is not good enough, at least when the prevented harms are much greater than the harms inflicted by the preventive war.

Just war theorists, including Crawford, might respond that too many countries will start wars if we tell them that wars might sometimes be permitted for humanitarian purposes, to enforce international law, or to spread democracy. This is far from obvious if other conditions limit such wars to clear and extreme cases, such as the rare cases where humanitarian wars meet consequentialist criteria. Moreover, even if publicly permitting such wars would lead to too much war, that is a reason not to build such permission into public rules of war. It shows nothing about the deep morality of war or about moral wrongness. That leaves no good reason to assume that self-defense is the only just cause that is adequate to justify war given other conditions.

In addition, the condition of self-defense needs to be interpreted carefully. Crawford, for example, claims that: 'A conception of the self that justifies legitimate preemption in self-defense must be narrowly confined to immediate risks to life and health within borders or to the life and health of citizens abroad.'[20]

A broader definition of the self might count war as self-defense when it is waged for the sake of 'economic well-being' and 'access to key markets and strategic resources.'[21] The Bush administration takes such a broad view of self-defense for the United States.

I grant that increasing the economic well-being of already prosperous nations, including the United States, is not true self-defense and could not justify war in any realistic scenario. However, if 'economic well-being' includes maintaining minimal economies for severely deprived people, then protecting economic well-being might count as self-defense. Perhaps such minimal economic well-being fits under 'life and health', but that just shows how economic well-being sometimes might be important enough to justify war.

It is also not clear why war could never be justified to protect 'strategic resources.' Strategic positions are ones that give an advantage, but resources are usually called strategic only when they are needed to be able to defend life and freedom. If we could not start a war to defend resources that are strategic in this narrower sense, then opponents who want to invade our country could cut off our strategic resources so as to make us unable to defend ourselves by the time they invaded.

By limiting self-defense to 'life and health', Crawford also implies that anticipatory war is never justified to protect our freedom at home or abroad. However, if it were morally wrong to start a war to defend our freedom, then it would be morally wrong to stop invaders who promised to keep us alive and healthy while taking over our government.

My most basic disagreement with Crawford and just war theory concerns method. Crawford announces that certain general kinds of values (life and health) are adequate and others (such as economic well-being) are not. However, particular instances of such general kinds vary along continua and are affected by circumstances. Freedom, health, and economic well-being come in endless degrees. The risk of attack can also vary from no chance to certainty. Whether a war is morally wrong depends on exactly where it falls along such continua. Most people's intuitions are not fine-grained enough for such complex questions. Hence, I see no reasonable alternative to the consequentialist position that whether a war is morally wrong depends on balance of probabilities of various values and disvalues among its consequences.

Imminence

We still need to ask whether prevention of future aggression is a just cause in the absence of any actual aggression at present. The traditional answer is that the future aggression must be imminent. This is the imminence condition. If the threat is imminent, the war is called preemptive. If it is not imminent, the war is called preventive. Traditional just war theory then forbids all preventive wars but not all preemptive wars.

A classic example of a preemptive war is Israel's Six Day War of 1967. Egypt was building up forces on its border with Israel, so it was credible that they would attack Israel very soon. Israel beat them to the punch by bombing Egyptian airfields while their planes were on the ground. Israel's attack was preemptive rather than preventive, because Egypt's attack was imminent. In contrast, a classic example of a preventive strike occurred when Israel bombed Iraq's Osirak nuclear reactor in 1981. The threatened attack was not imminent, because it would have been years before the reactor produced material for nuclear weapons.

When does an attack count as imminent? Some just war theorists specify a time period. Crawford, for example, answers that an attack is imminent when and only when it 'can be made manifest within hours or weeks.'[22] How many hours or weeks? Presumably, 'hours or weeks' must be shorter than a month. Crawford's formulation then suggests that Israel's bombing of Egyptian airfields at the start of the Six Day War met the condition of imminence, so it was not morally wrong, if the other conditions were met; but Israel's bombing of the Osirak reactor failed the condition of imminence, so it was morally wrong.

This condition makes moral wrongness depend on timing, but why does time matter? Several answers are common. First, by waiting until Egypt's attack was imminent, Israel gave Egypt an opportunity to forswear aggression. It might seem unfair to remove that chance to improve. Second, by waiting until Egypt's attack was imminent, Israel also waited until the probability of attack was high. Countries sometimes threaten aggression when they do not really mean it or at least will not really do it when push comes to shove. As time goes by, non-aggressive possibilities disappear and the preemptor gains more and stronger evidence (which increases the epistemic probability) of the feared attack. For such reasons, time is correlated with probability: When the attack is imminent, the probability of attack is usually higher than before it became imminent.

Consequentialists agree that probability can affect what is morally wrong, but usually they deny that time itself affects what is morally wrong. A test case would occur if time did not change probability (or did not change it enough to make a difference). Imagine that Israel had attacked Egypt in the same way as it did in 1967, but a month earlier. In this imaginary scenario, Israelis were just as certain about the impending attack by Egypt, and waiting a few weeks until the attack was imminent would not have made Israel more certain. Nevertheless, waiting would have made Israel's defense less likely to succeed and more costly in both Israeli and Egyptian lives. The imminence condition implies that this earlier anticipatory attack would have been morally wrong, because the threatened attack was not imminent. I find this position hard to believe. If the level of certainty is high enough a week in advance, the same probability should be high enough a month in advance. If waiting will not decrease the probability of aggression and will increase the costs to both sides (in innocent Israeli as well as Egyptian lives), then I see no reason to wait. Time itself provides no reason. Temporal imminence is not necessary for guilt, since Egypt was conspiring to attack Israel more than a month in advance. It might seem unfair not to grant Egypt a last chance to mend its ways, but Egypt would have had many such opportunities long before Israel's attack, even if that attack had come a month earlier. If every last opportunity had to be provided, then Israel would not have been justified in bombing even one minute before the Egyptian planes took off (or entered Israeli airspace). Even just war theorists do not believe that. Hence, temporal imminence cannot really be necessary for an anticipatory war to avoid being morally wrong.

This point also applies to Israel's attack on the Osirak reactor. Israel argued that, if they had waited, the reactor would probably have been used to make nuclear weapons. If they had waited to bomb it when it was active, then very many people in Iraq would have been killed by the explosion and nuclear fallout, whereas only a few people were killed when they bombed the reactor before it was active. The same reasoning might also apply to Bush's attack on Iraq. Imagine that Bush had allowed Saddam Hussein to develop more chemical and biological weapons and then to begin loading them into missiles while expressing the intention to shoot those missiles at the United States or our allies, such as Israel. If we had bombed their missiles at that later time, then the chemical and biological agents might have spread widely throughout Iraq and neighboring countries. This would have caused even more devastation to innocent civilians than the current war. I am not claiming and do not believe that these facts are accurate or that this scenario motivated Bush. My point is only that certain types of weapons—nuclear as well as biological and chemical—change the equation. . . . When threatened with weapons of these sorts, waiting can sometimes be much more dangerous for innocent people on both sides. I shall argue later that this affects what our public policies should be. For now the point is that it also affects whether preventive war can be morally justified.

My conclusion is that countries ought to wait when it is not too dangerous to wait, but sometimes waiting is too dangerous, and then preventive war might not be morally wrong. If so, time in itself makes no difference. What really matters are the likely benefits and costs of acting at one time as opposed to another, just as consequentialism suggests. . . .

A CONSEQUENTIALIST VIEW OF PREVENTIVE WAR

To determine whether preventive war is morally justified, just war theorists ask whether prevention of nonimminent aggression is a just cause. The answer is far from clear, partly because the question lumps together so many different circumstances. In contrast, consequentialism enables a more nuanced and insightful view of preventive war.

Because of its sensitivity to circumstances, consequentialism clearly implies that it is at least logically and physically possible for some preventive war to be morally justified. . . . A general rule against preventive war cannot hold in all possible cases if the moral wrongness of such wars depends on their consequences and the consequences of the available alternatives in the particular circumstances.

Preventive war still might never be justified in any actual case, according to consequentialism. However, we already saw a plausible example: Israel's preventive bombing of the Osirak reactor. Assuming that international negotiation and pressure would probably have failed, if Israel had waited for the reactor to start up, then they probably would have had to attack either an active reactor or a plant for building nuclear bombs. Either alternative would be likely to have spread nuclear radiation over a large area and harmed many more innocent people than the actual preventive bombing. On these facts, then,

consequentialism implies that this attack was morally justified.

The United Nations Security Council condemned Israel for bombing the Osirak reactor. However, that condemnation does not reveal any consensus that the bombing was immoral. It does not even show that the Security Council members shared that belief. They might have thought it useful to make such a public condemnation even though Israel's attack was justified. After all, the Security Council did nothing beyond making a statement. If they had really believed that the attack was morally wrong, then they should have done more than talk. Anyway, consequentialists can explain how public condemnation of Israel could be morally justified by the consequences of that public speech act, even if Israel's bombing was not morally wrong because of the beneficial consequences of that separate action.

I know of no actual case where a preventive war seems justified as defense against conventional weapons. An early preventive campaign against Hitler would have been a likely candidate, but Hitler had already attacked and was occupying several countries, so an early attack (say, in 1938) could have been justified as law enforcement or on humanitarian grounds rather than as prevention. That leaves no justified preventive war against conventional weapons. Why? Maybe because the cost of waiting until an attack is imminent is never actually too high with conventional weapons. It is possible that an early attack would prevent scattering of enemy weapons that would make a later attack less effective and more costly to both sides, and that these costs would outweigh the benefits of waiting; but this seems unlikely. The absence of actual cases supports this guess.

What about Bush's attack on Iraq? According to consequentialism, Bush's attack was morally wrong if any available alternative would have had better consequences overall for the world. The crucial question is not whether the attack was better than doing nothing at all to reduce terrorism. The critical question, instead, is whether any available alternative would have been better. One multipronged nonmilitary alternative has been proposed and supported forcefully by Bart Gruzalski:

Breaking up terrorist cells, arresting terrorists, putting terrorists on trial in a world court, negotiating with the Taliban, no longer propping up tyrannical Arab regimes, pulling U.S. troops out of Saudi Arabia, and even-handedly dealing with the Palestinian–Israeli conflict would have been a successful strategy both to protect Americans and to stop the spread of anti-American insurgents.[23]

More particularly,

Instead of invading Iraq, one alternative approach would have let Hans Blitz and the U.N. inspectors finish their job. . . . In addition . . . , the U.S. could have insisted on overflights with high altitude surveillance planes to check for weapons and military activity. . . . Since there was no military threat from Iraq [under such circumstances], the U.S. and the rest of the world could have lifted sanctions against Iraq and brought Iraq into the world trading community. . . . Instead of turning Iraq into a recruitment poster for al-Qaeda, the nonmilitary approach would foreseeably undermine the support for terrorism in the Islamic world.[24]

If this alternative would have been better overall than Bush's attack on Iraq, as I believe, then Bush's war was morally wrong according to consequentialism.

Bush's defenders might respond that Gruzalski's proposal would not have reduced terrorism. After all, many members and leaders of al-Qaeda have been rounded up since the war began. That, however, is no reason to assume that they would not have been rounded up without the war. Even before the attack on Afghanistan, many countries were already taking significant steps to break up terrorist cells and arrest terrorists.[25] These steps would be likely to have produced many arrests of al-Qaeda members without any attack on Iraq. Indeed, the US attack on Iraq (as well as treatment of terrorists in Guantanamo) squandered good will after September 11, led to less international cooperation, and thereby hurt the previous efforts to round up terrorists. The attack on Iraq also increased hatred of the United States among Arabs and seemed to confirm Bin Laden's claim that he is defending Islam against US aggression. For these reasons, instead of decreasing terrorism, Bush's Iraq War seems likely to increase terrorism against the United States and its allies in the long run.

This point applies even if one appeals to a US right to self-defense or if one gives up impartiality and appeals to interests of the United States in particular. Neither of these justifications works if Gruzalski and I are correct, because Bush's Iraq War does not help to defend the United States or serve US interests. This point becomes even clearer when we add the costs of the war on the US economy and on US civil rights.

Bush still might justify his Iraq attack as the only way to maintain US preeminence. Preeminence by itself is never enough for a consequentialist. Still, if US preeminence is the best means to achieve or maintain peace, then the best means to United States preeminence might be justified. However, many people (and I among them) doubt that US preeminence is the best means to peace. Then Bush's attack cannot be justified as a means to US preeminence.

Finally, Bush might defend his war as a way to bring to justice those responsible for the terrorist attacks on September 11. Then the war was not preventive. It was also not justified. Al-Qaeda had already been attacked in Afghanistan, and there were no clear connections between al-Qaeda and Iraq (or at least none has been found yet). Other proposed justifications, such as to spread democracy or to enforce international law, also fail, because there were better ways to achieve those goals, as Gruzalski argues.

My conclusion is that Bush's war in Iraq is morally wrong on consequentialist grounds. Of course, I am not certain. However, given such uncertainty, there is at least no adequate reason to believe that Bush's war was morally justified.[26] This lack of any adequate reason plus the presumption against war based on long and painful experience together support my conclusion that it was morally wrong to go to war in Iraq.

What about Bush's general policy of preventive war? Bush announced that the United States will engage in preventive war whenever it sees that step as necessary to defend itself. I doubt that such an unfettered policy is defensible. Politicians in the heat of the moment are too likely to err. However, as I argued, some preventive wars might not be morally wrong, although the only realistic cases are preventive wars against nuclear, chemical, biological, and possibly other unconventional threats. I also agree with Luban (2004) that the only realistic examples are rogue states. If that is correct, then we might benefit by acknowledging it. The United States could publicly renounce any preventive war against conventional threats but still reserve the right to use preventive attacks against threats by rogue states with unconventional WMD, though only when there is strong enough evidence that no other option will be less costly overall.

This policy could even be written into some enforceable international law. It would be very tricky to specify details, such as which states are rogue states, which weapons are conventional, when destruction is mass destruction, and when the evidence is strong enough. But partial solutions can be developed. The problem of inadequate evidence, for example, could be reduced (though not removed) if countries agreed not to engage in preventive war unless an impartial body agrees (unanimously or by a supermajority) that the evidence that the attacked country both has weapons of mass destruction and also is a rogue state are strong enough to justify preventive war. Reluctance to invoke the permission and engage in preventive war could be induced by agreeing to impose penalties (such as forced reparations) on countries that engage in preventive wars on the basis of evidence that is later discovered to be faulty, such as when it turns out that there were no weapons of mass destruction. Countries that want to start a preventive war will then have to decide whether they really believe that their evidence is strong enough for them to take the chance that they will be forced to pay reparations later.

This plan is admittedly idealistic, because many countries will be unwilling to accept or enforce such international laws. There are also bound to be significant disagreements about which policy would be best if adopted. Still, if some such policy could be worked out (and written into international law, applied by impartial courts, and enforced by some group of nations), then it might help to slow the spread of unconventional WMD and also deter the acts that get countries classified as rogue states. This kind of policy might then satisfy some of the Bush administration's legitimate concerns without being as dangerous as the current Bush policy.[27]

NOTES

1. I shall often refer to Bush as shorthand for his administration or troops carrying out his plans.

2. Some commentators suggest that whether an attack is preventive depends not on the attacker's goal but only on the nature of the capability, threat, or attack to which the attack responds. However, an attack does not respond in the relevant sense to a threat if the attacker's goal is not even partly to prevent that threat The attacker's goal, thus, determines what it is that the attacker responds to.

3. When a war has several purposes, we can ask whether a particular reason is good enough by itself to justify the war. That is my question here. It is fair, because most defenders of the war claim that the Iraq War's role as a preventive war is enough to justify it apart from any other reasons for the war.

4. United States, White House, National Security Council, *National Security Strategy of the United States of America* (September 2002), 16. http://www.white-house.gov/nsc/nss/2002/nss.pdf.

5. Jeff(erson) McMahan, 'The Ethics of Killing in War', *Ethics,* 114:4 (2004), 693–733. . . .

6. McMahan's phrase 'deep morality' does not refer to fundamental as opposed to derived principles. Instead, the point is that public rules need to use easily accessible markers in place of obscure factors that really determine what is morally wrong. The depth of deep morality is more like the depth of chemistry (which looks at the deep structure of chemicals instead of their superficial perceivable properties) than like the depth of axioms as opposed to theorems.

7. On consequentialism in general, see Walter Sinnott-Armstrong, 'Consequentialism,' in E. N. Zalta (ed), *The Stanford Encyclopedia of Philosophy* (2006). http://plato.stanford.edu/entries/consequentialism/. Consequentialist views of war have also been defended by Richard Brandt, 'Utilitarianism and the Rules of War', *Philosophy & Public Affairs,* 1: 2 (1971), 145–65; and Douglas Lackey, *The Ethics of War and Peace* (Englewood Cliffs, NJ: Prentice-Hall, 1989).

8. David Luban, 'Preventive War', *Philosophy & Public Affairs,* 32: 3 (2004), 207–48.

9. Isolated strikes can be kept secret, at least in some cases, but isolated strikes by themselves do not make a war.

10. See Walter Sinnott-Armstrong, 'Moral Intuitionism Meets Empirical Psychology,' in T. Horgan and M. Timmons (eds), *Metaethics After Moore* (New York: Oxford University Press, 2005).

11. See Walter Sinnott-Armstrong, 'Gert Contra Consequentialism,' in W. Sinnott-Armstrong and R. Audi (eds), *Rationality, Rules, and Ideals: Critical Essays on Bernard Gert's Moral Theory* (Lanham, MD: Rowman and Littlefield, 2002).

12. David Rodin, *War and Self-Defense* (Oxford: Clarendon Press, 2002), 11; compare his chapter 6 [Shue and Rodin (eds), *Preemption*, 143–70.]

13. I grant Rodin's methodological point that moral theories should explain not only what is immoral and why but also why certain cases seem obvious and others do not. My point is only that this consideration is only one among others and can be overridden in some cases, including this one.

14. Rodin, *War and Self-Defense,* 11.

15. See Rodin in this volume, p. 576.

16. Rodin, *War and Self-Defense,* 10.

17. Sinnott-Armstrong, 'Gert Contra Consequentialism,' 152–3.

18. Brian Orend, 'War', in E. N. Zalta (ed), *The Stanford Encyclopedia of Philosophy* (2003).

19. Neta Crawford, 'The Justice of Preemption and Preventive War Doctrines', in Mark Evans (ed.), *Just War Theory Revisited* (Edinburgh: University of Edinburgh Press, 2005).

20. Neta Crawford, 'The Slippery Slope to Preventive War', *Ethics and International Affairs,* 17: 1 (2003), 30–6.

21. See "The False Promise of Preventive War" in *Preemption,* Shue and Rodin, eds, pp. 89–125. by Crawford . . . quoting US government documents.

22. See Crawford, ibid., 119.

23. Bart Gruzalski, 'Some Implications of Utilitarianism for Practical Ethics: The Case Against the Military Response to Terrorism', in Henry West (ed), *Blackwell's Guide to Mill's Utilitarianism* (Oxford: Blackwell, 2005), pp. 249–69.

24. Ibid.

25. Ibid.

26. The way in which the war was conducted was also morally wrong in many ways. The initial strategy of Shock and Awe, e.g. violated just war theory and, more importantly, produced unnecessary bad effects.

27. For helpful discussion and comments on drafts, I thank Sue Uniacke, David Rodin, Henry Shue, Frances Kamm, Jeff McMahan, Bart Gruzalski, Peter Singer, Bernard Gert, Julia Driver, Nir Eyal, Anne Eaton, John Oberdick, Philip Pettit, Nan Keohane, Kim Scheppele, Steve Macedo, and others in audiences at the University of Oxford, the International Society of Utilitarian Studies, and the Princeton Center for Human Values. I would also like to thank the Oxford Leverhulme Program on the Changing Character of War and the Princeton University Center for Human Values for financial support while writing this chapter.

READING QUESTIONS

1. What does Sinnott-Armstrong mean in claiming that consequentialism represents a "deep" theory about the morality of war?
2. How does Sinnott-Armstrong reply to Rodin's claim that consequentialism is useless in addressing preventive war?
3. What objections does Sinnott-Armstrong raise against just-war theory appeals to just cause in addressing preventive wars?
4. Why does Sinnott-Armstrong claim that appeal to temporal imminence is problematic in distinguishing morally justified from unjustified anticipatory wars?

DISCUSSION QUESTIONS

1. Discuss whether Sinnott-Armstrong's responses to Rodin's objections to the act consequentialist approach to war are convincing.
2. Sinnott-Armstrong is critical of nonconsequentialist appeals to self-defense in objecting to preventive wars that define "self-defense" narrowly to rule out such considerations as economic well-being as part of a nation's self-defense. Discuss whether his objections to this conception of self-defense are plausible.

3. Sinnott-Armstrong claims that the imminence standard for distinguishing preventive from preemptive wars—a standard that relies on timing—is problematic. Discuss how a proponent of this standard might defend against Sinnott-Armstrong's objections.

Michael Walzer

Terrorism: A Critique of Excuses

After explaining the particular evil of terrorism and why it cannot be morally justified, Michael Walzer criticizes the typical "excuses" that are offered in defense of terrorist acts. The excuses include (1) terrorism is a last resort, (2) terrorist activities are needed because of weakness or other inability to mobilize a movement or nation, (3) terrorism is effective on behalf of oppressed groups, and (4) terrorism is a proper response to oppression. He then proceeds to consider ways of best responding to terrorism and concludes by examining the link between terrorism and oppression.

No one these days advocates terrorism, not even those who regularly practice it. The practice is indefensible now that it has been recognized, like rape and murder, as an attack upon the innocent. In a sense, indeed, terrorism is worse than rape and murder commonly are, for in the latter cases the victim has been chosen for a purpose; he or she is the direct object of attack, and the attack has some reason, however twisted or ugly it may be. The victims of a terrorist attack are third parties, innocent bystanders; there is no special reason for attacking them; anyone else within a large class of (unrelated) people will do as well. The attack is directed indiscriminately against the entire class. Terrorists are like killers on a rampage, except that their rampage is not just expressive of rage or madness; the rage is purposeful and programmatic. It aims at a general vulnerability: Kill these people in order to terrify those. A relatively small number of dead victims makes for a very large number of living and frightened hostages.

This, then, is the peculiar evil of terrorism—not only the killing of innocent people but also the intrusion of fear into everyday life, the violation of private purposes, the insecurity of public spaces, the endless coerciveness of precaution. A crime wave might, I suppose, produce similar effects, but no one plans a crime wave; it is the work of a thousand individual

From "Terrorism: A Critique of Excuses" by Michael Walzer in *Problems of International Justice*, ed. Steven Luper-Foy (Boulder, CO: Westview Press, 1988), pp. 237–247. Reprinted by permission of the author.

decisionmakers, each one independent of the others, brought together only by the invisible hand. Terrorism is the work of visible hands; it is an organizational project, a strategic choice, a conspiracy to murder and intimidate . . . you and me. No wonder the conspirators have difficulty defending, in public, the strategy they have chosen.

The moral difficulty is the same, obviously, when the conspiracy is directed not against you and me but against *them*—Protestants, say, not Catholics; Israelis, not Italians or Germans; blacks, not whites. These "limits" rarely hold for long; the logic of terrorism steadily expands the range of vulnerability. The more hostages they hold, the stronger the terrorists are. No one is safe once whole populations have been put at risk. Even if the risk were contained, however, the evil would be no different. So far as individual Protestants or Israelis or blacks are concerned, terrorism is random, degrading, and frightening. That is its hallmark, and that, again, is why it cannot be defended.

But when moral justification is ruled out, the way is opened for ideological excuse and apology. We live today in a political culture of excuses. This is far better than a political culture in which terrorism is openly defended and justified, for the excuse at least acknowledges the evil. But the improvement is precarious, hard won, and difficult to sustain. It is not the case, even in this better world, that terrorist organizations are without supporters. The support is indirect but by no means ineffective. It takes the form of apologetic descriptions and explanations, a litany of excuses that steadily undercuts our knowledge of the evil. Today that knowledge is insufficient unless it is supplemented and reinforced by a systematic critique of excuses. That is my purpose [here]. I take the principle for granted: that every act of terrorism is a wrongful act. The wrongfulness of the excuses, however, cannot be taken for granted; it has to be argued. The excuses themselves are familiar enough, the stuff of contemporary political debate. I shall state them in stereotypical form. There is no need to attribute them to this or that writer, publicist, or commentator; my readers can make their own attributions.[1]

THE EXCUSES FOR TERRORISM

The most common excuse for terrorism is that it is a last resort, chosen only when all else fails. The image is of people who have literally run out of options. One by one, they have tried every legitimate form of political and military action, exhausted every possibility, failed everywhere, until no alternative remains but the evil of terrorism. They must be terrorists or do nothing at all. The easy response is to insist that, given this description of their case, they should do nothing at all; they have indeed exhausted their possibilities. But this response simply reaffirms the principle, ignores the excuse; this response does not attend to the terrorists' desperation. Whatever the cause to which they are committed, we have to recognize that, given the commitment, the one thing they cannot do is "nothing at all."

But the case is badly described. It is not so easy to reach the "last resort." To get there, one must indeed try everything (which is a lot of things) and not just once, as if a political party might organize a single demonstration, fail to win immediate victory, and claim that it was now justified in moving on to murder. Politics is an art of repetition. Activists and citizens learn from experience, that is, by doing the same thing over and over again. He is by no means clear when they run out of options, but even under conditions of oppression and war, citizens have a good run short of that. The same argument applies to state officials who claim that they have tried "everything" and are now compelled to kill hostages or bomb peasant villages. Imagine such people called before a judicial tribunal and required to answer the question, What exactly did you try? Does anyone believe that they could come up with a plausible list? "Last resort" has only a notional finality; the resort to terror is ideologically last, not last in an actual series of actions, just last for the sake of the excuse. In fact, most state officials and movements militants who recommend a policy of terrorism recommend it as a first resort; they are for it from the beginning, although they may not get their way at the beginning. If they are honest, then, they must make other excuses and give up the pretense of the last resort.

The second excuse is designed for national liberation movements struggling against established and powerful states. Now the claim is that nothing else is possible, that no other strategy is available except terrorism. This is different from the first excuse because it does not require would-be terrorists to run through all the available options. Or, the second excuse requires terrorists to run through all the options in their heads, not in the world; notional finality is enough. Movement strategists consider their options and conclude that they have no alternative to terrorism. They think that they do not have the political strength to try anything else, and thus they do not try anything else. Weakness is their excuse.

But two very different kinds of weakness are commonly confused here: the weakness of the movement vis-à-vis the opposing state and the movement's weakness vis-à-vis its own people. This second kind of weakness, the inability of the movement to mobilize the nation, makes terrorism the "only" option because it effectively rules out all the others: nonviolent resistance, general strikes, mass demonstrations, unconventional warfare, and so on.

These options are only rarely ruled out by the sheer power of the state, by the pervasiveness and intensity of oppression. Totalitarian states may be immune to nonviolent or guerrilla resistance, but all the evidence suggests that they are also immune to terrorism. Or, more exactly, in totalitarian states state terror dominates every other sort. Where terrorism is a possible strategy for the oppositional movement (in liberal and democratic states, most obviously), other strategies are also possible if the movement has some significant degree of popular support. In the absence of popular support, terrorism may indeed be the one available strategy, but it is hard to see how its evils can then be excused. For it is not weakness alone that makes the excuse, but the claim of the terrorists to represent the weak; and the particular form of weakness that makes terrorism the only option calls that claim into question.

One might avoid this difficulty with a stronger insistence on the actual effectiveness of terrorism. The third excuse is simply that terrorism works (and nothing else does); it achieves the ends of the oppressed even without their participation. "When the act accuses, the result excuses."[2] This is a consequential argument, and given a strict understanding of consequentialism, this argument amounts to a justification rather than an excuse. In practice, however, the argument is rarely pushed so far. More often, the argument begins with an acknowledgment of the terrorists' wrongdoing. Their hands are dirty, but we must make a kind of peace with them because they have acted effectively for the sake of people who could not act for themselves. But, in fact, have the terrorists' actions been effective? I doubt that terrorism has ever achieved national liberation—no nation that I know of owes its freedom to a campaign of random murder—although terrorism undoubtedly increases the power of the terrorists within the national liberation movement. Perhaps terrorism is also conducive to the survival and notoriety (the two go together) of the movement, which is now dominated by terrorists. But even if we were to grant some means-end relationship between terror and national liberation, the third excuse does not work unless it can meet the further requirements of a consequentialist argument. It must be possible to say that the desired end could not have been achieved through any other, less wrongful, means. The third excuse depends, then, on the success of the first or second, and neither of these look likely to be successful.

The fourth excuse avoids this crippling dependency. This excuse does not require the apologist to defend either of the improbable claims that terrorism is the last resort or that it is the only possible resort. The fourth excuse is simply that terrorism is the universal resort. All politics is (really) terrorism. The appearance of innocence and decency is always a piece of deception, more or less convincing in accordance with the relative power of the deceivers. The terrorist who does not bother with appearances is only doing openly what everyone else does secretly.

This argument has the same form as the maxim "All's fair in love and war." Love is always fraudulent, war is always brutal, and political action is always terrorist in character. Political action works (as Thomas Hobbes long ago argued) only by generating fear in innocent men and women. Terrorism is the politics of state officials and movement militants alike. This argument does not justify either the officials or the militants, but it does excuse them all. We hardly can be harsh with people who act the way everyone else acts. Only saints are likely to act differently, and sainthood in politics is supererogatory, a matter of grace, not obligation.

But this fourth excuse relies too heavily on our cynicism about political life, and cynicism only sometimes answers well to experience. In fact, legitimate states do not need to terrorize their citizens, and strongly based movements do not need to terrorize their opponents. Officials and militants who live, as it were, on the margins of legitimacy and strength sometimes choose terrorism and sometimes do not. Living in terror is not a universal experience. The world the terrorists create has its entrances and exits.

If we want to understand the choice of terror, the choice that forces the rest of us through the door, we have to imagine what in fact always occurs, although we often have no satisfactory record of the occurrence: A group of men and women, officials or militants, sits around a table and argues about whether or not to adopt a terrorist strategy. Later on, the litany of excuses obscures the argument. But at the time, around the table, it would have been no use for defenders of terrorism to say, "Everybody does it," because there they would be face to face with people proposing to do something else. Nor is it historically the case that the members of this last group, the opponents of terrorism, always lose the argument. They can win, however, and still not be able to prevent a terrorist campaign; the would-be terrorists (it does not take very many) can always split the movement and go their own way. Or, they can split the bureaucracy or the police or officer corps and act in the shadow of state power. Indeed, terrorism often has its origin in such splits. The first victims are the terrorists' former comrades or colleagues. What reason can we possibly have, then, for equating the two? If we value the politics of the men and women who oppose terrorism, we must reject the excuses of their murderers. Cynicism at such a time is unfair to the victims.

The fourth excuse can also take, often does take, a more restricted form. Oppression, rather than political rule more generally, is always terroristic in character, and thus, we must always excuse the opponents

of oppression. When they choose terrorism, they are only reacting to someone else's previous choice, repaying in kind the treatment they have long received. Of course, their terrorism repeats the evil—innocent people are killed, who were never themselves oppressors—but repetition is not the same as initiation. The oppressors set the terms of the struggle. But if the struggle is fought on the oppressors' terms, then the oppressors are likely to win. Or, at least, oppression is likely to win, even if it takes on a new face. The whole point of a liberation movement or a popular mobilization is to change the terms. We have no reason to excuse the terrorism reactively adopted by opponents of oppression unless we are confident of the sincerity of their opposition, the seriousness of their commitment to a nonoppressive politics. But the choice of terrorism undermines that confidence.

We are often asked to distinguish the terrorism of the oppressed from the terrorism of the oppressors. What is it, however, that makes the difference? The message of the terrorist is the same in both cases: a denial of the peoplehood and humanity of the groups among whom he or she finds victims. Terrorism anticipates, when it does not actually enforce, political domination. Does it matter if one dominated group is replaced by another? Imagine a slave revolt whose protagonists dream only of enslaving in their turn the children of their masters. The dream is understandable, but the fervent desire of the children that the revolt be repressed is equally understandable. In neither case does understanding make for excuse—not, at least, after a politics of universal freedom has become possible. Nor does an understanding of oppression excuse the terrorism of the oppressed, once we have grasped the meaning of "liberation."

These are the four general excuses for terror, and each of them fails. They depend upon statements about the world that are false, historical arguments for which there is no evidence, moral claims that turn out to be hollow or dishonest. This is not to say that there might not be more particular excuses that have greater plausibility, extenuating circumstances in particular cases that we would feel compelled to recognize. As with murder, we can tell a story (like the story that Richard Wright tells in *Native Son,* for example) that might lead us, not to justify terrorism, but to excuse this or that individual terrorist. We can provide a personal history, a psychological study, of compassion destroyed by fear, moral reason by hatred and rage, social inhibition by unending violence—the product, an individual driven to kill or readily set on a killing course by his or her political leaders.[3] But the force of this story will not depend on any of the four general excuses, all of which grant what the storyteller will have to deny: that terrorism is the deliberate choice of rational men and women. Whether they conceive it to be one option among others or the only one available, they nevertheless argue and choose. Whether they are acting or reacting, they have made a decision. The human instruments they subsequently find to plant the bomb or shoot the gun may act under some psychological compulsion, but the men and women who choose terror as a policy act "freely." They could not act in any other way, or accept any other description of their action, and still pretend to be the leaders of the movement or the state. We ought never to excuse such leaders.

THE RESPONSE TO TERRORISM

What follows from the critique of excuses? There is still a great deal of room for argument about the best way of responding to terrorism. Certainly, terrorists should be resisted, and it is not likely that a purely defensive resistance will ever be sufficient. In this sort of struggle, the offense is always ahead. The technology of terror is simple; the weapons are readily produced and easy to deliver. It is virtually impossible to protect people against random and indiscriminate attack. Thus, resistance will have to be supplemented by some combination of repression and retaliation. This is a dangerous business because repression and retaliation so often take terroristic forms and there are a host of apologists ready with excuses that sound remarkably like those of the terrorists themselves. It should be clear by now, however, that counterterrorism cannot be excused merely because it is reactive. Every new actor, terrorist or counterterrorist, claims to be reacting to someone else, standing in a circle

and just passing the evil along. But the circle is ideological in character; in fact, every actor is a moral agent and makes an independent decision.

Therefore, repression and retaliation must not repeat the wrongs of terrorism, which is to say that repression and retaliation must be aimed systematically at the terrorists themselves, never at the people for whom the terrorists claim to be acting. That claim is in any case doubtful, even when it is honestly made. The people do not authorize the terrorists to act in their name. Only a tiny number actually participate in terrorist activities; they are far more likely to suffer than to benefit from the terrorist program. Even if they supported the program and hoped to benefit from it, however, they would still be immune from attack—exactly as civilians in time of war who support the war effort but are not themselves part of it are subject to the same immunity. Civilians may be put at risk by attacks on military targets, as by attacks on terrorist targets, but the risk must be kept to a minimum, even at some cost to the attackers. The refusal to make ordinary people into targets, whatever their nationality or even their politics, is the only way to say no to terrorism. Every act of repression and retaliation has to be measured by this standard.

But what if the "only way" to defeat the terrorists is to intimidate their actual or potential supporters? It is important to deny the premise of this question: that terrorism is a politics dependent on mass support. In fact, it is always the politics of an elite, whose members are dedicated and fanatical and more than ready to endure, or to watch others endure, the devastations of a counterterrorist campaign. Indeed, terrorists will welcome counterterrorism; it makes the terrorists' excuses more plausible and is sure to bring them, however many people are killed or wounded, however many are terrorized, the small number of recruits needed to sustain the terrorist activities.

Repression and retaliation are legitimate responses to terrorism only when they are constrained by the same moral principles that rule out terrorism itself. But there is an alternative response that seeks to avoid the violence that these two entail. The alternative is to address directly, ourselves, the oppression the terrorists claim to oppose. Oppression, they say, is the cause of terrorism. But that is merely one more excuse. The real cause of terrorism is the decision to launch a terrorist campaign, a decision made by that group of people sitting around a table whose deliberations I have already described. However, terrorists do exploit oppression, injustice, and human misery generally and look to these at least for their excuses. There can hardly be any doubt that oppression strengthens their hand. Is that a reason for us to come to the defense of the oppressed? It seems to me that we have our own reasons to do that, and do not need this one, or should not, to prod us into action. We might imitate those movement militants who argue against the adoption of a terrorist strategy—although not, as the terrorists say, because these militants are prepared to tolerate oppression. They already are opposed to oppression and now add to that opposition, perhaps for the same reasons, a refusal of terror. So should we have been opposed before, and we should now make the same addition.

But there is an argument, put with some insistence these days, that we should refuse to acknowledge any link at all between terrorism and oppression—as if any defense of oppressed men and women, once a terrorist campaign has been launched, would concede the effectiveness of the campaign. Or, at least, a defense of oppression would give terrorism the appearance of effectiveness and so increase the likelihood of terrorist campaigns in the future. Here we have the reverse side of the litany of excuses; we have turned over the record. First oppression is made into an excuse for terrorism, and then terrorism is made into an excuse for oppression. The first is the excuse of the far left; the second is the excuse of the neoconservative right.[4] I doubt that genuine conservatives would think it a good reason for defending the status quo that it is under terrorist attack; they would have independent reasons and would be prepared to defend the status quo against any attack. Similarly, those of us who think that the status quo urgently requires change have our own reasons for thinking so and need not be intimidated by terrorists or, for that matter, antiterrorists.

If one criticizes the first excuse, one should not neglect the second. But I need to state the second more precisely. It is not so much an excuse for oppression as an excuse for doing nothing (now) about oppression. The claim is that the campaign against terrorism has priority over every other political activity. If the people who take the lead in this campaign are the old oppressors, then we must make a kind of peace with them—temporarily, of course, until the terrorists have been beaten. This is a strategy that denies the possibility of a two-front war. So long as the men and women who pretend to lead the fight against oppression are terrorists, we can concede nothing to their demands. Nor can we oppose their opponents.

But why not? It is not likely in any case that terrorists would claim victory in the face of a serious effort to deal with the oppression of the people they claim to be defending. The effort would merely expose the hollowness of their claim, and the nearer it came to success, the more they would escalate their terrorism. They would still have to be defeated, for what they are after is not a solution to the problem but rather the power to impose their own solution. No decent end to the conflict in Ireland, say, or in Lebanon, or in the Middle East generally, is going to look like a victory for terrorism—if only because the different groups of terrorists are each committed, by the strategy they have adopted, to an indecent end.[5] By working for our own ends, we expose the indecency.

OPPRESSION AND TERRORISM

It is worth considering at greater length the link between oppression and terror. To pretend that there is no link at all is to ignore the historical record, but the record is more complex than any of the excuses acknowledge. The first thing to be read out of it, however, is simple enough: Oppression is not so much the cause of terrorism as terrorism is one of the primary means of oppression. This was true in ancient times, as Aristotle recognized, and it is still true today. Tyrants rule by terrorizing their subjects; unjust and illegitimate regimes are upheld through a combination of carefully aimed and random violence.[6] If this method works in the state, there is no reason to think that it will not work, or that it does not work, in the liberation movement. Wherever we see terrorism, we should look for tyranny and oppression. Authoritarian states, especially in the moment of their founding, need a terrorist apparatus—secret police with unlimited power, secret prisons into which citizens disappear, death squads in unmarked cars. Even democracies may use terror, not against their own citizens, but at the margins, in their colonies, for example, where colonizers also are likely to rule tyrannically. Oppression is sometimes maintained by a steady and discriminate pressure, sometimes by intermittent and random violence—what we might think of as terrorist melodrama—designed to render the subject population fearful and passive.

This latter policy, especially if it seems successful, invites imitation by opponents of the state. But terrorism does not spread only when it is imitated. If it can be invented by state officials, it can also be invented by movement militants. Neither one need take lessons from the other; the circle has no single or necessary starting point. Wherever it starts, terrorism in the movement is tyrannical and oppressive in exactly the same way as is terrorism in the state. The terrorists aim to rule, and murder is their method. They have their own internal police, death squads, disappearances. They begin by killing or intimidating those comrades who stand in their way, and they proceed to do the same, if they can, among the people they claim to represent. If terrorists are successful, they rule tyrannically, and their people bear, without consent, the costs of the terrorists' rule. (If the terrorists are only partly successful, the costs to the people may be even greater: What they have to bear now is a war between rival terrorist gangs.) But terrorists cannot win the ultimate victory they seek without challenging the established regime or colonial power and the people it claims to represent, and when terrorists do that, they themselves invite imitation. The regime may then respond with its own campaign of aimed and random violence. Terrorist tracks terrorist, each claiming the other as an excuse.

The same violence can also spread to countries where it has not yet been experienced; now terror is reproduced not through temporal succession but through ideological adaptation. State terrorists wage bloody wars against largely imaginary enemies: army colonels, say, hunting down the representatives of "international communism." Or movement terrorists wage bloody wars against enemies with whom, but for the ideology, they could readily negotiate and compromise: nationalist fanatics committed to a permanent irredentism. These wars, even if they are without precedents, are likely enough to become precedents, to start the circle of terror and counterterror, which is endlessly oppressive for the ordinary men and women whom the state calls its citizens and the movement its "people."

The only way to break out of the circle is to refuse to play the terrorist game. Terrorists in the state and the movement warn us, with equal vehemence, that any such refusal is a sign of softness and naiveté. The self-portrait of the terrorists is always the same. They are tough-minded and realistic; they know their enemies (or privately invent them for ideological purposes); and they are ready to do what must be done for victory. Why then do terrorists turn around and around in the same circle? It is true: Movement terrorists win support because they pretend to deal energetically and effectively with the brutality of the state. It also is true: State terrorists win support because they pretend to deal energetically and effectively with the brutality of the movement. Both feed on the fears of brutalized and oppressed people. But there is no way of overcoming brutality with terror. At most, the burden is shifted from these people to those; more likely, new burdens are added for everyone. Genuine liberation can come only through a politics that mobilizes the victims of brutality and takes careful aim at its agents, or by a politics that surrenders the hope of victory and domination and deliberately seeks a compromise settlement. In either case, once tyranny is repudiated, terrorism is no longer an option. For what lies behind all the excuses, of officials and militants alike, is the predilection for a tyrannical politics.

NOTES

1. I cannot resist a few examples: Edward Said, "The Terrorism Scam," *The Nation,* June 14, 1986; and (more

intelligent and circumspect) Richard Falk, "Thinking About Terrorism," *The Nation,* June 28, 1986.

2. Machiavelli, *The Discourses* I:ix. As yet, however, there have been no results that would constitute a Machiavellian excuse.

3. See, for example, Daniel Goleman, "The Roots of Terrorism Are Found in Brutality of Shattered Childhood," *New York Times,* September 2, 1986, pp. C1, 8. Goleman discusses the psychic and social history of particular terrorists, not the roots of terrorism.

4. The neoconservative position is represented, although not as explicitly as I have stated it here, in Benjamin Netanyahu, ed., *Terrorism: How the West Can Win* (New York: Farrar, Straus & Giroux, 1986).

5. The reason the terrorist strategy, however indecent in itself, cannot be instrumental to some decent political purpose is because any decent purpose must somehow accommodate the people against whom the terrorism is aimed, and what terrorism expresses is precisely the refusal of such an accommodation, the radical devaluing of the Other. See my argument in *Just and Unjust Wars* (New York: Basic Books, 1977), pp. 197–206, especially 203.

6. Aristotle, *The Politics* 1313–1314a.

READING QUESTIONS

1. Walzer examines excuses for terrorism while granting that terrorism cannot be morally justified. What is the distinction between a justification and an excuse?
2. Why does Walzer think that the third excuse depends on the success of the first or second?
3. What is the significance of Walzer's claim that an act of terror is a deliberate, free, and rational choice of a moral agent?
4. Why does Walzer think that the last-resort excuse is a pretense for both state officials and movement militants who recommend a policy of terrorism?

DISCUSSION QUESTIONS

1. Walzer's article was written prior to the 9/11 attacks. Do you think his critique of excuses is applicable to the type of terrorists involved in the 9/11 attacks? Why or why not?
2. Discuss the reasons one might give for claiming that all politics is a form of terrorism. Should terrorism be excused because terrorists are doing nothing different than what state officials sometimes do? Why or why not?
3. Do you agree with Walzer that the proper response to terrorism is to refuse to play the terrorists' game? Why or why not? If you agree, what alternative action do you propose? If you disagree, do you think counterterrorism can be morally justified or excused?

ANDREW VALLS

Can Terrorism Be Justified?

After defining "terrorism" so that by definition not all instances are necessarily morally wrong, Andrew Valls argues that "if just war theory can justify violence committed by states, then terrorism committed by nonstate actors can also, under certain circumstances, be justified by it as well." In defending this claim, Valls considers each of the provisions of just-war theory, with particular attention given to the provisions of just cause, legitimate authority, and discrimination.

Recommended Reading: the discussion of just-war theory in the introduction to this chapter.

[J]ust war theory, despite its ambiguities, provides a rich framework with which to assess the morality of war. But interstate war is only the most conventional form of political violence. The question arises, Is it the only form of political violence that may ever he justified? If not, how are we to assess the morality of other cases of political violence, particularly those involving nonstate actors? In short, does just war theory apply to terrorism, and, if so, can terrorism satisfy its criteria?

In the public and scholarly reactions to political violence, a double standard often is at work. When violence is committed by states, our assessment tends to be quite permissive, giving states a great benefit of the doubt about the propriety of their violent acts. However, when the violence is committed by nonstate actors, we often react with horror, and the condemnations cannot come fast enough. Hence, terrorism is almost universally condemned, whereas violence by states, even when war has not been declared, is seen as legitimate, if not always fully justified. This difference in assessments remains when innocent civilians are killed in both cases and sometimes when such killing

is deliberate. Even as thoughtful a commentator as Michael Walzer, for example, seems to employ this double standard. In his *Just and Unjust Wars,* Walzer considers whether "soldiers and statesmen [can] override the rights of innocent people for the sake of their own political community" and answers "affirmatively, though not without hesitation and worry" (1992, 254). Walzer goes on to discuss a case in point, the Allied bombing of German cities during World War II, arguing that, despite the many civilians who deliberately were killed, the bombing was justified. However, later in the book, Walzer rejects out of hand the possibility that terrorism might sometimes be justified, on the grounds that it involves the deliberate killing of innocents (1992, chapter 12). He never considers the possibility that stateless communities might confront the same "supreme emergency" that justified, in his view, the bombing of innocent German civilians. I will have more to say about Walzer's position below, but for now I wish to point out that, on the face of it at least, his position seems quite inconsistent.

From a philosophical point of view, this double standard cannot be sustained. As Coady (1985)

From: "Can Terrorism Be Justified?" by Andrew Valls in *Ethics in International Affairs*, ed. A. Valls (Lanham, MD: Rowman and Littlefield), pp. 65–79.

argues, consistency requires that we apply the same standards to both kinds of political violence, state and nonstate. Of course, it may turn out that there are simply some criteria that states can satisfy that nonstate actors cannot, so that the same standard applied to both inevitably leads to different conclusions. There may be morally relevant features of states that make their use of violence legitimate and its use by others illegitimate. However, I will argue that this is not the case. I argue that, on the most plausible account of just war theory, taking into account the ultimate moral basis of its criteria, violence undertaken by nonstate actors can, in principle, satisfy the requirements of a just war.

To advance this view, I examine each criterion of just war theory in turn, arguing in each case that terrorism committed by nonstate actors can satisfy the criterion. The most controversial parts of my argument will no doubt be those regarding just cause, legitimate authority, and discrimination, so I devote more attention to these than to the others. I argue that, once we properly understand the moral basis for each of these criteria, it is clear that some nonstate groups may have the same right as states to commit violence and that they are just as capable of committing that violence within the constraints imposed by just war theory. My conclusion, then, is that if just war theory can justify violence committed by states, then terrorism committed by nonstate actors can also, under certain circumstances, be justified by it as well. But before commencing the substantive argument, I must attend to some preliminary matters concerning the definition of *terrorism*.

DEFINITIONAL ISSUES

There is little agreement on the question of how *terrorism* is best defined. In the political arena, of course, the word is used by political actors for political purposes, usually to paint their opponents as monsters. Scholars, on the other hand, have at least attempted to arrive at a more detached position, seeking a definition that captures the essence of terrorism. However, there is reason, in addition to the lack of consensus, to doubt whether much progress has been made.

Most definitions of terrorism suffer from at least one of two difficulties. First, they often define terrorism as murder or otherwise characterize it as intrinsically wrong and unjustifiable. The trouble with this approach is that it prejudges the substantive moral issue by a definitional consideration. I agree with Teichman, who writes that "we ought not to begin by *defining* terrorism as a bad thing" (1989, 507). Moral conclusions should follow from moral reasoning, grappling with the moral issues themselves. To decide a normative issue by definitional considerations, then, ends the discussion before it begins.

The second shortcoming that many definitions of terrorism exhibit is being too revisionist of its meaning in ordinary language. As I have noted, the word is often used as a political weapon, so ordinary language will not settle the issue. Teichman (1989, 505) again is correct that any definition will necessarily be stipulative to some extent. But ordinary language does, nevertheless, impose some constraints on the stipulative definition that we can accept. For example, Carl Wellman defines *terrorism* as "the use or attempted use of terror as a means of coercion" (1979, 251) and draws the conclusion that when he instills terror in his students with threats of grade penalties on late papers, he commits terrorism. Clearly this is not what most of us have in mind when we speak of terrorism, so Wellman's definition, even if taken as stipulative, is difficult to accept.

Some definitions of terrorism suffer from both of these shortcomings to some degree. For example, those that maintain that terrorism is necessarily random or indiscriminate seem both to depart markedly from ordinary usage—there are lots of acts we call terrorist that specifically target military facilities and personnel—and thereby to prejudge the moral issue. (I will argue below that terrorism need not be indiscriminate at all.) The same can be said of definitions that insist that the aim of terrorism must be to terrorize, that it targets some to threaten many more. . . . As Virginia Held has argued, "We should probably not construe either the intention to spread fear or the intention to kill noncombatants as necessary for an act of political violence to be an act of terrorism"

(1991, 64). Annette Baier adds that "the terrorist may be ill named" because what she sometimes wants is not to terrorize but "the shocked attention of her audience population" (1994, 205).

With all of this disagreement, it would perhaps be desirable to avoid the use of the term *terrorism* altogether and simply to speak instead of political violence. I would be sympathetic to this position were it not for the fact that *terrorism* is already too much a part of our political vocabulary to be avoided. Still, we can with great plausibility simply define *terrorism* as a form of political violence, as Held does: "I [see] terrorism as a form of violence to achieve political goals, where creating fear is usually high among the intended effects" (1991, 64). This is a promising approach, though I would drop as nonessential the stipulation that terrorism is usually intended to spread fear. In addition, I would make two stipulations of my own. First, "violence" can include damage to property as well as harm to people. Blowing up a power plant can surely be an act of terrorism, even if no one is injured. Second, for the purposes of this chapter, I am interested in violence committed by nonstate actors. I do not thereby deny the existence of state terrorism. . . . However, for the purposes of my present argument, I assume that when a state commits terrorism against its own citizens, this is a matter for domestic justice, and that when it commits violence outside of its own borders, just war theory can, fairly easily, be extended to cover these cases. The problem for international ethics that I wish to address here is whether just war theory can be extended to nonstate actors. So my stipulative definition of *terrorism* in this chapter is simply that it is violence committed by nonstate actors against persons or property for political purposes. This definition appears to leave open the normative issues involved and to be reasonably consistent with ordinary language.

JUS AD BELLUM

It is somewhat misleading to speak of just war *theory,* for it is not a single theory but, rather, a tradition within which there is a range of interpretation. That is, just war theory is best thought of as providing a framework for discussion about whether a war is just, rather than as providing a set of unambiguous criteria that are easily applied. In what follows I rely on what I believe is the most plausible and normatively appealing version of just war theory, one that is essentially the same as the one articulated and developed by the preceding chapters. I begin with the *jus ad bellum* criteria, concerning the justice of going to war, and then turn to *jus in bello* criteria, which apply to the conduct of the war.

Just Cause

A just cause for a war is usually a defensive one. That is, a state is taken to have a just cause when it defends itself against aggression, where *aggression* means the violation or the imminent threat of the violation of its territorial integrity or political independence (Walzer 1992). So the just cause provision of just war theory holds, roughly, that the state has a right to defend itself against the aggression of other states.

But on what is this right of the state based? Most students of international ethics maintain that any right that a state enjoys is ultimately based on the rights of its citizens. States in and of themselves have value only to the extent that they serve some good for the latter. The moral status of the state is therefore derivative, not foundational, and it is derivative of the rights of the individuals within it. This, it seems, is the dominant (liberal) view, and only an exceedingly statist perspective would dispute it (Beitz 1979; Walzer 1992).

The right that is usually cited as being the ground for the state's right to defend itself is the right of self-determination. The state is the manifestation of, as well as the arena for, the right of a people to determine itself. It is because aggression threatens the common life of the people within a state, as well as threatening other goods they hold dear, that the state can defend its territory and independence. This is clear, for example, from Walzer's (1992, chapter 6) discussion of intervention. Drawing on John Stuart Mill (1984), Walzer argues that states generally ought not to intervene in the affairs of other states because to do so would be to violate the right of self-determination of the community within the state. However, once the right of self-determination is recognized, its implications go beyond a right against intervention or a right of defense. Walzer makes this clear as well, as his discussion of Mill's argument for nonintervention is followed immediately by exceptions to the rule, one of which is secession. When a secessionist movement has demonstrated that it represents the will of its people, other states may intervene to aid the secession because, in this case, secession reflects the self-determination of that people.

In the twenty years since Walzer presented this argument, a great deal of work has been done on nationalism, self-determination, and secession. Despite the range of views that has developed, it is fair to say that something of an overlapping consensus has formed, namely, that under certain circumstances, certain kinds of groups enjoy a right of self-determination that entitles them to their own state or at least to some autonomy in a federal arrangement within an existing state. The debate is mostly over what these circumstances are and what kinds of groups enjoy the right. For example, Allen Buchanan, in his important book *Secession* (1991), argues that the circumstances must include a historical injustice before a group is entitled to secede. Others are more permissive. Christopher Wellman (1995) and Daniel Philpott (1995) argue that past injustice is not required to entitle a group to secession and, indeed, that any group within a territory may secede, even if it is not plausibly seen as constituting a nation.

The modal position in the debate is, perhaps, somewhere between these positions, holding that certain groups, even absent a history of injustice, have a right to self-determination but that this applies not to just any group but only to "peoples" or "nations." This is essentially the position taken by Kymlicka (1995), Tamir (1993), Miller (1995), and Margalit and Raz (1990). There are, of course, important differences among these authors. Kymlicka argues that groups with "societal cultures" have a right to self-government but not necessarily secession. Margalit and Raz advance a similar argument, and their notion of an "encompassing group" is very close to Kymlicka's "societal culture." Tamir emphasizes that, in her view,

the right to self-determination is a cultural right, not a political one, and does not necessarily support a right to political independence. Miller does interpret the right of self-determination as a right to a state, but he hesitates to call it a right, for it may not always be achievable due to the legitimate claims of others. (His concern would perhaps be alleviated by following Philpott in speaking of a "prima facie" right.)

For the purposes of my present argument, I need not enter this important debate but only point out that any one of these views can support the weak claim I wish to make. The claim is that under some circumstances, some groups enjoy a right to self-determination. The circumstances may include—or, following Buchanan, even be limited to—cases of injustice toward the group, or, in a more permissive view, it may not. This right may be enjoyed only by nations or by any group within a territory. It may be that the right of self-determination does not automatically ground a right to political independence, but if some form of self-determination cannot be realized within an existing state, then it can, under these circumstances, ground such a right. For the sake of simplicity, in the discussion that follows I refer to nations or peoples as having a right of self-determination, but this does not commit me to the view that other kinds of groups do not enjoy this right. Similarly, I will sometimes fail to distinguish between a right of self-determination and a right to a state, despite realizing that the former does not necessarily entail the latter. I will assume that in some cases—say, when a federal arrangement cannot be worked out—one can ground the right to a state on the right to self-determination.

My conclusion about the just cause requirement is obvious. Groups other than those constituted by the state in which they live can have a just cause to defend their right of self-determination. While just war theory relies on the rights of the citizens to ground the right of a state to defend itself, other communities within a state may have that same right. When the communal life of a nation is seriously threatened by a state, that nation has a just cause to defend itself. In the case in which the whole nation is within a single state, this can justify secession. In a case in which the community is stateless, as with colonial rule, it is probably less accurate to speak of secession than national liberation.

This is not a radical conclusion. Indeed, it is recognized and endorsed by the United Nations, as Khatchadourian points out: "The UN definition of 'just cause' recognizes the rights of peoples as well as states," and in Article 7 of the definition of *aggression,* the United Nations refers to "the right to self-determination, freedom, and independence, as derived from the Charter, of *peoples* forcibly deprived of that right" (1998, 41). So both morally and legally, "peoples" or "nations" enjoy a right to self-determination. When that right is frustrated, such peoples, I have argued, have the same just cause that states have when the self-determination of their citizens is threatened.

Legitimate Authority

The legitimate authority requirement is usually interpreted to mean that only states can go to war justly. It rules out private groups waging private wars and claiming them to be just. The state has a monopoly on the legitimate use of force, so it is a necessary condition for a just war that it be undertaken by the entity that is uniquely authorized to wield the sword. To allow other entities, groups, or agencies to undertake violence would be to invite chaos. Such violence is seen as merely private violence, crime.

The equation of legitimate authority with states has, however, been criticized by a number of philosophers—and with good reason. Gilbert has argued that "the equation of proper authority with a lawful claim to it should be resisted" (1994, 29). Tony Coates (1997, chapter 5) has argued at some length and quite persuasively that to equate legitimate authority with state sovereignty is to rob the requirement of the moral force that it historically has had. The result is that the principle has become too permissive by assuming that any de facto state may wage war. This requirement, then, is too easily and quickly "checked off": If a war is waged by a state, this requirement is satisfied. This interpretation has meant that "the criterion of legitimate authority has become the most neglected of all the criteria that have been traditionally

employed in the moral assessment of war" (Coates 1997, 123). Contrary to this tendency in recent just war thinking, Coates argues that we must subject to close scrutiny a given state's claim to represent the interests and rights of its people.

When we reject the view that all states are legitimate authorities, we may also ask if some nonstates may be legitimate authorities. The considerations just adduced suggest that being a state is not sufficient for being a legitimate authority. Perhaps it is not necessary either. What matters is the plausibility of the claim to represent the interests and rights of a people. I would like to argue that some non-state entities or organizations may present a very plausible case for being a people's representative. Surely it is sufficient for this that the organization is widely seen as their representative by the members of the nation itself. If an organization claims to act on behalf of a people and is widely seen by that people as legitimately doing so, then the rest of us should look on that organization as the legitimate authority of the people for the purposes of assessing its entitlement to engage in violence on their behalf.

The alternative view, that only states may be legitimate authorities, "leads to political quietism [and is] conservative and uncritical" (Coates 1997, 128). Once we acknowledge that stateless peoples may have the right to self-determination, it would render that right otiose to deny that the right could be defended and vindicated by some nonstate entity. As Dugard (1982, 83) has pointed out, in the case of colonial domination, there is no victim state, though there is a victim people. If we are to grant that a colonized people has a right to self-determination, it seems that we must grant that a nonstate organization—a would-be state, perhaps—can act as a legitimate authority and justly engage in violence on behalf of the people. Examples are not difficult to find. Coates cites the Kurds and the Marsh Arabs in Iraq and asks, "Must such persecuted communities be denied the right of collective self-defense simply because, through some historical accident, they lack the formal character of states?" (1997, 128).

It must be emphasized that the position advocated here requires that the organization not only claim representative status but be perceived to enjoy that status by the people it claims to represent. This is a rather conservative requirement because it rules out "vanguard" organizations that claim representative status despite lack of support among the people themselves. The position defended here is also more stringent than that suggested by Wilkins, who writes that it might "be enough for a terrorist movement simply to claim to represent the aspirations or the moral rights of a people" (1992, 71). While I agree that "moral authority may be all that matters" (Wilkins 1992, 72), I would argue that moral authority requires not merely claiming to represent a people but also being seen by the people themselves as their representative.

How do we know whether this is the case? No single answer can be given here. Certainly the standard should not be higher than that used for states. In the case of states, for example, elections are not required for legitimacy, as understood in just war theory. There are many members of the international community in good standing that are not democratic regimes, authorized by elections. In the case of nonstate entities, no doubt a number of factors will weigh in, either for or against the claim to representativeness, and, in the absence of legal procedures (or public opinion polls), we may have to make an all-things-considered judgment. No doubt there will be some disagreement in particular cases, but all that is required for the present argument is that, in principle, nonstate organizations may enjoy the moral status of legitimate authorities.

Right Intention

If a national group can have a just cause, and if a nonstate entity can be a legitimate authority to engage in violence on behalf of that group, it seems unproblematic that those engaging in violence can be rightly motivated by that just cause. Hence, if just cause and legitimate authority can be satisfied, there seems to be no reason to think that the requirement of right intention cannot be satisfied. This is not to say, of course, that if the first two are satisfied, the latter is as well, but only that if the first two requirements are met, the latter can be. All that it requires is that the relevant actors be motivated by the just cause and not some other end.

Last Resort

Can terrorist violence, undertaken by the representatives of a stateless nation to vindicate their right of self-determination, be a last resort? Some have doubted that it can. For example, Walzer refers to the claim of last resort as one of the "excuses" sometimes offered for terrorism. He suggests that terrorism is usually a first resort, not a last one, and that to truly be a last resort, "one must indeed try everything (which is a lot of things), and not just once. . . . Politics is an art of repetition" (1988, 239). Terrorists, according to Walzer, often claim that their resort to violence is a last resort but in fact it never is and never can be.

Two problems arise concerning Walzer's position. First, related to the definitional issues discussed above and taken up again below when discrimination is treated, Walzer takes terrorism to be "an attack upon the innocent," and he "take[s] the principle for granted: that every act of terrorism is a wrongful act" (1988, 238). Given the understanding of terrorism as murder, it can never be a justified last resort. But as Fullinwider (1988) argues in his response to Walzer, it is puzzling both that Walzer construes terrorism this way, for not all terrorism is random murder, and that Walzer simply takes it for granted that nothing can justify terrorism. Walzer's position is undermined by a prejudicial definition of *terrorism* that begs the substantive moral questions, reflected in the fact that he characterizes arguments in defense of terrorism as mere "excuses."

The second problem is that again Walzer appears to use a double standard. While he does not say so explicitly in the paper under discussion, Walzer elsewhere clearly endorses the resort to war by states. Here, however, he argues that, because "politics is an art of repetition," the last resort is never arrived at for nonstate actors contemplating violence. But why is it that the territorial integrity and political independence of, say, Britain, justify the resort to violence—even violence that targets civilians—but the right of self-determination of a stateless nation never does? Why can states arrive at last resort, while stateless nations cannot? Walzer never provides an answer to this question.

The fact is that judgment is called for by all political actors contemplating violence, and among the judgments that must be made is whether last resort has been satisfied. This is a judgment about whether all reasonable nonviolent measures have been tried, been tried a reasonable number of times, and been given a reasonable amount of time to work. There will always be room for argument about what *reasonable* means here, what it requires in a particular case, but I see no justification for employing a double standard for what it means, one for states, another for nonstate actors. If states may reach the point of deciding that all nonviolent measures have failed, then so too can nonstate actors.

Probability of Success

Whether terrorism ever has any probability of success, or enough probability of success to justify embarking on a terrorist campaign, depends on a number of factors, including the time horizon one has in mind. Whether one considers the case of state actors deciding to embark on a war or nonstate actors embarking on terrorism, a prospective judgment is required, and prospective judgments are liable to miscalculations and incorrect estimations of many factors. Still, one must make a judgment, and if one judges that the end has little chance of being achieved through violence, the probability of success criterion requires that the violence not be commenced.

Does terrorism ever have any probability of success? There are differing views of the historical record on this question. For example, Walzer thinks not. He writes, "No nation that I know of owes its freedom to a campaign of random murder" (1988, 240). Again, we find that Walzer's analysis is hindered by his conception of what terrorism is, and so it is of little help to us here. To those who have a less loaded notion of terrorism, the evidence appears more ambiguous. Held provides a brief, well-balanced discussion of the issue. She cites authors who have argued on both sides of the question, including one who uses the bombing of the U.S. Marines' barracks in Beirut in 1982 (which prompted an American withdrawal) as an example of a successful terrorist attack. Held concludes that "it may be impossible to predict whether an act of terrorism will in fact have its intended effect" but notes that in this it is no different from other prospective judgments (1991, 71). Similarly, Teichman concludes that

the historical evidence on the effectiveness of terrorism is "both ambiguous and incomplete" (1989, 517). And Baier suggests that, at the least, "the prospects for the success of a cause do not seem in the past to have been reduced by resort to unauthorized force, by violent demonstrations that cost some innocent lives" (1994, 208). Finally, Wilkins (1992, 39) believes that some terrorist campaigns have indeed accomplished their goal of national independence and cites Algeria and Kenya as examples.

I am not in a position to judge all of the historical evidence that may be relevant to this issue. However, it seems clear that we cannot say that it is never the case that terrorism has some prospect of success. Perhaps in most cases—the vast majority of them, even—there is little hope of success. Still, we cannot rule out that terrorism can satisfy the probability of success criterion.

Proportionality

The proportionality criterion within *jus ad bellum* also requires a prospective judgment—whether the overall costs of the violent conflict will be outweighed by the overall benefits. In addition to the difficulties inherent in prospective judgments, this criterion is problematic in that it seems to require us to measure the value of costs and benefits that may not be amenable to measurement and seems to assume that all goods are commensurable, that their value can be compared. As a result, there is probably no way to make these kinds of judgments with any great degree of precision.

Still, it seems clear that terrorism can satisfy this criterion at least as well as conventional war. Given the large scale of destruction that often characterizes modern warfare, and given that some very destructive wars are almost universally considered just, it appears that just war theory can countenance a great deal of violence if the end is of sufficient value. If modern warfare is sometimes justified, terrorism, in which the violence is usually on a far smaller scale, can be justified as well. This is especially clear if the end of the violence is the same or similar in both cases, such as when a nation wishes to vindicate its right to self-determination.

JUS IN BELLO

Even if terrorism can meet all the criteria of *jus ad bellum,* it may not be able to meet those of *jus in bello,* for terrorism is often condemned, not so much for who carries it out and why but for how it is carried out. Arguing that it can satisfy the requirements of *jus in bello,* then, may be the greatest challenge facing my argument.

Proportionality

The challenge, however, does not come from the proportionality requirement of *jus in bello.* Like its counterpart in *jus ad bellum,* the criterion requires proportionality between the costs of an action and the benefits to be achieved, but now the requirement is applied to particular acts within the war. It forbids, then, conducting the war in such a way that it involves inordinate costs, costs that are disproportionate to the gains.

Again, there seems to be no reason to believe that terrorist acts could not satisfy this requirement. Given that the scale of the death and destruction usually involved in terrorist acts pales in comparison with that involved in wars commonly thought to be just, it would seem that terrorism would satisfy this requirement more easily than war (assuming that the goods to be achieved are not dissimilar). So if the means of terrorism is what places it beyond the moral pale for many people, it is probably not because of its disproportionality.

Discrimination

The principle of discrimination holds that in waging a war we must distinguish between legitimate and illegitimate targets of attack. The usual way of making this distinction is to classify persons according to their status as combatants and noncombatants and to maintain that only combatants may be attacked. However, there is some disagreement as to the moral basis of this distinction, which creates disagreement as to where exactly this line should be drawn. While usually based on the notion of moral innocence, noncombatant status, it can be argued, has little to do with innocence, for often combatants are conscripts, while those truly responsible for aggression are usually not liable (practically, not morally) to attack. Moreover, many who provide essential support to the war effort are not combatants.

For the moment, though, let us accept the conventional view that discrimination requires that violence be directed at military targets. Assuming the line can be clearly drawn, two points can be made about terrorism and discrimination. The first is that, a priori, it is possible for terrorism to discriminate and still be terrorism. This follows from the argument presented above that, as a matter of definition, it is implausible to define terrorism as intrinsically indiscriminate. Those who define terrorism as random or indiscriminate will disagree and maintain that "discriminate terrorism" is an oxymoron, a conceptual impossibility. Here I can only repeat that this position departs substantially from ordinary language and does so in a way that prejudges the moral issues involved. However, if my argument above does not convince on this question, there is little more to be said here.

Luckily, the issue is not a purely a priori one. The fact is that terrorists, or at least those called terrorists by almost everyone, in fact do often discriminate. One example, cited above, is the bombing of the barracks in Beirut, which killed some 240 American soldiers. Whatever one wants to say to condemn the attack, one cannot say that it was indiscriminate. Fullinwider cites the example of the kidnapping, trail, and killing of Aldo Moro by the Italian Red Brigades in 1978 and argues that, whatever else one might want to say about it, "there was nothing indiscriminate about the taking of Aldo Moro" (1988, 250). Coady (1985, 63) cites another example, that of an American diplomat in Uruguay who was targeted and killed in 1970 because of the assistance he was providing to the authoritarian regime. These may be the exceptions rather than the rule, but it clearly is not accurate to say that terrorists—and there was never any doubt that these were acts of terrorism—never discriminate.

It might be useful to look, one last time, at Walzer's position on this issue because, from the point of view I have developed, he errs on both the conceptual and the empirical question. Walzer maintains that "terrorism in the strict sense, the random murder of innocent people, emerged . . . only in the period after World War II" (1992, 198). Previously, non-state actors, especially revolutionaries, who committed violence did discriminate. Walzer gives several examples of this in which Russian revolutionaries, the Irish Republican Army, and the Stern Gang in the Middle East went to great lengths to not kill civilians. He also notes that these people were called terrorists. Yet he refuses to say that they *were* terrorists, insisting instead that they were not, really, and using scare quotes when he himself calls them terrorists. This is tortured analysis indeed. Why not simply acknowledge that these earlier terrorists were indeed terrorists while also maintaining, if evidence supports it, that today more terrorists are more indiscriminate than in the past? I suspect that Walzer and I would agree in our moral assessment of particular acts. Our main difference is that he believes that calling an act terrorism (without the scare quotes) settles the question.

All of this is consistent with the assumption that a clear line can be drawn between combatants and noncombatants. However, the more reasonable view may be that combatancy status, and therefore liability to attack, are matters of degree. This is suggested by Holmes (1989, 187), and though Holmes writes as a pacifist critic of just war theory, his suggestion is one that just war theorists may nevertheless want to endorse. Holmes conceives of a spectrum along which we can place classes of individuals, according to their degree of responsibility for an aggressive war. At one end he would place political leaders who undertake the aggression, followed by soldiers, contributors to the war, supporters, and, finally, at the other end of the spectrum, noncontributors and nonsupporters. This view does indeed better capture our moral intuitions about liability to attack and avoids debates (which are probably not resolvable) about where the absolute line between combatants and noncombatants is to be drawn.

If correct, this view further complicates the question of whether and when terrorism discriminates. It means we must speak of more and less discriminate violence, and it forces us to ask questions like, To what *extent* were the targets of violence implicated in unjust aggression? Children, for example,

would be clearly off-limits, but nonmilitary adults who actively take part in frustrating a people's right to self-determination may not be. With terrorism, as with war, the question to ask may not be, Was the act discriminate, yes or no? but, rather, How discriminate was the violence? Our judgment on this matter, and hence our moral appraisal of the violence, is likely to be more nuanced if we ask the latter question than if we assume that a simple yes or no settles the matter. After all, is our judgment really the same—and ought it be—when a school bus is attacked as when gun-toting citizens are attacked? Terrorism, it seems, can be more discriminate or less so, and our judgments ought to reflect the important matters of degree involved.

One final issue is worth mentioning, if only briefly. Even if one were to grant that terrorism necessarily involves the killing of innocents, this alone does not place it beyond the scope of just war theory, for innocents may be killed in a just war. All that just war theory requires is that innocents not be *targeted*. The basis for this position is the principle of double effect, which holds, roughly, that innocents may be killed as long as their deaths are not the intended effects of violence but, rather, the unintended (though perhaps fully foreseen) side effects of violence. So the most that can be said against my position, even granting that terrorism involves the killing of innocents, is that the difference between (just) war and terrorism is that in the former innocents are not targeted but (routinely) killed while in the latter they are targeted and killed. Whether this is a crucial distinction is a question that would require us to go too far afield at this point. Perhaps it is enough to say that if there are reasons to reject the principle of double effect, such as those offered by Holmes (1989, 193–200), there is all the more basis to think that terrorism and war are not so morally different from each other.

CONCLUSION

I have argued that terrorism, understood as political violence committed by nonstate actors, can be assessed from the point of view of just war theory and that terrorist acts can indeed satisfy the theory's criteria. Though stateless, some groups can nevertheless have a just cause when their right to self-determination is frustrated. Under such circumstances, a representative organization can be a morally legitimate authority to carry out violence as a last resort to defend the group's rights. Such violence must conform to the other criteria, especially discrimination, but terrorism, I have argued, can do so. . . .

It is important to be clear about what I have not argued here. I have not defended terrorism in general, nor certainly have I defended any particular act of violence. It follows from my argument not that terrorism can be justified but that if war can be justified, then terrorism can be as well. I wish to emphasize the conditional nature of the conclusion. I have not established just war theory as the best or the only framework within which to think about the moral issues raised by political violence. Instead I have relied on it because it is the most developed and widely used in thinking about violence carried out by states. I have done so because the double standard that is often used in assessing violence committed by states and nonstate actors seems indefensible. Applying just war theory to both, I believe, is a plausible way to bring both kinds of violence under one standard.

I have little doubt that most terrorist acts do not satisfy all of the criteria of just war theory and that many of them fall far short. In such cases we are well justified in condemning them. But the condemnation must follow, not precede, examination of the case and is not settled by calling the act terrorism and its perpetrators terrorists. I agree with Fullinwider that, while terrorism often fails to be morally justified, "this failure is contingent, not necessary. We cannot define terrorism into a moral corner where we do not have to worry any more about justification" (1988, 257). Furthermore, failure to satisfy the requirements of just war theory is not unique to acts of terrorism. The same could be said of wars themselves. How many wars, after all, are undertaken and waged within the constraints imposed by the theory?

The conditional nature of the conclusion, if the above argument is sound, forces a choice. Either both interstate war and terrorism can be justified or

neither can be. For my part, I must confess to being sorely tempted by the latter position, that neither war nor terrorism can be justified. This temptation is bolstered by pacifist arguments, such as that presented by Holmes (1989, chapter 6), that the killing of innocents is a perfectly predictable effect of modern warfare, the implication of which is that no modern war can be just. That is, even if we can imagine a modern just war, it is not a realistic possibility. Though the pacifist position is tempting, it also seems clear that some evils are great enough to require a response, even a violent response. And once we grant that states may respond violently, there seems no principled reason to deny that same right to certain nonstate groups that enjoy a right to self-determination.

REFERENCES

Baier, Annette. 1994. Violent Demonstrations. In *Moral Prejudices: Essays on Ethics.* Cambridge: Harvard University Press.

Beitz, Charles R. 1979. *Political Theory and International Relations.* Princeton: Princeton University Press.

Buchanan, Allen. 1991. *Secession: The Morality of Political Divorce from Fort Sumter to Lithuania and Quebec.* Boulder: Westview Press.

Coady, C. A. J. 1985. The Morality of Terrorism. *Philosophy* 60: 47–69.

Coates, Anthony J. 1997. *The Ethics of War.* Manchester: Manchester University Press.

Fullinwider, Robert K. 1988. Understanding Terrorism. In *Problems of International Justice,* ed. Steven Luper-Foy. Boulder: Westview Press.

Gilbert, Paul. 1994. *Terrorism, Security, and Nationality: An Introductory Study in Applied Political Philosophy.* New York: Routledge.

Held, Virginia. 1991. Terrorism, Rights, and Political Goals. In *Violence, Terrorism, and Justice,* ed. R. G. Frey and Christopher W. Morris. Cambridge: Cambridge University Press.

Holmes, Robert L. 1989. *On War and Morality.* Princeton: Princeton University Press.

Khatchadourian, Haig. 1998. *The Morality of Terrorism.* New York: Peter Lang.

Kymlicka, Will. 1995. *Multicultural Citizenship: A Liberal Theory of Minority Rights.* Oxford: Clarendon Press.

Margalit, Avishai, and Joseph Raz. 1990. National Self-Determination. *Journal of Philosophy* 87: 439–61.

Mill, John Stuart. 1984 [1859]. A Few Words on Non-Intervention. In *Essays on Equality, Law, and Education: Collected Works of John Stuart Mill,* Vol. 21, ed. John Robson. Toronto: University of Toronto Press.

Miller, David. 1995. *On Nationality.* Oxford: Oxford University Press.

Philpott, Daniel. 1995. In Defense of Self-Determination. *Ethics* 105: 352–85.

Tamir, Yael. 1993. *Liberal Nationalism.* Princeton: Princeton University Press.

Teichman, Jenny. 1989. How to Define Terrorism. *Philosophy* 64: 505–17.

Walzer, Michael. 1988. Terrorism: A Critique of Excuses. In *Problems of International Justice,* ed. Steven Luper-Foy. Boulder: Westview Press.

———. 1992 [1979]. *Just and Unjust Wars: A Moral Argument with Historical Illustrations.* 2nd edition. New York: Basic Books.

Wellman, Carl. 1979. On Terrorism Itself. *Journal of Value Inquiry* 13: 250–58.

Wellman, Christopher H. 1995. A Defense of Secession and Political Self-Determination. *Philosophy and Public Affairs* 24: 142–71.

Wilkins, Burleigh Taylor. 1992. *Terrorism and Collective Responsibility.* New York: Routledge.

READING QUESTIONS

1. According to Valls, what are the two difficulties that arise when one is trying to define "terrorism"? What final definition of the term does Valls stipulate that he will use in his arguments?

2. Valls's weak claim for just cause is that some groups enjoy a right to self-determination. Which groups, according to Valls, might enjoy such a right?

3. Valls argues that the legitimate authority requirement can be met by a nonstate organization under two conditions. First, the organization must claim to represent the rights and interests of a people. What is the second condition?

4. If the first two requirements of jus ad bellum are met, is entailment of the right intention requirement necessarily entailed? How does Valls answer that question?

5. Valls argues that there are two problems arising from Walzer's claim that terrorism never can be a last resort. What are those problems?

6. What is the difference in context between the proportionality requirement of jus ad bellum and the proportionality requirement of jus in bello?

7. Valls suggests that the question of discrimination between combatants and noncombatants be replaced with a question about the extent to which a violent act discriminates among targets along a continuum. What reasons does he give for this view?

DISCUSSION QUESTIONS

1. Various commentators claim that acts of violence need not be indiscriminate, or directed toward innocents, or intended to spread fear in order to be classed as acts of "terror." Discuss whether you think that each of these is or is not a necessary condition of "terrorism."

2. Someone might argue that although certain acts of terrorism may satisfy the criteria of jus ad bellum, they do not satisfy the criteria of jus in bello. Give an example (real or fictional) of such a case.

3. Valls claims that the decision to commit violence as a last resort is justified when all reasonable nonviolent measures have been tried, and there is always room for argument about what "reasonable" means. Think of an example of an act of state or nonstate violence and discuss whether and to what extent "reasonable" nonviolent measures were tried.

ALAN M. DERSHOWITZ

Should the Ticking Bomb Terrorist Be Tortured?

The "ticking bomb" case refers to a hypothetical situation in which only by torturing a terrorist who knows the whereabouts of a ticking bomb can the bomb be found and defused before it detonates and kills many innocent people. Should the ticking bomb terrorist be tortured? Dershowitz argues from an act utilitarian moral perspective for an affirmative answer to this question. He then argues that a democratic society governed by the rule of law should never declare some action to be absolutely wrong, yet knowingly allow the military or other public officials to engage in that activity "off the books." But if torture is morally permissible in extreme "necessity" cases such as the ticking bomb case, democratic governments ought to change existing law to accommodate this practice. Dershowitz proposes that a system of judicial "torture warrants" be instituted as part of a legal system regulating the practice.

Recommended Reading: consequentialism, chap. 1, sec. 2A, particularly act utilitarianism.

HOW I BEGAN THINKING ABOUT TORTURE

In the late 1980s I traveled to Israel to conduct some research and teach a class at Hebrew University on civil liberties during times of crisis. In the course of my research I learned that the Israeli security services were employing what they euphemistically called "moderate physical pressure" on suspected terrorists to obtain information deemed necessary to prevent future terrorist attacks. The method employed by the security services fell somewhere between what many would regard as very rough interrogation (as practiced by the British in Northern Ireland) and outright torture (as practiced by the French in Algeria and by Egypt, the Philippines, and Jordan today). In most cases the suspect would be placed in a dark room with a smelly sack over his head. Loud, unpleasant music or other noise would blare from speakers. The suspect would be seated in an extremely uncomfortable position and then shaken vigorously until he disclosed the information. Statements made under this kind of nonlethal pressure could not be introduced in any court of law, both because they were involuntarily secured and because they were deemed potentially untrustworthy—at least without corroboration. But they were used as leads in the prevention of terrorist acts. Sometimes the leads proved false, other times they proved true. There is little doubt that some acts of terrorism—which would have killed many civilians—were prevented. There is also little doubt that the cost of saving these lives—measured in terms of basic human rights—was extraordinarily high.

In my classes and public lectures in Israel, I strongly condemned these methods as a violation of core civil liberties and human rights. The response that people gave, across the political spectrum from

From Alan M. Dershowitz, *Why Terrorism Works: Understanding the Threat, Responding to the Challenge* (New Haven and London: Yale University Press, 2002). Reprinted by permission.

civil libertarians to law-and-order advocates, was essentially the same: but what about the "ticking bomb" case?

The ticking bomb case refers to a scenario that has been discussed by many philosophers, including Michael Walzer, Jean-Paul Sartre, and Jeremy Bentham. Walzer described such a hypothetical case in an article titled "Political Action: The Problem of Dirty Hands." In this case, a decent leader of a nation plagued with terrorism is asked "to authorize the torture of a captured rebel leader who knows or probably knows the location of a number of bombs hidden in apartment buildings across the city, set to go off within the next twenty-four hours. He orders the man tortured, convinced that he must do so for the sake of the people who might otherwise die in the explosions—even though he believes that torture is wrong, indeed abominable, not just sometimes, but always."[1]

In Israel, the use of torture to prevent terrorism was not hypothetical; it was very real and recurring. I soon discovered that virtually no one was willing to take the "purist" position against torture in the ticking bomb case: namely, that the ticking bomb must be permitted to explode and kill dozens of civilians, even if this disaster could be prevented by subjecting the captured terrorist to nonlethal torture and forcing him to disclose its location. I realized that the extraordinarily rare situation of the hypothetical ticking bomb terrorist was serving as a moral, intellectual, and legal justification for a pervasive *system* of coercive interrogation, which, though not the paradigm of torture, certainly bordered on it. It was then that I decided to challenge this system by directly confronting the ticking bomb case. I presented the following challenge to my Israeli audience: If the reason you permit nonlethal torture is based on the ticking bomb case, why not limit it exclusively to that compelling but rare situation? Moreover, if you believe that nonlethal torture is justifiable in the ticking bomb case, why not require advance judicial approval—a "torture warrant"? That was the origin of a controversial proposal that has received much attention, largely critical, from the media. Its goal was, and remains, to reduce the use of torture to the smallest amount and degree possible, while creating

public accountability for its rare use. I saw it not as a compromise with civil liberties but rather as an effort to maximize civil liberties in the face of a realistic likelihood that torture would, in fact, take place below the radar screen of accountability. . . .

THE CASE FOR TORTURING THE TICKING BOMB TERRORIST

The arguments in favor of using torture as a last resort to prevent a ticking bomb from exploding and killing many people are both simple and simple-minded. Bentham constructed a compelling hypothetical case to support his utilitarian argument against an absolute prohibition on torture:

> Suppose an occasion were to arise, in which a suspicion is entertained, as strong as that which would be received as a sufficient ground for arrest and commitment as for felony—a suspicion that at this very time a considerable number of individuals are actually suffering, by illegal violence inflictions equal in intensity to those which if inflicted by the hand of justice, would universally be spoken of under the name of torture. For the purpose of rescuing from torture these hundred innocents, should any scruple be made of applying equal or superior torture, to extract the requisite information from the mouth of one criminal, who having it in his power to make known the place where at this time the enormity was practising or about to be practised, should refuse to do so? To say nothing of wisdom, could any pretence be made so much as to the praise of blind and vulgar humanity, by the man who to save one criminal, should determine to abandon 100 innocent persons to the same fate?[2]

If the torture of one guilty person would be justified to prevent the torture of a hundred innocent persons, it would seem to follow—certainly to Bentham—that it would also be justified to prevent the murder of thousands of innocent civilians in the ticking bomb case. Consider two hypothetical situations that are not, unfortunately, beyond the realm of possibility. In fact, they are both extrapolations on actual situations we have faced.

Several weeks before September 11, 2001, the Immigration and Naturalization Service detained Zacarias Moussaoui after flight instructors reported suspicious statements he had made while taking flying lessons and paying for them with large amounts of cash.[3] The government decided not to seek a warrant to search his computer. Now imagine that they had, and that they discovered he was part of a plan to destroy large occupied buildings, but without any further details. They interrogated him, gave him immunity from prosecution, and offered him large cash rewards and a new identity. He refused to talk. They then threatened him, tried to trick him, and employed every lawful technique available. He still refused. They even injected him with sodium pentothal and other truth serums, but to no avail. The attack now appeared to be imminent, but the FBI still had no idea what the target was or what means would be used to attack it. We could not simply evacuate all buildings indefinitely. An FBI agent proposes the use of nonlethal torture—say, a sterilized needle inserted under the fingernails to produce unbearable pain without any threat to health or life, or the method used in the film *Marathon Man,* a dental drill through an unanesthetized tooth.

The simple cost-benefit analysis for employing such nonlethal torture seems overwhelming: it is surely better to inflict nonlethal pain on one guilty terrorist who is illegally withholding information needed to prevent an act of terrorism than to permit a large number of innocent victims to die. Pain is a lesser and more remediable harm than death; and the lives of a thousand innocent people should be valued more than the bodily integrity of one guilty person. If the variation on the Moussaoui case is not sufficiently compelling to make this point, we can always raise the stakes. Several weeks after September 11, our government received reports that a ten-kiloton nuclear weapon may have been stolen from Russia and was on its way to New York City, where it would be detonated and kill hundreds of thousands of people. The reliability of the source, code named Dragonfire, was uncertain, but assume for purposes of this hypothetical extension of the actual case that the source was a captured terrorist—like the one tortured by the Philippine authorities—who

knew precisely how and where the weapon was being brought into New York and was to be detonated. Again, everything short of torture is tried, but to no avail. It is not absolutely certain torture will work, but it is our last, best hope for preventing a cataclysmic nuclear devastation in a city too large to evacuate in time. Should nonlethal torture be tried? Bentham would certainly have said yes.

The strongest argument against any resort to torture, even in the ticking bomb case, also derives from Bentham's utilitarian calculus. Experience has shown that if torture, which has been deemed illegitimate by the civilized world for more than a century, were now to be legitimated—even for limited use in one extraordinary type of situation—such legitimation would constitute an important symbolic setback in the worldwide campaign against human rights abuses. Inevitably, the legitimation of torture by the world's leading democracy would provide a welcome justification for its more widespread use in other parts of the world. Two Bentham scholars, W. L. Twining and P. E. Twining, have argued that torture is unacceptable even if it is restricted to an extremely limited category of cases:

> There is at least one good practical reason for drawing a distinction between justifying an isolated act of torture in an extreme emergency of the kind postulated above and justifying the *institutionalisation* of torture as a regular practice. The circumstances are so extreme in which most of us would be prepared to justify resort to torture, if at all, the conditions we would impose would be so stringent, the practical problems of devising and enforcing adequate safeguards so difficult and the risks of abuse so great that it would be unwise and dangerous to entrust any government, however enlightened, with such a power. Even an out-and-out utilitarian can support an absolute prohibition against institutionalised torture on the ground that no government in the world can be trusted not to abuse the power and to satisfy in practice the conditions he would impose.[4]

Bentham's own justification was based on *case* or *act* utilitarianism—a demonstration that in a *particular case,* the benefits that would flow from the limited use of torture would outweigh its costs. The argument against any use of torture would derive from *rule* utilitarianism—which considers the implications of establishing a precedent that would inevitably be extended beyond its limited case utilitarian justification to other possible evils of lesser magnitude. Even terrorism itself could be justified by a case utilitarian approach. Surely one could come up with a singular situation in which the targeting of a small number of civilians could be thought necessary to save thousands of other civilians—blowing up a German kindergarten by the relatives of inmates in a Nazi death camp, for example, and threatening to repeat the targeting of German children unless the death camps were shut down.

The reason this kind of single-case utilitarian justification is simple-minded is that it has no inherent limiting principle. If nonlethal torture of one person is justified to prevent the killing of many important people, then what if it were necessary to use lethal torture—or at least torture that posed a substantial risk of death? What if it were necessary to torture the suspect's mother or children to get him to divulge the information? What if it took threatening to kill his family, his friends, his entire village? Under a simple-minded quantitative case utilitarianism, anything goes as long as the number of people tortured or killed does not exceed the number that would be saved. This is morality by numbers, unless there are other constraints on what we can properly do. These other constraints can come from rule utilitarianisms or other principles of morality, such as the prohibition against deliberately punishing the innocent. Unless we are prepared to impose some limits on the use of torture or other barbaric tactics that might be of some use in preventing terrorism, we risk hurtling down a slippery slope into the abyss of amorality and ultimately tyranny. Dostoevsky captured the complexity of this dilemma in *The Brothers Karamazov* when he had Ivan pose the following question to Alyosha: "Imagine that you are creating a fabric of human destiny with the object of making men happy in the end, giving them peace at least, but that it was essential and inevitable to torture to death only one tiny creature—that baby beating its breast with its fist, for instance—and to found that edifice on its unavenged tears, would you consent to be the architect on those conditions? Tell me the truth."

A willingness to kill an innocent child suggests a willingness to do anything to achieve a necessary result. Hence the slippery slope.

It does not necessarily follow from this understandable fear of the slippery slope that we can never consider the use of nonlethal infliction of pain, if its use were to be limited by acceptable principles of morality. After all, imprisoning a witness who refuses to testify after being given immunity is designed to be punitive—that is painful. Such imprisonment can, on occasion, produce more pain and greater risk of death than nonlethal torture. Yet we continue to threaten and use the pain of imprisonment to loosen the tongues of reluctant witnesses.

It is commonplace for police and prosecutors to threaten recalcitrant suspects with prison rape. As one prosecutor put it: "You're going to be the boyfriend of a very bad man." The slippery slope is an argument of caution, not a debate stopper, since virtually every compromise with an absolutist approach to rights carries the risk of slipping further. An appropriate response to the slippery slope is to build in a principled break. For example, if nonlethal torture were legally limited to convicted terrorists who had knowledge of future massive terrorist acts, were given immunity, and still refused to provide the information, there might still be objections to the use of torture, but they would have to go beyond the slippery slope argument.

The case utilitarian argument for torturing a ticking bomb terrorist is bolstered by an argument from analogy—an a fortiori argument. What moral principle could justify the death penalty for past individual murders and at the same time condemn nonlethal torture to prevent future mass murders? Bentham posed this rhetorical question as support for his argument. The death penalty is, of course, reserved for convicted murderers. But again, what if torture was limited to convicted terrorists who refused to divulge information about future terrorism? Consider as well the analogy to the use of deadly force against suspects fleeing from arrest for dangerous felonies of which they have not yet been convicted. Or military retaliations that produce the predictable and inevitable collateral killing of some innocent civilians. The case against torture, if made by a Quaker who opposes the death penalty, war, self-defense, and the use of lethal force against fleeing felons, is understandable. But for anyone who justifies killing on the basis of a cost-benefit analysis, the case against the use of nonlethal torture to save multiple lives is more difficult to make. In the end, absolute opposition to torture—even nonlethal torture in the ticking bomb case—may rest more on historical and aesthetic considerations than on moral or logical ones.

In debating the issue of torture, the first question I am often asked is, "Do you want to take us back to the Middle Ages?" The association between any form of torture and gruesome death is powerful in the minds of most people knowledgeable of the history of its abuses. This understandable association makes it difficult for many people to think about nonlethal torture as a technique for *saving* lives.

The second question I am asked is, "What kind of torture do you have in mind?" When I respond by describing the sterilized needle being shoved under the fingernails, the reaction is visceral and often visible—a shudder coupled with a facial gesture of disgust. Discussions of the death penalty on the other hand can be conducted without these kinds of reactions, especially now that we literally put the condemned prisoner "to sleep" by laying him out on a gurney and injecting a lethal substance into his body. There is no breaking of the neck, burning of the brain, bursting of internal organs, or gasping for breath that used to accompany hanging, electrocution, shooting, and gassing. The executioner has been replaced by a paramedical technician, as the aesthetics of death have become more acceptable. All this tends to cover up the reality that death is forever while nonlethal pain is temporary. In our modern age death is underrated, while pain is overrated.

I observed a similar phenomenon several years ago during the debate over corporal punishment that was generated by the decision of a court in Singapore to sentence a young American to medically supervised lashing with a cane. Americans who support the death penalty and who express little concern about inner-city prison conditions were outraged by the specter of a few welts on the buttocks of an American. It was an utterly irrational display of hypocrisy and double standards. Given a choice

between a medically administrated whipping and one month in a typical state lockup or prison, any rational and knowledgeable person would choose the lash. No one dies of welts or pain, but many inmates are raped, beaten, knifed, and otherwise mutilated and tortured in American prisons. The difference is that we don't see—and we don't want to see—what goes on behind their high walls. Nor do we want to think about it. Raising the issue of torture makes Americans think about a brutalizing and unaesthetic phenomenon that has been out of our consciousness for many years.[5]

THE THREE—OR FOUR—WAYS

The debate over the use of torture goes back many years, with Bentham supporting it in a limited category of cases, Kant opposing it as part of his categorical imperative against improperly using people as means for achieving noble ends, and Voltaire's views on the matter being "hopelessly confused."[6] The modern resort to terrorism has renewed the debate over how a rights-based society should respond to the prospect of using nonlethal torture in the ticking bomb situation. In the late 1980s the Israeli government appointed a commission headed by a retired Supreme Court justice to look into precisely that situation. The commission concluded that there are "three ways for solving this grave dilemma between the vital need to preserve the very existence of the state and its citizens, and maintain its character as a law-abiding state." The first is to allow the security services to continue to fight terrorism in "a twilight zone which is outside the realm of law." The second is "the way of the hypocrites: they declare that they abide by the rule of law, but turn a blind eye to what goes on beneath the surface." And the third, "the truthful road of the rule of law," is that the "law itself must insure a proper framework for the activity" of the security services in seeking to prevent terrorist acts.

There is of course a fourth road: namely to forgo any use of torture and simply allow the preventable terrorist act to occur.[7] After the Supreme Court of Israel outlawed the use of physical pressure, the Israeli security services claimed that, as a result of the Supreme Court's decision, at least one preventable act of terrorism had been allowed to take place, one that killed several people when a bus was bombed. Whether this claim is true, false, or somewhere in between is difficult to assess.[8] But it is clear that if the preventable act of terrorism was of the magnitude of the attacks of September 11, there would be a great outcry in any democracy that had deliberately refused to take available preventive action, even if it required the use of torture. During numerous public appearances since September 11, 2001, I have asked audiences for a show of hands as to how many would support the use of nonlethal torture in a ticking bomb case. Virtually every hand is raised. The few that remain down go up when I ask how many believe that torture would actually be used in such a case.

Law enforcement personnel give similar responses. This can be seen in reports of physical abuse directed against some suspects that have been detained following September 11, reports that have been taken quite seriously by at least one federal judge. It is confirmed by the willingness of U.S. law enforcement officials to facilitate the torture of terrorist suspects by repressive regimes allied with our intelligence agencies. As one former CIA operative with thirty years of experience reported: "A lot of people are saying we need someone at the agency who can pull fingernails out. Others are saying, 'Let others use interrogation methods that we don't use.' The only question then is, do you want to have CIA people in the room?" The real issue, therefore, is not whether some torture would or would not be used in the ticking bomb case—it would. The question is whether it would be done openly, pursuant to a previously established legal procedure, or whether it would be done secretly, in violation of existing law.

Several important values are pitted against each other in this conflict. The first is the safety and security of a nation's citizens. Under the ticking bomb scenario this value may require the use of torture, if that is the only way to prevent the bomb from exploding and killing large numbers of civilians. The second value is the preservation of civil liberties and human rights. This value requires that we not accept torture as a legitimate part of our legal system. In my debates with two prominent civil libertarians, Floyd Abrams and Harvey Silverglate, both have acknowledged that they would want nonlethal torture to be used if it could prevent thousands of deaths, but they did not want torture to be officially recognized by our legal system. As Abrams put it: "In a democracy sometimes it is necessary to do things off the books and below the radar screen." Former presidential candidate Alan Keyes took the position that although torture might be *necessary* in a given situation it could never be *right*. He suggested that a president *should* authorize the torturing of a ticking bomb terrorist, but that this act should not be legitimated by the courts or incorporated into our legal system. He argued that wrongful and indeed unlawful acts might sometimes be necessary to preserve the nation, but that no aura of legitimacy should be placed on these actions by judicial imprimatur.

This understandable approach is in conflict with the third important value: namely, open accountability and visibility in a democracy. "Off-the-book actions below the radar screen" are antithetical to the theory and practice of democracy. Citizens cannot approve or disapprove of governmental actions of which they are unaware. We have learned the lesson of history that off-the-book actions can produce terrible consequences. Richard Nixon's creation of a group of "plumbers" led to Watergate, and Ronald Reagan's authorization of an off-the-books foreign policy in Central America led to the Iran-Contra scandal. And these are only the ones we know about!

Perhaps the most extreme example of such a hypocritical approach to torture comes—not surprisingly—from the French experience in Algeria. The French army used torture extensively in seeking to prevent terrorism during a brutal colonial war from 1955 to 1957. An officer who supervised this torture, General Paul Aussaresses, wrote a book recounting what he had done and seen, including the torture of dozens of Algerians. "The best way to make a terrorist talk when he refused to say what he knew was to torture him," he boasted. Although the book was published decades after the war was over, the general was prosecuted—but not for what he had done to the

Algerians. Instead, he was prosecuted for *revealing* what he had done, and seeking to justify it.

In a democracy governed by the rule of law, we should never want our soldiers or our president to take any action that we deem wrong or illegal. A good test of whether an action should or should not be done is whether we are prepared to have it disclosed—perhaps not immediately, but certainly after some time has passed. No legal system operating under the rule of law should ever tolerate an "off-the-books" approach to necessity. Even the defense of necessity must be justified lawfully. The road to tyranny has always been paved with claims of necessity made by those responsible for the security of a nation. Our system of checks and balances requires that all presidential actions, like all legislative or military actions, be consistent with governing law. If it is necessary to torture in the ticking bomb case, then our governing laws must accommodate this practice. If we refuse to change our law to accommodate any particular action, then our government should not take that action.

Only in a democracy committed to civil liberties would a triangular conflict of this kind exist. Totalitarian and authoritarian regimes experience no such conflict, because they subscribe to neither the civil libertarian nor the democratic values that come in conflict with the value of security. The hard question is: which value is to be preferred when an inevitable clash occurs? One or more of these values must inevitably be compromised in making the tragic choice presented by the ticking bomb case. If we do not torture, we compromise the security and safety of our citizens. If we tolerate torture, but keep it off the books and below the radar screen, we compromise principles of democratic accountability. If we create a legal structure for limiting and controlling torture, we compromise our principled opposition to torture in all circumstances and create a potentially dangerous and expandable situation.

In 1678, the French writer François de La Rochefoucauld said that "hypocrisy is the homage that vice renders to virtue." In this case we have two vices: terrorism and torture. We also have two virtues: civil liberties and democratic accountability. Most civil libertarians I know prefer hypocrisy, precisely because it appears to avoid the conflict between security and civil liberties, but by choosing the way of the hypocrite these civil libertarians compromise the value of democratic accountability. Such is the nature of tragic choices in a complex world. As Bentham put it more than two centuries ago: "Government throughout is but a choice of evils." In a democracy, such choices must be made, whenever possible, with openness and democratic accountability, and subject to the rule of law.[9]

Consider another terrible choice of evils that could easily have been presented on September 11, 2001—and may well be presented in the future: a hijacked passenger jet is on a collision course with a densely occupied office building; the only way to prevent the destruction of the building and the killing of its occupants is to shoot down the jet, thereby killing its innocent passengers. This choice now seems easy, because the passengers are certain to die anyway and their somewhat earlier deaths will save numerous lives. The passenger jet must be shot down. But what if it were only *probable,* not certain, that the jet would crash into the building? Say, for example, we know from cell phone transmissions that passengers are struggling to regain control of the hijacked jet, but it is unlikely they will succeed in time. Or say we have no communication with the jet and all we know is that it is off course and heading toward Washington, D.C., or some other densely populated city. Under these more questionable circumstances, the question becomes *who* should make this life and death choice between evils—a decision that may turn out tragically wrong?

No reasonable person would allocate this decision to a fighter jet pilot who happened to be in the area or to a local airbase commander—unless of course there was no time for the matter to be passed up the chain of command to the president or the secretary of defense. A decision of this kind should be made at the highest level possible, with visibility and accountability.

Why is this not also true of the decision to torture a ticking bomb terrorist? Why should that choice of evils be relegated to a local policeman, FBI agent, or CIA operative, rather than to a judge, the attorney general, or the president?

There are, of course, important differences between the decision to shoot down the plane and the decision to torture the ticking bomb terrorist. Having to shoot down an airplane, though tragic, is not likely to be a recurring issue. There is no slope down which to slip. Moreover, the jet to be shot down is filled with our fellow citizens—people with whom we can identify. The suspected terrorist we may choose to torture is a "they"—an enemy with whom we do not identify but with whose potential victims we do identify. The risk of making the wrong decision, or of overdoing the torture, is far greater, since we do not care as much what happens to "them" as to "us." Finally, there is something different about torture—even nonlethal torture—that sets it apart from a quick death. In addition to the horrible history associated with torture, there is also the aesthetic of torture. The very idea of deliberately subjecting a captive human being to excruciating pain violates our sense of what is acceptable. On a purely rational basis, it is far worse to shoot a fleeing felon in the back and kill him, yet every civilized society authorizes shooting such a suspect who poses dangers of committing violent crimes against the police or others. In the United States we execute convicted murderers, despite compelling evidence of the unfairness and ineffectiveness of capital punishment. Yet many of us recoil at the prospect of shoving a sterilized needle under the finger of a suspect who is refusing to divulge information that might prevent multiple deaths. Despite the irrationality of these distinctions, they are understandable, especially in light of the sordid history of torture.

We associate torture with the Inquisition, the Gestapo, the Stalinist purges, and the Argentine colonels responsible for the "dirty war." We recall it as a prelude to death, an integral part of a regime of gratuitous pain leading to a painful demise. We find it difficult to imagine a benign use of nonlethal torture to save lives.

Yet there was a time in the history of Anglo-Saxon law when torture was used to save life, rather than to take it, and when the limited administration of nonlethal torture was supervised by judges, including some who are well remembered in history. This fascinating story has been recounted by Professor John Langbein of Yale Law School, and it is worth summarizing here

because it helps inform the debate over whether, if torture would in fact be used in a ticking bomb case, it would be worse to make it part of the legal system, or worse to have it done off the books and below the radar screen.

In his book on legalized torture during the sixteenth and seventeenth centuries, *Torture and the Law of Proof,* Langbein demonstrates the trade-off between torture and other important values. Torture was employed for several purposes. First, it was used to secure the evidence necessary to obtain a guilty verdict under the rigorous criteria for conviction required at the time—either the testimony of two eyewitnesses or the confession of the accused himself. Circumstantial evidence, no matter how compelling, would not do. As Langbein concludes, "no society will long tolerate a legal system in which there is no prospect in convicting unrepentant persons who commit clandestine crimes. Something had to be done to extend the system to those cases. The two-eyewitness rule was hard to compromise or evade, but the confession invited 'subterfuge.'" The subterfuge that was adopted permitted the use of torture to obtain confessions from suspects against whom there was compelling circumstantial evidence of guilt. The circumstantial evidence, alone, could not be used to convict, but it was used to obtain a torture warrant. That torture warrant was in turn used to obtain a confession, which then had to be independently corroborated—at least in most cases (witchcraft and other such cases were exempted from the requirement of corroboration).[10]

Torture was also used against persons already convicted of capital crimes, such as high treason, who were thought to have information necessary to prevent attacks on the state.

Langbein studied eighty-one torture warrants, issued between 1540 and 1640, and found that in many of them, especially in "the higher cases of treasons, torture is used for discovery, and not for evidence." Torture was "used to protect the state" and "mostly that meant preventive torture to identify and forestall plots and plotters." It was only when the legal system loosened its requirement of proof (or introduced the "black box" of the jury system) and when perceived threats against the state diminished that torture was no longer deemed necessary to convict guilty defendants against whom there had previously been insufficient evidence, or to secure preventive information.[11] . . .

Every society has insisted on the incapacitation of dangerous criminals regardless of strictures in the formal legal rules. Some use torture, others use informal sanctions, while yet others create the black box of a jury, which need not explain its common-sense verdicts. Similarly, every society insists that, if there are steps that can be taken to prevent effective acts of terrorism, these steps should be taken, even if they require some compromise with other important principles.

. . . In deciding whether the ticking bomb terrorist should be tortured, one important question is whether there would be less torture if it were done as part of the legal system, as it was in sixteenth- and seventeenth-century England, or off the books, as it is in many countries today. The Langbein study does not definitively answer this question, but it does provide some suggestive insights. The English system of torture was more visible and thus more subject to public accountability, and it is likely that torture was employed less frequently in England than in France. "During these years when it appears that torture might have become routinized in English criminal procedure, the Privy Council kept the torture power under careful control and never allowed it to fall into the hands of the regular law enforcement officers," as it had in France. In England "no law enforcement officer . . . acquired the power to use torture without special warrant." Moreover, when torture warrants were abolished, "the English experiment with torture left no traces." Because it was under centralized control, it was easier to abolish than it was in France, where it persisted for many years.[12]

It is always difficult to extrapolate from history, but it seems logical that a formal, visible, accountable, and centralized system is somewhat easier to control than an ad hoc, off-the-books, and under-the-radar-screen nonsystem. I believe, though I certainly cannot prove, that a formal requirement of a judicial warrant as a prerequisite to nonlethal torture would decrease the amount of physical violence directed against suspects. At the most obvious level, a double check is always more protective than a single check. In every instance in which a warrant is requested, a field officer has already decided that torture is justified and, in the absence of a warrant requirement, would simply proceed with the torture. Requiring that decision to be approved by a judicial officer will result in fewer instances of torture even if the judge rarely turns down a request. Moreover, I believe that most judges would require compelling evidence before they would authorize so extraordinary a departure from our constitutional norms, and law enforcement officials would be reluctant to seek a warrant unless they had compelling evidence that the suspect had information needed to prevent an imminent terrorist attack. A record would be kept of every warrant granted, and although it is certainly possible that some individual agents might torture without a warrant, they would have no excuse, since a warrant procedure would be available. They could not claim "necessity," because the decision as to whether the torture is indeed necessary has been taken out of their hands and placed in the hands of a judge. In addition, even if torture were deemed totally illegal without any exception, it would still occur, though the public would be less aware of its existence.

I also believe that the rights of the suspect would be better protected with a warrant requirement. He would be granted immunity, told that he was now compelled to testify, threatened with imprisonment if he refused to do so, and given the option of providing the requested information. Only if he refused to do what he was legally compelled to do—provide necessary information, which could not incriminate him because of the immunity—would he be threatened with torture. Knowing that such a threat was authorized by the law, he might well provide the information.[13] If he still refused to, he would be subjected to judicially monitored physical measures designed to cause excruciating pain without leaving any lasting damage.

Let me cite two examples to demonstrate why I think there would be less torture with a warrant requirement than without one. Recall the case of the alleged national security wiretap placed on the phones of Martin Luther King by the Kennedy administration in the early 1960s. This was in the days when the attorney general could authorize a national security wiretap without a warrant. Today no judge would issue a warrant in a case as flimsy as that one. When Zacarias Moussaoui was detained after raising suspicions while trying to learn how to fly an airplane, the government did not even seek a national security wiretap because its lawyers believed that a judge would not have granted one. If Moussaoui's computer could have been searched without a warrant, it almost certainly would have been.

It should be recalled that in the context of searches, our Supreme Court opted for a judicial check on the discretion of the police, by requiring a search warrant in most cases. The Court has explained the reason for the warrant requirement as follows: "The informed and deliberate determinations of magistrates . . . are to be preferred over the hurried action of officers."[14] Justice Robert Jackson elaborated:

> The point of the Fourth Amendment, which often is not grasped by zealous officers, is not that it denies law enforcement the support of the usual inferences which reasonable men draw from evidence. Its protection consists in requiring that those inferences be drawn by a neutral and detached magistrate instead of being judged by the officer engaged in the often competitive enterprise of ferreting out crime. Any assumption that evidence sufficient to support a magistrate's disinterested determination to issue a search warrant will justify the officers in making a search without a warrant would reduce the Amendment to nullity and leave the people's homes secure only in the discretion of police officers.[15]

Although torture is very different from a search, the policies underlying the warrant requirement are relevant to the question whether there is likely to be more torture or less if the decision is left entirely to field officers, or if a judicial officer has to approve a request for a torture warrant. As Abraham Maslow once observed, to a man with a hammer, everything looks like a nail. If the man with the hammer must get judicial approval before he can use it, he will probably use it less often and more carefully.

There are other, somewhat more subtle, considerations that should be factored into any decision regarding torture. There are some who see silence as a virtue when it comes to the choice among such horrible evils as torture and terrorism. It is far better,

they argue, not to discuss or write about issues of this sort, lest they become legitimated. And legitimation is an appropriate concern. Justice Jackson, in his opinion in one of the cases concerning the detention of Japanese-Americans during World War II, made the following relevant observation:

> Much is said of the danger to liberty from the Army program for deporting and detaining these citizens of Japanese extraction. But a judicial construction of the due process clause that will sustain this order is a far more subtle blow to liberty than the promulgation of the order itself. A military order, however unconstitutional, is not apt to last longer than the military emergency. Even during that period a succeeding commander may revoke it all. But once a judicial opinion rationalizes such an order to show that it conforms to the Constitution, or rather rationalizes the Constitution to show that the Constitution sanctions such an order, the Court for all time has validated the principle of racial discrimination in criminal procedure and of transplanting American citizens. The principle then lies about like a loaded weapon ready for the hand of any authority that can bring forward a plausible claim of an urgent need. Every repetition imbeds that principle more deeply in our law and thinking and expands it to new purposes. All who observe the work of courts are familiar with what Judge Cardozo described as "the tendency of a principle to expand itself to the limit of its logic." A military commander may overstep the bounds of constitutionality, and it is an incident. But if we review and approve, that passing incident becomes the doctrine of the Constitution. There it has a generative power of its own, and all that it creates will be in its own image.[16]

A similar argument can be made regarding torture: if an agent tortures, that is "an incident," but if the courts authorize it, it becomes a precedent. There is, however, an important difference between the detention of Japanese-American citizens and torture. The detentions were done openly and with presidential accountability; torture would be done secretly, with official deniability. Tolerating an off-the-book system of secret torture can also establish a dangerous precedent.

A variation on this "legitimation" argument would postpone consideration of the choice between authorizing torture and forgoing a possible tactic necessary to prevent an imminent act of terrorism until after the choice—presumably the choice to torture—has been made. In that way, the discussion would not, in itself, encourage the use of torture. If it were employed, then we could decide whether it was justified, excusable, condemnable, or something in between. The problem with that argument is that no FBI agent who tortured a suspect into disclosing information that prevented an act of mass terrorism would be prosecuted—as the policemen who tortured the kidnapper into disclosing the whereabouts of his victim were not prosecuted. In the absence of a prosecution, there would be no occasion to judge the appropriateness of the torture.

I disagree with these more passive approaches and believe that in a democracy it is always preferable to decide controversial issues in advance, rather than in the heat of battle. I would apply this rule to other tragic choices as well, including the possible use of a nuclear first strike, or retaliatory strikes—so long as the discussion was sufficiently general to avoid giving our potential enemies a strategic advantage by their knowledge of our policy.

Even if government officials decline to discuss such issues, academics have a duty to raise them and submit them to the marketplace of ideas. There may be danger in open discussion, but there is far greater danger in actions based on secret discussion, or no discussion at all.

NOTES

1. Michael Walzer, "Political Action: The Problem of Dirty Hands," *Philosophy and Public Affairs,* 1973.

2. Quoted in W. L. Twining and P. E. Twining, "Bentham on Torture," *Northern Ireland Legal Quarterly,* Autumn 1973, p. 347. Bentham's hypothetical question does not distinguish between torture inflicted by private persons and by governments.

3. David Johnston and Philip Shenon, "F.B.I. Curbed Scrutiny of Man Now a Suspect in the Attacks," *New York Times,* 10/6/2001.

4. Twining and Twining, "Bentham on Torture," pp. 348–49. The argument for the limited use of torture in the ticking bomb case falls into a category of argument known as "argument from the extreme case," which is a useful heuristic to counter arguments for absolute principles.

5. On conditions in American prisons, see Alan M. Dershowitz, "Supreme Court Acknowledges Country's Other Rape Epidemic," *Boston Herald,* 6/12/1994. . . .

6. John Langbein, *Torture and the Law of Proof* (Chicago: University of Chicago Press, 1977), p. 68. Voltaire generally opposed torture but favored it in some cases.

7. A fifth approach would be simply to never discuss the issue of torture—or to postpone any such discussion until after we actually experience a ticking bomb case—but I have always believed that it is preferable to consider and discuss tragic choices before we confront them, so that the issue can be debated without recriminatory emotions and after-the-fact finger-pointing.

8. Charles M. Sennott, "Israeli High Court Bans Torture in Questioning; 10,000 Palestinians Subjected to Tactics," *Boston Globe,* 9/7/1999.

9. Quoted in Twining and Twining, "Bentham on Torture," p. 345.

10. Langbein, *Torture and the Law of Proof,* p. 7.

11. Ibid., p. 90, quoting Bacon.

12. Langbein, *Torture and the Law of Proof,* pp. 136–37, 139.

13. When it is known that torture is a possible option, terrorists sometimes provide the information and then claim they have been tortured, in order to be able to justify their complicity to their colleagues.

14. *U.S. v. Lefkowitz,* 285 U.S. 452, 464 (1932).

15. *Johnson v. U.S.* 333 U.S. 10, 13–14 (1948).

16. *Korematsu v. U.S.* 323 U.S. 214, 245–46 (1944) (Jackson, J., dissenting).

READING QUESTIONS

1. Explain the case for why the ticking bomb terrorist should be tortured according to Dershowitz. How did his visit to Israel impact his views on this matter?

2. What is the strongest argument against the view that the ticking bomb terrorist should be tortured? Explain how the distinction between act and rule utilitarianism is relevant to this argument.

3. What is the biggest problem for an act utilitarian justification of torture according to Dershowitz? What is a "torture warrant" and how does Dershowitz believe torture warrants could be implemented in order to overcome the relevant problem?

4. What are the four ways that Dershowitz considers for how we can resolve the dilemma between the conflicting values of security and abiding by the law? Why are accountability and visibility in democracy important according to Dershowitz? Consider in particular the possible consequences of a lack of accountability in a democracy.

DISCUSSION QUESTIONS

1. Should we agree with Dershowitz that the introduction of torture warrants would result in fewer terrorist attacks as well as allow for more government accountability? Why or why not? Consider and discuss some of the potential problems that might arise with the introduction of such warrants. Are there any better or additional alternatives that could be implemented in order to prevent terrorist attacks that would also result in greater accountability in a democracy?

2. Consider and discuss whether the act utilitarian argument that Dershowitz gives for the justification of torture fails to provide adequate reasons to support his view. Is Bentham's hypothetical case different in any morally relevant ways from the case of the ticking bomb terrorist that Dershowitz considers? If so, how?

MARCIA BARON

The Ticking Bomb Hypothetical

In her essay, Marcia Baron claims that using the case of the ticking bomb terrorist to reject an absolute prohibition on torture is problematic. She asks why this is. Baron rejects the claim that such a ban is problematic just because the case is artificial. Artificial cases as used by philosophers doing ethics, she argues, can sometimes help one untangle moral complexities in order to focus on some particular moral issue; their artificiality does not matter. But, she claims, the ticking bomb hypothetical is different—its artificiality does matter—because it is intended to weaken a commitment to the absolutist position that torture should be banned in all circumstances. She defends this claim by examining in detail versions of the ticking bomb hypothetical, explaining why their artificiality is seriously misleading and should not be employed to justify torture in special circumstances.

1

2

Recent literature arguing for, or reaffirming, the impermissibility of torture has deplored the ticking bomb hypothetical and its frequent invocation. I have in mind in particular the work of David Luban and Henry Shue.[1] I share their views, by and large, but at the same time think that just what is so problematic about the hypothetical remains somewhat unclear.[2] This essay, while very much indebted to their work, aims to bring out more sharply how the focus on the ticking bomb hypothetical in the revived torture debates has led us astray.[3] I take issue not only with those who rely on the hypothetical to defend the use of interrogational torture,[4] but also with those who, while taking a much more nuanced view, insist on "the relevance and significance of the catastrophic case."[5] Oren Gross writes that "there are two perspectives from which we ought to approach the question of the use of preventive interrogational torture, namely, the general policy perspective and the perspective of the catastrophic case . . . . We can only focus on one to the exclusion of the other at our peril."[6] I see no peril in ceasing to take "the perspective of the catastrophic case."

When I presented a version of this paper at a conference, some expressed perplexity at my attention to empirical facts. Perhaps the expectation, given my strong Kantian leanings, was that I would focus on moral principles, and offer a Kantian argument against torture. But arguing against torture on Kantian grounds is unlikely to budge those who believe that moral opposition to torture needs to be tempered by (as they see it) realism. Indeed, one often comes across such phrases as "all but unabashed Kantians recognize" in discussions of torture, as in this: "the fact that all but unabashed Kantians recognize the difficulties presented by extreme cases to any absolutist position is taken as further evidence that an absolutist position with respect to a ban on torture is untenable."[7] To engage those who defend torture, or who believe that the ticking bomb hypothetical forces us to reconsider the ban on torture, it is crucial to meet them on their turf rather than invite them to consider the issue from a Kantian perspective.

I begin by quoting two versions of the ticking bomb hypothetical, the first by an opponent of torture, and the second by authors who defend it. Henry Shue presents it as follows in his classic 1978 article, "Torture":

> There is a standard philosopher's example which someone always invokes: suppose a fanatic, perfectly willing to die rather than collaborate in the thwarting of his own scheme, has set a hidden nuclear device to explode in the heart of Paris. There is no time to evacuate . . . the only hope of preventing tragedy is to torture the perpetrator, find the device, and deactivate it.[8]

Mirko Bagaric and Julie Clarke offer the following version:

> A terrorist network has activated a large bomb on one of hundreds of commercial planes carrying more than three hundred passengers that are flying somewhere in the world at any point in time. The bomb is set to explode in thirty minutes. The leader of the terrorist organization announces this via a statement on the Internet. He states that the bomb was planted by one of his colleagues at one of the major airports in the world in the past few hours. No details are provided regarding the location of the plane where the bomb is located. Unbeknownst to him, he was under police surveillance and is immediately apprehended by police. The terrorist leader refuses to answer any police questions, declaring that the passengers must die and will shortly.[9]

The conclusion, as Bagaric and Clarke see it, is clear. "Who would deny that all possible means should be used to extract the details of the plane and the location of the bomb?"[10]

So, just what is problematic about the hypothetical? Doesn't it test our intuitions, getting us to question our commitment to a principle that torture is always wrong? The idea in putting forward the example, David Luban writes, is to "force the liberal prohibitionist to admit that yes, even . . . she would agree to torture in at least this one situation. Once [she . . .] admits that, then she has conceded that her opposition to torture is not based on principle. Now that [she] has admitted that her moral principles can be breached, all that is left is haggling about the price."[11] Luban goes on to say that the ticking bomb example "bewitches" us, and I think he is right, though just how it bewitches us is somewhat elusive. But I can also see that this would sound pretty lame to those who defend torture, as if when confronted by an example that clinches their case (as they see it) we protest that there is some unfairness, some trickery, that we are being bewitched. We seem to be dodging the problem. Shouldn't we have to answer their question and say whether or not we think that torture in such a situation is permissible?

I don't think we should have to. I also don't think that granting that torture might be permissible in extraordinary circumstances would weaken the prohibitionist's case in the way Luban's remarks suggest. But before we get to that, and before I explain in what ways the hypothetical has misled us, we need to be clear on what the problem isn't.

Those who take the ticking bomb hypothetical very seriously sometimes suppose that opposition to it is merely opposition to "artificial cases" or "fantastic examples" in general.[12] This is not entirely surprising. Although both Shue and Luban provide excellent reasons for seeing the ticking bomb hypothetical as problematic in a way that distinguishes it from most "fantastic examples," some of their remarks, at least if read out of context, may leave the impression that the ticking bomb example is of the same ilk as other "artificial cases." Luban remarks that "artificial cases" such as those of "fat men thrown in front of runaway trolleys, blown out of mineshafts with bazookas, or impaled on pitchforks as they fall from windows" are "deeply cartoonish."[13] Shue writes that "There is a saying in jurisprudence that hard cases make bad law, and there might well be one in philosophy that artificial cases make bad ethics."[14]

Artificial cases are not all of a kind. Some help us focus on key issues, while others distract us from the real issues or distort a reality they purport to depict (or both). The ticking bomb hypothetical is artificial and dangerously misleading in a way that the examples Luban refers to are not.[15] There may be reasons for objecting to them, but the problem I wish to bring out is not a problem they share.[16]

Just as it is not the sheer "cartoonishness" or "artificiality" of the examples that is the problem, the objection to the reliance on the hypothetical is not that ticking bomb scenarios are so rare that it is unwise to let them shape our general policy regarding the use of torture (though that is closer).

3

So what is the problem? Partly this: as Shue has explained, it is almost impossible to be in the position depicted in ticking bomb hypotheticals and also to know that one is in such a position. But once again it may sound as if the claim is only that the hypothetical is unrealistic, and why does that matter, when many hypotheticals are unrealistic? To understand why it matters in this case yet not in general and to see in what way this hypothetical is aptly said to "bewitch" us, we need to reflect on the role of hypotheticals in philosophical discussion, and then examine how this hypothetical differs from others.

Normally when we are presented with a hypothetical, we accept it as a hypothetical and focus attention on whatever the person presenting the hypothetical asks us to consider. It is bad form to ask "Does it really work that way?" We are expected to accept the hypothetical as such. But if we do so, granting it for the sake of discussion, we may be granting assumptions that are highly implausible. Often in philosophy it doesn't matter that we are granting highly implausible assumptions for the sake of discussion; we bracket one thing in order to focus on another. With many hypotheticals, it is fruitful to do so. There is something to be gained by thinking about the issue without worrying about the details that we are agreeing not to question. The fantastic examples may provide (as they do in Thomson's "A Defense of Abortion")[17] a way to disentangle the various arguments against a particular practice or policy or individual choice and examine them more clearheadedly. In the case of the ticking bomb hypothetical, however, it is hard to see why it would be helpful to set aside relevant facts about torture, since the matter under discussion is the moral permissibility of the practice of interrogational torture.

In many discussions involving an implausible hypothetical, the person proffering it is not claiming or assuming that this is in fact something that happens (or that we had better be prepared to see happen or, if it is something we might want to see happen, that we can bring about). With the ticking bomb hypothetical, things are different; yet we may, if we treat the hypothetical as one normally treats a hypothetical, fail to recognize this. We may, in effect, be tricked by the ticking bomb hypothetical into thinking that we are only accepting it as a hypothetical, when in fact we are being led to view torture in a wholly inaccurate way.

It should now be somewhat clearer why the ticking bomb hypothetical is problematic in a way that other "artificial cases" are not, but more needs to be said to bring out how the former differs from the latter. Recall the runaway trolley, the fat man wedged in the mouth of a cave, the kidnapped violinist, and the people seeds that can drift into homes and take root in the upholstery. Or consider the cases involving killing someone—or, in another case, helping a starving person to die—so that his body can be used for medical research, or for "spare parts," or for making a serum from his dead body that will save several lives. Imagine someone objecting to one of the medical examples by saying, "Wait a minute, is it really possible to make a serum from someone's dead body that would then save several lives?" We would reply, "Don't worry about that; it doesn't matter whether it is possible," and we would then explain (supposing that we are discussing Philippa Foot's "Abortion and the Doctrine of Double Effect"[18]) that Foot's point was to contrast (a) our view that killing or allowing someone to die in order to save several people is clearly wrong to (b) our reaction to a case where a decision is made to withhold a life-saving drug that is in short supply from a patient who requires a massive dose, and instead to give it to several people who also require the drug, but for whom a much smaller dose will suffice. Note that her point in doing this was not to convince us of the wrongness or rightness of one medical policy or another, so her use of "fantastic examples" is strikingly different from the use

to which the ticking bomb hypothetical is put. Her aim, rather, was to consider whether the doctrine of double effect or a different principle better accounts for our judgments about such cases.

In the essays from which I've drawn these examples—Foot's "Abortion and the Doctrine of Double Effect" and Thomson's "A Defense of Abortion"—there is a distance between the example and the point in support of which the example is put forward, a distance that we don't have between the ticking bomb hypothetical and the claim it is intended to support. The relation between the example and the intended point is such that it makes no difference at all that the example is artificial, or unrealistic. But because the ticking bomb hypothetical is intended to weaken our commitment to prohibitions on torture and lend support to a (possibly very limited) practice of torture, it indeed does matter whether the hypothetical is realistic. Yet, perhaps because normally we do not question the realism of a hypothetical, many people pay little attention to whether the ticking bomb hypothetical is at all plausible.

4

Let's look more closely at a couple of versions of the ticking bomb hypothetical—versions put forward by those who believe the hypothetical should be taken seriously—to see in what way it is unrealistic, and in what way its being unrealistic leads us astray.

Recall the Bagaric and Clarke example. There we are asked to envision a situation where a leader of a terrorist organization has announced that a bomb has been placed on a passenger jet. The jet is now in flight, and the bomb is set to go off in thirty minutes. The terrorist leader was already under surveillance; we are asked to imagine that he is therefore apprehended quickly. We are to accept that he knows where the bomb is, that by torturing him (but by no other means[19]) we can extract the necessary information, that the pilots can then be contacted, and that it will be possible either to quickly land and evacuate the plane, or to locate the bomb on the plane and defuse it—all in less than thirty minutes. We are to accept, in short, that torture is the solution, and that the only thing standing in the way of saving the lives of over three hundred people is our moral scruples.

Or consider a version of the ticking bomb hypothetical put forward by Jean Bethke Elshtain. In her version, a bomb has been planted in one of several hundred elementary schools in a particular city. We don't know which school (though we know which city), but we are virtually certain that we have apprehended someone who is not only part of the plot, but who also knows in which school the bomb has been placed. The bomb is to go off within the hour. Officials know, Elshtain writes, that "they cannot evacuate all of the schools."[20] Curiously, it is considered a much surer thing to torture the suspect, extract the information, and then evacuate the school in question. If there is time to evacuate the school in question after the torture has extracted the information, why not skip the torture and immediately evacuate all the several hundred schools? That would be a much surer way to prevent loss of life.

These versions of the hypothetical stand in stark contrast to such cases as the runaway trolley and the drifting people seeds. To make sense of the hypothetical we accept, perhaps without fully realizing we are doing so, assumptions that in effect give the game away: that torture works, works very quickly, in some situations is the only thing that will work,[21] and moreover, that we can know when we are in a situation where torture, and only torture, will prevent a disaster. If we do not accept these assumptions, we will find the hypothetical baffling; if we accept it as a hypothetical and do not question the assumptions, most of the important issues about the moral permissibility of the practice of torture have been taken off the table. The only thing that has not been taken off the table is moral principles condemning torture; concern about these, however, is dismissed as a sort of prissiness, or moral narcissism.[22]

The ticking bomb hypothetical asks us to forget about the fact that we do not know that our prisoner actually has the information we need, and to ignore all the evidence that even if we do have the right person, torture is generally ineffective—certainly unreliable—as a way of obtaining the information we

need.[23] It invites us to conceive of torture as in effect a truth serum. Indirectly, it also prods us to ignore the evidence that torture is very difficult to contain. I'll say more about this shortly.

5

The ticking bomb hypothetical is marred by the very feature that is supposed to make it so compelling: that there is no time to lose. Torture is particularly unlikely to work when the bomb will go off within thirty minutes, or even a couple of hours. A determined terrorist is likely to be able to withstand the torture until the bomb goes off, and even this isn't necessary, since naming the wrong flight or school is as likely to end the torture as is naming the correct one.

A defender of torture might concede this, and put forward a different hypothetical, where there is more time. But when there *is* time for torture to have a somewhat better chance of working,[24] there is also time to try to gain the captive's trust; when one does, one generally learns far more than when one tortures. Some defenders of torture (e.g., Charles Krauthammer) find such suggestions preposterous; one would almost think from their scoffing that intelligence is generally obtained only via torture.[25]

Readers accustomed to such scoffing might find it helpful to hear something about how interrogators can successfully interrogate without relying on violence, humiliation, degradation, and in general breaking the person down so fully that (if he survives intact enough to be able to remember the information and communicate it) he blurts out whatever the interrogator wants to hear (which defenders of torture assume will be something true). Given space limitations, a brief summary drawn from Ali Soufan's Senate testimony will have to do.[26] The "Informed Interrogation Approach" is based on the following, Soufan explains: the interrogator turns "the fear that the detainee feels as a result of his capture and isolation from his support base" and the fact that people "crave human contact" to his advantage, "becoming

the one person the detainee can talk to and who listens to what he has to say, and uses this to encourage
the detainee to open up"; in addition, the kindness
he shows the detainee takes the detainee by surprise,
as the detainee (if a member of Al Qaeda, anyway)
is trained to resist torture, but not to resist kindness.
(Soufan's offer of sugar-free cookies to Abu Jandal,
whom he knew to be diabetic, is but one example
of the many ways he established the rapport that
quickly led Jandal to share with him extensive information, just after 9/11, on the 9/11 hijackers and the
structure of Al Qaeda.) The interrogator also takes
into account "the need the detainee feels to sustain
a position of respect and value to interrogator." In
addition, "there is the impression the detainee has of
the evidence against him. The interrogator has to do
his or her homework and become an expert in every
detail known to the intelligence community about
the detainee." This serves both "to impress upon the
detainee that everything about him is known and that
any lie will be easily caught" and to establish rapport.[27] Such expertise of course is also important in
other ways: without it, the interrogator is less likely
to ask the right questions and to pick up on details
that might otherwise not seem significant.[28]

6

I mentioned that the ticking bomb hypothetical
encourages us to view torture as something easily
contained. It suggests that torture can happen just
once, just for this particular emergency, without there
being a practice of torture, and without torture ever
being used again. But it is seriously misleading to
speak of a single instance of torture, necessary only
for this one emergency.

There are two reasons for this. To have any prospect of even occasional success, torture requires,
inter alia, training, manuals, equipment, practice at
torturing, personnel to assist in torturing, and medical personnel to revive the detainee às needed and
to advise on limits that need to be observed lest the
torture result in death or another state that precludes

extracting the needed information. So although it
would be an exaggeration to say that torture is impossible except as part of a practice of torture, we have
to assume that torture defended on the grounds that it
may be necessary, albeit only in rare circumstances,
for obtaining information needed to prevent a ticking bomb from detonating, will be not a "one time"
use of torture, but part of a practice. Any attempt to
justify interrogational torture for use only in rare circumstances will also either be, or require, a justification of torture as a practice.

The second reason torture needs to be viewed as
a practice concerns not what must have preceded
it if the contemplated torture is going to have any
chance of being effective, but what follows in its
train. As Rejali has meticulously documented and
Shue, Luban, and others have elaborated, it is virtually impossible for torture to be limited to just one
instance. Even when the plan is to allow it in only
very rare instances, soon other situations arise where
a catastrophe looms, even if not quite as huge a catastrophe, and torture is deemed necessary there, too;
and then, as we have seen in the conduct of the United
States in recent years, it is pointed out that we cannot
afford to wait until there is a ticking bomb, and need
to uncover terrorist plots before they are executed (a
sound thought so far!), and to that end—given the
seriousness of the calamity if we do not prevent it—
we must employ "enhanced techniques" of interrogation as an ongoing part of our war on terror.

Torture spreads. History shows that soldiers bring
it home, where it is used in police interrogations and
by prison guards.[29] Torture intended only for very
limited use (e.g., in Guantánamo) soon shows up in
U.S.-run prisons in Iraq and Afghanistan.[30] It spreads
not only geographically, but also from one accepted
purpose to a purpose that initially was not seen as
justifying it. As the torture equipment, training, and
personnel expand, and reports of the use of torture
spread, torture becomes "normalized," and the range
of instances where torture is deemed necessary (or
even just "worth a try") expands. The more torture
is viewed as the best way to get crucial intelligence,
the more the truly valuable techniques languish,
and intelligence-gathering skills deteriorate; torture
is then relied on all the more.[31] In addition, torture

initially justified only for intelligence gathering is soon used to express a sense of mastery, to humiliate . . . and to get the captive to say what one wants to hear (possibly to provide a pretext for some military action,[32] or to justify action already taken).

7

It might be objected that I have chosen to examine versions of the ticking bomb hypothetical that are stunningly stupid. It is true that they are—especially the one about the school. But that itself tells us something. It is very telling that those who take the hypothetical so seriously do not even notice that in the scenario they draw up, either the time frame is such that torture hardly stands a chance of working in time (as in the example of the bomb on the plane) or that there is another, far better solution, not involving torture (as in the case of the schools, where immediate evacuation of all the schools would be a much surer way of saving lives than torturing first, and then, relying on whatever one elicited from the captive, evacuating only the school in question). It is evidence of how mesmerized people are by the idea of a ticking bomb scenario that people with JDs or PhDs and a record of excellent scholarship can commit such a blunder. More specifically, it is evidence of the readiness on the part of many intelligent people to see torture as the best solution (if moral issues are set to one side), the most effective way (at least when time is of the essence) to deal with terrorism. The mindless way the topic of torture is discussed itself deserves our attention, and is part of the reason for the aptness of Luban's hyperbolic claim that the ticking bomb hypothetical has bewitched us.

Still, we might ask if these are just poor versions of the ticking bomb hypothetical. Will a better version avoid the problems I have noted? Shue's version fares somewhat better than those put forward by supporters of torture. In his version, it is an entire city that will be blown up, not just a school, so evacuation is not a very serious option (depending on the time frame, which is not indicated). Still, it is hard to imagine—even if we somehow know we have the (or a) perpetrator, and that the perpetrator knows where the bomb is—that we know with a reasonable degree of certainty that torture will extract the information and will do so in time for the bomb to be located and deactivated. If the terrorist is determined that the bomb go off, he is more likely to hold out or lie or otherwise gain time than to tell the truth.[33] This and other points made earlier apply to thoughtfully crafted ticking bomb hypotheticals, not only to Elshtain's and to Bagaric and Clarke's.

It may be countered that torture has worked—that there have been real ticking bomb scenarios, where torture succeeded in extracting the necessary information in time, where the bomb really would have gone off had the information not been extracted, and where there is very good reason to believe that nothing else would have worked. Those who have scrutinized the cases report that in fact it wasn't like that. In a case defenders of torture often cite, that of Abdul Hakim Murad, the torture—67 days of it!—may possibly have played a role in gleaning the information, though the information was provided not under torture, but only afterward, when the interrogators threatened to turn Murad over to the Israelis. But in fact, all the information that Murad eventually provided was on his laptop, which the interrogators had in their possession the entire time they were busy torturing Murad. Not only was torture unnecessary, but the information could have been obtained much more quickly if proper intelligence-gathering procedures were used. Rejali describes that interrogation as a textbook case of "how a police force is progressively deskilled by torture."[34] In another case often cited to show that torture does indeed work, Abu Zubaydah in fact revealed valuable information[35] only when the interrogators quit torturing and a new interrogator persuaded the captive that it was his religious duty to reveal the requested information.[36]

Rather than discuss further the question of whether there have been any authentic ticking bomb scenarios—where torture thwarted a major disaster that could not have been thwarted otherwise, and where those deciding to use torture believed on good evidence that torture and only torture would do the trick—I want to shift my focus and ask this question:

Suppose there really have been authentic ticking bomb scenarios. Or, even if there haven't been such cases, suppose there can be. What would that show?

I raise this question in part because I note in some of the literature with which I sympathize an eagerness to deny that a ticking bomb scenario could ever happen. The worry is that if we concede that it could, we'll be asked whether it is permissible to torture in such circumstances. And then, it is thought, we are in trouble. Luban writes (as noted earlier) that the idea in putting forward the ticking bomb hypothetical is to "force the liberal prohibitionist to admit that yes, even . . . she would agree to torture in at least this one situation. Once the prohibitionist admits that, then she has conceded that her opposition to torture is not based on principle. Now that [she] has admitted that her moral principles can be breached, all that is left is haggling about the price."[37] In the article from which I am quoting, it is not entirely clear whether Luban is agreeing that the concession really is this significant or simply explaining a strategy. But in his "Unthinking the Ticking Bomb," he makes it clear that he does think it quite significant: "After making the initial concession, any prohibition on torture faces significant dialectical pressure toward balancing tests and the unwelcome . . . conclusion that interrogational torture can be justified whenever the expected benefits outweigh the expected costs."[38]

But the problem is not as serious as that suggests. Switch for a moment from torture to rape. Suppose that in some very weird scenario, perhaps involving a demented character like Jack D. Ripper from *Dr. Strangelove*, a horrible catastrophe—the detonation of nuclear bombs—could be prevented only by raping or abetting a rape. (If it helps, add to the example that one has to rape a child, and has to do so in front of the child's family and one's own family.) We do not in any way deny that rape is impermissible—nor do we deny that our objection to it is based on principle—if we do not rule out the possibility that were this absolutely the only way to prevent a horrific catastrophe, and we knew it would prevent it, choosing to do so would not be wrong in those circumstances. The categories countenanced by Luban are too limited. It is not as if believing that X is wrong on principle—even horribly wrong—entails denying

that there could be a scenario in which X would be a permissible choice. That we allow this does not mean that X can be permitted any time the benefits of permitting it outweigh the costs.[39]

We are expected to be prepared to answer questions about whether we would torture, or want others to torture, in a ticking bomb scenario, yet are not expected to answer questions about whether we would be willing to rape someone, or order or abet a rape, if that were necessary to prevent a catastrophe of massive proportions. Both scenarios are very unlikely, but torture is treated differently. I believe it is treated differently only because we are still bedeviled into thinking that torture is generally effective and that therefore in a ticking bomb scenario, or perhaps even in a situation where we think there may be plans to bomb a city, torture is—from a strictly pragmatic standpoint—our best bet for obtaining the crucial information. We have not fully abandoned the idea that torture will work when nothing else will. Despite the fact that most of us really do know better, torture retains its status as the method of choice—as what you'll do if you really want to get the job done.

8

I have tried in my paper to bring out what is so misleading about the ticking bomb hypothetical, in the context of a discussion of the practice of interrogational torture, and to show that it is problematic in a way that other hypotheticals—the runaway trolley, etc.—are not. The latter in no way rely for their effectiveness on the case being realistic, whereas the ticking bomb hypothetical does. Relatedly, the ticking bomb hypothetical takes off the table most of the objections to torture, in effect asking us to ignore such facts as that torture is a very unreliable way to gather intelligence and that torture is both very difficult to contain and particularly unlikely to succeed if it is not part of an ongoing practice, involving assistants, equipment, and extensive training. It is thus not well suited to a "one time" or very occasional use that those who think it justifiable in ticking bomb scenarios envision.

I realize that some may find there to be something chilling about my attention to these pragmatic considerations, and in closing I want to emphasize that nothing I say should be construed as an indication that I think torture would be morally defensible if only it did work. As I noted at the outset, arguing against torture by focusing on its moral wrongness is very unlikely to budge those I hope to engage. Some defenders of torture believe that morality requires that we use torture in such a ticking bomb scenario; others do not, but hold that moral principles—or "scruples"—are a luxury that we cannot afford in an emergency. What is needed to convince those inclined to either position is to show how very misleading the ticking bomb hypothetical is.[40]

NOTES

1. David Luban, "Liberalism, Torture, and the Ticking Bomb," *Virginia Law Review* 91 (2005): 1425–61, and "Unthinking the Ticking Bomb," in *Global Basic Rights*, ed. Charles R. Beitz and Robert E. Goodin (New York: Oxford University Press, 2009), 181–206; and Henry Shue, "Torture in Dreamland: Disposing of the Ticking Bomb," *Case Western Reserve Journal of International Law* 37 (2005): 231–39. See also Bob Brecher, *Torture and the Ticking Bomb* (Malden, MA: Blackwell, 2007); Claudia Card, "Ticking Bombs and Interrogations," *Criminal Law and Philosophy* 2 (2008): 1–15; Elaine Scarry, "Five Errors in the Reasoning of Alan Dershowitz," in *Torture: A Collection* (revised ed.), ed. Sanford Levinson (New York: Oxford University Press, 2005): 281–98; Kim Lane Scheppele, "Hypothetical Torture in the 'War on Terrorism,'" *Journal of National Security Law and Policy* 1 (2005): 285–340; and Yuval Ginbar, *Why Not Torture Terrorists?* (Oxford: Oxford University Press, 2010).

2. This much, however, is very clear: employing the hypothetical to try to justify the use of torture by the United States during the administration of George W. Bush is deplorable. There torture was used (among other reasons, such as to humiliate, and to avenge killings) as a fishing expedition to uncover plots, *not* to prevent a ticking bomb from detonating. For more on the singular inappropriateness of trying to justify via the ticking bomb hypothetical the use of torture in the "war on terror," see Scheppele, "Hypothetical Torture."

3. That there is some confusion about just what the point is in dismissing ticking bomb hypotheticals as "artificial" is evident from Oren Gross, "The Prohibition on Torture and the Limits of Law," in Levinson, *Torture*, 229–55 at 234.

4. My focus throughout this paper is on interrogational torture (i.e., torture aimed at acquiring information crucial to preventing, or limiting the scope of, a catastrophe). I do not in this paper address instances of torture in direct self-defense or defense of others, where, say, someone is torturing my child and threatening to kill her, and for some reason the only way to get him to stop is to torture him (or his confederate . . . or his child). For discussion of such cases, see Sherry F. Colb, "Why Is Torture 'Different' and How 'Different' Is It?" *Cardozo Law Review* 30 (2009): 1411–73. Nor do I consider in this paper torture for purposes of obtaining information that could then be used to convict someone; I assume that readers of this volume would not regard that to be worth considering. Even those who think that torture might very occasionally be permissible presumably would not want the criminal justice system to rely on information obtained by torture. Indeed torture other than preventive interrogational torture or torture in direct self-defense (e.g., torture to extract confessions, exorcise demons, intimidate rebels, get revenge, or relieve boredom) I assume all readers of this volume, indeed all even moderately reasonable persons, agree is absolutely impermissible.

5. Gross, "Prohibition on Torture," 239.

6. *Ibid.*, 239–40.

7. *Ibid.*, 231.

8. Henry Shue, "Torture," *Philosophy and Public Affairs* 7 (1978): 124–43 at 141.

9. Mirko Bagaric and Julie Clarke, *Torture: When the Unthinkable Is Morally Permissible* (Albany: SUNY Press, 2007), 2.

10. *Ibid.*, 3.

11. Luban, "Liberalism," 1440.

12. See, e.g., Bagaric and Clarke, *Torture*, 3, where they write that "fantastic examples cannot be dismissed summarily merely because they are 'simply' hypothetical." I agree (though not with the implication that some opponents of torture dismiss the ticking bomb hypothetical solely on those grounds).

13. Luban, "Unthinking," 206.

14. Shue, "Torture," 141.

15. Clarification is in order concerning the content of the hypothetical. It is part of the content not only that a bomb will detonate soon unless we disable it and that we don't know where it is, but also that (a) we cannot find out in time except by torturing someone we have in captivity, (b) torturing him or her will indeed enable us to prevent the catastrophe, and (c) we know this. The clarification is

needed because some respond to claims that the hypothetical is extremely implausible by saying there is no doubt that ticking bomb scenarios do occur, pointing in support of their claim to a case where a suicide bombing was averted but where (not only was the bomb not yet ticking, but more importantly) there is no indication that torture was used in the interrogation that led to the disclosure of the planned bombing, let alone that torture was needed (and, moreover, known to be needed). See e.g., Stephen de Wijze's review of Karen Greenberg, ed., *The Torture Debate in America*, in *Democratiya* 7 (2006): 10–36, especially 21.

16. As this paper goes to press, Allen Wood points out to me ways in which some of the problems I single out as particularly problems with ticking bomb hypotheticals also afflict trolley examples. See his excellent "Humanity as End in Itself," in Samuel Scheffler (ed.), Derek Parfit, *On What Matters*, Volume 2 (Oxford: Oxford University Press, 2011), pp. 58–82.

17. Judith Jarvis Thomson, "A Defense of Abortion," *Philosophy and Public Affairs* 1 (1971): 47–66.

18. Philippa Foot, *Virtues and Vices* (Berkeley: University of California Press, 1978), Ch. 2.

19. Bagaric and Clarke do not specify that no other means will be effective, though "the terrorist leader refuses to answer any police questions" (*Torture*, 2) seems intended to indicate this. It is possible that they think that we should use an assortment of techniques, torture included, with the idea that by using "all means" we increase our chances of extracting information. But success is not increased by increasing the number of means used. Using torture seriously undermines the effectiveness of Army Field Manual techniques, since these are based on establishing some rapport. See Jane Mayer, *The Dark Side* (New York: Doubleday, 2008); Darius Rejali, *Torture and Democracy* (Princeton, NJ: Princeton University Press, 2007); and Sherwood Moran, "Suggestions for Japanese Interpreters Based on Work in the Field," excerpted in William F. Schulz, ed., *The Phenomenon of Torture: Readings and Commentary* (Philadelphia: University of Pennsylvania Press, 2007), 249–54. Someone might hold that torture can be justifiable other than as a last resort, but I do not think that view worth discussing, and so do not take it up here. See also note 21.

20. Jean Bethke Elshtain, "Reflection on the Problem of 'Dirty Hands'," in Levinson, ed. *Torture*, 78.

21. This assumes that we regard torture as something to be avoided if at all possible. Of course if one thinks that terrorists deserve to be tortured, it may not seem necessary, to justify torture, that it be the only way to prevent a catastrophe; it will matter more that we not make mistakes

and torture someone who (whether or not he or she has the information we need to prevent the catastrophe) is not a terrorist.

22. Elshtain asks us who we would want in a position of judgment in her hypothetical. Would we prefer a "person of such stringent moral and legal rectitude that he or she would not consider torture because violating his or her own conscience is the most morally serious thing a person can do? Or a person, aware of the stakes and the possible deaths of hundreds of children, who acts in the light of harsh necessity and orders the prisoner tortured? This second leader," Elshtain adds, "does not rank his or her 'purity' above human lives." Elshtain, "Reflection," 80–81.

23. See, among other sources, Rejali, *Torture and Democracy*, especially chaps. 21 and 22; the Senate testimony of former FBI agent Ali Soufan (who obtained extremely important information without using "enhanced" techniques and saw effective interrogations ruined when another agent insisted on torturing the detainee), Committee on the Judiciary, U.S. Senate, May 13, 2009. (Available at <http://www.judiciary. senate.gov/hearings/testimony.cfm?id=e655f9e2809e54768 62f735da14945e6&wit_id=e655f9e2809e5476862f735da1 4945e6–1-2>, accessed February 1, 2012; hereafter Soufan, "Testimony"), and his *New York Times* op-eds, in particular, "My Tortured Decision," (April 22, 2009), and "What Torture Never Told Us" (September 5, 2009); Mayer, *The Dark Side*; Jean Maria Arrigo, "A Utilitarian Argument against Torture Interrogation of Terrorists," *Science and Engineering Ethics* 10 (2004): 1–30; and the Army Field Manual.

24. Only somewhat, however, and only at enormous cost. It has a better chance of working in part because time provides an opportunity to interrogate many other people, and thereby confirm or disconfirm the information obtained. But once the notion that torture is the most effective way of obtaining information has taken hold, there is now an incentive for torturing an ever increasing number of people, and over a long period of time. As torture becomes an ongoing activity, torturing those whom one has no good reason to think have valuable information becomes increasingly common. For a vivid picture, see the literature on the use of torture by the French in Algeria (e.g., Rejali, *Torture and Democracy*, chap. 22, part of which is published, with some modification, as "Does Torture Work?" in Schulz, *Phenomenon of Torture*, 256–65).

Worth noting, too, is that it is not as if detainees will have reason to figure that any misinformation they provide will be easily detected; some misinformation will be hard to detect, particularly by agents focused on torturing rather than on understanding the political situation. A tactic when one is pressed for names of those plotting terrorist attacks is to name members of a rival, more moderate group. The effect is that those who might have helped to develop a compromise and end the violence are themselves destroyed or radicalized by torture; support for the more extremist, more violent group thus increases. This strategy was employed by the Algerian Front de Libération Nationale (FLN). As Rejali writes, the French soldiers, knowing little about the subtleties of Algerian nationalism, "helped the FLN liquidate the infrastructure of the more cooperative organization and tortured MNA [Movement National Algérien–Ed.] members driving them into extreme opposition" (Rejali, "Does Torture Work?" 256).

The other reason that prolonged torture is more likely to work than brief torture is that it is more likely to "break" the captive. Not to be forgotten, though, is that the captive may well not have the information sought, and if she does, may be so damaged by the torture as to be unable to recall or articulate the information. The particular horrors of prolonged torture need to be borne in mind here; they are hard to fathom, but we can get some sense of them from the film "Taxi to the Dark Side" (2007) and from memoirs of those who survived torture.

25. Charles Krauthammer, "Torture? No. Except . . . " op-ed, *Washington Post*, May 1, 2009.

26. Readers wanting more detail might read the full text of his statement in Soufan, "Testimony." See also Michael Isikoff, " 'We Could Have Done This the Right Way': How Ali Soufan, FBI Agent, Got Abu Zubaydah to Talk without Torture," *Newsweek* (April 25, 2009); the film *The Oath* (Laura Poitras, 2010); Sherwood Moran, "Suggestions for Japanese Interpreters" 249–54; Scott Pelley's interview with George Piro about his interrogations of Saddam Hussein, "60 Minutes," January 27, 2008, available at <http://www.cbsnews.com/video/watch/?id =4758713n&tag=mncol;lst;3>, accessed November 27, 2012; and Rejali, *Torture and Democracy*.

27. In his first interrogation of Zubaydah, Soufan asked him his name; Zubaydah replied with his alias, and Soufan responded, "How about if I call you 'Hani'?" 'Hani' being the name Zubaydah's mother nicknamed him as a child. "He looked at me in shock, said 'ok,' and we started talking," Soufan recounts. Soufan, "Testimony."

28. The need for interrogators to be very knowledgeable is put more starkly by an unnamed former CIA operative. Lamenting the interrogations in Afghanistan by people with "no understanding of Al Qaeda or the Arab World," the operative said that "the key to interrogation is knowledge, not techniques. We didn't know anything. And if you don't know anything, you can't get anything." Mayer, *The Dark Side*, 144.

29. See Rejali, *Torture and Democracy*, 436 and 178–80.

30. For details, see Scheppele, "Hypothetical Torture," and Mayer, *The Dark Side*, among others.

31. A further factor, difficult to assess, is that torture—it is reported by some who have taken part in torturing or in exercises designed to fortify soldiers in case they become victims of torture—is often quite intoxicating. See Jane Mayer, "The Experiment," *The New Yorker* (July 11, 2005); see also Rejali, *Torture and Democracy*, pp. 486–87.

32. See Mayer, *The Dark Side*, chaps. 6 and 7, and in particular her discussion of the interrogation of Ibn al-Shaykh al-Libi, who was speaking freely with FBI agents interviewing him in the traditional "rapport" based way, but then was forcibly removed by the CIA and taken to Egypt. There, under torture, he said what he gathered they wanted him to say, and thus provided the "intelligence" [CIA director George] Tenet relied on when he told [Secretary of State Colin] Powell that Al Qaeda and Hussein's secret police trained together in Baghdad, and that chemical and biological weapons were involved (137). See also the discussion of al-Libi in Rejali, *Torture and Democracy*, 504–505.

33. And if he does cave in and release the information, chances are that it is no longer accurate, since when terrorists suspect that a member of their cohort is in custody, they generally alter their plans and their own locations. This is a consideration worth bearing in mind in assessing claims one often hears along the following lines (paraphrased and quoted from Jeff McMahan's "Torture, Morality, and Law," *Case Western Reserve Journal of International Law* 37 (2006): 241–48 at 244): in some instances in which Israeli security forces captured persons in the process of making or transporting such bombs, those captured were then "tortured in order to force them to divulge information about other attacks . . . planned for the future." The information thereby obtained "then enabled the security forces to take preemptive action to thwart the planned attacks." This may be just what happened; it is hard to say because no specifics are provided. But given the standard practice of altering plans when a member of their cohort cannot be reached and is presumed to be in custody, one wonders if what thwarted the planned attacks was perhaps simply the capture of someone involved in, and informed about, the plan, rather than the intelligence gleaned through the torture.

34. Rejali, *Torture and Democracy*, 507. Another instructive example is that of an Algerian locksmith arrested by the French and tortured for three days. He had in his pocket "bomb blueprints with the address of an FLN bomb factory in Algiers." The "locksmith bought time, the bombers relocated, and the French raid three days later fell

on open air." "Had the soldiers been able to read Arabic, they would have found the bomb factory days earlier," and had they not been focused on torturing, they could have sought help with the Arabic. Ibid., 486.

35. Such as it was; the value of the information Abu Zubaydah provided is a matter of dispute. See Luban, "Unthinking," 189–90.

36. See details in ibid., 189. See also Ali Soufan, "My Tortured Decision." Soufan was one of Zubaydah's interrogators.

37. Luban, "Liberalism," 1440.

38. Luban, "Unthinking," 198.

39. It is worth noting here that Kant, despite his position that suicide is impermissible, raised the following question, to which he did not offer an answer: "A man who had been bitten by a mad dog already felt hydrophobia coming on. He explained, in a letter he left, that, since as far as he knew the disease was incurable, he was taking his life lest he harm others as well in his madness (the onset of which he already felt). Did he do wrong?" Immanuel Kant, *The Metaphysics of Morals*, Mary Gregor, ed. and trans. (New York: Cambridge University Press, 1996), 178 (AK 6: 423–24).

40. I am grateful to Scott Anderson and Sandra Shapshay for helpful comments, and to discussants at conferences at the University of Chicago Law School (2008) and at Washington University (2008) for stimulating discussion of earlier drafts of this paper.

READING QUESTIONS

1. In section 4, how does Baron object to the ticking bomb hypotheticals as described by Bagaric and Clarke and by Elshtain?
2. What is the "Informed Interrogation Approach" to interrogation?
3. What reasons does Baron give for rejecting the idea that interrogational torture can be limited in its use?
4. What point is Baron making in section 7 with the example of rape?

DISCUSSION QUESTIONS

1. Would Dershowitz's proposal involving torture warrants adequately address Baron's worries about limiting the use of interrogational torture?
2. Can interrogational torture in a ticking bomb terrorist case ever be justified by Kant's Humanity formulation of the categorical imperative?

ADDITIONAL RESOURCES

Web Resources

Amnesty International, <www.amnesty.org>. International organization that campaigns for recognition of human rights. A source of up-to-date news on torture.

Anti-War.Com, <www.antiwar.com>. Site devoted to opposition to war. Critical of current and past U.S. administration positions on wars.

CIA website, <www.cia.gov>. See "CIA & the War on Terrorism" link for the CIA's perspective on terrorism.

The World Organization Against Torture, <www.omct.org>. Information about and opposition to torture and other human rights violations.

Fiala, Andrew, "Pacifism," *Stanford Encyclopedia of Philosophy*, <http://plato.stanford.edu/entries/pacifism>. An overview of types of pacifism with discussion of consequentialist, deontological, and religious approaches to the topic.

Miller, Seamus, "Torture," *Stanford Encyclopedia of Philosophy*, <http://plato.stanford.edu/entries/torture/>. An overview of the torture debate.

Orend, Brian, "War," *Stanford Encyclopedia of Philosophy*, <http://plato.stanford.edu/entries/war/>. An overview of the ethics of war and peace. Includes an extended treatment of the provisions of just war theory.

Authored Books and Articles

Allhoff, Fritz, "Terrorism and Torture," *International Journal of Applied Philosophy* 17 (2003): 105–18. A defense of torture for certain purposes only, including obtaining information regarding significant threats.

Davis, Michael, "The Moral Justification of Torture," *International Journal of Applied Philosophy* 19 (2005): 161–78. Critical of using ticking bomb scenarios in arguments over torture.

Dershowitz, Alan M., *Why Terrorism Works: Understanding the Threat, Responding to the Challenge*. (New Haven and London: Yale University Press, 2002). A lively exploration of the causes of and recommended responses to recent state-sponsored terrorism.

Holmes, Robert L., *On War and Morality* (Princeton, N.J.: Princeton University Press, 1989). Holmes defends a historically informed version of anti-war pacifism.

May, Larry, "Torturing Detainees During Interrogation," *International Journal of Applied Philosophy* 19 (2005): 193–208. Argues against the torture of captured suspected terrorists.

Miller, Seamus, "Is Torture Ever Morally Justified?" *International Journal of Applied Philosophy* 19 (2005): 179–92. Defense of the moral justification but not legalization of torture.

Waldron, Jeremy, "Torture and Positive Law," *Columbia Law Review* 105 (2005): 1681–750. Argues against the legalization of torture.

Walzer, Michael, *Just and Unjust Wars*, 2nd ed. (New York: Basic Books, 1992). An important book defending a just-war approach.

Walzer, Michael, *Arguing about War* (New Haven and London: Yale University Press, 2004). A collection of Walzer's essays in which he appeals to a version of just war theory in examining a variety of issues including nuclear deterrence, humanitarian intervention, the recent wars in Afghanistan and Iraq, and terrorism.

Edited Collections

Cole, David (ed.), *The Torture Memos: Rationalizing the Unthinkable* (New York: The New Press, 2009). A collection of memos released by the U.S. Department of Justice describing interrogation techniques used by the CIA under the Bush administration.

Greenberg, Karen (ed.), *The Torture Debate in America* (Cambridge: Cambridge University Press, 2006). A collection of twenty essays, organized into four parts: "Democracy, Terror and Torture," "The Geneva Conventions and International Law," "On Torture," and "Looking Forward."

Levinson, Sanford (ed.), *Torture: A Collection* (New York: Oxford University Press, 2004). A collection of essays by different authors organized into four parts: (1) Philosophical Considerations, (2) Torture as Practiced, (3) Contemporary Attempts to Abolish Torture through Law, and (4) Reflections on the Post-September 11 Debate about Legalizing Torture. Part 4 includes articles by Elaine Scarry and Richard A. Posner that are critical of Dershowitz's views on the morality of torture.

Shue, Henry and David Rodin (eds.), *Preemption: Military Action and Moral Justification* (Oxford and New York: Oxford University Press, 2009). A collection of nine essays by scholars from the fields of history, law, political science, and philosophy debating the justifiability of preemptive war.

Sterba, James P. (ed.), *Terrorism and International Justice* (New York: Oxford University Press, 2003). A collection of essays by various authors covering basic questions about the natural causes and morality of terrorism.

14 } World Hunger and Poverty

The devastation caused by the Indian Ocean tsunami disaster in December 2004 prompted massive relief efforts by many nations including generous donations from many individuals. In 2005, parts of Alabama, Louisiana, and Mississippi were devastated by Hurricane Katrina, leaving many people without food, water, electricity, and shelter. More recently, in October 2012, Hurricane Sandy devastated portions of the Caribbean, as well as the mid-Atlantic, and northeastern United States, causing many deaths, destroying homes and businesses, and again leaving survivors without basic necessities. According to a 2014 report by the World Bank, 1.2 billion of the world's population lives in extreme poverty, which it defines as not having enough income to meet one's most basic needs. These disasters and the World Bank's statistics call attention to the fact that disease, famine, poverty, and displacement are widespread evils that especially afflict the economically disadvantaged and may afflict those who live in relatively wealthy countries. Moral reflection on hunger, poverty, and other such evils prompts the following questions about the obligations of those more affluent countries and their citizens:

- Are economically advantaged people morally required to participate in a scheme of redistribution so that some of their wealth goes to people who are severely economically disadvantaged?
- If so, what best explains this obligation?

One way in which we can think about these questions is by focusing on the widely recognized duty of **beneficence** or charity, which is roughly the duty to help those in dire need.

1. THE DUTY OF BENEFICENCE

Let us assume there is a duty of beneficence, and let us assume further that this duty is a requirement only for those who are in a position to help others. There are three questions we can raise about this duty. First, there is the question of *scope*—to whom is this duty owed? Assuming for the sake of simplicity that we are concerned just with members of the current world population who are in need of help, does this obligation extend to distant strangers? The second question is about the duty's *content*—for those who can afford to do so, how much are they morally required to sacrifice? The third question is about *strength*—how strong is one's obligation to help those in need when doing so conflicts with other moral duties (such as educating one's own children) and with various nonmoral reasons for action including the pursuit of, say, expensive hobbies or various artistic endeavors? One can imagine a very strong duty of beneficence according to which the economically advantaged have an obligation to all disadvantaged individuals worldwide, which requires not only that they sacrifice a great amount of what they now have in an effort to help those in need, but also that this obligation to help is as strong as any conflicting duty they might have. On the other hand, one can easily imagine a moral code that includes a much weaker duty of beneficence along one or more of the three dimensions just described.

2. THEORY MEETS PRACTICE

Three main theoretical approaches to the moral issues of hunger and poverty are represented in this chapter's selections: consequentialism, the ethics of prima facie duty, and Kantian moral theory. Let us consider them in order.

Consequentialism

A purely consequentialist moral theory of the sort described in chapter 1, section 2A, is going to imply that one's moral obligation to help those in need will depend on the likely consequences of doing so compared to not doing so. Consequentialists can and do disagree about likely consequences, because they often disagree about the root causes of hunger and poverty. Thomas Robert Malthus (1766–1834) claimed that population necessarily outruns economic growth, which in turn necessarily leads to famine. Neo-Malthusians, as they are called, follow Malthus in claiming that the level of economic growth needed to sustain increases in population cannot be maintained and that eventually unchecked population growth will lead to massive poverty and famine. This analysis of famine and poverty, together with a commitment to consequentialism, is the basis for Garrett Hardin's view that affluent countries and individuals have a moral obligation to *not* help those in overpopulated countries by giving food and other forms of aid. His claim is that doing so will in the long run likely be worse for humanity generally (including those who now have their basic needs met) than will be the likely consequences of refusing to help the needy in overpopulated countries. We can express Hardin's view on the morality of helping those in need by saying that for him, the scope, content, and strength of any such obligation depend entirely on the likely consequences on overall human welfare of engaging in such aid. Since the overall human welfare would likely be decreased by such aid, we have no obligation to help those in overpopulated countries; indeed, we have an obligation to not help.

Peter Singer also approaches the issue of helping those in need from a broadly consequentialist perspective—one that emphasizes one's moral obligation to reduce the level of human misery. On this basis, Singer reaches a different moral conclusion about giving aid from the one Hardin reaches. He argues that given the great evils of poverty and starvation, those who now enjoy an affluent life and who, by helping, would sacrifice nothing of genuine moral significance have a moral obligation to help those in need. As Singer points out, the scope, content, and strength of the duty to help would require a radical revision in how most people currently think about their obligations to others in need.

Another broadly consequentialist approach to moral questions about world hunger and poverty allows for the idea that rights in general and property rights in particular have intrinsic and not just instrumental value. (The idea that rights have only instrumental value is perhaps the most common view of rights held by consequentialists.) But, as Amartya Sen points out in one of our selections, recognizing the intrinsic value of a right does not rule out considering the consequences of adhering to the right. Sen's idea is that in thinking about our obligations to help those in need, we need to consider both the intrinsic value of holding some property right as well as the overall value of the consequences of adhering to that right. On this basis, Sen makes a case for the moral justification of redistribution of wealth in preventing famine.

Ethics of Prima Facie Duty

According to an ethics of prima facie duty, thinking about world hunger and poverty requires that we consider various competing prima facie duties. Suppose we grant that those living in affluence have a duty to help alleviate the evils of poverty and starvation. (Arguably, we might have this duty even if those to whom it is owed have no moral right against those who are in a position to help.) From this theoretical perspective, we have all sorts of prima facie duties—negative duties not to injure, lie, and break promises, as well as such positive duties as self-improvement and beneficence. When two or more of these prima facie duties conflict in some circumstance, we have to decide which of them is overriding and thus which of them is one's all-things-considered duty in that circumstance. This in turn requires that we think in detail about our circumstances and carefully weigh the relevant strengths of our prima facie obligations.

Kantian Moral Theory

Kant defended the claim that we have a duty of beneficence—a duty to help at least some of those in need on at least some occasions. Because it is up to those who are in a position to help to decide when and how to fulfill this duty—its fulfillment involves a good deal of latitude—Kant claimed that our duty of beneficence is a wide duty. (By contrast, duties to others to not inflict harm and duties to ourselves to not commit suicide are among the narrow duties—duties that do not involve the kind of latitude for choice that is characteristic of our wide obligations.)[1] What is the basis in Kant's theory for the wide duty of beneficence? In her article, Onora O'Neill explains that the Humanity formulation of Kant's fundamental moral principle—the categorical imperative—requires that we not treat others as mere means to our own ends and that we positively treat others as ends in themselves. It is this second, positive part of the categorical imperative that, according to O'Neill, is the basis for our wide duty of beneficence, which she explains and defends.

NOTE

1. For more on the distinction between wide and narrow duty in Kantian moral theory, see chapter 1, section 2C.

GARRETT HARDIN

Lifeboat Ethics

According to Hardin, in thinking about hunger and poverty as moral issues, it is useful to think of them in terms of the metaphor of a lifeboat. Each rich nation is to be thought of as occupying a lifeboat full of comparatively rich people, whereas each poor nation is thought of as a lifeboat containing mostly relatively poor people. Put in these terms, the question is what obligations do rich passengers in one boat have to their poorer counterparts in the less fortunate boats? Hardin rejects essentially Christian and Marxist approaches that would require rich nations to help poor ones, because he thinks that their approaches to solving problems of hunger and poverty—problems of overpopulation—will lead to what he calls "the tragedy of the commons." Taking an essentially consequentialist perspective, Hardin argues that given the likely disastrous overall consequences of rich countries aiding poor countries, the moral implication is that the affluent ought not to help people in countries where overpopulation cannot realistically be brought under control.

Recommended Reading: consequentialism, chap. 1, sec. 2A.

No generation has viewed the problem of the survival of the human species as seriously as we have. Inevitably, we have entered this world of concern through the door of metaphor. Environmentalists have emphasized the image of the earth as a spaceship—Spaceship Earth. Kenneth Boulding (1966) is the principal architect of this metaphor. It is time, he says, that we replace the wasteful "cowboy economy" of the past with the frugal "spaceship economy" required for continued survival in the limited world we now see ours to be. The metaphor is notably useful in justifying pollution control measures.

Unfortunately, the image of a spaceship is also used to promote measures that are suicidal. One of these is a generous immigration policy, which is only a particular instance of a class of policies that are in error because they lead to the tragedy of the commons (Hardin 1968). These suicidal policies are attractive because they mesh with what we unthinkingly take

to be the ideals of "the best people." What is missing in the idealistic view is an insistence that rights and responsibilities must go together. The "generous" attitude of all too many people results in asserting inalienable rights while ignoring or denying matching responsibilities.

For the metaphor of a spaceship to be correct the aggregate of people on board would have to be under unitary sovereign control (Ophuls 1974). A true ship always has a captain. It is conceivable that a ship could be run by a committee. But it could not possibly survive if its course were determined by bickering tribes that claimed rights without responsibilities.

What about Spaceship Earth? It certainly has no captain, and no executive committee. The United Nations is a toothless tiger, because the signatories of its charter wanted it that way. The spaceship metaphor is used only to justify spaceship demands on common

From Garrett Hardin, "Living on a Lifeboat," *Science* 24 (1974). Reprinted by permission.

resources without acknowledging corresponding spaceship responsibilities.

An understandable fear of decisive action leads people to embrace "incrementalism"—moving toward reform in tiny stages. As we shall see, this strategy is counterproductive in the area discussed here if it means accepting rights before responsibilities. Where human survival is at stake, the acceptance of responsibilities is a precondition to the acceptance of rights, if the two cannot be introduced simultaneously.

LIFEBOAT ETHICS

Before taking up certain substantive issues let us look at an alternative metaphor, that of a lifeboat. In developing some relevant examples the following numerical values are assumed. Approximately two-thirds of the world is desperately poor, and only one-third is comparatively rich. The people in poor countries have an average per capita GNP (Gross National Product) of about $200 per year; the rich, of about $3,000. (For the United States it is nearly $5,000 per year.) Metaphorically, each rich nation amounts to a lifeboat full of comparatively rich people. The poor of the world are in other, much more crowded lifeboats. Continuously, so to speak, the poor fall out of their lifeboats and swim for a while in the water outside, hoping to be admitted to a rich lifeboat, or in some other way to benefit from the "goodies" on board. What should the passengers on a rich lifeboat do? This is the central problem of "the ethics of a lifeboat."

First we must acknowledge that each lifeboat is effectively limited in capacity. The land of every nation has a limited carrying capacity. The exact limit is a matter for argument, but the energy crunch is convincing more people every day that we have already exceeded the carrying capacity of the land. We have been living on "capital"—stored petroleum and coal—and soon we must live on income alone.

Let us look at only one lifeboat—ours. The ethical problem is the same for all, and is as follows. Here we sit, say 50 people in a lifeboat. To be generous, let us assume our boat has a capacity of 10 more, making 60. (This, however, is to violate the engineering principle of the "safety factor." A new plant disease or a bad change in the weather may decimate our population if we don't preserve some excess capacity as a safety factor.)

The 50 of us in the lifeboat see 100 others swimming in the water outside, asking for admission to the boat, or for handouts. How shall we respond to their calls? There are several possibilities.

One. We may be tempted to try to live by the Christian ideal of being "our brother's keeper," or by the Marxian ideal (Marx 1875) of "from each according to his abilities, to each according to his needs." Since the needs of all are the same, we take all the needy into our boat, making a total of 150 in a boat with a capacity of 60. The boat is swamped, and everyone drowns. Complete justice, complete catastrophe.

Two. Since the boat has an unused excess capacity of 10, we admit just 10 more to it. This has the disadvantage of getting rid of the safety factor, for which action we will sooner or later pay dearly. Moreover, *which* 10 do we let in? "First come, first served"? The best 10? The neediest 10? How do we *discriminate?* And what do we say to the 90 who are excluded?

Three. Admit no more to the boat and preserve the small safety factor. Survival of the people in the lifeboat is then possible (though we shall have to be on our guard against boarding parties).

The last solution is abhorrent to many people. It is unjust, they say. Let us grant that it is.

"I feel guilty about my good luck," say some. The reply to this is simple: *Get out and yield your place to others.* Such a selfless action might satisfy the conscience of those who are addicted to guilt but it would not change the ethics of the lifeboat. The needy person to whom a guilt-addict yields his place will not himself feel guilty about his sudden good luck. (If he did he would not climb aboard.) The net result of conscience-stricken people relinquishing their unjustly held positions is the elimination of their kind of conscience from the lifeboat. The lifeboat, as it were, purifies itself of guilt. The ethics of the lifeboat persist, unchanged by such momentary aberrations.

This then is the basic metaphor within which we must work out our solutions. Let us enrich the image step by step with substantive additions from the real world.

REPRODUCTION

The harsh characteristics of lifeboat ethics are heightened by reproduction, particularly by reproductive differences. The people inside the lifeboats of the wealthy nations are doubling in numbers every 87 years; those outside are doubling every 35 years, on the average. And the relative difference in prosperity is becoming greater.

Let us, for a while, think primarily of the U.S. lifeboat. As of 1973 the United States had a population of 210 million people, who were increasing by 0.8% per year, that is, doubling in number every 87 years.

Although the citizens of rich nations are outnumbered two to one by the poor, let us imagine an equal number of poor people outside our lifeboat—a mere 210 million poor people reproducing at a quite different rate. If we imagine these to be the combined populations of Colombia, Venezuela, Ecuador, Morocco, Thailand, Pakistan, and the Philippines, the average rate of increase of the people "outside" is 3.3% per year. The doubling time of this population is 21 years.

Suppose that all these countries, and the United States, agreed to live by the Marxian ideal, "to each according to his needs," the ideal of most Christians as well. Needs, of course, are determined by population size, which is affected by reproduction. Every nation regards its rate of reproduction as a sovereign right. If our lifeboat were big enough in the beginning it might be possible to live *for a while* by Christian-Marxian ideals. *Might.*

Initially, in the model given, the ratio of non-Americans to Americans would be one to one. But consider what the ratio would be 87 years later. By this time Americans would have doubled to a population of 420 million. The other group (doubling every 21 years) would now have swollen to 3,540 million.

Each American would have more than eight people to share with. How could the lifeboat possibly keep afloat?

All this involves extrapolation of current trends into the future, and is consequently suspect. Trends may change. Granted: but the change will not necessarily be favorable. If—as seems likely—the rate of population increase falls faster in the ethnic group presently inside the lifeboat than it does among those now outside, the future will turn out to be even worse than mathematics predicts, and sharing will be even more suicidal.

RUIN IN THE COMMONS

The fundamental error of the sharing ethics is that it leads to the tragedy of the commons. Under a system of private property the man (or group of men) who own property recognize their responsibility to care for it, for if they don't they will eventually suffer. A farmer, for instance, if he is intelligent, will allow no more cattle in a pasture than its carrying capacity justifies. If he overloads the pasture, weeds take over, erosion sets in, and the owner loses in the long run.

But if a pasture is run as a commons open to all, the right of each to use it is not matched by an operational responsibility to take care of it. It is no use asking independent herdsmen in a commons to act responsibly, for they dare not. The considerate herdsman who refrains from overloading the commons suffers more than a selfish one who says his needs are greater. (As Leo Durocher says, "Nice guys finish last.") Christian-Marxian idealism is counterproductive. That it *sounds* nice is no excuse. With distribution systems, as with individual morality, good intentions are no substitute for good performance.

A social system is stable only if it is insensitive to errors. To the Christian-Marxian idealist a selfish person is a sort of "error." Prosperity in the system of the commons cannot survive errors. If *everyone* would only restrain himself, all would be well; but it takes *only one less than everyone* to ruin a system of voluntary restraint. In a crowded world of less than perfect human beings—and we will never know any other—mutual ruin is inevitable in the commons. This is the core of the tragedy of the commons....

WORLD FOOD BANKS

In the international arena we have recently heard a proposal to create a new commons, namely an international depository of food reserves to which nations will contribute according to their abilities, and from which nations may draw according to their needs. Nobel laureate Norman Borlaug has lent the prestige of his name to this proposal.

A world food bank appeals powerfully to our humanitarian impulses. We remember John Donne's celebrated line, "Any man's death diminishes me." But before we rush out to see for whom the bell tolls let us recognize where the greatest political push for international granaries comes from, lest we be disillusioned later. Our experience with Public Law 480 clearly reveals the answer. This was the law that moved billions of dollars worth of U.S. grain to food-short, population-long countries during the past two decades. When P.L. 480 first came into being, a headline in the business magazine *Forbes* (Paddock 1970) revealed the power behind it: "Feeding the World's Hungry Millions: How it will mean billions for U.S. business."

And indeed it did. In the years 1960 to 1970 a total of $7.9 billion was spent on the "Food for Peace" program, as P.L. 480 was called. During the years of 1948 to 1970 an additional $49.9 billion were extracted from American taxpayers to pay for other economic aid programs, some of which went for food and food-producing machinery. (This figure does *not* include military aid.) That P.L. 480 was a give-away program was concealed. Recipient countries went through the motions of paying for P.L. 480 food—with IOU's. In December 1973 the charade was brought to an end as far as India was concerned when the United States "forgave" India's $3.2 billion debt (Anonymous 1974). Public announcement of the cancellation of the debt was delayed for two months: one wonders why....

What happens if some organizations budget for emergencies and others do not? If each organization is solely responsible for its own well-being, poorly managed ones will suffer. But they should be able to learn from experience. They have a chance to mend their ways and learn to budget for infrequent but certain emergencies. The weather, for instance, always varies and periodic crop failures are certain. A wise and competent government saves out of the production of the good years in anticipation of bad years that are sure to come. This is not a new idea. The Bible tells us that Joseph taught this policy to Pharaoh in Egypt more than 2,000 years ago. Yet it is literally true that the vast majority of the governments of the world today have no such policy. They lack either the wisdom or the competence, or both. Far more difficult than the transfer of wealth from one country to another is the transfer of wisdom between sovereign powers or between generations.

"But it isn't their fault! How can we blame the poor people who are caught in an emergency? Why must we punish them?" The concepts of blame and punishment are irrelevant. The question is, what are the operational consequences of establishing a world food bank? If it is open to every country every time a need develops, slovenly rulers will not be motivated to take Joseph's advice. Why should they? Others will bail them out whenever they are in trouble.

Some countries will make deposits in the world food bank and others will withdraw from it: there will be almost no overlap. Calling such a depository-transfer unit a "bank" is stretching the metaphor of *bank* beyond its elastic limits. The proposers, of course, never call attention to the metaphorical nature of the word they use.

THE RATCHET EFFECT

An "international food bank" is really, then, not a true bank but a disguised one-way transfer device for moving wealth from rich countries to poor. In the absence of such a bank, in a world inhabited by individually responsible sovereign nations, the population

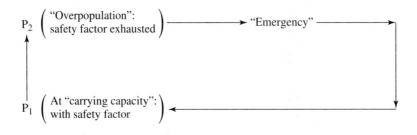

FIGURE 14.1

of each nation would repeatedly go through a cycle of the sort shown in Figure 14.1. P_2 is greater than P_1, either in absolute numbers or because a deterioration of the food supply has removed the safety factor and produced a dangerously low ratio of resources to population. P_2 may be said to represent a state of overpopulation, which becomes obvious upon the appearance of an "accident," e.g., a crop failure. If the "emergency" is not met by outside help, the population drops back to the "normal" level—the "carrying capacity" of the environment—or even below. In the absence of population control by a sovereign, sooner or later the population grows to P_2 again and the cycle repeats. The long-term population curve (Hardin 1966) is an irregularly fluctuating one, equilibrating more or less about the carrying capacity.

A demographic cycle of this sort obviously involves great suffering in the restrictive phase, but such a cycle is normal to any independent country with inadequate population control. The third century theologian Tertullian (Hardin 1969) expressed what must have been the recognition of many wise men when he wrote: "The scourges of pestilence, famine, wars, and earthquakes have come to be regarded as a blessing to overcrowded nations, since they serve to prune away the luxuriant growth of the human race."

Only under a strong and farsighted sovereign—which theoretically could be the people themselves, democratically organized—can a population equilibrate at some set point below the carrying capacity, thus avoiding the pains normally caused by periodic and unavoidable disasters. For this happy state to be achieved it is necessary that those in power be able to contemplate with equanimity the "waste" of surplus food in times of bountiful harvests. It is essential that those in power resist the temptation to convert extra food into extra babies. On the public relations level it is necessary that the phrase "surplus food" be replaced by "safety factor."

But wise sovereigns seem not to exist in the poor world today. The most anguishing problems are created by poor countries that are governed by rulers insufficiently wise and powerful. If such countries can draw on a world food bank in times of "emergency," the population *cycle* of Figure 14.1 will be replaced by the population *escalator* of Figure 14.2. The input of food from a food bank acts as the pawl of a ratchet, preventing the population from retracing its steps to a lower level. Reproduction pushes the population upward, inputs from the world bank prevent its moving downward. Population size escalates, as does the absolute magnitude of "accidents" and "emergencies." The process is brought to an end only by the total collapse of the whole system, producing a catastrophe of scarcely imaginable proportions.

Such are the implications of the well-meant sharing of food in a world of irresponsible reproduction....

To be generous with one's own possessions is one thing; to be generous with posterity's is quite another. This, I think, is the point that must be gotten across to those who would, from a commendable love of distributive justice, institute a ruinous system of the commons....

If the argument of this essay is correct, so long as there is no true world government to control reproduction everywhere it is impossible to survive in dignity if we are to be guided by Spaceship ethics. Without

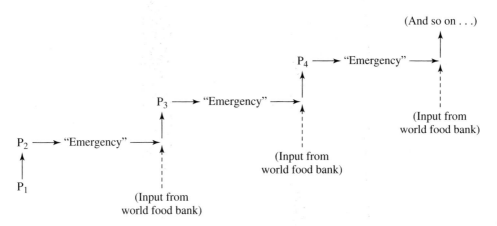

FIGURE 14.2

a world government that is sovereign in reproductive matters mankind lives, in fact, on a number of sovereign lifeboats. For the foreseeable future survival demands that we govern our actions by the ethics of a lifeboat. Posterity will be ill served if we do not.

REFERENCES

Anonymous. 1974. *Wall Street Journal,* 19 Feb.

Boulding, K. 1966. The economics of the coming spaceship earth. In H. Jarrett, ed. *Environmental Quality in a Growing Economy.* Johns Hopkins Press, Baltimore.

Hardin, G. 1966. Chap. 9 in *Biology: Its Principles and Implications,* 2nd ed. Freeman, San Francisco.

———. 1968. The tragedy of the commons. *Science* 162: 1243–1248.

———. 1969. Page 18 in *Population, Evolution, and Birth Control,* 2nd ed. Freeman, San Francisco.

Marx, K. 1875. *Critique of the Gotha program.* Page 388 in R. C. Tucker, ed. *The Marx-Engels Reader,* Norton, N.Y., 1972.

Ophuls, W. 1974. The scarcity society. *Harper's* 248 (1487): 47–52.

Paddock, W. C. 1970. How green is the green revolution? *Bioscience* 20: 897–902.

READING QUESTIONS

1. What are the problems with the metaphor of Earth as a spaceship according to Hardin?
2. Explain Hardin's lifeboat metaphor and the three possible responses that we might take toward the ethical problems it suggests.
3. Why does Hardin reject the first response to the ethical lifeboat problem? How does he respond to those who claim that the third possibility is unjust?
4. Why does Hardin think that an international food bank is an implausible solution to the problem of world hunger and poverty? What is the "ratchet effect" and how does it figure into his objections and proposed solution to the problem?

DISCUSSION QUESTIONS

1. Consider whether Hardin's lifeboat metaphor represents a plausible understanding of the way the nations of the world can or do operate. Are there any ways in which the metaphor could or should be modified?

2. Is Hardin correct to assume that the implementation of something like an international food bank would result in a vicious cycle of overpopulation accompanied by emergency scenarios? Consider some ways that a world food bank could operate more successfully in order to prevent such disasters.

PETER SINGER

The Life You Can Save

In this excerpt from his 2009 book, *The Life You Can Save*, Singer presents a basic argument for the claim that in not donating to human aid organizations, those in a financial position to do so are acting immorally—an argument he originally advanced in his influential 1972 article, "Famine, Affluence, and Morality." In the following selection, Singer presents recent empirical data about poverty and affluence, and he also responds to various objections to his basic argument that he has encountered over the years.

Recommended Reading: consequentialism, chap. 1, sec. 2A.

1. SAVING A CHILD

On your way to work, you pass a small pond. On hot days, children sometimes play in the pond, which is only about knee-deep. The weather's cool today, though, and the hour is early, so you are surprised to see a child splashing about in the pond. As you get closer, you see that it is a very young child, just a toddler, who is flailing about, unable to stay upright or walk out of the pond. You look for the parents or babysitter, but there is no one else around. The child is unable to keep his head above the water for more than a few seconds at a time. If you don't wade in and pull him out, he seems likely to drown. Wading in is easy and safe, but you will ruin the new shoes you bought only a few days ago, and get your suit wet and muddy. By the time you hand the child over to someone responsible for him, and change your clothes, you'll be late for work. What should you do?

I teach a course called Practical Ethics. When we start talking about global poverty, I ask my students what they think you should do in this situation. Predictably, they respond that you should save the child. "What about your shoes? And being late for work?" I ask them. They brush that aside. How could anyone consider a pair of shoes, or missing an hour or two at work, a good reason for not saving a child's life?

In 2007, something resembling this hypothetical situation actually occurred near Manchester, England. Jordon Lyon, a ten-year-old boy, leaped into a pond after his stepsister Bethany slipped in. He struggled to support her but went under himself.

From Peter Singer, *The Life You Can Save* (New York: Random House, 2009). Reprinted with permission of the author.

Anglers managed to pull Bethany out, but by then Jordon could no longer be seen. They raised the alarm, and two police community support officers soon arrived; they refused to enter the pond to find Jordon. He was later pulled out, but attempts at resuscitation failed. At the inquest on Jordon's death, the officers' inaction was defended on the grounds that they had not been trained to deal with such situations. The mother responded: "If you're walking down the street and you see a child drowning you automatically go in that water . . . You don't have to be trained to jump in after a drowning child."[1]

I think it's safe to assume that most people would agree with the mother's statement. But consider that, according to UNICEF, nearly 10 million children under five years old die each year from causes related to poverty. Here is just one case, described by a man in Ghana to a researcher from the World Bank:

> Take the death of this small boy this morning, for example. The boy died of measles. We all know he could have been cured at the hospital. But the parents had no money and so the boy died a slow and painful death, not of measles but out of poverty.[2]

Think about something like that happening 27,000 times every day. Some children die because they don't have enough to eat. More die, like that small boy in Ghana, from measles, malaria, and diarrhea, conditions that either don't exist in developed nations, or, if they do, are almost never fatal. The children are vulnerable to these diseases because they have no safe drinking water, or no sanitation, and because when they do fall ill, their parents can't afford any medical treatment. UNICEF, Oxfam, and many other organizations are working to reduce poverty and provide clean water and basic health care, and these efforts are reducing the toll. If the relief organizations had more money, they could do more, and more lives would be saved.

Now think about your own situation. By donating a relatively small amount of money, you could save a child's life. Maybe it takes more than the amount needed to buy a pair of shoes—but we all spend money on things we don't really need, whether on drinks, meals out, clothing, movies, concerts, vacations, new cars, or house renovation. Is it possible that by choosing to spend your money on such things rather than contributing to an aid agency, you are leaving a child to die, a child you could have saved?

Poverty Today

A few years ago, the World Bank asked researchers to listen to what the poor are saying. They were able to document the experiences of 60,000 women and men in seventy-three countries. Over and over, in different languages and on different continents, poor people said that poverty meant these things:

- You are short of food for all or part of the year, often eating only one meal per day, sometimes having to choose between stilling your child's hunger or your own, and sometimes being able to do neither.
- You can't save money. If a family member falls ill and you need money to see a doctor, or if the crop fails and you have nothing to eat, you have to borrow from a local moneylender and he will charge you so much interest as the debt continues to mount and you may never be free of it.
- You can't afford to send your children to school, or if they do start school, you have to take them out again if the harvest is poor.
- You live in an unstable house, made with mud or thatch that you need to rebuild every two or three years, or after severe weather.
- You have no nearby source of safe drinking water. You have to carry your water a long way, and even then, it can make you ill unless you boil it.

But extreme poverty is not only a condition of unsatisfied material needs. It is often accompanied by a degrading state of powerlessness. Even in countries that are democracies and are relatively well governed, respondents to the World Bank survey described a range of situations in which they had to accept humiliation without protest. If someone takes what little you have, and you complain to the police, they may not listen to you. Nor will the law necessarily protect you from rape or sexual harassment. You have a pervading sense of shame and failure because you cannot provide for your children. Your poverty traps you, and you lose hope of ever escaping from a life of hard work for which, at the end, you will have nothing to show beyond bare survival.[3]

The World Bank defines extreme poverty as not having enough income to meet the most basic human needs for adequate food, water, shelter, clothing, sanitation, health care, and education. Many people are familiar with the statistic that 1 billion people are living on less than one dollar per day. That was the World Bank's poverty line until 2008, when better data on international price comparisons enabled it to make a more accurate calculation of the amount people need to meet their basic needs. On the basis of this calculation, the World Bank set the poverty line at $1.25 per day. The number of people whose income puts them under this line is not 1 billion but 1.4 billion. That there are more people living in extreme poverty than we thought is, of course, bad news, but the news is not all bad. On the same basis, in 1981 there were 1.9 billion people living in extreme poverty. That was about four in every ten people on the planet, whereas now fewer than one in four are extremely poor.

South Asia is still the region with the largest number of people living in extreme poverty, a total of 600 million, including 455 million in India. Economic growth has, however, reduced the proportion of South Asians living in extreme poverty from 60 percent in 1981 to 42 percent in 2005. There are another 380 million extremely poor people in sub-Saharan Africa, where half the population is extremely poor—and that is the same percentage as in 1981. The most dramatic reduction in poverty has been in East Asia, although there are still more than 200 million extremely poor Chinese, and smaller numbers elsewhere in the region. The remaining extremely poor people are distributed around the world, in Latin America and the Caribbean, the Pacific, the Middle East, North Africa, Eastern Europe, and Central Asia.[4]

In response to the "$1.25 a day" figure, the thought may cross your mind that in many developing countries, it is possible to live much more cheaply than in the industrialized nations. Perhaps you have even done it yourself, backpacking around the world, living on less than you would have believed possible. So you may imagine that this level of poverty is less extreme than it would be if you had to live on that amount of money in the United States, or any industrialized nation. If such thoughts did occur to you, you should banish them now, because the World Bank has already made the adjustment in purchasing power: Its figures refer to the number of people existing on a daily total consumption of goods and services—whether earned or home-grown—comparable to the amount of goods and services that can be bought in the United States for $1.25.

In wealthy societies, most poverty is relative. People feel poor because many of the good things they see advertised on television are beyond their budget—but they do have a television. In the United States, 97 percent of those classified by the Census Bureau as poor own a color TV. Three quarters of them own a car. Three quarters of them have air-conditioning. Three quarters of them have a VCR or DVD player. All have access to health care.[5] I am not quoting these figures in order to deny that the poor in the United States face genuine difficulties. Nevertheless, for most, these difficulties are of a different order than those of the world's poorest people. The 1.4 billion people living in extreme poverty are poor by an absolute standard tied to the most basic human needs. They are likely to be hungry for at least part of each year. Even if they can get enough food to fill their stomachs, they will probably be malnourished because their diet lacks essential nutrients. In children, malnutrition stunts growth and can cause permanent brain damage. The poor may not be able to afford to send their children to school. Even minimal health care services are usually beyond their means.

This kind of poverty kills. Life expectancy in rich nations averages seventy-eight years; in the poorest nations, those officially classified as "least developed," it is below fifty.[6] In rich countries, fewer than one in a hundred children die before the age of five; in the poorest countries, one in five does. And to the UNICEF figure of nearly 10 million young children dying every year from avoidable, poverty-related causes, we must add at least another 8 million older children and adults.[7]

Affluence Today

Roughly matching the 1.4 billion people living in extreme poverty, there are about a billion living at a level of affluence never previously known except in the courts of kings and nobles. As king of France, Louis XIV, the "Sun King," could afford to build the most magnificent palace Europe had ever seen, but he could not keep it cool in summer as effectively as most middle-class people in industrialized nations can keep their homes cool today. His gardeners, for all their skill, were unable to produce the variety of fresh fruits and vegetables that we can buy all year-round. If he developed a toothache or fell ill, the best his dentists and doctors could do for him would make us shudder.

But we're not just better off than a French king who lived centuries ago. We are also much better off than our own greatgrandparents. For a start, we can expect to live about thirty years longer. A century ago, one child in ten died in infancy. Now, in most rich nations, that figure is less than one in two hundred.[8] Another telling indicator of how wealthy we are today is the modest number of hours we must work in order to meet our basic dietary needs. Today Americans spend, on average, only 6 percent of their income on buying food. If they work a forty-hour week, it takes them barely two hours to earn enough to feed themselves for the week. That leaves far more to spend on consumer goods, entertainment, and vacations.

And then we have the superrich, people who spend their money on palatial homes, ridiculously large and luxurious boats, and private planes. Before the 2008 stock market crash trimmed the numbers, there were more than 1,100 billionaires in the world, with a combined net worth of $4.4 trillion.[9] To cater to such people, Lufthansa Technik unveiled its plans for a private configuration of Boeing's new 787 Dreamliner. In commercial service, this plane will seat up to 330 passengers. The private version will carry 35, at a price of $150 million. Cost aside, there's nothing like owning a really big airplane carrying a small number of people to maximize your personal contribution to global warming. Apparently, there are already several billionaires who fly around in private commercial-sized airliners, from 747s down. Larry Page and Sergey Brin, the Google cofounders, reportedly bought a Boeing 767 and spent millions fitting it out for their private use.[10] But for conspicuous waste of money and resources it is hard to beat Anousheh Ansari, an Iranian-American telecommunications entrepreneur who paid a reported $20 million for eleven days in space. Comedian Lewis Black said on Jon Stewart's *The Daily Show* that Ansari did it because it was "the only way she could achieve her life's goal of flying over every single starving person on earth and yelling 'Hey, look what I'm spending my money on!'"

While I was working on this book, a special advertising supplement fell out of my Sunday edition of *The New York Times:* a sixty-eight-page glossy magazine filled with advertising for watches by Rolex, Patek Philippe, Breitling, and other luxury brands. The ads didn't carry price tags, but a puff piece about the revival of the mechanical watch gave guidance about the lower end of the range. After admitting that inexpensive quartz watches are extremely accurate and functional, the article opined that there is "something engaging about a mechanical movement." Right, but how much will it cost you to have this engaging something on your wrist? "You might think that getting into mechanical watches is an expensive proposition, but there are plenty of choices in the $500–$5000 range." Admittedly, "these opening-price-point models are pretty simple: basic movement, basic time display, simple decoration and so on." From which we can gather that most of the watches advertised are priced upward of $5,000, or more than one hundred times what anyone needs to pay for a reliable, accurate quartz watch. That there is a market for such products—and one worth advertising at such expense to the wide readership of *The New York Times*—is another indication of the affluence of our society.[11]

If you're shaking your head at the excesses of the superrich, though, don't shake too hard. Think again about some of the ways Americans with average incomes spend their money. In most places in the United States, you can get your recommended eight glasses of water a day out of the tap for less than a penny, while a bottle of water will set you back $1.50 or more.[12] And in spite of the environmental concerns raised by the waste of energy that goes into producing and transporting it, Americans are still buying bottled water, to the tune of more than 31 billion liters in 2006.[13] Think, too, of the way many of us get our caffeine fix: You can make coffee at home for pennies rather than spending three dollars or more on a latte. Or have you ever casually said yes to a waiter's prompt to order a second soda or glass of wine that you didn't even finish? When Dr. Timothy Jones, an archaeologist, led a U.S. goverment–funded study of food waste, he found that 14 percent of household garbage is perfectly good food that was in its original packaging and not out of date. More than half of this food was drypackaged or canned goods that keep for a long time. According to Jones, $100 billion of food is wasted in the United States every year.[14] Fashion designer Deborah Lindquist claims that the average woman owns more than $600 worth of clothing that she has not worn in the last year.[15] Whatever the actual figure may be, it is fair to say that almost all of us, men and women alike, buy things we don't need, some of which we never even use.

Most of us are absolutely certain that we wouldn't hesitate to save a drowning child, and that we would do it at considerable cost to ourselves. Yet while thousands of children die each day, we spend money on things we take for granted and would hardly notice if they were not there. Is that wrong? If so, how far does our obligation to the poor go?

2. IS IT WRONG NOT TO HELP?

Bob is close to retirement. He has invested most of his savings in a very rare and valuable old car, a Bugatti, which he has not been able to insure. The Bugatti is his pride and joy. Not only does Bob get pleasure from driving and caring for his car, he also knows that its rising market value means that he will be able to sell it and live comfortably after retirement. One day when Bob is out for a drive, he parks the Bugatti near the end of a railway siding and goes for a walk up the track. As he does so, he sees that a runaway train, with no one aboard, is rolling down the railway track. Looking farther down the track, he sees the small figure of a child who appears to be absorbed in playing on the tracks. Oblivious to the runaway train, the child is in great danger. Bob can't stop the train, and the child is too far away to hear his warning shout, but Bob can throw a switch that will divert the train down the siding where his Bugatti is parked. If he does so, nobody will be killed, but the train will crash through the decaying barrier at the end of the siding and destroy his Bugatti. Thinking of his joy in owning the car and the financial security it represents, Bob decides not to throw the switch.

The Car or the Child?

Philosopher Peter Unger developed this variation on the story of the drowning child to challenge us to think further about how much we believe we should sacrifice in order to save the life of a child. Unger's story adds a factor often crucial to our thinking about real-world poverty: uncertainty about the outcome of our sacrifice. Bob cannot be certain that the child will die if he does nothing and saves his car. Perhaps at the last moment the child will hear the train and leap to safety. In the same way, most of us can summon doubts about whether the money we give to a charity is really helping the people it's intended to help.

In my experience, people almost always respond that Bob acted badly when he did not throw the switch and destroy his most cherished and valuable possession, thereby sacrificing his hope of a financially secure retirement. We can't take a serious risk with a child's life, they say, merely to save a car, no matter how rare and valuable the car may be. By implication, we should also believe that with the simple act of saving money for retirement, we are acting as badly as Bob. For in saving money for retirement, we are effectively refusing to use that money to help save lives. This is a difficult implication to confront. How can it be wrong to save for a comfortable retirement? There is, at the very least, something puzzling here.

Another example devised by Unger tests the level of sacrifice we think people should make to alleviate suffering in cases when a life is not at stake:

> You are driving your vintage sedan down a country lane when you are stopped by a hiker who has seriously injured his leg. He asks you to take him to the nearest hospital. If you refuse, there is a good chance that he will lose his leg. On the other hand, if you agree to take him to hospital, he is likely to bleed onto the seats, which you have recently, and expensively, restored in soft white leather.

Again, most people respond that you should drive the hiker to the hospital. This suggests that when prompted to think in concrete terms, about real individuals, most of us consider it obligatory to lessen the serious suffering of innocent others, even at some cost (even a high cost) to ourselves.[16]

The Basic Argument

The above examples reveal our intuitive belief that we ought to help others in need, at least when we can see them and when we are the only person in a position to save them. But our moral intuitions are not always reliable, as we can see from variations in what people in different times and places find intuitively acceptable or objectionable. The case for helping those in extreme poverty will be stronger if it does not rest solely on our intuitions. Here is a logical argument from plausible premises to the same conclusion.

> First premise: Suffering and death from lack of food, shelter, and medical care are bad.
> Second premise: If it is in your power to prevent something bad from happening, without sacrificing anything nearly as important, it is wrong not to do so.
> Third premise: By donating to aid agencies, you can prevent suffering and death from lack of food, shelter, and medical care, without sacrificing anything nearly as important.
> Conclusion: Therefore, if you do not donate to aid agencies, you are doing something wrong.

The drowning-child story is an application of this argument for aid, since ruining your shoes and being late for work aren't nearly as important as the life of a child. Similarly, reupholstering a car is not nearly as big a deal as losing a leg. Even in the case of Bob and the Bugatti, it would be a big stretch to suggest that the loss of the Bugatti would come close to rivaling the significance of the death of an innocent person.

Ask yourself if you can deny the premises of the argument. How could suffering and death from lack of food, shelter, and medical care not be really, really bad? Think of that small boy in Ghana who died of measles. How you would feel if you were his mother or father, watching helplessly as your son suffers and grows weaker? You know that children often die from this condition. You also know that it would be curable, if only you could afford to take your child to a hospital. In those circumstances you would give up almost anything for some way of ensuring your child's survival.

Putting yourself in the place of others, like the parents of that boy, or the child himself, is what thinking ethically is all about. It is encapsulated in the Golden Rule, "Do unto others as you would have them do unto you." Though the Golden Rule is best known to most westerners from the words of Jesus as reported by Matthew and Luke, it is remarkably universal, being found in Buddhism, Confucianism, Hinduism, Islam, and Jainism, and in Judaism, where it is found in Leviticus, and later emphasized by the sage Hillel. [17] The Golden Rule requires us to accept that the desires of others ought to count as if they were our own. If the desires of the parents of the dying child were our own, we would have no doubt that their suffering and the death of their child are about as bad as anything can be. So if we think ethically, then those desires must count as if they were our own, and we cannot deny that the suffering and death are bad.

The second premise is also very difficult to reject, because it leaves us some wiggle room when it comes to situations in which, to prevent something bad, we would have to risk something *nearly* as important as the bad thing we are preventing. Consider, for example, a situation in which you can only prevent the deaths of other children by neglecting your own children. This standard does not require you to prevent the deaths of the other children.

"Nearly as important" is a vague term. That's deliberate, because I'm confident that you can do without plenty of things that are clearly and inarguably not as valuable as saving a child's life. I don't know what *you* might think is as important, or nearly as important, as saving a life. By leaving it up to you to decide what those things are, I can avoid the need to find out. I'll trust you to be honest with yourself about it.

Analogies and stories can be pushed too far. Rescuing a child drowning in front of you, and throwing a switch on a railroad track to save the life of a child you can see in the distance, where you are the only one who can save the child, are both different from giving aid to people who are far away. The argument I have just presented complements the drowning-child case, because instead of pulling at your heartstrings by focusing on a single child in need, it appeals to your reason and seeks your assent to an abstract but compelling moral principle. That means that to reject it, you need to find a flaw in the reasoning....

3. COMMON OBJECTIONS TO GIVING

Charity begins at home, the saying goes, and I've found that friends, colleagues, students, and lecture audiences express that resistance in various ways. I've seen it in columns, letters, and blogs too. Particularly interesting, because they reflect a line of thought prevalent in affluent America, were comments made by students taking an elective called Literature and Justice at Glennview High (that's not its real name), a school in a wealthy Boston suburb. As part of the reading for the course, teachers gave students an article that I wrote for *The New York Times* in 1999, laying out a version of the argument you have just read, and asked them to write papers in response.[18] Scott Seider, then a graduate student at Harvard University researching how adolescents think about obligations to others, interviewed thirty-eight students in two sections of the course and read their papers.[19]

Let's look at some of the objections raised by these varied sources. Perhaps the most fundamental objection comes from Kathryn, a Glennview student who believes we shouldn't judge people who refuse to give:

There is no black and white universal code for everyone. It is better to accept that everyone has a different view on the issue, and all people are entitled to follow their own beliefs.

Kathryn leaves it to the individual to determine his or her moral obligation to the poor. But while circumstances do make a difference, and we should avoid being too black-and-white in our judgments, this doesn't mean we should accept that everyone is entitled to follow his or her own beliefs. That is moral relativism, a position that many find attractive only until they are faced with someone who is doing something really, really wrong. If we see a person holding a cat's paws on an electric grill that is gradually heating up, and when we vigorously object he says, "But it's fun, see how the cat squeals," we don't just say, "Oh, well, you are entitled to follow your own beliefs," and leave him alone. We can and do try to stop people who are cruel to animals, just as we stop rapists, racists, and terrorists. I'm not saying that failing to give is like committing these acts of violence, but if we reject moral relativism in some situations, then we should reject it everywhere.

After reading my essay, Douglas, another Glennview student, objected that I "should not have the right to tell people what to do." In one sense, he's correct about that. I've no right to tell you or anyone else what to do with your money, in the sense that that would imply that you *have* to do as I say. I've no authority over Douglas or over you. On the other hand, I do have the right of free speech, which I'm exercising right now by offering you some arguments you might consider before you decide what to do with your money. I hope that you will want to listen to a variety of views before making up your mind about such an important issue. If I'm wrong about that, though, you are free to shut the book now, and there's nothing I can do about it.

It's possible, of course, to think that morality is not relative, and that we should talk about it, but that

SINGER • The Life You Can Save

the right view is that we aren't under any obligation to give anything at all. Lucy, another Glennview High student, wrote as follows:

> If someone wants to buy a new car, they should. If someone wants to redecorate their house, they should, and if they need a suit, get it. They work for their money and they have the right to spend it on themselves. . . .

Lucy said that people have a right to spend the money they earn on themselves. Even if we agree with that, having a *right* to do something doesn't settle the question of what you *should* do. If you have a right to do something, I can't justifiably force you not to do it, but I can still tell you that you would be a fool to do it, or that it would be a horrible thing to do, or that you would be wrong to do it. You may have a right to spend your weekend surfing, but it can still be true that you ought to visit your sick mother. Similarly, we might say that the rich have a right to spend their money on lavish parties, Patek Philippe watches, private jets, luxury yachts, and space travel, or, for that matter, to flush wads of it down the toilet. Or that those of us with more modest means shouldn't be forced to forgo any of the less-expensive pleasures that offer us some relief from all the time we spend working. But we could still think that to choose to do these things rather than use the money to save human lives is wrong, shows a deplorable lack of empathy, and means that you are not a good person. . . .

Libertarians resist the idea that we have a duty to help others. Canadian philosopher Jan Narveson articulates that point of view:

> We are certainly responsible for evils we inflict on others, no matter where, and we owe those people compensation...Nevertheless, I have seen no plausible argument that we owe something, as a matter of general duty, to those to whom we have done nothing wrong.[20]

There is, at first glance, something attractive about the political philosophy that says: "You leave me alone, and I'll leave you alone, and we'll get along just fine." It appeals to the frontier mentality, to an ideal of life in the wide-open spaces where each of us can carve out our own territory and live undisturbed by the neighbors. At first glance, it seems perfectly reasonable. Yet there is a callous side to a

philosophy that denies that we have any responsibilities to those who, through no fault of their own, are in need. Taking libertarianism seriously would require us to abolish all state-supported welfare schemes for those who can't get a job or are ill or disabled, and all state-funded health care for the aged and for those who are too poor to pay for their own health insurance. Few people really support such extreme views. Most think that we do have obligations to those we can help with relatively little sacrifice—certainly to those living in our own country, and I would argue that we can't justifiably draw the boundary there. But if I have not persuaded you of that, there is another line of argument to consider: If we have, in fact, been at least in part a cause of the poverty of the world's poorest people—if we are harming the poor—then even libertarians like Narveson will have to agree that we ought to compensate them. . . . There are many ways in which it is clear, however, that the rich *have* harmed the poor. Ale Nodye knows about one of them. He grew up in a village by the sea, in Senegal, in West Africa. His father and grandfather were fishermen, and he tried to be one too. But after six years in which he barely caught enough fish to pay for the fuel for his boat, he set out by canoe for the Canary Islands, from where he hoped to become another of Europe's many illegal immigrants. Instead, he was arrested and deported. But he says he will try again, even though the voyage is dangerous and one of his cousins died on a similar trip. He has no choice, he says, because "there are no fish in the sea here anymore." A European Commission report shows that Nodye is right: The fish stocks from which Nodye's father and grandfather took their catch and fed their families have been destroyed by industrial fishing fleets that come from Europe, China, and Russia and sell their fish to well-fed Europeans who can afford to pay high prices. The industrial fleets drag vast nets across the seabed, damaging the coral reefs where fish breed. As a result, a major protein source for poor people has vanished, the boats are idle, and people who used to make a living fishing or building boats are unemployed. The story is repeated in many other coastal areas around the world.[21]

Or consider how we citizens of rich countries obtain our oil and minerals. Teodoro Obiang, the dictator of tiny Equatorial Guinea, sells most of his country's oil to American corporations, among them Exxon Mobil, Marathon, and Hess. Although his official salary is a modest $60,000, this ruler of a country of 550,000 people is richer than Queen Elizabeth II. He owns six private jets and a $35 million house in Malibu, as well as other houses in Maryland and Cape Town and a fleet of Lamborghinis, Ferraris, and Bentleys. Most of the people over whom he rules live in extreme poverty, with a life expectancy of forty-nine and an infant mortality of eighty-seven per one thousand (this means that more than one child in twelve dies before its first birthday).[22] Equatorial Guinea is an extreme case, but other examples are almost as bad. In 2005, the Democratic Republic of the Congo exported minerals worth $200 million. From this, its total tax revenues were $86,000. Someone was surely making money from these dealings, but not the people of the Congo.[23] In 2006, Angola made more than $30 billion in oil revenue, about $2,500 for each of its 12 million citizens. Yet the majority of Angolans have no access to basic health care; life expectancy is forty-one years; and one child in four dies before reaching the age of five. On Transparency International's corruption perception index, Angola is currently ranked 147th among 180 countries.

In their dealings with corrupt dictators in developing countries, international corporations are akin to people who knowingly buy stolen goods, with the difference that the international legal and political order recognizes the corporations not as criminals in possession of stolen goods but as the legal owners of the goods they have bought. This situation is, of course, profitable for corporations that do deals with dictators, and for us, since we use the oil, minerals, and other raw materials we need to maintain our prosperity. But for resource-rich developing countries, it is a disaster. The problem is not only the loss of immense wealth that, used wisely, could build the prosperity of the nation. Paradoxically, developing nations with rich deposits of oil or minerals are often worse off than otherwise comparable nations without those resources. One reason is that the revenue from the sale of the resources provides a huge financial incentive for anyone tempted to overthrow the government and seize power. Successful rebels know that if they

succeed, they will be rewarded with immense personal wealth. They can also reward those who backed their coup, and they can buy enough arms to keep themselves in power no matter how badly they rule. Unless, of course, some of those to whom they give the arms are themselves tempted by the prospect of controlling all that wealth ... Thus the resources that should benefit developing nations instead become a curse that brings corruption, coups, and civil wars.[24] If we use goods made from raw materials obtained by these unethical dealings from resource-rich but money-poor nations, we are harming those who live in these countries.

One other way in which we in the rich nations are harming the poor has become increasingly clear over the past decade or two. President Yoweri Museveni of Uganda put it plainly, addressing the developed world at a 2007 meeting of the African Union: "You are causing aggression to us by causing global warming .... Alaska will probably become good for agriculture, Siberia will probably become good for agriculture, but where does that leave Africa?"[25]

Strong language, but the accusation is difficult to deny. Two-thirds of the greenhouse gases now in the atmosphere have come from the United States and Europe. Without those gases, there would be no human-induced global warming problem. Africa's contribution is, by comparison, extremely modest: less than 3 percent of the global emissions from burning fuel since 1900, somewhat more if land clearing and methane emissions from livestock production are included, but still a small fraction of what has been contributed by the industrialized nations. And while every nation will have some problems in adjusting to climate change, the hardship will, as Museveni suggests, fall disproportionately on the poor in the regions of the world closer to the equator. Some scientists believe that precipitation will decrease nearer the equator and increase nearer the poles. In any case, the rainfall upon which hundreds of millions rely to grow their food will become less reliable. Moreover, the poor nations depend on agriculture to a far greater degree than the rich. In the United States, agriculture represents only 4 percent of the economy; in Malawi it is 40 percent, and 90 percent of the population are subsistence farmers, virtually all of whom are dependent on rainfall. Nor will drought be the only problem climate change brings to the poor. Rising sea levels will inundate fertile, densely settled delta regions that are home to tens of millions of people in Egypt, Bangladesh, India, and Vietnam. Small Pacific Island nations that consist of low-lying coral atolls, like Kiribati and Tuvalu, are in similar danger, and it seems inevitable that in a few decades they will be submerged.[26]

The evidence is overwhelming that the greenhouse gas emissions of the industrialized nations have harmed, and are continuing to harm, many of the world's poorest people—along with many richer ones, too. If we accept that those who harm others must compensate them, we cannot deny that the industrialized nations owe compensation to many of the world's poorest people. Giving them adequate aid to mitigate the consequences of climate change would be one way of paying that compensation.

In a world that has no more capacity to absorb greenhouse gases without the consequence of damaging climate change, the philosophy of "You leave me alone, and I'll leave you alone" has become almost impossible to live by, for it requires ceasing to put any more greenhouse gases into the atmosphere. Otherwise, we simply are not leaving others alone.

America is a generous nation. As Americans, we are already giving more than our share of foreign aid through our taxes. Isn't that sufficient?

Asked whether the United States gives more, less, or about the same amount of aid, as a percentage of its income, as other wealthy countries, only one in twenty Americans gave the correct answer. When my students suggest that America is generous in this regard, I show them figures from the website of the OECD, on the amounts given by all the organization's donor members. They are astonished to find that the United States has, for many years, been at or near the bottom of the list of industrialized countries in terms of the proportion of national income given as foreign aid. In 2006, the United States fell behind Portugal and Italy, leaving Greece as the only industrialized country to give a smaller percentage of its national income in foreign aid. The average nation's effort in that year came to 46 cents of every $100 of gross national income, while the United States gave only 18 cents of every $100 it earned.

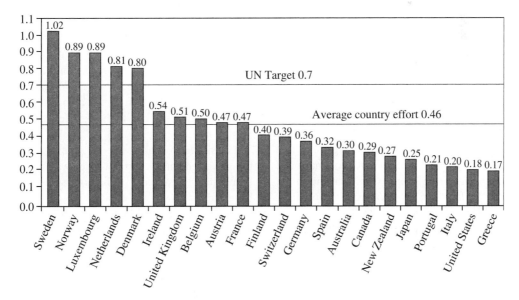

FIGURE 14.3 Official Aid as a Percentage of Gross National Income (2006)[27]

Philanthropic responses undermine real political change.

If those on the right fear that I am encouraging the state to seize their money and give it to the world's poor, some on the left worry that encouraging the rich to donate to aid organizations enables them to salve their consciences while they continue to benefit from a global economic system that makes them rich and keeps billions poor.[28] Philanthropy, philosopher Paul Gomberg believes, promotes "political quietism," deflecting attention from the institutional causes of poverty—essentially, in his view, capitalism—and from the need to find radical alternatives to these institutions.[29]

Although I believe we ought to give a larger portion of our income to organizations combating poverty, I am open-minded about the best way to combat poverty.[30] Some aid agencies, Oxfam for example, are engaged in emergency relief, development aid, *and* advocacy work for a fairer global economic order. If, after investigating the causes of global poverty and considering what approach is most likely to reduce it, you really believe that a more revolutionary change is needed, then it would make sense to put your time, energy, and money into organizations promoting that revolution in the global economic system. But this is a practical question, and if there is little chance of achieving the kind of revolution you are seeking, then you need to look around for a strategy with better prospects of actually helping some poor people.

Giving people money or food breeds dependency.

I agree that we should not be giving money or food directly to the poor, except in emergencies like a drought, earthquake, or flood, where food may need to be brought in to stop people from starving in the short term. In less dire situations, providing food can make people dependent. If the food is shipped in from a developed nation, for example the United States, it can destroy local markets and reduce incentives for local farmers to produce a surplus to sell. We need to make it possible for people to earn their own money, or to produce their own food and meet their other needs in a sustainable manner and by their own

work. Giving them money or food won't achieve that. Finding a form of aid that will really help people is crucial, and not a simple task, but as we'll see, it can be done.[31]

Cash is the seed corn of capitalism. Giving it away will reduce future growth.

Gaetano Cipriano contacted me after reading one of my articles because he thought that as an entrepreneurial capitalist, he could offer a helpful perspective. The grandson of immigrants to America, he owns and runs EI Associates, an engineering and construction firm based in Cedar Knolls, New Jersey, that has assets of around $80 million. "Cash is the seed corn of capitalism" is his phrase. Gaetano told me that he deploys his capital to the best of his ability to promote profits and enduring growth, and that giving more of it away would be "cutting my own throat." But he does not spend extravagantly. "I do not live in a splendid house," he told me. "I have no second home. I drive a 2001 Ford Explorer with 73,000 miles. I belong to a nice squash club, and have four suits and two pairs of black shoes. When I take vacations they are short and local. I do not own a boat or a plane." While he does give to charity, he does it "at a level which is prudent and balanced with sustainable growth." If he were to give much more money away, it would have to come out of sums that he now reinvests in his business. That, in turn, would reduce his future earnings and perhaps the number of people he is able to employ, or how well he can pay them. It would also leave him with less to give if, later in life, he decides that he wants to give more.

For similar reasons, we can agree that it's a good thing Warren Buffett did not give away the first million dollars he earned. Had he done so, he would not have had the investment capital he needed to develop his business, and would never have been able to give away the $31 billion that he has now pledged to give. If you are as skilled as Buffett in investing your money, I urge you to keep it until late in life, too, and then give away most of it, as he has done. But people with less-spectacular investment abilities might do better to give it away sooner. . . .

What if you took every penny you ever had and gave it to the poor of Africa...? What we would have is no economy, no ability to generate new wealth or help anybody.

This objection comes from Colin McGinn, a professor of philosophy at the University of Miami.[32] It isn't clear whether McGinn's "you" is you, the individual reader, or the group an American Southerner might refer to as "y'all." If you [insert your name], took every penny you ever had and gave it to the poor of Africa, our national economy would not notice. Even if every reader of this book did that, the economy would barely hiccup (unless the book's sales exceed my wildest dreams). If *everyone* in America did it, the national economy would be ruined. But, at the moment, there is no cause for worry about the last possibility: there is no sign of it happening, and I am not advocating it.

Because so few people give significant amounts, the need for more to be given is great, and the more each one of us gives, the more lives we can save. If everyone gave significantly more than they now give, however, we would be in a totally different situation. The huge gulf between rich and poor means that if everyone were giving, there would be no need for them to take every penny they ever had and give it all to Africa. As you'll see before the end of this book, quite a modest contribution from everyone who has enough to live comfortably, eat out occasionally, and buy bottled water, would suffice to achieve the goal of lifting most of the world's extremely poor people above the poverty line of $1.25 per day. If that modest contribution were given, we would no longer be in a situation in which 10 million children were dying from poverty every year. So whether a small number of people give a lot, or a large number of people give a little, ending large-scale extreme poverty wouldn't cripple our national economy. It leaves plenty of scope for entrepreneurial activity and individual wealth. In the long run, the global economy would be enhanced, rather than diminished, by bringing into it the 1.4 billion people now outside it, creating new markets and new opportunities for trade and investment.

People do have special relationships with their families, their communities, and their countries.

This is the standard equipment of humanity, and most people, in all of human history, have seen nothing wrong with it.[33]

—Alan Ryan, philosopher and warden of
New College, Oxford

It is true that most of us care more about our family and friends than we do about strangers. That's natural, and there is nothing wrong with it. But how far should preference for family and friends go? Brendan, a Glennview High student, thought that instead of going to aid for the poor, money "can be better spent helping your family and friends who need the money as well." If family and friends really *need* the money, in anything remotely like the way those living in extreme poverty need it, it would be going too much against the grain of human nature to object to giving to them before giving to strangers. Fortunately, most middle-class people in rich nations don't have to make this choice. They can take care of their families in an entirely sufficient way on much less than they are now spending, and thus have money left over that can be used to help those in extreme poverty. Admittedly, saying just where the balance should be struck is difficult....

Kiernan, another Glennview High School student, made a point similar to Alan Ryan's:

> [*Giving what we don't need to the poor*] *would make the world a better, more equal place. But it is like a little kid buying a pack of candy, keeping one piece, and giving the rest away. It just doesn't happen.*

The issue raised by all these remarks is the link between what we humans are (mostly) like, and what we *ought* to do. When Brendan O'Grady, a philosophy student at Queen's University in Ontario, posted a blog about this issue, he got the following response from another Canadian philosophy student Thomas Simmons:

> Of course I do not want people to die, but I just feel generally unattached to them. I have no doubt that if I were to take a trip to places where people are starving then I might think differently, but as it stands now they are just too far removed. In not making these donations, I am implicitly valuing the affluence of my own life over

the basic sustenance of many others. And, well, I guess I do. Am I immoral for doing so? Maybe.[34]

When O'Grady queried this, Simmons clarified his position: "I don't intend to make a moral defense, but rather just reveal my personal feelings—that is, just to explain how I feel." The distinction between describing how things are and saying how they ought to be is also relevant to what Kiernan and Alan Ryan are saying. The fact that we tend to favor our families, communities, and countries may explain our failure to save the lives of the poor beyond those boundaries, but it does not justify that failure from an ethical perspective, no matter how many generations of our ancestors have seen nothing wrong with it.

NOTES

1. BBC News, September 21, 2007, http://news.bbc.co.uk/2/hi/uk_news/england/manchester/7006412.stm.

2. Deepa Narayan with Raj Patel, Kai Schafft, Anne Rademacher, and Sarah Koch-Schulte. *Voices of the Poor: Can Anyone Hear Us?* Published for the World Bank by Oxford University Press (New York, 2000), p. 36.

3. This is a compilation of things said by the poor, cited in ibid., p. 28.

4. World Bank Press Release, "New Data Show 1.4 Billion Live on Less Than US$1.25 a Day, But Progress Against Poverty Remains Strong," August 26, 2008, http://go.worldbank.org/ T0TEVOV4E0. The estimate is based on price data from 2005, and does not reflect increases in food prices in 2008, which are likely to have increased the number below the poverty line. For the research on which the press release is based, see Shaohua Chen and Martin Ravallion, "The Developing World Is Poorer Than We Thought, But No Less Successful in the Fight Against Poverty," Policy Research Working Paper 4073, World Bank Development Research Group, August 2008, www.wds.worldbank.org/external/default/WDSContentServer/IW3P/IB/2008/08/26/000158349_20080826113239/Rendered/PDF/WPS4703.pdf.

For further discussion of World Bank statistics, see Sanjay Reddy and Thomas Pogge, "How *Not* to Count the Poor," www.columbia.edu/-sr793/count.pdf, and Martin Ravallion, "How *Not* to Count the Poor: A Reply to Reddy and Pogge," www.columbia.edu/-sr793/wbreply.pdf.

5. Robert Rector and Kirk Anderson, "Understanding Poverty in America," Heritage Foundation Backgrounder #1713 (2004), www.heritage.org/Research/Welfare/bg1713.

cfm. Rector and Anderson draw on data available from the 2003 U.S. Census Bureau report on poverty and on various other government reports.

6. United Nations, Office of the High Representative for the Least Developed Countries, Landlocked Developing Countries and the Small Island Developing States, and World Bank, World Bank Development Data Group, "Measuring Progress in Least Developed Countries: A Statistical Profile" (2006), tables 2 and 3, pp. 14–15. Available at www.un.org/ohrlls/.

7. United Nations Development Program, *Human Development Report 2000* (Oxford University Press, New York, 2000) p. 30; *Human Development Report 2001* (Oxford University Press, New York, 2001) pp. 9–12, p. 22; and World Bank, *World Development Report 2000/2001,* overview, p. 3, www.worldbank.org/poverty/wdrpoverty/report/overview.pdf, for the other figures. The *Human Development Reports* are available at http://hdr.undp.org.

8. James Riley, *Rising Life Expectancy: A Global History* (New York: Cambridge University Press, 2001); Jeremy Laurance, "Thirty Years: Difference in Life Expectancy Between the World's Rich and Poor Peoples," *The Independent* (UK), September 7, 2007.

9. "Billionaires 2008," *Forbes*, March 24, 2008, www.forbes.com/forbes/2008/0324/080.html.

10. Joe Sharkey, "For the Super-Rich, It's Time to Upgrade the Old Jumbo," *The New York Times,* October 17, 2006.

11. "Watch Your Time," Special Advertising Supplement to *The New York Times,* October 14, 2007. The passage quoted is on p. 40.

12. Bill Marsh, "A Battle Between the Bottle and the Faucet," *The New York Times,* July 15, 2007.

13. Pacific Institute, "Bottled Water and Energy: A Fact Sheet," www.pacinst.org/topics/water_and_sustainability/bottled_water/bottled_water_and_energy.html.

14. Lance Gay, "Food Waste Costing Economy $100 Billion, Study Finds," Scripps Howard News Service, August 10, 2005, www.knoxstudio.com/shns/story.cfm?pk=GARBAGE-08-10-05.

15. Deborah Lindquist, "How to Look Good Naked," Lifetime Network, Season 2, Episode 2, July 29, 2009. As relayed by Courtney Moran.

16. Peter Unger, *Living High and Letting Die* (New York: Oxford University Press, 1996).

17. For further discussion see Peter Singer, *The Expanding Circle* (Oxford: Clarendon Press, 1981), pp. 136, 183. For futher examples, see www.unification.net/ws/theme015.htm.

18. Peter Singer, "The Singer Solution to World Poverty," *The New York Times Sunday Magazine,* September 5, 1999.

19. Glennview High School is Seider's fictional name for the school, and the names of the students are also pseudonyms.

20. Jan Narveson, " 'We Don't Owe Them a Thing!' A Tough-minded but Soft-hearted View of Aid to the Faraway Needy," *The Monist,* 86:3 (2003), p. 419.

21. Sharon Lafraniere, "Europe Takes Africa's Fish, and Boatloads of Migrants Follow," *The New York Times,* January 14, 2008, and Elizabeth Rosenthal, "Europe's Appetite for Seafood Propels Illegal Trade," *The New York Times,* January 15, 2008.

22. See Leif Wenar, "Property Rights and the Resource Curse," *Philosophy & Public Affairs* 36:1 (2008), pp. 2–32. A more detailed version is available on Wenar's website: www.wenar.staff.shef.ac.uk/PRRCwebpage.html.

23. Paul Collier, *The Bottom Billion* (New York: Oxford University Press, 2007).

24. See Leonard Wantchekon, "Why Do Resource Dependent Countries Have Authoritarian Governments?" *Journal of African Finance and Economic Development* 5:2 (2002), pp. 57–77; an earlier version is available at www.yale.edu/leitner/pdf/1999-11.pdf. See also Nathan Jensen and Leonard Wantchekon, "Resource Wealth and Political Regimes in Africa," *Comparative Political Studies,* 37 (2004), pp. 816–841.

25. President Museveni was speaking at the African Union summit, Addis Ababa, Ethiopia, February 2007, and the speech was reported in Andrew Revkin, "Poor Nations to Bear Brunt as World Warms," *The New York Times,* April 1, 2007.

26. Andrew Revkin, op. cit., and "Reports from Four Fronts in the War on Warming," *The New York Times,* April 3, 2007; Kathy Marks, "Rising Tide of Global Warming Threatens Pacific Island States," *The Independent* (UK), October 25, 2006.

27. Organisation for Economic Co-operation and Development (OECD), *OECD Journal on Development: Development Co-operation Report 2007,* p. 134, www.oecd.org/dac/dcr. The table is reproduced by kind permission of OECD. See also *Statistical Annex of the 2007 Development Co-operation Report,* www.oecd.org/dataoecd/52/9/1893143.xls, Fig. 1e.

28. See, for example, Anthony Langlois, "Charity and Justice in the Singer Solution," in Raymond Younis (ed) *On the Ethical Life* (Newcastle upon Tyne: Cambridge Scholars, forthcoming); Paul Gomberg, "The Fallacy of Philanthropy," *Canadian Journal of Philosophy* 32:1 (2002), pp. 29–66.

29. Gomberg, *op. cit.*, pp. 30, 63–64.

30. See Andy Lamey's response to Anthony Langlois's paper in the volume referred to in n. 28, above.

31. Singer addresses the question of finding a form of aid that really works in chapter 7 of *The Life You Can Save*, "Improving Aid."

32. Colin McGinn, as quoted by Michael Specter in "The Dangerous Philosopher," *The New Yorker*, September 6, 1999.

33. Alan Ryan, as quoted by Michael Specter in "The Dangerous Philosopher," *The New Yorker*, September 6, 1999.

34. http://www.muzakandpotatoes.com/2008/02/peter-singer-on-affluence.html.

READING QUESTIONS

1. Explain what poverty and affluence are like today according to the information provided by Singer. Include in your explanation the World Bank's definition of "extreme poverty."

2. Describe the two main thought experiments utilized by Singer. Explain the differences between them.

3. What is Singer's basic argument for why failing to donate to aid organizations such as UNICEF is wrong? Why does Singer think that it is hard to reject each of the premises?

4. Describe a few of the common objections raised against the basic argument by high school students. How does Singer respond to each of these objections?

5. Explain the Libertarian view with respect to whether we have a duty to help others. How does Singer argue that wealthy nations and their citizens have caused harm to developing nations and their people?

DISCUSSION QUESTIONS

1. Are there any objections Singer fails to consider in response to his basic argument? Consider responses on his behalf to any further objections.
2. What do people spend money on what they either don't need or rarely use other than those things mentioned by Singer? What things might people be most easily convinced to do without?
3. How would you respond in the cases of the drowning child and the child on the train tracks? Consider and discuss differing reactions to these two thought experiments.

John Arthur

World Hunger and Moral Obligation

One of the premises in Peter Singer's basic argument from the previous selection states: *If it is in your power to prevent something bad from happening, without sacrificing anything nearly as important, it is wrong not to do so.* Arthur labels this premise Singer's "greater moral evil rule," pointing out that it is meant to capture the idea that morality involves giving equal consideration to the interests of all. However, as Arthur observes, such equality is only one part, and Singer's rule ignores other elements of our moral code including considerations of entitlement which involve both rights and desert. On the basis of considerations of entitlement, Arthur argues that our present moral code allows such considerations to qualify considerations of equality of interests. For example, our moral rights to life and to property represent entitlements that we can invoke as a moral justification for not helping strangers when the cost to us is substantial.

Of course, the fact that our current moral code includes such entitlements does not show that such entitlements are justified. Perhaps there is good reason to move to a new moral code that drops the sorts of entitlements mentioned above and includes Singer's greater moral evil rule. In the final section of his paper, Arthur considers this proposal and argues that an ideal moral code that is genuinely workable would include entitlements that justify the sort of rights to property that one can invoke as a moral justification for not helping strangers when the cost is substantial.

Recommended Reading: consequentialism, chap. 1, sec. 2A, see especially the discussion of rule consequentialism. Also relevant, the discussion of moral rights in chap. 1, sec. 2D, and Rawls's principles of justice in chap. 1, sec 2G.

INTRODUCTION

My guess is that everyone who reads these words is wealthy by comparison with the poorest millions of people on our planet. Not only do we have plenty of money for food, clothing, housing, and other necessities, but a fair amount is left over for far less important purchases like phonograph records, fancy clothes, trips, intoxicants, movies, and so on. And what's more we don't usually give a thought to whether or not we ought to spend our money on such luxuries rather than to give it to those who need it more; we just assume it's ours to do with as we please.

Peter Singer, in "Famine, Affluence, and Morality," argues that our assumption is wrong, that we should not buy luxuries when others are in severe need. But [is he] correct? . . .

He first argues that two general moral principles are widely accepted, and then that those principles imply an obligation to eliminate starvation.

The first principle is simply that "suffering and death from lack of food, shelter and medical care are bad." Some may be inclined to think that the mere existence of such an evil in itself places an obligation on others, but that is, of course, the problem which Singer addresses. I take it that he is not begging the question in this obvious way and will argue from the existence of evil to the obligation of others to eliminate it. But how, exactly, does he establish this? The second principle, he thinks, shows the connection, but it is here that controversy arises.

This principle, which I will call the greater moral evil rule, is as follows:

> If it is in our power to prevent something bad from happening, without thereby sacrificing anything of comparable moral importance, we ought, morally, to do it.[1]

In other words, people are entitled to keep their earnings only if there is no way for them to prevent a greater evil by giving them away. Providing others with food, clothing, and housing would generally be of more importance than buying luxuries, so the greater moral evil rule now requires substantial redistribution of wealth.

Certainly there are few, if any, of us who live by that rule, although that hardly shows we are *justified* in our way of life; we often fail to live up to our own standards. Why does Singer think our shared morality requires that we follow the greater moral evil rule? What arguments does he give for it?

He begins with an analogy. Suppose you came across a child drowning in a shallow pond. Certainly we feel it would be wrong not to help. Even if saving the child meant we must dirty our clothes, we would emphasize that those clothes are not of comparable significance to the child's life. The greater moral evil rule thus seems a natural way of capturing why we think it would be wrong not to help.

But the argument for the greater moral evil rule is not limited to Singer's claim that it explains our feelings about the drowning child or that it appears "uncontroversial." Moral equality also enters the picture. Besides the Jeffersonian idea that we share certain rights equally, most of us are also attracted to another type of equality, namely that like amounts of suffering (or happiness) are of equal significance, no matter who is experiencing them. I cannot reasonably say that, while my pain is no more severe than yours, I am somehow special and it's more important that mine be alleviated. Objectivity requires us to admit the opposite, that no one has a unique status which warrants such special pleading. So equality demands equal consideration of interests as well as respect for certain rights.

But if we fail to give to famine relief and instead purchase a new car when the old one will do, or buy fancy clothes for a friend when his or her old ones are perfectly good, are we not assuming that the relatively minor enjoyment we or our friends may get is as important as another person's life? And that is a form of prejudice; we are acting as if people were not equal in the sense that their interests deserve equal consideration. We are giving special consideration to ourselves or to our group, rather like a racist does. Equal consideration of interests thus leads naturally to the greater moral evil rule.

RIGHTS AND DESERT

Equality, in the sense of giving equal consideration to equally serious needs, is part of our moral code. And so we are led, quite rightly I think, to the conclusion that we should prevent harm to others if in doing so we do not sacrifice anything of comparable moral importance. But there is also another side to the coin, one which Singer ignore[s]. . . . This can be expressed rather awkwardly by the notion of entitlements. These fall into two broad categories, rights and desert. A few examples will show what I mean.

All of us could help others by giving away or allowing others to use our bodies. While your life may be shortened by the loss of a kidney or less enjoyable if lived with only one eye, those costs are probably not comparable to the loss experienced by a person who will die without any kidney or who is totally blind. We can even imagine persons who will actually be harmed in some way by your not granting sexual favors to them. Perhaps the absence of a sexual partner would cause psychological harm or even rape. Now suppose that you can prevent this evil without sacrificing anything of comparable importance. Obviously such relations may not be pleasant, but according to the greater moral evil rule that is not enough; to be justified in refusing, you must show that the unpleasantness you would experience is of equal importance to the harm you are preventing. Otherwise, the rule says you must consent.

If anything is clear, however, it is that our code does not *require* such heroism; you are entitled to keep your second eye and kidney and not bestow sexual favors on anyone who may be harmed without them. The reason for this is often expressed in terms of rights; it's your body, you have a right to it, and that weighs against whatever duty you have to help. To sacrifice a kidney for a stranger is to do more than is required, it's heroic.

Moral rights are normally divided into two categories. Negative rights are rights of noninterference. The right to life, for example, is a right not to be killed. Property rights, the right to privacy, and the right to exercise religious freedom are also negative, requiring only that people leave others alone and not interfere.

Positive rights, however, are rights of recipience. By not putting their children up for adoption, parents give them various positive rights, including rights to be fed, clothed, and housed. If I agree to share in a business venture, my promise creates a right of recipience, so that when I back out of the deal, I've violated your right.

Negative rights also differ from positive in that the former are natural; the ones you have depend on what you are. If lower animals lack rights to life or liberty it is because there is a relevant difference between them and us. But the positive rights you may have are not natural; they arise because others have promised, agreed, or contracted to give you something.

Normally, then, a duty to help a stranger in need is not the result of a right he has. Such a right would be positive, and since no contract or promise was made, no such right exists. An exception to this would be a lifeguard who contracts to watch out for someone's children. The parent whose child drowns would in this case be doubly wronged. First, the lifeguard should not have cruelly or thoughtlessly ignored the child's interests, and second, he ought not to have violated the rights of the parents that he helped. Here, unlike Singer's case, we can say there are rights at stake. Other bystanders also act wrongly by cruelly ignoring the child, but unlike the lifeguard they do not violate anybody's rights. Moral rights are one factor to be weighed, but we also have other obligations; I am not claiming that rights are all we need to consider. That view, like the greater moral evil rule, trades simplicity for accuracy. In fact, our code expects us to help people in need as well as to respect negative and positive rights. But we are also entitled to invoke our own rights as justification for not giving to distant strangers or when the cost to us is substantial, as when we give up an eye or kidney. . . .

Desert is a second form of entitlement. Suppose, for example, an industrious farmer manages through hard work to produce a surplus of food for the winter while a lazy neighbor spends his summer fishing. Must our industrious farmer ignore his hard work and give the surplus away because his neighbor or his family will suffer? What again seems clear is that we have more than one factor to weigh. Not only should we compare the consequences of his keeping it with his giving it away; we also should weigh the fact that one farmer deserves the food, he earned it through his hard work. Perhaps his deserving the product of his labor is outweighed by the greater need of his lazy neighbor, or perhaps it isn't, but being outweighed is in any case not the same as weighing nothing!

Desert can be negative, too. The fact that the Nazi war criminal did what he did means he deserves punishment, that we have a reason to send him to jail. Other considerations, for example the fact that nobody will be deterred by his suffering, or that he is old and harmless, may weigh against punishment and so we may let him go; but again that does not mean he doesn't still deserve to be punished.

Our moral code gives weight to both the greater moral evil principle and entitlements. The former emphasizes equality, claiming that from an objective point of view all comparable suffering, whoever its victim, is equally significant. It encourages us to take an impartial look at all the various effects of our actions; it is thus forward-looking. When we consider matters of entitlement, however, our attention is directed to the past. Whether we have rights to money, property, eyes, or whatever, depends on how we came to possess them. If they were acquired by theft rather than from birth or through gift exchange, then the right is suspect. Desert, like rights, is also backward-looking, emphasizing past effort or past transgressions which now warrant reward or punishment.

Our commonly shared morality thus requires that we ignore neither consequences nor entitlements, neither the future results of our action nor relevant events in the past. It encourages people to help others in need, especially when it's a friend or someone we are close to geographically, and when the cost is not significant. But it also gives weight to rights and desert, so that we are not usually obligated to give to strangers. . . .

But unless we are moral relativists, the mere fact that entitlements are an important part of our moral code does not in itself justify such a role. Singer . . . can perhaps best be seen as a moral reformer advocating the rejection of rules which provide for distribution according to rights and desert. Certainly

the fact that in the past our moral code condemned suicide and racial mixing while condoning slavery should not convince us that a more enlightened moral code, one which we would want to support, would take such positions. Rules which define acceptable behavior are continually changing, and we must allow for the replacement of inferior ones.

Why should we not view entitlements as examples of inferior rules we are better off without? What could justify our practice of evaluating actions by looking backward to rights and desert instead of just to their consequences? One answer is that more fundamental values than rights and desert are at stake, namely fairness, justice, and respect. Failure to reward those who earn good grades or promotions is wrong because it's *unfair;* ignoring past guilt shows a lack of regard for *justice;* and failure to respect rights to life, privacy, or religious choice suggests a lack of *respect for other persons.*

Some people may be persuaded by those remarks, feeling that entitlements are now on an acceptably firm foundation. But an advocate of equality may well want to question why fairness, justice, and respect for persons should matter. But since it is no more obvious that preventing suffering matters than that fairness, respect, and justice do, we again seem to have reached an impasse. . . .

ENTITLEMENTS AND THE IDEAL MORAL CODE

The idea I want now to consider is that part of our code should be dropped, so that people could no longer invoke rights and desert as justification for not making large sacrifices for strangers. In place of entitlements would be a rule regarding that any time we can prevent something bad without sacrificing anything of comparable moral significance we ought to do it. Our current code, however, allows people to say that while they would do more good with their earnings, still they have rights to the earnings, the earnings are deserved, and so need not be given away. The crucial question is whether we want to have such entitlement rules in our code, or whether we should reject them in favor of the greater moral evil rule....

I believe that our best procedure is not to think about this or that specific rule, drawing analogies, refining it, and giving counterexamples, but to focus instead on the nature of morality as a whole. What is a moral code? What do we want it to do? What type of code do we want to support? These questions will give us a fresh perspective from which to consider the merits of rules which allow people to appeal to rights and desert and to weigh the issue of whether our present code should be reformed.

We can begin with the obvious: A moral code is a system of rules designed to guide people's conduct. As such, it has characteristics in common with other systems of rules. Virtually every organization has rules which govern the conduct of members; clubs, baseball leagues, corporations, bureaucracies, professional associations, even *The* Organization all have rules. Another obvious point is this: What the rules are depends on why the organization exists. Rules function to enable people to accomplish goals which lead them to organize in the first place. Some rules, for example, "Don't snitch on fellow mafiosi," "Pay dues to the fraternity," and "Don't give away trade secrets to competing companies," serve in obvious ways. Other times the real purposes of rules are controversial, as when doctors do not allow advertising by fellow members of the AMA.

Frequently rules reach beyond members of a specific organization, obligating everyone who is capable of following them to do so. These include costs of civil and criminal law, etiquette, custom, and morality. But before discussing the specific purposes of moral rules, it will be helpful to look briefly at some of the similarities and differences between these more universal codes.

First, the sanctions imposed on rule violators vary among different types of codes. While in our legal code, transgressions are punished by fines, jail, or repayment of damages, informal sanctions of praise, blame, or guilt encourage conformity to the rules of morality and etiquette. Another difference is that while violation of a moral rule is always a serious

affair, this need not be so for legal rules of etiquette and custom. Many of us think it unimportant whether a fork is on the left side of a plate or whether an outmoded and widely ignored Sunday closing law is violated, but violation of a moral rule is not ignored. Indeed, that a moral rule has lost its importance is often shown by its demotion to status of mere custom.

A third difference is that legal rules, unlike rules of morality, custom, and etiquette, provide for a specific person or procedure that is empowered to alter the rules. If Congress acts to change the tax laws, then as of the date stated in the statute the rules are changed. Similarly for the governing rules of social clubs, government bureaucracies, and the AMA. Rules of custom, morals, and etiquette also change, of course, but they do so in a less precise and much more gradual fashion, with no person or group specifically empowered to make changes.

This fact, that moral rules are *in a sense* beyond the power of individuals to change, does not show that rules of morality, any more than those of etiquette, are objective in the same sense that scientific laws are. All that needs to happen for etiquette or morality to change is for people to change certain practices, namely the character traits they praise and blame, or the actions they approve and disapprove. Scientific laws, however, are discovered, not invented by society, and so are beyond human control. The law that the boiling point of water increases as its pressure increases cannot be changed by humans, either individually or collectively. Such laws are a part of the fabric of nature.

But the fact that moral rules, like legal ones, are not objective in the same sense as scientific ones does not mean that there is no objective standard of right or wrong, that one code is as good as another, or even that the "right thing to do" is just what the moral code currently followed in our society teaches is right. Like the rules of a fraternity or corporation, legal and moral rules can serve their purposes either well or poorly, and whether they do is a matter of objective fact. Further, if a moral code doesn't serve its purpose, we have good reason to think of a way to change it, just as its serving us well provides a good reason to obey. In important respects morality is not at all subjective.

Take, for example, a rule which prohibits homosexual behavior. Suppose it serves no useful purpose, but only increases the burdens of guilt, shame, and social rejection borne by 10% of our population. If this is so, we have good reason to ignore the rule. On the other hand, if rules against killing and lying help us to accomplish what we want from a moral code, we have good reason to support those rules. Morality is created, and as with other systems of rules which we devise, a particular rule may or may not further the shared human goals and interests which motivated its creation. There is thus a connection between what we ought to do and how well a code serves its purposes. If a rule serves well the general purposes of a moral code, then we have reason to support it, and if we have reason to support it, we also have reason to obey it. But if, on the other hand, a rule is useless, or if it frustrates the purposes of morality, we have reason neither to support nor to follow it. All of this suggests the following conception of a right action: Any action is right which is approved by an ideal moral code, one which it is rational for us to support. Which code we would want to support would depend, of course, on which one is able to accomplish the purposes of morality.

If we are to judge actions in this way, by reference to what an ideal moral code would require, we must first have a clear notion of just what purposes morality is meant to service. And here again the comparison between legal and moral rules is instructive. Both systems discourage certain types of behavior—killing, robbing, and beating—while encouraging others—repaying debts, keeping important agreements, and providing for one's children. The purpose which both have in discouraging various behaviors is obvious. Such negative rules help keep people from causing harm. Think, for example, of how we are first taught it is wrong to hit a baby brother or sister. Parents explain the rule by emphasizing that it hurts the infant when we hit him. Promoting the welfare of ourselves, our friends and family, and to a lesser degree all who have the capacity to be harmed is the primary purpose of negative moral rules. It's how we learn them as children and why we support them as adults.

The same can be said of positive rules, rules which encourage various types of behavior. Our own welfare, as well as that of friends, family, and others, depends on general acceptance of rules which encourage keeping promises, fulfilling contracts, and meeting the needs of our children. Just try to imagine a society in which promises or agreements mean nothing, or where family members took no concern for one another. A life without positive or negative rights would be as Thomas Hobbes long ago observed: nasty, brutish, and short.

Moral rules thus serve two purposes. They promote our own welfare by discouraging acts of violence and promoting social conventions like promising and paying debts, and second, they perform the same service for our family, friends, and others. We have reason to support a moral code because we care about our own welfare, and because we care about the well-being of others. For most of us the ideal moral code, the one we would support because it best fulfills these purposes, is the code which is most effective in promoting general welfare.

But can everyone be counted on to share these concerns? Think, for example, of an egoist, who only desires that *he* be happy. Such a person, if he existed, would obviously like a code which maximizes his own welfare. How can we hope to get agreement about which code it is rational to support, if different people expect different things from moral rules?...

There is also a line of reasoning which suggests that disagreement about which moral code to support need not be as deep as is often thought. What sort of code in fact *would* a rational egoist support? He would first think of proposing one which allows him to do anything whatsoever that he desires, while requiring that others ignore their own happiness and do what is in his interests. But here enters a family of considerations which will bring us back to the merits of entitlements versus the greater moral evil rule. Our egoist is contemplating what code to *support*, which means going before the public and trying to win general acceptance of his proposed rules. Caring for nobody else, he might secretly prefer the code I mentioned, yet it would hardly make sense for him to work for its public adoption since others are unlikely to put his welfare above the happiness of themselves and their families. So it looks as if the code an egoist would actually support might not be all that different from the ideal (welfare maximizing) code; he would be wasting his time to advocate rules that serve only his own interests because they have no chance of public acceptance.

The lesson to be learned here is a general one: The moral code it is rational for us to support must be practical; it must actually work. This means, among other things, that it must be able to gain the support of almost everyone.

But the code must be practical in other respects as well. I have emphasized that it is wrong to ignore the possibilities of altruism, but it is also important that a code not assume people are more unselfish than they are. Rules that would work only for angels are not the ones it is rational to support for humans. Second, an ideal code cannot assume we are more objective than we are; we often tend to rationalize when our own interests are at stake, and a rational person will also keep that in mind when choosing a moral code. Finally, it is not rational to support a code which assumes we have perfect knowledge. We are often mistaken about the consequences of what we do, and a workable code must take that into account as well.

I want now to bring these various considerations together in order to decide whether or not to reject entitlements in favor of the greater moral evil rule. I will assume that the egoist is not a serious obstacle to acceptance of a welfare maximizing code, either because egoists are, like angels, merely imaginary, or because a practical egoist would only support a code which can be expected to gain wide support. We still have to ask whether entitlements would be included in a welfare maximizing code. The initial temptation is to substitute the greater moral evil rule for entitlements, requiring people to prevent something bad whenever the cost to them is less significant than the benefit to another. Surely, we might think, total welfare would be increased by a code requiring people to give up their savings if a greater evil can be prevented.

I think, however, that this is wrong, and that an ideal code would provide for rights and would

encourage rewarding according to desert. My reasons for thinking this stem from the importance of insuring that a moral code really does, in fact, work. Each of the three practical considerations mentioned above now enters the picture. First, it will be quite difficult to get people to accept a code which requires that they give away their savings, extra organs, or anything else merely because they can avoid a greater evil for a stranger. Many people simply wouldn't do it: they aren't that altruistic. If the code attempts to require it anyway, two results would likely follow. First, because many would not live up to the rules, there would be a tendency to create feelings of guilt in those who keep their savings in spite of having been taught it is wrong, as well as conflict between those who meet their obligations and those who do not. And, second, a more realistic code, one which doesn't expect more than can be accomplished, may actually result in more giving. It's a bit like trying to influence how children spend their money. Often they will buy less candy if rules allow them to do so occasionally but they are praised for spending on other things than if its purchase is prohibited. We cannot assume that making a charitable act a requirement will always encourage such behavior. Impractical rules not only create guilt and social conflict, they often tend to encourage the opposite of the desired result. By giving people the right to use their savings for themselves, yet praising those who do not exercise the right but help others instead, we have struck a good balance; the rules are at once practical yet reasonably effective.

Similar practical considerations would also influence our decision to support rules that allow people to keep what they deserve. For most people, working is not their favorite activity. If we are to prosper, however, goods and services must be produced. Incentives are therefore an important motivation, and one such incentive for work is income. Our code encourages work by allowing people to keep a large part of what they earn, indeed that's much the point of entitlements. "I worked hard for it, so I can keep it" is an oft-heard expression. If we eliminate this rule from our code and ask people to follow the greater moral evil rule instead, the result would likely be less work done and so less total production. Given a choice between not working and continuing to work knowing the efforts should go to benefit others, many would choose not to work.

Moral rules should be practical in a third sense, too. They cannot assume people are either more unbiased or more knowledgeable than they are. This fact has many implications for the sorts of rules we would want to include in a welfare maximizing code. For example, we may be tempted to avoid slavish conformity to counterproductive rules by allowing people to break promises whenever they think doing so would increase total welfare. But again we must not ignore human nature, in this case our tendency to give special weight to our own welfare and our inability to be always objective in tracing the effects of our actions. While we would not want to teach that promises must never be broken no matter what the consequences, we also would not want to encourage breaking promises any time a person can convince himself the results of doing so would be better than if he kept his word.

Similar considerations apply to the greater moral evil rule. Imagine a situation where someone feels he can prevent an evil befalling himself by taking what he needs from a large store. The idea that he's preventing something bad from happening (to himself) without sacrificing anything of comparable moral significance (the store won't miss the goods) would justify robbery. Although sometimes a particular act of theft really is welfare maximizing, it does not follow that we should support a *rule* which allows theft whenever the robber is preventing a greater evil. Such a rule, to work, would require more objectivity and more knowledge of long-term consequences than we have. Here again, including rights in our moral code serves a useful role, discouraging the tendency to rationalize our behavior by underestimating the harm we may cause to others or exaggerating the benefits that may accrue to ourselves.

The first sections of this paper attempted to show that our moral code is a bit schizophrenic. It seems to pull us in opposite directions, sometimes toward helping people who are in need, other times toward the view that rights and desert justify keeping things we have even if greater evil could be avoided were we to give away our extra eye or our savings account. This apparent inconsistency led us to a further question: Is the emphasis on entitlements really defensible, or should we try to resolve the tension in our own code by adopting the greater moral evil rule and ignoring entitlements? In this section I considered the idea that we might choose between entitlements and the greater moral evil rule by paying attention to the general nature of a moral code; and in particular to the sort of code we might want to support. I argued that all of us, including egoists, have reason to support a code which promotes the welfare of everyone who lives under it. That idea, of an ideal moral code which it is rational for everyone to support, provides a criterion for deciding which rules are sound and which ones we should support.

My conclusion is a conservative one: Concern that our moral code encourages production and not fail because it unrealistically assumes people are more altruistic or objective than they are means that our rules giving people rights to their possessions and encouraging distribution according to desert should be part of an ideal moral code. And since this is so, it is not always wrong to invoke rights or claim that money is deserved as justification for not giving aid, even when something worse could be prevented by offering help. The welfare maximizing moral code would not require us to maximize welfare in each individual case.

I have not yet discussed just how much weight should be given to entitlements, only that they are important and should not be ignored. . . . Certainly an ideal moral code would not allow people to overlook those in desperate need by making entitlements absolute, any more than it would ignore entitlements. But where would it draw the line?

It's hard to know, of course, but the following seems to me to be a sensible stab at an answer. Concerns about discouraging production and the general adherence to the code argue strongly against expecting too much; yet on the other hand, to allow extreme wealth in the face of grinding poverty would seem to put too much weight on entitlements. It seems to me, then, that a reasonable code would require people to help when there is no substantial cost to themselves, that is, when what they are sacrificing would not mean *significant* reduction in their own or their families' level of happiness. Since most people's savings accounts and nearly everybody's second kidney are not insignificant, entitlements would in those cases outweigh another's need. But if what is at stake is trivial, as dirtying one's clothes would normally be, then an ideal moral code would not allow rights to override the greater evil that can be prevented. Despite our code's unclear and sometimes schizophrenic posture, it seems to me that these judgments are not that different from our current moral attitudes. We tend to blame people who waste money on trivia when they could help others in need, yet not to expect people to make large sacrifices to distant strangers. An ideal moral code thus might not be a great deal different from our own.

NOTE

1. Singer also offers a "weak" version of this principle which, it seems to me, is *too* weak. It requires giving aid only if the gift is of *no* moral significance to the giver. But since even minor embarrassment or small amounts of happiness are not completely without moral importance, this weak principle implies little or no obligation to aid, even to the drowning child.

READING QUESTIONS

1. What part of our moral code does Arthur think is being ignored by Peter Singer?
2. Explain Arthur's argument for why our moral code does not require the sort of heroism involved in actions such as giving up one's kidney or eye.
3. Explain the distinction between negative and positive moral rights according to Arthur. Give examples of each.
4. How does Arthur explain the difference between positive and negative forms of desert?
5. What two purposes do moral rules serve, according to Arthur?
6. Arthur mentions three ways in which a moral code must be practical. State those three ways.

DISCUSSION QUESTIONS

1. Does Peter Singer's greatest moral evil rule require that persons act in heroic ways or go above and beyond the call of duty as Arthur suggests?
2. How might Peter Singer respond to Arthur's claim that he has ignored the notion of entitlements in his argument for why we should give to charity?
3. In the final paragraph of his article, Arthur suggests that "to allow extreme wealth in the face of grinding poverty would seem to put too much weight on entitlements. It seems to me, then, that a reasonable code would require people to help when there is no substantial cost to themselves, that is, when what they are sacrificing would not mean *significant* reduction in their own or their families' level of happiness." How might one go about determining what counts as a "significant" reduction in one's level of happiness?

Amartya Sen

Property and Hunger

According to Sen, starvation and famine result from failures of entitlements to property that would otherwise provide the resources for the starving to afford life's necessities including food. This "entitlement" analysis suggests a redistributive economic policy to deal with famine that would increase the entitlements of severely deprived groups while reducing the entitlements of those in economically advantaged groups. Would such redistributive intervention represent a morally wrongful violation of the property rights of the advantaged? Does one's entitlement right to one's own property justify refusing to contribute to the alleviation of poverty and hunger of strangers? One might suppose that if rights have intrinsic value, then such redistribution is not justified. However, Sen proposes a moral system which, unlike a purely consequentialist view of rights, recognizes their intrinsic value, but like consequentialism insists that an overall moral assessment of any right must include a consideration of its likely consequences. If the value of the consequences of limiting or abridging a right are of very great benefit in helping to fulfill morally important goals, such limits are morally justified. The importance of avoiding starvation and famine is the basis for a moral claim or right not to be hungry, which can justify limiting the property entitlements of the economically advantaged. Sen concludes by exploring the likely practical implications of recognizing this right.

Recommended Reading: rights-focused approach to moral issues, chap. 1, sec. 2D. Also relevant is consequentialism, chap. 1, sec. 2A.

... [T]he claims of property rights, which some would defend and some ... would dispute, are not just matters of basic moral belief that could not possibly be influenced one way or the other by any empirical arguments. They call for sensitive moral analysis responsive to empirical realities, including economic ones.

Moral claims based on intrinsically valuable rights are often used in political and social arguments. Rights related to ownership have been invoked for ages. But there are also other types of rights which have been seen as "inherent and inalienable," and the American Declaration of Independence refers to "certain unalienable rights," among which are "life, liberty and the pursuit of happiness." The Indian constitution talks even of "the right to an adequate means of livelihood."[1] The "right not to be hungry" has often been invoked in recent discussions on the obligation to help the famished.

RIGHTS: INSTRUMENTS, CONSTRAINTS, OR GOALS?

Rights can be taken to be morally important in three different ways. First, they can be considered to be valuable *instruments* to achieve other goals. This is

From Amartya Sen, "Property and Hunger," *Economics and Philosophy* 4 (1988): 57–68. Reprinted by permission of Cambridge University Press.

the "instrumental view," and is well illustrated by the utilitarian approach to rights. Rights are, in that view, of no intrinsic importance. Violation of rights is not in itself a bad thing, nor fulfillment intrinsically good. But the acceptance of rights promotes, in this view, things that are ultimately important, to wit, utility. Jeremy Bentham rejected "natural rights" as "simple nonsense," and "natural and imprescriptible rights" as "rhetorical nonsense, nonsense upon stilts." But he attached great importance to rights as instruments valuable to the promotion of a good society, and devoted much energy to the attempt to reform appropriately the actual system of rights.

The second view may be called the "constraint view," and it takes the form of seeing rights as *constraints* on what others can or cannot do. In this view rights *are* intrinsically important. However, they don't figure in moral accounting as goals to be generally promoted, but only as constraints that others must obey. As Robert Nozick has put it in a powerful exposition of this "constraint view": "Individuals have rights, and there are things no person or group may do to them (without violating their rights)." Rights "set the constraints within which a social choice is to be made, by excluding certain alternatives, fixing others, and so on."[2]

The third approach is to see fulfillments of rights as goals to be pursued. This "goal view" differs from the instrumental view in regarding rights to be intrinsically important, and it differs from the constraint view in seeing the fulfillment of rights as goals to be generally promoted, rather than taking them as demanding only (and exactly) that we refrain from violating the rights of others. In the "constraint view" there is no duty to help anyone with his or her rights (merely not to hinder), and also in the "instrumental view" there is no duty, in fact, to help unless the right fulfillment will also promote some other goal such as utility. The "goal view" integrates the valuation of rights—their fulfillment and violation—in overall moral accounting, and yields a wider sphere of influence of rights in morality.

I have argued elsewhere that the goal view has advantages that the other two approaches do not share, in particular, the ability to accommodate integrated moral accounting including inter alia the intrinsic importance of a class of fundamental rights. I shall not repeat that argument here. But there is an interesting question of dual roles of rights in the sense that some rights may be *both* intrinsically important and instrumentally valuable. For example, the right to be free from hunger could—not implausibly—be regarded as being valuable in itself as well as serving as a good instrument to promote other goals such as security, longevity or utility. If so, both the goal view and the instrumental view would have to be simultaneously deployed to get a comprehensive assessment of such a right....

The instrumental aspect is an inescapable feature of every right, since irrespective of whether a certain right is intrinsically valuable or not, its acceptance will certainly have other consequences as well, and these, too, have to be assessed along with the intrinsic value of rights (if any). A right that is regarded as quite valuable in itself may nevertheless be judged to be morally rejectable if it leads to disastrous consequences. This is a case of the rights playing a *negative* instrumental role. It is, of course, also possible that the instrumental argument will *bolster* the intrinsic claims of a right to be taken seriously....

There are two general conclusions to draw, at this stage, from this very preliminary discussion. First, we must distinguish between (1) the intrinsic value of a right, and (2) the overall value of a right taking note inter alia of its intrinsic importance (if any). The acceptance of the intrinsic importance of any right is no guarantee that its overall moral valuation must be favorable. Second, no moral assessment of a right can be independent of its likely consequences. The need for empirical assessment of the effects of accepting any right cannot be escaped. Empirical arguments are quite central to moral philosophy.

PROPERTY AND DEPRIVATION

The right to hold, use and bequeath property that one has legitimately acquired is often taken to be inherently valuable. In fact, however, many of its defenses seem to be actually of the instrumental type, e.g., arguing that property rights make people more free to choose one kind of a life rather than another. But even if we do accept that property rights may have some intrinsic value, this does not in any way amount to an overall justification of property rights, since property rights may have consequences which themselves will require assessment. Indeed, the causation of hunger as well as its prevention may materially depend on how property rights are structured. If a set of property rights leads, say, to starvation, as it well might, then the moral approval of these rights would certainly be compromised severely. In general, the need for consequential analysis of property rights is inescapable whether or not such rights are seen as having any intrinsic value....

...I have tried to argue elsewhere...that famines are, in fact, best explained in terms of failures of entitlement systems. The entitlements here refer, of course, to legal rights and to practical possibilities, rather than to moral status, but the laws and actual operation of private ownership economies have many features in common with the moral system of entitlements analyzed by Nozick and others.

The entitlement approach to famines need not, of course, be confined to private ownership economies, and entitlement failures of other systems can also be fruitfully studied to examine famines and hunger. In the specific context of private ownership economies, the entitlements are substantially analyzable in terms, respectively, of what may be called "endowments" and "exchange entitlements." A person's endowment refers to what he or she initially owns (including the person's own labor power), and the exchange entitlement mapping tells us what the person can obtain through exchanging what he or she owns, either by production (exchange with nature), or by trade (exchange with others), or a mixture of the two. A person has to starve if neither the endowments, nor what can be obtained through exchange, yields an adequate amount of food.

If starvation and hunger are seen in terms of failures of entitlements, then it becomes immediately clear that the total availability of food in a country is only one of several variables that are relevant. Many famines occur without any decline in the availability of food. For example, in the Great Bengal famine

of 1943, the total food availability in Bengal was not particularly bad (considerably higher than two years earlier when there was no famine), and yet three million people died, in a famine mainly affecting the rural areas, through rather violent shifts in the relative purchasing powers of different groups, hitting the rural laborers the hardest. The Ethiopian famine of 1973 took place in a year of average per capita food availability, but the cultivators and other occupation groups in the province of Wollo had lost their means of subsistence (through loss of crops and a decline of economic activity, related to a local drought) and had no means of commanding food from elsewhere in the country. Indeed, some food moved *out* of Wollo to more prosperous people in other parts of Ethiopia, repeating a pattern of contrary movement of food that was widely observed during the Irish famines of the 1840s (with food moving out of famine-stricken Ireland to prosperous England which had greater power in the battle for entitlements). The Bangladesh famine of 1974 took place in a year of *peak* food availability, but several occupation groups had lost their entitlement to food through loss of employment and other economic changes (including inflationary pressures causing prices to outrun wages). Other examples of famines without significant (or any) decline in food availability can be found, and there is nothing particularly surprising about this fact once it is recognized that the availability of food is only one influence among many on the entitlement of each occupation group. Even when a famine *is* associated with a decline of food availability, the entitlement changes have to be studied to understand the particular nature of the famine, e.g., why one occupation group is hit but not another. The causation of starvation can be sensibly sought in failures of entitlements of the respective groups.

The causal analysis of famines in terms of entitlements also points to possible public policies of prevention. The main economic strategy would have to take the form of increasing the entitlements of the deprived groups, and in general, of guaranteeing minimum entitlements for everyone, paying particular attention to the vulnerable groups. This can, in the long run, be done in many different ways, involving both economic growth (including growth of food output) and distributional adjustments. Some of these policies may, however, require that the property rights and the corresponding entitlements of the more prosperous groups be violated. The problem, in fact, is particularly acute in the short run, since it may not be possible to engineer rapid economic growth instantly. Then the burden of raising entitlements of the groups in distress would largely have to fall on reducing the entitlements of others more favorably placed. Transfers of income or commodities through various public policies may well be effective in quashing a famine (as the experience of famine relief in different countries has shown), but it may require substantial government intervention in the entitlements of the more prosperous groups.

There is, however, no great moral dilemma in this if property rights are treated as purely *instrumental*. If the goals of relief of hunger and poverty are sufficiently powerful, then it would be just right to violate whatever property rights come in the way, since—in this view—property rights have no intrinsic status. On the other hand, if property rights are taken to be morally inviolable irrespective of their consequences, then it will follow that these policies cannot be morally acceptable even though they might save thousands, or even millions, from dying. The inflexible moral "constraint" of respecting people's legitimately acquired entitlements would rule out such policies.

In fact this type of problem presents a reductio ad absurdum of the moral validity of constraint-based entitlement systems. However, while the conclusions to be derived from that approach might well be "absurd," the situation postulated is not an imaginary one at all. It is based on studies of actual famines and the role of entitlement failures in the causation of mass starvation. If there is an embarrassment here, it belongs solidly to the consequence-independent way of seeing rights.

I should add that this dilemma does not arise from regarding property rights to be of intrinsic value, which can be criticized on other grounds, but not this one. Even if property rights *are* of intrinsic value, their violation may be justified on grounds of the favorable consequences of that violation. A right, as was mentioned earlier, may be intrinsically valuable and still be justly violated taking everything into account. The

"absurdum" does not belong to attaching intrinsic value to property rights, but to regarding these rights as simply acceptable, regardless of their consequences. A moral system that values both property rights and other goals—such as avoiding famines and starvation, or fulfilling people's right not to be hungry—can, on the one hand, give property rights intrinsic importance, and on the other, recommend the violation of property rights when that leads to better overall consequences (*including* the disvalue of rights violation).

The issue here is not the valuing of property rights, but their alleged inviolability. There is no dilemma here either for the purely instrumental view of property rights or for treating the fulfillment of property rights as one goal among many, but specifically for consequence-independent assertions of property rights and for the corresponding constraint-based approaches to moral entitlement of ownership.

That property and hunger are closely related cannot possibly come as a great surprise. Hunger is primarily associated with not owning enough food and thus property rights over food are immediately and directly involved. Fights over that property right can be a major part of the reality of a poor country, and any system of moral assessment has to take note of that phenomenon. The tendency to see hunger in purely technocratic terms of food output and availability may help to hide the crucial role of entitlements in the genesis of hunger, but a fuller economic analysis cannot overlook that crucial role. Since property rights over food are derived from property rights over other goods and resources (through production and trade), the entire system of rights of acquisition and transfer is implicated in the emergence and survival of hunger and starvation.

THE RIGHT NOT TO BE HUNGRY

Property rights have been championed for a long time. In contrast, the assertion of "the right not to be hungry" is a comparatively recent phenomenon. While this right is much invoked in political debates, there is a good deal of skepticism about treating this as truly a right in any substantial way. It is often asserted that this concept of "right not to be hungry" stands essentially for nothing at all ("simple nonsense," as Bentham called "natural rights" in general). That piece of sophisticated cynicism reveals not so much a penetrating insight into the practical affairs of the world, but a refusal to investigate what people mean when they assert the existence of rights that, for the bulk of humanity, are not in fact guaranteed by the existing institutional arrangements.

The right not to be hungry is not asserted as a recognition of an institutional right that already exists, as the right to property typically is. The assertion is primarily a moral claim as to what should be valued, and what institutional structure we should aim for, and try to guarantee if feasible. It can also be seen in terms of Ronald Dworkin's category of "background rights—rights that provide a justification for political decisions by society in abstract."[3] This interpretation serves as the basis for a reason to change the existing institutional structure and state policy.

It is broadly in this form that the right to "an adequate means of livelihood" is referred to in the Constitution of India: "The state shall, in particular, direct its policy towards securing…that the citizens, men and women equally, have the right to an adequate means of livelihood." This does not, of course, offer to each citizen a guaranteed right to an adequate livelihood, but the state is asked to take steps such that this right could become realizable for all.

In fact, this right has often been invoked in political debates in India. The electoral politics of India does indeed give particular scope for such use of what are seen as background rights. It is, of course, not altogether clear whether the reference to this right in the Indian constitution has in fact materially influenced the political debates. The constitutional statement is often cited, but very likely this issue would have figured in any case in these debates, given the nature of the moral and political concern. But whatever the constitutional contribution, it is interesting to ask whether the implicit acceptance of the value of the right to freedom from hunger makes any difference to actual policy.

It can be argued that the general acceptance of the right of freedom from acute hunger as a major goal has played quite a substantial role in preventing famines in India. The last real famine in India was in 1943, and while food availability per head in India has risen only rather slowly (even now the food availability per head is no higher than in many sub-Saharan countries stricken by recurrent famines), the country has not experienced any famine since independence in 1947. The main cause of that success is a policy of public intervention. Whenever a famine has threatened, a public policy of intervention and relief has offered minimum entitlements to the potential famine victims, and thus have the threatening famines been averted. It can be argued that the quickness of the response of the respective governments (both state and central) reflects a political necessity, given the Indian electoral system and the importance attached by the public to the prevention of starvation. Political pressures from opposition groups and the news media have kept the respective governments on their toes, and the right to be free from acute hunger and starvation has been achieved largely because it has been seen as a valuable right. Thus the recognition of the intrinsic moral importance of this right, which has been widely invoked in public discussions, has served as a powerful political instrument as well.

On the other hand, this process has been far from effective in tackling pervasive and persistent undernourishment in India. There has been no famine in post-independence India, but perhaps a third of India's rural population is perennially undernourished. So long as hunger remains non-acute and starvation deaths are avoided (even though morbidity and mortality rates are enhanced by undernourishment), the need for a policy response is neither much discussed by the news media, nor forcefully demanded even by opposition parties. The elimination of famines coexists with the survival of widespread "regular hunger." The right to "adequate means" of *nourishment* does not at all seem to arouse political concern in a way that the right to "adequate means" to *avoid starvation* does.

The contrast can be due to one of several different reasons. It could, of course, simply be that the ability to avoid undernourishment is not socially accepted as very important. This could be so, though what is socially accepted and what is not is also partly a matter of how clearly the questions are posed. It is, in fact, quite possible that the freedom in question would be regarded as a morally important right if the question were posed in a transparent way, but this does not happen because of the nature of Indian electoral politics and that of news coverage. The issue is certainly not "dramatic" in the way in which starvation deaths and threatening famines are. Continued low-key misery may be too familiar a phenomenon to make it worthwhile for political leaders to get some mileage out of it in practical politics. The news media may also find little profit in emphasizing a non-spectacular phenomenon—the quiet survival of disciplined, non-acute hunger.

If this is indeed the case, then the implications for action of the goal of eliminating hunger, or guaranteeing to all the means for achieving this, may be quite complex. The political case for making the quiet hunger less quiet and more troublesome for governments in power is certainly relevant. Aggressive political journalism might prove to have an instrumental moral value if it were able to go beyond reporting the horrors of visible starvation and to portray the pervasive, non-acute hunger in a more dramatic and telling way. This is obviously not the place to discuss the instrumentalities of practical politics, but the endorsement of the moral right to be free from hunger—both acute and non-acute—would in fact raise pointed questions about the means which might be used to pursue such a goal. . . .

NOTES

1. This is presented as a "Directive Principle of State Policy." It does not have a direct operational role in the working of the Indian legal system, but it has considerable political force.

2. Robert Nozick, *Anarchy, State, and Utopia* (New York: Basic, 1974), pp. ix, 166.

3. Ronald Dworkin, *Taking Rights Seriously* (Cambridge, Mass.: Harvard University Press, 1977), p. 93.

READING QUESTIONS

1. Explain how rights can be instruments, constraints, or goals according to Sen. What does he think the advantages of the goal view of rights are?
2. What are the two conclusions about rights that he draws from the distinction among the three different views? How does he distinguish between the intrinsic value of a right and the overall value of a right?
3. What is the best explanation for the cause of famines according to Sen? Explain the difference between endowments and entitlements.
4. Explain what Sen means when he talks about the right not be hungry. How does he use the notion of background rights to argue for his view?

DISCUSSION QUESTIONS

1. How does Sen's solution to the problem of world hunger compare to the others proposed in this chapter? Discuss whether there are any potential problems with his view that he fails to consider.
2. What are some of the ways that private citizens could work to implement the sort of strategies suggested by Sen?

ONORA O'NEILL

A Kantian Approach to World Hunger

O'Neill approaches questions about our obligations to the hungry and poor through Kant's Humanity formulation of his fundamental moral principle, the categorical imperative: *So act that you use humanity, whether in your own person or that of another, always at the same time as an end, never merely as a means.* In requiring that we never treat others merely as means, the principle in question imposes requirements of justice. But in requiring that we treat humanity as an end, it goes further and imposes requirements of beneficence. After explaining the rudiments of Kant's Humanity principle, O'Neill proceeds to explore the implications of Kantian justice and beneficence regarding obligations to help those in need.

   Recommended Reading: Kantian moral theory, chap. 1, sec. 2C, particularly the Humanity formulation of the categorical imperative.

We use others as *mere means* if what we do reflects some maxim *to which they could not in principle consent.* Kant does not suggest that there is anything wrong about using someone as a means. Evidently every cooperative scheme of action does this. A government that agrees to provide free or subsidized food to famine-relief agencies both uses and is used by the agencies; a peasant who sells food in a local market both uses and is used by those who buy it. In such examples each party to the transaction can and does consent to take part in that transaction. Kant would say that the parties to such transactions use one another but do not use one another as *mere means*. Each party assumes that the other has its own maxims of action and is not just a thing or prop to be used or manipulated.

   But there are other cases where one party to an arrangement or transaction not only uses the other but does so in ways that could only be done on the basis of a fundamental principle or maxim to which

the other could not in principle consent. If a false promise is given, the party that accepts the promise is not just used but used as a mere means, because it is *impossible* for consent to be given to the fundamental principle or project of deception that must guide every false promise, whatever its surface character. Those who accept false promises *must* be kept ignorant of the underlying principle or maxim on which the "undertaking" is based. If this isn't kept concealed, the attempted promise will either be rejected or will not be a *false* promise at all. In false promising the deceived party becomes, as it were, a prop or tool—a *mere* means—in the false promisor's scheme. Action based on any such maxim of deception would be wrong in Kantian terms, whether it is a matter of a breach of treaty obligations, of contractual undertakings, or of accepted and relied upon modes of interaction. Maxims of deception *standardly* use others as mere means, and acts that could only be based on such maxims are unjust.

From Onora O'Neill, "The Moral Perplexities of Famine and World Hunger," in Tom Regan, ed., *Matters of Life and Death,* 2nd edition, New York, Random House, 1986, pp. 322–329.

Another standard way of using others as mere means is by coercing them. Coercers, like deceivers, standardly don't give others the possibility of dissenting from what they propose to do. In deception, "consent" is spurious because it is given to a principle that couldn't be the underlying principle of *that* act at all; but the principle governing coercion may be brutally plain. Here any "consent" given is spurious because there was no option *but* to consent. If a rich or powerful landowner or nation threatens a poorer or more vulnerable person, group, or nation with some intolerable difficulty unless a concession is made, the more vulnerable party is denied a genuine choice between consent and dissent. While the boundary that divides coercion from mere bargaining and negotiation varies and is therefore often hard to discern, we have no doubt about the clearer cases. Maxims of coercion may threaten physical force, seizure of possessions, destruction of opportunities, or any other harm that the coerced party is thought to be unable to absorb without grave injury or danger. A moneylender in a Third World village who threatens not to make or renew an indispensable loan, without which survival until the next harvest would be impossible, uses the peasant as mere means. The peasant does not have the possibility of genuinely consenting to the "offer he can't refuse." The outward form of some coercive transactions may *look* like ordinary commercial dealings: but we know very well that some action that is superficially of this sort is based on maxims of coercion. To avoid coercion, action must be governed by maxims that the other party can choose to refuse and is not bound to accept. The more vulnerable the other party in any transaction or negotiation, the less their scope for refusal, and the more demanding it is likely to be to ensure that action is noncoercive.

In Kant's view, acts done on maxims that coerce or deceive others, so therefore cannot in principle have the consent of those others, are wrong. When individuals or institutions, or nation states act in ways that can only be based on such maxims they fail in their duty. They treat the parties who are either deceived or coerced unjustly. To avoid unjust action it is not enough to observe the outward forms of free agreement and cooperation; it is also essential to see that the weaker party to any arrangement has a genuine option to refuse the fundamental character of the proposal.

TREATING OTHERS AS ENDS IN THEMSELVES

For Kant, as for utilitarians, justice is only one part of duty. We may fail in our duty, even when we don't use anyone as mere means (by deception or coercion), if we fail to treat others as "ends in themselves." To treat others as "Ends in Themselves" we must not only avoid using them as mere means but also treat them as rational and autonomous beings with their own maxims. If human beings were *wholly* rational and autonomous then, on a Kantian view, duty would require only that they not use one another as mere means. But, as Kant repeatedly stressed, but later Kantians have often forgotten, human beings are *finite* rational beings. They are finite in several ways.

First, human beings are not ideal rational calculators. We *standardly* have neither a complete list of the actions possible in a given situation nor more than a partial view of their likely consequences. In addition, abilities to assess and to use available information are usually quite limited.

Second, these cognitive limitations are *standardly* complemented by limited autonomy. Human action is limited not only by various sorts of physical barrier and inability but by further sorts of (mutual or asymmetrical) dependence. To treat one another as ends in themselves such beings have to base their action on principles that do not undermine but rather sustain and extend one another's capacities for autonomous action. A central requirement for doing so is to share and support one another's ends and activities at least to some extent. Since finite rational beings cannot generally achieve their aims without some help and support from others, a general refusal of help and support amounts to failure to treat others as rational and autonomous beings, that is as ends in themselves. Hence Kantian principles require us not only to act justly, that is in accordance with maxims that don't coerce or deceive others, but also to avoid manipulation and to lend some support to others' plans and activities. Since famine, great poverty and powerlessness all undercut the possibility of autonomous action, and the requirement of treating others as ends in themselves demands that Kantians standardly act to support the possibility of autonomous action where it is most vulnerable, Kantians are required to do what they can to avert, reduce, and remedy famine. On a Kantian view, beneficence is as indispensable as justice in human lives.

JUSTICE AND BENEFICENCE IN KANT'S THOUGHT

Kant is often thought to hold that justice is morally required, but beneficence is morally less important. He does indeed, like Mill, speak of justice as a *perfect duty* and of beneficence as an *imperfect duty*. But he does not mean by this that beneficence is any less a duty; rather, he holds that it has (unlike justice) to be selective. We cannot share or even support *all* others' maxims *all* of the time. Hence support for others' autonomy is always selective. By contrast we can make all action and institutions conform fundamentally to standards of nondeception and noncoercion. Kant's understanding of the distinction between perfect and imperfect duties differs from Mill's. In a Kantian perspective justice isn't a matter of the core requirements for beneficence, as in Mill's theory, and beneficence isn't just an attractive but optional moral embellishment of just arrangements (as tends to be assumed in most theories that take human rights as fundamental).

JUSTICE TO THE VULNERABLE IN KANTIAN THINKING

For Kantians, justice requires action that conforms (at least outwardly) to what could be done in a given situation while acting on maxims neither of deception nor of coercion. Since anyone hungry or destitute is more than usually vulnerable to deception and coercion, the possibilities and temptations to injustice are then especially strong.

Examples are easily suggested. I shall begin with some situations that might arise for somebody who happened to be part of a famine-stricken population. Where shortage of food is being dealt with by a reasonably fair rationing scheme, any mode of cheating to get more than one's allocated share involves using some others and is unjust. Equally, taking advantage of others' desperation to profiteer— for example, selling food at colossal prices or making loans on the security of others' future livelihood, when these are "offers they can't refuse"—constitutes coercion and so uses others as mere means and is unjust. Transactions that have the outward form of normal commercial dealing may be coercive when one party is desperate. Equally, forms of corruption that work by deception—such as bribing officials to gain special benefits from development schemes, or deceiving others about their entitlements—use others unjustly. Such requirements are far from trivial and frequently violated in hard times; acting justly in such conditions may involve risking one's own life and livelihood and require the greatest courage.

It is not so immediately obvious what justice, Kantianly conceived, requires of agents and agencies who are remote from destitution. Might it not be sufficient to argue that those of us fortunate enough to live in the developed world are far from famine and destitution, so if we do nothing but go about our usual business will successfully avoid injustice to the destitute? This conclusion has often been reached by those who take an abstract view of rationality and forget the limits of human rationality and autonomy. In such perspectives it can seem that there is nothing more to just action than meeting the formal requirements of nondeception and noncoercion in our dealings with one another. But once we remember the limitations of human rationality and autonomy, and the particular ways in which they are limited for those living close to the margins of subsistence, we can see that mere conformity to ordinary standards of commercial honesty and political bargaining is not enough for justice toward the destitute.

If international agreements themselves can constitute "offers that cannot be refused" by the government of a poor country, or if the concessions required for investment by a transnational corporation or a development project reflect the desperation of recipients rather than an appropriate contribution to the project, then (however benevolent the motives of some parties) the weaker party to such agreements is used by the stronger.

In the earlier days of European colonial penetration of the now underdeveloped world it was evident enough that some of the ways in which "agreements" were made with native peoples were in fact deceptive or coercive or both. "Sales" of land by those who had no grasp of market practices and "cession of sovereignty" by those whose forms of life were prepolitical constitute only spurious consent to the agreements struck. But it is not only in these original forms of bargaining between powerful and powerless that injustice is frequent. There are many contemporary examples. For example, if capital investment (private or governmental) in a poorer country requires the receiving country to contribute disproportionately to the maintenance of a developed, urban "enclave" economy that offers little local employment but lavish standards of life for a small number of (possibly expatriate) "experts," while guaranteeing long-term exemption from local taxation for the investors, then we may doubt that the agreement could have been struck without the element of coercion provided by the desperation of the weaker party. Or if a trade agreement extracts political advantages (such as military bases) that are incompatible with the fundamental political interests of the country concerned, we may judge that at least some leaders of that country have been "bought" in a sense that is not consonant with ordinary commercial practice.

Even when the actions of those who are party to an agreement don't reflect a fundamental principle of coercion or deception, the agreement may alter the life circumstances and prospects of third parties in ways to which they patently could not have not consented. For example, a system of food aid and imports agreed upon by the government of a Third World country and certain developed countries or international agencies may give the elite of that Third World country access to subsidized grain. If that grain is then used to control the urban population and also produces destitution among peasants (who used to grow food for that urban population), then those who are newly destitute probably have not been offered any opening or possibility of refusing their new and worsened conditions of life. If a policy is imposed, those affected *cannot* have been given a chance to refuse it: had the chance been there, they would either have assented (and so the policy would not have been *imposed*) or refused (and so proceeding with the policy would have been evidently coercive).

BENEFICENCE TO THE VULNERABLE IN KANTIAN THINKING

In Kantian moral reasoning, the basis for beneficent action is that we cannot, without it, treat others of limited rationality and autonomy as ends in themselves. This is not to say that Kantian beneficence won't make others happier, for it will do so whenever they would be happier if (more) capable of autonomous action, but that happiness secured by purely paternalistic means, or at the cost (for example) of manipulating others' desires, will not count as beneficent in the Kantian picture. Clearly the vulnerable position of those who lack the very means of life, and their severely curtailed possibilities for autonomous action, offer many different ways in which it might be possible for others to act beneficently. Where the means of life are meager, almost any material or organizational advance may help extend possibilities for autonomy. Individual or institutional action that aims to advance economic or social development can proceed on many routes. The provision of clean water, of improved agricultural techniques, of better grain storage systems, or of adequate means of local transport may all help transform material prospects. Equally, help in the development of new forms of social organization—whether peasant self-help groups, urban cooperatives, medical and contraceptive services, or improvements in education or in the position of women—may help to extend possibilities for autonomous action. Kantian thinking does not provide a means by which all possible projects of this sort could be listed and ranked. But where some activity helps secure possibilities for autonomous action for more people, or is likely to achieve a permanent improvement in the position of the most vulnerable, or is one that can be done with more reliable success, this provides reason for furthering that project rather than alternatives.

Clearly the alleviation of need must rank far ahead of the furthering of happiness in the Kantian picture. I might make my friends very happy by throwing extravagant parties: but this would probably not increase anybody's possibility for autonomous action to any great extent. But the sorts of development-oriented changes that have just been mentioned may *transform* the possibilities for action of some. Since famine and the risk of famine are always and evidently highly damaging to human autonomy, any action that helps avoid or reduce famine must have a strong claim on any Kantian who is thinking through what beneficence requires. Depending on circumstances, such action may have to take the form of individual contribution to famine relief and development organizations, of individual or collective effort to influence the trade and aid policies of developed countries, or of attempts to influence the activities of those Third World elites for whom development does not seem to be an urgent priority. Some activities can best be undertaken by private citizens of developed countries; others are best approached by those who work for governments, international agencies, or transnational corporations. Perhaps the most dramatic possibilities to act for a just or an unjust, a beneficent or selfish future belong to those who hold positions of influence within the Third World. But wherever we find ourselves, our duties are not, on the Kantian picture, limited to those close at hand. Duties of justice arise whenever there is some involvement between parties—and in the modern world this is never lacking. Duties of beneficence arise whenever destitution puts the possibility of autonomous action in question for the more vulnerable. When famines were not only far away, but nothing could be done to relieve them, beneficence or charity may well have begun—and stayed—at home. In a global village, the moral significance of distance has shrunk, and we may be able to affect the capacities for autonomous action of those who are far away.

THE SCOPE OF KANTIAN DELIBERATIONS ABOUT FAMINE AND HUNGER

In many ways Kantian moral reasoning is less ambitious than utilitarian moral reasoning. It does not propose a process of moral reasoning that can (in principle) rank *all* possible actions or all possible institutional arrangements from the happiness-maximizing "right" action or institution downward. It aims rather to offer a pattern of reasoning by which we can identify whether *proposed action or institutional arrangements* would be just or unjust, beneficent or lacking in beneficence. While *some* knowledge of causal connections is needed for Kantian reasoning, it is far less sensitive than is utilitarian reasoning to gaps in our causal knowledge. The conclusions reached about particular proposals for action or about institutional arrangements will not hold for all time, but be relevant for the contexts for which action is proposed. For example, if it is judged that some institution—say the World Bank—provides, under present circumstances, a just approach to certain development problems, it will not follow that under all other circumstances such an institution would be part of a just approach. There may be other institutional arrangements that are also just; and there may be other circumstances under which the institutional structure of the World Bank would be shown to be in some ways deceptive or coercive and so unjust.

These points show us that Kantian deliberations about famine and hunger can lead only to conclusions that are useful in determinate contexts. This, however, is standardly what we need to know for action, whether individual or institutional. We do not need to be able to generate a complete list of available actions in order to determine whether proposed lines of action are not unjust and whether any are beneficent. Kantian patterns of moral reasoning cannot be guaranteed to identify the optimal course of action in a situation. They provide methods neither for listing nor for ranking all possible proposals for action. But any line of action that is considered can be checked.

The reason this pattern of reasoning will not show any action or arrangement the most beneficent one available is that the Kantian picture of beneficence is less mathematically structured than the utilitarian one. It judges beneficence by its overall contribution to the prospects for human autonomy and not by the quantity of happiness expected to result. To the extent that the autonomous pursuit of goals is what Mill called "one of the principal ingredients of human happiness" (but only to that extent), the requirements of Kantian and of utilitarian beneficence will coincide. But whenever expected happiness is not a function of the scope for autonomous action, the two accounts of beneficent action diverge. For utilitarians, paternalistic imposition of, for example, certain forms of aid and development assistance need not be wrong and may even be required. But for Kantians, whose beneficence should secure others' possibilities for autonomous action, the case for paternalistic imposition of aid or development projects without the recipients' involvement must always be questionable.

In terms of some categories in which development projects are discussed, utilitarian reasoning may well endorse "top-down" aid and development projects which override whatever capacities for autonomous choice and action the poor of a certain area now have in the hopes of securing a happier future. If the calculations work out in a certain way, utilitarians may even think a "generation of sacrifice"—or of forced labor or of imposed population-control policies not only permissible but mandated. In their darkest Malthusian moments some utilitarians have thought that average happiness might best be maximized not by improving the lot of the poor but by minimizing their numbers, and so have advocated policies of "benign neglect" of the poorest and most desperate. Kantian patterns of reasoning are likely to endorse less global and less autonomy-overriding aid and development projects; they are not likely to endorse neglect or abandoning of those who are most vulnerable and lacking in autonomy. If the aim of beneficence is to keep or put others in a position to act for themselves, then emphasis must be placed on "bottom-up" projects, which from the start draw on, foster, and establish indigenous capacities and practices of self-help and local action....

READING QUESTIONS

1. Under what circumstances does one individual use another as a means according to O'Neill? Explain why false promises and coercion involve using someone as a means.
2. How can we treat others as ends in themselves according to O'Neill? In what ways are human beings limited by their finitude?
3. Explain the role of justice and beneficence in Kant's thought. Why do justice and beneficence require helping the vulnerable?
4. What reasons does O'Neill give for thinking that a Kantian approach to the problem of hunger is less ambitious but more successful than the utilitarian approach?

DISCUSSION QUESTIONS

1. Is O'Neill right to claim that the Kantian approach does not face the same sorts of difficulties as the utilitarian approach to the problem of world hunger? Why or why not? What sorts of problems might the Kantian approach face that the utilitarian approach does not?
2. Consider and discuss whether the Kantian argument for helping the vulnerable is more or less convincing than the traditional utilitarian arguments. What kinds of arguments would be the most likely to persuade people to help those in need?

ADDITIONAL RESOURCES

Web Resources

Hunger Notes, <www.worldhunger.org>. Established in 1976 by the World Hunger Education Services features information about world hunger.

The World Bank, <www.worldbank.org>. The stated goals of this organization are to "end extreme poverty within a generation and boost shared prosperity."

The World Food Programme, <www.wfp.org>. A branch of the United Nations whose objectives include reducing hunger.

OXFAM, <http://www.oxfam.org/>. An international organization devoted to helping the world's poor.

Beauchamp, Tom, "The Principle of Beneficence in Applied Ethics," *Stanford Encyclopedia of Philosophy*, <http://plato.stanford.edu/entries/principle-beneficence>. A useful discussion of the place of a principle of beneficence in various ethical theories including those of Kant, Mill, and Hume, as well as how considerations of beneficence figures in discussions of applied ethics.

Authored Books and Articles

Cullity, Garrett, *The Moral Demands of Affluence* (Oxford: Oxford University Press, 2004). Cullity argues that the obligations of the affluent to help those in desperate need are modestly demanding.

Murdoch, William W. and Allan Oaten, "Population and Food: Metaphors and the Reality," *Bioscience* 25 (1975). A reply to Hardin's "lifeboat ethics."

O'Neill, Onora, *Faces of Hunger: An Essay on Poverty, Justice, and Development* (London and Boston: Unwin Hyman, 1986).

Pogge, Thomas, *World Poverty and Human Rights: Cosmopolitan Responsibilities and Reforms* (Cambridge: Polity Press, 2002). Pogge argues that our current economic order is morally indefensible and that those who are relatively economically well off are responsible for serious global injustices.

Sen, Amartya, *Poverty and Famines: An Essay on Entitlement and Deprivation* (Oxford: Oxford University Press, 1984). A penetrating analysis of the causes of poverty and famine.

Unger, Peter, *Living High and Letting Die: Our Illusion of Innocence* (Oxford: Oxford University Press, 1996). An examination of the incongruity between basic moral principles most people do accept and their attitudes toward those in need.

Edited Collections

Aiken, William and Hugh LaFollette, eds., *World Hunger and Moral Obligation*, 2nd ed. (Englewood Cliffs, NJ: Prentice Hall, 1996). An extensive and important collection of essays.

Crocker, David A, and Toby Linden (eds.), *Ethics of Consumption: The Good Life, Justice, and Global Stewardship* (Lanham, MD: Rowman & Littlefield, 1997). A collection of essays from renowned scholars from many disciplines that cover many aspects of morality and consumption.

15 } The Environment, Consumption, and Climate Change

At the 2015 Paris Climate Conference, 195 countries adopted a legally binding agreement—the "Paris Agreement"—to address climate change. Included among the key provisions of the agreement are the following four that pertain to reducing emissions:

- A long-term goal of keeping the increase in global average temperature to well below 2°C above pre-industrial levels
- To aim to limit the increase to 1.5°C, since this would significantly reduce risks and the impacts of climate change
- On the need for global emissions to peak as soon as possible, recognizing that this will take longer for developing countries
- To undertake rapid reductions thereafter in accordance with the best available science

Other provisions include: (1) countries periodically reporting progress toward the goals agreed to, (2) countries strengthening the abilities of societies to deal with the impacts of climate change, and (3) countries addressing actual and predictable loss and damage associated with changing climate. The agreement goes into effect once 55 countries that are responsible for 55 percent of global emissions have officially signed the agreement.

The urgency many feel for dealing with climate change is instrumental. That is, it is concern for human life, now and in the future, that drives concern over climate change. However, many environmentally concerned individuals think there is more to an ethical concern for the environment than how the welfare of human beings might be affected. Their thought is that at least some so-called lower forms of life (nonhuman and non-higher-animal life) have intrinsic value and thus some degree of **direct moral standing**. Their moral concern for the environment thus goes beyond a concern for how changing the environment might impact human beings. The moral claims of such environmentalists raise a number of fundamental ethical questions, including the following:

- Do biological entities other than humans and higher nonhuman animals have at least some degree of direct moral standing?
- What about nonliving things such as mountains and streams? What sort of direct moral standing (if any) do they have?
- If either some nonhuman biological creatures or nonliving things have direct moral standing, what does this imply about how human beings ought to treat such things?

In the remainder of this introduction, I will first explain some of the basic ideas and positions of those who address these three questions. After that, I will turn to the particular environmental issue of climate change.

1. EXPANDING THE SCOPE OF DIRECT MORAL STANDING?

As in the chapter on the ethical treatment of animals, the main philosophical issue in this chapter concerns what we are calling the scope of *direct* moral standing. You may recall that for something to be within the scope of direct moral standing is for it itself to count morally because of its own nature and not merely because it is of instrumental value to human beings or any other creature. If anything is clear in the realm of disputed moral issues it is that human beings have direct moral standing—each of us possesses a kind of standing that imposes requirements on others and how they treat us. We can put the point in terms of reasons: that your action would cause me serious injury is a reason for you not to do that action. Granted, there may be cases in which this reason is overridden by an even more important moral reason. But still, because of the fact that I am the sort of creature I am, I am of direct (not just indirect) moral concern.

Those who would ascribe moral rights to (at least some) nonhuman animals, or who would claim that human beings have obligations *to* nonhuman animals, advocate expanding the sphere of direct moral standing beyond the realm of human beings to include some nonhuman animals. As we shall see in this chapter, some philosophers propose that we expand the scope of direct moral standing even further and include a wider range of entities. These "expansionists" differ among themselves as to how inclusive this scope should be. In order to get a sense of the issues and arguments featured in some discussions about ethics and the environment, let us first introduce some terminology that is often used to pick out different positions one might take on this issue of scope, and then consider some of the arguments featured in debates over environmental ethics.

2. FOUR APPROACHES

Here, then, are four general approaches to questions about the scope of direct moral standing, organized from least to most inclusive:

- **Anthropocentrism:** The only beings who possess direct moral standing are human beings. All other beings (living and nonliving) are of mere indirect moral concern.
- **Sentientism:** All and only sentient creatures—creatures who have the capacity to experience pleasure and pain—have direct moral standing. Thus, morality includes requirements that include direct moral concern for all sentient beings.
- **Biocentrism:** All living beings *because they are living* possess direct moral standing. Thus, morality includes requirements that include direct moral concern for all living beings.
- **Ecocentrism:** The primary bearers of direct moral standing are ecosystems in virtue of their functional integrity. An **ecosystem** is a whole composed of both living and nonliving things including animals, plants, bodies of water, sunlight, and other geological factors. Hence, morality involves moral obligations to maintain the functional integrity

of ecosystems and because, according to this view, ecosystems are *primary* bearers of direct moral standing, their preservation takes moral precedence over concern for individual things and creatures that compose the system.

One basic difference between the first three approaches and ecocentrism is the contrast between **atomism** and **holism** regarding the primary bearers of direct moral standing—a distinction implicit in the previous characterizations. Atomism in this context is the view that the primary items of moral appraisal are individuals—only individuals can be properly judged as intrinsically valuable, or rights holders, or as having obligations. By contrast, holism maintains that wholes or collectives are bearers of value, or of rights, or of obligations. Of course, the view that wholes are bearers of direct moral standing is compatible with the atomistic view that individual members of a whole also have direct moral standing. Thus, one view, sometimes called **ecoholism,** maintains that both ecosystems and at least some individual items that make up an ecosystem have direct moral standing. But notice that the eco*centrist* makes a stronger holistic claim: the *only* bearers of direct moral standing are wholes, and not the individual items of which they are composed.

3. THE VERY IDEA OF AN ENVIRONMENTAL ETHIC

Having described four basic positions about the scope of moral concern, we are now in a position to clarify the very idea of an environmental ethic. Here it is important to distinguish between an ethic *of* the environment and an ethic *for the use of* the environment. The latter kind of "management ethic" for the environment is consistent with anthropocentrism, and so it does not count as an environmental ethic. Thus, an environmental ethic must accord direct moral standing to beings other than humans. But this minimum necessary condition is not enough—not sufficient—for an ethic to be an environmental ethic. After all, an ethical theory that accorded some direct moral standing to humans and to apes, but nothing else, would not, strictly speaking, count as an **environmental ethic**. So, with some modification, let us follow philosopher Tom Regan's characterization of an environmental ethic:

1. An environmental ethic must hold that there are nonhuman beings that have direct moral standing.
2. An environmental ethic must hold that the class of beings that have direct moral standing is larger than the class of conscious beings—that is, this sort of ethic must ascribe direct moral standing to nonconscious beings.[1]

This characterization of an environmental ethic, while perhaps not airtight, does at least properly categorize the three basic approaches we discussed in the previous section. Clearly, anthropocentric and sentientist accounts of direct moral standing ethic are ruled out by Regan's definition, even if they allow for a management ethic in dealing with environmental issues. However, both biocentric and ecocentric views do count as versions of an environmental ethic. So, on this way of understanding ethical issues concerning treatment of the environment, the fundamental issue is over the scope of those beings (including living, nonliving, individuals, and collectives) that possess direct moral standing. And this issue brings us in direct contact with one of the most fundamental questions of ethical theory: *In virtue of what does something have direct moral standing?*

4. CONSUMPTION AND CLIMATE CHANGE

Perhaps the most publicized contemporary ethical issue associated with the environment is that of climate change and, in particular, global warming. Many have recently argued that excessive human consumption that produces emissions of greenhouse gases (GHGs), including in particular high emission levels of carbon dioxide (CO_2),[2] has brought about certain undesirable climactic changes: global warming, severe weather, and changes in ocean currents. For instance, according to a 2007 report by the Intergovernmental Panel on Climate Change (IPCC).[3]

> Global atmospheric concentrations of CO_2, CH_4 and N_2O have increased markedly as a result of human activities since 1750 and now far exceed pre-industrial values determined from ice cores spanning many thousands of years. The atmospheric concentrations of CO_2 and CH_4 in 2005 exceed by far the natural range over the last 650,000 years. Global increases in CO_2 concentrations are due primarily to fossil fuel use, with land-use change providing another significant but smaller contribution. It is very likely that the observed increase in CH_4 concentration is predominantly due to agriculture and fossil fuel use. The increase in N_2O concentration is primarily due to agriculture.[4]

The IPCC report contains projections for the 21st century about the likely effects of climate change and global warming in particular on four categories of concern: (1) agriculture, forestry, and ecosystems; (2) water resources; (3) human health; and (4) industry, settlement, and society. These projections are based on the assumption that GHGs will continue to be emitted at the same rate or higher than 2007 emission levels. Figure 15.1 presents the 2007 IPCC report that summarizes their projections.[5] (Note: Reference to SRES scenarios [Special Report on Emissions Scenarios] in the top row of the second column refers to various possible projections regarding demographic, economic, and technological changes on the basis of which predictions about climate change are projected. For example, one of the four basic scenarios "assumes a world of very rapid economic growth, a global population that peaks in mid-century and rapid introduction of new and more efficient technologies."[6])

Three comments are in order here. First, notice that not all of the predicted effects mentioned in this table are negative. For instance, one likely human health benefit from warmer temperatures is a decrease in mortality rates from exposure to cold. Also, reduced energy demand for purposes of heating homes and increased yields in agricultural products in areas whose temperatures will increase are among the projected positive effects of global warming. However, when put side to side with the number of projected negative effects (some of them, e.g., increased energy demand for cooling), the likely positive effects seem to be seriously outweighed by the likely negative effects.

Second, although most experts seem to agree that climate change is a genuine phenomenon, questions have been raised about the accuracy of the predictions featured in the IPCC report. Some have argued that the projections are faulty or misleading. Such critics include those who argue that the severity of the projected negative effects are exaggerated, while others have argued that such projections are too conservative, that the IPCC report underestimates the harm that will likely result from global warming.[7] Questions have also been raised about the extent to which climate change is due to human activities and how much is due to other, naturally occurring factors.

Examples of major projected impacts by sector

Phenomena and direction of trend	Likelihood of future trends based on projections for 21st century using SRES scenarios	Agriculture, forestry, and ecosystems	Water resources	Human health	Industry, settlement, and society
Over most land areas, warmer and fewer cold days and nights, warmer and more frequent hot days and nights.	Virtually certain	Increased yields in colder environments; decreased yields in warmer environments; increased insect outbreaks.	Effects on water resources relying on snowmelt; effects on some water supplies.	Reduced human mortality from decreased cold exposure.	Reduced energy demand for heating; increased demand for cooling; declining air quality in cities; reduced disruption to transport due to snow, ice; effects on winter tourism.
Warm spells/heat waves. Frequency increases over most land areas.	Very likely	Reduced yields in warmer regions due to heat stress; increased danger of wildfire.	Increased water demand; water quality problems, e.g., algal blooms.	Increased risk of heat-related mortality, especially for the elderly, chronically sick, very young, and socially isolated.	Reduced quality of life for people in warm areas without appropriate housing; impacts on elderly, very young, and poor.
Heavy precipitation events. Frequency increases over most areas.	Very likely	Damage to crops; soil erosion, inability to cultivate land due to waterlogging of soils.	Adverse effects on quality of surface and groundwater; contamination of water supply; water scarcity may be relieved.	Increased risk of deaths, injuries, and infectious respiratory and skin diseases.	Disruption of settlements, commerce, transport and societies due to flooding: pressures on urban and rural infra-structures; loss of property.
Area affected by drought increases.	Likely	Land degradation; lower yields / crop damage and failure; increased livestock deaths; increased risk of wildfire.	More widespread water stress.	Increased risk of food and water shortage; increased risk of malnutrition; increased risk of water- and food-borne diseases.	Water shortage for settlements, industry and societies; reduced hydropower generation potentials; potential for population migration.
Intense tropical cyclone activity increases.	Likely	Damage to crops; windthrow (uprooting) of trees; damage to coral reefs.	Power outages causing disruption of public water supply.	Increased risk of deaths, injuries, water- and food-borne diseases; post–traumatic stress disorders.	Disruption by flood and high winds; withdrawal of risk coverage in vulnerable areas by private insurers; potential for population migrations; loss of property.
Increased incidence of extreme high sea level (excludes tsunamis).	Likely	Salinization of irrigation water, estuaries, and fresh-water systems.	Decreased fresh-water availability due to saltwater intrusion.	Increased risk of deaths and injuries by drowning in floods; migration-related health effects.	Costs of coastal protection versus costs of land-use relocation; potential for movement of populations and infrastructure.

FIGURE 15.1 Examples of possible impacts of climate change due to changes in extreme weather and climate events, based on projections to the mid- to late 21st century. These do not take into account any changes or developments in adaptive capacity. The likelihood estimates in column 2 relate to the phenomena listed in column 1.

Third, and finally, one should beware of politicians, pundits, and people with certain financial interests who outright deny the reality of climate change, despite the growing consensus among climate scientists that such change is real. I quote from a November 28, 2015, *New York Times* article, "Short Answers to Hard Questions About Climate Change" by Justin Gillis:

> *Why do people question climate change?*
>
> **Hint: ideology.**
>
> *Most of the attacks on climate science are coming from libertarians and other political conservatives who do not like the policies that have been proposed to fight global warming. Instead of negotiating over those policies and trying to make them more subject to free-market principles, they have taken the approach of blocking them by trying to undermine the science.*
>
> *This ideological position has been propped up by money from fossil-fuel interests, which have paid to create organizations, fund conferences and the like. The scientific arguments made by these groups usually involve cherry-picking data, such as focusing on short-term blips in the temperature record or in sea ice, while ignoring the long-term trends.*
>
> *The most extreme version of climate denialism is to claim that scientists are engaged in a worldwide hoax to fool the public so that the government can gain greater control over people's lives. As the arguments have become more strained, many oil and coal companies have begun to distance themselves publicly from climate denialism, but some are still helping to finance the campaigns of politicians who espouse such views.*

But assuming that climate change is a genuine phenomenon and assuming, too, that much of it is due to human activity including, for instance, the use of fossil fuels that emit high levels of CO_2 into the atmosphere, the main ethical questions are these:

- What makes addressing the threat of global climate change particularly challenging?
- What ethical implications does climate change have for individuals who live in a consumer society?
- What ethical implications does climate change have for governments, particularly those such as the United States whose consumer population apparently contributes a high percentage of the greenhouse gases that contribute to the phenomenon of global warming?

These questions receive attention from Stephen M. Gardiner, Walter Sinnott-Armstrong, and Bjørn Lomborg in their contributions to this chapter.

5. THEORY MEETS PRACTICE

Kantian moral theory extended

Many defenders of an environmental ethic base their view (whether biocentric or ecocentric) on the claim that intrinsic value is possessed by such things as nonsentient life forms, features of the environment, perhaps whole species, and the ecosystem itself. Thus, on their view, some or all of these items have direct moral standing. If we now add the idea that creatures and things having direct moral standing require that they be treated with an appropriate kind and level of respect, we arrive at a Kantian ethical theory, extended in scope.

Consequentialism

A consequentialist might go a number of ways with regard to an environmental ethic. If she follows the utilitarian tradition and accords direct moral standing only to sentient creatures—creatures who have the developed capacity to have experiences of pleasure and pain—then she is going to deny that nonsentient creatures and nonliving things have direct moral standing. This view will thus deny that there is or can be a genuine environmental ethic as we defined it earlier.

However, recall that the main consequentialist idea is that the rightness or wrongness of an action depends entirely on the net intrinsic value of the likely consequences of the various alternative actions or policies under consideration. It is open to a nonutilitarian consequentialist to hold that nonsentient creatures and perhaps nonliving things have intrinsic value and thus embrace the central tenets of an environmental ethic. If a consequentialist goes this route, there is still a difference between consequentialism so extended and a Kantian environmental ethic: the consequentialist maintains that what has intrinsic value is something *to be promoted,* while the Kantian holds that respecting what has intrinsic value is not simply a matter of promoting more of it. For instance, it is open to a Kantian to claim that proper respect for the environment requires of us that we *appreciate* and *preserve* it (or certain of its elements) where doing so is not a matter of (but may sometime include) promoting in the sense of increasing the items having intrinsic value.

Thus, consequentialists as such need not reject the main tenets of an environmental ethic, and those who do embrace such an ethic need not worry about collapsing their view into an essentially Kantian view.

Virtue Ethics

Suppose one is skeptical of the idea that nonsentient creatures and/or nonliving things have direct moral standing, and thus skeptical of the idea of an environmental ethic. And suppose one rejects any form of consequentialism, including utilitarianism. What sense might one make of the idea that responsible moral agents morally ought to have a certain noninstrumental regard for the environment? One answer is provided by a virtue-centered approach to ethics, according to which to fail to have a proper noninstrumental regard for the environment might involve one or more failures of character. This is the approach taken by Thomas E. Hill Jr. in his article included in this chapter.

Social Contract Theory

According to T. M. Scanlon's version of social contract theory (which he labels "contractualism"), one has a moral obligation to refrain from performing an action whenever it violates a general principle or rule that no one (suitably motivated) could reasonably reject as a public principle governing behavior of people in a society. In the selection "It's Not *My* Fault: Global Warming and Individual Moral Obligation," Walter Sinnott-Armstrong considers a variety of moral principles that one might attempt to use as a basis for arguing that it is morally wrong to, say, drive a gas-guzzling vehicle just for fun. He argues that neither the contractualist principle nor any of the other moral principles featured in leading moral theories can ground a plausible argument for wrongness of such an action.

NOTES

1. See Tom Regan, "The Nature and Possibility of an Environmental Ethic," *Environmental Ethics* 3 (1981): 19–34. I have broadened Regan's conception by not requiring that an environmental ethic attribute direct moral standing to conscious beings. Clearly, a holistic ethic of the sort described earlier counts as an environmental ethic, but it *need not* attribute any direct moral standing to the individuals (both living and nonliving) that compose a whole ecosystem. It should also be noted that Regan's conception of an environmental ethic excludes both anthropocentrism and sentientism from counting as environmental ethics. But other writers define "environmental ethics" more generally as the study of the ethics of human interactions with, and impact upon, the natural environment. On this broader definition, neither anthropocentrist nor sentientist views are excluded.

2. In addition to CO_2, other greenhouse gases include methane (CH_4), nitrous oxide (N_2O) and halocarbons (a group that includes hydrocarbons containing fluorine, chlorine, or bromine).

3. Established in 1988, the IPCC is a scientific intergovernmental body whose main task is to study the effects of human activity on climate.

4. From IPCC, *Climate Change 2007: Synthesis Report*, p. 15.

5. IPCC, *Climate Change 2007: Synthesis Report*, p. 31.

6. IPCC, *Climate Change 2007: Synthesis Report*, p. 44.

7. See, for instance, ch. 7 of the Wikipedia entry on the IPCC, "Criticisms of IPCC," <http://en.wikipedia.org/wiki/Intergovernmental_Panel_on_Climate_Change>.

WILLIAM F. BAXTER

People or Penguins: The Case for Optimal Pollution

William Baxter defends an anthropocentric approach to ethical issues concerning the environment by specifying four goals that are to serve as criteria for determining solutions to problems of human organization. On the basis of these "people-oriented" criteria, Baxter argues that we should view our treatment of the environment as a matter of various trade-offs whose aim is to promote human welfare. Two of Baxter's criteria appeal to the Kantian idea that all persons are to be treated as ends in themselves, and so his view represents one way in which Kant's ethics can be extended to environmental concerns.

Recommended Reading: Kantian moral theory, chap. 1, sec. 2C, particularly the Humanity formulation of the categorical imperative.

I start with the modest proposition that, in dealing with pollution, or indeed with any problem, it is helpful to know what one is attempting to accomplish. Agreement on how and whether to pursue a particular objective, such as pollution control, is not possible unless some more general objective has been identified and stated with reasonable precision. We talk loosely of having clean air and clean water, of preserving our wilderness areas, and so forth. But none of these is a sufficiently general objective: each is more accurately viewed as a means rather than as an end.

With regard to clean air, for example, one may ask, "how clean?" and "what does clean mean?" It is even reasonable to ask, "why have clean air?" Each of these questions is an implicit demand that a more general community goal be stated—a goal sufficiently general in its scope and enjoying sufficiently general assent among the community of actors that such "why" questions no longer seem admissible with respect to that goal.

If, for example, one states as a goal the proposition that "every person should be free to do whatever he wishes in contexts where his actions do not interfere with the interests of other human beings," the speaker is unlikely to be met with a response of "why." The goal may be criticized as uncertain in its implications or difficult to implement, but it is so basic a tenet of our civilization—it reflects a cultural value so broadly shared, at least in the abstract—that the question "why" is seen as impertinent or imponderable or both.

I do not mean to suggest that everyone would agree with the "spheres of freedom" objective just stated. Still less do I mean to suggest that a society could subscribe to four or five such general objectives that would be adequate in their coverage to serve as testing criteria by which all other disagreements might be measured. One difficulty in the attempt to construct such a list is that each new goal added will conflict, in certain applications, with each prior goal listed; and thus each goal serves as a limited qualification on prior goals.

Without any expectation of obtaining unanimous consent to them, let me set forth four goals that I generally use as ultimate testing criteria in attempting to frame solutions to problems of human organization.

From William F. Baxter, *People or Penguins: The Case for Optimal Pollution*, Columbia University Press, 1974, pp. 1–13. Reprinted with permission of the publisher.

My position regarding pollution stems from these four criteria. If the criteria appeal to you and any part of what appears hereafter does not, our disagreement will have a helpful focus: which of us is correct, analytically, in supposing that his position on pollution would better serve these general goals. If the criteria do not seem acceptable to you, then it is to be expected that our more particular judgments will differ, and the task will then be yours to identify the basic set of criteria upon which your particular judgments rest.

My criteria are as follows:

1. The spheres of freedom criterion stated above.
2. Waste is a bad thing. The dominant feature of human existence is scarcity—our available resources, our aggregate labors, and our skill in employing both have always been, and will continue for some time to be, inadequate to yield to every man all the tangible and intangible satisfactions he would like to have. Hence, none of those resources, or labors, or skills, should be wasted—that is, employed so as to yield less than they might yield in human satisfactions.
3. Every human being should be regarded as an end rather than as a means to be used for the betterment of another. Each should be afforded dignity and regarded as having an absolute claim to an evenhanded application of such rules as the community may adopt for its governance.
4. Both the incentive and the opportunity to improve his share of satisfactions should be preserved to every individual. Preservation of incentive is dictated by the "no-waste" criterion and enjoins against the continuous, totally egalitarian redistribution of satisfactions, or wealth; but subject to that constraint, everyone should receive, by continuous redistribution if necessary, some minimal share of aggregate wealth so as to avoid a level of privation from which the opportunity to improve his situation becomes illusory.

The relationship of these highly general goals to the more specific environmental issues at hand may not be readily apparent, and I am not yet ready to demonstrate their pervasive implications. But let me give one indication of their implications. Recently scientists have informed us that use of DDT in food production is causing damage to the penguin population. For the present purposes let us accept that assertion as an indisputable scientific fact. The scientific fact is often asserted as if the correct implication—that we must stop agricultural use of DDT—followed from the mere statement of the fact of penguin damage. But plainly it does not follow if my criteria are employed.

My criteria are oriented to people, not penguins. Damage to penguins, or sugar pines, or geological marvels is, without more, simply irrelevant. One must go further, by my criteria, and say: Penguins are important because people enjoy seeing them walk about rocks; and furthermore, the well-being of people would be less impaired by halting use of DDT than by giving up penguins. In short, my observations about environmental problems will be people-oriented, as are my criteria. I have no interest in preserving penguins for their own sake.

It may be said by way of objection to this position, that it is very selfish of people to act as if each person represented one unit of importance and nothing else was of any importance. It is undeniably selfish. Nevertheless I think it is the only tenable starting place for analysis for several reasons. First, no other position corresponds to the way most people really think and act—i.e., corresponds to reality.

Second, this attitude does not portend any massive destruction of nonhuman flora and fauna, for people depend on them in many obvious ways, and they will be preserved because and to the degree that humans do depend on them.

Third, what is good for humans is, in many respects, good for penguins and pine trees—clean air for example. So that humans are, in these respects, surrogates for plant and animal life.

Fourth, I do not know how we could administer any other system. Our decisions are either private or collective. Insofar as Mr. Jones is free to act privately, he may give such preferences as he wishes to other forms of life: he may feed birds in winter and do with less himself, and he may even decline to resist an advancing polar bear on the ground that the bear's appetite is more important than those portions of himself that the bear may choose to eat. In short my basic premise does not rule out private altruism to competing life-forms. It does rule out, however, Mr. Jones' inclination to feed Mr. Smith to the bear, however hungry the bear, however despicable Mr. Smith.

Insofar as we act collectively on the other hand, only humans can be afforded an opportunity to participate in the collective decisions. Penguins cannot vote now and are unlikely subjects for the franchise—pine trees more unlikely still. Again each individual is free to cast his vote so as to benefit sugar pines if that is his inclination. But many of the more extreme assertions that one hears from some conservationists amount to tacit assertions that they are specially appointed representatives of sugar pines, and hence that their preferences should be weighted more heavily than the preferences of other humans who do not enjoy equal rapport with "nature." The simplistic assertion that agricultural use of DDT must stop at once because it is harmful to penguins is of that type.

Fifth, if polar bears or pine trees or penguins, like men, are to be regarded as ends rather than means, if they are to count in our calculus of social organization, someone must tell me how much each one counts, and someone must tell me how these life-forms are to be permitted to express their preferences, for I do not know either answer. If the answer is that certain people are to hold their proxies, then I want to know how those proxy-holders are to be selected: self-appointment does not seem workable to me.

Sixth, and by way of summary of all the foregoing, let me point out that the set of environmental issues under discussion—although they raise very complex technical questions of how to achieve any objective—ultimately raise a normative question: what *ought* we to do? Questions of *ought* are unique to the human mind and world—they are meaningless as applied to a nonhuman situation.

I reject the proposition that we *ought* to respect the "balance of nature" or to "preserve the environment" unless the reason for doing so, express or implied, is the benefit of man.

I reject the idea that there is a "right" or "morally correct" state of nature to which we should return. The word "nature" has no normative connotation. Was it "right" or "wrong" for the earth's crust to heave in contortion and create mountains and seas?

Was it "right" for the first amphibian to crawl up out of the primordial ooze? Was it "wrong" for plants to reproduce themselves and alter the atmospheric composition in favor of oxygen? For animals to alter the atmosphere in favor of carbon dioxide both by breathing oxygen and eating plants? No answers can be given to these questions because they are meaningless questions.

All this may seem obvious to the point of being tedious, but much of the present controversy over environment and pollution rests on tacit normative assumptions about just such nonnormative phenomena: that it is "wrong" to impair penguins with DDT, but not to slaughter cattle for prime rib roasts. That it is wrong to kill stands of sugar pines with industrial fumes, but not to cut sugar pines and build housing for the poor. Every man is entitled to his own preferred definition of Walden Pond, but there is no definition that has any moral superiority over another, except by reference to the selfish needs of the human race.

From the fact that there is no normative definition of the natural state, it follows that there is no normative definition of clean air or pure water—hence no definition of polluted air—or of pollution—except by reference to the needs of man. The "right" composition of the atmosphere is one which has some dust in it and some lead in it and some hydrogen sulfide in it—just those amounts that attend a sensibly organized society thoughtfully and knowledgeably pursuing the greatest possible satisfaction for its human members.

The first and most fundamental step toward solution of our environmental problems is a clear recognition that our objective is not pure air or water but rather some optimal state of pollution. That step immediately suggests the question: How do we define and attain the level of pollution that will yield the maximum possible amount of human satisfaction?

Low levels of pollution contribute to human satisfaction but so do food and shelter and education and music. To attain ever lower levels of pollution, we must pay the cost of having less of these other things. I contrast that view of the cost of pollution control with the more popular statement that pollution control will "cost" very large numbers of dollars.

The popular statement is true in some senses, false in others; sorting out the true and false senses is of some importance. The first step in that sorting process is to achieve a clear understanding of the difference between dollars and resources. Resources are the wealth of our nation; dollars are merely claim checks upon those resources. Resources are of vital importance; dollars are comparatively trivial.

Four categories of resources are sufficient for our purposes: At any given time a nation, or a planet if you prefer, has a stock of labor, of technological skill, of capital goods, and of natural resources (such as mineral deposits, timber, water, land, etc.). These resources can be used in various combinations to yield goods and services of all kinds—in some limited quantity. The quantity will be larger if they are combined efficiently, smaller if combined inefficiently. But in either event the resource stock is limited, the goods and services that they can be made to yield are limited; even the most efficient use of them will yield less than our population, in the aggregate, would like to have.

If one considers building a new dam, it is appropriate to say that it will be costly in the sense that it will require x hours of labor, y tons of steel and concrete, and z amount of capital goods. If these resources are devoted to the dam, then they cannot be used to build hospitals, fishing rods, schools, or electric can openers. That is the meaningful sense in which the dam is costly.

Quite apart from the very important question of how wisely we can combine our resources to produce goods and services, is the very different question of how they get distributed—who gets how many goods? Dollars constitute the claim checks which are distributed among people and which control their share of national output. Dollars are nearly valueless pieces of paper except to the extent that they do represent claim checks to some fraction of the output of goods and services. Viewed as claim checks, all the dollars outstanding during any period of time are worth, in the aggregate, the goods and services that are available to be claimed with them during that period—neither more nor less.

It is far easier to increase the supply of dollars than to increase the production of goods and services—printing dollars is easy. But printing more dollars doesn't help because each dollar then simply becomes a claim to fewer goods, i.e., becomes worth less.

The point is this: many people fall into error upon hearing the statement that the decision to build a dam, or to clean up a river, will cost $X million. It is regrettably easy to say: "It's only money. This is a wealthy country, and we have lots of money." But you cannot build a dam or clean a river with $X million—unless you also have a match, you can't even make a fire. One builds a dam or cleans a river by diverting labor and steel and trucks and factories from making one kind of goods to making another. The cost in dollars is merely a shorthand way of describing the extent of the diversion necessary. If we build a dam for $X million, then we must recognize that we will have $X million less housing and food and medical care and electric can openers as a result.

Similarly, the costs of controlling pollution are best expressed in terms of the other goods we will have to give up to do the job. This is not to say the job should not be done. Badly as we need more housing, more medical care, more can openers, and more symphony orchestras, we could do with somewhat less of them, in my judgment at least, in exchange for somewhat cleaner air and rivers. But that is the nature of the trade-off, and analysis of the problem is advanced if that unpleasant reality is kept in mind. Once the trade-off relationship is clearly perceived, it is possible to state in a very general way what the optimal level of pollution is. I would state it as follows:

People enjoy watching penguins. They enjoy relatively clean air and smog-free vistas. Their health is improved by relatively clean water and air. Each of these benefits is a type of good or service. As a society we would be well advised to give up one washing machine if the resources that would have gone into that washing machine can yield greater human satisfaction when diverted into pollution control. We should give up one hospital if the resources thereby freed would yield more human satisfaction when devoted to elimination of noise in our cities. And so on, trade-off by trade-off, we should divert our productive capacities from the production of existing goods and services to the production of a cleaner, quieter, more pastoral nation up to—and no further than—the point at which we value more highly the next washing machine or hospital that we would have to do without than we value the next unit of environmental improvement that the diverted resources would create.

Now this proposition seems to me unassailable but so general and abstract as to be unhelpful—at least unadministerable in the form stated. It assumes we can measure in some way the incremental units of human satisfaction yielded by very different types of goods. . . . But I insist that the proposition stated describes the result for which we should be striving—and again, that it is always useful to know what your target is even if your weapons are too crude to score a bull's eye.

READING QUESTIONS

1. What are the four goals Baxter proposes in order to develop a solution to the problems of human organization?
2. How does Baxter respond to the objection that it is selfish to act as if one person counts as one unit of importance? Mention at least four of the six reasons he gives in defense of his starting position.
3. What are the four categories of resources mentioned by Baxter? What is the difference between resources and dollars according to Baxter?
4. Explain Baxter's argument for why there is no "morally correct" state of nature to which we should return.
5. What is the ultimate goal toward which we should be striving according to Baxter?

DISCUSSION QUESTIONS

1. Should we go along with Baxter and reject the idea that we should not strive to protect and preserve nature and the environment unless doing so is a benefit to humans?
2. Is there such a thing as an optimal state of pollution? Is Baxter right to claim that part of our goal should be to achieve some optimal state of pollution?
3. What should our goals be regarding nature and the environment other than the one Baxter mentions here?

ALDO LEOPOLD

The Land Ethic

This essay is from the final chapter of Aldo Leopold's classic in environmentalism, *A Sand County Almanac.* Leopold proposes an ecocentric ethic whose basic principle is "A thing is right when it tends to preserve the integrity, stability, and beauty of the biotic community [including soils, waters, plants, animals]. It is wrong when it tends otherwise."

When god-like Odysseus returned from the wars in Troy, he hanged all on one rope a dozen slave-girls of his household whom he suspected of misbehavior during his absence.

This hanging involved no question of propriety. The girls were property. The disposal of property was then, as now, a matter of expediency, not of right and wrong.

Concepts of right and wrong were not lacking from Odysseus' Greece: witness the fidelity of his wife through the long years before at last his black-prowed galleys clove the wine-dark seas for home. The ethical structure of that day covered wives, but had not yet been extended to human chattels. During the three thousand years which have since elapsed, ethical criteria have been extended to many fields of conduct, with corresponding shrinkages in those judged by expediency only.

THE ETHICAL SEQUENCE

This extension of ethics, so far studied only by philosophers, is actually a process in ecological evolution. Its sequences may be described in ecological as well as in philosophical terms. An ethic, ecologically, is a limitation on freedom of action in the struggle for existence. An ethic, philosophically, is a differentiation of social from antisocial conduct. These are two definitions of one thing. The thing has its origin in the tendency of interdependent individuals or groups to evolve modes of co-operation. The ecologist calls these symbioses. Politics and economics are advanced symbioses in which the original free-for-all competition has been replaced, in part, by co-operative mechanisms with an ethical content.

The complexity of co-operative mechanisms has increased with population density, and with the efficiency of tools. It was simpler, for example, to define the antisocial uses of sticks and stones in the days of the mastodons than of bullets and billboards in the age of motors.

The first ethics dealt with the relation between individuals; the Mosaic Decalogue is an example. Later accretions dealt with the relation between the individual and society. The Golden Rule tries to integrate the individual to society; democracy to integrate social organization to the individual.

There is as yet no ethic dealing with man's relation to land and to the animals and plants which grow upon it. Land, like Odysseus' slave-girls, is still property. The land-relation is still strictly economic, entailing privileges but not obligations.

From *A Sand County Almanac, with Other Essays on Conservation from Round River*, Aldo Leopold, Oxford: Oxford University Press (1949, reprinted in 1981). Reprinted by permission of Oxford University Press, Inc.

The extension of ethics to this third element in human environment is, if I read the evidence correctly, an evolutionary possibility and an ecological necessity. It is the third step in a sequence. The first two have already been taken. Individual thinkers since the days of Ezekiel and Isaiah have asserted that the despoliation of land is not only inexpedient but wrong. Society, however, has not yet affirmed their belief. I regard the present conservation movement as the embryo of such an affirmation.

An ethic may be regarded as a mode of guidance for meeting ecological situations so new or intricate, or involving such deferred reactions, that the path of social expediency is not discernible to the average individual. Animal instincts are modes of guidance for the individual in meeting such situations. Ethics are possibly a kind of community instinct in-the-making.

THE COMMUNITY CONCEPT

All ethics so far evolved rest upon a single premise: that the individual is a member of a community of interdependent parts. His instincts prompt him to compete for his place in that community, but his ethics prompt him also to co-operate (perhaps in order that there may be a place to compete for).

The land ethic simply enlarges the boundaries of the community to include soils, waters, plants, and animals, or collectively, the land.

This sounds simple: do we not already sing our love for and obligation to the land of the free and the home of the brave? Yes, but just what and whom do we love? Certainly not the soil, which we are sending helter-skelter downriver. Certainly not the waters, which we assume have no function except to turn turbines, float barges, and carry off sewage. Certainly not the plants, of which we exterminate whole communities without batting an eye. Certainly not the animals, of which we have already extirpated many of the largest and most beautiful species. A land ethic of course cannot prevent the alteration, management, and use of these "resources," but it does affirm their

right to continued existence, and, at least in spots, their continued existence in a natural state.

In short, a land ethic changes the role of *Homo sapiens* from conqueror of the land-community to plain member and citizen of it. It implies respect for his fellow-members, and also respect for the community as such.

In human history, we have learned (I hope) that the conqueror role is eventually self-defeating. Why? Because it is implicit in such a role that the conqueror knows, ex cathedra, just what makes the community clock tick, and just what and who is valuable, and what and who is worthless, in community life. It always turns out that he knows neither, and this is why his conquests eventually defeat themselves.

In the biotic community, a parallel situation exists. Abraham knew exactly what the land was for: it was to drip milk and honey into Abraham's mouth. At the present moment, the assurance with which we regard this assumption is inverse to the degree of our education.

The ordinary citizen today assumes that science knows what makes the community clock tick; the scientist is equally sure that he does not. He knows that the biotic mechanism is so complex that its workings may never be fully understood. . . .

SUBSTITUTES FOR A LAND ETHIC

When the logic of history hungers for bread and we hand out a stone, we are at pains to explain how much the stone resembles bread. I now describe some of the stones which serve in lieu of a land ethic.

One basic weakness in a conservation system based wholly on economic motives is that most members of the land community have no economic value. Wildflowers and songbirds are examples. Of the 22,000 higher plants and animals native to Wisconsin, it is doubtful whether more than 5 percent can be sold, fed, eaten, or otherwise put to economic use. Yet these creatures are members of the biotic community, and if (as I believe) its stability depends on its integrity, they are entitled to continuance.

When one of these non-economic categories is threatened, and if we happen to love it, we invent subterfuges to give it economic importance. At the beginning of the century songbirds were supposed to be disappearing. Ornithologists jumped to the rescue with some distinctly shaky evidence to the effect that insects would eat us up if birds failed to control them. The evidence had to be economic in order to be valid.

It is painful to read these circumlocutions today. We have no land ethic yet, but we have at least drawn nearer the point of admitting that birds should continue as a matter of biotic right, regardless of the presence or absence of economic advantage to us.

A parallel situation exists in respect of predatory mammals, raptorial birds, and fish-eating birds. Time was when biologists somewhat overworked the evidence that these creatures preserve the health of game by killing weaklings, or that they control rodents for the farmer, or that they prey only on "worthless" species. Here again, the evidence had to be economic in order to be valid. It is only in recent years that we hear the more honest argument that predators are members of the community, and that no special interest has the right to exterminate them for the sake of a benefit, real or fancied, to itself. . . .

Some species of trees have been "read out of the party" by economics-minded foresters because they grow too slowly, or have too low a sale value to pay as timber crops: white cedar, tamarack, cypress, beech, and hemlock are examples. In Europe, where forestry is ecologically more advanced, the non-commercial tree species are recognized as members of the native forest community, to be preserved as such, within reason. Moreover, some (like beech) have been found to have a valuable function in building up soil fertility. The interdependence of the forest and its constituent tree species, ground flora, and fauna is taken for granted.

Lack of economic value is sometimes a character not only of species or groups, but of entire biotic communities: marshes, bogs, dunes, and "deserts" are examples. Our formula in such cases is to relegate their conservation to government as refuges, monuments, or parks. The difficulty is that these communities are usually interspersed with more valuable private lands; the government cannot possibly own or control such scattered parcels. The net effect is that we have relegated some of them to ultimate extinction over large areas. . . .

To sum up: a system of conservation based solely on economic self-interest is hopelessly lopsided. It tends to ignore, and thus eventually to eliminate, many elements in the land community that lack commercial value, but that are (as far as we know) essential to its healthy functioning. It assumes, falsely, I think, that the economic parts of the biotic clock will function without the uneconomic parts. . . .

THE LAND PYRAMID

An ethic to supplement and guide the economic relation to land presupposes the existence of some mental image of land as a biotic mechanism. We can be ethical only in relation to something we can see, feel, understand, love, or otherwise have faith in.

The image commonly employed in conservation education is "the balance of nature." For reasons too lengthy to detail here, this figure of speech fails to describe accurately what little we know about the land mechanism. A much truer image is the one employed in ecology: the biotic pyramid. I shall first sketch the pyramid as a symbol of land. . . .

Plants absorb energy from the sun. This energy flows through a circuit called the biota, which may be represented by a pyramid consisting of layers. The bottom layer is the soil. A plant layer rests on the soil, an insect layer on the plants, a bird and rodent layer on the insects, and so on up through various animal groups to the apex layer, which consists of the larger carnivores.

The species of a layer are alike not in where they came from, or in what they look like, but rather in what they eat. Each successive layer depends on those below it for food and often for other services, and each in turn furnishes food and services to those above. Proceeding upward, each successive layer decreases in numerical abundance. Thus, for every carnivore there are hundreds of his prey, thousands of their prey, millions of insects, uncountable plants.

The pyramidal form of the system reflects this numerical progression from apex to base. Man shares an intermediate layer with the bears, raccoons, and squirrels which eat both meat and vegetables.

The lines of dependency for food and other services are called food chains. Thus soil-oak-deer-Indian is a chain that has now been largely converted to soil-corn-cow-farmer. Each species, including ourselves, is a link in many chains. The deer eats a hundred plants other than oak, and the cow a hundred plants other than corn. Both, then, are links in a hundred chains. The pyramid is a tangle of chains so complex as to seem disorderly, yet the stability of the system proves it to be a highly organized structure. Its functioning depends on the co-operation and competition of its diverse parts.

In the beginning, the pyramid of life was low and squat, the food chains short and simple. Evolution has added layer after layer, link after link. Man is one of thousands of accretions to the height and complexity of the pyramid. Science has given us many doubts, but it has given us at least one certainty: the trend of evolution is to elaborate and diversify the biota.

Land, then, is not merely soil; it is a fountain of energy flowing through a circuit of soils, plants, and animals. Food chains are the living channels which conduct energy upward; death and decay return it to the soil. The circuit is not closed; some energy is dissipated in decay, some is added by absorption from the air, some is stored in soils, peats, and long-lived forests; but it is a sustained circuit, like a slowly augmented revolving fund of life. There is always a net loss by downhill wash, but this is normally small and offset by the decay of rocks. It is deposited in the ocean and, in the course of geological time, raised to form new lands and new pyramids.

The velocity and character of the upward flow of energy depend on the complex structure of the plant and animal community, much as the upward flow of sap in a tree depends on its complex cellular organization. Without this complexity, normal circulation would presumably not occur. Structure means the characteristic numbers, as well as the characteristic kinds and functions, of the component species. This interdependence between the complex structure of the land and its smooth functioning as an energy unit is one of its basic attributes.

When a change occurs in one part of the circuit, many other parts must adjust themselves to it. Change does not necessarily obstruct or divert the flow of energy; evolution is a long series of self-induced changes, the net result of which has been to elaborate the flow mechanism and to lengthen the circuit. Evolutionary changes, however, are usually slow and local. Man's invention of tools has enabled him to make changes of unprecedented violence, rapidity, and scope. . . .

THE OUTLOOK

It is inconceivable to me that an ethical relation to land can exist without love, respect, and admiration for land, and a high regard for its value. By value, I of course mean something far broader than mere economic value; I mean value in the philosophical sense. . . .

The "key-log" which must be moved to release the evolutionary process for an ethic is simply this: quit thinking about decent land-use as solely an economic problem. Examine each question in terms of what is ethically and esthetically right, as well as what is economically expedient. A thing is right when it tends to preserve the integrity, stability, and beauty of the biotic community. It is wrong when it tends otherwise.

It of course goes without saying that economic feasibility limits the tether of what can or cannot be done for land. It always has and it always will. The fallacy the economic determinists have tied around our collective neck, and which we now need to cast off, is the belief that economics determines *all* land-use. This is simply not true. An innumerable host of actions and attitudes, comprising perhaps the bulk of all land relations, is determined by the land-users' tastes and predilections, rather than by his purse. The bulk of all land relations hinges on investments of time, forethought, skill, and faith rather than on investments of cash. As a land-user thinketh, so is he.

I have purposely presented the land ethic as a product of social evolution because nothing so important as an ethic is ever "written." Only the most superficial student of history supposes that Moses "wrote" the Decalogue; it evolved in the minds of a thinking community, and Moses wrote a tentative summary of it for a "seminar." I say tentative because evolution never stops.

The evolution of a land ethic is an intellectual as well as emotional process. Conservation is paved with good intentions which prove to be futile, or even dangerous, because they are devoid of critical understanding either of the land, or of economic land-use. I think it is a truism that as the ethical frontier advances from the individual to the community, its intellectual content increases.

The mechanism of operation is the same for any ethic: social approbation for right actions; social disapproval for wrong actions.

By and large, our present problem is one of attitudes and implements. We are remodeling the Alhambra with a steamshovel, and we are proud of our yardage. We shall hardly relinquish the shovel, which after all has many good points, but we are in need of gentler and more objective criteria for its successful use.

READING QUESTIONS

1. How does Leopold distinguish an ethic from a philosophical ethic? Explain the ethical sequence in terms of ecological evolution.
2. How does Leopold characterize the idea of a land ethic? What is the main substitute for a land ethic and what are its weaknesses according to Leopold?
3. Explain the land pyramid structure characterized by Leopold. What role does evolution play in this system?
4. How does Leopold suggest we change the way we think about land use?
5. When is an action considered right in Leopold's view?

DISCUSSION QUESTIONS

1. Leopold suggests that economics should not be our only concern when it comes to the use of land. To what extent should economic considerations play a part in our treatment of nature and the environment? Are there any situations in which economic concerns might trump environmental ones?
2. Should we adopt the land ethic suggested by Leopold? What sorts of difficulties might arise if we consider things like soil, water, and plants as members of the same moral community to which we belong?

THOMAS E. HILL JR.

Ideals of Human Excellence and Preserving the Natural Environment

Thomas Hill rejects those attempts to explain proper environmental concern that appeal either to rights, to intrinsic value, or to religious considerations. Rather, Hill advocates an alternative to such views that focuses on ideals of human excellence. In particular, Hill claims that insensitivity to the environment reflects either ignorance, exaggerated self-importance, or a lack of self-acceptance that are crucial for achieving the human excellence of proper humility. Hill's approach to environmental issues can be understood through the lens of a virtue ethics approach.

Recommended Reading: virtue ethics, chap. 1, sec. 2E. Also relevant are consequentialism, chap. 1, sec. 2A, and rights-based moral theory, chap. 1, sec. 2D.

I

A wealthy eccentric bought a house in a neighborhood I know. The house was surrounded by a beautiful display of grass, plants, and flowers, and it was shaded by a huge old avocado tree. But the grass required cutting, the flowers needed tending, and the man wanted more sun. So he cut the whole lot down and covered the yard with asphalt. After all it was his property and he was not fond of plants.

It was a small operation, but it reminded me of the strip mining of large sections of the Appalachians. In both cases, of course, there were reasons for the destruction, and property rights could be cited as justification. But I could not help but wonder, "What sort of person would do a thing like that?"

Many Californians had a similar reaction when a recent governor defended the leveling of ancient redwood groves, reportedly saying, "If you have seen one redwood, you have seen them all."

Incidents like these arouse the indignation of ardent environmentalists and leave even apolitical observers with some degree of moral discomfort. The reasons for these reactions are mostly obvious. Uprooting the natural environment robs both present and future generations of much potential use and enjoyment. Animals too depend on the environment; and even if one does not value animals for their own sakes, their potential utility for us is incalculable. Plants are needed, of course, to replenish the atmosphere quite aside from their aesthetic value. These reasons for hesitating to destroy forests and gardens are not only the most obvious ones, but also the most persuasive for practical purposes. But, one wonders, is there nothing more behind our discomfort? Are we concerned solely about the potential use and enjoyment of the forests, etc., for ourselves, later generations, and perhaps animals? Is there not something else which disturbs us when we witness the destruction or even listen to those who would defend it in terms of cost/benefit analysis?

Imagine that in each of our examples those who would destroy the environment argue elaborately that, even considering future generations of human beings and animals, there are benefits in "replacing" the natural environment which outweigh the negative utilities which environmentalists cite.[1] No doubt we could press the argument on the facts, trying to show that the destruction is shortsighted and that its defenders have underestimated its potential harm or ignored some pertinent rights or interests. But is this all we could say? Suppose we grant, for a moment, that the utility of destroying the redwoods, forests, and gardens is equal to their potential for use and enjoyment by nature lovers and animals. Suppose, further, that we even grant that the pertinent human rights and animal rights, if any, are evenly divided for and against destruction. Imagine that we also concede, for argument's sake, that the forests contain no potentially useful endangered species of animals and plants. Must we then conclude that there is no further cause for moral concern? Should we then feel morally indifferent when we see the natural environment uprooted? . . .

II

The problem, then, is this. We want to understand what underlies our moral uneasiness at the destruction of the redwoods, forests, etc., even apart from the loss of these as resources for human beings and animals. But I find no adequate answer by pursuing the questions, "Are rights or interests of plants neglected?" "What is God's will on the matter?" and "What is the intrinsic value of the existence of a tree or forest?" My suggestion, which is in fact the main point of this paper, is that we look at the problem from a different perspective. That is, let us turn for a while from the effort to find reasons why certain *acts* destructive of natural environments are morally wrong to the ancient task of articulating our ideals of human excellence. Rather than argue directly with destroyers of the environment who say, "Show me why what I am doing is *immoral*," I want to ask,

"What sort of person would want to do what they propose?" The point is not to skirt the issue with an ad hominem, but to raise a different moral question, for even if there is no convincing way to show that the destructive acts are wrong (independently of human and animal use and enjoyment), we may find that the willingness to indulge in them reflects the absence of human traits that we admire and regard morally important.

This strategy of shifting questions may seem more promising if one reflects on certain analogous situations. Consider, for example, the Nazi who asks, in all seriousness. "Why is it wrong for me to make lampshades out of human skin—provided, of course, I did not myself kill the victims to get the skins?" We would react more with shock and disgust than with indignation, I suspect, because it is even more evident that the question reveals a defect in the questioner than that the proposed act is itself immoral. Sometimes we may not regard an act wrong at all though we see it as reflecting something objectionable about the person who does it. Imagine, for example, one who laughs spontaneously to himself when he reads a newspaper account of a plane crash that kills hundreds. Or, again, consider an obsequious grandson who, having waited for his grandmother's inheritance with mock devotion, then secretly spits on her grave when at last she dies. Spitting on the grave may have no adverse consequences and perhaps it violates no rights. The moral uneasiness which it arouses is explained more by our view of the agent than by any conviction that what he did was immoral. Had he hesitated and asked, "Why shouldn't I spit on her grave?" it seems more fitting to ask him to reflect on the sort of person he is than to try to offer reasons why he should refrain from spitting.

III

What sort of person, then, would cover his garden with asphalt, strip mine a wooded mountain, or level an irreplaceable redwood grove? Two sorts of answers, though initially appealing, must be ruled out. The first is that persons who would destroy the environment in these ways are either shortsighted, underestimating the harm they do, or else are too little concerned for the well-being of other people. Perhaps too they have insufficient regard for animal life. But these considerations have been set aside in order to refine the controversy. Another tempting response might be that we count it a moral virtue, or at least a human ideal, to love nature. Those who value the environment only for its utility must not really love nature and so in this way fall short of an ideal. But such an answer is hardly satisfying in the present context, for what is at issue is *why* we feel moral discomfort at the activities of those who admittedly value nature only for its utility. That it is ideal to care for nonsentient nature beyond its possible use is really just another way of expressing the general point which is under controversy.

What is needed is some way of showing that this ideal is connected with other virtues, or human excellences, not in question. To do so is difficult and my suggestions, accordingly, will be tentative and subject to qualification.

The main idea is that, though indifference to nonsentient nature does not *necessarily* reflect the absence of virtues, it often signals the absence of certain traits which we want to encourage because they are, in most cases, a natural basis for the development of certain virtues. It is often thought, for example, that those who would destroy the natural environment must lack a proper appreciation of their place in the natural order, and so must either be ignorant or have too little humility. Though I would argue that this is not necessarily so, I suggest that, given certain plausible empirical assumptions, their attitude may well be rooted in ignorance, a narrow perspective, inability to see things as important apart from themselves and the limited groups they associate with, or reluctance to accept themselves as natural beings. Overcoming these deficiencies will not guarantee a proper moral humility, but for most of us it is probably an important psychological preliminary. . . .

Consider first the suggestion that destroyers of the environment lack an appreciation of their place in the universe. Their attention, it seems, must be focused on parochial matters, on what is, relatively speaking, close in space and time. They seem not to understand that we are a speck on the cosmic scene, a brief stage in the evolutionary process, only one among millions of species on Earth, and an episode in the course of human history. Of course, they know that there are stars, fossils, insects, and ancient ruins; but do they have any idea of the complexity of the processes that led to the natural world as we find it? Are they aware how much the forces at work within their own bodies are like those which govern all living things and even how much they have in common with inanimate bodies? Admittedly scientific knowledge is limited and no one can master it all; but could one who had a broad and deep understanding of his place in nature really be indifferent to the destruction of the natural environment?

This first suggestion, however, may well provoke a protest from a sophisticated anti-environmentalist. "Perhaps *some* may be indifferent to nature from ignorance," the critic may object, "but *I* have studied astronomy, geology, biology, and biochemistry, and I still unashamedly regard the nonsentient environment as simply a resource for our use. It should not be wasted, of course, but what should be preserved is decidable by weighing long-term costs and benefits." "Besides," our critic may continue, "as philosophers you should know the old Humean formula, 'You cannot derive an *ought* from an *is*.' All the facts of biology, biochemistry, etc., do not entail that I ought to love nature or want to preserve it. What one understands is one thing; what one values is something else. Just as nature lovers are not necessarily scientists, those indifferent to nature are not necessarily ignorant."

Although the environmentalist may concede the critic's logical point, he may well argue that, as a matter of fact, increased understanding of nature tends to heighten people's concern for its preservation. If so, despite the objection, the suspicion that the destroyers of the environment lack deep understanding of nature is not, in most cases, unwarranted, but the argument need not rest here.

The environmentalist might amplify his original idea as follows: "When I said that the destroyers of nature do not appreciate their place in the universe, I was not speaking of intellectual understanding alone, for, after all, a person can *know* a catalog of facts without ever putting them together and seeing vividly the whole picture which they form. To see oneself as just one part of nature is to look at oneself and the world from a certain perspective which is quite different from being able to recite detailed information from the natural sciences. What the destroyers of nature lack is this perspective, not particular information."

Again our critic may object, though only after making some concessions: "All right," he may say, "*some* who are indifferent to nature may lack the cosmic perspective of which you speak, but again there is no *necessary* connection between this failing, if it is one, and any particular evaluative attitude toward nature. In fact, different people respond quite differently when they move to a wider perspective. When *I* try to picture myself vividly as a brief, transitory episode in the course of nature, I simply get depressed. Far from inspiring me with a love of nature, the exercise makes me sad and hostile. You romantics think only of poets like Wordsworth and artists like Turner, but you should consider how differently Omar Khayyám responded when he took your wider perspective. His reaction, when looking at his life from a cosmic viewpoint, was 'Drink up, for tomorrow we die.' Others respond in an almost opposite manner with a joyless Stoic resignation, exemplified by the poet who pictures the wise man, at the height of personal triumph, being served a magnificent banquet, and then consummating his marriage to his beloved, all the while reminding himself, 'Even this shall pass away.'"[2] In sum, the critic may object, "Even if one should try to see oneself as one small transitory part of nature, doing so does not dictate any particular normative attitude. Some may come to love nature, but others are moved to live for the moment; some sink into sad resignation; others get depressed or angry. So indifference to nature is not necessarily a sign that a person fails to look at himself from the larger perspective."

The environmentalist might respond to this objection in several ways. He might, for example, argue that even though some people who see themselves as part of the natural order remain indifferent to nonsentient nature, this is not a common reaction.

Typically, it may be argued, as we become more and more aware that we are parts of the larger whole we come to value the whole independently of its effect on ourselves. Thus, despite the possibilities the critic raises, indifference to nonsentient nature is still in most cases a sign that a person fails to see himself as part of the natural order.

If someone challenges the empirical assumption here, the environmentalist might develop the argument along a quite different line. The initial idea, he may remind us, was that those who would destroy the natural environment fail to *appreciate* their place in the natural order. "Appreciating one's place" is not simply an intellectual appreciation. It is also an attitude, reflecting what one values as well as what one knows. When we say, for example, that both the servile and the arrogant person fail to *appreciate* their place in a society of equals, we do not mean simply that they are ignorant of certain empirical facts, but rather that they have certain objectionable attitudes about their importance relative to other people. Similarly, to fail to appreciate one's place in nature is not merely to lack knowledge or breadth of perspective, but to take a certain attitude about what matters. A person who *understands* his place in nature but still views nonsentient nature merely as a resource takes the attitude that nothing is *important* but human beings and animals. Despite first appearances, he is not so much like the pre-Copernican astronomers who made the intellectual error of treating the Earth as the "center of the universe" when they made their calculations. He is more like the racist who, though well aware of other races, treats all races but his own as insignificant.

So construed, the argument appeals to the common idea that awareness of nature typically has, and should have, a humbling effect. The Alps, a storm at sea, the Grand Canyon, towering redwoods, and "the starry heavens above" move many a person to remark on the comparative insignificance of our daily concerns and even of our species, and this is generally taken to be a quite fitting response.[3] What seems to be missing, then, in those who understand nature but remain unmoved is a proper humility.[4] Absence of proper humility is not the same as selfishness or egoism, for one can be devoted to self-interest while still viewing one's own pleasures and projects as trivial and unimportant. And one can have an exaggerated view of one's own importance while grandly sacrificing for those one views as inferior. Nor is the lack of humility identical with belief that one has power and influence, for a person can be quite puffed up about himself while believing that the foolish world will never acknowledge him. The humility we miss seems not so much a belief about one's relative effectiveness and recognition as an attitude which measures the importance of things independently of their relation to oneself or to some narrow group with which one identifies. A paradigm of a person who lacks humility is the self-important emperor who grants status to his family because it is *his,* to his subordinates because *he* appointed them, and to his country because *he* chooses to glorify it. Less extreme but still lacking proper humility is the elitist who counts events significant solely in proportion to how they affect his class. The suspicion about those who would destroy the environment, then, is that what they count important is too narrowly confined insofar as it encompasses only what affects beings who, like us, are capable of feeling.

This idea that proper humility requires recognition of the importance of nonsentient nature is similar to the thought of those who charge meat eaters with "speciesism." In both cases it is felt that people too narrowly confine their concerns to the sorts of beings that are most like them. But, however intuitively appealing, the idea will surely arouse objections from our nonenvironmentalist critic. "Why," he will ask, "do you suppose that the sort of humility I *should* have requires me to acknowledge the importance of nonsentient nature aside from its utility? You cannot, by your own admission, argue that nonsentient nature *is* important, appealing to religious or intuitionist grounds. And simply to assert, without further argument, that an ideal humility requires us to view nonsentient nature as important for its own sake begs the question at issue. If proper humility is acknowledging the relative importance of things as one should, then to show that I must lack this you must first establish that one *should* acknowledge the importance of nonsentient nature."

Though some may wish to accept this challenge, there are other ways to pursue the connection between humility and response to nonsentient nature. For example, suppose we grant that proper humility requires only acknowledging a due status to sentient beings. We must admit, then, that it is logically possible for a person to be properly humble even though he viewed all nonsentient nature simply as a resource. But this logical possibility may be a psychological rarity.

It may be that, given the sort of beings we are, we would never learn humility before persons without developing the general capacity to cherish, and regard important, many things for their own sakes. The major obstacle to humility before persons is self-importance, a tendency to measure the significance of everything by its relation to oneself and those with whom one identifies. The processes by which we overcome self-importance are doubtless many and complex, but it seems unlikely that they are exclusively concerned with how we relate to other people and animals. Learning humility requires learning to feel that something matters besides what will affect oneself and one's circle of associates. What leads a child to care about what happens to a lost hamster or a stray dog he will not see again is likely also to generate concern for a lost toy or a favorite tree where he used to live. Learning to value things for their own sake, and to count what affects them important aside from their utility, is not the same as judging them to have some intuited objective property, but it is necessary to the development of humility and it seems likely to take place in experiences with nonsentient nature as well as with people and animals. If a person views all nonsentient nature merely as a resource, then it seems unlikely that he has developed the capacity needed to overcome self-importance.

IV

This last argument, unfortunately, has its limits. It presupposes an empirical connection between experiencing nature and overcoming self-importance, and this may be challenged. Even if experiencing nature promotes humility before others, there may be other ways people can develop such humility in a world of concrete, glass, and plastic. If not, perhaps all that is needed is limited experience of nature in one's early, developing years; mature adults, having overcome youthful self-importance, may live well enough in artificial surroundings. More importantly, the argument does not fully capture the spirit of the intuition that an ideal person stands humbly before nature. That idea is not simply that experiencing nature tends to foster proper humility before other people; it is, in part, that natural surroundings encourage and are appropriate to an ideal sense of oneself as part of the natural world. Standing alone in the forest, after months in the city, is not merely good as a means of curbing one's arrogance before others; it reinforces and fittingly expresses one's acceptance of oneself as a natural being.

Previously we considered only one aspect of proper humility, namely, a sense of one's relative importance with respect to other human beings. Another aspect, I think, is a kind of *self-acceptance*. This involves acknowledging, in more than a merely intellectual way, that we are the sort of creatures that we are. Whether one is self-accepting is not so much a matter of how one attributes *importance* comparatively to oneself, other people, animals, plants, and other things as it is a matter of understanding, facing squarely, and responding appropriately to who and what one is, e.g., one's powers and limits, one's affinities with other beings and differences from them, one's unalterable nature and one's freedom to change. Self-acceptance is not merely intellectual awareness, for one can be intellectually aware that one is growing old and will eventually die while nevertheless behaving in a thousand foolish ways that reflect a refusal to acknowledge these facts. On the other hand, self-acceptance is not passive resignation, for refusal to pursue what one truly wants within one's limits is a failure to accept the freedom and power one has. Particular behaviors, like dyeing one's gray hair and dressing like those 20 years younger, do not *necessarily* imply lack of self-acceptance, for there could be reasons for acting in these ways other than the wish to hide from oneself what one really is. One fails to accept oneself when the patterns of behavior and emotion are rooted in a desire to disown and deny features of oneself, to pretend to oneself that they are not there. This is not to say that a self-accepting

person makes no value judgments about himself, that he likes all facts about himself, wants equally to develop and display them; he can, and should feel remorse for his past misdeeds and strive to change his current vices. The point is that he does not disown them, pretend that they do not exist or are facts about something other than himself. Such pretense is incompatible with proper humility because it is seeing oneself as better than one is.

Self-acceptance of this sort has long been considered a human excellence, under various names, but what has it to do with preserving nature? There is, I think, the following connection. As human beings we are part of nature, living, growing, declining, and dying by natural laws similar to those governing other living beings; despite our awesomely distinctive human powers, we share many of the needs, limits, and liabilities of animals and plants. These facts are neither good nor bad in themselves, aside from personal preference and varying conventional values. To say this is to utter a truism which few will deny, but to accept these facts, as facts about oneself, is not so easy—or so common. Much of what naturalists deplore about our increasingly artificial world reflects, and encourages, a denial of these facts, an unwillingness to avow them with equanimity.

Like the Victorian lady who refuses to look at her own nude body, some would like to create a world of less transitory stuff, reminding us only of our intellectual and social nature, never calling to mind our affinities with "lower" living creatures. The "denial of death," to which psychiatrists call attention, reveals an attitude incompatible with the sort of self-acceptance which philosophers, from the ancients to Spinoza and on, have admired as a human excellence. My suggestion is not merely that experiencing nature causally promotes such self-acceptance, but also that those who fully accept themselves as part of the natural world lack the common drive to disassociate themselves from nature by replacing natural environments with artificial ones. A storm in the wilds helps us to appreciate our animal vulnerability, but, equally important, the reluctance to experience it may *reflect* an unwillingness to accept this aspect of ourselves. The person who is too ready to destroy the ancient redwoods may lack humility, not so much in the sense that he exaggerates his importance relative to others, but rather in the sense that he tries to avoid seeing himself as one among many natural creatures. . . .

NOTES

I thank Gregory Kavka, Catherine Harlow, the participants at a colloquium at the University of Utah, and the referees for *Environmental Ethics,* Dale Jamieson and Donald Scherer, for helpful comments on earlier drafts of this paper.

1. When I use the expression "the natural environment," I have in mind the sort of examples with which I began. There is also a broad sense, as Hume and Mill noted, in which all that occurs, miracles aside, is "natural." As will be evident, I shall use "natural" in a narrower, more familiar sense.

2. T. Tildon, "Even This Shall Pass Away," in *The Best Loved Poems of the American People,* ed. Hazel Felleman (Garden City, New York: Doubleday, 1936).

3. An exception, apparently, was Kant, who thought "the starry heavens" sublime and compared them with "the moral law within," but did not for all that see our species as comparatively insignificant.

4. By "proper humility" I mean that sort and degree of humility that is a morally admirable character trait. How precisely to define this is, of course, a controversial matter; but the point for present purposes is just to set aside obsequiousness, false modesty, underestimation of one's abilities, and the like.

READING QUESTIONS

1. What is Hill's "strategy," mentioned in section II, for addressing cases that involve problematic treatment of the environment?
2. Why does Hill think that pointing to the shortsightedness or lack of proper concern with other people and animals does not really help explain what is morally problematic about the person who would cover his garden with asphalt, strip mine a wooded mountain, or level an irreplaceable redwood grove?
3. How does Hill understand the attitude of humility? What role does proper humility play in the case Hill makes for acknowledging the importance of nonsentient nature? How, according to Hill, does one learn to become humble?
4. Another theme in Hill's essay is the importance of self-acceptance. What does Hill mean by self-acceptance? How does he connect self-acceptance with preserving nature?

DISCUSSION QUESTIONS

1. Should we agree with Hill that considerations of self-acceptance are important in thinking about how we ought to treat the environment?
2. How might a utilitarian respond to Hill's appeals to humility and self-acceptance in explaining what is wrong with the person who would pave over his front yard in asphalt? Can a utilitarian appeal to these same sorts of considerations (humility and self-acceptance) in explaining on utilitarian grounds what is wrong with the person who paves over his garden? If so, would there be any significant difference between the views of Hill and the utilitarian with regard to how they would explain what is morally problematic about destroying (within one's rights) some part of the environment?

Stephen M. Gardiner

A Perfect Moral Storm: Climate Change, Intergenerational Ethics, and the Problem of Moral Corruption

According to Stephen M. Gardiner's analysis, climate change involves the convergence of three independently harmful factors: global, intergenerational, and theoretical. As he explains, the convergence of three make the ethical issues of climate change particularly challenging—"a perfect moral storm."

The most authoritative scientific report on climate change begins by saying:

> Natural, technical, and social sciences can provide essential information and evidence needed for decisions on what constitutes "dangerous anthropogenic interference with the climate system." At the same time, *such decisions are value judgments.*[1] . . . .

There are good grounds for this statement. Climate change is a complex problem raising issues across and between a large number of disciplines, including the physical and life sciences, political science, economics and psychology, to name just a few. But without wishing for a moment to marginalise the contributions of these disciplines, ethics does seem to play a fundamental role.

Why so? At the most general level, the reason is that we cannot get very far in discussing why climate change is a problem without invoking ethical considerations. If we do not think that our own actions are open to moral assessment, or that various interests (our own, those of our kin and country, those of distant people, future people, animals and nature) matter, then it is hard to see why climate change (or much

else) poses a problem. But once we see this, then we appear to need some account of moral responsibility, morally important interests and what to do about both. And this puts us squarely in the domain of ethics.

At a more practical level, ethical questions are fundamental to the main policy decisions that must be made, such as where to set a global ceiling for greenhouse gas emissions, and how to distribute the emissions allowed by such a ceiling. For example, where the global ceiling is set depends on how the interests of the current generation are weighed against those of future generations; and how emissions are distributed under the global gap depends in part on various beliefs about the appropriate role of energy consumption in people's lives, the importance of historical responsibility for the problem, and the current needs and future aspirations of particular societies.

The relevance of ethics to substantive climate policy thus seems clear. But this is not the topic that I wish to take up here.[2] Instead, I want to discuss a further, and to some extent more basic, way in which ethical reflection sheds light on our present predicament. This has nothing much to do with the substance

From *Environmental Ethics* 15 (2206): 397–413. Notes have been renumbered and edited.

of a defensible climate regime; instead, it concerns the process of making climate policy.

My thesis is this. The peculiar features of the climate change problem pose substantial obstacles to our ability to make the hard choices necessary to address it. Climate change is a perfect moral storm. One consequence of this is that, even if the difficult ethical questions could be answered, we might still find it difficult to act. For the storm makes us extremely vulnerable to moral corruption.

Let us say that a perfect storm is an event constituted by an unusual convergence of independently harmful factors where this convergence is likely to result in substantial, and possibly catastrophic, negative outcomes. The term "the perfect storm" seems to have become prominent in popular culture through Sebastian Junger's book of that name and the associated Hollywood film.[3] Junger's tale is based on the true story of the *Andrea Gail*, a fishing vessel caught at sea during a convergence of three particularly bad storms. The sense of the analogy is then that climate change appears to be a perfect moral storm because it involves the convergence of a number of factors that threaten our ability to behave ethically.

As climate change is a complex phenomenon, I cannot hope to identify all of the ways in which its features cause problems for ethical behaviour. Instead, I will identify three especially salient problems—analogous to the three storms that hit the *Andrea Gail*—that converge in the climate change case. These three "storms" arise in the global, intergenerational and theoretical dimensions, and I will argue that their interaction helps to exacerbate and obscure a lurking problem of moral corruption that may be of greater practical importance than any of them.

I. THE GLOBAL STORM

The first two storms arise out of three important characteristics of the climate change problem. I label these characteristics:

• Dispersion of Causes and Effects
• Fragmentation of Agency
• Institutional Inadequacy

Since these characteristics manifest themselves in two especially salient dimensions—the spatial and the temporal—it is useful to distinguish two distinct but mutually, reinforcing components of the climate change problem. I shall call the first "the Global Storm." This corresponds to the dominant understanding of the climate change problem; and it emerges from a predominantly spatial interpretation of the three characteristics.

Let us begin with the Dispersion of Causes and Effects. Climate change is a truly global phenomenon. Emissions of greenhouse gases from any geographical location on the Earth's surface travel to the upper atmosphere and then play a role in affecting climate globally. Hence, the impact of any particular emission of greenhouse gases is not realised solely at its source, either individual or geographical; rather impacts are dispersed to other actors and regions of the Earth. Such spatial dispersion has been widely discussed.

The second characteristic is the Fragmentation of Agency. Climate change is not caused by a single agent, but by a vast number of individuals and institutions not unified by a comprehensive structure of agency. This is important because it poses a challenge to humanity's ability to respond.

In the spatial dimension, this feature is usually understood as arising out of the shape of the current international system, as constituted by states. Then the problem is that, given that there is not only no world government but also no less centralised system of global governance (or at least no effective one), it is very difficult to coordinate an effective response to global climate change.

This general argument is generally given more bite through the invocation of a certain familiar theoretical model. For the international situation is usually understood in game theoretic terms as a Prisoner's Dilemma, or what Garrett Hardin calls a "Tragedy of the Commons."[4] For the sake of ease of exposition, let us describe the Prisoner's Dilemma scenario in terms of a paradigm case, that of overpollution. Suppose that a number of distinct agents are trying to decide whether or not to engage in a polluting activity, and that their situation is characterised by the following two claims:

(PDl) It is *collectively rational* to cooperate and restrict overall pollution: each agent prefers the outcome produced by everyone restricting their individual pollution over the outcome produced by no one doing so.

(PD2) It is *individually rational* not to restrict one's own pollution: when each agent has the power to decide whether or not she will restrict her pollution, each (rationally) prefers not to do so, whatever the others do.

Agents in such a situation find themselves in a paradoxical position. On the one hand, given (PDl), they understand that it would be better for everyone if every agent cooperated; but, on the other hand, given (PD2), they also know that they should all choose to defect. This is paradoxical because it implies that if individual agents act rationally in terms of their own interests, then they collectively undermine those interests.

A Tragedy of the Commons is essentially a Prisoner's Dilemma involving a common resource. This has become the standard analytical model for understanding regional and global environmental problems in general, and climate change is no exception. Typically, the reasoning goes as follows. Imagine climate change as an international problem and conceive of the relevant parties as individual countries, who represent the interests of their citizens in perpetuity. Then, (PD1) and (PD2) appear to hold. On the one hand, no one wants serious climate change. Hence, each country prefers the outcome produced by everyone restricting their individual emissions over the outcome produced by no one doing so, and so it is collectively rational to cooperate and restrict global emissions. But, on the other hand, each country prefers to free ride on the actions of others. Hence, when each country has the power to decide whether or not she will restrict her emissions, each prefers not to do so, whatever the others do.

From this perspective, it appears that climate change is a normal tragedy of the commons. Still, there is a sense in which this turns out to be encouraging news; for, in the real world, commons problems are often resolvable under certain circumstances, and climate change seems to fill these desiderata. In particular, it is widely said that parties facing a commons problem can resolve it if they benefit from a wider context of interaction; and this appears to be the case with climate change, since countries interact with each other on a number of broader issues, such as trade and security.

This brings us to the third characteristic of the climate change problem, institutional inadequacy. There is wide agreement that the appropriate means for resolving commons problems under the favourable conditions just mentioned is for the parties to agree to change the existing incentive structure through the introduction of a system of enforceable sanctions. (Hardin calls this "mutual coercion, mutually agreed upon"). This transforms the decision situation by foreclosing the option of free riding, so that the collectively rational action also becomes individually rational. Theoretically, then, matters seem simple; but in practice things are different. For the need for enforceable sanctions poses a challenge at the global level because of the limits of our current, largely national, institutions and the lack of an effective system of global governance. In essence, addressing climate change appears to require global regulation of greenhouse gas emissions, where this includes establishing a reliable enforcement mechanism; but the current global system—or lack of it— makes this difficult, if not impossible.

The implication of this familiar analysis, then, is that the main thing that is needed to solve the global warming problem is an effective system of global governance (at least for this issue). And there is a sense in which this is still good news. For, in principle at least, it should be possible to motivate countries to establish such a regime, since they ought to recognise that it is in their best interests to eliminate the possibility of free riding and so make genuine cooperation the rational strategy at the individual as well as collective level.

Unfortunately, however, this is not the end of the story. For there are other features of the climate change case that make the necessary global agreement more difficult, and so exacerbate the basic Global Storm.[5] Prominent amongst these is scientific uncertainty about the precise magnitude and distribution of effects, particularly at the national level. One reason for this is that the lack of trustworthy data about the costs and benefits of climate change at the national level casts doubt on the truth of (PDl). Perhaps, some nations wonder, we might be better off with climate change than without it. More importantly, some countries might wonder whether they will at least be relatively better off than other countries, and so might get away with paying less to avoid the associated costs.[6] Such factors complicate the game theoretic situation, and so make agreement more difficult.

In other contexts, the problem of scientific uncertainty might not be so serious. But a second characteristic of the climate change problem exacerbates matters in this setting. The source of climate change is located deep in the infrastructure of current human civilisations; hence, attempts to combat it may have substantial ramifications for human social life. Climate change is caused by human emissions of greenhouse gases, primarily carbon dioxide. Such emissions are brought about by the burning of fossil fuels for energy. But it is this energy that supports existing economies. Hence, given that halting climate change will require deep cuts in projected global emissions over time, we can expect that such action will have profound effects on the basic economic organisation of the developed countries and on the aspirations of the developing countries.

This has several salient implications. First, it suggests that those with vested interests in the continuation of the current system—e.g., many of those with substantial political and economic power—will resist such action. Second, unless ready substitutes are found, real mitigation can be expected to have profound impacts on how humans live and how human societies evolve. Hence, action on climate change is likely to raise serious, and perhaps uncomfortable, questions about who we are and what we want to be. Third, this suggests a *status quo* bias in the face of uncertainty. Contemplating change is often uncomfortable; contemplating basic change may be unnerving, even distressing. Since the social ramifications of action appear to be large, perspicuous and concrete, but those of inaction appear uncertain, elusive and indeterminate, it is easy to see why uncertainty might exacerbate social inertia.

The third feature of the climate change problem that exacerbates the basic Global Storm is that of skewed vulnerabilities. The climate change problem interacts in some unfortunate ways with the present global power structure. For one thing, the responsibility for historical and current emissions lies predominantly with the richer, more powerful nations, and the poor nations are badly situated to hold them accountable. For another, the limited evidence on regional impacts suggests that it is the poorer nations that are most vulnerable to the worst impacts of climate change.[7] Finally, action on climate change creates a moral risk for the developed nations. It embodies a recognition that there are international norms of ethics and responsibility, and reinforces the idea that international cooperation on issues involving such norms is both possible and necessary. Hence, it may encourage attention to other moral defects of the current global system, such as global poverty, human rights violations and so on.

II. THE INTERGENERATIONAL STORM

We can now return to the three characteristics of the climate change problem identified earlier:

- Dispersion of Causes and Effects
- Fragmentation of Agency
- Institutional Inadequacy

The Global Storm emerges from a spatial reading of these characteristics; but I would argue that another, even more serious problem arises when we see them from a temporal perspective. I shall call this "the Intergenerational Storm."

Consider first the Dispersion of Causes and Effects. Human-induced climate change is a severely lagged phenomenon. This is partly because some of the basic mechanisms set in motion by the greenhouse effect—such as sea level rise—take a very long time to be fully realised. But it also because by far the most important greenhouse gas emitted by human beings is carbon dioxide, and once emitted molecules of carbon dioxide can spend a surprisingly long time in the upper atmosphere.[8]

Let us dwell for a moment on this second factor. The IPCC says that the average time spent by a molecule of carbon dioxide in the upper atmosphere is in the region of 5–200 years. This estimate is long enough to create a serious lagging effect; nevertheless, it obscures the fact that a significant percentage of carbon dioxide molecules remain in the atmosphere for much longer periods of time, of the order of thousands and tens of thousands of years. . . .

The fact that carbon dioxide is a long-lived greenhouse gas has at least three important implications. The first is that climate change is a *resilient* phenomenon. Given that currently it does not seem practical to remove large quantities of carbon dioxide from the upper atmosphere, or to moderate its climatic effects, the upward trend in atmospheric concentration is not easily reversible. Hence, a goal of stabilising and then reducing carbon dioxide concentrations requires advance planning. Second, climate change impacts are *seriously backloaded*. The climate change that the earth is currently experiencing is primarily the result of emissions from some time in the past, rather than current emissions. As an illustration, it is widely accepted that by 2000 we had already committed ourselves to a rise of at least 0.5 and perhaps more than 1 degree Celsius over the then-observed rise of 0.6°C.[9] Third, backloading implies that the full, cumulative effects of our current emissions will not be realised for some time in the future. So, climate change is a *substantially deferred* phenomenon.

Temporal dispersion creates a number of problems. First, as is widely noted, the resilience of climate change implies that delays in action have serious repercussions for our ability to manage the problem. Second, backloading implies that climate change poses serious epistemic difficulties, especially for normal political actors. For one thing, backloading makes it hard to grasp the connection between causes and effects, and this may undermine the motivation to act, for another, it implies that by the time we realise that things are bad, we will already be committed to much more change, so it undermines the ability to respond. Third, the deferral effect calls into question the ability of standard institutions to deal with the problem. For one thing, democratic political institutions have relatively short time horizons—the next election cycle, a politician's political career—and it is doubtful whether such institutions have the wherewithal to deal with substantially deferred impacts. Even more seriously, substantial deferral is likely to undermine the will to act. This is because there is an incentive problem: the bad effects of current emissions are likely to fall, or fall disproportionately, on future generations, whereas the benefits of emissions accrue largely to the present.

These last two points already raise the spectre of institutional inadequacy. But to appreciate this problem fully, we must first say something about the temporal fragmentation of agency. There is some reason to think that this might be worse than the spatial fragmentation even considered in isolation. For there is a sense in which temporal fragmentation is more intractable than spatial fragmentation: in principle, spatially fragmented agents may actually become unified and so able really to act as a single agent; but temporally fragmented agents cannot actually become unified, and so may at best only act *as if* they were a single agent.

Interesting as such questions are, they need not detain us here. For temporal fragmentation in the context of the kind of temporal dispersion that characterises climate change is clearly much worse than the associated spatial fragmentation. For the presence of backloading and deferral together brings on a new collective action problem that adds to the tragedy of the commons caused by the Global Storm, and thereby makes matters much worse.

The problem emerges when one relaxes the assumption that countries can be relied upon adequately to represent the interests of both their present and future citizens. Suppose that this is not true. Suppose instead that countries are biased towards the interests of the current generation. Then, since the benefits of carbon dioxide emission are felt primarily by the present generation, in the form of cheap energy, whereas the costs—in the form of the risk of severe and perhaps catastrophic climate change—are substantially deferred to future generations, climate change might provide an instance of a severe intergenerational collective action problem. Moreover, this problem will be iterated. Each new generation will face the same incentive structure as soon as it gains the power to decide whether or not to act.[10]

The nature of the intergenerational problem is easiest to see if we compare it to the traditional Prisoner's Dilemma. Suppose we consider a pure version of the intergenerational problem, where the generations do not overlap.[11] (Call this the "Pure Intergenerational Problem" (PIP).) In that case, the problem can be (roughly) characterised as follows[12]:

> (PIP 1) It is *collectively rational* for most generations to cooperate: (almost) every generation prefers the outcome produced by everyone restricting pollution over the outcome produced by everyone overpolluting.
>
> (PIP2) It is *individually rational* for all generations not to cooperate: when each generation has the power to decide whether or not it will overpollute, each generation (rationally) prefers to overpollute, whatever the others do.

Now, the PIP is worse than the Prisoner's Dilemma in two main respects. The first respect is that its two constituent claims are worse. On the one hand, (PIP1) is worse than (PD1) because the first generation is not included. This means not only that one generation is not motivated to accept the collectively rational outcome, but also that the problem becomes iterated. Since subsequent generations have no reason to comply if their predecessors do not, noncompliance by the first generation has a domino effect that undermines the collective project. On the other hand, (PIP2) is worse than (PD2) because the reason for it is deeper. Both of these claims hold because the parties lack access to mechanisms (such as enforceable sanctions) that would make defection irrational. But whereas in normal Prisoner's Dilemma-type cases, this obstacle is largely practical, and can be resolved by creating appropriate institutions, in the PIP it arises because the parties do not coexist, and so seem unable to influence each other's behaviour through the creation of appropriate coercive institutions.

This problem of interaction produces the second respect in which the PIP is worse than the Prisoner's Dilemma. This is that the PIP is more difficult to resolve, because the standard solutions to the Prisoner's Dilemma are unavailable: one cannot appeal to a wider context of mutually-beneficial interaction, nor to the usual notions of reciprocity.

The upshot of all this is that in the case of climate change, the intergenerational analysis will be less optimistic about solutions than the tragedy of the commons analysis. For it implies that current populations may not be motivated to establish a fully adequate global regime, since, given the temporal dispersion of effects—and especially backloading and deferral– such a regime is probably not in *their* interests. This is a large moral problem, especially since in my view the intergenerational problem dominates the tragedy of the commons aspect in climate change. . . .

III. THE THEORETICAL STORM

The final storm I want to mention is constituted by our current theoretical ineptitude. We are extremely ill-equipped to deal with many problems characteristic of the long-term future. Even our best theories face basic and often severe difficulties addressing basic issues such as scientific uncertainty, intergenerational equity, contingent persons, nonhuman animals and nature. But climate change involves all of these matters and more.

Now I do not want to discuss any of these difficulties in any detail here. Instead, I want to close by gesturing at how, when they converge with each other and with the Global and Intergenerational Storms, they encourage a new and distinct problem for ethical action on climate change, the problem of moral corruption.

IV. MORAL CORRUPTION

Corruption of the kind I have in mind can be facilitated in a number of ways. Consider the following examples of possible strategies:
- Distraction
- Complacency
- Unreasonable Doubt
- Selective Attention
- Delusion
- Pandering
- False Witness
- Hypocrisy

Now, the mere listing of these strategies is probably enough to make the main point here; and I suspect that close observers of the political debate about climate change will recognise many of these mechanisms as being in play. Still, I would like to pause for a moment to draw particular attention to selective attention.

The problem is this. Since climate change involves a complex convergence of problems, it is easy to engage in *manipulative or self-deceptive* behaviour by applying one's attention selectively, to only some of the considerations that make the situation difficult. At the level of practical politics, such strategies are all too familiar. For example, many political actors emphasise considerations that appear to make inaction excusable, or even desirable (such as uncertainty or simple economic calculations with high discount rates) and action more difficult and contentious (such as the basic lifestyles issue) at the expense of those that seem to impose a clearer and more immediate burden (such as scientific consensus and the Pure Intergenerational Problem).

But selective attention strategies may also manifest themselves more generally. And this prompts a very unpleasant thought: perhaps there is a problem of corruption in the theoretical, as well as the practical, debate. For example, it is possible that the prominence of the Global Storm model is not independent of the existence of the Intergenerational Storm, but rather is encouraged by it. After all, the current generation may find it highly advantageous to focus on the Global Storm. For one thing, such a focus tends to draw attention toward various issues of global politics and scientific uncertainty that seem to problematise action, and away from issues of intergenerational ethics, which tend to demand it. Thus, an emphasis on the Global Storm at the expense of the other problems may *facilitate* a strategy of procrastination and delay. For another, since it presumes that the relevant actors are nation-states who represent the interests of their citizens in perpetuity, the Global Storm analysis has the effect of assuming away the intergenerational aspect of the climate change problem. Thus, an undue emphasis on it may obscure much of what is at stake in making climate policy, and in a way that may benefit present people.

In conclusion, the presence of the problem of moral corruption reveals another sense in which climate change may be a *perfect* moral storm. This is that its complexity may turn out to be *perfectly convenient* for us, the current generation, and indeed for each successor generation as it comes to occupy our position. For one thing, it provides each generation with the cover under which it can seem to be taking the issue seriously—by negotiating weak and largely substanceless global accords, for example, and then heralding them as great achievement—when really it is simply exploiting its temporal position. For another, all of this can occur without the exploitative generation actually having to acknowledge that this is what it is doing. By avoiding overtly selfish behaviour, earlier generations can take advantage of the future without the unpleasantness of admitting it—either to others, or, perhaps more importantly, to itself.[13]

NOTES

1. Intergovernmental Panel on Climate Change (IPCC) 2001a, p. 2; emphasis added.

2. For more on such issues, see Gardiner 2004b.

3. Junger 1999.

4. Hardin 1968. I discuss this in more detail in previous work, especially Gardiner 2001.

5. There is one fortunate convergence. Several writers have emphasised that the major ethical arguments all point in the same direction: that the developed countries should bear most of the costs of the transition—including those accruing to developing countries—at least in the early stages of mitigation and adaptation. See, for example, Singer 2002 and Shue 1999.

6. This consideration appears to play a role in U.S. deliberation about climate change, where it is often asserted that the U.S. faces lower marginal costs from climate change than other countries. See, for example, Mendelsohn 2001; Nitze 1994; and, by contrast, National Assessment Synthesis Team 2000.

7. This is so both because a greater proportion of their economies are in climate-sensitive sectors, and because—being poor—they are worse placed to deal with those impacts. See IPCC 2001b, 8, 16.

8. For more on both claims, see IPCC 2001a, 16–7.

9. Wigley 2005; Meehl et al. 2005; Wetherald et al., 2001.

10. Elsewhere, I have argued that it is this background fact that most readily explains the weakness of the Kyoto deal. See Gardiner 2004a.

11. Generational overlap complicates the picture in some ways, but I do not think that it resolves the basic problem. See Gardiner 2003.

12. These matters are discussed in more detail in Gardiner 2003, from which the following description is drawn.

13. This paper was originally written for presentation to an interdisciplinary workshop on *Values in Nature* at Princeton University. I thank the Center for Human Values at Princeton and the University of Washington for research support in the form of a Laurance S. Rockefeller fellowship. I also thank audiences at Iowa State University, Lewis and Clark College, the University of Washington, the Western Political Science Association and the Pacific Division of the American Philosophical Association. For comments, I am particularly grateful to Chrisoula Andreou, Kristen Hessler, Jay Odenbaugh, John Meyer, Darrel Moellendorf, Peter Singer, Harlan Wilson, Clark Wolf and an anonymous reviewer for this journal. I am especially indebted to Dale Jamieson.

REFERENCES

Gardiner, Stephen M. 2001. "The Real Tragedy of the Commons." *Philosophy and Public Affairs* **30**: 387–416.

Gardiner, Stephen M. 2003. "The Pure Intergenerational Problem." *Monist* **86**: 481–500.

Gardiner, Stephen M. 2004a. "The Global Warming Tragedy and the Dangerous Illusion of the Kyoto Protocol." *Ethics and International Affairs* **18**: 23–39.

Gardiner, Stephen M. 2004b. "Ethics and Global Climate Change." *Ethics* **114**: 555-600.

Hardin, Garrett. 1968. "Tragedy of the Commons." *Science* **162**: 1243–8.

Intergovernmental Panel on Climate Change (IPCC). 2001 a. *Climate Change 2001: Synthesis Report.* Cambridge: Cambridge University Press. Available at <www.ipcc.ch>.

Intergovernmental Panel on Climate Change (IPCC). 2001b. Summary for Policymakers. *Climate Change 2001: Impacts, Adaptation, and Vulnerability.* Cambridge: Cambridge University Press. Available at <www.ipcc.ch>.

Junger, Sebastian. 1999. *A Perfect Storm: A True Story of Men Against the Sea.* Harper.

Meehl, Gerald, Washington, Warren M., Collins, William D., Arblaster, Julie M., Hu, Aixue, Buja, Lawrence E., Strand, Warren G. and Teng, Haiyan. 2005. "How Much More Global Warming and Sea Level Rise?" *Science* **307**: 1769–72.

Mendelsohn, Robert O. 2001. *Global Warming and the American Economy.* London: Edward Elgar.

Nitze W.A. 1994. "A Failure of Presidential Leadership." In Irving Mintzer and J. Amber Leonard, *Negotiating Climate Change: The Inside Story of the Rio Convention.* Cambridge: Cambridge University Press: 189–90.

National Assessment Synthesis Team. 2000. *Climate Change Impacts on the United States: The Potential Consequences of Climate Variability and Change.* Cambridge: Cambridge University Press, 2000. Available at <www.usgcrp.gov/usgcrp/nacc/default.htm>.

Shue, Henry. 1999. "Global Environment and International Inequality." *International Affairs* **75**: 531–45

Singer, Peter. 2002. "One Atmosphere." In Peter Singer, *One World*: *The Ethics of Globalization.* New Haven, CT: Yale University Press: chapter 2.

Wetherald, Richard T., Stouffer, Ronald J. and Dixon, Keith W. 2001. "Committed Warming and Its Implications for Climate Change." *Geophysical Research Letters*, Vol. 28, No. 8, 1535–8, at 1535, April 15.

Wigley, T.M.L. 2005. "The Climate Change Commitment." *Science* **307**: 1766–9.

READING QUESTIONS

1. How does Gardiner make use of the game theoretic Prisoner's Dilemma to explain the "Global Storm"?
2. Why does Gardiner think that temporal considerations associated with the "Intergenerational Storm" are more problematic than the spatial considerations characteristic of the "Global Storm"?
3. What are the factors that contribute to what Gardiner calls the moral problem of corruption?

DISCUSSION QUESTION

1. In his 2011 book, *A Perfect Moral Storm: The Ethical Tragedy of Climate Change*, Gardiner writes that with respect to moral corruption, he is primarily concerned with "corruption that targets our ways of talking and thinking, and so prevents us from even seeing the problem in the right way" (301). He goes on to say, "my primary subject is the public discourse around climate change and the need to protect it against this threat. Hence, I say 'our main interest in moral corruption is really with how to fight it, not who to blame for it,' given that 'we are the ones vulnerable' to such distortion" (308). Focusing, then, on how to fight such ways of talking and thinking, how might this problem be addressed?

WALTER SINNOTT-ARMSTRONG

It's Not *My* Fault: Global Warming and Individual Moral Obligations

Walter Sinnott-Armstrong addresses the question: Given the enormity of the problem of global warming, what moral obligations does an *individual* (living in relative affluence) have in light of all this? To focus his question, he considers whether it is morally wrong for him to take a Sunday drive in a gas-guzzling car just for fun. In answering this question, Sinnott-Armstrong appeals to a wide range of moral principles, including principles familiar from consequentialist, natural law (double effect), Kantian, virtue ethics, and social contract traditions. He argues that applying the various principles does not imply that he (or similarly situated individuals) has a *moral obligation* to refrain from taking the Sunday drive. He admits, however, that it is still "morally better or ideal" for individuals not to engage in such activities. Governments, however, do have a moral obligation to address the problem of global warming partly because only they are in a position to help fix the problem.

Recommended Reading: consequentialism, natural law theory, Kantian moral theory, virtue ethics, and social contract theory chap. 1, secs. 2A, 2B, 2C, 2E, and 2G.

Previous chapters in *Perspectives on Climate Change* have focused on scientific research, economic projections, and government policies. However, even if scientists establish that global warming is occurring, even if economists confirm that its costs will be staggering, and even if political theorists agree that governments must do something about it, it is still not clear what moral obligations regarding global warming devolve upon individuals like you and me. That is the question to be addressed in this essay.

1. ASSUMPTIONS

To make the issue stark, let us begin with a few assumptions. I believe that these assumptions are probably roughly accurate, but none is certain, and I will not try to justify them here. Instead, I will simply take them for granted for the sake of argument.[1]

First, global warming has begun and is likely to increase over the next century. We cannot be sure exactly how much or how fast, but hot times are coming.[2]

Second, a significant amount of global warming is due to human activities. The main culprit is fossil fuels.

Third, global warming will create serious problems for many people over the long term by causing climate changes, including violent storms, floods from sea level rises, droughts, heat waves, and so on. Millions of people will probably be displaced or die.

Fourth, the poor will be hurt most of all. The rich countries are causing most of the global warming, but they will be able to adapt to climate changes more easily.[3] Poor countries that are close to sea level might be devastated.

Fifth, governments, especially the biggest and richest ones, are able to mitigate global warming.[4] They can impose limits on emissions. They can require or give incentives for increased energy efficiency. They can stop deforestation and fund reforestation. They can develop ways to sequester carbon dioxide in oceans or underground. These steps will help, but the only long-run solution lies in alternatives to fossil fuels. These alternatives can be found soon if governments start massive research projects now.[5]

Sixth, it is too late to stop global warming. Because there is so much carbon dioxide in the atmosphere already, because carbon dioxide remains in the atmosphere for so long, and because we will remain dependent on fossil fuels in the near future, governments can slow down global warming or reduce its severity, but they cannot prevent it. Hence, governments need to adapt. They need to build seawalls. They need to reinforce houses that cannot withstand storms. They need to move populations from low-lying areas.[6]

Seventh, these steps will be costly. Increased energy efficiency can reduce expenses, adaptation will create some jobs, and money will be made in the research and production of alternatives to fossil fuels. Still, any steps that mitigate or adapt to global warming will slow down our economies, at least in the short run.[7] That will hurt many people, especially many poor people.

Eighth, despite these costs, the major governments throughout the world still morally ought to take some of these steps. The clearest moral obligation falls on the United States. The United States caused and continues to cause more of the problem than any other country. The United States can spend more resources on a solution without sacrificing basic necessities. This country has the scientific expertise to solve technical problems. Other countries follow its lead (sometimes!). So the United States has a special moral obligation to help mitigate and adapt to global warming.[8]

2. THE PROBLEM

Even assuming all of this, it is still not clear what I as an individual morally ought to do about global warming. That issue is not as simple as many people assume. I want to bring out some of its complications.

It should be clear from the start that "individual" moral obligations do not always follow directly from "collective" moral obligations. The fact that your government morally ought to do something does not prove that "you" ought to do it, even if your government fails. Suppose that a bridge is dangerous because so much traffic has gone over it and continues to go over it. The government has a moral obligation to make the bridge safe. If the government fails to do its duty, it does not follow that I personally have a moral obligation to fix the bridge. It does not even follow that I have a moral obligation to fill in one crack in the bridge, even if the bridge would be fixed if everyone filled in one crack, even if I drove over the bridge many times, and even if I still drive over it every day. Fixing the bridge is the government's job, not mine. While I ought to encourage the government to fulfill its obligations,[9] I do not have to take on those obligations myself.

All that this shows is that government obligations do not "always" imply parallel individual obligations. Still, maybe "sometimes" they do. My government has a moral obligation to teach arithmetic to the children in my town, including my own children. If the government fails in this obligation, then I do take on a moral obligation to teach arithmetic to my children.[10] Thus, when the government fails in its obligations, sometimes I have to fill in, and sometimes I do not.

What about global warming? If the government fails to do anything about global warming, what am I supposed to do about it? There are lots of ways for me as an individual to fight global warming. I can protest against bad government policies and vote for candidates who will make the government fulfill its moral obligations. I can support private organizations that fight global warming, such as the Pew Foundation,[11] or boycott companies that contribute too much to global warming, such as most oil companies. Each of these cases is interesting, but they all differ. To simplify our discussion, we need to pick one act as our focus.

My example will be wasteful driving. Some people drive to their jobs or to the store because they have no other reasonable way to work and eat. I want to avoid issues about whether these goals justify driving, so I will focus on a case where nothing so important is gained. I will consider driving for fun on a beautiful Sunday afternoon. My drive is not necessary to cure depression or calm aggressive impulses. All that is gained is pleasure: Ah, the feel of wind in your hair! The views! How spectacular! Of course, you could drive a fuel-efficient hybrid car. But fuel-efficient cars have less "get up and go." So let us consider a gas-guzzling sport utility vehicle. Ah, the feeling of power! The excitement! Maybe you do not like to go for drives in sport utility vehicles on sunny Sunday afternoons, but many people do.

Do we have a moral obligation not to drive in such circumstances? This question concerns driving, not "buying" cars. To make this clear, let us assume that I borrow the gas-guzzler from a friend. This question is also not about "legal" obligations. So let us assume that it is perfectly legal to go for such drives. Perhaps it ought to be illegal, but it is not. Note also that my question is not about what would be "best." Maybe it would be better, even morally better, for me not to drive a gas-guzzler just for fun. But that is not the issue I want to address here. My question is whether I have a "moral" obligation not to drive a gas-guzzler just for fun on this particular sunny Sunday afternoon.

One final complication must be removed. I am interested in global warming, but there might be other moral reasons not to drive unnecessarily. I risk causing an accident, since I am not a perfect driver. I also will likely spew exhaust into the breathing space of pedestrians, bicyclists, or animals on the side of the road as I drive by. Perhaps these harms and risks give me a moral obligation not to go for my joyride. That is not clear. After all, these reasons also apply if I drive the most efficient car available, and even if I am driving to work with no other way to keep my job. Indeed, I might scare or injure bystanders even if my car gave off no greenhouse gases or pollution. In any case, I want to focus on global warming. So my real question is whether the facts about global warming give me any moral obligation not to drive a gas-guzzler just for fun on this sunny Sunday afternoon.

I admit that I am "inclined" to answer, "Yes." To me, global warming does "seem" to make such wasteful driving morally wrong.

Still, I do not feel confident in this judgment. I know that other people disagree (even though they are also concerned about the environment). I would probably have different moral intuitions about this case if I had been raised differently or if I now lived in a different culture. My moral intuition might be distorted by overgeneralization from the other cases where I think that other entities (large governments) do have moral obligations to fight global warming. I also worry that my moral intuition might be distorted by my desire to avoid conflicts with my environmentalist friends.[12] The issue of global warming generates strong emotions because of its political implications and because of how scary its effects are. It is also a peculiarly modern case, especially because it operates on a much grander scale than my moral intuitions evolved to handle long ago when acts did not have such long-term effects on future generations (or at least people were not aware of such effects). In such circumstances, I doubt that we are justified in trusting our moral intuitions alone. We need some kind of confirmation.[13]

One way to confirm the truth of my moral intuitions would be to derive them from a general moral principle. A principle could tell us why wasteful driving is morally wrong, so we would not have to depend on bare assertion. And a principle might be supported by more trustworthy moral beliefs. The problem is "which" principle?

3. ACTUAL ACT PRINCIPLES

One plausible principle refers to causing harm. If one person had to inhale all of the exhaust from my car, this would harm him and give me a moral obligation not to drive my car just for fun. Such cases suggest:

The harm principle: We have a moral obligation not to perform an act that causes harm to others.

This principle implies that I have a moral obligation not to drive my gas-guzzler just for fun "if" such driving causes harm.

The problem is that such driving does "not" cause harm in normal cases. If one person were in a position to inhale all of my exhaust, then he would get sick if I did drive, and he would not get sick if I did not drive (under normal circumstances). In contrast, global warming will still occur even if I do not drive just for fun. Moreover, even if I do drive a gas-guzzler just for fun for a long time, global warming will not occur unless lots of other people also expel greenhouse gases. So my individual act is neither necessary nor sufficient for global warming.

There are, admittedly, special circumstances in which an act causes harm without being either necessary or sufficient for that harm. Imagine that it takes three people to push a car off a cliff with a passenger locked inside, and five people are already pushing. If I join and help them push, then my act of pushing is neither necessary nor sufficient to make the car go off the cliff. Nonetheless, my act of pushing is a cause (or part of the cause) of the harm to the passenger. Why? Because I intend to cause harm to the passenger, and because my act is unusual. When I intend a harm to occur, my intention provides a reason to pick my act out of all the other background circumstances and identify it as a cause. Similarly, when my act is unusual in the sense that most people would not act that way, that also provides a reason to pick out my act and call it a cause.

Why does it matter what is usual? Compare matches. For a match to light up, we need to strike it so as to create friction. There also has to be oxygen. We do not call the oxygen the cause of the fire, since oxygen is usually present. Instead, we say that the friction causes the match to light, since it is unusual for that friction to occur. It happens only once in the life of each match. Thus, what is usual affects ascriptions of causation even in purely physical cases.

In moral cases, there are additional reasons not to call something a cause when it is usual. Labeling an act a cause of harm and, on this basis, holding its agent responsible for that harm by blaming the agent or condemning his act is normally counterproductive when that agent is acting no worse than most other people. If people who are doing "no" worse than average are condemned, then people who are doing "much" worse than average will suspect that they will still be subject to condemnation even if they

start doing better, and even if they improve enough to bring themselves up to the average. We should distribute blame (and praise) so as to give incentives for the worst offenders to get better. The most efficient and effective way to do this is to reserve our condemnation for those who are well below average. This means that we should not hold people responsible for harms by calling their acts causes of harms when their acts are not at all unusual, assuming that they did not intend the harm.

The application to global warming should be clear. It is not unusual to go for joyrides. Such drivers do not intend any harm. Hence, we should not see my act of driving on a sunny Sunday afternoon as a cause of global warming or its harms.

Another argument leads to the same conclusion: the harms of global warming result from the massive quantities of greenhouse gases in the atmosphere. Greenhouse gases (such as carbon dioxide and water vapor) are perfectly fine in small quantities. They help plants grow. The problem emerges only when there is too much of them. But my joyride by itself does not cause the massive quantities that are harmful.

Contrast someone who pours cyanide poison into a river. Later someone drinking from the river downstream ingests some molecules of the poison. Those molecules cause the person to get ill and die. This is very different from the causal chain in global warming, because no particular molecules from my car cause global warming in the direct way that particular molecules of the poison do cause the drinker's death. Global warming is more like a river that is going to flood downstream because of torrential rains. I pour a quart of water into the river upstream (maybe just because I do not want to carry it). My act of pouring the quart into the river is not a cause of the flood. Analogously, my act of driving for fun is not a cause of global warming.

Contrast also another large-scale moral problem: famine relief. Some people say that I have no moral obligation to contribute to famine relief because the famine will continue and people will die whether or not I donate my money to a relief agency. However, I could help a certain individual if I gave my donation directly to that individual. In contrast, if I refrain from driving for fun on this one Sunday, there is no individual who will be helped in the least.[14] I cannot help anyone by depriving myself of this joyride.

The point becomes clearer if we distinguish global warming from climate change. You might think that my driving on Sunday raises the temperature of the globe by an infinitesimal amount. I doubt that, but, even if it does, my exhaust on that Sunday does not cause any climate change at all. No storms or floods or droughts or heat waves can be traced to my individual act of driving. It is these climate changes that cause harms to people. Global warming by itself causes no harm without climate change. Hence, since my individual act of driving on that one Sunday does not cause any climate change, it causes no harm to anyone.

The point is not that harms do not occur from global warming. I have already admitted that they do. The point is also not that my exhaust is overkill, like poisoning someone who is already dying from poison. My exhaust is not sufficient for the harms of global warming, and I do not intend those harms. Nor is it the point that the harms from global warming occur much later in time. If I place a time bomb in a building, I can cause harm many years later. And the point is not that the harm I cause is imperceptible. I admit that some harms can be imperceptible because they are too small or for other reasons.[15] Instead, the point is simply that my individual joyride does not cause global warming, climate change, or any of their resulting harms, at least directly.

Admittedly, my acts can lead to other acts by me or by other people. Maybe one case of wasteful driving creates a bad habit that will lead me to do it again and again. Or maybe a lot of other people look up to me and would follow my example of wasteful driving. Or maybe my wasteful driving will undermine my commitment to environmentalism and lead me to stop supporting important green causes or to harm the environment in more serious ways. If so, we could apply:

The indirect harm principle: We have a moral obligation not to perform an act that causes harm to others indirectly by causing someone to carry out acts that cause harm to others.

This principle would explain why it is morally wrong to drive a gas-guzzler just for fun if this act led to other harmful acts.

One problem here is that my acts are not that influential. People like to see themselves as more influential than they really are. On a realistic view, however, it is unlikely that anyone would drive wastefully if I did and would not if I did not. Moreover, wasteful driving is not that habit forming. My act of driving this Sunday does not make me drive next Sunday. I do not get addicted. Driving the next Sunday is a separate decision.[16] And my wasteful driving will not undermine my devotion to environmentalism. If my argument in this chapter is correct, then my belief that the government has a moral obligation to fight global warming is perfectly compatible with a belief that I as an individual have no moral obligation not to drive a gas-guzzler for fun. If I keep this compatibility in mind, then my driving my gas-guzzler for fun will not undermine my devotion to the cause of getting the government to do something about global warming.

Besides, the indirect harm principle is misleading. To see why, consider David. David is no environmentalist. He already has a habit of driving his gas-guzzler for fun on Sundays. Nobody likes him, so nobody follows his example. But David still has a moral obligation not to drive his gas-guzzler just for fun this Sunday, and his obligation has the same basis as mine, if I have one. So my moral obligation cannot depend on the factors cited by the indirect harm principle.

The most important problem for supposed indirect harms is the same as for direct harms: even if I create a bad habit and undermine my personal environmentalism and set a bad example that others follow, all of this would still not be enough to cause climate change if other people stopped expelling greenhouse gases. So, as long as I neither intend harm nor do anything unusual, my act cannot cause climate change even if I do create bad habits and followers. The scale of climate change is just too big for me to cause it, even "with a little help from my friends."

Of course, even if I do not cause climate change, I still might seem to contribute to climate change in the sense that I make it worse. If so, another principle applies:

The contribution principle: We have a moral obligation not to make problems worse.

This principle applies if climate change will be worse if I drive than it will be if I do not drive.

The problem with this argument is that my act of driving does not even make climate change worse. Climate change would be just as bad if I did not drive. The reason is that climate change becomes worse only if more people (and animals) are hurt or if they are hurt worse. There is nothing bad about global warming or climate change in itself if no people (or animals) are harmed. But there is no individual person or animal who will be worse off if I drive than if I do not drive my gas-guzzler just for fun. Global warming and climate change occur on such a massive scale that my individual driving makes no difference to the welfare of anyone.

Some might complain that this is not what they mean by "contribute." All it takes for me to contribute to global warming in their view is for me to expel greenhouse gases into the atmosphere. I do "that" when I drive, so we can apply:

The gas principle: We have a moral obligation not to expel greenhouse gases into the atmosphere.

If this principle were true, it would explain why I have a moral obligation not to drive my gas-guzzler just for fun.

Unfortunately, it is hard to see any reason to accept this principle. There is nothing immoral about greenhouse gases in themselves when they cause no harm. Greenhouse gases include carbon dioxide and water vapor, which occur naturally and help plants grow. The problem of global warming occurs because of the high quantities of greenhouse gases, not because of anything bad about smaller quantities of the same gases. So it is hard to see why I would have a moral obligation not to expel harmless quantities of greenhouse gases. And that is all I do by myself.

Furthermore, if the gas principle were true, it would be unbelievably restrictive. It implies that I have a moral obligation not to boil water (since water vapor is a greenhouse gas) or to exercise (since I expel carbon dioxide when I breathe heavily). When you think it through, an amazing array of seemingly morally acceptable activities would be ruled out by the gas principle. These implications suggest that we had better look elsewhere for a reason why I have a moral obligation not to drive a gas-guzzler just for fun.

Maybe the reason is risk. It is sometimes morally wrong to create a risk of a harm even if that harm does not occur. I grant that drunk driving is immoral, because it risks harm to others, even if the drunk driver gets home safely without hurting anyone. Thus, we get another principle:

The risk principle: We have a moral obligation not to increase the risk of harms to other people.[17]

The problem here is that global warming is not like drunk driving. When drunk driving causes harm, it is easy to identify the victim of this particular drunk driver. There is no way to identify any particular victim of my wasteful driving in normal circumstances.

In addition, my earlier point applies here again. If the risk principle were true, it would be unbelievably restrictive. Exercising and boiling water also expel greenhouse gases, so they also increase the risk of global warming if my driving does. This principle implies that almost everything we do violates a moral obligation.

Defenders of such principles sometimes respond by distinguishing significant from insignificant risks or increases in risks. That distinction is problematic, at least here. A risk is called significant when it is "too" much. But then we need to ask what makes this risk too much when other risks are not too much. The reasons for counting a risk as significant are then the real reasons for thinking that there is a moral obligation not to drive wastefully. So we need to specify those reasons directly instead of hiding them under a waffle-term like "significant."

4. INTERNAL PRINCIPLES

None of the principles discussed so far is both defensible and strong enough to yield a moral obligation not to drive a gas-guzzler just for fun. Maybe we can do better by looking inward.

Kantians claim that the moral status of acts depends on their agents' maxims or "subjective principles of volition"[18]—roughly what we would call motives or intentions or plans. This internal focus is evident in Kant's first formulation of the categorical imperative:

The universalizability principle: We have a moral obligation not to act on any maxim that we cannot will to be a universal law.

The idea is not that universally acting on that maxim would have bad consequences. (We will consider that kind of principle below.) Instead, the claim is that some maxims "cannot even be thought as a universal law of nature without contradiction."[19] However, my maxim when I drive a gas-guzzler just for fun on this sunny Sunday afternoon is simply to have harmless fun. There is no way to derive a contradiction from a universal law that people do or may have harmless fun. Kantians might respond that my maxim is, instead, to expel greenhouse gases. I still see no way to derive a literal contradiction from a universal law that people do or may expel greenhouse gases. There would be bad consequences, but that is not a contradiction, as Kant requires. In any case, my maxim (or intention or motive) is not to expel greenhouse gases. My goals would be reached completely if I went for my drive and had my fun without expelling any greenhouse gases. This leaves no ground for claiming that my driving violates Kant's first formula of the categorical imperative.

Kant does supply a second formulation, which is really a different principle:

The means principle: We have a moral obligation not to treat any other person as a means only.[20]

It is not clear exactly how to understand this formulation, but the most natural interpretation is that for me to treat someone as a means implies my using harm to that person as part of my plan to achieve my goals. Driving for fun does not do that. I would have just as much fun if nobody were ever harmed by global warming. Harm to others is no part of my plans. So Kant's principle cannot explain why I have a moral obligation not to drive just for fun on this sunny Sunday afternoon.

A similar point applies to a traditional principle that focuses on intention:

The doctrine of double effect: We have a moral obligation not to harm anyone intentionally (either as an end or as a means).

This principle fails to apply to my Sunday driving both because my driving does not cause harm to anyone and because I do not intend harm to anyone. I would succeed in doing everything I intended to do if I enjoyed my drive but magically my car gave off no greenhouse gases and no global warming occurred.

Another inner-directed theory is virtue ethics. This approach focuses on general character traits rather than particular acts or intentions. It is not clear how to derive a principle regarding obligations from virtue ethics, but here is a common attempt:

The virtue principle: We have a moral obligation not to perform an act that expresses a vice or is contrary to virtue.

This principle solves our problem if driving a gas-guzzler expresses a vice, or if no virtuous person would drive a gas-guzzler just for fun.

How can we tell whether this principle applies? How can we tell whether driving a gas-guzzler for fun "expresses a vice"? On the face of it, it expresses a desire for fun. There is nothing vicious about having fun. Having fun becomes vicious only if it is harmful or risky. But I have already responded to the principles of harm and risk. Moreover, driving a gas-guzzler for fun does not always express a vice. If other people did not produce so much greenhouse gas, I could drive my gas-guzzler just for fun without anyone being harmed by global warming. Then I could do it without being vicious. This situation is not realistic, but it does show that wasteful driving is not essentially vicious or contrary to virtue.

Some will disagree. Maybe your notions of virtue and vice make it essentially vicious to drive wastefully. But why? To apply this principle, we need some antecedent test of when an act expresses a vice. You cannot just say, "I know vice when I see it," because other people look at the same act and do not see vice, just fun. It begs the question to appeal to what you see when others do not see it, and you have no reason to believe that your vision is any clearer than theirs. But that means that this virtue principle cannot be applied without begging the question. We need to find some reason why such driving is vicious. Once we have this reason, we can appeal to it directly as a reason why I have a moral obligation not to drive wastefully. The side step through virtue does not help and only obscures the issue.

Some virtue theorists might respond that life would be better if more people were to focus on general character traits, including green virtues, such as moderation and love of nature.[21] One reason is that it is so hard to determine obligations in particular cases. Another reason is that focusing on particular obligations leaves no way to escape problems like global warming. This might be correct. Maybe we should spend more time thinking about whether we have green virtues rather than about whether we have specific obligations. But that does not show that we do have a moral obligation not to drive gas-guzzlers just for fun. Changing our focus will not bring any moral obligation into existence. There are other important moral issues besides moral obligation, but this does not show that moral obligations are not important as well.

5. COLLECTIVE PRINCIPLES

Maybe our mistake is to focus on individual persons. We could, instead, focus on institutions. One institution is the legal system, so we might adopt.

The ideal law principle: We have a moral obligation not to perform an action if it ought to be illegal.

I already said that the government ought to fight global warming. One way to do so is to make it illegal to drive wastefully or to buy (or sell) inefficient gas-guzzlers. If the government ought to pass such laws, then, even before such laws are passed, I have a moral obligation not to drive a gas-guzzler just for fun, according to the ideal law principle.

The first weakness in this argument lies in its assumption that wasteful driving or gas-guzzlers ought to be illegal. That is dubious. The enforcement costs of a law against joyrides would be enormous. A law against gas-guzzlers would be easier to enforce, but inducements to efficiency (such as higher taxes on gas and gas-guzzlers, or tax breaks for buying fuel-efficient cars) might accomplish the same goals with less loss of individual freedom. Governments ought to accomplish their goals with less loss of freedom, if they can. Note the "if." I do not claim that these other laws would work as well as an outright prohibition of gas-guzzlers. I do not know. Still, the point is that such alternative laws would not make it illegal (only expensive) to drive a gas-guzzler for fun. If those alternative laws are better than outright prohibitions (because they allow more freedom), then the ideal law principle cannot yield a moral obligation not to drive a gas-guzzler now.

Moreover, the connection between law and morality cannot be so simple. Suppose that the government morally ought to raise taxes on fossil fuels in order to reduce usage and to help pay for adaptation to global warming. It still seems morally permissible for me and for you not to pay that tax now. We do not have any moral obligation to send a check to the government for the amount that we would have to pay if taxes were raised to the ideal level. One reason is that our checks would not help to solve the problem, since others would continue to conduct business as usual. What would help to solve the problem is for the taxes to be increased. Maybe we all have moral obligations to try to get the taxes increased. Still, until they are increased, we as individuals have no moral obligations to abide by the ideal tax law instead of the actual tax law.

Analogously, it is actually legal to buy and drive gas-guzzlers. Maybe these vehicles should be illegal. I am not sure. If gas-guzzlers morally ought to be illegal, then maybe we morally ought to work to get them outlawed. But that still would not show that now, while they are legal, we have a moral obligation not to drive them just for fun on a sunny Sunday afternoon.

Which laws are best depends on side effects of formal institutions, such as enforcement costs and loss of freedom (resulting from the coercion of laws). Maybe we can do better by looking at informal groups.

Different groups involve different relations between members. Orchestras and political parties, for example, plan to do what they do and adjust their actions to other members of the group in order to achieve a common goal. Such groups can be held responsible for their joint acts, even when no individual alone performs those acts. However, gas-guzzler drivers do not form this kind of group. Gas-guzzler drivers do not share goals, do not make plans together, and do not adjust their acts to each other (at least usually).

There is an abstract set of gas-guzzler drivers, but membership in a set is too arbitrary to create moral responsibility. I am also in a set of all terrorists plus me, but my membership in that abstract set does not make me responsible for the harms that terrorists cause.

The only feature that holds together the group of people who drive gas-guzzlers is simply that they all perform the same kind of act. The fact that so many people carry out acts of that kind does create or worsen global warming. That collective bad effect is supposed to make it morally wrong to perform any act of that kind, according to the following:

The group principle: We have a moral obligation not to perform an action if this action makes us a member of a group whose actions together cause harm.

Why? It begs the question here merely to assume that, if it is bad for everyone in a group to perform acts of a kind, then it is morally wrong for an individual to perform an act of that kind. Besides, this principle is implausible or at least questionable in many cases. Suppose that everyone in an airport is talking loudly. If only a few people were talking, there would be no problem. But the collective effect of so many people talking makes it hard to hear announcements, so some people miss their flights. Suppose, in these

circumstances, I say loudly (but not too loudly), "I wish everyone would be quiet." My speech does not seem immoral, since it alone does not harm anyone. Maybe there should be a rule (or law) against such loud speech in this setting (as in a library), but if there is not (as I am assuming), then it does not seem immoral to do what others do, as long as they are going to do it anyway, so the harm is going to occur anyway.[22]

Again, suppose that the president sends everyone (or at least most taxpayers) a check for $600. If all recipients cash their checks, the government deficit will grow, government programs will have to be slashed, and severe economic and social problems will result. You know that enough other people will cash their checks to make these results to a great degree inevitable. You also know that it is perfectly legal to cash your check, although you think it should be illegal, because the checks should not have been issued in the first place. In these circumstances, is it morally wrong for you to cash your check? I doubt it. Your act of cashing your check causes no harm by itself, and you have no intention to cause harm. Your act of cashing your check does make you a member of a group that collectively causes harm, but that still does not seem to give you a moral obligation not to join the group by cashing your check, since you cannot change what the group does. It might be morally good or ideal to protest by tearing up your check, but it does not seem morally obligatory.

Thus, the group principle fails. Perhaps it might be saved by adding some kind of qualification, but I do not see how.[23]

6. COUNTERFACTUAL PRINCIPLES

Maybe our mistake is to focus on actual circumstances. So let us try some counterfactuals about what would happen in possible worlds that are not actual. Different counterfactuals are used by different versions of rule-consequentialism.[24]

One counterfactual is built into the common question, "What would happen if everybody did that?" This question suggests a principle:

The general action principle: I have a moral obligation not to perform an act when it would be worse for everyone to perform an act of the same kind.[25]

It does seem likely that, if everyone in the world drove a gas-guzzler often enough, global warming would increase intolerably. We would also quickly run out of fossil fuels. The general action principle is, thus, supposed to explain why it is morally wrong to drive a gas-guzzler.

Unfortunately, that popular principle is indefensible. It would be disastrous if every human had no children. But that does not make it morally wrong for a particular individual to choose to have no children. There is no moral obligation to have at least one child.

The reason is that so few people "want" to remain childless. Most people would not go without children even if they were allowed to. This suggests a different principle:

The general permission principle: I have a moral obligation not to perform an act whenever it would be worse for everyone to be permitted to perform an act of that kind.

This principle seems better because it would not be disastrous for everyone to be permitted to remain childless. This principle is supposed to be able to explain why it is morally wrong to steal (or lie, cheat, rape, or murder), because it would be disastrous for everyone to be permitted to steal (or lie, cheat, rape, or murder) whenever (if ever) they wanted to.

Not quite. An agent is permitted or allowed in the relevant sense when she will not be liable to punishment, condemnation (by others), or feelings of guilt for carrying out the act. It is possible for someone to be permitted in this sense without knowing that she is permitted and, indeed, without

anyone knowing that she is permitted. But it would not be disastrous for everyone to be permitted to steal if nobody knew that they were permitted to steal, since then they would still be deterred by fear of punishment, condemnation, or guilt. Similarly for lying, rape, and so on. So the general permission principle cannot quite explain why such acts are morally wrong.

Still, it would be disastrous if everyone knew that they were permitted to steal (or lie, rape, etc.). So we simply need to add one qualification:

The public permission principle: I have a moral obligation not to perform an act whenever it would be worse for everyone to know that everyone is permitted to perform an act of that kind.[26]

Now this principle seems to explain the moral wrongness of many of the acts we take to be morally wrong, since it would be disastrous if everyone knew that everyone was permitted to steal, lie, cheat, and so on.

Unfortunately, this revised principle runs into trouble in other cases. Imagine that 1,000 people want to take Flight 38 to Amsterdam on October 13, 2003, but the plane is not large enough to carry that many people. If all 1,000 took that particular flight, then it would crash. But these people are all stupid and stubborn enough that, if they knew that they were all allowed to take the flight, they all would pack themselves in, despite warnings, and the flight would crash. Luckily, this counterfactual does not reflect what actually happens. In the actual world, the airline is not stupid. Since the plane can safely carry only 300 people, the airline sells only 300 tickets and does not allow anyone on the flight without a ticket. If I have a ticket for that flight, then there is nothing morally wrong with me taking the flight along with the other 299 who have tickets. This shows that an act is not always morally wrong when it would (counterfactually) be disastrous for everyone to know that everyone is allowed to do it.[27]

The lesson of this example applies directly to my case of driving a gas-guzzler. Disaster occurs in the airplane case when too many people do what is harmless by itself. Similarly, disaster occurs when too many people burn too much fossil fuel. But that does not make it wrong in either case for one individual to perform an individual act that is harmless by itself. It only creates an obligation on the part of the government (or airline) to pass regulations to keep too many people from acting that way.

Another example brings out another weakness in the public permission principle. Consider open marriage. Max and Minnie get married because each loves the other and values the other person's love. Still, they think of sexual intercourse as a fun activity that they separate from love. After careful discussion before they got married, each happily agreed that each may have sex after marriage with whomever he or she wants. They value honesty, so they did add one condition: every sexual encounter must be reported to the other spouse. As long as they keep no secrets from each other and still love each other, they see no problem with their having sex with other people. They do not broadcast this feature of their marriage, but they do know (after years of experience) that it works for them.

Nonetheless, the society in which Max and Minnie live might be filled with people who are very different from them. If everyone knew that everyone is permitted to have sex during marriage with other people as long as the other spouse is informed and agreed to the arrangement, then various problems would arise. Merely asking a spouse whether he or she would be willing to enter into such an agreement would be enough to create suspicions and doubts in the other spouse's mind that would undermine many marriages or keep many couples from getting married, when they would have gotten or remained happily married if they had not been offered such an agreement. As a result, the society will have less love, fewer stable marriages, and more unhappy children of unnecessary divorce. Things would be much better if everyone believed that such agreements were not permitted in the first place, so they condemned them and felt guilty for even considering them. I think that this result is not unrealistic, but here I am merely postulating these facts in my example.

The point is that, even if other people are like this, so that it would be worse for everyone to know that everyone is permitted to have sex outside of marriage with spousal knowledge and consent, Max and Minnie are not like this, and they know that they are not like this, so it is hard to believe that they as individuals have a moral obligation to abide by a restriction that is justified by other people's dispositions. If Max and Minnie have a joint agreement that works for them, but they keep it secret from others, then there is nothing immoral about them having sex outside of their marriage (whether or not this counts as adultery). If this is correct, then the general permission principle fails again.

As before, the lesson of this example applies directly to my case of driving a gas-guzzler. The reason why Max and Minnie are not immoral is that they have a right to their own private relationship as long as they do not harm others (such as by spreading disease or discord). But I have already argued that my driving a gas-guzzler on this Sunday afternoon does not cause harm. I seem to have a right to have fun in the way I want as long as I do not hurt anybody else, just like Max and Minnie. So the public permission principle cannot explain why it is morally wrong to drive a gas-guzzler for fun on this sunny Sunday afternoon.[28]

One final counterfactual approach is contractualism, whose most forceful recent proponent is Tim Scanlon.[29] Scanlon proposes:

The contractualist principle: I have a moral obligation not to perform an act whenever it violates a general rule that nobody could reasonably reject as a public rule for governing action in society.

Let us try to apply this principle to the case of Max and Minnie. Consider a general rule against adultery, that is, against voluntary sex between a married person and someone other than his or her spouse, even if the spouse knows and consents. It might seem that Max and Minnie could not reasonably reject this rule as a public social rule, because they want to avoid problems for their own society. If so, Scanlon's principle leads to the same questionable results as the public permission principle. If Scanlon replies that Max and Minnie "can" reasonably reject the anti-adultery rule, then why? The most plausible answer is that it is their own business how they have fun as long as they do not hurt anybody. But this answer is available also to people who drive gas-guzzlers just for fun. So this principle cannot explain why that act is morally wrong.

More generally, the test of what can be rejected "reasonably" depends on moral intuitions. Environmentalists might think it unreasonable to reject a principle that prohibits me from driving my gas-guzzler just for fun, but others will think it reasonable to reject such a principle, because it restricts my freedom to perform an act that harms nobody. The appeal to reasonable rejection itself begs the question in the absence of an account of why such rejection is unreasonable. Environmentalists might be able to specify reasons why it is unreasonable, but then it is those reasons that explain why this act is morally wrong. The framework of reasonable rejection becomes a distracting and unnecessary side step.[30]

7. WHAT IS LEFT?

We are left with no defensible principle to support the claim that I have a moral obligation not to drive a gas-guzzler just for fun. Does this result show that this claim is false? Not necessarily.

Some audiences[31] have suggested that my journey through various principles teaches us that we should not look for general moral principles to back up our moral intuitions. They see my arguments as a "reductio ad absurdum" of principlism, which is the view that moral obligations (or our beliefs in them) depend on principles. Principles are unavailable, so we should focus instead on particular cases, according to the opposing view called particularism.[32]

However, the fact that we cannot find any principle does not show that we do not need one. I already gave my reasons why we need a moral principle to back up our intuitions in this case. This case is controversial, emotional, peculiarly modern, and likely to be distorted by overgeneralization and partiality. These factors suggest that we need confirmation for our moral intuitions at least in this case, even if we do not need any confirmation in other cases.

For such reasons, we seem to need a moral principle, but we have none. This fact still does not show that such wasteful driving is not morally wrong. It only shows that we do not "know" whether it is morally wrong. Our ignorance might be temporary. If someone comes up with a defensible principle that does rule out wasteful driving, then I will be happy to listen and happy if it works. However, until some such principle is found, we cannot claim to know that it is morally wrong to drive a gas-guzzler just for fun.

The demand for a principle in this case does not lead to general moral skepticism. We still might know that acts and omissions that cause harm are morally wrong because of the harm principle. Still, since that principle and others do not apply to my wasteful driving, and since moral intuitions are unreliable in cases like this, we cannot know that my wasteful driving is morally wrong.

This conclusion will still upset many environmentalists. They think that they know that wasteful driving is immoral. They want to be able to condemn those who drive gas-guzzlers just for fun on sunny Sunday afternoons.

My conclusion should not be so disappointing. Even if individuals have no such moral obligations, it is still morally better or morally ideal for individuals not to waste gas. We can and should praise those who save fuel. We can express our personal dislike for wasting gas and for people who do it. We might even be justified in publicly condemning wasteful driving and drivers who waste a lot, in circumstances where such public rebuke is appropriate. Perhaps people who drive wastefully should feel guilty for their acts and ashamed of themselves, at least if they perform such acts regularly; and we should bring up our children so that they will feel these emotions. All of these reactions are available even if we cannot truthfully say that such driving violates a moral "obligation." And these approaches might be more constructive in the long run than accusing someone of violating a moral obligation.

Moreover, even if individuals have no moral obligations not to waste gas by taking unnecessary Sunday drives just for fun, governments still have moral obligations to fight global warming, because they can make a difference. My fundamental point has been that global warming is such a large problem that it is not individuals who cause it or who need to fix it. Instead, governments need to fix it, and quickly. Finding and implementing a real solution is the task of governments. Environmentalists should focus their efforts on those who are not doing their job rather than on those who take Sunday afternoon drives just for fun.

This focus will also avoid a common mistake. Some environmentalists keep their hands clean by withdrawing into a simple life where they use very little fossil fuels. That is great. I encourage it. But some of these escapees then think that they have done their duty, so they rarely come down out of the hills to work for political candidates who could and would change government policies. This attitude helps nobody. We should not think that we can do enough simply by buying fuel-efficient cars, insulating our houses, and setting up a windmill to make our own electricity. That is all wonderful, but it does little or nothing to stop global warming, nor does this focus fulfill our real moral obligations, which are to get governments to do their job to prevent the disaster of excessive global warming. It is better to enjoy your Sunday driving while working to change the law so as to make it illegal for you to enjoy your Sunday driving.

NOTES

1. For skeptics, see Lomborg (1998, chapter 24) and Singer (1997). A more reliable partial skeptic is Richard S. Lindzen, but his papers are quite technical. If you do not share my bleak view of global warming, treat the rest of this essay as conditional. The issue of how individual moral obligations are related to collective moral obligations is interesting and important in its own right, even if my assumptions about global warming turn out to be inaccurate.

2. See the chapters by Mahlman, Schlesinger, and Weatherly in Sinnott-Armstrong and Howarth (eds.), *Perspectives on Climate Change*.

3. See the chapter by Shukla in Sinnott-Armstrong and Howarth (eds.), *Perspectives on Climate Change*.

4. See the chapter by Bodansky in Sinnott-Armstrong and Howarth (eds.), *Perspectives on Climate Change*.

5. See the chapter by Shuc in Sinnott-Armstrong and Howarth (eds.), *Perspectives on Climate Change*.

6. See the chapter by Jamieson in Sinnott-Armstrong and Howarth (eds.), *Perspectives on Climate Change*.

7. See the chapter by Toman in Sinnott-Armstrong and Howarth (eds.), *Perspectives on Climate Change*.

8. See the chapter by Driver in Sinnott-Armstrong and Howarth (eds.), *Perspectives on Climate Change*.

9. If I have an obligation to encourage the government to fulfill its obligation, then the government's obligation does impose some obligation on me. Still, I do not have an obligation to do what the government has an obligation to do. In short, I have no parallel moral obligation. That is what is at issue here.

10. I do not seem to have the same moral obligation to teach my neighbors' children when our government fails to teach them. Why not? The natural answer is that I have a special relation to my children that I do not have to their children. I also do not have such a special relation to future people who will be harmed by global warming.

11. See the chapter by Claussen in Sinnott-Armstrong and Howarth (eds.), *Perspectives on Climate Change*.

12. Indeed, I am worried about how my environmentalist friends will react to this essay, but I cannot let fear stop me from following where arguments lead.

13. For more on why moral intuitions need confirmation, see Sinnott-Armstrong (2005).

14. Another difference between these cases is that my failure to donate to famine relief is an inaction, whereas my driving is an action. As Bob Fogelin put it in conversation, one is a sin of omission, but the other is a sin of emission. But I assume that omissions can be causes. The real question is whether my measly emissions of greenhouse gases can be causes of global warming.

15. Cf. Parfit (1984, pp. 75–82).

16. If my act this Sunday does not cause me to drive next Sunday, then effects of my driving next Sunday are not consequences of my driving this Sunday. Some still might say that I can affect global warming by driving wastefully many times over the course of years. I doubt this, but I do not need to deny it. The fact that it is morally wrong for me to do all of a hundred acts together does not imply that it is morally wrong for me to do one of those hundred acts. Even if it would be morally wrong for me to pick all of the flowers in a park, it need not be morally wrong for me to pick one flower in that park.

17. The importance of risks in environmental ethics is a recurrent theme in the writings of Kristin Shrader-Frechette.

18. Kant (1785/1959, p. 400, n. 1).

19. *Ibid.*, 424. According to Kant, a weaker kind of contradiction in the will signals an imperfect duty. However, imperfect duties permit "exception in the interest of inclination" (421), so an imperfect obligation not to drive a gas-guzzler would permit me to drive it this Sunday when

I am so inclined. Thus, I assume that a moral obligation not to drive a gas-guzzler for fun on a particular occasion would have to be a perfect obligation in Kant's view.

20. *Ibid.*, 429. I omit Kant's clause regarding treating others as ends because that clause captures imperfect duties, which are not my concern here (for reasons given in the preceding note).

21. Jamieson (n.d.).

22. Compare also standing up to see the athletes in a sporting event, when others do so. Such examples obviously involve much less harm than global warming. I use trivial examples to diminish emotional interference. The point is only that such examples share a structure that defenders of the group principle would claim to be sufficient for a moral obligation.

23. Parfit (1984, pp. 67–86) is famous for arguing that an individual act is immoral if it falls in a group of acts that collectively cause harm. To support his claim Parfit uses examples like the Harmless Torturers (p. 80). But torturers intend to cause harm. That's what makes them torturers. Hence, Parfit's cases cannot show anything wrong with wasteful driving, where there is no intention to cause any harm. For criticisms of Parfit's claims, see Jackson (1997).

24. Cf. Sinnott-Armstrong (2003) and Hooker (2003).

25. Cf. Singer (1971).

26. Cf. Gert (2005). Gert does add details that I will not discuss here. For a more complete response, see Sinnott-Armstrong (2002).

27. The point, of course, depends on how you describe the act. It would not be disastrous to allow everyone "with a ticket" to take the flight (as long as there are not too many tickets). What is disastrous is to allow everyone (without qualification) to take the flight. Still, that case shows that it is not always morally wrong to do X when it would be disastrous to allow everyone to do X. To solve these problems, we need to put some limits on the kinds of descriptions that can replace the variable X. But any limit needs to be justified, and it is not at all clear how to justify such limits without begging the question.

28. The examples in the text show why violating a justified public rule is not sufficient for private immorality. It is also not necessary, since it might not be disastrous if all parents were permitted to kill their children, if no parent ever wanted to kill his or her children. The failure of this approach to give a necessary condition is another reason to doubt that it captures the essence of morality.

29. Scanlon (1998).

30. Scanlon's framework still might be useful as a heuristic, for overcoming partiality, as a pedagogical tool, or as a vivid way to display coherence among moral intuitions at different levels. My point is that it cannot be used to justify moral judgments or to show what makes acts morally wrong. For more, see Sinnott-Armstrong (2006, chap. 8).

31. Such as Bill Pollard in Edinburgh.

32. Developed by Dancy (1993, 2004). For criticisms, see Sinnott-Armstrong (1999).

ACKNOWLEDGMENTS

For helpful comments, I would like to thank Kier Olsen DeVries, Julia Driver, Bob Fogelin, Bernard Gert, Rich Howarth, Bill Pollard, Mike Ridge, David Rodin, Peter Singer, and audiences at the University of Edinburgh, the International Society for Business, Economics, and Ethics, and the Center for Applied Philosophy and Public Ethics in Melbourne.

REFERENCES

Dancy, J. (1993). *Moral reasons.* Oxford: Blackwell.

Dancy, J. (2004). *Ethics without principles.* New York: Oxford University Press.

Gert, B. (2005). *Morality: Its nature and justification* (Revised ed.). New York: Oxford University Press.

Hooker, B. (2003). Rule consequentialism. In: *The Stanford Encyclopedia of Philosophy.* Available at: http://plato.stanford.edu/entrics/consequentialism-rule

Jackson, F. (1997). Which effects? In: J. Dancy (Ed.), *Reading Parfit* (pp. 42–53). Oxford: Blackwell.

Jamieson, D. (n.d.). When utilitarians should be virtue theorists. Unpublished manuscript.

Kant, I. (1959). *Foundations of the metaphysics of morals* (L. W. Beck, Trans.). Indianapolis. IN: Bobbs-Merrill. (Original work published in 1785).

Lomborg, B. (1998). *The skeptical environmentalist.* New York: Cambridge University Press.

Parfit, D. (1984). *Reasons and persons.* Oxford: Clarendon Press.

Scanlon, T. (1998). *What we owe to each other.* Cambridge, MA: Harvard University Press.

Singer, M. (1971). *Generalization in ethics.* New York: Atheneum.

Singer, S. F. (1997). *Hot talk, cold science.* Oakland, CA: The Independent Institute.

Sinnott-Armstrong, W. (1999). Some varieties of particularism. *Metaphilosophy, 30,* 1–12.

———. (2002). Gert contra consequentialism. In: W. Sinnott-Armstrong and R. Audi (Eds.), *Rationality, rules, and ideals: Critical essays on Bernard Gert's moral theory* (pp. 145–163). Lanham, MD: Rowman and Littlefield.

———. (2003). Consequentialism. In: *The Stanford Encyclopedia of Philosophy*. Available at: http://plato .stanford.edu/entries/consequentialism.

———. (2005). Moral intuitionism and empirical psychology. In: T. Horgan and M. Timmons (Eds.), *Metaethics after Moore* (pp. 339–365). New York: Oxford University Press.

———. (2006). *Moral skepticisms.* New York: Oxford University Press.

READING QUESTIONS

1. How does Sinnott-Armstrong argue that individual moral obligations do not always follow directly from collective moral obligations (e.g., obligations of the government)?

2. What is the harm principle, and how does Sinnott-Armstrong argue that it does not imply that he has a moral obligation not to drive his gas-guzzler just for fun? Why does he think the principle implies this only if his driving the gas-guzzler is both unusual and done with the intent to harm?

3. One of Sinnott-Armstrong's objections to the risk principle is that it is too restrictive, and one possible response to this objection involves distinguishing significant from insignificant risks. What is the risk principle, and what does Sinnott-Armstrong believe is wrong with this response to his objection?

4. How does Sinnott-Armstrong interpret Kant's means principle, and why does he think the principle cannot explain why he has no moral obligation not to drive his gas-guzzler just for fun?

5. In his discussion of the group principle, Sinnott-Armstrong presents a hypothetical case where the president sends everyone a $600 check. What is the group principle, and how is Sinnott-Armstrong's case supposed to show that the group principle fails?

6. What is the contractualist principle, and how does Sinnott-Armstrong use the case of Max and Minnie to show that the principle cannot explain why driving gas-guzzlers just for fun is wrong?

7. How does Sinnott-Armstrong argue that we cannot know whether driving gas-guzzlers just for fun is wrong unless we can provide a defensible general moral principle that implies that it is wrong?

DISCUSSION QUESTIONS

1. Is Sinnott-Armstrong right that the virtue principle "cannot be applied without begging the question"? How might one argue, without begging the question, that driving gas-guzzlers just for fun is contrary to virtue?

2. Sinnott-Armstrong suggests that there is no contradiction in claiming that (i) people who drive wastefully should feel guilty and ashamed for doing so and that (ii) there is no moral obligation not to drive wastefully. But how could it be the case that one *should* feel guilty and ashamed for doing something even when what one did violates no moral obligation?

BJØRN LOMBORG

Let's Keep Our Cool about Global Warming

Bjørn Lomborg argues that the drastic reductions in CO_2 emissions that some have proposed as a way of curbing global warming are not politically realistic. Instead he advocates a balanced approach to the problem that involves economically feasible taxing of CO_2 emissions along with expenditures on the research and development of noncarbon emitting technologies.
    Recommended Reading: consequentialism, chap. 1, sec. 2A.

There is a kind of choreographed screaming about climate change from both sides of the debate. Discussion would be on much firmer ground if we could actually hear the arguments and the facts and then sensibly debate long-term solutions.

Man-made climate change is certainly a problem, but it is categorically not the end of the world. Take the rise in sea levels as one example of how the volume of the screaming is unmatched by the facts. In its 2007 report, the United Nations estimates that sea levels will rise about a foot over the remainder of the century.[1] While this is not a trivial amount, it is also important to realize that it is not unknown to mankind: since 1860, we have experienced a sea level rise of about a foot without major disruptions.[2] It is also important to realize that the new prediction is lower than previous Intergovernmental Panel on Climate Change (IPCC) estimates and much lower than the expectations from the 1990s of more than two feet and the 1980s, when the Environmental Protection Agency projected more than six feet.[3]

We dealt with rising sea levels in the past century, and we will continue to do so in this century. It will be problematic, but it is incorrect to posit the rise as the end of civilization. We will actually lose very little dry land to the rise in sea levels. It is estimated that almost all nations in the world will establish maximal coastal protection almost everywhere,

simply because doing so is fairly cheap. For more than 180 of the world's 192 nations, coastal protection will cost less than 0.1 percent GDP and approach 100 percent protection.[4]

The rise in sea level will be a much bigger problem for poor countries. The most affected nation will be Micronesia, a federation of 607 small islands in the West Pacific with a total land area only four times larger than Washington, D.C.[5] If nothing were done, Micronesia would lose some 21 percent of its area by the end of the century (Tol 2004, 5). With coastal protection, it will lose just 0.18 percent of its land area. However, if we instead opt for cuts in carbon emissions and thus reduce both the sea level rise and the economic growth, Micronesia will end up losing a larger land area. The increase in wealth for poor nations is more important than sea levels: poorer nations will be less able to defend themselves against rising waters, even if they rise more slowly. This is the same for other vulnerable nations: Tuvalu, the Maldives, Vietnam, and Bangladesh. The point is that we cannot just talk about CO_2 when we talk about climate change. The dialogue needs to include both considerations about carbon emissions and economics for the benefit of humans and the environment. Presumably, our goal is not just to cut carbon emissions, but to do the best we can for people and the environment.

We should take action on climate change, but we need to be realistic. The UK has arguably engaged in the most aggressive rhetoric about climate change. Since the Labour government promised in 1997 to cut emissions by a further 15 percent by 2010, emissions have *increased* 3 percent.[6] American emissions during the Clinton/Gore administration increased 28 percent. Look at our past behavior: at the Earth Summit in Rio in 1992, nations promised to cut emissions back to 1990 levels by 2000 (UNFCCC 1992, 4.2a). The member countries of the Organisation for Economic Cooperation and Development (OECD) overshot their target in 2000 by more than 12 percent.

Many believe that dramatic political action will follow if people only knew better and elected better politicians.[7] Despite the European Union's enthusiasm for the Kyoto Protocol on Climate Change—and a greater awareness and concern over global warming in Europe than in the United States—emissions per person since 1990 have remained stable in the U.S. while E.U. emissions have increased 4 percent (EIA 2006). Even if the wealthy nations managed to rein in their emissions, the majority of this century's emissions will come from developing countries—which are responsible for about 40 percent of annual carbon emissions; this is likely to increase to 75 percent by the end of the century.[8]

In a surprisingly candid statement from Tony Blair at the Clinton Global Initiative, he pointed out:

> I think if we are going to get action on this, we have got to start from the brutal honesty about the politics of how we deal with it. The truth is no country is going to cut its growth or consumption substantially in the light of a long-term environmental problem. What countries are prepared to do is to try to work together cooperatively to deal with this problem in a way that allows us to develop the science and technology in a beneficial way. (Clinton Global Initiative 2005, 15)

Similarly, one of the top economic researchers tells us: "Deep cuts in emissions will only be achieved if alternative energy technologies become available at reasonable prices" (Tol 2007, 430). We need to engage in a sensible debate about how to tax CO_2. If we set the tax too low, we emit too much. If we set it too high, we end up much poorer without doing enough to reduce warming.

In the largest review of all of the literature's 103 estimates, climate economist Richard Tol makes two important points. First, the really scary, high estimates typically have not been subjected to peer review and published. In his words: "studies with better methods yield lower estimates with smaller uncertainties." Second, with reasonable assumptions, the cost is very unlikely to be higher than $14 per ton of CO_2 and likely to be much smaller (Tol 2005).[9] When I specifically asked him for his best guess, he wasn't too enthusiastic about shedding his cautiousness—as few true researchers . . . are—but gave the estimate of $2 per ton of CO_2.[10]

Therefore, I believe that we should tax CO_2 at the economically feasible level of about $2/ton, or maximally $14/ton. Yet, let us not expect this will make any major difference. Such a tax would cut emissions by 5 percent and reduce temperatures by 0.16°F. And before we scoff at 5 percent, let us remember that the Kyoto Protocol, at the cost of 10 years of political and economic toil, will reduce emissions by just 0.4 percent by 2010.[11]

Neither a tax nor Kyoto nor draconian proposals for future cuts move us closer toward finding better options for the future. Research and development in renewable energy and energy efficiency is at its lowest for twenty-five years. Instead, we need to find a way that allows us to "develop the science and technology in a beneficial way," a way that enables us to provide alternative energy technologies at reasonable prices. It will take the better part of a century and will need a political will spanning parties, continents, and generations. We need to be in for the long haul and develop cost-effective strategies that won't splinter regardless of overarching ambitions or false directions.

This is why one of our generational challenges should be for *all nations to commit themselves to spending 0.05 percent of GDP in research and development of noncarbon emitting energy technologies.* This is a tenfold increase on current expenditures yet would cost a relatively minor $25 billion per year (seven times cheaper than Kyoto and many more times cheaper than Kyoto II). Such a commitment could include all nations, with wealthier nations paying the larger share, and would let each country focus on its own future vision of energy needs, whether that means concentrating on renewable sources, nuclear energy, fusion, carbon storage, conservation, or searching for new and more exotic opportunities.

Funding research and development globally would create a momentum that could recapture the vision of delivering both a low-carbon and high-income world. Lower energy costs and high spin-off innovation are potential benefits that possibly avoid ever stronger temptations to free-riding and the ever tougher negotiations over increasingly restrictive Kyoto Protocol-style treaties. A global financial commitment makes it plausible to envision stabilizing climate changes at reasonable levels.

I believe it would be the way to bridge a century of parties, continents, and generations, creating a sustainable, low-cost opportunity to create the alternative energy technologies that will power the future.

To move toward this goal we need to create sensible policy dialogue. This requires us to talk openly about priorities. Often there is strong sentiment in any public discussion that we should do *anything* required to make a situation better. But clearly we don't actually do that. When we talk about schools, we know that more teachers would likely provide our children with a better education.[12] Yet we do not hire more teachers simply because we also have to spend money in other areas. When we talk about hospitals, we know that access to better equipment is likely to provide better treatment, yet we don't supply an infinite amount of resources.[13] When we talk about the environment, we know tougher restrictions will mean better protection, but this also comes with higher costs.

Consider traffic fatalities, which are one of the ten leading causes of deaths in the world. In the U.S., 42,600 people die in traffic accidents and 2.8 million people are injured each year (USCB, 2006, 672). Globally, it is estimated that 1.2 million people die from traffic accidents and 50 million are injured every year (Lopez, Mathers, Ezzati, Jamison, and Murray 2006, 1751; WHO 2002, 72; 2004, 3, 172).

About 2 percent of all deaths in the world are traffic-related and about 90 percent of the traffic deaths occur in third world countries (WHO 2004, 172). The total cost is a phenomenal $512 billion a year (WHO 2004, 5). Due to increasing traffic

(especially in the third world) and due to ever better health conditions, the World Heath Organization estimates that by 2020, traffic fatalities will be the second leading cause of death in the world, after heart disease.[14]

Amazingly, we have the technology to make all of this go away. We could instantly save 1.2 million humans and eliminate $500 billion worth of damage. We would particularly help the third world. The answer is simply lowering speed limits to 5 mph. We could avoid almost all of the 50 million injuries each year. But of course we will not do this. Why? The simple answer that almost all of us would offer is that the benefits from driving moderately fast far outweigh the costs. While the cost is obvious in terms of those killed and maimed, the benefits are much more prosaic and dispersed but nonetheless important—traffic interconnects our society by bringing goods at competitive prices to where we live and bringing people together to where we work, and lets us live where we like while allowing us to visit and meet with many others. A world moving only at 5 mph is a world gone medieval.

This is not meant to be flippant. We really could solve one of the world's top problems if we wanted. We know traffic deaths are almost entirely caused by man. We have the technology to reduce deaths to zero. Yet we persist in exacerbating the problem each year, making traffic an ever-bigger killer.

I suggest that the comparison with global warming is insightful; we have the technology to reduce it to zero, yet we seem to persist in going ahead and exacerbating the problem each year, causing temperatures to continue to increase to new heights by 2020. Why? Because the benefits from moderately using fossil fuels far outweigh the costs. Yes, the costs are obvious in the "fear, terror, and disaster" we read about in the papers every day.

But the benefits of fossil fuels, though much more prosaic, are nonetheless important. Fossil fuels provide us with low-cost electricity, heat, food, communication, and travel.[15] Electrical air conditioning means that people in the U.S. no longer die in droves during heat waves (Davis, Knappenberger, Michaels, and Novicoff 2003). Cheaper fuels would have avoided a significant number of the 150,000 [deaths] in the UK since 2000 due to cold winters.[16]

Because of fossil fuels, food can be grown cheaply, giving us access to fruits and vegetables year round, which has probably reduced cancer rates by at least 25 percent.[17] Cars allow us to commute to city centers for work while living in areas that provide us with space and nature around our homes, whereas communication and cheap flights have given ever more people the opportunity to experience other cultures and forge friendships globally (Schäfer 2006).

In the third world, access to fossil fuels is crucial. About 1.6 billion people don't have access to electricity, which seriously impedes human development (IEA 2004, 338–40). Worldwide, about 2.5 billion people rely on biomass such as wood and waste (including dung) to cook and keep warm (IEA 2006, 419ff). For many Indian women, searching for wood takes about three hours each day, and sometimes they walk more than 10 kilometers a day. All of this causes excessive deforestation (IEA 2006, 428; Kammen 1995; Kelkar 2006). About 1.3 million people—mostly women and children—die each year due to heavy indoor air pollution. A switch from biomass to fossil fuels would dramatically improve 2.5 billion lives; the cost of $1.5 billion annually would be greatly superseded by benefits of about $90 billion.[18] Both for the developed and the developing world, a world without fossil fuels—in the short or medium term—is, again, a lot like reverting back to the middle ages.

This does not mean that we should not talk about how to reduce the impact of traffic and global warming. Most countries have strict regulations on speed limits—if they didn't, fatalities would be much higher. Yet, studies also show that lowering the average speed in Western Europe by just 5 kilometers per hour could reduce fatalities by 25 percent—with about 10,000 fewer people killed each year (WHO, 2002, 72; 2004, 172). Apparently, democracies in Europe are not willing to give up on the extra benefits from faster driving to save 10,000 people.

This is parallel to the debate we are having about global warming. We can realistically talk about $2 or even a $14 CO_2 tax. But suggesting a $140 tax, as Al Gore does, seems to be far outside the envelope. Suggesting a 96 percent carbon reduction for the OECD by 2030 seems a bit like suggesting a 5 mph speed limit in the traffic debate. It is technically doable, but it is very unlikely to happen.

One of the most important issues when it comes to climate change is that we cool our dialogue and consider the arguments for and against different policies. In the heat of a loud and obnoxious debate, facts and reason lose out.

NOTES

1. (IPCC, 2007b:10.6.5). Notice that the available report (IPCC 2007a) has a midpoint of 38.5 cm.

2. Using (Jevrejeva, Grinsted, Moore, and Holgate 2006), 11.4 inches since 1860.

3. 1996: 38–35 cm (IPCC and Houghton 1996:364), 1992 and 1983 EPA from (Yohe and Neumann 1997, 243; 250).

4. (Nicholls and Tol 2006, 1088), estimated for 2085. Notice low-lying undeveloped coasts in places such as Arctic Russia, Canada and Alaska are expected to be undefended. Notice that the numbers presented are for loss of dry land, whereas up to 18 percent of global wetlands will be lost.

5. "Micronesia" (CIA 2006).

6. Labour has urged a 20 percent CO_2 emission cut from 1990 in 2010 in three election manifestos (BBC Anon. 2006a); this translates into a 14.6 percent reduction from 1997 levels. From 1997 to 2004, CO_2 emissions increased 3.4 percent (EIA 2006).

7. Take, for instance, both Gore's "we have to find a way to communicate the direness of the situation" and Hansen's "scientists have not done a good job communicating with the public" (Fischer 2006).

8. Developing countries emitted 10.171 Gt of the global 26 Gt in 2004 (IEA, 2006, 513, 493), OECD counties 51 percent in 2003 (OECD 2006, 148), Weyant estimates 29 percent from industrialized countries (1998, 2286), IPCC emission scenarios from 23 in the business-as-usual A1 to 36 percent (Nakicenovic and IPCC WG III 2000).

9. Based on a cost of $50 per ton of carbon (Tol 2005:2071).

10. From the Environmental Assessment Institute we asked him in July 2005: "Would you still stick by the conclusion that $15/tC seems justified or would you rather only present an upper limit of the estimate?" He answered: "I'd prefer not to present a central estimate, but if you put a gun to my head I would say $7/tC, the median estimate with a 3 percent pure rate of time preference" ($7/tC = $1.9/tCO_2$). This is comparable with Pearce's estimate of $1–2.5/tCO_2$ ($4–9/tC) (2003:369).

11. There are many advantages to taxes over emission caps, mainly that with taxes, authorities have an interest in collecting them (because it funds the government), whereas with caps, individual countries have much less interest in achieving goals with such an effort, because the benefits are dispersed (global) and the damages localized (to local industries).

12. (Akerhielm 1995; Angrist and Lavy 1999; Graddy and Stevens 2005). Of course, this could be modified in many ways, such as by focusing on paying teachers better, more resources for books, computers, etc. It is also important that we should be saying "more teachers will at least not make schools worse and will likely make them better," as most studies show some or no effect from extra resources but very few show negative results.

13. E.g., (Fleitas et al. 2006; Gebhardt and Norris 2006). On the other hand, it is less clear that (after a certain limit) more doctors and bed space is the answer, since they may just make for more visits and increase the possibility of infections and harm (Weinberger, Oddone, and Henderson 1996; Wennberg et al. 2004).

14. (WHO 2002, 129) puts it second, whereas (WHO 2004, 5) puts it third.

15. This only looks at the marginal benefit of fossil fuels—which is the relevant one for our discussion. On a basic level, though, it is important to remember that they have fundamentally changed our lives. Before fossil fuels, we would spend hours gathering wood, contributing to deforestation and soil erosion—as billions in the third world still do today (Kammen 1995). We have electric washing machines that have cut domestic work dramatically. The historical economist Stanley Lebergott wrote only semi-jokingly: "From 1620 to 1920 the American washing machine was a housewife" (Lebergott 1993, 112). In 1900, a housewife spent seven hours a week laundering, carrying 200 gallons of water into the house and using a scrub board. Today, she spends 84 minutes with much less strain (Robinson and Godbey 1997, 327). We have a fridge that has both given us more spare time and allowed us to avoid rotten food and eat a more healthy diet of fruit and vegetables (Lebergott 1995, 155). By the end of the nineteenth century human labor made up 94 percent of all industrial work in the U.S. Today, it constitutes only 8 percent (Berry, Conkling, Ray, and Berry 1993, 131). If we think for a moment of the energy we use in terms of "servants," each with the same work power as a human being, each person in Western Europe has access to 150 servants, in the U.S. about 300, and even in India each person has 15 servants to help (Craig, Vaughan, and Skinner 1996:103).

16. Steve Jones, "Help the Aged," said: "Many pensioners still agonize about whether or not to heat their homes in the cold weather. In the world's fourth richest country, this is simply shameful" (BBC Anon. 2006b).

17. The World Cancer Research Fund study estimates that increasing the intake of fruit and vegetables from an average of about 250 g/day to 400 g/day would reduce the overall frequency of cancer by around 23 percent (WCRF 1997:540).

18. Mainly from fewer deaths and less time use.

REFERENCES

Akerhielm, K. 1995. "Does class size matter?" *Economics of Education Review* 14(3), 229–41.

Angrist, J. D., and V. Lavy. 1999. "Using Maimonides' rule to estimate the effect of class size on scholastic achievement." *Quarterly Journal of Economics* 114(2), 533–75.

BBC Anon. 2006a, March 28. UK to miss CO_2 emissions target. BBC. Available at http://news.bbc.co.uk/2/hi/science/nature/4849672.stm. Accessed January 29, 2007.

———. 2006b, October 27. "Winter death toll" drops by 19%: Deaths in England and Wales fell to 25,700 last winter, a decline of 19% on the previous year. BBC Web site. Available at http://news.bbc.co.uk/2/hi/uk_news/6090492.stm. Accessed November 13, 2006.

Berry, B. J. L., E. C. Conkling, and D. M. Ray. 1993. *The Global Economy: Resource Use, Locational Choice, and International Trade.* Englewood Cliffs, N.J.: Prentice Hall.

CIA. 2006. *CIA World Fact Book.* Central Intelligence Agency, December 12.

Clinton Global Initiative. 2005, September 15. Special Opening Plenary Session: Perspectives on the Global Challenges of Our Time. Available at http://attend.clintonglobalinitiative.org/pdf/transcripts/plenary/cgi_09_15_05_plenary_1.pdf. Accessed January 29, 2007.

Craig, J. R., D. J. Vaughan, and B. J. Skinner. 1996. *Resources of the Earth: Origin, Use and Environmental Impact.* Upper Saddle River, N.J.: Prentice Hall.

Davis, R. E., P. C. Knappenberger, P. J. Michaels, and W. M. Novicoff. 2003. "Changing heat-related mortality in the United States." *Environmental Health Perspectives* 111(14), 1712–18.

EIA. 2006. International Energy Annual 2004. Energy Information Agency. Available at http://www.eia.doe.gov/iea/. Accessed November 30, 2006.

Fischer, D. 2006, December 15. Gore urges scientists to speak up. *Contra Costa Times.* Available at http://www.truthout.org/cgi-bin/artman/exec/view.cgi/67/24524. Accessed January 29, 2007.

Fleitas, I., et al. 2006. The quality of radiology services in five Latin American countries. *Revista Panamericana de Salud Publica-Pan American. Journal of Public Health* 20(2–3), 113–24.

Gebhardt, J. G., and T. E. Norris 2006. Acute stroke care at rural hospitals in Idaho: Challenges in expediting stroke care. *Journal of Rural Health* 22, 88–91.

Graddy, K., and M. Stevens. 2005. The impact of school resources on student performance: A study of private schools in the United Kingdom. *Industrial & Labor Relations Review* 58(3), 435–51.

IEA. 2004. World Energy Outlook 2004: IEA Publications.

———. 2006. World Energy Outlook 2006: IEA Publications.

IPCC. 2007a. Climate Change 2007: WGI: Summary for Policymakers.

———. 2007b. Climate Change 2007: WGI: The Physical Science Basis. Cambridge (UK): Cambridge University Press.

IPCC and J. T. Houghton. 1996. Climate Change 1995: The Science of Climate Change. Cambridge and New York: Cambridge University Press.

Jevrejeva, S., A. Grinsted, J. C. Moore, and S. Holgate. 2006. Nonlinear trends and multiyear cycles in sea level records. *Journal of Geophysical Research-Oceans* 111(C9).

Kammen, D. M. 1995. Cookstoves for the Developing-World. *Scientific American* 273(1), 72–75.

Kelkar, G. 2006, May 8. The Gender Face of Energy. Presentation at CSD 14 Learning Centre, United Nations. Available at http://www.un.org/esa/sustdev/csd/csd14/lc/presentation/gender2.pdf. Accessed January 30, 2007.

Lebergott, S. 1993. Pursuing Happiness: American Consumers in the Twentieth Century. Princeton, N.J.: Princeton University Press.

———. 1995. Long-term trends in the US standard of living. In J. Simon (Ed.), State of Humanity (pp. 149–60). Oxford: Blackwell.

Lopez, A. D., C. D. Mathers, M. Ezzati, D. T. Jamison, and C. J. L. Murray. 2006. Global and regional burden of disease and risk factors, 2001: systematic analysis of population health data. *Lancet* 367(9524), 1747–57.

Nakicenovic, N., and IPCC WG III. 2000. Special Report on Emissions Scenarios: A Special Report of Working Group III of the Intergovernmental Panel on Climate Change. Cambridge and New York: Cambridge University Press.

Nicholls, R. J., and R. S. J. Tol. 2006. "Impacts and responses to sea-level rise: a global analysis of the SRES scenarios over the twenty-first century." *Philosophical Transactions of the Royal Society A—Mathematical Physical and Engineering Sciences* 364(1841), 1073–95.

OECD. 2006. *OECD Factbook* 2006 (p. v.). Paris: Organization for Economic Co-operation and Development.

Pearce, D. 2003. "The social cost of carbon and its policy implications." *Oxford Review of Economic Policy* 19(3), 362–84.

Robinson, J. P., and G. Godbey. 1997. *Time for Life: The Surprising Ways Americans Use Their Time.* University Park, PA.: Pennsylvania State University Press.

Schäfer, A. 2006. "Long-term trends in global passenger mobility." *Bridge* 36(4), 24–32.

Tol, R. S. J. 2004. The double trade-off between adaptation and mitigation for sea level rise: an application of FUND. Hamburg University and Centre for Marine and Atmospheric Science, Hamburg.

———. 2005. "The marginal damage costs of carbon dioxide emissions: An assessment of the uncertainties." *Energy Policy* 33(16), 2064–74.

———. 2007. "Europe's long-term climate target: A critical evaluation." *Energy Policy* 35(1), 424–32.

UNFCCC. 1992. United Nations Framework Convention on Climate Change.

USCB. 2006. Statistical Abstract of the United States: 2007. U.S. Census Bureau. Available at http://www.census.gov/prod/www/statistical-abstract.html. Accessed January 30, 2007.

WCRF. 1997. *Food, Nutrition and the Prevention of Cancer: A Global Perspective.* Washington, D.C.: World Cancer Research Fund & American Institute for Cancer Research.

Weinberger, M., E. Z. Oddone, and W. G. Henderson. 1996. "Does increased access to primary care reduce hospital readmissions?" *New England Journal of Medicine* 334(22), 1441–47.

Wennberg, J. E., et al. 2004. "Use of hospitals, physician visits, and hospice care during last six months of life among cohorts loyal to highly respected hospitals in the United States." *British Medical Journal* 328(7440), 607–610A.

WHO. 2002. The world health report 2002—reducing risk, promoting healthy life. World Health Organization.

———. 2004. World report on road traffic injury prevention: World Health Organization.

Wigley, T. M. L. 1998. "The Kyoto Protocol: CO_2, CH_4 and climate implications." *Geophysical Research Letters* 25(13), 2285–88.

Yohe, G., and J. Neumann. 1997. "Planning for sea level rise and shore protection under climate uncertainty." *Climatic Change* 37, 243–70.

READING QUESTIONS

1. How will climate change affect the poorest countries like Micronesia? How will it affect the richest countries? Where should our focus be regarding climate change according to Lomborg?
2. Why does Lomborg think we need to be more realistic about climate change? How have current governments failed with respect to their past promises to reduce emissions?
3. What two points does Lomborg raise for the statistical research that has been done so far on the costs of reducing CO_2 emissions? What should the goal of each nation be according to Lomborg? How does he think the nations of the world can achieve this goal?
4. Explain the traffic analogy considered by Lomborg. How does this case illustrate why it is unlikely that the nations and people of the world will be able to meet the reduced emissions goals set by Al Gore?

DISCUSSION QUESTIONS

1. Lomborg claims that climate change is not the end of the world but that it will be bad for some people. How realistic is this claim? What reasons could be offered in support of the view that climate change does pose a significant threat to the majority of people in the world?
2. Lomborg suggests that we need to consider arguments for and against different policies in order to combat the effects of climate change successfully. Is he right to suggest that the nations of the world are not currently engaged in this type of project? Why or why not? Are there any sorts of policies that deserve more consideration than others? What kinds of policies should be rejected?

ADDITIONAL RESOURCES

Web Resources

Global Issues, <www.globalissues.org/>. Site featuring many articles on global ethical issues (most of them written by the site's creator, Anup Shah).

The World Watch Institute, <www.worldwatch.org>. Features independent research on the environment and its protection.

Wikipedia, <http://en.wikipedia.org/wiki/Main Page>. Contains useful entries on global warming and on the International Panel of Climate Change (IPCC).

Brennan, Andrew and Yeuk-Sze Lo, "Environmental Ethics," *Stanford Encyclopedia of Philosophy*, <http://plato.stanford.edu/entries/ethics-environmental/>. An overview of the topic including a discussion of traditional ethical theories and environmental ethics.

Authored Books and Articles

Attfield, Robin, *Environmental Ethics: An Overview for the Twenty-First Century* (Cambridge: Polity Press, 2003). An introduction to environmental ethics that usefully surveys major positions and defends what the author calls "biocentric consequentialism."

Brown, Donald, *Climate Change Ethics: Navigating the Perfect Storm* (London: Routledge, 2012). The author examines why ethical principles have not had much effect on policy formation and makes proposals for ensuring that climate change policies do respond to ethical concerns.

Gardiner, Stephen M., "Ethics and Global Climate Change," *Ethics* 114 (2004): 555–600. A critical evaluation of the arguments by Lomborg and other like-minded skeptics.

Gardiner, S. M., *A Perfect Moral Storm*: *The Ethical Tragedy of Climate Change* (New York: Oxford University Press, 2011).

Gardiner, S. and D. Weisbach, *Debating Climate Ethics* (New York: Oxford University Press, 2016). The authors of this book debate the relevance of ethics to the issue of global climate policy.

Gore, Al, *An Inconvenient Truth* (Emmaus, PA: Rodale Books, 2006). Former U.S. vice president's book version of his documentary film of the same name about the dangers of global warming.

Houghton, John, *Global Warming: The Complete Briefing*, 4th ed. (Cambridge: Cambridge University Press, 2009). An undergraduate textbook that provides a comprehensive scientific guide to global warming.

Lomborg, Bjørn, *Cool It: The Skeptical Environmentalist's Guide to Global Warming* (New York: Random House, 2007, reprinted: Vintage, 2008). An overview by an economist and statistician of the problems produced by global warming and how best to address them. This book and Lomborg's previous books on global warming have stirred much controversy.

Anthologies

Hayward, Tim and Carol Gould (eds.), *The Journal of Social Philosophy* 40 (2009), special issue: The Global Environment, Climate Change, and Justice. Eight articles exploring ethical and political implications of global climate change, including issues of intra- and intergenerational justice.

Jamieson, Dale (ed.), *A Companion to Environmental Philosophy* (Oxford: Blackwell Publishing, 2003). Contains thirty-six articles written for this volume, which covers a wide variety of cultural, legal, political, and ethical issues relating to the environment.

Kaufman, Frederick, A. (ed.), *Foundations of Environmental Philosophy* (New York: McGraw-Hill, 2003). Combines text written for students with selected readings covering a wide range of topics, including biocentrism, ecocentric ethics, anthropomorphism, deep ecology, and ecofeminism.

Light, Andrew and Rolston Holmes III (eds.), *Environmental Ethics: An Anthology* (London: Blackwell, 2002). Classical and contemporary selections covering a wide range of topics organized into six parts: (1) What Is Environmental Ethics?, (2) Who Counts in Environmental Ethics?, (3) Is Nature Intrinsically Valuable?, (4) Is There One Environmental Ethics?, (5) Focusing on General Issues, and (6) What on Earth Do We Want? Human Social Issues and Environmental Values.

*Philosophy and Public Issue*s (New Series), (2013): 89–135. A special issue with papers discussing Gardiner's book, *A Perfect Moral Storm: The Ethical Tragedy of Climate Change*, with replies by Gardiner.

Pojman, Louis P., *Environmental Ethics: Readings in Theory and Application,* 4th ed. (Belmont, CA: Wadsworth, 2004). A collection of eighty-two articles debating most every aspect of ethical concern for the environment including new articles for this edition on ecorealism, world hunger, population, and city life.

Sandler, Ronald and Philip Cafaro (eds.), *Environmental Virtue Ethics* (Lanham, MD: Rowman & Littlefield, 2005). Thirteen essays organized into four parts: (1) Recognizing Environmental Virtue Ethics, (2) Environmental Virtue Ethics Theory, (3) Environmental Virtues and Vices, and (4) Applying Environmental Virtue Ethics.

Schmidtz, David and Elizabeth Willott (eds.), *Environmental Ethics: What Really Matters, What Really Works* (New York: Oxford University Press, 2001). This comprehensive anthology features sixty-two selections organized into two major parts: (1) What Really Matters: Essays on Value in Nature, and (2) What Really Works: Essays on Human Ecology.

Glossary

Each entry in the glossary indicates the chapter and section in which the term is first introduced and, in some cases, additional places where the term occurs. Cross-references are in italics.

Abolitionist   Someone who is opposed to the death penalty and advocates its abolition. (chap. 12, intro.)

Abortion   Cases in which a pregnancy is intentionally interrupted and involves (as part of the process or aim of interruption) the intentional killing of the fetus. (chap. 10, sec. 2)

Acceptance value   The value of the consequences that would likely be brought about through the acceptance of some rule. (chap. 10, sec. 7) See *rule consequentialism*. (chap. 1, sec. 2; chap. 13, sec. 4)

Act consequentialism   Any version of *consequentialism* according to which it is the net intrinsic value of the consequences of particular alternative actions open to an agent in some situation that determines the rightness or wrongness of those alternative actions. See *rule consequentialism*. (chap. 1, sec. 2A)

Active euthanasia   Cases of euthanasia in which one party actively intervenes to bring about the death of another. See *euthanasia, passive euthanasia*. (chap. 8, sec. 1)

Addiction   A type of compulsive behavior involving dependence on some substance or activity that is undesirable. It is common to distinguish between physical and psychological addiction. (chap. 5, sec. 2)

Adult stem cell   Stem cell of a fully formed individual. See *stem cell*. (chap. 11, sec. 1)

Adultery   The act of voluntary sexual intercourse between a married person and someone other than his or her legal spouse. (chap. 3, sec. 3)

Anthropocentrism   The view that the only beings who possess *direct moral standing* are human beings. All other beings (living and nonliving) are of mere indirect moral concern. (chap. 15, sec. 2)

Anticosmopolitanism   The denial of cosmopolitanism. See *cosmopolitanism*. (chap. 7, sec. 2)

Antiwar pacifism   The view that wars are always or nearly always morally wrong. (chap. 13, sec. 4)

Assisted suicide   A suicide in which another party helps an individual commit suicide by providing either the information or the means, or by directly helping the person who commits the act. See *suicide.* (chap. 8, sec. 2)

Atomism   The view according to which the primary items of moral appraisal are individuals—it is only individuals that can be properly judged as intrinsically valuable, or rights holders, or as having obligations. (chap. 15, sec. 2)

Basic right   Any right of particular importance within the realm of rights. So, for instance, the right to life is a basic right. (chap. 1, sec. 2D)

Beneficence, duty of   The duty to help those in dire need. (chap. 14, intro. and sec. 1)

Biocentrism   The view that all living beings, because they are living, possess *direct moral standing.* Thus, morality includes requirements of direct moral concern for all living beings. (chap. 15, sec. 2)

Categorical imperative   The fundamental moral principle in the moral theory of Immanuel Kant. As this principle is employed in reasoning about moral issues, it takes two forms: the *Universal Law* and the *Humanity* formulations. (chap. 1, sec. 2C)

Clone   An individual that comes about as a result of cloning. Also referred to as an *SCNT individual.* (chap. 11, sec. 1)

Cloning   The process of "asexually" producing a biological organism that is virtually genetically identical to another organism. (chap. 11, sec. 1)

Cold war   A conflict over ideological differences carried on by methods short of sustained overt military action and usually without breaking off diplomatic relations. (chap 13, sec. 1)

Consequentialism (C)   A type of moral theory according to which the rightness and wrongness of actions is to be explained entirely in terms of the intrinsic value of the consequences associated with either individual concrete actions or rules associated with actions. See *act consequentialism, rule consequentialism, intrinsic value, utilitarianism, perfectionist consequentialism.* (chap. 1, sec. 2A)

Consequentialist theory of punishment   A theory of punishment according to which (C1) punishment as a response to crime is morally justified if and only if this practice, compared to any other response to crime, will likely produce as much overall intrinsic value as would any other response, and (C2) a specific punishment for a certain crime is morally justified if and only if it would likely produce at least as much overall intrinsic value as would any other alternative punishment. See *retributive theory of punishment.* (chap 12, sec. 2)

Conservatism   A political ideology that maintains that it is proper for a government to advocate and sometimes enforce a particular conception of the good life. This ideology tends to attach great importance to various cultural traditions, in contrast to Liberal ideology. See *Liberalism.* (chap. 4, sec. 2)

Conservative position on some issue   A moral position on some issue which, in contrast to moderate and liberal positions, is restrictive in what it holds to be morally permissible behavior with regard to the issue. For example, with regard to issues of sexual morality, a typical conservative position holds that sexual intercourse is morally wrong except between married couples of the opposite sex. (chap. 3, sec. 1; chap. 10, sec. 5) See *liberal position, moderate position*. (chap. 10, sec. 5)

Cosmopolitanism   The idea that all human beings, regardless of political affiliation, are part of a single human community, which should be cultivated. (chap. 7, sec. 2)

Cyberpornography   Pornography available on the Internet (chap. 3, sec. 1)

Deterrence   Someone is deterred from committing murder by the threat of the death penalty only if his recognition of the death penalty as a possible consequence of committing murder explains why he does not commit it. (chap. 12, sec. 2)

Direct moral standing   For something to have direct moral standing is for it to possess features in virtue of which it deserves to be given moral consideration by agents who are capable of making moral choice. See *indirect moral standing*. (chap. 9, sec. 1; chap. 10, sec. 3; chap. 15, sec. 1)

Doctrine of double effect (DDE)   This doctrine is composed of a set of provisions under which it is morally permissible to knowingly bring about evil in the pursuit of the good. DDE is associated with *natural law theory*. (chap. 1, sec. 2B; chap. 13, sec. 4)

Drug   Any chemical substance that affects the functioning of living organisms. See also *psychotropic drug*. (chap. 5, sec. 1)

Drug abuse   Excessive nonmedical use of a drug that may cause harm to oneself or to others. (chap. 5, sec. 2)

Drug criminalization/decriminalization The former refers to having legal penalties for the use and possession of small quantities of drugs; the latter refers to not having such legal penalties. (chap. 5, sec. 4)

Drug prohibition/legalization The former refers to having legal penalties for the manufacture, sale, and distribution of large quantities of drugs; the latter refers to lack of such penalties. (chap. 5, sec. 4)

Duty-based moral theory   Any moral theory that takes the concept of duty to be basic and so characterizes or defines right action independently of considerations of intrinsic value and independently of considerations of moral rights. Examples include the ethics of prima facie duty and Kantian moral theory. Duty-based moral theories contrast with *value-based moral theories* and with *rights-based moral theories*. (chap. 1, sec.1)

Ecocentrism   The view according to which the primary bearers of *direct moral standing* are ecosystems in virtue of their functional integrity. Hence, morality involves moral obligations to maintain the functional integrity of ecosystems, and because, according to this view, ecosystems are primary bearers of direct moral standing, their preservation takes moral precedence over concern for individual things and creatures that compose the system. See *ecosystem, ecoholism*. (chap. 15, sec. 2)

Ecoholism   The view that both ecosystems and at least some individual items that make up an ecosystem have direct moral standing. (chap. 15, sec. 2)

Ecosystem   A whole composed of both living and nonliving things including animals, plants, bodies of water, sunlight, and other environmental factors. See *ecocentrism*. (chap. 15, sec. 2)

Embryo   The term used to refer to a stage in prenatal development which in humans begins at roughly the second week of pregnancy and lasts until roughly the eighth week. See *zygote, fetus*. (chap. 10, sec. 1; chap. 11, sec. 1)

Embryonic stem cell   Stem cells found in an embryo. See *stem cell*. (chap. 11, sec. 1)

Environmenal ethics   The view that (1) there are nonhuman beings that have direct moral standing, and (2) the class of such beings is larger than the class of conscious beings. (chap. 15, sec. 3)

Erotica   The depiction of erotic behavior (as in pictures or writing) intended to cause sexual excitement, but that either does not describe or portray sexual behavior that is degrading or does not endorse such degrading behavior. See *pornography*. (chap. 4, sec. 1)

Ethics of prima facie duty   A moral theory, originally developed by W. D. Ross, that features a plurality of moral principles that express *prima facie duties*. (chap. 1, sec. 2F)

Eugenics, human   The aim of improving the human race through genetic manipulation. (chap. 11, sec. 3)

Euthanasia   The act or practice of killing or allowing someone to die on grounds of mercy. (chap. 8, sec. 1)

Explanatory power, principle of   A principle for evaluating how well a moral theory does at satisfying the *theoretical aim* of such theories. According to this principle, a moral theory should feature principles that explain our more specific considered moral beliefs, thus helping us to understand why actions and other items of evaluation have the moral status they have. See *theoretical aim*. (chap. 1, sec. 3)

Extrinsic value   Something has extrinsic value when its value (good or bad) depends on how it is related to something having *intrinsic value*. (chap. 1, sec. 1)

Fetus   Used in a strict biological sense, a fetus is an unborn vertebrate animal that has developed to the point of having the basic structure that is characteristic of its kind. This stage is characterized by growth and full development of its organs. Also spelled "foetus." See *zygote, embryo*. (chap. 10, sec. 1)

Genetic enhancement   The process of manipulating genetic material in order to enhance the talents and capacities of living creatures. See *cloning*. (chap. 11, sec. 3)

Golden rule   Do unto others as you would have them do unto you. (chap. 1, sec. 2C)

Harm principle   A liberty-limiting principle according to which a government may justifiably pass laws to limit the liberty of its citizens in order to prohibit individuals from causing harm to other individuals or to society. See *liberty-limiting* principle. (chap. 4, sec. 2; chap. 5, sec. 3)

Hate speech   Language (oral or written) that expresses strong hatred, contempt, or intolerance for some social group, particularly social groups classified according to race, ethnicity, gender, sexual orientation, religion, disability, or nationality. (chap. 4, sec. 4)

Hedonistic utilitarianism (HU)   A version of *utilitarianism* featuring a hedonistic theory of intrinsic value. See *value hedonism.* (chap. 1, sec. 2A)

Holism   The view that wholes or collectives are bearers of value, or of rights, or of obligations. (chap. 15, sec. 2)

Homosexual behavior   Sexual activity, particularly intercourse, between members of the same sex. (chap. 3, sec. 3)

Hot war   A conflict involving actual fighting. (chap. 13, sec. 1)

Humanity formulation   A particular formulation of Kant's categorical imperative according to which an action is morally permissible if and only if (and because) the action treats humanity (whether in oneself or others) never as a mere means but as an end in itself. (chap. 1, sec. 2C)

Human rights   Moral rights that are universally shared by all human beings, including rights to life, liberty, and well-being. (chap. 1, sec. 2D).

In vitro fertilization (IVF)   The process through which a sperm fertilizes an egg outside a woman's body and is later implanted in a woman's uterus. (chap. 11, intro.)

Indirect moral standing   For something to have indirect moral standing is for it to deserve moral consideration only because it is related to something with direct moral standing. See *direct moral standing.* (chap. 9, sec. 1; chap. 10, sec. 3; chap. 15, sec. 1)

Induced pluripotent stem cells (iPSC)   Adult stem cells that have been genetically reprogrammed so as to have the capacity to develop into cells of most any type. (chap. 11, notes)

Interrogational torture   Torture whose aim is to gain information from the victim. See *torture.* (chap. 13, sec. 3)

Intrinsic value   To say that something has intrinsic positive value—that it is intrinsically good—is to say that its goodness is grounded in features that are inherent in that thing. Similarly for intrinsic negative value. See *extrinsic value.* (chap. 1, sec. 1)

Involuntary euthanasia   Euthanasia in which the individual has expressed a desire not to be the subject of euthanasia, but others act in violation of that desire, that is, *against* the individual's consent. See *euthanasia, voluntary euthanasia, nonvoluntary euthanasia.* (chap. 8, sec. 1)

Jus in bello   That part of *just-war theory* that sets forth moral requirements for military activities within a war. (chap. 13, sec. 4)

Jus ad bellum   That part of *just-war theory* that sets forth moral requirements for going to war. (chap. 13, sec. 4)

Just-war theory   A moral theory about the conditions under which a government is morally justified in going to war (*jus ad bellum*) and what military activities are morally permissible within a war (*jus in bello*). (chap. 13, sec. 4)

Just-war pacifism   The moral view that all or nearly all wars fail to meet the demands of just-war theory and are therefore morally wrong. (chap. 13, sec. 4)

Kantian moral theory   A type of moral theory first developed by German philosopher Immanuel Kant (1724–1804) that features the notions of respect for persons and universality. These two guiding ideas are expressed in Kant's *Humanity formulation* of his fundamental moral principle—*the categorical imperative*—and in the *Universal Law formulation,* respectively. (chap 1, sec. 2C)

Legal moralism principle   A liberty-limiting principle according to which a government may justifiably pass laws to limit the liberty of its citizens in order to protect common moral standards, independently of whether the activities in question are harmful to others or to oneself. See *liberty-limiting principle.* (chap. 4, sec. 2; chap. 5, sec. 3)

Legal paternalism principle   A liberty-limiting principle according to which a government may justifiably pass laws to limit the liberty of its citizens in order to prohibit individuals from causing harm to themselves. See *liberty-limiting principle.* (chap. 4, sec. 2; chap. 5, sec. 3)

Legal punishment   Punishment administered by a legal authority. (chap. 12, sec. 1)

Legal rights   Rights that result or come into existence as the result of the activities of a legal statute or some other form governmental activity. To be contrasted with *moral rights.* (chap. 1, sec. 2D)

Lex talionis (law of retribution)   A principle of punishment for specific offenses according to which the appropriate punishment for a crime involves doing to the wrongdoer the same kind of action that he or she did to his or her victim(s). See *retributive theory of punishment.* (chap. 12, sec. 2)

Liberal position on some issue   A moral position on some issue which, in contrast to conservative and moderate positions, is not as restrictive in what it holds to be morally permissible behavior with regard to the issue. For example, on issues of sexual morality, a typical liberal position holds that sexual intercourse is morally permissible so long as those involved do not violate any general moral rules such as rules against deception and coercion. See *conservative position, moderate position.* (chap. 3, sec. 1; chap. 10, sec. 5)

Liberalism   A political ideology that puts strong emphasis on liberty and equality of individuals, maintaining in particular that proper respect for the liberty and equality of individuals requires that governments remain as neutral as possible over conceptions of the good life. See *conservatism.* (chap. 4, sec. 2)

Liberty-limiting principle   A principle that purports to set forth conditions under which a government may be morally justified in passing laws that limit the liberty of its citizens. (chap. 4, sec. 2; chap. 5, sec. 3)

Moderate position on some issue   A moral position on some issue which is less restrictive than a conservative position and more restrictive than a liberal position. For example, with regard to issues of sexual morality, a typical moderate, in contrast to a typical conservative, will hold that marriage is not a necessary condition for morally permissible sexual intercourse. In contrast to a typical liberal, a moderate will hold that there are such requirements as being committed to a relationship with one's sexual partner that must be observed in order for sexual intercourse to be morally permissible. See *conservative position, liberal position.* (chap. 3, sec. 1; chap. 10, sec. 5)

Moral criteria   Features of an action or other item of evaluation in virtue of which the action or item is morally right or wrong, good or bad. Moral criteria for an action's rightness or wrongness are often expressed in *principles of right conduct,* while criteria for something's being intrinsically good or bad are often expressed in *principles of value.* (chap. 1, sec. 1)

Moral judgment   An acquired skill at discerning what matters the most morally speaking and coming to an all-things-considered moral verdict, where this skill cannot be entirely captured by a set of rules. (chap. 1, secs. 2D and 2F)

Moral nihilism (regarding war)   The view that morality does not apply to war. (chap. 13, sec. 4)

Moral principle   A general statement that purports to set forth conditions under which an action or other item of evaluation is right or wrong, good or bad, virtuous or vicious. (chap. 1, sec. 1)

Moral rights   Rights that an individual or group has independently of any legal system or other conventions. Such rights have also been called "natural rights." To be contrasted with *legal rights*. (chap. 1, sec. 2D)

Moral standing   See *direct moral standing, indirect moral standing.*

Moral theory   An attempt to provide well-argued-for answers to general moral questions about the nature of right action and value. Typically, answers to such questions are expressed as *moral principles.* See *theory of right conduct, theory of value.* (chap. 1, intro. and sec. 1)

Natural law theory   A type of nonconsequentialist moral theory that attempts to ground morality on objective facts about human nature. See *doctrine of double effect, consequentialism.* (chap. 1, sec. 2B)

Natural right   See *moral right.* (chap. 1, sec. 2D)

Negative right   A right corresponding to a negative duty on the part of rights addressees to refrain from certain actions that would violate the right in question. For instance, the right to free speech is a negative right demanding that others not interfere with one's attempt to express oneself in speech. (chap. 1, sec. 2D)

Nonconsensual pornography (NCP)   Distribution by one party of sexually explicit images of another party without the latter's consent. This includes distribution that is motivated by revenge—"revenge porn"—though this term is sometimes used more broadly to refer to such distribution regardless of motive. (chap. 3, sec. 1)

Nonvoluntary euthanasia   Euthanasia in which the individual has not given his consent to be subject to euthanasia because he has not expressed a view about what others may do in case, for example, he goes into a persistent vegetative state. See *euthanasia, voluntary euthanasia, involuntary euthanasia.* (chap. 8, sec. 1)

Offense principle   A liberty-limiting principle according to which a government may justifiably pass laws to limit the liberty of its citizens in order to prohibit individuals from offending others. See *liberty-limiting principle.* (chap. 4, sec. 2; chap. 5, sec. 3)

Oocyte   An unfertilized egg whose fertilization results in a *zygote.* (chap. 11, sec. 1)

Pacifism (regarding war)   See *antiwar pacifism.*

Passive euthanasia   Euthanasia in which the death of the individual in question resulted from (or was hastened by) withholding or withdrawing some form of treatment which, had it been administered, would likely have prolonged the life of that individual. See *euthanasia, active euthanasia.* (chap. 8, sec. 1)

Perfectionist consequentialism   A version of *consequentialism* that accepts a perfectionist theory of value. See *value perfectionism*. (chap. 1, sec. 2A)

Pornography   The depiction of erotic behavior (as in pictures or writing) intended to cause sexual excitement. See *erotica*. (chap. 4, sec. 1)

Positive right   A right corresponding to a positive duty on the part of rights addressees to perform certain actions called for by the right in question. For instance, the right to an education corresponds to an obligation, presumably of a state, to engage in certain activities to help ensure that its citizens receive (or have the opportunity to receive) an education. (chap. 1, sec. 2D)

Practical aim (of a moral theory)   To offer *practical guidance* for how we might arrive at correct or justified moral verdicts about matters of moral concern. See *theoretical aim*. (chap. 1, sec. 1)

Practical guidance, principle of   A principle for evaluating how well a moral theory does at satisfying the practical aim of such theories. According to this principle, a moral theory should feature principles that are useful in guiding moral deliberation toward correct or justified moral verdicts about particular cases which can in turn be used to help guide choice. See *practical aim*. (chap. 1, sec. 3)

Preemptive war   A war initiated by a state as a response to a clear imminent threat of attack by another state. (chap. 13, sec. 1)

Prevention   For example, someone is prevented by execution from committing a particular murder only if, had the individual not been executed, he or she would have committed the murder. (chap. 12, sec. 2)

Preventive war   A war initiated by one state as a response to an action of a potential aggressor who does not yet pose an imminent threat. (chap. 13, sec. 1)

Prima facie duty   An action which (1) possesses a duty-relevant feature where (2) this feature is a defeasibly sufficient condition for the action being an all-things-considered duty. (chap. 1, sec. 2F)

Principle of proportionality   A principle of punishment according to which the appropriate moral measure of specific punishments requires that they be in "proportion" to the crime: that the severity of the punishment should "be commensurate" with the gravity of the offense. See *retributive theory of punishment*, *lex talionis*. (chap. 12, sec. 2)

Principle of right conduct   A general moral statement that purports to set forth conditions under which an action or a practice is morally right and, by implication, when an action is morally wrong. (chap. 1, sec. 1)

Principle of utility   The fundamental moral principle of the utilitarian moral theory, according to which (in its "act" version) an action is morally right (not wrong) if and only if (and because) it would likely produce as high a utility as would any available alternative action open to the agent. See *utility*. (chap. 1, sec. 2A)

Principle of value   A general statement that purports to set forth conditions under which some item of evaluation (a person, experience, or state of affairs) is intrinsically good and, by implication, when any such item is intrinsically bad (or evil). See *intrinsic value, moral theory*. (chap. 1, sec. 1)

Psychotropic drug   A drug that produces changes in mood, feeling, and perception, including opiates, hallucinogens, stimulants, cannabis, and depressants. (chap. 5, sec. 1)

Racism   Racial prejudice or discrimination based on a belief that race is the primary determinant of human traits and capacities and that racial differences produce an inherent superiority of a particular race. (chap. 6, sec. 1)

Reparation   Activities involved in making up for past wrongs. (chap. 6, sec. 2)

Reproductive cloning   Cloning whose main purpose is to produce an individual member of the species. Human reproductive cloning has as its aim the production of a child. See *cloning, therapeutic cloning.* (chap. 11, intro.)

Retentionist   Someone who favors the death penalty and wants states that have it to retain it. (chap. 12, intro.)

Retributive theory of punishment   A theory of punishment according to which (R1) what morally justifies punishment of wrongdoers is that those who break the law (and are properly judged to have done so) *deserve* to be punished, and (R2) the punishment for a particular offense against the law should "fit" the crime. See *lex talionis, principle of proportionality.* (chap. 12, sec. 2)

Revenge porn   *See nonconsensual pornography.*

Right   An entitlement (either moral or legal) to be free to engage in some activity or exercise some power or to be given something. See *legal rights, moral rights, negative rights, positive rights, rights addressee, rights content, rights holder.* (chap. 1, sec. 2D)

Rights   See *moral rights.*

Rights-based moral theory (R)   A type of moral theory according to which moral rights (claims) are the basis for explaining the rightness and wrongness of actions. See *moral rights, rights-focused approach.* (chap. 1, sec. 2D)

Rights-focused approach   An approach to moral issues that focuses primarily on moral rights. Such an approach need not be committed to a rights-based moral theory. See *moral rights, rights-based moral theory.* (chap. 1, sec. 2D)

Rights addressee   The individual or group against whom a right is held and who thus has an obligation toward the holder of the right. (chap. 1, sec. 2D)

Rights content   What a moral or legal right is a right to. (chap. 1, sec. 2D)

Rights holder   The individual or group that possesses rights. (chap. 1, sec. 2D)

Rights infringement   An action that goes against the rights of a rights holder but which in the circumstances is justified. A moral rights infringement is morally justified, a legal rights infringement is legally justified. (chap. 1, sec. 2D)

Rights, strength of   The strength of a right corresponds to how strong the moral or legal justification must be in order for the right to be justifiably overridden. The stronger the right, the stronger the justification must be in order to override the right. See *rights infringement.* (chap. 1, sec. 2D)

Rights violation   An action that goes against the rights of a rights holder and which is either not morally justified (and hence a moral wrong) or not legally justified (and hence illegal). (chap. 1, sec. 2D)

Rule consequentialism (RC)   Any version of consequentialism according to which the rightness or wrongness of some particular action that is (or might be) performed in some situation depends on the *acceptance value* of the rule corresponding to the action in question. A right action is one falling under a rule with at least as high an acceptance value as any other rule governing the situation in question. See *act consequentialism.* (chap. 1, sec. 2A)

SCNT individual   An individual produced through the process of *somatic cell nuclear transfer.* (chap. 11, sec. 1)

Sentience   The developed capacity to have experiences of pleasure and pain. (chap. 10, sec. 1)

Sentientism   The view that all and only sentient creatures—creatures who have the capacity to experience pleasure and pain—have *direct moral standing.* Thus, morality includes requirements of direct moral concern for all sentient beings. (chap. 15, sec. 2)

Sexism   Prejudice or discrimination based on sex, especially prejudice and discrimination against women. (chap. 6, sec. 1)

Social contract theory of morality   A species of moral theory according to which (roughly) correct or justified moral rules or principles are ones that result from some sort of social agreement—whether the agreement in question is conceived of as having actually taken place or (more likely) is hypothetical. (chap. 1, sec. 2G)

Somatic cell Any cell other than an egg or sperm (gametes). (chap. 11, notes)

Somatic cell nuclear transfer (SCNT)   Process of asexually producing an individual in which the nucleus of an unfertilized egg (oocyte) is replaced by the nucleus of a donor cell. This is the process involved in cloning. See *cloning.* (chap. 11, sec. 1)

Speciesism   The systematic discrimination against the members of some species by the members of another species. (chap. 9, sec. 2)

Stem cell   A cell found throughout the body that is significant because of its capability of developing into any kind of cell or tissue in the body. See *adult stem cell.* (chap. 11, sec. 1)

Suicide   Intentionally and thus voluntarily ending one's own life. (chap. 8, sec. 2)

Terrorism   The use of threat or violence against innocent people to elicit terror in them, or in some other group of people, in order to further a political objective. See *interrogational torture, terrorist torture.* (chap. 13, sec. 2)

Terrorist torture   Torture whose aim is to punish, coerce, or derive sadistic satisfaction. See *terrorism, torture.* (chap. 13, sec. 3)

Theoretical aim (of a moral theory)   To discover those underlying features of actions, persons, and other items of moral evaluation that *make* them right or wrong, good or bad, and thus *explain why* such items have the moral properties they have. Features of this sort serve as *moral criteria* of the right and the good. See *practical aim.* (chap. 1, sec. 1)

Therapeutic cloning   Cloning that aims only at producing an embryo which might then be used for medical purposes. See *cloning, reproductive cloning.* (chap. 11, intro.)

Torture   Activities involving the infliction of intense pain (either physical, psychological, or both) on a victim with the aim of punishing, coercing, or deriving sadistic satisfaction. See *terrorist torture* (chap. 13, sec. 3)

Universal Law formulation   A formulation of Kant's *categorical imperative* which states that an action is morally permissible if and only if the maxim associated with the action is universalizable. (chap. 1, sec. 2C)

Utilitarianism   A consequentialist moral theory according to which happiness has positive intrinsic value in terms of which actions are right or wrong. See *consequentialism, hedonistic utilitarianism, act consequentialism, rule consequentialism.* (chap. 1, sec. 2A)

Utility   A technical term introduced in connection with *utilitarianism* to refer to the net intrinsic value (positive or negative) of the consequences of some action or rule, where what has intrinsic positive value for the utilitarian is happiness and what has intrinsic negative value is unhappiness. (chap. 1, sec. 2A)

Value hedonism   A theory of intrinsic value according to which only states of pleasure possess positive intrinsic value (are intrinsically good) and only states of pain possess negative intrinsic value (are intrinsically bad or evil). This theory of value is featured in *hedonistic utilitarianism.* (chap. 1, sec. 2A)

Value perfectionism   The view that certain forms of human perfection have intrinsic value, the most general being knowledge and achievement. See *perfectionist consequentialism.* (chap. 1, sec. 2A)

Value-based moral theory   Any moral theory according to which the concept of intrinsic value is more basic than the concept of right action, and so right action is characterized or defined in terms of intrinsic value. Value-based theories are contrasted with *duty-based moral theories* and with *rights-based moral theories. Consequentialism* is one clear example of a value-based moral theory. (chap. 1, sec. 1)

Viability   The stage in fetal development wherein it is possible for the fetus to survive outside the uterus. (chap. 10, sec. 2)

Vice   A trait of character or mind that involves dispositions to act, feel, and think in certain ways, and is central in the negative evaluation of persons. See *virtue, virtue ethics.* (chap. 1, sec. 2E)

Virtue   A trait of character or mind that involves dispositions to act, feel, and think in certain ways, and is central in the positive evaluation of persons. See *vice, virtue ethics.* (chap. 1, sec. 2E)

Virtue ethics (VE)   A type of moral theory that makes considerations of virtue and vice the basis for explaining the rightness and wrongness of actions. See *virtue, vice.* (chap. 1, sec. 2E)

Voluntary euthanasia   Euthanasia in which the party has consented to the active bringing about of her death or to some means of passively allowing her to die. See *euthanasia, nonvoluntary euthanasia, involuntary euthanasia.* (chap. 8, sec. 1)

War   A state of usually open and declared armed hostile conflict between states or nations. (chap. 13, sec. 1)

Zygote   A fertilized ovum. Also called a "conceptus." See *embryo, fetus.* (chap. 10, sec. 1; chap. 11, sec. 1)